KU-304-900

WITHDRAWN

LIVERPOOL JMU LIBRARY

3 1111 01443 6610

A

Philip E. Lilienthal (signature)

BOOK

The Philip E. Lilienthal imprint
honors special books
in commemoration of a man whose work
at University of California Press from 1954 to 1979
was marked by dedication to young authors
and to high standards in the field of Asian Studies.
Friends, family, authors, and foundations have together
endowed the Lilienthal Fund, which enables UC Press
to publish under this imprint selected books
in a way that reflects the taste and judgment
of a great and beloved editor.

Vietnam

FROM INDOCHINA TO VIETNAM:
REVOLUTION AND WAR IN A GLOBAL PERSPECTIVE
Edited by Fredrik Logevall and Christopher E. Goscha

Vietnam

*State, War, and Revolution
(1945–1946)*

———

David G. Marr

UNIVERSITY OF CALIFORNIA PRESS
Berkeley   Los Angeles   London

University of California Press, one of the most distinguished university presses in the United States, enriches lives around the world by advancing scholarship in the humanities, social sciences, and natural sciences. Its activities are supported by the UC Press Foundation and by philanthropic contributions from individuals and institutions. For more information, visit www.ucpress.edu.

University of California Press
Berkeley and Los Angeles, California

University of California Press, Ltd.
London, England

© 2013 by The Regents of the University of California

Ch 3 is reprinted by permission of the publisher from "Creating Defense Capacity in Vietnam, 1945–1947" in THE FIRST VIETNAM WAR: COLONIAL CONFLICT AND COLD WAR CRISIS, edited by Mark Atwood Lawrence and Fredrik Logevall, pp. 74–101, Cambridge, Mass.: Harvard University Press, Copyright © 2007 by The President and Fellows of Harvard College.

Library of Congress Cataloging-in-Publication Data
Marr, David G.
    Vietnam : state, war, and revolution, 1945–1946 / David G. Marr.
        p.   cm.
    Includes bibliographical references and index.
    ISBN 978-0-520-27415-0 (cloth : alk. paper)
    1. Vietnam (Democratic Republic)—History.   2. Indochinese War, 1946–1954.   I. Title.
    DS560.6.M37 2013
    959.704ʹ1—dc23

                                                    2012036193

Manufactured in the United States of America

22   21   20   19   18   17   16   15   14   13
10   9   8   7   6   5   4   3   2   1

In keeping with a commitment to support environmentally responsible and sustainable printing practices, UC Press has printed this book on Rolland Enviro 100, a 100% post-consumer fiber paper that is FSC certified, deinked, processed chlorine-free, and manufactured with renewable biogas energy. It is acid-free and EcoLogo certified.

For our grandchildren
Grace, Billy, Jimmy, and Ella

CONTENTS

ILLUSTRATIONS

MAPS

FIGURES

FOREWORD

David G. Marr's scholarship on modern Vietnam needs no introduction. In a series of path-breaking studies published by the University of California Press, Marr has provided definitive accounts of Vietnamese anticolonialism, socio-cultural change, and revolution. Now, in *Vietnam: State, War, and Revolution (1945–46)*, Marr draws on a wide array of Vietnamese-language memoirs, news-papers, and government archives captured by the French to provide the first full-length study of the emergence and formation of the postcolonial state of the Democratic Republic of Vietnam (DRV). Through a series of thematic chapters, Marr shows in masterful detail how a state emerged in Vietnamese hands, one capable of mobilizing people and allocating resources as well as preparing an army for war with a French government determined to reestablish colonial sovereignty, first in the south, then in the north.

Whereas many scholars have focused on the invisible hand of the Vietnamese communists operating from on high, Marr takes us down below to follow intermediary civil servants, hardly any of them communists, as they did their best to keep the DRV functioning. The communist leadership, including Ho Chi Minh, receive careful attention as well, but Marr shows that the communists were much weaker at the time than they and their detractors would like to admit later. In addition, Marr provides important insights into the conceptualization of Vietnam's first constitution and the difficult yet fascinating debates that went into it and the creation of the country's first National Assembly in 1946. Of equal importance is the attention he pays to policing and to the economy, neither of which has received sustained treatment in the existing historiography.

In Marr's hands, contingency and incoherence become as important to understanding this fledgling state's early evolution as the revolution from which it was born and the war that the French hoped would allow them to shut it down. Those readers interested in modern Vietnam in general and the DRV in particular will be richly rewarded, as will those working on the wars for Vietnam, postcolonial state formation, and decolonization. It is an honor and a pleasure to be able to introduce this volume to our readers and to count it among the titles in our series.

Christopher E. Goscha, Université du Québec à Montréal
Fredrik Logevall, Cornell University

PREFACE

I began my encounter with Vietnam in the 1960s, wondering why so many people talked with such excitement about where they were and what they were doing in 1945–46. Vietnamese materials about that era proved very hard to find, however. There was almost nothing in Saigon libraries or bookshops. I located a left-wing book store in Hong Kong that sold subscriptions to Hanoi periodicals, notably *Nghiên Cứu Lịch Sử (Historical Research)*. One day in 1964 two FBI agents came to our Berkeley graduate student apartment to ask why I was receiving enemy propaganda in the mail. The following year, while researching student political agitation in Saigon, I was given a stack of confiscated Hanoi publications by Colonel Phạm Ngọc Liễu, chief of the Republic of Vietnam's National Police. These whetted my appetite, but were hardly the makings of a PhD project.

My 1968 dissertation and first book focused on the minority of Vietnamese who contested French occupation and colonization during the late nineteenth and early twentieth centuries.[1] They left a legacy of failures tinged with heroism, as well as a blunt challenge to the new generation of French-educated youth to learn from their mistakes. My second book pursued the intelligentsia of this generation as it debated issues of ethics and politics, language and literacy, the status of women, lessons from the past, harmony and struggle, knowledge power, and political praxis.[2] These lively exchanges took place amidst rapid socioeconomic change, repeated changes in French colonial policy, and finally the turmoil of World War II. Not solely intellectuals, but other Vietnamese as well became convinced that life was not preordained, liberation and modernity were open to all peoples of the world, and one could join with others to force change.

My third book tried to bring alive the events and explain the significance of what Vietnamese still call the August Revolution of 1945.[3] First I canvassed the previous five years, when Vichy French, Japanese, Chinese, Americans, British, Free French, Vietnamese communists, and Vietnamese nationalists all tried to control or influence events in Indochina. On 9 March 1945, the Japanese Army overturned the French colonial administration, which meant that France was removed from the contest for a vital six months. Vietnamese quickly discovered they could publish, organize, and demonstrate in favor of national independence, so long as they did not hinder Japanese defense preparations. The anti-Japanese Vietnam Independence League (Việt Nam Độc Lập Đồng Minh), or Việt Minh, continued to extol Allied victories and denounce the "dwarf bandits" (giặc lùn), but mostly avoided confrontation in favor of popular proselytizing and preparations for eventual revolt. In some localities peasants raided rice granaries, seized landlords' properties, incarcerated village headmen, and caused district mandarins to flee for their lives.

News of Tokyo's capitulation to the Allies on 15 August spread quickly across Vietnam, triggering scores of exuberant demonstrations, seizures of government offices, burning of documents, and formation of revolutionary committees. Indochinese Communist Party (ICP) members took control in Hanoi, Huế, Saigon, and some provincial towns in the name of the Việt Minh, while elsewhere bands of young men and women accomplished much the same thing of their own volition. It was a moment when everything seemed possible, when people felt they were making history, not just witnessing it. Some Japanese commanders made available to local Vietnamese groups stocks of arms and ammunition they had seized from the French. Việt Minh cadres, having identified themselves with the Allies, now enjoyed a major propaganda advantage over groups that previously had cooperated with the Japanese. As a result, most youth groups were soon waving Việt Minh flags and repeating available Việt Minh slogans, even though they had no contact with higher Việt Minh echelons and no familiarity with the overall Việt Minh platform.

Vietnam 1945 ends on 2 September, when big crowds gathered in Hanoi and Saigon to celebrate Vietnamese national independence. In Hanoi, Hồ Chí Minh, provisional president of the new Democratic Republic of Vietnam (DRV), read a short independence declaration designed for international as well as domestic consumption. Loudspeakers ensured that the audience not only heard what Hồ and others had to say, but responded loudly and eagerly on numerous occasions. After Hồ brought the meeting to a close, Việt Minh contingents marched downtown, disbanded, and joined in the general merriment until the hour of curfew. In Saigon, however, members of the Southern Provisional Administrative Committee had just finished addressing the crowd when shots rang out on the periphery, people stampeded, and mobs proceeded to hunt down French civilians, killing several, beating up others, and terrorizing the rest. These two denouements, one orderly, the other anarchic, showed how the popular upheavals of August could propel Vietnam in starkly different directions. People sensed that their lives had changed irrevocably, yet no one could predict what the next week might bring, much less subsequent months and years.

This book focuses on events of the next sixteen months, when Vietnam's future course was largely determined. Between September 1945 and December 1946, the DRV state began to function, a national army was created, the Japanese, British, Americans and Chinese faded from the Indochina power equation, and France and the DRV maneuvered vigorously to gain advantage. A second famine was mostly averted, French properties were appropriated, and informal fundraising campaigns were used alongside formal tax levies. The ICP gradually extended its control over local Việt Minh groups, then pressured other parties to either accept ICP hegemony or be treated as traitors. Millions of men, women, and children joined local associations for the defense and development of the nation. Hồ Chí Minh spent the summer of 1946 in Paris trying to negotiate a settlement, but tensions increased at home. This culminated in French seizure of Haiphong in November, and DRV attacks in Hanoi and elsewhere on 19 December. The First Indochina War would last another seven and a half years.

The DRV survived and eventually prevailed largely due to the unprecedented participation of ordinary citizens, most of whom never fired a shot in anger. Why and how people took part are questions I approach from multiple angles. Clearly individuals had other aspirations besides defeating the enemy. The DRV state took on many functions that had no direct bearing on the armed struggle, although it usually justified these expansions in resistance terms. The ICP also used the war to justify its grabs for power. Amidst all these attempts to control affairs, war and revolution produced a host of unintended consequences that Vietnamese had to live with for decades thereafter.

Often I have asked myself the same question that Thomas Carlyle did when he embarked on his history of the French Revolution: What was it like to be there? Lacking Carlyle's dramatic flair, I cannot evoke a Vietnamese Mirabeau or Robespierre. Well-known personages like Hồ Chí Minh, Võ Nguyên Giáp, and Trường Chinh do tread the stage here, yet I'm equally interested in the teenage Việt Minh activist, the aggrieved village petitioner, the provincial committee chairman, the former colonial *fonctionnaire*, the eager journalist, and the high school pupil heading south to fight the French, armed only with a machete.

Archival dossiers, newspapers, and books generated in 1945–46 have motivated me for years to get up each morning, tackle inconsistent evidence, find patterns but also contradictions, and then try to craft an historical narrative of human beings responding to and making events at this particular place and time. Most exhilarating has been the gouvernement de fait (GF) collection at the

Archives national d'outre-mer (ANOM) in Aix-en-Provence, seventy-eight cartons of DRV documents captured by the French Army in Hanoi in late 1946.[4] It is one measure of the high-level confusion bedeviling the DRV on 19 December 1946 that government clerks were still at their desks in Hanoi only two hours before Vietnamese attacks began; they then failed to destroy thousands of dossiers lodged in the basement of the Northern Region Office (Bắc Bộ Phủ) before leaving.

If it had been feasible to write this book twenty years ago, Vietnam watchers would quickly have recognized the political rhetoric, the policy assumptions, and attitudes of people carried over from the late 1940s. Now a lot has changed. Amidst today's mobile phones, vibrant markets, foreign investors, Nike shoe factories, and nouveau riche families, stories of war and revolution may seem embarrassingly antiquated. For young Vietnamese it is still necessary to learn enough about the anti-French resistance to pass school examinations, but beyond that the period appears distant and inconsequential. For many young scholars of Vietnam in the West there seems to be an assumption that amidst all the Communist Party propaganda nothing of continuing significance can be found out about the DRV, the Việt Minh, or the resistance. Yet many of the state institutions created in the late 1940s remain intact in Vietnam today, as do popular beliefs in modernity, efficiencies of scale, and centralization of power. Just below the surface, fears of foreign intervention or manipulation persist as well. The party continues to justify its dictatorship by reference to alleged achievements in the August 1945 Revolution and anti-French resistance. Critics of the party sometimes harken back to the relatively open press of 1945–46, the January 1946 national elections, the Democratic Party, and the November 1946 constitution, yet they lack detailed knowledge of events.

My debts to friends, colleagues, archivists, librarians, research assistants, and students in regard to this book extend back almost half a century, starting in 1965 with staff at the Institute of Ancient History in Saigon who let me photograph a 1945 newspaper. From 1969, I had help and guidance in Paris from Georges Boudarel, Pierre Brocheux, Daniel Hémery, and Christian Rageau. From 1974, members of the Institute of History in Hanoi shared publications, ideas, and personal contacts—above all Dương Trung Quốc, more recently a vigorous member of Vietnam's National Assembly. In 1983, I made my first of seven trips to the archives in Aix-en-Provence, where François Bordes, Lucette Vachier, and Sylvie Clair gave me unparalleled access and encouragement. During the 1990s, Phan Huy Lê, head of the Vietnam Studies Center at Hanoi National University, introduced me to his history colleagues and sponsored my entry to the Vietnam National Archives, Center No. 3. Phạm Thế Khang, director of Vietnam's National Library, facilitated my multiple sojourns among 1945–1946 periodicals and resistance-era monographs.

Many colleagues have graciously loaned or given me publications, forwarded documents, and provided valuable source leads, including Đào Hùng, Phan Huy Lê, Phạm Khiêm Ích, the late Đặng Phong, Andrew Hardy, Christopher Goscha, Stein Tønnesson, Đinh Xuân Lâm, Nguyễn Văn Kự, Ben Kerkvliet, Hùynh Kim Khánh, Christophe Dutrône, Howard Daniel III, John Kleinen, Tony Reid, Phạm Mai Hùng, Rob Hurle, François Guillemot, Paul Sager, Michael Di Gregorio, and Martin Grossheim. On each visit to Hanoi I walked up Tin Street, climbed three flights of stairs, and was invited by Trần Tấn Cảnh, owner of the Hiệu Sách Cũ bookshop, to drink strong tea, chat, and peruse stacks of publications.

Jennifer Brewster, Đỗ Quý Tấn, Nguyễn Thanh, Nguyễn Thị Hương Giang, Đỗ Thiện, Nguyễn Điền, and Nguyễn Thị Hồng Hạnh gave excellent support as research assistants in Canberra, Paris, and Hanoi. Their notes will fuel writing projects beyond this book.

William Turley and Stein Tønnesson read each chapter draft as it appeared, reacting promptly and constructively. Bùi Đình Thanh gave me verbal observations on chapters each time we met in Hanoi. Portions of the manuscript were read by Ben Kerkvliet, Mark Selden, Marilyn Larew, Nile Thompson, and John Spragens Jr. David Elliott and Christopher Goscha provided valuable comments after reviewing the manuscript for the University of California Press.

Hoàng Oanh Collins took each of my chapter penscripts and with professional flair turned them into sterling typescripts. She handled subsequent drafts with equal precision. Without her experience with Vietnamese fonts it would have been impossible to employ full diacritics in the text and endnotes of this book.

During 2005–8 I received a grant from the Australian Research Council; I am thankful to our division administrator, Dorothy MacIntosh, for taking care of its procedural intricacies on my behalf. Karina Pelling, of Cartographic & GIS Services, Australia National University, created the two vital maps that follow this preface, using data collected by me over the decades. At the University of California Press, Niels Hooper, Kim Hogeland, and Mari Coates piloted the book through its many requisite stages. I especially appreciated the professional care and friendly disposition of my assigned copyeditor, Caroline Knapp.

Chapter 3, "Defense," is a revised and expanded version of my contribution to Mark Atwood Lawrence and Fredrik Logevall, editors, *The First Vietnam War* (Cambridge, MA: Harvard University Press, 2007). Part of Chapter 6, "Material Dreams and Realities," appeared originally in Christopher E. Goscha and Benoît De Tréglode, editors, *Naissance d'un État-Parti: Le Viêt Nam depuis 1945* (Paris: Les Indes Savantes, 2004). Both are used by permission.

A few words about terminology. To make the text more friendly to nonspecialists, I employ English translations of Vietnamese organizational names, administrative titles, and the like, while providing the original Vietnamese in parentheses on first mention. One exception is "Việt Minh," introduced above. Although formally an organization established in 1941 by the ICP, the term "Việt Minh" came to be used spontaneously by hundreds if not thousands of local revolutionary, anticolonial groups in late 1945. To complicate matters, the ICP, following its "self-dissolution" in November, employed "Việt Minh" as a cover name to signify patriotic commitment above and beyond party affiliation. The Việt Minh General Headquarters (Tổng Bộ Việt Minh) issued public statements as if it was in charge, but actually left the job of gaining control over local Việt Minh groups to the underground ICP. Among the public at large, "Việt Minh" gradually became conflated with the DRV state. The French called their opponents "*les Vietminh*," never the DRV or National Guard. I try to alert readers to which meaning of Việt Minh I am referring.

I have chosen not to homogenize regional designations, since the way in which these geographical terms were employed tells us something about the times and the people involved. Readers thus need to know from the outset that: Tonkin=Bắc Bộ=northern Vietnam; Annam=Trung Bộ=central Vietnam; and Cochinchina=Nam Bộ=southern Vietnam. When it comes to provincial identifications, we are fortunate that after four decades of renaming provinces and creating new ones, the Socialist Republic of Vietnam in 1989–96 decided to return mostly to the provincial names and borders of 1945. Most Vietnamese place names come in two separated syllables, for example, Lạng Sơn, Nam Định, Đà Nẵng, Nha Trang, and Cần Thơ. However, I conflate syllables in the following place names: Vietnam, Hanoi, Haiphong, Saigon, and Dalat.

Some Vietnamese personalities in this era employed a variety of aliases. I have used the name by which an individual was best known in the late 1940s, be it his or her given name, pen name, code name, or revolutionary pseudonym.[5] I introduce each individual by full name, then follow Vietnamese practice by referring to a person's given name rather than surname. Thus, within a given paragraph Huỳnh Thúc Kháng is identified subsequently as Kháng. One exception is Hồ Chí Minh, who is always Hồ and never Minh. Individuals with no middle name, for example Phan Anh or Trường Chinh, are allowed to keep their full names.

Throughout this period, the Bank of Indochina (BIC) piastre continued to dominate Vietnamese as well as French financial calculations and transactions. One piastre (1$00BIC) was valued at seventeen francs in late 1945. One franc was worth less than one cent American, and the franc declined further for years thereafter. When the DRV began to issue its own money in 1946 it hoped one *đồng* would be exchanged for one piastre, but that proved a chimera. Many DRV documents use *đồng* to mean the BIC piastre without spelling this out, which creates a monetary minefield for unwary researchers. With this awareness, I reserve *đồng* for the few values that are explicitly in DRV currency

As I strove to impart structure to this book, I was reminded of a particular type of bark cloth I came upon in Đắk Tô (Kontum province) in 1962, with rough strips that were dark and light, wide and thin. My nine chapters here constitute the warp, while the ideas, beliefs, and behavior of Vietnamese during these sixteen months make up the weft. Terms like "independence," "nation," "the people," "struggle," "revolution," "reactionary," and "resistance" appear in different circumstances. Some preoccupations vanish or go underground, perhaps to emerge a decade or five decades later.

When the Vietnam History Association organized a seminar in Hanoi in 1995 to discuss my *Vietnam 1945* book, the passage to which a number of participants took exception was the assertion that "the only truth in history is that there are no historical truths, only an infinite number of experiences." By contrast, only one person criticized me for underrating the role of the ICP in events, while several others chose to recount personal experiences in 1945 that supported my argument, without saying so explicitly. Today, younger generations in Vietnam seem less wedded to historical truths, more willing to question dogma. I look forward to lively discussions.

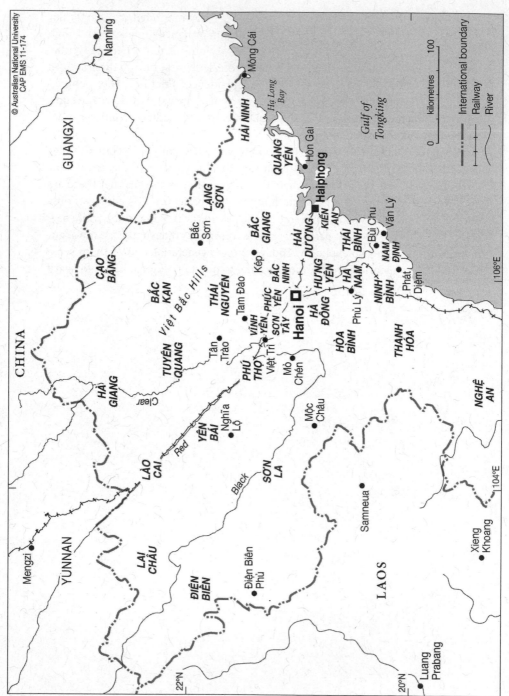

© Australian National University
CAP EMS 11-174

MAP 1. Northern Vietnam.

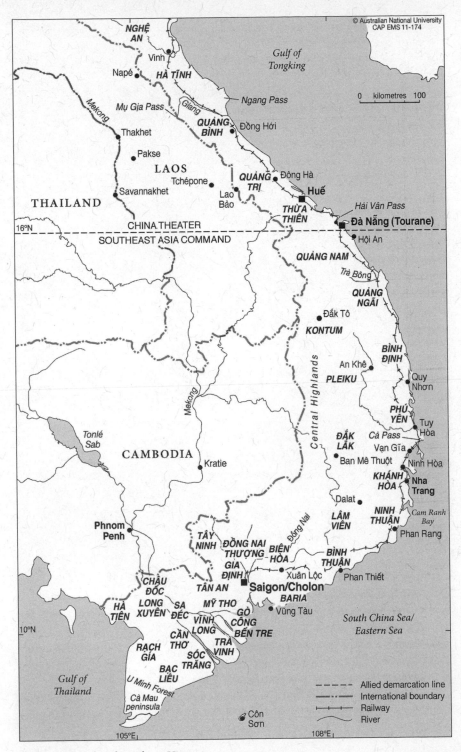

MAP 2. Central and southern Vietnam.

Introduction

This book is about the birth of the Vietnamese nation amidst war and revolution. The story bears comparison with the American Revolution (or War of Independence), although I don't pursue that line of inquiry here. Proclaimed in Hanoi in early September 1945, the Democratic Republic of Vietnam (DRV) rapidly gained popular support. However, the provisional government had to deal immediately with centrifugal revolutionary impulses, the arrival of Chinese Nationalist troops in the north, and British-French units driving DRV adherents out of Saigon. No foreign government recognized the DRV's existence. Food deficits threatened a repeat of the terrible famine of early 1945. The army was miniscule. Some citizens remained more focused on settling old scores and seizing property than becoming part of a national movement. Yet the DRV not only survived these challenges but proceeded to mobilize millions of citizens to defend the country against French reconquest.

In 1945, Vietnam possessed about twenty million inhabitants, at least 90 percent of whom lived in the countryside. Vietnam's long north-south configuration and mountainous backbone created substantial problems of communication and political integration. Earlier, France had chosen to establish the three distinct administrations of Tonkin, Annam, and Cochinchina, which it then combined with Cambodia and Laos to form the Indochina Federation. Vietnamese patriots vehemently rejected those demarcations, arguing that 80 percent of the population of Vietnam (Tonkin-Annam-Cochinchina) spoke the same language, and independent Vietnamese monarchies had for centuries ruled territories that crossed the later French borders. They also pointed proudly to recent enhancements in Vietnamese political and social consciousness, culminating in the upheavals of summer 1945.

France in 1945 refused to concede the existence of a Vietnamese identity, much less acknowledge a state of Vietnam. Across the French political spectrum there was agreement that French sovereignty over Indochina had to be reasserted, if necessary by force. With few exceptions, French analysts viewed August 1945 as the work of disgruntled intellectuals, former political prisoners, and social outcasts. For six months no French government statement contained the terms "Vietnam" or "Vietnamese." The unrecognized DRV was labeled the "Annamite government," while DRV adherents were "Annamite rebels." In March 1946, France did recognize the "Republic of Vietnam" as a free state within the Indochina Federation and French Union, yet it proved impossible in subsequent months for leaders of France and the DRV to agree on what this formula meant in practice.

With the advent of full-scale hostilities at the end of 1946, French authorities concentrated on neutralizing armed rebellion against their constituted authority. French forces had complete control of the air and almost complete control of the sea. President Hồ Chí Minh declared nationwide resistance against "French reactionary colonialists," until such time as Vietnam was completely independent and reunified. Hồ did not exclude the possibility of a favorable change in government in Paris, but meanwhile it was "20 million [Vietnamese] against 100,000 colonialists," with the former "bound to win."[1] The equation was not nearly that clear cut, as Hồ surely realized. And no one imagined that thirty years of sacrifice, death, and destruction lay ahead.

REVOLUTION

On news of Japan's surrender in mid-August 1945, millions of Vietnamese joined in a grand festival of revolution. Popular exuberance and patriotic euphoria swept the countryside as well as cities and towns. Farmers who had never ventured beyond the nearest marketplace now leaped at the opportunity to march on their province seat and beyond. With French colonial rule eliminated earlier by the Japanese, the Vietnamese monarchy ended, and an independent Vietnam declared, people wanted to make their own break with the past too. Liberation meant freeing the country, but it also meant trashing symbols of the evil past, seizing property from alleged traitors, humiliating village notables, and punishing gamblers, opium dealers, and prostitutes. It justified sons and daughters in leaving home to join new organizations, despite opposition from parents and clan elders. In some localities revolution also involved violent contests for power, kidnappings, and revenge killings. Everywhere it was young people who took the initiative, speaking directly, ignoring taboos, refusing to worry about personal safety, exuding confidence. Alongside the iconoclasm and bravado there was a longing to identify with something certain, to find new order within oneself and throughout the universe. Youthful heroics and the wish for order came together in the rush to join militia *(tự vệ)* units, where inventiveness and bravery counted for more than social origin, schooling, or wealth.[2]

Revolution *(cách mạng)* had been debated vigorously in Vietnam since the 1911 Chinese Revolution. Broadly speaking, two ideas took shape among the intelligentsia: First, we must be masters in our own house of Vietnam; and second, our house is in desperate need of improvement, if not demolition and rebuilding. In 1929–30 and again in 1940, communist and nationalist revolutionaries tried separately to overthrow the French colonial regime, with disastrous results both times. Meanwhile, proponents of wholesale modernization who had put their hopes in Franco-Vietnamese cooperation became increasingly pessimistic. By 1940, advocates of an "antifeudal" revolution accepted the necessity of national independence. During the Pacific War, Japan tantalized Vietnamese anticolonialists with talk of independence, only to stand aside when the French cracked down on nascent opposition. As Japan's military fortunes waned, people paid more attention to propaganda from pro-Allied organizations. The Vietnam Nationalist Party (Việt Nam Quốc Dân Đảng) preached political independence, yet had almost nothing to say about socioeconomic or cultural transformations. The Indochinese Communist Party (ICP) also put independence first, via the pronouncements of its front group, the Vietnam Independence League (Việt Minh). However, Việt Minh advocacy of a national liberation revolution was understood by Vietnamese intellectuals versed in Marxist dialectics to mean the first step on the road to socialist revolution. Although Việt Minh statements downgraded class struggle and deferred redistribution of land to poor peasants, they promised to achieve other antifeudal goals under the rubric of "new democracy" *(tân dân chủ)*.

August 1945 saw a spontaneous welling up of social revolutionary sentiments and behavior in Vietnam, whatever the intentions of leaders of the political insurrection. In some rural localities, tax records were burned, landlords thrown out of their homes, employees of the former colonial regime beaten up and incarcerated, and alleged counterrevolutionaries killed. In the cities some French civilians were molested and their houses pillaged under the placid gaze of Japanese soldiers. Restraints on non-state violence which had already frayed during earlier months now stretched to the breaking point. At mass meetings around the country, speakers celebrated revolutionary justice and equality, the abolition of colonial taxes, confiscation of French properties, and the end of exploitation of man by man. For many participants, such meetings were ecstatic, life-changing experiences. Subsequent demonstrations could turn ugly. News of mob violence spread widely, striking fear among people who had yet to witness any such behavior. Some instigators of August takeovers tried to reason with rampaging youths, especially by arguing that any internal Vietnamese chaos would be exploited by foreign powers. ICP newspapers accused anarchists and enemy agents of fomenting divisions and disorder. Nonetheless, the revolutionary crowd remained a vital political weapon for Việt Minh organizers. The art was to focus mass energy on objectives identified by government or Việt Minh leaders. Later, participants recalled nostalgically the passion, idealism, and high expectations of the early revolution, often in implicit contrast to the frustrations and disappointments that followed. Some individuals came to realize they had played their revolutionary roles by chance, not by choice or design.

Vietnamese revolutionaries believed they were driving events forward collectively, yet sometimes had to acknowledge that events were driving them. There was a sense of revolutionary destiny, but in reality no guiding hand. People often placed their hopes in Hồ Chí Minh, yet he understood he could not determine the future. Hồ wanted to avoid being painted into a policy corner, meanwhile developing options and choosing favorable moments to act in the quest for independence and modernity. I hope to convey the uncertainty and contingency, as well as the coherency and momentum, of revolutionary events in 1945–46.

STATE FORMATION

When Hồ Chí Minh asserted to the Hanoi crowd on 2 September 1945 that Vietnam "has become a free and independent country," he was making a profession of faith rather than a statement of fact. Hồ insisted that France had lost any claim to be "protector" of Indochina's inhabitants by its record of eighty years of crass exploitation, plus proceeding to sell the territory twice to Japan. Nonetheless, appreciating that a new state required not only commitment from citizens but confirmation by other states of its right to exist, Hồ called upon the Allied powers to recognize the Democratic Republic of Vietnam in the spirit of the 1943 Teheran and May 1945 San Francisco conferences. Soon afterward, when French troops arrived with British forces in Saigon, and the United States and China moved to recognize French sovereignty over Indochina, Hồ understood that the DRV state would have to survive under constant threat of attack and dismemberment. He hoped for the best, a mutually advantageous Franco-Vietnamese treaty, but instructed his lieutenants to plan for the worst—a war in which the DRV would have to survive without allies.

At the same Independence Day meeting in Hanoi on 2 September, Võ Nguyên Giáp, the new interior minister, foreshadowed democratic elections to a national assembly, which would then devise a constitution and provide a legal government. The army would be developed, the economy rebuilt, and education given higher priority. Giáp warned that such goals required "loans, subscriptions, and income taxes," a prospect offensive to many revolutionaries. More openly than Hồ, Giáp appealed to the United States and China for support, but then emphasized that if no help was forthcoming the Vietnamese nation, united, would have to go it alone. Under such circumstances, Giáp warned ominously, "division, doubt, and apathy are all a betrayal of the country." Nguyễn Lương Bằng, representing the Việt Minh General Headquarters, spoke briefly on the need for unity and struggle. Paraphrasing Lenin (without attribution), Bằng asserted that retaining power was more difficult than gaining it in the first place. Taking a more intractable position than either Hồ or Giáp, Bằng insisted that it would be necessary to fight the French, and that Vietnam "should not rely (ỷ lại) on anyone else."[3]

The kind of state aspired to by educated Vietnamese possessed a defined territory, hard borders, a centralized hierarchy of power, a common identity and culture, and, above all, undivided sovereignty. This state model was communicated to regional and province revolutionary committees in a blitz of provisional DRV government decrees issued during the first three weeks of September. However, no decree announced the territorial and maritime boundaries of Vietnam. Only a mid-October national election decree that listed participating provinces and cities offered official guidance. No DRV claims were made on neighboring territories, nor was there any mention of possible claims by neighbors on Vietnamese territory.

All outgoing official correspondence began with the new letterhead: "Democratic Republic of Vietnam. Independence, Freedom, Happiness." Within weeks, almost all incoming messages contained that identical heading, and within a few months citizen petitions and even private letters followed suit. The government ordered all Vietnamese employees of the former colonial state to remain in position, and most complied. Members of the former Civil Guard were encouraged to join the new national army as individuals, not units. ICP members took custody of the Sûreté (police) headquarters in Hanoi, but found that most Vietnamese staff had vanished. The new Ministry of Information and Propaganda ordered all newspaper and book publishers to continue submitting copy to former colonial censors. Post, Telegraph and Telephone (PTT) personnel stayed on the job, enabling the new state authorities to communicate with most localities above the sixteenth parallel. Radio Hanoi provided a separate channel for transmitting edicts and other official messages, as well as broadcasting regular news bulletins. The "wiring" of the colonial state had largely survived, to be used by new masters.

The DRV's strong preference for centralized government was the result of ten centuries of monarchical rule, eighty years of French statism, and twenty years of intellectual fascination with the Soviet Union, Italy, and Germany. Montesquieu's arguments in favor of separating executive, legislative, and judicial powers had been canvassed earlier by Vietnamese literati, then largely ignored by the new intelligentsia. Historians knew that monarchs had been compelled to make significant concessions to Vietnam's tortuous geography, ethnic differences, and locally powerful clans, yet such complications were regarded by modernists as "feudal remnants" to be stamped out by the independent nation-state. As we shall see, the central DRV authorities did achieve impressive policy momentum in late 1945. Three regional committees also functioned, although the southern committee was forced to flee Saigon for the countryside in late September. Province committees became the linchpin of the DRV administrative hierarchy. The National Assembly elections promised by Võ Nguyên Giáp duly took place in early January 1946, contributing to state legitimacy. However, elections to provincial and commune people's councils took longer, and the councils often failed to exercise authority over administrative committees as intended. On the military front, a high command and general staff headquarters was established in Hanoi, soon to be followed by specialized communications, intelligence, medical, and officer-training units. Military logistics remained chaotic, with regular army units often obliged to rely on province committees and Việt Minh groups for food, shelter, and clothing

Proud of having a central Vietnamese government—and anxious not to be accused of obstructionism or worse—local committees tried to understand and apply most of the edicts coming from Hanoi. This became apparent in early September after Hanoi angrily ordered all committees to stop illegal assaults and confiscations, and the number of such incidents dropped off significantly. A month later, facing the threat of another major famine, the DRV issued production and distribution instructions to committees, also reprinted in Việt Minh newspapers. Although food riots seemed imminent at one point, and starvation was not prevented entirely, the terrible mass deaths that had taken place one year earlier were not repeated. By May 1946, most local committees could report a bountiful rice crop about to be harvested. On other policy fronts however, district, commune, or village committees sometimes managed to ignore, evade, or selectively apply orders from the center. Punishments were often meted out locally without reference to central laws or judicial oversight.

During 1945–46, ideas about the nation which had excited the Vietnamese intelligentsia during the 1920s and 1930s spread among the public at large. Most important was patriotism, which meant loving one's land and people as a whole, as opposed to traditional fidelity to king and parents. A true patriot was willing to risk his life and personal happiness for "the nation" (quốc gia; nước), a concept which incorporated both "the people" (quốc dân) and "the state" (chính quyền; nhà nước). More emotionally, the nation became "the Fatherland" (Tổ Quốc). Mystical notions like "unity of hearts" (đồng tâm) and "great unity" (đại đồng) were also freely invoked. For several years people enjoyed calling each other "comrade" (đồng chí), a usage reminiscent of citoyen in 1789 France and tovarich in 1917 Russia. Finally, there was the term dân tộc, a neologism meant to conjure up a centuries-old Vietnamese peoplehood which was ethnic and cultural-linguistic in content. Simultaneously, *dân tộc* was placed in front of the names of dozens of ethnic groups (Nùng, Thái, Mường, Rhadé, etc.) who were expected to become (minority) members of the nation of Vietnam.

The legal concept of sovereignty, so important to the Westphalian state system long dominant in Europe, was unknown to most Vietnamese. Several lawyers trained in France took responsibility for explaining to the public what sovereignty meant, and how the DRV must gain international recognition of Vietnam's unity and territorial integrity. When French and Vietnamese representatives sat down to explore parameters for a peaceful resolution of their differences, it became painfully clear that both sides would need to accept something less than full sovereignty. Given sufficient time, a formula might have been found, but meanwhile the question of Cochinchina (Nam Bộ) ate like a cancer into relations between the DRV and France. For Vietnamese patriots, French aggression in Cochinchina in September 1945 and the subsequent refusal by Paris to acknowledge that Nam Bộ was an integral part of Vietnam made them suspicious of the entire negotiating process. From there it was only a short step to regarding negotiations as a mere tactical expedient, a means to gain time in which to improve the DRV's fighting capabilities.

Members of the ICP had played key roles in the August 1945 insurrection, and the ICP's Standing Bureau worked hard to translate that influence into real political power. Indeed, the Communist Party's goal was to control the entire Vietnamese nation, both people and state. Following Soviet precedent, the party would become the font of all power, authority, and legitimacy. These ambitions were no secret to politically alert Vietnamese, and they continued to be espoused by some party members in print after Hồ Chí Minh instructed the ICP to declare its dissolution in November. The Vietnam Nationalist Party roundly condemned the ICP's Leninist dictatorial ambitions, yet it too displayed similar proclivities if not abilities. Noncommunists, who made up the vast majority of DRV civil officials and military officers in 1946, tended to admire the discipline and self-sacrifice of their ICP peers while discounting their expertise and ideology. ICP members working inside specific civil or military bodies often identified with the needs of that institution rather than paying close attention to party pronouncements. The ICP's greatest advantage was that members in different localities could communicate and plan secretly with each other without being accused of disloyalty or treason—a privilege that no other political party could exercise by late 1946 without risking arrest.

The committee hierarchy which emerged in late 1945 came to define the DRV state, and remains in operation today. Tensions between the center and localities persisted, sometimes to the system's advantage. Local committees gave the state a depth and resilience that no amount of top-level edicts could provide. On the other hand, without instructions from above, committees might well have marched in quite different directions, cancelled each other out, or even fought each other. Local-level vitality imposed certain de facto limitations on central power, much to the irritation of many central leaders. When full-scale hostilities with France exploded in late 1946, it was the local committees that saved the DRV from extinction. "The Center" (Trung ương) was unable to communicate with most localities throughout 1947, yet more than a year of prior experience gave members of province, district, and communal committees the confidence to continue basic state operations. By 1948 the hierarchy was largely restored, although contact with the south (Nam Bộ) remained episodic. The DRV regular army went through a similar process, mostly disaggregating to the local level in 1947, recombining to battalion and occasional regimental size in 1948, establishing one infantry division in late 1949, and forming artillery, engineering, and other specialized units with Chinese assistance in 1950.

WAR

Amidst the revolutionary euphoria of August 1945, Vietnamese assumed they were leaving war behind, and certainly did not anticipate that they were about to face a new war. The fighting in Saigon in late September sent angry shockwaves throughout the country. Suddenly the eager rhetoric about defending Vietnamese independence took on dire implications. Several thousand young men promptly headed south with no idea of what combat entailed, only to be shot down or compelled to flee in disarray. In the Mekong delta, other resistance groups had to abandon one town after another to advancing French forces. In late January 1946, the French encircled more than a thousand armed Vietnamese ten kilometers west of Nha Trang, then bombarded them with naval guns. Survivors fled into the forest. At this point the French decided to halt their ground offensive in favor of negotiating with Chinese Nationalist authorities for a return to the north (Tonkin) via the port of Haiphong. Amidst all these debacles for the DRV, the northern press insisted on claiming a succession of Vietnamese victories, although any reader with access to a map could judge otherwise. After the 6 March Franco-Vietnamese Preliminary Accord reduced the chances of early French attack above the sixteenth parallel, Nam Bộ became the symbol of nationwide resistance to French attempts to recolonize Vietnam. When southern DRV adherents gradually worked out tactics capable of sustaining rural and jungle resistance despite French assaults, this gave the government in Hanoi confidence that forced evacuation from the capital could be weathered, and the fight carried on from the hills and countryside if required.

The reality of war in the south and threat of war in the north changed the nature of the Vietnamese revolution and the DRV state. Aspirations to transform society, end exploitation, develop the economy, and create a new culture had to defer to protection of the new political order against enemies both foreign and domestic. The antifeudal agenda was never abandoned publicly, and some modernizing components were subsumed within the anticolonial agenda, notably literacy and public hygiene, but in practice the vision of Vietnam catching up with advanced societies had to be deferred indefinitely. War and revolution fed upon each other, heightening suspicions, escalating fears, making life (and death) quite unpredictable. The dichotomies of we/they, friend/enemy, and patriot/traitor dominated public discourse. Vietnam had no one in the world to call on for help. France appeared to be pursuing the traditional strategy of divide-and-rule, first establishing the "Republic of Cochinchina," then announcing several "autonomous countries" in areas inhabited by ethnic minorities. The number of Vietnamese serving in French forces increased each year. Eventually, France reached agreement with former emperor Bảo Đại on formation of the Associated State of Vietnam as competition to the DRV. Civil war now intersected with the war between the DRV and France. In early 1950, the Cold War was added to this equation, as China and the Soviet Union recognized the DRV, and the United States and Great Britain recognized the Associated State of Vietnam. The DRV now had friends, at a price yet to be determined.

War made harsh demands on Vietnam's economy. During the Pacific War, Indochina had already taken on many characteristics of a war economy, including regulatory edicts, rationing, scarcities, and a black market. Inured to the state exercising minute economic controls, many Vietnamese were not surprised when the fledgling DRV government announced similar regulations for distribution of rice and other essential commodities. However, when the government decided to continue most former colonial taxes, this met with widespread complaints and noncompliance. A patchwork regime emerged, with provinces trying to collect some taxes but not others, depending on local circumstances.

The alternative was for the government to ask people for voluntary contributions. National defense proved the most convincing rationale, as youth teams moved from house to house seeking donations of rice or money, assuring citizens that contributions would go to purchasing firearms and feeding combatants. The government launched two national fundraising campaigns to protect Vietnam's independence and to support the Nam Bộ resistance. Local committees sometimes retained a portion of the proceeds for their own purposes. With one committee or another approaching citizens every few weeks to ask that they demonstrate their patriotism in cash or kind, people gradually became less forthcoming. Receipt slips were displayed to prove prior donations. In April 1946, the government declared a defense contribution, to be collected from every citizen between eighteen and sixty-five years of age. One key objective was to remove the need for regular army units to obtain food directly from local citizens, a practice which had raised the traditional spectre of soldiers living off the land. By one means or another, civilian committees took responsibility for feeding the military.

With chances of a Franco-Vietnamese diplomatic settlement sliding away in late 1946, DRV and Việt Minh leaders tried to condition the populace to protracted conflict. Every citizen had wartime responsibilities, and the total contribution would be greater than the sum of its parts. While few overt comparisons were made in print, it seems clear that Vietnamese writers drew inspiration from the French Revolution, a story familiar to all former high school students. Colonial textbooks had focused on the storming of the Bastille and later Napoleonic glories, but Vietnamese intellectuals readily found alternative accounts that stressed class conflict, the contributions of Robespierre, or the role of the *levée en masse* in the birth of modern warfare. The term "people's war" had been invented by Clausewitz during the Napoleonic wars, but most Vietnamese saw it first in articles about Chinese Red Army operations during the anti-Japanese resistance. In 1946, a cascade of books and articles appeared in Vietnam celebrating the Soviet people's victory over German invaders, which writers used to bolster confidence in the anti-French resistance.

MASS MOBILIZATION

Revolution, state formation, and war intersected to produce the largest, most intense mobilization of human resources ever seen in Vietnam. Ordinary Vietnamese worked harder and longer, turned over a higher proportion of their produce, transported more supplies to designated points, and joined in more political campaigns than anyone could have imagined before. Most citizens also denied information or succor to the enemy. Young men strove to shoot a rifle, absorb basic tactics, and test their mettle in battle. Young women sought military training as well, only to find themselves assigned jobs as cooks, nurses, clerks, runners, or spies. In Vietnam's thousands of villages, meanwhile, men, women and children participated in a range of new groups, each meant to appeal to a particular constituency, heighten patriotic commitment, and provide practical support to the resistance.

Today, so far away from these events, it is hard to convey the idealism, romanticism and sheer energy of the Vietnamese generation of 1945 as it confronted the future. One point of entry is the vibrant press of September 1945 to December 1946. As mentioned earlier, scores of new newspapers appeared across the country during this time, generally instigated by intellectuals in their early thirties who had come to prominence during the heady Popular Front era of the late 1930s. Most reporters were in their twenties, and the reading audience included literate teenagers. While almost every paper declared support for the DRV, not all were affiliated with Việt Minh groups, and those identifying themselves as Việt Minh showed significant editorial variations. During these sixteen months about eight hundred books and booklets were published as well, exhibiting a wider range of content than the newspapers. Publications often were passed from one reader to another or placed on a shelf for group members to peruse. More importantly, public speakers, roving propaganda teams, and convenors of small group discussions routinely relied on the press for their verbal ammunition. With up to 90 percent of the populace still unable to read, mass mobilization could only be advanced by myriad oral encounters.

While the press of the late 1940s and surviving archival materials can tell us a great deal about what the literate minority was thinking, how do we understand the attitudes of the farmers, artisans, laborers, and traders who made up the vast majority of Vietnam's population? Something can be learned from thousands of citizen petitions, many dictated by illiterates to local scribes, and forwarded to President Hồ Chí Minh or DRV ministries. For the most part, however, we must depend on what journalists and government personnel wrote about "the people," whether collectively or more usefully in their descriptions of encounters with specific individuals or small groups. Even my most skeptical reading of available evidence leads me to conclude that most Vietnamese believed in national independence and wanted to contribute in some way to making that independence a reality. Voluntarist engagement was highest during the August 1945 insurrection and following months, when people not only went to a host of meetings and donated to the cause, but joined associations that required focused effort. Taking part in those groups brought a sense of pride, honor, and solidarity. Even individuals who felt foreboding or revulsion towards the revolution proceeded to enroll in national salvation associations out of self-protection or hopes that the nation would shift course.

For some people the idealism and enthusiasm of August 1945 persisted for years, for others it faded during 1946. Individual emotional investment in "the nation" soon ranged from continuing passionate commitment to watery fidelity. Spontaneous voluntarism gave way to peer pressure, obedience to instructions, and conditioning to the new revolutionary order. Enjoyment of the moment of liberation was replaced by concentration on what needed to be done. Given the continuing revolutionary context, citizens had to prove their patriotic credentials again and again, whatever their private thoughts. To drop out of the independence struggle meant ostracism, harassment, and eventually punishment. Subsequently there was the option of moving to a French-controlled town, yet even there underground Việt Minh members would come routinely to collect "donations" and warn against collaboration with the

enemy. Those who ignored such warnings knew that their families in the countryside might face trouble.

State building did not slow as voluntarism withered. Local committees expanded their ambit of responsibilities, nudging citizens to help the army and
police, the local militia, hungry compatriots, literacy teachers, and propaganda
teams. Each material contribution was small—characteristically, enough rice to
fill an empty condensed milk can—yet the cumulative drain was large for families enduring economic disruption and then wartime stringencies. Villagers also
billeted soldiers, sewed uniforms, stood guard, carried supplies, dug up roads to
inhibit enemy movement, and reported any suspicious behavior to the authorities. In the new revolutionary state, citizens were exhorted to advance beyond
mere compliance and periodic voting to active cooperation with committees, the
military, and the police. To meet wartime demands, local Việt Minh and government operations were subsequently combined to form "resistance-administration
committees" (ủy ban kháng chiến hành chính).

THE INDOCHINESE COMMUNIST PARTY

Vietnamese communists continue to insist that their party led the revolution
from 1930, planned and implemented the entire August 1945 insurrection, directed the DRV state from its inception, and masterminded the anti-French resistance. Available evidence does not support such assertions. In the summer of
1945, ICP leaders did indeed have a plan for insurrection and were making preparations, yet when the opportune moment came in mid-August the party lacked
the capacity to engineer widespread takeovers. Instead, unaffiliated youths took
the initiative on their own, often shouting Việt Minh slogans and waving the
Việt Minh flag, but otherwise acting according to local circumstances. The ICP,
with only five thousand members, many of whom had yet to make contact, had
no hope of controlling the DRV state. Instead, the party's small party Standing
Bureau, headed by Trường Chinh, concentrated first on placing senior communists in the central government, taking over the Hanoi police bureau, upgrading
the Cứu Quốc (National Salvation) newspaper as the central organ of the Việt
Minh, and liaising with ICP members in provincial people's committees. The
Standing Bureau also moved to resolve internal disputes within some party
branches, and began the difficult task of converting hundreds of self-styled Việt
Minh groups into organizations willing to accept central ICP authority.

In November 1945, the Standing Bureau suddenly announced the self-
dissolution of the ICP, to "destroy all misunderstandings, foreign and domestic"
that might hinder the liberation of Vietnam. Hồ Chí Minh had insisted on this
statement, designed to respond to Vietnam Nationalist Party charges that the
DRV was a front for communists, and to reduce the chances of Nationalist Chinese

usurpation. The party continued to function as before, except that its name was removed from the list of Việt Minh adherents and members were instructed to conduct party business secretly. This had the effect of reinforcing colonial-era clandestine behavior and making the party unaccountable to the government for its actions. In the name of the Association to Research Marxism in Indochina, Trường Chinh used the *Sự Thật (Truth)* weekly to communicate the party line openly, although it appears that copies failed to circulate beyond towns or very far down the coast. On hearing of the self-dissolution, many party members in central and southern Vietnam were left confused and demoralized for months.

In late May 1946, Việt Minh newspapers carried a statement by a list of public intellectuals declaring their intention to form a new Vietnam National Alliance (Hội Liên Hiệp Quốc Dân Việt Nam), to embrace each and every patriotic organization in the country. In reality, the ICP was putting all non-Việt Minh organizations on notice that they must join what became known as the Liên Việt or be labeled antipatriotic, even treasonous. The Vietnam Nationalist Party was the principal target, and soon its leaders had to decide whether to flee towards China, risk elimination, or submit to ICP direction camouflaged as Liên Việt participation. Political dissent now equaled disloyalty to the nation—except when ICP leaders themselves published criticisms of DRV policies. When Hồ Chí Minh called repeatedly for "unity, great unity," he had some ICP members in mind as well as more obvious sources of discord. By late 1946, the ICP had overcome most of its own internal divisions and brought the bulk of local Việt Minh branches under its control. However, ICP authority within the state apparatus was still quite limited.

It is questionable whether Hồ Chí Minh wanted the ICP to extend its power over every aspect of Vietnamese life in the manner of Stalin's Communist Party of the Soviet Union. However, Hồ's capacity to control the ICP was limited by the fact that he had been out of the country when men like Trường Chinh were consolidating their leadership. As we shall see, Hồ did impose his will during the volatile days of March 1946, to the point of negating opposition from some ICP leaders. But no sooner had Hồ departed for France on 31 May than the party began taking actions that impinged on DRV government operations and had the effect of narrowing policy options. When Hồ finally returned on 20 October, he had barely been briefed on intervening events and taken part in the second session of the National Assembly when the French Army attacked DRV units in Haiphong on 20 November. During the tense days of mid-December, when decisions about going to war or not were being debated vigorously, it remains unclear whether Hồ had the last say.

During 1945–46 individual ICP members participated in local committees and militia groups, but because communication with the Standing Bureau in Hanoi was so infrequent they relied more on instructions via civil or military channels. Party members high in civil and military hierarchies rarely took part in Standing Bureau activities. Importantly, there was no ICP central committee. Towards the end of 1946, the Standing Bureau did insinuate itself into the state decisionmaking process. After both the DRV central government and the ICP Standing Bureau took refuge in the hills north of Hanoi, Hồ Chí Minh seems deliberately to have conducted government affairs without routinely consulting the Standing Bureau.

HỒ CHÍ MINH AS NATIONAL ICON

So desperate was the popular need in 1945 for a Vietnamese national leader that a number of individuals other than Hồ Chí Minh could have filled that role. Hồ was almost completely unknown when he stepped up to the microphone in Ba Đình square on 2 September. Word had swept through Hanoi that an elderly patriot headed the new government. Some said he had roamed the world in search of enlightenment and ways to expel the French colonialists. Hồ chose to present himself to the people in a faded Sun Yat-sen jacket, deliberately eschewing either the traditional Vietnamese black tunic and turban or a Western suit and tie. His accent revealed that he was from Nghệ An province in Trung Bộ. The text of the independence declaration which Hồ read was concise and devoid of Sino-Vietnamese rhetorical flourishes. There was an air of mystery about this gentleman that allowed people to imagine their own ideal leader of the new Vietnam.

Hồ Chí Minh spoke over Voice of Vietnam on occasion, but realized that the paucity of radio receivers meant that few people would hear him even if the broadcast was announced in advance. At large meetings he employed a microphone and loudspeaker skillfully, but preferred to engage with smaller groups, asking individuals about their families, encouraging them to keep the faith, to work harder for the cause. He enjoyed walking amidst a crowd of ordinary citizens, establishing personal rapport, much to the concern of his security escort. Hồ's surprise visits to government bureaus and army units became legendary. On an average day, half a dozen delegations from the provinces might come to President Hồ's office, present him with simple gifts, perhaps receive an autographed photo in return. Hồ made a point of passing received gifts on to other deserving persons, thus promoting a symbolic chain of reciprocity.

Far more people encountered Hồ Chí Minh indirectly, through stories communicated by word of mouth or through his proclamations and homilies in the press. While the content of Hồ's written pronouncements owed something to Sun Yat-sen, he kept the text simple, brief, and often aimed at a specific audience. Citizens who could not read savored the photos and ink drawings of Hồ printed in newspapers or posted on bulletin boards. Việt Minh groups gave photos of Hồ to high achievers, but the same images could also be purchased in the marketplace. Large paintings of Hồ were auctioned to wealthy citizens at public fund-raising events. Hồ's image could be found on locally printed promissory notes even before the DRV Finance Ministry issued the first legal tender bearing his likeness. People of diverse backgrounds wanted someone pure, wise, and unself-ish to look up to. Clearly Hồ met Max Weber's concept of charisma, in which the impact of a visionary leader transforms the outlook of his followers and induces them to identify with him from a humble distance.

Hồ Chí Minh's prior Comintern identification as Nguyễn Ái Quốc was kept out of the press, although rank-and-file ICP members soon learned by word of mouth that the two persons were indeed one. Those who met Hồ found him politely un-willing to discuss his past. It was not until 1948 that a published account of Hồ's life began to circulate within the party, authored by Hồ himself under a pseudonym, and designed to evoke Hồ's simultaneous patriotic and communist credentials.

THE CONTEXT AND CONTENT OF THIS BOOK

While the First Indochina War (1945–54) has been the object of scores of serious accounts over the past half-century, this is the first study in English or French about formation of the DRV state, the lively newspaper culture, and the 1945–46 activities of Việt Minh groups and other organizations. In early 1954, Bernard Fall produced an admirable description of the DRV's structure and modus ope-randi at that moment, but offered readers little as to origins.[4] In Vietnamese, one can find thousands of articles recalling the excitement and mass engagement of 1945–46, but censors labor hard to enforce a single political line that assigns all agency to the Communist Party. Nguyễn Tố Uyên in 1999 managed to ignore a number of party shibboleths when he published a well-researched history of the DRV's formation.[5] Sadly Uyên died soon afterward, and his pathbreaking work in the DRV archives, national gazette (Công Báo), and 1945–46 periodicals has yet to be advanced by Vietnamese scholars.

Chapter 1 of this book describes the creation and early operations of the DRV government, from the central ministries to the three regional committees (north, center, south), then on to province, district, and commune committees below. The first few weeks saw scores of urgent decrees dispatched downward and local leaders sending lively reports upward. The whole system of official communica-tion and compliance could not have functioned without the participation of thousands of former colonial administrators and clerks, who nonetheless en-dured taunts from fellow citizens and soon had to find ways to survive minus traditional pay and allowances. Chapter 1 concludes with a description of the national and local elections meant to confirm the DRV's democratic legitimacy.

Chapter 2 portrays the first and second sessions of the DRV National Assem-bly. It also elucidates debates over a national constitution, and takes a close look at three centrally controlled institutions: the education system, the judiciary, and the postal system. From May 1946, the executive branch of the DRV increasingly finessed or appropriated legislative and judicial powers—a circumstance which continues to the present day. Chapter 2 concludes with a characterization of center-locality relations at the end of 1946.

In Chapter 3, I focus on DRV efforts to defend the fledgling nation from foreign assault.[6] These began with frantic, chaotic attempts to resist the British-French takeover of Cochinchina and Annam below the sixteenth parallel. Simultaneously, a command and general staff headquarters was being fashioned in Hanoi, and a variety of company-size units were made part of the regular army, or National Guard. This left hundreds of militia groups spending more time in revolutionary agitation than in preparing for combat. Over time local committees and the National Guard managed to gain authority over many of these groups, but the continuing autonomy of others jeopardized agreements negotiated between DRV and French representatives. As Franco-Vietnamese relations deteriorated in November 1946, the state was slow to prepare military and civilian echelons for guerrilla warfare.

Franco-Vietnamese negotiations during 1945–46 are the focus of chapter 4. Both sides took the quest for a peaceful settlement more seriously than many general histories would have us believe. Besides benchmark deliberations in Hanoi (March 1946), Dalat (April–May 1946), and Paris-Fontainebleau (July–September 1946), I describe the eye-opening visit of DRV parliamentarians to France in April 1946, and examine cease-fire encounters which took place as early as October 1945 and as late as December 1946. I also canvass Vietnamese press opinion on the vital issue of peace or war.

Chapter 5 depicts Vietnamese efforts to understand the world beyond their borders, and the desperate attempt to find foreign governments and peoples willing to support DRV independence. Highest priority went to courting the United States and Nationalist China, followed by South Asia and Southeast Asia, the Soviet Union, and the United Nations. All of these endeavors proved unsuccessful, and the DRV had no choice but to face the French alone. Yet both the government and many citizens continued to believe that foreign assistance would be forthcoming. They would have to wait three years or more.

Chapter 6 addresses Vietnam's tenuous economic circumstances in 1945–46, particularly the scarcity of food, conflicts over property, and the struggle to secure the means to build an army and keep the state functioning.[7] I look at taxes and donations; little-known attempts to continue the colonial salt, alcohol, and opium monopolies; and the gradual introduction of a DRV currency. Amidst tough demands of the moment and gathering war clouds, the government remained committed to an ambitious peacetime development agenda.

All revolutions assume the existence of internal enemies that must be outma-neuvered, isolated, and if necessary eliminated. In chapter 7, I examine the DRV's detention of alleged opponents, the construction of a feared security apparatus, and the state's cavalier attitude towards legal due process. I then look at how the authorities treated suspect political and religious groups, including Đại Việt par-ties, Trotskyists, the Vietnam Revolutionary League, the Vietnam Nationalist Party, and the Catholic Church.

The Indochinese Communist Party and the Việt Minh Front come under scru-tiny in chapter 8. I first examine how some ICP veterans worked outside the DRV government to try to achieve party control of the state, while local party members labored to reorganize and direct disparate Việt Minh groups. The role of the prin-cipal Việt Minh newspaper, Cứu Quốc, in propagating a single revolutionary line is given particular attention. I introduce the little-known Democratic Party, showing how it tried to project a separate identity under the Việt Minh umbrella. Contrary to almost all prior studies, I argue that the ICP Standing Bureau at the end of 1946 still did not have operational custody of either the DRV government or the national army, and suggest that Hồ Chí Minh was content with that state of affairs.

In chapter 9, I address mass mobilization, the single most important factor ex-plaining the DRV's capacity to withstand formidable foreign and domestic chal-lenges. No single ideological platform or government policy impelled millions of Vietnamese to become involved in the resistance that began on the streets of Sai-gon in September 1945. Rather, a volatile mix of patriotic sentiment, behavioral conditioning, and self-interest drove people to immerse themselves in a grueling crusade that lasted far longer than anyone could have imagined.

In a brief epilogue I describe how the DRV survived French Army attacks in 1947 and went on three years later to drive the enemy from the northern frontier region. Vietnam's revolution, state construction, and mass mobilization com-bined to prevent France from either defeating the DRV militarily or quelling the will to resist of millions of civilians. With the arrival of Chinese Communist forces at the border in late 1949 the DRV finally had a powerful ally. However, Paris and former emperor Bảo Đại had finally found a formula whereby an alter-native state could begin to function, with support from the United States. Viet-nam was now locked into the Cold War.

Forming the DRV Government

Amidst the revolutionary tumult of August 1945, a new Vietnamese government began to take shape. Although the young Việt Minh activists who took custody of public buildings in Hanoi on 19 August had almost no experience at governing, they knew enough to use the Post, Telegraph and Telephone (PTT) system to demand and receive allegiance from most northern province offices, and then to blitz the region with edicts demonstrating their authority. On 24 August, *Cứu Quốc (National Salvation)*, the principal Việt Minh newspaper, announced formation of a national "Provisional People's Government," composed almost entirely of ICP members. Hồ Chí Minh countermanded this decision when he arrived two days later, insisting that five ICP members step aside in favor of five hastily recruited "eminent personalities" *(nhân sĩ)*. This Provisional Government of the Democratic Republic of Vietnam met for the first time on 27 August and decided to fix Sunday, 2 September, as National Independence Day. It also released a statement that first identified the provisional government with the National People's Congress convened earlier by the Việt Minh in the hills north of Hanoi, then took a different tack, emphasizing Hồ's instructions to broaden Cabinet membership beyond the Việt Minh.[1]

SEPTEMBER DECREES

September set the tone of DRV administrative action for the next fifteen months. At least forty-one decrees were promulgated during the first three weeks.[2] Martial law was declared over Hanoi on 1 September, then lifted nine days later. Vietnamese citizens were prohibited from enrolling in the French armed forces, selling food to the French military, or otherwise becoming "lackeys" *(tay sai)* of the French. The police were given twenty-four hours to investigate suspects before turning them over to the courts. However, another decree authorized the police to dispatch persons "dangerous to the DRV" directly to detention camps *(trại an trí)*. Four existing political organizations were pronounced illegal (see chapter 7). Anyone wishing to mount a demonstration had to notify the relevant local people's committee twenty-four hours in advance. The royal mandarinal hierarchies for education, administration, and justice were abolished, while Mr. Vĩnh Thụy (formerly Emperor Bảo Đại) was appointed advisor to the DRV provisional government. The Empire of Vietnam's yellow standard with the red Chinese character *ly* was abolished, and the Việt Minh's red banner with its yellow star was declared the national flag.

Reflecting the government's parlous finances, another early edict contradicted prior Việt Minh promises of sweeping tax relief by retaining until further notice all colonial-era imposts, with the exception of the especially detested head tax. A national Department of Customs and Indirect Taxes was established; its responsibilities included supervision of continuing salt and opium monopolies, which Hồ Chí Minh and other anticolonialists had been denouncing for decades. Mindful that people might evade existing taxes, the government announced a new Independence Fund to encourage voluntary patriotic contributions (see chapter 6). The government also was authorized to requisition vital materials from private owners, with recompense offered at market prices. Longstanding restrictions on sale and transport of rice were terminated in northern Vietnam, yet the government reserved the right to punish rice "speculators." In a diplomatic nod to the victorious Allies, the government abolished former Governor General Decoux's December 1941 sequestration of American, Dutch, and British properties.

Five decrees in early September promoted national education. Top priority was assigned to achieving literacy within one year among all persons nine years and above. Literacy classes were to be free and compulsory for illiterates; fines would be levied on those who failed to learn to read and write Vietnamese (*quốc ngữ*). Instruction costs would be borne by province- and commune-level people's committees. Night classes were ordered for farmers and workers. A national Department of Popular Education was created, with responsibilities and funding unspecified.[3]

Procedures to establish a National People's Assembly (Quốc Dân Đại Hội) were decreed on 8 September. All Vietnamese citizens eighteen years or older—men and women alike—would have the right to vote and to stand for election, with the exception of individuals stripped of citizen rights or persons not of sound mind. A committee would formulate regulations for the first national election, to take place within three months. Another committee was to put together a draft constitution to present to the elected legislature of three hundred

FIGURE 1. First DRV Cabinet, September 1945. First row, left to right: Võ Nguyên Giáp, Vũ Dình Hòe, Hồ Chí Minh, Trần Huy Liệu, Nguyễn Văn Tố. Second row: Nguyễn Mạnh Hà, Hoàng Tích Trí (acting health minister), Vũ Trọng Khánh, Dương Đức Hiền. Third row: Phạm Văn Đồng, Hoàng Minh Giám, Cù Huy Cận. In *X&N* 11 (Jan. 1995): 31. Courtesy of Vietnam Historical Association.

delegates, which alone had authority to determine the final content of the DRV constitution. Twelve days later the seven-person constitution drafting committee was announced, composed almost entirely of ICP and Việt Minh members.[4] Notably, no decree specified the geographical territory to which the DRV laid claim. Citizens were left to assume that the borders of colonial Tonkin, Annam, and Cochinchina with China, Laos, and Cambodia now constituted Vietnam's national boundaries. This assumption was strengthened by the mid-October national election decree (discussed below) which specified seventy-one electoral units, all within former Tonkin, Annam, and Cochinchina.[5]

The format of these early DRV decrees owed a great deal to colonial administrative precedent, although the content was less prolix. Hanoi bureaus also dispatched hundreds of official telegrams *(công điện; télégramme officiel)* to subordinate units or local people's committees. All outgoing messages were headed with the words "Democratic Republic of Vietnam. Independence, Freedom, Happiness." Local bodies quickly picked up this formula, and soon many citizens followed suit. Each outgoing or incoming message was assigned a number and recorded in a logbook; on 2 September, a line was drawn across the page of each logbook and a new numbering sequence begun, but communication procedures remained unchanged. Old French file folders were turned upside down and given new subject headings. The blank back sides of old colonial documents were used to type out new messages, reports, and memoranda.

The provisional government employed the press to try to convey basic principles, structures, and policies to the public. Selected decrees were dispatched to newspapers for obligatory publication. In early September, Việt Minh papers told citizens to act only on orders from the government. One editorial claimed that "the Vietnamese people (dân tộc) know how to respect discipline, how to obey orders from higher authority".[6] Only two weeks prior the authors of these words had been exhorting everyone to overthrow the existing regime. The new interior minister, Võ Nguyên Giáp, held a press conference to explain how government functions needed to be delineated from Việt Minh activities at all levels.[7] Later, Giáp spent two hours with journalists critiquing the behavior of local people's committees. He urged citizens to forward complaints to a "political inspectorate" being established in his ministry. Giáp also promised to meet regularly with committee chairpersons, open training courses, and promote "New Vietnam Model Communes." It was obvious from his remarks, however, that many local committees were still following their own revolutionary trajectories.[8]

Cứu Quốc launched a vitriolic attack on "some people's committees," accusing members of behaving like feudal-era officials, detaining and terrorizing their fellow citizens without reason, shooting into the air to scare people, and confiscating private property unlawfully. "Revolutionary mandarins" *(quan cách mạng)* were shouting orders, cursing, forcing defendants to kneel down in front of them. If a particular committee failed to represent the people, then *Cứu Quốc* averred that "the people could possibly overthrow it." On the other hand, editors cautioned citizens to avoid "divisiveness," first joining together to present their grievances to the committee and, if this didn't work, petitioning higher authority. This policy of "criticizing in order to repair" would strengthen cooperation between the people and the government, the editors concluded hopefully.[9] Readers must have wondered what chance a delegation of villagers would have when presenting their complaints to a band of violent youths. It took months of persistent effort before central government legitimacy could be translated into administrative authority in most provinces of northern and north-central Vietnam. Further south, authority continued to vary dramatically from one locality to another.

PERSONNEL IN TRANSITION

Hồ Chí Minh and his lieutenants wanted the former colonial administrative apparatus to continue functioning under their control, subject to whatever modifications they thought necessary. Working hours for government employees were announced as six thirty to eleven in the morning, followed by a midday break from eleven to two, then an afternoon session from two to five. Saturday morning was work time as well, for a total of forty-two working hours per week. Government personnel were encouraged to use their midday breaks to practice marching, to disassemble and assemble firearms, and to listen to lectures on military tactics. The threat of French return in force hung over everyone. Early in September, Võ Nguyên Giáp alerted all DRV administrative echelons that French troops had reentered Indochina at several places and were proceeding "to butcher our people." Localities facing French assault were to react by destroying roads, culverts, and telegraph lines, and by implementing a policy of "empty gardens and vacant houses" *(vườn không nhà trống)*.[10] This ominous term, used previously by Việt Minh groups evading enemy sweeps in the northern hills, would become painfully familiar to all citizens in due course.

Former colonial employees who had taken part in exciting meetings, demonstrations, and group organizing during the heady days of August fully expected to continue such political activities in September. The DRV provisional government, while accepting that all citizens had both a right and a duty to be politically engaged, wanted civil servants to resume their tasks promptly. Nguyễn Xiển, chair of the new Northern Region People's Committee, instructed heads of bureaus and local committees to focus staff attention back on their jobs, to make sure that at least one person remained on duty whenever everyone else was authorized to attend a political event, and to require staff members enrolling in external military or youth training courses to obtain prior permission from superiors.[11] Võ Nguyên Giáp complimented government employees for having formed political organizations, "for example [Việt Minh] national salvation groups," but then ordered them to abandon all decisionmaking roles and limit themselves to offering advice.[12] Younger employees in particular came to regard their day-to-day paper-pushing tasks with quiet frustration, given the continuing revolutionary fervor beyond office windows. Some would soon find ways to transfer to the nascent national army.

Reading through September correspondence files, one often notes civil servants using old categories and trying to conduct business as before, even as new realities pushed in relentlessly. Staff often searched for regulations or precedents to justify specific decisions, only to be left in quandaries about which was onerous colonial residue and which timeless administrative wisdom. Sometimes the safest response was to forward the file to another office for decision. The press routinely chided government employees for attitudes of dependency *(ỷ lại)*. Nguyễn Xiển accused many employees of "retaining an indifferent, risk-averse attitude, demonstrating listlessness and timidity in the face of rapid changes in the government system." He exhorted staff to throw aside such outdated behavior, work faster, and above all be punctual—the latter attribute being a preoccupation of provisional President Hồ Chí Minh.[13] Nguyễn Xiển himself possessed an elitist, hierarchical approach to operations, in which the idea that the government belonged to the people had few if any practical consequences. Hoàng Minh Chính, general secretary of the Democratic Party, criticized the government for being "entirely distant from the populace" after a group of petitioners were refused entry to Xiển's office.[14]

The DRV provisional government had taken possession of individual personnel files from the colonial era, plus a batch of departmental rosters compiled for the Japanese following the 9 March 1945 *coup de force*. The PTT roster, for example, listed over 2,400 employees headed by forty-one "cadres européens" (who in fact were indigenous), and 124 senior Indochinese staff members. The Public Instruction Directorate roster included 118 indigenous "cadres européens" and 127 senior Indochinese members, mostly tertiary and secondary teachers.[15] Many government employees based in province or district towns had vacated their worksites hastily during the August upheavals; when they returned, it was usually on terms set by local people's committees, at least until contact was reestablished with departmental superiors in Hanoi.[16]

In early October the government allocated fifty-seven departments, bureaus, courts, and agencies of the former Gouvernement général de l'Indochine to the twelve new DRV ministries.[17] The Ministry of Communications and Transport received the most employees, notably those belonging to the PTT and the Indochina Railways Department. The Interior Ministry acquired the sensitive police and political services divisions, minus staff who had departed in July or early August and not returned. As it became obvious that some former Gouvernement général units no longer had a reason to exist, employees were transferred elsewhere, until only a few caretaker staff remained, pending final disposition. All these personnel shifts caused headaches for pay clerks, leading the Finance Ministry to urge that transferred employees continue to be paid temporarily by their prior organizations.[18]

DRV ministerial offices in Hanoi were not large, a reflection of their newness and the government's decision to decentralize some operations to regional and provincial levels. In September–October 1945, only about three hundred staff members were spread across twelve offices. Four ministries possessed 58 percent of total staff reported: Communications and Transport; National Economy; National Education; and Interior.[19] Some ministerial offices quickly proved much more active than others. By mid-November, the Interior Ministry's roster had more than doubled, to sixty-five staff members organized into a directorate (3), secretariat (3), gazetteer office (2), press office (5), legal bureau (13), personnel bureau (10), politics and police bureau (12), and messenger pool (17).[20] The Interior Ministry used the telegraph system five times more than the Information and Propaganda Ministry, fifty-seven times more than the National Economy Ministry, and two thousand times more than the nascent Health Ministry.[21] With few exceptions, neither DRV ministers nor former senior colonial employees had ever witnessed a ministerial system in action.

REGIONAL COMMITTEES

The next administrative echelon below the DRV provisional government comprised three regional committees—for the north (Bắc Bộ; Tonkin), center (Trung Bộ; Annam), and south (Nam Bộ; Cochinchina). A Provisional Northern Region Revolutionary People's Committee had been announced on 20 August, with the word "Revolutionary" dropped nine days later, and "People's" changed to "Administrative" at the end of 1945. The chairman, Nguyễn Xiển, introduced above, had obtained a graduate mathematics degree in France, taught school in Hanoi together with Võ Nguyên Giáp, helped to edit *Tạp chí Khoa Học (Science Magazine)*, and been employed in the Indochina Bureau of Meteorology until August.[22] Immediately under the committee was the Northern Region Office (Bắc Bộ Phủ), with 146 staff divided into seven departments: secretariat (22), personnel (16), taxation (14), finance (31), information and propaganda (38), administration (18), and economy (7).[23] Eleven bureaus *(sở)* and services *(nha)* reported to the committee: public works, land registration, primary schools, health, veterinary, economy, agriculture, water and forests, labor, prisons, and taxation.[24] Bureaus and services possessed offices in most northern provinces, where staff had experienced the upheavals of August firsthand, some being abused as lackeys of the old regime, others allowed to assist local committees on an unpaid basis. In its end-of-year report, the Northern Region Committee was unable to claim many achievements for its subordinate bureaus and services, and advised that staff numbers were being cut back severely. Yet the committee still aimed to retain these multiple hierarchies extending down to province and sometimes district levels.[25]

Establishing the Hanoi-Province Relationship

On 1–2 September 1945, a remarkable meeting of Northern Region officials and representatives from thirteen provincial revolutionary committees took place in Hanoi.[26] Northern Region officials particularly wanted each province *(tỉnh)*, district *(huyện)*, and commune *(xã)* to designate a single legitimate political body that would bear the standardized name of "people's committee," consist of five to seven members (appointed or elected "depending on conditions"), and be more broadly representative than appeared to be the case with many committees at that moment. Officials also warned that the central government was unable to dispense funds to cover local expenses, hence each province had to use whatever resources they already possessed with extreme care, and mount patriotic fundraising campaigns urgently. After provincial participants were invited to state their own priorities, most did so with alacrity, ranging from Nam Định's concern about losing income from likely termination of the salt monopoly, to Sơn Tây's pressing need for additional youths to guard military equipment obtained from the Japanese. The sober discussion came back repeatedly to questions about which taxes would be abandoned and which retained, how victims of the recent floods could be fed, what sort of criteria should be applied when confiscating or requisitioning property, and how to keep former French enterprises functioning to Vietnamese benefit.

Exactly one month later another such meeting took place, this time with representatives from twenty-one northern provinces and cities attending.[27] On this occasion the Northern Region Office prepared an agenda, and most items listed received due attention. Opening the meeting, Nguyễn Xiển first welcomed the interior minister, Võ Nguyên Giáp, then took the trouble to introduce each province chairman around the table. Giáp proceeded to give everyone a brief national appraisal, commenting that central government contacts with the northern region were "partly firm," but that communication with the south remained slow and erratic. With fighting having broken out in Saigon only one week prior, and anti-French feelings running high in Hanoi, Giáp nonetheless eschewed patriotic hyperbole, instead telling those around the table to "work methodically and resolutely to consolidate national foundations (nền tảng quốc gia), [thus] forming a strong bloc in support of our fellow country people in the south." For Giáp, state building and national defense went hand in hand.

After Nguyễn Xiển's formal report to the meeting, Võ Nguyên Giáp asked each province chairman to summarize achievements so far, especially in regard to establishing effective people's committees at province, district, and commune levels. The responses were frank and to the point, probably because most province chairmen present were ICP members who appreciated that local knowledge carried more weight at this particular encounter than political rhetoric. Only one province people's committee had been elected (in Vĩnh Yên). The others had made efforts to diversify during September, and now mostly claimed united front representation.[28] Some province committees had slightly more Việt Minh than non-Việt Minh members, while for others it was the reverse. Several committee chairmen added that non-Việt Minh members were assigned less sensitive jobs like justice or social welfare. At one point in the discussion, Nguyễn Khang, who had been delegated by the Interior Ministry to inspect certain localities, revealed that it had been necessary to order reorganization of a couple of province committees because they included only town dwellers, no members from surrounding rural districts. Participants in the meeting also distinguished between those province committee members who were government employees receiving a salary, and those who received local food donations and ate collectively. Within two months, inflation had further reduced the purchasing value of government salaries, compelling more collective eating, yet the distinction between government employees and nonemployees persisted.

A number of province chairmen took credit for organizing district people's committees in their jurisdiction, yet the situation remained patchy. In Hà Đông province, Đặng Kim Giang had shifted members of district committees to other districts, while always keeping such outsiders in the minority. Some districts still lacked a committee as of late September, while other existing district committees were being refused recognition by province leaders. Below the district level, canton (tổng) offices were reported by most province chairmen to be out of action; in November, cantons would be abrogated by decree. Very little was reported about commune people's committees. Three provinces stated that about half of their communes possessed committees. Two provinces mentioned receiving requests from villages (thôn) to secede from their commune or to join an adjacent commune, but such initiatives were being discouraged.

In the afternoon of 1 October, eight directors of Northern Region bureaus and services met with the province committee chairmen to explain their operations and make requests. The Public Works Department needed province help in repairing dikes broken in the mid-August flood, and hoped that help would take the form of rice to feed workers. The director also asked that documents removed from local Public Works offices in August be returned. Somewhat reluctantly the director accepted that province committees would decide which local Public Works staff to retain and which to lay off. The director of Water and Forests asked that province committees help to stop rampant burning of forests, and facilitate continued collection of resource taxes. The Economic Services director outlined efforts to foster production and distribution of rice, coal, cooking oil, and textiles. The PTT director pleaded with province chairmen to help crack down on highly disruptive thefts of telegraph and telephone wire, and offered to assign replacements for any local PTT employees considered unacceptable. The Primary Schools director apologized that a new curriculum would not be available soon, but foreshadowed a weekly periodical of value to teachers if provinces could help pay printing and postal costs. Finally, the Popular Education director asked province committees to assist in rural literacy efforts, as the government lacked the means to pay literacy teachers or provide paper and pens to pupils. By this point province chairmen must have wondered how they could support even a fraction of government services previously funded from Hanoi.

The next morning's session began with a lively discussion led by Hoàng Hữu Nam of the Interior Ministry on how to classify and deal with Vietnamese traitors (see chapter 7). This was followed by an agitated exchange with the finance minister, Phạm Văn Đồng, after he specified that the central government intended to allocate its meager funds to the army, leaving provinces to find their own ways to support essential staff and run top priority projects. Đồng reaffirmed that locally based employees of Northern Region bureaus and services would be laid off unless local committees took up responsibility for their pay and food rations. He did not reveal that the Hanoi branch of the Bank of Indochina was honoring DRV Treasury drafts, probably because he doubted this practice would last. BIC payments to Treasury reached twenty-two million piastres before French officials halted payments on 23 October.[29]

On the afternoon of 2 October, four additional government ministers arrived to explain to province chairmen how their portfolios functioned, and to highlight recent decrees, edicts, and public announcements needing the attention of local committees. The minister for information and propaganda, Trần Huy Liệu, sent a letter to alert everyone to training courses then underway for advance propaganda teams. He would be giving course graduates letters of introduction to present to province committees. Liệu cautioned that teams would bring with them predetermined propaganda programs, and were not permitted to go beyond those instructions. Who would feed and house these teams was not explained.

That evening, Võ Nguyên Giáp returned with several of his Interior Ministry associates to lead a discussion on organization of commune-level people's committees, taking as precedent the Việt Bắc liberation zone experience in June–August 1945. A proposal to establish "model villages" (làng kiểu mẫu) was debated, but there is no record of such villages materializing in later months. There was an underlying assumption at the meeting that commune committees ought to be the foundation on which district and province committees were built, yet as we have seen the latter still only had a vague idea of what the former were doing. In reality an administrative gap remained between many commune committees formed in August and higher echelons.[30]

Central and Southern Regional Committees

When Việt Minh activists in Huế announced formation of a revolutionary people's committee on 23 August, it was in the name of Thừa Thiên province, not central Vietnam (Trung Kỳ; Annam).[31] Việt Minh seizure of power in Huế had national importance, as it triggered the abdication of Emperor Bảo Đại, but the regional implications remained unclear. Throughout the central region in August, the revolutionary center of gravity was at the province level, with only limited knowledge of more distant events. ICP members played significant roles in forming province committees, but they did so mostly on their own initiative, without instructions from party leaders. Indeed, throughout the summer of 1945 the party had been unable to reconstitute its Central Region Committee (Xứ Ủy Trung Kỳ), while communications with top echelons in the north remained erratic at best. Not until 31 August were party members from eighteen central provinces able to meet at the office of the former Annam résident supérieur in

Huế. They declared a new regional party executive committee, headed by Hoàng Quốc Việt, a northerner, who then immediately departed for Saigon to try to resolve serious differences within the southern branch of the party. In practice, Nguyễn Chí Thanh, newly appointed head of the Trung Bộ Việt Minh Committee, took on regional party leadership as well.[32]

Two days following the party meeting, Trần Hữu Dực, recent leader of the uprising in Quảng Trị province, was selected to chair the new Provisional Central Region Revolutionary People's Committee, based in Huế. The same men who had just dealt with party and Việt Minh matters now discussed the business of government, about which they knew very little. According to Dực, the meeting "went around in circles for a whole session, still feeling at a loss," before it agreed to set a target of one month for organizing a viable administrative structure from region to province, district, and commune.[33] The staff of the former *résidence superieure* insisted that Dực remain cloistered until tailors could fit him out with a Western suit, tie, hat, and leather shoes to replace the battered shorts, shirt, and sandals he had worn since leaving jail.[34] Dực then addressed senior employees of the former administration and met members of the royal family. Eventually the Central Region Committee was able to convene, with Nguyễn Duy Trinh as deputy chair, Nguyễn Chánh responsible for defense, and ten other members supervising the existing regional bureaus and services which also were meant to report to ministries in Hanoi. In early 1946, the committee was pared down to five members, but with an unwieldy total of twenty-one directors of specialized bureaus reporting to it. Dực managed to travel to all eighteen provinces under his jurisdiction, although after January 1946 it was no longer possible to go further south than Phú Yên, due to French military advances.[35]

Meanwhile, the DRV central government dispatched thousands of national decrees, edicts, instructions, and letters to the Central Region Committee in Huế. One of the first messages from Hanoi instructed each regional committee to prepare a realistic budget, to contact province-level committees urgently, to devote special attention to repairing roads and bridges, and to account to the government for any funds drawn from local Treasury (Kho Bạc) offices.[36] It appears from the files that most correspondence addressed to the regional committee was routed directly to one of the specialized bureaus for action. Outgoing traffic also showed little evidence of regional committee involvement. The Northern Region Committee in Hanoi sometimes dispatched messages directly to province committees in the central region, bypassing the Trung Bộ committee in Huế, a practice not permitted in the north.[37] Clearly the Central Region Committee exercised much less authority over specialized bureaus and province committees than was true of the Northern Region Committee in Hanoi.

Communications specialists in Huế maintained regular contact with all central region provinces until early 1946, when committees from Phú Yên southward had to flee French attack. The telegraph system functioned as far south as Đà Nẵng in April, but soon after that Huế itself became terminus of the telegraph line running through the coastal provinces from Hanoi. Telephone connections were more erratic, although the line between Vinh and Hanoi functioned well.[38] The main Huế radio transmitter was employed to send Morse code traffic to local committees and military units, including some operating behind French lines. A number of provinces kept their own rudimentary internal telegraph and telephone networks operating. The official mail system continued to reach most provinces and districts in central Vietnam, although foot couriers and boats often had to substitute for erratic train or motor transport.

In central Vietnam, the demarcation between DRV civil administration and ICP-Việt Minh operations was often blurred or ignored, whereas in northern Vietnam the distinction was taken seriously throughout 1945–46 and beyond. ICP activists in all regions often showed their dislike and distrust of employees of the former colonial regime, although particularly in the north they might accept grudgingly the need to use some temporarily. Not surprisingly, this reduced the effectiveness of cooperation between employees, and led some to switch their services back to the French when the opportunity presented itself. Even those Trung Bộ ICP members who encouraged old regime personnel to continue working saw nothing counterproductive about Việt Minh committees seizing public property, levying informal taxes, meting out their own punishments, and otherwise duplicating or negating the functions of government. By the summer of 1946 the party seemed to be trying to separate administrative committee and Việt Minh responsibilities. Nguyễn Duy Trinh, deputy chairman of the Trung Bộ Administrative Committee and an ICP member, managed to reduce overlaps at regional level.[39] At the province level and below, however, confusion persisted.

The Southern Region Committee received packets from Hanoi containing the early DRV decrees outlined above and managed to forward copies to some Mekong delta provinces before being forced to flee Saigon in late September 1945 (see chapter 3).[40] The committee subsequently regained two-way shortwave radio contact with Hanoi, while some other southern venues possessed receivers capable of picking up Voice of Vietnam transmissions in Morse code. We know from documents captured by the French army in late 1945 that DRV adherents in southern provinces as distant as Hà Tiên and Rạch Giá were employing government nomenclature identical to that found in central and northern Vietnam. Very soon, however, the Southern Region Committee felt the need to innovate, for example designating three "political inspectors" for eastern, central, and western Nam Bộ. It then sought to delineate responsibilities for "resistance committees" (*ủy ban kháng chiến*) that had formed separately from local people's committees.[41] This issue arose wherever it became necessary to engage the French in battle. In 1947, based partly on prior Nam Bộ experience, the central DRV government would decree the merger of military and civil bodies into "resistance and administrative committees" *(ủy ban kháng chiến hành chính)* at province, district, and commune levels.

Phạm Văn Bạch, chairman of the Southern Region Committee, made a frantic attempt to bring together communist, Catholic, Hòa Hảo (Buddhist), and Cao Đài faithful to sustain armed struggle against French reoccupation of Cochinchina.[42] In early 1946, another well-known lawyer, Phạm Ngọc Thuần, was designated deputy chairman of the Southern Region Committee. Three months prior, the French Sûreté had put Thuần under house arrest, but he soon escaped Saigon by bicycle to join the maquis. Thuần found himself under heavy suspicion until he and a physician friend built a workshop to make grenades and mines to give to local combatants. When offered membership in the ICP, Thuần arranged for his initiation ceremony to take place on Bastille Day 1946.[43] Noted professionals like Bạch and Thuần retained the respect of some former colonial public servants, religious leaders, and businessmen. Bạch was ordered north in February 1946 to represent the south in government deliberations, chaired the Southern Resistance Committee in Phú Yên from late 1946, and did not return to Nam Bộ until 1948.[44]

Other Southern Region Committee members were scattered across the Mekong delta, mostly keeping in touch by courier. On one occasion the committee did manage to convene a meeting of representatives from all provinces of Nam Bộ.[45] Amidst the fighting and moving, however, the committee was in no position to direct the region's administration, which devolved to leaders of the eastern, central, and western subregions (now numbered as *khu* 7, 8, and 9). Nonetheless, with DRV adherents in the south cut off from the national government in the north for months at a time, the roles of regional committee members remained significant. The committee put its name to public declarations and to correspondence with foreign organizations which in the north were the prerogatives of President Hồ Chí Minh. Finally, the Southern Region Committee offered a visible alternative to the "Cochinchina Republic" being pieced together by the French.

STANDARDIZATION OF LOCAL GOVERNMENT

In November 1945, the DRV provisional government issued a decree on composition of people's councils *(hội đồng nhân dân)* and administrative committees *(ủy ban hành chính)* which has continued to shape local government in Vietnam to the present day.[46] A committee headed by Võ Nguyên Giáp had prepared a draft to discuss with province heads, then present to the Cabinet. While affirming the "great success" of the local committees that had sprung up during the August Revolution, conditions were now said to be sufficiently stable and the form of government *(chính thể)* sufficiently clear that it was time "to organize the people's authority in a unified, rational manner, and to demarcate powers transparently."[47] At the commune and province levels, people's councils selected by popular election would have the authority to issue resolutions, choose the administrative committee at the same level, set a budget, collect fees, own or rent property, and participate in business enterprises of public benefit. Administrative committees would function at commune, district, province, and regional levels, thus eliminating the canton *(tổng)* and prefectural *(phủ)* levels of local government that had existed for hundreds of years.[48] Relatives were prohibited from sitting on the same administrative committee, and not all committee members had to be natives of the territory encompassed—both clauses designed to reduce the propensity to form local cliques. The public had the right to attend people's council sessions but not to raise questions from the floor. Administrative committees would normally meet behind closed doors.

Although this November 1945 decree intended that councils and committees serve the interests of inhabitants of the specific territory involved, it simultaneously placed each council and committee under extensive scrutiny from higher echelons, and provided punishments for any body that contradicted government decrees, edicts, or instructions. The outcome of all council and committee elections had to be ratified from above. Budgets had to be approved, as did any proposal to buy or sell property, set new fees, borrow money, let contracts, or initiate lawsuits. If a people's council issued a resolution contrary to higher authority, it would be told to rescind or correct the document. If it refused, the council could be dissolved and new elections ordered. Administrative committees were instructed bluntly to "carry out the orders *(mệnh lệnh)* of higher echelons." If they did not, the committee could be discharged and offending individuals removed from council membership. The constitutional principle of dual accountability had yet to be formulated, but local committees already faced the problem of how to satisfy both their constituents and the state.

By the end of 1945, thousands of local committees had already conformed to government instructions and changed their name to "administrative committee."[49] From the government's point of view, these committees were still only provisional, pending people's council elections which would lead to selection and ratification of proper administrative committees. As we shall see, some council elections did take place during 1946, at least in northern Vietnam, yet in many cases councils failed to gain control over their administrative committees, whose members had been working together since the August Revolution.

PUBLIC SERVICE CUTBACKS

Phạm Văn Đồng's early October warning that the central government lacked funds to pay public servants appears not to have been heeded. Some heads of departments and committees probably thought the minister of finance was bluff-ing. In late October, a number of province committees warned Hanoi that most of their remaining funds would be consumed if they met that month's salary obligations.[50] The government reacted by ordering all public servants employed for thirty years or more, and all those aged fifty-five and older to retire immedi-ately. It also discontinued severance pay for retirees, and froze all personnel promotions until further notice.[51] Shortly thereafter the government encouraged employees to consider applying for six-months leave without pay, with the pos-sibility of extension. Behind this latter initiative lay the expectation that many individuals taking formal leave would continue to work, relying on a combina-tion of family ingenuity and popular donations, until such time as the govern-ment's financial situation improved and pay could be resumed.

In following weeks each administrative unit submitted a roster to the Interior Ministry that indicated who wished to take leave without pay, who was retiring outright, and who had moved to another unit. The Northern Region Office man-aged to reduce its own complement from 155 to 103, although only four were retiring and eleven taking leave without pay (or with half-pay), compared to thirty-one transfers.[52] The sixteen bureaus and services under its supervision had much less success in reducing staff numbers. Among eleven units reporting, with a total complement of 3,875 employees, only 163 individuals were retiring, 37 taking leave without pay (or with half-pay), and 68 transferring elsewhere. Add-ing thirty dismissals and one death, this still amounted to a meager 2.6 percent reduction in staff.[53] Province-level staff cutbacks were more substantial, yet the number of employees who remained was still well beyond the capacity of prov-ince committees to pay them.[54] Provinces told the Interior Ministry that essen-tial employees were threatening to resign, and warned that further reductions could cripple operations entirely. Hundreds of employees sent petitions to Hanoi to complain that inflation was making life extremely difficult for them at current pay levels.[55]

Sometime in December the central government quietly accepted that locally negotiated pay reductions were preferable to large-scale resignations or dismiss-als. The large amount of work that province offices had put in to make recommen-dations for keeping or dropping individual employees was largely wasted. Many employees were prepared to stay if adequate food was provided from a combina-tion of state and local sources. As they were for the most part former members of the colonial system, these employees also regarded participation in the DRV ad-ministration as offering protection against revolutionary harassment.

At the local level, however, government employment proved no guarantee against harsh treatment. In late December, Trần Văn Của, director of the North-ern Region Public Works Department, wrote a caustic letter to superiors on behalf of his exasperated senior engineers: "They are routinely belittled and terrorized.

For example, Mr. Trường has been arrested without cause. Mr. Khánh is currently detained without anyone knowing the reason, or who is responsible. At present my ranking employees are all confused and discouraged, and I lack any authority with which to offer them encouragement."[56] Của concluded that most of his engineers nonetheless did want to continue working, despite such local maltreatment and despite considerable material sacrifice. Tax collectors and customs officers often found themselves in similar circumstances (see chapter 6).

Many northern province committees had retained former district mandarins as "advisors" in August, and subsequently employed them as "specialists." When there were calls to dismiss these former district mandarins or force them to retire, a number of province committees raised objections. In early November, the Interior Ministry told lower echelons to select only a few former mandarins to remain on new contracts at lower pay. Better yet, former mandarins could work without any pay, "like many Ministers and other persons helping the Government in its endeavors."[57] A month later the Finance Ministry ordered all former mandarins to sign new contracts that included a 25 percent pay reduction. This met some opposition, not on financial grounds, since inflation was eating relentlessly into everyone's pay packet, but because it meant former mandarins being singled out.[58]

In its end-of-year report, the Northern Region's Office of Personnel admitted that it had barely begun to process employee requests to retire, although it had arranged for five hundred pre-August retirees to continue receiving their pensions. Simultaneously it was trying to identify worthy employees and keep them working at lower pay. Many individuals who had abandoned their provincial posts hastily in August and congregated in Hanoi now wished to resume duties, but the Finance Ministry had yet to reply about funding. The end-of-year report concluded with a blunt assessment: inflation was turning salaried employees into paupers, yet those suddenly instructed to resign were finding themselves even worse off.[59] Meanwhile, presumably on ideological grounds, the wages of working-class state employees had been increased, not reduced.[60] All other government employees had had to accept lower pay or take leave without pay and continue working, perhaps in a different unit. By January 1946, many employees had sent their dependents to ancestral villages to subsist, while they themselves ate together with office mates.[61] This solution to feeding government employees would persist for years to come.

On several occasions the Vietnam General Association of Government Employees tried to intercede with the provisional DRV government about pay and conditions, but its leaders were tainted by prior associations with French and Japanese officials. Newspapers carried scores of letters from continuing or retrenched employees describing their economic plight. Claiming not to be bitter, a fired employee in Huế accepted that he had "done wrong in the past and needed reeducation." He now took part eagerly in political demonstrations and participated in several organizations, but remained unemployed.[62] Another contributor to the same paper argued that professional expertise was less important for government employment than virtue and "loyalty to people's interests."[63] In January 1946, the Interior Ministry felt it necessary to deny rumors that a further round of sackings was imminent.[64] In February, the principal Việt Minh paper foreshadowed election of national office bearers to the alternative General Association of Government Employees for National Salvation.[65] Several months later, two hundred people met in Huế to form the Thừa Thiên Government Employees Association.[66]

PROVINCE COMMITTEES: THE ADMINISTRATIVE LINCHPIN

In precolonial Vietnam, province seats had exuded state gravitas compared to the modest prefect and district offices immediately below them. The colonial authorities reinforced this tradition when they placed a French *résident* in each province to supervise Vietnamese personnel down to commune level. Most provinces also possessed specialized units that reported to Gouvernement général de l'Indochine offices in Hanoi. The French had also increased the number of provinces to sixty-five compared to the thirty-one delineated by Emperor Minh Mang in 1834.[67] When declaring independence in early September 1945, the DRV provisional government was content to retain colonial-era province names and territorial demarcations. A number of province committees preferred new revolutionary designations, usually the name of a local anticolonial martyr, and they proceeded to employ this identification in messages sent to Hanoi. However, none of those name changes gained central endorsement. Within several months they faded from province-initiated correspondence, although they were often retained in local speeches, banners, and poetry.

We have seen how the Northern Region People's Committee called in province chairmen in early September to discuss vital issues. At that meeting province chairmen were also instructed to submit semimonthly reports to Hanoi. The reports of the next four months proved to be blunt and concise, yet wide-ranging. Province chairmen admitted their inexperience to higher authorities, but often showed discomfort at relying on local functionaries carried over from the colonial regime. They wanted feedback and guidance from above and they expected material support as well. It soon dawned on them, however, that individuals at the "center" *(trung ương)* possessed no more experience at governing than they did. Some of the hundreds of orders coming down had little or no relevance to their province. Most sobering of all, Hanoi could not provide most of the funding, supplies, and equipment required to fulfill locally the tasks expected.[68]

Obeying classic bureaucratic principles, the Interior Ministry soon promulgated a detailed checklist that each province chairman had to consult when writing his periodic report. This list categorized knowledge in a manner appealing to the center, yet also had the effect of discouraging chairmen from raising unique or unexpected developments. With Hanoi determined to standardize administrative procedures and homogenize terminology, it should not surprise us that province reports soon became more ritualistic in form and cautious in content. Submitting a vague report in time was preferable to sending a precise report late. Tardiness triggered tart reminders, and sometimes provoked a barrage of onerous questions from superiors. Thus, when a Bắc Giang periodic report was late, the Northern Region Committee demanded to know exactly how the 1,780,000$BIC left by the Japanese had been used, what amount of money had been allocated to support National Guard units based in the province, and how "foreign guests" (presumably Chinese army units) were being handled.[69] We do not know how Bắc Giang responded, but reading through other files it is apparent that standardized reporting increasingly obscured the effervescence, heterogeneity, and contingency of revolution in the provinces.

Province chairmen learned how to evade and sometimes ignore stern questioning from above. For example, only twelve out of twenty-seven northern provinces bothered to respond to government requests for a comparison of province office employee numbers before and after the August 1945 Revolution.[70] Perhaps some province chairmen did not wish to be seen as ignoring Hanoi's instructions to cut staff numbers. More generally, local leaders now understood the value of keeping some information to themselves, although this was not without risk.

The DRV government reserved the right to dismiss province committee chairmen, or indeed entire committees. In September, the Hưng Yên province chairman, Học Phi, was accused by unnamed persons of having countenanced "terror" (khủng bố) after taking power the previous month. Hundreds of citizens then proceeded to sign petitions in support of Học Phi, praising his revolutionary initiative, blaming the violence on others, or suggesting that fellow activists slow to move in Hưng Yên in mid-August were jealous of Học Phi's popularity. A Northern Region official who reviewed these petitions in Hanoi acknowledged that Học Phi enjoyed local esteem, yet still recommended that he be stood down as a signal to Hưng Yên inhabitants that "terror and persecutions" would not be allowed to return.[71] This begs the questions of why Học Phi was singled out for removal, when Việt Minh leaders in other provinces were vulnerable to similar charges yet remained in office. It appears that Học Phi led an ICP cell which relied on Democratic Party support when taking power in Hưng Yên and establishing the new province administration. This Democratic Party connection may have been the main reason for Học Phi's removal in late September (see chapter 8). Whatever the cause, Học Phi's dismissal served as warning to other province chairmen about limits on their tenure.[72]

Late 1945 saw several other interventions by Hanoi in provincial leadership. The Northern Region Committee cut the membership of the Thái Bình province committee from fourteen to seven, but this was part of wider efforts to streamline committee functions at all levels.[73] In early November, the head of the Yên Bái branch of the National Treasury accused the Yên Bái province chairman of withdrawing twenty thousand piastres to purchase rafts to rent to the Chinese Army for personal gain. Within days the Interior Ministry had dismissed the entire Yên Bái committee and ordered someone else to form a new committee.[74] This incident probably had more to do with the DRV loss of Yên Bái town to the Vietnam Nationalist Party than to official peculation. Until June 1946, several other province seats along the Red River corridor remained in Nationalist Party hands, with DRV province committees compelled to retreat to the countryside or to adjacent provinces (see chapter 7). In December, the Ninh Bình province chairman was replaced after only two weeks in office, most likely due to late November discussions between senior government representatives and the Catholic Church (see chapter 7).[75]

By early 1946, most province committees in northern and north-central Vietnam were functioning as the vital link between the DRV government and the populace at large. Province committees took responsibility for: recruiting young men to join the National Guard; organizing province-level militia; securing rice to feed both military and civilian personnel; coordinating tax collections; supervising requisitioned properties and facilities; resolving local disputes; detaining enemies of the state; and keeping markets, roads, and waterways open. Hanoi decrees, edicts, and instructions went down to province offices, which then brought them to the attention of district and village committees. More than that, province authorities had an obligation to monitor lower-level performance and enforce compliance on behalf of the central government. It was rare for Hanoi to bypass the province and interact directly with district or village committees. Citizen petitions sent to President Hồ Chí Minh or cabinet ministers in Hanoi would normally be logged in, read by someone, then routed back down to the relevant province committee with instructions to investigate, resolve, and report. In special cases, as we shall see, Hanoi dispatched its own investigator to a locality, deliberately bypassing intervening echelons. The ICP communicated up and down the geographical hierarchy separately from the civil administration. Overall, however, central leaders accepted that it was difficult to penetrate, fathom, and change local realities without province leaders playing a key coordinating role.

On at least two occasions the DRV government canvassed all province committees about a sensitive policy issue. In May 1946, provinces were asked whether

Catholic and Buddhist priests and nuns should perform obligatory labor *(tạp dịch)* and stand guard duty like other citizens. The question had originated with the Quảng Nam province committee in central Vietnam. At least fourteen northern provinces responded with a wide variety of opinions. In September the Interior Ministry exempted priests and nuns from obligatory labor; a month later it excused them from guard duties as well.[76] About this same time province committees were asked a series of questions about village allocations of "public land" *(công điền)* to serving soldiers and their families. The answers from twenty northern provinces were quite nuanced and diverse, a reflection of different local land customs as well as the policy preferences of respondents. In this case the government does not appear to have followed up with a national decree, probably due to the sheer complexity of current land practices, and uncertainty about what to do in the many villages that no longer possessed public land to distribute.[77] The problem of supporting families of soldiers became more acute after full-scale hostilities commenced in December. Eventually this was one justification for ordering radical land redistributions.

The questions of just *who* was responsible for *what* inevitably led to some pulling and tugging between province committees and higher authorities. This was particularly apparent on economic matters. In January 1946, the Haiphong committee asked the government whether or not local merchants should be permitted to export rice and cement. The Economics Ministry reply asserted its prerogative to issue export licenses and levy taxes. The Finance Ministry then heard that Haiphong's committee was blocking exports on the grounds that domestic needs deserved priority. Eventually the Northern Region Committee admitted to Finance that it had issued a secret order to Haiphong forbidding rice exports, but denied there was any restriction on cement exports.[78] Coal from Hòn Gai district became the object of bureaucratic competition, with Hanoi fixing allocations at the beginning of 1946, but Hòn Gai itself more interested in selling output to the highest bidder. In May, the Bắc Bộ Regional Committee ordered the Hòn Gai committee to dispatch six thousand tons of coal per month to the main Hanoi electric power plant before selling to anyone else.[79] The salt monopoly occasioned voluminous correspondence and some disputation between Hanoi and province committees, with each echelon aiming to garner the revenue (see chapter 6). Price-setting was another regular source of contestation. In June, for example, Bắc Giang innocently requested a list of official rental charges for rickshaws, bicycles, ox carts, and boats, then offered to set rates locally if no national list existed. This query and others eventually led to an October government edict fixing prices for motor transport (e.g., 2$00BIC per kilometer for trucking one ton), but inviting each province to forward its own proposed rates on rickshaws, bicycles, and ox carts. Boats were left for later consideration.[80] Attempted micromanagement of the economy began long before the ICP gained control of the state.

Noneconomic responsibilities also provoked testy exchanges between Hanoi and province committees. As the rainy season approached in the north, the Northern Region Committee became increasingly concerned that some Red River delta provinces were not devoting sufficient attention to dike repairs. In early May, Nguyễn Xiển, the Northern Region chairman, sent a blistering telegram to the Hải Dương committee: "[Repair of the] Hải Dương dike is slow and poor, because the supervisory committee is inefficient, tardy, and lazy. Mr Nguyễn Xuân Mẫn must take principal responsibility. The chairmen of local administrative committees are also indifferent, especially Vĩnh Bảo [district]. Request province administrative committee resolutely fulfill duty. Northern Office wants to purge ruthlessly incapable elements and punish bad elements."[81] These tough words reflected Hanoi's concern that a dike breach in one province could harm others, but it is doubtful Nguyễn Xiển was in a position to carry out his threat.

During 1946, the DRV government tried to get some province committees to return confiscated properties. One example serves to highlight the difficulties involved. Before the August Revolution, a Mr. Vui of Hòa Bình town had rented a building to the Japanese, then leased it to Chinese troops a few months later. When the Chinese departed, the Hòa Bình province committee took custody and the building became police headquarters. In September 1946, the Northern Committee, after pointing out to Hòa Bình that provinces lacked authority to confiscate property, ordered that Mr. Vui's building be returned to him. Two months later Hòa Bình continued to justify its action, on grounds that the building was not Mr. Vui's personal residence.[82] It is highly unlikely that Mr. Vui received his property back prior to the outbreak of hostilities in December.

Province administrators took delight in catching Hanoi issuing contradictory orders. In June 1946, the Northern Region Office distributed a model identification card to all northern provinces, with instructions to print copies and issue them to local citizens. Many provinces began to comply, but three months later the Interior Ministry distributed a different national identity card model, provoking considerable confusion. In early November, the Northern Committee told provinces to continue using its ID version until printed stocks ran out, thus not wasting money. A host of province queries ensued. Hưng Yên, having printed 235,000 ID cards, now wanted to know exactly how to number and stamp each card, and what fee to charge recipients. Four other provinces quoted chapter and verse from various edicts to demonstrate to Hanoi that conflicting instructions existed about whether to extract payment for ID cards and, if so, how much.[83] War in December halted efforts to distribute citizen cards, leaving people to rely on a variety of letters of introduction and permits signed by local authorities.

Each month province committees appeared to operate with more confidence and purpose. Realizing that district and commune committees might not report embarrassing information, province chairmen traveled from one place to another, asking questions and making on-the-spot decisions. Local Việt Minh groups were often most forthright in pushing for change. However, many citizens chose to send petitions to President Hồ Chí Minh or ministerial offices when they had accusations to make against district and commune committees. In most cases these petitions were routed back to the relevant province committee, which then was expected to get to the bottom of complaints, resolve them, and report back to Hanoi. Often three or four levels of administration exchanged information over several months, with mixed results.

Charges of unfair arrest and torture by local committees continued to be made throughout 1946. Three different petitions accused the "secret investigation section" *(ban trinh sát)* of Giao Thủy district (Nam Định) of systematic torture. In response, Hanoi authorities merely told the province committee to replace the investigators if the torture charges proved to be true.[84] Chairmen of commune committees were occasionally arrested and taken away by persons who refused to identify themselves. A small but increasing number of petitions accused local officials of embezzlement. Thus, the chairman of the Ý Yên district committee (Nam Định) was alleged to possess seven sets of clothes, four pairs of shoes, a hat, a watch, and a fountain pen, whereas on taking office a year earlier he had owned only one set of clothes.[85] Many if not most accusations against local committees appear not to have been resolved, with case files ending up in "pending" boxes at one administrative level or another.[86]

Disputes between administrative echelons received more sustained attention. Some controversies had their roots in the tumult of August 1945. At that time, for example, revolutionaries in Hiệp Hòa district (Bắc Giang) had seized two boats containing 127 oil drums, managing to hide most of the drums before Japanese troops arrived. Thirty-five drums were turned over to the new district people's committee, but the DRV's Department of Minerals and Industry insisted that all drums be located and surrendered to them. As of August 1946 the thirty-five drums had reached a provincial warehouse, but the remaining drums failed to materialize. Questioned again, the Bắc Giang province committee told Hanoi that it could not fix responsibility for this loss, because in the heady excitement of late 1945 no one had thought about the implications of confiscation, and armed units moved from one place to another constantly.[87] In Hưng Yên province, after a former village head *(lý trưởng)* accused local revolutionary authorities of extorting 120,000 piastres from him, the Interior Ministry instructed the province committee to investigate the charge and, if true, punish the extortionists. Six months later the Hưng Yên committee chairman replied in an aggrieved tone that the money had been seized legitimately at a district office during the August

Revolution and two-thirds allocated to the province's Việt Minh headquarters.[88] The former village head may well have been punished locally for daring to raise the matter.

In Thái Nguyên province in October 1945, the province police arrested two members of a plantation management committee at the request of a district committee chairman. When the case went to court, the proceedings resulted in the district chairman being dismissed from office, yet the two accused remained under detention. The Northern Region Committee told Thái Nguyên to release the two if insufficient evidence existed to convict them. Months later, Thái Nguyên accused the two of crimes amounting to treason, yet still failed to move towards a trial. Five days later, a visiting Northern Region official apparently engineered their release.[89] Almost surely this dispute involved the interests of plantation tenants versus those of nearby villagers who previously had sold land to French plantation owners (sometimes under duress) and now wanted it back. It was possible for a resolute local committee to outmaneuver even a national ministry, as we shall see later.

PETITIONS AND SPECIAL INVESTIGATORS

When revolutionaries took over the imperial delegate's office in Hanoi on 19 August 1945, they found among other things almost one thousand unanswered petitions. A new surge of several thousand petitions arrived in the mail from as far away as the Mekong delta in subsequent weeks.[90] Dispatching petitions to state officials was familiar practice from the colonial era, although never in such quantity. Petitioners probably discussed their problems extensively before deciding to act, then might pay (or obtain a favor from) someone to compose the text in appropriate language and format. While individuals learned the new format quickly, it would take longer to master the new language of citizenship. By mid-September, the vast majority of petitions began with the words "Democratic Republic of Vietnam. Independence, Liberty, Happiness." A few gave their petition a lunar calendar date. Others proudly proclaimed "First Year of the Democratic Republic," in imitation of French Revolutionary custom, but most simply wrote the solar calendar date. Petitions were generally addressed to "Elder Hồ" (Cụ Hồ) or "President Hồ" (Hồ Chủ Tịch), while a minority were addressed to a government office, particularly the Interior Ministry or the Northern Region Office. The petitioner then stated his/her name, explained the problem, and signed at the bottom, usually in roman script (quốc ngữ), but sometimes in Chinese characters.[91]

Each petition that arrived in the daily mail was given a date stamp, recorded in a logbook, and viewed by one or more officials, who often scribbled marginalia and marked specific passages.[92] A routing slip was then typed up, sometimes including specific questions to guide local investigators or reminders about which government decrees were relevant to the case.[93] Most petitions then went to a province committee, with instructions to "investigate and report." The province might pass the petition down to the district committee, send a query to the relevant commune, or dispatch an individual to investigate on the spot. Persons had to be questioned, perhaps a solution worked out, and an answer formulated for transmission to Hanoi. Delay often triggered a reminder from Hanoi, which also reserved the right to send an inspector directly to the scene. The amount of effort involved was extraordinary. However, given the large number of petition routing slips sitting in Hanoi files with no evidence of resolution, one can guess that less than half the cases were ever closed. The system may also have become less effective with time. Especially at the province level, officials must have felt harassed, with papers piling up making complaints that individually did not seem momentous. District officials generally knew more about a case than their province superiors, and commune officials knew the most, yet all were reluctant to commit precise answers to paper. When pressed, they developed the art of explaining local particulars using the generalizing rhetoric of government decrees and edicts.

Early on the DRV provisional government recognized the necessity of occasionally bypassing the administrative hierarchy by sending its own special investigators to get to the bottom of problems revealed by petitions or other sources of information. Already on 3 September 1945, Nguyễn Tuân Nghĩa was given a paper authorizing him to travel anywhere in northern Vietnam "to resolve any and all political questions." Local people's committees were ordered to assist him in every way possible. Nghĩa traveled with an aide, and both carried pistols.[94] In October, the Interior Ministry dispatched a political inspector to correct the "mistaken behavior" of a district people's committee in Phú Thọ province.[95] The papers issued to these early DRV inspectors are reminiscent in plenipotentiary tone to those given to "commissioners of the republic" in the French Revolution, which probably was no accident. In practice, an inspector usually set out with a dispatch case full of petitions and telegrams relating to a variety of cases, which he was supposed to solve before returning to Hanoi, not remaining as an alternative source of authority to the local committees.

In late November, Hồ Chí Minh decreed establishment of a national Special Inspectorate (Ban Thanh Tra Đặc Biệt), with authority to seize evidence and question members of any people's committee or government office, as well as to suspend or incarcerate any official pending court proceedings.[96] A month later the Ministry of Information and Propaganda alerted the public to the Special Inspectorate's existence, and specifically encouraged citizens to address complaints (khiếu nại) to Elder Hồ's office.[97] Bùi Bằng Đoàn, former royal court mandarin, and Cù Huy Cận, Democratic Party leader and DRV minister of agriculture, were appointed to head the Special Inspectorate.[98] Meanwhile, the Northern Region Committee had quietly formed its own Political and Administrative

Inspectorate (Ban Thanh Tra Chính Trị và Hành Chính).[99] The Special Inspectorate appeared to limit itself to processing petitions to forward to the Northern
Region Committee and to composing instructions on routing slips destined for
central Vietnam provinces. By contrast, the Political and Administrative Inspectorate routinely dispatched members to northern provinces to investigate and attempt to resolve cases. Two inspectors, Đào Văn Biểu and Nguyễn Duy Thân,
traveled constantly between January and August 1946. Biểu, troubleshooter par
excellence, moved from province to province to deal with Vietnamese-Chinese
altercations, disputes with Vietnam Nationalist Party branches, election irregu-
larities, local detentions, and disappearances. If Biểu failed to get local cooperation, he sometimes arranged for his superiors to order the responsible province
chairman to come immediately to Hanoi for a dressing-down. Police could also
be dispatched to continue the investigation

In Hanoi, inspectorate staff built up substantial files on each province administration, subdivided by district. Many an incoming petition received its own
folder, into which clerks added copies of routing slips, telegrams, and internal
memos. Files were opened on particular long-running disputes, poorly functioning committees, cases of flagrant misuse of power, and tensions between local
leaders and specialized bureaus. President Hồ Chí Minh perused some fraction
of the thousands of petitions addressed to him; if he commented on a specific
case, it immediately received priority attention. For example, a long series of petitions from the family of a sixty-year-old merchant, Đỗ Đình Thiểm, eventually
came to the notice of the president, who urged subordinates to get to the bottom
of Hải Dương province assertions that Thiểm had escaped jail and disappeared.
The Northern Region Inspectorate threatened Hải Dương with unspecified
sanctions if it turned out that that information was false.[100]

When a province committee failed to respond to a specific inspectorate query,
reminders were sent. If a province response was deemed unsatisfactory, further
correspondence ensued. After several months the tone of inspectorate messages
became peremptory. In February 1946, the Special Inspectorate sent an urgent and
secret *(khẩn mật)* letter to the Hà Nam province committee, threatening to apply
"resolute methods" against it if repeated queries about the killing of the former
province mandarin, Đàm Duy Huyến, were not answered satisfactorily within
ten days.[101] Perhaps there was an answer, as one month later an unnamed staff
member placed a summary note on the file which was headed: "The killing of
Đàm Duy Huyến, greedy official who sabotaged the revolutionary movement."
In the meantime, however, the Northern Region Committee sent down a blistering criticism of Hà Nam's general behavior, ranking it as "the province with the
most citizen complaints of all," and characterizing it as burdened with a committee that failed to do its job properly and a leadership that oppressed its own people.
Regarding one specific commune, problems had been brought to the attention of

the Hà Nam committee five months prior, yet there was no evidence that anyone had looked into the case, much less taken remedial action.[102]

At province level and below, some committees resented the right of citizens to petition the central government directly. Already in October 1945, the chairman of the Hanoi suburban committee was telling subordinates that petitions ought to go through the committee hierarchy, not around it. Local committees deserved respect because they represented the people and the government. "Only if a committee misuses its power and oppresses the people should people consider complaining to Higher Authority (Thượng Cấp)," the chairman concluded.[103] The Hà Đông committee chairman grumbled that relatives of prisoners were "causing trouble with investigations" because Hà Đông's proximity to Hanoi enabled them to submit petitions quickly.[104] Some provinces organized their own censorship offices and proceeded to tamper with the mail, including outgoing petitions. In Hải Dương, censors tore up three registered letters containing petitions on behalf of one detainee, an action which the province chairman criticized as "anarchistic and antipolitical behavior."[105] Hanoi had already ordered local committees to leave mail surveillance to the PTT.

By March 1946, far too many citizen petitions were coming in for the existing administrative system to handle them. Especially at the province level, committee staff must have felt overwhelmed, with papers piling up on hundreds of complaints, pressure persisting from Hanoi, and district and commune committees unable or unwilling to provide necessary information. In Hanoi, the Northern Region Committee proposed to the government that its inspection capacities be upgraded and renamed the Northern Region Inspectorate.[106] Probably this proposal was approved, as two months later an edict divided the northern region into four zones, each to be given its own special inspectorate.[107] However, the files make no further mention of these zone inspectorates, which suggests they never materialized. In October, the Northen Committee requested that Đào Văn Biểu and Nguyễn Duy Thân be detached from the Northern Region Inspectorate and returned to their former responsibilities, as local administration had improved and hence diminished the need for roving inspectors.[108] It seems more likely that someone had decided to reduce the political profile of the Northern Region Inspectorate in favor of routine processing of case files. One month later, an internal note referred to dissolution of the Northern Region Inspectorate, with some of its tasks taken by new offices for internal deportation, prison inspection, and petitions.[109]

Meanwhile, the national Special Inspectorate had its own problems. From its establishment in January 1946, the Special Inspectorate seems to have subsisted financially on ad hoc transfers from other central government units.[110] In August, the Finance Ministry gave the Interior Ministry 20,000$BIC to establish an inspection service, probably a sign that the autonomy previously enjoyed by the

Special Inspectorate was at an end.[111] Petitions continued to arrive addressed to Elder Hồ or President Hồ, and he may have resumed reading some of them following his return from France in late October, but the overall handling of citizen petitions had been demoted to just another administrative function. Cù Huy Cận became a valued DRV bureaucrat, while Bùi Bằng Đoàn was elected chair of the National Assembly's Standing Committee in late 1946.[112]

ELECTIONS: NATIONAL

Although the early September promise of National Assembly elections within three months seemed like a chimera to some observers, the DRV provisional government proceeded resolutely to draft the necessary electoral rules and implementing instructions. In mid-October, the election date of 25 December was announced, then modified to 23 December a few weeks later. Regulations were promulgated concerning voter and candidate eligibility, preparation of voter rolls, issuing of voter identification cards, formation of provincial electoral boards, restrictions on campaigning, ballot counting procedures, rights of complaint, and announcement of results.[113] It was an incredibly ambitious bureaucratic agenda, especially in regard to completing voter rolls and issuing voter cards, tasks which were assigned to village and urban neighborhood committees. Committees too were expected to compile lists of citizens excluded from voting, which included the insane (điên), professional beggars, individuals under permanent institutional care, and criminals not pardoned by the existing government. Assembly candidates did not have to reside in the province where they stood for election; they could compete individually or join with others in an electoral slate. The time and place of each campaign meeting to attract voters had to be given to the local people's committee one day in advance. Meetings could be disbanded if they appeared to jeopardize "independence and public order." Candidate posters, banners, and leaflets had to be checked in advance by local committees.

Each province or city was assigned a specific number of National Assembly seats to be contested in the election, based more or less on population statistics. Nam Định, Thanh Hóa, and Quảng Nam received the largest number of seats (fifteen each), while five provinces were allocated only one seat.[114] The total number of seats came to 329,[115] with thirty of these being reserved for ethnic minority delegates who would come from twenty-seven different provinces.[116] On election day, voters could cast their ballots for as many candidates as there were seats being contested in their province. A candidate had to receive more than 50 percent of votes cast to be elected. If not enough candidates exceeded 50 percent then a second election would be organized in the province affected. In early November the Interior Ministry disseminated further details on how candidate lists and voter rolls should be filled out, the proper design for voter identification cards, and the exact wording for election result forms. The ministry admitted that communication limitations and paper shortages would impede election arrangements, yet could only suggest to province committees that they dispatch teams to each locality to explain the importance of the National Assembly election and proper procedures for implementation.[117]

Newspapers were slow to pick up the national election story, probably mindful that delicate negotiations were underway between Việt Minh, Nationalist Party, and Revolutionary League leaders about not only election modalities, but also the future state system in general (see chapter 7). From early December, however, editorials and articles about an impending election proliferated, nudged on by the Ministry of Propaganda and Việt Minh activists. Banner headlines (sometimes in red ink) were spread across front pages, urging people to vote; electoral procedures were explained in detail. The purpose of the whole exercise, as one paper put it, was to select good representatives who would draft a constitution and elect an executive government. Beyond that, the people of Vietnam would be participating in the widest possible exercise of voting rights, a feat allegedly accomplished by only one other country—the Soviet Union.[118] Another paper warned that people who did not vote were putting themselves "on a par with the insane, beggars, and criminals who have lost this right of citizenship." Then it added darkly, "to vote for an unworthy candidate is to sell one's rights cheaply, to sell liberty and happiness cheaply, to commit a crime against the Fatherland."[119] Two days before the election this Huế paper alerted voters to "evil, spurious *(tà ngụy)* influences wanting to force their way into the people's heart." These elements had to be struggled against, and only persons of talent and virtue elected. "We only listen to our own kind *(ta chỉ nghe ta),*" the writer concluded tellingly.[120] How to identify the best candidates remained an issue. More boldly than most, one Hanoi weekly contrasted "revolutionary" and "political" candidates, suggesting that many (but not all) revolutionaries were only good for tearing things down, whereas Vietnam now was entering the phase of building things up. On the other hand, many politicians had reaped personal benefit from the colonial system and taken part in the farcical theatrics of colonial assemblies, which the forthcoming National Assembly definitely had to avoid.[121]

The registration of candidates proceeded slowly in most provinces, with only a handful able to dispatch certified lists to the central government by the third week in December. On 18 December, Hồ Chí Minh decreed postponement of the election from 23 December to 6 January 1946.[122] While this was presented as a concession to the Nationalist Party and Revolutionary League, leading up to the 24 December agreement signed by Hồ Chí Minh, Vũ Hồng Khanh, and Nguyễn Hải Thần (see chapter 7), a delay probably would have been required on administrative grounds alone. As candidate lists came in, worries evaporated (at least in northern and north-central Vietnam) that some provinces would lack sufficient candidates for the number of seats available. Remarkably, Thái Bình had eighty-eight candidates to contest thirteen seats, Kiến An sixty persons for seven seats, and Hanoi city seventy-four persons for six seats.[123]

How candidates were to convey themselves to voters in the short time available remained problematic. The 7 October election decree, described above, required candidates to present their propaganda materials to local people's committees before distribution, and to obtain committee permission before scheduling any public meetings. We don't know how many candidates obeyed these rules, or how rigorously the rules were enforced. In mid-December, one writer criticized candidates for being too slow to convene meetings to present their platforms to voters. He also urged candidates to take questions from the audience, for example on how best to fight the French in the South, how to define "protracted resistance," when the world was going to recognize Vietnam's independence, or how to expand economic output.[124] Later an unnamed candidate in Nam Định province was congratulated for organizing a meeting to talk about the August Revolution, the future constitution, the international situation, and the role of youth and women in building the country.[125]

Such single candidate meetings do not seem to have occurred often, however. It was more common for the people's committee, the local office of the Propaganda Ministry, or the local Việt Minh branch to invite all or some candidates to present their platforms to a public audience. Although chairmen tended to discourage questions from the floor, interjections were common. Candidates sometimes traded accusations. One newspaper chided candidates for putting nasty labels on each other at the drop of a hat, for example calling an opponent "reactionary" or "Fourth [International]," the latter a coy reference to Trotskyism. On the other hand, one candidate became outraged when another candidate simply raised his voice, leading the journalist to question rhetorically whether it had become a crime to speak loudly.[126]

Haiphong city paid attention to the upcoming national election earlier than most places. Already in the third week of November the local Việt Minh daily newspaper, *Dân Chủ (Democracy)*, reprinted the official candidate and voter registration forms for people to fill out and submit.[127] In early December, the Haiphong People's Committee publicized the names of the city's thirteen ward heads *(trưởng khu)*, as well as addresses where citizens could register. *Dân Chủ* editors placed a notice on their front page: "Whether you are Việt Minh, not Việt Minh, or opposed to the Việt Minh, every citizen go ahead and take part in the National Assembly Election."[128] On 16 December, the people's committee convened a public meeting at the Opera House square, where candidates were given five minutes each to sway the audience. According to *Dân Chủ*: "One gentleman focused on people's livelihood (Dương Duy Mão), another sided with the poor and with women (Dr. Vịnh), still another wanted to foster a sports movement

(Phạm Quang Chất). Pharmacist Vũ Công Thuyết emphasized his ability to make explosives. Some stressed that they belonged to no party." People listened attentively, but did not take a visible or vocal position for or against any particular candidate. The reporter considered this a very positive sign, demonstrating how citizens were preoccupied with national solidarity.[129] Several Haiphong candidates selected their own speaking venues, publicized their intentions, obtained loudspeakers, and spoke to audiences without seeking permission from the authorities.[130]

Two days following the Haiphong Opera House meeting the national election was postponed to 6 January 1946, which led the city people's committee to reopen candidate registrations and accept five more contestants. Ward representatives now were sent to family residences to inscribe the names of voters and issue voter identification cards. On the other hand, voter rolls at work sites and headquarters of organizations were discontinued, perhaps to reduce the danger of duplication. There was considerable organizational confusion, but also growing propaganda momentum. Haiphong voters were urged not to listen to those who urged them to write in President Hồ's name on their ballot, as he was standing for election only in Hanoi. Front-page woodcuts showed a wife waking up her lazy husband to go to vote together, citizens led by a soldier and a minority woman eagerly approaching a ballot box, and a scale balancing ballots and bullets. Most vividly, one cartoon depicted ballots being fed into a cannon to blast French soldiers holding a tricolor, with the following caption: "Ballots are ammunition to wipe out aggressors (giặc)." As election day approached, Haiphong residents were urged to fly the national flag and affix leaflets to the front of their homes stating "6 January 1946. Go to Vote".[131]

Nam Định was slower to focus on the election than Haiphong, but by the third week of December the local office of the Propaganda Ministry and the local Việt Minh branch had taken up the cause energetically. The weekly Việt Minh paper, Nam Tiến (Southern Advance), invited all province candidates to respond to a set of questions, then printed twelve of the answers in abbreviated fashion. Not surprisingly the paper gave editorial preference to Đặng Châu Tuệ, chairman of the Nam Định administrative committee, who had joined the Revolutionary Youth League in the late 1920s and subsequently spent considerable time in colonial jails. Reflecting a central ICP policy decision, Tuệ and other Việt Minh Front members were not identified as such in the election.[132] At least six non-Việt Minh candidates had their edited answers printed.[133] Meanwhile, the Propaganda Ministry office asked the fifteen individuals running for Nam Định city seats to address a public meeting, and all but two accepted. Ms. Nguyễn Khoa Diệu Hồng was invited to go first, but before she could speak several members of the audience asked her why the Việt Minh had yet to dissolve itself, now that a national unity government was being established. She replied that because the Việt Minh's work was far from complete, the issue of dissolution had yet to arise, a response that was said to have received cheers and applause from the audience.[134] The meeting continued for two and a half hours, with all thirteen candidates present apparently able to take the rostrum.[135]

Several newspapers in Hanoi became election vehicles for specific slates or individual candidates, a media practice common during the colonial era. *Tương Lai (Future)* touted the slate headed by its publisher, Trương Văn Minh, which included one of his feature writers, two journalists from other papers, a high school teacher, an architect, and a landlord. *Tương Lai* criticized unnamed competitors who aped the self-seeking "Mr. Assembly Man" (Ông Nghị) of colonial times, when they should be putting the needs of the nation ahead of individual or party political interests. "We don't want a new class to materialize," the writer concluded.[136] Another periodical, *Bạn Gái (Women's Friend)*, published a special issue just prior to the election to promote the candidacy of Ms. Đoàn Tâm Đán, with much of the front page taken up by a woodcut of Ms. Đán wearing the traditional northern head scarf.[137] *Đồng Minh*, the organ of members of the Revolutionary League prepared to work with the existing government, touted four members recently returned from China, describing their past patriotic endeavours in detail but saying nothing about their policy platforms as candidates. They stood for election in four northern provinces, and publicly opposed the deal whereby the League would receive twenty nonelected seats in the National Assembly.[138]

The publishers of the *Dân Sinh (People's Livelihood)* newspaper compiled a preelection booklet containing the names, occupations, and home addresses of the seventy-four individuals standing for election in Hanoi, as well as self-promotions provided by seventeen of the candidates.[139] The occupations of the Hanoi candidates were as follows: public servants (16), merchants/manufacturers (15), teachers/principals (11), physicians (7), writers/journalists (6), people's committee members (5), DRV ministers (3), landowners (3), engineers (2), and other (6). From the biographical data and brief platforms provided, we catch a glimpse into the multitudinous backgrounds, ideas, and assumptions that characterized Hanoi's political aspirants at the end of 1945. Viet Minh adherents were mixed together with members of the Vietnam Nationalist Party and Vietnam Revolutionary League. Former employees of the French administration offered their expertise to the new independent state. Political statements were deliberately vague and nonconfrontational, reflecting the public push for national unity at this time. Despite Vietnam's grim economic circumstances, some merchants and manufacturers promised to open trade with the United States, end unemployment, apply the latest scientific methods to cultivate rice, and create a national airline. There was no discussion by candidates about how the future National Assembly ought to conduct its business, or what should be the content of the future constitution.

Some provinces ignored provisional President Hồ's 18 December postponement decree and organized voting on 23 December, rather than wait until 6
January. In Kiến An, only three candidates received more than 50 percent of
the vote each, necessitating a runoff one month later for the remaining four
seats.[140] A number of central and southern provinces also appear to have voted
on 23 December.

National Election Day, 6 January 1946, took on the character of a traditional
festival in many villages and urban neighborhoods, with drums alerting everyone early, individuals putting on their best clothing, flag-bearing youths marching from one street to another, and people converging on the community hall
(đình) or headquarters of the local administrative committee. Contrary to regulations, activists circulated among those waiting to vote, calling out the names of
their favored candidates. It is unlikely that voter rolls had been completed in
most venues, much less voter cards distributed. Ballots did not have the names of
candidates printed on them, so literate voters wrote down their selections, and
illiterate voters received assistance from a relative or anyone else available. Việt
Minh youths stood by to help, with predictable results. In the contest for the six
Hanoi city seats, there was concern that voters might not write in the full name
of Hồ Chí Minh, instead complying with traditional name-avoidance customs
for Vietnamese monarchs.[141] Young men conducting the election in one Hanoi
neighborhood dumped the ballots without bothering to count them, then reported a 99.9 percent vote for Hồ Chí Minh.[142] In Huế, voters were told to write
only given names on the ballot, not surnames, and often encouraged to vote for
"Yên Phộc," a corruption of "Ông Phiệt," meaning Tôn Quang Phiệt, chairman
of the Thừa Thiên province committee.[143] Anything approximating Phiệt's name
probably was accepted by ballot scrutineers, as he easily won election.

The scant information obtained about election preparations and voting in
faraway southern Vietnam was published eagerly in northern and central region
newspapers.[144] Allegedly twenty thousand voter cards had been issued to citizens
in Saigon-Cholon, despite French occupation of the city.[145] Later the press reported that forty-two cadres had died in the south while organizing the vote, and
that scores of citizens going to the polls in two provinces had been killed or injured
by French aircraft assaults.[146] A unit of Vietnamese trying to resist the French advance in Laos found time to cast ballots in Tchépone, each trooper receiving in
return a glutinous rice cake and a pack of cigarettes.[147]

Two days after the national election, the Northern Region Committee requested voting statistics from all twenty-eight provinces and cities under its jurisdiction. Specifically it wanted the number of candidates, the number of people
who went to the polls, the number of legal ballots cast, the names of successful
candidates, and the number of votes received by each.[148] Any formal protests had
to go to the relevant provincial election supervisory board, whose decision was

FIGURE 2. Hanoi electees to the National Assembly meet the public. From left to right: Hoàng Văn Đức, Hồ Chí Minh, Trần Duy Hưng, Nguyễn Văn Luyện, Vũ Đình Hòe, and Mme Nguyễn Thị Thục Viên. Photo given to me by Hoàng Văn Đức, whose image was airbrushed from later reproductions.

final.[149] Available archive files lack any provincial responses, leaving us with a handful of statistics reprinted in newspapers. In Hanoi, 176,765 ballots were cast from among 187,880 registered voters, an impressive 92 percent turnout. Hồ Chí Minh received 98.4 percent of the vote, the highest in the country. Trần Duy Hưng, chairman of the Hanoi city committee, received 73 percent, closely followed by Vũ Đình Hòe (minister of national education) with 72.6 percent, then Nguyễn Văn Luyện (public intellectual) with 61.4 percent, Nguyễn Thị Thục Viên (a girl's school principal) with 55.4 percent, and Hoàng Văn Đức (Democratic Party secretary) with 52.2 percent.[150] Hanoi thus filled all six allocated seats without the need for any runoff election.

In Haiphong, 88 percent of the 543,089 registered voters cast ballots on 6 January, at sixty-nine polling stations around the city. After counting was completed, ballot boxes and certified tallies were delivered to the election board at the Opera House for consolidation. Three candidates easily obtained more than half the votes and were thus declared elected. Trương Trung Phụng, a member of the Revolutionary League who had sided with the DRV government, received

LIVERPOOL JOHN MOORES UNIVERSITY
LEARNING SERVICES

91 percent voter support, probably a reflection of how anxious people were to see an end to party political disputation. Nguyễn Đình Thi, a prominent young Việt Minh writer, garnered 88.1 percent of the vote, while Nguyễn Sơn Hà, a Haiphong industrialist, obtained 69.1 percent.[151] It is very unlikely that all provinces around the country were able to imitate Hanoi and Haiphong in providing the central government with detailed voting statistics. In late January, the Northern Region Committee reminded provinces which had yet to send certified results to do so immediately, as the government wanted National Assembly delegates to arrive in Hanoi by 20 February. We don't know how many provinces had to conduct runoff elections due to an insufficient number of candidates obtaining more than 50 percent of votes.[152] It appears that some of these runoff elections for National Assembly seats were conducted simultaneously with subsequent elections for province people's councils (see below), while some never occurred at all.

In late January, the *Sự Thật (Truth)* newspaper asserted that 95 percent of Vietnam's eligible citizens had participated in the national election.[153] This figure must have been pulled out of thin air, as no national count of registered voters existed, much less a total vote count. Most localities had not been able to issue voter cards. Already in early December, Hanoi officials had noted that voter registrations were lagging far behind the number of citizens likely to come to polling stations on election day. This, rather than a deliberate stuffing of ballot boxes, probably explains why some provinces reported more ballots tallied than the number of voters registered.[154]

French officials were not impressed by the 6 January National Assembly elections. Sûreté agents in Tonkin claimed that Annamites had shown little interest in the proceedings, a reflection of more general political lassitude. A later analysis considered the elections a parody of popular consultation, "neither national nor democratic."[155] Vietnamese sources from the period point to widespread public interest in the elections, and serious attempts by the DRV administration to follow correct electoral procedures. In northern and north-central Vietnam, most results were credible, if not achieved in full compliance with relevant government edicts. In the south, administrative confusion and French counteraction prevented a similar outcome. Predictably, the Propaganda Ministry asserted total, enthusiastic southern participation in the elections. No ministry encouragement was required for the press to take the same line. People wanted to believe in the territorial integrity of Vietnam, and the 6 January 1946 elections were considered proof positive.[156] Philippe Devillers judged the DRV elections no less authentic than contemporary electoral efforts in France by General de Gaulle and Georges Bidault.[157] In the teeth of war, recent famine, and dire poverty, without prior organizing experience, 6 January nonetheless proved to be the fairest election the DRV/SRV has experienced to the present day.

ELECTIONS: LOCAL

The DRV government regarded election of people's councils *(hội đồng nhân dân)* at province and commune levels to be another important step in legitimizing the overall political system. Councils were meant to provide local democratic representation, and more particularly, to select the smaller administrative committees. No sooner were the national elections completed on 6 January 1946 than the Interior Ministry instructed all provinces to conduct people's council elections before 15 February. Messages relating to election procedures now increased to at least 25 percent of total Bắc Bộ Phủ outgoing and incoming traffic.[158] While Hanoi authorities propounded a single procedure for implementing province council elections, many province committees preferred to make adjustments of their own. There were province proposals to modify the number of council seats up for election, to restrict individuals from standing for election outside their home district, and to exclude government employees from running for election. The Interior Ministry rejected these proposals and others, yet it seems likely that local disparities persisted. When it became apparent that many provinces were experiencing administrative difficulties, Hanoi extended the province council election deadline to the end of February. Two provinces were ordered to cancel their election results of 14 February and send voters to the polls again on 28 February. The content of these messages, as well as the sheer volume, demonstrate that both central government and province committees took council elections seriously.

One hefty file on the province people's council election in Tuyên Quang, northwest of Hanoi, offers us a unique view of voter rolls, candidate lists, ballot tallies, and election results.[159] Some communes had managed to compile registration lists containing each voter's name and age, and sometimes place of birth, occupation, and literate/illiterate status. In early February 1946, a total of 40,742 Tuyên Quang province voters made their choices from district slates ranging from four to twelve candidates. Voter turnout ranged from 76 percent to 99.5 percent in the countryside, and was 69 percent in Tuyên Quang town. Town officials had managed to mimeograph tally sheets for their neighborhood clerks to fill in, while rural commune clerks had to draw up their own tally sheets from a national model. Town voters had a choice of twelve candidates for three province council seats. Of 5,943 registered voters in town, 4,106 cast votes, but 103 ballots were declared invalid, leaving 4,003 valid ballots. Nguyễn Công Bình easily won a seat with 2,863 votes, but no one else obtained more than 50 percent, forcing a runoff election at which only 2,519 persons bothered to vote. When all candidates scored below 50 percent in this runoff, the two top candidates, with 47.3 percent and 44 percent of the vote, were declared elected per government rules designed to avoid yet another runoff. In Hồng Thái district the top candidate received forty-six more votes than the total number of valid ballots cast, yet no one appears to have pointed out this discrepancy. Nonetheless, the overall impression is one of formalities being observed with remarkable care, and commune clerks laboring long hours to achieve results.[160]

February 1946 came and went, but most provinces had yet to conduct people's council elections. Hanoi had conceded too much in January when it authorized provinces to "reorganize" their administrative committees without waiting for people's councils to elect official committees.[161] The DRV government had far more pressing problems in March, as we shall see, but starting in April it pressured recalcitrant provinces to hold people's councils elections urgently. One by one the provinces of the Red River delta complied, and sent their election results for scrutiny in the capital. When Bắc Ninh reported two candidates with identical vote counts, the Northern Region Committee instructed it to check birth certificates and declare the elder candidate elected, a notable bow to tradition. Someone at the center was cross-checking results carefully, as when Kiến An province was told to exclude one winning candidate because he had already been elected in Bắc Giang. Once Hanoi had approved the outcome of a particular province people's council election, attention shifted to getting the council to elect a new administrative committee. Hanoi also had to scrutinize results of these administrative committee elections, although here approval seemed to be almost automatic. There is ample evidence that the composition of province administrative committees changed little, and that people's councils often failed to exercise the oversight role delineated for them in government decrees.

Elections to the Hanoi and Haiphong people's councils, both originally scheduled for 24 February, were seen by experienced observers as better tests of democratic procedure than either the 6 January 1946 national election or the provincial people's council elections. In Hanoi on 12 February, the deputy chair of the city's administrative committee, Khuất Duy Tiến, called a meeting of more than one hundred candidates, where he encouraged them to organize their own gatherings, print leaflets, paint banners, and circulate through town with loudspeakers mounted on autos. However, Tiến cautioned candidates against "individual" (cá nhân) street demonstrations. Everyone present at the meeting is said to have agreed not to launch personal attacks or to engage in other behavior "damaging to the reputation or rights of fellow candidates." Then Tiến revealed that because the Hanoi Administrative Committee lacked sufficient funds to print two hundred thousand ballots, candidates would need to make financial donations.[162] One wing of the Vietnam Revolutionary League took the Hanoi election seriously, publicizing its slate of three merchants, one industrialist, and one government employee.[163] However, the authorities found it necessary to postpone the Hanoi election to 10 March, then to defer it indefinitely.[164] In Haiphong, representatives of the Việt Minh, Democratic Party, Nationalist Party, and Revolutionary League met on 9 February to discuss the Việt Minh idea of a unity slate containing three candidates from each organization. Five days later, however, the Nationalist Party withdrew its participation in the election and denounced Việt Minh manipulation of the proceedings. On 23 February, the Haiphong Administrative Committee deferred the election to 10 March, then again to 16 March. On 11 March, however, the election was "postponed until new orders."[165] The DRV government offered no explanation for these failures of democratic process, which probably first reflected the capacity of opposition parties and independents to challenge Việt Minh primacy in the cities, then the chaos surrounding the 6 March Preliminary Accord and arrival of French troops (see chapters 3 and 4).

Elections to Hanoi's five ward councils *(ủy ban khu phố)* in June 1946 incurred no postponements. Candidates hoisted banners and distributed leaflets, but attendance at meetings was sparse and most newspapers ignored the proceedings. On 16 June, markets closed for the morning, flags were displayed, and citizens walked to the same polling stations as for the 6 January election. Because of the high number of candidates, and the requirement that victors receive more than 50 percent of votes cast, three out of five wards needed a follow-up election on 30 June to secure a full council. Noting that many illiterate voters had stayed away from the first election, Việt Minh groups promised them assistance from literate youths on polling day. Some citizens tried unsuccessfully to have a family member serve as substitute voter.[166] At the Opera House on 7 July, acting DRV President Huỳnh Thúc Kháng presided over swearing-in ceremonies for all members of the five Hanoi ward councils.[167]

As of late July, people's councils had still not been elected in six northern provinces. Four province seats had only recently been wrested from the Vietnam Nationalist Party or were still being contested. Hải Ninh had been partly controlled by the Revolutionary League, while Lai Châu had been out of touch with Hanoi for more than a year, and was now occupied by French troops.[168] A month later, three provinces still remained without people's councils: Lào Cai, Hải Ninh, and Lai Châu.[169] Meanwhile, the Haiphong administrative committee formally requested a further delay in organizing its people's council election, and this was approved.[170] In central Vietnam, it seems that some provinces elected people's councils, but details are lacking. In Thừa Thiên province, adjacent to Huế, an election took place in April, and the council subsequently selected Hoàng Anh over Hoàng Phương as chairman, by a vote of sixteen to three.[171]

Commune people's councils, conceived of as the foundational level of democratic government, proved far more difficult to implement than national or provincial councils. Often commune administrative committees were in no hurry to answer to an elected people's council. More fundamentally, modernists saw village and commune Vietnam as infested by parochialism, petty intrigue, vendettas, and perpetual status competition. Factionalism *(óc bè phái)* was endemic.

According to this view, if a commune election was called, candidates would go house-to-house making promises, criticizing their opponents, ignoring the common cause. In this polluted atmosphere, virtuous, well-qualified villagers would not seek office.[172] For these commentators, the more acquainted people were with each other the less able they were to achieve a good electoral result. Nationalist Party writers took this argument a step further, calling for communal administrative committees to be appointed by higher echelons rather than elected by people's councils. This position was vehemently rejected by Việt Minh writers, who however admitted that an extended period of political education was required before local government could function properly.[173] By July 1946, only one northern province (Bắc Giang) had submitted results of commune people's council elections to Hanoi for approval. The Northern Region Committee set a deadline of 15 August to complete the process, yet it must have known this was unrealistic.[174]

In July 1946 the Northern Region Committee proposed to the DRV government that it set a date for election of the three regional administrative committees (north, center, south), as specified in the November 1945 decree. Mindful of their own provisional status after almost one year of labor, members of the northern committee argued that election of "official" *(chính thức)* regional committees would complete the structure of "people's power" *(chính quyền nhân dân)* in Vietnam.[175] By their own prior admission, however, people's councils had yet to be elected in many northern communes. More importantly, French control over much of Nam Bộ and French troop advances up the south-central coast made DRV regional elections there quite impractical. Even arranging for each northern province or city people's council to vote on a roster of regional administrative committee candidates was too much to ask in late 1946.

By mid-1946, the DRV civil apparatus was proving its effectiveness north of the sixteenth parallel. Decrees and other instructions composed by central ministries and bureaus made their way to regional, province, district, and commune committees, where they received serious attention if not always compliance. Lower echelons responded to specific queries, sent in periodic reports, and generated their own requests or propositions. Desirous that most former colonial civil servants continue working, but lacking money to pay them, the DRV government encouraged continuing employees to find their own "temporary" means of sustenance, and many did so. As we have seen, the authorities gave considerable attention to organizing national and local elections, not as mere propaganda exercises, but with the serious intent of creating representative government. The next chapter looks at DRV efforts to write a constitution, create a legislative branch of government, and develop education, justice, and communication systems.

The Government at Work

With the DRV administrative hierarchy erected and national elections realized, attention shifted to convening the National Assembly, ending the government's provisional status, drafting a constitution, and enhancing Hanoi's capacity to direct local affairs. During February and March 1946, Hồ Chí Minh had to concentrate on negotiations with the French and Chinese (see chapter 4), yet he found time to guide domestic discussions leading to a new cabinet and meet delegations from the countryside. It was a considerable disappointment to most Assembly delegates when their inaugural session lasted only four hours. Nguyễn Văn Tố, chair of the new Assembly Standing Committee, tried unsuccessfully to get the executive to recognize his standing and to help him build contacts with dispersed delegates and local citizens. Tố's failure is one of the untold stories of DRV history. Political debate surrounding Vietnam's first constitution peaked on the floor of the Assembly in early November, a lively event deliberately ignored by later propaganda czars. Meanwhile the DRV executive took more powers unto itself. I look at three centrally controlled bodies that were meant to extend operations to every province in the country—the education system, the judiciary, and the postal service. While education was starved of funds and justice faltered, the former colonial PTT gave valuable service to the new authorities.

CONVENING THE NATIONAL ASSEMBLY

Three days after the 6 January 1946 national elections, Hồ Chí Minh decreed that the National Assembly would convene in Hanoi on 3 March.[1] This decision preempted Vietnam Nationalist Party proposals for quicker Assembly convocation and selection of a new cabinet. When the Nationalist Party publicly objected to the "delay," ICP writers quoted chapter and verse from the 17 October 1945 election decree, which specified complicated procedures for tallying results, hearing complaints, conducting runoff elections, forwarding delegate names to Hanoi, and securing cabinet approval. They also pointed to the time it would take for southern delegates to travel to the capital.[2] Six weeks following the election, all but four northern provinces had forwarded Assembly delegate names to Hanoi.[3] Processing of results in Trung Bộ above the sixteenth parallel also went well, but the outcome below the sixteenth parallel remained fragmentary. Beyond these operational requirements, however, we may surmise that Hồ Chí Minh wanted time to try to reach some sort of understanding with French and Chinese interlocutors before the National Assembly met.[4]

During the lead-up to the 6 January elections there had been scant public discussion of what delegates going to the National Assembly would be expected to do beyond deliberating the draft constitution and ratifying a new cabinet. In early January, the propaganda minister, Trần Huy Liệu, gave a speech on the history and general characteristics of the legislative branch of government.[5] Provisional President Hồ Chí Minh told a Nam Định audience that they soon would have their own representatives, but that the National Assembly belonged to the entire country, not to Nam Định or the northern region.[6] The principal Việt Minh newspaper in central Vietnam positioned the National Assembly within the "new democratic revolution" (cách mạng tân dân chủ), which in this context meant that the minority must obey the majority, and lower elected bodies must obey higher ones. The editors assumed that the Assembly's Standing Committee would exercise considerable power, but that if it "acted wrongly" (làm bậy) the Assembly could override it. And if the Assembly failed in its duties, the people could take direct action, either peaceful or violent in nature.[7] Since the Việt Minh and ICP persistently claimed to represent "the people," these words constituted a blunt warning to future legislators.

The day after the 6 January elections, a committee to prepare convocation of the National Assembly was named, although whether it actually met is uncertain.[8] At the end of January, Việt Minh newspapers began to urge delegates to meet local citizens and solicit from them issues to be raised at the National Assembly's first session. Among topics mooted were the draft constitution, taxes, lowering land rents, increasing agricultural production, resolving the "party problem" (vấn đề đảng phái), implementing democratic rights, punishing traitors, building up the army, mobilizing resistance, wiping out illiteracy, revising school curricula, encouraging cultural renaissance, and improving the health system. The overriding question of peace or war was not yet specified, although there was reference to "setting foreign policy."[9] The DRV Interior Ministry instructed provincial administrative committees to assist National Assembly delegates in canvassing public opinion. Delegates were told to obtain identity and travel papers from province committees, to carry at least three hundred piastres and a change of clothes, and to arrive in Hanoi no later than 1 March. Living expenses were to be borne either by the individual delegate or by his provincial committee. "While delegates are in Hanoi, the political, administrative, and military work of localities must continue to run normally," the ministry added, thus acknowledging the large number of cadres and government employees who had been elected to the Assembly.[10] There was more than a hint of executive condescension towards fledgling legislators in these ministry instructions, which some Assembly delegates must have noticed. On the other hand, three hundred piastres for accommodation and food expenses seemed to foreshadow a National Assembly session of several weeks duration, not the mere half-day encounter which eventuated.

During February the readiness of some newly elected National Assembly delegates to meet their constituents helped to foster lively public discussion, questioning, and voicing of grievances. Newspapers urged people to get to know their delegates and to offer them support. When Haiphong delegate Nguyễn Sơn Hà met writers and other intellectuals to debate vital issues, the group is said to have agreed that the army be unified, war declared, the entire country mobilized to "kill the enemy" *(giết giặc)*, and a command economy established.[11] The Hanoi University Student Union newspaper asked readers to consider whether the National Assembly should be "an instrument to urge the nation-people *(dân tộc)* in a previously determined direction, or a helmsman with sufficient powers to pursue its own conscience and mission?" Rather than try to answer that important constitutional question, the editors coyly concluded, "Perhaps it is hard to say in advance."[12] ICP Secretary General Trường Chinh urged more meetings where citizens could give policy proposals to delegates for Assembly floor debate. He clearly expected the constitution to be deliberated.[13] The announcement on 25 February that Việt Minh, Nationalist Party, and Revolutionary League negotiators had reached agreement on a new unity Cabinet to present to the National Assembly sparked hope that domestic disputes could be resolved calmly and sensibly (see chapter 7).

As National Assembly delegates converged on Hanoi, journalists sought members out and published abbreviated interviews. Especially prized were delegates arriving from distant battlefields. Y Nông, introduced as a Rhadé minority delegate, described the fighting at Ban Mê Thuột in the central highlands, then added that he was upset by the amount of public dissent he observed in Hanoi. A delegate from Quảng Ngãi evoked the zeal of revolutionary people's courts when dealing with traitors, and told of women who cut their hair short and volunteered for combat further south. Đào Thiện Thi recounted acts of heroism at Nha Trang, but also told of the terrible power of the heavy cruiser *Richelieu* to destroy all Vietnamese defenses within range of its guns (see chapter 3). A Hà Tĩnh delegate claimed recent victories against the French in Laos. Closer to the capital, Đặng Việt Châu of Vĩnh Yên called for villages to be consolidated into big communes of seven thousand to eight thousand people to facilitate mass mobilization, as France had in 1791 or China in 1937. Đỗ Đức Dục of Hà Đông foreshadowed a number of questions for National Assembly consideration, including whether to declare war on France, whether to order military conscription and nationalization of economic resources, how to unify the army, and what special measures ought to be taken against pro-French elements.[14] Dục, a prominent member of the Democratic Party, clearly expected the first Assembly session to address and debate momentous issues.

Because of the possibility of surprise French assault, or an abrupt reversal of Chinese occupation policy, the DRV Interior Ministry prepared two different venues for the National Assembly to meet: the Hanoi Opera House and the village of Đình Bảng, across the Red River in Bắc Ninh province. The 1 March issue of Sự Thật foreshadowed Assembly convocation two days later as "a glorious page in the history of Vietnam."[15] On 1 March, however, Hồ Chí Minh decided to convene the Assembly one day early. Growing pressure from both French and Chinese interlocutors may have been one reason, although Hồ could not know that the French fleet was preparing to depart Cap St. Jacques for Haiphong the following day. Revolutionary League leaflets calling for a boycott of the 3 March meeting probably influenced Hồ's decision as well. Late on 1 March, meeting organizers told elected Assembly delegates to enter the Opera House at seven the next morning. According to one source, at five in the morning on 2 March, Hồ Chí Minh arrived unannounced at the joint headquarters of the Nationalist Party and Revolutionary League, invited the seventy nonelected delegates to participate, and personally accompanied those who agreed to the Opera House. There he asked them to wait in an anteroom until he formally requested the elected delegates to accept the fifty Nationalist Party and twenty Revolutionary League nominees.[16] However, a number of nonelected delegates may not have been informed of Hồ's rescheduling of the Assembly session, or chose not to attend. Nguyễn Hải Thần, head of the Revolutionary League, and due to be nominated as the country's vice president, was nowhere to be seen.

The National Assembly which gathered at the Opera House on the morning of 2 March was an extraordinary organizational achievement, except when it came to getting southern delegates to Hanoi. Northern Vietnam was almost entirely represented, the only province missing being Lai Châu. Central Vietnam had delegates listed from all provinces and cities, although Bình Thuận and Lâm Viên members failed to make it to Hanoi. Southern Vietnam had only seven out of twenty provinces listed in the National Assembly roster, suggesting that local authorities in thirteen provinces had been unable to conduct even rudimentary election exercises from whence delegate names might have been transmitted by radio to Hanoi. Only one Nam Bộ delegate was present when the Assembly convened: Huỳnh Bá Nhung, from Rạch Giá. Another seventeen Nam Bộ delegates were listed as absent, and some of these would arrive months later. Saigon-Cholon was meant to elect five delegates, yet only one could be found on the absentee list.[17] Despite undoubted efforts to produce at least the semblance of participation from Nam Bộ, the National Assembly convening on 2 March represented only two-thirds of the country.

The Opera House auditorium had been draped with banners containing the words "Independence," "Resistance," "Nation Building," and "Long Live Independent Vietnam." Behind the podium was the Việt Minh-DRV flag containing a yellow star on red field, which the Nationalist Party still refused to accept as national standard. Party flags were hung to the left and right. In the gallery sat invited dignitaries, foreign and Vietnamese, together with a number of journalists. A total of 242 elected Assembly delegates were present. Each delegate had a badge with number on it, but no further identification. The eldest delegate, Catholic businessman Ngô Tử Hạ, assumed the chair, flanked by two of the youngest delegates, Nguyễn Đình Thi and Đào Thiện Thi, who would serve as secretaries. At nine o'clock, provisional President Hồ Chí Minh and members of his cabinet were invited to take the stage, amidst much clapping, cheering, and patriotic music from the military band present.[18] After stressing the unprecedented nature of this meeting in the history of Vietnam, President Hồ requested and received Assembly approval to add seventy "Vietnamese revolutionary comrades from overseas who had not had time to participate in our people's general election." Nationalist Party and Revolutionary League members were then escorted into the auditorium amidst loud calls of "Unity, Unity!" Hồ Chí Minh then presented a brief account of his provisional government's achievements, acknowledged that many important matters had needed to be deferred, and concluded by assigning highest priority to preparing the nation for protracted resistance. After formally returning executive powers to the National Assembly, Hồ sat down and listened to Nguyễn Đình Thi offer effusive thanks for his government's leadership in extremely difficult times.[19]

The chairman, Ngô Tử Hạ, then proposed that the Assembly proceed to elect a national president and vice president, who would be responsible for forming a Cabinet and presenting it to the Assembly. Đỗ Đức Dục of the Democratic Party asked if the impending votes were to be taken by secret ballot or open show of hands, to which the minutes record the Assembly as unanimously agreeing to the latter. The chairman immediately nominated Hồ Chí Minh and Nguyễn Hải Thần for president and vice president. As there were no other nominations, both men were elected by acclamation, although Thần was not present "due to ill health." After Hồ left the auditorium to gather his Cabinet, one delegate complained to the

FIGURE 3. Hồ Chí Minh presenting the new Cabinet to the National Assembly, 2 March 1946. From left to right: Trương Đình Tri, Đặng Thai Mai, Chu Bá Phượng, Nguyễn Tường Tam, Huỳnh Thúc Kháng, Hồ Chí Minh, Vĩnh Thụy, Lê Văn Hiến, Phan Anh, Vũ Đình Hòe, Trần Đăng Khoa, and Bồ Xuân Luật. In *X&N* 74 (April 2000): 10. Courtesy of Vietnam Historical Association.

chair about all the noisy cheering and exclamations at what was supposed to be a solemn occasion. This provoked a chorus of protests, causing the chair to call a fifteen-minute recess. During the morning a huge crowd filled the Opera House square and Tràng Tiền Street down to the lake.

At 10:10 a.m., President Hồ led his new cabinet back into the room and introduced each member individually.[20] Supreme Advisor Vĩnh Thụy (Bảo Đại) was presented as head of the Advisory Group, and Võ Nguyên Giáp and Vũ Hồng Khanh (Nationalist Party) were introduced as chairman and vice chairman of the Resistance Committee, a last-minute compromise designed to address the issue of armed forces unification. The Assembly then stood up while President Hồ read the oath of office to the cabinet plus Vĩnh Thụy, Võ Nguyên Giáp, and Vũ Hồng Khanh. All swore fidelity to the Fatherland (Tổ Quốc), as symbolized by an ancestral altar positioned at the back of the stage.

Ngô Tử Hạ again turned the floor over to Nguyễn Đình Thi, this time to deliver the National Assembly's formal recognition of the Resistance Coalition Government (Chính Phủ Liên Hiệp Kháng Chiến). In a phrase pregnant with future meaning, Thi affirmed that the Assembly "passes power to that Government." Following collective cheers of "Long Live Independent Vietnam!" the doors opened to admit a citizens' contingent from various Hanoi national salvation organizations—an unmistakable assertion of Việt Minh primacy that must have infuriated Nationalist Party and Liberation League members present. The chairman then tabled a resolution calling on the political parties immediately to implement unification of the army, the civil administration, and the propaganda services, which passed promptly by a show of hands. Nguyễn Đình Thi read out an Assembly proclamation for release to the public, as well as a batch of telegrams to dispatch to soldiers at the front, minority peoples, Vietnamese in France, the United Nations, Generalissimo Chiang Kai-shek, the people of China, the people of Laos, the pope, the people of France, and all the peoples of the world.

In what must have been disconcerting news to many delegates present, Ngô Tử Hạ then informed everyone that, "In face of the current grave circumstances, the National Assembly cannot prolong this session and must adjourn today." Given such a severe time limitation, the most pressing business was to establish a National Assembly Standing Committee and a Constitution Drafting Committee. The chair then for the first time invited delegates to speak, which triggered more than an hour of animated debate concerning the powers of the Standing Committee. Twenty-six delegates spoke up, keeping Nguyễn Đình Thi very busy trying to summarize opinion and achieve a suitable outcome.[21] This was not mere political theater, but Vietnam's first attempt at representative government.

Proposals were read out that empowered the Standing Committee to "resolve" government draft laws, inspect government activities, decide administrative and judicial issues, and reconvene the Assembly "whenever the situation becomes calm again." Some speakers considered these powers too sweeping, while others argued that all Assembly powers should devolve to the committee between Assembly sessions. Cù Huy Cận (Hà Đông) warned that if full powers went to the committee, it might then reassign them to a smaller body, which could end in dictatorship. Hồ Chí Minh offered a very different set of Standing Committee functions: to contribute opinions to the government, to "appeal to the nation-people" if the government ignored committee criticisms, and to agree to convene the National Assembly on request of the government. Đoàn Phú Tứ (Nam Định) immediately opposed Hồ's formulation, because it meant "the Government will have powers greater than the Standing Committee, thus greater than the National Assembly." Several speakers then brought up the Resistance Committee chaired by Võ Nguyên Giáp as a third authority to be reckoned with, notably on momentous issues of declaring war or ceasing hostilities. A Quảng Ngãi delegate insisted that war and peace powers be left to the government, as there would not be time to convene the Assembly. Another delegate rejected all talk of peace until Vietnam's independence was secured. When Cù Huy Cận offered Russian and French historical examples of peace negotiations being the appropriate response, a delegate interjected that French examples should not be used. Nguyễn Văn Chi (Khánh Hòa) insisted that resistance was the only route to independence.

At this point, Hồ Chí Minh asserted his prerogative on matters of war and peace. The Resistance Committee, he said, was to focus entirely on enhancing resistance capacity. The Assembly's Standing Committee would be consulted before declaring war or ceasing hostilities, "but the power of decision must be delegated to the Government or else it will never be possible to resolve the matter." Đỗ Đức Dục interjected, "What if the people want to spill their last drop of blood?" Hồ replied, "There are many confidential circumstances the people cannot understand. If you want the job to be accomplished then the person entrusted must be given the necessary powers. Responsibility has to be accompanied by authority." Rather than try to put this weighty question to a vote, Nguyễn Đình Thi simply stated, "It has been decided that the powers of declaring war and ceasing hostilities reside with the Government."

Nguyễn Đình Thi then proceeded to resummarize the powers of the Standing Committee as a motion. The Standing Committee would contribute views to the government, be consulted on issues of war and peace, and approve treaties with foreign countries. It could "appeal to the nation" *(hiệu triệu quốc dân)* if the government acted contrary to national interests. And a majority vote of Standing Committee members could convene the National Assembly. Thi then called for a vote, and the minutes record that "All delegates raised their hands in favor [of the motion], thus ending the Standing Committee question." Thi then read a list of fifteen nominees to fill the fifteen Standing Committee positions, plus three alternates. A Buddhist priest requested that his name be withdrawn, leading Phạm Văn Đồng to nominate a minority delegate. Each nominee was introduced by an acquaintance, the list was put to a vote, and the Assembly gave its unanimous approval.[22]

As Nguyễn Đình Thi proceeded to the remaining business of forming a Constitution Drafting Committee, an unnamed delegate stood up to insist that the question of Vietnam's flag and national anthem be addressed. He continued, "The red flag with yellow star is only temporary; if the nation accepts this as fait accompli, I fear it amounts to compulsion." Rather than ask that the issue be debated and put to a vote, however, he proposed that the red banner with yellow star be accepted while a subcommittee of the Constitution Drafting Committee proceeded to research the matter, together with the national anthem question. Opening the flag issue to floor discussion would have unleashed a direct confrontation between Việt Minh and Nationalist Party delegates. The minutes simply state that the motion for a subcommittee was "passed by a majority," not unanimously as with previous matters. Thi then read a list of eleven nominees for the eleven positions on the Drafting Committee, and the slate was approved quickly.[23]

Ngô Tử Hạ then reiterated that, "because of the grave circumstances it is necessary temporarily to adjourn the National Assembly." Everyone was told to return to their localities to continue the resistance, and to reconvene at a favorable opportunity. After Hạ had led the Assembly in yelling six different slogans, he turned the floor over to Hồ Chí Minh for the last word. President Hồ urged members to carry home a spirit of unity, resistance, determination, and will to succeed in their mission. With this Assembly meeting achieved, and a government dedicated to resistance formed, Hồ expressed the hope that the next time would see a "Victory Assembly and Victory Government." Finally, he led everyone in cheering "Victorious resistance!" "Successful nation-building!" and "Long live Vietnamese independence!"

It is doubtful that Hồ Chí Minh had any particular time in mind for reconvening the National Assembly. So long as delicate, difficult negotiations continued with the French, he was content to consult with a few members of the Standing Committee, rather than risk acrimonious disputes on the Assembly floor. Once Hồ left for France at the end of May, neither the Standing Committee nor most delegates around the country saw much point in convening the Assembly before his return. However, the effect of meeting for only four hours, then dispersing indefinitely, proved very damaging to the National Assembly as a nascent political institution. There had been no opportunity for delegates to get acquainted, or to discuss even a fraction of the issues they had canvassed locally prior to arrival in the capital. Undoubtedly some officials in Hanoi were glad to see the backs of National Assembly delegates. However, this does not mean that the national elections and convocation of the Assembly had been conceived and implemented as a mere propaganda exercise. Both communist and noncommunist activists believed that Vietnam required a functioning legislature. How high a political priority would be given to this objective remained to be seen.

THE NATIONAL ASSEMBLY STANDING COMMITTEE

Two days following adjournment of the National Assembly, the Standing Committee met and elected as chairman Nguyễn Văn Tố, a respected historian and minister of social relief in the 28 August 1945 provisional government. A five-person Standing Bureau (Ban Thường Vụ) was selected, also chaired by Tố.[24] Some time later the names of four southern Việt Minh activists were added to the parent Standing Committee, although it is unlikely any of them attended meetings in Hanoi before October.[25] Nguyễn Văn Tố attended the extraordinary 6 March expanded meeting of the cabinet, at which Hồ Chí Minh presented the text of his preliminary accord with Jean Sainteny and received endorsement (see chapter 4).[26]

As senior officer of the DRV's legislative branch when the National Assembly was not in session, Nguyễn Văn Tố took his job seriously and expected the executive branch to acknowledge his standing. The Interior Ministry did quickly assign several staff members to assist him. Tố thought it natural for him to build contacts with localities without necessarily going through the Interior Ministry or the regional administrative committees. He probably tried to correspond with

National Assembly delegates who had returned home. Tố dispatched a circular to all province committees asking them to liaise with the Assembly's Standing Committee twice a month, so that "it can know the aspirations and opinions of local people."[27] Soon the Standing Committee was receiving scores of letters and petitions from citizens seeking assistance in dealing with local authorities or redress of grievances. In late April, a DRV cabinet circular went to province committees urging them to, "try hard to help members of the National Assembly's Standing Committee to ease their work and gather documentation so they can give views to the Government." This message caused dissatisfaction in the Interior Ministry and Northern Region Office, however. Someone in the latter office scribbled on his copy of this circular that many Standing Committee interventions "are without foundation," and noted that the Interior Ministry shared his opinion. He then proceeded to open up a file designed to prove his case when the opportunity arose.[28]

If Nguyễn Văn Tố had confined himself to receiving complaints and forwarding them to appropriate bureaus for action, a dispute could have been avoided. However, Tố gave his opinion on cases, proposed solutions, and reminded bureaus when they failed to respond to his correspondence. Administrators jumped whenever President Hồ Chí Minh forwarded a petition and requested action, but most were not prepared to do the same for a former employee of the École française d'Extrême-Orient with no revolutionary credentials. More fundamentally, officials at the Interior Ministry and Northern Region Office did not want to acknowledge a role for the National Assembly's Standing Committee in making policy and implementing decisions. In early June, the Northern Region Office used a disputed commune committee election in Hải Dương province to question the legitimacy of any Standing Committee intervention in such cases. According to these officials, the Standing Committee had been hoodwinked by disgruntled petitioners employing fictitious names, whereas the relevant district administrative committee had certified the commune election as clean and legal. Shortly thereafter, officials circulated a memo that asked rhetorically, "Does the National Assembly Standing Committee have the authority to send directives (chỉ thị) to localities, and must localities obey the Standing Committee?" The memo then referred back to the minutes of the 2 March Assembly meeting to argue that the Standing Committee was only authorized to contribute views to the government, not compel localities to carry out those views. "The Standing Committee can only 'appeal to the nation,' it is not the higher administration (thượng cấp hành chánh)," the memo concluded.[29]

It is doubtful that Nguyễn Văn Tố saw this overstated memo, but he certainly would have been aware of growing opposition to his activities. Already in late April he had been passed over in favor of Phạm Văn Đồng to lead a ten-person National Assembly delegation to France (see chapter 4). In early June, Tố would have been pleased to see the position of chairman of the Standing Committee placed second only to national president in the government's protocol roster. However, Tố's request to the Interior Ministry to locate a building in Hanoi large enough to accommodate four hundred delegates when the National Assembly reconvened, as well as to lodge Standing Committee staff all year round, seems to have been shelved indefinitely.[30] The National Assembly would have to wait many decades for its own accommodation.

Nguyễn Văn Tố's found his capacity to intervene increasingly circumscribed, yet that did not stop him from trying. This was particularly evident in relation to National Assembly delegates who faced harassment or arrest. In early May, Tố had become aware of the arrest in Ninh Bình of Nguyễn Bạch Vân, a Nationalist Party delegate. Tố's intervention with the Interior Ministry triggered a release order to the Ninh Bình committee, which replied by telegraph: "Sufficient proof reactionary. Request allow incarceration. Cable directive immediately." Hanoi answered: "Send documents immediately so Interior can negotiate (thương lượng) with National Assembly." The Standing Committee then met in extraordinary session to discuss this arrest of an Assembly member, concluding that the accusations against Nguyễn Bạch Vân were too vague, his alleged reactionary acts unspecified. Yet the committee merely asked for more information before proceeding further.[31] The file ends here, but from what we know of other police moves against Nationalist Party members it seems likely that Vân was moved to a deportation camp in the hills (see chapter 7). Three months later, Nguyễn Văn Tố interceded for another Nationalist Party delegate, Nguyễn Đồng Lâm, detained in Hải Dương for "generating antigovernment propaganda".[32]

Nguyễn Văn Tố continued to take up cases of maltreatment and injustice. For example, when Cầm Văn Lương of Sơn La province asserted that four persons had killed his unarmed father, brother, and two nephews without cause, Tố requested an investigation. The presiding judge of Sơn La court acknowledged that a National Guard unit had been ordered to kill traitors just prior to arrival of French troops in the area, and that the petitioner's relatives had indeed been taken for execution without explanation to anyone. On 17 December, two days before hostilities exploded in Hanoi, the Interior Ministry forwarded this information to Nguyễn Văn Tố, without comment.[33]

During the summer of 1946, Nguyễn Văn Tố still had the ear of newspaper editors. Aware of heightened domestic tensions, Tố in early July dispatched an open letter to the Việt Minh, the Nationalist Party, Democratic Party, and Revolutionary League, professing delight that the entire nation had responded vigorously in the face of French threats, "with non-Catholics and Catholics of one heart and mind and political parties putting the Fatherland above all else."[34] Tố remained silent following police and Việt Minh assaults on Nationalist Party offices a week later (see chapter 7). In September he protested French capture in the south of

Nguyễn Ngọc Bích, a member of the National Assembly Standing Committee.[35] Inside officialdom, however, Tố was being isolated and degraded. He formally complained when the Northern Region Office listed his Standing Committee below four other government bodies, contrary to President Hồ Chí Minh's instructions. Memos flew back and forth on this issue for a month.[36] At the second session of the National Assembly, Tố would be replaced by a more malleable colleague.

WHAT KIND OF CONSTITUTION?

As mentioned in the previous chapter, shortly after its formation in early September 1945 the provisional DRV government named a Constitution Drafting Committee composed almost entirely of Việt Minh adherents. Given other pressing responsibilities of committee members, however, responsibility for compiling the preliminary draft was probably given to several sympathetic lawyers. During the 1920s, many Vietnamese writers had explored constitutional history and advocated various constitutional models for Vietnam, but the topic declined in significance as France continued to rule Indochina by decree and showed no signs of granting autonomy, much less independence, to the colony. People in late 1945 were thus poorly informed about constitutional questions, and the press focused on other matters. One exception was *Tương Lai (Future)* weekly, which began to serialize an essay on general constitutional principles, relevant legal terminology, different forms of government, and the rights and responsibilities of citizens.[37]

On 9 November 1945, the provisional government released the text of a draft constitution, which was promptly serialized in a number of newspapers.[38] The preamble listed three fundamental goals for Vietnam's constitution: to build a completely independent democratic republic; to preserve domestic tranquillity as well as peace and friendship with foreign countries; and "to bring people along the road of progress and national construction, thus catching up with civilized countries." In the draft constitution's political system, the legislative branch held sway over the executive. A unicameral People's Assembly (Nghị Viện Nhân Dân) would select from among its members the DRV president (Chủ tịch nước) and cabinet (Nội các), who together constituted the Government (Chính phủ). When not in session, the People's Assembly would delegate considerable powers to a fifteen-member Standing Committee, including being able to abrogate government decisions and to declare war. As we have seen, troubles emerged between the head of the Standing Committee and some executive officials during the summer of 1946, before the DRV had a constitution. The judicial branch received scant attention in this draft constitution, setting a DRV precedent that can still be felt today. The draft did uphold freedoms of the press, assembly, belief *(tín ngưỡng)*, and travel. People's Assembly sessions were to be open to the press and public, and proceedings would be published in the *National Gazette (Công Báo)*.

All DRV citizens had a duty to defend the Fatherland, respect the constitution, obey the law, protect public property, and serve in the armed forces. Any citizen committing treason would be severely punished under the law.

The provisional government encouraged citizens to send proposed constitutional amendments to the Justice Ministry by no later than 15 December 1946, which hardly gave much time for public discussion. Presumably the plan was to have a revised text to present to the National Assembly, which at that time was scheduled to be elected on 23 December, and might be expected to convene a month later. The press ignored such time constraints, beginning a modest yet revealing constitutional discourse that percolated until late 1946. The first question to attract attention was whether to favor separation of powers (*phân quyền*) or concentration of powers (*tập quyền*). Most commentators tilted towards concentration, but differed over whether the legislature or the executive ought to be assigned preeminence. The necessity of responding quickly and decisively to wartime threats or diplomatic opportunities weighed heavily. As one writer put it: "If the executive and legislative branches are put in opposition (*đối lập*) to each other, they will lose much time trying to reach agreements, when what is needed is establishment of essential organizations. In those circumstances, the government will be perpetually jostled and confused internally, and with regard to foreign affairs not able to cope propitiously."[39] On the other hand, Đoàn Phú Tứ, a prominent journalist, argued that the draft constitution's concentration of powers already risked Vietnam becoming a dictatorship.[40] Several Việt Minh writers wanted to see rights of popular referendum and recall introduced as guards against government misdeed.[41]

The future system of voting for delegates to the National Assembly and the internal dynamics of the Assembly, came in for detailed press attention. The relative merits of putting candidates on the ballot by party slate versus individual listing were presented by one knowledgeable writer, who then declared his own preference for a third choice: proportional representation.[42] There appeared to be consensus that the national president be elected from among the parliamentary membership for a fixed term, although differences remained over whether the term duration should be four, five, or six years.[43] How the National Assembly might be dissolved occasioned debate, with some writers uncomfortable about giving the Standing Committee that power. One writer suggested that the Assembly also have the power to dissolve the Standing Committee.[44]

One article analyzing the draft constitution stands out for its sweep and political frankness.[45] Two Huế writers employing pseudonyms saw five principles at work in the draft. First, the interests of all the people (*nhân dân*) underpinned everything. Secondly, there were to be no distinctions by ethnicity, gender, class, or religion. Thirdly, democratic centralism was to prevail, thus ensuring that state machinery functioned vigorously and expeditiously. The authors contrasted democratic centralism with separation of powers, which would "make the state weak, prone to run awry, tardy, and vulnerable to exploitation by big capitalists." At this time of danger, the authors emphasized, it would be suicidal for the legislature to interfere constantly in executive matters, as was proven in the current French political system. Fourthly, there should be provision for amendment or even complete replacement of the constitution, thus taking into account future progress *(tiến hóa).* Finally, central and local powers should be coordinated *(điều hòa),* with province and commune people's councils able to issue their own instructions and to elect administrative committees, while having both councils and committees subject to higher level orders. The statist assumptions behind these principles were shared by many non-Việt Minh adherents, and would be reflected in the constitution eventually agreed upon.

In the lead-up to convocation of the National Assembly in early March 1946, it was widely presumed that the draft constitution would be tabled, debated, amended, and possibly even a final text would be approved. Once again, newspapers offered commentary and suggestions. Hải Sinh, one of the December analysts, now claimed that the draft was more democratic in content than the British, French, or American constitutions.[46] Readers in Haiphong and its vicinity were encouraged to discuss and offer opinions on whether the existing flag and anthem should be retained, whether Vietnam should take a unicameral or bicameral path, and whether separation of powers or concentration of powers should prevail. The editors also asked whether in resistance circumstances it was necessary to restrict democratic freedoms, and if so, how?[47] For a major Việt Minh newspaper some of these questions were rhetorical, and no reader responses were published before the National Assembly convened six days later, yet the fact that such choices still were being mooted is significant. A non-Việt Minh writer argued vigorously for independence of the judiciary from both legislative and executive branches, "and indeed from the populace as well." Judges should not participate in politics or belong to any party. "They must obey the law and nothing or no one else," he emphasized.[48] Editors of a Revolutionary League paper wanted the constitution to say more about economic issues, notably the right to private property, the right to work, and the right of farmers to arable land. They also recommended that the executive be given more powers, that appointment of ministers from outside the legislature be permitted, and that the minimum voting age be raised to twenty-one or even twenty-three, rather than eighteen.[49] Sixteen days after the National Assembly had adjourned, the periodical of the Hanoi Student Union offered an item by item discussion of the draft constitution.[50] As discussed above, the most the Assembly could do in early March was to appoint from among its members another constitution drafting committee. Media interest in the constitution faded until the early October announcement that the National Assembly would be reconvening at the end of the month.

During early 1946, several intriguing political philosophy essays were published by Nguyễn Bằng, drawing extensively from French precedent, but mindful that Vietnam faced different challenges than France had in 1789, 1848, or 1940.[51] Bằng began from the premise that Vietnamese were no longer the compliant colonial subjects of 1926 or 1936, but from 1945 had woken up to their rights as citizens, and now demanded to take part in local deliberations, to vote members of people's councils in or out, and to elect their own delegates to the National Assembly. He explored sympathetically the option of a federal system that would recognize how socioeconomic conditions varied substantially around Vietnam, and help to prevent too many powers being concentrated at the capital. However, Bằng insisted that foreign affairs, finance, and the armed forces be controlled by Vietnam's central government, and he believed the people would willingly concede further powers to the state in times of foreign invasion or internal chaos (nội loạn).

Nguyễn Bằng placed great emphasis on the National Assembly, which needed to convene often, be able to demand confidential documents from the executive, and call ministers to account. Assembly delegates had to feel free to express themselves on the floor with no fear of arrest, except by the Assembly itself. Bằng wanted delegates to represent the interests of their constituents, but never to the detriment of the republic. Indeed, delegates should be prepared to "sacrifice the freedom of the group (đoàn thể) in order to scheme the freedom of the masses (quần chúng)."[52] He offered two examples of how this principle applied in 1946 Vietnam. First, delegates representing workers should not push for an eight-hour day or oppose compulsory transfers to armament factories. Second, delegates representing landlords should deny their right to grow glutinous rice to make liquor, when people instead required ordinary rice to eat. Bằng vehemently rejected bicameralism, arguing that upper houses always tried to protect special interests. Unicameralism did not foster arbitrary despotism, as bicameralists claimed, unless a minority gained control and refused to hold elections. Bằng was eager to promote discussion of Vietnam's political culture well beyond immediate policy issues, as evidenced by his translation of Machiavelli's The Prince.[53] Most of what Bằng wanted to debate was buried by the demands of war and then communist party dictatorship, yet his writings remain to be considered by future generations.[54]

CENTRAL GOVERNMENT OPERATIONS

By May 1946, the DRV central government and Northern Region Office possessed procedural momentum and sense of confidence that contrasted with the extreme uncertainty of two months prior, when armed confrontation seemed almost inevitable in and around Hanoi. The 3 April Franco-Vietnamese military

FIGURE 4. Hồ Chí Minh standing outside the Northern Region
Office. Photo taken by British photographer, 14 March 1946.
Copyright Imperial War Museums (SE 7020).

staff agreement and the 18 April opening of bilateral discussions in Dalat appeared to presage a period of relative calm that the government could use to
consolidate operations and attempt serious planning.

The Interior Ministry was restructured into seven bureaus: secretariat, inspectorate, personnel and accounting, legal affairs, information and propaganda,
police, and ethnic minorities. The message logs of the Interior Ministry show
that incoming mail traffic doubled between March and July, then increased another 20 percent by early October. Incoming telegraph messages doubled in
volume. Outgoing routing slips showed a similar growth. The types of problems
addressed also became more diverse.[55]

The Military Commission (Quân Sự Ủy Viên Hội), headed by Võ Nguyên Giáp, was by early May functioning from five offices: general operations, military staff, politics, general command, and the Central Vietnamese-French Military Commission for Liaison and Control. The Resistance Committee, which in March had brought Giáp together with Nationalist Party leader Vũ Hồng Khanh, was no longer mentioned. There also was a Sino-Vietnamese Liaison Committee, dedicated to coordinating interactions with remaining Chinese military units and the overseas Chinese community (see chapter 5). Efforts were made to rationalize the military court system, which had functioned haphazardly so far. The Northern Region Office now had eight specialized departments (sở) under its jurisdiction: education, land registration, police, health, labor, hydraulics and forestry, public works, and information and propaganda. Administration of the capitol, Hanoi, had been shifted to Interior Ministry jurisdiction.[56] The government pay system had failed to keep up with transfers of offices and individuals, so that the Bắc Bộ Phủ in particular was still paying hundreds of employees who now worked for central ministries and bureaus. Although the problem was brought to the attention of the Interior Ministry in early May, and more urgently in late June, no answer had been received by the Northern Region Office as of mid-July.[57] Payrolls were only one facet of the bureaucratic overlap between ministries and the Northern Region Office that persisted to the end of 1946.

Day-to-day office routine in Hanoi still reflected longstanding colonial practice. By mid-1946, scores of French language forms had been translated into Vietnamese, printed, and put into circulation. There were personnel forms; legal affidavits; applications; licenses; property inventories; health and veterinary certificates; school diplomas; permits to travel, transport goods, purchase petrol, and cut timber; and certificates of birth, marriage, and death.[58] Each office possessed several financial receipt books, often pasted together laboriously from colonial-era scrap paper. One batch of thirty receipts signed by individual staff members prior to undertaking official travel added up to only 151$BIC, an example of the extraordinary attention to detail of procedure whenever money was involved.[59] Each office also maintained a duty officer ledger and an approved signature list for responsible individuals at the locations it communicated with regularly. Each outgoing communication was recorded in a logbook, approved for transmission by a responsible officer, and retained as a carbon copy on file. There was also a logbook for recording the loan of dossiers to other offices.[60]

Nonetheless, dossiers did go missing. The most serious case involved several hundred personnel file folders that were found stripped of all contents. A report on this incident described how a much larger quantity of personnel files had been taken to the basement in early March 1946 for destruction in the event of enemy attack. When security fears subsided, no coolies could be found to carry the files back upstairs. "We even asked the director of prisons for some convicts to help, but it still took a long time," the report explained. Amidst this labor, one pile of files had been left outside a door. The report concluded that the papers had probably been sold for scrap, not stolen for any "political motive." The case was referred to the police, who suspected several office messengers but failed to find any evidence at their homes.[61]

The mailroom of the Northern Region Office submitted monthly reports to superiors that summarized administrative activities in general, based on a reading of all incoming and outgoing communications. Clearly the quantity of work continued to increase, although not enough of these reports survive to comment on their quality. In November 1946, the mailroom complained gently that its employees were overworked.[62] The growing threat of war in late November and early December did not disrupt administrative routine, as can be seen from the abundant message traffic, internal processing, circulation of memos, minutes of meetings, personnel rosters, and requests for office supplies. Between 5 November and 19 December, the Confidential Office (Văn Phòng Mật) of the Northern Region Committee sent out an average of 10.5 items per day.[63] The office's last letter on 19 December was sent to Sơn Tây province, conveying a negative reply from the Defense Ministry concerning an inquiry into the fate of Đỗ Văn Mẽ, who had disappeared following the August 1945 general uprising.[64]

Firm administrative procedures had their merits, but they also tended to breed complacency. It was not uncommon for an urgent problem to be raised at some level, only to become bogged down in a welter of correspondence and internal memos. On 26 May 1946, several Chinese Army trucks removed batches of steel from a government depot across the river from Hanoi, probably to take to the Haiphong docks for transport to Manchuria. DRV members of the Sino-Vietnamese Liaison Committee persuaded Chinese officers to defer taking away more, while the head of the Government Buildings Committee strongly advised the government to transport the remaining fifty tons of steel elsewhere before the Chinese returned. On 6 June, the Department of Public Works said that the cost of the required twenty truck trips was not covered in its budget. By 11 May, the Northern Region Office had commandeered trucks, but it took another two days for Public Works to allocate funds to buy fuel and to pay workers to load and unload the cargoes. Fortunately the Chinese bureaucracy proved slower to react than the Vietnamese one, apparently enabling Vietnamese workers to shift the steel to the countryside a few days later.[65]

Also in late May 1946, Chinese units began to withdraw from scores of buildings in Hanoi, causing a scramble for custody between French and DRV organizations, and simultaneous competition among Vietnamese ministries and bureaus for newly available space. Because French and DRV organizations both occupied buildings opportunistically as soon as they saw the Chinese vacating, the situation could have descended into acrimonious disputation or even armed hostilities. Instead, some sort of understanding appears to have been reached with minimum fuss by French and Vietnamese staff officers.[66] The notable exception was the former governor general's palace, which the French seized on 26 June, triggering a Vietnamese general strike (see chapter 4).

The tussle for space among DRV organizations began in mid-May with a host of ambit claims being submitted, followed by an energetic exchange of memos. Most government units carried over from the colonial era were reasonably well-endowed, with seven to ten buildings each, yet they were not averse to requesting more. By contrast, units only existing since September 1945 had been forced to rent or to borrow office space scattered around the capital. They now called for substantial reallocations. Most assertive was the Defense Ministry, which began its claim with a dig at other ministries for relying on colonial precedent. Defense wanted its ten bureaus (*cục*) to receive an average of fifteen rooms each, plus twenty rooms for the ministry's secretariat—a total of 170 rooms. It also asked for another twenty Hanoi buildings to serve as storehouses, workshops, and medical facilities. Meanwhile, the Northern Region police office defended its men having occupied a building vacated by the Chinese, and told the Hanoi mayor's office to stop sending representatives asking them to move out. Trần Duy Hưng, chairman of the Hanoi Administrative Committee, labelled the police occupation "improper," and insisted that the building was already earmarked for the Ministry of National Education. The finance minister, Lê Văn Hiến, chided unnamed organizations for having "already shifted location in a very disorderly fashion," and pointedly reminded everyone of his request for full inventories of state property, a massive task if taken seriously. Several organizations asked for residential quarters for employees and their families, a practice that became prevalent in subsequent years.

On 17 June, the newly formed interministerial Committee to Allocate Housing and Government Buildings met to try to resolve all these competing claims. It was agreed that each ministry would first endeavor to rationalize its own space by consolidating geographically, trying to avoid rental properties, and giving preference for space to ordinary staff over ministers and ranking officials. A long list of specific building allocations was then tabled, provoking "lively discussion." In the end, the Interior Ministry and the Northern Region Office continued to share the large building on Lý Thái Tổ Street across from the Métropole Hotel. The Defense Ministry received the Hanoi horse racing track and the Bạch Mai airstrip, plus four buildings for National Guard use. The Justice Ministry had to make do with one modest building, yet another example of the government's inattention to judicial matters. Five "associations" (*hội*) were listed as appropriate for space allocations, but only the Veterans and Invalids Association and the National Construction Committee received buildings. Seven newly available properties had been donated by private owners to the government's Independence

Fund. There is no record of the interministerial committee convening again, suggesting that each organization was left to fend for itself—until everyone fled the city in late December.

In late May 1946, the Northern Region Committee began a two-month intensive training course for province and district level administrators. Thirty-eight students (including one female) came from seventeen northern provinces, their ages ranging from twenty-two to forty. Eleven instructors lectured on legal theory and practice, government structure (colonial and DRV), public finance, socioeconomic conditions, and applied administration. Visits were arranged to Hanoi bureaus, where staff explained functions and helped students familiarize themselves with office procedure, printed forms, logbooks, routing of correspondence, dispatch, and archiving. Based on this experience, the Interior Ministry ordered establishment of an administrative training school in each of the country's three regions. The Northern Committee started to organize a second intensive course, to begin in October, but it failed to materialize.[67]

Education

The men who took power in Hanoi in August 1945 considered a new education system vital to Vietnam's future. Precolonial rulers had imported Chinese texts, conducted civil examinations, and maintained a modest tertiary institute attached to the court, but then left most schooling to the initiative of local elites. The French discontinued the civil exams, organized French language instruction for a small native elite, and experimented with various basic education schemes that still left 90 percent of the population illiterate. Vietnamese nationalists, mindful of mass education achievements in Europe, America, and Japan, castigated the colonial regime for locking Vietnam out of the quest for modernity. Now DRV leaders promised unparalleled educational opportunities. Ordinary citizens, seeing study as a means of personal as well as national advancement, leapt at the opportunity to participate in classes. However, expectations far exceeded the capacity of the nascent state to meet demand. Informal schooling resumed its traditional importance, with the state still determined to control educational content.

In early September, provisional President Hồ Chí Minh met with his minister for national education, Vũ Đình Hòe, to kick-start the government's ambitious tertiary, secondary, primary, and popular literacy programs.[68] Hòe had been selected for the education portfolio because of his publication three months earlier of a comparison of overseas pedagogical methods and reforms.[69] In keeping with Việt Minh policy priorities, the first item on the meeting's agenda was mass literacy. Hòe tabled a draft decree specifying that "within one year, all Vietnamese people over eight years of age must know how to read and write the national script (quốc ngữ)." Those persons failing to meet this goal would have to pay a fine. The cost of literacy classes was the responsibility of province and commune committees. A second decree established a new Bureau of Mass Education (Nha Bình Dân Học Vụ) within the Education Ministry.[70]

The second item on Vũ Đình Hòe's agenda was a requirement that Vietnamese language be used in all classes from the start of the new school year, to include university courses. Hồ Chí Minh praised the intent, but asked whether such a quick change from French might be precipitous. Hòe called on Nguyễn Văn Huyên and Ngụy Như Kontum, new directors of tertiary and secondary studies respectively, to respond.[71] They described how the *Science Magazine* (*Tạp chí Khoa Học*) group had compiled and published a Franco-Vietnamese scientific glossary, and how Hoàng Xuân Hãn, national education minister in the short-lived Imperial Vietnam government, had initiated the shift to Vietnamese language during the summer of 1945.[72] According to Hòe's memoirs, President Hồ authorized him to proceed with this major language transition, yet there is no record of a decree being issued, nor any newspaper announcement. A few days earlier the University Student Union had requested that upcoming examinations be conducted in French as before, and Hòe agreed.[73] The opening of the new school year was postponed to mid-November, giving the university time to distribute Franco-Vietnamese glossaries, and teachers a chance to convert some lectures to Vietnamese. However, the job of standardizing new words and publishing textbooks in Vietnamese would take years.

Before closing the meeting on education, Hồ Chí Minh reminded Hòe to concentrate first on organizing the Mass Education Bureau and promoting nationwide literacy efforts.[74] Hồ must have been concerned that these well-educated professionals would gravitate towards what they knew best—tertiary and secondary instruction. Nonetheless, Hồ also wanted to be seen to embrace higher education as part of Vietnam's overall modernizing agenda, and to offer practical incentives for the colonial, educated elite to commit themselves to the DRV.

The DRV Ministry of National Education drew its staff mainly from the former Direction de l'instruction publique en Indochine. The ministry's tertiary studies bureau also became responsible for public libraries, museums, and the École française d'Extrême-Orient.[75] Later a bureau for youth and sports was added to the education ministry, absorbing some staff from the discontinued youth ministry.[76] Vũ Đình Hòe eliminated all school fees, announced scholarships for needy secondary pupils, and foreshadowed establishment of dozens of secondary school dormitories (*ký túc xá*) in provincial towns. None of these edicts indicated where necessary funds would come from, however. Many teachers had not received their salaries or allowances since June or July. When payment did arrive, it had already been undercut by continuing inflation. Some primary schools had run out of paper and pens or pencils.[77] By December, teachers complained that inflation had reduced them and their families to eating rice gruel. In

practice, many teachers now had to depend on modest food allocations from local administrative committees. This provoked testy exchanges between local
committees and the Education Ministry, which earlier had warned committees
not to become involved in teaching matters.[78]

The jewel in the DRV's educational crown was to be Vietnam University (the
former Indochina University), modelled unmistakably on Western institutions
like the Sorbonne or Oxford. An autonomous fund was created, into which it was
hoped that not only central government allocations but local government contributions and private donations would flow as well. The university was to be gov-
erned by a board of trustees chaired by the Education Ministry's director of tertiary studies, and including deans, faculty representatives, a student representative,
and three eminent individuals from outside. The board would recommend to the
government for approval the annual university budget, curriculum, teaching
staff, establishment of research facilities, scholarship awards, and grants to study
overseas.[79] Faculties of medicine, science, and art would carry over from the Indochina University structure, while the law faculty would be transformed into a
faculty of politics and society, with courses in civil law, public law, constitutional
law, economics, commerce, public finance, administration, and international
relations. Students would be required to learn one of three foreign languages:
Chinese, English, or Russian.[80] An entirely new faculty of letters was to be established, in order to train secondary school teachers and to "Raise up Vietnam's
literature to be worthy of an independent country and to keep up with the advanced countries of the world." That faculty's curriculum would include courses
in philosophy, Vietnamese literature, Chinese literature, history, and geography,
with sociology and anthropology to be added later.[81]

Vietnam University opened its doors on 15 November 1945, with the inaugural
ceremony attended by provisional President Hồ Chí Minh, other cabinet members, and several Chinese officials. Nguyễn Văn Huyên, director of tertiary studies, gave the principal address. With emotion, Huyên emphasized how both
teachers and students wanted to show the world that "the Vietnamese people,
besides conducting a blood and bones struggle on the battlefield, are also striv-
ing to participate in the cultural advance of humanity." Huyên continued: "We
want this university to become a citadel in the protracted fight to restore all our
national territory and to liberate our people's spirit. We are a civilized people
(dân tộc văn hiến) with more than a thousand years of independent history, during which time we built a unique civilization in this corner of the Pacific." Huyên
complimented students who had recently passed their secondary graduation or
university end-of-year exams, then expressed the fervent hope that a just peace
would return so that currently serving soldiers, southern youths, and Cambodian and Lao youths could safely enroll. Turning to the assembled teaching staff,
Huyên characterized it as an effective blend of age and youth, modern and classi-

cal expertise. Together with holders of advanced degrees, the university had also recruited to its staff individuals possessing international relations, political, or cultural experience. Drawing on his own Confucian classical training, and knowing that he risked alienating radicals in the audience, Huyên suggested that the university's mission was to create "superior persons" *(quân tử)* capable of both conceptualizing complex matters and taking appropriate action in real life.[82]

Except for this inaugural ceremony, the university received almost no press attention, perhaps because highly educated organizers like Nguyễn Văn Huyên felt uncomfortable about publicizing their cause, or because most newspaper editors saw the university as expensive window dressing or pandering to the colonial-era elite. Sixty years later, Vũ Đình Hòe still felt the need to defend restarting the university amidst French aggression, incipient famine, an empty treasury, and youthful preoccupations with immediate mobilization.[83] Appointment of the university's provisional board of trustees received no newspaper coverage whatsoever.[84] The science faculty appears to have made the transition from colonial to postcolonial instruction with minimal fuss. Fourteen science staff members continued to teach twenty-four courses in mathematics, physics, chemistry, biology, zoology, botany, and geology. The politics and society faculty possessed twelve teachers offering courses in law, international law, economics, finance, commerce, English, and Russian.[85] In the new faculty of letters, a stunning roster of twelve teachers offered fourteen courses in history, geography, literature, philosophy, and anthropology.[86] Most of these men would contribute to the intellectual life of Vietnam for the next thirty or forty years, albeit under conditions unimagined in 1946.

On 18 February 1946, all university classes, with the exception of English and Russian language instruction, suddenly were suspended so that students could "participate in practical tasks in current circumstances." This was a time of great tension and uncertainty in Hanoi, and students were more likely to be engaged in military drills or talking politics than coming to class (see chapter 3). However, the university suspension persisted after relative calm had returned to the capital in late March.[87] Medical and dental classes resumed in April, and the student dormitory remained open for all, but most courses had not reconvened by May, when it was almost time for the regular summer break. For some faculty members the university suspension may have been a relief, as they already were dividing their time between two or three different activities. Thus, Tạ Quang Bửu, besides teaching physics and English, became assistant minister of defense in March and then a member of the negotiating delegation to France at the end of May.[88] Đặng Thái Mai replaced Vũ Đình Hòe as education minister in March, published articles on contemporary China, and played a key role in the Việt Minh National Salvation Cultural Association. Nguyễn Văn Huyên took part in the Dalat conference in May and the Fontainebleau conference thereafter.

Vietnam University's second academic year began on 1 October 1946. Administrative formalities, plans for a university library, and new dormitory regulations were spelled out by the acting education minister, Ca Văn Thỉnh.[89] The press continued to ignore the university, and neither the *Công báo* nor archival files mention course offerings, enrollments, or faculty meetings. In early November, Nguyễn Văn Huyên was promoted to minister of education (the fourth individual to hold that office in fifteen months), but not much could be done on the university front before fighting exploded in Hanoi on 19 December. Tertiary classes would reopen in the northern hills and in Thanh Hóa province in 1949–50.

Secondary or "middle" schools *(trung học)* were slow to reopen following the summer 1945 break and tumultuous events of August. Many teenagers now regarded political engagement as far more important than mere book learning. Teachers came under political scrutiny. Some teachers committed themselves to the revolution, others found the behavior of pupils shocking and wondered how they might restore authority in the classroom. No one seemed to know when salaries would be paid. In October, Chinese Army units took over secondary and primary school buildings in towns north of the sixteenth parallel. Later that month, the education ministry gave permission for two prestigious secondary schools to reopen: Chu Văn An in the Hanoi suburbs, and Nguyễn Trãi in Nam Định city. However, only sciences and foreign languages were to be taught, not history or literature. Queries about pay were referred to the finance ministry. When Phú Thọ secondary school received permission to reopen, it was on the condition that the province cover most costs.[90] The Northern Region Committee's budget submission for 1946 listed only 2.2 percent of its total expenditures to be divided among six secondary schools.[91]

The education ministry ordered all secondary schools to nominate "oversight councils," chaired by a representative of the ministry, but only Khải Định school in Huế seems to have complied. Officials in Huế were the first to propose special teacher-training courses in Vietnamese literature, to replace the colonial-era curriculum.[92] With no new text books to use, however, such proposals went nowhere. In April 1946, the education minister announced formation of a national Textbook Council chaired by Dương Quảng Hàm, longtime teacher of Vietnamese literature at the Collège du Protectorate in Hanoi, and currently inspector of secondary schools. The size and membership of this council gives us some idea of the pedagogical gravity attached to selecting exactly what schoolchildren would be required to read nationwide. There were four university professors, five secondary school principals or teachers, five ministry officials, an artist, a writer, and the assistant minister of communications and public works. Eventually four textbooks were approved for use in secondary school classes: two in mathematics and one each in chemistry and classical Chinese.[93]

During the summer of 1946, many province committees submitted proposals to open a secondary school. Mindful of budget stringencies, the education ministry circulated a plan to set up "model" secondary schools in a few additional provinces.[94] However, a number of northern provinces had already collected donations from citizens and were recruiting teachers for the 1946–47 school year, regardless of what the education ministry had in mind. In central Vietnam, three "semipublic schools" *(trường bán công)* were being upgraded to public secondary schools, for which the education ministry insisted that the Central Region Committee in Huế take "total budget responsibility." When it came time to report to the National Assembly however, the education ministry blandly claimed jurisdiction over twenty-five public and semipublic secondary schools containing 194 teachers and 7,514 pupils.[95] While such figures represented an improvement over secondary school teacher and pupil numbers in the late colonial era, they also concealed a host of intractable financial and administrative problems that would take many years to resolve.

The education ministry also received a number of applications to establish private secondary schools. In Quảng Ngãi province, noted for its revolutionary zeal, a member of the National Assembly collected the impressive amount of three hundred thousand piastres to establish a private primary-secondary school, then proceeded to hire eleven teachers and secure temporary quarters in the town's marketing cooperative building. A local paper proudly claimed this to be the largest private school in south-central Vietnam.[96] In Hải Dương province, the overseas Chinese community submitted a detailed proposal to open a private secondary school.[97] The most extraordinary private education initiative came from Đặng Thái Mai, Việt Minh cultural luminary and briefly education minister, who announced formation of his own primary-secondary school in Hanoi. This flew in the face of both ICP and noncommunist intelligentsia convictions about state monopolization of education. Yet *Cứu Quốc*, the principal Việt Minh daily, carried repeated advertisements for Đặng Thái Mai's school.[98] Dương Đức Hiền, director of the education ministry's bureau of youth and sports, took the unusual step of issuing his own official statement of patronage for the school.[99] Full-scale war might loom, yet some Việt Minh intellectuals still devoted time and energy to private schooling.

The DRV's ambition was to make free primary education available to every child. This meant helping to pay existing teachers, setting a new curriculum, training a new generation of teachers, supervising performance, and conducting examinations to determine who advanced to secondary schooling. Remarkably, the Northern Region Committee allocated 55 percent of its total 1946 budget to primary school and village school *(hương sư)* instruction.[100] As 1946 progressed, only a fraction of this funding for primary education actually materialized, yet when combined with local fees, donations, and volunteer teaching the result was far more children attending school than previously. Evidence for this assertion is more anecdotal than statistical, as provinces seldom bothered to report enrollments to Hanoi. In late October, Hanoi city had twenty primary schools operating, with 2,930 pupils enrolled. Only one of these Hanoi schools was for girls.[101] In November, the education ministry claimed 5,654 primary schools nationwide, with 280,789 pupils and 6,757 teachers, which on average amounted to 50 pupils and 1.2 teachers per school.[102]

New primary teaching materials were slow to appear. The government wanted to avoid using colonial textbooks or teacher guides, but no one gave priority attention to compilation and approval of new publications. In September 1946, the education ministry's textbook council approved six primary school texts for use throughout the country. The two titles dealing with children's games, and those dealing with mathematics, geometry, and physical exercise *(luyện chí)* could not have aroused much controversy. The sixth, a Vietnamese literature book, may have occasioned debate over how to treat fiction and poetry of recent decades. No agreement was reached, however, on appropriate textbooks for "citizen's education" *(công dân giáo dục)*, history, or geography.[103]

In August 1946, the DRV acting president, Huỳnh Thúc Kháng, signed decrees foreshadowing a new national education structure. There would be an "elementary level" *(bậc học cơ bản)* of four years duration, followed by one year designed to differentiate general and vocational pupils, then two separate tracks to produce university students or skilled workers. Children from seven to eleven years of age would receive free elementary schooling (with provision for older pupils to enroll as well). Each commune was expected to establish and fund its own elementary school, with possible help from province or regional budgets. Boys and girls would have separate classes, and be instructed by teachers of their own sex. Private or group *(đoàn thể)* elementary schools were permitted as well, but they had to follow education ministry rules and be subject to government inspection. Elementary schooling would be made compulsory by 1950.[104]

One month later, the education ministry issued an extremely ambitious thirteen thousand word, four-year elementary school curriculum, presumably designed to compensate for the continuing absence of teacher retraining courses, pedagogical manuals, or textbooks.[105] Twelve courses would be taught: moral education *(đức dục)*, citizen's education, Vietnamese language, maths, general science, agriculture and industry, hygiene, history, geography, drawing, handicrafts, and physical education. This list was almost identical to the previous six-year colonial primary school program, with the notable omission of French language instruction. Accompanying notes suggest that pedagogical techniques also remained almost the same. Moral education retained a strong Confucian orientation, beginning with family relationships, then moving to friends, strangers, and the state. In place of loyalty to the king or the French motherland, children were to be taught their responsibilities to the Vietnamese Fatherland, and how to "place the interests of the nation *(quốc gia)* over the interests of the individual." In the syllabus on citizen's education, teachers were told to use the flag-raising ceremony, national anniversaries, and visits to the offices of local people's councils to reinforce classroom descriptions of the DRV government, cooperatives, and the New Life movement.[106] Hygiene had been part of the colonial curriculum too, but now it was linked to "rebuilding the race" *(cải tạo nòi giống)* as well as to personal and neighborhood gain. In the final year, pupils were introduced to parasites, germs, infectious diseases, epidemics, and first aid practices.

The history course aimed to teach elementary school children the origins of the country of Vietnam and to encourage them "to love and to fulfil their duties towards the Fatherland." Teachers were provided with a list of thirty-eight patriotic heroes to introduce to pupils, beginning with Phù-Đổng Thiên-Vương, the mythical boy-giant who drove away foreign invaders, and concluding with Hồ Chí Minh, "the collective grandfather of [Vietnamese] children." The geography course began with local orientation, then moved on to descriptions of the students' district and province or city. In the third year, pupils learned the geography of Vietnam, Laos, Cambodia, and Thailand, while in the last year they were introduced to China, Japan, India, and the five oceans and continents. When it came to physical education, teachers were told first to eradicate their own disparaging attitudes towards exercise and fitness. They also were given an elaborate extracurricular program of youth activities based explicitly on Boy Scout principles and practices.

Almost as an afterthought, the education ministry included a curriculum section on training of girls, which focused on housecleaning, hygiene, going to market, sewing, and infant care (final year). Teachers were told to limit their instruction to what girls could use in a practical way at home, not to tax them with "theoretical" matters. Such a traditional attitude towards the education of young women already had been challenged publicly from the 1930s, and it blithely ignored participation of young women in the August 1945 insurrection and subsequent mobilization. Vietnamese women still had a long ways to go in consolidating a new position for themselves in a male-controlled system.

At the second session of the National Assembly in late October, the education minister tried to respond to probing, critical questions from the floor and made some florid promises. When war intervened seven weeks later, education ministry personnel scattered and school supervision devolved to zone and province levels. Nonetheless, the detailed decrees and ambitious initiatives of 1946 remained DRV government policy, to be readdressed when conditions improved. The state refused to concede its commitment to a modern, comprehensive educational system.

Justice

Among expected governance responsibilities, the DRV state of 1945–46 gave least attention to the administration of justice, setting a precedent that persists to the present day. In imitation of the French and Russian revolutions, the DRV's first judicial decree mandated establishment of nine military courts *(tòa án quân sự)* to try persons accused of "endangering independence." Each court would possess a presiding judge chosen from the fledgling National Guard, a member nominated by the local people's committee, and a member from the local civilian court of appeals.[107] The Hanoi military court convened first, with Trần Độ the presiding judge, Phan Mỹ the judicial member, and Lê Giản the prosecutor.[108] The Huế military court followed soon afterward, taking cases from as far south as Nha Trang. Then came the Haiphong court, presided over by Lê Quang Hòa, deputy head of Military Region 3. In Nam Bộ, French offensive operations compelled several military courts to move covertly from one venue to another.[109] In January 1946, the crimes of kidnapping, extortion, and assassination were added to the jurisdiction of military courts. A February decree tried to define the roles of Interior and Justice ministries in managing military courts, while the Defense Ministry remained uninvolved except for providing judges from the National Guard. Separate courts martial *(tòa án quân đội)* were to be formed to try military personnel.[110] Although military courts continued to deal primarily with perceived political threats, some criminal cases carrying a potential death penalty came their way as well (see chapter 7).

Meanwhile, the wider DRV judicial system remained confused, understaffed, and demoralized. In early October 1945, Hồ Chí Minh signed a decree retaining colonial laws, rules, and regulations until such time as a new legal code was enacted for the entire country.[111] Officially this meant that DRV officials and courts would continue to enforce the different codes that had grown up previously in Tonkin, Annam, and Cochinchina, not to mention separate arrangements for Hanoi, Haiphong, and Tourane/Đà Nẵng. In practice, the October decree was largely ignored. It seemed to contradict the DRV's fundamental assertions of national independence and territorial integrity. And local people's committees were not about to surrender to former colonial magistrates, court clerks, and interpreters the dispensing of summary justice. The justice minister, Vũ Trọng Khánh, found it hard to gain the attention of President Hồ Chí Minh and the Cabinet. Other experienced lawyers who enjoyed the confidence of the president much preferred to work in foreign affairs or administration, not the drafting of new civil or criminal law codes. Younger graduates of the Hanoi Law Faculty, observing public resentment directed at colonial laws and legal procedures, sought employment elsewhere. Those who stayed with the Justice Ministry took the unusual step of carpeting Khánh with a list of grievances.[112]

In early January 1946, Vũ Trọng Khánh presented to the Cabinet a draft decree on DRV courts and magistrates. In his accompanying argument, Khánh stated that the Cabinet had already endorsed three guiding principles: separation of courts from the administration; central government appointment of all magistrates; and incorporation of people's assessors *(phụ thẩm nhân dân)* to court room proceedings. He hoped that both "old government employees" and "new persons" would apply to become magistrates, with the selection committee looking for individuals who possessed both legal knowledge and virtue. After courts and magistrates were in place, Khánh professed confidence that issues of jurisdiction, law suits, procedure, and civil and criminal codes could be resolved too, "thus bringing about general order and protection of democratic rights." He added that prospective foreign investors would first look at the DRV's legal system to see if their interests were likely to be protected.[113] Khánh also called a press conference to explain the difficulties being encountered in establishing the national judicial system. He insisted that the judiciary be able to guard its independence, well aware that many Việt Minh adherents rejected this notion. On the most pressing problem of finding good magistrates, Khánh at first excluded individuals who had served the French or Japanese, but later averred that former officials who had not "exploited the people" ought to be eligible too. Khánh recommended special courses of one or two year's duration designed to reorient colonial holdovers and provide basic legal instruction to newcomers.[114]

The resulting decree on courts and magistrates signed by President Hồ in late January described an elaborate judicial hierarchy based on French precedent, with barely a nod to the political transformations of previous months.[115] Starting at the bottom level, the decree affirmed the composition of commune judicial subcommittees, but then endeavored to circumscribe their authority by limiting fines to a paltry six piastres, prohibiting property confiscations, and requiring detainees to be transferred or released within twenty-four hours. District courts were to be composed of one magistrate, one clerk, and one or more secretaries. Province and city courts had already been given top priority by Vũ Trọng Khánh in earlier statements, who cited current case backlogs at that level, travel impediments, and the extreme scarcity of magistrates. Each province or city court would possess a presiding judge, two magistrates, a chief clerk, multiple secretaries, and a roster of prospective people's assessors provided by the relevant administrative committee.[116] A court in session would hear from the accused, witnesses, the prosecutor, and again the accused in rebuttal, after which the judge, magistrates, and two people's assessors would reach a decision by majority vote. Above the province and city level, the decree specified establishment of three regional courts of appeal, in Hanoi, Huế, and Saigon. No mention was made of a national court, nor did the decree acknowledge the military courts already in operation. The decree's penultimate clause recognized that it could only be "implemented gradually," which proved a considerable understatement.

Desperate for magistrates, the Justice Ministry canvassed other government bodies for prospects. The Northern Region Committee forwarded sixty-three personnel dossiers, with more dribbling in later.[117] A high-ranking committee screened incoming files and applications.[118] Meanwhile, a Hanoi court of appeals had begun to function, with twenty-four cases on its calendar as of 13 February.[119] It took more than three months to select and appoint only five new magistrates to province- and city-level courts in northern Vietnam. Other persons had either withdrawn their applications or been refused permission to transfer by parent bureaus. By October the Justice Ministry could report a total of eighty-six district court magistrates functioning in eighteen northern provinces, fifty-seven of whom had just been appointed.[120] The following month it reported that a total of thirty-one provincial- and city-level magistrates had been appointed to seventeen courts in the north. Central Vietnam now also had a court of appeals at Huế, provincial and city courts in ten provinces plus Đà Nẵng, and seventy-nine district magistrates operating from Thanh Hóa province down the coast to Phú Yên.[121]

Although these late 1946 figures for province and district magistrates look promising, they mask a plethora of problems that prevented courts from functioning effectively. Justice Ministry salaries and allowances for magistrates were undercut by inflation, and payments sometimes failed to arrive at all. Hundreds of former colonial court clerks, secretaries, and judicial police (tư pháp công an) applied to work again, but the Finance Ministry was slow to earmark the necessary funds, some individuals proved averse to being posted to rural districts, and many Việt Minh activists doubted such persons were capable of redemption at all.[122] District courts sometimes lacked paper, pens, and ink, much less a typewriter or reference books. The Ministry's schedules of fines and court costs to be levied were ludicrously low.[123] Magistrates had to plead with local administrative committees for food rations. Inevitably stories began to circulate of magistrates taking bribes, as in colonial times. In May, the Huế court of appeals warned all Trung Bộ magistrates to uphold the sanctity of their office, maintain probity and composure, and restrict their interactions with other government bodies to judicial matters. Later the Justice Ministry ordered all court personnel not to receive guests inside their offices, not to talk informally with interested parties or their relatives, and above all not to accept any money or gifts.[124] In October, a magistrate was charged with taking 9,500$BIC in bribes from prisoners, tried by the Hanoi Court of Appeals, and sentenced to five years jail.[125]

Military courts enjoyed more respect and received far more resources than ordinary courts, much to the displeasure of Justice Ministry officials and provincial magistrates. Jurisdictional disputes led President Hồ Chí Minh to order the formation of three regional councils to "demarcate the competence of military courts, special courts, and ordinary courts."[126] If two courts continued to disagree over jurisdiction, the case file had to be forwarded to a national council for decision. In practice, however, if a military court wanted a case the ordinary court usually deferred. In July, Chu Văn An, deputy chair of the Hanoi Suburban Administrative Committee, was brought before the Hanoi military court to face widely publicized charges of illegal property confiscation, misappropriation, and embezzlement. An was defended by Vũ Văn Hiền, a Paris-trained lawyer and finance minister in the short-lived Imperial Vietnam government. Nineteen persons testified for the prosecution, the defendant apparently refused to admit guilt, and the court sentenced him to ten years hard labor.[127] In another case, Vĩnh Yên province authorities, after detaining fourteen men on charges of murdering a husband and wife in a botched robbery, suggested to Hanoi that the accused be tried by a military rather than ordinary court, because the gang had "used the Việt Minh name as cover." This proposal was endorsed by the Northern Region police, yet as of late August the accused were still not listed on the Hanoi Military Court's trial calendar.[128]

The largest proportion of judicial matters continued to be decided by administrative committees, not the courts. Committees detained citizens, interrogated them, levied hefty fines, confiscated property, and occasionally executed individuals, often ignoring basic principles of justice. Committee members assigned to judicial tasks lacked relevant training or prior experience.[129] As the Interior Ministry gradually gained more oversight of local committees the most obvious miscarriages of justice diminished, yet this was an administrative achievement, not a judicial one. Interior actively protected committees against the Justice Ministry and local magistrates. In February 1946, the Hà Đông provincial court executed an arrest warrant against the chairman of the Thạch Bích commune committee, who was believed to be hiding the murderers of Nguyễn Văn Kinh. Coming to Hà Đông court to seek his colleague's release, the commune deputy chairman, whose son was one of the alleged killers, threatened to mount a protest demonstration. The Hà Đông magistrate informed the Hanoi court of appeals of this interference, warning that the prestige of the entire judicial system was on the line. The Justice Ministry then complained to the Northern Region Committee, which queried the province committee. Six weeks later the Hà Đông committee finally replied, stating that it had received numerous petitions and a delegation from Thạch Bích commune protesting the arrest of their chairman. In the opinion of the Hà Đông committee, the commune chairman was not implicated in the death of Kinh, and his continued detention prevented him from collecting important taxes from villagers. The Northern Committee sided with the Hà Đông committee, as did the interior minister, Huỳnh Thúc Kháng, who added that government officers should only be arrested when "really necessary."

Kháng then asked the Northern Committee to warn all subordinate committees to respect the authority of the Justice Ministry.[130] This waffle by Kháng, who also was acting DRV president at the time, could hardly disguise the blow to Justice Ministry authority. With the outbreak of full-scale war a few months later, many ordinary courts ceased to function.

Postes, Télégraphes, et Téléphones (PTT)

The most valuable institution left behind by the French colonial regime was the PTT, which had continued to provide communication services first for the Imperial Vietnam government (from April to August 1945) and then for the DRV. The telegraph system possessed hubs in Hanoi and Saigon; a main north-south line going through Vinh, Huế, Đà Nẵng, and Nha Trang; and links to all provinces. Most districts were not connected by telegraph, but there were dedicated lines to military posts, mines, plantations, and French hill stations (Sapa, Tam-đảo, Dalat). PTT radios were used as backup to the telegraph in the event of storm damage, floods, or sabotage. The telephone system was much less extensive, with no line connecting Hanoi and Saigon. During the late 1930s, Hanoi had about two thousand phone numbers, Haiphong five hundred, Nam Định two hundred, and other northern towns less than fifty each. The mail system extended down to district and commune level, with provision for registered mail, parcels, printed matter, cash transfers, and savings accounts. Stamps were expensive for ordinary Vietnamese: in 1939 a four *xu (sou)* stamp to mail a simple letter cost the equivalent of 1.3 kilograms of rice. A modest telegram would set one back 20 kilograms of rice.[131] All of the PTT equipment that came into the hands of the DRV in August 1945 dated to the 1930s or earlier, and the tropical climate imposed further maintenance problems. International and regional PTT connections had been cut during the Pacific War, with the exception of telegraph and radio links to Vientiane and Phnom Penh.

More important than the PTT's physical infrastructure was the Vietnamese staff of up to six thousand persons, most of whom obeyed orders to continue working after two hundred French staff members were removed during the summer of 1945. While personnel numbers declined substantially in later months, telegraph contact was sustained most of the time between Hanoi and province seats in Bắc Bộ and northern Trung Bộ.[132] Long-distance telephone connections were more limited, yet it was generally feasible for towns as distant as Lạng Sơn, Vinh, and Thanh Hóa to talk with Hanoi. Nonpriority official mail *(công văn)* travelled by train, boat, auto, bicycle, horse-cart, or foot courier.[133] However, Lai Châu province in the far west of Bắc Bộ had already lost all contact with Hanoi in March 1945; official mail sent faithfully from the capital to Lai Châu was returned unopened for the next twenty-two months. In October 1945, provisional

President Hồ Chí Minh apologized publicly to the inhabitants of Lào Cai province (just east of Lai Châu) for not being able to communicate with them.[134]

In Hanoi, the PTT processed each day up to a thousand incoming and outgoing messages and letters for government bureaus. Meticulous logbooks helped to ensure that items were not lost in transit, and that each could be linked to previous and subsequent correspondence. Each outgoing telegraph log listed the intended recipient, message number, word count, time accepted, time dispatched, and the name of the originating bureau. PTT clerks totalled up monthly outgoing word totals and billed each bureau accordingly. The Hanoi central telephone exchange timed long-distance calls and billed users accordingly. The number of telephones in use declined substantially in late 1945, with French civilian phones apparently all disconnected and many business phones lying idle. A government-compiled Hanoi telephone list from circa 1946 contains only eighty-three active numbers, of which fifty-four (65 percent) are DRV bureaus, eight are nationalized companies, twelve national salvation (Việt Minh) offices, eight newspapers, and one private home.[135] However, we know from newspaper ads and business stationery that some Hanoi stores and professionals retained active telephones too. And even towns as small as Thái Nguyên, Sơn Tây, and Phủ Lý possessed switchboards linking ten to fifteen phones.

The PTT's biggest problem was theft of telegraph and telephone wire. During the colonial era, village heads were punished if anyone tampered with wires passing through their jurisdiction. This system eroded during the summer of 1945, and during August some insurrectionaries made a point of removing long stretches of wire and digging up poles.[136] While the new DRV government was quick to order all local committees to protect telegraph and telephone lines, the PTT continued to report numerous outages due to removed wire. In September 1945, all four existing telephone lines between Hanoi and Haiphong were cut simultaneously. Inside the capital, seven hundred meters of telephone wire were stolen off the poles.[137] The PTT's national director, Nguyễn Tường Thụy, complained that "since the second change of regime," local authorities no longer had guards protecting the telegraph and telephone lines.[138] This politically noncommittal turn of phrase, in an instruction sent to all subordinate PTT units, would have infuriated some Việt Minh adherents, particularly given Thụy's family connections (see below). The stakes were raised when Chinese troops occupying northern Indochina in late September and October lodged protests each time their own use of telegraph or telephone communications was blocked by wire removals. DRV government authority was now literally on the line.

During November and December, PTT crews repaired twenty-two major telephone or telegraph line cuts, each requiring replacement of hundreds or even thousands of meters of lost wire. The Interior Ministry forwarded to the

Northern Region Committee details of two particularly serious losses, then warned that local committees must take "complete responsibility." In turn, the Northern Committee pressured province committees, suggesting that some of their subordinate committees knew exactly who was stealing the wire but chose to look the other way. Local committees were ordered to form special guard units, explain to people how important the lines were to national defense preparations, and identify perpetrators who could be put on trial and punished severely as a deterrent. Losses persisted however, with for example Hanoi–Phủ Lý telephone communications being knocked out and wire looted three times in the last days of December.[139] In January, the press condemned persons responsible for sabotage of communication lines and called for the death penalty. One paper carried a front-page public notice titled "Will Be Executed," addressed to anyone who had stolen, transported, or purchased electric power lines, telephone, or telegraph wire. Guilty parties had five days to sell these items to the government or face dire punishment.[140] In some cases PTT teams were blocked physically from carrying out their task of restoring poles and restringing wire. In late January, a district committee in Hà Đông province was ordered to detain and punish anyone impeding a PTT team, and to actively assist in repairing the Hanoi–Phủ Lý line.[141]

To be able to carry out so many replacements the PTT must have possessed a fair reserve of colonial-era telephone and telegraph wire. However, by January 1946 supplies were running short. Although U.S. Army surplus stocks of wire were known to be on sale in Bangkok, Manila, and Hong Kong, the DRV's paltry quantities of hard currency and gold had to be spent on higher priority items like firearms, ammunition, and radio equipment. When Chinese troop units began to depart from Indochina from April onward, they appear to have sold some of their own rolls of wire to overseas Chinese associates (see chapter 5). In late April, Vũ Gia Thụy, PTT director for Bắc Bộ, learned that 14,200 meters of wire was available in Quảng Yên town, fifteen kilometers northeast of Haiphong. Thụy notified the Northern Region Committee, which quickly instructed the Quảng Yên province committee to make certain the wire did not go to private buyers, as it badly needed for "defense purposes." Whether a price was negotiated or the DRV government simply confiscated the wire is not revealed in the archives.[142] By May, the incidence of wire theft seems to have dropped off to manageable proportions, if the absence of government correspondence or newspaper warnings is a reliable indicator. In September, telephone wire theft was still listed by police among six priority crimes to be addressed, along with counterfeiting, armed robbery, burglary, extortion, and kidnapping.[143] However, the PTT had found ways to keep the telephone network functioning most of the time.

The PTT endured substantial reductions in personnel during the transition from colonial to postcolonial operations. One source indicates that PTT numbers dropped from almost six thousand persons in August 1945 to three thousand one year later.[144] Some of the five hundred local post offices existing in August were forced to close, while others cut back staff. Rather than resigning, many PTT staff applied for retirement or long-term leave without pay, in hopes of receiving a pension or continuing to work in exchange for food rations from local administrative committees.[145] Specialists—telegraphers, technicians, repairmen, typists, and code clerks—were mostly encouraged to remain on the job. The PTT section devoted to monitoring the content of private cables and mail appears to have expanded compared to colonial times.[146] In March 1946, the Finance Ministry allocated the significant sum of twenty-five thousand piastres to pay per diems and incidental expenses to PTT technicians and repairmen.[147] Some militia groups sought specialized training from the PTT, with haphazard results.[148] In late November, the PTT began to assign telephones and special lines to militia units expected to help defend the capital (see chapter 3).[149]

The sensitive nature of some government information being transmitted through PTT facilities inevitably meant that DRV security services and self-appointed Việt Minh agents would start to investigate the backgrounds and current behavior of PTT personnel. Suspicion focused particularly on individuals who previously had worked closely with French staff. This probably accounts for fourteen higher-level PTT employees being dismissed without benefits between November 1945 and February 1946.[150] The most notorious PTT dismissal was that of its general director, Nguyễn Tường Thụy, a story which extended over many months. In December 1945, the police arrested Thụy, only to release him without charge the next day, claiming it was all a mistake. Thụy angrily submitted his resignation, arguing that he was being victimized because his brother, Nguyễn Tường Tam, had a leading role in the Vietnam Nationalist Party. The government refused to accept Thụy's resignation, and indeed reaffirmed his status as general director by DRV decree three months later. However, in September the government designated Vũ Gia Thụy to the general directorship during such time as Nguyễn Tường Thụy was "unable to fulfil his responsibilities."[151] In fact, Thụy had just been arrested, and three months later he was still in jail awaiting his fate (see chapter 7).

A significant minority of Vietnamese had learned how to utilize the PTT during the colonial era, and more found it handy as DRV citizens in 1945–46. Unfortunately we lack statistics for postal processing. It seems that specialized services such as cash transfers, savings accounts, and registered mail dropped off rapidly. Large parcels had to be refused due to transport difficulties. A few letters managed to travel from south to north and reach their destinations. Above the sixteenth parallel, the posting of newspapers and books expanded substantially.[152] Persons wishing to send ordinary letters were pleased to see the price of postage stamps falling well below general inflation. Official letters dispatched to and

FIGURE 5. 1946 postage stamps, showing DRV overprints of colonial stamps, the first Hồ Chí Minh stamp, and an early France Outre-Mer Indochine stamp. Author's collection.

from Hanoi had to bear stamps as well, with each clerk keeping meticulous records of stamps purchased and used.[153]

   Unable to locate a suitable color printing press for the production of new stamps, the government instructed the PTT to overprint the less controversial among the colonial stamps with the words "Việt Nam Dân Chủ Cộng Hòa" (DRV) plus a new price, then to sell these hybrids to customers as a stopgap. In January 1946, the minister of communications and public works authorized overprinting and use of the Villes Martyres stamp, featuring the Orleans cathedral.[154] In April, the État français stamps that pictured Emperor Bảo Đại and Empress Nam Phương were approved for DRV use, with part of the proceeds to go to a national relief fund.[155] Four months later the image of the Bishop of Adran, who had assisted Nguyễn Ánh to fight the Tây Sơn in the 1790s, was subject to overprinting, with some stamp proceeds to go to the Association for Invalid Soldiers and the National Defense Fund.[156]

Immediately after the August 1945 Revolution, however, it seems that a number of local PTT offices had already moved on their own volition to ink the new nation's name onto sheets of whatever colonial stamps happened to be available. Some citizens must have been angered to see images of the same French admirals who had invaded Vietnam, French governors general, and Marshal Philippe Pétain, the Vichy head of state. There was even a stamp of an Indochina youth proudly making the fascist salute. Besides the stamps bought, pasted, and cancelled on envelopes as postage, citizens apparently were encouraged to purchase sheets of uncancelled stamps in support of various government causes. Calls to wipe out illiteracy and join the New Life movement could be found overprinted on other colonial stamps.[157] Finally, in late August 1946, the acting DRV president, Huỳnh Thúc Kháng, decreed the first original DRV postage stamp, naturally bearing the image of President Hồ Chí Minh.[158]

As the National Guard increased in numbers, and units moved further from their home provinces, many soldiers looked to the PTT mail system in order to keep in touch with their families and friends. Illiterate soldiers asked literate comrades to read or write letters for them. Unit political officers encouraged such correspondence, while cautioning everyone against revealing military secrets. Some letters made their way into the press. Mail to and from Laos appears to have come through more often than mail to or from the south.[159]

DRV authorities were proud of the PTT system and tried hard to keep it functioning. Despite disruptions, communication was sustained between Hanoi and almost all province seats north of Đà Nẵng. At the district level, much depended on whether committees were willing to feed post office personnel. PTT operations were thrown into chaos following the outbreak of full-scale war in December 1946, yet zones not occupied by the French soon managed to resume internal telegraph and telephone links. Nam Bộ and southern Trung Bộ had already demonstrated how couriers could carry official correspondence to almost any location.

THE SECOND SESSION OF THE NATIONAL ASSEMBLY

During the summer of 1946, some members of the National Assembly worried that the longer the Assembly failed to reconvene, the more the executive branch would take control of affairs. In June, the constitution subcommittee reported that it would soon be able to forward its draft to the Assembly's Standing Committee.[160] Month by month, however, the absence of President Hồ Chí Minh in France seemed sufficient cause to delay reconvening. News of the 14 September Franco-Vietnamese modus vivendi, and Hồ's subsequent sea voyage home, triggered preparations for the Assembly's second session. Nguyễn Văn Tố, head of the Standing Committee, announced his intention to have the committee first discuss the modus vivendi urgently, but this meeting apparently did not take place.[161] On 9 October, Acting President Huỳnh Thúc Kháng formally requested that the National Assembly reconvene; two days later Tố dispatched instructions to delegates around the country to arrive in Hanoi by 23 October. Twelve days notice was wildly impractical for those delegates below the sixteenth parallel, who would need to travel through French-controlled territory. The Finance Ministry allocated a modest ten thousand piastres for immediate expenses to convene the Assembly.[162] Not until after the Assembly adjourned in November did the government authorize travel passes, allowances, and per diems for Assembly members' attendance.[163] In many cases delegates had to pay their own way or be assisted financially by local committees.

Early October saw an upsurge of press interest in constitutional issues, government policy options, and possible cabinet changes. Sensing a political opening, dissident papers tried to canvass questions such as unicameral versus bicameral legislative systems, protecting democratic freedoms, the national flag, and deficiencies in the modus vivendi. Government censors reacted by chopping out huge sections in articles and editorials.[164] DRV police and armed Việt Minh squads rounded up and incarcerated several hundred alleged enemies of the state (see chapter 7). After some National Assembly delegates belonging to the Nationalist Party were arrested, others had to decide whether to flee or hope the Assembly could protect their parliamentary immunity. When Hồ Chí Minh finally stepped ashore in Haiphong on 21 October, after twenty weeks abroad, he had only one week to reacquaint himself with domestic issues, consult with colleagues, and prepare for Assembly business. Hồ and Huỳnh Thúc Kháng invited all delegates to a reception the day before the Assembly reconvened.[165] With so many local activists and national leaders converging on the Hanoi Opera House the next morning, DRV security units looked for signs of a French coup, aware that the enemy had plotted such preemptive action before.

The second session of the National Assembly opened at eight o'clock on the morning of Monday, 28 October, with American, British, Chinese, and Swiss consuls present, as well as a representative of General Louis Morlière, commander of French forces in northern Indochina and interim commissioner of the republic. A bevy of foreign correspondents also observed the first day's proceedings. Of the total of 400 Assembly delegates accredited nationwide, 290 were present on 28 October, including thirty-eight of the seventy Nationalist Party and Revolutionary League members who had been invited to join the Assembly in March.[166] Meeting organizers had decided to divide the chamber into "Left," "Center," and "Right" seats, in imitation of the French National Assembly. On the Left they placed fourteen Marxists, twenty-four Socialists, and forty-five Democrats. In the Center there were eighty Việt Minh and ninety nonparty or independent delegates. On the Right, Nationalist Party and Revolutionary League delegates were meant to sit. Socialist Party delegates wore dark red ties, while a prominent Democratic Party delegate, Đỗ Đức Dục, sported a half red and half blue tie.[167] In reality, Marxists, Socialists, and Democrats all belonged to the Việt Minh Front, but at this meeting it would have been impossible for ICP leaders to enforce a single policy line. Besides, the image of political diversity might deflect criticism about arrests of dissidents that had taken place earlier. Differentiation also gave the Việt Minh four times as many speaking opportunities.

Election of a member to chair National Assembly proceedings quickly revealed the extent of Việt Minh dominance. Phạm Văn Đồng nominated Bùi Bằng Đoàn, former court mandarin and current delegate from Hà Đông province, but Đoàn declined for alleged health reasons. Someone then proposed Tôn Đức Thắng, a senior ICP activist from Nam Bộ, who accepted the nomination on grounds of national unity. Nguyễn Văn Tố, chair of the Assembly's Standing Committee, also was nominated, only to be roundly defeated by Thắng. Next came election of four delegates to join Thắng in the chairman's group. After seven individuals were nominated, Phạm Văn Đồng (ICP) received the highest vote, followed by Đỗ Đức Dục (Democratic Party), Trần Hữu Dực (ICP), and Ngô Tử Hạ, the Catholic businessman and eldest delegate who had chaired the first session of the National Assembly in March. The three unsuccessful nominees came from the Nationalist Party, the Revolutionary League, and the Catholic Church.[168] It soon became apparent that Tố was being nudged to the sidelines. The next day he was criticized for letting the Interior Ministry control issuing of passes to the press and public, and the Assembly voted to expand the number of passes.[169] The final blow to Tố came towards the end of the second session, when he was omitted from the new Standing Committee elected by the Assembly. Tố's insistence on Standing Committee prerogatives during the summer had garnered him enemies within the ICP and among senior DRV administrators. As consolation, Hồ Chí Minh made him a minister without portfolio in the new cabinet.

Franco-Vietnamese tensions hung over National Assembly proceedings. On the first day, Nguyễn Văn Tạo, delegate from Rạch Giá, was given the floor to speak at length about French terror campaigns in the south, popular resistance, and the importance of defending Nam Bộ as an integral part of Vietnam. Tạo concluded his address: "The day will come soon when we can relive the radiant days of the August Revolution, when every town and village will be free to shout these happy salutations: Long Live President Hồ! Long Live Vietnamese Independence!"[170] According to reporters, this speech brought tears to the eyes of delegates from all over the country, and President Hồ rushed up to embrace and kiss Tạo.[171] All delegates were mindful that a Franco-Vietnamese cease-fire was supposed to begin on 30 October (see chapter 4). The press noted the arrival in Hanoi of French officials to discuss implementation of the cease-fire and other modus vivendi provisions. Return of the Pasteur Institute to France was reported as evidence of DRV good faith. During National Assembly deliberations, however, no one made the case for a special relationship with France, nor was there any mention of France or the French Union in the text of the DRV Constitution approved on 8 November. On that same day the Assembly instructed the new DRV government not to give in on the Haiphong customs issue "at any price," an order which increased the chances of armed confrontation.[172]

From the Assembly's first day, Nationalist Party delegates objected strenuously to being seated on the "far Right," arguing that they had as much commitment to political and social reform as the Democrats or Socialists. Nor should they be labelled conservatives *(bảo thủ)*, as they possessed no more property or money to conserve than others present.[173] On 30 October, Nguyễn Văn Tố revealed that he had favored letting each delegate sit wherever he or she preferred, but others had wanted seating by "tendency" *(khuynh hướng)*. Another member of the Standing Committee accepted responsibility for seating arrangements, claiming he had simply responded to letters sent in by political parties. Xuân Thủy, from the "centrist" Việt Minh, said the original idea was to seat delegates by their province or city electorates, but that failed to accommodate the Nationalist Party and Revolutionary League delegates, who had been admitted en bloc at the Assembly's first session in March. Trần Huy Liệu, a senior Việt Minh member, commented that the political tendency of delegates would be recognized by what they said, not by where they sat. In Vietnam's immediate circumstances, he added, "the correct position is to be neither left nor right." Eager to move on to other matters, the chair, Trần Hữu Dực, sought and received assent to his faintly ironic summing up: "The sense of this meeting is that the National Assembly has neither left nor right, in the same way that Vietnam has no Trung Bộ, Nam Bộ, and Bắc Bộ."[174]

Government question time, which began on Thursday morning, 31 October, and extended until midnight, represented a novel political experience for everyone present. Among hundreds of telegrams sent by "the people" *(dân chúng)* to the Assembly, thirty-two were read out in the spirit of direct democracy. Then sixty-two written questions from Assembly delegates were tabled, with another twenty-six questions coming later in the sitting. President Hồ stood up first to reply to questions about three government members not present; the status of the economics minister, Chu Bá Phượng; and Vietnam's foreign policy. He criticized Vice President Nguyễn Hải Thần, Foreign Minister Nguyễn Tường Tam, and Deputy Resistance Commissioner Vũ Hồng Khánh for abandoning their posts earlier in the year, but professed readiness to welcome them back if they recanted. Hồ deflected criticism of Phượng, his only remaining Nationalist Party minister, and reiterated his defense of the modus vivendi. Next, Võ Nguyên Giáp, chairman of the Military Commission, fielded questions about the commission's imminent merger with the Defense Department, the clash with French troops at Bắc Ninh in early August, and first reports on the Franco-Vietnamese cease-fire in Nam Bộ (see chapter 4).[175] Interior Minister Huỳnh Thúc Kháng spoke a few words, then turned the floor over to his deputy, Cù Huy Cận, who answered questions about the arrest of four Assembly members who belonged to the Nationalist Party. According to Cận, all four delegates had "directly or indirectly participated in kidnappings and extortions," and the arrests had been agreed to by the Assembly's Standing Committee.

Taking the floor to respond to a batch of legal questions, Vũ Đình Hoè, minister of justice, insisted that all foreign nationals must obey Vietnamese laws, noted that French property was the object of current Franco-Vietnamese deliberations, and foreshadowed tougher punishments for bribery. Finance Minister Lê Văn Hiến fielded questions on new taxes, the 1946 budget, introduction of DRV currency, and the Franco-Vietnamese dispute over Haiphong customs duties. Chu Bá Phượng, the minister for national economy, had just begun to answer submitted questions when he was interrupted repeatedly from the floor concerning scarcities of rice, salt, and sugar. Eventually Phượng invited his interrogators to come to his office to examine relevant records. Trần Đăng Khoa, minister of transport and public works, answered queries about particular bridges, power plants, and irrigation sluices needing to be rebuilt. Minister for Agriculture Bồ Xuân Luật had only tackled a couple of questions when the chair called a halt for dinner. Reconvening at eight in the evening, the chair recognized Trương Đình Tri, minister for health and society, who announced that more doctors would need to be conscripted to the National Guard, regretted the absence of controls on the import and sale of medicines, and doubted that the extreme shortage of rural health facilities could be rectified soon. Finally, Ca Văn Thỉnh, the outgoing minister for national education, attempted to deal with a host of questions about preschools, primary schools, teacher training, literacy classes, and even the Fine Arts Academy in Hanoi. He revealed that the government had an ambitious plan to create and maintain fifty thousand primary schools by 1954.[176]

At ten o'clock, the Assembly chair, Đỗ Đức Dục gave nine delegates twenty minutes each to raise further questions and comment on government activities to date. Seven of these speakers belonged to the Việt Minh Front, two were nonaligned, and none belonged to the Nationalist Party or Revolutionary League. A Socialist group member demanded that "certain elements" who had been hiding behind party labels to sow antigovernment rumors, sabotage rail lines, murder compatriots, and obey foreign powers be brought to justice. These allegations—obviously directed at the Nationalist Party—received repeated bursts of applause. A nonaligned delegate complained about confusion in government economic policies, with some officials advocating cooperatives, others promoting limited liability companies, and still others wanting the state to buy up plantations and factories. Khuất Duy Tiến, of the Marxist group, criticized those who continued to assert that internationalism and nationalism were incompatible. He then attacked "false revolutionaries and cynical traitors" (to applause), and urged the government to stop allocating ministries on the basis of political party. Nguyễn Đình Thi stressed that the Việt Minh was a front *(mặt trận)*, not a party, and that it had been the first to oppose the French colonialists and Japanese fascists. He supported the government's clemency policy, which had "averted dangerous confrontations" and made it possible to "receive people who previously we thought could never march side by side with us." Nguyễn Sơn Hà, an independent Haiphong entrepreneur, asked why his detailed economic proposal submitted to the government had been ignored.

Trần Huy Liệu launched a critique of government negotiations with the French, asking if the modus vivendi was founded on the principle of equality, then answering his own question in the negative. He warned that France must adhere strictly to the cease-fire, while the DRV had to retain (French-owned) strategic enterprises, control customs duties, and have the right to issue currency. Liệu's speech concluded, "The Vietnamese and French peoples must unite to oppose French reactionaries and secure Vietnam's complete independence and territorial integrity." Huỳnh Văn Tiểng, of the Democratic group, labelled the modus vivendi a "misfortune," supported calls for Saigon to be renamed Hồ Chí Minh City, and equated the city's future liberation with those of Stalingrad in 1943 and Paris in 1944. Xuân Thủy, of the Việt Minh group, defended the modus vivendi as reflecting realities of the moment. Finally, Nguyễn Văn Tạo, of the Marxist group, castigated the most recent public statement by the French high commissioner, Admiral d'Argenlieu.

President Hồ Chí Minh now took the floor to speak on behalf of the government Cabinet. First he quashed any further discussion of changing the national flag, saying that the existing banner was already soaked in the blood of heroic fighters in the south, and had been flown proudly and saluted officially "from Asia to Europe and back again." Rather than condemn opposition elements, Hồ chose to mock their ineffectiveness. Yet when it came to freedom of the press and other citizen rights, Hồ argued that amidst current stressful conditions it was necessary to circumscribe some individual liberties in the interests of the collective. Concerning the modus vivendi, Hồ stated bluntly that the cabinet disagreed with Trần Huy Liệu's interpretation. Both sides had made concessions. While he readily acknowledged that there were good and bad French persons, Hồ insisted that "the majority of French people today favor our independence and territorial unity." Employing a unique metaphor, Hồ suggested that "when an egg cracks it's a misfortune, yet from that event a bird emerges." Finally, Hồ warned delegates that "not everything can be accomplished by military means".[177] He was determined not to abandon the diplomatic path, despite obvious skepticism among Assembly delegates concerning the modus vivendi. It is worth noting here that Phạm Văn Đồng, who had headed the DRV delegation to France, at no time during the second session of the Assembly took the floor to support his president's position on negotiations.

At the conclusion of his speech, President Hồ announced resignation of the Cabinet and return of executive powers to the Assembly. The Assembly then invited Hồ to form a new nonparty government. In his brief acceptance speech, Hồ stressed how much needed to be accomplished, his disinterest in personal power, and his commitment to all-people, nonparty government. "I declare before the Assembly, before the people, and before the world, I have only one party, the Vietnam Party," Hồ concluded.[178]

For some weeks the public had been speculating about cabinet changes. With the Nationalist Party and Revolutionary League decimated, it was assumed that the Việt Minh would secure most ministerial appointments. *Cứu Quốc*, the principal Việt Minh daily, called for more talented ministers and more southern representation, and asserted that there was no further need to achieve a balance across political parties.[179] The new cabinet which Hồ presented to the Assembly on 3 November contained a mix of ICP stalwarts and nonaligned professionals, plus one token member each from the Nationalist Party and the Revolutionary League. Huỳnh Thúc Kháng (independent) remained as interior minister. Võ Nguyên Giáp (ICP) replaced Phan Anh (independent) as defense minister while continuing as army commander. Lê Văn Hiến (ICP) stayed as finance minister. Most independent ministers were backed up by an ICP vice minister *(thứ trưởng)*. Aiming to provide some representation from Nam Bộ in the cabinet, Hồ made Nguyễn Văn Tạo (ICP) minister of labor, Ngô Tấn Nhơn minister of agriculture, and kept the Economics Ministry vacant for a southerner.[180] Democrats and Socialists were largely excluded from the cabinet, a decision that provoked discontent well into 1947.

Deliberating the Draft Constitution

The National Assembly began work on the DRV constitution on 2 November, the galleries packed with attentive citizens. Delegates only received copies of the draft constitution on entering, and had one hour to digest the contents. When presenting the drafting committee's report, Đỗ Đức Dục harkened back to the 1789 French and 1917 Russian revolutions, sketched some of political choices available, but then eschewed advocating a particular line, leaving the draft to speak for itself. Not a lot had changed from the draft constitution circulated one year earlier. The chair, Phạm Văn Đồng, invited each "group" in the chamber to make a preliminary assessment of the draft. Commentary moved along with only minor reservations until the Nationalist Party spokesperson, Trần Trung Dung, tried to make the case for representative rather than direct democracy, bicameralism rather than unicameralism, and the current necessity of defending freedom of the press and freedom of association. Dung encountered ever more hostile interjections from the floor, and eventually Đồng told him to sit down. A female delegate from Nam Bộ, Ngô Thị Huệ, challenged Dung's assertion that the Vietnamese people were not yet ready for full-fledged democracy. Khuất Duy Tiến accused Dung of "offending Vietnam's national sovereignty." When Dung sought the rostrum to be able to respond, scores of delegates objected loudly, and Đồng decided to finesse the situation by instructing the secretary to read some telegrams coming from the provinces. Then he adjourned the meeting for lunch.[181]

Opening the 2 November afternoon session, Phạm Văn Đồng gave the floor to a series of independent delegates to comment on the draft constitution. Favorable remarks by several ethnic minority delegates and a Catholic priest, Phạm Bá Trực, received particularly vigorous applause. Then it was time to deliberate each article of the draft in succession. Article one, stating that "all power in the country belongs to the entire Vietnamese people *(nhân dân)* without distinction of ethnicity, gender, wealth/poverty, class, or religion," quickly received approval by a show of hands. The same happened with article two, specifying that "the land of Vietnam is a center-south-north bloc that cannot be divided." When the chair came to article three, which designated Vietnam's flag, anthem, and capital location, Phan Tử Nghĩa, delegate from Thái Bình, called on everyone to stand, face the flag and sing "Tiến quân ca" ("Advancing Army"). The vote was a foregone conclusion.

Moving on to the articles dealing with responsibilities and rights of citizens, delegates of both sexes applauded women as well as men being available for military service. Article nine, stating that "women are equal to men in every aspect," was subject to an amendment deleting the words "in every aspect," but the amendment failed. Nguyễn Sơn Hà, from Haiphong, sought to add "freedom to engage in business" to the other citizen rights specified, but his proposal appears to have been ignored. When a Catholic delegate proposed adding "freedom of education," this provoked an extended debate over the status of public schools, with opponents of the amendment arguing that education was a collective rather than individual matter. By a vote of 110 for, 100 against, and 34 abstentions, the Assembly decided to refer this contentious topic to a subcommittee.[182]

On the morning of Monday, 4 November, Trần Hữu Dực chaired the continuing deliberation on civil liberties. An amendment to extend the right of private property beyond individual Vietnamese citizens to legal entities was defeated. Article thirteen, stating that "the rights of manual and intellectual workers are guaranteed," was roundly criticized as vague and inadequate. However, others argued that current circumstances demanded conciliation between workers and managers in the interests of national unity. This was clearly the government's position, and the original wording prevailed. Article fifteen, making primary education obligatory and free, requiring private schools to follow the state curriculum, and allowing ethnic minorities to use their own languages in primary classes, was passed after considerable discussion of detail. Articles concerning the franchise, recall, and referendum passed with little debate. It was agreed that candidates for election to the National Assembly must read and write Vietnamese, but this ought not be obligatory for candidates to local people's councils. An amendment was tabled specifying that serving military personnel had the right to vote and to run for office. When delegates suggested this was redundant because soldiers were already citizens, Đỗ Hữu Du, a National Guard officer, pointed out that some countries had laws withholding the franchise from soldiers. After further discussion, the amendment was voted upon affirmatively.[183]

Attention now turned to the chapter in the constitution regarding the National Assembly itself.[184] The chair gave the floor to a delegate who first offered a legal history of unicameral and bicameral experiences in the West, then argued the merits of a second house of review and warned that a lone house for Vietnam risked dictatorship. To this a Socialist Party member retorted that the upper house in a bicameral system always defended the ruling classes, then added: "With a popularly elected unicameral house, if conditions require a dictatorship then at least it belongs to the people, whereas a bicameral system will oppose the interests of the people."[185] Phạm Gia Độ, a lawyer and the only Nationalist Party member to have served on the constitution drafting committee, stated flatly that unicameralism meant "dictatorship by the majority." When Nguyễn Đình Thi (Việt Minh) countered that in Vietnam's current dangerous circumstances it was vital to possess a strong central power capable of making decisions quickly, an opponent interjected, "Just like the dictatorship of the [French] Convention of 1792." Thi shot back, "There is no fear of that here, as the Assembly is only legislative, whereas the executive is in the hands of the Government." This reply by Thi misconstrued the constitution text being considered, yet accurately foreshadowed what happened soon after the Assembly adjourned. After some additional debate, the chair called for a vote: two hundred delegates supported unicameralism and ten bicameralism.[186]

Armed with a massive majority, the chair now decided to push through with little discussion a series of articles delineating Assembly procedures and powers. Article twenty-five, specifying that "delegates do not only represent their localities but also represent the entire people," would soon be used by the executive to secure routine policy approvals from the Assembly Standing Committee. The provision in the November 1945 draft for printing of Assembly proceedings in the National Gazette was dropped. Articles defining the work of the Standing Committee did trigger a wider debate about legislative versus executive powers. Some delegates insisted that the Assembly had the right to control the executive, while others said that it should only critique executive actions, and if necessary call a new election. Several votes confirmed the latter position. Nonetheless, Assembly powers remained substantial, which helps to explain why ICP leaders made sure that a solid majority of Việt Minh members were elected to the Standing Committee at the end of the Assembly's second session.[187] For the next seven years there was no possibility of reconvening the National Assembly, so a few members of the Standing Committee who resided in the Việt Bắc hills together with the executive performed a quasi-legitimizing function.

The issue of parliamentary immunity stimulated considerable Assembly debate, which is not surprising considering that some Nationalist party delegates had already been jailed and others wondered about their fate once the second session ended. The majority of speakers argued that Assembly delegates caught in the act of committing a crime (cas de flagrant délit) could be arrested by the police, but there was much confusion in trying to delineate which criminal offences rated such serious action. Some speakers wanted blanket immunity for anything that a delegate said or voted upon inside the Assembly, while others argued this should not extend to high treason. Lê Trọng Nghĩa, a Democrat, worried that a party with members in the government might order the arrest of members of another party just long enough to prevent them from voting on important legislation. At one point the chair moved to end debate, but this was rejected by a vote of 109 to 58, indicating that not only Nationalist Party delegates wanted clarification. In the end, it was agreed that a delegate could not be prosecuted for anything said or voted upon in the Assembly, which turned out to be no protection whatsoever during the many years when the Assembly did not convene. Another clause stated that the government could not arrest and try any delegate without prior agreement of the Assembly or the Standing Committee (when the Assembly was not in session), but further language allowed the government to arrest a delegate "caught in the act," and then to notify the Standing Committee for determination.

Functions of the government (Chính phủ) received only a fraction of the attention that delegates had given to the National Assembly, probably out of respect for the incumbent president, plus a growing desire to uphold central authority in the face of escalating tensions with France. The president was made commander-in-chief of the armed forces, an increase in power from the November 1945 constitution draft, in which the president had authority only to select general officers. He could not be removed during his five-year tenure except if convicted of treason by a special court convened by the Assembly. All government decrees (sắc lệnh) were to be signed by the president, which in the absence of Assembly sessions to enact laws (luật) gave him clear authority over the prime minister and cabinet. However, declarations of war or cessation of hostilities were to be shared between the president, cabinet, and Standing Committee (the latter when the Assembly was not in session). A Marxist deputy argued that the president should not be compelled to subject himself to popular election like other Assembly members, but this was opposed by other delegates, and it certainly would have been countered by Hồ Chí Minh himself. A substantive debate ensued over whether the prime minister should be chosen by the Assembly, or be selected by the president from among Assembly members and presented to the Assembly for approval. Proponents of the latter position argued that in current circumstances it was the president who could best guard the interests of the nation. They prevailed, with only six dissenting votes. A provision remained whereby the Standing Committee or one-quarter of Assembly delegates could call for a vote of confidence on the prime minister, the cabinet, or any specific minister. Assistant ministers could be appointed from outside the Assembly, a significant change from the November 1945 draft.

From 6 November onward, the National Assembly appeared under pressure to conclude its deliberations as soon as possible. Discussion of local people's councils and administrative committees was quite short, considering the importance of these bodies to overall government performance. Some delegates argued that meetings of councils and committees should be closed to the public. Others urged that higher echelons be empowered to dismiss lower echelon bodies. Still others sought a compromise between strong central direction and local initiative. As approved, however, the six articles on local administration simply summarized the decree issued one year earlier (see above). The DRV judicial system also received scant Assembly attention. Provisions contained in the November 1945 constitution draft remained intact, except for the addition of a people's assessor to each court. A proposal to establish an autonomous supreme court, similar to that in the United States, was voted down. The last article in the draft dealt with procedures to amend the constitution, with two-thirds of the Assembly required to agree on changes, followed by submission to the national electorate for majority approval or rejection. Democratic Party delegates wanted a further article specifying that Vietnam's democratic republican system of government never be altered, but this was rejected by the Assembly as contrary to the principle of popular democracy. Notably, no one proposed an article on the role of political parties, leagues, associations, or fronts in the DRV.

On the morning of Friday 8 November, a preamble to the constitution was tabled by a subcommittee. The Assembly discussed the text at some length and made a few changes. The first portion of the preamble offers a concise view of Vietnam's immediate past and future:

> The August Revolution regained the country's sovereignty, freedom for the people *(nhân dân)*, and the foundations of a Democratic Republic. After eighty years of struggle the Vietnamese people *(dân tộc)* have escaped from colonial oppression and simultaneously cast aside monarchism.

The country *(nước nhà)* has stepped onto a new path.

The responsibility of our people in this era is to protect all territory, achieve full independence, and build the nation *(quốc gia)* on democratic foundations.

During this sitting, Nguyễn Sơn Hà took the floor to reiterate that the constitution needed a paragraph on the economy, one which specifically upheld entrepreneurial freedom. A majority voted against reopening this question and Hà reluctantly resumed his seat.[188]

Trần Hữu Dực, the chair of this sitting, then invited a representative of each "group" in the chamber to make a concluding statement regarding the draft constitution. Speaking for independent delegates, Lê Tu Lảnh approved the text and particularly mentioned support for unicameralism, a democratic republic, and the current flag and national anthem. Phan Tử Nghĩa, on behalf of Socialist Party delegates, continued to oppose private schools and to favor a command economy, but said that the Socialists would vote in favor of the draft. Hồ Đức Thành, of the Revolutionary League, accepted the draft with no reservations. Đỗ Đức Dục, Democratic Party spokesperson, gave the most reflective concluding speech of all. The constitution's content had not changed significantly from the first draft a year earlier, he commented, and it still failed to give adequate weight to the two principles of direct democracy and concentration of political power. Dục chided delegates for being reluctant to enhance their own powers, or to strengthen the Assembly's right to free speech and free determination. But he understood this reticence to reflect the spirit of "Vietnamese combatants forgetting themselves for the country, and only knowing how to 'sacrifice one's life for the people.'" Dục was unhappy that the proposal to make the democratic republican system immune from future constitutional amendment had been rejected, but he and his Democratic Party comrades accepted the current draft constitution.[189] Dục's argument, poorly constructed in places, unwittingly demonstrated how war and revolution would make operation of the National Assembly impossible.

Phạm Gia Độ spoke at length for the Nationalist Party, reasserting the need to protect individual liberties, especially freedom of expression, opposing dictatorship even if backed by the vast majority, repeating arguments for bicameralism, and calling for heads of local administrative committees to be appointed by the central government. Hoàng Anh, delegate from Thừa Thiên, speaking on behalf of the Việt Minh, warmly recalled President Hồ's pledge before the Assembly that "I have only one party, the Vietnam Party." Then Anh reminded everyone that their compatriots in the south were at that moment fighting and dying for the nation. Khuất Duy Tiến, representing the Marxists, lauded the draft constitution as the "child of the August Revolution," then criticized the Nationalist Party's preoccupation with civil liberties, arguing that "liberty given to the individual should not prejudice the interest of the group." Perhaps influenced by the vigorous applause, Tiến continued, "We have always fought and will continue to fight to achieve a society from which all human exploitation will be banished."

There being no other delegates wishing to speak, the chair moved to a vote on the entire draft constitution. First he asked whether delegates wanted a secret ballot or simple show of hands; a clear majority supported the latter. With 242 delegates present, 240 voted in favor and two against the constitution, with no abstentions. On the motion of one delegate, and joined by a packed balcony of citizens, the Assembly then rose to sing the national anthem.[190] Phạm Gia Độ was the only Nationalist Party delegate to vote against the constitution; some others probably chose not to be present. Nguyễn Sơn Hà was the other negative vote, and his choice provoked an angry backlash in Haiphong. One week later a public meeting was called at the Haiphong Opera House, where Hà tried to explain his position on freedom of business enterprise, and his frustration when the Assembly failed repeatedly to debate the matter. Members of the Opera House audience began interjecting aggressively, leading Nguyễn Đình Thi, also present on stage, to urge that the meeting not be turned into a court interrogation. The crowd proceeded to whistle, yell, and bang chairs, causing Thi to halt the meeting and escort his fellow Assembly member away.[191]

On Saturday morning, 9 November, with Đỗ Đức Dục in the chair, the National Assembly discussed the troubling implications of article twenty-one, which required a popular referendum on the constitution before it became law. Members readily agreed that it was impossible in current tense conditions to organize a nationwide referendum. Some delegates favored a formal announcement that both the referendum and elections to a new Assembly would take place as soon as possible, and that meanwhile the present Assembly would continue to function. Other delegates argued that the people had already spoken in support of the constitution by means of rallies and demonstrations, as well as via their elected representatives. As one speaker put it, other countries might experience "diverse, perplexing differences concerning constitutional issues," resulting in no solid majority one way or another, but in Vietnam 240 Assembly delegates had just approved this constitution text, with only two members dissenting. Therefore, no referendum was needed. A motion to this effect was eventually put to delegates, and it triumphed by a vote of 227 to 8. Another vote, deciding that the constitution should not yet be enacted by government decree, and foreshadowing elections to a new Assembly when circumstances improved, gave mixed signals,.[192] As Stein Tønnesson has concluded, "Formally this meant that the National Assembly violated the terms of the constitution immediately after having voted on it."[193]

On the afternoon of 9 November, President Hồ congratulated the Assembly on effecting the "very first constitution in the history of Vietnam, and one of the earliest beacons in East Asia's constitutional history." He added that the constitution was "not yet perfect, but the result of practical exigencies." The constitution declared to the world that Vietnam was "already independent," yet a few sentences later Hồ urged all citizens to join with the government "to achieve independence, territorial unity, a strong country, and a wealthy populace."[194] Tôn Đức Thắng, deputy chair of the new Standing Committee, thanked President Hồ for his address, summarized the accomplishments of the previous thirteen days, and then led the entire hall in cheers of "Long Live President Hồ! Long Live Unification! Long Live Independence!" The national anthem was sung accompanied by the National Guard band, the second session of the assembly was declared closed, and everyone cheered President Hồ and the cabinet as they left the chamber.[195] The Assembly would not reconvene until December 1953.

The DRV constitution of 8 November 1946 was substantially influenced by French legal precedent, but more so by that of the pre-World War II Third Republic than that of the Fourth Republic that was taking shape in France during 1946. As we have seen, the first DRV constitution draft appeared in November 1945, and that content remained quite visible in the constitution approved by the Assembly one year later. Almost surely the 1946 drafting committee canvassed the French constitution that had been defeated by popular referendum on 5 May, and managed to peruse the text of the constitution that was eventually ratified on 27 October. However, the Fourth Republic constitution had two legislative chambers rather than one, and provided for a much stronger judiciary than the DRV constitution. It also contained provisions regarding the legislative process, annual budget, auditing, and citizenship not found in the DRV constitution. And it contained twenty-three articles concerning the new French Union which had no echo whatsoever in the DRV constitution. There were a few borrowings from the Soviet constitutional model in the DRV text, notably people's councils and administrative committees meant both to serve their constituency and to obey directives from above. One Việt Minh delegate scolded those speakers who had used foreign legal precedent to argue their case, saying that "the constitution is for Vietnam, not Russia or the United States." Nonetheless, delegates had emerged from the second session certain that they had not "betrayed the people (dân chúng)," and that the constitution would "take the people (dân tộc) to a radiant future."[196]

This second session of the National Assembly has proved to be the most wide-ranging, substantive public deliberation by an official body ever to take place in Vietnam to date. It was not an entirely free discussion, given that some Nationalist Party delegates had already been arrested, and that everyone else was mindful that punishment might befall those who pursued contrary opinions beyond still ill-defined parameters. According to French intelligence, Phạm Gia Độ was incarcerated a few weeks later, and some independent delegates found police agents and Việt Minh activists scaring away their friends or trying to ensnare them in financial improprieties.[197] Still, during the second session, delegates across the political spectrum believed they were debating important questions and setting good parliamentary precedents. The ICP did not enforce a party line on Việt Minh adherents, and indeed was in no position to do so. Hồ Chí Minh made his will felt at some junctures, but as head of state, not ICP leader. On many occasions it was the Democratic Party and some Socialists who held the initiative in the Assembly. War soon made it impossible for the Assembly to function, and within a few years the Democrats and Socialists became policy mimics for the ICP/Workers' Party. Since then, the story of the second session has been almost entirely ignored in Vietnam, and the National Assembly has not come close to emulating the intense, far-reaching discourse of late 1946. In recent years, Vietnamese critics of the existing political system have sometimes harkened back to the 1946 DRV constitution without discussing publicly why it failed to be taken seriously.

THE GOVERNMENT AND GROWING
FRANCO-VIETNAMESE CONFLICT

As National Assembly delegates headed home in mid-November, they knew that Franco-Vietnamese talks were underway in Hanoi on implementation of the military provisions of the modus vivendi, and that at the same time the dispute in Haiphong over customs controls seemed to be escalating (see chapter 4). The DRV government had compiled plans for peacetime economic development, and a team headed by Phan Anh and Phạm Khắc Hoè was preparing position papers for each of the Franco-Vietnamese mixed commissions stipulated by the modus vivendi.[198] The DRV civil administration continued to function routinely at central, regional, and local levels. The General Staff (Tổng Tham mưu) of the National Guard had drafted war plans during the summer based on several different scenarios, although nothing was communicated down the chain of command. At the end of September, an ICP document urged correction of military deficiencies, and preparations to take the offensive. Two weeks later, ICP members from some military units and Việt Minh committees met to try to find practical solutions. Hồ Chí Minh sought peace, but he also wanted improved DRV military readiness. Meanwhile, Việt Minh newspapers stepped up their calls on the populace to get ready for protracted armed resistance (see chapter 9). Only a handful of activists in the north had witnessed the bloodshed in southern and south-central Vietnam. The rest were propelled to fight by visions of ancient Vietnamese warriors and stories from the French, Russian, and Chinese revolutions.

The massive French attack in Haiphong on 23 November caught both DRV leaders and Việt Minh activists by surprise. Hồ Chí Minh tried desperately to reach the French government in Paris to restore prior conditions. He deliberately did not put the DRV government and army on a war footing, aware this would torpedo any remaining chances for peace. But Hồ did upgrade confidential ICP-led efforts to shift rice, salt, and equipment into the hills southwest and north of Hanoi. The Northern Region Committee also began to acquire seventeen hundred tons of grain from various Red River delta provinces in order to ship them south to Thanh Hóa province, yet by 19 December it seems that no more than several hundred tons of paddy had made it beyond the Nam Định railroad yards.[199] The government was slow to assist civilians fleeing the carnage in Haiphong, and conveyed mixed signals to Hanoi residents trying to decide whether to remain or evacuate to the countryside. On 24 November, the long-planned First All-Country Cultural Conference convened in the capital, only to have its agenda cut down to one day instead of the eight days originally intended.[200] On the other hand, DRV administrators were determined not to let the French disrupt office activities. They continued to dispatch and receive telegrams and mail, process personnel files, keep petty cash receipts, compile reports, and route citizen petitions to appropriate venues.

Concerned that the French might try to decapitate the DRV by seizing or killing the president, security advisors convinced Hồ Chí Minh to reduce public engagements, keep his itinerary secret, and sleep in one of several villages just west of Hanoi. Hồ's time at the Bắc Bộ Phủ was now limited to receiving foreign officials or journalists, plus chairing several hasty cabinet meetings. It became impossible for most ministers and senior staff to gain the ear of the president, who in any event was now almost completely occupied with issues of peace or war. On 28 November, Hồ appealed publicly for calm, yet the same day *Cứu Quốc*, the principal Việt Minh newspaper, quoted the Nam Bộ military commander, Nguyễn Bình, as arguing that "only guns and bullets can stop the French reactionaries." The next day, *Cứu Quốc* urged citizens to ferret out and punish compatriots who disseminated false rumors that the enemy employed to undermine Vietnamese morale.[201] In early December, Hồ was hit by an attack of malaria, making it all the more difficult for him to exercise leadership, much less regain strategic momentum. Militia units in the Haiphong area now felt justified in sniping at French troops, and this behavior soon spread to other locations. French soldiers also fired at *"les Viets"* without provocation, and their officers often turned a blind eye.[202]

The DRV government neglected to prepare lower echelons for what to do in the event of French attacks extending to the capital. The only exception I have found is an urgent, secret letter dispatched by the Northern Region Committee to bureau chiefs on 3 December, which assumed that the government would withdraw from Hanoi, yet implicitly ruled out any attempt to relocate bureaus intact to the countryside. Instead, staff members were to present themselves individually to province chairmen and accept whatever jobs were offered. Province committees would be told to provide public servant evacuees with either a salary or food rations. The letter concluded with a warning that no government employee consider serving the French.[203] Some employees had already sent their families to live with relatives outside the capital, and more did this as Franco-Vietnamese tensions escalated. On the morning of 19 December, the Interior Ministry addressed a confidential letter to the chairman of the Northern Committee, formally authorizing immediate evacuation of employee families, and outlining how public servants would be utilized in wartime. Some would join combat units. Others would withdraw to the countryside, whether to serve the central government once it resumed operations, to put themselves at the disposal of authorities in their natal villages, or to volunteer as mass mobilization (dân vận) cadres pending employment by province or district committees. The Interior Ministry foreshadowed establishment of rural "production camps" (trại sản xuất), where unemployed public servants would receive priority membership. This letter, signed by assistant minister Hoàng Hữu Nam, made its way to several bureaus inside the Northern Region Office on 19 December before staff hastily exited the building that evening.[204]

The content of mail and telegrams arriving at and departing from the Northern Region Office in the week prior to 19 December differed little from previous weeks. At 10:25 A.M. on 19 December the telegraph office dispatched a message to Hải Dương acknowledging its promise to send seventy-six tons of rice to Thanh Hóa, part of the central government's tardy effort to create a defense stockpile outside the Red River delta.[205] Later in the day, Economics Bureau staff received a circular instructing them to remain at their desks if they heard gunfire around the city, but noting that if they heard fire before coming to the office they had permission to stay home until it ceased, then report to work.[206] One office continued its routine of archiving copies of newspapers, so that later researchers are blessed with seven different Hanoi papers dated 18 December, and even one 19 December paper.[207] Another office examined the offer by M. Saissac in Huế to sell his three hundred hectares plantation in Ninh Bình for four hundred thousand piastres.[208] The last outgoing telegram copy filed away dealt with working hours for public servants from 23 December onward. The last encrypted telegram dispatched from the Northern Region Committee, at 5:50 P.M. on 19 December, was regarding Đỗ Văn Mẽ, who as we saw earlier had disappeared fifteen months earlier.[209]

While the option of attacking the French first, rather than waiting to be attacked, was one of the scenarios developed months earlier by the National Guard's General Staff, it was the late November Haiphong conflagration which triggered orders to prepare for such an operation (see chapter 3). From 15 December the French position hardened, and some Vietnamese militia groups became more belligerent. During the night of 18–19 December, Hồ Chí Minh met with his lieutenants and it was decided to launch an all-country, anti-French resistance struggle, but the date and time of attack remained unspecified. As of the morning of 19 December, Hồ withheld dissemination of the attack order, which helps to explain the business-as-usual atmosphere within DRV government offices throughout the day.[210] That morning Phạm Khắc Hoè, the Foreign Ministry's Cabinet director, met Assistant Minister Hoàng Minh Giám, who told him that talks with the French were continuing. At three in the afternoon, however, Hoè heard about instructions to sleep in the suburbs that night. Hoè chose to ignore this information and was completely surprised when the lights went out at 8:03 P.M., and the blackout was followed by gunfire (see chapter 3).[211] Meanwhile, the finance minister, Lê Văn Hiến, was informed by Võ Nguyên Giáp at four in the afternoon that the attack was going ahead that evening. Hiến gave Giáp a large quantity of newly printed DRV currency, then at five thirty departed the capital for a previously designated venue, shepherding cartloads of additional currency.[212] Some cabinet ministers escaped Hanoi the next day.

Others were not so fortunate. Đặng Phúc Thông, assistant minister of communications and public works, was captured by French troops. Phạm Khắc Hoè was detained on 21 December and found himself placed by the Sûreté in a "VIP cell" at Hỏa Lò prison, together with five other prominent individuals. Conversing over a tray of food, they quickly came to the conclusion that the DRV had started the fighting, as the French would have chosen to attack in daylight.[213] Nguyễn Văn Luyện, member of the first National Assembly Standing Committee, was killed along with his son in the Hanoi fighting.[214] Several thousand government employees caught by surprise by the shooting hid at home, fled the city, or joined local militia groups. Staff on duty at the Northern Region Office failed to destroy thousands of dossiers in the basement, leaving them to be captured by the French and exploited for intelligence purposes. This was in spite of the fact that there was ample time to burn everything, as two National Guard platoons defended the building until six in the evening on 20 December.[215] High-level indecision over peace or war had translated into poor contingency planning and implementation at lower levels.

3

Defense

Contrary to popular belief, the new regime in Hanoi did not commit itself to guerrilla resistance following the example of several hundred Liberation Army members who had descended from the northern hills in late August 1945. Instead, the provisional DRV government declared its intention to build a modern regular army capable of defending the entire territory of Vietnam, from the Sino-Vietnamese frontier to the Cà Mau peninsula. It was a matter of national honor that the army be able to protect both state and citizenry from foreign attack. This obligation came under quick challenge when hastily formed units in Saigon proved incapable of defending the city and surrounding countryside from British-French attack. Further defeats ensued, compelling local resistors to teach themselves guerrilla tactics, and to rely entirely on local citizens for provisioning. Meanwhile, however, the central government hewed to its regular armed forces agenda, even planning for a navy and air force. This reflected the influence of those few cadres who possessed officer or noncommisioned officer experience in the French and Chinese armies, but also the wider realization that it was less difficult to teach new recruits basic conventional tactics than the subtle demands of guerrilla struggle, which required initiative, flexibility, and guile. Either way, in a nation born amidst war and revolution, consolidation of armed force would have to take place while fighting.

While the Vietnamese revolution began immediately following Japan's violent termination of French colonial administration on 9 March 1945, the Japanese military had no interest in fostering a Vietnamese national army, although it did arm a few paramilitaries and foster martial spirit among proliferating youth groups. With the sudden announcement five months later of Tokyo's surrender to the Allies, both paramilitaries and youth groups moved eagerly to seize the trappings of power, including leftover French firearms, uniforms, and other military equipment. The Japanese continued to protect disarmed French soldiers and most French civilians from Vietnamese assault, pending the arrival of Allied forces.

The tyranny of geography, poor transport, severe economic constraints, a paucity of specialized staff, and enemy counteractions meant that the DRV central government could not exercise the degree of command and control over armed groups scattered around the country that it wished. Hanoi's writ increased rapidly in northern Vietnam, improved slowly in the center, and remained minimal in the south. Even in the north, the province rather than the region remained the vital territorial level for recruiting, outfitting, and sustaining regular army regiments or battalions. Often the relationship between local administrative committees and local military commanders was uneasy. A favorable rice harvest in May and June 1946 and subsequent tax collections meant that both Hanoi and provincial committees gained more leverage over armed groups and were able to expand the formal military system. However, the actions of many local militia (tự vệ) groups remained volatile and unpredictable, despite affirmations of allegiance to the DRV and growing interactions with the state.

The Indochinese Communist Party (ICP) was determined to control both the national army and these militia groups, yet the degree of party mastery varied from total to nonexistent. This reflected the ICP's very small membership base, its perceived need to distribute cadres across every sector of society, and the DRV government's desire to keep the party's profile low. As events unfolded, some nonparty leaders who demonstrated prowess in fighting the enemy advanced quickly to command of larger contingents. The government, if not the party, appreciated that good battlefield commanders did not necessarily make good politicians. With everyone learning by doing, exciting opportunities opened in the army for committed youths of diverse origins.

.This chapter opens with a description of early armed confrontations between DRV adherents and British-Japanese-French forces below the sixteenth parallel, which culminated in a shattering Vietnamese defeat at Nha Trang in late January 1946. These clashes, and the popular response to them, helped to shape the course of Vietnam's entire independence struggle, yet they have never received serious attention from historians. Next I examine simultaneous DRV endeavors north of the sixteenth parallel to put together a defense ministry and national army, beginning with the General Staff headquarters, communications bureau, contacts with dozens of local detachments (chi đội) seeking recognition, and an itemization of military resources. These initial steps to fashion a DRV defense capacity were only possible because the Chinese occupation authorities prevented French forces from returning to northern Indochina for six months. Although this circumstance changed dramatically in March 1946, with Sino-French and Franco-Vietnamese agreements allowing nonviolent return of French forces above the sixteenth parallel, the DRV went on constructing its national army, including specialized branches, training facilities, and a program to rationalize disparate combat detachments into battalions and regiments. The continuing existence of hundreds of smaller militia groups offered both opportunities for mass mobilization and risks of disobedient behavior. I conclude with brief accounts of ongoing armed resistance to the French south of the sixteenth parallel, the November fighting in Haiphong and Lạng Sơn, and the outbreak of full-scale hostilities in late December.[1]

SEPTEMBER 1945

On 2 September 1945, Hồ Chí Minh warned potential enemies that "the entire Vietnamese people are determined to mobilize all their physical and mental strength, to sacrifice their lives and property, in order to safeguard their freedom and independence."[2] Perhaps more than any other Vietnamese individual, however, Hồ apprehended the raw power of the foreign forces descending on the fledgling DRV even as he spoke. Chinese soldiers were marching on Hanoi and Haiphong from the north. British units were approaching Saigon from the south. The French government had restated its intention to send troops from the *métropole*, and some twelve thousand French colonial soldiers under Japanese detention anticipated early release. French commandos were already operating in Laos and on the islands adjacent to Haiphong. Japanese forces in Indochina, totaling about seventy thousand, had to be taken into account as well.

At that moment, Hồ Chí Minh and his lieutenants had no idea how many fellow citizens were armed and willing to defend the new nation. The Liberation Army (Giải Phóng Quân) unit that had just marched into Hanoi from the northern hills numbered about two hundred, out of a total of no more than twelve hundred members trained and occasionally tested during the previous nine months. Former Garde Indochinoise/Civil Guard (Bảo An Binh) personnel had been given the choice of joining the Liberation Army or turning over their weapons and returning home; probably several thousand took the former option. Larger numbers of young men had come into possession of firearms during the August Revolution and were declaring their readiness to fight and die for the Fatherland. The government told them to form militia units and report to the nearest people's committee or Việt Minh branch. Meanwhile, hundreds of thousands of men and women of all ages wielded bamboo spears, machetes, and wooden guns to participate in military drills and armed demonstrations at countless venues around the country.

The government's immediate priority was to convince all these armed citizens not to provoke conflict with incoming Allied forces. Already, along the Chinese frontier, Việt Minh adherents had sniped at Chinese troops and tried to mount food boycotts. Other Việt Minh groups skirmished with Vietnam Nationalist Party and Vietnam Revolutionary League groups that accompanied Chinese forces (see chapter 7). However, once it became apparent that General Lu Han, the Chinese commander, was not going to depose summarily the provisional DRV government headed by Hồ Chí Minh, anger at Chinese occupation changed to wary observation. When word circulated that the Chinese were rejecting French requests for colonial troops interned in Yunnan and Guangsi since April 1945 to recross the frontier, people north of the sixteenth parallel breathed a sign of relief.

· The British, however, chose to take a company of French troops along with their own four companies when flying into Saigon's Tân Sơn Nhứt airport on 12 September. The British commander, General Douglas Gracey, refused to deal with the DRV-affiliated committee that had taken power in Saigon in late August. Instead, he declared martial law, then rearmed fourteen hundred French colonial soldiers to assist him in throwing Vietnamese out of administrative buildings, police stations, post offices, and government warehouses on the night of 22 September. French civilians as well as soldiers took this opportunity to run amok, cursing, beating up, detaining, and otherwise offending any native encountered. Vietnamese bands retaliated on the night of 24 September, killing over one hundred civilians of French nationality (see chapter 4). Pending arrival of battle-hardened French regiments from the *métropole*, the British ordered Japanese infantry battalions to join British-Indian units in quelling Vietnamese opposition. Fires destroyed whole neighborhoods of Saigon, civilians fled the city, and most armed Vietnamese retreated to the adjacent countryside by late October. During the next three months, French gunboats coursed up and down the tributaries of the Mekong, armored columns dashed to all corners of the delta, and Vietnamese resistance proved minimal. On 5 February 1946, the French commander, General Jacques Philippe Leclerc, declared rashly that "the pacification of Cochinchina is entirely achieved."[3]

Early Southern Actions

In early September 1945, the Southern Region Provisional Administrative Committee (Lâm Ủy Hành Chánh Nam Bộ) had divided Saigon city into five "fronts" composed of thirteen "subregions" containing more than three hundred armed "groups"—reflecting the fluid, tense conditions of the moment.[4] As it became obvious from international news reports that the British intended to assist French armed forces to return to Indochina, bitter arguments broke out among southern activists about whether to try to reach an understanding or instead attack the enemy before it had time to build up its forces. ICP leaders, having touted their alleged Allied credentials to gain political primacy ten days earlier, had little

FIGURE 6. Allied flags (minus The French) festoon Saigon's former Hôtel de Ville, headquarters of the DRV Southern Region Committee in early September 1945. Germaine Krull photo, courtesy of Philippe Devillers.

choice but to push for negotiations—only to be told by incoming British officers that all Vietnamese were to be disarmed.[5]

Four Vietnamese army divisions *(sư đoàn)* formed in the Saigon region. The First Division, led by a former French Army lieutenant, was composed mostly of former Garde Indochinoise members.[6] Cao Đài adherents made up the Second Division. The Third and Fourth Divisions were led by Japanese-trained police officers, and contained a mélange of anticolonial groups.[7] At this point no ICP activist seems to have led any armed group larger than one hundred or two hundred men, reflecting the low priority given to military preparations by southern communists before the August Revolution. Garde Indochinoise members had basic military training and years of colonial garrison duty, but no combat experience. Some Cao Đài and Vanguard Youth members had several months of paramilitary training under Japanese auspices. No one had ever commanded a unit in battle, no overall plan of operations had been agreed upon, and provisions for communication and resupply under fire were nonexistent. The Southern Region Committee told citizens to prepare to mount a general strike for 17 September, followed by armed resistance if the French tried to seize power, yet to avoid harming Allied personnel in the process.[8] In the wake of the British-French coup of 22–23 September, and while French personnel were still rampaging through Saigon, the Southern Administrative Committee met to decide how to react. Trần Văn Giàu had already drafted a call to armed resistance and expected quick endorsement. However, Hoàng Quốc Việt, representing the Tổng Bộ Việt Minh, insisted that permission be obtained first from Hanoi. Some at the meeting favored fighting and negotiating simultaneously. Others reported that local militia groups had already started to fight back. Everyone could hear hundreds of people outside the building calling for battle. Arguing that "border generals could not always wait for royal orders," Giàu took personal responsibility for the fight, adding that he was prepared to lose his head if the "king" judged him to be wrong. Giàu put his text to a vote, it passed, and within hours thousands of leaflets were spread across the city, calling upon all southerners, old and young, men and women, to "grab weapons and rise up to drive out the invading forces." Henceforth the first responsibility of all citizens was to "wipe out the French bandits, wipe out their collaborators."[9]

Several days later Hoàng Quốc Việt issued a less virulent statement, emphasizing the Saigon general strike and calling for destruction of roads, encirclement of the enemy, and exposure of traitors—but not open warfare. The British were accused of conspiring with the French to violate Allied instructions, yet no guidance was offered to citizens about how to respond to expanding British-Indian troop operations. The Japanese, now being used by the British for more dangerous missions, were not mentioned in the statement.[10] Meanwhile, the number of violent skirmishes increased, more Vietnamese and Chinese noncombatants fled to the suburbs, and stocks of latex, rice, and tobacco went up in flames.[11]

On 1 October 1945, General Gracey and his political advisor met with members of the Southern Administrative Committee for the first time, securing their agreement to a truce and to discussions with Jean Cédile, the French commissioner of the republic for Cochinchina. This was a major reversal for the committee, probably on instructions from Hanoi. The ceasefire was set for six in evening on 2 October, at which point skirmishing did indeed drop off substantially; three Franco-Vietnamese meetings took place during the next six days, without any

FIGURE 7. Poorly armed patriots face British-Indian-French
force in the south. *Dân Quốc* 53 (6 Nov. 1945). Courtesy of
Vietnam National Library.

agreement being reached (see chapter 4). Meanwhile, a French armored unit
disembarked in the port of Saigon, and General Gracey's own forces went from
a vulnerable fifteen hundred men up to more than twelve thousand troops
equipped with artillery, armored cars, and trucks. The British told the Southern Administrative Committee on 9 October that it had twenty-four hours
from midnight to lay down arms and stop obstructing Allied forces. They also
informed the committee of Allied plans to expand territorial control substantially, in the first instance occupying the northern suburbs of Gò Vấp and Gia
Định.[12]

In the urgent Vietnamese deliberations that followed this meeting the weight
of opinion shifted decisively to resumption of armed resistance. On the evening

of 10 October, a small British-Indian convoy coming from Tân Sơn Nhứt airport to the city was ambushed, with a British captain and three Indian soldiers killed before six survivors were rescued by Gurkha and Japanese troops. This incident convinced General Gracey to begin hostilities in earnest. There were several other Vietnamese assaults the same night, yet no coordinated offensive materialized.[13] In reality, once fighting had begun on 23 September, no Vietnamese leader controlled more than a fraction of the combatants in and around Saigon, so it was impossible either to sustain a ceasefire or to organize a general counterattack.

First Assistance from the Center and North

Hanoi received foreign news accounts of the 23 September 1945 French assaults in Saigon that same morning. An urgent confidential message arrived too from the ICP's Southern Committee chaired by Trần Văn Giàu, requesting central instructions, but also reporting that armed resistance had already been decided locally and was indeed underway.[14] This was a grave blow to the DRV's policy of avoiding conflict with Allied forces. Whatever the French provocations, it must have vexed provisional President Hồ Chí Minh and others to be presented with a fait accompli. The evening of 23 September, Hồ expressed frustration to Archimedes Patti, the American Office of Strategic Services (OSS) representative in Hanoi, that relevant Vietnamese leaders in Saigon were either not receiving his instructions or disregarding them.[15] Yet to disavow southern actions was out of the question. The next day, central state and party bureaus allegedly telegraphed approval to their counterparts in the outskirts of Saigon, and told provincial committees throughout northern and central Vietnam to support their southern brethren.[16] Hoàng Văn Thái, Liberation Army chief of staff, traveled to at least six northern provinces during the next few days to start mobilizing contingents to go south.[17] Not until 26 September did Hồ Chí Minh go on the radio to praise the "resolute patriotic spirit of southern countrymen," and to promise that the government and citizens everywhere would assist them in their "sacrifice and struggle to hold firm the independence of the country." As an implied rebuke for the murders of the night of 24 September, Hồ urged the people of the south to treat French prisoners mercifully (khoan hồng), so that the world at large and the French public in particular would understand that Vietnamese were "more civilized than the gang that goes around killing people and stealing countries."[18] In France, however, news of the killing of French women and children in Saigon had already provoked public outrage. Saigon's violent confrontations of late September strengthened the hands of those in both Paris and Hanoi who insisted that no negotiated solution was possible.

Word of French assaults in Saigon spread quickly among the people of northern and central Vietnam, sparking anger, fear, and urgent discussion. For many, the euphoria of August was now replaced by trepidation that war might be inevitable. The date "23 September" became a metaphor for national danger. It galvanized public opinion and provided a focal point for action that transcended local revolutionary preoccupations or organizational affiliations. Without waiting for instructions from above, small groups of young men headed down the coast by train, local committees outfitted armed groups of thirty to two hundred men, and people began to donate money, clothing, medicine, and food to support the anti-French resistance in Nam Bộ. The first organized, reasonably well-armed, company-sized unit arrived across the river from Saigon on 25 September. It had come from Quảng Ngãi province, where violent revolutionary struggle had broken out four months earlier than in any other province in central Vietnam, and mass mobilization was intense.[19] This Quảng Ngãi contingent, and perhaps several others arriving soon after, joined southern forces in their attempted blockade of Saigon, then retreated with them to the Mekong delta in late October.

The first northern unit to head towards Saigon was Detachment 3 (Chi Đội 3), a unit of the Liberation Army that had been forged in the Việt Bắc hills before the August Revolution.[20] Initially composed mostly of upland minority soldiers, Detachment 3 added a platoon of thirty-two Hanoi high school students, then two platoons from Thanh Hóa and Nghệ An, before everyone boarded a train at Vinh on 27 September, just before the Chinese Army took control of the railway down to the sixteenth parallel (Đà Nẵng).[21] The unit's political officer was Nam Long, a tall, twenty-four-year-old Tày minority graduate of a military training course in China, and briefly head of Hồ Chí Minh's security guard. In Quảng Ngãi, a company from Huế was added to Detachment 3, making it a symbolically rich, multiregional, multiethnic unit of perhaps seven hundred men. Whether such diversity complicated command and control remained to be seen. At several points below Quảng Ngãi, breaks in the railway made it necessary to shuttle by truck or march on foot. Japanese officers approached to parley on several occasions, but did not try to turn the unit back. Detachment 3 arrived in Biên Hòa on 6 October, where Nam Long met urgently with Trần Văn Giàu, Hà Huy Giáp, and other southern leaders—all of whom he particularly noticed wore Western suits and shifted to French when arguing.

Detachment 3's first mission was to neutralize the rotating arch of the Bình Lợi bridge over the Saigon river, which carried both rail and road traffic between the city and points north. Former Garde Indochinoise platoons of unknown loyalty were said to be based on either side of the seven-arch, 270-meter bridge, and a few Japanese soldiers manned guard posts at each end. The plan was for one company to assault the north side, followed immediately by a second company chugging across the bridge by train, accompanied by a bridge technician who knew how to open the rotating arch and then sabotage the machinery located on the southern side. Borrowing old work clothes to reconnoiter the bridge up close on 9 October, Nam Long suddenly saw a British-Indian team drive to the middle of the bridge, scrutinize the surroundings with binoculars, then withdraw. The Vietnamese plan was speeded up, with a squad catching the four Japanese guards on the northern side by surprise, disarming them, then letting them walk across to the southern side. Perhaps because Detachment 3 was under orders to maintain the 2 October cease-fire, no Vietnamese troops followed the guards, a night passed, and not surprisingly a British-Indian unit was in position the next morning and began to fire a heavy machine gun at the northern side. Detachment 3 returned fire, soldiers ran the full length of the bridge and destroyed the Japanese guard post, yet failed to rotate the bridge and destroy the machinery before withdrawing.[22]

The next morning, 11 October, a British-Indian-Japanese force took firm control of the southern side of Bình Lợi bridge and hit the northern side with mortars. This force was part of the same British brigade accompanied by three Japanese detachments *(butai)* that occupied Gia Định and prepared to move into Gò Vấp the next day. Remarkably, Vietnamese commanders continued to allow Japanese trucks to use the bridge, providing no weapons were transported out of Saigon and no food carried in. Vietnamese leaders were confused as to Japanese intentions, while British and French commanders believed that some Japanese officers were secretly directing Vietnamese operations and committing their own men to attacks.[23]

Fighting continued along the Saigon river until 15 October, when a Japanese captain alerted Hà Huy Giáp and Nam Long that a British major had parachuted to the Japanese headquarters at Long Thành to order them immediately to attack the Vietnamese from the rear. Because the Japanese were estimated to possess thirty-six hundred troops, Hà Huy Giáp and Nam Long felt they had no choice but to withdraw from the river front as urged by the captain. In the retreat, companies quickly lost contact with each other, a Japanese unit prevented anyone carrying weapons from crossing the Biên Hòa bridge, and the presence of thousands of refugees intensified the chaos. One company commander requested to remain in the area and convert his unit to guerrilla operations, but this was refused. Another company commander was captured by an Indian unit and put before a firing squad. He was about to yell "Long live Hồ Chí Minh!" by way of last words when he was untied and allowed to escape.[24] Nam Long attempted to regroup Detachment 3 in the forest adjacent to Biên Hòa, while some southern groups withdrew upriver. Elsewhere during the week of 11–18 October, Vietnamese forces suffered heavy losses. Several banzai-style charges against Gurkha positions on Khánh Hội island, adjacent to the Saigon docks, withered under expert machine-gun fire. In the early morning hours of 13 October, Vietnamese fighters penetrated the British-Indian perimeter around Tân Sơn Nhứt airport, almost reaching the parked aircraft and radio transmitter facility before being driven out. Up to four hundred men, some armed with bows and poison arrows, unsuccessfully attacked Gurkha defenders of a bridge on the night of 15 October. Two Vietnamese platoons defending the Thị Nghè bridge between Saigon and Gia Định died to the last man.[25] Vietnamese forces lacked dynamite, detonators, and individuals skilled at placing explosive charges, especially on bridges.

On 17 October, the third and last brigade of General Gracey's 20th Division arrived in Saigon and soon moved to occupy the Thủ Đức–Biên Hòa–Thủ Dầu Một triangle with little opposition. The British increased pressure on Japanese commanders to track down, disarm, or kill Vietnamese resistors. The French Expeditionary Force, now numbering 4,575 men, launched armored assaults deep into the Mekong delta, supported by British and Japanese units, attacks which caught local Vietnamese organizations entirely by surprise.[26] By the end of October, the four Vietnamese military "divisions" had disintegrated, with some elements fleeing to the swamps, others roaming through villages in search of food and booty, and still others looking for ways to accommodate with the French. Some former colonial employees and village officials offered their services again to the victorious foreigners. Even so, the French found it difficult to extend their control beyond delta towns, main roads, and waterways. Within three or four months the shock of defeat wore off for continuing DRV supporters, and better resistance tactics began to be employed in Nam Bộ.

FIGHTING THE JAPANESE

On 23 October 1945, the day before British armored cars swept into Biên Hòa, Detachment 3 received orders to withdraw to Xuân Lộc, fifty kilometers to the east. A number of southern groups joined this retreat of about three thousand men total—taking them all further away from Saigon and the Mekong delta.[27] For the northern and central members of Detachment 3 and a Quảng Ngãi contingent, the fight at Bình Lợi bridge had brought them to within twelve kilometers of the Saigon train station, yet it would be another thirty years before Nam Long and a handful of surviving comrades were able to stand victoriously in downtown Saigon.

From early 1945 the Japanese Army had constructed defense fortifications at Xuân Lộc, to be used in the event of Allied invasion. As many as ten thousand rubber plantation workers lived in the area, some of whom had formed militia groups. Detachment Vy, recruited in Ninh Bình province, had also just arrived from the north. In the last days of October, perhaps five thousand men were available to take a stand at Xuân Lộc, yet apparently no overall commander had been designated, nor had a defense plan been formulated. Nothing was done about the small Japanese garrison in the middle of town. The plantation workers provided food and chopped down trees to impede enemy vehicles.[28]

Alerted by the Japanese garrison at Xuân Lộc of the Vietnamese buildup, a British-Japanese column set out from Biên Hòa on 29 October, encountering few road obstacles and no ambushes amidst the rubber plantations. Few Vietnamese took advantage of the old Japanese trenches, and they were caught by surprise when the Japanese mounted a banzai charge at night, screaming and throwing grenades liberally. When Detachment 3's machine guns jammed, only a few former colonial soldiers knew how to clear them in the dark. One Vietnamese unit dared to counterattack and fight hand-to-hand. The British reported at least one hundred Vietnamese killed and a quantity of arms seized, at the cost of one British soldier killed in action, but no mention of Japanese casualties. After several sharp engagements the next day resulted in further heavy Vietnamese losses, survivors straggled in the direction of Phan Thiết, another 108 kilometers to the east. In terrain notoriously dry and sparsely settled, water and food soon ran out, with the wounded suffering most of all.[29]

Phan Thiết was even more chaotic than Xuân Lộc, with new groups arriving from Quảng Ngãi, Thừa Thiên, and Quảng Bình intent on pressing further south, only to hear shocking stories from battle survivors wandering in. The Phan Thiết civilian administration tried to feed everyone, but some groups went for days without rations. A hungry delegation marched on the office of the Phan Thiết resistance committee, with some participants firing their rifles into the air and threatening to go to Hanoi to petition President Hồ Chí Minh. A new special regional committee was formed, chaired by Đào Duy Kỳ (a native of Thanh Hóa recently released from Côn Sơn prison), with the highly ambitious objective of unifying forces in order to mount a counteroffensive to liberate Saigon. Amazingly the small Japanese garrison in Phan Thiết was left alone, but it radioed its anxiety to Saigon.

Đào Duy Kỳ called a meeting of all units at the Phan Thiết sports field. The threat of an enemy flank attack from the sea or by land (via Dalat or Ban Mê Thuột) does not appear to have been discussed. A proposal was tabled to reorganize so that every platoon would contain members from the center, south, and north of the country. This idea was opposed by Việt Phương, a seventeen-year-old student from Hanoi, who argued that enemy attack was too imminent to accomplish such a radical amalgamation in time. Instead, they needed urgently to find a more effective way to fight, or else everyone would be compelled to retreat again and again, leaving more comrades dead on each occasion. Following this meeting, Nam Long agreed to let Việt Phương and one comrade travel to the capital to report to the president. They were received instead by Võ Nguyên Giáp, who praised the bravery exhibited at Bình Lợi bridge and Xuân Lộc, then instructed them to return immediately to their unit, as the central leadership already selected comrade Nguyễn Sơn to take charge in the south.[30] It was at this moment in early November that Giáp told a Hanoi press conference that the DRV must plan and prepare for the possibility that war would spread to the north, "because imperialist ambitions have no limits."[31]

On 9 November, a Japanese battalion arrived by sea at Phan Thiết under British orders to disarm all natives in the area. After three days of combat in and around the railroad station, hospital, power plant, and administration building, Vietnamese units were forced into the countryside, where some joined with local militia to learn how to fight guerrilla-style, while others headed up the coast. Arriving in Phan Rang, Detachment 3 (now renamed Detachment Nam Long) spearheaded methodical assaults on Japanese positions, relying on two machine guns and a quantity of grenades. The Japanese slipped away towards Dalat on the night of 23 November, leaving ten killed in action plus a quantity of arms and ammunition behind. People poured into Phan Rang to congratulate the victors, there were speeches and a three-gun salute to honor fallen comrades (including a company commander), followed by a banquet the next day that featured local delicacies, songs from local children, banners, drums, and the ringing of temple and church bells. Soldiers felt proud to have driven the enemy away for the first time. However, Detachment Nam Long was now exhausted, having fought four battles in six weeks, taken heavy casualties, and been reduced from 700 to only 250 men. On 27 November it withdrew towards Nha Trang, only to be thrown into action the next day.[32]

THE NAM TIẾN MOVEMENT

During November a number of additional military units had come down the coast as far as Khánh Hòa and Phú Yên provinces, in what was now popularly dubbed the Nam Tiến (Southern Advance) movement. This term had long been used by Vietnamese historians to characterize the migration of ethnic Kinh from the Red River delta to the Mekong delta over a period of seven hundred years, in the process vanquishing the Cham and Khmer peoples. Nationalists of the early twentieth century, influenced by Social Darwinism, glorified the Nam Tiến as evidence of Vietnamese superiority compared to neighboring "races" (chủng tộc). From late 1942, ICP organizers along the Sino-Indochina border had given the Nam Tiến label to several armed groups and spoken of a Nam Tiến strategy, sometimes meaning an advance on Hanoi, at other times dreaming of liberating the entire country to the Cà Mau peninsula.[33] In late 1945, Nam Tiến evoked heroic images of northern and central forces coming to the aid of their beleaguered countrymen in the south. As we have seen, the first groups departing in late September moved down the coast quickly and arrived in time to fight in or near Saigon in October. Subsequent Nam Tiến groups encountered crowds at each major railroad station along the route—young women offering free food and drink, officials making speeches, slogans yelled in unison, and soldiers joining in

FIGURE 8. "Southern Advance" volunteers at Tuy Hòa station, October 1945. Nguyễn Bá Khỏan photo, courtesy of Vietnam National Library.

patriotic songs. Local youths tried to sign up and jump aboard. The mood was light-hearted and joyful, a festival of revolution. Only at Quảng Ngãi station did everyone notice a stern, no-nonsense atmosphere. Young men were stunned to see Quảng Ngãi's all-female military units, with hair cut short, skin darkened by the sun, and weapons wielded with confidence.[34] Three teenage girls coming from Huế to volunteer as nurses were lucky not to be shot as spies, and were instead packed aboard the next train northward.[35]

From early October, Nam Tiến groups had to obtain permission from the Chinese to board trains, always minus their firearms, which were dispatched separately by boat or occasionally hidden in freight cars. While Chinese forces always enjoyed transport priority, Vietnamese railroad staff sometimes added a car or two to the back of an existing train. A transport altercation at the Huế station was resolved by a Vietnamese commander who spoke Chinese. DRV flags had to be removed from the front of trains occasionally. Chinese liaison officers accompanied each Vietnamese contingent. One Chinese officer, observing local youths trying to hop the train south, commented wryly that in his country, men had to be abducted into the military.[36] Below Đà Nẵng, small Japanese units gave old French weapons and ammunition to Nam Tiến groups in exchange for food or money.[37] However, these Japanese units also reported Vietnamese activities to Saigon until the British gave them permission to withdraw to Nha Trang at the end of October.[38]

Most Nam Tiến groups possessed a mixture of French, Japanese, Chinese, and American rifles of different vintages, plus a sprinkling of carbines, shotguns, and muskets. Company commanders and platoon leaders sported pistols of all sorts. Finding ammunition for such a variety of firearms became a major problem, and much old ammunition proved unreliable. Soldiers counted themselves lucky to be allotted twenty to twenty-five cartridges of any age. Grenades became valued weapons, and Japanese grenade launchers were especially prized. However the detonators of locally produced grenades prove not only unreliable but dangerous. Mines and TNT had yet to be found. Although detachments carried machine guns of different sizes and origin, paucity of ammunition limited their deployment. The same applied to the few mortars and small artillery pieces available.[39]

Eager to give Nam Tiến groups a regular army appearance, organizers tried to outfit them in proper uniforms at a time when cloth was extremely scarce. Detachment Thu Sơn boasted one company wearing French Army khaki, and another possessing uniforms of blue and brown cloth obtained from the Nam Định textile mill.[40] Detachment Vi Dân began its move south with nondescript clothing, but in Phú Yên it raffled a big portrait of Hồ Chí Minh at a public meeting and used the proceeds to outfit members with uniforms. Detachment Hoa Lư from Ninh Bình received a full complement of khaki uniforms, forage caps, and leather boots from the Defense Ministry when its name was upgraded to Detachment Độc Lập 1 (Independence 1) in January 1946. Other Nam Tiến organizers were content to concentrate on standardized headgear, usually forage caps, but sometimes Japanese cloth caps or colonial-era pith helmets. After a month or two in the field, however, individual soldiers took on berets, felt fedoras, or straw hats. Commanders set themselves apart with their pistols and occasionally a Japanese sword; some possessed binoculars, compasses, or map cases as well.[41] Most detachments were named after their commanders, reflecting both French and Japanese military traditions, as well as the personal leadership style of the day. Even some companies and platoons were known by their leader's name. One contemporary observer described the typical platoon leader as "something of a modern samurai," with a "rather pale face adorned with a fine moustache, carrying a long sword and wearing hobnail boots".[42]

Former Garde Indochinoise members were well represented in Nam Tiến units, and former French Army *tirailleurs* (infantry) to a lesser degree. Many had no desire to return in disgrace to home villages, wished to demonstrate loyalty to the DRV, and took pride in being able to impart skills to the majority of volunteers who were ignorant of military matters. A high proportion of platoon and squad leaders were former members of the Garde Indochinoise. Detachment Thu Sơn had one company commander of *tirailleur* origin. Formed in Hanoi, Detachment Vi Dân possessed a former French Army lieutenant, Phạm Văn Thọ, who first took responsibility for training, then became chief of staff when the unit reached the front. However, no Nam Tiến detachment-size unit was commanded by a former Garde Indochinoise or French Army member, in contrast to what had occurred in the south in September.[43] Perhaps Liberation Army headquarters in Hanoi managed to preclude any such selection. Some former colonial soldiers had second thoughts en route to the south. Detachment Vi Dân lost one-third of its entire complement due to desertions among these men. In Phú Yên, when all remaining members of Detachment Vi Dân were offered a last chance to return home, a veteran *tirailleur* stepped forward and then was followed by twenty other members. At this point the commander exploded, causing all except four men (including the *tirailleur*) to return to ranks.[44] Once in battle, there is no evidence that former colonial soldiers skulked, malingered, went absent without leave, or deserted in higher numbers than anyone else.

Earlier, some Nam Tiến participants had undergone paramilitary training at the French Youth Academy in Phan Thiết, the Vanguard Youth School in Huế, or less formal programs initiated by local Japanese commanders. Boy Scouts joined as well. Many Việt Minh adherents had taken part in drills during the summer of 1945 that ranged from simple village marching with wooden guns to vigorous tactical exercises. Most prestigious were three classes that had been organized at the Anti-Japanese Military-Political Resistance School in the Việt Bắc hills, each lasting fifteen days. Class 4 convened in the new national capital, Hanoi, in late September. In early October, seventy-two graduates of the school went south; forty-six of these entered Nam Tiến units and twenty-six walked via the rubber plantations north of Saigon to join groups in the Mekong delta. Following graduation of Class 5 on 15 November, Trần Văn Giàu delivered a fiery oration to the assembly, evoking the desperate resistance struggle in the south and emphasizing the vital importance of the Nam Tiến movement. All four hundred graduates declared their readiness to depart south immediately, which must have concerned the central leadership, as other priority organizing was underway in the north. Sixty-four graduates were selected to accompany Huỳnh Tấn Phát (who had come north with Trần Văn Giàu) to the south. Arriving in Khánh Hòa at the end of November, it was decided to dispatch a first group of twenty-five via Ban Mê Thuột, just at the moment when a French armored column was approaching from the southwest (see below).[45]

In early December, provisional President Hồ Chí Minh dispatched his labor minister, Lê Văn Hiến, as special government commissioner to central and southern Vietnam, with instructions to evaluate conditions, resolve problems where possible, and refer major issues back to Hanoi. At each province head-quarters below Huế, Hiến tried to obtain troop numbers. Together Đà Nẵng city and the provinces had dispatched 2,390 soldiers south and 100 men to Laos, while keeping 5,000 at home.[46] This did not include units coming from elsewhere or prior Quảng Ngãi commitments, so it is impossible to estimate totals. Several locations emphasized to Hiến that only one-third to one-half of their in-province soldiers possessed firearms, whereas their Nam Tiến units were better endowed.

Commanders tried to arrange brief training courses for their men while they were en route to the south, or waiting to be ordered into battle. The most rudimentary skills came first: weapons disassembly and assembly, cleaning and dry firing, squad movements, taking cover and signaling, utilizing the terrain, entrenching, and bivouacking. However, because instructors came from very different military traditions—French, Japanese, Chinese, American—drills could be quite confusing to new recruits. Some commanders possessed French Army small unit training manuals, which they used to prepare lectures or to make partial translations to give to platoon and squad leaders. The Detachment Vi Dân commander treasured a copy of *The Art of War (Ping Fa)* by Sun-tzu, and recited long memorized passages in class. Maps were extremely scarce, and those who knew how to read a map were held in awe.[47]

Discipline appears to have been lax. There was no censorship when soldiers used the PTT to send letters to their families. Halted in Quảng Ngãi for several weeks, former Hanoi students chafed at base regulations, and jumped the fence to hit the town and seek the attentions of local women. One student was jailed for taking the commander's motor vehicle on a joyride. After this particular prank, the entire unit was lined up and criticized for treating war like a holiday or a Boy Scout camp. Soldiers of working-class background proved better than students at obeying regulations. Later, lack of guard discipline caused several units to be caught by surprise at night.

Detachment and company commanders tended to rely on a small team of comrades for advice and support—usually men with whom they shared prerevolution or August Revolution experiences. It was common for members of a platoon to elect their own platoon leader, both when first coming together, and again if the incumbent was killed, wounded, or transferred. Aware of their own inadequacies, members often selected a former Garde Indochinoise comrade, perhaps pairing him with a "political officer" *(chính trị viên)* possessing some sort of revolutionary credentials.[48] The platoon was the vital level of organization in detachments of late 1945, with members usually recruited from the same location, sharing daily routines, marching together, and being less likely to lose touch with each other in battle. Communication between units was almost entirely by runner.

Even before the August Revolution it was assumed that Vietnam's national army should possess political officers side by side with combat commanders, as in the Chinese Nationalist Army as well as the Russian Red Army. However, few Nam Tiến participants understood what a political officer was meant to do. Units from the Việt Bắc hills had ICP political officers who reported faithfully up the ICP hierarchy. Detachment Vi Dân's political officer was a thirty-eight-year-old ICP member by the name of Nguyễn Văn Trình, known affectionately as "Old Grandmother Trình," reflecting his advanced age and his preferred role as counselor and welfare officer. When Detachment Vi Dân later merged with a Phú Yên province group, the senior political officer was a non-ICP former colonial administrator.[49] Each platoon of Detachment 3 elected its own political officer, only a handful of whom were ICP members. Not until early 1946 did Detachment 3 get its first party cell, suggesting a rather faint ICP footprint.[50] Most Nam Tiến units raised along the north-central coast had no ICP cell at all.

Command and control of Nam Tiến operations above the detachment level ranged from chaotic to nonexistent. This first became apparent when Nam Bộ leaders and Nam Tiến groups failed to coordinate neutralization of the Bình Lợi bridge. As various elements retreated to Xuân Lộc, then Phan Thiết and Phan Rang, consultation between leaders occurred haphazardly, the relationship of military units to local people's committees was uncertain, and coherent orders failed to arrive from above. Stunned by battlefield reversals and lacking a unified command or higher echelon instructions, several detachments dispatched their own delegations to Hanoi to try to explain the grim situation and trigger top-level response.[51] Although the DRV provisional government apparently designated Nguyễn Sơn as chairman of the Southern Resistance Committee (Ủy Ban Kháng Chiến Miền Nam) from late September, his headquarters did not start functioning in Bình Định until two months later. By this time the government had also dispatched Nguyễn Bình to the rubber plantations just north of Saigon to begin reorganizing resistance in Nam Bộ.[52]

From a strictly military point of view, it would have made sense after October to withdraw Nam Tiến elements all the way from Biên Hòa to Nha Trang, destroying rail and road communications along the way and avoiding Japanese posts. Even assuming a successful position defense, Vietnamese forces were very vulnerable to flank attack, isolation, and piecemeal destruction. However, the idea of surrendering such large chunks of the Fatherland to the enemy without a fight went contrary to the entire spirit of nationwide struggle against the foreign invader. In addition, southern groups that had retreated up the coast together with Nam Tiến contingents would have been outraged and might have accused the DRV government of abandoning the south entirely. Another option was to break down into smaller elements, link up with provincial militia, and mount guerrilla operations. This did happen for some groups, whether deliberately or by accident. Unfortunately the region between Xuân Lộc and Phan Rang was lightly settled, deficient in food, and far behind regions further north when it came to

FIGURE 9. Southern militia group. Photo courtesy of Christophe
Dutrône.

political mobilization. Besides, the DRV government and most military leaders
remained committed to conventional strategies and tactics, with guerrilla warfare as a fallback option.

Finance Minister Lê Văn Hiến traveled from Khánh Hòa southward by boat
to Baria, where he found that relations among some resistance groups had deteriorated to the point that they were physically surrounding or forcibly detaining
each other. A January 1946 meeting tried to delineate responsibilities, stop confiscations of private property, and improve judicial procedures. Hiến was invited
to review a Bình Xuyên parade, which included modest artillery, antiaircraft,
and motor transport contingents. He also was introduced to some thirty Japanese soldiers who had joined the fight against the French. After reading pronouncements from President Hồ Chí Minh and Interior Minister Võ Nguyên
Giáp to the formation, Hiến declared Bình Xuyên units to be part of the national

army. That same day, however, the French launched Operation Gaur, which jeopardized the entire DRV position in south-central Vietnam (see below). Hiến received an urgent message to return to Hanoi instead of continuing to the Mekong delta as planned.[53] From this point onward, south-central and southern theaters had to function on their own.

Nha Trang and Ban Mê Thuột

Nha Trang, the largest town along the south-central coast of Vietnam, remained under Japanese control for three months following Allied victory in mid-August, although a DRV-affiliated people's committee was allowed to function and militia groups trained enthusiastically. General Leclerc wanted British-Indian troops to take over Nha Trang, and General Gracey included this in his original occupation plan, but the provision seems to have been dropped on the insistence of Admiral Lord Louis Mountbatten, head of South East Asia Command. Several thousand wounded and ill Japanese personnel who had been evacuated from Burma were being cared for in Nha Trang, and at least five hundred French colonial soldiers and civilians remained under Japanese guard there as well. Vietnamese Nam Tiến groups heading down the coast from late September could readily bypass Nha Trang because the north-south train line and road ran several kilometers west of town. In early October, the Khánh Hòa province committee designated one of its members to create a defense line anchored on the train junction, from whence an attack might be launched east along the rail spur into Nha Trang. Spirits were high, yet the Khánh Hòa force possessed only an assortment of platoon-sized units equipped with two 75 mm field cannon, one 81 mm mortar, one 25 mm antiaircraft gun, a handful of machine guns, and a mélange of rifles, muskets, and spears. Sensing danger, the Vietnamese population of Nha Trang began evacuating to the countryside.[54]

On 20 October, two platoons of French marines landed in Nha Trang under Japanese protection. On British orders, French colonial soldiers were released and rearmed by the Japanese. Two days later, Japanese patrols tested Vietnamese positions, triggering fire fights. Early the next morning Vietnamese forces attacked eastward, seizing the Nha Trang train station and destroying the power plant, but they were compelled to withdraw two days later under heavy bombardment from French warships. Two smaller French vessels tried to tie up at the Nha Trang pier, but were driven away by Vietnamese fire. The French L-19 observation planes, nicknamed "old madams" (đầm già) by the Vietnamese, enabled French gunners to begin accurate pounding of Vietnamese defenses. Construction began on a more ambitious Vietnamese trench line three kilometers further from the coast, with more than a thousand villagers and Nha Trang evacuees doing most of the digging. Local women cooked and delivered food to front-line units. Young women from Huế and Quảng Ngãi served as medics and organized evening songfests.

On 19 November, a French infantry battalion of twelve hundred men landed at Nha Trang under cover of fire from the cruiser *Triumphant* and strafing by French Spitfires. Squads of Vietnamese soldiers defended solidly constructed churches, villas, and administrative buildings until each was reduced to rubble. Some Japanese units refused to take orders from the French, and several score Japanese appear to have crossed over to the Vietnamese side. French forces moved inland behind rolling fire from the *Triumphant*. On the night of 30 November, Vietnamese forces counterattacked, but without heavy weapons it proved impossible to break through. From early December the French chose to stay on the defensive, awaiting developments elsewhere. Vietnamese units west of Nha Trang dug more trenches and bunkers, determined to prevent the French from cutting off movement of soldiers and supplies from north to south.[55] Meanwhile, a dispute had arisen between the Khánh Hòa People's Committee chairman and the military front commander, which Labor Minister Lê Văn Hiến, arriving on his travels as DRV commissioner, tried to resolve. Hiến urged both men to curb their "hot-tempered manner," show mutual sympathy *(thông cảm)*, and focus on the grave threat from the French.[56] Complicating matters further, contradictory operational orders continued to descend from Hanoi, Huế, and the ICP's Central Region Committee.

A new front emerged on 1 December when a French armored column abruptly approached the central highland town of Ban Mê Thuột, having moved swiftly from the Mekong delta up Route 14, encountering only a handful of felled trees and ditches. A platoon of Detachment Vì Dân which had only arrived from the coast the previous day was surprised and cut down. Another platoon led by Sơn Nam arrived the next day to find the French gone. Burying scores of bodies (among them civilians) and welcoming the twenty-five graduates from Hanoi's Class 5 who were en route south, Sơn Nam then ordered preparation of a defense line southwest of town, behind a bridge set with explosives. However, when the French returned in force on 6 December the explosive charge failed and armored vehicles tore through Vietnamese lines, killing Sơn Nam and twenty-nine others.[57] In early January Vietnamese units counterattacked into Ban Mê Thuột, where Lê Văn Hiến read letters of encouragement from President Hồ and Võ Nguyên Giáp. Hiến also witnessed animosity between ethnic Vietnamese (Kinh) and Rhadé (Ê Đê) peoples, and knew from his 1930s experience in Kontum prison how the French could take advantage of this. The French launched armored raids east along Route 21, while Vietnamese units sustained resistance in the adjacent forest, supplied by several old buses and five elephants. Nam Long was compelled to withdraw his detachment headquarters eastward on four occasions in the face of French artillery fire guided from the air and assaults by jungle-trained commandos.[58]

On 25 January, a large French armored column swept along Route 21 all the way into Ninh Hòa town. The French capture of Ninh Hòa was one half of Operation Gaur, the other being an armored sweep through Dalat and Phan Rang, then up the coast to Nha Trang. This daring pincers offensive made the ten kilometers of trenches that Vietnamese had dug just west of Nha Trang quite useless, and indeed threatened to trap all units in a French meatgrinder. Many soldiers fled in panic. Detachment Bắc Bắc, which had just arrived at the Nha Trang front and was preparing to attack French positions, suddenly received orders to retreat northward to Phú Yên, barely escaping the encirclement.[59] Two companies of Detachment Thu Sơn managed to escape inland, then march north across the hills to Phú Yên, covering more than 150 kilometers in one week with no map, no guides, and only three days' rations. Survivors of Detachment Nam Long wandered along footpaths used by local Rhadé people, trading personal effects for food. Some stragglers were killed by minority men and their heads turned in to the French for bounty. Others joined local militia groups that would combat the French in Khánh Hòa province until 1954. Those who made it to Phú Yên province in early February were offered fields of sugarcane to chop down and savor for Tết.[60] In Hanoi, President Hồ Chí Minh asked an officer coming from the front why it had not been possible to destroy roads sufficiently to block or slow down French armored vehicles. He received no answer.[61]

Between 18 January and 5 February, Võ Nguyên Giáp traveled to south-central Vietnam to convey the determination of leaders in Hanoi to back armed resistance to the French invaders. Giáp also aimed to evaluate the current military situation, appraise Vietnamese combat capacity, and canvas strategic options. Moving down the central coast by auto, he was impressed by the patriotic commitment of ordinary people, observing them drilling in Vinh, bidding farewell to sons and brothers boarding a train in Đồng Hới, caring for the wounded in Huế, and looking for enemy agents in Quảng Nam. In Quảng Ngãi, Giáp's car sped by a militiaman standing guard, only to hear the hiss of bullets overhead and be compelled to stop. Trần Hữu Dực, chairman of the Central Region Administrative Committee, who was accompanying Giáp, showed the guard his official letter of introduction, to which the guard responded angrily, "Where is this Central Region village located?" After some explanation, the guard allowed them to go.[62]

At a meeting with soldiers on the frontline facing Nha Trang, Giáp lauded their having prevented the enemy from breaking out of the city for 101 days, thus giving other locations time to prepare for protracted struggle against the invaders.[63] Giáp seemed to think it was still feasible to move weapons and troops from north to south along the coast, a capacity the French had eliminated a few days later.[64] The Nha Trang front was the first time Giáp had ever seen combat of any magnitude, complete with French naval gunfire, artillery, and air attacks. His arrival coincided with the moment when the two French armored columns from Ban Mê Thuột and Phan Rang closed in on Nha Trang, and Giáp received a cable from Hồ Chí Minh directing him to return to Hanoi. En route back to the capital, Giáp detoured to An Khê, Pleiku, and Kontum in the central highlands—places he realized could be strategically important in the near future.[65] In an article probably written by Giáp as he passed through Huế, the loss of Ban Mê Thuột was ascribed not only to French armor and artillery, but also to "our Rhadé brothers not being organized yet," and to lowland Vietnamese unfamiliarity with the terrain. Such conditions were no grounds for pessimism, he insisted. According to Giáp, "Protracted resistance routinely involves the loss of territory," as had been demonstrated early in the war against Germany and Japan.[66] At a 15 February press conference in Hanoi, Giáp stated that the French had "bought off" some minority people in Ban Mê Thuột. He also criticized the decision at Nha Trang to dig trenches and face off with the French, while neglecting to destroy roads and bridges, mobilize the populace, or begin to learn guerrilla tactics.[67]

As it happened, the French chose to concentrate on Tonkin from late February 1946, leaving Vietnamese forces in the center (Annam) precious time to regroup, tie in better with local organizations, and learn different tactics. Huế and Quảng Ngãi became focal points of military organizing and training. The ambition to build larger-scale units was by no means abandoned, but resistance in French-occupied areas would need to be conducted by other means.

MILITARY ORGANIZING IN THE NORTH

In Hanoi from late August 1945, DRV leaders assigned high priority to constructing a national army, whatever their day-to-day preoccupations with the Chinese, Americans, British, French, or Japanese. Already the first step had been taken in April, when heads of small Việt Bắc armed groups were brought together with ICP Standing Bureau members working in the Red River delta to devise a plan of action. All of Vietnam was divided into seven battle zones, of little practical consequence at the time, yet the demarcations showed strategic foresight and appreciation of the country's geographical peculiarities. In May, the two principal armed contingents led by Võ Nguyên Giáp and Chu Văn Tấn were merged to form the Vietnam Liberation Army.[68] On 25 August, as revolutionaries celebrated the end of the old order, the Northern Region Revolutionary People's Committee ordered all armed groups to disband themselves and enroll in the Liberation Army. How this was to be done remained unspecified. Meanwhile, the northern headquarters of the Civil Guard (formerly the Garde Indochinoise) was allowed to continue functioning, with Liberation Army cadres moving into adjacent offices and adopting the same bureaucratic procedures.[69] When corresponding, the Liberation Army used old Résident superieure stationery with new DRV rubber stamps. Intriguingly, on 18 September 1945 it requested that one hundred ballots be printed for an election of Liberation Army senior officers.[70]

On 28 August, Chu Văn Tấn was named minister of defense in the provisional cabinet of the DRV, while Võ Nguyên Giáp became minister of the interior.[71] Giáp was also de facto commander of the Liberation Army, although this was not announced. At that moment there was little for a commander or general command headquarters *(bộ tổng chỉ huy)* to do, as designated units of the Liberation Army were still few in number. Probably for this reason, first priority was given on 7 September to establishing a general staff headquarters, headed by Hoàng Văn Thái.[72] Two days later, the army's Office of Communication and Liaison was set up in the same building, headed by Hoàng Đạo Thúy, a respected teacher and Boy Scout leader.[73]

Meanwhile, the fledgling Defense Ministry blitzed other organizations with action messages, sent mostly via the Northern Region Office and PTT networks.[74] On 4 September, each northern province was instructed to send about ten men to a platoon leaders course, bringing along their own weapons, paper, pens, clothing, and twenty days' rations. Likewise all northern province revolutionary people's committees were told to dispatch their "military commissioners" *(ủy viên quân sự)* to a Hanoi meeting on 7 September. The Northern Minerals Bureau was asked what quantities of relevant chemicals it possessed for making gunpowder. A government decree assigned manufacturing of arms and ammunition to the former colonial Minerals and Industry Service, and authorized it to requisition the necessary factories and material. On 11 September, probably reacting to the arrival of Chinese troop units, the government put all Hanoi offices on combat alert and told them to be ready to evacuate files by motor vehicle on short notice. Two days later, a government circular to Liberation Army units (also published in the *National Gazette*) prohibited them from frisking women while on patrol or initiating house searches. Any person detained by the military was to be turned over quickly to the police for proper investigation. The same day, Hồ Chí Minh signed a decree establishing military courts to try persons charged with harming DRV independence. One week later, all northern provinces were ordered to provide within seven days a detailed report including: the number of soldiers in their jurisdiction, divided between "assault militia" *(tự vệ xung phong)* and former Civil Guard; the names of unit commanders and political officers; numbers and types of weaponry; quality of ammunition; method of food supply; and "how the problem of uniforms is being dealt with." The Defense Ministry thus asserted its authority to consolidate data on all armed groups and, by implication, to control their subsequent activities.

Provincial responses to Hanoi's request for details on armed elements came in very erratically. Thái Bình had already reported three hundred "official troops" in the province town, unspecified numbers at district seats, and "lots of militia." In mid-November, Thái Bình made an extraordinary claim to one hundred thousand militia, yet six weeks later stated that each district had only twenty "fighting militia" *(tự vệ chiến đấu)*.[75] Bắc Giang province reported more than one thousand soldiers organized into three detachments, "not counting district militia." Like many other province committees, Bắc Giang put in a plea for food, clothing, and blankets for the troops, but already understood that firearms were a local responsibility.[76] Hòa Bình gave Hanoi a list of the ninety-three firearms it possessed for its five small units.[77] Thái Nguyên itemized eight platoons, one composed of "Chinese-Vietnamese" (Hoa-Việt). A count of weapons revealed 416 firearms, including eight heavy machine guns, ten light machine guns, and a total of 13,129 cartridges (that is, only thirty-two per firearm).[78] Hà Đông reported 135 soldiers in the province town, twenty men in each district, and a total of 302 firearms, 42,200 cartridges, 340 detonators, and 545 grenades.[79] Sơn Tây province stressed that it had to support a Liberation Army unit of 342 men possessing almost enough firearms and 16,000 cartridges, but desperately in need of shoes, socks, and belts. Its own town unit had 160 men and 96 firearms. A Japanese unit in Sơn Tây had turned over 380 guns and 70 oxcarts before departing. Quảng Yên described an impressive 728-man province unit, among whom 463 were former colonial soldiers, 150 sailors, 29 policemen, and 86 workers. It estimated its 1946 province military expenses would amount to 2.2 million piastres, including 330,000$BIC for weapons purchases—clearly hoping that the central government would come up with most of that amount.[80]

From early days the Defense Ministry and other central offices also received a host of unsolicited messages from below about military matters that required attention.[81] On 7 September, the Hanoi branch of the Vietnam Democratic Party, a Việt Minh affiliate, requested permission to conduct military classes at the Chu Văn An School, in the Bạch Mai suburbs. Permission was granted six days later, with the organizers asked to provide a copy of their syllabus. As urgent queries came in from local committees about feeding, arming, and outfitting military units, the Northern Region People's Committee ("Revolution" had been dropped from its title) informed the Interior Ministry on 9 September that it needed one million piastres immediately just to feed soldiers, and proposed the Finance Ministry take responsibility. Nine days later Interior was queried again. On 20 September, the committee asked the Finance Ministry directly if province committees could obtain funds from Treasury offices or draw from local Independence Fund donations. Ninh Bình province asked Hanoi bluntly, "Where do soldiers look to for survival?"

Haiphong city had strategic significance second only to Hanoi, which may explain why the chairman of the Northern Region People's Committee gained Võ Nguyên Giáp's approval to send a "secret order" *(mật lệnh)* to the Treasury office in Haiphong and the Haiphong Bank for an account to be opened in the name of the chairman of the Haiphong People's Committee, containing five hundred thousand piastres for provisioning army units in the city.[82] Revolutionaries could cut across the existing system this way, yet the wider problem of how to finance the armed forces remained. Already in early September the finance minister, Phạm Văn Đồng, had told first the cabinet and then province committee chairmen that everyone had to find their own means of support, as the treasury was nearly bare.

On 13 September, Hưng Yên province sent eleven military questions to Hanoi, which were mostly answered twenty-five days later by Nguyễn Văn Trân, a key member of the Northern Region Committee. According to Trân, province committees had to cover the expenses of Liberation Army units until the Defense Ministry "unified arrangements for the whole country." Design of uniforms and insignia for the entire army would be spelled out by the Ministry. Firearms permits were to be issued by province and city-level people's committees upon written application and a letter of introduction from the relevant national salvation association—a trenchant example of how government and Việt Minh operations overlapped, although this was not official policy. Women were not yet to be recruited into the army (an answer that ignored some women already serving). Soldiers could not take autos belonging to others without paying for them. Private vehicles were not permitted to fly the national flag. Printed education materials on military subjects were available for purchase (with a list being provided to Hưng Yên). A question about how much soldiers should be paid per month for "matches and tobacco" was left unanswered.[83]

The government simultaneously launched public campaigns to convince citizens to increase overall food production, to donate money or goods to patriotic funds *(qũy)*, and to volunteer their time to a variety of defense projects. In early September, a Military Provisions Committee (Uỷ Ban Binh Lương) was formed in Hanoi, and first tasked to gain jurisdiction over rice granaries guarded by the Japanese. Here, however, arriving Chinese forces quickly took precedence. The committee did manage to purchase some rice, cloth, petrol, grease, and weapons. However, with only a small staff, no prior commercial experience, and very limited funds, the committee's efforts benefited only units in the capital and several adjacent provinces.[84] In practice, severe shortages of food in northern Vietnam until the May 1946 rice harvest limited expansion of the regular army more than any other factor. If local committees taxed farmers too heavily in the name of increasing troop numbers, they risked not only loss of popular support but more deaths by starvation than actually occurred (see chapter 6).

Communications

While Liberation Army leaders in August–September 1945 appreciated the need to build a reliable, expeditious military communications system, they had no idea how long this would take. Throughout late 1945 and 1946 the military had to rely mostly on civilian organizations for communications support. Mail and messages initiated by the military traveled via PTT channels in much the same way as other official traffic. Over time, some National Guard units acquired their own internal telephone hookups, while continuing to rely on the PTT for calls to and from other units. Radios were the most highly sought-after communications device, yet almost all radio operators and technicians remained within the former Indochina Radio Bureau, now assigned to the Interior Ministry after a brief turf dispute with the Northern Region People's Committee.[85] Radio Bạch Mai in the Hanoi suburbs took responsibility for both public voice broadcasts and official Morse transmissions and receptions. By 13 September, staff at Radio Bạch Mai had established contact with Radio Saigon, the Central Region Revolutionary Military Committee in Quảng Ngãi, radio station VN3G in Huế, and the patrol boat *Crayssac*, which had been captured from the French in Hòn Gai one week earlier.[86] The Interior Ministry also requisitioned the former Air France transmitter, as well as a transmitter which previously had linked up French mines in Tonkin.[87] Two experts trained in Paris before the Pacific War led the reconditioning of a variety of smaller transmitters and receivers.[88]

On 15 September, a newly arrived Chinese Army unit occupied the radio bureau's repair facility before Vietnamese staff could remove parts and equipment. This sparked hasty evacuation of all movable material from other facilities. Within two weeks, however, when it was apparent that General Lu Han would permit the provisional DRV government to operate Radio Bạch Mai, the material was brought back and activities resumed. Soon the government gave the Defense Ministry top priority in radio operations, and allowed it to requisition civilian technicians and equipment from the radio bureau.[89] Radio Bạch Mai handled both military and civil administrative traffic, with each employing the same wavelengths at different times of day. Subsequently the National Guard acquired several smaller transmitters, some electric generators, and a wide variety of commercial receivers.[90] It also located former colonial army radio operators and convinced them to join up. Classes cropped up to teach Morse code to selected army recruits. However, as late as October 1946 many commanders still had no idea how to employ a communications section effectively, and some individuals assigned to communication duties had not been told what to do.[91]

Prior to August 1945 the very small Liberation Army had developed its own rudimentary courier network in the hills north of Hanoi. This was now expanded to link fledgling military units in the Red River delta, and down the north-central coast. In September, the Northern Police Bureau donated eight Ford V-8 autos and drivers to the army's Communication and Liaison Bureau for courier duties, but these vehicles were soon lost to local commanders who claimed they had greater need.[92] Bicycles donated by better-off urban families were used by teenage recruits to carry information from one unit to another. Foot couriers were required beyond roads and tracks. Although all army couriers carried identification papers and travel permits, such documents often failed to convince guards at local checkpoints. Many hours or even days might be lost while local authorities sought verification from higher authority. A system eventually evolved whereby an individual army courier would be received by a local liaison cadre who then escorted him or her to the next locality in turn. Although intricate, this courier system proved its utility when French forces came to control all the main communication routes and it became necessary to go around them.

The DRV was very slow to develop reliable cryptographic capabilities, whether military or civilian. Apparently the French had excluded Vietnamese from all colonial cryptographic facilities, although Vietnamese radio operators must have received communications security training, and some junior officers or noncommissioned officers may have utilized French one-time pads (by which each message is enciphered uniquely by the sender, and may be deciphered by someone possessing exactly the same materials). In early September 1945, Hanoi radio staff proposed to Saigon that both utilize the *Tale of Kiều*, by Nguyễn Du, as basic cipher. Saigon favored Mendalaev's periodic table of elements instead. To find a better alternative, Hoàng Văn Thái selected Tạ Quang Đệ, former colonial district mandarin and scoutmaster, to head a code bureau within the army's Communications and Liaison Office. Armed with one book, *Eléments de Cryptographie*, by Captain Baudouin, and fond memories of cipher games played in high school and at Scouting jamborees, Đệ and several youths produced a Vietnamese language code in only one week. The cipher was then carried by team members to radio units in various northern locations for communications testing. It soon became clear that the code could be broken easily, which led to modifications. Five or six unit commanders sent individuals to Hanoi to learn how to use the code. In October, Hoàng Quốc Việt carried a cipher copy south and gave it to members of the ICP's Southern Region Committee.[93] Within a month or two French experts were breaking Vietnamese codes routinely, yet Vietnamese counterintelligence personnel failed to notice. The French thus acquired valuable information about the movement of personnel between Nam Bộ and Hanoi, Trần Văn Giàu's efforts to garner support in Thailand, and policy differences between the central government and southern leaders concerning when to fight and when to negotiate. By April 1946, the French were routinely deciphering local radio messages as well, for example between the Defense Ministry and a troop unit in Sơn La province, between Mộc Châu and Qui Nhơn, and even between the

Vietnam Nationalist Party headquarters in Hanoi and subordinates at Việt Trì.[94] Meanwhile, Vietnamese security cadres convinced themselves that some National Guard radio operators were traitors transmitting secret information to the French.[95]

After the flight of Vietnamese forces from Saigon city at the end of September 1945, only one transmitter in the south managed to sustain contact with Hanoi, with messages relayed by the Quảng Ngãi station. Operating from Mỹ Tho until it was forced to evacuate in late October, the transmitter ended up in the U Minh forest near the tip of the Cà Mau peninsula, far from most other surviving DRV groups in the Mekong delta. Gradually a small delta radio net was pieced together, using equipment purchased secretly in Saigon and two transmitters seized in an attack on Tân Sơn Nhứt airport. Not until early March 1946 was the Southern Command headquarters, now better located in Thủ Dầu Một province north of Saigon, able to establish regular radio communication with General Staff headquarters in Hanoi, although it was still necessary to relay traffic via Quảng Ngãi or Huế.[96]

Other Specialized Military Branches

On 15 September 1945, an Arms Office (Phòng Quân Giới) was established within the Defense Ministry. For some months most collection or purchasing of arms continued to take place at the army unit or province committee level. However, the Arms Office did succeed in purchasing two train-car loads of weapons from the Chinese, which were promptly dispatched down the coast. Ammunition was stolen from a Chinese ammunition dump. An Arms Office team seized one thousand sticks of dynamites, black powder canisters, and detonators from a Quảng Ninh plantation.[97] Machine shops repaired firearms, made detonators for grenades and mines, and tried without much success to fashion their own rifles, submachine guns and antitank weapons. On 25 October, the French-owned Star company in Hanoi was requisitioned and renamed the Vietnam Army Engineering Department, concentrating on arms repair and manufacturing of grenades.[98] Workers at the requisitioned Mai Trung Tâm factory managed to rebuild six French artillery pieces. Beyond Hanoi, the Arms Office played little role. Instead, artisans acted on their own, then sought support from a local army unit, people's committee, Việt Minh branch, or ICP cell. A former French Army cartridge works in Tuyên Quang was revived and expanded. Fabrication of reliable gunpowder, TNT, and mercury detonators proved the biggest bottlenecks. There were numerous horrible accidents.[99]

Defense Ministry employees aggressively sought out raw materials of military importance. The Fontaine distillery was "requested" to provide unspecified quantities of mercury, nitric acid, sulfur, and copper. Ten days later it was instructed to turn over 3.5 tons of copper ingots, four hundred kilograms of aluminum, and eight tons of cast iron. Citizens volunteered information about discarded French or Japanese ammunition to local committees, which notified higher echelons. One village committee claimed to possess "many thousands" of mortar casings and artillery shells. Even the disposition of 155 rounds of rifle ammunition, found by Mrs. Phạm Kim Thạch in a pond while collecting snails, became the object of a petition by her husband and the exchange of official messages between committees. On 21 November, the Defense Ministry heard that the Ban Mê Thuột People's Committee, far to the south, had taken possession of 328 bombs, 28 cases of incendiary devices, and many 81 mm and 60 mm mortar shells.[100] We do not know if some of these munitions were shifted to the forest before a French armored column entered Ban Mê Thuột nine days later. Some months later, DRV officials conceived a plan to barter coal for arms in China, at a rate of four tons of coal for one U.S. rifle and one hundred rounds of ammunition. A target of sixty thousand imported rifles was set. French countermeasures at the coal mines and in Haiphong probably forestalled this project or reduced it to a dribble.[101]

Establishing a national military school was another high government priority. Already during June–August 1945 in the Việt Bắc hills, three short classes for platoon leaders and political officers had graduated 234 students. Early in September, the new General Staff headquarters organized the Vietnam Military-Political Academy (Trường Quân Chính Việt Nam), directed by Nguyễn An (a.k.a. Trương Văn Lĩnh), with Trần Tử Bình as political officer.[102] The young men sent from northern provinces, mentioned earlier, were screened at the Lycée Đỗ Hữu Vị near the Citadel. On 15 September, Class 4 began a three-week course, with a high proportion of its 156 students coming from Hanoi secondary schools. Some participants still only carried wooden rifles. A mix of Việt Bắc cadres and former Civil Guard officers and NCOs constituted the teaching staff. Besides rifle familiarization, dry firing, parade drills, forced marches, and PE, some hours were devoted to map reading, terrain assessment, small-unit movement, and guerrilla tactics. Political lectures treated the current situation in Indochina and the world at large, the "liberation revolution," principles of leadership, and how to guide the thinking of subordinates. President Hồ Chí Minh visited the Academy, inspected the mess hall and lavatories, gave a short speech, and reviewed Class 4 in drill formation. When the ranks presented arms by thrusting their bayonet-tipped rifles forward (a practice begun in the Việt Bắc hills), President Hồ advised the army to change to a nonthreatening vertical rifle presentation, as soldiers would be drilling in front of the Vietnamese people, not the enemy. After Class 4 graduated, those not sent south were mostly assigned to units in provinces adjacent to Hanoi and Haiphong.[103]

With Chinese army units at the nearby Citadel watching everything, it was decided to shift the Academy to the Cité Universitaire and give it the more innocuous name of Vietnam Cadre Training School (Trường Huấn Luyện Cán Bộ Việt Nam). Province-level Việt Minh committees from Huế northward nominated men for an expanded one-month course, with 525 being selected for Class 5, which began training on 15 October. Additional former French Army and Civil Guard personnel joined the teaching staff, while prominent ICP members like Trường Chinh, Võ Nguyên Giáp, Phạm Văn Đồng, and Hoàng Hữu Nam came to lecture as well. The first ICP cell was formed among Academy staff, headed by Trần Tử Bình. Nonetheless, some university-trained enrollees to Class 5 proceeded openly to criticize Việt Minh activities, provoking intense reeducation efforts from political instructors and expulsion of a few recalcitrants. Henceforth screening and selection of students prior to entry was made more rigorous. Food for staff and students alike became very scarce by the end of October, compelling the Academy to borrow rice from other army units and to "mobilize" (vận động) donations from citizens. Hồ Chí Minh addressed Class 5 at graduation, urging them never to give up studying and to research both victories and defeats.

With the Ministry of Education reopening Hanoi University, and Military Academy staff eager to find space for live firing and tactical maneuvers, attention focused on Sơn Tây, thirty-five kilometers west of Hanoi, a place of military significance for centuries. Chinese troops had moved out of the former French Air Force billets at Sơn Tây, taking all the furniture and leaving garbage and excrement everywhere. After cleaning up, making repairs, and scrounging for desks, chairs, and beds, in early December the Academy welcomed Class 6, composed of 314 students from all three regions of the country, to Sơn Tây. Each student received one former Civil Guard uniform, a forage cap, and a pair of leather shoes, plus use of a kapok mattress, mosquito net, and wool blanket. Instructors demonstrated live grenade throwing, but students threw only wooden replicas. Towards the end of Class 6, each student fired one live round at the rifle range. Class 7, which began on 15 February 1946 with 327 students and lasted two months, had the luxury of three live rounds per student, plus instruction in use of the machine gun, 60 mm mortar, compass, topographical map, and binoculars. During Class 7's last week, its two units maneuvered against each other, practicing encampment, infiltration, ambush, attack, and defense. Members were also called upon to explain the meaning of the 6 March 1946 Preliminary Accord to civilians in the area (see chapter 4), a practical test of "popular mobilization" (dân vận). With departure of Class 7 on 16 April, the Academy could count a total of fifteen hundred small-unit command and political officers who had graduated since the previous June.[104]

In subsequent months, Academy graduates serving around the country sent hundreds of letters to their former teachers, expressing gratitude and describing recent favorable experiences, but also criticizing comrades or superior officers by name, and even requesting that Academy staff intervene on their behalf to gain redress or to obtain transfers. In September the Academy's management board addressed an extraordinary open letter to former students, emphasizing that, "We can be your friend or advisor, but no longer your commander." The board further counseled that "there will always be injustices, yet repeated wrongs will eventually be found out." Graduates were also advised that promotion to company or battalion commander was more likely to come from week-to-week performance, reading of available books and newspapers, and frank discussion with peers, rather than necessarily attending further formal courses. Finally, the board expressed the hope that graduates of all seven classes could enjoy a big reunion someday—an aspiration unfulfilled for more than thirty years.[105] Board members appreciated how bonds had formed between teachers and students, and between members of the same Academy class, but at this moment they wanted to instill respect for the chain of command, a readiness to accept disliked jobs, and habits of self-study.

Establishment of an army medical corps proved more difficult. Units arriving from the Việt Bắc hills in late August 1945 possessed one former medical student, who simply dispensed available pills. In late September 1945, Dr. Vũ Văn Cẩn set up a medical facility for army units in Hanoi, and within weeks physicians in Haiphong and Phúc Yên followed suit. Hospital attendants and orderlies volunteered for service elsewhere. All army enrollees were supposed to undergo health examinations, but standards were lax. Most ill soldiers were referred to civilian hospitals and clinics. Dr Cẩn's office in Hanoi began a series of courses to train army medics, each lasting thirty to forty-five days. On 19 October, the Northern Region Committee founded a civilian First Aid Association (Hội Cứu Thương) to recruit and train personnel, some of whom later enrolled in the army. Women first-aid volunteers joined armed groups heading south, yet no team of physicians, nurses, and orderlies appears to have been dispatched. Despite hearing of heavy casualties in the south, and though mindful that fighting might break out elsewhere, the Army General Staff still failed to prepare medically for combat conditions. Then suddenly in late November 1945, the government ordered conscription of all doctors (y sĩ) and pharmacists (dược sĩ) to serve either the Ministry of Health or the Defense Ministry. Younger specialists would be called up first, with no deferrals accepted, and unspecified "stern punishment" for those who disobeyed.[106] This was the only attempt at conscription in the early life of the DRV, and it proved unsuccessful. While some doctors and pharmacists had already volunteered, others objected to being the only citizens singled out for conscription. The Vietnam Nationalist Party criticized the decree, garnering some support from within the medical profession. As of early 1946, the National Guard possessed only fifteen doctors on its rolls.[107] In July, the National Gazette published a list of eighty-three physicians (bác sĩ) who had graduated from the Hanoi

Medical School and would now "gradually be conscripted to assist the Army Medical Bureau" founded six months prior.[108] As of November, the DRV health minister could only report 32 out of 182 doctors in the north enrolled in the National Guard. Any young doctors remaining outside would be conscripted soon, he insisted.[109]

In June 1946, the Army Medical Bureau began to publish a fortnightly paper called *Vui Sống (Joy in Life)*, designed mainly to promote public health and hygiene, but also to link up doctors, nurses, and medics within the National Guard. An inaugural article admitted that medical examinations of army inductees revealed a disconcerting proportion of health problems, but that because of the imperatives of national defense only a limited number of men were rejected. An article by a physician making the rounds of National Guard camps naively insisted that every soldier should receive nutritious food, ten minutes rest per hour when marching, protection from excessive heat, daily ablutions, and mercurochrome to daub on cuts or scratches. By contrast, an article by a surgeon working among combatants in south-central Vietnam described the soldiers' single tattered set of clothes, the lice, the malaria, and the lack of anesthetic when operating. Meanwhile, the surgeon concluded sourly, some people in Hanoi were enjoying a life of luxury and talking of perpetual peace. In July, the defense minister, Phan Anh, spoke at the graduation ceremony for the third class of National Guard medics, some forty in number. On 21 November, President Hồ Chí Minh inaugurated the Army Medical School. Army medical personnel committed themselves to raising medicinal plants, vegetables, and livestock. A facility was opened at Sầm Sơn beach in Thanh Hóa for seriously injured and ill patients. One writer evoked the plight of soldier amputees, then quoted one young man who was missing an arm as telling his female caregiver, "My only wish is not to be pitied."[110]

THE CHINESE MILITARY PRESENCE

From 10 September 1945 until March 1946, the DRV government had to deal on a day-to-day basis with a profusion of Chinese Army commanders and staff officers. Although it soon became evident that the overall commander, General Lu Han, was not going to allow the French to participate in occupation duties, the degree to which the Chinese would insert themselves into Vietnamese affairs remained unclear until the end of 1945. At Hồ Chí Minh's first meeting with Lu Han, on 16 September, attention focused on currency exchange rates, feeding the Chinese Army, repairing roads, and maintaining order (see chapter 5). Lu Han demanded to know the numbers, organization, and disposition of DRV armed elements. Hồ Chí Minh reluctantly agreed to provide this information, even though at this point he himself possessed only fragmentary data. Following this meeting, Hồ shifted most of the still-small Hanoi armed contingent out of the city and decided to drop the emotive title of Liberation Army in favor of the modest name of National Guard (Vệ Quốc Đoàn).[111] Hồ understood that Lu Han could shove aside the DRV government in Hanoi at any time he wished, but then would have to allocate a fair number of Chinese troops to trying to quell opposition in the countryside. On 22 September, the day after General Gracey declared martial law in Saigon, Lu Han assured Hồ Chí Minh that he had no intention of following the British precedent, providing the government maintained public order in both Hanoi and the countryside.[112]

The next evening, shaken by news of French seizure of key positions in Saigon and the outbreak of fighting, Hồ Chí Minh told the OSS representative in Hanoi, Archimedes Patti, that he was considering withdrawal to the jungle in anticipation of French invasion of the north.[113] Paris had been pressing the Chinese government in Chongqing to allow French forces to share northern Indochina occupation duties, and Hanoi was awash with rumors that the forty-five hundred French nationals interned in the Citadel would be rearmed. French commandos were probing from Hạ Long Bay in the east and Laos in the west. The possibility of a French airborne attack (staged via Pakse airport in Laos) could not be dismissed. Already in October, Chongqing had plans to withdraw Chinese forces as soon as a satisfactory treaty was negotiated with Paris, which in the event did not occur until the end of February 1946. Meanwhile, Lu Han and other officers convinced President Chiang Kai-shek that to permit French troops to share occupation responsibilities was to court violence and jeopardize local order.[114] The Chinese government thus gave the DRV five valuable months of de facto protection from serious French attack north of the sixteenth parallel.

The Chinese price for this protection was unfettered exploitation of the northern Vietnamese economy and DRV acceptance of significant political roles for the Vietnam Nationalist Party and Vietnam Revolutionary League. Top-level discussions on the latter issue proceeded correctly but slowly (see chapter 7). Behind the scenes, the ICP was determined to block national army leadership roles for cadres from those organizations, some of whom possessed considerable military experience in southern China. An armed standoff soon developed along the three main routes from Hanoi to China, with Nationalist and Revolutionary League units controlling the towns (Lào Cai, Yên Bái, Phú Thọ, Việt Trì, Vĩnh Yên, Lạng Sơn, Móng Cái), and DRV loyalists controlling most of the surrounding countryside. Chinese officers in the towns probably discouraged their Nationalist and Revolutionary League friends from launching attacks on nearby militia or National Guard positions, while DRV leaders explained to aggressive local adherents the dangers of Chinese retaliation and the larger strategic necessity of focusing on the French threat.

With Hồ Chí Minh determined to proceed with national elections in early January, a tenuous Hanoi power-sharing agreement was hammered out in late December. In a preelection roster, Chu Văn Tấn remained as defense minister and Võ Nguyên Giáp as interior minister.[115] However, in the list presented to the new National Assembly on 2 March 1946 and quickly approved, Tấn and Giáp were replaced by two prominent "nonparty" intellectuals, Phan Anh and Huỳnh Thúc Kháng.[116] Another body was created, the Resistance Committee, which reported directly to the Cabinet and issued commands (via General Staff headquarters) to units of the National Guard. Võ Nguyên Giáp was designated chairman of this commission, while the head of the Nationalist Party, Vũ Hồng Khanh, became deputy chairman. Khanh was soon boxed out of operations, however: he received no access to confidential communications and was avoided by most National Guard cadres.[117]

THE FRENCH RETURN TO THE NORTH

In late October 1945, French Army units that had fled to Yunnan in March and April made preparations to return to Indochina. The Chongqing government was receptive, but Chinese generals in Hanoi restated the danger of Franco-Vietnamese confrontations. In early November, the number of ethnic Vietnamese deserting from French units in Yunnan increased dramatically. Capt. Nguyễn Duy Viên took his fully armed company of *tirailleurs* across the frontier to Hà Giang town and a rousing welcome from Vietnam Nationalist Party adherents. Other Nationalist Party groups prepared to defend Lào Cai and Lai Châu against the French. Meanwhile, the DRV's National Guard declared a northwest front, and nine northern province committees sent modest armed groups to Sơn La. In early January 1946, Chongqing gave the French permission to enter Indochina in western Tonkin and use Lai Châu as a staging point to move into Laos. About two thousand Rhadé, Lao, Thái, Thổ (Tày), and Vietnamese who had remained loyal joined fourteen hundred French troops in the subsequent march to Lai Châu. Ignoring Chinese wishes, the main French Army contingent then continued down the right bank of the Black River. Both Nationalist Party and DRV National Guard units skirmished repeatedly with the French, the former eventually retreating to Lào Cai, the latter to Sơn La. The French were poised to attack Sơn La when they were restrained by the 6 March Preliminary Accord (see chapter 4). Following withdrawal of the last Chinese units from this area in May, the French tightened their control, resumed relations with local clan leaders, and talked of forming an autonomous "Thái Federation."[118] Fighting would ebb and flow through this region until final French defeat at Điện Biên Phủ in 1954.

French military representatives tried repeatedly to convince the Chinese authorities to give them access to Hanoi airport and to allow colonial troops in the Citadel to be rearmed. The French Air Force strove frantically to obtain more C-47 Dakota aircraft from British or American sources in order to be able to transport a combat force from Saigon to Hanoi via Pakse in Laos.[119] The French had in mind a coup d'état against Hồ Chí Minh's government, providing that reinforcements could be flown in and that Chinese forces agreed to stand aside. Vietnamese leaders must have appreciated this threat, but we have no evidence about what precautions were taken. Such a coup would have meant bitter street fighting in Hanoi, with unarmed civilians, both Vietnamese and French, suffering the most. The Chinese continued to refuse French requests, causing the latter to focus increasingly on a more substantial seaborne entry at Haiphong.[120]

By mid-February, DRV leaders knew that Chinese and French negotiators were moving towards an agreement that included French troops relieving Chinese troops north of the sixteenth parallel. Fundamental strategic choices now pressed down relentlessly, amidst which the government had to factor in the capacity of the National Guard and the local militia to take or not take specific actions (see chapter 4). We don't know when President Hồ Chí Minh heard from Chinese sources that the French expected to land at Haiphong, but Hoàng Văn Thái and his general staff could have deduced that substantial French entry by land via China or Laos was unlikely, and there were no signs of a French advance north from Nha Trang. That left either a French airborne descent on Hanoi, a landing at Haiphong, or both. National Guard units were placed on high alert, and by the end of February the public in Hanoi and Haiphong sensed that events might soon take a dramatic, possibly dangerous turn. Hồ understood that the Chinese held the high cards. If he ignored the 28 February Sino-French agreement and ordered armed resistance to the arriving French, the Chinese probably would have deposed him and moved to disarm Vietnamese units, compelling the remnant DRV government to take to the hills in very unfavorable circumstances. Hồ chose to negotiate the least onerous agreement with the French, with some help from Chinese generals. However, there remained the possibility that on arrival of French forces some National Guard and militia elements might disobey orders to withhold fire, or fail to receive clear-cut orders, resulting in armed conflict. If this happened, and the DRV government showed itself incapable of terminating confrontations quickly, then the Chinese and French together would have put an end to the DRV.

Because Hồ Chí Minh had kept the content of his negotiations secret to all but a few confidants, word of the 6 March arrival of French forces at Haiphong and the signing of the Franco-Vietnamese Preliminary Accord in Hanoi came as a general shock. The country was soon awash with speculation, and Việt Minh leaders took conflicting positions in public. Arguments ensued among members of National Guard units, and some local militia groups talked of ambushing French "bandits" *(giặc)*. Supporters of the 6 March Accord appeared much in the minority. At this moment Hồ Chí Minh and DRV government faced their greatest test of legitimacy. Yet no cases of outright military disobedience were reported. No militiamen sniped at French soldiers as they took up Chinese-assigned positions in Haiphong. In Hanoi, General Raoul Salan renewed the French project to fly weapons to Gia Lâm airport, actually loading ten Dakotas in Saigon and putting them into the air before again being rebuffed by the Chinese command.[121] If the Chinese had allowed those firearms to make it to Gia Lâm airport, and word had spread through the city of French efforts to shift them to the Hanoi Citadel in order to rearm colonial soldiers, a violent confrontation would have been inevitable.

In the military annex to the 6 March Preliminary Accord, the French were given overall command of a twenty-five-thousand-man "relief force," composed of fifteen thousand of their own men and ten-thousand Vietnamese troops commanded by Vietnamese officers "subject to the orders of the military authorities

FIGURE 10. Curbside reviewing stand for Franco-Vietnamese military parade in Hanoi, 22 March 1946. Võ Nguyên Giáp in his fedora is flanked on the left by General Leclerc and General Valluy, on the right by an officer who may be General Lu Han, then by Jean Sainteny and General Salan. In Hội Khoa Học Lịch Sử Việt Nam, *Ký Ưc*, 138. Courtesy of Vietnam Historical Society.

of Vietnam." Unit movements, positioning, and missions would be dealt with at subsequent combined staff meetings.[122] On 22 March, four days after the arrival of Gen Leclerc's 220-vehicle column in Hanoi, a joint military parade was organized that included one well-drilled, green-uniformed, leather-booted Vietnamese battalion marching six abreast, singing revolutionary songs as it went. Officers boasted swords and men carried rifles with fixed bayonets. In front of Leclerc and Giáp on the reviewing stand, each platoon executed "eyes right!" much to the delight of the Vietnamese crowd. Then, however, the French came past with U.S. Greyhound armored cars, half-tracks, and even a synchronized flyby of Spitfires, leaving the crowd somber.[123] On 3 April, French and Vietnamese officers reached a general staff agreement which specified venues and troop allocations for each side, outlined movement protocols, and established a Mixed Central Commission for Liaison and Control. Within a week, however, the French prepared to mount a coup d'etat at multiple locations, collecting intelligence, forming undercover hit teams, and planning commando assaults.[124] They soon discovered that reviving clandestine operational capacity in the north was far more difficult than it had been in the south during previous months. Meanwhile, Vietnamese representatives to the Mixed Commission politely deflected French urging to implement the single command and General Staff structure. Nothing in the Accord prevented the DRV National Guard from continuing to build up units outside their ten-thousand-man contribution to the relief force.

THE 1ST BATTALION HANOI REGION

We know a lot about one particular National Guard unit, the 1st Battalion of the Hanoi Region, because it was based at the Northern Region Office, some of whose records were captured by the French in late 1946. At the end of May 1946, the 1st Battalion possessed 438 men and 404 firearms of nineteen different types, from the prestigious Thompson submachine gun to lowly bird rifles. Most men with rifles had been issued about eighty cartridges each, with additional rounds in the armory for some makes of weapon. However, at a practice firing session for Company 2 on 2 June, a disconcerting 154 out of 440 rounds misfired (35 percent). Company 2 also had 145 grenades (69 Japanese, 19 French, 57 Vietnamese), of which two were demonstrated successfully at the 2 June practice. Battalion headquarters boasted a British 7.92 mm Bren gun.

Company personnel sheets contain fifteen categories of information on each battalion member: name (including pseudonyms), age, rank and position, birthplace, date of enlistment, prior occupation, parents' names, parents' occupations, parents' current location, marital status and number of children, firearm type, serial number and cartridges issued, grenades, battle experience, prior organizational affiliation, and educational level. For example, Bùi Đình Phùng, Company 1 commander, was born in 1920 in Vĩnh Yên to a farming family, enlisted on 2 January 1945, had a wife and no children, was armed with a Chinese "Bat" pistol (serial number 840B20) and seventy-two rounds, also carried two grenades, had fought the Japanese at Tam Đảo (16 July 1945) and Thái Nguyên (21–24 August 1945), and possessed some primary schooling. Company 1 members originated from many different northern provinces, but most had enlisted in Hanoi in August and September 1945, asserted that they had some classroom education, and lacked any battle experience. Under "Prior organizational affiliation," twelve different names appear, including a variety of militia groups, Việt Minh national salvation associations, and the Democratic Party.[125]

The 1st Battalion developed a garrison routine familiar to military men everywhere, with training sessions, inspections, drills, work assignments, transfers, awards, and punishments. On 30 May 1946, each company was instructed to contribute one well-equipped, carefully inspected squad to the honor guard for President Hồ Chí Minh as he departed Gia Lâm airport for France the next morning. Other squads were sent to guard three administrative buildings. On four different occasions the battalion commander, Siêu Hải, forbade off-duty soldiers from wearing their uniforms on the street, the last time threatening company commanders and platoon leaders with punishment if the practice persisted. Everyone was warned to upgrade security by carefully controlling entry and exit to bases, watching for unusual behavior, checking identification papers, keeping documents locked up, and limiting access to confidential materials. "It is not enough to watch the enemy, one must also prevent the enemy from watching us," Siêu Hải concluded.[126] The battalion political officer, Vi Ngô, bestowed heroic historical names on the battalion and one of its company, stressed the importance of voting in eventual Hanoi People's Council elections, and urged all commanders and political officers to attend a 19 June talk by Trần Huy Liệu.[127]

In early July, all battalion officers were told to go out and find more recruits, who had to be between eighteen and thirty-five years old; stand at least 1.55 meters tall; and possess a birth certificate, a good conduct endorsement from their local people's committee, and a doctor's affirmation. They also had to agree to serve three years. Several days later, however, the battalion political officer criticized shoddy recruitment standards, especially that some enlistees were too young, and some had not been told the "political context" of enlistment, presumably a reference to obeying the Việt Minh line.[128] Perusing these many messages, one gets the feeling of young men trying hard to "be military," with the battalion commander and political officer wanting to supervise and teach everything, when in fact they too were learning army behavior day to day like everyone else.

First Battalion also received numerous orders from Hoàng Văn Thái, in charge of General Staff headquarters, and from Lê Quảng Ba, commander of National Guard units in Hanoi. Units were warned about acquiring items and selling them to "stay alive"; henceforth they needed to inform Hanoi command in advance, get approval, and forward 70 percent of the proceeds upward. "Any unit disobeying this order is guilty of 'localism' *(địa phương chủ nghĩa)*, a very dangerous offense in the military," the message concluded. A soldier who had gone absent without leave on more than one occasion was imprisoned for fifteen days and then expelled from the National Guard. All units were encouraged to send their men to the Opera House to view a new film, "Vietnamese Compatriots in France," making sure that no weapons were carried. A political training syllabus condemned the United States for giving war materials to the French Army and for joining with the British to "repress nations opposing capitalism (Soviet Union, small countries)."[129]

In late June, Trần Độ, political officer for the Hanoi command, informed all battalions that the French attitude had become more pugnacious, due, he said, to Hồ Chí Minh being away and to recent French election results. The French Army was occupying more positions; most notably, on the previous day they had seized the governor general's palace (see chapter 4). Trần Độ summarized the DRV position to the troops: "We remain calm, not committed to fighting. Whenever the order is issued we are determined to fulfill the duty of a Revolutionary soldier and uphold the flag of the Vietnam Fatherland."[130] Two weeks later, following violent altercations at Hòn Gai and French occupation of positions at Lạng Sơn, the 1st Battalion was ordered to be on special lookout for saboteurs and secretly to scout enemy positions in Hanoi. Soldiers were given a new set of slogans to memorize, most importantly, "The National Guard swears a life-and-death oath not to abandon Hanoi."[131]

Orders issued during late July and August 1946 reflect increasing tensions and uncertainty. On 24 July, General Staff headquarters distributed instructions to roadblock personnel on how to stop French trucks, politely ask a few questions, gain intelligence, wave them on, and report results quickly. The message concluded: "We must remember carefully that according to the Preliminary Accord we have to brush against *(đụng chạm)* the French for another five years, unless an agreement in Paris determines differently." That same day, however, French jeeps fired on several guard põsts, which led to new orders for National Guard personnel to keep under cover where possible, not congregate, and stay out of uniform on streets where the French were numerous.[132]

Remarkably, the 1st Battalion commander, Siêu Hải, issued his own written "appeal" or "call" *(hiệu triệu)* to his troops, assessing the Fontainebleau conference as a "stormy quarrel" because neither the French negotiating position nor French negotiators had changed since the abortive Dalat conference two months prior. Hence the battalion had to be ready for a sudden French attack, and be prepared to die for Hanoi and ultimate victory. In the next sentence, however, Siêu Hải insisted that "the new Vietnam and the new France will succeed in their efforts at cooperation." Such a typed message from a mere battalion commander reflected the personal leadership style of the period, although one can assume the content derived from higher-level briefings. Meanwhile, the 1st Battalion political officer, Vi Ngô, criticized company commanders for not teaching their men about U.S. imperialism and the fraudulent democratic rhetoric of President Truman. If company commanders did not shape up soon, Vi Ngô intimated, they would be replaced.[133] In August, the chief of general staff criticized National Guard commanders for lacking sangfroid amidst French provocations, losing contact, allowing their units to "run in all directions," opening fire without authorization, and being afraid of circling aircraft. While the French had a plan of aggravation, DRV government policy was not yet to open hostilities, hence, "We must curb our feelings, respect discipline, remain calm, persevere—but not forget to prepare and be vigilant."[134] At the end of August, however, General Staff headquarters contributed to the nervousness by distributing a questionable warning to look out for seven aircraft that the French had painted with the DRV emblem (yellow star on red background) and were using for black operations.[135]

RATIONALIZING AND EXPANDING
THE NATIONAL GUARD

Throughout the summer of 1946, the Defense Ministry and Central Military Commission worked hard to fashion the National Guard into a standing army of credible proportions. Policy documents had been prepared earlier. In March, President Hồ Chí Minh signed a decree outlining military structure, ranks, uniform, and insignias. The anticipated structure bore a striking resemblance to the U.S. Army: squad, platoon, company, battalion, regiment, brigade, division, corps, and army. Regimental commanders would designate privates, division commanders would decide on sergeants, the General Command would commission company officers (úy), the minister of defense would award field ranks (tá), and the president would decree generals (tướng). A single khaki uniform was described, but permission was granted to utilize other clothing temporarily. Insignia resembled that of the French Army. Specialized units such as engineers, artillery, or medical corps would have their own emblems, to be determined later. Political officers would have a black background to their rank insignia.[136] Except for three or four battalions under direct central command, there was no immediate attempt to implement this ambitious decree.

In late May, President Hồ Chí Minh issued regulations for a National Armed Forces (Quân Đội Quốc Gia), a work which dealt meticulously with organization, recruitment, ranks, promotion, discipline, awards, offenses, punishments, and ceremonies.[137] Enlistees had to be between eighteen and thirty years old, be declared fit by an army doctor, and know how to read and write quốc ngữ. There was no mention of only males being accepted, nor of the need for character clearance from either local Việt Minh or administrative committee officials. However, province authorities were directed to compile personal history files on every soldier, as would their units subsequently. The decree set minimum periods of time in each rank, treated medical personnel as a special branch, and precluded political officers from outranking their commanders. Surprisingly, the decree allowed for individual transfers to be arranged between the two commanders involved, without reference to higher echelons.

Military awards, offenses, and punishments were spelled out meticulously in the May decree. Orders from superiors had to be obeyed without hesitation, criticism, or complaint, although provision was made for discussion and criticism at a later point, when everyone had equal rights to express their opinions. Political officers were to help commanders to consider options, but they were not to give orders or take military responsibility. Commanders had to agree with their political officer on "matters of a political nature." On the delicate issue of personal pronouns, superiors were to call their men *anh* (older brother), while those below called those in higher ranks *ông* (grandfather) or *anh* depending on circumstance. When on duty no one was to use the familiar *mày* (you) and *tao* (me), even if both speakers were of equal status. When reporting, a soldier was to address the commander by his position, for example "regimental commander, sir" *(thưa trung đoàn trưởng)*, while referring to himself or herself in the first-person *(tôi)*. This military employment of the impersonal first-person "I" was potentially quite significant, as it avoided the need for quasi-familial pronoun dyads such as "elder brother/younger brother" *(anh em)* or "senior uncle/nephew" *(bác cháu)*.

Twelve "ordinary" military offenses were listed in the May 1946 decree—from sloppy uniform to rudeness towards one's superiors—for which there were eight possible punishments ranging from reprimand in front of the unit to dismissal. Fourteen "grave" offenses were specified, to be punished by fixed-term imprisonment, life at hard labor, or execution. With courts martial yet to be established to handle these grave cases, commanders could either incarcerate offenders on base or in civilian prisons. Many provisions in this May decree seem to have been left to the future. In July, the government established a central commission to scrutinize all officer rank proposals coming up from military units and to make case-by-case recommendations to approve or reject them.[138]

In July 1946, the Defense Ministry submitted to the Cabinet a budget request for 170,000,000\$BIC, surely more than the Finance Ministry could hope to provide.[139] The Defense Ministry now contained the following specialized bureaus: military production, arms manufacturing, politics, administration, training, engineering and transport, justice, supply, and medicine. Phan Anh and Tạ Quang Bửu deliberately chose non-ICP bureau heads, the only exception being Vũ Anh, in charge of supply. The Central Military Commission included operations,

General Staff, politics, the Vietnam Relief Force Command, and the Vietnamese-French Mixed Central Commission for Liaison and Control.[140] Hoàng Văn Thái expanded the General Staff headquarters to include sections for operations, intelligence, research, communications, cryptography, maps, training, and personnel. Intelligence remained General Staff's weakest link. The section head, Hoàng Minh Đạo, reported establishment of twenty-six "enemy observation posts" north of the sixteenth parallel. However, local personnel still had to be taught how to collect, communicate, and update French order-of-battle details. In Hanoi, section members needed to learn how to compile and evaluate data, then compose timely intelligence reports. Assessing higher-level French military intentions proved especially difficult.[141]

Military communication between Hanoi and key locations was substantially improved by the purchase of American radio equipment from withdrawing Chinese forces. Morse code traffic flowed routinely between Hanoi and seven headquarters as far south as Quảng Ngãi, with Quảng Ngãi also relaying messages to and from Nam Bộ, Phan Thiết, and Thailand. Smaller MK2 and MK15 transmitters with hand-cranked generators were allocated to northern "war zones" (chiến khu) and regiments, but new equipment sometimes languished until radio operators could be trained. A network of relay stations for military couriers was established, with particular attention to back routes in case the enemy controlled the roads. Civilian telegraph and telephone lines continued to be employed by central military bureaus to communicate with subordinate echelons as far south as Phú Yên.[142] Cryptographic practices still lagged far behind communication capacity. Not until September did the General Staff organize the first cryptography training course. By November, most northern war zones and regiments possessed cryptography teams, but commanders often used these men for other tasks, which undermined morale and led some to seek reassignment.[143] The issue of enhancing cryptographic security against French deciphering still had not been addressed.

Artillery remained the National Guard's most telling deficiency. In late June 1946, three old French 75 mm antiaircraft guns were consolidated into one artillery battery for the capital.[144] Doãn Tuế, formerly of the colonial artillery, was put to work translating a French artillery manual, coining Vietnamese terms along the way.[145] Also in June, a team began to design an imitation of the American 2.5-inch bazooka, for use against armored vehicles, reinforced bunkers, and river boats. The self-propelled shell with its shaped charge posed the biggest challenge. Powder had to come from captured enemy artillery shells. In October, Hồ Chí Minh brought back from Paris a German-trained scientist, Trần Đại Nghĩa, who joined the bazooka team in Thái Nguyên to produce fifty prototype projectiles and four tubes. When tested, the projectiles failed to penetrate. In March 1947, an improved model was used in battle for the first time.[146] However, the lack of medium and heavy weapons would continue to restrict Vietnamese tactical options until 1950.

By August 1946, the Defense Ministry had convinced most local arsenals to abandon attempts to produce rifles and submachine guns in favor of upgrading their output of black powder, ammunition, detonators, grenades, mines, and mortars. Plans were afoot to shift some arms manufacturing away from the Red River delta to upland locations. Already the Thái Nguyên arsenal employed about six hundred workers, including one hundred or more Japanese deserters.[147]

The National Guard in the north could count seventeen infantry regiments and nine separate infantry battalions by September 1946. All regiments were province based, and depended on province committees for provisioning.[148] By contrast, all but one of the battalions were under direct Military Commission control—five positioned in or near Hanoi and three to the northeast in War Zone 12. The relationship between province-based regiments and war zone commanders had yet to be spelled out.[149]

In May 1946, the Vietnam Cadre Training School at Sơn Tây was renamed the Trần Quốc Tuấn Military Academy and enrolled 288 students for a six-month officer course designed to produce qualified platoon leaders.[150] Students came from diverse class backgrounds and were not subject to rigorous political screening, a practice later criticized by the ICP. At the opening ceremony, President Hồ Chí Minh presented the Academy with a red banner on which the following slogan was embroidered in yellow: "Loyal to the Country, Grateful to the People."[151] Lesson materials were still taken from French Army and Chinese Nationalist Army sources, plus some writings by Hồ on guerrilla tactics. Towards the end of the course, the entire class took part in a two-hundred-kilometer march and tactical exercise. After graduating on 8 December, most students immediately returned to their parent units, while a limited number were assigned to the Defense Ministry or remained as instructors at the Academy. A few graduates later deserted to the French side.[152] Meanwhile, in Bắc Sơn district (Lạng Sơn), a smaller military-political school limited its enrollees explicitly to ICP and Việt Minh cadres.[153]

Military Socialization

Turning young men of diverse origins and temperament into soldiers is a challenge in any country. In Vietnam, the absence of a professional army meant that almost everyone learned from scratch. High school students were eager to wield a rifle, but found the physical exertion and material privations of army life very demanding. Farm boys could not read instructions and became homesick for village life. Recruits of all backgrounds were told to accept that: "Once you are in the army you cannot ask to be discharged to take care of family duties. If your father or mother dies, so be it. If your wife or child is ill, too bad. You must break completely from your family after you enlist."[154] National Guard enlistment forms explicitly obligated individuals to "voluntarily emancipate *(thoát ly)* yourself from the family."[155]

Marching back and forth with a wooden stick had been part of August 1945 revolutionary effervescence, but once young men were put into platoons and former colonial army NCOs or Chinese military school graduates assigned to drill them, the mood turned relentless. Each unit learned to fall in, form ranks, count off, march in unison, shoulder arms, present arms, and honor the national flag. Each trooper had to stay clean, wash his own clothing, salute crisply, answer the instructor's questions succinctly, memorize the soldier's oath, and treat his rifle as his wife or girlfriend.[156] For units lacking a drill instructor there were former Boy Scouts and participants in the colonial youth movement who taught the basics. Newspapers carried columns dealing not only with drills but also map reading, terrain evaluation, squad tactics, weapons operation, and fire discipline.

Newspapers aimed more specifically at National Guard and militia readers made a point of exposing sloppy or improper military behavior. Hoàng Minh Thảo chose to castigate poor comportment, failure to salute, smoking or talking in the ranks, groveling before superiors, falling asleep on watch, neglecting to patrol vigorously, and failing to press an attack.[157] Other writers condemned poor security procedures, sleeping in class, dirty ammunition, wild shooting at night, troopers on furlough who failed to pay for public transport, and soldiers who held up a train for fifteen minutes so they could finish their lunch. At a more subtle level, one commentator criticized the tendency of soldiers to form their own groups within a unit in order to eat, sleep, and amuse themselves separately. "From group to clique is not far," he concluded ominously.[158]

As late as October 1946, one observer reported several different forms of military salute at a single flag-raising ceremony, a lack of uniformity which should not be allowed to persist. Calls for spiffy, standardized salutes usually were accompanied by warnings that foreign officers would look down on a Vietnamese army that neglected to follow international military convention. Once foreign officers were no longer in physical proximity the practice of saluting faded within the National Guard. The use of insignia to designate military rank was often insisted upon. As one writer maintained, rank insignia "enabled everyone to know who commanded whom."[159] On the other hand, Trần Độ, political officer of the Hanoi military region, denounced the deferential military hierarchy of the colonial era as represented by language as well as insignias. Độ favored the egalitarian "comrade" *(đồng chí)* or, when necessary, the identification of cadres according to position rather than rank. One combatant writing from Laos mocked unit leaders who devised their own insignias to impress Lao women and be able to tell them *"moi lieutenant,"* or *"moi capitaine."*[160] After 1946, insignia tended only to be displayed on formal occasions, not in the field. Neatness of uniform also declined in military significance, but not crisp deportment or personal cleanliness.

As in every army, the National Guard faced problems of soldiers deserting or going absent without leave (AWOL). Desertion was widespread in south and south-central Vietnam as units reeled under sustained French attack, yet seems to have declined after February 1946. Above the sixteenth parallel, prospective deserters realized that local administrative committees or the police would probably catch them, with harsh punishment to follow. On the other hand, first time AWOLs were often allowed simply to return to their unit promptly for summary "correction." Following the 6 March Preliminary Accord and opening of the Dalat conference, a wave of AWOLs and resignations hit the National Guard. Some young men, having volunteered to fight the aggressor, not to become professional soldiers, now wanted to return to their former occupations or resume studies. One man allegedly told Trần Huy Liệu, "I became a soldier to drink the enemy's blood," to which Liệu replied, "As long as the nation is not completely independent, you have plenty to do."[161] Other writers pointed to continuing French military operations south of the sixteenth parallel to convince soldiers not to leave the service.[162] Trần Độ repeatedly urged his comrades to stay in the ranks, and to rededicate themselves to obeying the Hồ Chí Minh government. "In life we serve as Independent citizens, in death we became Fighting Ghosts," Độ intoned.[163] After the 14 September modus vivendi there was another resignation scare, with some former students wanting to take on civilian economic challenges, and other troopers hoping to rejoin their families in time for the rice harvest. They were told that "to ask to resign is to sacrifice half-way, to drop drumsticks in midbeat, to fail to fulfill the historical responsibility conveyed to us . . ."[164] A Quảng Ngãi newspaper stated flatly that "resignations are out of the question." Given French violations of previous agreements, every soldier should "commit himself to harder training and heightened vigilance."[165]

Despite such concerns, by late 1946 the National Guard was a remarkably disciplined, socially coherent organization compared to the confusion of one year prior. A small minority possessing prior military experience had trained a majority brimming with naïve enthusiasm. Fearless adventurers combined with diligent, patient problem-solvers to create an institution greater than the sum of its parts.[166] However, most units had yet to experience combat. A few officers who had held up well under the French hammer blows at Nha Trang and Khánh Hòa were brought north for extended debriefings. In a May interview in Hanoi, Nam Long, the magnetic detachment commander, evoked the bitter contest in January for Route 21 between Ban Mê Thuột and Ninh Hòa. When asked about the morale of his men, Nam Long asserted that "as long as I am alive, the spirit of my soldiers remains high; they believe in me, based on prior accomplishments."[167]

Such personalization of command did not endear Nam Long to higher echelons, and perhaps explains why he was never given charge of a division.

Unfortunately we lack information on the social composition of National Guard units, with the exception of the 1st Battalion Hanoi Region, discussed above, and one unnamed regiment based in Quảng Ngãi in August 1946. This regiment had a complement of 898 persons, of which 568 (63 percent) were identified as peasants or agricultural laborers, 237 (26.5 percent) as workers, and 93 (10.5 percent) as members of the bourgeoisie or petit bourgeoisie. Among that third category were thirty-four school pupils *(học sinh)*, plus an unquantified assortment of merchants, shopkeepers, and "industrialists" *(kỹ nghệ gia)*. Neither landlords nor former colonial government employees were mentioned. Sixteen women served in supply, cooking, medical, and sewing capacities, "because women are not allowed to be soldiers."[168] These numbers suggest a regiment put together from decimated units, perhaps some early Quảng Ngãi rural contingents, some Nam Tiến platoons, and some volunteers from coastal towns like Tuy Hòa, Quy Nhơn, and Đà Nẵng. With battle attrition, illness, and perhaps desertions, the proportion of rural enlistees had already increased substantially compared to late 1945.

Political officers were supposed to play a vital role in transforming a disparate bunch of young men into a coherent, motivated military unit. However, as noted previously in regard to early Nam Tiến detachments, most political officers had no idea what they were supposed to do beyond give patriotic pep talks and listen to the grumblings of individual soldiers.[169] Political officers were to promote "self-aware discipline," whereby each member of a unit was free to express his opinion at the appropriate time, but also ensure that collective understanding of the "just cause" *(chính nghĩa)* guaranteed that "when the order comes to attack, you attack."[170] According to Hoàng Minh Thảo, unlike the German or Japanese armies, which relied on harsh punishments to maintain discipline, the Vietnamese army, born of revolution and patriotic commitment, could depend on voluntary readiness to unite to fight the enemy. If a soldier was ill-disciplined, "it hurt not only him but also the group and the nation." A wider failure of discipline, Thảo concluded forebodingly, could "cause the organization to disintegrate, ruin the Revolution, and bring about our [collective] death."[171]

Intellectuals like Hoàng Minh Thảo, who had read about the October 1917 Revolution, pointed to the Russian Red Army's urgent use of political officers to heighten consciousness, sustain morale, and ferret out ex-Czarist traitors. Without saying so, Thảo and other ICP activists wanted all political officers to be Communist Party members, even if this meant assigning young men without prior vetting or indoctrination. However, most aspiring youths with a bit of education wanted to be commanders or, failing that, to obtain a staff assignment.

Throughout 1946 political officers received low marks in the press. One writer criticized them for organizing events at the wrong time (for example when the commander had assigned the men to dig bunkers), trying to alter punishments meted out by the commander, talking endlessly, arranging amusements like a scoutmaster, and "hoping to train everyone else to be a political officer." According to another writer, some political officers aimed to maintain their prestige by keeping distant from the troops, while others were too familiar, lax in discipline, and even spoke ill of the commander. Too many political officers lectured mechanically from notebooks and didn't even bother to adjust their language to the local accent.[172] There was general agreement that the political officer's role should complement, not overlap with or contradict the commander's role, yet published assessments made it clear that this balance had yet to be achieved. By the end of 1946, most battalion and company political officers probably were ICP members, although they were often only recently admitted and without ideological instruction.

THE MILITIA: DOUBLE-EDGED SWORD

In early September 1945, there were thousands of groups in Vietnam calling themselves "militia" *(tự vệ)* or similar titles. These groups ranged from eager villagers drilling with spears, to excited youths who had acquired firearms when taking power at district or provincial levels, to previously existing clandestine organizations now armed and expecting to play key political roles in the cities. In Saigon, many militia groups joined the four military "divisions," then fell back on their own resources or disintegrated entirely under French attack. In the north and center, as we have seen, several score local groups headed south to fight the French. Among the vast majority of militia groups that remained behind, some were accepted on a unit basis into the National Guard, although the General Staff 's preference was to induct individuals and place them under separately selected platoon leaders and company commanders. At province and district levels, many militia groups liked to call themselves part of the Liberation Army or National Guard, yet were not recognized as such by the Defense Ministry or General Staff. In Hanoi, a City Militia Command bureau was established as an umbrella for the dozen or more militia groups in the capital, but the fact that its office was open only one hour per day suggests not much was being accomplished.[173] Just outside Hanoi, a plan was devised to rename more than twenty militia groups as companies *(đại đội)* and place them under a single "Suburban Militia" command, with the potential to expand to one hundred companies.[174]

Militia groups in late 1945 not only were preparing to fight foreign invaders but also were intimately involved in local revolutionary upheavals and ongoing struggles for power. The central government expected province committees to be aware of this turmoil and take action where necessary. However, aggrieved parties had the right to petition the president or regional committees for redress, so a small portion of the conflicts or altercations involving militia groups show up in the central files. Thus, the national salvation militia of one village in Hà Đông province complained bitterly when village authorities sent one hundred men to seize all militia weapons, pull down its flag, and force it to disband. According to the militia's petition, the village committee was engaged in shady land transactions, had compelled every citizen to pay a monthly tax of two *hào* (o$2oBIC), and had arbitrarily banned demonstrations.[175] In another Hà Đông village, militia petitioners protested prefecture orders to arrest village committee members.[176] A batch of petitions from Ninh Bình province accused a district propaganda commissioner of using armed militiamen to repress citizens and extort money.[177] About the same time, a self-styled "military police" *(cảnh binh)* unit in Ninh Bình was ordered to stop using the National Guard arm patch.[178] Elsewhere citizens were encouraged to report anyone wearing military uniform or insignia but unable to present a valid ID. On numerous occasions *Việt Nam,* principal paper of the Vietnam Nationalist Party, accused local militia groups of aping the traditional goon squads maintained by mandarins or village head men—the only difference being that they saluted rather than kowtowed to their boss.[179]

During 1946, provincial authorities increasingly took responsibility for incorporating selected militia groups into province-supported regiments which aspired to "regular army" *(quân chủ lực)* recognition by Hanoi. However, this still left several thousand militia groups connected to a wide variety of other organizations, whether local administrative committees, Việt Minh associations, the Vietnam Nationalist Party (until it was suppressed), or religious leaders (Catholics in the north and center, Hòa Hảo and Cao Đài in the south). With the arrival of French forces in Haiphong and Hanoi in March, and especially their spread to other locations from April through June, the behavior of militia groups took on new significance for the DRV government. If militia sniped at French guards, abducted soldiers, or ambushed convoys, the strategy of "compromise in order to advance" could be jeopardized. Some such incidents did indeed occur, and were duly used by the French to question the DRV's capacity to maintain law and order.[180] DRV officials and military commanders managed gradually to convince more militia groups that they could better restrict French actions by serving as guards, police auxiliaries, intelligence agents, porters, and builders of defense works.

The French learned the term *tự vệ* (militia) quickly, used it in their reports, and monitored militia activities wherever possible. In May, for example, the Sûreté noted that there were two thousand militia members preparing defense works in Haiphong in case of collapse of the Preliminary Accord, while militia members in Hanoi assisted police in restricting circulation of certain types of

piastre currency. The next month, after French officials protested violent altercations with militia groups in Hanoi, the Vietnamese police raided buildings and
detained militia suspects, but then apparently released them several days later.[181]
Cứu Quốc, the principal Việt Minh paper, denounced a "few" militia for "falling
into the trap of reactionaries and threatening the French," but it denied rumors
that the DRV government intended to disband a major militia group inside the
capital.[182] When Vietnamese authorities did move to disband certain militia
groups, they sometimes got bogged down in voluminous exchanges of paperwork
between administrative echelons.[183] When a militia group confiscated files from
the railroad office in Việt Trì town, including dossiers needed for repair of bridges,
the issue had still not been resolved four months later.[184] The Interior Ministry issued new regulations in June designed to restrict militia patrolling and prevent
militias from harassing ordinary citizens. The DRV government also discussed
putting all militias under Central Military Commission authority, inserting
National Guard cadres into militias, and intensifying military training.[185] In September, newspapers published an order from Võ Nguyên Giáp requiring the National Guard to assist militia units to strengthen discipline and improve their
technical skills—in the spirit of "army-citizen unanimity" (quân-dân nhất trí).[186]
In practice, however, such efforts were left to civilian provincial committees to
coordinate. Trần Huy Liệu, while acknowledging that the National Guard was
gradually "regularizing" (chính qui hóa) itself, clearly wanted more attention devoted to local militias, which he insisted were proving their value in Nam Bộ just
as they had in the Soviet Union and China during World War II.[187]

Some local militia groups dared to harass agents of higher Vietnamese authority, especially tax collectors. By September 1946, the Northern Region Tax
Department had forwarded enough complaints to the Northern Region Committee to compel the latter to issue a warning to all province committees. "Some
local militia units have shown themselves lacking in a spirit of discipline, too
enamored of personal interests," the message intoned. When tax officers showed
up, the militia were to "maintain law and order, join in constructing the nation,
and place the interests of the Fatherland above all else."[188] A serious incident occurred in Nam Định in October, when armed tax agents intercepted four boats
loading salt for illegal export, then moved to impound a row of salt-laden oxcarts
on the shore as well. The agents were surrounded by militia members from the
adjacent village, subjected to taunts and threats by a growing crowd, tied up, and
eventually allowed to flee the area. The Tax Department now warned the government that soon it would be impossible to collect salt at all. Despite the director's
urgent, aggrieved tone, the Northern Region Committee merely instructed all
provinces to remind militia groups of its previous message.[189] Yet this was the
time when the government was trying to collect and transport salt to upland
warehouses ahead of the prospect of full-scale hostilities with the French.

From June 1946, the Northern Region Committee began to form separate civilian guard units *(đội cảnh vệ)* to take routine security tasks off the hands of the National Guard. The committee expected twelve million piastres from the defense budget for this purpose, with province committees again supposed to make up the difference. Probably the government aimed to absorb existing militia groups into these new guard units. Four months later the number of civilian guards had grown to five thousand, which the Northern Committee chairman believed to be quite inadequate, particularly in upland provinces and places where "bandits" *(thổ phỉ)* were still active.[190] In November, the committee began to form a special five-hundred-man civilian guard unit for Hanoi, with its own camp and training schedule.[191] Provincial guard units were also used to move groups of prisoners. Province committees sought permission to buy weapons from Defense Ministry arsenals to outfit their guard units. The Thái Bình province guard arranged with an arms facility to buy rifles, pistols, machine guns, and grenades, suggesting they had more than routine security duties in mind. As of 13 December, however, permission had still not been received from the Defense Ministry.[192]

SOUTH-CENTRAL VIETNAM

Following collapse of the Nha Trang front at the end of January 1946, those Vietnamese combatants who had managed to evade French encirclement and retreat northward to Phú Yên were badly in need of encouragement and reorganization. Nguyễn Sơn gathered together one thousand survivors to revive morale, consolidate units, and issue new orders. Nationwide, no one possessed more war experience than Nguyễn Sơn, accumulated during fifteen years in China with various CCP units. Shortly after the meeting, Nguyễn Sơn summoned Nam Long, the most charismatic leader to emerge during five months of fighting and retreating, to share his vision of the immediate future. After first making sure that Nam Long consumed three bowls of phở, Nguyễn Sơn opined that current negotiations between China, France, and the DRV would result in French forces going to the north, which would give central Vietnam precious time to build its military capabilities.[193] Nam Long was given command of a reconstituted detachment, which immediately received new uniforms to replace tattered shirts and shorts. Then it marched proudly through Sông Cầu town and took part in a soccer match against the local team.[194]

Attempts by survivors of the debacle in south-central Vietnam to draw lessons occasionally spilled over to the press. One well-informed writer criticized the practice of forming a defense line, losing it, then forming another, without joining with the populace to strike behind enemy lines and cut enemy communications. The public had been willing to help with food and labor, yet still regarded resistance as a job for the regular army. The writer pointed out that soldiers wearing uniforms had a hard time hiding amidst the people. Four months of brave fighting and retreating had exposed leadership deficiencies, which were often connected to the fact that "each unit has been recruited and trained separately, each province and region has a different approach." This problem became acute as units were consolidated, and higher-level commanders realized they knew little about most of the men under them.[195] This writer, and others, did not call for a shift to guerrilla warfare, but rather much closer interaction between the regular army and the people. How to achieve this remained a matter of debate.

In April, Nguyễn Sơn declared establishment of three brigades, each containing three or four regiments. While the late March government decree on military structure had listed brigades, Nguyễn Sơn was the only regional commander who tried to build them in 1946. We don't know the reasoning behind his decision, but it soon proved too ambitious. One of Nguyễn Sơn's brigades, the 27th, responsible for the area from Tuy Hòa town all the way south to Bình Thuận, probably never took shape at all. There, French forces retained the tactical initiative, scattering DRV detachments, and capturing a number of local leaders.[196] The other two brigades, one based in Quảng Nam and Quảng Ngãi and the other in Bình Định, appear to have possessed only skeleton headquarters staff, without radio communications and with only a handful of supporting personnel (logistics, engineering, medical).[197] It may be that some of the Japanese officers who had deserted to the Vietnamese side and clustered in Quảng Ngãi worked hardest to implement Nguyễn Sơn's brigade structure. A traincar-load of rifles and ammunition arrived from Hanoi in May, but was earmarked for further transport by boat to Nam Bộ.[198]

The Bình Định 23rd Brigade, with four thousand men but only fifteen hundred rifles, had its better units operating in the central highlands. In anticipation of another French offensive, trenches were dug around Pleiku and Kontum, and Route 14 was severed in places. However, the minority peoples of the region were slow to join in road destruction efforts, and the terrain often made it possible for vehicles to go off road. Vietnamese defenders still lacked the capacity to destroy moving armored vehicles. On 21 June, French forces struck northward from Ban Mê Thuột, and within days took both Pleiku and Kontum. Over objections from some of his staff, Nguyễn Sơn ordered a general withdrawal from the highlands to concentrate on defense of An Khê pass, a point of strategic significance since the eighteenth century. Subsequent fighting around An Khê was intense, with several Vietnamese units holding fixed positions to the death rather than retreat. Whatever Nguyễn Sơn's experience in China, he had not taught his troops how to mount a mobile defense or to employ reserves in counterattack. After six days of combat, the French captured An Khê on 2 July. Meanwhile, another French force moved northward from Nha Trang to seize Cả pass and advance into Tuy Hòa town. Again some Vietnamese units bypassed by the French chose not to retreat northward, instead joining with local militia and resistance committees to mount guerrilla actions in later months and years. Already in November 1946, a report from Khánh Hòa province claimed success in eliminating traitors, spreading leaflets, hoisting the DRV flag, and conducting unspecified guerrilla and "terror" *(khủng bố)* operations.[199]

After taking An Khê, the French found it impossible to advance the remaining seventy kilometers to Qui Nhơn, due to thousands of Bình Khê district residents participating in wholesale destruction of the road, and helping to build a series of trenches and redoubts in depth. Six months later, on 21 December, French forces tried to resume their advance, backed up by 155 mm howitzers firing from An Khê. Although civilian casualties were heavy, Vietnamese forces had learned how to retreat tactically and then counterattack, as well as to dispatch units behind An Khê to ambush supply trucks along Route 19.[200] Repeated French efforts to seize Qui Nhơn did not bear fruit until March 1954, ironically just at the moment that Vietnamese forces began to draw the noose around Điện Biên Phủ far to the north.

The 31st Brigade had two regiments in Quảng Ngãi to guard against possible French amphibious landings or parachute drops, and two regiments in Quảng Nam to watch the French "relief" contingent in Đà Nẵng. Quảng Ngãi remained the revolutionary heartland of central Vietnam, dispatching units to the south, west, and north; training cadres; repairing firearms; manufacturing grenades and mines; and providing a rear headquarters for the Southern Resistance Committee. Nguyễn Sơn now possessed enough radios to sustain contact with regiments and battalions, but many communications personnel preferred to rely on colonial-era telegraph and telephone lines.[201] As many as two hundred Japanese deserters gravitated to Quảng Ngãi, where Nguyễn Sơn put them to work as instructors, members of his staff, weapons technicians, engineers, mechanics, radio operators, and medics.[202]

Nguyễn Sơn's most lasting contribution to the anti-French resistance was his establishment in June 1946 of the Quảng Ngãi Ground Forces Secondary Academy, which immediately enrolled four hundred students, and continued to function long after his departure in November.[203] About half the trainees had already fought in the south, while the other half were newly recruited high school students or young civil servants. Trainees were divided into four companies, each commanded by a Japanese instructor. The course was designed to produce qualified small-unit leaders after one year, with tactical lessons on map reading, reconnaissance, camouflage, use of terrain, communications-liaison, and night assaults. Nguyễn Sơn lectured regularly at the Academy, focusing on logistics, training techniques, and command. At the end of each day's instruction, companies

FIGURE 11. Refilling cartridges. Photo courtesy of Christophe Dutrône.

marched back to base singing revolutionary songs. As it became apparent in November that the course would have to be cut short, companies were sent out in four directions to test what they had learned, a demonstration which included attacks on mock enemy forts—and at least one real assault against an enemy position.[204] Following graduation ceremonies, students received their unit assignments and said their farewells, some going as far south as the Mekong delta, others taking the train north to Đà Nẵng, Vinh, or Hanoi. One graduate, suddenly recalling his Larousse dictionary with its cover image of a young woman blowing on a dry flower and uttering the words *"Je sème à tout vent"* (I scatter seed far and wide), wondered if he would ever meet any of his schoolmates again.[205]

The curriculum of the Quảng Ngãi Academy seems to have been resolutely conventional in character, even though Nguyễn Sơn had firsthand exposure to CCP guerrilla war doctrine, and would go on later to translate some of Mao Zedong's treatises into Vietnamese. Perhaps he believed the DRV could build a modern national army fast enough to prevent French reconquest, despite early reversals and his own failure to hold An Khê in late June 1946. If so, he was badly mistaken. Or Nguyễn Sơn may have assumed that squad- and platoon-level tactics, properly mastered, would serve equally well in either conventional or guerrilla combat. However, to fill out the three-brigade structure that Nguyễn Sơn had ordered would have required many of the first four hundred Academy graduates to command companies, serve on battalion or regimental staffs, or take responsibility for forming specialized units (logistics, heavy weapons, engineering, communications, counterintelligence). It would be another three years before DRV armed forces reached this level of organization. Nguyễn Sơn may simply have felt that constructing a conventional military hierarchy was less difficult than teaching everyone to survive and prevail amidst the enemy without regular orders or provisioning. Ultimately guerrilla warfare could not be taught; it had to be learned through harsh experience.

Meanwhile, some Japanese instructors aimed to convince their Vietnamese students that spirit could overcome matter, that suicide units could defeat French armor, artillery, and aircraft.[206] This idea undoubtedly appealed to zealous young patriots in 1946. At the battle of An Khê, for example, some Vietnamese defenders fired on the advancing enemy to their penultimate cartridge, then directed the last bullet at themselves. A few wounded combatants unable to be evacuated used their last grenade to kill themselves, hoping to catch several unwary enemy soldiers as well.[207] Such actions were glorified by political officers and featured in newspaper accounts. Việt Minh propaganda asserted that idealistic sacrifice for the just cause would vanquish the evil imperialists. Yet Quảng Ngãi Academy students knew that Japan had lost its war, whatever its spiritual commitment. The Japanese mystification of warrior death did not have a Vietnamese counterpart. Commanders sometimes asked for volunteers on what amounted to suicide missions, and many youths stepped forward, but if they could accomplish the job and still come back alive it was cause for celebration.

Following provisions in the 6 March 1946 Preliminary Accord, one thousand French soldiers arrived in Đà Nẵng to share "relief" duties with the specially formed 96th Vietnamese Regiment. Two battalions were fitted out with full uniforms and leather shoes, much to the delight of Đà Nẵng townsfolk, "proud to see their army on a par with the French, fulfilling international responsibilities as recognized by Allied forces."[208] Tall, French-speaking students were located and made up into teams that patrolled for three hours each evening with their French counterparts. Each Sunday, the two Vietnamese battalion commanders, each wearing the temporary rank of major, met French officers at the riverside Morin hotel (now the Bạch Đằng hotel), where they exchanged pleasantries and sized each other up. More substantive discussions were handled by Mixed Commission officers. Each side hosted the other at banquets on several occasions, with the Vietnamese receiving a subvention of three thousand packs of MIC cigarettes per month from the Đà Nẵng Administrative Committee to sell on the market in order to cover socializing costs. Ordinary soldiers were under instructions not to accept Philip Morris cigarettes from their French counterparts. On Bastille Day 1946, soldiers politely refused French entreaties to share sweets and champagne. However, the Vietnamese command did agree to contribute one company to the Bastille Day parade, after practicing marching beforehand, and apparently making a good impression on viewers.[209]

The ICP seems to have exercised little influence over Đà Nẵng regiment operations. Although the regimental political officer was a party member, as late as July 1946 he had only managed to locate four other members in subordinate units. It was the ICP's Đà Nẵng city committee which took the initiative to form these men into a cell and start looking for candidate members in the regiment. Most company and platoon political officers still were not ICP members. In following months, enough candidate members were recruited to form party cells within each of the three battalions and some companies, but there was no time before the outbreak of hostilities in late December to construct a parallel party hierarchy, much less try to replace nonparty individuals in positions of authority.[210]

By November 1946, the Đà Nẵng regiment was an amalgam of men from many different origins and post-August 1945 experiences. A number of Japanese manned heavy machine guns. Most remarkably, some Vietnamese *tirailleurs* from the metropolitan French Army, who had been allowed to demobilize and return to Vietnam by October, proceeded to join the Đà Nẵng regiment.[211] Nguyễn Bá Phát, regimental commander from late November, had previously served six years in the French Navy, mostly as a kitchen boy, but also acquiring knowledge of gunnery and explosives.[212] On 5 December, the French landed a Foreign Legion battalion at Đà Nẵng without consulting the DRV, and the Đà Nẵng regiment retaliated by cutting the road to Huế.[213]

In late November, the DRV government decided to recall Nguyễn Sơn to Hanoi, to cancel his three-brigade structure, and to downgrade the Southern Resistance Committee.[214] Phạm Văn Đồng was designated central government representative for south-central Vietnam, based in Quảng Ngãi (his province of origin), but the region itself was divided into two zones: War Zone 5 (Quảng Nam south to Bình Định), and War Zone 6 (Phú Yên down to Bình Thuận).[215] I have yet to find any published explanation for these dramatic changes. Indirect evidence suggests that Nguyễn Sơn had built up his command and made operational decisions with little reference to Hanoi, thus raising the ire of some within the central leadership. Replacing him with Phạm Văn Đồng, probably Hồ Chí Minh's closest lieutenant, would help to ensure that the ongoing struggle in south-central Vietnam served national strategic interests. On the other hand, Hồ may have summoned his most experienced officer back to the capital to help prepare a nationwide battle plan, a need made especially urgent by the outbreak of bitter fighting at Haiphong starting on 20 November. There was no chance of Nguyễn Sơn being given the top military position, as several weeks earlier the National Assembly had approved Võ Nguyên Giáp to head the combined Defense Ministry and General Command.[216] However, Nguyễn Sơn could have been offered a northern command position or Hoàng Văn Thái's job as chief of the General Staff. Instead Hồ put Sơn in charge of the Military Training Bureau, telling him to reorient officer training immediately towards guerrilla warfare and to initiate a one-month crash course at the Sơn Tây academy. Sơn departed for Sơn Tây on 3 December, thus taking no part in the Hanoi battle planning and combat of following weeks.[217]

NORTH-CENTRAL VIETNAM

While south-central Vietnam endured repeated confrontations with French forces advancing up the coast and through the central highlands, north-central Vietnam escaped attack thanks to Chinese prohibitions on French entry. Nonetheless, no one could assume that such tranquility would persist. As we have seen, north-central provinces contributed a number of armed groups to the Nam Tiến movement in late 1945. Appreciating the vulnerability of their territory to attack from the sea, province revolutionary committees mobilized thousands of people to dig rudimentary fortifications at key coastal locations.

However, it was mostly towards the west that north-central revolutionaries looked for military action. Aware that the Japanese after March 1945 had not managed to eliminate all French resistance in Laos, poorly armed Vietnamese groups probed westward along Routes 7, 8, and 9. In September, a Nghệ An group attacked a French post in Xieng Khoang province, while a combined Nghệ An–Hà Tĩnh group assaulted the post at Napé.[218] The provisional DRV government now gave north-central provinces principal responsibility for linking up with anticolonial groups along both sides of the Mekong River in Laos and northeastern Thailand. So long as the Chinese occupation command blocked the French Army from returning in force to Laos north of the sixteenth parallel, anticolonial groups retained the upper hand. Thừa Thiên province sent four platoons to Laos in late 1945.[219] Assuming other provinces contributed similar numbers, it is possible that six hundred to seven hundred north-central fighters joined with overseas Vietnamese and some Lao to contest French return to Laos.

Soon after the 28 February 1946 Sino-French agreement was signed in Chongqing, French Army units supported by Spitfires attacked Việt Minh and Lao Issara positions in Savannakhet, then overran Thakhet one week later. Several hundred defenders were killed, with survivors joining thousands of Vietnamese and Lao civilians in fleeing across the Mekong River to Thailand.[220] Newspapers in Vietnam provided highly colored accounts of operations, but they could not hide the fact that anti-French forces had been pushed out of the Mekong plain.[221] Back in Vietnam, parent military units publicly commemorated comrades who had fallen in battle in Laos.[222] Chiến Sĩ (Fighter) newspaper accorded a two-column, black-bordered obituary to Lương Phan Ngọc, former student and company commander, who had fought courageously on the Laos front, returned home to recover from malaria, but then died in hospital.[223] Between June and September, the French occupied a number of key upland positions in Laos, yet found it impossible to eliminate small forest-based guerrilla units composed of Vietnamese and their local allies.[224]

In Vietnam, the relative quiet in north-central provinces provided a good opportunity to organize military training courses. In mid-November 1945, the Huế

Political-Military School graduated its first class of 160 prospective political offi-cers and squad leaders. The second class followed its two weeks of course work with a one-week march and operational exercise around Lăng Cô, adjacent to Hải Vân pass. *Chiến Sĩ* printed a wealth of training material, ranging from the most basic techniques to abstruse strategic concepts. Readers were told the exact thickness of materials required to protect themselves from a rifle bullet fired from fifty meters away (ranging from one meter of clay soil to 1.2 centimeters of steel plate). Another article described the sounds of different kinds of explosions. There were technical details on different firearms, ammunition, and grenades; a serialized explanation of scores of military terms; and an essay canvassing tech-niques for advancing under enemy fire.[225] A column titled "Listen and Watch" featured firsthand combat experiences from soldiers to the south or in Laos. A number of Chinese texts were translated and serialized, including a long inter-view with General Zhu De, a discourse by Zhou Enlai on political work while fighting, a guerrilla war tactical manual, and extensive excerpts from Sun-tzu's classic *The Art of War*. Most surprisingly, sections from three English-language books were translated and serialized, dealing with the Russian Army, Wingate's Raiders in Burma, and the Normandy landings.[226]

On 29 March 1946, the French dispatched an armored column from Laos across the hills to Huế, roaring into the city much to the shock of the public.[227] Vietnamese forces along the route held their fire, possibly on orders from above, although provisions for stationing 950 French "relief" soldiers in Huế (in accor-dance with the 6 March Preliminary Accord) had yet to be finalized in Hanoi. For the next eight months, the two sides coexisted uneasily in Huế, with the Trần Cao Vân Regiment, commanded by Hà Văn Lâu, providing "relief" units in much the same way as the 96th Regiment was in Đà Nẵng. In July, Nguyễn Chí Thanh convened a meeting of ICP and Việt Minh representatives from through-out Thừa Thiên province to step up preparations for war. Soon emplacements were being dug at street intersections and alongside waterways.[228] As of August, Zone 4, extending from Thừa Thiên north to Thanh Hóa, possessed five regi-ments and one battalion, all still province-based.[229]

Huế served as medical center to receive seriously wounded soldiers from both the Laos and south-central fronts. In February 1946, more than three hundred military patients were being treated in Huế. Two months later, additional build-ings had been requisitioned and the call went out for more hospital volunteers. Civilian Việt Minh delegations visited the wounded routinely, trying to enhance morale with talk of battlefield successes. Stacks of books and periodicals were donated for patients to read. However, some war-injured soldiers could be seen begging on the streets of Huế. One amputee offered himself as a human bomb against the enemy. The authorities politely declined, urging him instead to help raise public donations for the patriotic cause.[230] In May, an Association to Assist

Disabled Soldiers was formed with royal family sponsorship and talk of setting up branches elsewhere.[231]

SOUTHERN VIETNAM

In early March 1946, when the best French combat units departed Cochinchina for Haiphong, a window of opportunity presented itself to leaders of anti-French armed groups in southern Vietnam who had undergone six months of demoralizing reversals. The last British combat units had gone in late January, and Japanese units, awaiting Allied ships to take them home, no longer took part in military operations. Although the failure of Hồ Chí Minh to gain French recognition of Nam Bộ as an integral part of Vietnam in the 6 March Preliminary Accord angered many southerners, the French promise of a future referendum highlighted the need for DRV adherents to gain influence over as many people as possible in coming months. The French in March still possessed thirty thousand soldiers on the ground in Cochinchina and southern Annam. They also had succeeded in recruiting thousands of Vietnamese "partisans" to accompany French units on patrol, share guard duties, and collect intelligence.[232] French commanders and Sûreté officers made contact with leaders of independence groups to propose ceasefire terms that amounted to either capitulation or turning their weapons against DRV followers. As we shall see in chapter 4, a French colonel even met with representatives of Nguyễn Bình, commander of War Zone 7, but discussions quickly foundered. The French government of the day had no intention of recognizing any DRV legitimacy or role below the sixteenth parallel, which became obvious as Admiral d'Argenlieu moved to establish a separate state of Cochinchina and then a "Möi" territory in the central highlands.

Prominent Vietnamese participants in d'Argenlieu's separatist scheme quickly became targets for assassination, starting with Trần Tấn Phát, member of the Cochinchinese Council, shot in front of his house on 29 March.[233] Nguyễn Bình had earlier taken personal responsibility for developing a network of urban commando teams, even slipping into Saigon-Cholon several times himself to assess conditions firsthand. There were plenty of commando volunteers, especially among workers and teenage students. Nguyễn Bình approved team leaders and liaison agents, selected targets, debriefed participants, and rewarded heroes (or their families).[234] The most spectacular commando feat was blowing up the large French ammunition dump located in downtown Saigon on 8 April, a mission which also destroyed or damaged a number of adjacent headquarters buildings and the Radio Saigon transmission tower.[235] In August, commandos succeeded in torching five hundred pallets of crepe rubber awaiting export—a practical warning to metropolitan interests considering reinvestment in Indochina.[236] Urban commandos tied down French police and intelligence specialists who would have been useful elsewhere, and the threat of assassination caused Vietnamese former colonial officials, professionals, and intellectuals to think twice before accepting French offers to collaborate. The persona of Nguyễn Bình took on almost mythical proportions in the minds of friends and foes alike. Psychologically, the effects of urban struggle were more visible and readily communicated than confrontations in the villages and forests.

Nonetheless, the conflict in the Nam Bộ countryside was more important militarily than commando and anticommando operations in Saigon-Cholon. Once it became obvious that Admiral d'Argenlieu demanded obedience to his particular vision of a Cochinchinese state, and that the French Army required all Vietnamese armed groups to submit or be treated as "bandits," anticolonial leaders scattered around the Mekong delta tried once again to cooperate with each other. At Nguyễn Bình's instigation, a new Unified National Front (Mặt Trận Quốc Gia Liên Hiệp) was formed on 10 April. No one expected this uneasy alliance of Việt Minh, Bình Xuyên, Cao Đài, Hòa Hảo, and Catholic adherents to result in a military counteroffensive, yet there was a renewed sense of purpose that translated into more killings of Vietnamese notables who had allied with the French, sniping at enemy posts, mining of roads, and occasional ambushes of French patrols.[237] One communist source describes with remarkable frankness how armed units dealt with villages where the majority of inhabitants had followed the enemy: "We blocked all exits so that no one could flee to inform the French, reprimanded the reactionaries, and then compelled everyone in the village—old and young, male and female—to join a national salvation association, listen to our explanation of current affairs, and participate in training sessions. After that, we restructured the village administration and eliminated the worst elements."[238] Meanwhile, Nguyễn Bình managed to sustain a modest "liberated zone" in Thủ Dầu Một province, while Võ Văn Đức did likewise in the isolated U Minh forest (Cà Mau). Both maintained contact with supporters and DRV representatives in Thailand. Several detachments of resident Vietnamese from Cambodia and Thailand made their way east to the lower Mekong delta, and were celebrated as "overseas troops."[239]

By August 1946, French reports on the pacification of rural Cochinchina were distinctly less optimistic than they had been four months prior, pointing to rebel bands that managed to reconstitute themselves rapidly after each tactical setback, and Việt Minh initiatives that paralyzed the French-installed administration. Rather than demanding absolute obedience, some Việt Minh leaders had now adopted the more flexible policy of obtaining the "semi-complicity of the population," probably a reference to the practice of allowing village notables to declare allegiance to France publicly while covertly assisting the anti-French effort.[240] General Leclerc was disturbed at partisans on the French side conducting "frequent acts of pillage." General Valluy spoke of young French replacement soldiers who committed "certain blunders and extortions" that Việt Minh propagandists seized upon quickly. Valluy stressed the need in Cochinchina to cut off enemy access to outside cadres, weapons, and ammunition. He also urged *"jaunissement"* of French forces and creation of a Cochinchinese Republican Guard—two policies that would be taken up in following years.[241]

Despite Nam Bộ being placed in political limbo by the 6 March 1946 Preliminary Accord, the DRV government never ceased to affirm that the south was an integral, nonnegotiable part of Vietnam, a position punctuated by numerous mass meetings, demonstrations, radio broadcasts, and newspaper articles. Not until late September, however, did the government publicly acknowledge the existence of southern National Guard units operating under orders from Hanoi. Võ Nguyên Giáp published a "daily order" to all "southern fighters worthy of the Vietnam Fatherland" to tighten their ranks, defend the rights of the people, and obey orders from above—thus "assuring territorial unity and protecting the government."[242] Beyond such exhortations, however, communications between Giáp and Nguyễn Bình remained very tenuous (and subject to French decryption). No reliable chain of command extended yet to the majority of armed independence groups operating in the southern countryside. In cases where larger-scale attacks were contemplated, it was most typical for several group leaders to reach agreement and then perhaps find additional participants to join them in launching an assault numbering three hundred to five hundred men.[243]

STRATEGIC DELIBERATIONS

During the summer of 1946, as talks in France seemed to be going nowhere, the ICP Standing Bureau evaluated the DRV's overall strategic position and began contingency deliberations for full-scale war. At the end of July, Trường Chinh organized a Central Cadres Conference to discuss both military and political dimensions. The concluding conference resolution began by asserting grandly that the international balance of forces between the Soviet Union and the imperialists had shifted substantially in favor of the former, and that Indochina had become a cockpit for revolutionary confrontation. The French Army in northern Vietnam was said to be intent on improving its tactical position short of outright hostilities, for example by establishing a "Nùng Autonomous Region" along the border with China, and once again preparing a possible coup d'état in Hanoi. However, most of the conference resolution focused on Vietnam's perceived internal problems, notably poor ethnic minority relations, parlous government finances, sluggish expansion of the united front beyond the Việt Minh, petty leadership disputes (especially in central Vietnam), and lax discipline within the ICP. A long list of military deficiencies followed, perhaps simply copied from conference minutes of discussion: the DRV armed forces were not unified, they

lacked specialized units, their commanders lacked experience, there was insufficient political work among soldiers, no coherent military strategy existed, and
sabotage missions often failed. "Main force units" had been squandered in Saigon in October 1945, mobilization of minority peoples in the central highlands
had miscarried, the strategic initiative had been lost, too much faith was being
placed in the 6 March Preliminary Accord, and preparations to take the offensive
received little attention.[244] Despite this litany of military weaknesses, the overall
tone of the resolution exuded confidence that each problem could be overcome in
turn. Almost nothing was said about Franco-Vietnamese talks. The possibility
that sabotage operations or offensive preparations could in themselves speed up
the clock ticking towards war was not considered.

Strategic and tactical discussions were not only the prerogative of a few ICP
members meeting secretly, however. The press in 1946 was replete with articles
about the international context of Vietnam's independence struggle, the relative
merits of negotiating or fighting, and the best way to prepare for possible full-
scale war. On the latter topic, *Cứu Quốc* published an order from Võ Nguyên
Giáp to the National Guard to "advance on the road to regularization" while
simultaneously retaining the "qualities of a guerrilla army." To this end, he said,
the army would help militia units to improve their discipline and technique, and
would incorporate them in practice maneuvers.[245] A less complacent view emerged
from Quảng Ngãi, where an anonymous but well-informed author argued that
Vietnamese tactics had been wrong from the beginning, with overly large units
being smashed by the enemy, towns torched when they could have made good
defense positions against enemy armor, units responding much too slowly to
adversity, and operational communications sometimes breaking down completely.[246] In late October, Trần Huy Liệu complemented the army for being
larger, better equipped, and better trained than it had been, but then added that,
"Everyone knows we are in an extremely tight spot, with everything dependent
on our own resources and ingenuity." If full-scale war came, an outcome which
Liệu clearly believed was most likely, then "the entire people have to be prepared
for a long, difficult struggle."[247]

The concept of "protracted resistance" *(trường kỳ kháng chiến)* had come
from China to Vietnam in the late 1930s, although writers would soon point to a
Vietnamese precedent in the ultimately successful fifteenth-century struggle
against the Ming. Trần Huy Liệu in October 1945 predicted a protracted resistance
against the French, and reaffirmed that belief on numerous later occasions.[248] For
Liệu, protracted resistance was linked to reliance on guerrilla warfare, as demonstrated in Nam Bộ. Liệu's goal was to wear down the enemy to the point that it
would concede that losses outweighed any possible gains and withdraw—
however long this might take. That was not the opinion of Võ Nguyên Giáp, who
probably was more familiar than Liệu with the history of guerrilla failures as

well as occasional triumphs. On witnessing the collapse of position defenses at Nha Trang in February, Giáp was quick to encourage local resort to guerrilla tactics, but he was more intent on reconstituting viable battalion- and regiment-sized units from the demoralized soldiers who had fled north to Tuy Hòa. At no point did Giáp accept that the regular army be disaggregated to company- or platoon-sized units at the district or commune level, although he would have to make temporary concessions in that direction in 1947. Giáp wanted French commanders to taste defeat on the battlefield. There remained the question of how long it would take for protracted resistance to succeed. In March one writer predicted that "our generation will yet see victory."[249] No one said that it might take two or three generations.

From late August to early November 1946, Võ Nguyên Giáp and the new French commander for northern Indochina, General Louis Constant Morlière, appeared to share a desire to prevent local clashes from escalating into war.[250] However, the failure of the 14 September modus vivendi to address vital issues in dispute meant that both sides stepped up military preparations. In mid-October, an ICP All-Country Military Conference met outside Hanoi to discuss continuing issues of command, cadre selection, logistics, political work, and day-to-day altercations with the French Army. The conference resolution urged that the Defense Ministry and Central Military Commission be merged to form the Defense Ministry–General Command, a proposal duly passed by the National Assembly soon afterward. This simplified the central military structure and made contests for leadership less likely, yet it also meant that civilians could not be appointed as future ministers of defense. The ICP conference also favored a reduction in the total number of regular soldiers, while strengthening militia units. Reference was still made to "brigade" (đại đoàn) formations, but these were abandoned six weeks later. The Finance Ministry was pressed to simplify defense budget procedures, to allow the Defense Ministry to audit its own accounts, and to increase defense allocations in line with inflation.[251] The ICP clearly wanted the DRV government to be responsible for feeding regular National Guard units, yet the central administration already had great difficulty meeting costs of weapons, ammunition, clothing, and shoes. Food for the troops would remain largely a province obligation.

When the DRV National Assembly met in Hanoi in late October 1946, delegates had a sense that peace was problematic yet full-scale war not inevitable. On strategic questions, Hồ Chí Minh showed every intent of continuing peaceful negotiations with the French, while making it clear to the Assembly that Vietnam's independence and territorial integrity would never be bargained away. The constitution gave the National Assembly the authority to declare war by a two-thirds vote of members present; when the Assembly was unable to meet, that power was delegated to its Standing Committee together with the government.

The president was made commander in chief of the armed forces. In Hồ Chí Minh's new cabinet, Võ Nguyên Giáp was defense minister and Tạ Quang Bửu assistant minister.[252] With the exception of Hoàng Hữu Nam, assistant interior minister, none of the other twenty-one members of the new cabinet had been involved in developing DRV defense capacity. Merger of the defense ministry and general command, and placement of the General Staff directly underneath the new merged command, resolved some of the duplications and demarcation disputes that had troubled military expansion to date.[253] Giáp and Hoàng Văn Thái, chief of the General Staff, now forged an effective partnership that lasted for decades.

One year earlier, Võ Nguyên Giáp had emphasized to General Staff personnel the importance of thinking nationally while not trying to centralize operations prematurely. While this perhaps made a virtue of necessity, no one was content in October 1946 that the National Guard remained unified in name only, with most regimental commanders still dependent on provincial committees for provisioning and militia coordination. The General Staff had yet to secure reliable data on many local units. In hopes of promoting interprovincial cooperation, the central government reorganized war zones (chiến khu) throughout the country. It proved impossible to bring zone leaders together in Hanoi for discussion. Two experienced ICP troubleshooters were dispatched down the coast, Phạm Văn Đồng to coordinate War Zones 5 and 6 (south-central Vietnam), and Lê Duẩn to reorganize resistance in Nam Bộ.[254]

Hồ Chí Minh's confidential thoughts on DRV strategic options following his return from France on 20 October are difficult to ascertain. He undoubtedly was watching the volatile French political scene closely and hoping the 10 November general election would produce a better climate for further negotiations scheduled for January 1947. On 5 November, however, Hồ prepared tough personal notes which have come down to us with the title of "Urgent Work Now." The first section merely outlines the personnel required to carry out a variety of military, economic, political, and communications tasks, with particular attention to selecting good party members and young men and women who have demonstrated their potential in action. The second section deals entirely with "protracted resistance"—arguing why Vietnam will emerge victorious from what is certain to be a harsh, bitter conflict. Hồ expects that the enemy will fight ferociously even when near defeat, aware that his entire imperialist inheritance is at stake. The enemy will send troop reinforcements ("not more than 100,000"), aircraft, and tanks, proceeding to ravage and terrorize, hoping to spread fear among the people until they surrender. "But we must understand," he continued, "that's the extent of enemy power. We resolutely resist to get through that 'blitzkrieg' (chớp nhoáng), the enemy will run out of steam, and we will win. So, we must possess, and cause our people to possess, inner confidence and inner determination."

For Hồ it does not matter if the cities have to be evacuated, as the entire countryside will be held. Here he offers up Nam Bộ as example, where preparations admittedly had been inadequate, the terrain difficult, yet resistance had persisted for more than a year already. He concludes, "We have good terrain and more forces, we can certainly resist for some years *(mấy năm)*, until victory."[255] Hồ Chí Minh was overoptimistic about controlling the entire countryside, and he chose to ignore the likelihood that the French would recruit increasing numbers of Vietnamese to their ranks, yet his overall conceptualization proved valid. Notably, Hồ did not limit DRV resistance to guerrilla operations.

Shifting Supplies and Equipment to the Countryside

Despite the threat of a French coup d'état that had hovered over the DRV state since March 1946, it was not until October that serious efforts began to establish bases away from Hanoi, bases where central institutions could continue to function if required. How to do this was not immediately obvious, however. The National Guard still lacked a logistics branch capable of acquiring, shifting, and storing supplies. The Ministry of Communications and Public Works relied mostly on private trucks and boats, whose owners had other commitments and might not maintain confidentiality. It was decided to give two senior ICP cadres responsibility for base creation, partly because they knew the relevant terrain well, partly because a party operation might be kept secret from the French. Nguyễn Lương Bằng was assigned to move rice, salt, machinery, raw materials, and currency. Trần Đăng Ninh recruited people to prepare several "safe zones" *(an toàn khu)*. Already the village of Vạn Phúc, adjacent to Hà Đông town, provided a venue for leaders to meet away from direct French observation. Twenty-five kilometers to the southwest of Hanoi, a more ambitious safe zone began to form in November, eventually including communication links, storage facilities, accommodation huts, and defense works.[256] One key position was Chinê plantation, which possessed its own electric power and machine shop, and was owned by Đỗ Đình Thiện, a wealthy entrepreneur who supported the DRV cause.[257] Trần Đăng Ninh kept each work group isolated from the others and checked often for security breaches.[258] This Hà Đông–Sơn Tây safe zone had ready access to the heavily populated Red River delta provinces to the east, plus back routes south to Thanh Hóa and north to Phú Thọ and Tuyên Quang. If this position proved untenable, serious attention was given to moving the central government to Thanh Hóa, thus facilitating communication with distant Nam Bộ and south-central Vietnam—an idea not discarded until Hồ Chí Minh returned from a brief trip to Thanh Hóa in late February 1947.[259]

The second safe zone was located in Thái Nguyên–Tuyên Quang, from whence the small Liberation Army had emerged in late August 1945. This zone had the advantage of preexisting Việt Minh networks, which the regional commander,

Chu Văn Tấn, had continued to nurture after his brief stint as defense minister in Hanoi. On the other hand, the entire Việt Bắc area was furthest away from the rest of the country, and the possibility of Chinese Nationalist attack from the rear had to be considered. Once Thanh Hóa was rejected and the Hà Đông–Sơn Tây safe zone came under increasing French pressure, however, a government move north to Thái Nguyên–Tuyên Quang was inevitable.[260]

Movement of bulk supplies to these safe zones proved difficult. Bắc Bộ's November 1946 rice crop was good, and many local administrative committees entered the rice market aggressively, buying cheaply, stockpiling some of their purchases, allocating some to army units and state employees, and selling the remainder at higher prices to merchants carrying permits from elsewhere. Assuming that Nguyễn Lương Bằng's confidential agents were well endowed with Indochina piastres (BIC), they presumably purchased paddy at market rates and began to transport it by boat, truck, or oxcart to the two safe zones. President Hồ Chí Minh also optimistically instructed Bằng to move twenty thousand tons of salt from Nam Định warehouses to the hills, for use not only by the army and evacuees, but also as currency in dealings with upland minorities, notably when purchasing opium. The government ordered ten thousand tons of salt be shipped to Phú Thọ and Tuyên Quang provinces, yet as late as 12 December the Customs Bureau was still searching for boats. Transport up the Red River continued for some weeks after full-scale hostilities commenced, but it seems unlikely that more than five thousand tons of Nam Định salt reached its destination.[261]

The ICP sent instructions to factory workers to dismantle equipment and move it to a safe zone, but not much happened until the crisis exploded on 19 December. Because fighting began a month earlier in Haiphong, workers there did evacuate some machines, tools, and spare parts to the adjacent countryside, where material often sat for months before someone decided where it should go. Later it was claimed that the Vietnamese working class had moved a total of thirty-eight thousand tons of machinery and raw materials to "free areas" (vùng tự do) by the end of January 1947.[262] Much of this fell prey to the elements before a use could be found for it.

FIGHTING AT HAIPHONG AND LẠNG SƠN

On 20 November 1946, French security personnel took custody of a Chinese-owned junk unloading gasoline drums in Haiphong harbor, Vietnamese police attempted to reverse this action, shooting broke out, and Mixed Commission officers obtained a temporary ceasefire. Haiphong had been the scene of numerous such altercations earlier in the year, and each time a way had been found to defuse the situation. On this occasion, however, the French commander expanded the confrontation dramatically, dispatching armored cars to the city center and demanding that Vietnamese forces pull out of the Chinese quarter and dismantle all barricades. Shooting intensified until General Morlière intervened by telephone from Hanoi, yet French troops remained in their new positions. Vietnamese reinforcements moved into Haiphong. On 23 November, the French launched a full-scale attack, including rolling naval gunfire and artillery barrages. Although many civilians had fled Haiphong earlier, this massive shelling killed several thousand people, including hundreds of refugees in Kiến An town to the south, which the French also bombarded from the sea.[263]

Despite months of warning, the Vietnamese defense of Haiphong was poorly prepared and ineffective. Diplomatic objectives had ruled out digging extensive fortifications inside the city. National Guard units remained mostly in the suburbs. Militia groups erected barricades and took up positions in key buildings, but command and communication links across the city were fragile, and the on-again, off-again character of the armed encounter left everyone confused. Some militia squads did succeed in holding up the French advance for hours. A group of militiamen armed with two Sten guns, six rifles, and an ample supply of grenades became national heroes by holding the Haiphong Opera House for most of one day, yelling slogans and singing patriotic songs between bursts of fire. Retreating to the top floor for their last stand, eight men were killed, several escaped, and several were captured.[264] The French shelling on 23 November eliminated any chance of citywide resistance, but there were several desperate counterassaults and attempts to burn down buildings before withdrawing. On 25 November, National Guard units attacked Cát Bi airfield southeast of the city, destroying the ammunition dump and petrol stocks before withdrawing two days later under attack by a paratroop unit dispatched from Saigon.[265] Loss of Haiphong was a heavy blow to the DRV government, and might have provoked a call for immediate nationwide resistance to the French. However, Hồ Chí Minh was still intent on making contact with whatever government materialized in Paris as a result of the 10 November elections (see chapter 4).

Independent of events in Haiphong, a dispute arose in Lạng Sơn town over control of the old stone citadel. Shots were exchanged on 21 November, a ceasefire was arranged, but then the French commander occupied the train station and post office. On 25 November, a French fighter plane strafed Vietnamese positions inside the citadel, a howitzer blew a hole in the wall, and French troops overwhelmed the defenders. Three days later, on instructions from General Valluy in Saigon, General Morlière foreshadowed to Võ Nguyên Giáp the extension of French control from Lạng Sơn eastward to the sea.[266] Vietnam's territorial integrity was now gravely jeopardized in the north, just as had happened previously in the southern and south-central regions of the country. Only if a new French government reversed decisions taken in November by French officials in Saigon could the DRV government avoid opting for all-out war.

FIGURE 12. Võ Nguyên Gíap in
the Việt Bắc. Photo courtesy
of Christophe Dutrône.

Võ Nguyên Giáp states that Vietnam's armed forces totaled about eighty-two thousand men in early December 1946.[267] Unfortunately neither Giáp nor any other available DRV/SRV source disaggregates this figure. The closest we have is a list of thirty-two regiments and eleven independent battalions for northern and central Vietnam, from which we might extrapolate a "regular army" of about forty thousand men (including unlisted specialized services).[268] French intelligence estimated the Vietnamese army to total forty to forty-five thousand men as of October 1946.[269] No estimates are available for Nam Bộ in late 1946, but it is unlikely that Nguyễn Bình could count on more than five thousand troops obeying his orders. French forces throughout Tonkin, Annam, and Cochinchina totaled almost seventy-four thousand at the end of October, with 70 percent of them still located in Cochinchina and southern Annam.[270]

As the Vietnamese General Staff assessed unit capacities and battle scenarios in early December, their attention focused first on the Hanoi–Hải Dương–Bắc Ninh triangle, where perhaps five thousand National Guard troops were under direct central command, and another fifteen thousand province-based troops were available, but had yet to operate outside their own localities. All battle plans included missions for militia groups, which meant a considerable amount of liaison with local committees and militia leaders. Once mobilized, a militia had to be provisioned, tied in with adjacent units, and told where to acquire additional ammunition.[271] Stunned by how quickly the French had overcome obstacles to armored vehicles in and around Haiphong, the General Staff looked for new techniques to destroy roads and culverts.[272] Although plans were prepared for assaults on specific French positions, the overall strategy remained defensive. Despite upgraded attention to guerrilla warfare, and deliberately keeping some regular units in reserve, the DRV government and General Command had no intention of conceding cities and towns to the French without a fight.

HANOI

The fate of Hanoi, the DRV capital, had obvious political and psychological significance. As Vương Thừa Vũ and Trần Độ made the rounds of every neighborhood from late October 1946, taking stock of available forces and considering tactical options, they understood that overt military preparations risked French protests and preemptive strikes, whereas refusing to act risked being taken by surprise and losing all chance of resistance. The compromise was to begin working inside buildings and in back alleys, bashing holes in walls to facilitate covert movement, using the sewers to move under streets, constructing bunkers, and stockpiling supplies. There were plans to tunnel under the Métropole Hotel and the Majestic Theater in order to blow them up at the right moment.[273] Trees had holes bored in them, so as to be ready to drop them across streets with black powder charges. Special attention was given to machine-gun emplacements, as Võ Nguyên Giáp had been impressed in August 1945 by the way Japanese gunners held up the Liberation Army advance into Thái Nguyên town, and recent reports of how the Haiphong militia group had utilized its two Sten guns on the top floor of the Opera House.[274] From late November, defense preparations proceeded more openly, with trucks, oxcarts, and cyclos bringing sand and dirt into Hanoi to fill sandbags and build fortifications, and street obstacles. Noncombatants were encouraged to evacuate the city, and tens of thousands did so.[275]

A Japanese officer given the Vietnamese name of Ái Việt (Love Vietnam) presented a detailed battle plan to a meeting of the General Staff. His plan involved defending three fortified lines in sequence, from downtown Hanoi to positions eight miles south and southwest of the city. After lively debate, this idea was rejected as beyond current Vietnamese military capacities, and as failing to take advantage of some eight thousand Hanoi militia ready and willing to fight on the terrain they knew best. Vương Thừa Vũ submitted an alternative plan which divided the city into three combat zones, the most important one centered on the tightly packed "36 Streets" district between the Red River and the Citadel, held by the French. Five National Guard battalions, totaling 2,250 men, would attack selected French troop positions and destroy key installations, notably the Pont Doumer/Long Biên bridge, power and water plants, petroleum tanks, and airport facilities. Simultaneously, militia groups would assault smaller French posts, throw up more barricades, plant mines and position snipers—turning Hanoi into a deadly obstacle course. Then one National Guard battalion would join three thousand militia men and women inside the 36 Streets perimeter, while the other four battalions took up blocking positions in the Hanoi suburbs, and launched support attacks into the city when so ordered. Vương Thừa Vũ's plan was designed to wreak as much havoc as possible in the first phase, then tie down French forces for as long as possible without risking the loss of more than one regular battalion. This would give the DRV government and armed forces time to regroup for protracted war in the countryside. Hoàng Văn Thái expressed concerns to Vũ about communication-liaison capacities, and Võ Nguyên Giáp urged him to coordinate closely with the civilian administration of Hanoi, but by late November the plan had been approved and was being implemented.[276] Two weeks later, when asked by Hồ Chí Minh how long Hanoi could be held, Giáp replied, "From one month upward." Subsequently President Hồ passed the word to Hanoi combatants that he'd be satisfied if they tied down the enemy for one to two weeks.[277]

On 13–14 December, outside Hanoi, Võ Nguyên Giáp chaired meetings with relevant military commanders and staff officers.[278] Hoàng Văn Thái summarized the National Guard's overall strengths and weaknesses. An average infantry company now had two-thirds of its men carrying firearms, compared to less than one-third twelve months prior. Ammunition remained a big problem. Militia groups still mostly wielded spears, swords, locally produced grenades, and a smattering of old firearms. Each war zone was endeavoring to stockpile two months' supply of grain for soldiers. Giáp chose to focus his remarks on the element of surprise. The French had caught Vietnam by surprise in Saigon in September 1945, and then again in Haiphong in November 1946. That must not be allowed to happen again, Giáp insisted. The minute the all-country open-fire order was issued, National Guard and militia units had to mount surprise attacks. Following those assaults, Giáp continued, units needed to keep the French bottled up in towns for as long as possible, prevent them from moving reinforcements from one region to another, and wear them down while preserving Vietnam's strength. Vương Thừa Vũ, in his report on combat preparations in the capital, reiterated Giáp's point about not giving the enemy the advantage of surprise. Giáp was then able to meet with four war zone leaders who had finally made it to Hanoi. He particularly told the War Zone 3 leader to be ready to destroy bridges between Haiphong and Hanoi. Continuing deficiencies in military intelligence and communication do not appear to have been discussed at these meetings.

Throughout early December 1946, senior Vietnamese and French officials maintained almost daily communication in Hanoi.[279] The French position hardened from 15 December, while some Vietnamese militia groups became increasingly pugnacious, perhaps encouraged by opponents of further talks with the French. Local altercations over barricades, transport, mixed guard operations, and inspections multiplied. On 18 December, French soldiers occupied two DRV government buildings (without opposition), and Major Jean Julien Fonde gave Hoàng Hữu Nam a letter threatening French takeover of all responsibilities for the "maintenance of order in Hanoi from 20 December 1946, at the latest." During the night of 18–19 December, an "expanded" ICP Standing Bureau met in Vạn Phúc village, chaired by Hồ Chí Minh. The meeting may have resolved to launch an all-country anti-French resistance struggle, but with no time or date being specified yet. Inside Hanoi, on the morning of 19 December, militia "suicide squads" *(đội quyết tử)* were told that rockets would go off at 6:45 P.M. to signal the attack.[280]

In the hours that followed, National Guard units and militia groups received a series of orders and heard rumors that left many bewildered about what was expected of them. This was due partly to last-minute attempts by Hồ Chí Minh to restart talks with French officials in Hanoi, and to make contact with Leon Blum, the new Socialist prime minister in Paris (see chapter 4). At about one o'clock, General Staff headquarters cabled coded orders to attack at eight that evening.[281] Three hours later, however, a message went out to Hanoi units not to attack unless the order came personally from Võ Nguyên Giáp or one of his two principal assistants. Not all units received this message. Some Hanoi militia groups heard informally about a postponement, yet chose to ignore it as likely enemy misinformation, or market rumor. At least one militia group in downtown Hanoi was told to attack that night if the lights went out. Meanwhile many units beyond Hanoi had yet to receive the one o'clock order specifying an eight o'clock P.M. attack, or lacked the means to decode what they received. The reasons for this extreme confusion on 19 December have never been discussed publicly by those Vietnamese leaders in a position to know. Clearly, lack of command experience, fragile communications, and the combustible psychological environment made conduct of such a diplomatic/military pas de deux extremely difficult if not impossible. Policy differences within the DRV government, ICP, and Việt Minh general headquarters further complicated events. We may never know whether key individuals disobeyed or chose to ignore orders, but there is abundant evidence of militia ill-discipline and gratuitous violence.

At 8:03 P.M. on 19 December the lights went out in downtown Hanoi, followed soon after by shots from a cannon positioned in the suburbs. The word had reached at least some units that these actions represented authentic signals for the attack. Workers at the Yên Phụ power plant had managed to smuggle explosives past French guards and detonate them almost on time.[282] Rifle fire and parachute flares followed soon after, mostly coming from the French. Railway workers positioned a train across several streets and disabled it. Tram drivers did likewise (presumably pushing the trams, without electricity). Militia groups multiplied the number of barricades, planted mines, and positioned snipers at key intersections. Small teams attacked the houses of French civilians, some of whom had recently been armed by the Sûreté and tried to defend themselves; at least twenty civilians were killed and two hundred taken prisoner.[283] The sharpest fighting on the night of 19–20 December took place at the Northern Region Office, with a company of French Legionnaires attacking from the Métropole Hotel, backed up by two 75 mm cannon, tanks, and armored cars. A National

Guard company held them off for twelve hours before the political officer, Lê Gia Định, ordered survivors to escape while he prepared a bomb to kill additional Legionnaires. The bomb failed to explode and Định was cut down, becoming one of Hanoi's first resistance heroes.[284]

Aside from damaging a power station and the water plant, none of the other priority targets in Hanoi appear to have suffered. The Citadel may have received a few artillery rounds, but there was no Vietnamese assault, and indeed French units came and went repeatedly. The same was the case with two other French bases. Most seriously, a 250 kilogram explosive charge failed to destroy the Long Biên bridge, which connected the French in Hanoi to Haiphong. French defenses at Gia Lâm airport and Shell oil tanks proved too strong for the Vietnamese units available, although a smaller oil and ammunition dump at Cửa Đông was destroyed. Considering that each of the five National Guard battalions had been assigned four to six different missions to accomplish, this failure is not surprising.[285] It is also likely that some battalions did not go into action promptly at eight on 19 December. On 22 December, Võ Nguyên Giáp committed another battalion to the southern suburbs, and the following day attacks were launched from the suburban perimeter inward, partly to facilitate the 101st Battalion withdrawing into the 36 Streets defensive complex with the militia. Some suicide volunteers wielding shaped charges on wooden poles managed to destroy French armored vehicles—and quickly came to symbolize the Hanoi resistance in DRV propaganda.[286]

Beyond Hanoi, poor communications and chain of command complications prevented National Guard forces from mounting attacks at eight on 19 December. Later that night, with surprise lost, units did attack French positions in the towns of Hải Dương, Bắc Ninh, Nam Định, Vinh, and Huế. As Tết 1947 approached, no one could predict how long it would take to break the enemy's will. Existing provincial management of many National Guard units became a distinct operational advantage, at least in the short term. Guerrilla techniques had to be mastered by everyone. Nonetheless, the catchphrase "protracted resistance" did not signify blanket reliance on guerrilla tactics. Instead, with patience and perseverance, National Guard units and militia groups together would make it harder for French forces to penetrate "free zones," eventually gaining the ability to attack the French on a larger scale.

4

Peace or War?

The DRV Faces France

As Hồ Chí Minh and his lieutenants put together a provisional government at the end of August 1945 and prepared to declare Vietnam's independence, they had ample reason to expect vigorous French opposition. Five months earlier, the provisional government of Charles de Gaulle had announced to the world its intention to form an "Indochina Federation" within a "French Union," with metropolitan hegemony over foreign affairs and defense, the right of the French Constituent Assembly to determine conditions of participation in the French Union, and the right of a governor general to arbitrate between different parts of the Indochina Federation. This 24 March Declaration also foreshadowed treatment of Tonkin, Annam, and Cochinchina as three separate "countries."[1] Vietnamese with access to shortwave receivers heard the declaration explained repeatedly on Radio Tananarive (Madagascar), most currently in the wake of Japan's sudden capitulation on 15 August. On 16 August, listeners were told that General de Gaulle had appointed Admiral Georges Thierry d'Argenlieu as high commissioner for Indochina. General de Gaulle then used his 22–24 August visit to Washington to beam to Indochina a call from "the Mother Country addressed to her children," and to reaffirm bluntly at a press conference that "France means to recover its sovereignty over Indochina." De Gaulle's plan was to establish a powerful French presence in Indochina *before* proceeding to talk with assorted native groups about the future.[2] As French intelligence agencies acquainted themselves with recent startling events in Hanoi, Saigon, and the provinces, they found their superiors preoccupied instead with military logistics, transport, and command relationships.

INITIAL FRENCH CHALLENGES

The first audacious attempt to restore French authority over Indochina involved parachuting "commissioners of the republic" into Tonkin, Annam, Cochinchina, and Cambodia in late August. The Tonkin commissioner, Pierre Messmer, was captured by Việt Minh adherents forty-five kilometers north of Hanoi and did not make it to the city until late October, by which time he had been made redundant.[3] A similar parachute drop in Annam resulted in four French participants being killed and two survivors incarcerated until June 1946. In Cochinchina, Commissioner Jean Cédile after hitting the ground found himself surrounded by Vietnamese farmers, stripped naked by arriving Japanese soldiers, driven in the back of a truck through the streets of Saigon, put under loose detention, then permitted to meet Trần Văn Giàu and other members of the Southern Provisional Administrative Committee on 27 August. When Cédile simply repeated the terms of the 24 March Declaration, Giàu concluded he was stalling for time until British and French troops arrived.[4]

A more serious challenge to the nascent DRV government was posed by the fifty-six hundred French colonial troops who had fled to southern China following the Japanese coup of 9 March, and now prepared to recross the frontier. The French commander, General Marcel Alessandri, was shocked to be told by Allied officials that Chinese forces alone would take the Japanese surrender in northern Indochina, and that no French units would be permitted to accompany them. French commando teams attempting to evade these instructions were turned back forcibly by Chinese units. Two French patrol boats already in Hạ Long Bay did manage to thread their way through Allied-planted mines into Haiphong harbor, but this triggered angry Vietnamese demonstrations, sporadic gunfire, and a Japanese decision to place the crews of both boats under arrest.[5] General Jacques Philippe Leclerc, newly designated commander of French forces in the Far East, ascertained that the only way to get troops into Indochina north of the sixteenth parallel was by parachute or landing craft.[6]

On 19 September 1945, General Alessandri flew to Hanoi to try to convince General Lu Han, commander of newly arrived Chinese forces, to relax the ban on French participation in occupation duties. He also sought release of almost forty-five hundred colonial prisoners of war still under Japanese guard at the Hanoi citadel. Three days earlier, however, Lu Han had informed Hồ Chí Minh that Chinese forces possessed sole responsibility for taking the Japanese surrender, and that he planned not to interfere in civil affairs unless there was a breakdown of public order.[7] When news arrived in Hanoi of the 23 September French rampage through Saigon (see below), Lu Han felt that the wisdom of his decision to exclude French participation north of the sixteenth parallel had been confirmed. In preparing the 28 September ceremony to take the Japanese surrender,

Chinese organizers placed Alessandri at number 106 on their guest list and ruled out any display of French flags, causing an angry Alessandri to boycott the proceedings. Ironically, Hồ Chí Minh also declined Lu Han's invitation to attend the ceremony because of he had been assigned a low guest status and the absence of a national flag. That same day, Hồ invited Alessandri to his office to discuss the possibility of going to China or India to meet Admiral Thierry d'Argenlieu, newly appointed high commissioner of France for Indochina. Although Alessandri liked this idea, it seems to have run afoul of de Gaulle's continuing ban on early deliberations with native groups.[8]

One French official who had taken Hồ Chí Minh and the Việt Minh seriously for months was Jean Sainteny, head of the Gaullist intelligence mission in southern China. In July, Sainteny had flown back to Paris to secure new orders concerning penetration of Indochina, yet found his superiors preoccupied by other matters. Immediately following Japan's 15 August capitulation, Sainteny formed a team to fly from Kunming to Hanoi, only to be blocked by Chinese troops surrounding his aircraft. On 22 August, Sainteny and four subordinates managed to obtain seats on the first Allied plane to Hanoi, carrying a larger American OSS team headed by Major Archimedes Patti. Sainteny immediately tried to bring in French reinforcements from Kunming, but Patti convinced China Theater superiors that this would almost surely provoke violent confrontations with Việt Minh adherents. The Japanese snubbed Sainteny because he lacked official accreditation from his own government, not to mention any authorization from the China theater commander, General Albert Wedemeyer. This anomaly did not prevent Hồ Chí Minh from dispatching Võ Nguyên Giáp to meet Sainteny on 27 August. Giáp's attempts to get Sainteny to explain what he meant by "Franco-Annamite cooperation" produced only vague generalizations.[9]

Minus credentials or authorization to negotiate anything, Sainteny spent most of September in Hanoi collecting information, dispatching confidential assessments to superiors in Calcutta, and trying to attend to the needs of French civilians. His young assistant, Lieutenant François Missoffe, walked brashly into the DRV's Northern Region Office and talked at length with Hồ Chí Minh and Hoàng Minh Giám, Hồ's aide for foreign relations. Missoffe emerged deeply impressed by Hồ and convinced that negotiations were possible. Some of Sainteny's reports advocated talks with the DRV (which the French dubbed the "Gouvernement révolutionnaire Annamite," or GRA), while others recommended holding back.[10] Meanwhile, Hồ told the first two Western journalists to reach Hanoi that he would "accept even French advisors so long as they come to Viet Nam as friends and not as conquerors."[11] In Paris, General de Gaulle now grudgingly acknowledged to a Chinese visitor the existence in Tonkin of "more or less improvised bodies going by the name of Annamite governments."[12] However, de Gaulle instructed Admiral d'Argenlieu not to make any promises to the Việt Minh, and above all not to "deal with our subjects" via a third party, whether British, Chinese, or American.[13]

ANGLO-FRENCH ARRIVALS IN SAIGON

The first challenge to the future of the DRV erupted in Saigon in mid-September 1945, as British forces arrived to take the Japanese surrender south of the sixteenth parallel. As we have seen, General Douglas Gracey, the British commander, no sooner landed at Tân Sơn Nhứt airport on 13 September than he ordered his Gurkha escort to accompany a Japanese unit to evict the Vietnamese Southern Provisional Committee from the former governor general's palace. British personnel relieved Japanese guards at ammunition depots, docks, and military warehouses, then promptly turned the facilities over to members of a small French unit that also had arrived from India. The next day, Gracey talked at length with French Commissioner Jean Cédile, but refused to meet Vietnamese of any political persuasion.[14]

Southern ICP leaders who had come to power in Saigon claiming a special relationship with the victorious Allies now found themselves acutely vulnerable to Trotskyist, Cao Đài, and Hòa Hảo calls to attack Gracey's modest contingent (at that moment thirteen hundred men, mostly support units), before tens of thousands of British and French infantry, artillery, and armored personnel arrived by sea. In the event of such a Vietnamese assault, militants hoped that Japanese commanders would ignore British orders to protect Allied personnel, yet those in favor of attack had to admit that their losses would be heavy if the Japanese obeyed General Gracey. After bitter argument, the Southern Committee took a middle path—announcing a general strike for Monday 17 September.[15] Gracey reacted to the strike by proclaiming martial law, including a nighttime curfew, a ban on all demonstrations or public meetings, and an order against carrying of arms (including "sticks, staves, bamboo spears, etc.") unless authorized by him. Gracey also ordered Japanese commanders to help him enforce martial law or face Allied retribution.[16]

Responding to repeated urgings from Cédile, General Gracey on 22 September authorized the arming of about fourteen hundred French prisoners of war and civilians to assist him in taking control of remaining Việt Minh positions in Saigon. These men then proceeded the next morning to rage through the city, cursing, beating up, detaining, and otherwise offending any native encountered. Although General Gracey angrily disarmed the former French internees as punishment, Vietnamese armed bands struck back ruthlessly on the night of 24–25 September, killing over one hundred civilians of French nationality, many of them women and children. Gracey then rearmed the French former internees.[17] As the hatred and bloodshed escalated, no leader—British, French, or Vietnamese—was in a position to reverse the cycle. Pending the arrival of battle-hardened French regiments from the *métropole*, Gracey employed Japanese and newly arrived British-Indian infantry battalions to quell Vietnamese opposition. Civilians fled the city, fires destroyed whole neighborhoods, groups of poorly armed youths mounted nightly counterassaults, and the Southern Committee tried to reconstitute resistance in the nearby countryside.[18]

In Hanoi, Hồ Chí Minh tried to follow day-to-day developments in Saigon, clearly frustrated by his inability to exercise any leadership. News of General Gracey's 13 September eviction of the Southern Administrative Committee from the former governor general's palace reached Hanoi quickly, sparking a mass demonstration the following day. The Saigon general strike of 17 September received unanimous endorsement in the Hanoi press. However, the lack of any secure means of communication between Hanoi and either the Southern Administrative Committee or the ICP's Southern Regional Committee (Xứ Ủy Nam Bộ) meant that Hồ Chí Minh could not receive timely confidential reports or dispatch precise instructions. When OSS Major Patti gave Hồ a French copy of the Southern Administrative Committee's 16 September declaration of public protest over Great Britain's refusal to recognize its legitimacy, Hồ commented that his worst fears were being realized. "If only there was a way to stop the inevitable onslaught," Hồ added with an air of resignation. He harkened back to the Atlantic Charter, issued by President Roosevelt and Prime Minister Churchill in 1941, which promised that the Allies would "respect the right of all peoples to choose the form of government under which they will live." Hồ now doubted the British had meant what they said.[19] Meanwhile, the Vietnamese press was outraged to hear General de Gaulle declare that the French Army was being sent to what he called "our country" [Indochina], in order to "eliminate a fanatical minority."[20]

FRANCO-VIETNAMESE TALKS IN SAIGON

Disturbed by news of the violence and destruction in Saigon, Admiral Lord Louis Mountbatten, head of South East Asia Command, summoned General Gracey and Commissioner Cédile to Singapore on 28 September 1945. Above all, Mountbatten wanted to avoid further British-Indian participation in combat against the Vietnamese, yet Japanese units would only go into action alongside British-Indian units, not the French. The French alone might be unable to hold out against resolute Vietnamese counterattack. Mountbatten therefore instructed General Gracey to contact the Vietnamese and tender his good offices for urgent talks with the French. It was hoped that these talks would produce a lull in the fighting, at least until French reinforcements steamed up the Saigon River in seven to ten days' time.[21] Besides armed confrontations, daily life was being made difficult for the British and French because of the Vietnamese general strike, food

blockade, torching of warehouses, and disruption of water and electricity supplies. Surprisingly, southern Vietnamese leaders accepted Gracey's offer, probably hoping that it signaled a change in British policy. On 1 October, a Vietnamese delegation arrived at Gracey's headquarters to be told by the general to "stop
molesting Allied nationals" and to cease armed activities, in return for which
Gracey's representative would sit in on subsequent Franco-Việt Minh discussions. Gracey's political advisor, Harry Brain, disingenuously assured the delegation that it was not the mission of British forces to reinstate the French administration by force, nor to be used for any political purposes whatever. It was
agreed that a ceasefire would take effect the evening of 2 October and talks would
begin the next day.[22]

At eleven o'clock on 3 October, General Gracey welcomed the French and
Vietnamese delegations to his office suite, introduced Brain to everyone, then
excused himself. The initial atmosphere was stiff, but gradually the participants
relaxed and talked readily, helped along by British tea, biscuits, and cigarettes.
Two hours on, however, the only practical outcome was a verbal undertaking to
release hostages, exchange prisoners, and look for the body of OSS Colonel Peter
Dewey (see chapter 5). That afternoon the key Vietnamese participant, Dr. Phạm
Ngọc Thạch, requested and received a private appointment with Brain, and the
two spoke alone in French for two hours. When Dr. Thạch asserted Vietnam's
right to be free, Brain accused the Việt Minh of having relied on the Japanese
enemy to gain political advantage. Brain then went further, arguing that Annam
was bound to France by treaties that could not be voided simply because Emperor
Bảo Đại had abdicated. Thạch asked Brain what he would do if their positions were
reversed, to which Brain replied that he would drop demands for immediate independence and "try to secure some promise of eventual self-government, if possible
with a fixed date." Following Thạch's departure, Brain gave Gracey his opinion
that faceless armed men determined to fight overshadowed any efforts by Việt
Minh political negotiators.[23]

On 6 October, a second Franco-Vietnamese meeting took place, with Brain
again present as General Gracey's representative. The French team consisted of
Commissioner Cédile, Colonel Répiton-Preneuf (General Leclerc's chief of staff),
and Major Paul Mus, the only member possessing Indochina expertise. The Vietnamese team was led by Phạm Văn Bạch, chair of the Southern Administrative
Committee, with Dr. Thạch doing most of the talking. The third member, Hoàng
Quốc Việt, who was introduced as a government representative from Hanoi, said
almost nothing.[24] Cédile used the highly publicized arrival of General Leclerc the
previous day to stress French determination to ensure law and order. Dr. Thạch
read a long statement; Cédile demanded to know what had happened to French
hostages; and Brain intervened to suggest that if the Việt Minh were unaware
of these hostages, that would confirm their administrative incapacity. Thạch

pointed out that tensions had been heightened by arrival of the cruiser *Triomphant*, carrying a portion of the 5th Colonial Infantry Regiment. Bạch said his delegation needed to refer all political questions to the central government in Hanoi. It was agreed to reconvene in two days' time, but meanwhile the Southern Administrative Committee urged Saigon residents to evacuate the city while the ceasefire lasted.[25]

When the 8 October Franco-Vietnamese talks achieved nothing, General Gracey decided to issue the Việt Minh an ultimatum. His deputy commander, Brigadier Hirst, summoned Việt Minh representatives on 9 October to reiterate Gracey's 21 September martial law proclamation. Specifically, if Việt Minh groups did not lay down their arms, stop obstructing Allied forces, and allow Saigon to return to normal, they would be put at the mercy of British armored cars, artillery, mortars, and aircraft. Hirst then drew for his listeners a grim word-picture of Việt Minh "half-trained levies" going up against British forces, "the finest trained troops in the world today." "You are fools if you think your troops can oppose [British forces] successfully," Hirst added. He informed the Vietnamese that British units would very soon be moving into Saigon's northern suburbs, whatever the Việt Minh response to General Gracey's ultimatum, which gave them until midnight 10–11 October to comply.[26]

This dressing-down from Brigadier Hirst ended Vietnamese hopes that British policy might change for the better. There could be no justification now for continuing to observe the ceasefire in the face of steady British and French augmentation of forces and readiness to deploy them offensively. In fact the ceasefire was already coming apart at the seams. Nonetheless, it seems that provisional President Hồ Chí Minh was still urging negotiations. On 9 October, General Leclerc told Admiral Lord Mountbatten and General Gracey of an intercepted radio message from Hanoi to the Việt Minh in the south which ordered continuation of negotiations for as long as possible. Leclerc expressed puzzlement, as prolongation of negotiations benefited the French more than the Annamites.[27] A southern self-criticism, published four years later, asserted that a number of cadres had been "overoptimistic" in October 1945 when they judged France too weak to mount a long campaign, and hence likely to make concessions to Vietnam either immediately or following a few months of fighting.[28]

The night of 9–10 October saw a number of Việt Minh attacks launched in different parts of Saigon. One ambush of a British-Indian engineer reconnaissance party near the airport left a British captain and three Indian soldiers dead. Furious at this particular encounter, General Gracey took satisfaction in issuing final orders for combined Japanese and British-Indian advances into Saigon's northern suburbs.[29] Gracey also dropped leaflets over the city that held the Việt Minh responsible for breaking the ceasefire. The Southern Administrative Committee acknowledged orders from the DRV government not to attack

British-Indian or Japanese forces, but argued a right of self-defense when British-Indian units opened fire first, and especially when French army units were allowed to insinuate themselves into British operations and make trouble: "We are compelled to fight against the French return because the British refuse to acknowledge Vietnam's sovereignty and allow the French army to precipitate bloodshed in Saigon [. . . .] The French Imperialists are our enemies because they use force to violate Vietnam's sovereignty."[30] Neither side would attempt to initiate further talks in southern Vietnam until after the 6 March 1946 Preliminary Accord (see below), by which time the British were no longer part of the equation.

The Franco-Vietnamese talks of early October 1945 in Saigon never had much of a chance, yet the poor choice of delegates on each side made matters worse. Rotund Commissioner Cédile had all the airs of an old colonial official, despite his claim to represent the "New France," He had no authority to deviate from the 24 March Declaration, so that he was simply marking time until arrival of High Commissioner d'Argenlieu on 31 October. If General Leclerc had come a week earlier he might have made a difference, but Leclerc chose to time his appearance by air to coincide with the arrival by sea of Colonel Jacques Massu's armored cars. Phạm Văn Bạch and Phạm Ngọc Thạch were thrust into this onerous diplomatic assignment because of their confident grasp of French language and culture, the public respect accorded them as nonparty professionals, and the disinclination of any other Southern Administrative Committee members to be seen treating with the enemy. Trần Văn Giàu, who had taken personal responsibility for the call to arms of 23 September, was soon ordered to Hanoi to explain himself. On at least one occasion, Bạch and Thạch were accompanied by Hoàng Quốc Việt, who possessed ICP credentials in the north, but not necessarily in Saigon. None of these three men were in a position to have their instructions obeyed by most of the armed Vietnamese groups that made up the shaky united front. Hồ Chí Minh, trying unsuccessfully to influence events from distant Hanoi, must have renewed his determination to take personal charge of DRV foreign affairs.

MARKING TIME DIPLOMATICALLY

In Hanoi, Commissioner Sainteny finally managed to meet provisional President Hồ Chí Minh on 15 October, yet neither of them seemed in any hurry to table specific proposals. Three days earlier, Sainteny had met Nguyễn Hải Thần, head of the anticommunist Vietnam Revolutionary League, who was trying to convince the Chinese generals to shove aside the provisional DRV.[31] For the next three months, Hồ needed to devote his diplomatic skills mostly to placating the Chinese (see chapter 5). His greatest fear continued to be that China would join with Britain and France to eliminate the DRV.[32] Meanwhile, there was not much point in trying to talk seriously with the French while various combinations of British-Indian, French, and Japanese units swept out of Saigon in all directions, taking Mỹ Tho (24 October), Xuân Lộc (29 October), Cần Thơ (30 October), Tây Ninh (8 November), and part of Nha Trang (19 November).[33] This certainly represented an impressive show of force, yet General de Gaulle would not be satisfied until the French Army was able to accomplish such feats on its own. British-Indian troops began disengaging and were mostly gone by the end of January 1946.[34] In late January, as described in the previous chapter, two French armored columns swept into Khánh Hòa province to smash the Vietnamese siege of Nha Trang. That might have been the opportune moment for de Gaulle to announce a serious diplomatic offensive, but he had just resigned as provisional president of France.[35]

In Saigon, Admiral d'Argenlieu was busy trying to give substance to the Indochina Federation specified in the 24 March 1945 Declaration. On 1 November, he announced establishment of a Federal Government Council, with himself as president, General Leclerc as vice-president, and a permanent secretariat composed of men who had accompanied him from India. Cédile was made commissioner of the republic for Southern Annam, foreshadowing French plans to take control of all territory south of the sixteenth parallel. However, d'Argenlieu's principal practical achievement came in Cambodia, when he exchanged letters of recognition in mid-November with young King Norodom Sihanouk. Laos remained contested, with Chinese troops allowing Vietnamese and Lao anticolonialists to organize north of the sixteenth parallel, while a Franco-Lao unit took control of Pakse south of the Allied demarcation line.[36] Meanwhile, Cédile had found a few Vietnamese landowners and professionals prepared to join a new Parti cochinchinois, dedicated to achieving autonomy within the Indochina Federation and French Union. On 27 November, d'Argenlieu announced creation of an advisory Council of Representatives from the Indochinese Countries, with members to be selected by the high commissioner.[37] Although these organizations remained on paper, d'Argenlieu's intentions were unmistakable: he would find people in each *pays* (country/region) willing to participate on his terms, according to his timetable.

As it became apparent by early January that a deal could be struck with Chungking for Chinese withdrawal from northern Indochina, General Leclerc and his staff began to consider how best to establish a French military presence there. As we have seen, Chinese generals continued to exclude movement of French units from Yunnan to the Red River delta. They also warned repeatedly against any sudden French descent from the air, or any attempt to rearm colonial soldiers languishing in the Hanoi citadel. This left debarkation at Haiphong as the only option, although port facilities were in bad shape and the adjacent waters littered with Allied mines. Leclerc set a target of late February or early March, and began to accumulate the necessary shallow-draft landing craft. While both Leclerc and d'Argenlieu might have preferred to administer a short, sharp lesson to any armed Vietnamese standing in the way, this ran the risk of Chinese reprisals and escalation of hostilities. D'Argenlieu was mindful too of the harmful effect on international and French public opinion of Leclerc's troops becoming embroiled in a bloody conflict following arrival in Tonkin. He reluctantly accepted the need to negotiate with *"des chefs annamites du Tonkin,"* but opposed adamantly any recognition of "GRA" (DRV) claims to Cochinchina or any dilution of Indochina Federation principles. Commissioner Sainteny was assigned responsibility for negotiating with Hồ Chí Minh without necessarily reaching any agreement, since Leclerc expected Hồ to become more tractable once a Sino-French accord was signed and French troops were on the ground.[38]

Probably aware by late December that Sino-French talks were starting to make headway, Hồ Chí Minh understood the danger of the DRV being ignored by both parties, and the need to reach some agreement with France before troops arrived, purportedly to replace Chinese units. On 6 January 1946, the day of DRV general elections, Hồ emphasized to a French journalist his government's desire "not to break the bonds that unite our two peoples," and his readiness to compromise, but then warned that "we are determined to fight to the end if forced to."[39] Early January saw a spate of violent attacks on unarmed French in Hanoi, sometimes instigated by Chinese or Vietnam Revolutionary League elements anxious to sabotage both Sino-French and Franco-Vietnamese rapprochement. The Hanoi director of the Bank of Indochina, Jean Baylin, was fatally shot in front of his home. General Leclerc again contemplated a coup from the air, but General Valluy worried that any troop arrival involving armed conflict would provoke a French civilian bloodbath. Hồ made a point of visiting injured French at Lanesson Hospital in Hanoi during the Tết holidays of early February.[40]

French nationals had feared for their lives since the Japanese coup of 9 March 1945. The Japanese Army concentrated most French civilians in a dozen urban centers, locking up some personnel but exercising only loose surveillance over others, which left the latter vulnerable to vilification, extortion, robbery, and assault.[41] During the August upheavals, any French national not already regrouped to a city was in grave danger; fragmentary evidence suggests that several dozen individuals were killed in diverse locations.[42] Following Tokyo's 15 August capitulation, Japanese soldiers continued to guard French military detainees until relieved by British or Chinese units, but they often ignored the plight of French civilians. French homes were ransacked by Vietnamese in search of hidden weapons or radios, or simply to confiscate valuables in the name of the revolution. Frenchwomen going in search of food and firewood found themselves turned away from marketplaces. Vietnamese wives or mistresses of Frenchmen were subject to special abuse. The sight of thousands of Vietnamese marching down the street yelling anti-imperialist slogans petrified French witnesses, even though very few of these demonstrations degenerated into assaults on French nationals. On some occasions when rumors of new French threats swept the Vietnamese populace, scores of French nationals were detained, interrogated, admonished, and then usually released. In Saigon on 2 September, several shots fired at a mass meeting sparked mass hysteria, with Vietnamese youths storming French neighborhoods; breaking into houses; assaulting men, women, and children; and taking away two hundred or so "suspects," almost all of whom were released the next day. Three weeks later, as noted earlier, more than one hundred unarmed civilians of French nationality were murdered in one of those same neighborhoods.

No such outrages befell French nationals in other cities and towns, yet the fear of being massacred gripped them all until French Army units arrived.[43] In October 1945, responding to news of French aircraft dropping bombs in the south, the DRV information and propaganda minister, Trần Huy Liệu, publicly threatened the lives of French nationals in Hanoi. Việt Minh youths proceeded to assault French civilians on the street and in the Đồng Xuân market. Hồ Chí Minh reacted by sacking the ICP secretary for Hanoi, Hoàng Tùng and, we may assume, delivering a rebuke to his propaganda minister.[44] North of the sixteenth parallel in late 1945, French intelligence calculated 17,611 "nationaux et ressortissants français" in seven locations, and 4,711 disarmed military personnel at three venues.[45] Admiral d'Argenlieu stated his resolute opposition to any evacuation of French citizens: "It is the presence of these thousands of French nationals that offers the most palpable sign of the rights and obligations of France in Indochina. Any large-scale departure will be exploited by the international press as a renunciation and a manner of capitulation."[46] The high commissioner was holding his compatriots hostage to the French future in Indochina.

In early October, Commissioner Sainteny's small staff began to produce an information sheet ambitiously titled *Volonté indochinoise* for distribution to beleaguered French nationals in Hanoi and Haiphong. The DRV authorities quickly objected, but an agreement was struck by which a four-page daily titled *l'Entente* could be published, provided it excluded all news or comment about Indochina affairs and was submitted to the censor like all other papers.[47] The vast majority of articles focused on metropolitan France and the world at large, trying to make up for the five years when readers had been forced to rely on Japan's Dōmei News Agency and surreptitious monitoring of Allied radio broadcasts. Some news in *l'Entente* was so current and so detailed that it seems likely Sainteny's team had managed to bring in a couple of teletypewriters to connect to their shortwave receivers. Other less immediate articles may have been cribbed from French magazines carried in by visitors. Atomic bombs, United Nations deliberations,

American politics, and the upcoming Nuremberg trials received special attention. A number of issues featured meticulous drawings of Allied aircraft, a not-so-subtle allusion to the technologically superior French forces that were on their way.

L'Entente aimed to sustain local French morale in trying conditions. Announcements of musical recitals, weddings, funerals, and masses at the Catholic cathedral in Hanoi offered a sense of normality. In the evening, one could go ballroom dancing at the Grand Hôtel Métropole, or view a newly arrived, "unedited" Hollywood film at the Cinéma Majestic. There was modest financial assistance for French employees of overseas companies who had not been paid, and newly-arrived condensed milk to be distributed according to regulations of the Office du Lait. The classified ads were mostly offers to sell bicycles, electrical appliances, phonographs, furniture, sets of china, books, and the occasional motor vehicle. Vendors often needed cash for daily necessities, but more and more French residents also intended to leave Indochina behind. In mid-January, the French Repatriation Commission urged prior applicants to consult departure lists posted at two venues in Hanoi. The Chinese authorities supervised transport of French passengers down the Red River by launch to Haiphong, with each individual instructed to carry three days' food and drinking water. Steamers stopped in Saigon, where passengers were permitted to purchase and transport home substantial quantities of goods still rationed in France. In late June, some two thousand French nationals congregated at Haiphong, from whence the *Suffren* would take them to the *métropole*.[48] The harrowing stories told by these returnees must have convinced some home listeners that the natives needed to be taught a harsh lesson.

From Vietnamese police records we know that French civilians in Hanoi and Haiphong continued to be preyed upon by armed robbers and thieves. In January 1946, Génin Andre lost property valued at eight thousand piastres; wanted posters went up around Hanoi for the accused criminal. In June, someone attempted to murder M. Pourtean in Haiphong. In September, three men were accused of killing Louis Bernard Achille. French nationals continued to depart northern Vietnam.[49] Those who remained often looked on their Vietnamese neighbors with a combination of fear and distaste. Colloquially Vietnamese were called "*gnac*" or "*nhaké*," French corruptions of *nhà quê* (boorish peasant).[50] Võ Nguyên Giáp recounted to a French officer how a Frenchwoman at a local shop in Hanoi demanded loudly to be served before "*les nha qué*."[51]

IN SEARCH OF SUITABLE TERMINOLOGY

By early February 1946, French officials in Indochina had accepted the necessity of dealing with Hồ Chí Minh, at least as head of the de facto native administration in Tonkin and northern Annam. Léon Pignon pointed out the dangers of French forces arriving in the north with no Annamite party in a position to restrain popular hostility. On 8 February, General Raoul Salan told Hồ that French landings were "imminent," to which a startled Hồ warned that resulting mass outrage could mean the killing of many French women and children. Nonetheless, Salan emerged from the meeting convinced that some sort of tactical accord could be struck. Although Hồ told Salan that the 24 March 1945 Declaration was quite outmoded, he avoided making "independence" a precondition to discussions. He also intimated to Salan that continued Chinese occupation was more harmful to Vietnamese interests than accepting peaceful arrival of French Army replacements as prelude to negotiating a longer-term relationship with the "New France."[52] Hồ may have been making a purse out of a sow's ear here, recognizing that the Chinese were likely to concede French return to the north whatever he said or did. Four days later, Admiral d'Argenlieu reluctantly acknowledged that Hồ was politically astute and enjoyed widespread popular support. He instructed Sainteny to reach an entente with the "Gouvernement Annamite d'Hanoi" that did not concede territorial unity of the three *kỳ* (Tonkin, Annam, Cochinchina), and did not mention the word "independence." D'Argenlieu had no objection to Annamites employing the term *"độc lập,"* asserting (inaccurately) that it possessed no French-language equivalent. He also would accept the English term "self-government."[53] Perhaps d'Argenlieu wished to emphasize the temporary nature of any entente by using alien words rather than French, the language of international law.

Vietnamese would continue to use *độc lập* among themselves, whatever the diplomatic maneuvering. In the popular mind—and expressed constantly in newspapers and public oratory—Vietnam had achieved its national independence in August 1945. From that moment onward, all citizens had an obligation to defend and enhance that independence. However, Hồ Chí Minh and most members of his government understood that Vietnam's independence had to be recognized by at least some of the Allied powers, or else the country would be in perpetual jeopardy. Since this Allied recognition had not materialized, nor did it seem likely to occur soon, some governmental concept short of independence had to be accepted in any deliberations with the French. It is interesting that d'Argenlieu did not tell Sainteny to press for "autonomy" (*tự trị* in Vietnamese), probably because he knew it would be unacceptable to Hồ in the context of the admiral's recent use of the term in relation to Cambodia and Cochinchina.

Only hours after d'Argenlieu departed for consultations in the *métropole*, General Leclerc, as acting high commissioner, cabled Paris to state his preference for the word "independence," on the grounds that Annamites used it in the same way as the French did "autonomy.". Leclerc probably knew this was not the case, yet semantics were incidental to his main point: "At present we have reaffirmed

French sovereignty and power, restored order in Cochinchina, Cambodia, and in parts of Laos and Annam, and we are just about to arrive in force at the gates of Tonkin. Now we can talk to the Annamites and make concessions, as a sovereign power and on the terms most favorable to us."[54] Without invoking General de Gaulle's name, Leclerc was saying that a sufficient show of force had almost been achieved, hence it was time to display magnanimity. Besides, two months earlier General Salan had estimated that fifty thousand troops would be necessary to storm the Haiphong–Hanoi–Nam Định triangle, a force Leclerc had no hope of mobilizing in early 1946.[55] Leclerc did not want Hồ Chí Minh taking to the hills to mount armed resistance.

DRV leaders faced ever more pressure to make difficult strategic decisions as the likelihood of a Sino-French agreement increased. By mid-February it was clear the French were coming, one way or another. To resist French reentry into northern Indochina before Chinese troops evacuated could mean fighting them both, at a time when Vietnamese armed forces were quite unprepared to fight either. To refuse to negotiate, and perhaps withdraw the DRV government from Hanoi as the French advanced, risked losing the initiative to Nationalist Party or pro-French elements. To negotiate with the French risked losing popular support for the DRV, and the possibility of no French concessions eventuating. Hồ Chí Minh chose not to deliberate these momentous choices within the DRV cabinet or the ICP Standing Bureau. The editors of *Cứu Quốc,* daily organ of the Tổng Bộ Việt Minh, seem to have been left out of the loop entirely (see chapter 8).

FORMAL TALKS BEGIN

On 16 February, Jean Sainteny and Hồ Chí Minh met in secret to explore the overall situation and then focus on terms for a possible accord. Hồ seemed willing to drop the word "independence" in favor of "self-government," he accepted Vietnam's integration into the French Union, and he urged Sainteny to come back soon with a French government proposal in writing. Hồ apparently made no comment when Sainteny posed the principle that Cochinchina decide its own future. In Paris on 20 February, the Interministerial Committee for Indochina delegated Admiral d'Argenlieu to dispatch instructions to Sainteny, in which d'Argenlieu for the first time referred to the DRV as "Vietnam." However, he re-emphasized that dealing officially with the "Hanoi government" did not mean that France accepted the unity of the three Annamite regions, most notably in reference to Cochinchina, but also when it came to Annam.[56] D'Argenlieu wanted a minimalist accord that promoted nonviolent entry of French troops to the north without in any way jeopardizing his vision of an Indochina Federation. It was left to Sainteny to find some formula acceptable to Hồ and those around him before the French fleet arrived off Haiphong in early March. Three French members of the Section française de l'Internationale ouvrière (SFIO) long resident in Indochina moved back and forth between the two negotiating teams, conveying information informally and looking for ways to overcome particular sticking points.

General Lu Han's staff probably told Hồ Chí Minh something about the French operational timetable, but at the 16 February meeting Sainteny did not mention the early March landing deadline, nor did Hồ seek details. News of the meeting itself leaked out quickly, provoking turmoil among Việt Minh adherents and sharp criticism from Nationalist Party leaders (see chapter 7). For several days provisional DRV President Hồ canvassed the idea of swapping positions with Supreme Advisor Bảo Đại in the interests of national solidarity, but this may have been a ploy to silence opposition within the ICP. Instead, on 24 February, Hồ gained Nationalist Party and Revolutionary League agreement to a new Cabinet of "Unity and Resistance" to present to the National Assembly in the first days of March. Hồ then felt sufficiently confident to announce to the public on 26 February that discussions were proceeding with Sainteny whereby France would recognize the right of Vietnam to possess its own government, parliament, army, and finances within the French Union, and an armistice would be implemented on all fronts. Hồ's announcement made no mention of French troops arriving in the north, however.[57] Two days later the Sino-French agreement was reached in Chungking. In exchange for French troops relieving Chinese units north of the sixteenth parallel, China obtained a free port at Haiphong, customs-free transit of goods to the port, and special status for Chinese nationals residing in Indochina.[58] The 28 February agreement completely ignored the existence of a Vietnamese authority, much to the embarrassment of both Hồ Chí Minh and the nationalists who had depended on Chinese support. The Vietnamese press had only Reuters news agency to rely on when it came to alerting the public to this ominous turn of events.[59] At the brief session of the new DRV National Assembly on 2 March there was no formal discussion of the Sino-French agreement or Franco-Vietnamese deliberations, but a great deal of speculation took place in the corridors.

Among Vietnamese, only a handful of individuals around Hồ Chí Minh were well informed about the intense negotiations of early March 1946. National Guard and militia units were on high alert, the country was awash with dark rumors, and prominent Việt Minh cadres took contradictory positions in public. On 3 March the ICP Standing Bureau drafted a seven page "Instruction" to party members that favored making concessions instead of fighting. No assistance could be expected from either the Soviet Union or the United Nations, yet it still was possible to foil the "white Chinese, Vietnamese reactionaries, and fascist French" who plotted to isolate the DRV and compel it to fight many enemies at once. The "Instruction" admitted military setbacks in Nam Bộ and some loss of political influence among citizens nationwide. "Traitors" and "reactionaries" who took advantage of such vulnerabilities would be eliminated.[60] With hindsight, we can see that the 3 March "Instruction" overrated Chinese intentions to remain, placed too much hope in the French Left, and set the bar too high when insisting that France immediately acknowledge Vietnam's independence and unity.

On the evening of 3 March 1946, SFIO intermediaries presented a revised text of the prospective Franco-Vietnamese accord to Hoàng Minh Giám and Hoàng Hữu Nam, two of Hồ Chí Minh's closest associates. In the long discussion that followed between these men, the status of Cochinchina, the modalities of French armed arrival in Hanoi, and the venue for a subsequent diplomatic conference remained unresolved. Also on 3 March, General Salan told General Ma Ying, his principal contact within the Chinese occupation command, that French troops would disembark on 6 March at Haiphong, while twelve C-47 Dakota transports would land at Gia Lâm airport filled with weapons to rearm the French colonial units still under Chinese guard at the Hanoi Citadel. When General Ma objected strongly to both moves, Salan decided to concentrate on gaining agreement to the much larger Haiphong disembarkation. At a meeting on the evening of 4 March, General Ma insisted that any disembarkation be postponed until the French and Vietnamese had signed an agreement, while General Salan continued to argue that the tides made entry to Haiphong harbor impossible after 7 March. At noon on 5 March a French staff officer sent a hasty note to Sainteny arguing that the only hope for accomplishing the Haiphong disembarkation the next day lay with prior announcement of a Franco-Vietnamese accord, even if it meant disavowing certain clauses subsequently. Simultaneously the deputy commander of the Chinese 53rd Army pressured Hồ to reach agreement with Sainteny. Both Hồ and Sainteny did make concessions at their meetings on 5 March, the former probably in regard to the clause on Cochinchina, and the latter concerning provisions within the military annex to the convention. Shortly before sunrise on 6 March, Hồ dispatched Giám to Sainteny's residence to state that the signing ceremony could proceed. However, when French landing craft approached the Haiphong docks that morning they were fired upon by Chinese forces. The French chose not to return fire, took casualties, then returned fire as they withdrew down river to await developments.[61]

In Hanoi, the DRV National Assembly's new Standing Committee met with Hồ Chí Minh and his cabinet on the morning of 6 March to discuss the Franco-Vietnamese accord. It was too late to make any changes, which must have irked some participants, but if anyone spoke against approval of the accord there is no record.[62] The signing ceremony took place in the late afternoon, with Vũ Hồng Khanh, head of the Vietnam Nationalist Party, contributing his signature along with Hồ and Sainteny. Almost surely the Chinese occupation authorities prevailed on Khanh to front up for what must have been a very distasteful act.[63]

THE 6 MARCH PRELIMINARY CONVENTION

The 6 March 1946 Preliminary Convention opens with France recognizing the "Republic of Vietnam" as a "free state," a term devoid of historical precedent in either French (*état libre*) or Vietnamese (*quốc gia tự do*).[64] It seems that Hồ Chí Minh had leaned towards "*état libre*" instead of "self-government" in the last minutes of bargaining with Sainteny, perhaps hoping this empty conceptual bottle could be filled creatively at the subsequent diplomatic conference, which the accord stated would take place in Hanoi, Saigon, or Paris. The accord then proceeds to acknowledge that Vietnam would have its own government, parliament, army, and finances, exactly as Hồ had publicized eight days prior. Vietnam would be part of the Indochina Federation as well as the French Union, something Hồ had chosen to omit earlier. On the most thorny issue of Cochinchina, it appears that Hồ convinced Sainteny to avoid mention of the territory itself, instead stating that France agreed to accept the results of a future popular referendum concerning "reunion of the three *Ky* (regions)." Vietnam agreed to greet amicably French Army units coming to relieve the Chinese north of the sixteenth parallel. Elsewhere, both sides promised to cease hostilities, maintain their troops in place, and "create the necessary favorable climate for immediate opening of friendly and frank negotiations." The military annex to the preliminary convention, signed by Sainteny, Salan, and Võ Nguyên Giáp, provided that ten thousand Vietnamese troops would join fifteen thousand French troops in relieving the Chinese, with the combined relief force commanded by French officers "assisted by Vietnamese delegates." One-fifth of French troops on Vietnamese territory would be relieved each year by the Vietnamese army, resulting in full relief after five years.[65] Finally, France promised not to utilize Japanese prisoners for military ends, as British forces had done south of the sixteenth parallel. Limits set on the number of French troops allowed in the north and how long they could stay represented major concessions from the French side, made at the last minute amidst fears of confrontation with Chinese forces. When selling the accord to ICP doubters, Hồ Chí Minh allegedly remarked, "Better to sniff French crap for five years than have to eat Chinese crap forever."[66]

The first indication that ordinary citizens had of the 6 March decisions was when, the next morning, proclamations were affixed to lampposts and walls in Hanoi and Haiphong, signed simply "Leclerc" and "Hồ Chí Minh," calling on people to receive French forces amicably according to the wishes of the Vietnamese government.[67] A different Vietnamese government communiqué was distributed on flyers around Hanoi, claiming that Vietnamese-French negotiations had achieved "results favorable to moving to full independence," and requesting citizens to "sustain a respect for discipline that will guarantee the future of the Fatherland."[68] Public reaction ranged from quiet relief to vocal outrage. Later on

7 March, Võ Nguyên Giáp, Vũ Hồng Khanh, and then Hồ Chí Minh addressed a large audience in front of the Hanoi Opera House, at what may have been the most critical meeting of the Vietnamese revolution. Combining passion and cold logic, Giáp rated France's recognition of Vietnam as a free country to be better than autonomy, but certainly not yet independence, which remained the government's resolute objective (frantic applause). Concerning Cochinchina, Giáp misconstrued the accord by claiming that France had accepted reunification of the three *kỳ* by means of a referendum of all the people of Vietnam. As for the arrival of French troops, the government realized that they would have come anyway without an accord, when the country was not ready for war, whether long or short. That left negotiations as the only alternative.[69] The accord with France gave the government time to organize the country's administration, strengthen its military capacity, develop the economy, and improve the people's standard of living. The present policy, Giáp concluded, was "Compromise in order to Advance" *(Hòa để tiến)*, with total independence still the strategic aim.[70] Khanh spoke next, also emphasizing that complete independence was the ultimate objective, but it could not be achieved in a single leap.[71]

When President Hồ Chí Minh approached the rostrum in front of the Opera House, he is said to have received a long ovation that he eventually calmed by raising both hands. Hồ insisted that Vietnam had achieved independence in substance in August 1945, yet reminded listeners that no foreign powers had acknowledged that fact, hence this preliminary convention with France opened the way to international recognition. Somewhat disingenuously, Hồ stated that French troops had arrived under Allied orders, and that they would remain only for five years. "Why in fact sacrifice fifty thousand or one hundred thousand men when we can by means of negotiation attain independence, perhaps in five years?" he argued. Hồ claimed that China continued to support Vietnam, "like lips and teeth." He concluded by putting his own reputation on the line: "I, Hồ Chí Minh, have always led you on the road to liberty. I have struggled all my life for independence of our Fatherland. You know I would prefer to die rather than sell our country. I swear to you I have not betrayed you."[72] Jean Sainteny, who was present at the meeting, sensed that Hồ's sincere, emotional tone carried the crowd with him.[73]

Nonetheless, the chances of a violent backlash kept everyone on edge.[74] Nationalist Party members, stunned by Vũ Hồng Khanh's signing of the 6 March Accord, needed time to figure out what to do next. The immediate danger was that unruly youths would attack French civilians, or that rogue militia groups would shoot at arriving French soldiers. Extensive patrolling by Chinese troops helped to prevent this from happening. In Haiphong harbor, with Sino-French "misunderstandings" resolved, French units began debarking on 7 March, with four thousand men ashore by the next evening.[75] On 8 March, Võ Nguyên Giáp

came to meet General Leclerc aboard the *Sénégalais* in Haiphong harbor, determined to size up this vaunted professional soldier whom General de Gaulle had
deputed to restore French power in Indochina. Giáp sought to identify beliefs
and experiences they might have in common, for example love of country or the
recent epic struggle against fascism, but it seems Leclerc was unimpressed by this
man who had yet to command more than a company-sized unit in combat. As
they parted, Leclerc warned Giáp that when it came to dealing with Vietnamese
aspirations he would remain "always French."[76]

On 9 March, the ICP Standing Bureau produced a second "Instruction," titled
"Compromise in order to Advance," not coincidentally the catchphrase that Võ
Nguyên Giáp had employed at the Hanoi Opera House two days earlier. This
document circulated widely among party branches and remained current for at
least five months. The Franco-Vietnamese preliminary accord had been necessary, according to the authors, because Vietnam was surrounded by enemies and
needed time to "rest and consolidate" before progressing to a new revolutionary
period. While the ICP authors acknowledged that the DRV had yet to gain full
independence, and predicted that reactionary French colonialists would try to
sabotage the accord, starting with the question of Nam Bộ/Cochinchina, they
also saw a "new France with a new spirit of freedom," which by implication should
be given an opportunity to prove itself. Therefore, the party's slogan of "Oppose
French colonial aggression" was now to be replaced by "Ally as equals with New
France." Two different public attitudes had to be combated: both patriotic indignation at not being able to shoot French colonialists and the naïve belief that
Franco-Vietnamese diplomacy could resolve everything. In current circumstances armed struggle had to be replaced by political, economic, and cultural
struggle, but that did not mean slowing down military development. Preparations for protracted resistance needed to continue, albeit conducted in secret, "to
avoid any misunderstanding between us and the French."[77] Although the word
compromise in the title of this 9 March instruction referred to dealings outside
the party, the text also reflected accommodation inside the ICP between those
who wanted seriously to explore a new relationship with the French and those
who considered war inevitable. However, in deciding to negotiate and to prepare
for war simultaneously, party leaders may not have considered how each effort
would intrude upon the other.

The degree of public shock at the 6 March Accord can best be measured in
Huế, where censorship was more relaxed than in Hanoi or Haiphong. Local citizens and especially soldiers based in Huế voiced distress, anger, sadness, and
confusion. At one hospital, amputees threatened to go on a hunger strike. One
writer expressed deep indignation that so many lives had been lost for the mere
status of "free state" within the Indochina Federation and French Union, and no
clarification about Nam Bộ. He doubted if sincere cooperation could ever be

achieved between France and the DRV.[78] At a public meeting of some five hundred people in Huế, a Việt Minh leader relied on President Hồ's personal promise to justify signing of the 6 March Accord. However, from the press account it is apparent that some in the audience regarded the accord as an ignominious defeat, others expected only perfidy from the French, and still others questioned whether the United States or China would ever recognize the DRV due to its communist leaders. Another published response mapped out a DRV negotiating position that left nothing for France except perhaps the recovery of a few French firms, whose management would be required to obey Vietnamese laws. Yet another reaction was quickly to protest French nonimplementation of the accord, an objection which was the theme of a Việt Minh-organized march through the streets of Huế by an alleged thirty thousand armed men and women.[79]

Within days of the preliminary convention being signed, Admiral d'Argenlieu began to signal limitations on its application. The high commissioner regarded agreement with Hồ Chí Minh as a distasteful but necessary move in order to be able to insert French armed forces north of the sixteenth parallel without facing immediate resistance. However, he was not about to allow any provisions of the agreement to jeopardize his grand design of an Indochina Federation composed of "autonomous states." In a 9 March speech, d'Argenlieu referred to the DRV as "the Hanoi government," and compared its status with that of autonomous Cambodia.[80] On 12 March, the commissioner for Cochinchina, Jean Cédile, publicly characterized the 6 March Accord as merely a "local convention" for the north, and insisted that no referendum would be held relating to Cochinchina until complete order had been restored. In a confidential message to Paris, d'Argenlieu strongly objected to a verbal assurance by Sainteny to Hồ that negotiations would take place in Paris. D'Argenlieu also did not intend to permit any representatives from the Hanoi government to come to Cochinchina to help implement the ceasefire. On these matters the high commissioner received quick, firm support from Paris, with the Interministerial Committee also objecting to any staged withdrawal of French troops north of the sixteenth parallel over a five-year period. The minister of overseas France, Marius Moutet, confirmed that Cochinchina would be treated as a separate state.[81] As evidence surfaced of French recoil from provisions of the 6 March Accord, Hồ Chí Minh came under renewed criticism from Vietnamese sources. In a 14 March radio speech aimed at both Vietnamese and French audiences, Hồ alleged specific French violations of the accord and called for a speedy opening of definitive negotiations. Banners and placards at a large, well-organized meeting at the Cité Universitaire featured calls to "Oppose Deceitful Policies of the French Colonialists," "Immediately Open Talks in Paris," and promote "Sino-Vietnamese Friendship."[82]

LECLERC ARRIVES IN HANOI

On 18 March, General Leclerc led 1,200 troops and 220 vehicles into Hanoi to the relief and delight of thousands of French civilians who had gathered along Paul Bert/Tràng Tiền Street to cheer them, wave French flags, and sing the "Marseillaise." Colonial soldiers at the Citadel were rearmed, and Leclerc stood on a balcony to declare Hanoi the "last step of Liberation after Fezzan, Paris, Strasbourg, and Berchtesgaden."[83] On the morning of 18 March, *L'Entente* printed a large drawing of Leclerc, his complete career history, and an appeal by Leclerc to French military and civilian personnel to uphold the dignity of their own "great Nation," exercise strict discipline, and be mindful that any provocation of Vietnamese (not Annamite) personnel would be punished severely.[84] While an obvious balm to French pride, above all for the civilians and unarmed soldiers who had feared for their lives ever since the Japanese coup de force in March 1945, it is hard to imagine a ceremonial arrival in Hanoi more likely to lacerate Vietnamese patriotic sensitivities. Only the pairing of French and Vietnamese flags on several arriving vehicles offered muted counterpoint. Four days later, Leclerc and Giáp placed flowers at the two monuments to French and Vietnamese war dead, then reviewed a joint military parade.[85] Writers complained bitterly about packs of French soldiers and civilians surging down the street, singing, yelling, making rude remarks towards Vietnamese, and refusing to pay their restaurant or cyclo bills.[86]

General Leclerc's sortie into Franco-Vietnamese diplomacy was rudely cut short by Admiral d'Argenlieu. At a reception in Saigon honoring visiting King Sihanouk of Cambodia, the high commissioner was heard to equate the 6 March Accord with the 1938 Munich agreement with Hitler.[87] On 24 March, d'Argenlieu insisted that Hồ Chí Minh come to his warship anchored in Hạ Long Bay, where naval pomp and ceremony prevailed over substantive discussion. The high commissioner had already decided that formal negotiations should take place in Dalat, "where one can work in a calm, serene atmosphere, sheltered from all crowd demonstrations either spontaneous or organized."[88] Hồ pushed hard for Paris, but d'Argenlieu would only concede to a Vietnamese parliamentary delegation visiting France as guests of the Constituent Assembly (see below). A week later Hồ reluctantly agreed to preparatory negotiations in Dalat, while d'Argenlieu accepted the principle of Paris talks at some unspecified date in the future. General Leclerc, furious at his cavalier treatment at the hands of d'Argenlieu, dispatched a long report to General de Gaulle (already out of power for two months), defending the 6 March Accord given the limited military resources available to him, and predicting that France would be more able to assert itself politically in northern Indochina as Chinese forces withdrew. However, it was the presence of Chinese forces that had compelled French and Vietnamese parties to sign the 6 March

FIGURE 13. French residents of Hanoi welcome Leclerc convoy,
18 March 1946. Photo courtesy of Christophe Dutrône.

Accord, so once the Chinese departed it did not necessarily follow that either side would become more yielding in negotiations.[89]

L'Entente newspaper suddenly took a vigorous political tone following arrival of Free French forces in Hanoi on 18 March 1946. General Leclerc became the great deliverer, who personally awarded medals to members of the previously incarcerated 9th Colonial Infantry Regiment. L'Entente published the frequencies and listening times in French of foreign radio stations, rebuffing DRV attempts to gain custody over private radio receivers. It initiated a "News of Indochina" column, followed by a column titled "Perusing the Vietnamese Press." This sparked vigorous rejoinders from Vietnamese newspapers, led by Hanoi Soir and Le Peuple. Now possessing their own printing press and independent access to newsprint, editors of l'Entente could ignore calls by Vietnamese papers that they obey DRV censorship regulations like everyone else. *L'Entente* targeted Francophone Vietnamese readers fully as much as French nationals remaining in the north. By late May, *l'Entente* was dividing its front page between rebuttals of *Hanoi Soir* and long verbatim reprints of speeches by Admiral d'Argenlieu. In June, on the sixth anniversary of de Gaulle's London radio address to his compatriots, *l'Entente* carried a big drawing of the general and a serialization of the current Gaullist political platform.[90] With the DRV government no longer able to censor *l'Entente,* Việt Minh newspapers used it as a foil to highlight differences between Vietnam and France. At one juncture, *l'Entente* editors appeared to reconsider their polemical mission, asserting that it ought to be feasible to achieve mutual comprehension, since both France and Vietnam had broken definitively from the past.[91] However, each side continued to speak past the other, not seeking points of understanding, much less agreement.

Although the 6 March Accord stated that both sides should cease hostilities and maintain troops in place, it offered no elucidation about where this provision applied. Sainteny had meant to limit its application to northern Indochina, while Hồ Chí Minh aimed to extend its implications south of the sixteenth parallel. French troops did stop advancing along the Black River in the vicinity of Sơn La. Armed confrontations along the frontier between Laos and north-central Vietnam dropped off briefly. Agreement was reached for a French battalion to debark at Đà Nẵng (Tourane) on 26 March, only seven kilometers north of the sixteenth parallel. Three days later, as mentioned in the previous chapter, a French column drove from Laos along Route 9 and entered Huế to the cheers of French civilians gathered in front of the Morin hotel, and "great consternation" among Vietnamese.[92] French vehicles later paraded loudly through Huế neighborhoods, roughing up those who objected. Nonetheless, for the next eight months the two sides avoided violent incidents in and around the former royal capital.[93]

A BRIEF CEASEFIRE ENCOUNTER IN NAM BỘ

At Võ Nguyên Giáp's first meeting with General Leclerc, on 8 March, he proposed that a DRV delegation be flown to Saigon to facilitate a ceasefire in Cochinchina, only to be told bluntly that Cochinchina was none of the Hanoi government's business until a referendum was undertaken. Nonetheless, on 11 March Giáp radioed the Southern Region Committee that a delegation was preparing to fly to Saigon, and *Cứu Quốc* newspaper named the delegates.[94] Meanwhile, local French commanders in Cochinchina spread leaflets instructing all armed Vietnamese bands to turn in their weapons and accept French authority. When this had little effect, new leaflets distinguished native Cochinchinese who might be accepted into French-controlled militia units from alien Tonkinese who had to withdraw northward immediately or face dire consequences. The French commander of the Biên Hòa region, Lieutenant Colonel Fehler, dispatched a letter to Vietnamese units in the vicinity, proposing a meeting. Nguyễn Bình, head of Military Region 7 (to the north and east of Biên Hòa), immediately convened his staff to consider options. The majority favored accepting Fehler's offer as a means to ascertain French intentions following the 6 March Accord. One person dissented and urged Bình to contact "the Center" (Hanoi) to let them decide. Bình did send a radio message, but meanwhile moved to select a delegation.[95]

On the morning of 10 April, a French staff officer received the Vietnamese delegation at Thiền Quang, and Lieutenant Colonel Fehler arrived shortly thereafter, wearing all his medals and the vaunted "Rhine and Danube" insignia. Vietnamese delegates brought along a uniformed platoon with members chosen for their height and ability to sing a bevy of antifascist songs. Rituals over, Fehler expressed disappointment that Nguyễn Bình could not attend, then presented the Vietnamese with a typed set of "propositions." Nguyễn Bình (no title) was to accept responsibility for delivering to the French all arms, munitions, radio equipment, and printing presses. Cochinchinese personnel had the choice of receiving a French laissez-passer to go home or being sent north. "Les Tonkinois" were to be repatriated to Tonkin without delay, unless they had resided in Cochinchina before the 9 March 1945 Japanese coup and now requested to remain. All Japanese were to be dispatched to the holding camp at Cap St Jacques (Vũng Tàu). Nguyễn Bình, his family and retinue were to be transferred by boat to Biên Hòa, then flown to Tonkin. All troops under Nguyễn Bình were to present themselves under the white flag at places to be designated. If the Vietnamese side did not accept these propositions by noon on 12 April, the French command would "resume its liberty of action".[96]

Phạm Thiều told Lieutenant Colonel Fehler that the terms of his document amounted to capitulation, then asked Fehler if he was authorized to discuss relevant political questions, for example French Army reinstallation of colonial-era village notables, or French terrorist acts committed against Vietnamese civilians.[97] When Fehler asserted a French right to protect the notables, Thiều declared the Vietnamese government's right to execute them as traitors. Thiều then took up the ceasefire provisions of the 6 March Accord, claiming that Nguyễn Bình had tried to implement them, whereas the French had continued their assaults. Fehler replied that Cochinchina was not covered by the accord, which must have raised the question in Vietnamese minds of why they were meeting at all. Fehler brought up the matter of Japanese nationals in the ranks of Nguyễn Bình's forces; the Vietnamese readily admitted their participation, and compared them to the French Foreign Legion. When Phạm Thiều equated Vietnamese resistance to the invading French with French resistance to the Germans, Fehler vehemently rejected the comparison, saying "We were in Indochina with you before the Japs arrived."

At the afternoon session, Lieutenant Colonel Fehler tried to concentrate on the issue of evicting armed northerners from Cochinchina, while members of the Vietnamese delegation proudly identified themselves as coming from north, center, and south. The Vietnamese tabled their own "propositions," calling for early diplomatic resolution of the status of Nam Bộ, formation of a mixed military commission in the south, French Army noninvolvement in Vietnamese civil administration, and establishment in Nam Bộ of a "neutral government with French councilors" pending higher level negotiations between the DRV and France.[98] These proposals being completely unacceptable to Fehler, he urged the Vietnamese delegation to introduce him to a ranking military officer able to address his demands. A second meeting was set for 15 April, but French attacks north of Biên Hòa from 12 April scuttled that plan. In addition, Nguyễn Bình had finally received a reply from Hanoi which discouraged any local meetings with the French. On 17 April, the DRV government informed the Southern Committee that the Nam Bộ issue definitely would be raised at the Dalat conference (see below), with a key objective being extension of ceasefire provisions to that part of the country.[99]

CEASEFIRE DISCUSSIONS IN SOUTH-CENTRAL VIETNAM

In Annam below the sixteenth parallel, the French were somewhat more inclined than in Cochinchina to involve Hồ Chí Minh's government in facilitating a ceasefire with armed Vietnamese opponents. Although in considerable disarray following the heavy defeat west of Nha Trang, some Vietnamese units had begun to reconsolidate in Phú Yên province, while others survived in the foothills of Khánh Hòa province. At the end of March, Nguyễn Chánh, of the South-Central Region Resistance Committee, traveled from Quảng Ngãi to head the delegation to meet the French in Nha Trang. With the delegation determined not to enter the city on mere bicycles or in a truck, Khánh Hòa activists retrieved from the hills a black Ford V8 sedan, smuggled gasoline from Nha Trang, and found a qualified driver. Flying a DRV flag on the fender, the delegation was driven in style twenty-five kilometers to the Nha Trang post office. There, the head of the French delegation, Colonel Penicaut, requested a lifting of the Vietnamese blockade on food to the city, to which Nguyễn Chánh agreed. However, Penicaut's proposal that colonial-era village notables be restored to authority was flatly rejected. The meeting then formed a Franco-Vietnamese liaison group, and discussed positioning of joint teams.[100]

On 6 April, the French flew Hoàng Quốc Việt, Phan Tử Nghĩa, and Ngô Tử Hạ from Hanoi to Nha Trang to take part in the "Mixed Armistice Commission for Southern Annam," one outcome of a general staff agreement reached in Hanoi three days prior (see below).[101] They were accompanied by a Captain Felix, who was ordered to make sure that commission members never approached the Cochinchina frontier, and that no French member discussed events in the central highlands.[102] Colonel Lorillot, commander of the Nha Trang sector, briefed the commission on the current military situation, after which the commissioner of the republic for Southern Annam gave them a civilian account. Vietnamese members chose to delay their response. Hoàng Quốc Việt was introduced to Hà Văn Lâu from the local mixed liaison group, and through him managed to meet privately with Khánh Hòa province leaders. Việt clearly intended to take advantage of this trip to acquaint himself with current political as well as military circumstances, especially given the poor state of communications between Hanoi and southern Trung Bộ. That evening, however, Việt took Lâu aside to urge him to withdraw from the liaison group because it conflicted with his continuing duties as Khánh Hòa front commander, and because the French might decide to detain or eliminate him. Việt was speaking from years of clandestine experience with the Sûreté, and Lâu soon withdrew from the proceedings.[103]

The next morning, Colonel Lorillot tabled a long list of "Hostile activities of V.N. forces," including dissemination of anti-French tracts, convening of anti-French meetings, incitement of Foreign Legionnaires to desert, threatened reprisals against persons using BIC currency, punishment of merchants doing business with French troops, targeting of native Catholics, detention or killing of persons having contact with the French administration, and tearing up railroad tracks. Lorillot then proposed military force regroupments and diminution of "hostile spirit," thus reducing the chances of a "dangerous incident." Phan Tử Nghĩa spoke for the Vietnamese side, emphasizing the mixed commission's responsibility to visit localities in order to "calm the population and achieve a real ceasefire." He agreed in principle on force regroupments, which would require the commission to make contact with the Vietnamese military sector headquarters in Tuy Hòa (Phú Yên). As discussion continued, the exclusion of political matters was questioned repeatedly by the Vietnamese. For example, the entire 6 March Accord needed to be explained to the masses properly in order for a lasting military armistice to be achieved. Eventually the French accepted that commission members might make "political contacts," but only for military ends. At the afternoon session, Hoàng Quốc Việt tabled a list of French hostile activities, including distribution of leaflets injurious to implementation of the 6 March Accord, conscription of Vietnamese Catholics into the French Army, the issuing of travel permits on colonial "Protectorat de l'Annam" stationery, and detention of six family members of M. Chanh, a DRV official.

On the morning of 8 April, the Mixed Armistice Commission drove in French vehicles up the coastline fifty-five kilometers to the small town of Vạn Giã, only to find no Vietnamese commander or liaison officer there to meet them. While waiting, Vietnamese and French members continued the debate about political contacts, eventually agreeing to encounters with local leaders but not public meetings. On the way back to Nha Trang the commission witnessed an attack by some fifty irregulars on a nearby French post, with bullets flying overhead and French commissioners citing the incident as a flagrant Vietnamese violation of the 6 March Accord. The next day the commission returned to Vạn Giã, where Vietnamese members had only thirty minutes to talk with local representatives. As the military commander lacked authority to agree on armistice provisions, the commission once again returned to Nha Trang.

The key encounters took place in Ninh Hòa town on 12 April, with Trần Công Khanh coming from Tuy Hòa, meeting Hoàng Quốc Việt and Phan Tử Nghĩa privately for several hours, then together presenting proposals to the French. They particularly wanted the commission to travel south to Phan Rang and Phan Thiết, and for armistice parameters to be extended beyond the coastal provinces to the central highlands. They also proposed rules concerning military bases, movement along roads, and the status of Vietnamese "partisans" (serving the French). The French side made no comment on travel south or extending the armistice to the highlands, choosing instead to probe critically the Vietnamese armistice propositions and to advance alternatives.

The next morning Colonel Lorillot received a message from Saigon which ruled out any commission visit to Phan Rang and Phan Thiết, ignored the highlands request, and directed an early return of the mixed commission to Hanoi. When the two sides reconvened, Colonel Lorillot told the Vietnamese they need not concern themselves with provinces to the south of Khánh Hòa because "the situation has been well-regulated already." Discussions about particular armistice provisions continued into 14 April, with the French now excluding certain items as "political," protesting alleged Vietnamese reinforcements arriving from points north, and complaining about Vietnamese propaganda inciting French soldiers to desert. Hoàng Quốc Việt (with Phan Tử Nghĩa interpreting) asserted vehemently that the DRV was adhering strictly to the 6 March Accord, and that President Hồ Chí Minh himself had given orders to respect French persons and property. At this tense moment, Lorillot suggested an adjournment for several hours, but not before announcing that the six members of the family of M. Chanh had been released.

When the meeting reconvened, the Vietnamese first expressed thanks to Colonel Lorillot for the release of M. Chanh's family, then Hoàng Quốc Việt requested air transport back to Hanoi, and Lorillot made the necessary arrangements. The *Cứu Quốc* newspaper blamed the failure of these talks on French efforts to reestablish the pre-1945 administrative system, and on the manner in which the French obstructed contacts between the DRV delegation and the public.[104] In late April, Lorillot demanded that the Vietnamese immediately return Foreign Legionnaires who had deserted or face attack. French assaults in Khánh

Hòa resumed on May Day and soon forced the retreat of two Vietnam National Guard detachments into Phú Yên.[105] We do not know if either side proposed to reconvene the Mixed Armistice Commission of Southern Annam, but it seems unlikely. The French in particular may have decided they were doing the Vietnam government too much of a favor by making central government representatives available at the local level. Nor was it clear that Hanoi representatives could convince local anti-French groups to implement unpalatable armistice provisions.

THE 3 APRIL GENERAL STAFF AGREEMENT

It was north of the sixteenth parallel that the military annex of the 6 March 1946 Accord had a serious chance of success. On 3 April, a General Staff Agreement was signed in Hanoi which spelled out positioning of French and Vietnamese "relief troops," procedures for troop movement, and the creation of a mixed liaison commission.[106] More than three-quarters of French forces were to be based in Hanoi, Haiphong–Hòn Gai, and along the Sino-Indochina frontier, although the latter postings would need to await Chinese authorization. By contrast, Vietnamese forces were to be spread across a host of locations stretching from the northern frontier to Đà Nẵng. In Hanoi, French relief troops would greatly outnumber Vietnamese, 5,000 compared to 952. French forces did not have to share Haiphong–Hòn Gai or Điện Biên Phủ, a provision that must have fed proprietary instincts of later consequence. On the other hand, Vietnamese forces were alone at seven venues, giving the French no excuse for military reconnaissance or bivouacking there. Supply convoys were not to have more than sixty armed men accompanying them. The Vietnamese government was to be informed forty-eight hours in advance of any troop movement, so that it could "notify the population in order to avert incidents, insofar as possible." It was agreed to dispatch an armistice commission to southern Annam, which as we have seen departed Hanoi for Nha Trang soon afterward. However, the French refused repeatedly to allow a similar commission to go to Cochinchina.

It was a matter of Vietnamese national honor to bring units assigned to the "Relief force" (Tiếp phòng quân) up to regular army standing. To head the force, Hồ Chí Minh selected Lê Quốc Vọng, a comrade from two decades prior in Canton who had studied at Whampoa Academy and then risen to the rank of colonel in the Nationalist Chinese Army, where his duties included command of a motor transport battalion. President Hồ gave Vọng the new name of Lê Thiết Hùng and the rank of brigadier general, considered sufficient status when dealing with French and Chinese counterparts. The next priority was to find enough cloth of suitable type, measure each soldier, and rely on hundreds of women volunteers to sew uniforms. Units then had to drill extensively, improve military bearing, show discipline, and keep their quarters neat and clean, especially when they were based next to a French unit. Vietnamese soldiers were instructed to salute French officers and to salute the French flag when it was raised in the morning—unthinkable practices only a few months earlier.[107] One can imagine young Vietnamese soldiers watching adjacent French troops very closely, with a mixture of suspicion, awe, and desire to learn.

The Central Mixed Commission for Liaison and Control was charged with facilitating and monitoring application of the 3 April General Staff Agreement.[108] Head of the commission's Vietnamese contingent was Hoàng Hữu Nam, who had been recruited by the British in Madagascar and parachuted to the Việt Bắc hills in September 1944, where he quickly put his training and radio equipment to Việt Minh purposes. Nam's deputy was Phan Mỹ, an early Việt Minh activist in Hanoi and younger brother of Phan Anh, the nonparty minister of defense. Their French counterparts were Colonel H. Répiton-Preneuf and Commandant Jean Julien Fonde. From Fonde's memoirs it seems that considerable mutual respect developed between these men, yet the two sides had very different instructions from their superiors, and the Central Mixed Commission functioned in parallel hierarchies, never as a combined body.[109] Vietnamese members tried to limit the activities of French forces as much as possible, whereas French members often treated the Commission as a legitimizing device for operational expansion. The first call on the Commission's time was a request from the DRV's Northern Region Public Works Bureau for the French to pay for "substantial damage" to the Long Biên/Doumer bridge caused by General Leclerc's tracked vehicles as they crossed the Red River into Hanoi on 18 March.[110] Before the Central Mixed Commission began to operate, the DRV government had told northern administrative committees to report regularly on French Army encampments so that details could be conveyed to a nascent Vietnamese military liaison group.[111]

Besides the Central Mixed Commission, the 3 April agreement specified formation of subordinate mixed commissions at each of the seven venues shared by Vietnamese and French "relief forces." French commanders readily assigned liaison officers to these local bodies, but Vietnamese commanders responded slowly or not at all. Most Vietnamese fluent in French tried to avoid a commission assignment, as it often meant restraining truculent fellow citizens and left the officer vulnerable to charges of being pro-French. Government orders to administrative committees to provide local mixed commissions with necessary facilities and services also met with resistance. It was bad enough having a French force in one's backyard, but worse to render upkeep, no matter how limited. Cadastre employees in Nam Định protested at being compelled to share their building with the local mixed commission, on grounds that French members might pry into their maps and property records.[112] Summing up the first month of mixed commission activities, a DRV government report pointed to French members seizing several office buildings in Haiphong, taking over an auto repair facility in

Hanoi, pushing to increase French military use of waterways, and wanting to investigate deaths and disappearances of French nationals dating back to the Japanese coup in March 1945. Former French colonial employees had also approached the mixed commissions for assistance in regaining private property in the provinces. Writers of this Vietnamese report made only passing mention of mixed commission investigations of local shooting incidents, a major French concern.[113]

The DRV government hoped the mixed commissions could channel and thus restrict French Army contacts with the civil administration and the Vietnamese public at large. For example, when the government objected to the French launching their own investigations into missing persons, Colonel Fonde submitted to Hoàng Hữu Nam a list of eighteen French soldiers who had disappeared since 25 December 1945. Nam gave the list to the Northern Region Police Bureau, which may have forwarded queries to relevant localities.[114] Later Fonde wanted information about specific missing Vietnamese wives and métis children of French nationals, as well as alleged detentions of particular métis French citizens. Local Vietnamese police and administrative committees regarded such queries with suspicion and generally ignored them unless pressed by superiors. In late April, a number of French soldiers and civilians were attacked, some fatally, causing accusations of culpability to fly in all directions. The perpetrators probably ranged from disgruntled Chinese troopers to Vietnamese of either Việt Minh or Nationalist persuasion who refused to accept the 6 March Accord. On 20 April, British Major Peter Simpson-Jones was ambushed on the road between Haiphong and Hòn Gai. A week later, four French soldiers were killed in a Haiphong attack, followed soon after by a senior French customs official.[115] The mixed commissions proved powerless to deal with such incidents.

In May 1946, a French C-47 Dakota airplane crashed in the village of Vân Canh (Hà Đông), eleven kilometers west of the capital. The Hanoi region mixed commission quickly took charge of rescuing French casualties, but it was left to the Hà Đông province committee to seek an indemnity of 107,000 piastres for the death of one villager, injuries to seven others, and associated destruction of property. Six weeks later, the French replied that owners of the Dakota were prepared to pay only for clearing away aircraft debris.[116] Vietnamese members of the mixed commission did not try to get anything further for Vân Canh inhabitants.

French Army food requirements trumped official Vietnamese efforts to restrict French contacts with the public. Initial attempts to negotiate sale of rice to French units via local administrative committees fell by the wayside. Overseas Chinese wholesalers soon bypassed mixed commissions to deal directly with French supply officers. Vietnamese retail merchants followed suit, although they were often compelled to register with the DRV police and pay a tax. Some Việt Minh cadres continued to rail against "trading with the enemy," but the marketplace prevailed. For a time the Ministry of Agriculture issued monthly quotas for the slaughter and sale of buffalo, cattle, and goats to the French at specific venues, orders which local committees were expected to enforce. In practice, some committees negotiated animal numbers and prices with French quartermasters, while elsewhere slaughterhouse owners had the upper hand.[117] When disputes arose between Vietnamese workers and French personnel, the mixed commissions were sometimes called in.

THE DALAT CONFERENCE

Having acceded to Admiral d'Argenlieu's demand for a preparatory conference in Dalat, Hồ Chí Minh found a way to use the meeting to domestic advantage, lining up some twenty prominent Vietnamese intellectuals to participate as delegates or advisors. None of these men (there were no women among them) possessed diplomatic experience, but they did know how to analyze issues, formulate arguments, speak publicly (almost all of them in French as well as in Vietnamese), and use informal encounters with French delegates to advantage. Up until mid-April, DRV diplomacy had been handled by Hồ himself, sometimes working through Hoàng Minh Giám and Hoàng Hữu Nam, but none of them would go to Dalat. Hồ convinced Foreign Minister Nguyễn Tường Tam to lead the delegation, in the spirit of Việt Minh-Nationalist Party solidarity when facing the French.[118] However, everyone understood that the most important member was Võ Nguyên Giáp, deputy head of the delegation, a status marked early by the single armed, uniformed guard who never strayed from Giáp's side during the airplane trip to Dalat. The other delegates and advisors ranged across the political spectrum, among them some individuals whose attitude towards the French return to Indochina remained uncertain or ambiguous.[119] All would be exposed at Dalat to the harsh reality of Franco-Vietnamese contestation. Being intellectuals, there was the risk they would spend endless hours debating options and find it impossible to formulate collective negotiating positions.

Ongoing Vietnamese commando attacks in Nam Bộ complicated DRV government efforts to gain diplomatic headway. While Vietnamese newspapers in the north lauded each southern sabotage or assassination report, the French media condemned the civilian killings, indiscriminate grenade assaults, and bombs placed in buildings frequented by off-duty French personnel. On 10 April, Hồ Chí Minh sent a confidential radiogram to southern commanders to reduce terrorist operations immediately. Despite this instruction, Nguyễn Bình informed Hanoi on 25 April that he would "support the conference in Dalat" by intensifying attacks on all fronts.[120] On more than one occasion it was necessary for embarrassed DRV negotiators to disavow the bomb-throwers in Saigon. Privately they worried that Nguyễn Bình was a loose cannon.

From mid-March, a committee to analyze the implications of the 6 March Accord had functioned under the DRV Foreign Ministry. Nguyễn Mạnh Tường suspended his legal practice to prepare a policy paper for the Dalat meeting.[121] On 15 April, the delegation met President Hồ Chí Minh and other members of the Cabinet to receive its final instructions. Hồ himself had never participated in a diplomatic meeting, although in 1919 he had circulated on the fringe of the Versailles Conference, later took part in Comintern meetings, and always tried to keep astride of international politics. Hồ told delegates to be united, meticulous, confidential, self-critical, and willing to discuss together each declaration before forwarding it to the French. When no agreement could be reached with the French on a particular issue, Hồ told the delegation not to inform the French that the government's view was being sought in Hanoi, as that would bind the government to the Dalat talks. Hồ expected that certain vital issues would prove too difficult to handle, and considered this precisely the reason why the subsequent state-to-state conference should take place in Paris. Hồ specified that any Indochina Federation should be limited to economic matters, that the future French Union should not preclude Vietnam from establishing diplomatic relations with other countries, and that Vietnam must have its own bank and currency—all points on which he would have to make concessions himself in Paris five months later. The interior minister, Huỳnh Thúc Kháng, asked Hồ what should be done about Nam Bộ. Hồ replied, "Don't raise the armistice problem," an instruction the delegation quickly proceeded to ignore in Dalat, as we shall see.[122] When Hồ said farewell to the delegation the next morning, his parting words were, "Tense but no breaking."[123]

At eight o'clock on the morning of 16 April, two French planes took off from Gia Lâm airport carrying the Vietnamese delegation, advisors, radio operators, and a large transmitter, as well as several French escorts. This was the first opportunity for all or most Vietnamese passengers to see their country from the air, and it made an indelible impression. Võ Nguyên Giáp was moved by the blue sea, the green canopy of the Trường Sơn range, and a snake-like river reflected in the sun. The scene brought to Giáp's mind ancestral references to Vietnam's mountains and rivers looking like a "piece of beautiful embroidery."[124] Hoàng Xuân Hãn eagerly recognized islands and estuaries as they flew southward, then identified features of his home province of Hà Tĩnh before the pilot turned west to the Mụ Gịa pass and Laos. "The more my patriotic feelings welled up," Hãn recalls, "the more I thought anxiously about our loss of country (mất nước)."[125]

After the planes landed at Pakse for refueling, the Vietnamese were informed that the three-engine Ju-52 Junker had developed engine trouble that would necessitate staying overnight until a replacement craft arrived from Saigon. Some delegates feared a plot to incarcerate them, but such thoughts were alleviated when the local French officer in charge allowed everyone to walk freely around

Pakse town. Falling behind the main group, Hoàng Xuân Hãn overheard French soldiers remarking that "two grenades would finish off negotiations," and "all of them should be tied to execution posts." Managing to engage the soldiers in conversation, Hãn realized they were raw, mischievous arrivals from the *métropole*, quite unlike the brutish, red-beret paratroopers he had encountered in Hanoi. That night in the rudimentary Pakse guest house, the delegation discussed individual tasks at the conference, Giáp regaled everyone with tales of the Việt Bắc maquis (1941–45), and then Nguyễn Mạnh Tường lightened things up by starting a quest to find a partner for Giáp, whose wife had died in a French prison four years earlier. Early the next afternoon a replacement Junker did arrive, the delegation endured a very bumpy, nauseous ride to Dalat, and everyone was then driven to the Langbian Hotel, except for the head of the delegation, Nguyễn Tường Tam, who was taken to a suite at the more prestigious Hotel du Parc. The Vietnamese were proud to see French and DRV flags of equal size flying over both hotels.[126]

Diplomatic foreplay began immediately, with the Vietnamese delegation learning that Admiral d'Argenlieu had invited them to his palace the next morning to be introduced to the head of the French delegation, Max André, and the rest of his team. This was regarded as a maneuver by the high commissioner to place himself above both delegations, hence the Vietnamese refused to come to the palace on the morning of 18 April, much to the confusion of waiting journalists and photographers. Following several hours of heated discussion, the two sides agreed that d'Argenlieu would style himself the head of the delegation just long enough to meet Nguyễn Tường Tam, then introduce André as his replacement. Also, rather than the high commissioner opening the first session of the conference, as he had planned, the banquet hosted by d'Argenlieu the afternoon of 18 April served as the agreed substitute. Following d'Argenlieu's welcoming speech in French, Tam replied in Vietnamese, to the growing discomfort of some Frenchmen around the table. Nguyễn Mạnh Tường stood up to provide a sparkling French interpretation, which lightened the atmosphere. During subsequent relaxed conversation, one French delegate remarked humorously to Hoàng Xuân Hãn that Tường and most other Vietnamese present seemed "more French than the French," which should make negotiations easy. Hãn replied, "With you gentlemen I'm sure there's no difficulty, but with the French government I don't know how matters will go."[127]

On the morning of 19 April, Vietnamese and French delegations convened at the austere Lycée Yersin to make opening statements and form working committees. Max André was a National Assembly member belonging to the Mouvement Républicain Populaire (MRP), the new Catholic party whose main leader was Georges Bidault. Accompanying André from Paris were five specialists, the most important being Pierre Messmer, whom we met earlier parachuting into Tonkin,

FIGURE 14. At the Dalat Conference, two delegations in front of the Lycée Yersin. From left to right: Bousquet, Pierre Messmer, Võ Nguyên Giáp, General Salan, Gonon, Nguyễn Tường Tam, Max André, Léon Pignon, Jean Bourgoin, Trịnh Văn Bính, Pierre Gourou, Nguyễn Mạnh Tường, and Dương Bạch Mai. From Raoul Salan, *Mémoires*, vol. 1. Tous droits réservés.

and who was now *chef de cabinet* of the minister of overseas France. Six delegates came from the Indochina High Commission in Saigon, most significantly Léon Pignon, who could boast seven months experience dealing with Vietnamese personalities across the political spectrum. General Salan, commander of French troops in northern Indochina, came to the delegation as military expert. Overall, the French delegation had a distinct bureaucratic tilt, making it ill-equipped to deliberate the political issues that hung over the conference. The Vietnamese delegation was politically more astute, yet needed to learn the ins and outs of conference procedure before it would be able to score any significant advances.

As delegates prepared to focus on committee organization, Dương Bạch Mai took the floor to propose that the conference publicly commit itself to a general ceasefire, thus helping the meeting to proceed in a peaceful atmosphere. Max André replied that the French delegation had no authorization to discuss a ceasefire, nor could the Dalat conference be converted into an armistice commission. Someone in the French delegation asserted that hostilities had ended in Cochinchina, leaving only routine police operations. This brought an angry response from Võ Nguyên Giáp, who reaffirmed the right of Vietnam National Guard units to be in Nam Bộ, condemned the continuation of French attacks despite the 6 March Accord, and called for an armistice commission to meet promptly in Saigon. With the French delegation refusing to budge, and the Vietnamese under instructions not to break up the conference, the two sides agreed merely to refer the matter back to the two governments. Mai's immediate raising of a Nam Bộ armistice had not been discussed in advance by the delegation; it seems he did it on his own initiative, despite Hồ Chí Minh's admonition.[128]

The meeting then moved on to establish four working committees, for politics, economics and finance, military affairs, and culture. The Vietnamese delegation agreed internally that Nguyễn Tường Tam ought not attend committee meetings, only the plenary sessions, presumably to continue making the point about his having a higher official status than Max André (who took part in meetings of two committees). This, together with his placement alone in the Hôtel du Parc, put Tam out of touch with much that was happening.[129] It quickly became evident that much of the discussion would remain hypothetical until some progress was made on the political and military fronts. At the first meeting of the political committee, on 20 April, the two delegations tabled different agendas, then spent hours defending their choices. By the end of the day they had agreed to discuss Vietnam's relations with other countries and with the French Union, the Indochina Federation, and the referendum on unification of the three regions. That evening, Vietnamese delegates dissected these issues, divided into mock Vietnamese and French teams to debate each other, then prepared multiple scenarios to refer to in subsequent encounters with André and his colleagues. The French may well have planted microphones in some hotel rooms occupied by the Vietnamese delegation, and it became apparent that some Vietnamese hotel employees were reporting to the Sûreté. Võ Nguyên Giáp suspected that one member of the Vietnamese delegation was reporting internal Vietnamese discussions to the French.[130]

On Sunday, 21 April, Dr. Phạm Ngọc Thạch arrived suddenly at the Langbian Hotel, having been driven from Saigon to Dalat by a physician friend, accompanied by Nguyễn Văn Sâm, the short-lived southern region viceroy appointed by Emperor Bảo Đại on 14 August 1945. Although Thạch had been listed on the DRV delegation, d'Argenlieu informed Hồ Chí Minh that Thạch was unacceptable due to his involvement in violent activities in Cochinchina. For two days the delegation hid Thạch in a hotel room, bringing him food from the marketplace, and listening to his upbeat report on resistance efforts in the south.[131] Võ Nguyên Giáp used Thạch's information at the second meeting of the political committee on 22 April, and compared current southern anti-French resistance to French resistance to the Nazis in 1940–44. When Giáp's renewed call for a ceasefire as specified in the 6 March Accord was again rejected by Max André and Pierre

Messmer, Nguyễn Mạnh Tường suggested a compromise whereby the committee would simply study armistice methods and report its findings to the two governments. This too met French opposition, and Messmer as chair referred the matter to a later plenary session.[132]

The morning of 23 April, André handed Nguyễn Tường Tam a note complaining that certain persons had come to Dalat in order to engage in "clandestine politics," clearly referring to Thạch and Sâm. At a meeting of the Vietnamese delegation shortly thereafter, Thạch argued that they must be determined to push the Nam Bộ issue, or else "the south will reproach its brothers in the north." Võ Nguyên Giáp replied that to break off negotiations now would leave Vietnam vulnerable to charges of intransigence. Tam then recalled President Hồ's instructions to mount a "tense" argument but not to the point of "snapping" negotiations completely. At this point Nguyễn Văn Huyên wrote in his notebook, "I feel Thạch is dissatisfied." Soon afterward a French Army captain and two plainclothes men seized Thạch and drove him back to Saigon. Tam tried to meet d'Argenlieu to protest this action, but was referred to André. Vietnamese delegation members were furious, with some feeling that it was time to pack up and return to Hanoi. However, Giáp insisted that such provocations by the French colonial faction should be met calmly, and other delegates pointed to particular French delegates who appeared to be sympathetic to Vietnamese aspirations. At the second plenary session the next day, Tam stood up immediately to protest Thạch's seizure. André replied that Thạch had not been arrested, merely "taken back" for having come to Dalat in a clandestine manner. Giáp then moved the plenary debate on to other questions.[133]

Also on 23 April, Admiral d'Argenlieu sent Nguyễn Tường Tam a diplomatic note requesting that the Vietnamese delegation's radio transmitter be turned off until the French government granted permission to use it. In the meantime, d'Argenlieu added coyly, "the French government will be happy to take responsibility for communications between Hanoi and the delegation." This challenge to Vietnamese sovereignty enraged many delegates. For Hoàng Xuân Hãn the timing seemed remarkably clumsy, given French talk in conference committees about the benefits of future cooperation within the French Union. Two telegraphers had come with the delegation to transmit daily stenographic notes to Hanoi and receive urgent government instructions. Since French intelligence could intercept most of this traffic, it seems that the high commissioner simply wanted to assert his authority over Indochina's airwaves. The Vietnamese delegation decided not to reply to d'Argenlieu's "request," the transmitter continued to operate, and nothing more was heard of this issue for the duration of the conference.[134] The DRV government remained unaware that the French had cracked its codes, although National Guard radio operators in both Dalat and Hanoi were reprimanded sharply for inventing their own simplified cipher to speed up transmission.[135]

Conference Deadlock

At the 24 April 1946 plenary session, Léon Pignon proposed that the two governments establish a committee outside the Dalat conference format to "resolve the armistice question and create a conciliatory atmosphere throughout the five regions of Indochina." The Vietnamese delegates considered reference to five regions totally unacceptable, and insisted that plenary meetings be adjourned indefinitely. When the delegation met back at the hotel to assess the conference impasse, Nguyễn Tường Tam spoke emotionally of how external adversity had caused Nationalist Party and Communist Party delegates to understand each other and work together in the national interest. During the next three days, Giáp met informally with key French delegates, and discussions within the cultural committee and the economics and finance committee made some progress.[136] Another gathering of the Vietnamese delegation on 27 April concluded that no substantial agreement could come out of the Dalat conference, yet that did not mean negotiations should be broken off. A request to Hanoi for new instructions went unanswered. Tam became ill and remained in his room.

The 3 May Franco-Vietnamese plenary session exposed raw emotions on both sides and effectively concluded negotiations, although the conference limped on for another eight days. Nguyễn Tường Tam, chair for this session, indicated that the first item of business would be Vietnam's reply to Pignon's armistice committee proposal eight days prior. However, Max André jumped up to announce that three hours earlier Trần Văn Thạch, a member of the Cochinchina Consultative Council, had been assassinated in Saigon. André praised Thạch's contribution to Franco-Vietnamese amity and condemned the assassins as well as those who incited them. Dương Bạch Mai then stood up to castigate "those persons in Nam Bộ who sell out their country." Pierre Messmer produced the text of an order from Nguyễn Bình to mount a general offensive "in support of the Dalat conference," and Bình's glowing report on the 8 April destruction of the huge French ammunition dump in downtown Saigon, which Messmer emphasized had killed many innocent civilians. Võ Nguyên Giáp replied bluntly that if the French army did not agree to a ceasefire the Vietnamese army had to protect itself and fire back.[137]

On 4 May, the Vietnamese invited the French delegation to a reciprocal banquet at the Hôtel du Parc, where the French particularly complimented the spring rolls (chả giò), and cross-table conversation was boisterous and convivial. Towards the end of the evening, Nguyễn Tường Tam raised his glass to wish André good luck in the constitutional referendum being held the next day in France. André thanked Tam, then launched an attack that stunned his Vietnamese hosts, labeling as murderers those persons who had conspired to kill Trần Văn Thạch, asserting that the French side had already made a lot of concessions at the conference, and warning that today's France was not the France of Munich in 1938.

Offended by such discourtesy from a guest, who also represented a country famous for its good manners, the Vietnamese nonetheless chose not to respond.
The next day, just before departing for the *métropole*, André gave Giáp an unad-
dressed, misdated note that bluntly affirmed the intention of New France to persist in the work of stimulating and coordinating Indochina's technology, economy, diplomatic affairs, and defense. France also refused "to abdicate its cultural
mission."[138]

Although no one had expected any agreements to be signed at Dalat, the discussions did serve to clarify positions. In the cultural committee, the Vietnamese side accepted French teachers, educational materials, and diploma programs,
but refused to acknowledge French as the first language of tertiary or secondary
instruction, nor would the government refund France for existing school buildings
and equipment. In the economics and finance committee, Vietnam was happy to
receive French capital, technical assistance, and expert advice, but it reserved the
right to nationalize key economic units, and it withheld comment on French demands to compensate owners for properties lost or damaged. The French insisted
on a single Indochinese currency, while the Vietnamese reserved the right to employ Vietnamese currency as well. In the military affairs committee, Võ Nguyên
Giáp accepted General Salan's offer of equipment, instructors and training programs, and reiterated that French bases were welcome for a specific time period,
but he argued that any combined general staff or unified command structure
should be limited to times of mobilization against a common enemy. In the political committee, the French insisted that the Indochina Federation must have
wide political powers, while the Vietnamese were determined to limit the federation to economic matters. Vietnamese delegates angrily disputed French claims
to protect the interests of ethnic minorities within the federation. They disagreed that all customs duties be directed to the federal budget, or that France
take sole responsibility for conducting the future referendum. Little was said
about the French Union, as defeat of the proposed French constitution had left its
status up in the air.[139]

At the final plenary session on 11 May, the issue of Cochinchina and unification of the three regions came to the fore again, and speeches became ever more
emotional. Léon Pignon quoted the refusal of the Cochinchina Consultative
Council to accept unification. Giáp stated flatly that, "If Nam Bộ is lost, the Vietnamese people will fight until it is regained." Nguyễn Mạnh Tường asserted that
"Nam Bộ's flesh is our flesh, its blood is our blood," words which soon were inscribed on banners around the country. Nguyễn Văn Huyên said, "It's not that
Nam Bộ belongs to Vietnam, but rather Vietnam belongs to Nam Bộ." Hoàng
Xuân Hãn stood up to give the concluding Vietnamese speech, although he
found it hard to talk. Suddenly Hồ Hữu Tường leapt up, tears in his eyes, and
walked out of the room. Giáp then grasped his briefcase and followed Tường,

slamming the door as he went. Hãn was determined to finish reading his speech, then everyone filed quietly out of the room, the French surprised to see some of the Vietnamese crying.[140]

Next morning, Vietnamese delegation members boarded two planes to fly back to Gia Lâm airport. On 13 May, the delegation met the DRV Cabinet to report. Nguyễn Tường Tam said it had been a tense struggle with the French, but the Vietnamese side had not allowed the conference to disintegrate. Delegates had worked hard, and emerged from the experience understanding each other better and feeling more united. Võ Nguyên Giáp gave the cabinet a harsh summary of French strategic objectives: "to reestablish colonial power via the Indochina Federation; to use Vietnamese lackeys to exercise direct rule over Nam Bộ; and to utilize their army to restrict our self-government in the north." Hồ Chí Minh apparently chose not to chastise the delegation for ignoring his instruction to eschew the armistice issue. The delegation then met alone for the last time to assess activities with an eye to doing better at the upcoming Paris conference. Giáp criticized interpersonal relations, secretariat operations, and committee organization. Vũ Văn Hiền felt that delegates had often become so preoccupied by detail that they lost sight of broader issues. Nguyễn Mạnh Tường pointed out that the delegation had failed to cultivate the press or private observers. That evening, Hồ and Huỳnh Thúc Kháng gave a dinner for the delegation, and inevitably Hồ asked if any members had composed poetry at Dalat. Only Hoàng Xuân Hãn, at the urging of Cù Huy Cận, recited one of his Dalat poems to the gathering.[141]

Vietnamese newspapers which tried to follow proceedings at Dalat encountered many difficulties. The French exercised control over accreditation of reporters, travel to and from Dalat, and the transmission of article copy. The DRV delegation did not routinely distribute press releases, which left papers mostly reliant on foreign radio broadcasts. A notable exception was *Cứu Quốc* daily, which must have been given copies of some of the radio messages from the delegation in Dalat, in order to enable it to publish exclusive reports. The French detention of Phạm Ngọc Thạch sparked media outrage. The inaugural issue of *Dân Mới (New Citizen)* in Nghệ An province carried a big front-page headline: "Violently protest the French Army's seizure of Mr. Phạm Ngọc Thạch."[142] Dương Bạch Mai's militant speeches on Nam Bộ received much favorable comment. Lacking detail on day-to-day meetings in Dalat, newspapers offered background articles on topics they knew would come up, for example the currency issue, customs duties, French-owned companies, the Indochina Federation, and the French Union. Nguyễn Văn Tố contributed an essay on the meaning of federalism.[143] A Việt Minh journal aimed at intellectuals praised the Dalat delegation's performance, but then commented that Paris was a better place to talk with the leaders of New France.[144] More critically, *Gió Mới (New Wind)* opined that Dalat had been torpedoed by the "dark cloud of events" in Nam Bộ, south-central

Vietnam, and Laos, as well as by left-wing setbacks in France. The two delegations had talked past each other, not reaching a modicum of understanding, much less friendship.[145]

THE DRV PARLIAMENTARY DELEGATION
TO FRANCE

On 16 April 1946, the same day the DRV negotiating delegation departed Hanoi for Dalat, a DRV parliamentary goodwill delegation boarded another plane to go to Paris as guests of the French National Constituent Assembly. This first direct Vietnamese encounter with the French *métropole* in six years has been largely ignored by historians. Headed by Phạm Văn Đồng, diligent lieutenant to Hồ Chí Minh, the delegation encompassed ICP and Democratic Party members, southerners, journalists, and nonparty professionals trained in France during the 1930s.[146] Arriving at Le Bourget airport on 25 April, the Vietnamese received official honors and attention befitting legislators of a sovereign state, not a mere local, de facto regime as Admiral d'Argenlieu would have preferred. In the airport reception area, the delegation was stunned to find not only French officials but two score photographers, one hundred police, and several hundred excited Vietnamese residents in France. Beyond the airport boundary, another thousand Vietnamese greeted the delegation with banners declaring "Long Live Complete Vietnamese Independence!" and "Long Live Hồ Chí Minh!"

At a planning meeting in Cairo prior to arrival, delegation members had agreed that, due to continuing unstable political circumstances in France, everyone should exercise prudence when talking with politicians, civil servants, journalists, and other opinion makers. They aimed to make formal contact with all major political parties, starting deliberately with the Christian democratic group, the Mouvement Républicain Populaire (MRP). The delegation also requested to meet with the important Comité Interministériel de l'Indochine (Comanindo); four such meetings did eventuate, including reciprocal banquets at a Chinese restaurant where the proprietor's wife was Vietnamese. After Jean Sainteny made a public statement in Paris to which the Vietnamese delegation took exception, it was decided to rebut Sainteny at a press conference. Further throwing caution to the wind, the delegation accepted an invitation from the Confédération Générale du Travail (CGT) to participate in the first May Day parade since the end of World War II. From the reviewing stand, delegates applauded more than one million people filing by, including the Vietnamese branch of the CGT carrying DRV flags and banners demanding implementation of the 6 March Accord, release of Vietnamese under detention in France, and the right of Vietnamese to return to their homeland.[147]

The delegation delayed meeting with the Parti Communiste Français (PCF) until 7 May, and this encounter lasted only one hour. Besides PCF leaders Maurice Thorez and Jacques Duclos, delegation members were introduced to André Marty, the most famous participant in the 1919 Black Sea mutiny within the French Navy. This was particularly significant to Tôn Đức Thắng, as he claimed to have participated in the same mutiny.[148] Amidst the whirl of formal receptions, political rituals, and excursions, delegation members also divided up to talk with writers, artists, teachers, scientists, and physicians. Overall, the delegation's combination of Francophonia and Vietnamese patriotism impressed many French interlocutors. Admiral d'Argenlieu dispatched a Cochinchinese information mission to Paris to try to neutralize the impact of the DRV delegation, but it arrived late and was largely ignored.[149]

Each member of the parliamentary delegation was meant to take responsibility for different tasks. Nguyễn Mạnh Hà used his 1930s sojourn in Paris to renew acquaintances with prominent French intellectuals and overseas Vietnamese professionals. Mme Hà, a French national, accompanied the delegation from Hanoi and readily accepted roles as facilitator and office manager. As the daughter of Georges Marrane, founding member of the PCF and National Assembly delegate from Ivry-sur-Seine, Mme. Hà helped to open many doors on the left for the delegation. Phạm Văn Đồng made all official pronouncements on behalf of the delegation and fielded difficult questions from journalists. Huỳnh Văn Tiểng evoked the armed struggle in Nam Bộ, while nondelegate [Ngô] Xuân Diệu described cultural transformations and political mobilization underway throughout Vietnam. Đỗ Đức Dục coordinated press relations and regularly telegraphed news of the delegation back to Vietnam, where its progress was reported widely in the press. Nguyễn Tấn Gi-Trọng sought out books, serials, pamphlets, and typescripts to carry home. Whatever money the delegation received from the DRV government seems to have run out halfway through the trip, which meant relying on overseas Vietnamese groups and individuals for assistance. Two rental cars had to be returned for lack of petrol ration tickets.[150]

This was the first opportunity for Vietnamese living in France to meet DRV representatives, a moving experience on both sides. The government had already compiled information on Việt Kiều (overseas Vietnamese) prior to the parliamentary delegation's departure from Hanoi. It estimated that there were twenty-two thousand Việt Kiều in France, including seven thousand soldiers, ten thousand workers, two thousand merchant mariners, and six hundred students. *Cứu Quốc* reported that Việt Kiều had raised ten million francs to send to the DRV government.[151] As noted above, the delegation received an enthusiastic Việt Kiều reception at the airport, but it soon became evident that many overseas Vietnamese were disturbed by the 6 March Accord, especially its failure to recognize

Nam Bộ/Cochinchina as an integral part of Vietnam. Soon after arrival, the delegation met privately with four Việt Kiều leaders to explain the government's position, urge them to restrain "extremists," and make sure that subsequent public meetings were conducted in an orderly manner. At a subsequent meeting of one hundred representatives of the Alliance of Overseas Vietnamese in France (Việt Kiều Liên Minh tại Pháp), Phạm Văn Đồng read out letters from President Hồ Chí Minh, the National Assembly, and the Hanoi branch of the Việt Minh. He then presented the Alliance with an autographed photo of Hồ plus other keepsakes, and urged it to help make sure the French government stuck to its promises in the 6 March accord. In his trip diary, Nguyễn Tấn Gi-Trọng judged this "an important meeting, bringing our overseas brethren inside the framework of Vietnamese citizenship, obeying and supporting the government, especially in regard to the 6 March Preliminary Convention."[152]

Nguyễn Tấn Gi-Trọng overestimated the degree of political consensus and organizational unity among Việt Kiều in France in April 1946. Soldiers, workers, intellectuals and professionals possessed diverse viewpoints and group affiliations, plus a lively history of disputation. Of particular concern to ICP members within the DRV delegation were Việt Kiều adherents of the Fourth International, popularly titled Trotskyists, who accused the Vietnamese government of selling out the working class in cahoots with international imperialism. On 5 May, a parliamentary delegation contingent took the train to Marseille to visit a French military camp for Vietnamese worker conscripts. More than one thousand workers marched in review, the DRV flag was saluted, and statements were read by both sides. On returning to Paris, two delegates boarded a plane with a French general to fly to an army base at Lake Constance, on the German-Swiss border. Here too there was a Vietnamese march in review and a flag-raising ceremony, followed by an overnight stay and discussion about events at home.[153] According to newspaper reports in Vietnam, soldiers at Lake Constance denounced a French military apparatus that could shift so rapidly from liberating Europe to attacking independent Vietnam.[154]

In Paris, Vietnamese groups of students, health professionals, Catholic clergy, and even French wives of Việt Kiều met with delegation members. A remarkable 120 Vietnamese intellectuals resident in France added their names to a motion, passed by fellow intellectuals in Hanoi five weeks prior, that protested French attempts to detach Nam Bộ and otherwise limit the sovereignty of the state of Vietnam.[155] Cultural exhibits, musical performances, and movie screenings took place. The artist Mai Trung Thứ directed and produced a film about Việt Kiều life in France and the 25 April reception of the delegation at the airport, in time for it to be carried back to Vietnam. As they prepared to board the plane to return to Hanoi, the National Assembly delegation sang both "Tiến quân ca" ("Advancing Army"), the DRV national anthem, and the "Marseillaise" for their

French hosts.[156] The parliamentary tour proved excellent preparation for the extraordinary campaign to woo the French public and the Việt Kiều that was launched by Hồ Chí Minh soon afterward. Landing back at Gia Lâm on 23 May, delegation members had one week to brief the negotiating team before it departed for France. They also carried with them stacks of letters from Vietnamese in France to loved ones at home—their first opportunity to make contact in six years.[157]

The parliamentary delegation surely also brought home a somber, much talked about article by Trần Đức Thảo on the causes of Franco-Vietnamese conflict.[158] For Thảo, a number of key words [in French] failed to carry the same meaning for Vietnamese and French users, so that sincere attempts at discussion usually ended amidst accusations of bad faith. Thus, the average French citizen was quite convinced that General Leclerc's army had gone to Indochina to set its people on the road to progress and freedom—within the French community. The French assumed that Vietnamese were incapable of governing themselves, so that if France left Indochina the country would soon be torn apart by faction fighting, or fall under the domination of another power. By contrast, Vietnamese saw the possibilities of an independent Vietnam, free to industrialize itself, to establish as many schools as it wished, "to send students to all the universities of Europe and America, to bring into play the law of competition, buying and selling at the best price." The two peoples also interpreted Vietnam's precolonial and colonial histories in very different ways. While the French continued to believe in their mission to defend and to ensure the happiness of Indochina's inhabitants, Thảo insisted that Vietnamese had never asked for these favors, nor were they asking for them now. All Vietnamese wanted was for the French "not to attack them and not to turn the country into a bloodbath." Any dialogue was "a perpetual misunderstanding on both sides, a misunderstanding which is total and irremediable."

In weeks leading up to departure of President Hồ Chí Minh and the negotiating delegation for France, the Vietnamese press opened up to reveal significant divergences of opinion on how much the French could be trusted, which issues were nonnegotiable, and what chances really existed for peaceful resolution of Franco-Vietnamese differences. Some writers remained convinced that the French really only understood raw power, that they would take advantage of any weakness and hold off only when faced with strength. The litmus test was Nam Bộ and southern Trung Bộ, where the French had shown no inclination to negotiate because they felt they had the upper hand.[159] In a Huế newspaper, a Vietnamese soldier described listening to his political officer talk about the New France and explain how democratic, progressive French citizens wanted to enjoy friendly ties with Vietnam. Why then, the soldier asked, were these French friends not helping right now to fight the fascists in Saigon who were determined to keep

Vietnam divided? Without such help, this soldier was convinced that his place was in the south, exchanging bullet for bullet with the enemy. "Weeds must be torn out from the roots, starting now," he concluded.[160] Clearly this soldier had an inflated opinion of what Vietnamese arms could accomplish in the south, probably due to reading wildly misleading combat accounts in the press.

At the other end of the spectrum, believers in negotiations argued that it was feasible and indeed essential to bypass the old colonialists in Saigon and engage the New France in Paris itself. During the summer of 1946, the French left might well strengthen its political position. Vietnamese delegates could also meet the press in Paris, and thus influence the public. As a Nghệ An writer enthused, "Paris citizens have the revolutions of 1789, 1830, 1848, and 1870 to be proud of." Vietnamese could show these revolutionary descendants that "we are not cowering colonized subjects, but citizens of a free country." Mutual benefits contained in a Franco-Vietnamese agreement might "lessen the pain of French mothers and wives who have lost men senselessly in Nam Bộ and Laos."[161] The author seemed unaware that most French socialists and communists had supported restoration of French sovereignty over Indochina.

The majority of Vietnamese commentators in late May and June 1946 stood somewhere between bellicosity and trust. They felt that talks in Paris were worth a try, but meanwhile everyone at home should remain vigilant and prepare for adversity. The Dalat experience compelled Vietnam to be cautious. French progressives might join Vietnamese in opposing French reactionaries, yet Vietnam's struggle for independence might still have to persist well beyond the Paris talks.[162] Just as Vietnamese popular resistance had led to President Hồ being invited to France, it was Vietnam's underlying strengths that would facilitate a favorable diplomatic settlement. French negotiators found this position offensive. They would have taken particular exception to one newspaper's summary characterization: "Believing in the struggle capacity of all the people, we will never again endure life as slaves with bird shit dropping on us."[163]

ONWARD TO PARIS

Not all ICP leaders favored President Hồ Chí Minh's trip to France. Some who had spent many years in jail or evading Sûreté capture worried that French agents might detain or poison their president.[164] Others felt that the president should apply himself to mass mobilization and defense preparations at home, leaving negotiations in Paris to the official Vietnamese delegation. Ironically, it was probably Admiral d'Argenlieu who silenced such critics when, on his first visit to Hanoi in 18–19 May, he tried to persuade Hồ not to go, citing the 2 June general election in France and possible delays in forming a new French government.[165] In Haiphong the next day, d'Argenlieu was serenaded by a Việt Minh chorus with a song known to all French schoolchildren, "En passant par la Lorraine," to make the point that Vietnam's south was treasured like France's Alsace-Lorraine.[166] Meanwhile, Hồ was making final choices for the delegation. At least one newspaper reported that Võ Nguyên Giáp would accompany the president to Paris.[167] On 29 May, the names of twelve delegates and five advisors were announced. As DRV foreign minister, Nguyễn Tường Tam would head the delegation, and Phạm Văn Đồng would be deputy head. Seven of the seventeen individuals named had been to Dalat. Two key additions were: Phan Anh, the defense minister, but more important for this mission, a lawyer with considerable debating and courtroom experience; and Hoàng Minh Giám, closest aide to the president on external affairs.[168] On 29 or 30 May, Nguyễn Tường Tam suddenly fled Hanoi for China (see chapter 7).

Hồ Chí Minh's departure for France on 31 May became a major DRV state ceremony, with citizens and militia guards lining the road to the Long Biên/ Doumer bridge before dawn, groups presenting flowers to the president at the Gia Lâm airport terminal, the president reviewing Vietnamese and French troops together with General Valluy, and a moving farewell from the acting president, Huỳnh Thúc Kháng, and other members of Cabinet.[169] Journalists interviewed members of the negotiating delegation, while one reporter obtained from the president a handwritten exhortation, "Unity, Discipline, Mission" (Đoàn kết, Kỷ luật, Công tác), which was photographically reproduced on the front page of the Việt Minh newspaper in Haiphong.[170] Hồ's parting counsel to the acting president came as a classical Sino-Vietnamese expression, "Cope with constantly shifting circumstances by adhering to fundamental principles" (dĩ bất biến, ứng vạn biến), which quickly spread among the populace as "Be ready for any eventuality", or "Always be prepared." Some French officials cited Hồ's remark as proof of his double-dealing, on the one hand preaching Franco-Vietnamese friendship and compromise, on the other hand preparing for war.[171] According to this reasoning, the DRV should have been content to rely entirely on the good graces of France.

Two Dakotas took off from Gia Lâm at 7:40 A.M. on 31 May, with the Vietnamese contingent accompanied by General Salan, Lieutenant Colonel Émile Tutenges (who had also travelled with the parliamentary delegation), and several civilian French officials. Perhaps at Hồ Chí Minh's insistence, Arthur Trevor-Wilson, senior British intelligence officer in Indochina, came along as implicit guarantor against French subterfuge. It was in Cairo that Hồ heard on the radio that Admiral d'Argenlieu had approved formation of the Autonomous Republic of Cochinchina on 1 June. Hồ angrily asked General Salan why no one had bothered to tell him officially. "Don't make Cochinchina another Alsace-Lorraine, or we'll have a Hundred Years war," he told Salan, and then asked to return to Hanoi.[172] Hồ calmed down, and on 9 June the travelers were invited to relax at Cannes until a new French government was formed following the 2 June elections. The next day their invitation was changed to the more isolated town of Biarritz, adjacent to the Spanish border. When they finally landed at Parme-Biarritz airport on 12 June there was no one to greet them, although lodging had been arranged at the Carlton, the best hotel in town. Hồ thanked the French flight crews warmly and presented each member with an ornate ivory tobacco/opium pipe.[173]

Jean Sainteny was assigned to host Hồ Chí Minh in Biarritz until the new government of Georges Bidault was prepared to welcome him in Paris. With Hồ still talking of return to Hanoi, Sainteny insisted disingenuously that the 6 March Accord's provision for a referendum trumped the high commissioner's "temporary" move. Sainteny found ways to amuse his guest, including a pilgrimage to Lourdes, visits to nearby villages, a successful fishing expedition on the Bay of Biscay, and relaxing at a beach villa belonging to Sainteny's sister, where Hồ enjoyed playing "uncle" to her children. Within a day of arriving at Biarritz, overseas Vietnamese began to come to pay their respects to the president. Hồ received them cordially, then relied on delegates to listen to their stories, accept gifts, and decide who was likely to be useful to the DRV cause. Soon delegation members who had studied in France in the 1930s departed Biarritz for Paris on various political missions, much to the irritation of Sainteny.[174]

Finally, on 22 June, Hồ Chí Minh was flown to Le Bourget airport, where he was met officially by Marius Moutet, the continuing minister of overseas France, not by Prime Minister Bidault. Nonetheless, Vietnamese were pleased to see their own flag displayed next to the tricolor, and they noted that Hồ was given full state-to-state honors before being driven to the Royal-Monceau hotel on Avenue Hoche. Hồ was willing to be guided on official engagements by the French head of protocol, but not to the detriment of his unpretentious persona. He retained his simple Sun Yat-sen tunic and canvas sandals for every occasion, while the DRV delegation was always seen in Western suit-and-tie. When Hồ was driven in an open limousine up the Champs-Elysées to lay a wreath at the Tomb of the Unknown Soldier, someone in the vehicle commented on the large crowd who had come to watch the procession, to which Hồ laughingly replied, "Why of course, everyone wants to see the Vietnamese version of Charlie Chaplin!" At the hotel, Hồ always rose early and received his first visitors at six in the morning, startling those who did not expect engagements before noon.[175]

Pleased with his Dalat precedent, Admiral d'Argenlieu proposed and Prime Minister Bidault accepted that negotiations take place not in Paris, but rather at Fontainebleau, sixty kilometers distant, to reduce the chance of popular demonstrations. D'Argenlieu himself took only forty hours to fly from Saigon to Paris, in contrast to Hồ's thirteen days to get to Biarritz. Back in Indochina, French forces seized Pleiku and Kontum on 21 June, completing their occupation of the "Plateaux Moïs" (south-central highlands). Four days later they took control of the governor general's palace in Hanoi as it was vacated by the Chinese, an act which triggered vigorous Vietnamese protests. This was d'Argenlieu's way of putting his mark on the Fontainebleau talks before they began, without having consulted the new French government.[176] Much of what Hồ Chí Minh and the DRV delegation had experienced since taking off from Hanoi five weeks earlier seemed designed by their hosts to demonstrate that France held the strategic initiative, and that Vietnam had no choice but to remain reliant on France, as demonstrated in many practical ways: transport, communications, overseas expenses, diplomatic protocol, and general tutelage in modernity. Bidault's decision not to appoint a Cabinet member as head of the French delegation, or indeed include any government minister, signaled that certain political issues might be excluded from discussion, and also made it impossible from a protocol point of view for Hồ Chí Minh to participate at Fontainebleau.

Fontainebleau

The Fontainebleau conference opened on 6 July 1946 with an anodyne welcoming speech from Max André, again head of the French delegation.[177] Phạm Văn Đồng responded with a blistering condemnation of Admiral d'Argenlieu's actions, notably the 1 June proclamation of a Cochinchina government and the more recent military offensive in the south-central highlands. As the two sides met in plenary session to agree on a conference agenda, the differences evident at Dalat surfaced once again. On 11 July, the French tabled a paper regarding the French Union which rejected a "simple association of interests" in favor of subordination to common institutions and laws.[178] Practically speaking, the French could not present a clear idea of what Vietnam had to gain from membership in the French Union since the Union did not yet exist. The next day the Vietnamese delegation countered with the idea of a voluntary alliance of free states.[179] In Paris, Hồ Chí Minh called a press conference to urge a bilateral treaty based on common interests. He also signaled that Vietnam's participation in the Indochina Federation would be "essentially economic," and promised security for French capital investments in Vietnam. On the issue of Nam Bộ, Hồ argued that "even before Corsica became French, Cochinchina was Vietnamese."[180] Léon Pignon was now alarmed at the favorable effect that Hồ Chí Minh and the DRV delegation were having on French public opinion. Privately he referred to his opposite numbers as the enemy, for the moment engaging France in battle by nonviolent means.[181] Gaullists reproached Prime Minister Bidault for permitting President Hồ to be officially present at the Bastille Day parade in Paris.[182]

Between 13 and 30 July, delegates at Fontainebleau met in four working committees, as at Dalat, to wrestle over specific issues. Amidst all the powers that French delegates aimed to assign to the Indochina Federation, the Vietnamese accepted only an *institut d'emission* (mint) and a money exchange office, while

FIGURE 15. Young "Vietnam" offers the 6 March 1946 Preliminary Accord to Marianne, "France," in exchange for something
more lasting. Prices are listed for "Federation," "Self-rule," and
"Free State," but "Independence" is marked "Not for Sale." In *Dư
Luận* 9 (16 June 1946). Courtesy of Vietnam National Library.

specifically rejecting taxation authority. In the military committee, the Vietnamese repeated their objections to a unified Franco-Vietnamese command structure in peacetime, and renewed their acceptance of French troops and bases until
1951 only. The French continued to insist on a unified command, and now retracted
their agreement to withdraw by 1951. Regarding diplomatic representation, France
offered Vietnam the right to station consular officers overseas, provided that all
other foreign contacts were handled at the French Union level. In the economic
committee, Vietnam once again insisted on its right to nationalize certain enterprises, while France not only wanted all French properties returned but also
wanted compensation for damages incurred since the March 1945 Japanese coup.
Vietnam agreed to give priority to French technicians, while France accepted
that not all technicians had to be recruited via the French government. Discussion over Cochinchina failed to make any progress, causing Dương Bạch Mai to
warn that the entire conference could collapse as a result, followed by the end of
Franco-Vietnamese friendship and peace and order in Vietnam.[183]

On 25 July, Admiral d'Argenlieu seized the initiative again, announcing in
Saigon that he would convene on 1 August a second conference at Dalat that included delegates from Cambodia, Laos, and Cochinchina, as well as observers
from southern Annam and the south-central highlands. At Fontainebleau, Phạm
Văn Đồng accused France of violating the 6 March Accord and dispatched a

formal note of protest to the French government. Prime Minister Bidault, who had not been informed in advance by d'Argenlieu, failed to respond promptly to Đồng's protest, which led the Vietnamese delegation to break off negotiations on 1 August.[184] The Vietnamese also became aware in late July that d'Argenlieu was blocking transmission of encrypted telegrams from the DRV government in Hanoi to the delegation in France. When this was brought to the attention of the French government, Hồ Chí Minh was told merely that a policy decision on encrypted messages was pending.[185] D'Argenlieu's hand was strengthened when a serious armed confrontation occurred in early August at the town of Bắc Ninh, just north of Hanoi, with twelve French soldiers killed and forty-two wounded (see below). French commanders assigned all blame to Vietnamese forces, the French press accused the DRV government of bad faith, and there were calls to terminate negotiations. However, Bidault and particularly Marius Moutet, minister of overseas France, still wanted some sort of agreement with Hồ Chí Minh. Max André assured Đồng that the second Dalat conference was merely consultative, the Bắc Ninh incident was set aside, and the Vietnamese agreed to resume negotiations.[186]

The French delegation at Fontainebleau was divided over what position it should take on key issues, notably the status of Cochinchina, powers to be vested in the Indochina Federation, and even whether or not the DRV was a suitable negotiating partner. In a confidential meeting of the delegation on 25 July, Pierre Messmer suggested that it ought to be possible to find a formula whereby Hanoi received guarantees that Cochinchina was part of Vietnam and yet a degree of autonomy remained. Others doubted this arrangement was possible or desirable. Six days later, Léon Pignon attacked the "Messmer thesis" for holding out the prospect of future tranquility, when in fact the Hanoi government's sole preoccupation was "to struggle against France until it has destroyed the last vestiges of French influence." Already, Pignon added, the French in Indochina questioned the commitment of the *métropole* and were thinking of repatriating their capital. Clearly Pignon was content to see an end to negotiations.[187] On 8 August, Marius Moutet sought to gain control, criticizing the "lack of national discipline during sensitive negotiations," reiterating a government commitment to the 6 March Accord, and disputing the need to rely on force to obtain basic French objectives.[188]

Unfortunately we have no access to similar records of private meetings of the Vietnamese delegation at Fontainebleau. Phạm Văn Đồng was in charge of delegation business, although he reported regularly to Hồ Chí Minh and received instructions. Đồng spoke most at the plenary sessions, with other delegates called on for supporting remarks. Phan Anh took his responsibility as *rapporteur* seriously, and could be depended upon to phrase legal issues properly. As the Cochinchina issue came to dominate proceedings, Dương Bạch Mai spoke more frequently. His volatile rhetoric played into the hands of Pignon, seeming to deny Messmer's assertion that a compromise could be secured over Cochinchina. Vietnamese delegates were upset to find PCF and Socialist Party delegates sometimes taking more rigid negotiating positions than their right-wing colleagues, apparently because the Left did not wish to be perceived as jeopardizing the French national interest as yet another National Assembly election approached.[189]

Subsequent weeks saw discussion continue at two levels: between Hồ Chí Minh and Marius Moutet; and within a select committee of Vietnamese and French delegates at Fontainebleau. While Hồ and Moutet appeared determined to identify points of correspondence that could lead to a limited accord, the select committee ranged across all issues once more. At a pivotal meeting on 3 September, French delegates spoke about property guarantees, cultural concerns, technicians, currency, and taxes. At the end of each presentation, Đồng simply replied "no objection in principle," probably because he wanted to get to the two issues that the Vietnamese side had placed on the agenda: independence and Cochinchina. Phan Anh made the case for French recognition of Vietnam's independence, to which Pignon replied that only France's council of ministers was empowered to consider the question. Then Đồng took up Cochinchina, which sparked sharp exchanges between Mai and Đồng on one side and Pignon and Albert Torel on the other. When Mai argued that his government had made the ultimate concession by agreeing to a referendum at all, since Cochinchina remained most definitely a part of Vietnam, Pignon replied that it was France that had made the concession since Cochinchina was French territory. Đồng said that the only way to convince people to stop fighting was to set a date for the referendum, but Torel commented that before any referendum, the population needed first to understand the reasons for Franco-Vietnamese cooperation.[190]

Moutet now assigned Pignon, together with Henri Laurentie from the ministry of overseas France, to negotiate a new memorandum (*note verbale*) with Hồ Chí Minh, the results of which were presented to a plenary session of the Fontainebleau conference on 10 September. To the surprise of the French delegation, Phạm Văn Đồng proposed reopening discussion of the entire accord text, and specifically insisted that the date and modalities of a referendum be inserted. Max André, presiding, declared an adjournment, but that proved to be the last meeting of the two delegations.[191] Students of diplomacy might see in French internal divisions and growing Vietnamese suspicions a prescription for failure, irrespective of what leaders on either side wanted.

Three days later the Vietnamese delegation left Paris by train for Marseille, where they boarded the *Pasteur* for Haiphong, along with 1,686 of their compatriots. Hoàng Minh Giám and Dương Bạch Mai were left behind with Hồ Chí Minh. As no account has surfaced of internal deliberations of the Vietnamese delegation, we can only speculate that some members took adamant exception to

FIGURE 16. Hồ Chí Minh and Marius Moutet shaking hands after signing the modus vivendi, with Lord Buddha as witness. In *France Illustration* 52 (28 September 1946): 295. Tous droits réservés.

the absence of any referendum date for Cochinchina or any French commitment to Vietnam's future independence. Without delegation consensus, it was left to President Hồ to decide whether some very limited agreement was worth signing or not. With the authorities having informed Hồ that his time as a guest of the French government was at an end, he departed the Royal Monceau hotel to become a houseguest of Raymond Aubrac, engineer, PCF member, and hero of the French Resistance.[192] After a flurry of meetings and exchanges of text, Hồ and Moutet signed a modus vivendi in Moutet's bedroom in the small hours of 15 September, backdating the document to 14 September.[193]

By way of context to the modus vivendi, a joint declaration reaffirmed the 6 March Accord, asserted that limited diplomatic progress had since been made, specified that neither a date nor the modalities of a referendum had been fixed yet, and presaged resumption of conference proceedings in January 1947. The text of the modus vivendi appeared to address a wide range of disputed issues, yet in most cases the internal contradictions and complexities were devolved to a mixed commission to resolve subsequently.[194] French nationals were to enjoy the same property rights and freedom of trade as Vietnamese nationals. Confiscated French property had to be returned (but with no mention of reparations). French schools were to operate freely; French nationals could conduct research throughout Vietnam; and the Pasteur Institute and Ecole française d'Extrême-Orient would resume activities. The DRV was to give priority to French advisors, technicians, and experts. Pending a future currency accord, only piastres issued by the (French-owned) Bank of Indochina would circulate in the DRV. As a member of the Indochina Federation, the DRV agreed to join a customs union which would set common export and import taxes and exclude internal tariffs. DRV consular officials would be permitted to function overseas once a mixed commission made arrangements.

Much subsequent attention focused on Article 9 of the modus vivendi, dealing with restoration of public order in Cochinchina and southern Annam, to include a ceasefire, coordination between French and Vietnamese military staffs, release of political prisoners, guarantee of democratic liberties, cessation of hostile propaganda, and neutralizing nationals of ex-enemy powers (a reference to Japanese deserters). In a rather plaintive passage, Vietnam guaranteed that no act of violence would be tolerated against persons by reason of their attachment or loyalty to France, while the French government guaranteed likewise in regard to persons by reason of their attachment to Vietnam. Finally, the DRV would designate an individual, acceptable to the French government, who would work with High Commissioner d'Argenlieu "to establish the cooperation indispensable to executing the current accord," which Article 9 declared would come into force on 30 October 1946.

D'Argenlieu was furious at the way Article 9 conceded to Hanoi some rights to participate in the affairs of Cochinchina and southern Annam. The French military was angry that Hồ Chí Minh had managed to exclude any requirement for non-Cochinchinese units to withdraw northward or be disarmed locally. Anticipating these objections, Moutet sent political instructions to d'Argenlieu focused mostly on Article 9. In them, Moutet reasserted his conviction that Cochinchina was "the very pivot of our whole Indochina policy." France had to succeed rapidly in Cochinchina, not excluding individuals who favored Vietnamese unity. He warned the high commissioner that a policy of force would almost certainly prove unsuccessful, because "our military means are and will remain limited."[195] Ten days later, the Defense General Staff in Paris dispatched a different interpretation of Article 9 to Admiral d'Argenlieu, declaring that the article did not supersede the standing objective of "disarming rebels originating in Cochinchina and southern Annam, and returning to Tonkin and northern Annam elements originating in those territories." As for the individual representing the DRV who would come south, the General Staff explained this as a minor French concession made when refusing Hồ Chí Minh's insistence on a mixed commission to implement the ceasefire.[196]

As he prepared to return to Vietnam, Hồ Chí Minh could not help but feel dejected at the meager diplomatic results expressed in the modus vivendi. He hoped that a more sympathetic French government would come to power follow-ing the second constitutional referendum, scheduled for 13 October, and subse-quent national elections. Separate from his negotiating efforts, Hồ had wooed the French political elite and the public at large. At a reception held in Jean Sain-teny's townhouse, Hồ was introduced to a range of politicians, including Albert Sarraut, former governor general of Indochina and minister of colonies, who is said to have exclaimed: "Well! Here you are, you old brigand. I have you within reach at last! What a good part of my life I've spent pursuing you!"[197] Several times Hồ asked Sainteny to arrange for him to meet General de Gaulle, yet he must have known that was unlikely. Hồ encountered General Leclerc once on a social occasion, but his attempts to meet privately were rebuffed, presumably reflecting Leclerc's suspicions, expressed since May, that Hồ was not sincere in his quest for peace. The French Right appears to have become quite mistrustful of Hồ by the end of his visit, partly due to his simultaneous courting of PCF leaders, and partly due to the efforts of some members of the DRV delegation to mobilize rank-and-file communist support for outright Vietnamese independence.[198] These left-wing contacts would prove valuable to the DRV when the PCF later took a position in opposition to the Indochina War. Thanks to French newspapers, radio broad-casts, and cinema newsreels, Hồ managed to reach ordinary French citizens, conveying to many a sense of firm patriotic purpose that did not negate Franco-Vietnamese friendship.

The presence in France of Hồ Chí Minh and the negotiating delegation caused considerable excitement amongst Việt Kiều (overseas Vietnamese). With the Vietnam National Assembly delegation having prepared the ground in April–May 1946, and one thousand Việt Kiều greeting Hồ at Le Bourget airport on 22 June, Hồ and delegation members had many subsequent opportunities to face Việt Kiều audiences, explain the DRV platform, share refreshments, and listen to the concerns of longtime residents in France. Mai Trung Thứ and Phạm Văn Nhân were able to film Hồ over the fourteen weeks he was in France, making a series of short documentaries that screened in both France and Vietnam.[199] Or-ganizations sprang up to assist the delegation in raising funds, disseminating information, and proselytizing amongst French friends and workmates. Some of the most trusted helpers in 1946 had come to France as servicemen or workers during World War I, then joined the PCF in the 1920s. They and other Việt Kiều now castigated the PCF for allowing the MRP and Socialist Party to sustain such a negative coalition position on Vietnamese independence and unity. Some Việt Kiều also criticized the DRV for giving in to so many French demands. Several score professionals volunteered to return to Vietnam to accept whatever positions were offered. Not everyone liked the ICP role in the DRV, yet the overriding sentiments were pride that Vietnam was no longer a French colony and admiration for President Hồ as he grappled with the likes of Sarraut, Bidault, and Moutet.

Even before signing the modus vivendi, Hồ Chí Minh had insisted that he go home by sea rather than air, citing health reasons. Jean Sainteny repeatedly tried to change his mind, as he was convinced that "extremists" had gained the upper hand in Hanoi and that only Hồ could reverse this trend before disaster struck.[200] Both Sainteny and Hồ knew that Admiral d'Argenlieu was likely to pursue his own hard-line agenda from Saigon in subsequent weeks. I suspect Hồ was shaken by the frantic last-minute negotiations, discouraged by the outcome, and anxious to be assisted by Phạm Văn Đồng and other members of the delegation when it came to arguing inside Vietnam for the merits of persisting with diplomatic efforts to avoid full-scale conflict. The DRV delegation had already departed by sea, and would reach Haiphong on 3 October.[201] Meanwhile, Hồ tried to get the text of the modus vivendi sent to Phạm Văn Đồng aboard the *Pasteur*, as well as to Acting President Huỳnh Thúc Kháng in Hanoi, but French agencies proved very slow to assist with transmission. Aboard the *Pasteur*, French intelligence agents copied or purloined documents belonging to the delegation. At Cap St Jacques, six tons of delegation luggage was "misdirected" to Saigon. When the luggage eventually arrived in Haiphong, the most important radio equipment had been damaged.[202]

THE VIETNAMESE PRESS FOLLOWS
NEGOTIATIONS IN FRANCE

It was much easier for Vietnamese papers to report the summer 1946 deliberations in France than those at Dalat. The high commissioner was not able to muzzle communications. Western news agencies showed more interest in the Fontainbleau proceedings, and Hồ Chí Minh knew how to generate stories that made their way around the world. Agence France Presse (AFP) and Reuters news bulletins could be heard on the radio throughout Vietnam. Editors in Hanoi and Haiphong also now had access to a range of metropolitan French papers arriving by air. Vietnamese were vastly more interested in the Franco-Vietnamese negotiations than metropolitan French citizens, most of whom had little understanding of the issues at stake.

In June and July, editors focused on issues that had arisen at Dalat, notably the status of Nam Bộ, the disposition of French properties, and the nature of an Indochina Federation. All newspapers (outside French-occupied Saigon) rejected any proposition that the south be separated from central and northern Vietnam. The prospect of a referendum in Nam Bộ remained unpopular, yet most papers accepted its inclusion in a comprehensive agreement, providing a ceasefire was in force and a joint DRV-French commission prepared and supervised the poll. As *Cứu Quốc* put it, "If certain people *(người ta)* wish to ask Vietnamese if they are Vietnamese, then the experiment can proceed, but it must be conducted fairly."[203] Most papers opposed any compensation for French losses prior to 19 August 1945 and insisted on the right of the DRV to nationalize selected enterprises. For some writers there was an acceptable trade-off between France investing substantially in the economic future of Vietnam and French claims for restitution being acknowledged and processed equitably.[204] As for the Indochina Federation, no Vietnamese paper accepted a formula whereby France stood above other members, much less Admiral d'Argenlieu's design to carve Vietnam into multiple memberships *(pays)*. However, several papers did investigate the historical concept of federation, looking for cases where the sovereignty of members had been respected. The idea of a wider French Union found readier Vietnamese acknowledgment than the Indochina Federation, yet writers looked in vain for relevant expositions in the metropolitan French press. They were intrigued by the British Commonwealth, with its combination of dominions and free states. If the DRV within a future French Union could operate like Canada or Australia within the British Commonwealth, that might work.[205] For both the Indochina Federation and the French Union, Vietnamese commentators wanted accession to be voluntary, and for it to carry with it the right to withdraw.

The Vietnamese press was outraged by Admiral d'Argenlieu's 25 July announcement that a conference of prospective Indochina Federation members would convene on 1 August in Dalat. How could the French government permit an appointee like d'Argenlieu to preempt Franco-Vietnamese deliberations in the *métropole*? Editorials backed Phạm Văn Đồng's suspension of the Fontainebleau talks until Paris disavowed the high commissioner's actions. Then, on 3 August in Bắc Ninh town, just across the river from Hanoi, a serious armed confrontation developed between French and Vietnamese forces (see below). These two events were linked in the Vietnamese press, and from then on editorial opinion on negotiations became more pessimistic. Coinciding with patriotic celebrations surrounding the first anniversary of the August Revolution and the 2 September declaration of independence, writers affirmed that if necessary Vietnam would fight the French alone. The cover illustration of one Independence Day special edition featured an armed National Guardsman standing triumphantly over a cowering French soldier.[206] The last remaining Nationalist Party publication stated flatly that if France refused to respect the territorial demarcation of Vietnam that was in existence as of 19 August 1945, then an entire generation had only the choice of shedding all its blood "for our beloved and respected mother: Tổ Quốc Việt Nam."[207]

Word of the Fontainebleau negotiations adjourning on 10 September, and the Vietnamese delegation preparing to sail home, confirmed press concerns that the window of opportunity for a peaceful solution might be closing. Võ Nguyên Giáp met reporters on 12 September to discuss the implications of adjournment. When one reporter asked why they had not signed a temporary agreement, Giáp simply answered that the Vietnamese delegation wanted a comprehensive accord.[208] On 14 September, a long *Cứu Quốc* editorial was titled: "How will the French reactionaries deal with Vietnam? Is there a Vietnamese-French conflict?" The editors opined that France, still recovering from World War II, lacked the strength to mount a war throughout Vietnam, and that French reactionaries faced opposition from the French people. Therefore the reactionaries would need to encroach gradually, as they had been doing since the 9 March accord, and most recently, when seizing the customs houses in Haiphong (see below). *Cứu Quốc* editors concluded: "We don't want war, the French people and government don't want war, but if the French reactionaries persist in using military force to achieve their aims, one locality at a time, then certainly the Vietnamese have to oppose them in self-defense."[209] Significantly, *Cứu Quốc* published this analysis and warning ahead of any DRV official pronouncement about the end of talks, other than Giáp's brief press remarks, an indication of growing policy drift.

Other Vietnamese writers now advanced beyond the routine reactionary/progressive dichotomy to an analysis of Vietnamese and French national interests. For "V. H," Fontainebleau demonstrated that Vietnam would reject any Indochina Federation which was a disguised colony, while France refused to accept equal powers for federation members. Given such differences, what both sides now needed was *time* to allow logic to be applied and surrounding circumstances to change, so that new negotiating formulas could emerge.[210] Clearly V. H. believed that avoidance of full-scale war favored DRV interests. The editors of *Độc Lập* focused on the need for DRV adherents to increase their strength in Nam Bộ, so that when talks resumed the separatist option would carry no weight.[211] *Dư Luận* editors ascribed suspension of Fontainebleau to "French refusal to acknowledge our life-and-death convictions." While waiting for talks to resume, Vietnam should try to build bridges with the French people, "but we cannot allow attacks to continue."[212] This was the DRV's strategic dilemma in a nutshell.

The unexpected news that President Hồ Chí Minh had signed a new agreement with the French appeared as a brief communiqué in Vietnamese papers on 16 September. It then took ten days for the DRV government to receive the official text of the modus vivendi, leaving everyone to decide how much to rely on French news sources. *Cứu Quốc* readily used Reuters, Radio Saigon, and *l'Entente*, identifying each source meticulously. An editorial of 18 September concluded that Vietnamese would have to push the reactionaries to desist while simultaneously preparing for the worst.[213] *Dân Chủ* in Haiphong took a more sanguine position, arguing that unlike the 6 March Accord's preoccupation with military questions, the modus vivendi addressed a wide range of other issues as well.[214] *Dư Luận* offered its own translation of the modus vivendi and promised a series of essays analyzing the cultural, economic-financial, political, and military implications of the accord. However, following the first promising article by Hoàng Xuân Hãn, editors felt compelled to stop due to possible "unfavorable diplomatic influences."[215]

Dư Luận's reticence may have been in response to a 23 September general order from censors to desist from commenting on the modus vivendi.[216] If so, the order was widely ignored. *Độc Lập,* the Democratic Party daily, complained that Vietnam had conceded much on the economic and cultural fronts, while France had given nothing in return, at which point the remainder of the editorial was excised by censors.[217] The Nationalist Party weekly went further, saying "It is now quite clear that France intends to restore the old colonial system gradually, while hoping to wear down the Vietnamese spirit." Faced with that perceived threat, the editors insisted, "We will not let any people steal our right to exist."[218] In distant Quảng Ngãi, editors emphasized that Moutet's signing of the modus vivendi and actual French implementation were not the same thing, hence everyone had to be ready to deal with unforeseen actions and await orders from the central government and National Guard headquarters.[219] Papers had little to say about the ceasefire provisions contained in Article 9 of the modus vivendi, which Hồ Chí Minh probably considered his principle last-minute achievement with Moutet.

In a wide-ranging essay at the end of September, *Cứu Quốc* editors remained pessimistic about implementing the modus vivendi, yet optimistic about the wider circumstances, citing worldwide setbacks for the forces of reaction, the favorable reception that President Hồ and the delegation had received in France, and the readiness of citizens at home to gather round the president and the government to "ward off each obstacle and advance to victory."[220] Following the return of Phạm Văn Đồng and delegation from France, *Cứu Quốc* took a more modest line, explaining that the modus vivendi had been signed because neither side wanted to cut off liaison, and because both sides appreciated the need for a minimum level of agreement to sustain matters until negotiations resumed. It added that the world situation was complex, and "even France itself is not yet stable," hence Vietnam too was still unable to "resolve definitively every problem."[221] Phan Anh, a delegation member, revealed to Hoàng Xuân Hãn that some participants had returned upset and no longer believing in any peaceful resolution of Franco-Vietnamese differences, whereas President Hồ retained a calm, controlled attitude.[222] Marking time on the diplomatic front left both Vietnamese and French governments poorly equipped to deal with further armed confrontations.

ARMED ALTERCATIONS IN THE NORTH

Following the 6 March 1946 Accord, confrontations above the sixteenth parallel between French soldiers and armed DRV adherents were rare for about ten weeks. French Army and National Guard officers liaised routinely, with both sides seemingly committed to resolving incidents or misunderstandings expeditiously. In Hanoi starting in late May, however, there was an increase in disturbances between French soldiers and Vietnamese militia and civilians. A *Cứu Quốc* editorial called for "calm readiness" in the face of recent French provocations and assaults, but several weeks later the same paper admitted that armed Vietnamese were instigating some of the incidents. On 9 June, a huge protest in the capital against Admiral d'Argenlieu's proclamation of a Republic of Cochinchina managed to steer clear of resident French nationals. On 18 June, members of the mixed commission were called to resolve a seemingly minor fray at a bar, then departed. In the early morning, however, French soldiers were fired upon as they walked from the bar to their vehicles. DRV police, backed by National Guardsmen, arrested thirty Vietnamese suspects and seized guns and ammunition. Trouble persisted into a second night, causing Huỳnh Thúc Kháng, acting DRV president, to threaten Vietnamese perpetrators with severe punishment for damaging Vietnamese-French friendship. *Cứu Quốc* still blamed French soldiers for starting the fight, claimed that *l'Entente* had blown everything out of proportion, and inferred that the only Vietnamese fault was carrying firearms without a permit. Four days later, *Cứu Quốc* intimated that French soldiers were under orders to provoke incidents, which caused the head of the French Army press office to demand a retraction. *Cứu Quốc* stood by its accusation.[223] In Haiphong about the same time, armed militiamen arrested three young Eurasians at the train station, triggering a French Army rescue operation, sustained shooting, and the death of one Eurasian and several Vietnamese. A mixed commission team brought firing to a halt; henceforth the French Army and National Guard mounted joint guard over the train station.[224]

Late June was the moment when Chinese forces evacuated scores of buildings in Hanoi, triggering a Franco-Vietnamese competition for occupancy. The biggest prize was the former governor general's palace. At dawn on 25 June, just as General Lu Han departed the palace to fly to China on a plane provided by the French, General Jean-Étienne Valluy ordered his men to take armed custody.[225] Perhaps more than any other event, this seizure convinced ordinary Vietnamese that the French were determined to reassert sovereignty over Indochina. Both Huỳnh Thúc Kháng and Võ Nguyên Giáp issued statements linking French occupation of the palace with the recent assault on the Haiphong train station and the capture of Pleiku in the central highlands. *Cứu Quốc*, after accusing the French military of escalating to a policy of "flagrant transgression," called on citizens to "determine to struggle enthusiastically *(phấn đấu)* but with discipline," and urged the DRV government to eschew an attitude of business-as-usual. A general strike followed in Hanoi two days later (see chapter 9).[226]

Franco-Vietnamese altercations in Hanoi appear to have ceased with announcement of the opening of the Fontainebleau conference on 6 July—or else the press was under strict government orders not to report them. Throughout most of July, *Cứu Quốc* turned its attention instead to condemning the Vietnam Nationalist Party and publicizing the results of 12 July attacks on Nationalist Party buildings (see chapter 7). Northeast of Haiphong, however, a bitter clash had taken place in the town of Hòn Gai, with a French Army unit backed up by gunboats driving out Vietnamese militia and destroying whole neighborhoods in the process.[227] On 8 July, a French convoy drove from Hanoi to the key border town of Lạng Sơn by prior agreement with the DRV authorities, but then troops advanced into adjacent villages in a manner not previously agreed upon.[228] Not until late July did DRV censors allow newspapers to condemn French actions at Lạng Sơn. *Cứu Quốc* asked in a big headline "Must Vietnamese People Prepare to Face a Surprise Clash with France?" and followed it the next day with the question, "Do the French plan to blame us for something they do?"[229] On 26 July, the National Guard's General Staff headquarters issued explicit instructions to road checkpoints on how to stop French trucks, ask a few questions politely, then wave them on, and report to superiors. Aware that every such encounter was prone to misunderstanding or worse, the General Staff reminded soldiers that the 6 March Accord allowed the French Army to remain until 1951.[230]

A major armed confrontation did indeed occur on 3 August 1946, casting a new cloud over Franco-Vietnamese relations. A French convoy of fifty-eight vehicles en route from Hanoi to Lạng Sơn came under sustained machine-gun and rifle fire as it passed through Bắc Ninh town, causing the long column to split into six segments. The first and largest segment, of twenty-four vehicles, quickly continued north across the Đáp Cầu bridge. A second segment of eighteen vehicles managed soon to disengage itself and follow the first. However, the remaining sixteen vehicles in four segments took fire and suffered heavy casualties until a French armored relief column from Hanoi arrived five hours later, firing into Bắc Ninh town and causing inhabitants to flee. Before that, two junior members of the Central Mixed Commission had tried to achieve a ceasefire. Their respective superiors, Jean Julien Fonde and Phan Mỹ, subsequently managed to halt the shooting and arrange the evacuation of French wounded. French losses came to fifteen dead and more than thirty wounded; Vietnamese losses were reported as eleven dead and seventeen wounded, with more expected to be found.[231] In retaliation, the French seized and fortified several buildings in Bắc Ninh town and used Spitfires the next day to strafe the adjacent neighborhood, causing additional civilian casualties.[232]

Why did such a confrontation happen at this particular time and place? The 3 April 1946 military agreement had provided for joint relief of Chinese forces in the northern border region, but failed to specify troop numbers or positioning. As the Chinese withdrew in June, French and Vietnamese commands moved separately to take their place. The most sensitive venue was Lạng Sơn, where ethnic Vietnamese, Nùng, and resident Chinese jockeyed for position. On 2 July, Võ Nguyên Giáp inspected Lạng Sơn town and vicinity.[233] On 8 July, as mentioned above, the first French force moved by road from Hanoi to Lạng Sơn. Additional French convoys followed, containing troops, arms, food, and equipment well beyond the amount that DRV leaders believed necessary for joint implementation of the 3 April agreement. On 1 August, a confidential ICP analysis concluded that the French intended to seize the region between Lạng Sơn and Móng Cái on the coast, in order to establish a "Nùng Autonomous Republic" to add to Admiral d'Argenlieu's Indochina Federation.[234] Unable to match the French buildup, National Guard commanders, local militia leaders, and ICP cadres probably considered ways they might inhibit French movement along the Hanoi–Lạng Sơn route, ranging from mass demonstrations at key junctures, to digging up the road, to outright attack on a convoy. Already in late July, French soldiers were reported to be firing randomly from trucks, and Vietnamese militia sniping at vehicles driving by. On 1 August, a lone French Army truck returning from Lạng Sơn to Hanoi refused to wait at the Đuống bridge checkpoint while its lack of papers was queried by telephone to National Guard headquarters, and instead allegedly shot several Vietnamese guards and civilians as it sped towards Gia Lâm.[235]

The French convoy of fifty-eight vehicles that approached Bắc Ninh at 6:45 A.M. on 3 August was capable of dealing with sniper fire or the occasional road blockage, but not a sustained assault. The column possessed no tank or armored car, only one half-track, one tractor equipped with a 57 mm cannon, five lightly armored jeeps, and one scout car.[236] A mere ten infantrymen accompanied all the specialized personnel. French headquarters had authorized a foreign AP reporter to go along, another sign that no trouble was anticipated. The convoy was allowed to stretch out four or five kilometers in length, with vehicles as much as one hundred meters apart, hardly sensible defense procedure. No armored unit was on standby in Hanoi, so that when the convoy's first radio alert arrived it took a couple of hours to put together and dispatch a relief column.

On the other hand, the Vietnamese attack hardly amounted to a credible ambush. No unit took control of or tried to destroy the Đáp Cầu bridge just northeast of Bắc Ninh town. No civilians were mobilized to dig up the road in advance. The only road obstacles were a cart filled with cinder blocks and some trees felled behind the column. No mortars were employed, only machine guns, rifles, and grenades. No infantry attempted to overrun one or more of the French convoy segments. Possibly the initiative to attack came not from National Guard headquarters in Hanoi but from some senior ICP members linking up with an army unit based in Bắc Ninh and local militia. Or the original plan may have specified limited harassment fire, but then spun out of control as local militia joined in from all directions. In his memoir, Võ Nguyên Giáp hinted at spontaneous behavior at Bắc Ninh, of "our people, burning with pent-up anger against the French invaders [and] liable to fight back at once."[237] Nonetheless, it is hard to imagine that discussion and preparations for the Bắc Ninh action could have escaped the attention of Hanoi headquarters only thirty kilometers away.

Major Fonde provided the first written report on the Bắc Ninh incident to French higher echelons.[238] After narrating what Hoàng Hữu Nam and Phan Mỹ had said to him about the incident, Fonde listed eight reasons why the Vietnamese attack was premeditated and French forces had reacted in good faith. Unless sanctions were imposed, pressures to limit the French presence at Lạng Sơn would intensify, and people in and around Bắc Ninh would regard the French as weak. A much more detailed report was produced six days later by General Valluy's headquarters in Hanoi.[239] They offered thirteen proofs of Vietnamese premeditation, some rather far-fetched. Neither Fonde nor Valluy's staff blamed a specific Vietnamese echelon or individual for the attack. Valluy's deputy, Colonel Crépin, suggested that Bắc Ninh be put in the context of some Vietnamese government members wishing to engage in combat before the return of Hồ Chí Minh, while other members preferred continuing preparations for conflict while hoping that the diplomatic negotiations would succeed. Crépin placed Giáp at the head of the latter group, adding that it was not certain his view would prevail.[240] In the opinion of the French Sûreté, Giáp had ordered the Bắc Ninh attack, yet a paragraph later it stated that Giáp was trying to avoid conflict until the return of President Hồ. The war party was said to be led by Nguyễn Lương Bằng and other "orthodox Marxists" in the Việt Minh General Headquarters.[241]

On 4 August, the bridge at Kép, thirty-four kilometers further up the road from Bắc Ninh, was destroyed. The next day, another French convoy was fired upon seventy-two kilometers short of Lạng Sơn, resulting in three men killed and four wounded. Spitfires strafed nearby buildings in retaliation.[242] In Hanoi, French soldiers in jeeps swept along downtown streets, shooting wildly and throwing at least one grenade.[243]

Vietnamese newspapers were not permitted to publish about the Bắc Ninh incident for several days. The eventual press coverage included publication of a Franco-Vietnamese mixed commission's plea for soldiers and the public to remain calm, and "to avoid fights that jeopardize joint efforts to promote peace," together with a Vietnamese government statement expressing "very much regret" over the shooting at Bắc Ninh.[244] However, Cứu Quốc editors insisted that the 1 August French shooting at Đuống bridge had triggered the much bigger confrontation two days later. They asked rhetorically if events at Bắc Ninh represented

a deliberate French provocation on orders from above. Soon *Cứu Quốc* was reporting "French aggressions" further up the same road, as well as fighting in
Lạng Sơn town itself, where citizens were cutting down trees to impede French
vehicles, and there had been "many casualties."[245] *Độc Lập* newspaper provided a
skewed description of the Bắc Ninh confrontation, then suggested that French
violent behavior had to be seen in the context of the earlier Hòn Gai assault, Admiral d'Argenlieu's pseudo-conference at Dalat, and the adjournment of Fontainebleau negotiations. According to *Độc Lập* editors, some French officers were
now resorting to Hitler-like tactics to try to demoralize the Vietnamese people,
but they would fail. The DRV National Assembly's Standing Committee chairman, Nguyễn Văn Tố, dispatched an open letter to President Hồ in Paris, asking
him to convey to the French government the Assembly's strong protest regarding
French actions at Bắc Ninh.[246] The Bắc Ninh incident then disappeared from the
newspapers, and no further violent confrontations were reported in the north for
many weeks.

The French military was quick to dispatch its version of the Bắc Ninh incident to the *métropole*, which was then used by opponents of the *"politique
d'accords"* to charge the DRV with rank duplicity—on the one hand "assassi-
nating French soldiers," on the other having its delegates play to the gallery in
Paris. French nationals also sent scores of telegrams and letters from Indochina to the French government, urging it to take stronger measures against
the Việt Minh.[247] The ability of generals, officials, and French civilians in Indochina to use the telegraph and radio to influence opinion and decisionmaking in
Paris was demonstrated vividly. They would refine this capacity four months
later after full-scale fighting broke out in Hanoi. Meanwhile, DRV officials remained at the mercy of the French-controlled external communications system.

In his 12 August report on the political situation in Tonkin, Colonel Crépin
declared that the French Army's response to the Bắc Ninh provocation had delivered a "very harsh lesson" to the Vietnamese government: it could not stop
French military ascendancy or the resumption of French relations with minorities. More than that, according to Crépin, the Vietnamese government was losing the "war of nerves," by which it tried to agitate the population with defense
preparations, orders to evacuate, and announcements of imminent combat,
which then had to be cancelled and the process renewed. When it came to Bắc
Ninh, he claimed popular disinterest. On the other hand, a number of "brighter
Annamites" were now saying to the French, "You are the strongest, what are you
waiting for, drive out the Viet Minh government and put us in its place."[248]

When General Louis Morlière arrived in Hanoi on 17 August as replacement
for General Valluy (who had been promoted to succeed General Leclerc), he
committed himself to achieving French government objectives without resort
to combat, which meant reaching an understanding with Võ Nguyên Giáp in

particular, so that neither side felt the necessity to take offensive action. This suited Giáp's objectives, at least until the return of President Hồ from France, and it accounts for a striking reduction in Franco-Vietnamese confrontations. Giáp moved to assert more control over National Guard units and militia groups, achieving more success with the former than the latter. The Bắc Ninh incident had the short-term effect of awakening both sides to their lack of readiness to deal with a sudden armed confrontation so close to Hanoi. For three months, it helped to reduce the chances of another such incident. In the longer term, however, Bắc Ninh reduced the chances of diplomatic settlement. Both sides came to the conclusion that they were contesting the same space, and aiming to control the same people. In such circumstances, only French and Vietnamese leadership at the highest levels could keep peace alive.

THE MODUS VIVENDI FIZZLES OUT

When departing France by sea on 18 September 1946, Hồ Chí Minh left behind his closest foreign policy associate, Hoàng Minh Giám, in hopes that practical discussions on implementation of the modus vivendi could proceed. On learning of this, Admiral d'Argenlieu immediately objected that such Vietnamese representation in France had not been specified in the agreement. The Bidault government concurred, although it allowed Giám and three colleagues to remain in France in a private capacity. Giám soon realized he was being boxed out by French officialdom, but he could not arrange a return to Hanoi until November.[249]

As described earlier, Article 9, the most important clause in the modus vivendi, specified a 30 October ceasefire in Cochinchina and southern Annam. Not surprisingly, both French and Vietnamese forces sought to expand their areas of control in the weeks leading up to the ceasefire. Admiral d'Argenlieu must not have been happy with the results, as already on 25 October he instructed subordinates to prepare for a resumption of hostilities in January 1947, aimed at "neutralizing the Hanoi government and thus facilitating pacification of the South."[250] The DRV government had decided to make adherence to the ceasefire on 30 October a test of its capacity to control armed groups in the south and influence southern behavior in general. Nguyễn Bình, now designated commissioner for military affairs in the Nam Bộ Administrative Committee, received orders from Hanoi to adhere to the ceasefire and stop furnishing arms and ammunition to groups that refused to submit to his authority. Similar orders were sent via ICP channels. The Administrative Committee instructed province committees to help implement the ceasefire. Most effectively, leaflets were distributed in the countryside, and Saigon newspapers sympathetic to the "unionist" cause published Nguyễn Bình's proclamation to cease hostilities at midnight on 29–30 October.[251] The day before the ceasefire, Võ Nguyên Giáp sent yet another order from Hanoi, reiterating the exact time and instructing units to keep their positions secret, remain vigilant, and only shoot if attacked, but "absolutely avoid provocative actions."[252] The French command also issued ceasefire orders to its units and broadcast instructions over Radio Saigon. The next day, with much fanfare, Admiral d'Argenlieu released 150 political detainees.[253]

French and Vietnamese sources agree that shooting stopped on cue at midnight, and that the ceasefire held throughout Nam Bộ for several days. In some places it persisted for a couple of weeks. Several times Nguyễn Bình reiterated orders not to attack, but to be prepared to repel any French attack. Soon he was distributing to Saigon newspapers lists of alleged French violations.[254] On 3 November, talks began in Hanoi between Hoàng Hữu Nam, representing the DRV Military Commission, and General Georges Nyo, commander of French forces in Cochinchina and southern Annam.[255] While Nam proposed consolidating an in-place ceasefire in ways that amounted to legitimizing the DRV presence in the south, General Nyo revived the requirement that all Vietnamese soldiers originating from outside Cochinchina and southern Annam be ordered to withdraw, and all southern "rebels" be disarmed. Indeed, on 30 October General Nyo had already ordered his troops to maintain law and order across the entire region, and be prepared for larger operations against "armed bands." The French rejected DRV urgings that a "joint ceasefire subcommittee" be dispatched from Hanoi to Nam Bộ.[256] Given such a wide disparity in ceasefire conceptions, the Hanoi talks achieved nothing and armed confrontations soon multiplied again in the south.

On 29 October the DRV government put forth Phạm Văn Bạch, chairman of the Nam Bộ Administrative Committee, as its representative to work with the high commissioner in execution of the modus vivendi. Hồ Chí Minh must have known that Admiral d'Argenlieu would reject Bạch, as his nomination amounted to de facto recognition of the Administrative Committee. On the other hand, d'Argenlieu would also have opposed a northern nominee, as signifying DRV legitimacy in Cochinchina. D'Argenlieu cabled Hồ that "nothing was less probable" than Paris approving Bạch. On 7 November, d'Argenlieu told Hồ that the activities of the committee were contrary to both the 6 March Accord and the 14 September modus vivendi. Hồ replied that the committee had existed since 25 August 1945, and that both the 6 March and 14 September 1946 agreements were founded on preservation of de facto arrangements until the referendum. D'Argenlieu quickly retorted that Cochinchina was French territory; its status could only be altered by decision of the French National Assembly. On 14 November, Hồ insisted that Cochinchina was a part of Vietnam where the presence of French military forces created a special de facto situation.[257] This rapid exchange of messages summarized the most important issue at stake between the two sides. Occurring at this moment, such raw exposure of differences over

Cochinchina offered justification for escalation of the conflict, which may well have been d'Argenlieu's intention.

On 13 November, Admiral d'Argenlieu departed Saigon for Paris, determined to ask the French government for suspension of the modus vivendi. Prior to leaving, d'Argenlieu gave General Valluy a letter instructing him not to "exclude the possibility that one might be forced to have recourse to a direct, forcible action against the Hanoi government."[258] As noted above, d'Argenlieu previously had alerted subordinates to prepare for operations of this kind in January. Now, however, he was moving the timetable forward, quite possibly because he had just received word that the Left had scored significant gains in the 10 November French National Assembly elections. The capacity of the DRV government and its adherents in Cochinchina to convince disparate armed groups to maintain the 30 October ceasefire, if only for a few days or a week, must have disturbed the high commissioner as well, although he could not have been entirely surprised, given prior intelligence reports on expanding unionist activities. He certainly would have been shocked by the 10 November suicide of Nguyễn Văn Thinh, the most credible participant in d'Argenlieu's Cochinchinese Council.[259]

FATHOMING POLITICAL DEVELOPMENTS IN FRANCE

Following the armed confrontation at Bắc Ninh, and then the meager diplomatic outcome at Fontainebleau, continuing Vietnamese hopes for peace focused on possible improvements in the French political environment. The "reactionary" epithet tended to obscure more than it revealed when applied to the French National Assembly. Except for the Gaullists, Vietnamese writers seemed confused as to who deserved that pejorative in the Assembly. Trần Huy Liệu, Vietnam's Jeremiah when it came to Franco-Vietnamese relations, demanded that Paris renounce its colonial reveries, especially in regard to Cochinchina, before resistance fighters would put aside their arms.[260] By that reckoning, many French socialists and communists would have to be lumped together with the Gaullists and the MRP as requiring thorough historical and ideological cleansing.

France's second, successful vote on a Fourth Republic constitution, on 13 October, attracted more informed attention in Vietnam. Editorials noted that Gaullists had opposed key passages in this constitution, so perhaps it was an improvement over the May 1946 text. However, one writer pointed out how the provision for negotiation of treaties between French Union members had been dropped from this text, thus giving the French National Assembly sole power to determine union bylaws and the precise status of different union members. If applied to Vietnam's prospective membership, the author concluded that the new constitution's section on the French Union "creates many difficulties, possibly leading to an impasse."[261] The passage in the constitution's preamble which declared,

"Faithful to her traditional mission, France intends to lead the people whom she has taken care of to the freedom to administrate themselves . . . ," was treated with derision by other writers. Vietnamese intellectuals were now taking the time to scrutinize texts relevant to the negotiations, even as their hopes for peace may have been receding.

With the French constitution now in force, and 10 November set for election of a new National Assembly, Vietnamese newspapers tried to report the campaign from the limited range of sources available to them. Nguyễn Văn Luyện published an ambitious analysis of the overall political situation in France, arguing that the MRP might well capture the "moderate middle" vote, composed not only of bourgeois, petit bourgeois, and working-class Catholic citizens, but also many intellectuals truly committed to democratic freedoms. Luyện predicted that the PCF vote might have peaked, and the Socialist (SFIO) vote was unlikely to increase.[262] As it transpired, the PCF secured the largest number of seats in the Assembly, much to the delight of some Việt Minh papers.[263] However, the Democratic Party weekly soon published a detailed analysis of election results which concluded that the implications for Vietnam were contradictory. PCF gains increased the chances of "democratic and equal deliberations," but the "Far Right" had gained too, thus offering succor to colonial reactionaries. The author predicted that French parties which had shown sympathy for "our people" (dân tộc ta) would now be less circumspect, while the reactionaries would "not dare act as automatically as before."[264] Both predictions proved wrong. As Stein Tønnesson has summarized, "With the timid exception of the Parti Communiste Français (PCF), the main political forces in France agreed that Vietnam should not be given full independence, and that the Viet Minh should under no circumstances be allowed to take control of Cochinchina."[265] The PCF occasionally was subjected to critical Vietnamese scrutiny. When a reader asked Dư Luận if French policy would change greatly if the PCF took power, the editors answered: "Putting hope in others often leads to disappointment. We should only believe and place hope in ourselves."[266] A paper published by members of the Northern Region Police devoted two pages to a biting cartoon condemning France's Indochina Federation scheme. We see a demure Vietnamese woman being walled in by a mason named d'Argenlieu, who completes the edifice with a heavy, locked door marked "Autonomy," then prances around, sword in hand, declaring "If you show your neck outside, you're a dead woman!"[267]

HAIPHONG

Even before taking power in August 1945, Hồ Chí Minh and his lieutenants understood that, second only to Saigon, Haiphong was most vulnerable to French counterassault, occupation, and employment as a base to recolonize Vietnam.

French arrival in Haiphong was delayed by Chinese occupation, but the 28 February 1946 Sino-French accord foreshadowed French control of Haiphong port so that a special zone for free transit of merchandise to and from China could be organized. The 6 March Accord finessed Franco-Vietnamese armed confrontation over Haiphong, but the French military could now proceed to repair port facilities, stake out encampments, and amass supplies and equipment sufficient to mount a variety of armed scenarios. French commanders did not run the city, instead sharing it with DRV civil and military authorities. In May, General Valluy formally complained to President Hồ about the failure of the Haiphong Administrative Committee to collect garbage, unblock the sewers, or even retrieve dead bodies from the streets.[268] Increasingly the French made themselves felt in the European quarter of Haiphong, while the National Guard and local militia made preparations against a possible French coup de force aimed at taking the Chinese and Vietnamese quarters as well.[269]

With the bulk of Chinese troops withdrawn by June 1946, the French began moves to gain control over collection of customs duties in Haiphong. On 7 July, the local French commander, Colonel Pierre Debès, tried unsuccessfully to persuade the Chinese consul to tell Chinese citizens to ignore DRV customs collectors and accept French military protection. Ten days later, however, when Vietnamese officials prevented a Chinese cargo ship from being unloaded, the Chinese consul protested, citing the Sino-French accord that waved duties on Chinese goods. This citation was irrelevant to the Vietnamese, as their government had not been party to the 28 February accord. In August, after a group of Chinese merchants complained to the French about Vietnamese confiscations, Debès occupied DRV customs buildings and jailed a number of Vietnamese customs officers and police. DRV negotiators returned the confiscated goods in exchange for release of the prisoners, but the underlying dispute persisted.[270] On 10 September, General Morlière announced that France would take control of all import and export activity in Haiphong from 15 October. The 14 September modus vivendi committed Vietnam to joining a customs union together with other countries of the Indochinese Federation, and foreshadowed meetings to accomplish this objective. However, before any such meetings could take place, Admiral d'Argenlieu ordered implementation of French controls.[271] Both sides knew that traders could and often did evade export or import duties by employing smaller transit points along the coast, yet that was ignored. The key issue was not effective revenue collection but the exercise of national authority.

On 9 October, French tanks and armored cars surrounded two DRV police bureaus in Haiphong, roughed up the occupants, and took away documents, money, and equipment. The Haiphong Việt Minh committee reacted by organizing demonstrations and a half-day general strike which linked French provocations in Haiphong with the ongoing occupation of Nam Bộ. Editors of the principal Việt Minh newspaper accused "French reactionaries" in Haiphong of violating both the 6 March Accord and the 14 September modus vivendi, of plotting to exclude the DRV from foreign trade, and of putting Vietnamese opponents in a secret jail. They asked, "Does France wish to cooperate with the Vietnamese people in gaining a secure livelihood, or rather to destroy its own economic prospects in Vietnam?"[272] The DRV central government, slow to recognize the gravity of Haiphong events, now had acting President Huỳnh Thúc Kháng dispatch a letter to the French president warning that implementation of General Morlière's order could "very possibly result in a regrettable clash taking place."[273] Into this volatile setting on 20 October came President Hồ aboard the *Dumont d'Urville,* yet he had no time to grapple with the issue locally before taking the train to Hanoi (see chapter 9). On 30 October, Colonel Debès distributed sealed envelopes to subordinates containing orders for seizing control of Haiphong. During this period Vietnamese commanders put their men on high alert and stood them down repeatedly.[274] Debès seems to have reveled in this war of nerves, hoping to goad the Vietnamese into an undisciplined piecemeal assault which he could then use as justification for opening the envelopes and mounting a full-scale attack with armor and artillery.

When the DRV National Assembly on 8 November instructed the new cabinet not to give in on the customs issue "at any price," Admiral d'Argenlieu and General Valluy had their prospective casus belli. President Hồ on 11 November took a different tack than the Assembly by simply protesting to d'Argenlieu over the creation of a French customs office in Haiphong.[275] On 17 November, however, the DRV customs bureau in Hanoi announced that all goods not declared to its officers in Haiphong for taxation were considered contraband, with perpetrators facing confiscation, a fine equal to the value of the goods, and up to three years jail. The announcement concluded, "In the current situation, the Government is paying special concern to finances and the prestige of the nation. Heavy punishments are specified. Absolutely no compromise."[276] This announcement was no less contrary to the modus vivendi than French moves to take over all Haiphong customs activity had been. Almost surely President Hồ had not been consulted, an indication of his inability to manage all aspects of the Franco-Vietnamese encounter at this most sensitive juncture. Hồ may also not have appreciated yet how d'Argenlieu, Valluy, and Debès were targeting Haiphong customs as an excuse to seize the city. His main French interlocutor in Hanoi, General Morlière, gave no hint of these intentions.

If ranking members of the Central Mixed Commission had been dispatched to Haiphong in mid-November it might have been possible to forestall an armed confrontation. Instead, Jean Julien Fonde was sending messages to Hoàng Hữu Nam protesting removal of bronze ornaments on the French war memorial in downtown Haiphong. Fonde asserted that the ignoble defacement had taken place just prior to French return in early March 1946. The DRV authorities in Hanoi hoped to establish that the bronze had been removed before the August 1945 Revolution, and was perhaps melted down by the Japanese. On 18 November, the Haiphong Administrative Committee received an instruction to investigate these French charges and report back.[277] Whatever French grievances about damage to this monument to compatriots fallen in the Great War, one cannot help but wonder if Fonde's protest was designed to preoccupy Vietnamese mixed commission members amidst the brewing customs crisis.

The violent 20 November Franco-Vietnamese altercation over a Chinese junk entering Haiphong harbor could have been defused by the city's mixed commission. Instead, Colonel Debès implemented his attack plan, first targeting the Haiphong Opera House and dispatching tanks into the Chinese quarter. General Morlière, in Hanoi, told Debès to halt offensive action while his political advisor met urgently with Hoàng Hữu Nam to agree on a ceasefire and the dispatch of Central Mixed Commission members to Haiphong. The next afternoon in Haiphong, Nam and a French staff officer signed a ceasefire which specified immediate withdrawal of French armor. However, General Valluy in Saigon told Debès to order all Vietnamese forces to evacuate the city, and if that order was ignored, to capture, disarm, and if necessary destroy the Vietnamese regular garrisons. Morlière's strong objections, especially over intended use of artillery, were rejected by Valluy, who claimed that the Vietnamese army no longer obeyed the DRV government and hence needed to be taught a "severe lesson." At six in the morning on 23 November, Debès gave Vietnamese commanders an ultimatum to withdraw from named sections of the city. Receiving no reply by the specified time, Debès launched his assaults, backed up by heavy artillery and naval barrages.[278]

Vietnamese newspapers immediately grasped the gravity of events in Haiphong. On 21 November *Cứu Quốc* carried a huge headline: "French Troops Have Instigated a Major Conflict in Haiphong." For the next week *Cứu Quốc* gave Haiphong top priority, including news from reporters on the spot, claims of Vietnamese counterattacks, references to heavy civilian losses, and editorials urging citizens elsewhere to prepare for trouble.[279] On 23 November, *Cứu Quốc* published a captured copy of Colonel Debès's secret order of 30 October, taken as indelible proof of French premedication. *Cấp Tiến*, a nonaligned paper in Hanoi, headlined its coverage of Haiphong, "We Categorically Protest the Aggressive and Provocative Attitude of the French Army."[280] *Độc Lập chủ nhật* offered evidence that the French Army was working to a predetermined plan, not only in Haiphong but also in Lạng Sơn to the north and in Phan Rang down the coast. Editors opined that the French Army wanted to present a fait accompli to Paris before a new government could be formed in which the Left held an important position. In these dire circumstances, the paper urged citizens to prepare to "stop the reactionary gang by every means," while also counseling the DRV government to protest vigorously to the French government and the French people.[281]

The Việt Minh General Headquarters published a rousing declaration which assumed that war was inevitable. "The blood of northerners is now mixed with the blood of their southern and south-central countrymen," the authors intoned. Unless Vietnamese wished to lose their country once again, it was essential to fight in self-defense. The statement concluded: "We believe that final victory cannot go to those who specialize in oppressing people, but rather to those with the legitimate cause *(chính nghĩa)*."[282] Trần Huy Liệu focused his personal remarks on French premeditation, the Vietnamese heroes who fought and died at the Haiphong Opera House, and his conviction that "only strength talks in foreign relations."[283] The last remaining Vietnam Nationalist Party paper offered a lead editorial headed, "The Army and the People are as One," but much of the content was blanked out.[284] A Catholic paper pronounced vaguely that in the face of peril, "We must serve the Fatherland according to practical needs of the moment," then lost most of the article's substance to the censors.[285] *Dư Luận* published a careful discussion of the origins of the Franco-Vietnamese confrontation in Haiphong. Hoàng Xuân Hãn, a key *Dư Luận* participant, ruminated privately with Phan Anh about French officials and commanders who understood the ancient tactic of "acting first and then talking, encroaching gradually, making us react, then accusing us of provocation."[286] *Kháng Chiến,* in distant Quảng Ngãi, was pleased by the way members of youth organizations in Haiphong had refused to evacuate with the general population. Editors printed a Việt Minh General Headquarters pronouncement bluntly challenging President Hồ's continuing efforts to ward off war: "We call on those with responsibility for interacting with the French to heed the will of the people *(quốc dân)*: no more concessions. Willpower can take on planes, tanks and those who specialize in stealing countries."[287]

HANOI

Before ordering the offensive at Haiphong, General Valluy already had staff advice that sufficient French forces were available to seize and hold the road westward and take control of Hanoi. However, Valluy and the high commissioner's political deputy, Léon Pignon, worried that such action would be disavowed in Paris. Instead, the plan was to pressure Hồ Chí Minh to break with his "extremist" lieutenants, acknowledge French primacy, and accept whatever deal he could get in the circumstances. If Vietnamese extremists took rash, violent action under pressure, this could be immediately publicized in the *métropole*, thus removing objections to Valluy employing overwhelming force in retaliation. While waiting for Admiral d'Argenlieu to lessen obstacles in Paris, Valluy dispatched Jean Sainteny to Hanoi to exploit his personal relationship with Hồ in ways that might provoke a split within the Vietnamese leadership, one that would be favorable to French interests.[288] Sainteny complained to Saigon that he knew too little about the internal dynamics of the Vietnamese leadership, despite the covert efforts of three different French intelligence services. As we have seen in the Vietnamese press, French behavior in Haiphong strengthened opinion that diplomatic efforts had failed, hence that war was probably unavoidable. Contrary to French assumptions about an extremist clique, however, those in the Vietnamese leadership who thought their president was tilting at diplomatic windmills dared not oppose his decision to give peace another, probably final chance.

Hồ Chí Minh must have understood that Admiral d'Argenlieu sometimes acted in a manner not reflecting the views of his superiors, yet was not brought to heel. French seizure of Haiphong told Hồ that the high commissioner, fearing that a new government would clip his wings or dismiss him outright, had decided to escalate French intervention north of the sixteenth parallel in ways the next French prime minister and Cabinet would find hard to reverse. D'Argenlieu, knowing that the main threat to his Indochina policy was at home, remained in Paris to lobby furiously.[289] By the same token, Hồ knew that his only chance of averting war was to reach the politicians who were putting together the new French government. Why did d'Argenlieu's mission succeed and Hồ's fail?

Admiral d'Argenlieu first made sure that the DRV had no one of stature to represent it in Paris. The DRV's informal representative, Trần Ngọc Danh, was snubbed by French officials, and had to assume that all of his communications with superiors were monitored. All telegraph traffic to and from Hanoi went through Saigon, where it could be delayed or even "lost" in transit. Historians have paid much attention to Hồ Chí Minh's 15 December message to Léon Blum being held back by Sainteny or Valluy for three days, yet Vietnamese negotiators since the April–May Dalat conference had come to expect such French behavior.

Radio was the alternative. On 8 December, Hồ Chí Minh did make a radio appeal to the French National Assembly and the French government, asking that French troops return to the positions they held in Haiphong before 20 November. This appeal was printed by Le Populaire in Paris on 9 December, the same day that Blum was entrusted with forming a new government. The next day, Le Populaire published an article by Blum that endorsed "sincere agreements on the basis of independence," rather than trying to take back Indochina by force of arms. Blum also foreshadowed policymaking capacity being taken away from military authorities or colonial settlers.[290] Perhaps if Hồ and Blum had been able to exchange a series of radio messages over the next week the descent into war could have been halted. However, conducting diplomacy by public radio was unprecedented, and would have been resisted staunchly by French officialdom. Why did Hồ not back up by radio broadcast the long 15 December letter to Blum that he entrusted to Sainteny for dispatch? Perhaps he thought that confidential transmission would give the letter more credence. As it was, Blum only received the letter on 20 December, accompanied by a critique from Valluy.

Hồ Chí Minh also appreciated the value of communicating proposals to third-party diplomats and foreign journalists, in hopes the content would reach relevant actors in France. Although bedridden in early December, Hồ insisted on receiving Abbot Low Moffat, head of the U.S. State Department's Division of Southeast Asian Affairs, who emerged deeply impressed by Hồ but constrained by the U.S. government from playing any substantive role (see chapter 5). The American consul in Hanoi, James O'Sullivan, transmitted to Washington the gist of Hồ's 15 December letter to Blum, which then reached the U.S. ambassador to France on 18 December, probably making him the only person in Paris to know the contents before fighting exploded in Hanoi on 19 December.[291] The Chinese consul in Hanoi was also being informed of developments, and soon after the fighting began his government floated the idea of British, American, and Chinese consuls in Hanoi interceding with a view to securing a ceasefire, to no avail.[292]

Unfortunately for Hồ Chí Minh, foreign correspondents were notably thin on the ground in Indochina during late November and early December. Most overseas newspapers relied on the AFP, which was closely controlled by the French authorities. No Western journalist was present in Haiphong to report the massacre of civilians by artillery and naval gunfire, which meant that French officials could simply issue flat denials of reports appearing in the Vietnamese and Chinese press, refer to Haiphong as a mere "incident," and insist that matters were under control.[293] With France preoccupied by other matters, not even papers of the Left bothered to dispatch a correspondent to Indochina. Nor did either the PCF or the Socialist Party send their own investigators, despite suspicions that the high commissioner, the French Army, Comonindo, and Prime Minister Bidault were engaged in obfuscation and fabrication. As Sainteny and Valluy stepped up pressure on Hồ and the DRV, the chances of altering political opinion in Paris in time to avert a clash in Hanoi looked unpromising indeed. Several Hanoi newspapers argued that the Blum government was just a holding operation, incapable of changing course in Indochina. Moutet continued to support d'Argenlieu, who clearly wanted war. *Dân Thành* editors concluded, "The establishment of a Léon Blum Cabinet brings no sunlight to Vietnam whatsoever."[294]

At their only meeting, Sainteny informed Hồ Chí Minh that Vietnamese troops must be withdrawn from Cochinchina, Haiphong was to remain under French control, Radio Bạch Mai should be relinquished, and France would be free to suppress all terrorism. Sainteny then told O'Sullivan that the Việt Minh edifice would "come tumbling down at the first serious defeat," ignoring how the DRV had weathered major reversals in Nam Bộ and Nha Trang. Most French analysts now assumed that the Vietnamese state could not survive a flight from the capital. As we have seen, actual DRV preparations to relocate to the countryside or hills were slow to materialize. In early December, Hồ would have worried that overt DRV readying for war could jeopardize his démarche with Blum. At some point, however, diplomacy could impede military capability.

In early December in Hanoi, both General Morlière and Võ Nguyên Giáp had available a variety of offensive and defensive plans, to be refined daily and upgraded or downgraded as circumstances warranted. Besides inferior firepower, the biggest Vietnamese weakness was uncertain command and control. National Guard officers were still learning how to formulate orders, communicate them unambiguously, and make sure they were executed faithfully. High levels of illiteracy meant that written orders meant nothing to some unit leaders. Most commands were delivered orally, by runner. Militia groups showed enthusiasm and resourcefulness, yet orders often needed to be explained and argued, even when time was of the essence. Rumors of imminent French attack or DRV orders to attack swept the city.

Cứu Quốc, the principal Việt Minh daily, tried to explain to readers what was happening, yet the editorial mood fluctuated wildly. On 4 December, war was imminent because French reactionaries believed they had to strike before a new government was formed in Paris. A week later, however, it looked like war might be averted when Socialist Party leader Blum was quoted as supporting Indochinese independence. On 15 December, in an editorial titled "Mr. Léon Blum and the Policy of Vietnamese-French cooperation," *Cứu Quốc* argued, "We must struggle *(tranh đấu)* with the French reactionaries to carry out Blum's ideas." Three days later, a headline asked ominously, "Does the French Army want to provoke a major confrontation in Hanoi?" *Cứu Quốc*'s last circulated issue in Hanoi, on the morning of 19 December, reported French seizure of several DRV government buildings and another urgent message from Hồ to Blum. In a small box it printed a newsflash as of 9:15 the previous evening: "The French military wants to put its hand into public security in Hanoi."[295] One more issue of *Cứu Quốc* was printed for distribution on 20 December but failed to appear. It spoke of armed preparations, but had nothing on the attack that had commenced in Hanoi the previous evening.[296]

Why did DRV adherents attack first? Emotionally, many Vietnamese felt anger and shame at their country and people having undergone eighty years of French aggression and exploitation. August 1945 was meant to exorcise that bitter history. However, after 23 September 1945 in Saigon it often appeared that the fledgling DRV was caught in a defensive vortex, compelled to endure repeated French provocations without being able to strike back effectively. Learning from that sorry experience, most recently in Haiphong, Võ Nguyên Giáp told his lieutenants on 13 December that the army must not be surprised again. From a General Staff perspective, given the diversity of Vietnamese participating forces and the fragile communication system, it was less difficult to plan and execute an offense than a defense. That left the question of whether to issue an ultimatum first or try to achieve a surprise attack. Surprise was chosen, although as it transpired on the evening of 19 December many Vietnamese units were just as surprised as the French. In a move that caused greater peril, the French Army quickly denounced the Vietnamese attacks publicly as perfidious and barbaric, labeling them the "Tonkin Vespers of 19 December," an allusion to the Sicilian Vespers of 1292 in which thousands of French inhabitants were massacred. Four days later, the French National Assembly voted unanimously to let the government transfer funds so that reinforcements could be dispatched to Indochina. Although Hồ Chí Minh must have worried about how a Vietnamese surprise attack would affect public opinion overseas, he seriously underrated the ability of d'Argenlieu, Valluy, and Pignon to mount a press campaign in the *métropole* that insured National Assembly underwriting of war operations for months, if not years, to come.

Stein Tønnesson, after analyzing the events of 19 December 1946 meticulously, concludes that Võ Nguyên Giáp as National Guard commander fell into a French trap. According to Tønnesson, "[Giáp] could not know it at the time, of course, but we now know that the French would *not* have launched any major attack if the Vietnamese had kept calm."[297] It is clear from Vietnamese sources that the DRV government, the National Guard command, the press, and Hanoi militia groups took seriously French threats delivered in writing on 18 December and the morning of 19 December. Most ominously, the French announced 20 December as the day they would neutralize the DRV police, clear away all barricades, and disarm the militia if the government failed to accede to a series of draconian demands.[298] For months the French Army strategy had been to ratchet up the pressure until the DRV fractured or disintegrated under the strain. As we have seen, the Vietnamese press understood French intentions as well as the DRV leadership. As the French now focused on the capital and appeared to set a date, there clearly was fear that the strategy might succeed. It seemed impossible now for the DRV to both talk and resist. If so, the best defense was to attack.

On 18 December, there was a top-level Vietnamese decision to get ready to attack nationally, no later than 20 December, unless a sudden breakthrough in negotiations occurred. Orders to this effect went out early on the morning of 19 December, employing both National Guard and ICP channels. After sunrise, Hoàng Minh Giám carried a short letter from Hồ Chí Minh to Jean Sainteny in Hanoi, urging immediate local talks to alleviate the tense atmosphere, pending a "decision from Paris." Sainteny refused to meet Giám. When Hồ received this news at twelve thirty that afternoon, he is reported to have frowned, pondered the situation for a few moments, then stated simply, "Huh! Then [we] fight" (*Hừ! Thì đánh).*[299] The National Guard General Staff headquarters proceeded to cable the attack order for eight that evening. Around three, however, Hồ received word that the Blum Cabinet had decided to dispatch Moutet urgently to Indochina.[300]

New orders may have gone out to postpone the attack. If so, they failed to have the desired effect.

As described in the previous chapter, workers at the Yên Phụ power plant cut the lights to Hanoi at 8:03 P.M. on 19 December, and soon after, a National Guard cannon fired several shots also taken by some to be a signal to arms. The attacks that followed were poorly coordinated and mostly failed to achieve their objectives. Hồ Chí Minh probably still hoped that a ceasefire could be arranged amidst anticipated talks with Moutet. This might have been possible in Hanoi, but as word spread throughout the country there was a sense of release from restraint and desire to strike at the enemy by whatever means. On 14 or 15 December, Hồ had penned an undated national call to armed resistance and sent it first to Võ Nguyên Giáp and then to Trường Chinh on 19 December for comment. Trường Chinh made several pen amendments, probably changing "We must make concessions" to "We made concessions," and adding the date 20 December. That night, typed copies of the text were sent to the telegrapher and to the printer. The morning of 20 December, Radio Vietnam, now located at Trầm pagoda outside Hanoi, had a staff member read Hồ's proclamation over the air.[301] The die was cast, whatever Hồ's intentions.

Why did the quest for peace fail? Above all, it took place amidst a clash of two political forces intent on regaining or gaining national honor and a sense of collective purpose. France, already humiliated by World War II, and in 1945–46 undergoing a protracted constitutional crisis, would not accept loss of sovereignty over any part of Indochina. At no time did Paris consider the DRV as equal negotiating partner. At a time of revolving-door governments, a Gaullist high commissioner in Saigon knew what he wanted and pursued his goals relentlessly. On the Vietnamese side, the revolution begun during the summer of 1945 possessed a vehement anti-French component which undermined DRV efforts to negotiate and implement interim agreements reached with representatives of "New France." Vietnamese local organizations had also expropriated large amounts of French property, which officials on both sides understood would be extremely hard to restore. Hồ Chí Minh was willing to stake his political existence on seeking a compromise with France, but support for this endeavor among his compatriots was never strong, and Paris never put someone of Hồ's caliber across the table, to give peace a chance.

Seeking Foreign Friends

Between 1940 and the summer of 1945, Indochina endured five years of isolation, except for the coming and going of Imperial Japanese forces and news filtered by Vichy French and Japanese censors. With the sudden capitulation of Japan to the Allied powers in mid-August 1945, Vietnamese in both town and countryside wanted to find out what had been happening in the world at large, and then try to understand how their lives might be altered as a result. Newspaper editors were quick to assign staff to listen to Allied radio stations in New Delhi, Chungking, Kunming, San Francisco, and Tananarive (Madagascar); transcribe news reports; and compose articles in Vietnamese. Foreign news availability expanded dramatically after the Japanese Army relinquished control of Radio Hanoi to DRV representatives in late August. Anyone in the Red River delta or north-central coast with access to a radio could receive Hanoi news bulletins broadcast several times a day, then proceed to repeat the information orally or in print. Radio Saigon's Vietnamese-language service also came under the control of DRV adherents for about three weeks before they were ejected from the facility by British troops.[1]

Once Allied soldiers began to arrive in Indochina in September, they provided another source of information on the world outside. Vietnamese crowds gathered to watch Chinese, British, Indian, or French units set up camp, prepare food, stand guard, clean their weapons, play cards, and otherwise occupy their time. The small American contingents in Hanoi and Saigon attracted special interest each time they emerged from their requisitioned villas. Francophone Vietnamese sought out Allied personnel capable of communicating in French, querying them about conditions in their homeland, the policy of their government regarding Indochina, and the motives of metropolitan French units arriving under the Allied umbrella. Few Allied soldiers could answer such questions in detail, having been away from home for some time. Most were in the dark about high-level purposes for dispatching them to Indochina, other than to "take the Japanese surrender." This hardly discouraged Vietnamese from striking up conversations at every opportunity.

Members of the provisional DRV government were in a somewhat better position to assess world affairs than the man in the street. They had ready access to intellectuals who had lived in Europe during the 1930s, as well as anticolonialist activists with years of experience in China, Siam, and Laos. Nonetheless, external events had moved very fast since the surrender of Nazi Germany in May, and especially since President Truman on 15 August designated Allied commanders to receive the Japanese surrender in different regions of Asia and the Pacific. Hồ Chí Minh thenceforth spent much of his time trying to keep up with day-to-day Allied developments as they affected Indochina. He clearly hoped that the United States would provide counterweight to Chinese and British ambitions, yet nothing learned in late August or early September offered room for optimism.[2] Most ICP members assumed that the victorious Soviet Union would come to the aid of the DRV in the name of national liberation from colonial oppression, yet no one could find evidence that Moscow even noticed Vietnam's August Revolution. More encouraging were radio reports of a new independent state of Indonesia, as well as the upsurge of independence activity in India and Burma. News of the United Nations organization starting to function led some DRV ministers to wonder if the United States and the Soviet Union could be convinced to put Vietnam or Indochina on the UN agenda. Based on his October–November 1945 observations in Saigon and Hanoi, however, the American journalist Harold Isaacs summed up the DRV position as follows: "The tiny Viet Nam Republic stood very feeble and very alone in the world. It had nothing but the will of its people behind it and a profound moral conviction of the justice of its cause. These were assets that could buy little on the world political markets after the end of the great war."[3]

This chapter looks at Vietnamese efforts to understand events beyond their borders, encounters with Chinese occupation forces, the search for external support of DRV independence aspirations, and the eventual realization that threats from France would have to be faced alone. As Vietnamese followed events in Europe, the Middle East, and Asia, they pondered whether the triumphant Allies would remain united, fragment, or recombine into two massive blocs led by the United States and the Soviet Union. Each eventuality suggested a different policy response from Vietnam. There were also domestic political implications, with the Vietnam Nationalist Party arguing for a tilt towards Washington, and the ICP eager to seek support from the "new democracies" led by Moscow. Violent suppression of the Nationalist Party during the summer of 1946 left the ICP free to tout its New Democracy platform unchallenged, even though Moscow still showed no interest in aiding its comrades in Vietnam. Meanwhile, DRV efforts to find support in Asia yielded many expressions of sympathy but very little practical aid. Yet Vietnamese interest in the world at large did not diminish. The government was committed to making its survival a matter of international consequence. Hồ Chí Minh in particular understood that the assertion of national independence did not create the reality. Vietnam's independence would need to be recognized by at least some states of consequence, no matter how long this might take.

CATCHING UP ON WORLD AFFAIRS

Reflecting the public's desire to understand what had been happening overseas since 1940, Vietnamese newspaper editors allocated considerable space to articles about the recent European War, relations between the Allied powers, formation of the United Nations, and the global upsurge of movements of national liberation. When discussing the European War, periodicals of all political persuasions gave top priority to the epic confrontation between Nazi Germany and the Soviet Union. Stories about the Battle of Stalingrad were carried widely. Most impressive was Độc Lập's translation of Constantin Simonov's novel about the Battle of Stalingrad, which it serialized for months. A Việt Minh newspaper in distant Quảng Ngãi province somehow obtained and serialized the story of "Nastia," a Russian war heroine.[4] Russo-German tank battles and the general development of tank warfare during World War II fascinated another author.[5] The Western front of the European conflict received almost no attention, one exception being Dư Luận's serialized account of the June 1944 Normandy landings by American, British, and French forces.[6] Tito's partisans in Yugoslavia attracted repeated praise, and Wingate's Raiders in Burma made a spirited entrance.[7] Nazi atrocities were described graphically, and the Nuremberg war crimes trials upheld.[8]

By far the most international coverage was provided by the Hanoi weekly Thời mới (New Times), successor to Trung Bắc Chủ Nhật (Sunday Center-North), which had been published during the latter months of the Pacific War by a group of teachers, lawyers, and other professionals. Already by early October, Thời mới had canvassed postwar problems emerging in Greece, Lebanon-Syria, Algeria, Egypt, India, Indonesia, China, and Korea. Writers noted how the wartime Four Power alliance appeared to be unravelling, the UN organization had yet to make any impact, and a host of independence movements had emerged across Asia and the Middle East. "All the oppressed peoples of East and South Asia have risen up to oppose the colonialists, and they are determined to win," one contributor exalted. He added ominously, "Those states that try to hold on to their colonies risk provoking World War III."[9] Thời mới editors denounced a London conference on Far Eastern issues for not including Vietnamese, Korean, and other Asian representatives. By way of antidote, *Thời mới* called for the convening of an inter-Asian conference committed to eliminating British, French, and Dutch colonialism.[10] The United States was praised for granting independence to the Philippines, and both the United States and the Soviet Union were complimented for committing themselves to Korean independence. On the other hand, *Thời mới* was disturbed by the growing tussle between the United Kingdom and the Soviet Union over Persia (Iran). *Thời mới* suddenly ceased publication at the end of December 1945, leaving other Hanoi periodicals to compete for the best international coverage (see chapter 9).

In the weeks preceding lunar new year observances in early February 1946, each newspaper editor compiled a special Tết edition, which by convention always included articles summing up the recent past, both international and domestic. One Việt Minh paper in Huế offered readers an impressive six-page chronology of events in Europe and the Far East over the previous five years. Huế's other Việt Minh paper chose to focus on five key global events: the outbreak of war in 1940–41; the Battle of Stalingrad; the April 1945 San Francisco Conference, which founded the United Nations; the defeat of Japan; and the growing confrontation in China between Nationalist and Communist forces.[11] A Catholic periodical chose to itemize the terrible loss of life that had occurred during World War II, not the grand historical junctures.[12]

As Vietnamese editors and writers tried to understand the relative positions of the big powers, differing viewpoints emerged. The United Kingdom was generally seen as a declining power, although some pointed to London's capacity to reassert its national interests in the Mediterranean, Persia, and Hong Kong, as well as to assist the Dutch in returning to Indonesia and the French to southern Indochina. Everyone perceived the United States and the Soviet Union as principal beneficiaries of the recent war, and many then questioned whether Washington and Moscow could possibly continue to cooperate with each other. On the vital issue of support for national self-determination, some Vietnamese authors considered U.S. credentials more credible, others favored the Soviet Union, while still others questioned whether either great power was prepared to let people make up their own minds freely. In a blunt expression of realpolitik, one Việt Minh paper chided readers who hoped the French public would get rid of General de Gaulle, that the Soviet Union would recognize Vietnam's independence, or that the Allied powers would compel France to stop attacking the DRV. On the contrary. "Each country has been worrying about itself since the defeat of fascism, so can hardly put Vietnam's problems above its own." In such circumstances, the editors concluded grimly, "We will have to lose a lot more blood before the enemy desists, the world notices us, and recognition is guaranteed."[13] While this dogged prediction proved remarkably accurate, these young men could not imagine in late 1945 just how long and decimating a struggle would ensue.

News that the foreign ministers of the Soviet Union, United States, and United Kingdom would meet in Moscow in December 1945 to deliberate Far Eastern issues was received expectantly in Vietnam. Perhaps the participants would agree to reassert Allied responsibilities in southern Indochina, rather than standing by as the British moved to cede authority to the French colonialists. The Indochina question appears to have been ignored at the eleven-day conference. More unsettling, however, the French were invited by the Soviet Union, United States, and United Kingdom to join a new Far Eastern commission, implicitly legitimizing France's position in Indochina. The only Asian delegates on the commission would be Chinese, Indian, and Filipino. Several Việt Minh papers tried to put a favorable spin on the Moscow proceedings, particularly noting the mutual Soviet and American commitment to reestablishment of Korea as an independent state.[14] Not long after, it became obvious that Moscow and Washington could not agree on terms for installation of a single provisional Korean government, which led to de facto partition.

During late 1945 and early 1946, Việt Minh newspapers offered a variety of views on the United States, reflecting both the different backgrounds of writers and the mixed signals being projected by Americans. It was still possible to admire the United States, but no Việt Minh adherents took the further step of criticizing the Soviet Union publicly. By contrast, Nationalist Party periodicals condemned Stalin as an imperialist, and accused the ICP of being a willing tool of Moscow. *Việt Nam* took a realpolitik position when assessing U.S.-USSR relations overall, then suggested that America had more to offer Vietnam in the long run.[15] Another Nationalist Party paper acknowledged that Moscow voiced support for national liberation movements in Western colonies, but meanwhile it enforced communism and violent class struggle in Eastern European countries occupied by the Red Army.[16] An independent Hanoi paper worried that "Russia's Communist Third International" government might come into open conflict with the United States, United Kingdom, and China, thus jeopardizing world peace.[17] According to an overseas Chinese newspaper, Americans believed that, "If colonialists don't answer oppressed peoples with something better than artillery, they will push one billion people into the arms of the communists."[18]

Whether the United States and the Soviet Union would go to war with each other or not cropped up repeatedly in the Vietnamese press during 1946. The Red Army was seen as superior to any combination of Western armies, but the United States had the atomic bomb. In January, one Việt Minh paper reported that Russia (Nga) possessed an atomic bomb "much more powerful than any U.S. or British device," citing the Reuters news agency as its source.[19] Actually the Soviet

FIGURE 17. "International situation": Stalin and Uncle Sam face off, with the British and Chinese trying to restrain them, and a Gaullist "bug" stuck in the middle. In *Dư Luận* 25 (6 October 1946). Courtesy of Vietnam National Library.

Union did not test its first atomic weapon successfully until 1949, yet ICP members in particular wanted to believe they were on the global winning side. When Moscow's possession of the bomb was not confirmed, Việt Minh writers condemned the existence of atomic weapons, and called for nuclear disarmament. One writer accepted that the Hiroshima and Nagasaki bombs had "helped to bring peace to the world," but now such weapons were a threat to everyone.[20] The same paper that previously had claimed Moscow's nuclear superiority now asserted that the strength of people united in a just cause was greater than any atomic bombs.[21] The independent newspaper *Dư Luận* described the frightening destructive power of nuclear weapons and called for international inspection and control.[22] Papers reported favorably on President Truman's statement that the world would manage to get through its current crises, and praised Marshal Stalin's subsequent comment that "war cannot occur yet."[23]

In August, Minh Tranh published *The Far East Yesterday and Today,* probably Vietnam's first international relations primer.[24] After characterizing the Far East historically as "a huge imperialist marketplace," Minh Tranh devoted chapters to India, Indonesia, Vietnam, the Philippines, Japan, and China. In each place, first the feudal class and then the bourgeois class had tried but failed to mobilize the masses effectively against the European colonialists.[25] Minh Tranh then claimed that popular antifascist forces in China, Vietnam, India, Indonesia, and the Philippines had contributed greatly to defeating the Japanese fascist imperialists, yet made no effort to substantiate this myth in the making. He was on firmer ground when describing how national liberation movements had seized the initiative throughout the Far East immediately following Tokyo's capitulation. Minh Tranh focused especially on China, knowing that events there often impacted Vietnam directly. However, he was uncertain about the outcome. At one point he insisted that "the socialist movement is spreading from Yan'an and other liberated zones to encompass all China, smashing the antiprogressive forces." Elsewhere he asserted that "fascists, imperialists, and reactionaries" within the Guomindang had demolished hopes for peace, triggering fierce fighting that "may be the fuse for a Third World War."

Minh Tranh concluded his book on a global note, arguing that "the world is now clearly divided into two blocs, the imperialists versus the Soviet Union combining with the oppressed peoples." It was vital to Minh Tranh's argument, however, that the imperialists also be rejected by citizens within their own countries. Behind his final words one can almost hear the music of the "Internationale": "People worldwide—including those living in the United States, France, Holland, and Great Britain—will not permit the gang of plutocrats *(bọn tài phiệt)* to wreak disaster on humanity. They will throw the monied oligarchy out, enabling humankind to advance towards peace and happiness."[26]

The bipolar geopolitical vision of ICP writers like Minh Tranh in the summer of 1946 was not shared by either Hồ Chí Minh in Paris or many members of the DRV government in Hanoi. As we have seen in the previous chapter, Hồ was trying to negotiate a compromise acceptable to both the French government of the day and his followers back home, thus avoiding what he knew would be a devestating, harrowing war. Meanwhile, the DRV government labored to sustain correct if not cordial relations with Chinese and U.S. officials (see below), and deliberately avoided taking positions on foreign issues that had no bearing on Vietnam's current fate. For the DRV to have followed ICP ideologues like Minh Tranh and proceeded to declare allegiance to a Soviet-led bloc would have been foolish in the extreme, ruining whatever chances existed for peaceful relations with France, the United States, or Nationalist China, and gaining nothing from Moscow in exchange. Marshal Stalin aimed to have the French Communist party achieve parliamentary and then executive dominance in metropolitan

France. French Communist Party leaders endorsed French sovereignty over Indochina, in the interests of attracting more voters. They made only occasional attempts in Cabinet or within the French negotiating delegation to soften French demands. We don't know if President Hồ attempted to educate ICP ideologues about Stalin and the French Communist Party after his return to Vietnam, but Hồ's subsequent actions suggest that he retained a multilateral view of the world until 1949.

CHINA AND THE CHINESE OCCUPATION OF NORTHERN INDOCHINA

Allied leaders meeting in Potsdam in late July 1945 had given China Theater responsibility for Indochina down to the sixteenth parallel. Neither President Chiang Kai-shek nor his American chief of staff, General Albert Wedemeyer, aimed to launch any offensive in that direction. Three weeks later, however, they suddenly had Allied authorization to take the Japanese surrender in northern Indochina. Chiang had three reasons for dispatching substantially more troops to Indochina than necessary to disarm and intern the Japanese pending repatriation. The operation enhanced his status as an Allied Big-Four leader. He could route some troops through Haiphong to board American ships for Taiwan and Manchuria. And he could siphon off Yunnan divisions in anticipation of mounting a coup against the governor of that province. Chiang assigned a Yunnanese general, Lu Han, to command the occupation forces.[27]

On 28 August, Yunnanese and Chinese central government divisions began to pour across the Indochina border at Lào Cai. Using segments of the Kunming–Hanoi railway, and the road paralleling the Red River, advance Chinese units arrived at Yên Bái town a week later, where they were greeted by a local Việt Minh committee. Soon, however, the Việt Minh group was forced out of town by a Vietnam Nationalist Party contingent travelling with the Chinese. To the east of Yên Bái, in Tuyên Quang province, a new people's committee pleaded for help from Hanoi to deal with the influx of Chinese troops demanding food, and asked for advice concerning Nationalist Party cadres who wanted to join the committee. Further to the east, Chinese units crossing from Guangxi province entered Lạng Sơn town, accompanied by Vietnam Revolutionary League members intent on asserting authority. Several hundred Việt Minh adherents were surrounded, then compelled to relinquish their firearms, ammunition, watches, and fountain pens before being allowed to leave town. They retaliated by mounting an economic blockade of Lạng Sơn, which was only lifted following a complaint from Lu Han's staff to the DRV in Hanoi.[28] As Chinese soldiers entered the heavily populated Red River delta, mostly on foot, Vietnamese villagers were stunned by their emaciated bodies, tattered clothing, and seeming lack of organization.

In early 1945, northern and north-central Vietnam had suffered its worst famine in half a century, with about one-tenth of the population starving to death. Those few villagers who in September possessed a rice surplus took umbrage when Chinese quartermasters demanded to purchase it with alien currencies of dubious value.

U.S. C-47 Dakota aircraft brought the Chinese advance group from Kunming to Hanoi in early September. On 9 September, a well-dressed, disciplined Yunnan regiment led the way across the Long Biên (Doumer) bridge into the city, followed by increasingly bedraggled units well into the night.[29] Vietnamese observers commented how the supposedly victorious Chinese troops appeared quite inferior to the defeated Japanese units. Stories soon circulated about the clouds of flies hovering over Chinese troop columns, and the number of soldiers who dragged themselves along on limbs swollen by beri beri.[30] Several weeks later at a surrender ceremony in Nam Định town, thousands of Vietnamese watched as Japanese and Chinese units faced each other, the Japanese commander barked a command to "Present arms!" prior to laying down weapons, and suddenly Chinese soldiers broke ranks and fled in panic, believing they were about to be mowed down.[31] Whatever their initial disparagement of Chinese troops, however, Vietnamese soon learned they had no choice but to accept the Chinese presence. Estimates vary greatly on how many Chinese soldiers entered northern Indochina, but their numbers at any one time probably peaked at about one hundred thousand by the end of 1945, then declined as units were shipped out by sea or withdrawn to Yunnan or Guangxi.[32] Along with the soldiers were at least twenty thousand Chinese porters, camp followers, and petty merchants.

General Lu Han arrived in Hanoi by air on 14 September, going directly to his command headquarters at the former governor general's palace, from where his advance team had ejected French commissioner Jean Sainteny four days prior. On 16 September, Lu summoned Hồ Chí Minh to the palace to discuss currency exchange rates, feeding the Chinese Army, repairing roads, the size of the Vietnamese Army, and the importance of maintaining order. Lu arbitrarily declared that one "Chinese gold unit" (*guan jin*; CGU) would be worth one and a half Indochina piastres, a gross overvaluing of the Chinese currency. Fearful of Chinese swooping into local markets to buy up rice with these bank notes, Hồ promised Lu that the DRV government would supply his troops with grain. Lu may originally have planned to impose Chinese military government in northern Indochina, but now he was prepared to test Hồ's assurances that the Vietnamese government could keep the peace. On 22 September, the day after General Gracey declared martial law in Saigon, Lu assured Hồ that he had no intention of following the British precedent, so long as public order persisted in both Hanoi and the countryside.[33] Nevertheless, Lu's exchange rate decree demonstrated how he could insert himself into Vietnamese government affairs at any moment.

FIGURE 18. General Lu Han in Hanoi, 14 March 1946. Copyright Imperial War Museums (SE 7021).

On 1 October, General He Yingqin, commander-in-chief of the Chinese Army, arrived in Hanoi to be briefed by General Lu Han on occupation progress. Overseas Chinese and Vietnamese youths hoisted banners and waved flags to welcome General He, who talked with reporters but chose not to meet provisional President Hồ Chí Minh.[34] The principal non-Việt Minh newspaper in Hanoi counselled China to understand the impossibility of "safeguarding peace in Asia and opposing British-French colonialism" without the active participation of Vietnam, Burma, Malaya, Thailand, and India.[35] General He's real reason for coming to Hanoi was to convince General Lu not to oppose the forcible removal by Generalissimo Chiang Kai-shek of the governor of Yunnan, Long Yun, who was Lu's patron and relative. Chiang's Kunming coup began on 2 October, Lu remained uninvolved, and Long Yun conceded defeat three days later. Lu retained his command over occupation forces, and appears to have convinced General He to counsel Chiang against any early return of French troops to northern Indochina.[36]

From the moment Chinese troops arrived, Vietnamese began to speculate about when or if they would depart. For supporters of the fledgling DRV, many day-to-day grievances against the Chinese could be stomached so long as the Chinese did not interfere in government or allow French forces to return north of the sixteenth parallel. Rumors of Sino-French negotiations began in September. One month later a Huế newspaper protested that, "If Chongqing has signed an antidemocratic deal with the French, it must accept responsibility before the Allies, the Chinese people, and all freedom- and independence-loving humanity."[37] Subsequent Reuters news reports of an imminent Sino-French accord produced both pained concern and patriotic implacability in the Vietnamese press. As one paper stated, the Chinese would be contradicting repeated professions of friendship, and any such Sino-French collusion would have somber consequences. Either way, the writer concluded grimly, "The Vietnamese people will not allow any Allied country to disregard Vietnam's sovereignty."[38] As suspicions grew about Chinese intentions, editors did not alter their opinion that "the main foe remains French colonialism."[39]

We get some idea of the problems caused by the Chinese occupation when perusing early periodic reports from DRV province-level administrative committees. In the uplands north and west of Hanoi, Chinese troops mostly walked through but left a company-sized garrison at each province seat. In Thái Nguyên, for example, a sizeable Chinese contingent arrived on 13 September, the province people's committee made some grain available, and the Chinese quartermaster promised to pay. Trouble occurred when soldiers descended on the marketplace with Chinese currency, shopkeepers refused to accept it, the soldiers made threats, and the entire market closed down in protest. Most of the troops departed two weeks later, to include the quartermaster who had not paid the unit's grain bill.[40] Two hundred kilometers to the west, in the province seat of Sơn La, Vietnamese former officials of the colonial regime sought and received Chinese help in expelling the recently created Việt Minh committee. Several weeks later, however, a different Việt Minh group convinced the commander of the small Chinese garrison to let them share guard duties, at which point the former colonial officials felt compelled to withdraw. Amidst these contestations, the Chinese seized ninety thousand piastres from the Sơn La treasury and commandeered 70 tons of rice, 14 tons of cattle, 150 horses, 150 saddles, and 20 floor mats.[41] Further west, in Lai Châu province, where as yet there was no DRV or Việt Minh presence, Chinese troops became involved in a power struggle between Nguyễn Văn An, an ethnic Việt former colonial prefect, and Điêu (Đèo) Văn Trì, a White Thái leader who had also enjoyed French support. According to reports received in Hanoi, the Chinese seized An, confiscated his property, and demanded one hundred thousand piastres for his release. Somehow this money was raised and An was allowed to go, only to be seized again when the Chinese heard that he owned several houses in Hanoi. Meanwhile, with Chinese support, Trì began levying contributions of cash and opium from subordinate officials. He also was said to be condemning the Việt Minh publicly and promising that the Thái people would never be ruled over by the Việt.[42]

In the Red River delta some provinces had to endure much larger numbers of Chinese soldiers. A spate of early brutalities went unpunished, but on 18 September a Chinese commander summarily executed two of his soldiers, who were accused of killing three Vietnamese in the town of Bắc Ninh, immediately northeast of Hanoi. One newspaper commented that, after a number of such incidents where Chinese perpetrators had gone untouched, "people are happy to see a change."[43] Vietnamese police took testimony from twenty-three Bắc Ninh residents who said they had been attacked and pillaged by Chinese on the night of 18 September. Nguyễn Văn Thể reported four soldiers breaking into his house, seizing clothes and rice, and uncovering one hundred piastres hidden behind his ancestral altar. Other citizens in the neighborhood had been tied up, and one elderly man died amidst the tumult.[44] In Sơn Tây province, just west of Hanoi, several thousand Chinese occupied the former colonial military base at Tống, the adjacent airstrip, and all school buildings in town. Three Chinese soldiers in Vietnamese clothing shot and killed three civilians and wounded others. Militiamen captured two of the Chinese, then "had difficulty restraining people's anger at the culprits." Chinese officers insisted that the two men be turned over to them, and it appears this was done.[45] In Hà Đông province seat, just southwest of Hanoi, a spate of Chinese troop outrages in November provoked scores of citizen petitions to central government officials. The Chinese were accused of raping women, beating up men, seizing personal property, occupying some private dwellings, and burning down others. One petitioner complained that "conditions are now more wretched than under the French and Japanese." DRV authorities dispatched a delegation to Hà Đông, after which they expressed hope "the situation has been resolved."[46] Northwest of Hanoi, the town of Phúc Yên faced repeated waves of Chinese troops coming through. One Chinese unit appeared suddenly, fired shots in the air, seized buildings, confiscated property, and killed two civilians. The province people's committee presented the unit headquarters with a request for compensation, but heard nothing back before the unit departed. Immediately thereafter, a bigger unit of five thousand men arrived and the quartermaster demanded the province committee provide four tons of rice per day, plus two tons of corn for the five hundred horses and mules. When some Chinese soldiers deserted, Vietnamese quietly fed and assisted them on their way.[47]

Hanoi and Haiphong were the most sensitive occupation venues. To show goodwill, and also to demonstrate the new government's capacity to mobilize public sentiment, the DRV authorities tried to organize big welcomes for Chinese forces entering both cities. Citizens were told to make Chinese and American flags out of paper. Newspapers listed officially authorized slogans. Banners carrying other slogans would be confiscated. When Chinese troops marched into Hanoi, however, no crowds welcomed them. In Haiphong, the audience appeared to be mostly overseas Chinese contingents of elders, merchants, women, and young men carrying Chinese flags and big images of Sun Yat-sen and Chiang Kai-shek.[48]

It quickly became clear that avoiding major altercations in Hanoi and Haiphong between Chinese soldiers and Vietnamese citizens was the main hurdle, not exhibiting goodwill. Only three days after General Lu Han and provisional President Hồ Chí Minh reached their understanding, Chinese soldiers provoked a fracas in downtown Hanoi that left two Vietnamese dead and ten badly injured. According to the newly established Hanoi Sino-Vietnamese Liaison Committee, Chinese officers quickly apologized, made compensation of thirty-three hundred "gold units," and turned over ten Vietnamese they had detained. Emotions still ran high, however, with city officials and policemen repeatedly encountering Hanoi residents who wanted to retaliate for this incident and others.[49] Entire Chinese platoons sometimes moved into upper-class Vietnamese residences, compelling families either to flee or retreat upstairs.[50] In Haiphong, the commander of the newly arrived Chinese 62nd Division gave his troops a long list of prohibitions (cấm) when dealing with local people. No soldier could enter anyone's home without military orders, no individual should be forced to accept Chinese currency, and it was a capital offense to seize Vietnamese or overseas Chinese property without authorization.[51] Nonetheless, a plethora of neighborhood-level altercations occurred in the early days of Chinese occupation of Haiphong, with the chair of the city people's committee pleading for residents to remain disciplined in the face of "minor disagreements." Haiphong's Việt Minh paper urged citizens to stop saying or doing things "not conducive to Sino-Vietnamese friendship," and to cease condemning Vietnamese officials for their handling of the issue.[52] No particular Sino-Vietnamese confrontation was ever described in the Haiphong press.

Vietnamese newspapers did convey general public fears about entry of Chinese troops. Articles recalled the early-fifteenth-century occupation of Vietnam by Ming dynasty forces, which lasted two decades. Elderly Vietnamese who had experienced Chinese Black Flag depredations of the early 1880s now repeated their stories to worried countrymen. Writers pointed out that rapacious warlords controlled some Chinese troop units, and the Chinese military in general had a reputation for treating civilians badly.[53] However, government censors made sure that no overtly anti-Chinese articles appeared. Việt Minh newspapers urged the public to remain calm, and to accept at face value Chinese government assurances that it had no territorial ambitions in Vietnam. A frantic search ensued for examples of Chinese sympathy towards Vietnamese independence, including a 1943 speech made in front of Việt Minh trainees in Guangxi, a 62nd Army leaflet distributed well before Japanese capitulation, and a recent Kunming radio broadcast. Papers asserted that Generalissimo Chiang Kai-shek respected Vietnamese sovereignty, which was not the case. "Today's China is not the same as feudal China," one editorial emphasized. China had suffered humiliation at the hands of Western imperialists, undergone the 1911 Revolution, and heroically resisted Japanese aggression. According to one editorial, China and Vietnam shared the same culture and ancestry *(huyết thống)*. "We will defend our territory in the same way China defended its territory," the editors insisted, which could be taken as a warning.[54]

The DRV Foreign Ministry warned the cabinet that Chinese Army ill-discipline in Haiphong, combined with a wide range of Sino-Vietnamese "misunderstandings" and repeated altercations, had produced a "very troublesome situation" in the city. Just to the northeast of Haiphong, in Hòn Gai town, Chinese troops imprisoned fifty individuals, broke into buildings, and seized a range of public and private property. In the nearby hills, local Chinese bands claiming to belong to the Chinese Army collected protection money from some villages and wreaked havoc on others.[55]

Chinese Army units commandeered scores of buildings, starting with barracks, offices, and warehouses used by the Japanese, but then moving on to eject DRV personnel from other venues, as well as taking over French dwellings. The Haiphong People's Committee was inundated with complaints from families whose homes had been seized by Chinese troops. In late September, the Việt Minh daily paper stated that the Chinese were acting according to custom in their own homeland, whereby troops arriving in any locality simply took the housing they required. It then urged people to "put the nation above the housing issue," accept their duty as citizens, and help make government responsibilities for housing and feeding the Chinese Army less onerous. The next day the newspaper had to print an apology for "mistakenly giving the impression that the Government does not concern itself with the rights of citizens." When the Chinese Army acted illegally in regard to housing, citizens should petition the people's committee, which would then refer the matter to the Sino-Vietnamese Liaison Commission for "immediate intercession."[56] Few newspaper readers would have considered this an adequate response. Government legitimacy must have suffered as Chinese moved in wherever they wished.

The Chinese Army took control of the Yunnan railway between Hanoi and Kunming, although it continued to depend on Vietnamese employees and some Japanese technicians to keep segments of the line functioning. The Vietnamese railway director accused Chinese troops of seizing coal and wood for their cooking fires, compelling staff to exchange money at ridiculous rates, and ordering trains to depart at incorrect times.[57] A Chinese Army unit also took over the Sauvage shipping company, which owned and operated three ships plus a number of smaller river craft. All employees were given a ten percent pay hike, and sailors also received free food and lodging. The Chinese civilian manager brought in by the army agreed to pay monthly rent to the DRV government, but the three Vietnamese ministries involved could not agree whether Sauvage vessels and facilities should be confiscated or merely "supervised" pending future developments.[58] Chinese troops occupied the Northern Region Veterinary Service experimental farm long enough to round up the horses and shoot the cows for meat. Valuable breeding horses were harnessed to overloaded carts, and several animals were beaten to death when they failed to perform. Chinese soldiers later returned to appropriate four thousand vials of veterinary vaccines.[59]

Despite Hồ Chí Minh's proposal on 16 September 1945 to supply rice to the Chinese Army, immediately thereafter the Chinese Army's quartermaster corps seized a number of rice warehouses in Haiphong.[60] This event seems to have caused DRV committees elsewhere to disperse and hide grain stocks, as no further reports of Chinese confiscations appear in the files until 30 October, when Chinese units descended on two Hanoi warehouses belonging to the Cereals Department, taking the modest total of twelve tons of paddy and thirty tons of milled rice, but more importantly acquiring 144,861 gunny sacks and thirty-seven weighing scales.[61] Quartermasters also took control of some salt stocks (see chapter 6). Early Chinese seizure of cloth stocks in Haiphong failed to alert DRV authorities in Hanoi to the danger, as one month later Chinese quartermasters located and requisitioned 43,742.5 meters of cloth from the warehouse of a French company, leaving it empty.[62] Liberation Army authorization to obtain 8,900 meters of cloth from the Bourgoin Meiffre company warehouse arrived one day after the Chinese Army requisitioned the lot. The Chinese then proceeded to occupy the spinning and weaving mills in Nam Định, taking some of the cotton and silk cloth warehoused there. Overall, half the cloth stocks reported to the Vietnamese authorities in early September probably were lost to the Chinese by late October.[63] Unlike grain stocks, no one had thought to disperse and hide cloth upon hearing of the first Chinese seizure.

With motor vehicles very scarce in northern Indochina, Chinese forces immediately took custody of all trucks and automobiles used by the Japanese Army, then moved to commandeer former colonial government vehicles and private autos belonging to French civilians. Nine trucks belonging to the DRV Northern

Region Materials Bureau were surrendered to the Chinese.[64] In an assertion of authority that must have galled Vietnamese observers, the Chinese military police instructed the DRV government to register all its motor vehicles with them. Thus, on 19 October, President Hồ's prewar Ford sedan (old license plate TH52; new license plate BB-6) was issued Chinese permit number 6249. The Interior Minister, Võ Nguyên Giáp, received a permit for his Ford the same day, while the minister of information and propaganda, Trần Huy Liệu, had yet to register his Renault. As of 29 October, fifteen autos used by the Bắc Bộ Phủ still lacked Chinese permits, and would not be allowed to exit the parking lot until this omission was rectified.[65] With vehicle repair facilities at a premium, it is notable that the Société Transports Automobiles Indochine (STAI) managed to avoid being commandeered by the Chinese Army, perhaps because the mechanics would have taken their tools and skills elsewhere. However, the Chinese did block a request that the STAI repair shop on the border at Lào Cai be relocated to Hanoi.[66]

The ongoing Chinese demand for rice carried more serious consequences than the loss of buildings or the day-to-day humiliations of army occupation. In mid-August 1945, flood waters had breached the dikes along the Red River, destroying or damaging about one-third of Tonkin's summer rice crop.[67] Chinese officers flew to Saigon in September to organize shipments of rice to Haiphong for their troops, yet by November they apparently had convinced the British to let them purchase and transport only two thousand tons. Rumors circulated that another twelve thousand tons would follow, but the French were in no hurry to see this happen.[68] Meanwhile, local Chinese troop commanders demanded that DRV province and city committees provide rice to feed their troops or they would take their Chinese currency into the marketplace, thus driving up the price paid by everyone else. In Haiphong, the commander of the 52nd Division offered to buy rice from the city at a mutually agreed-upon price. When this did not work, he dispatched an officer to the city committee on 3 October to "request" five hundred tons of rice by 10 October. After being told that all such allocations were being handled by the central DRV government, the officer insisted on two hundred tons by 15 October or he'd take "forceful measures in the marketplace." The city committee then convinced two Chinese and two Vietnamese merchant associations to provide fifty tons of rice quickly, without hiking the price. However, the merchants insisted the DRV government bear the unfavorable exchange rate when the 52nd Division paid them in Chinese "gold units."[69]

In mid-December, the DRV government agreed to sell to the Chinese Army two thousand tons of rice before the end of the month, with another four thousand tons to follow in January. The price of rice had dropped somewhat following the November harvest, but was expected to climb again from February. General Lu Han had secured a forty million piastre loan from the Bank of Indochina to pay occupation expenses, yet his representatives refused to pay the DRV the current market price of 6,500–7,000 piastres per ton, insisting that the Vietnamese accept 5,000 piastres per ton. Assuming that Chinese Army quartermasters had one hundred thousand mouths to feed, at a quantity of twenty-five kilograms of milled rice per person per month, they required twenty-five hundred tons of rice each month. The DRV government dispatched officials to six delta provinces to agree on quotas, and it was the responsibility of province committees to purchase and deliver the rice to one of three collection points. In return, the Chinese promised not to enter local markets to purchase rice with their "gold units," a practice that had triggered numerous public protests and altercations.[70] Meanwhile, many Vietnamese families had to subsist on corn, yams, and beans, saving their tiny supply of rice for ritual occasions.

During the Anti-Japanese War in China, the Chinese Army often had been much more ruthless towards its own citizens than proved to be the case among Vietnamese civilians. Even as Lu Han's divisions marched into the Red River delta in late 1945, other Chinese Army units were descending like locusts on Guangdong's coastal cities, seizing food, property, and women at will. Such comparisons offered no solace to Vietnamese on the receiving end of Chinese ravenous behavior, yet ICP and Nationalist Party cadres who had witnessed the war in China would have perceived the difference. And Chinese commanders in northern Indochina probably felt they were exercising commendable restraint.

Considering the grievances that Vietnamese accumulated as a result of Chinese Army occupation, it is notable how few acts of violence against Chinese personnel occurred. In late October 1945 in Haiphong, the Chinese 62nd Division complained about Vietnamese violent behavior directed against its men, and the city people's committee promised to take appropriate action.[71] In December, a DRV National Guard platoon tried to rescue their leader from Chinese detention, losing one soldier killed in action and seven captured. The Hải Dương province committee managed to gain release of all but three prisoners and thirteen firearms.[72] About this time, a delegation of Việt Minh activists from Phú Thọ, escorted by Trần Huy Liệu, sought permission from President Hồ Chí Minh to attack vexatious Chinese troops in their province. Hồ gave them a stern geopolitical lesson, chided Liệu for having encouraged such foolishness, and sent them packing.[73] In early January 1946, it was reported that ten Chinese soldiers and twenty-two overseas Chinese had been shot and killed by local militia in Ninh Bình province. The message was quickly routed to the Foreign Affairs Ministry for action by Hồ Đức Thành, special commissioner for Sino-Vietnamese affairs, but the archives fail to reveal what happened then. A month later, another commissioner went to Ninh Bình to investigate a charge that Vietnamese soldiers had destroyed an automobile and killed seven overseas Chinese occupants. These may have been false alarms, yet the DRV government took them quite seriously.[74]

On 6 March 1946, in An Dương district (Kiến An), Vietnamese stopped a Chinese Army truck coming from nearby Haiphong, abducted and apparently killed six occupants, and carried away boxes of clothing, shoes, leather belts, soap, and ammunition. Word quickly reached DRV authorities in Hanoi, who dispatched special commissioners Đào Văn Biểu and Hồ Đức Thành to investigate what became known as the Ro-Nha village incident. Three persons were soon arrested by Vietnamese police, and the 60th Chinese Army commander demanded the death penalty. President Hồ Chí Minh told the special commissioners that, providing no DRV government personnel were involved in the crime, the accused could be turned over to the Chinese together with a formal letter of apology, "thus assuaging China." Two days later, however, the Kiến An provincial court tried the accused and sentenced them to death, with Chinese officers invited to attend the execution. President Hồ refused to commute the sentences. and it appears two of those convicted were executed. The family of the third person, Mai Trung Diễm, had raised questions about his guilt, supported by petitions from fellow villagers. His sentence was reduced to a hefty fine to be paid forthwith by his father, or else the execution would proceed. Meanwhile, the 60th Army had demanded a large compensation payment from the DRV for loss of life and property. As of 2 April, the government hoped the Chinese Army would accept 70,000 piastres for the lives lost and 225,000 Chinese "gold units" for the missing supplies. Six weeks later, Diễm's alleged wife was pleading for her husband to be allowed out of jail temporarily for medical treatment.[75] While it was rare for Hồ Chí Minh to intervene overtly in a case of this kind, he obviously saw maintenance of correct relations with the Chinese Army as paramount. On the other hand, even Hồ could not prevent the local authorities from modifying the outcome.

It was more common for local Việt Minh groups to find money to purchase arms and ammunition from Chinese soldiers who had retained surrendered Japanese stocks, instead of forwarding them to prescribed collection points. Lacking money, adventurous youths tried and occasionally succeeded in stealing Chinese weapons. Chinese commanders might then retaliate locally or forward complaints to the DRV government, which dutifully dispatched commissioners to investigate each incident.[76] In June 1946, two machine guns and four rifles were stolen from a Chinese unit at Đồ Sơn (Kiến An). The Chinese commander took hostage members of the Đồ Sơn committee and police force, which apparently facilitated capture by the Chinese of the six thieves and weapons. The Đồ Sơn committee then collected a boat and six thousand piastres from families of the perpetrators to gain their release from Chinese custody—only to spend part of the money on a lavish party and gratuities for Vietnamese said to have helped resolve the incident.[77]

Overseas Chinese

Many Vietnamese regarded the overseas Chinese (Hoa Kiều) as having received favorable treatment by the French colonial authorities that enabled them to get rich at the expense of the Kinh (Việt) majority. Admittedly the Japanese had treated some overseas Chinese badly after overthrowing the French administration in March 1945. With the arrival of the Chinese Army in September, however, Vietnamese immediately suspected the overseas Chinese of linking up with the occupation authorities for mutual gain. They were bitter when overseas Chinese draped Chinese government flags, rather than DRV flags, outside residences. Overseas Chinese pride in China's new status as a Big Four member sometimes translated into overbearing behavior towards Vietnamese, who could never be more than citizens of a small country. Nonetheless, overseas Chinese came to realize that the Chinese Army might not remain for long in Indochina, in which case careful account needed to be taken of the DRV government on the one hand, and returning French forces on the other. Overseas Chinese appreciated Hồ Chí Minh's efforts to sustain relations with the Chinese government beyond the occupation period, but often doubted the DRV's capacity to withstand French pressure. The growing confrontation between Guomindang and Communist forces in China also reverberated among overseas Chinese in Indochina.

In late September 1945, Vietnamese and overseas Chinese alike across Indochina expressed outrage at British-French actions in Saigon-Cholon. Both nationalities endured casualties, torched properties, and destroyed merchandise. Both fled for their lives to the southern countryside. The Chinese government sent protests to London and Paris, and newspapers in China denounced renewed Western colonial ambitions. Chinese-language newspapers in Hanoi and Haiphong vehemently condemned French atrocities in Cochinchina, even to the point of proposing reprisals against French nationals in the north.[78] Chinese associations in the north made donations to a range of DRV welfare initiatives. President Hồ Chí Minh reciprocated by meeting overseas Chinese representatives, encouraging formation of local Sino-Vietnamese friendship associations, and making sure that the 10 October anniversary of the 1911 Revolution in China was observed prominently. In Haiphong, a big commemoration of "Double Ten Day" took place in front of the Opera House, complete with massed Việt Minh groups, flags of both countries, speeches by the chairman of the city people's committee and a member of the Chinese General Staff, and the singing of both national anthems. A Dân Chủ editorial, after explaining the history of Double Ten and Sun Yat-sen's Three Principles of the People, declared euphorically that "Chinese and Vietnamese brothers are closer together, genuinely equal, and truly supportive of each other."[79]

An unknown number of overseas Chinese had their property commandeered by local Việt Minh groups during the August 1945 Revolution. Those who chose to petition the government for redress received urgent attention from the Interior Ministry's Sino-Vietnamese Bureau (Ty Hoa-Việt). Provincial people's committees were ordered to investigate, and the files suggest that petitioners eventually received at least partial satisfaction. Mr. Ung Ngan Nhie, absentee owner of a plantation in Vĩnh Yên province, petitioned for return of twenty water buffaloes, three tons of rice, one bicycle, two rifles (registered), and a stack of office files. Ung added that the Việt Minh group had threatened to confiscate his November rice harvest, and even to redistribute plantation land to local villagers. The Foreign Ministry took charge of this case, instructing the Northern Region Committee to order the Bình Xuyên district committee to obtain restoration of Ung's property. A month after lodging his petition, Ung reported that 60 percent of his property had been restored. He wished to waive further restitution, and promised to donate three tons from the upcoming rice harvest to the Bình Xuyên district Liberation Army unit, as "my expression of Sino-Vietnamese friendship." The Northern Region Committee thanked Ung and separately instructed the district committee to protect Ung's upcoming harvest.[80]

Some overseas Chinese behavior caused substantial difficulties for the DRV. Overseas Chinese accepted proposals from French factory owners to lease or purchase enterprises at cut-rate prices, thus cutting across DRV plans to requisition or manage French enterprises. Others recruited Chinese soldiers to accompany them into Vietnamese enterprises to demand that merchandise or even the building itself be sold in exchange for highly inflated Chinese "gold units." Overseas Chinese merchants routinely ignored DRV edicts banning export of rice, gold, or opium. They also evaded customs duties on legitimate imports and exports, sometimes employing Chinese soldiers to keep DRV inspectors away.[81] DRV government efforts to continue wartime controls on scarce commodities like cloth, condensed milk, soap, and medicines were now sometimes ignored by overseas Chinese merchants. When the Northern Region Economic Bureau instructed an overseas Chinese wholesaler to turn over 3000 of his remaining 3,266 cakes of scented soap, it was informed that the entire stock had already been donated to the Chinese Army.[82]

Continuing the colonial practice of opening civilian mail, DRV censors concentrated their diminished resources on the Haiphong postal exchange, which saw as many as two hundred outgoing Chinese language letters per day. Lacking a staff member able to read these letters, the Haiphong chief censor carried a daily stack over to the head of the city's Việt-Hoa Friendship Committee for help. Many correspondents pointed out the cheap price of rice in Vietnam compared to that in southern China. Some complimented the "docility" of Vietnamese. Other letters called the Vietnamese "cowards," or expressed fear of being poisoned by them. These uncomplimentary letters the censor held back or destroyed.[83] The files contain no cases of poisoning, but Vietnamese did physically assault overseas

Chinese, steal their property, and even burn their homes. In late November, General Lu Han dispatched a formal complaint to the DRV government which itemized by date and venue a series of such criminal acts. Lu concluded, "We have many times raised these matters [with you], yet still no appropriate action has been taken".[84] It must have been a relief to the DRV government that Lu did not order Chinese Army retaliation for these violent incidents directed at overseas Chinese.

The position of overseas Chinese became more complicated once it became clear in early 1946 that the Chungking government was negotiating with France over the terms for Chinese troop withdrawal. In early February, a group of overseas Chinese in Hanoi obtained government permission to start a Vietnamese language *(quốc ngữ)* daily newspaper titled *Trung Việt Tân Văn (China-Vietnam News)*. It lasted only eleven issues before closing without explanation, probably a victim of the 28 February Sino-French Agreement. Việt Minh newspapers continued to call for Vietnamese and overseas Chinese solidarity in resisting the French colonialists. In Huế, both Việt Minh papers told the story of an overseas Chinese father grieving for his son killed in action in Laos, yet allegedly not regretting that two of his other sons had now joined the fight.[85] After arrival of French troops in the north, however, overseas Chinese mostly avoided further affirmations of anticolonial resistance in favor of support for DRV education, health, and welfare programs. In Haiphong, for example, an overseas Chinese owner of five movie theatres volunteered to donate the proceeds of a series of screenings to the *quốc ngữ* literacy campaign.[86] A well-traveled overseas Chinese writer, after expressing great admiration for President Hồ Chí Minh and recounting DRV achievements, concluded philosophically: "All of us live in a time when good and bad deeds will be recorded in history."[87]

If overseas Chinese were particularly concerned about how to avoid violence, DRV officials often focused their attention on evidence of overseas Chinese economic manipulation and tax avoidance. The Hải Ninh People's Committee asserted that wealthy overseas Chinese had seized two-thirds of all arable land in the province, leaving little for Vietnamese, Nùng, or other ethnic groups.[88] The mayor of Hanoi blamed the escalation of rice prices in March and early April on overseas Chinese speculators and Chinese soldiers roaming the city, buying, and selling at will.[89] In June, even as Chinese troop units were departing Hanoi, soldiers still were being hired as protection for illicit trading. When customs officers moved to impound 118 jerry cans of gasoline and 88 containers of oil, a Chinese soldier tried to ward them off by firing his pistol into the air. Police arrested the overseas Chinese merchant but apparently allowed the soldier to escape.[90] As Chinese forces withdrew, people increasingly rejected "gold units." Some province committees were left with large quantities of this currency, which presumably could no longer be exchanged.[91] During the summer of 1946, the

DRV government attempted to shift the wholesale rice trade away from the big overseas Chinese merchants and towards a host of smaller dealers, each authorized to buy in a specific province. However, big traders still accounted for 94.5 percent of rice delivered to the city of Hanoi in October.[92]

The Franco-Vietnamese customs dispute simmering in Haiphong during the summer of 1946 placed overseas Chinese in an increasingly precarious position. Each side employed carrot-and-stick tactics to induce the overseas Chinese to move into its camp. From September, the French military intensified its checking of imports and exports, giving overseas Chinese engaged in foreign trade little choice but to register with French customs authorities. In retaliation, the DRV police arrested some overseas Chinese merchants on charges of failing to pay Vietnamese duties.[93] DRV customs on 17 November publicly threatened Chinese merchants and others with up to thirty-six months imprisonment for not declaring goods.[94] Meanwhile, the Chinese consulate in Hanoi complained confidentially to the DRV government that Vietnamese soldiers and police elsewhere had been "making it very hard for Chinese in recent months."[95]

The fighting which exploded in Haiphong for five days from 20 November ended with overseas Chinese inhabitants of the city under French control. Hostilities also erupted in Lạng Sơn town from 21 November, where there is no doubt that most of the five thousand overseas Chinese inhabitants wanted French protection. Earlier the overseas Chinese had affirmed their own identity vis-à-vis the more numerous Nùng and Thổ (Tày) ethnic groups.[96] The French also recruited a "partisan" group that included overseas Chinese. Following French seizure of the town on 25 November, eight hundred overseas Chinese met with French officers to receive a quantity of firearms and discuss how best to guard themselves against Vietnamese National Guard and militia units which remained in the adjacent countryside. At other locations in Lạng Sơn province, the French instructed overseas Chinese to fly a Chinese government flag whenever a French plane approached.[97]

Throughout late 1945 and 1946, the DRV made no attempt to define by law or decree the status of overseas Chinese in Vietnam. In practice they were considered citizens of China but subject to Vietnamese authority wherever feasible. There was no policy to recruit overseas Chinese to the National Guard, although a few Chinese youths volunteered and were accepted. As the French moved to assert sovereignty north of the sixteenth parallel, they naturally claimed the right to protect and manage the overseas Chinese. After the last Chinese troops departed in September, Chinese diplomats in Hanoi and Haiphong tried to intercede with DRV and French officials on behalf of overseas Chinese under growing pressure from both sides. Increasingly, however, overseas Chinese families had to make their own difficult choices to avoid being caught in the crossfire. Most sought refuge behind French lines, yet this did not give them immunity from

DRV exactions. They still had to pay taxes and utter the correct slogans when approached by underground DRV or Việt Minh cadres.

Fathoming the Chinese Revolution

Political and social upheavals in China had captured the attention of neighboring Vietnamese from the 1900s onward. Three generations of Vietnamese intellectuals read the essays of Kang Youwei and Liang Qichao, followed events of the 1911 Revolution and May 4th 1919 Movement, and partook of the science and democracy debates of the 1920s. During the mid-1920s in Canton, young Vietnamese activists rubbed shoulders with dissidents from Korea, India, Indonesia, and Japan who were enrolled in the Whampoa Military Academy, and listened to a thirty-five-year-old Comintern agent named Nguyễn Ái Quốc outline antiimperialist strategies. Following the 1927 violent confrontation in Guangzhou between Guomindang and Communist party adherents, Vietnamese could be found on both sides. Militants who crossed back to Indochina encountered returnees from France and the Soviet Union with whom to debate revolutionary theory and praxis—often inside French colonial prisons. After the outbreak of the Sino-Japanese War in 1937, the possibility loomed of Indochina becoming embroiled in regional or global conflict. For awhile, colonial censors allowed newspapers to report events in China freely, and even cleared booklets that extolled Chinese Communist Party policies of united front, mass mobilization, people's war, and protracted resistance.

Following French arrest and imprisonment of thousands of Vietnamese anticolonial activists in 1939–40, southern China became a relative haven in which to try to pick up the pieces, with nationalists and communists competing for support from Guomindang generals and staff officers. Hồ Chí Minh took advantage of two years' experience working among CCP cadres in Yan'an and Hunan to formulate a strategy for seizing power in Indochina, which he presented for approval at the pivotal Eighth Plenum of the ICP Central Committee in May 1941. Prior to being arrested by local Chinese authorities in August 1942, Hồ composed a forty-three-page training manual on "Guerilla Fighting Methods," which drew heavily from Chinese Red Army precedents.[98] Although there would be very little fighting against French or Japanese forces for the next three years, the Việt Minh "armed propagandists" who survived enemy sweeps, hunger, and malaria to emerge from the forest in the summer of 1945 had learned their guerilla lessons well, and also taught basic people's-war doctrine to citizens of the six-province region adjacent to the Chinese frontier.

The new DRV army accepted Vietnamese who had served in diverse Chinese units during the Anti-Japanese War, the best known individuals being Nguyễn Sơn of the Red Army and Lê Thiết Hùng of the Nationalist Army. The Vietnam Nationalist Party and Vietnam Revolutionary League possessed members

FIGURE 19. "Vietnamese-Chinese Amity" poster. SHD 10H 2369(1). Tous droits réservés.

experienced in Chinese civil administration, Guomindang organizing, and army staff work. Whatever their political preferences, Vietnamese who had lived through the revolutionary violence, intensity, and vastness of China in the 1930s and early 1940s could not help but be affected.

The Vietnamese press in late 1945 quickly resumed its fascination with the Chinese revolution, after being muzzled by French and Japanese censors for five years. Sun Yat-sen, already the object of six *quốc ngữ* biographies during the 1920s, now was introduced to a new generation of Vietnamese in both National-ist Party and Việt Minh publications.[99] Sun's widely circulated pronouncement, the Three Principles of the People, resonated favorably with many Vietnamese, perhaps because it presumed to integrate the best in East Asian and Western political philosophies. For some, Sun's three-stage revolutionary program, moving from military rule to political tutelage to constitutional government, appeared germane to the Vietnam of 1945–46. According to one prominent writer, the DRV's foundation motto of "Independence, Freedom, and Happiness" could be compared favorably with Sun's formula of "Nationalism, Democracy, and Equalization/Livelihood."[100] Hồ Chí Minh drew extensively from Sun's rhetoric when issuing statements designed to reach the widest audience possible.

There is a peripatetic flavor to Vietnamese publishing about China in 1946, due to the scarcity of current sources. One newspaper translated and serialized a 1937 French book on China which obviously said nothing about the traumatic years of war.[101] A 1930s story by Pearl Buck about the tenuous lives of poor Chinese farmers was serialized.[102] Several out-of-date typologies of Chinese political parties were offered. The journal of the Hanoi University Student Union serialized a lively history of Chinese student contributions to the anti-Japanese struggle. China's "new literature" *(tân văn nghệ)* efforts received a glowing tribute.[103] In *Tiên Phong,* the Việt Minh's fortnightly journal for intellectuals, Đặng Thái Mai relayed information on China's "New Culture" movement that he had obtained years earlier, while Học Phi was able to locate and describe several more recent articles from China outlining "culture responsibilities" in the era of resistance and nation building.[104]

During the Pacific War, Yan'an in northern China had taken on magical importance for ICP members, nurtured by glowing radio and word-of-mouth descriptions. During 1946, any printed materials about the Yan'an "liberated zone" which reached Vietnam were quickly translated and published. A French journalist's account of Yan'an, "the Chinese communist capital," communicated to readers a revolutionary utopia.[105] The only work by Mao Zedong to be published in 1946 was a collection of articles and speeches on Yan'an's economy and finances.[106] Trần Huy Liệu and Minh Tranh found time to translate *One Month in Yan'an,* by Zhao Chauguo, published to coincide with the first anniversary of Vietnam's August Revolution.[107] One month later a Việt Minh group in Huế published *A Trip to Yan'an,* by Huang Yan, who had flown from Chongqing to Yan'an in June 1945 as member of a delegation hoping to promote peaceful resolution of CCP/KMT differences.[108] Huang waxed euphoric about Yan'an's skilful workers, well-stocked state stores, clean streets, nascent university, healthy citizens, and dedicated "vanguard medics" *(y sĩ xung phong).* Mao himself took Huang to the People's Hall of Education to address a large, attentive audience. Many Vietnamese, not only ICP members, would have been impressed by Huang's evocation. If full-scale war had to come to Vietnam, Yan'an seemed to represent what could still be achieved in liberated zones.

Touting the CCP was one way for ICP writers to argue the communist case in Vietnam without making a mockery of the party's self-dissolution in November

1945. Thus, a 1938 Shanghai book, *The Chinese Communist Party and Revolutionary War,* was deemed worthy of translation and publication in 1946.[109] In his preface, the Vietnamese translator suggested that while the CCP experience was meaningful to all proletarians, it was especially valuable to those small nationalities *(dân tộc)* "engaged in armed struggle to recover their homelands." Sections of the book dealing with Lenin, the Soviet Union, leadership, political officers in the army, staff work, logistics, transport, and military industries would have been read enthusiastically by ICP cadres in 1946. The Democratic Party's daily paper serialized in translation a more recent essay titled "The Current Policy of the Chinese Communist Party".[110] As had happened during the late 1930s, a number of articles were published in 1946 on Chinese guerrilla tactics. An extended essay by Zhou Enlai, "Political Work in Time of Resistance," was serialized by a Huế newspaper.[111]

Vietnamese with a sense of history understood that political and military developments inside the giant neighbor to the north would influence their own fate. Newspapers tried to follow China's "Nationalist/Communist problem" *(vấn đề Quốc-Cộng)* as closely as sources would permit. In September 1945, Việt Minh and non-Việt Minh papers alike lauded Chiang Kai-shek and Mao Zedong for meeting together to seek a peaceful, negotiated resolution of differences. One commentator contrasted the present favorable united-front environment with the volatile, ultimately disastrous united front of 1924–27. Mao had confirmed publicly that CCP ideology did not conflict with Sun Yat-sen's Three Principles of the People. Mao's "sole refusal," according to this writer, occured when Chiang insisted that the Red Army be placed under central government command. This surely was a major stumbling block, yet one month later the same writer claimed substantial progress towards cooperation between Nationalists and Communists, and indeed chided Vietnam's "recently returned revolutionary leaders" for not emulating the Chinese experience.[112] General George Marshall's late 1945 mediation effort in China was reported favorably. At the end of January, in the spirit of Tết, several Vietnamese papers saw hope for a peaceful settlement.

By May 1946, however, Vietnamese papers had to report that Nationalist/Communist talks were stalled and fighting was escalating in northern China. Non-Việt Minh papers worried about the consequences for Vietnam of prolonged civil war in China.[113] Việt Minh papers now leaned openly toward the CCP and asserted that the Red Army was holding its own despite the large amounts of U.S. aid being provided to the "Central Army."[114] I suspect that President Hồ Chí Minh had insisted the press avoid siding with either Chinese Nationalists or Communists, but once he departed for France at the end of May some ICP leaders chose to ignore Hồ's wishes. *Cứu Quốc* increasingly associated the DRV with the CCP under the rubric of "new democratic" forces in Asia. In late August, a remarkably different editorial appeared in *Cứu Quốc,* arguing that neither side in China could wipe out the other, hence the civil war might continue indefinitely, endangering peace in Asia and the world. According to this writer, because Vietnam had a relationship like "lips and teeth" with China, it would surely suffer ill effects from a protracted Chinese civil war, to include the conflict spilling into Vietnam. All the author could offer by way of remedy, however, was for Vietnam to encourage Chinese Nationalists and Communists to reconcile (hòa giải).[115] Next day, the principal Democratic Party newspaper featured an article titled, "Oppose White Terror: The Chinese Guomindang Have Used Poison Gas to Attack the Communists." The article offered no evidence for this claim, simply using it to declare support for the CCP and Red Army.[116] Minh Tranh accused reactionaries and fascists within the Guomindang of deliberately wrecking the negotiations, thereby making fierce conflict inevitable, and even risking triggering a Third World War.[117]

By the summer of 1946, Vietnamese newspapers enjoyed regular, up-to-date news from China. Editors commissioned detailed evaluations of the military strengths and weaknesses of Nationalist and Communist forces.[118] Maps of Manchuria appeared on front pages, complete with unit designations, troop movements, and battle venues. Zhou Enlai was quoted as ruling out a resumption of talks and predicting a CCP military victory. A Catholic newspaper focused on General Marshall's reluctant abandonment of mediation and return to the United States.[119]

Chinese Army occupation of northern Indochina had been traumatic for many ordinary people, and it was a relief to see the last units depart in September 1946. Yet the Chinese troop presence had prevented the French Army from taking aggressive action against the DRV north of the sixteenth parallel. As the probability of full-scale Franco-Vietnamese conflict increased dramatically in November, the DRV could not expect any help from the Nanjing government, much less the CCP regime in faraway Yan'an. Nonetheless, it was still vital to convince China not to cooperate with France in strangling the DRV. Meanwhile, the DRV would try to upgrade its covert contacts in southern China to obtain more weapons, ammunition, radios, medicines, and other supplies necessary to sustain war with France.

THE UNITED STATES: FROM HOPE TO ACCUSATIONS
OF COLONIAL CONNIVANCE

Educated Vietnamese had long been fascinated by America (Mỹ), partly in order to make comparisons with France, but also because the United States seemed to symbolize so many of the promises and pitfalls of modernity. In the early decades of the twentieth century, Confucian literati saw America as a great Social Darwinian success story, demonstrating what collective struggle and the genius of men like Benjamin Franklin, George Washington, and Abraham Lincoln could accomplish. For Phan Châu Trinh, the Americans were "truly a civilized race," who had resisted the oppressive English; developed schools, factories, and commerce; and achieved "peace and security" in all directions.[120] In 1925, Nguyễn Ái Quốc quoted favorably from America's Declaration of Independence and credited the United States with a successful "capitalist revolution," but insisted that America's exploited workers and farmers still aimed to achieve a second "comprehensive revolution."[121] The new intelligentsia generation of the 1920s and 1930s ruminated upon American materialism, pragmatism, ingenuity, technological prowess, and industrial momentum. Young urban men and women were drawn equally to Hollywood films in the local cinema and American popular music available on song sheets or RCA records. Just prior to the Pacific War, several textbooks for learning English were published.[122] The ICP, which earlier had resolutely condemned American imperialism, from 1941 declared its allegiance to a grand democratic, antifascist front led by the Soviet Union and the United States.

No Vietnamese intellectual had spent time in America and come back to explain its mysteries, unlike the many returnees from France and China (plus a handful from the Soviet Union). During the Pacific War, a few individuals risked imprisonment to listen to Allied radio broadcasts, including the powerful American station in San Francisco. Hồ Chí Minh haunted the Liuzhou bureau of the U.S. Office of War Information (OWI) during the summer of 1944, reading periodicals and news bulletins, and chatting with available Americans. The OWI tried unsuccessfully to gain Washington's permission to dispatch Hồ to San Francisco to broadcast news in Vietnamese. Other Vietnamese activists in southern China cultivated contacts among OSS and State Department personnel.[123] The first chance for Vietnamese inside the country to observe Americans and try to understand what they said occurred in late July 1945, at Hồ Chí Minh's headquarters at Tân Trào in the Việt Bắc hills, where an OSS team began to train one hundred men in preparation for assaults on Japanese communication lines. This also happened to be the moment when ICP cadres and Việt Minh luminaries began to arrive at Tân Trào for long-anticipated national meetings. While all were impressed by American weapons and equipment, as well as the OSS team's cordiality and desire to fight the Japanese, opportunities to share ideas were cut short by news of Japan's 15 August capitulation. The OSS team was then observed by thousands of Vietnamese as it marched to the delta together with the Việt Minh trainees, eventually reaching Hanoi on 9 September.[124]

Americans in Hanoi

Meanwhile, another OSS team had flown to Hanoi on 22 August, headed by Major Archimedes Patti. More than any other person, Patti influenced Vietnamese opinion about America in the early days of the DRV. The fact that Patti arrived two weeks before any Chinese officers led people to assume that the United States was taking the lead in Allied occupation duties. Although a mere major, Patti rose to the occasion in almost proconsul fashion, taking part in a whirl of meetings, banquets, and public ceremonies.[125] As one Vietnamese observer recalled, "in a city plastered with slogans and banners denouncing imperialism, Major Patti's jeep, flying its American flag, was constantly mobbed by people who simply wanted to see and touch the representative of the United States of America."[126] In encounters with Vietnamese journalists, Patti's words of sympathy were taken to mean that the U.S. government opposed France's return to Indochina and favored Vietnamese independence, neither of which was true. Even if Patti had been more cautious in his pronouncements, however, Việt Minh newspaper editors were determined to argue that recent Vietnamese-American cooperation in fighting the Japanese gave the DRV special status with the Allies, above all the United States. Hồ Chí Minh, who had met Patti already in southern China, knew that such reasoning could not carry his fledgling government very far. Above all, Hồ sought from Patti a way to communicate with the U.S. president, the secretary of state, or their authorized representatives. Patti did forward several letters from Hồ addressed to President Truman, none of which reached the Oval Office, or were even acknowledged. Hồ also plied Patti with questions about current U.S. policy on Indochina. Patti queried his OSS superiors for up-to-date formulations, only to be scolded for exceeding his brief by discussing political matters with Hồ.[127]

On 16 September, Vietnamese were delighted to see an American general officer arrive in Hanoi. This was Bridagier General Philip Gallagher, head of the U.S. Military Advisory and Assistance Group attached to General Lu Han's command, but taking orders from Major General Robert McLure, deputy commander of U.S. Army Forces, China Theater. Hồ Chí Minh immediately invited Gallagher to attend a mass fundraising rally in downtown Hanoi, and the next day's papers featured Gallagher's participation. However, Gallagher had instructions from McLure to facilitate French participation in the occupation. One of Gallagher's first actions was to sponsor the arrival from China of General Marcel Alessandri, who was determined to clear the way for return of his colonial troops to northern Indochina. Patti's earlier warnings that arrival of French troops could spark widespread violence were no longer being heeded by China Theater.[128] As we have seen, General Lu Han decided to rebuff Alessandri and prohibit movement of his troops across the frontier, as well as to reject French requests to rearm soldiers detained in the Hanoi Citadel. One month later, Gallagher raised with Lu Han the option of deposing the provisional DRV government, to no avail.

One of Gallagher's principal responsibilities was to coordinate with the U.S. Navy the loading of tens of thousands of Chinese troops destined for Manchuria or Taiwan. Not wishing to see French forces arriving precipitously by sea, Gallagher convinced the Navy to limit mine clearing to the outer approaches to Haiphong harbor. Chinese troop embarkations took place at Đồ Sơn, twenty kilometers southeast of the Haiphong docks.[129] In November and December, Gallagher stepped forward to mediate the Sino-French dispute which had erupted after High Commissioner d'Argenlieu banned circulation of some five-hundred-piastre notes throughout Indochina. Thanks to Gallagher's efforts, the Chinese released two detained Bank of Indochina officials, the French rescinded the ban north of the sixteenth parallel, and the Vietnamese lifted their boycott on selling to French nationals.[130]

Within a week of General Gallagher's arrival, Hồ Chí Minh understood that Gallagher was much less important to him than General Lu Han. All the same, Hồ continued to meet privately with Gallagher, hoping that his reports to higher echelons would be both positive and persuasive. The content of Gallagher's reports ranged from populist admiration for the patriotism of ordinary Vietnamese, to conviction that the country was not ready for self-government and would lose out in competition with other countries. Nonetheless, Gallagher remained of considerable symbolic value to the DRV until his departure in mid-December. He readily accepted invitations to public gatherings and showed every sign of enjoying himself among crowds of Vietnamese. Whatever Gallagher said publicly was embroidered in the Vietnamese press, yet he never appears to have sought corrections from editors. When Gallagher's superior, General McLure, visited Hanoi in early October, he was quoted as saying, "The United States is always ready to support those countries wanting to implement a democratic system," which editorialists took as endorsement of Vietnamese independence.[131]

General Gallagher encouraged OSS officers to work with Việt Minh members to set up the Vietnam-American Friendship Association, including helping to draft the Association's bylaws.[132] Gallagher made a point of attending the 17 October inaugural meeting of the Association, together with DRV Supreme Advisor Vĩnh Thụy (Bảo Đại). Invited to respond to the chairman's address, Gallagher concluded his brief remarks by endorsing a proposal to exchange students, thus promoting greater cultural understanding.[133] Following songs from a group of Vietnamese young women, Gallagher was easily convinced to sing several American songs for a delighted audience.

The DRV Interior Ministry had already approved the Vietnam-American Friendship Association's bylaws before the inaugural meeting, and the press had published a list of its acting committee members.[134] Trịnh Văn Bình, the acting chairman, had graduated from the Hautes études commerciales in Paris, and was currently director of the DRV customs service. Lê Xuân, acting vice chairman, was a journalist employed by Gallagher, well known to the French Sûreté for his anticolonial activities.[135] The Association's plan included organizing language courses, starting a lecture series, translating Vietnamese materials into English (and vice versa), publishing a monthly magazine, and building a library. Such an ambitious agenda could only be implemented with American financial help, although there is no record that money was advanced. Association membership was limited to Vietnamese, but others could sign up as honorary members, and some American personnel did so. Attendance at Association meetings grew to "nearly six thousand," if Lieutenant Commander Carleton Swift, Patti's OSS replacement, is to be believed.[136] Three issues of the *Vietnamese-American Magazine (Việt-Mỹ Tạp Chí)* appeared between October 1945 and February 1946, and then the publication seems to have ceased. One article praised the rapid arrival after August of new American films, beginning with "Blondie Goes to Town."[137] Another article envisaged Vietnam as a new market for American commodities, the construction of a Ford Motor factory, and the arrival of teachers, engineers, and technicians from America.[138] A Hanoi newspaper touted possible Vietnamese exports to the United States, citing fifteen-year-old statistics.[139] In 1946, when hopes for early bilateral DRV-U.S. relations had paled, the Vietnam-American Friendship Association continued to serve as quasi-official host for representatives of American companies scouting prospects in northern Indochina.[140]

The third American officer of significance to the DRV was Colonel Stephen Nordlinger, who arrived in Hanoi on 28 August at the head of a small U.S. Army civil affairs and military government (G-5) detachment. Nordlinger's orders were to locate and aid Allied POWs, and to "do everything possible to secure humanitarian treatment of all elements of the civil community." Finding few American or British POWs, Nordlinger concentrated on the 4,450 French POWs still under Japanese guard at the Hanoi Citadel. First his men collected vital statistics and identified persons needing urgent medical attention. With the Citadel hospital already holding 350 patients in a facility designed for 150, and six or seven men dying daily, Nordlinger went to Hồ Chí Minh to secure agreement for some patients to be transferred to a civilian hospital.[141] On 5 September, the government instructed the Đồn Thủy hospital director to accept and care for 150 ill French POWs about to arrive under American escort. If no Japanese soldiers were available, the director was to request members of the former Civil Guard (Bảo An Binh) to guard the prisoners in hospital.[142] Nordlinger also dispatched a G-5 team to Haiphong to locate and assess the much smaller group of French POWs there. On 11 September, the Haiphong People's Committee had an unspecified altercation with the American Dr. Bernard Margolis about shifting ill prisoners, which apparently was resolved soon afterward.[143] Nordlinger obtained DRV approval for French civilian medical personnel to resume positions in Hanoi and Haiphong hospitals, although it is unlikely many did so. With U.S. aircraft bringing in quantities of medicine, sterile dressings, hospital equipment, and powdered milk,

Nordlinger used these very scarce supplies to bargain for better treatment of French patients and staff alike.

Shortly after arrival in Hanoi, Colonel Nordlinger initiated a procedure at the Citadel whereby each day two hundred to three hundred POWs with families living in the city received passes to exit the premises until nightfall. From 12 September, Nordlinger apparently stopped the pass system and doubled the Japanese guard, in response to radio news reports that French units had accompanied British forces to Saigon, and French POWs there were being released and rearmed. On 13 September, a POW hoisted the French tricolor over Hanoi Citadel, which quickly attracted an angry Vietnamese crowd. Nordlinger's demand that the flag be removed was obeyed by the POWs. The pass system was resumed, and on 26 September POWs roamed downtown streets tearing down DRV posters addressed to French nationals, and allegedly assaulting Việt Minh members passing out pamphlets. Tạ Quang Bửu, representing Interior Minister Võ Nguyên Giáp, delivered a strong protest and warning to Major Patti. Within the hour, Patti, Gallagher, and Nordlinger were at the office of General Lu Han, who told them that Chinese patrols were already rounding up and returning POWs to the Citadel. Lu also "requested" that Gallagher withdraw all passes until calm was restored. Patti quickly phoned Bửu, and a potentially serious confrontation was averted.[144]

Nordlinger was criticized by General Gallagher for going beyond the French POWs to try to help all French nationals in the area. Patti, in his memoirs, labelled Nordlinger a "World War I francophile." Nordlinger recommended to Gallagher that the Việt Minh be disarmed so they could no longer "terrorize" French civilians. On the other hand, he rejected French entreaties that soldiers in the Citadel be rearmed.[145] Hồ Chí Minh must have known of Nordlinger's French sympathies, yet still met repeatedly with him to make the case for Vietnamese independence. Hồ and Nordlinger went together to several meetings that highlighted the plight of poor and undernourished Vietnamese, where symbolic amounts of U.S. food were distributed. Even Patti admits that Nordlinger became as concerned about Vietnamese humanitarian dilemmas as he was for the French POWs and civilians.[146] Provisional President Hồ Chí Minh encouraged Supreme Advisor Vĩnh Thụy (Bảo Đại) to accompany him to formal encounters with the Americans, where General Gallagher insisted on drinking toasts "to the health of His Majesty Bảo Đại." Bảo Đại also met socially with American officers, who enjoyed talking with him about big-game hunting, golf, tennis, and airplanes. On one occasion Bảo Đại was invited to inspect P-38 Lightning fighters parked at Gia Lâm airport. The idea of Bảo Đại travelling to the United States as DRV goodwill ambassador was mooted, but not pursued officially.[147]

Within days of the Pacific War ending, U.S. military teams were looking for MIA personnel in places around Asia previously controlled by the Japanese. In

FIGURE 20. Colonel Stephen Nordlinger attending an antifamine rally. From left to right: Nguyễn Văn Tố, Nordlinger, Vĩnh
Thụy/Bảo Đại (behind), Hồ Chí Minh, and Ngô Tử Hạ. Courtesy
of John Nordlinger.

Haiphong, two Americans asked the city people's committee to provide a boat
and crew to take them forty-five kilometers northeast to Hòn Gai in search of a
missing American. The committee sought and received quick authorization
from Hanoi.[148] In Thái Nguyên on 20 October, an American major, a European
woman claiming to be his wife, and two U.S. soldiers asked the provincial committee for help in locating the remains of three U.S. airmen downed in 1943,
about fourteen kilometers from town. Within five hours the crash site was located, the remains collected, and each helper given sixty piastres. The province
committee hosted the American team for dinner, then telegraphed Hanoi to report the mission "accomplished perfectly."[149] Two months later a more official
U.S. MIA search team arrived in Hanoi, whereupon the Interior Ministry in-

structed local committees to send it any available information concerning the remains of downed aviators. The American team offered rewards for any bodies recovered.[150] Forty years later, similar instructions would be issued concerning MIAs from the Second Vietnam War, and other U.S. teams dispatched to many more localities.

Saigon Futility

Far to the south, in Saigon, another U.S. officer arrived on 4 September 1945, only to be killed twenty-two days later. Lieutenant Colonel Peter Dewey headed an OSS team coming from Ceylon with orders to repatriate American POWs, protect U.S. property, and gather intelligence on southern Indochina. Dewey was immediately approached by adherents of the DRV who had formed the Southern Provisional Executive Committee ten days prior. The committee gave Dewey a letter of welcome meant to be shared with representatives of other Allied powers, notably the British, who landed their first detachment at Tân Sơn Nhứt airport on 6 September. The welcome letter tried to sum up the case for independence in a few vehement words:

> The VIET-MINH, i.e. the Democratic Front for the Independence of the [sic] VIET-NAM, having fought during four years against French domination, and against Japanese militarism, has been brought to power, by peaceful revolution, from North to South by the unanimous will of the Annamese people to live in freedom and independence under the sign of New Democracy [. . . .] All the hope of the Provisory [sic] Government of the Republic of VIET NAM is going toward you, the Representatives of the Allied Powers, because you will go to explain to your own nations, the will of our people![151]

However, Dewey quickly learned that a schism existed between the Việt Minh-dominated Executive Committee, who were determined to try to cooperate with incoming Allied forces, and the International Communist League (Trotskyists), who were calling for the populace to be armed to fight the imperialist British and French.[152]

From monitoring Radio Delhi and Radio Tananarive, the Southern Provisional Executive Committee knew that Great Britain intended to assist the French to return to Indochina, and heard the French foreshadowing their imminent arrival. The committee may have presumed, or at least hoped, that arrival of Colonel Dewey and his OSS team ahead of the British signaled that the United States was destined to play a significant role in Allied operations south of the sixteenth parallel. We don't know what Dewey told his two principal interlocutors, Phạm Ngọc Thạch and Phạm Văn Bạch, but it had to be disconcerting, as he was in no position to promise them a more substantial American presence, or even provide a response from OSS superiors to their pointed questions. Following arrival of

General Douglas Gracey on 13 September, Thạch and Bạch would quickly observe how the British excluded Dewey from all matters political. In fact, Gracey summoned Dewey to warn him to restrict his mission to checking U.S. property and assisting British counterintelligence with their war crimes investigations. Dewey ignored Gracey's admonition, remained involved in the talks between Bạch and Jean Cédile, French commissioner for Cochinchina, and dispatched daily reports to OSS Kandy (Ceylon) as well as to Patti in Hanoi.[153] Dewey at one point volunteered to spirit Thạch out of Saigon to talk with officials in Washington.[154] After the Executive Committee called a general strike for 17 September which closed down much of Saigon, Cédile asked Dewey to meet committee members and urge them to call off the strike. Dewey did this on the evening of 18 September, but the Vietnamese were in no mood to cooperate with the increasingly assertive French.[155] After hearing this news from Dewey, Cédile held a press conference to call off the talks, and to denounce the Việt Minh as politically unrepresentative and incapable of maintaining order.

Dewey was now being watched so relentlessly by both French and British agents that it was impossible for him to meet further with Executive Committee members. On the evening of 21 September, Dewey sent Captain Herbert Bluechel and George Wickes (who spoke some Vietnamese) to meet Phạm Ngọc Thạch, who gave them an appeal addressed to President Truman and revealed preparations to mount a demonstration on 23 September. When Bluechel pointed out that any such demonstration was illegal under the martial law just enacted by Gracey, Thạch replied that the committee fully expected the British and French to repress the demonstration violently, causing many casualties, but this would bring world attention to the Vietnamese as "peaceful, freedom-loving martyrs." As described earlier, Cédile proposed and Gracey approved the rearming of fourteen hundred French POWs, who during the early morning of 23 September seized public buildings and hoisted French flags everywhere. French civilians then joined the soldiers in roaming through Vietnamese neighborhoods, breaking down doors, and assaulting men, women, and children. Dewey went to Gracey's office to protest, but the general refused to see him. The next day, Gracey declared Dewey persona non grata, and ordered him to leave.[156]

Dewey could have disobeyed Gracey's order and sought higher-level U.S. intercession, meanwhile continuing to collect information and dispatch reports. Instead he made arrangements on 24 September to fly out on 26 September, then dispatched his own apocalyptic assessment, "Cochinchina is burning, the French and British are finished here, and we ought to clear out of Southeast Asia."[157] Dewey probably aimed to find his way back to Washington and make his opinions known at the highest level, not an unrealistic aspiration given his family's political connections.[158] On the night of 24–25 September, Vietnamese mobs struck back in Saigon, assaulting, torturing, kidnapping, and killing French civilians. On 25 September, OSS Captain Joseph Coolidge was badly wounded at a Vietnamese roadblock when returning from a day trip to Dalat.

Dewey was ambushed and killed by Vietnamese assailants the next day. When Hồ Chí Minh heard this news, he expressed his profound regret to General Gallagher, adding that any such incident would take place in the north "only over my dead body."[159] Hồ also gave Patti a letter of condolence addressed to President Truman that promised to search for and punish Dewey's killers, although it added that "it is impossible to investigate into the matter now, Saigon being still in the hands of the Franco-British troops." More remarkably, Phạm Ngọc Thạch sent a letter to Dewey's father in Illinois, especially recalling Dewey's friendly smile, which for Thạch represented an "illuminating light that came with the spirit of chivalry, and it was from the bottom of his heart, trying to understand us and with his great intelligence and his great sensitiveness for our cause." Dewey's father tried to send a reply to Thạch, only to have it returned by the U.S. War Department as likely to cause "misunderstanding and recrimination."[160] Dewey's body was never found. If the Southern Executive Committee managed to ascertain who killed Dewey, that information was not revealed. Finally, half a century later, a former member of the Southern Executive Committee, Huỳnh Văn Tiểng, revealed that a Gò Vấp guerrilla group had ambushed Dewey's jeep thinking he was French. Fearing repercussions, the committee then radioed Hanoi that the French had killed Dewey.[161]

In subsequent months the OSS unit in Saigon was cut back, and by March 1946 only two members remained under cover positions within the American consulate, much to the distaste of Consul Charles Reed. Alexander Edeleanu compiled the consulate's daily press review and dispatched intelligence reports to the Strategic Services Unit (SSU) of the War Department. George Sheldon was listed in the consulate's message center, but spent most of his time talking with French and Vietnamese contacts around Saigon.[162] In his final report, Edeleanu gave Sheldon five pages to characterize French and Annamite attitudes and behavior—much to the detriment of the former. Sheldon concluded that Hồ Chí Minh was "recognized and desired by most of the people of Cochinchina," the Annamites were "politically quite advanced," and the undercover resistance would "survive and succeed in the end."[163] Towards the end of 1946, Sheldon published an article that summarized developments in Vietnam during the previous sixteen months. He described the DRV administrative system favorably, lauded the literacy campaign, and concluded that a "workable and equitable" collaboration was possible between Vietnam and France.[164] One day after Sheldon's article appeared, full-scale war broke out. Returning to Indochina as a United Press correspondent, Sheldon was noted by the French police in 1947 to be seeking out members of the Vietnam-American Friendship Association to talk with.[165]

In Hanoi, following Major Patti's abrupt departure on 1 October 1945, all U.S. personnel were under high-level instructions to reduce their interactions with

DRV officials and to refer Vietnamese policy queries to General Lu Han. The OSS team continued to feed intelligence reports to Chongqing, some of which were forwarded to Washington. At least four more communications from Hồ Chí Minh to President Truman or Secretary of State Byrnes were accepted by American personnel in Hanoi and transmitted. One radio teletype message appears to have traveled from Hanoi via RCA links directly into the White House, which referred it to the State Department.[166] In late September, the State Department believed there were only nineteen American nationals there, though the number probably exceeded one hundred.[167] By November, however, numbers were dropping fast, and by early 1946 only skeleton teams remained.

In early March 1946, Major Frank White arrived in Hanoi under SSU orders to report current political developments in the absence of any other official American presence. PFC George Wickes accompanied White as a Vietnamese speaker, as well as a radio operator with one-time cryptographic pads. White rented two rooms on the top floor of the Métropole Hotel, then sent his card to President Hồ Chí Minh requesting an audience. Following the 6 March Franco-Vietnamese Preliminary Accord, Hồ invited White and Wickes to the cavernous salon of the Bắc Bộ Phủ, where they sat together and talked in English for two hours: "There were no interruptions, no secretaries, no telephone calls, no messengers. This by itself was strange, given the conflict and tumult outside. At one juncture a male servant produced tea and left. Ho wore the traditional high buttoned tunic, [and] floppy pants of the same khaki material. His beard was then wispy and his manner curiously detached. I was unprepared for a person so slight."[168]

White began by offering to transmit messages to Washington, but Hồ politely demurred. Instead Hồ ranged across Vietnam's history of resistance to foreign aggression, the prospects for a settlement with France, and his reasons for coming to believe in communism. Then Hồ delivered his principle message: the Soviet Union was in no position to help build a new Vietnam in the near future, whereas the United States could do so if it wished. However, Hồ doubted this would happen, as Vietnam was a small, faraway country, and could not be expected to loom large in the preoccupations of the United States.[169] Wickes was overwhelmed by Hồ. In a letter sent to his parents soon afterward, Wickes portrayed Hồ as an ascetic holy person totally dedicated to his people, a combination of St. Francis of Assisi and Abraham Lincoln.[170]

White had no sooner returned to the Métropole than he received an invitation from Hồ Chí Minh to attend a reception that evening, which turned out to be a banquet also attended by General Leclerc and his entourage, two Chinese generals, and Lieutenant Colonel Arthur Trevor-Wilson, the senior British officer in Hanoi. As the most junior officer present, White held back until everyone else was seated, then was stunned to be placed next to Hồ. The French said little during dinner, the Chinese got drunk, and White quietly offered the comment to Hồ that some guests might resent the seating arrangements. Hồ replied, "Yes. I can see that. But who else could I talk to?" If White took this to mean that Hồ wanted eventually to advance beyond pleasantries to talk with him about Vietnam–– U.S. relations, he would be disappointed. White received an autographed photograph from Hồ and encountered him again on several public occasions, but Hồ was now concentrating on bilateral relations with the French.[171] An American diplomat had also taken up residence in Hanoi (see below).

Hồ Chí Minh and the U.S. Government

Hồ Chí Minh realized early on that U.S. Army officers like Patti, Gallagher, and Nordlinger were useful sounding boards and informal providers of information, but they could not deliver what he wanted most: recognition by the U.S. government. On 30 August 1945, Hồ began his campaign by drafting a rather disjointed note to President Truman requesting that Vietnam have a representative on a commission for the Far East being discussed by the United States, Soviet Union, United Kingdom, and China. Major Patti dared not use his radio to communicate with Washington, but did agree to send the note to Ambassador Patrick Hurley in Chongqing, who apparently filed it away. At this meeting with Hồ, Patti cautioned that the United States had no plans to interfere in the internal affairs of Indochina, yet also reaffirmed President Roosevelt's commitment to self-determination for the Indochinese peoples.[172] In another letter to President Truman seven weeks later, Hồ reiterated Vietnam's claim to a seat on the newly announced UN Advisory Commission for the Far East, arguing that the presence of France and the absence of Vietnam on the commission led to the completely erroneous conclusion that France could represent the Vietnamese people.[173] Three days later, Hồ told Truman that France had lost its sovereignty over Vietnam in late 1941, when the Vichy regime signed an agreement with the Japanese military. Now the French were trying to take Vietnam back by force, starting by "treacherously attack[ing] us in Saigon on September 23rd." Hồ warned Truman that the Vietnamese people were determined to fight French troops coming from any direction under any circumstances.[174] In a more detailed letter to Secretary of State James Byrnes, Hồ maintained that the critical situation in south Vietnam called for "immediate interference on the part of the United Nations". He acknowledged that the French had obtained from Great Britain "a tacit recognition of their sovereignty and administrative responsibility," but that did not prevent the "whole Vietnamese nation [rising] up as one man against French aggression." Hồ specifically urged Byrnes to support a Vietnamese delegation to the first meeting of the UN Far East Commission; send a commission of inquiry to the south; and agree that the "full independence of Vietnam should be recognized by the United Nations."[175]

Hồ Chí Minh's messages to Truman and Byrnes ended up at the U.S. State Department's Division of Southeast Asian Affairs, headed by Abbot Low Moffat, who filed them away because any written response would mean implicit U.S. recognition of the DRV.[176] Presumably Hồ soon comprehended the reason why he had not received even a pro forma acknowledgment, yet he continued to send the occasional letter to Truman as a matter of principle. Sovereignty remained the overriding issue. In May 1945, Truman had confirmed to Paris his government's recognition of French sovereignty over Indochina, but had made no public statement to that effect. In August, General de Gaulle used his state visit to Washington to tell the press that "France means to recover its sovereignty over Indochina," yet again no coherent American position materialized. A month later, some French officials believed that the OSS was carrying out a secret plot to prevent France from regaining its sovereignty. In October, General Gallagher told reporters that the Allies had not yet recognized French sovereignty over Indochina.[177] Given the continuing absence of any U.S. policy statement, Hồ Chí Minh could be forgiven for remaining cautiously hopeful.

On 20 October 1945, John Carter Vincent, head of the State Department's Office of Far Eastern Affairs, gave a speech to the Foreign Policy Association in New York that contained the first public elucidation of U.S. policy on Indochina for many months.[178] The U.S. government did not question French sovereignty, Vincent stated. On the other hand, the United States had "no intention to assist or participate in forceful measures for the reimposition of control" by France. Vincent also offered American diplomatic mediation should it be requested by the parties involved, well aware that France would make no such request. Two days later, the principal Việt Minh paper in Hanoi headlined its article on Vincent's speech, "America Recognizes Vietnam's Independence," which was either a deliberate misinterpretation or a very loose extrapolation from Vincent's reference to mediation between the parties involved. According to Cứu Quốc, Vincent had also refused to speak in terms of the restoration of French sovereignty, which was perhaps a garbled version of America declining to assist or participate in forceful measures.[179]

Hồ Chí Minh would have taken a much more sober view of Vincent's speech. With the United States openly affirming French sovereignty, and the Chinese government likely to follow suit, Hồ had no choice but to regard France as his principal diplomatic interlocutor. Even Vincent's promise that the United States would not assist France in reimposing control had to be questioned, given reports Hồ was receiving of American Dakota aircraft, motor vehicles, weapons, and ammunition being employed by French troops in Nam Bộ.[180] During late 1945 and 1946, State Department officials insisted that the United States was pursuing a policy of "neutrality" in Indochina, but it hardly looked that way to Hồ and his lieutenants. The United States recognized French, not Vietnamese, sovereignty, it communicated officially with one party and not the other, and it provided the means of war to only one side.[181]

Starting with Hồ Chí Minh's earliest encounters with Americans in southern China, he was asked routinely about his communist affiliations, and he generally offered individuals just enough information to sustain his credibility. Hồ had to be more forthcoming when questioned by Archimedes Patti in Kunming in April 1945, as Patti had spent months perusing relevant OSS and State Department files.[182] Patti clearly did not believe that Hồ's communism should impede U.S.-Việt Minh cooperation in fighting the Japanese, nor preclude Washington from supporting Vietnam's subsequent self-determination. However, other OSS and army officers disagreed, and their reports increasingly gained a hearing in Washington. From the U.S. Embassy in Moscow, George Kennan argued that the Soviet Union would use the Chinese and French communist parties to try to gain control over Indochina. Some commentators asserted that the Việt Minh was 100 percent communist, and as such could be at the service of Soviet expansionism. During the last months of 1945, as Stalin probed for hegemony in Persia/Iran and Turkey, many U.S. policymakers turned resolutely against the Soviet Union.[183] Hồ could not gauge such seismic shifts of attitude in Washington, but the radio waves and foreign press were filled with evidence of growing tension between the United States and Soviet Union. The "self-dissolution" of the ICP in November was meant mainly to assuage China, yet Hồ surely hoped it would be noticed in Washington too. Hồ Chí Minh's communist background did not loom large in Washington's actions (or inaction) over Indochina in late 1945, however. If General Lu Han had ejected Hồ in favor of an anticommunist Vietnamese leader equally opposed to French sovereignty, the United States would still have deferred to Paris in deciding how to deal with that replacement.

In mid-February 1946, painfully aware that Paris and Chongqing were moving towards an agreement that would allow French troops to return to northern Indochina, Hồ Chí Minh dispatched what turned out to be his last letter to President Truman. Hồ accused Truman of making lofty declarations of principal before the United Nations, then failing to stop the French colonialists from "waging on us a murderous and pitiless war in order to reestablish their domination." Warming to this theme, Hồ asserted: "The French aggression on a peace-loving people is a direct menace to world security. It implies the complicity, or at least the connivance of the Great Democracies. They ought to interfere to stop this unjust war, and to show that they mean to carry out in peacetime the principles for which they fought in wartime."[184] As before, the State Department provided no acknowledgement. Hồ's castigation of the "Great Democracies" applied to the Soviet Union as well, a signal that Hồ understood the DRV would have to face the French alone.

American Consular Offices

In early 1946, the State Department sent Charles S. Reed to Saigon to open a consulate accredited to the French government. Aside from managing routine correspondence, hosting American businessmen, and fielding specific queries from Washington, Reed compiled and sent reports on Cochinchina political developments. He became quite concerned at violent French repression of Vietnamese who demonstrated against separation of Cochinchina from the rest of Vietnam. Reed also supervised opening of a U.S. Information Service (USIS) office in Saigon, although this was inhibited by French customs agents intercepting reading materials and films, as well as police intimidating local staff and harassing Vietnamese who visited the premises. Nonetheless, several thousand Vietnamese are said to have used the library each month, and even more attended the film series that promoted American education, technological ingenuity, and health care. The French allowed Radio Saigon to broadcast American music.[185]

In late March, Reed dispatched his deputy, James O'Sullivan, to Hanoi to appraise relations between the Chinese Army, the newly arrived French forces, and the DRV government. Two weeks later, the State Department authorized Reed to post O'Sullivan to Hanoi on temporary duty, with a stingy per diem of seven dollars plus expenses. Unlike Frank White of the OSS/SSU, O'Sullivan had no radio transmitter, although at some point he did acquire cryptographic capability from the U.S. consulate in Nanjing. He could not dispatch messages via the DRV's PTT service, as that would imply U.S. recognition. O'Sullivan began by using the reestablished French radiotelegraph facility, but it interfered with his communications so often that O'Sullivan switched to the Chinese Army post, where he could send and receive messages via the U.S. consulate in Kunming.[186] O'Sullivan readily made informal contact with members of the DRV Ministry of Foreign Affairs, but did not talk with Hồ Chí Minh prior to the latter's departure for France at the end of May. O'Sullivan's first opportunity to make a splash in Hanoi was when he organized an official Fourth of July reception for seventy French, Vietnamese, Chinese, and American guests, at a total cost of 1,713$80BIC. Much of O'Sullivan's time was taken up with routine consular duties, notably American business inquiries and turning back Vietnamese who wished to study in the United States— but also caring for an elderly American nun, returning the personal effects of two deceased P-38 aviators, and visiting an American arrested for emission of false bills.[187] With a U.S. military jeep, O'Sullivan traveled around the Red River delta and northern hills, where the French noted that he paid particular attention to phosphate and tin mines.[188]

In late July, O'Sullivan heard from Washington that the French Foreign Office had agreed to let the United States open a full-fledged consulate in Hanoi. Soon O'Sullivan was looking at numerous French buildings that owners were offering at discount prices. However, the State Department would only pay in American war surplus goods. More particularly, "either the Vietnam or the French government would pay the owner in piasters and would receive a credit (at the official rate of exchange) for the purchase of such surplus materials." One floor of the eventual building was to be set aside for a USIS office and library, with supplies of books, periodicals, and films to come via China, probably to circumvent French customs.[189] The possibility of the Vietnamese government being party to this elaborate transaction, and even permitted to receive American war surplus equipment, suggests that the U.S. policy of nonrecognition was still open to creative reinterpretation by at least some State Department officials in Washington.

In Hanoi, O'Sullivan had to navigate constantly between French and Vietnamese interests. In June, when returning to the DRV Foreign Ministry a letter they had sent to General Douglas MacArthur concerning repatriation of Vietnamese students from Japan, O'Sullivan informed the ministry that such matters had to be handled through the French mission to MacArthur's headquarters in Tokyo. At another juncture O'Sullivan recommended that all Vietnamese applications for U.S. visas be held, pending agreement between France and the DRV on passports and foreign exchange regulations. If the consulate granted a student visa, for example, O'Sullivan predicted that the French authorities would refuse to release U.S. dollars for the Vietnamese student to travel to America.[190] On the other hand, O'Sullivan agreed to look into a request from the Foreign Ministry that the Vietnam Medical Service purchase directly from the United States a consignment of pharmaceuticals and surgical instruments, thus reducing Vietnamese dependence on French supplies.[191]

On 16 August, an American Graves Registration Service team moving under French military guard was fired upon at a mountain site just south of the sixteenth parallel, withdrawing with one member wounded. O'Sullivan opposed the American team's plan to return to the site under heavier French protection, as DRV officials told him they considered the area to be a combat zone. If the American unit insisted on going ahead, the Vietnamese offered to escort it from Tourane (Đà Nẵng), just north of the sixteenth parallel. O'Sullivan concluded: "I believe attempt should not be made. If it must, then from Tourane."[192]

In late October 1946, the State Department ordered Reed and O'Sullivan to establish the consulate in Hanoi which had been foreshadowed three months earlier. Seals, stamps, coat of arms, cryptographic material, and initial office supplies would be sent via Saigon. O'Sullivan was to "inform local authorities Hanoi of establishment consulate and that awaiting receipt exequatur his provisional recognition has been requested." Although the telegram is worded ambiguously, I assume O'Sullivan was being told to inform the DRV Foreign Ministry ("local authorities Hanoi") of his formal status as consul, while making it clear that the French government would issue the exequatur. As of early January 1947, French recognition of O'Sullivan as consul still had not materialized. Amidst the fighting, O'Sullivan worked together with the Chinese and British consuls to facilitate safe passage of thousands of people from Hanoi. O'Sullivan decided to tell Jean Sainteny, in English, that "as of 9 January, the American Consulate [is] established," although he had yet to open the premises to the public.[193]

The Bloom Is Off the Rose

During 1946, Vietnamese media attention directed at Americans and the United States fell off dramatically. The expectations of August–September 1945 that Washington would oppose the return of French forces to Indochina had become a sick joke. China had shown more anticolonial resolution than the United States, at least until it signed the 28 February 1946 agreement with Paris. Nonetheless, the press avoided condemnation of American behavior. Việt Minh newspapers, which a few months earlier had claimed a special American relationship with Liberation Army units and the provisional DRV government, now simply went silent on the United States, even though privately some ICP members had never trusted the Americans in the first place. It seems likely that Hồ Chí Minh gave ICP leaders, newspaper editors, and propaganda ministry censors his reasons why contacts with the United States needed to be sustained, whatever one's sense of disappointment or ideological reservations. For Hồ, neither French nor U.S. policy towards Vietnam was fixed in stone; there were still ways to probe for improvements. The government continued to explain its position to Americans, both locally and overseas.[194]

There were limits to Vietnamese silence, however. Responding to a Radio Saigon report that France and the United States had signed an agreement about the Saigon-Hanoi air route, the DRV Foreign Ministry insisted that "the U.S. government understand that any agreement involving Vietnam which does not have the consent of self-governing *(tự chủ)* Vietnam lacks all value."[195] A Việt Minh paper in Huế accused "Anglo-American imperialism" of trying to undermine and impede the Soviet Union.[196] From June onward, some Vietnam National Guard political officers castigated the United States in their confidential talks to soldiers. The political officer of the battalion defending the Bắc Bộ Phủ in Hanoi lectured the troops on contradictions between the United States and Soviet Union, American help to the Chinese Nationalist side in its confrontation with CCP forces, U.S. leadership of world capitalist exploitation, and the difference between "real and fake democracy." Closer to home, the political officer accused the United States of supplying war material to French units positioned in Hanoi.[197] Critical press commentary about America now slipped past the censor more often. A Vietnam Nationalist Party paper asserted grimly that Vietnam must "save itself first" before either the United States or China would extend assistance.[198] A new book by the son of President Roosevelt, recalling how often his father had remarked that France had no right to return to Indochina, was cited by *Cứu Quốc* as rebuke to President Truman. In late November, there was brief mention that "reactionaries" had emerged victorious in the recent U.S. Congressional elections.[199] Nonetheless, after a DRV trade team met with visiting American businessmen, a follow-up questionnaire was forwarded to northern provinces, and efforts made to compile relevant economic data.[200]

The 6 December 1946 visit to Hanoi of Abbot Low Moffat, head of the State Department's Division of Southeast Asian Affairs, revealed how unlikely it was that the United States and Vietnam could find any common ground. Moffat had been one of the strongest advocates of pressuring France to accept international mediation of its conflict with the DRV. Once that idea was shelved, he continued to look for ways the United States could nudge Franco-Vietnamese negotiations along. Jean Sainteny opposed allowing Moffat to come to Hanoi and, failing that, tried to micromanage Moffat's itinerary. Moffat was repelled by Võ Nguyên Giáp's immobile face and stony replies to questions, which for Moffat symbolized "the typical Commie—the cartoon Commie."[201] By contrast, Moffat liked Hoàng Minh Giám, but considered him extremely naïve to be offering trade preferences and a base at Cam Ranh Bay in exchange for supporting Vietnam's independence.[202] Moffat may have suggested informally to Giám that Vietnam lodge an appeal with the United Nations. French intelligence intercepted a Vietnamese document which made this assertion, triggering a high-level French query to Washington.[203]

Moffat had long wanted to meet Hồ Chí Minh, and requested instructions from the State Department about what to say during an eventual meeting, but these failed to arrive. Moffat decided to see Hồ anyway, which infuriated Sainteny, as this was not part of the agreed itinerary. When Giám escorted Moffat and James O'Sullivan into Hồ's office, they found him in bed ill, but lucid and preferring to speak in English. Mindful of American apprehensions about his communist affiliations, Hồ said that he'd be content in his lifetime to secure Vietnam's independence, then added, "Perhaps fifty years from now the United States will be communist; then they will not object if Vietnam is also."[204] In Moffat's testimony to the Fulbright Committee in 1972, he deeply regretted the lack of instructions from Washington, adding that, "It seemed [Hồ] was hoping that I would have some message for him and I was miserable not to be able to say anything." Moffat told Senator Fulbright, "I had a feeling just that I was in the presence of somebody who was great, and I don't know how you quite define it." To which Fulbright replied, "I know [. . .] it doesn't happen too often."[205] Moffat and O'Sullivan would be the last American diplomats to meet Hồ, who remained president of the DRV until his death twenty-two years later.

When Moffat saw his State Department instructions after returning to Saigon, he probably was relieved not to have been compelled to follow them when meeting Hồ Chí Minh. Acting Secretary of State Dean Acheson first warned Moffat to "keep in mind Ho's clear record as agent international communism." Acheson then told Moffat to urge Hồ to make concessions to the French on Cochinchina, and to recognize that diplomatic "intransigence" could only retard the economic rehabilitation of Indochina. Moffat was to avoid giving the impression that the United States was making any formal intervention, and to eschew publicity of any kind.[206] In Mofatt's report to Washington, he argued that DRV leaders were above all nationalists, using the techniques of communism in their struggle for national independence. He did not believe there would be any all-out war, as both parties wished to avoid it.[207] Moffat seemed unaware that French military commanders were engaging in brinksmanship that would lead to war only one week later.

SOUTH AND SOUTHEAST ASIA

Soon after Japan's mid-August 1945 capitulation, Vietnamese newspapers ran brief but enthusiastic reports of national independence initiatives in Indonesia, India, Burma, and the Philippines.[208] Editorials began to assert that the peoples of South and Southeast Asia faced similar threats, experienced common emotions, and should thus look to each other for support. However, it proved impossible to acquire regular information about what exactly was happening in Jakarta, Surabaya, Delhi, Calcutta, Rangoon, or Manila, much less to establish bilateral contacts and contemplate cooperation. Most news came via Allied shortwave broadcasts. Otherwise, the French worked hard to keep Vietnamese as isolated from their neighbors as possible. Ironically, this meant that independence movements elsewhere could be magnified and idealized as encouragement to Vietnamese action. For some years the *idea* of regional anticolonial solidarity proved more powerful than any practical interaction.

Indonesia captured Vietnamese attention first, after snippets were picked up on the airwaves concerning Sukarno's proclamation of independence on 17 August and subsequent mass meetings and demonstrations. British forces arrived in Jakarta at the end of September, one week after General Gracey drove DRV adherents out of Saigon, but Vietnamese papers withheld comment. In mid-October, however, *Cứu Quốc* juxtaposed articles on British-French forces in Nam Bộ employing Japanese troops to attack DRV adherents with stories about British-Dutch units doing the same thing with Japanese units in Semarang and Surabaya. *Thời mới* insisted that even two hundred thousand Dutch troops would not be able to reestablish colonial rule over fifty million Indonesians.[209] Drawing on fragmentary radio reports, Vietnamese papers reported the death by sniper fire of British General Mallaby in Surabaya, the massive British retaliation, and the hordes of villagers wielding bamboo stakes and machetes who threw themselves against British machine guns. Editorials now made explicit comparisons with the fighting in Nam Bộ, then argued that resolute anticolonial resistance in one country was certain to undermine colonial resolve in the other.[210] It was at this moment that provisional President Hồ Chí Minh sent a confidential letter to the new Indonesian government, proposing a joint Vietnam-Indonesia declaration condemning French and Dutch efforts to restore colonial tutelage by force of arms. The Indonesian prime minister, Sutan Sjahrir, chose not to reply, concerned that the Dutch would use Hồ's communist background to discredit the Indonesian nationalist revolution.[211]

In February 1946, a Việt Minh paper in Huế reported that the Indonesia issue had been raised at the United Nations, an option that some hoped might apply to Vietnam as well.[212] Australian popular support for the independence struggle of the Indonesian people was lauded. Growing American pressure on the Dutch to negotiate an agreement with the Indonesian Republic seems to have been missed by Vietnamese editors, or else they were under instructions from the censor to avoid invidious comparisons with U.S. de facto support for the French in Indochina. In July, Vietnamese journalists obtained detailed Indonesian government materials that served to supplement their radio transcripts. One long proclamation from Yogyakarta was translated and published in full, followed by Indonesian statements accusing the Dutch of rank betrayal (phản bội).[213] Three months later one paper serialized a "History of Liberation Struggle in Indonesia," beginning with the early-twentieth-century formation of Budi Utomo and Sarekat Islam, and concluding with the Indonesian-Dutch negotiations that produced the 12 November Linggajati Agreement, whereby both sides pledged to work towards a United States of Indonesia.[214] Vietnamese hopes of a similar agreement with Paris were dealt what proved to be a fatal blow by French attacks in Haiphong in late November. Empathy with the Indonesian revolution remained strong, and was sometimes expressed in florid Vietnamese poetry.[215]

India attracted Vietnamese attention in different ways from Indonesia. It had long been acknowledged as a center of classical civilization. Rabindranath Tagore and Mohandas Gandhi had sparked interest among Vietnamese intellectuals of the 1920s and 1930s. India's independence movement seemed better organized than any other in Asia. During the Pacific War, Việt Minh writers extolled the antifascist position of the Communist Party of India and denounced the Indian National Congress as representing outdated feudal and bourgeois interests. In September 1945, Việt Minh papers chose to ignore India rather than try to explain the charisma of Gandhi, criticize his commitment to nonviolence, or admit that the Congress Party possessed a mass following. However, Thời mới, the most prominent independent paper, chose from its first issue to serialize a glowing narrative of Gandhi's life, emphasizing his self-sacrifice, fearless opposition to British imperial exploitation, and ability to inspire countrymen of all ages and backgrounds.[216] Jawaharlal Nehru, Gandhi's protégé, declared Congress Party support for independence movements in Southeast Asia, although the independence aspirations of India itself remained stalled throughout late 1945 and 1946. The fact that Indians constituted a large proportion of British troop units arriving in Saigon was noted by Vietnamese papers in Hanoi, yet there was no move to condemn them as colonial lackeys or encourage them to desert. Việt Minh adherents in the south did leaflet Indian troops, asking why they shed blood on behalf of the colonizer instead of recognizing the need for Vietnamese and Indian peoples to help each other struggle against the common enemy.[217] Radio reports indicated that Nehru was pushing the British for early return of Indian soldiers from Southeast Asia; by early 1946 they were gone from Nam Bộ.

In early February 1946, Cứu Quốc, the principal Việt Minh daily, splashed the following headline across its front page: "India Supports Resistance in Indochina and Indonesia." This asserted more than the Congress Party was willing to deliver. Closer to the mark was a Cứu Quốc headline six weeks later quoting Nehru: "The Era of Imperialism and Colonialism is Dead." Other articles discussed British Labour Party policy on India, the prospects for early Indian independence, and growing Hindu-Muslim tensions.[218] During July, stories about independence demonstrations in India were featured almost daily in Cứu Quốc, and were clearly designed to show Vietnamese readers that they were not alone in facing up to a major colonial power. Very little coverage was given to communist-led peasant insurgencies in some states of India or to the escalation of communal violence. The prolific Việt Minh writer Minh Tranh reopened the ideological question by arguing that Indian feudal and bourgeois classes, having failed miserably to mobilize the masses to liberate the country from British imperial rule, now had no choice but to accept Indian working-class leadership, in solidarity with New Democracy forces worldwide. Eventually, however, Minh Tranh had to acknowledge that India's provisional government was in the hands of the Congress Party and Nehru, not the Communist Party of India.[219]

In September 1946, Nehru launched his plan for an All-Asia Conference to take place in Delhi in early 1947, then made a point of announcing that invitations were being sent to Hồ Chí Minh and Sukarno. This news garnered front-page, uniformly positive coverage in Vietnam.[220] Nehru's public affirmation of friendship with Vietnam and Indonesia a few weeks later garnered equal enthusiasm, whereas his stated intention to set up a consulate in Saigon was greeted with silence. Saigon was in French hands, and it would become apparent that Nehru's definition of friendship did not include actions likely to embroil India in altercations with France. Nonetheless, Hồ Chí Minh must have been delighted with Nehru's invitation to the All-Asia Conference and professions of India-Vietnam amity. As he headed home from Paris on a French ship, carrying only a stopgap modus vivendi, Hồ needed evidence that the DRV was not totally alone. India's moral support was deeply appreciated precisely because of Vietnam's otherwise parlous international circumstances.

The Philippines received far less attention in the Vietnamese press than Indonesia or India. A decade earlier, newspapers had reported Washington's granting of commonwealth status to the Philippines, and its promise of full independence in ten years. However, prewar commentators remained sceptical that the United States would give up its military bases and considerable economic privileges. Võ Nguyên Giáp also pointed to Japanese designs on the Philippines, symbolized by Tokyo's covert support to Sakdalist and Islamic anticolonialist groups.[221] Immediately after the end of the Pacific War, no one tried to describe how the Philippines had fared, although news must have been available from American radio stations. In December 1945, *Thời mới* did tell readers that "very soon the Philippines will be completely independent," adding that Paris should emulate the American example.[222] It seems that Spanish Dominicans subsequently communicated news about the Philippines to Vietnamese clergy, as brief reports occasionally surfaced in Catholic papers. A Filipino poem dedicated to Vietnamese patriots was translated and published on the front page of *Đa Minh*.[223] Several papers noted the 4 July 1946 ceremony in Manila which inaugurated the Philippine Republic. One editorial claimed grandly that four hundred years of Filipino anticolonial struggle had compelled the Americans to concede independence. The U.S. experience should thus serve as a sober lesson to France in regard to Indochina.[224] Minh Tranh's *Far East Yesterday and Today*, mentioned earlier, lauded the guerrilla operations of the communist-led Hukbalahap during the Pacific War, yet the author seemed unaware that the newly-elected president, Manual Roxas, had ordered the Philippine constabulary against Huk adherents in Luzon. Minh Tranh emphasized that the Philippines remained far from fully independent of the United States.[225] Readers in August and September 1946 would have understood Minh Tranh to be cautioning the DRV government against making too many diplomatic concessions to the French.

Malaya was almost entirely ignored by the Vietnamese press in late 1945–46. This is curious, as the Malayan People's Anti-Japanese Army (MPAJA) was remarkably similar to the Việt Minh in some ways. It had been established by communists during the Pacific War, had cooperated with Allied intelligence organizations, and had moved to take power in August 1945. However, MPAJA members were mostly ethnic Chinese, with few Malay or Indian participants. When arriving British commanders called upon the MPAJA to disband, Malayan Communist Party (MCP) leaders obeyed and turned in some weapons, while retaining the objective of Malayan independence from Great Britain. ICP members must have been shocked by those MCP concessions, yet they were disinclined to discuss circumstances in Malaya for fear of encouraging similar thoughts in Vietnam. This does not explain why non-Việt Minh papers failed to report events in

Malaya, however. The ICP and MCP did sustain covert contacts, which would become more significant in 1948, when the MCP, under its new secretary-general, Chin Peng, decided it had no choice but to take up armed struggle.[226]

Thailand, like Malaya, was seldom mentioned in the Vietnamese press. In late September 1945, *Thời mới* did report that tensions had developed between Great Britain and the United States over the future of Thailand. It characterized London as pursuing a colonialist policy and Washington a policy of national liberation. Limited by sparse information, *Thời mới* missed the nuanced maneuvering over the fate of Thailand.[227] No Vietnamese newspaper discussed French moves to retake the two Cambodian provinces lost to Thailand in 1941. In May 1946, the French launched a small but bloody assault on the disputed areas, Thailand threatened to retaliate, and the United States stepped in to mediate an agreement in November that distinctly favored France.[228] Vietnamese censors apparently warned editors against publishing anything detailed or inflammatory about Thailand or Cambodia during this period. The only exceptions I have found appeared in a Quảng Ngãi paper in September, and include descriptions of fighting in contested Siem Reap province, French manipulations of the Cambodian government, and criticism of the Vietnamese resistance for not seeking out comrades in Cambodia.[229]

During this period, Bangkok became the DRV's most important external operational venue, where regional friends could be cultivated, weapons purchased, intelligence exchanged, and propaganda disseminated in multiple foreign languages. The Thai government of the day, headed by Pridi Banomyong, supported Vietnam's independence from French rule. Behind the scenes, Thai leaders provided valuable introductions, permissions, cover papers, and physical protection to DRV adherants. When French victories in Laos in March 1946 caused the flight of tens of thousands of Vietnamese across the Mekong river, Thai authorities allowed them sanctuary and did not object to Việt Minh groups retaining firearms, uniforms, and radios. In August, the first official DRV delegation managed to make it to Bangkok from Hanoi. Phạm Ngọc Thạch presented Pridi with a letter from President Hồ Chí Minh that mooted the idea of mutual diplomatic recognition. The Thai government, although furious at French reconquest of the two Cambodian provinces, did not want to derail the American-mediated negotiations then underway, or to jeopardize Bangkok's application to join the United Nations. It thus agreed only to a DRV "representative delegation," well short of an embassy or legation. Yet this made it possible for the Vietnamese rapidly to expand and coordinate a variety of overt and covert operations into Indochina and overseas. Trần Văn Giàu, who had known Pridi in France in the late 1920s, took advantage of the glut of war surplus arms, ammunition, and equipment available in Bangkok to purchase and transport consignments by land or sea to Vietnam.[230]

THE SOVIET UNION

As noted earlier, Vietnamese marveled at what they heard about stubborn Russian resistance to German invasion, the climactic battle of Stalingrad, and the final crushing of Hitler's regime in the spring of 1945. During the 1930s, many noncommunist as well as communist intellectuals had praised the Russian Revolution, and looked to the Soviet socialist model when imagining a future independent Vietnam. These views resurfaced in late 1945. The independent paper *Thời mới*, for example, contrasted the great French and Russian revolutions with the mere *putches* engineered by Mussolini in Italy and Hitler in Germany.[231] Another independent paper serialized a history of Russian foreign policy since 1237 A.D., asking in conclusion whether the Soviet Union's assertive Third Internationalism could continue to coexist with the policies of the United States, China, and Great Britain.[232]

What many Vietnamese expected in late 1945, however, was Soviet support for Vietnam's national liberation. When this failed to materialize, ICP members were most disappointed, and some expressed outright bitterness. One communist told Harold Isaacs that "the Russians are nationalists for Russia first and above all," not interested in helping the ICP unless it served their own purpose, which was not the case at the time. Trần Văn Giàu told Isaacs that the Russians went in for "an excess of ideological compromise." He expected no help from Moscow, not even verbal support. Isaacs's Vietnamese communist interlocutors also spoke contemptuously of Maurice Thorez, head of the PCF, and derided the small French communist group in Saigon.[233] No ICP member voiced these opinions in print, but the absence of any news from Moscow about Indochina issues would have been noticed by readers. One Việt Minh paper completely ignored the Soviet Union when canvassing the chances of friendship with specific big powers.[234] A journalist recently returned to Hanoi from the fighting in Nam Bộ opined that both Russia and the United States would merely offer distant, verbal support, whereas China was a close friend.[235]

Hồ Chí Minh tried to contact Stalin on two occasions in late 1945. In a brief generic letter sent in September to other heads of state as well, Hồ informed Stalin of establishment of the "Vietnam Republic" with himself as president, and requested aid to stave off famine in the wake of serious flooding in the Red River delta. In late October, Hồ dispatched a longer message specifically to Stalin that outlined events in Indochina since 1940, culminating with the formation of the independent DRV. Hồ then stressed to Stalin the DRV's commitment to principles contained in the Atlantic Charter and United Nations Charter, in stark contrast to the French, who had flagrantly violated those principles by attacking Saigon on 23 September, and who now were making plans to invade the entire country. If the French tried to carry out those plans, the Annamite people would "resolutely struggle and resist them." Hồ received no acknowledgment that either message had been received, much less a substantive reply. Neither missive was brought to Stalin's attention by subordinates—instead both were simply filed away.[236] It is doubtful that anyone in Moscow at the time realized that the person signing these messages ("Hotchimin" and "Hotrimin" in transliterated Russian) was the former senior Comintern agent Nguyễn Ái Quốc, although a small amount of staff work would have made the connection.

One Russian residing in Hanoi in late 1945 met Hồ and knew his prior identity. Stéphane Solovieff claimed to be representing Soviet interests in Indochina, and somehow managed to sustain good relations with Japanese, Vietnamese, Chinese, and French officials alike. When asked by Archimedes Patti about Soviet intentions regarding Indochina, particularly given the sudden ascent to power in Hanoi of an old comrade, Solovieff replied that "Mother Russia" required time to recover and rebuild before asserting itself in Southeast Asia. Solovieff also thought the French were needed to guide the Vietnamese towards self-government.[237] By early 1946, Solovieff was cooperating closely with Jean Sainteny, who in June facilitated his travel to France, where he soon linked up with the Soviet embassy.[238] Assuming that Solovieff operated in Hanoi under instructions from Moscow (however infrequently communicated), his behavior must have strengthened Hồ Chí Minh's doubts that any help could be expected from the Soviet Union in the foreseeable future. With the only Russian communist in town talking about the need for French tutelage, one might have expected ICP writers to tone down their praise for the Soviet Union, but the reverse turned out to be the case.

By the spring of 1946, scores of contemporary French-language publications about the Soviet Union had made their way to Vietnam, and they triggered a spate of Vietnamese translations. New Century Publishing House in Hanoi offered books on Leninism (two volumes), Soviet proletarianism, women and children in the Soviet Union, and Soviet principles of property and equality.[239] Another publisher released a booklet titled *Russian Women and the Soviet Revolution*, based on the contentious writings of Alexandra Kolontai, the world's first female ambassador (to Sweden, in 1943). The booklet's cover depicted a Russian woman in army uniform, standing at attention.[240] An independent paper obtained and translated parts of a biography of the famous Russian revolutionary anarchist, Peter Kropotkin (1842–1921), which must have angered ICP members.[241] Vietnamese papers occasionally translated pronouncements by Marshal Stalin, for example his order commemorating the twenty-eighth anniversary of the founding of the Red Army, or a foreign policy speech that editors headlined "A Bell Sounding for Peace."[242] Even the French-language paper controlled by Jean Sainteny contributed a cautiously favorable editorial on Stalin.[243] An article from *Ce Soir* (Paris) praising the Soviet economy was featured in Haiphong's Việt Minh daily. The same Vietnamese paper ran a long, serialized essay on Soviet accomplishments in the realm of health and hygiene.[244] In the town of Vinh, a Việt Minh paper extolled Lenin's famous dictum that "Socialism is Soviet power plus electrification of the whole country." The same issue claimed that the Soviet Union was currently donating food to needy countries like Poland, Romania, Finland, and India.[245] Moscow might be ignoring Vietnam, but most Vietnamese editors still wanted to say only good things about the Soviet Union.

Bucking the tide, papers belonging to the Vietnam Nationalist Party and the Catholic Church insisted that Stalin was an evil dictator who aimed to engineer a communist takeover of the entire world. Having made such assertions, however, Vietnamese anticommunists possessed very little current information about Stalin or the Soviet Union from which to build their case. Thus, a Nationalist Party weekly ran a serial on "Red Fascism" that narrated Stalin's climb to power, his elimination of old comrades, and his alleged control over communist parties worldwide, yet the editors had nothing to tell readers about postwar developments.[246] Vietnamese were warned once again about communist nationalization of private property and the perverse promises of "World Harmony" (Thế Giới Đại Đồng).[247] A Catholic weekly serialized a strange essay that claimed a major religious revival in the Soviet Union in the late 1930s.[248] It seems that anticommunist groups in France either were not publishing much in 1946, or were not bothering to dispatch materials to their contacts in Indochina.

During the summer of 1946, ICP writers and editors began openly to campaign for the DRV to align itself with the Soviet Union. Trần Huy Liệu insisted that the contradiction between the Soviet Union and the United States had become a "principal factor in world affairs," influencing almost every other issue. For Liệu, Moscow led the legions of progress, Washington the legions of reaction. More particularly, smaller and weaker peoples had to line up with the "forces of peace and democracy, in opposition to the imperialist gang that seeks to foment war and reconquer lost colonies." Liệu implored his readers to recognize the impossibility of separating the Vietnamese struggle against French colonialism from "the Nationalist/Communist issue in China, the Philippine civil war, the question of the Jews in Palestine, the contest in India, and many other problems worldwide."[249] He did not attempt to explain how joining the global revolutionary alliance headed by the Soviet Union would bring concrete benefits to endangered Vietnam. In late July, someone managed to locate an article in a Russian paper that condemned Admiral d'Argenlieu's creation of the Autonomous Cochinchina Republic.[250] Beyond that, Moscow remained silent.

Undaunted, Vietnamese editors took advantage of the increasing amount of material about the Soviet Union being obtained (mostly from France) to expand their coverage. A favorite topic was education and the mobilization of youth in the Soviet Union, which attracted non-Việt Minh as well as Việt Minh editors. In distant Quảng Ngãi, a glowing essay about Russian revolutionary literature was translated and published.[251] Maxime Gorki was mentioned often, and one of his short stories printed.[252] In November, the editors of *Kháng Chiến* newspaper in Quảng Ngãi compiled a Russian Revolution commemorative issue. Their lead editorial stated that, despite many obstacles, Russian revolutionaries had still achieved "complete victory." They concluded: "We are still in the national liberation stage, and will also face many difficulties, so the Russian Revolution is a shining beacon for us."[253]

In mid-November, *Dân Chủ* daily in Haiphong announced gleefully that Vietnam's National Salvation Youth Association had received greetings from the quasi-official USSR Youth Union.[254] However, Hồ Chí Minh, who had returned from France three weeks earlier, undoubtedly explained to ranking cadres that neither the ICP nor the DRV government should anticipate Soviet support any time soon. Stalin was content to delegate the Indochina question to the PCF, which was preoccupied with electoral politics in the *métropole*. In 1947–48, DRV representatives would make contact with Soviet diplomats in several European and Southeast Asian capitals, and Moscow would become better informed about the Franco-Vietnamese conflict. As the international Cold War intensified, the 1946 two-camp analysis of Trần Huy Liệu and Minh Tranh came to seem more credible, and expectations increased of Vietnam receiving concrete assistance from New Democracy countries. What price Vietnam was prepared to pay in return for this help became an issue in 1949–50.

THE UNITED NATIONS

Vietnamese attitudes towards the United Nations went from naïve hope to firm skepticism in less than a year. At the time of the April–May 1945 conference in San Francisco which established the United Nations, Hồ Chí Minh tried unsuccessfully to petition the organizers on behalf of Vietnamese independence, much as he had done at the Versailles Peace Conference in 1919. Upon hearing of the Allied decision to rely on Chinese and British forces to occupy Indochina, a Việt Minh spokesman in Kunming urged his OSS contacts to intercede with the United Nations to name alternatives. On 1 September, in Hanoi, Hoàng Minh Giám lectured Major Patti on the failure of the United States to raise the issue of Indochinese self-determination at the San Francisco conference.[255] The principal non-Việt Minh paper in Hanoi insisted that the new government secure Vietnam's representation at the United Nations, adding, "We can probably put our faith in the UN's liberation policy."[256] Such thoughts were quickly challenged by the failure of any country to raise the Indochina issue at the United Nations in the wake of British-French assaults on Việt Minh adherents in Nam Bộ. In January 1946, Hồ sent a telegram to Henri Spaak, chairman of the UN General Assembly, requesting that the Vietnam issue be placed on the agenda for investigation, but apparently received no reply.[257] Newspapers reported United Nations news regularly, yet readers were left to wonder why Vietnam's case was being ignored.

In early February 1946, the newspaper of the pro-DRV wing of the Vietnam Revolutionary Alliance reported a Chinese source asserting that the United Nations would soon discuss the Indochina question.[258] This provoked a negative outburst from Độc Lập, the Democratic Party's standard-bearer, which warned that China or someone else was likely to propose a UN trusteeship for Vietnam. Trusteeships might be appropriate for "backward people like in Africa or the Pacific," Độc Lập editors averred, but not for Vietnam, which had four thousand years of history, eighty years of anticolonial struggle, and French abdication of authority to the Japanese in 1941. The editors seemed unaware that the French government had vehemently opposed American proposals of trusteeship in April 1945, and that no one had tried to revive the idea since. Độc Lập insisted on Vietnam's right to decide its own future.[259]

Editors of Haiphong's Việt Minh paper, having observed how the United Nations dealt with issues elsewhere, declared that it would be folly to rely on the United Nations because its principals, as expressed in the UN charter, bore little or no relationship to the big-power politics at work in the backrooms and corridors.[260] One of those big powers, France, was warning other UN members that it would use its veto power in the Security Council to prevent Indochina being placed on the agenda. The Soviet Union, China, or the United States could have put France's threat to the test, but chose not to. Despite all these obstacles, domestic as well as international, Trường Chinh, secretary general of the ICP, still supported government efforts to convince the United Nations to send an inspection team to Indochina to help ward off war.[261]

Vietnamese newspapers continued to report UN debates on other international hot spots, notably Indonesia, Iran, Trieste, and Palestine. One paper offered readers a dispassionate description of the United Nation's structure and modus operandi, followed later by a favorable account on the UN Relief and Rehabilitation Administration.[262] In August, the New York Times reported that five unnamed political parties in Indochina had written to the United Nations charging France with repeated violations of agreements and asking for UN intervention.[263] No mention of this démarche appeared in the Vietnamese press, suggesting that approaching the United Nations remained a contentious issue. What was Hồ Chí Minh's position? While in Paris during the summer of 1946, Hồ must have noted how apprehensive the French government became at any mention of a UN role in Indochina. Immediately after arriving back in Hanoi, Hồ circulated to all members of the cabinet a six-page draft of an appeal to the United Nations, for study and comment.[264] Possibly Hồ aimed for this appeal to be issued in the name of Vietnam's National Assembly, which convened on 28 October. That did not happen. In subsequent weeks, only a Catholic weekly gave any attention to the United Nations, first wondering whether the United Nations could help the United States and Soviet Union resolve their differences before the world headed towards another global conflagration, then claiming (without substantiation) that the United Nations was becoming a more powerful organization. A key section of this article was censored, perhaps because it called on the DRV and France to go to the United Nations before full-scale hostilities broke out—as happened only four days later.[265]

ISOLATED BUT NOT RECLUSIVE

The high hopes for foreign support of Vietnam's independence which marked public opinion in late August and early September 1945 were dashed in subsequent months. Shock and anger swept the country as British and French troops seized Saigon and occupied most towns in southern and south-central Vietnam. The United States refused to intervene or even mediate the conflict. In late February 1946, China moved to transfer its occupation duties north of the sixteenth parallel to the French, which compelled Hồ Chí Minh to either receive French troops peacefully or face both Chinese and French retaliation. The Soviet Union remained silent. The new UN organization was powerless to do anything, given France's right of veto in the Security Council. Only among organizations elsewhere in Asia also struggling for an end to colonial subjugation did Vietnam receive expressions of support. The most important affirmations came from leaders in India and Indonesia, although they remained either unable or unwilling to advance concrete assistance.

Hồ Chí Minh understood the importance of a foreign public. He made himself readily available to foreign visitors and dispatched scores of messages overseas. Reports of his diverse encounters in Paris were featured in the Vietnamese press. There was an unspoken relationship between political credibility abroad and moral authority at home. Vietnamese wanted to be respected in the world at large, and Hồ gave them that sense of respect vicariously.

Some ICP comrades were exasperated by the amount of time and effort that Hồ Chí Minh devoted to cultivating the United States and China. They wanted an early declaration of alliance with New Democracy forces led by Marshal Stalin. By February 1946, Hồ must have realized that neither the United States nor China was going to help the DRV in its upcoming negotiations with France, nor perhaps even restrain France from taking unilateral action. Even so, Hồ tried to sustain official contacts with the United States and China at whatever level was feasible. In the short-term this might give the French pause when considering violent overthrow of the DRV government. And there was always the possibility that policies might change in Washington or Nanjing. Hồ's many talks with foreign journalists and unofficial visitors were also designed to reach beyond governments to influence world public opinion. Providing the DRV could survive and continue to make its struggle known, some nations eventually would find reason to offer assistance and diplomatic recognition. In the meantime, Hồ had to see whether a reasonable understanding could be negotiated with the French.

This coherent effort by Hồ Chí Minh to maintain contacts across the international political spectrum was not understood by the Việt Minh rank-and-file, who preferred to divide the world into anticolonial and colonial, progressive and reactionary. After their expectations that the Allies would recognize DRV independence had been dashed, many Việt Minh adherents turned inward, insisting grimly that the Vietnamese people could defeat the colonialists and reactionaries alone. Over time, however, the argument of ICP and Democratic Party publicists that Vietnam identify itself with New Democracy forces gained more weight, despite continuing deafening silence from Moscow.

It is worth asking whether DRV efforts to cultivate foreign friends were undermined by revolutionary calls for blood to be spilled, for the French colonialists to be expelled by force, for the country to enroll in the New Democracy alliance. A proper answer to this question would require more study of overseas reactions to Indochina developments as revealed in archival and newspaper collections. The U.S. and Chinese governments reendorsed French sovereignty with no reference to the status of the DRV. Việt Minh armed militancy and eventual support from the Soviet Union and CCP made it less likely this endorsement would be reconsidered in Washington or Nanjing. In India and Southeast Asia, some independence leaders remained wary of publicizing militant Việt Minh statements or being seen to associate closely with communist Vietnamese. Nonetheless, the level of media criticism of French actions and support for Hồ Chí Minh appears to have increased throughout Asia.

Vietnamese fascination with the world beyond Vietnam remained high too, despite repeated setbacks in DRV efforts to find foreign friends. Both Việt Minh and non-Việt Minh periodicals continued not only to cover events globally, but to comment on them in editorials. A small country like Vietnam had no choice but to keep abreast of international developments, draw lessons, and look for advantage. From the summer of 1946, however, Việt Minh papers painted an ever-rosier picture of the Soviet Union and CCP-held regions of China, while non-Việt Minh newspaper editors either limited their commentary or had their articles censored.

Growing Việt Minh press coverage of Yan'an, the CCP, and the Chinese Red Army started a trend that would culminate in excited reports of 1948 Red Army victories over "Chiang Kai-shek puppet forces," translations of Mao Zedong's speeches, and paeans to the People's Republic of China established in October 1949. ICP leaders could now assert that 1946 praise for the CCP and Yan'an had been prescient and fully justified. Everything the United States and Nationalist China had done in 1945–46 was now denounced as a failed imperialist plot. The fact that Hồ Chí Minh had consorted with the enemy was treated as a mere tactical exercise designed to gain time before inevitable full-scale war. The bipolar world of antiimperialists and imperialists, progressives and reactionaries, would frame DRV public discourse for decades to come, without necessarily determining all decisions within the ruling Communist Party.

Material Dreams and Realities

In times of revolution, hopes are aroused of great abundance, an end to fear about where the next meal will come from, an ability to enjoy the fruits of one's labor, and membership in a much larger effort to create a new order of production, exchange, and community welfare. In Vietnam, material aspirations became linked with ideas of progress and modernity. In this future life, farmers would obtain pumps, manual laborers become truck drivers, merchants offer a cornucopia of commodities at fair prices, engineers alter the physical landscape, and scientists contribute to world knowledge.

However, revolution also releases fury at those countrymen who are seen to have profited from the colonial system, who live in comfort while others starve. People subject to such accusations lose property, even their lives. Or they may be allowed to show remorse, contribute resources to the revolution, learn the latest political slogans, and gain admission to a patriotic association. Much depends on local circumstance. Meanwhile, everyone must face scarcities of food and other essentials, pay taxes, and accept that the country's future is replete with uncertainties. The government tries to increase output, manage some allocations, and ensure that the nascent army receives top resource priority. Long after the events of a revolution, archive dossiers sometimes allow us to tune in on village property disputes, small-scale commodity transactions, and neighborhood collection of taxes and donations.

EARLY DAYS

Amidst the euphoria of seizing power in August 1945, young militants turned to the general public to give them food and shelter. They expected well-off families to donate property or money, and they canvassed merchants to obtain scarce supplies of cloth, medicines, office supplies, and cigarettes. In the name of the revolution, youth groups also felt free to confiscate the rice stores, oxen, bicycles, typewriters, furniture, and occasionally dwellings of persons they labeled exploiters or reactionaries. Property belonging to the former colonial regime was routinely expropriated. French nationals, having already lost some possessions following the 9 March 1945 Japanese coup, now found that anything beyond their immediate urban dwelling was likely to be taken.

The provisional DRV government, uncomfortable about reports of thousands of groups collecting donations spontaneously, soon attempted to institute a system of formal reporting and delivery of proceeds. It also called a halt to further confiscations without state authorization, but was disinclined to expend political capital on trying to reverse the property seizures of previous weeks. Hundreds of petitions for restitution of property began to arrive at central government offices, and were dutifully noted in logbooks, their texts routed to relevant people's committees and then often ignored. Central authorities did press local committees to take seized property away from nondeserving perpetrators. Sometimes Hanoi knew that the people's committee was synonymous with the miscreants, yet the principle still was to assert public over private advantage. Recalcitrant groups were warned that the newly independent nation and people of Vietnam would not tolerate self-seeking, lawless behavior.

From its earliest pronouncements, the DRV government coupled preservation of national independence with building a strong, modern economy. Provisional President Hồ Chí Minh repeatedly called on citizens to build the country as well as oppose foreign aggressors. The two words "resistance" (kháng chiến) and "construction" (kiến thiết) were paired together on street banners and in speeches and newspaper editorials. Material progress appealed to urban and rural Vietnamese alike. In previous decades, townsfolk had become familiar with electric lights, tap water, vitamin injections, streetcars, cinemas, dance halls, scented soap, and gâteaux, although many lacked the means to enjoy such icons of modernity in person. Villagers observed railroad trains, trucks, river steamers, steamshovels, and dredges in action. They might see airplanes flying overhead, and hear about tractors, pumps, and jackhammers. Country folk could sometimes afford to purchase kerosene lanterns, matches, rubber sandals, factory-made cloth, and cigarettes. A favored few Vietnamese traveled overseas on big ships and perhaps viewed a suspension bridge, hydraulic dam, or skyscraper first hand. The Vietnamese intelligentsia explained to readers that industrialization was the path to the highest forms of productivity, and that modernization demanded use of the most advanced technologies. However, the French had deliberately chosen to withhold such opportunities from their Indochinese colonial subjects. Marxist writers voiced such convictions at every opportunity, yet most non-Marxists drew the same conclusions.

Immediately following World War I, a tiny Vietnamese bourgeoisie had tried to assert itself, hoping in particular to eliminate French and Chinese monopolies, and more generally to loosen civil and economic restrictions. During the 1920s, a small but strategically placed working class emerged in the dockyards, mines, and plantations. By the early 1930s, however, it appeared to many observers that neither the Vietnamese bourgeoisie nor the Vietnamese proletariat could grow very large under French colonial rule.[1] Whether one favored a capitalist, socialist, or communist future for Vietnam, national independence had to be achieved first. This argument gained more converts following collapse of the French Popular Front and the ruthless colonial repression of 1939–40.

In May 1941, ICP leaders deferred working-class and poor peasant demands in favor of crafting a united front to achieve national liberation. For the next four years the ICP had very little to say about future economic transformations, concentrating instead on political proselytizing and organization. In early June 1945, Hồ Chí Minh began preparations for a national people's congress, which might well have turned its attention to economic issues. However, the congress convened just as Japan was capitulating to the Allies on 15 August. Its agenda was cut back to one day and a National Liberation Committee hastily elected, none of whose members possessed any experience in economic matters.[2]

Eleven days later, the fifteen-man Cabinet that Hồ Chí Minh convened in Hanoi contained only one individual with economic experience—Nguyễn Mạnh Hà, appointed minister for national economy. Hà had graduated from the Institut des sciences politiques in Paris, and held a doctorate in law. However, during the early 1940s he had served in the labor office of the Haiphong Municipal Council, and by the summer of 1945 was head of the Tonkin Economic Service in Hanoi. These positions gave Hà considerable knowledge of the Indochinese wartime economy, especially the plethora of French and Japanese controls, although his awareness of policy alternatives was limited to book learning and his residence in France during the 1930s.[3] Three other ministries had obvious economic relevance: finance, labor, and communications and public works. Phạm Văn Đồng, the finance minister, was soon being employed by provisional President Hồ as troubleshooter on other fronts. The labor minister, Lê Văn Hiến, had come to national attention in 1938 for his memoir about abysmal conditions at Kontum prison. Hiến would become finance minister in March 1946, and serve in that capacity until 1951. The communications and public works minister, Đào Trọng Kim, was a respected civil engineer.

Wartime economic controls initiated by Governor General Jean Decoux in 1940–41 had been condemned by ICP and Việt Minh writers as designed solely to protect and enhance the interests of French colonialists and Japanese fascists, while exploiting everyone else. Other Vietnamese complained about Decoux's perpetuation of business syndicates and monopolies that discriminated against native entrepreneurs. Even so, because imports from Europe were cut off, Decoux allowed Chinese and Vietnamese inventors, manufacturers, and entrepreneurs to apply their talents without fear of intruding on traditional French business privileges. As a result, some families garnered considerable wealth in only two or three years. Small firms cropped up to make machine tools, spare parts, pharmaceutical substitutes, carbonate of soda for soap, potassium chlorate for matches, low-quality bicycle tires, and tire retreads for motor vehicles.[4] As goods became more scarce, however, the colonial government's prior penchant for paperwork increased relentlessly. Separate forms were required in order to purchase, transport, store, or sell rice, corn, salt, cooking oil, cloth, coal, matches, and water filters. In Tonkin, the Service économique enforced a maze of regulations through the government hierarchy and via private companies authorized to trade in specific wares. Ration tickets were issued to French nationals. Not surprisingly, the black market proliferated. By early 1945, the control system was clogged by huge quantities of telegrams, letters, commodity samples, price lists, internal memos, and formal complaints requiring investigation—all inscribed on paper of degenerating quality due to the absence of chemicals and spare parts. None of these controls were able to ward off the terrible famine of early 1945 in Tonkin and northern Annam. Indeed, the controls may have made the famine worse.[5]

OPEN MARKET

In early September 1945, Võ Nguyên Giáp, on behalf of the provisional president, signed a decree abrogating all previous restrictions on the sale and transport of rice in northern Vietnam, and declaring that henceforth the DRV government would purchase whatever rice it needed from private sources *(tư gia)*. With these statements the government seemed to recognize that official curbs on the rice trade had distorted the market badly. It certainly acknowledged the degree to which farmers detested the private syndicates *(liên đoàn)* which had collected tax rice for the colonial regime. However, Giáp's decree went on to warn that anyone hoarding rice or "plotting speculation" would be punished by martial law and have their property confiscated.[6] Such a draconian admonition placed question marks over the decree's promise of free trade in rice, especially since no definitions were offered for "hoarding" or "speculation." Later in September, President Hồ decreed the abolition of six preferential business associations for agriculture and fisheries, industry, minerals, trade (foreign and domestic), transport, and banking.[7]

In an extraordinary blitz of edicts, the national economy minister, Nguyễn Mạnh Hà, freed specific commodities—including cattle, vegetable oils, peanuts, coconuts, fish oil, cotton seed, dyes, lumber, wood products, turpentine, and paper—from restrictions on production, trade, and transport. He then eliminated regulations that required persons trading in industrial or craft products to obtain government permission to open, expand, move, or sell their enterprises.[8] It seems that Hà's prior management of economic controls had turned him into the new government's prime advocate of an open market. Inspectors and clerks who had handled the previous labyrinthine apparatus must have worried about their future. A Hanoi reporter interviewed a trader carrying liquor who enthused, "Now I can sell freely. Anyone can sell whatever they want, not like under the French previously." But a fifty-year-old merchant was still scared from the time he had been jailed by the French for eight days for selling soap above the fixed price.[9] In fact, neither alcohol nor soap had been released from government restrictions, nor had salt, opium, cloth, coal, and some other commodities.

At the important early October 1945 meeting of provincial committee leaders with central government officials, discussed earlier, the representative from Nam Định, Đặng Châu Tuệ, described the recent muddle over salt, with everyone first assuming termination of the salt monopoly, producers in his province then being told not to sell to anyone except customs agents, and speculators making lots of money amidst the confusion. The customs official present at the meeting attacked moves to "liberate salt," saying this would "favor four thousand salt producers at the expense of nine million ordinary citizens in the north." Tuệ retorted, "Then please immediately arrest dealers in contraband salt." Other province representatives expressed surprise that salt had not been liberated. As his punch line, the customs official pointed out that the French authorities had taken eight million piastres per year in revenue from the salt monopoly, but only because they "captured the illegals selling on the market."[10] The new government would have to decide whether or not to follow French precedent and rely on monopolies for most of its income. If the DRV state went down the monopoly path, could black market competitors be eliminated?

Two weeks later, Phan Tử Nghĩa, commissioner for economics and finance in the Northern Region People's Committee, dispatched a remarkable message to the minister of national economy, affirming that sweeping DRV reforms meant that "the command economy is gradually giving way to the free economy (kinh tế tự do)." As a result, he enthused, trade, industry, and agriculture would be able to develop openly, not be "held down as during the period of French rule." Nghĩa then appended specific proposals for the elimination of restrictions on the selling and transport of salt, cloth, tobacco, and other goods. However, someone in the ministry office then scribbled, "Brother Phan Tử Nghĩa was able to be informed clearly, and agreed to cancel this message."[11] Had Nghĩa simply overstepped his position? More likely, Nguyễn Mạnh Hà was under criticism at that moment, and did not want to expose his dilemma in a reply message. Nghĩa's non-message turned out to be the high point of "free economy" advocacy. About the same time, the DRV tax director castigated local people's committees for not helping him to collect taxes on salt, liquor, opium, and foreign cigarettes, and instead claiming that their constituents were engaged in innocuous buying and selling.[12] A textile wholesaler proposed retention of the preferential business association for cloth, so as to be able to prevent Chinese and Indian retailers from jacking up the price to consumers by huge margins.[13] However, because state-fixed prices on cotton as well as cloth had fallen so far behind general inflation, farmers were not bothering to deliver raw cotton to the spinning mill in Nam Định.[14]

By November 1945, the policy pendulum had swung away from encouragement of a market economy towards a return to state controls. The most important reason was the necessity of averting another famine. No one was prepared to rely on the market to ensure that available rice reached the people most in need. Already in early October, President Hồ had banned the export of paddy, rice, corn, and beans on the grounds that a domestic famine was threatening. A subsequent decree prohibited production, storage, and consumption of Vietnamese-style liquors *(rượu ta)* made from grain, while saying nothing about continuing production of French-style liquors under monopoly.[15] Besides food shortages, the outbreak of fighting in Nam Bộ raised the specter of nationwide combat, which would require moving to a full-fledged war economy. Even assuming peacetime conditions, however, the government had decided that it needed to keep some monopolies as a tax-raising device (see below). The first evidence was an edict from the finance minister, Phạm Văn Đồng, adding salt, raw cotton, cloth, gold, and silver to the export ban list.[16]

Support for open-market operations was always paper thin. Neither precolonial Vietnamese governments nor the French colonial system had left much room for unfettered production and commerce. The few Vietnamese entrepreneurs who made a name for themselves had to accept conditions set down by the French. While some professionals and intellectuals in 1945 did want to explore and advocate the benefits to independent Vietnam of free commerce, competition, and specialization, they had only a couple of months to make their case before the door closed.[17] Ex-colonial civil servants perpetuated the commodity paper chase, protected by the intelligentsia's faith in state management of the economy. Coal was the only exception, with officials advocating purchase at open-market rates in grudging recognition that French managers and technicians would be required to get coal mines operating again.[18]

FIGHTING THE HUNGER BANDIT

Warding off another mass famine was both the provisional DRV government's first economic challenge, and a key test of its capacity to rule. Although the June

1945 rice harvest had ended widespread starvation in northern and north-central Vietnam, many families continued to survive on one meal a day, worrying constantly that their meager resources would not get them to the next harvest in November. In mid-August, floods destroyed approximately one-third of that prospective November crop in the Red River delta.[19] Tens of thousands of draft animals also perished. One of the new government's first acts in late August was to take control of warehouses containing tax grain previously promised by the imperial delegate to the Japanese military. Japanese commanders released or sold some of their wartime grain stocks to provincial people's committees, although stories also circulated of Japanese units dumping rice into rivers. Urgent government telegrams went to Saigon, where rice supplies were abundant. President Hồ placed mass hunger at the top of his list of state problems tabled at the first DRV Cabinet meeting following Independence Day celebrations. His two immediate proposals were to mount a campaign to plant supplementary crops like corn and yams, and to urge countrymen to fast one meal every ten days towards a fund to feed the poor.[20] There was one grim reason for optimism not mentioned by anyone: the number of mouths to feed had dropped by more than one million as a result of the early 1945 deaths.

With Allied aircraft no longer attacking coastal shipping or rail lines, it was assumed in late August 1945 that Nam Bộ could resume its role of supplying rice to rice-deficient regions to the north, preferably in exchange for anthracite coal from Hòn Gai and salt from Nam Định. An initial plan to utilize five French cargo vessels sequestered on the Mekong River proved impossible to implement. However, word arrived in Hanoi during the first days of September that 150 junks carrying 4,850 tons of rice were enroute to Haiphong, only to learn a week later that many of these boats had been intercepted by unidentified groups along the coast and forced to relinquish their cargoes. When reprimanded by the DRV government, people's committees replied lamely that locals had assumed the rice to be Japanese. From 15 September, trains departed Saigon for Vinh carrying 200–240 tons of rice each day. Fifty thousand jute sacks were collected in the north for dispatch southward.[21] On 23 September, the British-French coup against the Southern Executive Committee in Saigon terminated these rail shipments and put further junk traffic in jeopardy. Only six hundred tons of additional Nam Bộ rice managed to reach the north before the French occupied Nha Trang, and made even modest shipments impractical.[22]

On 11 October 1945, the DRV's campaign to "Contribute Rice to Wipe Out the Hunger Bandit" officially opened in Hanoi, with President Hồ, Supreme Advisor Vĩnh Thụy, and American Colonel Stephen Nordlinger in attendance. In a remarkably blunt speech, Mai Văn Hàm, prominent Catholic entrepreneur, told everyone by loudspeaker that with flood waters still receding slowly and farmers needing to hold back some seed rice to replant, many people would die in coming months unless others shared what food they had. As a practical measure, Hàm calculated that if each citizen of Hoàng Diệu (Hanoi) contributed three butter tins of rice per month, they could save forty thousand lives. President Hồ stepped forward to place the first amount of rice in a collection basket, followed by Vĩnh Thụy, several government ministers, and Colonel Nordlinger. The next day, young men and women fanned out across the city to collect rice in earnest.[23] In following weeks the collection campaign spread to Haiphong, Nam Định, and other towns. As far south as Huế, soldiers were reported to be abstaining from lunch to be able to help famine victims in the north.[24] Inmates at the Hanoi Central Prison agreed to fast three days each month to help famine victims, with the first two occasions in October yielding a total of 589.225 kilograms of rice and 1,196$58BIC cash.[25] Over a period of forty days in October and November, the inhabitants of Hanoi contributed 57.5 tons of rice and 32 tons of salt to help those in need, not an impressive amount if divided by the total population of the city.[26]

After watching the market price of rice climb ominously through October, the Northern Region Committee urged President Hồ in writing to convene immediately a meeting of relevant government ministers and bureau heads to grapple with food supply issues.[27] Government employees on fixed salaries were finding it impossible to make ends meet, and workers in enterprises and mines pushed openly for wage increases. In November, the Hanoi price of rice exceeded eight hundred piastres per tạ (one hundred kilograms), more than double the August price. Some provinces reported one thousand piastres per tạ. The minister of national economy, Nguyễn Mạnh Hà, banned the making of rice wine or rice confections for three months, and even tried to close down restaurants and pastry shops.[28] Northern provinces that had escaped the August flood endured a drought in September and October which caused some crops to wither and die. Almost surely several tens of thousands of people died of starvation during this period before serious relief efforts got underway and before what remained of the summer-autumn rice crop could be harvested.[29] The reaction of most local people's committees to food shortages and skyrocketing rice prices was to prohibit movement of rice out of their jurisdiction, which only helped to drive prices even higher. Instead of reiterating its early September decree eliminating all restrictions on the sale and movement of rice, which would have fallen on deaf ears, the government went back to the imperial delegate's practice of requiring written permits for purchase and transport of any amount of rice exceeding fifty kilograms. It also cajoled those localities that had not suffered flood or drought losses to sell quantities to provinces most in need. In the wake of the modest November harvest, prices dropped to 620–640$BIC per tạ, then rose again to 650–700$BIC by February 1946.[30]

Cultivating spare plots of land and planting faster-growing substitutes for rice would prove the most effective way to attack the "Hunger Bandit." President Hồ

FIGURE 21. The Nationalist Party mocks Hồ Chí Minh seeking rice donations, accompanied by Vĩnh Thụy/Bảo Đại and Ngô Tử Hạ. Note the (Việt Minh) gunman for additional persuasion. In *Thiết Thực* (Hanoi) 4 (29 Nov. 1945). Courtesy of Vietnam National Library.

revived the neo-Confucian slogan: "An inch of land equals an ounce of gold" *(Tấc đất, tấc vàng).*[31] As of late October, however, this strategy had saved no lives, since newly planted yams could only be dug up in January, and corn and beans harvested in February. Minister Nguyễn Mạnh Hà worried publicly that deaths due to starvation during the next seven months might exceed the terrible losses of early 1945. Two weeks later he revealed the internal calculation of how many tons of paddy had been lost during flooding in August, pinpointed March through May 1946 as the period of greatest famine danger, and again urged farmers to plant fast-growing substitute crops. People's committees were told to get vacant land into cultivation by any means necessary, although Hà also chastised some committees for mistreating landlords (see below). He suggested that committees auction usage rights on abandoned land, keeping the money to give to owners if they returned, or putting it into village coffers if they did not.[32] Hà was not alone in his apocalyptic visions: the agriculture minister, Cù Huy Cận, worried that the rice harvested in the north in November would run out by February.[33]

The Vietnam Nationalist Party began to criticize provisional DRV government handling of the food crisis from late November 1945, focusing especially on the plight of Hanoi residents unable to pay extraordinarily high prices for rice. Numerous stories were published of residents traveling to the countryside to purchase modest quantities of rice for their families, only to be detained by local people's committees and forced to turn over their sack in exchange for a confiscation receipt. Local "revolutionary mandarins" *(quan cách mệnh)* allegedly meted out the same treatment to Vietnamese rice traders from Hanoi, but dared not touch foreigners (presumably a reference to Chinese merchants). One angry correspondent accused some local committee personnel of being economic terrorists. Another called on fellow Hanoi inhabitants to march on the Northern Region Office to remonstrate, and suggested that citizens' groups be formed to help protect rice traders in their travels. However, yet another writer argued that traders be removed entirely from the equation and farmers possessing a surplus be ordered to sell it to the government.[34]

Criticism of the government's handling of the food crisis surfaced in other newspapers as well. *Tương Lai* weekly, after calculating food needs for an average family, demonstrated how inflation was making it increasingly difficult for people to survive. It also censored landlords who failed to plant all their available land, and called for "elimination of hoarders."[35] Reporters discovered that police were turning away some merchants carrying rice into Hanoi, to which the Northern Region Committee replied that it wanted to restrict rice destined for French nationals, and also to foil speculators.[36] *Thời mới* published a biting exposé of a relief camp set up in the Hanoi suburbs and controlled from within by two hundred men and women "as strong as elephants," who ate voraciously and then doled out miserly portions to everyone else. The camp had begun with five thousand inhabitants, but in November it was down to half that number, with 789 persons having died and others who had allegedly exited the premises more gaunt than when they arrived. Other desperate people hovered outside the camp, hoping to be admitted, yet could not do so unless they paid the elephants first. Most recently, the writer claimed, a load of rice destined for the camp had been hijacked.[37] The next issue of *Thời mới* featured on its cover the photo of a naked adolescent boy, badly emaciated yet still standing and staring at the camera. The caption read, "Rescuing [people] from starvation is a way to save the country at this moment."[38]

Thái Bình, one of the provinces hardest hit in the early 1945 famine, and then the victim of 70 percent flooding in August, faced a particularly perilous food emergency toward the end of 1945. Already the province people's committee had "borrowed" five hundred thousand piastres from the local branch of the Treasury to purchase paddy from elsewhere, but that would enable only about ten thousand people to survive for one month. In early December, the Thái Bình committee reported to Hanoi that the crop just harvested was "not good," and help was not arriving from any other direction. The committee had dispatched a large wad of one-hundred-piastre and twenty-piastre notes to Thanh Hóa province in order to purchase rice, but not only did Thanh Hóa decide not to send any rice, it returned the purchase amount in five-hundred-piastre notes, which the French high commissioner had recently declared no longer legal tender (see below). "This really made us indignant," the Thái Bình committee remarked. Another province, Nam Định, not only did not help, but grabbed rice destined for Thái Bình as it passed through, claiming that the originating province owed it money. The Northern Committee had promised one hundred tons of rice to Thái Bình, but this had yet to arrive. Meanwhile, three thousand Japanese troops and eight hundred Chinese soldiers were still eating Thái Bình rice, and seed grain was desperately needed to plant the June crop. "Although Thái Bình's famine is still worthy of deep concern, has this information really penetrated the Government?" the province committee concluded with more than a hint of exasperation.[39] Another Thái Bình report calculated that its people would require 108,000 tons of paddy to survive between January and June 1946, clearly an exaggeration.[40]

The permit system for the purchase and transport of rice was already well known to people from wartime French practices. At the end of November, the Northern Region Committee outlined an ambitious plan, whereby a district permit would be required for more than fifty kilograms of rice to travel from one village to another, a province permit to move from one district to another, and an interprovincial committee permit to go from one province to another. Those persons not obeying the system would see their rice confiscated.[41] Although the files contain no evidence that such a system was implemented between villages or between districts in subsequent months, province committees already issued a permit that enabled individuals to go to another specified province to purchase a certain quantity of rice at a certain price. Often the purchaser also took the precaution of obtaining a permit from the Northern Economic Office, to bolster his or her credentials, but this was not yet a requirement.

Being armed with a purchase permit by no means guaranteed results. Officials at the selling end often reduced the quantity to be sold, insisted on a higher price, or turned back the buyer entirely. For example, after Quảng Yên province officials had given permission for two boat owners to buy 1.6 tons and 0.9 tons of rice from merchants in adjacent Bắc Giang province, and the owners had secured permits from the Northern Economic Office as well, the people's committee of Đức Lai village in Bắc Giang only allowed the boats to carry away 0.5 tons each.[42] Some local committees refused to allow even amounts under fifty kilograms to leave their jurisdictions, which the Northern Committee angrily labeled as "playing into the hands of the reactionaries."[43] Thái Nguyên province bluntly told Hanoi that it had forbidden any of its own paddy or rice to be sold outside the province, in order that its poor could be assured of food and also to prevent speculation.[44] To further complicate matters, some National Guard units ordered everyone within their area of operations to obtain military permits to carry rice, under penalty of being turned back at checkpoints.[45]

The position of the DRV government regarding sale and transport of rice remained inconsistent, reflecting divergent viewpoints and interests. Several times it repeated the policy of free movement within Vietnam, while simultaneously allowing, even ordering, restrictions. In one case the Finance Ministry was unaware that the Northern Committee had secretly ordered the Haiphong Administrative Committee to prevent all movements of rice above fifty kilograms.[46] The central government entered the market routinely to obtain rice for the National Guard or state employees, and occasionally to help deficient provinces, but because it usually wanted to pay less than the market price, disagreements were inevitable with wholesale merchants and local committees alike. Province committees also became rice operators, deciding which merchants to work with, where to sell surpluses, and how much of the province budget to allocate to rice purchases.[47] Bắc Giang felt free to reduce down to a mere ten tons of rice a Northern Committee instruction to supply Hòn Gai, saying it was already committed to send larger amounts to Quảng Yên and Lạng Sơn.[48]

Hanoi city, as the largest single northern consumer of rice (fifty-four hundred tons per month), regularly complained about province administrators who arbitrarily crossed out quantities specified in permits in favor of smaller amounts. Provinces also forced Hanoi merchants to cool their heels for many days, thus driving up the price to end consumers. The Hà Nam province committee replied by accusing Hanoi of issuing too many permits. At one point the Northern Committee instructed the Hanoi city committee to limit its permits to three provinces. Hanoi responded that prices were higher in those provinces, and the three might decide to reduce access, leaving city dwellers in real danger. In the surrounding delta provinces, meanwhile, committee members remembered vividly how only one year earlier country folk had starved to death in far greater numbers than city folk.

In April 1946, the Hanoi chairman, Trần Duy Hưng, submitted a revealing report on rice to the Northern Committee. City dwellers were quite worried about market volatility, with prices sometimes changing two or three times a day. They called often for a "free system" (chế độ tự do) that would cause the price of rice to drop. Nonetheless, Hưng urged that restrictions be maintained on other grounds. First, the Chinese Army, in league with Chinese merchants, had been speculating in rice, and now the French also were sending out "Vietnamese traitors" to buy up and stockpile rice. Some big Vietnamese landlords and merchants wanted to stockpile rice in Hanoi to await further price rises. To this threat, the city committee had reacted by dispatching Việt Minh groups and policemen to apply pressure on Vietnamese merchants. Given all this stockpiling, to declare an open market would not necessarily result in cheaper rice to the consumer. Finally, Hưng argued that it was unwise strategically to warehouse a lot of grain in Hanoi: if war broke out, the National Guard might not be able to use those food stocks.[49] Even as Hưng submitted that report, the wholesale price of rice was starting to drop in Hanoi, mainly in anticipation of a reasonable June harvest. Anyone still holding grain stocks from the previous harvest now unloaded on the market. Also, with the BIC piastre declining in value, landlords preferred to loan rice rather than money to their tenants. And the fall in the Chinese "gold dollar" reduced incentives to export rice to China.[50]

By early May, signs of a favorable harvest were multiplying, and on 4 June the northern director of supply went so far as to inform the DRV cabinet that "the rice supply problem has been solved for all the nation's people."[51] A number of delta provinces reported modest surpluses for the June crop. Hà Nam, for example, stated that 120,000 *mẫu* had produced 48,000 tons of paddy, of which 40,000 was needed for local consumption and 2,400 tons for seed, leaving a surplus of 5,600 (13 percent of the crop).[52] The Ministry for Society proposed that each province establish a paddy reserve storehouse of about one-thousand-ton capacity as protection against disasters, with unused stock to be sold towards the end of the season, when prices generally were higher. Eventually the Northern Committee gave wary support to this idea, providing everyone understood that such state storehouses were entirely different from earlier French and Japanese compulsory paddy collection points, that landowners would not be pressured to contribute, and that full market price would be paid.[53]

Yams, corn, and beans ripening from January 1946 onward largely averted the famine feared before the June rice harvest. According to a published source, 145,600 hectares planted with those supplementary crops resulted in 614,000 tons of food, which largely compensated in the north for the deficient November 1945 rice total of 500,000 tons (half of 1938–43 averages). The number of hectares planted in yams, corn, and beans tripled compared to the colonial era, and yields per hectare were said to have increased by one-third as well.[54] Roughly calculated, 614,000 tons of these carbohydrates minus any rice could have kept 5.6 million people alive for five months.[55] Nonetheless, famine did claim lives during the first half of 1946. The Northern Committee requested that all provinces report the number of citizens who had died of starvation between January and June. Eventual replies from six provinces added up to 11,458 deaths.[56] Four provinces flooded in August 1945 did not reply, notably Thái Bình and Sơn Tây, each of which had suffered 70 percent inundation. It seems likely, therefore, that at least twenty thousand persons starved to death. Although sufficient food may well have been available in total, some people who could not afford to pay were missed by relief cadres and volunteers, usually in more remote villages.

One way or another, the specter of another mass famine that had haunted northern Vietnamese in September 1945 was driven away by June 1946. There had been deaths from starvation, but only a small fraction of those lost one year prior.[57] Nor had there been food riots, violent altercations with the Chinese Army over grain, or hundreds of thousands of emaciated citizens wandering desperately from place to place in search of sustenance. The expanding army and police force had enough to eat, and modest stockpiling was possible starting in mid-1946. DRV government and Việt Minh publicists took credit for all this, and many Vietnamese probably equated President Hồ Chí Minh with the traditional beneficent king able to "feed his people." Nonetheless, the heavens had favored the north with better weather than the previous year, and many local groups had acted on their own initiative to cultivate empty land. The struggle against the "famine bandit" also tossed up problems for the fledgling DRV state that would continue far beyond 1946, notably command versus market forces in food production and distribution, central versus local administrative controls, and the degree of protection to be offered to private land.

ORDER AND CHAOS: EVOLUTION OF A RICE SYSTEM

In July 1946, the price of rice fluctuated in the range of 415–460$BIC per *tạ* in Hanoi, with variations above and below that level persisting in the provinces.[58] A government meeting calculated minimum daily wages for workers in terms of amounts of rice, eventually settling on 0.75 kilograms per day for adults, 0.6 for youths aged fifteen to eighteen years old and 0.45 for working children aged twelve to fifteen.[59] The communications and public works minister met with a delegation of railway workers for four hours to discuss a possible wage supplement due to the high price of rice.[60] Rice price reports received from province committees were broadcast regularly on Voice of Vietnam radio, to serve as the basis for calculating employee allowances in each locality.[61] Nonetheless, localities still requested the Northern Committee to cable them current rice prices, and the committee responded, probably a device to facilitate local salary or allowance agreements.[62]

Haiphong rice dynamics were unique, due to the presence there of numerous overseas Chinese merchants, the DRV government's determination to block rice exports, and a city committee bent on controlling rice transactions down to the household level. In April and May 1946, the Haiphong authorities stepped up their interception of rice on the move without proper papers. In one case agents swooped on a line of boats containing forty tons of rice and confiscated the lot. The city committee donated this contraband rice to the prison, the public hospital, and the relief association.[63] Not coincidentally the price of rice escalated in Haiphong, at a time when prices were starting to decline elsewhere in the north. The Haiphong committee reacted by issuing a raft of purchasing permits that allowed small-scale traders *(hàng sáo)* to travel to adjacent provinces, only to find that local committees refused to honor these pieces of paper, instead issuing their own sale and transport permits to other traders.[64] The city committee then convened a meeting of neighborhood representatives at the Haiphong Opera House, where it was decided that each of the thirteen neighborhood committees would draw up a list of households and rice needs. Based on a meager average requirement of twenty kilograms of rice per household per month, each neighborhood committee was to submit its total calculation to city auditors, who would then authorize the committee to purchase and distribute said amounts to households.[65] This was a wildly unrealistic plan for mid-1946 Haiphong, perhaps for anywhere, yet we see here the germ of what later became the DRV's state supply system.

In following weeks the price of rice in Haiphong climbed back up to six hundred piastres per *tạ*, provoking the local Việt Minh daily to feature an ominous editorial titled "Rice! Rice! Rice!" across its front page. The editors complained especially about deficient controls and weak distribution mechanisms, which allowed black marketeers to flourish and citizens to suffer. They proposed formation of neighborhood cooperatives *(hợp tác xã)*, which could only sell rice to members, not beyond. And it might be necessary to apply the death penalty to illegal traders, the editors added grimly.[66] No cooperatives emerged, however, nor were death sentences applied. In October, the Haiphong Administrative Committee announced new rice regulations: a handful of wholesalers would be licensed to transport up to ten tons at a time; two hundred other merchants would receive cards authorizing them to carry up to two hundred kilograms; and retailers had to limit their sales to no more than fifteen kilograms per customer. The communiqué promised that transactions would be "based on the market price," yet it simultaneously warned that inspectors would monitor markets and, if necessary, fix prices. These rules applied to overseas Chinese as well as Vietnamese traders, the communiqué concluded.[67] In a city where the population needed at least fifteen hundred tons of rice per month to survive, such schemes could not possibly work.

The November 1946 rice crop in the north was good, and many farmers then proceeded to plant yams in order to be able to harvest them before transplanting the next rice seedlings in early 1947.[68] At all levels, administrative committees entered the rice market aggressively, buying cheaply, stockpiling some, selling some at below-market prices to National Guard units and state employees, and offering the remainder at higher prices to merchants presenting permits from elsewhere. Hanoi became concerned about how much economic power was being consolidated at the province level in particular. Only one day before the outbreak of full-scale hostilities, the Northern Committee sent a sharp rebuke to the Vĩnh Yên committee, accusing it of trying to monopolize all rice transactions in its jurisdiction, as distinct from scrutinizing and signing permits.[69]

In early December, the Hanoi Administrative Committee expressed relief to the Northern Committee that prices had not exploded as the result of heightened tensions with the French and evacuation of civilians from the city. However, it complained that merchants still controlled most of the city's rice trade, setting prices to their own advantage. In hope of promoting competition, the city committee was now issuing more permits than needed in its dealings with neighboring provinces. It added, "If everyone had freedom to trade, the city would not be short of rice and not have to buy dearly"—a statement quite at odds with the one it made eight months prior.[70] In practice, terms like "free trade" or "control" were bandied about at the rhetorical level, meaning different things to different people, with few if any attempts at analysis or explanation. Meanwhile, problems associated with implementation of a command economy were surfacing already.

With favorable reports coming in for the November 1946 rice harvest, the Northern Committee commissioned a specialist to assess food conditions over the previous twenty months. Causes of the early 1945 famine were analyzed, and deaths due to starvation estimated at one million in the north and three hundred thousand in central Vietnam. Additional deaths caused by the August 1945 flood in the north were calculated at 11,458 persons. DRV policies to prevent another famine had included trying to transport rice from southern and central regions to the north, seeking aid from overseas without success, limiting individual transport of rice to fifty kilograms, banning rice exports, permitting interprovince trade by authorized persons or groups (đoàn thể), and increasing food production overall. Finally, according to this specialist, the development of a "government distribution network" meant that those citizens in dire need did not have to buy food at cut-throat prices.[71] Perhaps this was a reference to the doling out of relief grain obtained from voluntary contributions, since even the military had yet to establish a food supply network. In contrast to this writer's upbeat view, another unnamed specialist predicted that, despite the favorable November 1946 harvest, up to one-quarter of the population of the north would still face hunger during the first six months of 1947. He urged the government to consider migration as a longer-term priority.[72]

THE AGRICULTURE MINISTRY

The provisional DRV cabinet formed on 28 August 1945 did not include a minister for agriculture, an omission rectified eleven weeks later with appointment of forestry engineer Cù Huy Cận to that position.[73] A number of units belonging to the former Gouvernement général were soon subsumed within the agriculture ministry, including river patrol, veterinary services, animal husbandry, fisheries, forestry, and agricultural credit.[74] Much effort was spent defining responsibilities, at a time when the budget allocated by the DRV finance ministry was only a fraction of that available during the colonial era. One of the ministry's most lively members was Hoàng Văn Đức, appointed director of the bureau for research, agricultural extension, land clearing and settlement, "village action" (xã dân công tác), seed propagation, and agronomy.[75] However, hundreds of other ministry personnel had to retire early, take long-term leave without pay, or rely on local committees for food and shelter. A forest research committee was established mainly to accommodate senior staff compelled by French Army occupation to vacate their posts in southern or south-central Vietnam.[76] The DRV government reasserted the royal and colonial policy that all forests were national property; therefore no one could cut down trees, make charcoal, or burn sections of forest without written permission from the forestry bureau. Criticism was leveled at "the people and ethnic minority countrymen" for destroying forests and exploiting them illegally.[77]

In late August 1945, the provisional DRV government was informed by former colonial accountants of the existence of six "popular credit funds," the most significant of which was dedicated to making loans to farmers. Progressive Vietnamese had long criticized the colonial Crédit Populaire for ignoring the needs of poor farmers. The agriculture credit fund's overriding problem, however, was that almost all existing capital had been loaned out prior to the Japanese coup in March 1945, and the DRV's other budget priorities precluded it from adding new capital. By early 1946, many loans had passed their repayment deadlines, so the fund concentrated on debt collection. By October, the overall default level had risen to 67 percent, with Ninh Bình farmers the worst offenders at 99.7 percent overdue. Several province committees had already declined to assist in collection because all local records of loans had been lost in the August 1945 flood or in political upheavals. The Nam Định province committee banned the agricultural fund representative from its meetings, and told local committees to ignore him.[78] Because these loans dated back to the colonial era, many farmers felt no obligation to pay, and local committees had no desire to be put in the role of debt collectors.

As a result of the early 1945 famine and August flood, northern Vietnam faced a huge deficit of draft animals and beef cattle. It would take years to regenerate the water buffalo and ox populations. In early September, the Northern People's Committee cabled the "Chef Gouvernement Laos" to seek authorization to purchase five hundred oxen, five hundred buffaloes, and one thousand piglets on behalf of Nam Định province, to use as breeding stock and beasts of burden.[79] Six weeks later the Northern Economic Bureau could report its own purchase of Lao cattle, adding that other organizations were doing this as well.[80] The national economy minister removed all restrictions on the rearing, purchase, movement, and processing of cattle.[81] Traditionally, Thanh Hóa and Nghệ An to the south, and Lạng Sơn in the north had supplied cattle for slaughter at Tonkin abattoirs. As of November, Thanh Hóa was providing the Hanoi abattoir with only two hundred steers per month. The Nghệ An committee refused to allow animals out of the province, but butchers in Hanoi managed to acquire some anyway. While nothing was available yet from Lạng Sơn, Thái Nguyên now possessed a market moving four hundred to five hundred head of draft animals and beef cattle each week.[82] Thái Bình province in the delta asserted that it was short ten thousand draft animals; buffaloes in particular remained expensive, at two thousand to three thousand piastres a head.[83]

The DRV government definitely wanted more draft animals instead of animals for meat, and most officials did not believe the market could achieve this. In late December 1945, the agriculture minister forbade the slaughter of male cattle from two to five years of age, and all females except those ill or unable to bear calves. All slaughter of buffaloes, oxen, calves, and horses had to take place at an abattoir under veterinary supervision.[84] When local committees failed to enforce this edict vigorously, the central government tried other approaches. The day before President Hồ Chí Minh departed for France in May 1946, he signed a decree closing abattoirs for one day each week, during which time no meat could be sold in the marketplace. Each of the north's twenty-seven provinces and two cities was allocated a quota of buffaloes and oxen to be slaughtered per month, ranging from 942 animals in Hanoi to only eleven in Hòa Bình.[85] In October the Economic Office rejected Hải Dương province's request to exceed its slaughter quota of 120 cattle so as to feed French soldiers as well as its own people. "Let them eat pigs, chickens, and ducks," the Economic Office commented, "rather than exacerbate the extreme shortage of draft animals".[86] Much slaughtering of cattle undoubtedly continued to take place outside abattoirs. One farmer was jailed for five days and fined 180$BIC for slaughtering his own buffalo so that village elders and office-bearers could celebrate the first anniversary of Vietnam's independence.[87] Some upland province committees complained to Hanoi that too many of their cattle were being purchased and taken to the lowlands for slaughter, undermining local efforts to grow sufficient food. Sơn La, after recalling how much it had already suffered from "French flight, Japanese arrival, Japanese withdrawal, Chinese arrival," warned that its people could not till the land unless the sale of buffalo to the lowlands was stopped. It also accused National Guard units of using newly formed "cooperatives" to profit from buffalo sales rather than to raise food.[88] Meanwhile, Lạng Sơn province was gradually recovering its status as supplier of cattle to the delta, with 150–200 head going through its market each week. In October, the Lạng Sơn committee suddenly banned further sale of draft animals. However, cattle traders soon complained to the central government about Lạng Sơn officials and police taking bribes in exchange for permits to buy and move livestock. Other buyers protested the reemergence of a livestock trade monopoly.[89]

The Minister of Agriculture was the only official authorized to block movement of livestock, most often on advice from the Veterinary Bureau, to try to isolate specific disease outbreaks. Many Vietnamese members of the Indochina-wide colonial veterinary service had continued to inspect villages and abattoirs after departure of their French supervisors in March 1945. Issues of the *National Gazette* in 1946 contain hundreds of announcements of irruptions of rinderpest, anthrax, surra, and barbone, each message in the form of an edict signed by the Agriculture Minister requiring counteraction. Rinderpest *(peste bovine)*, an acute, usually fatal disease of cattle, appears to have been far more prevalent than the other three ailments, or else veterinarians paid it closest attention. Reports were published from as far south as Kontum and Quảng Ngãi. A confidential ICP resolution asserted that 80 percent of cattle in Quảng Bình province had been lost due to disease.[90] Because animal vaccines and most veterinary medicines had long since been used up in Indochina, the most authorities could do was to quarantine cattle in the locality affected. The Agriculture Minister also occasionally ordered temporary closure of abattoirs as a health measure.

PROPERTY CONFLICTS

Every revolution sees some people taking property, others losing it. Almost always force or the threat of force is involved. Emotions run high. Takers justify their actions, losers may or may not seek redress. In Vietnam, this process began soon after the March 1945 Japanese coup. By August, there was a property upheaval underway from below that no government could control. However, provisional DRV government orders to cease confiscations did cause local revolutionaries to think twice before proceeding with further seizures, and led many dispossessed persons to petition the authorities for restitution. Thanks to hundreds of these petitions now housed at the archives in Aix-en-Provence, we can get some idea of who was taking from whom, how people perceived what was happening, and what, if anything, the government did in response.

French plantation owners were the first to face the prospect of dispossession. Following the Japanese coup, most relocated hastily to the nearest city or town, leaving plantation affairs in the hands of Vietnamese managers. Some tenants saw the opportunity to renegotiate rents or land tenure. On the other hand, villagers adjacent to plantations might push for the return of land alienated during the colonial era, which put them in competition with current tenants. Sensing a declining asset, French owners started to look for Vietnamese buyers. Already at the end of May 1945, the (Vietnamese) head of the Hanoi cadastre office asked the imperial delegate, Phan Kế Toại, to rule whether such property transfers, often occurring under duress, should be considered definite or not. A draft response said no, but this passage was crossed out in favor of a simple instruction to continue entering into the official register the purchases of French property by Vietnamese.[91] Some French men transferred ownership to their Vietnamese wives or métis children. M. and Mme Lemeur chose to donate their plantation in Sơn Tây to a Vietnamese order of Catholic nuns, to help care for orphans and abandoned children.[92] René Gilles, owner of a plantation in Hải Dương province, was challenged by villagers who asserted they had been forced to sell thirty-five hectares to him in 1932, which left only 158 hectares to sustain village members.[93]

By July, Vietnamese plantation owners were starting to come under pressure as well. A canton chief in Nam Định province found adjacent villagers demanding back twenty-seven hectares he had acquired from them a decade earlier.[94] The owner of a 224-hectare plantation in Phú Thọ province first lost a number of his water buffaloes, then in July witnessed nearby villagers tilling portions of his land without permission. This dispute, and others like it, would carry over to the DRV era.[95]

August and early September 1945 saw an explosion of property seizures across Vietnam. For many people, "liberation" (giải phóng) meant redressing long-standing material grievances, dispossessing enemies, or taking control of scarce resources in the name of the revolution. French-owned plantations remained the most obvious targets, with Vietnamese managers often fleeing for their lives, movable property being cleaned out, and buildings dismantled or destroyed. A Việt Minh group stormed a French plantation at Cầu Lác (Hưng Yên), confiscating everything that could be shifted and distributing parcels of land to local peasants.[96] Vietnamese landlords felt the heat too, often being compelled to surrender movable property to self-styled Việt Minh groups. Vũ Thi submitted to authorities a list of more than one hundred items taken from his residence in Hòa Bình, including a trunk of clothing, a pistol, and 740$BIC.[97] Nguyễn Văn Long, owner of the Cổ Phúc plantation in Yen Bái province, protested that on 5–6 September a band of armed men had seized his two firearms, ten tons of rice, eighty containers of honey, seventy-eight buffaloes, one hundred water jars, and quantities of clothing. The band had also forced his four small children to walk 140 kilometers from Yên Bái to Hanoi. Long admitted to holding French citizenship, but insisted he had done nothing wrong, and declared his support for the new government.[98] Other landlords thought it prudent to "donate" tracts of land to the revolution, leaving Việt Minh activists temporarily nonplussed about what to do with them.[99]

Down the central coast, in Quảng Nam province, youths confiscated the property of absent French nationals and "Vietnamese traitors," pressured landlords to reduce rents, and sometimes reallocated communal land.[100] In adjacent Quảng Ngãi, persons hauled in front of "people's courts" and sentenced to death also had their family property confiscated or sealed pending future disposal.[101] In the Mekong delta, both ICP and Vanguard Youth groups quickly confiscated property belonging to absent French colonials or to Vietnamese families regarded as lackeys of the French or the Japanese. Some of the most substantial confiscations took place around the town of Cần Thơ, including thousands of hectares of French-owned plantation land, tens of thousands of tons of paddy or rice stored in warehouses, several thousand head of cattle, and all the boats and ferries belonging to the Société d'exploitation forestiére de l'ouest. Peasants also seized the land, rice stores, and agricultural equipment of some Vietnamese landlords. Once taken, there was no consistency as to what to do next with the property—whether, for example, to nationalize it or simply distribute parcels to worthy followers. ICP members urged peasants to keep calm and "wait for directions from higher echelons," often in vain.[102]

The provisional DRV government opposed unauthorized property seizures. Even before formal declaration of independence on 2 September, the Northern Region People's Committee had instructed all provinces to halt requisitioning *(trưng thu)* of property, whether fixed or movable, and to return to owners whatever possessions remained intact. A bit later it told people's committees to preserve all plantations intact, whether foreign or Vietnamese owned.[103] On 20 September, the Northern Committee chairman, Nguyễn Xiển, adopted a more personal tone with subordinate committees, first revealing that his office was being inundated with petitions that protested arrests and property confiscations, than entreating committees to investigate carefully before detaining anyone, and to leave property alone pending legal proceedings. "I urgently call upon you *(anh em)* to exercise caution in meting out punishments in these times," Nguyễn Xiển pleaded. He also asked them to consider that "the old cliquish mentality is still strong in the countryside. Individual grudges, schemes to grab rank and status, etc., are bedeviling many places."[104]

The view from below differed significantly from that of Nguyễn Xiển in Hanoi. A 30 September report from one province committee portrayed outright class conflict, with rich people *(phú hào)* upset about confiscations of land, homes, and movable property, while the poor wanted immediate division of communal lands and early return of land "exploited away" from them in the past. To this report an anonymous Northern Office member appended a memo to his superiors advising more vigorous patriotic solidarity campaigns in the countryside and a halt to illegal confiscations, but also "punishment of traitors to prevent their reorganization."[105] At the early October meeting between province committee chairmen and DRV officials, Nghiêm Xuân Yểm of the Northern Office spoke of a "land revolution" underway, with many poor people expecting to receive land soon. While it was up to the DRV Cabinet to decide whether division of property would occur or not, the immediate need according to Yểm was to foster cultivation of every available plot of land. Regarding plantations in particular, Yểm urged province leaders to travel to each venue, convince people to stop destroying property, and make local committees responsible for promoting production.[106] The Thái Nguyên committee proceeded to request central funds in order to employ twenty-two persons to administer seven French plantations within its province, one way of saying that it had higher priorities to deal with.[107]

In Phúc Yên, the province committee dispatched one of its members to visit each village, to deal with the volatile "agrarian problem." He first reported struggles over fields, communal land division, rights to fish in the river, and hamlets wanting to break away from existing villages. Two weeks later, Hanoi was told that: "Disagreements continue between traditionalist and progressive factions, between people's committees and old village despots (cường hào). Our poor peasant brothers (anh em) have misunderstood the word *freedom*, thus exceeding their prerogatives and fostering antipathies with rich peasants."[108]

The Tuyên Quang province committee referred to an "ultra-leftist struggle among peasants that has yet to be resolved."[109] Back in Hanoi, the national economy minister, Nguyễn Mạnh Hà, publicly criticized people's committees "in a few locations" for menacing landlords, confiscating their grain, and ruining property. On the other hand, Hà ordered all landlords to report to village committees any arable land not being planted before Tết (early February 1946), thus enabling the committee to assign someone else to cultivate such fields for one season only. Noncompliant landlords could be fined fifty piastres, hardly a large sum for them.[110]

What was the ICP doing amidst all the turmoil over land holdings? In 1941, the ICP had insisted that any initiatives to expropriate property be limited to "national enemies," a term which at that time referred to the French, the Japanese, and a "small number of Vietnamese traitors." Overthrowing other landlords would quickly push them into the enemy camp, harming the primary fight for national liberation. Poor peasants would thus need to defer any broad struggle for land to a later stage of the revolution.[111] This moderate land policy remained in effect into the August 1945 Revolution, yet at this point many ICP members either failed in their efforts to implement policy, or eagerly joined local bands in driving landlords out of homes, confiscating goods, and taking over fields in the name of enhancing national production. Senior ICP members inside the provisional DRV government mostly left it to noncommunists like Nguyễn Xiển, Nghiêm Xuân Yểm, and Nguyễn Mạnh Hà to criticize citizens who seized property without authorization. ICP leaders outside the government also said nothing publicly, although they may have hosed down some ICP firebrands on confidential trips through the provinces. In Huế, Việt Minh editors published a disclaimer of rumors that rice fields and other possessions were to be divided equally. They also helped to organize a meeting of landlord and peasant representatives, who allegedly agreed to subordinate their differences so that the "interests of all the people can be resolved."[112]

The Vietnam Nationalist Party condemned the DRV government, people's committees, and especially ICP/Việt Minh activists for bad treatment of landlords, warning that it would increase the likelihood of famine and make longer-term development of agriculture almost impossible. *Việt Nam* daily, published by the Nationalist Party, pointed to ongoing physical assaults on landlords, burning of houses, confiscation of seed grain, and occupation of fields. Such treatment made landlords as a group fearful of their future, and reluctant to invest in seed grain, new equipment, or repair of irrigation facilities. On the other hand, encouraging poor people to occupy fallow land without money for seed grain or basic implements would hardly produce bumper harvests.[113] Nationalist Party criticism like this was embarrassing to the DRV government, which was trying to convince landlords that the "excesses" of August and September would no longer be tolerated and that "patriotic landlords" were valued members of the national united front against resurgent French colonialism.

Although most tenants probably would have preferred plantation owners and landlords to disappear for good, they sometimes faced serious challenges to their own user rights from adjacent villages who protested that land had been unfairly alienated during colonial times. Thus, members of a commune adjacent to the Marty plantation in Hưng Yên province petitioned for return of two hundred *mẫu* "lost" during the colonial period, only to be jailed when they tried to present their case to the prefectural committee. Twenty villagers then petitioned President Hồ Chí Minh, emphasizing their peaceful intent.[114] Two other villages now joined the push for land retrieval from the Marty plantation, apparently threatening cadastral officers who arrived in February 1946 to survey. The Northern Region Committee ordered the Hưng Yên committee to "step in immediately and, if necessary, arrest the gang *(bọn)* that is disturbing order."[115] Elsewhere in Hưng Yên, a village committee proposed to buy back seventy-two *mẫu* of land "forcibly taken from us by French bandits," and now in the hands of the Thái Bình Catholic diocese, but petitioners doubted the bishop would accept the price being offered.[116]

Once the shock of August–September 1945 receded and government promises to respect private property were disseminated, some landlords petitioned Hanoi for return of their possessions. Trần Anh, owner of a sixty-mẫu property in Bắc Ninh, protested Việt Minh paddy seizures in July, his incarceration and loss of movable property in August–September, and his discovery on release that some of his land had been occupied illegally. After extensive correspondence between four levels of administration, the Northern Region Inspectorate concluded that: Anh's paddy had fed August uprising units legitimately; he had been detained on charges (subsequently dropped) of denouncing Việt Minh members to the Japanese police; the local district committee had supervised return of much of Anh's movable property; and the land dispute was before the provincial court.[117] In Tuyên Quang province, after Nguyễn Văn Tự protested his detention in August and loss of movable property, the local committee replied that Tự had been regarded initially as a reactionary but then released, while his possessions were taken away by Chinese troops. Tự rebutted this account, naming persons "jealous of my wealth" who had detained him and seized his goods before Chinese arrival. Eventually Tự was invited to the Inspectorate office in Hanoi, where he promised to provide a list of property items lost.[118] Đặng Thị Châu petitioned the

Agriculture Ministry in November 1945 to reaffirm her ownership and right to control cultivation of the 550-mẫu Tuấn Lương plantation in Hưng Yên. After discovering that Châu's land had been taken by others, the agriculture minister urged the Interior Ministry to see that her rights were restored in time for planting of the early 1946 rice crop. Interior ordered the Hưng Yên committee to act accordingly, but as of January the relevant local committee had yet to report compliance.[119]

Anxious to acquire enough rice to feed the National Guard and civil administration, the DRV government aimed to strike a tacit bargain with landlords. It encouraged tenants to turn over rents to landlords in return for landlords selling paddy at reasonable prices to state agents or designated merchants. Landlords were also more likely than tenants to pay the land tax which was reintroduced in 1946. Where plantation owners or landlords had fled their properties, the government sometimes endeavored to collect rents on their behalf, naturally taking a hefty commission.[120] Landlords were also called upon to reduce rents by one-quarter, but there was no attempt to enforce this policy yet. We have almost no evidence about how tenants felt about the state-landlord bargain. In late 1945, three farmers petitioned Trần Huy Liệu, minister of information and propaganda, recounting how landlords had taken land from them and extorted rents and taxes for many years—until the Việt Minh said otherwise. Then, however, the new village committee had come armed with guns and made them pay 6$90BIC per mẫu, claiming that it was going to be "offered to the top level (cúng lên thượng cấp)." And yet, they asked, why had adjacent villages not paid? The petition concluded, "We are just stupid peasants, so please convey our petition to President Hồ so he can check on our behalf."[121]

Vietnamese landlords continued to come under pressure from tenants, adjacent villagers, and local committees. In Hà Đông, relatives of a landlord detained by villagers submitted documents, including tenant contracts, that helped to convince the Northern Committee to instruct the province committee to gain release of the landlord and return of his property. Several weeks later the province committee reported that both had been accomplished.[122] A landlord in Ninh Bình complained that a group of harvesters backed by the local committee was forcing itself upon him at exorbitant rates and preventing others from doing the job.[123] Nguyễn Văn Long, whom we met in September 1945 petitioning for restitution of movable property, now complained that two village committees were chasing away tenants attempting to plant his fields, and refusing to return his possessions valued at three hundred thousand piastres. The agriculture minister, Cù Huy Cận, took up Long's cause, adding that such local committee behavior had a bad influence on public opinion, and was "very detrimental to government efforts to increase production." The Interior Ministry routed Cận's letter to the Yên Bái provincial committee, together with a stern cover note instructing them to investigate and punish those responsible, if necessary by confiscating property belonging to the village chairmen.[124] Despite repeated government calls to respect current property rights, villagers continued throughout 1946 to petition the authorities for restoration of lands lost during colonial times.

In mid-May 1946 the interior minister, Huỳnh Thúc Kháng, dispatched a resolute message to every administrative committee in northern and central Vietnam, stating that in some places there were people not working, calling themselves proletarians and either waiting to be given land, buffaloes, and seed, or seizing these things from landowners, causing serious disorder. Kháng ordered committees to tell people to respect personal property rights, and warned that any local committee failing to stop illegal land or grain appropriations would face "complete responsibility."[125] Once again, a noncommunist member of cabinet was put in the position of upholding landowners and criticizing poor peasants, while ICP ministers remained silent. Local disputes over property persisted, although not at the levels evident in late 1945. In October, members of a village in Bắc Ninh demanded return of sixty-five mẫu from a local landlord, threatening to march three hundred strong on his house and shed blood if necessary. The Interior Ministry ordered the relevant local committee to tell people they would be punished severely if government directives were disobeyed. "Only in this way," the message concluded "can production expand and local authorities increase their prestige (uy tín)."[126] Elsewhere, landlords complained to Hanoi that their tenants were still refusing to pay rents. In some cases district committees negotiated agreements whereby tenants turned over some rent immediately and promised to pay the remainder later.[127]

French plantation owners, having withdrawn fearfully to towns during the summer of 1945, saw nothing favorable in the advent of the DRV in September. Vietnamese managers, already finding it difficult to collect rents from tenants, now faced outright hostility and sometimes incarceration. In Thái Nguyên, the manager of the Keppler plantation was jailed by villagers, who accused him of earlier forcing them to sell paddy to the Japanese, and more recently threatening them with return of French forces. Following a query from Hanoi, villagers reluctantly agreed to release the accused pending judicial due process.[128] The owner of a Yên Bái concession, Mme Trimbours, received a visit in Hanoi from her distraught manager, who described how the province committee had seized her property, then allowed it to be trashed by locals. Mme Trimbour's complaint received no reply.[129] Few French petitioners tried a second time. A notable exception was Alfred Lévy, owner of a plantation in Chinê (Hà Nam), who petitioned the Interior and Foreign Affairs ministries repeatedly for release of his manager, Trịnh Văn Nghiêm, as well as return of cattle, coffee beans, paddy, butter, and cheese seized by soldiers. To one petition Lévy appended on article from Cứu Quốc affirming that plantations would be protected. Foreign Affairs assured

Lévy that instructions had gone to Chinê to restore Nghiêm as manager. Two months later Lévy complained that nothing had happened.[130]

Vietnamese wives or métis children of French nationals also sometimes petitioned the DRV authorities for return of property or financial compensation. Suzanne Croibier, the métis daughter of Emile Croibier-Huguet, recently deceased, applied to be recognized as owner of her father's concession in Hưng Yên province. The relevant district committee objected vehemently, first describing how the plantation had been sealed up as "imperialist property" because M. Croibier-Huguet had loaned money at exorbitant interest rates, then explaining that the plantation's future income was "needed very much to support the locality." Finally, the committee argued that Mlle Croibier ought to be ruled out as owner because of her French citizenship.[131] As we have seen above, Mlle Croibier tried again two months later under the name of Đặng Thị Châu, gaining the agriculture minister's endorsement, yet apparently obtaining no better result. Mme Nguyễn Thị Ninh, wife of M. Saint Carpier, applied for transfer of title on nineteen mẫu of land from their son, Jean Carpier, on grounds he was mentally incompetent. The relevant prefectural committee argued that any decision be postponed until the Vietnamese and French governments achieved a general property agreement.[132] Mme Nguyễn Thị Liên, wife of Alfred Gilet, sought return of sixty-nine mẫu seized from her during the August 1945 tumult. The village committee implicated in the takeover explained that it had acted to prevent others from occupying the property. Liên was free to return to claim her land and paddy, "yet for some unknown reason she has refused to do so."[133]

PROPERTY APPROPRIATED BY THE STATE

The DRV central government showed no hesitation about taking over key private buildings, equipment, and supplies, even as it was trying to restrict local committees from doing the same thing. The Interior Ministry quickly requisitioned the Hanoi waterworks, the Air France radio facility, a metalworks plant, and l'Action printery. The Association pour la formation intellectuelle et morale des Annamites (Hội Khai Trí Tiên Đức) was dissolved and its property confiscated on the grounds that it had served French and Japanese imperial interests.[134] The French Yunnan Railway Company was requisitioned in early September, an act ignored by the Chinese Army. Already during the summer, local people had encroached on railway land, and now local committees did likewise.[135] A mixture of Vietnamese, Chinese, Japanese, and French personnel kept the trains running between Hanoi and the Chinese frontier at Lào Cai. The large train repair facility at Vinh was commandeered, and some workers and machines redirected to weapons production. An early DRV decree explained the necessity of requisitioning private materiel that was both extremely scarce and urgently needed, then promised vaguely to pay owners the "current price in compensation."[136] Most private automobiles appear to have been requisitioned or acquired at knock-down prices by one state organization or another. When an auto taken from the Grands Travaux Marseille company broke down in September, the Northern Committee not only asked the firm for a replacement, but requested that it pay the driver's wages as well.[137]

Many French villas requisitioned by the Japanese after their March 1945 coup came into the hands of DRV organizations after August, only to be relinquished to Chinese Army units a few weeks later. Some wealthy Vietnamese families saw their houses appropriated by one side or another as well. Trần Văn Chương, prominent colonial-era lawyer and foreign affairs minister in the short-lived Imperial Vietnam government, had his Hanoi villa confiscated by Việt Minh adherents in August, returned by the city people's committee in early September, then "loaned" to the government a few weeks later as headquarters for the Ministry of Information and Propaganda.[138] Hồ Đắc Diễm, former provincial governor, saw his Hà Đông villa sealed up by the province committee, after which he agreed to let the Northern Committee transport his furniture to Hanoi to be used in an official reception building. Diễm also "donated" (cúng) fifty tons of paddy to Hà Đông, which then agreed to let the National Economy Ministry borrow it in order to supply Chinese forces.[139] In Haiphong, the civil court ordered "expropriation in the common interest" of land belonging to sixty-two different owners in order to be able to construct a new road and housing area. Lots varied in size from 4,020 meters squared to a mere three meters squared. Expropriation proceedings had begun with an edict from Governor General Decoux in January 1945, been reaffirmed by the imperial delegate just prior to the August Revolution, and the final court order promulgated at the end of November—a striking example of administrative continuity across three disparate regimes.[140]

A number of French enterprises continued to function in late 1945, albeit under various degrees of DRV control or scrutiny. A rather tentative October decree authorized foreign companies to continue operating pending new laws, providing they accepted government supervision, if necessary by means of undefined "specialized committees."[141] French firms providing goods or services to the central government sent their invoices in triplicate to the Northern Economic Office, complete with tax stamps on each copy. One of the most active was the Boillot company, at 1 rue Paul Bert, which serviced motor vehicles. In early January, Boillot presented bills totaling almost fifteen thousand piastres, some dating back to July. The Société Transports Automobiles Indochinois (STAI) was the only French enterprise to type invoices in Vietnamese, beginning at the top with "Democratic Republic of Vietnam, Year 1." Each of its invoices was stamped by Mai Văn Việt, chairman of the Hanoi Workers Committee, probably evidence that the company had been requisitioned.[142]

Smaller French-owned shops were vulnerable to predatory local committees. Whenever the Northern Committee heard that a local committee was putting up a French enterprise for sale, it fired off an order to desist immediately. "French properties must be protected for them," one early message asserted flatly.[143] By the end of 1945, the status of hundreds of requisitioned or confiscated properties, Vietnamese as well as French, was the object of extensive administrative exchange and political wrangling, reflecting the different attitudes and interests of parties involved. Another government decree specified which officials were authorized to issue requisition orders, outlined a formula for restitution, and threatened fines or jail for property owners who refused a legitimate requisition order.[144] In January 1946, authority to requisition was delegated to the DRV's three regional administrative committees; seven months later, province and city committees could requisition as well.[145]

The vast majority of property disputes were handled via administrative committees and specialized bureaus, not the DRV court system, which was slow to reorganize after the August Revolution and had difficulty asserting its legitimacy. It was rare for property owners, tenants, local committees, or other interested parties to lodge complaints with the courts, although officials sometimes threatened court action if parties refused administrative resolution. In practice the Northern Committee took on substantial powers of legal arbitration, basing its decisions on relevant decrees and edicts. In the countryside, province committees often bore de facto responsibility for mediating lower-level land aspirations on the one hand, and central government desires to maximize grain production on the other.

Throughout 1946, local registrars continued to process property valuations, title searches, sales contracts, and mortgages. A fair number of title deeds had been destroyed or lost during the tumultuous events of the previous summer. In line with colonial decrees of 1925 and 1939, the *National Gazette* published "announcements of lost title deeds" by both Vietnamese and French real estate owners, as part of the process of reregistration. Fifty-one Vietnamese, twenty-one French, and three probable Chinese individuals, mostly located in Hanoi or Haiphong, detailed their own title claims. For example, Trần Văn Cúc asserted ownership of seven different properties in Haiphong, while Dương Văn Lược in Hanoi shared three properties with his wife and a fourth with both his wife and his concubine. Agnès-Marie Vacher declared ownership of a building at No. 1 Vọng Đức Street in Hanoi, stemming from the estate of one J. C. Wilken.[146] Some French claimants clearly were hoping to reaffirm title pursuant to selling out and returning to the *métropole*.

Franco-Vietnamese property issues received detailed airing at both the May 1946 Dalat and July–September Fontainebleau conferences. The 14 September modus vivendi gave French nationals the same property rights as Vietnamese nationals, and stated that confiscated French property would be returned. However, Vietnamese newspapers at home took a much tougher line, especially in regard to reparations. If anything, editors insisted, France should compensate Vietnam for eighty years of crass exploitation, for letting the Japanese into Indochina, and for continuing to wreak death and destruction in Nam Bộ. Most papers were ominously silent on return of French property. In Quảng Ngãi, a senior military officer drew a distinction between concessions which the colonial regime had passed out to favorites for almost nothing, and enterprises like the Nam Định textile mill which had required significant French capital investment. By implication, most concessionaires did not deserve to receive back their holdings.[147] Earlier the DRV minister of communications and transport, Trần Đăng Khoa, had stated that the Yunnan Railway as far as Lào Cai had been nationalized and would remain so.[148] If Franco-Vietnamese negotiations had resumed in early 1947, as foreshadowed in the modus vivendi, all such property questions would have been vetted again. Reversing property seizures of 1945–46 would have proven impossible in many cases.

French owners and DRV administrators continued to deal with each other right up to 19 December 1946. M. de Heulme, owner of the eight thousand hectare Chesney concession in Bắc Giang and Thái Nguyên provinces, managed from Hanoi to keep in touch with cultivation activities and likely harvest results. In late October, de Heulme offered to sell most of his estimated fifty-seven-hundred-ton November crop to the Vietnam National Guard if it would help with harvesting. The Defense Ministry's quartermaster corps quickly expressed interest in acquiring one thousand tons of paddy, yet the Northern Committee delayed four weeks before asking the opinion of the two province committees, especially in regard to current landlord-tenant relations. Thái Nguyên responded that only several hundred mẫu of the rice fields in question were located inside its territory. Bắc Giang had still not responded by early December, when harvesting should have been completed.[149] It seems likely that district committees had already struck purchasing deals with many of the tenants and did not want de Heulme, the quartermaster corps, or the Northern Committee to get involved. In another case, M. Saissac, currently living in Huế, sought government assistance in selling his plantation in Ninh Bình province. For his three hundred *ha* of land, one brick house, twenty-five thousand coffee trees, twenty-five thousand tea bushes, and one hundred cattle, Saissac was asking four hundred thousand piastres. The Central Region Economic Office in Huế even offered to represent the Agricultural Ministry or Northern Committee in a government purchase. No one in Hanoi appears to have taken action for two months. The very last item dispatched by the Northern Economic Office on 19 December, just hours prior to the outbreak of fighting in Hanoi, was the Huế message being routed to another bureau in the same building.[150]

TAXES OR NO TAXES?

No facet of French colonialism was more detested than the multifarious tax system. Việt Minh propaganda had promised abolition of colonial taxes and Việt Minh adherents had made life difficult for Imperial Vietnam tax collectors during the summer of 1945.[151] On taking power in August, some local activists declared an end to all existing taxes, while others banned those they disliked the most, starting with the head tax *(thuế thân)*. On 23 August, the Northern Committee abolished the market tax and the abattoir tax. In the popular imagination, revolution or liberation included release from onerous state impositions. Indeed, some farmers wanted the new government to reimburse them for past taxes unfairly collected by village headmen. On the other hand, provisional DRV government members saw an overriding need for resources to build an army, feed civil administrators, repair public facilities, and implement a national development program.

At the first meeting in Hanoi of Northern Office and provincial committee members on 1–2 September, each province reported which specific tax collections had already been terminated in their jurisdiction. The head tax was mentioned most often, followed by the market tax and the ferry-crossing tax. Two provinces had announced to the public no further collection of existing taxes, two said they had retained [only?] the tax on commerce, and one spoke vaguely of eliminating more than ten types of tax. Several representatives commented that their people were upset about recent press reports that colonial laws would remain in force until the government specified otherwise.[152] The meeting agreed that the government should quickly declare which taxes were to be collected, which ones dropped. It was also agreed that each province set up a National Salvation Fund (Qũy Cứu Quốc) to receive donations, issue receipts, and report results to Hanoi. However, only the central government could issue promissory notes, public bonds, or currency.[153]

On 7 September, a DRV decree eliminated the head tax nationwide. Three days later, the Customs and Indirect Tax Bureau was established to supervise the salt and opium monopolies, collect import and export duties, and gather such other taxes as mandated subsequently.[154] At the second meeting between government officials and northern province committee chairmen, on 1–2 October, Võ Nguyên Giáp, the interior minister, reaffirmed "elimination of taxes" *(bỏ thuế)* in line with previous Việt Minh promises, yet then offered no further policy details, except that unexpectedly quick assumption of state authority prevented a progressive income tax from taking the place of the defunct head tax. Phạm Văn Đồng, the finance minister, then told everyone bluntly that the center lacked funds for everything except the army, so each province had to follow the principle of "self-sufficiency" *(tự cấp tự túc)*. When this statement met with considerable consternation, especially in regard to paying state employees at provincial and district levels, Đồng retorted: "One shouldn't grumble a lot. This was accomplished earlier in the [Việt Minh] war zone. You need to solve the problem yourself, you must." Later in the meeting Đồng encouraged province committees to apply any kind of tax not yet abrogated by government decree, then negotiate with the Northern Office concerning how much to remit to the center, and how much to retain for local use. After the director of customs arrived at the meeting, he revealed that many tax collectors had abandoned their posts in the countryside, while the rest had no idea whether they would receive their next salary payment or not.[155]

Within days of this Hanoi meeting it became clear that customs employees and people's committees would have difficulty working together. Central tax officials accused local committees of refusing to cooperate with tax collectors, of harassing them, of blocking operations entirely. When customs agents fingered black marketeers and requested assistance in making arrests, committee members questioned the accusations or claimed that police were preoccupied with other tasks. In one case involving hundreds of tons of salt, the customs director asked the Northern Committee rhetorically, "Are these law-abiding citizens deserving of local people's committee protection, or offenders to be tracked down and punished?" He was determined to apply the 18 October 1921 colonial law on fines for illegal sale of opium, to arrest anyone producing or selling liquor beyond small amounts needed for family use, and to investigate operations at the large Nam Định salt pans. Responding to the director's complaints, the Northern Committee merely reiterated to provinces that customs taxes remained in force.[156] Most provinces preferred to decide for themselves which taxes to retain, who would be selected to collect them, and how much revenue to keep and how much to remit to Hanoi.

Meanwhile, President Hồ received hundreds of complaints about the continuation of colonial taxes. Local committees him sent requests for clarification that amounted to tax indictments.[157] Merchants and shopkeepers protested the continuation of commercial license fees (thuế môn bài) in particular. When the Hanoi City People's Committee announced an end to commercial licenses, the Northern Committee disagreed vehemently, arguing that licenses would bring five million piastres to government coffers. The Interior Ministry sided with the Northern Committee, despite the flood of complaints coming from other localities as well. A DRV decree then abolished commercial licenses for the smallest traders, but dissent persisted.[158] Nam Định province commented that with Hanoi newspapers openly opposing commercial licenses it was hard to collect fees from merchants.[159] Phúc Yên reported that when it tried to collect, merchants protested that the fee was four times what the French had charged in 1944. This was the sole justification Phúc Yên offered for admitting that "truthfully, we haven't been able to collect a cent."[160] By contrast, Thái Nguyên reported that it had obtained 9,835$BIC from the issuing of 369 commercial licenses, 79 percent of total taxes collected over three weeks in October and November. Thái Nguyên also secured 1,992$BIC from timber-cutting licenses, and two other provinces followed suit, causing a Water and Forestry employee to complain to his superiors in Hanoi that no one was declaring for what purpose this revenue was being put.[161] The colonial practice of rewarding tax agents financially for any tax arrears and fines they collected was also resented.[162]

The provisional DRV government's volte-face on colonial taxes and the public's angry reaction received hardly any attention in the press, except for the brief flap in Hanoi over commercial licenses mentioned above. Perhaps editors had been warned off by the censors. A Việt Minh newspaper in Huế did print a letter from Quảng Bình province describing people's joy in August at the prospect of all taxes disappearing. The writer himself accepted the necessity of taxation, but urged radical simplification.[163] Tax protests continued to arrive in Hanoi from local committees. In mid-November, Bắc Kạn province reported that people remained quite upset about taxes, explaining that: "The Government announced complete elimination of imperialist taxes, yet now there are orders to collect them. At present the populace is poor, yet has to bear (chịu) a lot of monthly charges and support donations. Collections of the land tax this year will be difficult because from one family to the next finances are in crisis."[164] It soon became clear that total receipts would be way down from previous years.

Donations

Amidst the excitement of declared independence, popular donations of money, rice, time, and labor to the national cause provided a prospective alternative or at least complement to traditional taxes. Solicitation techniques had been developed by Việt Minh activists during 1941–44, then applied more ambitiously during the summer of 1945 when carving out a six-province liberation zone north of Hanoi. The ICP objective there was to form "national salvation" groups in each village, through which cadres would motivate members to part with grain or other valuables. Normally donors saw their amounts recorded carefully in a ledger, and received a small receipt if paper was available. Reasons for contributing ranged from humane altruism to fear of retribution if one refused (see chapter 9). With the massive proliferation of local revolutionary groups in August, each needing some degree of material support, citizens soon faced a bewildering range of solicitations. How were people to judge who was genuine, who was using scarce resources most effectively?

On 4 September 1945, the government announced formation of an Independence Fund (Qũy Độc Lập) to receive public donations in patriotic support of the Democratic Republic. People's committees at every level were instructed to select one person responsible for fund propaganda, collection, and accounting.[165]

Amounts collected were to be forwarded to a special office in Hanoi, there to be used exclusively for national defense, which undoubtedly enhanced the fund's credibility. However, province committees immediately began to ask if money could be taken from Independence Fund collections to meet local defense requirements, especially buying firearms and feeding soldiers.[166] When pressed hard by province chairmen in early October, Phạm Văn Đồng agreed that provinces encountering financial difficulties could withdraw increments of ten thousand piastres or less from their Independence Fund collections, providing the money was used for defense and the central government was informed each time. Haiphong asked to set up its own Independence Fund account, but was politely refused.[167]

Considerable popular enthusiasm surrounded the Independence Fund, at least in its early months of operation. Newspaper coverage, Việt Minh meetings, and people's committee prodding combined to foster a psychological climate of mass donation for a worthy cause. A striking woodblock print was used to promote the fund visually, featuring many hands passing bricks up to a bricklayer, with the DRV flag in the background.[168] Photographs of President Hồ were distributed to Independence Fund facilitators to present to more generous donors. At one point the Propaganda Ministry banned shops from selling images of President Hồ and gave the monopoly of such sales to the Independence Fund.[169] State employees were expected to lead by example with their donations. At the Northern Office, employees quickly subscribed one day's salary, writing their names and amounts on bureau rosters and being given in return a colorful receipt stating that the donor was "contributing to the building of national independence."[170] Fifty-three members of the PTT General Directorate contributed 837$50BIC, led by the director, Nguyễn Tường Thụy (brother of Nguyễn Tường Tam).[171] Five officers of the remnant Civil Guard contributed a total of 156$80BIC, while Company 3 (Region I) of the Liberation Army donated 400$54. Members of the Northern Region Investigation Bureau donated 2154$21, the Agricultural Office 292$, and the Ecole française d'Extrême-Orient, headed by Nguyễn Văn Huyên, a total of 482$.[172]

Province committees were very slow to report their Independence Fund collections, causing the finance minister to launch a query in mid-October. Several provinces subsequently brought collections directly to the Northern Office. Hải Dương reported 127,213$BIC collected as of 31 October, and deposited it in the local branch of the state bank as per central instructions.[173] Other provinces preferred to report only donations from prominent members of the old regime. Thus, Hà Đông itemized contributions from former governor Hồ Đắc Diễm, including seventy thousand notebooks, five thousand student copybooks, stationery, dinnerware, and furniture. Most of these items were sold for cash, but Hà Đông neglected to mention the amount of money garnered or where it had been directed.[174] Hưng Yên secured a pledge of thirty tons of paddy from former governor Trần Lưu Vy, with the first eight tons directed to the leper colony in Thái Bình, but the remaining twenty-two tons still not materializing seven months later.[175] Starting in late December, the Defense Ministry began to supervise the fund, instructing all provinces to convert cash to grain, store it carefully, and report details.[176] As late as February 1946, however, the Finance Ministry was still trying to find out how much each province had collected for the fund and how much had already been used. Some provinces now simply listed fund receipts as part of provincial income.[177] Occasionally fund donations came to the Northern Office directly from individual villages, probably because villagers distrusted intervening district or province committees.[178]

The Independence Fund had been operating for less than two weeks when the government began "Gold Week" *(Tuần lễ vàng)*, during which tables were set up in public venues to receive donations of jewelry, gold leaf, and other precious items from patriotic citizens. At the 16 September inauguration ceremony in front of Hanoi Opera House, President Hồ promised to give a gold medal he had received from overseas Vietnamese admirers to the highest donor during Gold Week.[179] Hanoi's leading independent periodical, *Thời mới*, recalled the classical exhortation to "scorn gold and honor righteousness" *(khinh vàng, trọng nghĩa)*, then warned that "anyone putting gold ahead of the Fatherland lacks patriotism, perhaps is a traitor."[180] Here was an opportunity for older women in particular to step forward publicly, present their jewelry, and receive patriotic recognition. Gold Week actually lasted for two weeks, with Supreme Advisor Vĩnh Thụy (Bảo Đại) presiding over the closing ceremony on 30 September.[181]

Most newspapers declared Gold Week a resounding success, yet no collection total was provided to the public, nor could I find a total in the Northern Office files. In Hanoi, Mme Vương Thị Lài won President Hồ's medal with a contribution of 109.872 taels (4.15 kilograms) of gold.[182] Apparently by the end of October 1945, few if any provinces had reported collection amounts, much less delivered the gold and other valuables to Hanoi. At a 4 November meeting, government officials reminded northern provincial chairmen of this obligation and received promises to deliver the goods within ten days.[183] The only province report I found on Gold Week collections is from Quảng Yên, as follows: Vietnamese gold, 2.882 kilograms; Western gold, 0.185 kilograms; silver, 40.925 kilograms; and currency, 1,083$35BIC. The province committee calculated all this to be worth 6,930$BIC, but said nothing about where it was going.[184] The only open criticism of Gold Week came later from the Vietnam Nationalist Party daily, which reported a village committee chairman yelling out, "Whoever donates gold is patriotic, whoever still wears gold wants to be a traitor!" Women hastily took off their jewelry and gave it to the chairman, receiving no receipts in return.[185] In early December, the principal Việt Minh daily paper claimed that Gold Week had netted valuables worth seven million piastres, which went into the Independence Fund to be "used in a worthy manner," and mentioned how much each rifle and cartridge might cost by way of example.[186] *Cứu Quốc* may have been reacting to rumors circulating about the gold from Gold Week being used to make ornate opium pipes for Chinese generals. From the fragmentary evidence available, I doubt if Gold Week pulled in more than three million piastres, and that mostly from better-off urban families. Much later, the historian Đặng Phong stated that the Independence Fund and Gold Week together obtained 370 kilograms of gold and twenty million piastres, roughly equivalent to annual head tax and land tax proceeds under the French.[187] If so, this was an impressive achievement, given the straitened conditions of late 1945.

A host of other funds materialized to solicit money and goods from the public. Most pervasive were the "national salvation funds" organized by scores of Việt Minh groups around the country. Each Việt Minh periodical called for national salvation donations to be sent to its editorial office, then printed the names of those who contributed and the amounts.[188] Teenage Việt Minh adherents made the rounds of homes in their neighborhood or village, often asking for only one condensed-milk can of rice per dwelling. Armed propaganda teams or militia squads approached merchants, landlords, and well-off farmers to request more substantial contributions. Việt Minh collections did not have to be justified or even reported to government administrators. The government only intervened in Việt Minh activities if it received a citizen complaint, in which case it normally referred the matter to local administrators for mediation. By contrast, Nationalist Party members going door-to-door in quest of contributions were at constant risk of police arrest on charges of extortion.

Two Việt Minh newspapers published in Huế offer us a rare glimpse into fundraising activities in late 1945. The owner of the Thanh Hóa town theater offered his premises free for a song and drama troupe to present a performance of "Patriotic Soul," with 1,117$BIC in audience donations going to the Liberation Army Fund. A list of priority items needed by the army was printed, including maps, binoculars, bicycles, clothing, paper, pencils, and books and serials for a mobile library. Donations would be gratefully accepted at three addresses in Huế.[189] Published lists of contributions to support the Việt Minh generally ranged from one-half to fifty piastres, with the occasional typewriter, pig, glutinous rice confections, or box of bread rolls recorded as well.[190] Mme Phạm Thị Chẩm of Đà Nẵng gave six thousand piastres to the National Guard. In Huế, "Mme Supreme Advisor Vĩnh Thụy," better known as former empress Nam Phương, donated five hundred piastres to a neighborhood Women's National Salvation group. In Quảng Trị province, National Guard propaganda teams collected 36,346$03BIC, plus quantities of clothing, blankets, rice, corn, and medicine. The National Guard headquarters in Huế organized an "American-style public benefit," where the fountain pen of French Lieutenant Antoine Budyneck, killed in action in Laos, was auctioned off for twenty-five hundred piastres. Fundraisers appreciated that the public was much more likely to donate to support the military than the civil government or the Việt Minh. Four National Guard regiments in central Vietnam reciprocated the fundraising activities of *Chiến Sĩ* weekly by donating money to purchase newsprint and ink.[191]

Following the outbreak of hostilities in Saigon in late September 1945, the provisional DRV government in Hanoi established a "Southern Resistance Fund" to coincide with popular outrage at British-French behavior. Initially, contributions were solicited at mass rallies and ceremonies to bid farewell to National Guard units heading south. It is hard to assess results from the fragmentary evidence found in the files. At the end of November, five locations reported contributions that totaled 13,883$47BIC, the smallest amount being 74$90 from Bắc Ninh prison. During the first half of December, Quảng Yên collected 6,180$BIC.[192] To step up public involvement, the Interior Ministry ordered each province in the north and center of the country to form a Committee to Support the Southern Resistance. Besides collecting money, clothing, and weapons, these committees were expected to organize meetings, send letters and books to the front, and assist families whose members had gone to battle or returned wounded.[193] One month later the name was changed to Committee to Support the Resistance, reflecting the spread of armed conflict to south-central Vietnam as well. In February, *Cứu Quốc* reported that local committees to support the resistance were indeed functioning. Committee collection totals to date ranged from 50$BIC to 15,668$75BIC, the latter achieved at the market adjacent to the Đáp Cầu paper mill.[194] After two further fundraising drives in May and June 1946, the Northern Committee reminded provinces to send in the money they had collected. At least seven provinces responded, with proceeds ranging from Haiphong's impressive 143,508$90BIC to Hà Nam's dismal 56$BIC. Donations of Chinese currency, rice, corn, clothing, medicine, and blankets were also reported. Radio Hanoi announced each province's contribution to the Resistance Fund, probably hoping to embarrass laggards.[195] The government's failure to announce national totals for this and other fundraising campaigns, or to tell the public exactly how the proceeds were being spent, may have caused people to contribute smaller amounts over time. The Vietnam Nationalist Party criticized the government for conflating public fundraising with highly partisan Việt Minh propaganda and accused local Việt Minh cadres of pocketing donations.[196]

Fundraising campaigns had certain advantages over standard tax collections: they were not colonial holdovers; each fund could be targeted to a popular government endeavor (building the army, famine relief, helping the south) as distinct from recurrent state expenditures; and they took advantage of the psychological intensity, mass meetings, and political fervor of the era. Contributions were also patriotic markers, with donors husbanding receipts in order to be able to verify allegiance if challenged. Better-off citizens in particular could be seen to donate significant sums to the cause, and they may have hoped thus to alleviate popular grievances over ill-gotten gains. However, it was hard to make government plans based on fundraising totals that varied dramatically by time and place. Donations of rice, clothing, blankets, or medicine required someone to inventory, store, and distribute all these goods. Reliance on thousands of voluntary fundraisers also risked threat or coercion being applied to extract contributions, as well as amounts being withheld by individual collectors or local groups.

The Land Tax

No land taxes (thuế điền thổ) could be collected until after the November 1945 rice harvest, giving the government several months to try to convince farmers of the necessity of continuing this traditional impost. A Finance Ministry edict reduced the land tax by 20 percent and exempted provinces badly flooded in August.[197] Nonetheless, dissatisfaction persisted in the countryside, and initial collection efforts were haphazard. The government relied in part on private tax collectors operating on a commission, often the same individuals who had done this under the French. The principal agent in Thái Bình claimed to have put two hundred thousand piastres of his own money into collecting 350 tons of paddy, which was then damaged by two storms. Not only did the state tax bureau reject the grain and refuse any financial restitution, but the agent was arrested as well.[198] Some local committees relied on Việt Minh groups to help them collect the land tax, but this too had its price when groups retained a portion of the grain for their own activities. A petition from a village on the outskirts of Hanoi denounced members of the Peasant National Salvation Association for harvesting rice from nonmembers and taking it away. The allegation was confirmed by investigators from the Northern Office, but the file is silent as to any followup action.[199]

From the first days of January 1946, the Northern Committee badgered province committees for November harvest details, including paddy totals, estimated surpluses, amounts collected for taxes, and arrangements for transport to government warehouses. Several provinces were chastised for permitting district committees arbitrarily to reduce land tax obligations. If Northern Committee message traffic throughout January is a reliable indicator, the land tax occupied more attention than any other issue.[200] Bắc Giang province posed the most problems. When tax collectors arrived at the large plantation of Lê Thuận Quát in Bắc Giang, they discovered that tenants had received a 25 percent reduction in rents as per government policy, half of the grain surplus had already been sold to the Defense Ministry, and most of the remainder had been donated to the Independence Fund. Eventually agents extracted a mere twenty tons in land tax.[201] When the Bắc Giang committee requested to Hanoi that private tax collectors be paid their commission of 24,030\$BIC, the Northern Committee replied that first the received taxes, in the amount of 1,782,342\$, must be deposited in the bank, per Finance Ministry orders.[202] Following a special visit to Bắc Giang in late March, Đào Văn Biểu, the Northern Office's principal roving investigator, reported that the province's land tax payments for the November harvest were still way behind.[203]

In May, the government issued land tax schedules for the remainder of the year. For northern Vietnam, one mẫu (thirty-six hundred square meters) of top-quality rice field was assessed at twelve piastres per annum, descending to ten and eight piastres for second- and third-grade fields. Non-rice land was taxed from twelve piastres down to 0\$10BIC per mẫu. Plantations continued to follow a 1940 colonial edict and were measured in hectares (mẫu tây), with the highest assessment being twenty piastres per hectare.[204] In central Vietnam, rice fields that benefited from state irrigation services were assessed from 35 percent to 56 percent higher than ordinary rice fields, and everyone was instructed to continue temporarily to apply colonial-era methods of categorization, reporting, and legal redress. A separate decree reduced the land tax by 15 percent in south-central provinces (Quảng Nam, Quảng Ngãi, Bình Định, and Phú Yên), presumably as incentive to defend against further French Army encroachment.[205]

After the June 1946 rice harvest, implementation of the land tax encountered fewer difficulties than a half year earlier, if the paucity of local complaints or telegraph traffic is a reliable indicator. Nonetheless, people continued to denigrate, evade, and occasionally obstruct tax collectors. In Ninh Bình province, when a National Guard unit was reported to be exceeding its authority by stopping tax collectors, the Northern Office simply asked the province committee to investigate and report.[206] Village chairmen skilled at levying taxes came to be prized by higher-level committees. During the summer of 1946, a number of provinces recommended reduction of the land tax, eventually provoking a rebuttal from Hanoi's Office of Direct Taxation.[207] In October, when Nguyễn Xiển presented his report on Northern Committee operations since August 1945, he listed land tax receipts at 32,150,439\$41BIC, or 77 percent of total tax collections.[208] While Xiển gave a positive spin to land tax proceeds, they amounted to only three piastres per capita. In defense of the ordinary peasant, some Việt Minh activists were quite content to see land tax collections remain low.[209]

Land tax collections following the November 1946 harvest are barely mentioned in Northern Office records. Some of the seventeen hundred tons of paddy frantically acquired for intended transport to Thanh Hóa in early December may have been tax grain. In its monthly report for November, the Bắc Kạn committee criticized itself for tardy tax remittances, due to village committees needing to wait until farmers converted their surpluses to cash.[210] After the French seized Haiphong and Lạng Sơn in late November, both farmers and local committees throughout the north may have been more likely to hold on to harvested paddy or cash derived from selling paddy rather than oblige the tax collector.

Much Effort for Modest Return

The DRV government was determined to collect a host of other taxes besides the land tax, despite the obvious reluctance of people to pay, and the many administrative complications. In early 1946, the Finance Ministry warned the public that all commercial and income taxes remained in force; persons not meeting the 1 March deadline for submission would be punished. A new tax was introduced on cinemas, music and dance halls, circuses, and geisha houses.[211] The newspaper of the General Union of Students proposed a tax on engagement and wedding ceremonies, which provoked negative reader response.[212] Another paper suggested rescinding the September 1945 decree limiting commercial licenses, and claimed this idea had Finance Ministry backing. Workers should be willing to pay income taxes, yet another paper opined.[213] The Customs Bureau reminded merchants and carriers that a 1944 colonial decree taxing foreign imports would be enforced vigorously. All persons transporting foreign goods inside Vietnam had to present customs authorization papers. Vendors at the Đồng Xuân market in Hanoi had to pay a monthly stamp duty on specific goods, notably pork, beef, soup (phở), silk, metals, and leather products.[214] Despite all these official warnings and media exhortations, tax receipts remained low. The Northern Committee's report of October 1946, mentioned above, itemized proceeds from eleven taxes besides the land tax. Together the abattoir tax, commerce tax, and commercial licenses garnered a disappointing 6,071,006$BIC (14.5 percent of total collections). The remaining eight taxes under Northern Committee jurisdiction took in miniscule percentages of total receipts, as follows: building tax (2.46), transport tax (1.75), entertainment tax (1.49), general profits tax (1.12), vehicle tax (0.90), mining tax (0.64), boat tax (0.08), and salary and benefits tax (0.03).[215]

Already by March 1946 it was clear to Finance Ministry officials that essential government expenditures far outweighed income derived from donations, taxes, and monopolies. People were getting fed up with being asked every month for two or three different donations. Public resistance to taxation remained high, and the capacity to collect receded as experienced government personnel took early retirement or leave without pay. Preparations were underway to print DRV money, but this action carried significant economic and diplomatic risks (see below).

In April, the government ordered a new "Defense Contribution" (Đảm Phụ Quốc Phòng) to be levied for only one year, both directly on every citizen between eighteen and sixty-five years of age, and indirectly as a supplement to certain existing taxes.[216] The preamble to the decree admitted that current taxes were not meeting national needs, then admitted that the system could not be overhauled yet. Citizens making a living quietly in rear areas had to help out at a time when soldiers were "putting their bones and blood forward to protect the country." The direct defense contribution was a flat five piastres per citizen, with exemptions for the poor or disabled, serving soldiers, and parents or spouses of soldiers killed in action. Rosters based on electoral rolls were to be drawn up and displayed in every village, with fines for local authorities who left people off the list or individuals who failed to pay the five piastres. Simultaneously, existing taxes directed at landlords, building owners, mine owners, holders of commercial licenses, state employees, and workers on wages would incur a defense contribution surcharge on a progressive scale. Thus, a small landlord assessed forty piastres in land tax would pay an additional 60 percent defense contribution, while a big landlord assessed three thousand piastres paid a further 200 percent, or nine thousand piastres in total. A minor state employee earning fifteen hundred piastres per annum would be levied a defense contribution of 0.50 percent, whereas a ranking official who received nine thousand piastres per annum was to pay 3 percent.

Cứu Quốc, the principal Việt Minh daily, was quick to publish a series of editorials designed to put the defense contribution in context.[217] The government needed "hundreds of millions" to arm, feed, and clothe the National Guard; to develop factories, mines, plantations, ports, and railways; and to pay state employees. It had to rely on the people, yet according to *Cứu Quốc* most taxes had been abrogated [sic], and all funds donated following the August Revolution were spent. Printing money would take time, and Vietnamese-French economic cooperation and foreign loans were matters for future negotiation. The editors urged readers to appreciate the difference between abusive colonial taxes and "shouldering responsibility in an independent country." It was impossible to build a nation based on voluntary donations. The DRV defense contribution was similar to special levies in European countries during World War II, to safeguard the nation, "much like the threat we face today."[218]

One month later other newspapers began to urge citizens to make their defense contributions. In Haiphong, *Dân Chủ* described a meeting between district committee members and local notables and landlords, who suggested a target amount to be raised for the defense contribution.[219] When upholding the defense contribution, *Gió Biển* insisted that "each citizen must consider himself/herself like a screw in a big machine, which is the DRV. The machine will run fast or slow, advance or stop short, depending on those screws, depending on all our countrymen."[220] In Vinh, *Dân Mới* gave readers a quick history of government budget constraints since September 1945, then emphasized that the defense contribution was "not an ordinary tax, but directed at a single purpose for several years, to achieve independence, freedom and happiness—which will bring benefits to families and individuals." In traditional fashion, a Nghệ An scholar offered a poem in support of the defense contribution.[221] In Huế, citizens were told to check the electoral rolls and then warned that anyone trying to evade their defense contribution responsibility would be hit with a fine ten times as large as the amount owed. A cartoon pictured citizens placing money bags on one side of a scale marked defense contribution, and Vietnamese tanks, ships, aircraft, and soldiers shooting on the other side.[222] In Kiến An, a National Guard newspaper stated that the defense contribution was required to "build an army that can stand beside armies of the world's major powers."[223] The Finance Minister, Lê Văn Hiến, made most of the arguments outlined above, then added that cessation of the defense contribution depended on fashioning a progressive income tax, which he admitted was extremely complicated.[224]

The defense contribution hardly ever appears in the Northern Office files, which is puzzling given the decree's requirement that province rosters be forwarded to regional committees, and that the Finance Ministry supervise the entire effort. Nguyễn Xiển's October 1946 report for the Northern Committee details revenues for twelve taxes down to the last piastre, but then simply states "the defense contribution is being collected." Perhaps data on five-piastre direct payments was sent on to the Finance Ministry, and no record has survived. If the defense contribution indirect surcharges on existing taxes are included in Nguyễn Xiển's figures, then collection results were even more disappointing. According to a later study, many persons eligible for exemption from the five-piastre levy insisted on paying as a patriotic signal.[225] Nonetheless, the absence of defense contribution figures from both the Northern Office files and subsequent Hanoi publications makes one wonder if the entire campaign faltered, or if perhaps amounts collected from citizens got no further than the province committees.

In June 1946, Xuân Thủy, editor of Cứu Quốc, addressed weaknesses in the tax collection system at its base.[226] Bad memories of colonial taxes remained fresh, Xuân Thủy acknowledged, yet he believed that people would be happy to remit taxes as citizens of self-governing Vietnam—providing the authorities collected in a fair manner. Then he pointedly asked local committee members nine questions. Was any tax income going for banquets, ceremonies, or personal aggrandizement? Was the issuing of receipts being ignored? Were illiterate citizens being deceived? Were personal enemies being accused unfairly of not paying taxes? Was peculation camouflaged by claims that someone had stolen a portion of tax proceeds? Were citizens treated poorly when they came to pay? Were armed militia sent out to collect? Did collectors insult people? And finally, did committee members use their taxation powers to gain revenge? Only if committee members were able to answer all nine questions with a resounding "No!" Xuân Thủy concluded, could they live up to President Hồ's requirement that public servants be incorruptible (liêm chính).[227]

Xuân Thủy's nine questions could equally have been asked of local Việt Minh groups and armed militia, who persisted in soliciting donations in kind or money throughout 1946 and beyond. Although in principle no one was obligated to give, and no government decree was violated by saying no, in practice collectors of informal donations had considerable psychological, social, and physical powers at their disposal. Over time, activists did find it necessary to come up with new fundraising techniques and to exercise more care when accounting for proceeds. Cultural evenings which engaged the audience were more likely to result in donations than having to listen to endless political speeches. The National Guard's Region III headquarters, based in Kiến An near Haiphong, organized a two-day sports and physical education carnival which generated considerable excitement and netted them fifty-nine hundred piastres, a large bronze lion (sư tử), silver and bronze sport cups, shoes, and a box of fifty bird-rifle cartridges.[228] As winter approached, a campaign to obtain knitted sweaters and blankets for soldiers generated good results among women's groups. In November, at the Hanoi Opera House, a program of solemn martial observances and light-hearted cultural performances was capped by President Hồ taking off his clothes to be auctioned— the winning bid coming in at thirty-five thousand piastres.[229]

Local newspapers became more assiduous when reporting individual and group donations to specific funds. Vui Sống, bimonthly publication of the National Guard's Medical Corps, itemized contributions to the central military hospital of meat from butchers, fresh milk from a dairy (ten bottles per day), and rice, flour, fried rolls, paper fans, and sandals from various shops. Individual readers pledged to donate specific amounts of money on a monthly basis. Cash contributions arrived at the editor's office from as far away as Thanh Hóa and Vinh.[230] In Huế, Quyết Thắng meticulously listed donations to five different causes: helping combatants in Nam Bộ, the Independence Fund, northern famine relief, the National Guard Support Fund, and assistance to disabled soldiers. Most donations now ranged between five and two hundred piastres. The National Guard Support Fund was particularly favored. During one short period it received 369 blankets, 136 trousers, 460 sweaters, 35 pairs of shoes, 15 straw mats, 12 conical hats, and one flask of medicinal oil. On another occasion workers in Huế gave this Fund 8,293$30BIC and a variety of goods and services.[231] In Nghệ An, district-level Việt Minh groups raised money to assist families of soldiers fighting in Laos and Nam Bộ. In some cases the families thanked the donors, then redonated the money to a resistance fund.[232] Quảng Ngãi province on the south-central coast reported remarkable levels of donations to patriotic causes, reflecting a revolutionary militancy that included public executions of alleged traitors. Some Quảng Ngãi citizens abstained entirely from Tết festivities in early February in order to give to military units.[233] In one eight-day period in April, 100,073$68BIC was collected in Quảng Ngãi to help combatants at the front and their families at home. Perusal of donation details, however, reveals that 91,000$ of the total came from five well-off individuals.[234] While citizens in Quảng Ngãi probably experienced the highest degree of compulsion to contribute, such pressures were far from absent elsewhere. The Nationalist Party newspaper, *Việt Nam*, leveled this accusation routinely against the Việt Minh. Very occasionally, Việt Minh papers admitted that force or the threat of force had been applied to collect "donations." One author pointed the finger at unnamed National Guard units which had used overt force rather than verbal persuasion to secure food from villagers. Worse yet, a unit in Nam Bộ was said to have reacted to the absence of rations by surrounding the local administrative committee office and threatening to shoot.[235] In late October 1946, when National Guard units were told to help villagers harvest the November crop in the Red River delta, troops were explicitly forbidden to accept any material support or gifts in return.[236]

MONOPOLIES

On taking power in late August 1945, the provisional DRV government had to decide what to do with the long-established colonial monopolies on salt, alcohol, and opium. Given popular dislike of the monopolies, and earlier Việt Minh promises to eliminate them, it was widely assumed that opium production and distribution would be banned outright, while salt and alcohol would either be put on the free market (subject to taxation) or sold privately at prices set by the government. In his 2 September independence declaration, Hồ Chí Minh denounced French sale of opium and alcohol as designed to "weaken our race." Eight days later, however, he signed a decree to "retain temporarily General Inspectorate rules and regulations on salt and opium," avoiding use of the term "monopoly" *(độc quyền)*.[237] Alcohol was treated differently, as described below. Faced with a near-empty treasury and smooth-talking customs officers, the government decided to retain monopolies at least until the wider tax system was transformed. Yet the government failed to prevent illegal sale of salt, alcohol, and opium despite issuing a host of decrees, granting considerable powers to the Customs and Indirect Tax Bureau, and threatening heavy penalties for noncompliance. As problems multiplied, the government amended regulations, adjusted collection procedures, and hiked prices to try to keep up with inflation. Administrative costs ate up most of the revenues, yet for some officials the state could not be seen to back down. Meanwhile the press had little to say about monopolies, pro or con.

Salt

Salt was the most important monopoly by far, reflecting its vital role in Vietnamese daily life, not only as a condiment but in food preservation. Inelastic price properties made control of salt attractive to both precolonial Vietnamese rulers and the French colonial regime. Salt was extracted from sea water evaporating in pans along the northern and central coast. In northern Vietnam, the majority of salt was produced in the Văn Lý quarter of Nam Định province. At the end of September 1945, contradicting the 10 September decree that had reiterated colonial salt and opium monopolies, the Finance Ministry suddenly told the Customs Bureau to "cease all restrictions and supervision of salt pans at Văn Lý," stop compelling producers to sell to the state, and limit customs activity to weighing, recording amounts, and purchasing salt for the government at a "reasonable price."[238] This instruction may have been a free-market salvo in the September–October intragovernment debate, described above, or a move aimed at making it less likely the Chinese Army would seize and exploit the salt monopoly. Either way, the Nam Định customs office proceeded to ignore the Finance Ministry edict and levy a "fine" on all boats transporting salt away from Văn Lý. This tax began at one hundred piastres (BIC) per ton, and soon escalated to seven hundred piastres per ton. As of early November, warehouses at Văn Lý and three smaller sites contained a total of twelve thousand tons of salt, guarded only by local people's committees. Salt not warehoused was being sold by workers on the open market.[239]

During this period the domestic price of salt soared well over one thousand piastres per ton, mainly due to exports to China. Chinese Army quartermasters and civilian traders used their inflated Chinese "gold dollars" to purchase and transport salt to Yunnan in particular.[240] Often they appear to have paid a fee to either customs officials or local committees. The Haiphong customs office reported that 76 percent of its October revenues derived from salt sales, and 56 percent of its November revenues.[241] The Hòn Gai city committee requested permission to export salt, or else it would not have money to pay its monthly expenses.[242] The Finance Ministry placed salt on its list of commodities banned for export and published official salt prices.[243] No one seems to have paid much attention to the fixed prices, nor did local committees feel obliged to help customs officers collect taxes on salt. In mid-January 1946, the minister of the interior, Võ Nguyên Giáp, felt it necessary to request that the three regional committees increase assistance to customs officers, who were encountering "many problems." As an example of appropriate action, Giáp cited the seizure on 24 December of seventeen boats carrying thirty-five tons of contraband salt.[244]

On 12 November 1945, DRV police arrested the former director of the Văn Lý Customs Bureau, Phạm Hữu Dược, on charges of corruption. The Northern Committee's senior investigator, Đào Văn Biểu, was dispatched urgently to Nam Định. Dược was accused of conspiring with the current director of the Northern Region Customs and Indirect Tax Bureau, Hoàng Văn Đông, to purchase five hundred tons of salt "outside the rules" and sell it for personal gain. Đông also had given a monopoly on salt transport to Stanley Lee of the Sino-Indochinois Development Corporation. The alleged salt transaction involved large Chinese "gold dollar" exchanges, so probably the government ban on salt exports was being violated as well. In March 1946, Đông was allowed a visit in prison from his father, who then wrote a letter to President Hồ stating that his son admitted to exchanging money for personal gain, but not to profiting from the salt transaction itself. Đông's face was swollen and he was coughing up blood, his father reported plaintively. Shortly thereafter the DRV Special Investigation Commission recommended that Đông and Dược be put on trial. However, Đào Văn Biểu, after pointing out that only forty-three tons of salt had actually been sold before discovery, proposed that the culprits repay that amount and be sacked from the public service rather than face trial and imprisonment. Biểu also suggested that Đông's superior, Trịnh Văn Bính, DRV general director of customs, be reprimanded but not sacked. There was a hint that Phạm Văn Đồng, finance minister in late 1945, should accept some responsibility as well. A dossier containing fifty-three documents was forwarded to the Hanoi court, but as of November 1946 Đông and Dược had yet to go to trial.[245] This was the highest level corruption case to embarrass the DRV government in its early years, and it must have further undermined the status and credibility of the Customs Bureau. Censors made sure that the case received no press attention.

In mid-January 1946, the Northern Region Economic Office warned the Northern Committee that salt stocks had been depleted to the extent that first-quarter allocations to provinces might not be met. Total stocks now amounted to 17,800 tons of salt, but with little hope of replenishment unless illegal sales could be stopped. "If Customs lacks the will, let us do it," the Economic Office suggested tartly. The Economic Office proposed to allocate 5,130 tons for January–March distribution at subsidized prices to the north's twenty-one provinces and two cities, compared to the normal requirement of 9,900 tons. The Northern Committee then informed everyone that allocations to lowland and midland provinces would be cut back 40 to 50 percent, while upland provinces would be reduced only slightly or not at all. Shortages were caused by large amounts of salt "being sold outside control of the Government," the committee admitted. It then urged all committees to help the Customs Bureau crack down on black marketeers.[246] In reality, many province committees had already made their own deals with private wholesalers, purchasing salt and then reselling to retailers at a profit. At one point the Northern Committee urged district committees to assume full responsibility for salt distribution, but this received a cool reception from province committees. Bắc Ninh's committee criticized continuation of the "French and Japanese monopoly system," instead advocating reliance on private traders subject to official supervision. If private salt traders undercut deals struck by province committees, however, they risked confiscation and fines.[247] The central government urged formation of local salt cooperatives, and some were duly established, but they usually turned out to be no more than renamed private enterprises.

Largely boxed out of province-level salt transactions, the Customs Bureau devoted itself to setting and resetting prices for whatever quantities of salt it still controlled. A similar salt regime existed in central Vietnam, but with seven smaller production sites scattered down the coast, and official prices set somewhat lower than in the north.[248] The Finance Ministry allocated seventy-five thousand piastres to repairing salt warehouses, particularly at Văn Lý.[249] Salt prices declined during the summer of 1946, perhaps due to a drop in exports following departure of most Chinese troops. Indeed, some salt began to arrive from coastal Chinese production sites, causing consternation among DRV officials trying to protect the state monopoly.[250] The conviction persisted that the state should and could micromanage salt production, pricing, and distribution, no matter what the complications.

From September 1946, the price of salt started to climb again. Province committees were stockpiling salt, preventing transport beyond province boundaries, and raising the price to retailers so as to help meet their growing operational budgets. The cost of officially authorized salt now exceeded the open-market price. In central Vietnam, customs announced monopoly salt prices that amounted to a 400 percent markup between producer and consumer.[251] In early October, the Northern Committee earmarked 9,108 tons of salt for distribution in the last quarter of the year and informed each province of its allocation. When specifying where to collect the salt, each message urged early action "due to the changing situation," presumably a reference to growing Franco-Vietnamese tensions.[252] This cautionary phrase would have caused province committees to tighten controls over salt even further. One month later the Northern Committee sent a vexed telegram to all provinces, pointing out that the open-market price of salt had shot up, causing trouble for citizens and exacerbating tax evasion. The message concluded, "Tell us if you are prepared to buy from us and sell cheaply to people. If not, we'll have to sell on open market to try to control price."[253] No province responded directly to the Northern Committee's question, and soon the proposal to release government salt on the open market was overtaken by the decision urgently to transport stocks from Nam Định to the northern hills, on defense grounds (see chapter 3).

Opium

Although most Vietnamese opposed opium smoking on moral, health, and economic grounds, the DRV provisional government nonetheless resolved to continue the opium monopoly for financial reasons, and because strategically positioned ethnic minority groups depended on opium growing for their livelihood. Revolutionaries routinely harassed opium smokers, and newspapers carried essays and short stories condemning the practice. At one point the Northern Committee ordered province committees to compile lists of all public servants addicted to opium and send that information to Hanoi. Only one reply came in, from Bắc Kạn, reporting no addicts.[254] A prison guard was summarily dismissed after he was discovered selling opium to inmates.[255]

What to do about opium smokers and opium parlors triggered divergent government responses. In Huế, newspapers reprinted a central region police message to all provincial police units ordering them to raid opium houses, issue heavy fines, put a placard on the chest of each user, and march the offenders around town. Anyone caught smoking a third time was to be dispatched to a deportation camp indefinitely. On learning of this initiative, the interior minister, Huỳnh Thúc Kháng, sent a stinging reprimand to the Central Region Administrative Committee and the national police director, pointing out that even courts did not have the right to set their own penalties, only to implement the law faithfully. Placard humiliation and indefinite detention "violate personal honor and individual freedom," Kháng insisted. In the absence of new laws, the police had to limit themselves to enforcing old laws still in place, for example by bringing to justice anyone who opened an opium parlor illegally.[256] Two very different visions of the Vietnamese revolution were being invoked here. The Nghệ An province committee had yet another suggestion: put an addiction tax of one hundred piastres per annum on each opium smoking pallet.[257]

The Customs Bureau was supposed to control opium purchase, transport, and sale, yet success was unlikely without help from local committees, where sympathy was minimal. Although few statistics are available on DRV opium monopoly operations, anecdotal evidence suggests poor results compared to the colonial era. The Haiphong customs office reported a collapse in revenue due to inadequate quantities of opium arriving via Hanoi.[258] The Customs Bureau proposed that upland province committees acquit their salt monopoly deficits with raw opium, "providing it is of good quality, smokable, and contains at least 10 percent morphine content."[259] In April 1946, as poppy plants neared harvest time in Laos, Customs requested border provinces to assist in tracking down and capturing smugglers. In particular, customs agents might need to call on local committees for armed force. Ly Quang Hiou was authorized by Customs to carry firearms and travel to Samneua to purchase raw opium. Another purchasing team showed up unannounced in Mộc Châu, causing the Sơn La province committee to query Hanoi as to its bona fides.[260]

One argument in support of continuing the opium monopoly was that otherwise illegal operators would rake in all the profits instead of the state. In practice, however, illegal trade in opium flourished side by side with the state monopoly. More than one province committee pointed this out when critiquing customs behavior. A few Việt Minh groups trafficked in opium to fund their activities, or for personal gain. In late 1945, a Việt Minh leader in Hà Đông province was arrested for keeping some opium from an amount seized from smugglers when assisting customs agents. Eight months later a military court ordered the man to remain in jail until he made restitution.[261] Missing quantities of captured opium could trigger a long paper chase. In December 1945, the customs director demanded to know what had happened to 3.41 kilograms of opium seized in Bắc Ninh. After extensive correspondence and investigations down to neighborhood level, the opium was located five months later in possession of customs personnel in Bắc Ninh.[262] The Finance Ministry possessed its own opium inspectorate, probably to look for mismanagement and corruption within the Customs Bureau.[263]

As French Army and civilian intelligence organizations resumed contact with ethnic minority leaders in upland provinces during the summer of 1946, the DRV opium monopoly came under further challenge. So'n La province appeared particularly vulnerable. In June, the So'n La committee reported that a "Việt Tiến cooperative" claiming to be part of the Finance Ministry, was ordering people to sell opium to it alone or face confiscation. Hanoi replied that unless the claimants possessed clear authorization from the Customs Bureau, they should be arrested and punished. In August, the customs director targeted So'n La as a hotbed of illegal opium activity, insisting that local committees jail traffickers and also fine them at least three thousand piastres per kilogram, slightly below the current market value of thirty-nine hundred piastres. The So'n La committee may have provoked this customs outburst by reporting individuals being relieved of five kilograms of contraband opium, but then proceeding to release the culprits for lack of a jail cell or rice to feed prisoners.[264]

In August 1946, the Finance Ministry and the Ministry for Society began to study ways to cut back both cultivation and smoking of opium. The Customs Bureau pointed out that the colonial law of 18 October 1921 was still in force, granting only the Mèo [Hmong] minority the right to grow poppies and collect the sap to make opium. Gradually reducing poppy cultivation in the highlands could reduce smoking in the lowlands. Equally, "if smoking is curtailed then poppy growers will not be able to sell the sap." In September, the Interior Ministry informed both northern and central region committees that a decree was being drafted to permit only "traditional locations" to continue growing poppies until substitute crops could be introduced. The Northern Committee copied this message to relevant provinces, inviting comment. Only one response appears in the files, from Hà Giang province, where mostly Mèo residents of three districts along the Yunnan border grew poppies for seven months and corn for the remaining five months. Providing there was not too much or too little rain, the province chairman estimated that Hà Giang produced four to five tons of opium sap per year. "For local people, opium sap is currency and corn is the principal food," the chairman stressed. He did not explain who processed the opium, simply stating that most opium was sold to the Chinese, not smoked locally. While he agreed that opium should be controlled with an eye to eventual eradication, the chairman mainly warned of the political dangers of removing Mèo liveli-hood before a substitute crop of equal value could be introduced.[265] No decree dealing with opium was issued before the outbreak of war. Meanwhile, the con-test for control of opium intensified between DRV and French organizations.

Alcohol

As during the French colonial era, the DRV Customs Bureau faced major prob-lems trying to enforce the alcohol monopoly at village level. Unlike salt or opium, many farmers possessed the means to make alcoholic beverages on their own. Also, there was a strong tradition of offering distilled rice "wine" *(rượu đế)* to one's ancestors on numerous occasions each year. Nonetheless, amidst the very real shortage of grain in late 1945, there seems to have been considerable popular sentiment for abstaining from fermentation and distillation until the food crisis was over. As mentioned earlier, at the end of October the government banned the making of rice wine. The November meeting of northern province committee chairmen with central government officials agreed to prohibit citizens from distill-ing alcohol, except in the uplands, where "superstition" *(mê tín)* had to be given precedence.[266] One week later, however, provisional President Hồ Chí Minh signed a decree banning not only production of traditional rice wine nationwide, but storage and consumption as well. Any person possessing rice wine had to declare it to Customs, which would seal and store the bottles or jars "until further no-tice." Fines for violations ranged from ten to two thousand piastres.[267] Recalling detested colonial practices, this decree appears to have been widely ignored or evaded. Results would have been different if President Hồ had instead exhorted farmers to defer distillation and donate the grain saved to famine relief. How-ever, some officials were more interested in restarting the alcohol monopoly, cit-ing fiscal necessity.

Controls on "Western alcohol" *(rượu tây)* and "Chinese alcohol" *(rượu tầu)* remained in effect based on colonial laws. The Chinese Army took control of French-owned distilleries in Hải Dương and Nam Định provinces.[268] In De-cember 1945, the Finance Minister declared both Western and Chinese spirits to be "luxuries" *(xa-xỉ phẩm)* subject to a supplementary tax.[269] Undaunted, a num-ber of entrepreneurs submitted applications to produce Western or Chinese spirits under customs license, complete with chemical analyses of contents and hand-drawn color samples of bottle labels.[270] Beer made a comeback in 1946, with the government fixing wholesale, pretax prices for Brasseries et Glacières de l'Indochine at 1$70BIC for a large bottle and 278$ for a one-hundred-liter keg.[271] Fontaine Distillery, which previously had been licensed to run the colonial alco-hol monopoly, now was allowed to resume modest production, focusing on in-dustrial alcohol. A French employee was granted laissez-passer papers, together with his wife and two children, so that he could work at the company's facility in

Nam Định.[272] The Société française des Distilleries de l'Indochine produced alcohol to power motor vehicles, with a pretax selling price set by the government at 579$BIC per one hundred liters.[273]

The ban on traditional rice wine may have been ignored in most localities, but if customs agents chose to enter a specific village or itinerant market in search of contraband spirits, the results could be contentious. After a customs agent uncovered a cache of rice wine in Hải Dương province in January 1946, he was set upon and injured by villagers allegedly led by an administrative committee member. The Hải Dương committee was ordered to investigate with an eye to court proceedings.[274] As the Customs Bureau forwarded other reports like this to superiors, it must have become evident to the government that local committees were mostly siding with the moonshiners rather than the revenuers. In May, without any explanatory preamble, President Hồ signed a decree abrogating the 10 November 1945 ban.[275] Now it was the turn of the Customs Bureau to evade orders, claiming that President Hồ's abrogation had not ended the validity of a 1921 French edict forbidding people from distilling spirits. Customs agents continued to search for and confiscate bootleg liquor (rượu lậu), sometimes backed up by specific Northern Committee or Interior Ministry instructions. In August, the Customs Bureau requested the Northern Committee to order the Hưng Yên committee to stop unfettered distilling of spirits in the province. Instead, three days later, the Northern Committee told all provinces that farmers could distill rice wine.[276]

This was not the end of the story, however, as customs agents continued to pursue local distillers. Thus, at nine in the morning on 5 October, the head of the Phu-Lô customs post in Phúc Yên province accosted twenty persons selling spirits in front of the pagoda at Thai Phù commune, ordering them to accompany him to his post. Instead, a member of Thai Phù committee allegedly insulted the agent and assisted the liquor vendors to disperse. In his report the same day, the customs agent condemned the whole group as reactionaries and requested they be punished as an example to others. "If everywhere we go we encounter reactionary forces like this, we might as well fold our hands," the agent concluded. Based on this report, the Northern Committee told the Phúc Yên committee to bring the offenders to justice and cashier the village committee member, despite the August permission for farmers to distill.[277] Clearly there were contradictory opinions and policies at work within the government, with some wanting to enforce a prohibition on local production of spirits, others wanting to focus on petty traders, and still others content to accede to popular custom. In some places a compromise was worked out, whereby local distillers sought and received customs permission to operate in exchange for a tax payment.[278] This was fertile ground for bribery or extortion, as some in the government must have realized.

Many Vietnamese revolutionaries wanted to stamp out all use of opium and alcohol on moral grounds. They preached state bans and, if that didn't work, then humiliation of smokers and imbibers in public. Việt Minh intellectuals called for a nationwide New Life Campaign that would consign addicts and imbibers to the dustbin of history (see chapter 9). Some revolutionaries may have supported the opium and alcohol monopolies as interim devices to cut back on popular consumption, ignoring the fact that Customs needed consumers to be able to justify its existence. While we lack DRV customs statistics on opium or alcohol monopoly revenue in 1946, indirect evidence suggests income was meager. Ironically, the presence of foreign military personnel drinking spirits and beer may have provided the Customs Bureau with its one financial success.

CURRENCY

For Vietnamese patriots, national independence and possession of a national currency went hand in hand. They felt ashamed to have to rely on a foreign currency, above all on the notes and coins of the former colonial exploiters. At the early October meeting of province chairmen with central officials, the minutes record one local representative stating bluntly, "We must print our own money quickly," and another pointing out how in China during the anti-Japanese resistance, even guerrilla zones printed money by lithograph. A Finance Ministry participant replied that the government had yet to control a suitable printing press. The newly appointed treasurer, Nguyễn Văn Khoát, focused on the more immediate problem of Vietnam being inundated with Chinese "gold dollars."[279] Periodic reports from province committees often mention popular puzzlement and frustration over the absence of DRV currency. The Hải Dương committee, for example, reported that while people believed in the government, and were ready to fight foreign aggressors, they worried about the currency situation and wanted a national bank to help unify the country.[280] Many people assumed that the new government could pay its way largely by printing money which all Vietnamese would accept as legal tender, a financial remedy occasionally stated in the press as well.

The DRV leadership possessed no experience in state finance, money supply and demand, or foreign currency dynamics. However, almost everyone had gone through depreciation of the Indochina piastre during the Pacific War, and those resident in China had seen what hyperinflation and rampant printing of bank notes could do to society. We don't know what deliberations took place on the question of issuing Vietnamese currency, but it is likely that some advisors warned the Cabinet that to print new notes on poor paper and make it an offense to refuse to accept the bills might undermine rather than strengthen the government. "Fiat money," which derives value from government promulgation, had proven a disastrous choice in some countries. Vũ Văn Hiền, finance minister in the Imperial Vietnam Cabinet of May through early August 1945, had a sound grasp of the checkered international history of unsecured bank notes, and appears to have remained on good terms with some DRV Cabinet members.[281] A confidential decision was made to stick with the piastre issued by the Bank of Indochina as an interim necessity, while moving to strike coins and print paper money for release at a time yet to be determined. Commitment to a national currency was symbolized by announcement of a Hanoi mint, although it possessed no staff or budget yet.[282]

The obvious place to produce paper money was the Imprimerie de l'Extrême-Orient (IDEO) in Hanoi, which had an offset press used by the Bank of Indochina to print piastre notes in increasing quantities from 1939 to August 1945.[283] However, the Chinese Army seized the IDEO facility in September and apparently released it to the French Army in June 1946. DRV attention then shifted to the Taupin lithograph printery in Hanoi, but first, teams of artists had to be recruited and paper and ink of sufficient quality located. Meanwhile a coin striking machine was found in the basement of a colonial museum, which soon was producing 2 hào (0.20 đồng) and 5 hào (0.50 đồng) aluminum coins bearing a star image and the words Việt Nam Dân Chủ Cộng Hòa (Democratic Republic of Vietnam). On 1 December 1945, the Finance Ministry announced release of the two-hào coin "in order to resolve the problem of worn out, torn, inconvenient paper money facing citizens engaged in commerce." The five-hào coin followed seven weeks later.[284] The paper notes referred to here were small-denomination BIC bills, which often had to be torn in half to provide small change. Economically speaking, the DRV coins were being insinuated within existing French currency, a precedent that would persist to some degree until 1954. Coins had played an important role in the Indochina colonial economy until gathering war clouds in 1939 caused first silver and then copper-nickel and nickel-brass alloy coins to disappear from circulation.[285] The two DRV coins appeared not to have circulated widely in the 1946 marketplace, probably due to insufficient quantity and to the fact that returning French forces brought with them a new batch of aluminum and copper-nickel coins marked République Française, Union Française, and Indochine Française.[286]

Southern Vietnam (Nam Bộ) probably saw the first printing and distribution of DRV-identified paper currency, in the form of "trust notes" (tín phiếu) given to citizens in exchange for BIC piastres, rice, and other necessities. This was not a new practice, having long been employed by Vietnamese political organizations when seeking material support, usually accompanied by a promise of redemption following victory. Now the Southern Region Executive Committee and some southern province committees issued trust notes of various denominations in the name of the DRV. Similar trust notes were soon being printed in Zone 5 (south-central Vietnam), with denominations ranging from one đồng to one thousand đồng. Each note carried a serial number, usually stamped after print-ing.[287] We don't know how often these trust notes—also known colloquially as "supply notes" *(phiếu tiếp tế)* or "exchange notes" *(phiếu đổi chác)*—moved from one citizen to another. Mainly they were seen by the populace as a political re-ceipt, to be displayed if one's patriotic commitment was questioned, not as a reli-able mode of exchange in the marketplace. Meanwhile, southern committees employed a red stamp to overprint BIC notes with the DRV name and province designation.[288]

By the end of 1945, four teams of artists in Hanoi were designing and etching DRV Finance Ministry notes of various denominations. Denominations were expressed in Vietnamese, Chinese, Khmer, and Lao, while the title DRV was in Vietnamese and Chinese. All carried the solemn image of President Hồ on one side and workers, farmers, or women and children on the other. Test printings were then conducted on paper of diverse quality and colors.[289] At the end of January 1946, President Hồ authorized the issue of "Vietnam paper money" in central Vietnam south of the sixteenth parallel. The idea was to test usage in an area out of reach of Chinese or French meddling. Responsibility for implementa-tion was assigned to the Central Region Administrative Committee in Huế.[290] However, it was the chairman of the Quảng Ngãi province committee who first burned a one-hundred-piastre note to symbolize the end of dependence on colo-nial currency, then issued to the public DRV notes featuring the image of Presi-dent Hồ. According to an official study, members of the audience were deeply moved to be able to hold in their own hands authentic Vietnamese currency. "Heavens, it's Elder Hồ money, our money!" people told each other.[291] Sources fail to tell us whether this money had been produced in Hanoi and transported down the coast, or printed locally. Not until March did the Finance Ministry es-tablish a management committee for the Vietnam mint. In April, the mint was assigned a respectable budget of three hundred thousand piastres per month.[292] Money continued to be printed experimentally at one of several small lithograph outlets until the government purchased the Taupin printshop from its French owner.[293]

The decision to put President Hồ on DRV paper money presumably occa-sioned internal government discussion, yet nothing of it has surfaced from the archives or in later publications. In 1946, so far as I can ascertain, no other state in the world featured the living head of state on its paper currency. During World War I, the United Kingdom had placed a profile of King George V on its Treasury bills, but discontinued the practice at war's end.[294] There was no precedent among French banknotes, metropolitan or colonial. The Republic of China pictured the deceased Sun Yat-sen, not Generalissimo Chiang Kai-shek. Marshal Stalin re-mained absent from Soviet Union money. The presidents on American greenbacks

FIGURE 22. One-hundred đồng DRV "finance note," with Hồ Chí Minh on one side and images representing the fights against illiteracy, foreign aggression, and famine on the other. In *100 Năm Tiền Giấy Việt Nam,* 153. Courtesy of Vietnam National Library.

were long deceased. Coins were completely different, with Alexander the Great, Augustus Caesar, and Edward the Confessor setting precedents for living representation that still resonated for some twentieth-century heads of state. In September 1946, Acting President Huỳnh Thúc Kháng decreed the striking of a one đồng aluminum coin with President Hồ featured in profile.[295] However, this coin quickly paled in significance compared to "Elder Hồ paper money" *(Đồng bạc Cụ Hồ)* representations. No one seems to have worried about Elder Hồ becoming wrinkled, dirty, smelly, and torn as bills passed across many hands and were carried on many bodies. The first issuing of Elder Hồ paper money in Quảng Ngãi was sufficiently favorable for the central leadership to instruct Hanoi engravers and printers to move ahead on a larger scale. President Hồ must have approved use of his face as a national icon.

In August 1946, Acting President Huỳnh Thúc Kháng instructed the Finance Ministry, Interior Ministry, Justice Ministry, and Central Region Committee to issue Vietnam paper currency in central Vietnam north of the sixteenth parallel. Anyone counterfeiting or otherwise "acting to sabotage the value of Vietnam's currency" would be prosecuted before a military court.[296] This was the first official reference to monetary value, without elucidation. Verbally, citizens were informed that one Vietnam đồng equaled one BIC piastre. Already in July, bank branches in Thanh Hóa, Vinh, and Huế had started to exchange đồng for piastres at parity. Government bureaus in Hanoi also began to pay employees a portion of their salaries in đồng, causing some confusion and disgruntlement.[297] The government held back from promulgating any decree making the đồng legal tender nationwide, partly due to logistical limitations, partly because currency was the subject of negotiation in Paris. In late August, however, the Finance Ministry defended expanding currency circulation across the country as the "legitimate act of a self-governing country." It assured citizens that the currency was guaranteed by the government, while also condemning unnamed reactionaries "who spread rumors designed to reduce the value of Vietnam's money."[298]

As DRV notes began to circulate in northern as well as central Vietnam, the press asked a number of questions. Were state organs obliged to accept đồng? Could đồng be used to pay taxes? Were there limitations on exchange? Soon a decree authorized payment of DRV taxes in Vietnam currency, BIC piastres, gold, or silver. Then the Finance Ministry stated that province-level Treasury offices could give anyone đồng in exchange for piastres, but to obtain piastres in exchange for đồng it would be necessary to fill out application forms at one of three bank locations (Hanoi, Haiphong, Nam Định).[299] No one said anything official about the exchange rate. The main Haiphong newspaper eventually claimed blithely that the two currencies had equal value, but urged citizens to use the đồng out of national pride.[300] A senior military officer in Quảng Ngãi told readers incorrectly that the 14 September modus vivendi did not restrict circulation of Vietnamese currency.[301]

In early November 1946, the currency question came up for public discussion that coincided with reconvening of the National Assembly. *Dân Chủ* (Haiphong) called for Vietnam's money to be issued nationwide. "The people want it," editors claimed, adding that DRV currency "can be a weapon of economic struggle." BIC notes were said to be "temporary and not guaranteed in value." The next day, the National Assembly affirmed that Vietnam's currency should circulate throughout the country. Two weeks later, in an unusual act of lobbying, employees of the

Finance Ministry met and called for the government to proceed immediately with a nationwide currency issue and payment of all public servant salaries in đồng.[302] At this same time, as a hedge against widened Franco-Vietnamese conflict, Finance Ministry personnel were shifting a portion of the money-printing operation to Chinê plantation, forty kilometers southwest of Hanoi.[303] Aluminum coins were already being struck at a facility in the Thái Nguyên hills, north of the capital.[304] Amidst all this printing and striking, no one cautioned against the possibility of a rapidly depreciating đồng and the consequences for the economy or public opinion.

Stacks of new DRV notes had already reached many northern provinces before the 8 November National Assembly vote of approval. The Bắc Giang committee complained that notes were so poorly printed that people feared they were counterfeit. Bắc Kạn promised to begin paying government employee salaries in DRV notes and coins from December.[305] However, the Northern Committee wanted all provinces to use the notes to acquire BIC currency from the populace, not to meet current expenses. Warnings to this effect accompanied each consignment of new DRV bills sent to the provinces, together with an explanation that BIC cash was needed for the resistance. The monetary amounts of currency dispatched to each province at this time were not large, ranging between five hundred thousand and three million đồng.[306] This probably reflected transport and security limitations, as well as uncertainty about public readiness to part with BIC currency. As Franco-Vietnamese tensions escalated in Hanoi in early December, the DRV Treasury encouraged civilian evacuees to exchange their BIC piastres for DRV notes, much to the irritation of French observers, who spoke disparagingly about "*la monnaie Ho Chi Minh.*"[307] Whether farmers would accept the new money from evacuees in payment for rice remained to be seen.

The French authorities took an energetic part in currency affairs as well, beginning with the French Army carrying large amounts of new BIC notes and Indochine Française coins to Saigon in late September 1945.[308] The Indochina high commissioner, Admiral d'Argenlieu, would have liked to demonetize all BIC currency printed in Indochina after the 9 March 1945 Japanese coup, but the job of separating all those notes from precoup notes was nigh impossible. Instead, d'Argenlieu focused solely on the five hundred piastre note, the largest denomination in circulation, in the process giving the DRV government a harsh lesson in currency politics.

On 17 November 1945, the high commissioner decreed five-hundred-piastre notes no longer legal tender throughout Indochina. Those five-hundred-piastre notes printed between 9 March and 23 September 1945 lost all value, while those printed earlier could be exchanged at 70 percent of value if deposited in a recognized bank by 25 November. The Chinese command in Hanoi objected strongly to d'Argenlieu's unilateral decree, arguing that it threatened public order in their zone of occupation. An internal Chinese report also estimated that one-third of all five-hundred-piastre notes in circulation were held by Chinese civilians. On 26 November, a crowd gathered in front of the Hanoi branch of the Bank of Indochina to protest the French decree and to demand that the bank exchange their five-hundred-piastre notes for other BIC denominations. Shots were fired, resulting in six Vietnamese and Chinese fatalities, closure of the bank, growing threats directed at French civilians around the city, and Chinese Army arrest of the BIC general manager and Hanoi branch manager. American Brigadier General Philip Gallagher then mediated a deal whereby d'Argenlieu rescinded the withdrawal of five-hundred-piastre notes north of the sixteenth parallel and the Chinese Army released the two BIC officials.[309] South of the sixteenth parallel, people had no choice but to exchange their precoup five-hundred-piastre notes at a 30 percent discount, then find someone buying postcoup notes for shipment north. In February 1946, French intelligence reported postcoup notes still being purchased at 200–250$BIC in Saigon, for transport to Hanoi in Chinese trucks.[310]

Bank of Indochina branches in Hanoi and Haiphong threw up bureaucratic hurdles for anyone wishing to exchange five-hundred-piastre notes. People had to wait a long time and fill out multiple documents. Others went instead to the DRV Treasury, or exchanged notes at a discount on the street. An employee of the Northern Office sent his pregnant wife to the Treasury to exchange two five-hundred-piastre notes, but she kept being pushed aside by others before reaching the counter. He petitioned his superiors for time off to accomplish the transaction.[311] Province committees tried to pay their bills with five-hundred-piastre notes, thus passing the exchange problem to someone else. Some provinces were less skilled at this than others: Thái Bình claimed to have nothing but five-hundred-piastre notes left in its account in April 1946.[312] The Irrigation Bureau reported some dike repair contractors refusing to accept five-hundred-piastre notes in payment.[313] The Hanoi city committee worked out a roster whereby each neighborhood was given a time for residents to present their five-hundred-piastre notes to swap for smaller denominations.[314]

Painfully aware that France continued to crank out new currency to help finance its operations in Indochina, the DRV government declared invalid and subject to confiscation all BIC notes issued after the 6 March 1946 Preliminary Accord. The Finance Ministry then specifically banned circulation of new printings of the old one-hundred-piastre "Dupleix" note, and the entirely new one-hundred-piastre note that pictured Angkor Wat statues on one side and five Vietnamese women shouldering goods on the other side.[315] Three months later, the ministry banned the new fifty-piastre note as well.[316] A few newspapers tried to explain to readers which BIC notes were now legitimate tender and which not, but the message was confusing.[317] Most merchants and shopkeepers appear to have ignored these DRV bans. A different form of control, begun earlier in the south, was to overstamp BIC notes with the national title "Democratic Republic of Vietnam," plus a regional or provincial designation. BIC notes not possessing that stamp could be confiscated.[318]

Counterfeiting had bothered past French colonial authorities on occasion, and it vexed the short-lived Imperial Vietnam government during the summer of 1945.[319] All BIC notes contained a stern written warning that forced labor was the punishment for falsifying bank notes. The DRV government, having committed the country to using BIC currency, was then put in the uncomfortable position of admonishing citizens against printing or passing counterfeit BIC bills, and occasionally punishing perpetrators. At one point a notice was sent to northern provinces threatening to label as traitor anyone who failed to destroy counterfeit BIC notes.[320] Việt Minh newspapers sometimes accused the Vietnam Nationalist Party of printing and circulating fraudulent BIC notes, and DRV police listed counterfeiting as one crime justifying arrest of Nationalist Party members in July 1946.[321] Newspapers printed Treasury descriptions of specific false BIC notes to enlist the public in identification.[322] In May 1946, the Yên Bái province committee included among twenty-one persons recommended for dispatch to a deportation camp a number of alleged passers of counterfeit money. The Hà Nam police intercepted persons in possession of sixty counterfeit twenty-piastre bills and detained them for trial.[323] Đặng Thị Hưng, wife of the Gia Lâm assistant train station master, was put on trial in June on charges of circulating counterfeit currency.[324] None of these communications addressed the question of witting versus unwitting possession of false bills. Nor were there any reports of uncovering plates or a printing press used in counterfeiting.

All DRV currency printed in 1946 carried the following warning: "By Vietnam Government decree, anyone counterfeiting or acting to sabotage (phá hoại) the Government's paper money will be punished according to military law." This imitated the French injunction but widened it, possibly to include burning, defacing, tearing, or even undermining the value of DRV notes. A "currency war" developed from 1947 onward, and included each side counterfeiting the other's money.

CLOTH

Cloth occupied the attention of DRV administrators more than any other commodity except rice. Output from textile mills in Nam Định and Haiphong had declined steadily during the Pacific War. The French authorities closely regulated raw cotton, yarn, and cloth production and distribution. By 1944 it was difficult for ordinary Vietnamese to obtain even two or three meters of cloth per year. By early 1945, poor rural inhabitants in the north had been reduced to wearing mats or woven grass coverings. Yet the government prevented mills and cloth wholesalers from selling significant stocks in their possession.

In early September 1945, the Northern Office compiled figures on the quantities of cloth currently in state or private warehouses, coming up with preliminary totals of 417,082 meters of cotton cloth and 121,549 meters of silk.[325] These were hardly large amounts if divided by the total northern population of ten million, yet mill managers and some wholesalers advised against unloading hundreds of thousands of meters of cloth on the market, for fear that prices would drop precipitously. The DRV government also wanted to give the Liberation Army top priority in cloth allocations. The army immediately received 37,057 meters of better quality cloth, plus 147,266$BIC in receipts from recent cloth sales. Another 3,700 meters of cloth previously reserved by the French to go to prisons in Laos and Guangzhouwan was turned over to the army. The Hanoi People's Committee obtained 20,000 meters of cloth, adjacent provinces received 19,000 meters total, and quantities were earmarked for other provinces. From late September, however, Chinese Army units seized large quantities of cloth before DRV adherents had the presence of mind to shift and hide stocks elsewhere.

The main DRV government response on cloth was to ask all ministries and bureaus urgently to submit their own fabric requests. This triggered a frenzy of applications, allocation decisions, occasional remonstrations, and issuing of acquisition permits. Often there was ambiguity about whether a unit was being given cloth or was expected to pay for it. When challenged by the Northern Economic Bureau to pay, units might back out, seek a lower price, or buy on credit. The Foreign Ministry requested 186 meters of "English khaki" to outfit its thirty-one employees, but received 155 meters of ordinary cotton cloth instead. Two hundred meters of cloth for street banners and an unspecified quantity for flags was needed by the Propaganda Ministry. Instead it was authorized to buy 300 meters of hemp cloth. Phạm Văn Đồng sent a vague request for mosquito nets and wool pullovers for Vietnam Military Academy students. Phan Tử Nghĩa (Northern Economic Bureau) asked Đồng about quantities and mode of payment. Đồng told him he needed 405 nets and pullovers, but said nothing about payment. Nghĩa allocated the Academy 4,860 meters of netting and cloth. When the Yunnan Railway submitted a list of 205 members of its Hanoi repair facility in order to obtain cloth, an Economic Bureau clerk calculated that a total of 717.5 meters would be needed to make one shirt and one pair of shorts for each worker. Later the railway was told that 5,000 additional meters of cloth had been reserved for its other employees, provided that each unit sent in rosters "to facilitate control and distribution." Rosters duly materialized and were processed. The Hanoi Industrial School was authorized 1,500 meters to clothe its pupils, contingent on pupil rosters being submitted. Seven drivers at the central motor pool reminded the Economic Bureau that the previous authorities had given them one set of winter clothing each October. They were provided with slips to buy five meters of cloth each. The Boy Scout Association was approved to purchase 850 meters of green and 1,400 meters of white cloth. Some organizations complained that the cloth they received was moldy or had been nibbled by rats.

By the end of October 1945, most applicants for cloth were being told by the Economic Bureau that remaining quantities were reserved for the army. In November, the Indian-owned Muthurama Company reported that it had dispatched 8,800 meters of cloth to Faifo (Hội An) and Quảng Ngãi, and offered to send more. The Army Quartermaster Corps purchased an additional 8,700 meters from Muthurama and notified Huế authorities. Perhaps hearing of these transactions, the Bình Thuận province committee further south asked if restrictions on sale of cloth had been lifted, adding that "we're in a war situation and may need special handling." A Yunnan Railway request for 340 meters of cloth to make oil rags was rebuffed, but it made its case twice again, and finally received a permit to purchase from a private source.[326] Those applicants who failed to receive any cloth included the Interior Ministry, Labor Ministry, Garage Aviat, and two orphanages. Some cloth remained available on the black market, provoking citizen complaints about high prices. At least one merchant ventured to Savannakhet in order to buy cloth that may have been Thai, agreeing on return to turn over to the government 23 percent of acquired stocks as tax.[327]

Production of new cloth received only a tiny fraction of government attention, compared to time spent on allocation of existing cloth. The Nam Định province committee's report for September 1945 states that the Société française annamite de textile (SFATE) textile mill produced 34,353 meters of cloth during the first two weeks of the month, but was running short of the raw materials normally supplied from provinces down the coast. The SFATE mill counted 417 workers, sixty-one Vietnamese office staff, ten Westerners, and four métis whom the Nam Định committee recommended be sent elsewhere.[328] Towards the end of 1945, the French manager of the SFATE mill advanced 472,282$BIC to purchase 27.781 tons of Nha Trang cotton, but the Nam Định province committee resold most of the cotton before it reached the mill and used the money for "defense purposes." In May 1946, the Northern Region Committee told Nam Định to repay the money, and in September it repeated this instruction, but the files contain no response.[329] We can surmise that the cotton had been distributed to handicraft spinners and weavers in Nam Định, in part to make uniforms.

With the DRV government trying to maintain wartime controls on buying and selling of raw cotton, supplies continued to decline. In March 1946, the Commerce Bureau recommended that controls be abrogated, new cotton growing cooperatives and private enterprises be encouraged, and more cotton purchased from central Vietnam. "We need new ideas," the Commerce Bureau concluded plaintively. However, the Northern Committee continued to uphold controls in the name of fighting inflation and opposing speculators. As long as textile mills in Nam Định and Haiphong remained under Chinese Army supervision, the committee added, available raw cotton was better directed to handicraft weavers.[330] Later in the year, when the Chinese were gone, the Northern Committee acknowledged that the Nam Định mills had a "raw material problem," then stated enigmatically that the Nam Định committee was in a position to restore supplies, perhaps a reference to raw cotton diversions to local weavers.[331] In late November the National Economy Ministry asked the Northern Committee to ascertain how many facilities besides those in Nam Định had the capacity to convert Indian raw cotton into yarn, and how many northern villages specialized in weaving cloth. Cables went out, but there were few responses, all negative.[332]

From September 1946, the Northern Economic Bureau told everyone that it was no longer distributing cloth, nor was it authorized to intercede with private companies on behalf of government employees seeking cloth. Nonetheless, scores of requests for cloth continued to come in. The Yên Bái province committee requested 450 meters of red and 50 meters of gold cloth to make national flags in order to replace paper flags that fell apart after one use.[333] Trần Duy Hưng, chairman of the Hanoi city committee, asked for 6,000 meters of khaki cloth to outfit 1,110 policemen before winter set in. Hưng offered the following political justification: "Police ought to be highly regarded by foreigners and respected by the public. They are loyal subjects (hiền thần) of law and order. Symbolic of government by the people, police apparel needs to be smart."[334] This request was routed to the Nam Định committee with a recommendation that the amount of cloth be reduced to 5,500 meters. It would take a lot more than uniforms for the police to gain popular respect. In October, the French mill managers raised cloth prices, claiming the French authorities were levying a tax. The Nam Định committee protested, but had to accept the higher prices.[335] Cloth paperwork continued right up to 19 December, an incredible expenditure of time and effort for such small returns.[336] It was also harbinger of the state allocation system that was reasserted in the early 1950s and persisted for forty years.

COAL

As a commodity, coal stood fourth behind rice, cloth, and salt when it came to DRV government attention. The coal mines developed during the colonial era in northeastern Tonkin fueled rail and water transport, ran the electric power stations and water pumping plants, and provided consumers with charcoal briquettes for cooking. For lack of petrol during and immediately following the Pacific War, all motor vehicles, hydraulic pumps, generators, and turbines continued to run on either charcoal gas or alcohol. The first decision of the government regarding coal involved a boat owner named Trương Đức Âm, whose prior contract to move coal from the coast to Hanoi and Đáp Cầu was renewed on 1 September 1945 by Đào Trọng Kim, communication and public works minister. One of Âm's boats that had been detained by a Việt Minh group in Bắc Ninh was quickly released, and all of his fifteen vessels received new operating permits.[337] A few days later, M. Max Xorius of Hanoi was authorized to transport five hundred tons of coal from Haiphong to Saigon by sea, but it is unlikely this got underway before British-French forces mounted their 23 September coup in Saigon.[338] Soon Chinese Army units were helping themselves to coal stocks and encouraging overseas Chinese to take over several mines in Quảng Yên province. The latter met opposition from Việt Minh groups, who had allowed French supervisors and technicians to remain on site in hopes of sustaining output.[339] Coal arriving in Hanoi was allocated first to the two power stations and the water works, then to Bạch Mai hospital, the Pasteur Institute, the central motor vehicle depot, and the Hanoi City People's Committee.[340]

In November, a Northern Committee edict declared production, transport, and sale of coal to be free of longstanding controls, while reserving the right to supervise quality and "if necessary" to fix a price for amounts needed by the government.[341] Even this modest move towards an open market in coal was resisted, however. The Economic Bureau acknowledged the edict, then commented, "But we still are responsible for securing enough coal for public facilities and transport."[342] In January 1946, the Water and Forestry Bureau calculated that DRV ministries and Bắc Bộ bureaus and departments would need 59,892 tons of coal (per annum?), with Defense requiring 11,000 tons (18.4 percent of the total) and Communications and Transport 12,200 tons (20.4 percent). By March, the Water and Forestry Bureau was making its own charcoal briquettes from timber and distributing some to ministries and bureaus. The price of coal climbed from six piastres per cubic meter in November 1945 to at least fifteen piastres in March 1946. Complaints poured in that coal was unavailable, of poor quality, or too expensive.[343] State distribution of briquettes made from coal dust functioned side by side with private distribution, a pattern that would spread to other commodities in coming months and years.

Problems began at the coal mines themselves. The Hòn Gai city committee stated that coal mines in its vicinity were not producing much. Thái Nguyên province reported that the Phấn Mễ coal mine was flooded and no pumping could be accomplished yet. There were 150 workers on site, but no manager or engineer.[344] The Northern Office received a complaint that the people's committee adjacent to the Phấn Mễ mine was failing to protect it: "Papers are being burned, account ledgers destroyed, valuable equipment smashed." With the French mine director no longer present, the petitioner pleaded for help in preserving the site so it could supply coal to the railway.[345] The Public Works Bureau warned that the growing shortage of coal was going to pose "real problems for electricity generation in particular."[346] The best-quality anthracite was going to China at considerable profit to those involved.[347] From January 1946, the Minerals and Industry Bureau began compiling files on each coal mine, detailing its previous history and the current status of its workers, technicians (if any), equipment, and financial accounts. Amidst all the messages trying to deal with week-to-week difficulties there was underlying appreciation of the importance of coal to Vietnam's future. The Economic Bureau negotiated a deal to exchange coal for firearms from China, at the rate of four tons coal for one U.S. rifle and one hundred rounds of ammunition.[348]

Following the March 1946 arrival of the French Army in Haiphong and Hanoi, French managers and technicians returned to more coal mines, and indeed were encouraged to do so by the DRV authorities. However, they found the workers better organized than before, and often determined to share in decisionmaking. Following withdrawal of most Chinese troops in June, French managers became more assertive about setting wages, controlling mine records, and selecting buyers. Nonetheless, they could not prevent workers from siphoning off coal for private sale, and at open pit mines it was common for local villagers and other "illegals" to carry away coal as well. With the French Army usually not in a position to intervene, owners and managers took their complaints to the DRV central government in Hanoi, which generally referred the matter to the relevant provincial committee.

A major controversy erupted at the Mao Khê mine in Hải Dương province, where by Franco-Vietnamese agreement a DRV National Guard unit was posted to "maintain order." The Hải Dương committee approached the Mao Khê manager to demand two thousand to three thousand tons of coal per month in payment for this service. General Jean-Étienne Valluy, commander of French forces in northern Indochina, protested this action to Hoàng Văn Thái, chief of the National Guard's General Staff, saying that it resembled the predatory behavior of Chinese troops. Assuming a pedagogic tone, General Valluy added: "This request [for payment] is inconceivable on the part of a democratic army. It is not for personal profit that such an army is charged by its Government to assure order, but on behalf of the collectivity and for general prosperity."[349] The Hải Dương committee denied Valluy's charge, saying that he had been deceived by the French administrators at Mao Khê, in particular M. Richard, who circulated this story after losing a large amount of money on the black market. The DRV government also vehemently rejected General Valluy's assertion, but it soon learned that the Hải Dương committee had indeed made such a request. Hoàng Văn Thái was furious, telling the Northern Committee, "I strongly object to the Hải Dương committee having used the army to enhance its finances (public? private?), thus wounding the prestige of the Government and the reputation of the National Army." Soon after, the French owners of the Mao Khê mine offered the Hải Dương committee five thousand piastres per month to "assure security," which apparently did not bother General Valluy. Not until two months later did the

Interior Ministry request that the Northern Committee "reprimand severely" the Hải Dương committee for this episode. Other problems persisted, however, with the Minerals and Industry Bureau criticizing Hải Dương for "ignoring the national need to reduce the coal shortage," and for authorizing groups to mine who were not approved by the bureau. As of mid-November, it appears that French nationals had withdrawn from five coal mines in Hải Dương due to increasingly volatile conditions.[350]

During the summer of 1946, total output of coal appears to have increased significantly, yet this did not translate into more coal for the state. Hanoi city remained short of its requirement of six thousand tons per month. Repeatedly the government instructed the Hòn Gai, Quảng Yên, and Hải Dương committees to give the capital top priority. In July, twenty-five boats transported coal upriver to Hanoi, the largest vessel carrying 753 tons, the smallest 35.[351] Trương Đức Âm, who we met earlier receiving the first shipping authorization in September 1945, now reported that his boats encountered time-consuming delays, mainly due to bigger foreign vessels getting priority at the loading facility, and occasionally because a boat was seized by pirates (thổ phỉ) until ransom was paid.[352] Clearly French coal companies were now exporting coal without consulting the DRV government. Hanoi also refused to pay open-market prices for coal, and chastised the Haiphong city committee in particular for doing so.[353] Meanwhile, requests were denied from province committees needing help in repairing electric generators because no coal was available to fuel the equipment.

By September 1946, the French Army was assisting French coal companies in trying to replace recalcitrant miners with workers from elsewhere. A DRV labor investigator, recalling unsuccessful attempts by the French in 1936 to bring five hundred miners from China, recommended that the Foreign Affairs Ministry approach the Chinese government to forestall this option now. The Haiphong police stopped a recruiter escorting forty laborers from Nam Định to a mine near Hòn Gai. DRV attempts to discuss wage rates with the French were rebuffed repeatedly. As the investigator pointed out, it did not help that the government had delayed issuing any decree setting a national minimum wage.[354] Adult underground miners were being paid 2$40BIC per day, adolescents 1$26. Adult male open-cut miners received 1$68BIC per day, adult females 1$43, and adolescents 1$05.[355] Many miners seemed content to leave the DRV government out of any struggle for better wages and conditions.

DEVELOPMENT PLANS

During 1946, the DRV government accumulated data on all sectors of the economy, prepared background papers for use at the Dalat and Fontainebleau conferences, and took a few development initiatives, yet the material dreams that had inspired revolutionaries in August 1945 seemed no closer to realization. At the beginning of the year, a forty-person Committee to Research a Construction Plan was announced, the membership of which reads like a who's-who of Vietnamese intellectuals, professionals, and acceptable former officials. Positioned directly under provisional President Hồ Chí Minh, the committee was to be given its own budget and support staff, and authorized to collect documentation from all government ministries and branches.[356] The committee's inaugural meeting on 10 January was opened by President Hồ, after which Võ Nguyên Giáp introduced everyone to the cabinet.[357] No further evidence has surfaced about this committee. If it received any funding or staff, the *National Gazette* is uncharacteristically silent. Perhaps some ICP leaders took exception to the membership. In late March, more than fifty academics, lawyers, and representatives from various bureaus of the Economy Ministry met to establish an Economic Commission, choosing medical doctor Hoàng Cơ Bình to chair the organizing subcommittee.[358] This was probably the brainchild of the minister of economy, Chu Bá Phượng, a Nationalist Party member of cabinet. It also seems to have gone nowhere. Both memberships were very light on private entrepreneurs, company managers, or others with business experience.

Government files contain a great deal of information on commodities other than those discussed above, again mostly focusing on use of existing supplies rather than plans to expand production and circulation. In the agricultural sector, besides grain and cattle, there were reviews if not full-fledged studies of vegetable oils, peanuts, fish sauce, sugar, and tea. Phosphate mines near the Chinese border were canvassed, but appear to have remained closed for lack of equipment and specialists.[359] Dike repair was given high priority in the north during the spring and early summer of 1946 (see chapter 9), but dredging of waterways and servicing of irrigation channels had to be deferred. Domestic producers of consumer merchandise like soap, matches, cigarettes, kitchenware, leather goods, medicinals, and paper, who had improvised solutions during the Pacific War, now faced a resurgence of imports, especially from China. DRV Customs Bureau efforts to restrict such imports had little effect. Light bulbs were the most precious commodity of all. In February 1946, the main Hanoi power plant swapped sixty light bulbs for a substantial quantity of industrial alcohol in the possession of the Northern Office, which proceeded meticulously to distribute each bulb to subordinate offices.[360] Most venues had to rely on peanut oil lamps until foreign kerosene gradually showed up again in the marketplace.

In June 1946, the National Economy Ministry asked the three regional administrative committees to forward to all provinces a questionnaire about current economic circumstances and prospects, focusing especially on agriculture, commerce, and industry. The files contain no responses from the central or southern regional committees, and nothing came back via the Northern Committee until the ministry reminded it in October. A few northern provinces then offered considerable detail, even broken down by district, while other provinces sent perfunctory replies or nothing at all. Traders appeared to be hundreds of times more numerous than "industrialists" *(nhà kỹ nghệ)*. However, Bắc Giang proudly listed five manufacturing sites, for paper, mercury, ceramic tiles, ceramic bowls, and leather tanning. To the question, "How many persons have applied to open a new manufacturing enterprise?" all province respondents answered "None."[361] The DRV Supply Bureau requested that each province provide regular statistics showing which commodities it needed and which it possessed in abundance — perhaps dreaming of a Soviet-style state supply system.[362]

On the other hand, the second half of 1946 saw several score limited liability companies receiving DRV authorization to operate. Again, most companies intended to engage in banking or commerce, not industry, mining, transport, or agricultural processing. Each company's announcement in the *National Gazette* listed an office address, a place where the bylaws could be consulted, a business purpose, the amount of capital to be raised, the value of each share, the manner in which profits would be allocated, and provisions for annual general meetings. The largest new enterprise, at least on paper, was the Việt Commerce Company based in Huế, with a capital subscription objective of thirty million piastres, and ambitions for one hundred million. Its diffuse business objective involved trading domestically and overseas, and "contributing to the growth of [Vietnam's] agriculture, industry, and commerce." The bylaws listed nineteen founders residing from Thanh Hóa down to Saigon.[363] The Vietnam Commercial Bank, announced in Hanoi in early July, was more carefully conceived. Trịnh Văn Bô, the prime initiator, had turned his house over to Hồ Chí Minh and his comrades in late August 1945, and Bô's family had contributed large amounts during Gold Week. As of the end of August 1946, more than half of the ten-million-piastre capital objective for the bank had been raised, from 249 individuals. The first general meeting proceeded to elect a twelve-member executive committee, which presented revised bylaws to the Hanoi court in late September.[364]

To put together new companies in the Vietnam of 1946 required considerable effort, as well as faith that war could be averted. The Pacific Trading Association increased its capital quest from 350,000$BIC to 1,000,000$BIC, aiming to build a hotel and to rebuild port facilities as well as engage in export-import.[365] South Asia United Company founders asked the Northern Committee to help it establish official contacts overseas, particularly in France and Hong Kong. The founders received a polite response, congratulating them on their participation in national economic development and expressing "readiness to help where possible."[366] New companies appeared in Haiphong, Phú Thọ, Nam Định, and Quảng Ngãi as well as Hanoi. Besides the plethora of banking and commerce initiatives, there were several transport companies, a lumber mill, a sugar mill, a chemical plant, and two printshops. Trịnh Văn Bô decided to invest in the new Hưng Việt export-import company as well as the bank. Hưng Việt shareholders meeting in October were told that half the necessary capital of five hundred thousand piastres had been raised, and that the remaining shares would be sold by 31 December.[367] They ran out of time.

In early December 1946, the DRV government began another, more detailed effort to collect economic data. Province committees were told to compile and forward agriculture statistics under sixty different categories, beginning with population, grain stocks, anticipated harvest, average harvest, current prices, salt, livestock, meat prices, textiles, peanut oil, lumber, tea, fish sauce, and potatoes. Then came a second batch of forty questions on industry, mining, and commerce. Answers were required no later than 25 December.[368] The Agriculture Ministry drew up and sent out 1947 production targets for specific provinces. Castor oil targets due to be dispatched to thirteen northern provinces were resting on a clerk's desk in the Northern Office on the afternoon of 19 December. The last Economic Bureau telegrams to depart Hanoi on 19 December were exhortations to fourteen provinces to "increase production."[369] We don't know what triggered this urgent demand for statistics, considering that Haiphong had already fallen to the French and Hanoi was under increasing threat. Perhaps the DRV cabinet was determined to continue development planning whatever the odds that war would explode. Or perhaps it was simple bureaucratic momentum, with officials in Hanoi wanting to extract information out of the provinces in anticipation of some grandiose five-year plan.

The Vietnamese press in late 1946 was replete with calls for a command economy. Nghiêm Xuân Yểm, respected agronomist and member of the Democratic Party, called for everyone to abandon individual quests for wealth in favor of "absorption to a common struggle program, a single development plan." Yểm argued that the financial and economic concession made by President Hồ in the modus vivendi meant that Vietnamese must try twice as hard to keep economic sovereignty from falling into the hands of others. Either Yểm disliked the idea of receiving aid and loans from the French, or he doubted they would ever materialize. Unlike most Vietnamese modernists, who talked of big industries, ships, dams, and electricity grids, Yểm wanted a plan which began from existing resources and skills.[370] Nguyễn Văn Luyện, physician and nonparty essayist, favored securing foreign aid and loans if possible, but also committing to tight domestic organization and restriction of individual rights in order to achieve rapid economic development. "In my opinion, Vietnam must introduce a socialist economy to be able to retain the August Revolution's spirit of new democracy," Luyện concluded.[371] Neither author considered where the limited liability companies cropping up in Vietnam in 1946 might fit within a command economy. Nor did anyone try to calculate how much time and energy was being expended in state paper-pushing.

Three years earlier, in the hills north of Hanoi, Phạm Văn Đồng had evoked his dream for Vietnam. Peasants would have enough land, workers would be fully employed. In countryside as well as city, there would be schools, hospitals, cinemas, electric lights, automobiles, social clubs, and homes for the elderly. Upland minorities could receive rice from Saigon and fish sauce from Quảng Yên. Women would be equal to men, and nationalities would "emulate each other to make our country stronger and richer."[372] Subsequent Việt Minh propaganda promised general happiness, dramatic improvements in living standards, and national wealth and power. In late 1946 it was clear that another terrible famine had been averted, and that northern Vietnam could survive without rice from the south. There was adequate food to support the growing national army, as well as increasing numbers of Việt Minh cadres and some public servants. The DRV had acquired sufficient revenue while denied access to most import-export duties, the most common source of income for emerging states. However, the government had hardly proved itself an effective economic manager. There also remained contradictions between the desire of many citizens to redress grievances and the state's ambition to expand production. As war swept the entire country, local committees assumed increasing responsibility for material decisions. Hopes for early development receded, yet the belief persisted that only a centralized command economy could achieve the vision conjured up by Phạm Văn Đồng and others.

Dealing with Domestic Opposition

Amidst the revolutionary exaltation of August 1945, no feeling was more widespread than national solidarity—the joy experienced when "the people" *(dân chúng; nhân dân)* join together as never before to build and defend "the nation" *(quốc gia)*, or, more colloquially, "our country" *(nước ta)*. Vietnamese who had never met before saluted each other as "comrade" *(đồng chí)*, shared food and drink, marched side by side in demonstrations, and joined with persons from other localities to form a range of patriotic organizations. Public speakers and newspaper writers insisted ceaselessly that only with unity and self-sacrifice could Vietnam's newly won independence be safeguarded from foreign predators.

Simultaneously, however, rumors of sedition swept Vietnam's towns and villages. Alleged "Vietnamese traitors" *(Việt gian)* and "reactionaries" *(kẻ phản động)* were detained, humiliated, beaten up, and sometimes killed. Many of these actions appear to have been unpremeditated, the dark side of mass excitement bordering on hysteria. But in other cases people sought revenge for past injustices, or pursued particular social revolutionary objectives such as eliminating landlords, redistributing property, or punishing those who gambled, drank alcohol, smoked opium, or engaged in extramarital sex. Several preexisting political organizations took advantage of the turmoil of late August and September to pull out lists of enemies to be detained or killed. Indochinese Communist Party (ICP) security squads proved most implacable at carrying out this task, but Vietnam Nationalist Party and Vietnam Revolutionary League teams rounded up and occasionally eliminated opponents as well.

When Hồ Chí Minh stood before a Hanoi crowd on 2 September to declare the independence of Vietnam, he directed considerable venom at the French colonialists, but said nothing about domestic enemies. In the speech immediately following, however, Võ Nguyên Giáp told the audience that if no Allied power warded off forceful French return, then the united Vietnamese nation would have to go it alone, in which case "division, doubt, and apathy are all a betrayal of the country."[1] Towards the end of the meeting, when Hồ was given the ceremonial sword of former emperor Bảo Đại, he joked that henceforth it would be employed to "cut off traitor's heads" rather than oppress the people as before.[2] In subsequent weeks, no DRV leader bothered to advance a public definition of sedition, much less insist that judicial due process be adhered to for those accused of this most serious crime.

Clearly affirmation of national solidarity did not preclude identification and punishment of political deviants. During nine hundred years of monarchist rule (in the tenth to nineteenth centuries A.D.), Vietnamese subjects understood that the king, royal court, and local officials remained perpetually vigilant for any signs of conspiracy, disloyalty, or heresy. Subjects charged with such grave crimes had scant opportunity to plead innocence; their best chance was to acknowledge guilt and throw themselves at the mercy of the monarch. Subsequent French colonial rulers opened the door to limited public criticism, notably via consultative councils and the print media, yet definitions of antigovernment behavior were ominously broad and punishments left to executive discretion. Vietnamese who voiced dissent faced a minefield of warnings from the colonial censor, police visits, threats, and abuse. If dissidents formed a political organization they were likely to end up in jail, exile, or clandestinity—where they encountered hardened revolutionaries dedicated to destroying the colonial system.

By the early 1940s, tens of thousands of politically alert Vietnamese had endured harsh lives in prison, survived as émigrés in China or Thailand, or hidden from arrest inside Indochina. Some had weathered all three experiences, making the acquaintance of bandits, racketeers, black marketeers, opium dealers, and informers along the way. The line between "political" and "criminal" behavior was blurred. Anticolonial organizations, in their efforts to avoid colonial penetration and eradication, developed techniques of compartmentalization, secrecy, deception, counterintelligence, internal punishment, and elimination of enemies. The ICP acquired its clandestine skills from Comintern experts, although that did not save it from near annihilation on two occasions. Vietnam Nationalist Party members who survived their own 1929–30 debacle picked up security skills from Chinese nationalist associates, who in turn owed much to Leninist practices. Northern Đại Việt groups learned covert methods from Japanese contacts, while some southern nationalists were put on the Kenpeitai payroll. Each of these clandestine organizations possessed special internal security units that answered only to the top leadership, and were much feared by the general membership. This legacy of jails, suspicion, subterfuge, and extra-legal action was bound to color the politics of the early DRV, whatever the commitment to national solidarity or the magnitude of threats from outside.

If the major chord in early revolutionary Vietnam was idealistic dedication to independence, an unmistakable minor chord made people fearful of holier-than-thou patriots, vigilante groups, and undercover security agents. If witchhunts were allowed to proliferate, and domestic violence persist beyond control of the fledgling DRV government, foreign schemers would take advantage of the accruing animosities to divide and rule Vietnam once again. Indeed, fratricide helps to explain why British-Japanese-French forces encountered only limited resistance in Saigon and the Mekong delta in late 1945, and why the French subsequently could forge tactical alliances with some religious and secular nationalist groups.

WHAT TO DO WITH DETAINEES

At the first meeting of province representatives with the Northern Region People's Committee, on 1–2 September 1945, there was detailed discussion about confiscating property from Vietnamese traitors (as well as black marketeers and "imperialists"), but only passing mention of physical detentions and executions.[3] Shortly thereafter, someone in the Hanoi office drafted a message to all subordinate committees instructing them to examine carefully the cases of persons jailed following the August insurrection, with an eye particularly to releasing those who were victims of private vendettas, while also compiling dossiers on the others for forwarding to provincial judicial commissions.[4] Already hundreds of petitions were coming in to the provisional DRV government from relatives of persons who had been detained or had disappeared. On 13 September, a batch of presidential decrees were issued that attempted to address security issues, including rules for detention and deportation (see below). The interim government also informed local committees that 466 prisoners "from previous regimes" had already been released from Hanoi Central Prison, and that the Northern Committee wanted to discharge more. However, because the Justice Ministry worried that additional releases would create local problems, given the paucity of police to maintain surveillance, remaining prisoners would need to be screened and a probation system worked out.[5] The continuing profusion of petitions from below led the chairman of the Northern Committee, Nguyễn Xiển, to urge local committees not to detain anyone further without careful prior investigation, and to release immediately those for whom evidence was lacking. Traitors could only be tried by a military court; other charges needed to be taken to judicial commissions for evaluation.[6] Xiển neglected to mention that such judicial commissions had yet to be formed.

At the same time that Nguyễn Xiển urged local people's committees to calm down, reconsider detentions, and leave serious cases to higher echelons, the ICP's principal newspaper, *Cờ Giải Phóng (Liberation Flag)* was publishing a list of traitors arrested and calling for sweeping purges of those who had served the French or Japanese. It chided "a number of Việt Minh cadres" for being soft-hearted and forgiving, thus allowing into the Front persons who had oppressed compatriots and "licked the heels" of foreigners. The newspaper alleged that some cadres had even dared to propose that Đại Việt adherents and Trotskyists be allowed to join Việt Minh committees.[7]

Nguyễn Xiển could admonish people's committees one way, and the editors of *Cờ Giải Phóng* exhort readers another way, but government orders had to come in the form of a decree signed by Hồ Chí Minh, or an edict from the minister of interior, Võ Nguyên Giáp. Hồ did send a confidential letter to "comrades" in his home province of Nghệ An, criticizing them for abuse of punishment powers: "I accept that a person must be punished *(trừng trị)* when there is clear proof of treason. However, we should not dig up old stories and turn them into new convictions. For those persons who are not particularly dangerous we should apply a policy of conversion and leniency, avoiding haphazard arrests and nonsensical confiscations of property, which cause much alarm among the public."[8] Not until mid-October did Hồ decide to chide all DRV people's committees publicly about their excessive arrests and punishments.[9] Hồ was not squeamish about capital punishment for traitors: in a later list of ten crimes warranting execution, number one was "consorting with the enemy, betraying the country."[10] Yet neither Hồ nor Giáp had bothered to define in government pronouncements what constituted sufficient evidence of treason for either arrest or conviction.

The matter of Vietnamese traitors received detailed, lively attention at the second meeting of province leaders with government ministers and members of the Northern Committee, on 1–2 October.[11] Hoàng Hữu Nam, Giáp's deputy at the Interior Ministry, defined traitors as: "Those who harm the people and country, those who are lackeys of foreign states. Previously they opposed the revolution. Now they oppose the Government, they have contact with the French to harm independence." Nam then underscored the need for evidence on each person accused: if it was "light" they ought to be released; if it was "heavy" the local committee still could not prosecute them, as that was the prerogative of the Interior Ministry. Deportations also required authorization from the top. Nam emphasized that pro-French elements *(bọn)* were the most dangerous, whereas pro-Japanese types could now be left alone. Nam then shifted tack, stating that truly evil mandarins and canton officials should be eradicated as well, so that people understood that the government intended to eliminate everything menacing to them. This broadening of the concept of treason had ominous implications for thousands of former colonial employees.

Following Hoàng Hữu Nam's comments on treason, province leaders at this early October meeting waded in with alacrity. Hòa Bình and Thái Bình representatives argued that province committees would "lose face" *(mất cả thể diện)* if they were not permitted to judge traitors. Nam replied that military courts would operate locally, thus upholding the prestige of provinces. He reiterated that arrests had to be based on evidence; a lot of people were complaining about injustice, and that was hurting the government. At this point Nguyễn Xiển interjected: "Any person damaging independence or opposing *(phản đối)* the government should be considered a traitor and arrested." Whether everyone present agreed or not with this sweeping definition of treason, the discussion shifted abruptly to the topic of deportation camps. Representatives of four upland provinces offered former colonial concentration camps *(tập trung dinh)*, adding the qualification that they did not possess the resources to restore buildings, provide guards, or feed the inmates. Hoàng Hữu Nam gave priority to rural venues where regular inhabitants were discreet and of proven loyalty, then revealed that the government had identified a place in Thái Nguyên which could be provisioned from neighboring Bắc Giang. The representative from Thái Bình still favored each province possessing its own deportation camp, but others argued that escape was too easy from delta locations. Two members of the Northern Committee urged that first attention be given to placing persons under forced residence *(quản thúc)* in their home villages, or perhaps dispersed in small groups to trustworthy villages, rather than creating and maintaining camps that would be a drain on the central budget. Nguyễn Khang, another Northern Committee member, seemed to think that two different solutions were on the table. However, Nam proceeded to ask which provinces wanted to offer camp venues, and made a vague promise about the government reimbursing them for costs. The discussion then moved on to ascertaining the current number of French detainees in each province.

CONSTRUCTING THE DRV SECURITY APPARATUS

As committed Leninists, ICP leaders were determined to make the police a "dictatorial instrument" *(công cụ chuyên chính)* of the revolutionary state.[12] While all had personal experience on the receiving end of colonial police operations, that did not mean they could suddenly reverse roles and become effective police commanders, much less fashion a new police force quickly. It is possible the ICP had a few members who had worked covertly within the Sûreté, but they were far outnumbered by the scores of party adherents who had worked elsewhere in the colonial administration.

When French Sûreté officers were interned following the 9 March 1945 Japanese coup, most Vietnamese employees of the Sûreté obeyed Japanese orders to continue working. As popular anticolonial sentiment became more overt in April and May, and the Japanese allowed thousands of political prisoners to be released, native members of the Sûreté must have realized their future was on the line. Some joined pro-Japanese political organizations, others quietly cultivated contacts with pro-Allied groups, still others shuffled files from one desk to another and hoped to avoid trouble. By June and July, ICP "honor teams" (*đội danh dự*) were tracking down and killing native Sûreté agents who had terrorized them in the past. Scores of Sûreté employees resigned in late July and early August.[13]

At the pivotal 17 August meeting in Hanoi called by the General Association of Government Employees, neither the Sûreté nor the Civil Guard units present chose to intervene when a Việt Minh armed squad seized the podium, cut down the royal government flag, harangued the crowd, and initiated a march through downtown streets. Two days later, as Việt Minh adherents took control of government buildings, the Northern Region Sûreté director convened sixty of his men to take part in formal turnover ceremonies, although control of Hanoi Central Prison was not transferred until 23 August. The new Northern Region Revolutionary People's Committee instructed all government employees to remain on the job, and specifically ordered the Sûreté (Liêm Phóng) and the ordinary police (Cảnh Sát) to arrest and punish "a lot of characters carrying weapons and collecting money in our name."[14]

Down the coast in central and southern Vietnam, we know far less about what happened to native employees of the Sûreté in the period between March and August 1945. The royal government based in Huế appears to have discouraged province-level Sûreté units from continuing their pursuit of political opponents, however defined. When Quảng Ngãi province exploded in revolutionary violence from late March, the Japanese tried to contain it, with minimal success. In Cochinchina, the Kenpeitai retrained some existing Sûreté and police units, as well as recruiting its own native auxiliaries. In July, the Japanese appointed Huỳnh Văn Phương, a 1930s Trotskyist activist, as chief of the Cochinchina Sûreté, while Nguyễn Hòa Hiệp, former secret society member and wartime Kenpeitai associate, was made head of the Saigon Sûreté. On the evening of 24 August, Vanguard Youth units, now identifying themselves loosely with the Việt Minh, occupied Saigon's local police stations.[15] The southern Sûreté was renamed the National Self-Defense Bureau (Quốc Gia Tự Vệ Cuộc), with Dương Bạch Mai (ICP) as Nam Bộ head, and Nguyễn Văn Trấn (ICP) director for Saigon-Chợ Lớn.[16]

From October 1945 in Cochinchina, French Sûreté officials managed to reestablish contact with a fair number of their former native employees, but further north in 1946 this proved a far more difficult task. Meanwhile, ICP counterintelligence teams had gained custody of colonial files in Hanoi and Huế that greatly facilitated their background investigations of former colonial employees, undercover agents, political prisoners (including ICP members), and other persons of interest (see chapter 8).[17]

Acknowledging the ICP's almost complete absence of members with professional police experience, the provisional DRV government in Hanoi reconfirmed

Chu Đình Xương as director of the Northern Region Security Service, with Lê Giản (ICP) appointed deputy director. At the first formal staff meeting after the Việt Minh's policy of leniency towards former enemies had been enunciated, each security service member was ordered to write down a complete record of his own past crimes, following which he was to expose the crimes of each colleague as well. These confessions were then set beside colonial files and other information, so that the Security Service would be able to pursue "dangerous elements" both inside itself and beyond.[18] The Interior Ministry instructed the three regional directors of the Security Service to compile two lists of current personnel: those considered to be diligent, meritorious, and healthy; and those not. The former list went to Interior for further scrutiny, while persons on the latter list were to be dismissed with two months of severance pay.[19]

Security Service members listed for dismissal had reason to worry about their future, since the public might well lump them together with previous "dangerous elements" who had been killed or arrested, or who had fled the scene. As of the end of October, however, only twenty-three members of the Northern Region Security Service had been dismissed, leaving 186 employees. When some of those removed sought jobs elsewhere in the government, the current Security Service director recommended that none be assigned to investigation or inspection positions. However, they could be considered for "social work," such as literacy instruction or welfare.[20]

While this gradual weeding out process was underway, Lê Giản and his small ICP team proceeded to recruit scores of young men and women from Việt Minh groups to learn from experienced Sûreté staff the arts of investigation, interrogation, weighing evidence, composing reports, typing, filing data, and maintaining accounts. Some fresh recruits were thrown into tough political missions almost immediately, with unpredictable results. For at least five months, however, old regime staff provided operational continuity. Among the seven office heads within the Northern Region Security Service in late 1945, only two appear to have been ICP members.[21] If formal reports are to be believed, the workload was not overwhelming. Thus, in the month up to 15 October, the Political Affairs Office interrogated seventy-seven persons, incarcerated fourteen, and released twenty-two prior detainees. The Investigations Office searched twelve houses, arrested twenty-three persons (seventeen "political" and six "economic"), and maintained surveillance over an unspecified number of "dangerous traitors."[22]

"Secret investigation" *(trinh sát)* units crop up occasionally in DRV government files, with various meanings. The term had originally piqued the curiosity of 1930s readers of spy novels, and was used by some early 1940s anticolonial organizations to identify their security and assassination squads. The Northern Region Revolutionary People's Committee of late August 1945 had a secret investigation committee responsible among other things for confiscating firearms and issuing gun permits, a highly sensitive job at the time. Two of its early gun permits were issued to members of a separate "self-defense secret investigation squad."[23] Several weeks later the head of secret investigations within the Central Police Bureau was instructed to return a Browning pistol to Hung Chan Ho, an overseas Chinese.[24] Localities also possessed their own secret investigation units. The Hanoi Suburbs People's Committee formed its squad to guard against traitors and black marketeers. The Phú Thọ secret investigation committee reported increasing success in eradication *(trừ diệt)* of political parties possessing "reactionary characteristics." The Hưng Yên squad was told to investigate covertly whether the chairman of the Yên Mỹ district people's committee had in fact buried alive the husband of Hoàng Thị Bổ, as she asserted in a petition to Hanoi. If so, the persons guilty of this "barbarous killing" were to be punished immediately.[25]

Thái Bình province boasted at least three different secret investigation units in late 1945. The main committee reported enthusiastically on its daily arrests, including a Đại Việt Duy Tân cadre from Hanoi who was in possession of a pistol and seven cartridges, and a man who spoke badly of the Việt Minh and praised Nguyễn Hải Thần, head of the Vietnam Revolutionary League. In the excited tones of spy fiction, the head of this committee described members pursuing a seven-person "secret party" which was disguised yet all wore the same brown clothing. "Our investigation is proceeding very intensively," he concluded. The committee also kept track of voluntary contributions from citizens, and confiscated Western medicine in order to give it to army units heading south. A second Thái Bình secret investigation committee pursued hoarders, speculators, and black marketeers, although the head of this unit was arrested in late October for "misusing his position." A third committee took shape more slowly, and was designed to include at least one covert member in each district, who would study the background of each people's committee member and report regularly on their behavior. Members of this committee had to be "awakened peasants" *(nông dân đã giác ngộ)* who were also upright, politically savvy, agile, and healthy.[26]

From internal evidence, as well as details provided later by communist historians, we can be confident that many of these secret investigation units included experienced ICP members working together with young Việt Minh adherents. The ICP itself possessed a central secret investigation committee, headed by Trần Đăng Ninh, which worked to insert ICP members into local investigation units.[27] However, "secret investigation" was not simply a cover name for ICP cells, or else reports on their operations would not have gone routinely to nonparty officials. From early 1946, the DRV government tried via the police to exercise more control over local-level secret investigation units. Provincial Security Service secret investigation units began to appear.[28] No later than July 1946 the Northern Public Security Bureau included an Office of Political Secret Investigation.[29] More complaints about secret investigators were coming in. Thus, the secret investigation committee of Giao Thủy district (Nam Định) was accused of unfair arrests and torture of prisoners, yet the Northern Region Committee merely ordered replacement of perpetrators if the charges were true. A member of the Bắc Ninh secret investigation unit was accused of "crooked dealings."[30] Only one newspaper, published by the Nationalist Party, condemned secret investigation units for striking fear in citizens, ignoring due process, and siphoning off resources better allocated to the military.[31]

In mid-September 1945, five important security decrees were signed by provisional President Hồ Chí Minh and promulgated. The first decree ordered a review of all cases of persons still in prison whose sentence had begun before 19 August, with the expectation of that most of these prisoners would be released pending later pardon procedures.[32] A second decree gave the Security Service and the police twenty-four hours to decide whether a detained person had a case to answer or not. If affirmative, the appropriate court had to be notified; if negative, the individual was to be released.[33] A third decree foreshadowed establishment of military courts to try persons accused of "endangering the independence of the DRV." A fourth decree authorized the Security Service to arrest persons "dangerous to the DRV" with the expectation of deporting them (đưa đi an trí), although it would be up to the three regional committees to decide exactly whom to deport and for how long.[34] Finally, a fifth decree instructed anyone wishing to organize a public demonstration to request permission from the relevant people's committee twenty-four hours in advance.[35]

Taken together these five decrees of 13 September projected conflicting signals. The release of pre-19 August prisoners suggested that the interim government wanted to begin with a clean slate, to judge people on their present and future actions, not the past. The twenty-four-hour investigative reporting rule promised something akin to habeas corpus. On the other hand, military courts presaged separate handling of high crimes against the state, with the Justice Ministry demoted and civilian courts finessed. The deportation decree overtly violated habeas corpus and excluded judicial authorities entirely. As for the decree on public demonstrations, its preamble admitted that freedom of assembly was a principle of democratic republics, then argued that current special conditions required supervision of demonstrations so as to avoid "unexpected situations that might have unfortunate influences on domestic order (nội trị) or foreign relations."

Five weeks later, the formula for release of pre-19 August prisoners was altered so as to discriminate between "genuine revolutionaries" from the colonial era, who would be amnestied, and "lackeys of the Japanese" convicted by the French or "lackeys of the French" convicted by the Japanese—both of whom had "acted to the detriment of our country's independence" and hence were traitors.[36] This decree obviously contradicted the policy of leniency towards former enemies.

More specifically, it made the pre-19 August actions of alleged pro-Japanese or pro-French Vietnamese a continuing crime of treason. In practice, such individuals were very unlikely to have remained in prison throughout the transmutations of March–August 1945, yet the 20 October decree stigmatized them officially, and indeed offered implicit grounds for jailing them once again. Subsequently the chief judge and the prosecutor of the Hanoi court of appeals seemed to distance themselves from the new decree by arguing that the royal amnesty of 17 May 1945 was still valid for those who had benefited from it. They also washed their hands of further judicial efforts to ascertain which colonial political prisoners were genuine revolutionaries and which were traitors, stating coyly that only people's committees possessed sufficient resources and documentation to pursue such matters.[37]

Military Courts

Military courts became a significant vehicle for punishing past "enemies of the revolution" and for delineating what constituted treason against the new democratic republic. Semantically they should have been styled "political courts," but that failed to convey the desired sense of national emergency and threat of war. Nine military courts were decreed in September 1945, yet it took some months to select judges and begin taking cases. Meanwhile, in Thái Nguyên, a "people's court" convened on the town's sports field in front of several thousand citizens to try Cung Đình Vận, former province mandarin, on charges of torturing and killing numerous revolutionaries over the years. Although Vận claimed to have urged villagers in August to support the Việt Minh, and said he had turned over weapons and property to the provisional government, the highly emotional testimony of seven witnesses sealed his fate. Phạm Văn An, whom Vận had dispatched to the Côn Sơn prison island for seven years, proposed that Vận's liver be cut out and eaten with rice wine, a gourd of which An displayed to the court. Vận was sentenced to death by firing squad, and the sentence implemented promptly in front of the crowd.[38]

Perhaps the first trial by a legitimately constituted military court took place in Huế in December, with the feature culprit among four being Nguyễn Tiến Lãng, writer, mandarin, and director of former emperor Bảo Đại's Cabinet. Lãng also was the son-in-law of Phạm Quỳnh, the prominent author, editor, and court mandarin who had been killed earlier in Huế by the ICP city committee. Condemned as a French lackey, Lãng was sentenced to six years' imprisonment and the loss of two-thirds of his property.[39] Phan Văn Đạt, a political activist arrested by the French in 1938, had allegedly assisted the Sûreté in destroying the underground network of his former comrades. He received ten years' jail. Ung Tập, proctor of the Huế Industrial School, was sentenced to eight years' jail and loss of two-thirds of his property for informing on his students to the Sûreté, leading to many arrests and incarcerations. Trần Đình Diểm, accused of fraudulently collecting money in the name of the Việt Minh during the August uprising in Huế, received three years' imprisonment. Court proceedings were open to the public, with attendance peaking at the sentencing session.[40]

Two months later the DRV government finally issued rules for military court proceedings. The accused had the right to represent himself or to rely on a lawyer or other person. In special circumstances court sessions could be held *in camera*, but all sentences had to be pronounced before the public. Punishments included confiscation of some or all property, imprisonment from one to twenty years, or execution. Only a sentence of execution could be appealed—to the DRV president.[41] Over time the crime of "endangering the independence of the DRV" came to be interpreted by prosecutors more broadly, and lower administrative committees and courts felt more inclined to refer potential capital punishment cases to military courts.

I have not been able to find information on the overall number of cases heard by military courts, the judgments reached, or the punishments meted out. All we have are some case files and a few press reports. A former gendarme arrested in November 1945 languished in jail for eight months until the local court decided he should be dispatched to the Hanoi military court on the charge of "having worked as a police agent *(mật thám)* against the interests of Vietnam."[42] A former canton head in Hưng Yên province accused of "maltreating people" and turning in Việt Minh adherents before the August uprising was sentenced by the Hanoi military court to five years' prison and loss of half his property.[43] Nguyễn Xuân Xứng, former employee of the French résident of Hà Nam province, who had been sentenced to death by unknown parties following the August uprising, had his punishment reduced to indefinite imprisonment, and then waited while his wife blitzed the central government with petitions. Eventually Xứng's case was sent to the Hanoi military court, at which point his wife told authorities verbally that he had been an ICP member since 1930. The Justice Ministry replied that Xứng would be released if this claim was verified. However, Xứng's case was still pending as of March 1946.[44] The Huế military court punished a number of former district mandarins with terms ranging from twenty years' hard labor to three years' suspended sentence.[45]

Military courts soon fell behind in their 1946 case calendars. Families of accused individuals awaiting trial sent hundreds of petitions to Hanoi asking for information. In some cases families had no idea what had happened from the moment their relative was arrested and taken away, causing the Justice Ministry to reiterate to all echelons the twenty-four-hour disposition rule announced in September 1945.[46] As of late November 1946, northern region prisons held fifty-nine inmates recently tried and sentenced in military courts, and seventy-six accused persons awaiting military court appearances.[47] A few cases were handled more expeditiously. In August, the Hanoi military court condemned a National Guard political officer to death for burning houses, killing women and children, seizing property illegally, using confiscated property improperly, and giving false evidence. The execution was carried out immediately, "for political impact," and all Hanoi National Guard units were told to take this punishment as object lesson.[48]

As this trial suggests, an increasing number of military court cases in the second half of 1946 dealt with acts taking place after establishment of the DRV, not before. Police force deserters occasionally went before a military court. Nguyễn Văn Thọ awaited military court appearance on charges of "plotting to overthrow the government" in Hòn Gai town. A Việt Minh workers' group stood accused of assassination. A member of the Kim Động district committee (Hưng Yên) was charged with illegal torture of detainees. Elsewhere committee members had allegedly absconded with public funds.[49] A group of Nam Định farmers who protested women having to pay land taxes was arrested for "creating disorder." According to Nam Định authorities, Ms. Đinh Thị Huệ then incited a crowd to assault local administrative committee members. More arrests were made, and a French flag allegedly found in one home. Now the culprits were labeled "reactionaries" and five ringleaders dispatched to the Hanoi military court on 26 July. A raft of citizen petitions protesting innocence had already preceded them.[50]

Hanoi Central Prison

The Hanoi Central Prison stood at the apex of the DRV's incarceration system, as it had for the French, under the title of Maison centrale. Inmates included persons under police investigation, those accused and awaiting trial or deportation, convicts serving their terms, and individuals sentenced to execution. The Central Prison held about two thousand inmates before the 19 August insurrection, more of them common criminals than political prisoners. That total had fallen to six hundred by the end of September, leading the minister of justice, Vũ Trọng Khánh, to propose unsuccessfully that one wing of the prison be converted to a literacy school and another to a weaving and sewing school for women.[51] On 3 October, 118 prisoners escaped when the gate opened to enable a garbage truck to depart. Remarkably, only three old regime guards were sacked; five days later the old regime director, Captain Nguyễn Văn Thừa, was thanked for his services and replaced by Lê Văn Ngọ. The twenty-three remaining guards were reinforced by six young recruits working without pay, but most of the Central Prison's firearms had been taken by a Việt Minh National Salvation unit in August and not returned. Ngọ did succeed in segregating the opium addicts, began literacy classes for inmates, and had cholera shots administered to both guards and prisoners.[52]

On 20 October, Lê Văn Ngọ requested that a guard be sacked for using a trustee to extort shoes and money from prisoners' families. Four days later a

Central Prison guard anonymously petitioned the government to complain about unfair imprisonments, inmates unable to tell families of their location, and the practice of Security Service staff taking bribes to release some of the accused while maltreating others. "Ah, what justice is there like money justice," the guard lamented. Soon after, the director reported that he had abolished the prisoner trustee system, as "they usually are bullies and strike deals with guards." Ngọ encouraged prisoners to come directly to him if treated unfairly. Nonetheless, a lot of "stealing and exploitation" persisted, and outside food contractors sometimes failed to live up to their commitments.[53] Refusing to be daunted, Ngọ requested free use of the Opera House on 17 November so that a popular song group and members of the prison staff could give a concert to raise money for a handicraft instruction facility for the prisoners.[54]

By the end of November 1945, inmate numbers at the Central Prison had climbed back over twelve hundred, mostly due to political prisoner arrivals from late October onward. The director asked for only two additional guards, probably aware of how desperate government finances were at the time.[55] Calculating that grain provided by the Cereals Office in late October would run out by 6 December, Lê Văn Ngọ requested an additional twenty tons of rice, yet apparently only received six tons of paddy—enough to feed 1,250 persons (guards and prisoners) for ten days at most.[56] These were worrisome times in regard to overall food availability in northern Vietnam, but clearly Central Prison inmates could not be allowed to starve. We can speculate that some prisoners received food parcels from their families, while others survived on reduced rice rations, gruel, and manioc until conditions improved. Sometime in early 1946, Director Ngọ received a letter of commendation from the Northern Committee, which praised the prison's improved hygiene, the initiation of political and military classes for convicts, and Ngọ's arrangement with the Railway Service by which damaged train seats were brought in for repair. As the commendation enthused, "In the future the jail will become a cathedral (giáo đường) to convert those who made the mistake of breaking the law."[57]

Deportation Camps

In late 1945, there was no DRV consensus over who was a "traitor," how many persons should be detained on political grounds, or for how long. Deportation camps represented the DRV government's main response to the reality of thousands of people being confined—mostly at village and district levels—and the incapacity of the police and judicial system to investigate all these cases, much less decide who was to be charged, put on trial, and declared guilty or innocent. Local committees may have freed up to half of those detained in August and early September within weeks, in response to interrogations, family entreaties, logistical imperatives, and exhortations from above. However, they did not want to see the others released. As we have seen from the 2 October Northern Office discussion about traitors, some province committees wanted to consolidate lower-level detainees at the province level, provided the central government covered costs. That idea was rejected in favor of deporting an unspecified number of detainees to out-of-the-way locations. Concerned that some local committees might choose to kill detainees rather than free them, DRV leaders probably saw deportation camps as part of the wider state effort to curb "spontaneous" revolutionary excesses. Those left behind might be placed under movement restrictions or local surveillance *(quản thúc)*.

Most province committees managed to ignore Hanoi requests to supply political detainee numbers and locations. Thái Bình reported "more than one hundred" detainees in the province jail, including twenty-four political cases already judged and sentenced, but offered no information on district or village numbers. Hà Đông reported 142 in the province jail, of which 60 were "political prisoners and suspected traitors being investigated."[58] Hải Dương claimed it had only six former Sûreté agents and one member of the Vietnam Revolutionary League in jail. Haiphong Prison sent a list of inmates carried over from before 19 August, but nothing about subsequent incarcerations.[59] In December, two provinces sent lists of political prisoners.[60] Some province committees probably had no reliable numbers on district- or village-level detentions, hence chose not to reply rather than expose their ignorance. Meanwhile, the Security Service tried with minimal success to compile records on false arrests and missing persons.[61]

The term "deportation camp" *(trại an trí)* derived from the precolonial practice of dispatching miscreant officials to distant, undesirable venues as punishment.[62] The first DRV deportation camp may have been at Cần Lưu in Thái Nguyên province, although no specific information about Cần Lưu is available until mid-1946. In late October 1945, Phú Thọ province reported establishment of a camp at Yên Lập, with thirty current occupants, sufficient food, and permission for relatives to visit twice a month.[63] In December, the Northern Region Security Service compiled a list of fifty-one political prisoners "dangerous to the Democratic Republic of Vietnam" who were to be dispatched to an unnamed camp in Thái Nguyên. The prisoners originated from thirteen different provinces or cities, and their average age was twenty-six. Although no political identifications accompanied each person's name, age, and place of birth, a cover letter mentioned the Đại Việt Quốc Dân Đảng, Vietnam Revolutionary League, and Trotskyists.[64] At least one deportation camp was located in Bắc Kạn province, and two in Sơn Tây. One of the Sơn Tây camps was at Chùa Bồ plantation, fourteen kilometers outside the province seat. Ethnic minority ("Mọi") men had pillaged the property, and twenty Liberation Army soldiers remained to guard against their return. On 26 October, Nguyễn Xiển, chairman of the Northern Region Committee, signed a contract with the plantation's owner whereby the government agreed to feed 150–200 deportees until they were released, at which time the owner might negotiate their remaining as tenants or agricultural laborers.[65] Fragmentary evidence also points to at least five deportation camps in central Vietnam: in Thanh Hóa, Quảng Trị, Thừa Thiên, Quảng Nam, and Quảng Ngãi.

The only deportation camp for which I possess detailed data is Mỏ Chén, a coffee plantation in Sơn Tây province. Mỏ Chén buildings and equipment had been completely destroyed by the same ethnic minority group that pillaged Chùa Bồ, yet the presence of tens of thousands of unpicked coffee bushes induced the Northern Committee to approve dispatch of inmates from Hanoi Central Prison. In early November, Nguyễn Xiển provided the prospective camp director, Nguyễn Đức Tố, with a letter to carry around to Hanoi merchants and neighborhood committees asking for donations in kind, to establish "a deportation and agricultural facility for persons with bad records." About fifty donors provided bamboo, nails, wire, rope, tin cans, cooking ware, and medicines—all carefully recorded in a ledger. On 16 November, six trucks carried to Mỏ Chén 164 prisoners, twenty-eight militia men, seven tradesmen, five camp administrators, and the donated supplies. Apparently the main supply of rice failed to arrive by separate means, so prisoners were immediately reduced to one meal a day. The entire camp awoke at five in the morning, saluted the flag, worked eight hours with a midday break, saluted the flag again, ate dinner at six thirty, and went to bed at nine. There were plans for politics and literacy classes, and learning patriotic songs, but these unraveled as people came down with malaria and food rations remained meager, at least for the prisoners.[66]

Five days after arrival, two prisoners died. By 2 December the prisoner count had dropped to 147, with three more dead and twelve transferred to the hospital in Sơn Tây town. On 5 December, ten more prisoners arrived from Hanoi. Every few days, two to ten sacks of paddy or rice came from town, presumably carried up by oxcart. The Northern Office instructed the veterinary bureau to dispatch thirty buffaloes, twenty-one sheep, and four horses or donkeys to Mỏ Chén, but camp records do not mention these animals arriving. The temperature dropped, and few prisoners had blankets. Prisoners now formally protested overall conditions, and tried to send a petition to Hanoi. On 18 December, when three camp administrators disputed decisions made by Director Tố, he cut their food rations. A National Guard platoon arrived, together with a political officer, to bolster the militia personnel.

On 21 December, Tố was arrested on unknown charges and replaced by Nguyễn Văn Bình. The number of administrators had now doubled and there were fifteen carpenters, masons, buffalo herders, coffee cultivators, rice millers, and cooks who consumed available food as well. Prisoner numbers were down to 119, with about two-thirds too ill with malaria or beriberi to work. Administrators recorded the exact amounts of paddy received, the rice consumed each day, prisoner work assignments, the number of ill prisoners, the name of each prisoner who died or was taken to Sơn Tây hospital, and the names of five prisoners who escaped. During the second half of December, prisoners received two rice meals per day, but starting in early January part of the ration was composed of manioc. Fifteen prisoners died between 21 December and 15 January, while sixteen more were sent to Sơn Tây hospital, where several died subsequently. On 25 January, National Guard trucks transported eighty-three prisoners from Mỏ Chén back to Hanoi Central Prison. The next day, an administrator penned two exquisite copies of a list of twenty-one office items returned from the deportation camp, including dossiers, ledgers, chops, ink, and unused paper.[67]

Examining these extensive records of Mỏ Chén, I suspect that a few young intellectuals or clerks recently recruited to the Northern Region Security Service submitted the deportation camp proposal to Nguyễn Xiển, who approved it providing there was little or no cost to his Northern Committee budget. In late 1945, the idea of reforming prisoners by means of manual labor, political lectures, songs, and literacy classes was widespread. The prospect of substantial quantities of coffee beans being delivered to the government must have motivated Nguyễn Xiển and camp organizers alike, although it seems that no administrator had experience with coffee cultivation. Indeed, the records make no mention of prisoners working among the rows of coffee bushes; instead they labored in the fields, gathered firewood, cut fodder for horses, cleaned latrines, and assisted the cooks (on one day, 55 percent of prisoners not ill were listed as "working in the kitchen").

Camp organizers seem to have expected that the Sơn Tây People's Committee would provide adequate amounts of paddy or rice for everyone at Mỏ Chén, yet this was a time when the overall food situation was so precarious that provincial leaders regularly restricted the movement of rice. Even if the Mỏ Chén control committee had had money to pay for rice, this would not necessarily have convinced Sơn Tây to release sufficient grain. Initially rice came in small amounts. On 29 December, the second camp director, Nguyễn Văn Bình, presented Sơn Tây with 25,000 piastres, and over the next two weeks 4.3 tons of rice, worth 23,428.60 piastres, made its way in increments to Mỏ Chén. That should have been enough to feed everyone until at least the end of January, if the rice was unspoiled and distributed fairly. And yet prisoners were getting part of their ration in manioc, and continuing to die.

On 29 March 1946, President Hồ Chí Minh signed a decree labeled "Protection of Individual Freedom," which ironically dealt almost entirely with various forms of detention, including deportation. Article 7 gave chairmen of the northern, central, and southern regional committees authority to deport to special camps "persons who by their words or actions may damage the struggle to preserve independence, the democratic system, public security, and national unity."

In urgent circumstances, province chairmen were authorized to detain persons "dangerous to the maintenance of order," providing they reported details within fifteen days to their regional committee for ultimate disposition. Lists of persons in deportation camps were to be submitted to regional committees each month, and every three months a regional council appointed by the minister of interior would review all cases.[68] Review councils for the central region and the northern region were announced some weeks later.[69] The Central Region Review Council was headed by the chief of police, Nguyễn Văn Ngọc, who thus was in the position of evaluating his own prior deportation actions. The Northern Review Council included two members of the Political and Administrative Inspectorate who routinely perused hundreds of petitions from relatives of detained or deported individuals, and had authority to investigate any government echelon or bureau, including the police.

The Northern Committee ordered all provinces to provide lists of deportees, names of persons deserving release, and recommendations for additional persons to dispatch to camps. Responses on existing deportees came in very slowly, partly because many persons had been sent to camps in other provinces and contact with them lost. The government had to repeat its instructions several times, and some provinces never seem to have answered.[70] Provinces were quicker to propose additional persons for deportation. Phú Thọ, for example, sent a list of twenty-eight persons to be deported for two years, three years, or "until the country is tentatively quiet *(tạm yên)*." Yên Bái ignored the March decree's definition of persons warranting deportation, instead sending Hanoi a list of alleged thieves, passers of counterfeit money, reactionaries, and fomenters of rebellion *(phiến loạn)*.[71] An increasing number of common criminals were now going to deportation camps, charged with murder, theft, racketeering, black marketeering, or vagabondage *(lưu manh)*. Lý Tạ Dũng, who allegedly specialized in organizing cock fights from well back in the French period, was recommended by the Hanoi police for deportation.[72]

Occasionally Hanoi was tougher about deportations than the provinces. One person who had been arrested for making provocative remarks and pounding the village ballot box at the early 1946 National Assembly elections was released by the Hưng Yên Administrative Committee, only to be slated for deportation by someone in the Northern Office.[73] A court sentence fining five thousand piastres for the crime of attempted murder in one case was changed by the minister of interior to deportation to a camp in Phú Thọ.[74] The Northern Region Police Director, Đào Xuân Mai, tried to have five persons finishing their jail terms dispatched to a deportation camp, only to be told they had already been released.[75] When Phạm Lê Bổng, prominent entrepreneur and publisher, was proposed for release from camp, a member of the Interior Ministry's Special Inspectorate vehemently opposed the idea: "He is totally pro-French. If released he may immediately join the French."[76] Phạm Lê Bổng was released at some point and collaborated with the DRV until 1952, when he joined the Bảo Đại cause.[77]

Deportation camps were public knowledge, not secret government business. *Việt Nam* daily, published by the Nationalist Party, criticized the policy of deportation and made reference to comrades who had been deported.[78] The monthly journal of the Northern Region Police Bureau listed the names of prisoners who had escaped from various deportation camps, including Mỏ Chén, described above.[79] *Cứu Quốc* publicized the results of the eighth meeting of the Northern Review Council, which decided to release six persons from deportation camps, shift two persons from deportation to forced residence, and release one individual from forced residence.[80] In late October, President Hồ instructed relevant organizations to reexamine prisoner dossiers with an eye to amnesties coinciding with the second session of the National Assembly. One month later *Cứu Quốc* gave the names of two dozen deportees released, although many still were subject to residence restrictions.[81] However, this same period saw a new wave of political arrests (see below).

HANOI TRIES TO ENFORCE DETENTION STANDARDS

Some members of the DRV cabinet appointed at the first meeting of the National Assembly in early March 1946 were clearly disturbed at the government's continuing incapacity to implement a single national policy concerning powers of arrest, investigation, detention, trial, and punishment. Huỳnh Thúc Kháng, the prominent literatus, publisher, and newspaper editor whom President Hồ Chí Minh had convinced to become interior minister, took the lead in composing regulations designed both to replace French colonial laws and to eliminate disturbing practices that had cropped up since the August 1945 insurrection. The 29 March decree on "Protecting Individual Freedoms," mentioned above, specified that while persons caught in the act of committing a crime should be arrested forthwith, all other arrests required a written warrant from a judge. All persons arrested had to be brought before a judge for questioning within twenty-four hours. Those charged with minor crimes could be detained for up to one month prior to trial, those charged with major crimes for up to three months, although courts could approve two extensions on these detention periods.

The second section of the 29 March decree, titled "Special Precautionary Measures," detailed provisions for deportation, as discussed above, as well as mentioning the lesser procedure of forced residence. A third section attempted to rule out informal detentions at village and district levels by stating that only province jails or Interior Ministry venues could hold suspects, convicted criminals, or "persons subject to precautionary arrest by administrative organs." However, an escape clause was provided whereby local places of detention other than province jails were reviewed periodically by regional councils. Torture to extract confessions was forbidden at any venue. Echoing colonial practice in regard to political prisoners, the decree specified that, unlike ordinary prisoners *(thường phạm)*, detainees subject to "special precautionary measures" could receive food, reading matter, and visits from their relatives. The 29 March decree's final section specified punishments for government employees or other persons who violated its provisions, ranging from two to ten years' imprisonment and one thousand to one hundred thousand piastre fines. If torture resulted in death or disability of a detainee, the perpetrator could be tried and punished for that crime.

Four days following promulgation of the 29 March 1946 decree, Huỳnh Thúc Kháng dispatched a circular to the chairmen of the three regional committees emphasizing their personal responsibility for approving or rejecting all cases of deportation or forced residence. His words were remarkably forthright: "I want to remind you of President Hồ's words: "The past is completely dead" *(dĩ vãng đã chết hẳn)*. Use that as your precept when examining the behavior of each individual. Only *present* behavior as demonstrated by *words* or *actions* can possibly justify the application of special precautionary measures."[82] Most newspapers chose to ignore the 29 March decree. *Cứu Quốc* reprinted it on an inside page without comment. *Dân Chủ* editors headlined their summary description as follows: "When Capturing Traitors, Pay Heed."[83] Clearly detainees still were considered guilty, with little opportunity to prove their innocence.

Despite the efforts of Huỳnh Thúc Kháng and others to impose standards and discipline on the treatment of political detainees, there is ample evidence that localities continued to ignore government decrees and circulars. One of the most flagrant cases involved the alleged escape of fourteen ranking deportees being trucked from Thái Nguyên to Bắc Kạn on 15 March 1946. Hanoi authorities only learned of the incident when petitions poured in from relatives of the deportees asking about their fate. According to province officials, the fourteen had made a run for it after a tire had blown out and the truck halted at an isolated spot. However, considering that some of the detainees were of advanced age, and apparently none were recaptured, Hanoi officials must have entertained suspicions.[84] By May, enough other cases of alleged escape had piled up on the desks of Northern Special Investigation Committee members to warrant a blunt message to all northern provinces and cities, which concluded: "After careful examination, [we] discern many cases where prisoners have not escaped, but in reality have been executed secretly. This must stop. If someone does escape, then those responsible must be punished."[85] Nonetheless, this message contained no order to investigate past disappearances and punish the perpetrators.

Faced with a plethora of petitions arriving at Hanoi offices that pointed to multiple illegalities in regard to detainees, special investigators were occasionally dispatched to localities to try to get to the bottom of things. Following numerous petitions from residents of Đồ Sơn (Kiến An) alleging police extortion, unfair arrests, and torture, two investigators arrived unannounced with authority to question anyone. A pregnant woman accused of selling opium had been subjected to electric torture until both she and her unborn child were dead. The deputy head of police had been thrown into jail by his boss, but managed to gain the attention of the two investigators and give them a four-page statement corroborating some of the petition allegations. An initial contributing factor involved someone stealing firearms from Chinese troops stationed at Đồ Sơn, which provoked Chinese retaliation and threats to do more if the thieves were not found and punished.[86] Quite possibly the thieves were Việt Minh activists.

Cases of National Guard units detaining people improperly came to the attention of Hanoi as well. In early May, the minister of defense, Phan Anh, felt the need to instruct the National Guard on the contents of the 29 March decree regarding detention. Anh accepted that circumstances would arise where military personnel suddenly had to decide whether to arrest someone or were called to respond to a civilian organization's request for assistance in carrying out an arrest. In the latter case it was important to check the bona fides of the civilian organization. Commanders were authorized to detain a suspect without ill treatment for up to twenty-four hours, making sure they could not escape but recognizing that it was forbidden to kill them "except in self-defense."[87] Several weeks later the Interior Ministry still felt it necessary to remind Defense about the need for soldiers to adhere to the detention rules set down in the 29 March decree, and for National Guard units to join with the police to "resolve immediately" all prior detentions.[88]

In late February 1946, the DRV government merged the Security Service and various police units to become the Vietnam Public Security Department (Việt Nam Công An Vụ), which we will call the Công An.[89] This consolidation of investigation and public order responsibilities had been discussed in previous weeks by Lê Giản, the Security Service deputy director, and Trần Đăng Ninh, representing the ICP leadership. Lê Giản was made interim director of the Công An, pending the outcome of sensitive negotiations to form a new Cabinet of national union.[90] The eventual agreement reached between political parties included Huỳnh Thúc Kháng accepting the position of interior minister, as an explicitly nonparty member of cabinet. Kháng then selected Nguyễn Dương as Công An national director, and Đào Hùng as head of the Công An's vital northern bureau. Dương, a teacher from the same province (Quảng Nam) as Kháng, had taught together with Võ Nguyên Giáp at Hanoi's Thăng Long private secondary school prior to the Pacific War. Hùng, also a secondary school teacher, was suspected by ICP members of leaning towards the Vietnam Nationalist Party.[91] In support of the new interior minister and his appointees, the Northern Committee instructed all local branches of the Công An to obey the orders of

Nguyễn Dương and Đào Hùng.[92] Nonetheless, ICP members remained in charge of key offices, and if called upon young Việt Minh recruits were expected to obey ICP orders rather than the top Công An officials. The ICP called this tactic "painting the head white," meaning that they were only accepting independent Công An leadership at the top and superficially.[93]

During April 1946, a quiet but intense struggle for control of the Công An persisted, at least in Hanoi and vicinity. Not unaware of ICP tactics, Đào Hùng made some appointments of his own and sacked a few ICP members. In late April, Bùi Đức Minh (ICP), head of the Công An's secret political investigation office, arrested a group of Nationalist Party activists and put them in Hanoi Central Prison. Hùng wrote an order for release of the detainees, which the prison warden (ICP) took to Minh for confirmation. It was decided to release the Nationalist Party group, but then use Công An autos to rearrest them quickly and take them to a different jail. Đào Hùng now insisted that Nguyễn Dương use his authority as general director to order their re-release, but Dương's only response was to tighten control over Công An motor vehicles. Night-time altercations escalated, with more Nationalist Party members ending up in jail, and Nationalist Party leaders pressuring Dương to assert himself. Instead Dương submitted his resignation to the interior minister. At some point Huỳnh Thúc Kháng became so irritated by this internecine conflict that he may have offered his resignation to President Hồ Chí Minh; if so, it was not accepted. However, Dương's resignation was accepted, and soon after, Đào Hùng went the same route. Lê Giản became national director, while Đào Xuân Mai (ICP) was promoted from the Nam Định Công An to be director of the Northern Region. As Lê Giản concludes sardonically in his memoir, "The attempt to render the Công An impartial had come to an end." Lê Giản also says he consulted almost daily with Hồ Chí Minh, Võ Nguyên Giáp, and Huỳnh Thúc Kháng.[94] Certainly Hồ made no effort to stop the ICP from gaining full control of the Công An, and indeed may have wanted the issue resolved before he headed overseas at the end of May.

TRAITORS AND REACTIONARIES

Pervasive public calls for national unity and denunciations of division raised the question of when it was acceptable for citizens to voice criticism or to place other needs ahead of the collectivity. Not while the country was under French attack, came the vehement answer from the south. In late 1945, the model of soldiers fighting and dying on the southern front was contrasted with conditions behind the lines, where people were said to be "bickering and splitting into political cliques, interrogating each other, wasting time and ink to show off this theory or that position." Only when Vietnam's sovereignty was secure could everyone "propagate their own theories to heart's content," Huế editors concluded with a hint of sarcasm. In the meantime, efforts of "certain elements" to deceive the populace had to be stamped out.[95] *Cứu Quốc,* in an editorial headlined "Don't Divide Any More!" praised groups for joining the Việt Minh and condemned others that stood outside "in order to provoke misunderstanding, confusion and disunion."[96] Left ambiguous was the question of whether one had to join the Việt Minh in order to be patriotic. The DRV propaganda minister, Trần Huy Liệu, accused an unnamed Vietnamese party of adopting the Western practice of cursing and insulting opponents, which he said was quite alien to East Asians. Nonetheless, Liệu intended to take up the challenge.[97] This was just at the moment when Hồ Chí Minh, under pressure from the Chinese occupation authority, was trying to reach tactical agreement with the Nationalist Party and Revolutionary League over formation of a government of national union.

Southern preoccupations with alleged traitors reverberated northward. The peremptory killing of former collaborators in Saigon in September 1945 was justified as a means to keep the French from using such people again. For the same reason it had been deemed necessary in Huế to kill two prominent mandarins, Phạm Quỳnh and Ngô Đình Khôi.[98] Northern readers were told that some locations in the south regarded persons who sold food to the enemy as traitors, and punished them accordingly. A member of the Mỹ Tho military court visiting Hanoi delineated three types of Vietnamese traitor: intellectuals who accepted appointment to French councils; uneducated persons who received guns from the French and then lorded over others, raping and stealing; and individuals who sought revenge for past events.[99] The arrival of French troops in Haiphong and Hanoi in March 1946 provoked frantic calls to uncover and eliminate traitors before they could serve the enemy. "Anyone who aims to divide the nation is a traitor," *Cứu Quốc* warned.[100] The term *đảng phái* (parties and groupings), which previously had been a descriptive noun, now took on distinctly pejorative connotations, meaning factional, narrow-minded, or partisan. Four months before, the standing bureau of the Central Region Việt Minh, based in Huế, had criticized some comrades for accusing persons of treason if they chose not to join the Việt Minh. "The Việt Minh does not have a monopoly on patriotism," the statement emphasized.[101] Such modesty did not last long.

The epithet "reactionary" *(phản động)* carried less grave implications than "traitor," yet could still result in a person being killed or detained indefinitely. Previously, "reactionary" had targeted those who rejected modernity and hoped to reassert "feudalism" in Vietnam. Now however, reactionary could mean almost any negative behavior, including gambling, usury, mistreating tenants, spreading superstition, or ignoring government orders. During early 1946, Việt Minh and Nationalist Party newspapers fired "reactionary" accusations at each other. One paper called on both groups to stop using the term, as it made the public apprehensive and confused.[102] *Việt Nam,* the Nationalist Party daily, later accused Việt Minh leaders of calling anyone a reactionary who disagreed with their platform, refuted their assertions, or criticized government mistakes. "The word belongs to a dictatorship," *Việt Nam* asserted, whereas in a democratic republic there were laws and courts to delineate illegal behavior.[103] This was in July, when the Nationalist Party could no longer look to the Chinese Army for protection. Eight days later the Công An and Việt Minh militia assaulted the Nationalist Party headquarters and took prisoners (see below).

THE ROLE OF POLITICAL PARTIES IN THE DRV

Three days following the 2 September 1945 independence declaration, the DRV interim government decreed dissolution of two political parties on the grounds that they had plotted actions harmful to national independence. The Greater Viet National Socialist Party (Đại Việt Quốc Xã Hội Đảng) was accused of consorting with foreigners in order to harm independence, while the Greater Viet Nationalist Party (Đại Việt Quốc Dân Đảng) had allegedly schemed to damage the country's economy as well as its independence. Any member of these parties who continued activities would be "dealt with severely according to law."[104] A week later, two northern youth associations received the same treatment.[105] Newspapers quickly identified these four organizations as "pro-Japanese," although no one explained why they had been singled out from among the many groups that had fraternized with the Japanese in previous months. Also, Japan was no longer a threat to Vietnamese independence, so why focus on outdated enemies? Whatever the answer to these questions (to which we will return), DRV leaders were conveying a broader message: they intended to determine which domestic organizations represented threats to national security and hence needed to be repressed.

Histories of the 1925–45 period in Vietnam tend to portray communist and noncommunist organizations as mortal enemies of each other. Much of this represents a reading backwards of 1945–54 hatreds, betrayals, and killings, applying that stance to an earlier era when political activists of varying ideological persuasions possessed similar educational backgrounds, interacted routinely, and sometimes were related to each other by blood or marriage. Organizations with different platforms shared information (selectively), signed public statements together, and formed and dissolved tactical coalitions without rancor. During 1924–27 in southern China, Vietnamese of diverse anticolonial persuasions interacted with each other as well as with Chinese, Koreans, and other nationals.[106] In the 1930s, a number of left-wing and centrist organizations inside Indochina joined in the push for fundamental reforms of the colonial system. Most remarkable of all was the 1933–37 political alliance in Cochinchina between Comintern adherents ("Stalinists") and members of the Fourth International ("Trotskyists")[107] During

1941–44 in southern China, the ICP, Vietnam Nationalist Party, and Vietnam Revolutionary League participated in the same anti-Japanese front groups, occasionally denouncing someone to their mutual Chinese sponsors, but not kidnapping or killing each other.[108] It was the competition for recruits, donations, and Chinese patronage that increased tensions between émigré organizations, more than ideological differences.[109]

The 9 March 1945 Japanese coup compelled Vietnamese organizations across the political spectrum to reassess their behavior and prospects. Those organizations that had been particularly close to the French ceased to function, and their leaders took as low a profile as possible. Those persons who had worked for the Japanese, or been given Japanese protection against French arrest, proceeded to go public, form organizations, initiate newspapers, convene meetings and test the parameters of Japanese indulgence. Those organizations committed to the Allied cause tried to prepare for a possible American amphibious landing in Indochina or a Chinese ground invasion from the north, meanwhile condemning groups who collaborated with the Japanese. All anticolonial organizations took advantage of considerable confusion within the Indochina Sûreté as the result of French personnel being interned. As indicated earlier, the level of political violence increased by July, yet political leaders and public intellectuals of different propensities continued to meet, swap rumors, and talk of patriotic coalitions. The remainder of this chapter takes a roughly chronological approach, discussing opposition groups in the order that the DRV or ICP moved against them. By August 1946, with the notable exception of the Catholic Church, opposition had been crushed, neutered, or forced into exile.

Đại Việt Parties: Immediate Suppression

In May 1945, members of several Japanese-associated Đại Việt parties crossed into China to meet with Vietnam Nationalist Party leaders. This led to formation of the Đại Việt Quốc Dân Đảng, a coalition aimed particularly at coordinating domestic and émigré operations in the event of Chinese invasion of Indochina. This proved to be a disastrous strategic choice for the Nationalist Party, not because it necessarily compromised the organization in the eyes of Chinese Nationalist patrons, but because the agreement left Nationalist Party leaders content to rely on Đại Việt capacities inside Vietnam rather than infiltrate their own personnel, as the ICP had been doing for some time already. When Japan unexpectedly surrendered in mid-August, armed Đại Việt groups in Hanoi, Haiphong, and Hải Dương had to act entirely on their own, without help from armed Nationalist Party units across the frontier in Guangxi and Yunnan, who were waiting for Chinese authorization to enter Indochina.

Trương Tử Anh, the most effective Đại Việt leader, marched a unit of 250 men into Hanoi on the evening of 17 August, just as some royal government officials were trying to stiffen the resolve of Civil Guard and Security Service units to block an impending takeover by Việt Minh adherents. However, none of these elements offered resistance on the morning of 19 August when Việt Minh-led crowds moved on government buildings. That evening in Hanoi, a crisis meeting of Đại Việt and local Nationalist Party members failed to agree on a plan to mount an immediate countercoup.[110] With provincial reinforcements held up by flooding of the Red River, this proposition soon faded, and Đại Việt units withdrew east and west of Hanoi to await developments. It was in this context that the DRV interim government outlawed the Đại Việt Quốc Dân Đảng on 5 September, aware that it could not ban the Nationalist Party without offending the Chinese military, whose first troop units reached Hanoi on 9 September. The ICP was also mindful that French officials were portraying the Việt Minh as a creation of the Japanese, hence there was utility in continuing to expose and punish alleged lackeys of the Japanese, as a way of reaffirming Allied credentials.

During September and October 1945, various DRV or Việt Minh organizations probably killed or detained several hundred alleged Đại Việt members. On 1 September, an armed Việt Minh unit attacked a Đại Việt Duy Tân group in Ninh Bình province, killing eight, capturing eleven, and collecting three firearms. Additional Đại Việt suspects were arrested in Ninh Bình in subsequent weeks, duly investigated, and reported to be all released by the end of October.[111] Tuyên Quang province committee reported several Đại Việt groups active in early September, but their presence was of no consequence compared to the difficulties of dealing with Chinese troops pouring into the province.[112] Thái Bình reported that a Đại Việt Quốc Gia organization which had caused trouble for Việt Minh adherents before 19 August had now broken up. Nonetheless, Đại Việt members were among many alleged traitors captured locally, and in some cases killed without authorization. In Phú Thọ, twenty-four Đại Việt members were arrested, with only four still detained as of late October. Meanwhile, the local Đại Việt organization was said to have disbanded.[113] In Hưng Yên, Nguyễn Thị Trang Nghiêm was arrested on 1 December for passing out reactionary leaflets in a restaurant, and deported seventeen days later. Her father and sister were members of the Đại Việt Quốc Gia Liên Minh.[114]

Trương Tử Anh managed to sustain a clandestine Đại Việt network despite police pursuit, while consistently warning Nationalist Party leaders against negotiating any power-sharing deal with the ICP.[115] Throughout 1946 the Công An continued to chase Đại Việt adherents. On 8 March, for example, the husband of Bùi Thị Dịu was taken away by a militia team without explanation; her subsequent district-level inquiries and petitions to Hanoi were ignored. In May, Dịu's husband was charged with being an active Đại Việt Duy Tân cadre and his case conveyed to the Hanoi Military Court.[116] Even those persons suspected of Đại Việt affiliations but released had to face intense suspicion, ostracism, and possible rearrest. On the other hand, a few former colonial employees who had been sacked by the French for membership in the Đại Việt Dân Chính proceeded to apply to the DRV for reemployment and were accepted. Thus, Nguyễn Huy Thành, who had been fired in 1942 for trying to indoctrinate his colleagues at the Phúc Yên Résidence, was restored to government employment in September 1946.[117]

Largely due to skilful Việt Minh propaganda, the term "Đại Việt" became a metaphor for crass collaboration with the Japanese occupier, in contrast to heroic Việt Minh endeavors to liberate the country from these "dwarf" *(lùn)* fascist imperialists. Prior to 9 March 1945, however, few Vietnamese had close relations with Japanese forces, and if the Việt Minh struggled with anyone it was the French. After 9 March, Vietnamese across the entire political spectrum—including some Việt Minh adherents—came into nonviolent contact with Japanese military and civilian personnel. As for the Việt Minh claim to have fought the Japanese, this vastly inflated a few ambushes in the northern hills. To heighten the myth of the Liberation Army combating the Imperial Japanese Army, it helped to present a despicable domestic deviation marked Đại Việt.

Trotskyists: The ICP's "Left Opposition"

Soon after Đại Việt parties were banned, alleged Trotskyists faced denunciation as enemies of the DRV. Third International (ICP) and Fourth International adherents had long accused each other of serving imperialist interests. The dispute remained largely confined to periodicals, leaflets, and oratory until August 1945 in Saigon, where it quickly escalated to public confrontations over power, how to deal with the Allies, and whether class struggle should be encouraged or not. Meetings to form a southern Vietnam revolutionary united front degenerated into slanging matches, followed by press recriminations that widened the impact and made compromise less likely. The Fourth International "Struggle" group (La Lutte) and the International Communist League condemned the Việt Minh for putting any faith in the Allied powers, who all remained profoundly imperialist, hence certain to try to quash an independent Vietnam rather than recognize its right to exist. The obvious strategy, according to both Trotskyist groups, was to arm the masses and attack the first British and French units to arrive in the south, rather than attempt to negotiate some compromise while ever more enemy troops poured in. When Trần Văn Giàu, ICP leader and chair of the Southern Provisional Administrative Committee, met a French representative, the Trotskyists accused him of betraying the revolution, following which he denounced them as enemy provocateurs. Even so, when the first planeload of British personnel flew into Tân Sơn Nhứt airport on 6 September, the Southern Committee selected four Struggle members to be the welcoming delegation—and they accepted.[118] Three days later Giàu stepped aside in favor of a nonparty lawyer, Phạm Văn Bạch, and several Trotskyists were invited to join an enlarged Southern Committee.

On 7–8 September in the Mekong delta, however, some Trotskyists had apparently joined with followers of the charismatic Hòa Hảo leader, Huỳnh Phú Sổ, in a bloody, unsuccessful attack on Việt Minh adherents in Cần Thơ town. Dương Bạch Mai (ICP), the Southern Committee's head of security, began incarcerating Trotskyists in the infamous Maison central prison in Saigon, where British troops found them on the night of 22 September and turned them over to the French. British-French attacks of that night sparked the call by Trần Văn Giàu for total armed struggle against imperialists and collaborators, sounding remarkably like the Trotskyists one month earlier. Trotskyists fought alongside other groups, and opposed the British-inspired ceasefire that lasted from 3 to 9 October (see chapter 4). During the mid-October general retreat from Saigon, ICP squads systematically tracked down and detained Trotskyists, subsequently killing at least two dozen leaders. Phan Văn Hùm, one of the most respected southern political figures from the 1930s, was executed aboard a train north of Phan Thiết, and his body dumped in a river. Other Trotskyists found refuge with armed Hòa Hảo and secular nationalist groups in the Mekong delta.[119] This ICP decision to wipe out an entire Marxist anticolonial cohort in the south shocked politically alert Vietnamese throughout the country, and has remained a source of condemnation to this day.

In northern Vietnam, Fourth International adherents had never been as influential as in the south. During the Pacific War, several Trotskyists remained active in the Hàn Thuyên publishing group in Hanoi, where diverse leftist intellectuals continued to deliberate the merits of "permanent revolution" versus a "two-stage revolution." Some miners, stevedores, and textile workers continued to favor Trotskyist arguments about class struggle and proletarian control of worksites. In August 1945, workers at Cẩm Phả northeast of Haiphong formed committees to operate the coal mines, railroad line, and telegraph system, but made no Fourth International claims. Lương Đức Thiệp, Trotskyist sympathizer, continued to publish booklets on materialism and petit bourgeois individualism.[120] The status of China in the global imperialist struggle had been part of lively debates between the Third International and the Fourth International in the 1930s, yet no Trotskyists stepped forward now in the north to call for immediate armed resistance to impending Nationalist Chinese occupation, unlike the comparable situation with the British in Saigon. Nonetheless, ICP and Việt Minh newspapers in the north put Trotskyists on their list of dangerous adversaries to be rooted out and neutralized (see chapter 8).

Trotskyists were never the object of a DRV proscription edict. Instead, provincial people's committees were ordered to report regularly on any Trotskyists uncovered and dealt with. In early September, the Haiphong People's Committee reported "immediate suppression" of unspecified Trotskyists in the city.[121] In October, Hưng Yên province told of ferreting out "Trotskyist reactionaries" in possession of copies of Chiến Đấu (Combat) newspaper, yet only two persons were arrested. Under the mandatory reporting category of "reactionaries," Quảng Yên affirmed vaguely that "a couple of fledgling Trotskyists have been awakened (giác ngộ)."[122] In October, Nguyễn Công Tính was arrested in Hà Đông as a "Fourth International Communist" and turned over to the Thái Nguyên security service, who took him to a Bắc Kạn deportation camp. In April 1946, his mother petitioned to be told of his whereabouts and disposition, but Bắc Kạn had no record of his existence.[123] Hải Dương province reported that a Trotskyist group had been "smashed."[124] Two men were arrested in Hanoi in December, accused of being Trotskyists and deported to Bắc Kạn. Six months later they petitioned for release, admitting to "previously possessing Communist Forth International tendencies" of a political but nonviolent nature, and promising no future opposition to the government.[125]

Minutes of a late November 1946 meeting of DRV Communications and Propaganda Bureau cadres state that among Vietnamese returning from France to Hải Dương province there were "some extreme Trotskyists active but with insignificant results."[126] Other than that one report, 1946 official files contain nothing further on Trotskyism. Either the government no longer included Trotskyists on its hit list, or localities had no more alleged Trotskyists to report under the category of "reactionaries." In the press the Trotskyists epithet continued to appear, most often as a warning to employees who complained publicly about the failure of wages to keep up with rampant inflation, or who dared to push for workers' control over enterprises. Interestingly, the 1930s leader of the Octoberist Fourth International group, Hồ Hữu Tường, was appointed to the Hanoi University Board of Trustees in December 1945, taught social sciences in the Faculty of Letters, and worked with Việt Minh-affiliated intellectuals in preparing for a national cultural congress.[127]

Vietnam Revolutionary League: Divide and Dismantle

During much of World War II, the Vietnam Revolutionary League (Việt Nam Cách Mệnh Đồng Minh Hội) had served as umbrella under which anticolonial organizations in southern China obtained recognition and support from General Zhang Fakui, commander of the Fourth Army Area (Guangxi-Guangdong). From about May 1945, however, Hồ Chí Minh had chosen to conduct Việt Minh operations across the border in northern Tonkin without reference to the Revolutionary League, much to the irritation of General Xiao Wen, General Zhang's subordinate responsible for Indochina affairs. General Xiao proceeded to enhance the status of Nguyễn Hải Thần, a sixty-seven-year old emigré nationalist respected for his early association with the revered Phan Bội Châu (1867–1940).

Hundreds of émigré Vietnamese clustered around Thần in expectation that he would lead them across the frontier together with Fourth Army area forces to attack the Japanese. However, when Japan suddenly capitulated to the Allies in mid-August 1945, Generalissimo Chiang Kai-shek in Chungking decided to assign the job of occupying northern Indochina to Yunnan General Lu Han, rather than General Zhang. General Lu had no reason to favor the Guangxi-based Revolutionary League over the Vietnam Nationalist Party or the Việt Minh, although he did accept General Xiao to his occupation staff.[128]

By 20 August 1945, Revolutionary League units could be found with advance Chinese units crossing into Cao Bằng and Lạng Sơn provinces. Indeed, one Revolutionary League unit popped up that day, eighty-five kilometers south of the frontier, in Tuyên Quang province.[129] On 1 September, a substantial Revolutionary League group accompanying Chinese troops into the coastal town of Móng Cái announced a "National Provisional Government of Vietnam," headed by Nguyễn Hải Thần.[130] Twelve days later the Revolutionary League unit in Lạng Sơn informed Hanoi that its banner was recognized by the Chinese government and the Allies as "the flag of all Vietnamese revolutionary parties." It even provided a drawing of the Revolutionary League flag: horizontal white and blue stripes in the upper left corner on a red field.[131] As Chinese troops trudged in the direction of Hanoi and Haiphong, division commanders instructed Revolutionary League cadres to leave civil affairs teams at each town en route, which made it impossible for Thần to concentrate his forces for political effect. When Thần made it to Hanoi on 16 September, he had only a modest guard element and probably little idea of what to expect.[132]

On 30 September, Nguyễn Hải Thần led a large Revolutionary League delegation to meet General Xiao Wen to try to discuss removal of the DRV provisional government and suppression of the ICP. According to a DRV police informant, Hsiao asked the Revolutionary League group sarcastically how many soldiers and firearms they possessed to accomplish the overthrow, and chided them for assuming that communists had to be eliminated rather than accepted as part of a national united front (Guomindang-CCP talks were then underway in Chongqing).[133] Xiao's deprecating remarks must have infuriated Thần, yet he was in no position to break with the Chinese. Thần was further embarrassed in late October when seven of his Revolutionary League subordinates signed with five Việt Minh members a "unity procedure" *(Biện pháp đoàn kết)*, which upheld "common struggle against French aggression in order to defend the liberty and independence of the Democratic Republic of Vietnam."[134] One Revolutionary League endorser of the "unity procedure," Trương Trung Phụng, was kidnapped by the Nationalist Party on 25 November, but released sixteen days later.[135] Another Revolutionary League endorser, Đinh Trương Dương, accepted a DRV mission to travel to central Vietnam.[136] However, several other League endorsers abrogated their involvement within days, and Thần publicly denounced the role of the ICP in the DRV. In Hanoi, a series of violent street clashes between Revolutionary League and Việt Minh adherents shocked the public and taxed the patience of Chinese commanders.[137]

As General Xiao Wen stepped up pressure on all parties to form a government of national union, Hồ Chí Minh found it tactically expedient to cultivate Nguyễn Hải Thần at the expense of Nationalist Party leaders. Thần could harken back to his comradeship with Phan Bội Châu and cite his lifelong refusal to collaborate with the French colonialists. Chinese leaders from Generalissimo Chiang downward showed public respect for Thần, although Vietnamese sometimes mocked him for having lost the ability to speak his native language properly. Thần demonstrated little capacity to build a domestic power base, which made him a suitable vice president in Hồ's eyes. Việt Minh activists played on divisions inside the Revolutionary League, much to the irritation of the Nationalist Party.[138]

While Việt Minh, Nationalist Party, and Revolutionary League leaders shook hands and haggled over legal definitions, ministerial appointments, and joint pronouncements, a bitter struggle persisted between newspaper editors, recruiters, fundraisers, and armed enforcers. The DRV Ministry of Information and Propaganda planted in various newspapers fictitious letters to the editor that criticized Nguyễn Hải Thần for not contributing Revolutionary League personnel to fight in the south, and accused him of making deals with the French.[139] Newspapers routinely accused opponents of rank extortion of vulnerable citizens. The DRV police repeatedly arrested Revolutionary League members for alleged shakedowns, especially of overseas Chinese.[140] Việt Minh and Revolutionary League adherents tore down each other's posters, made physical threats, and sometimes broke up opponents' meetings. Bồ Xuân Luật, a Revolutionary League cadre who had parted company with Nguyễn Hải Thần, was encouraged by DRV leaders to start his own newspaper. Ten days later in downtown Hanoi, Luật was ambushed by two carloads of armed men, and was lucky to escape with only two bullet wounds.[141] His *Đồng Minh (Alliance)* newspaper continued to publish until November 1946.

Revolutionary League units in towns from the Chinese border down to the Red River delta had no difficulty holding their positions, at least until Chinese forces began withdrawing starting in April 1946. Local teachers, civil servants, and police officers had to decide whether to show loyalty to the Revolutionary League, to attempt neutrality, or to withdraw from town. A late 1945 Hanoi Education Department report on four provinces stated that some school buildings had been occupied by Chinese troops, while other schools had discontinued classes due to "bothering" of teachers, students, and local citizens by Revolutionary League members.[142] The Revolutionary League occasionally had to extend de facto recognition to DRV authorities, as when it requested government permission to purchase and transport twenty tons of salt.[143]

As part of the tripartite accord reached 23 December 1945, Nguyễn Hải Thần was designated DRV vice president in a provisional coalition government duly announced to the public on 1 January 1946, five days before the national elections.[144] Following on the 23 December agreement, twenty Revolutionary League members were made deputies to the National Assembly by executive order. They were not assigned to geographical locations as regular National Assembly candidates were.[145] Several other Revolutionary League members chose to stand for election. Hồ Đắc Thành made sure that his personal details were published together with those of other candidates in Nam Định, and was duly elected to the National Assembly from that province.[146] Bồ Xuân Luật won election from Hưng Yên province and soon was made DRV vice minister of agriculture.[147] When the National Assembly convened at the Hanoi Opera House on 2 March 1946, Hồ Chí Minh had to inform deputies that Nguyễn Hải Thần was "unwell" and unable to attend. Nominating a government Cabinet to the Assembly, Hồ by prior arrangement proposed Thần as vice president and another Revolutionary League member, Trương Đình Tri, as minister of society (which would include health, welfare and labor), characterizing Dr. Tri as a "well-known specialist in the medical field."[148]

Hovering over everyone in the first days of March, however, were the critical, highly-charged negotiations between the DRV, France, and China. Revolutionary League members must have been shaken on hearing of the 28 February Sino-French agreement, by which Chungking accepted imminent French return to northern Indochina and withdrawal of Chinese forces. Hồ may have sought Nguyễn Hải Thần's participation in discussions with the Chinese and French, and he certainly tried to gain Thần's cosignature to the 6 March Preliminary Accord, but Thần was nowhere to be found, having already departed Hanoi several days prior.

Overshadowed by the Nationalist Party, and increasingly bedeviled by internal disputes, the Revolutionary League lost coherence during March 1946. Some members focused on defending towns north of Hanoi, others switched over to the Nationalist Party, and still others accepted de facto subordination to the Việt Minh. Some of the attacks on French soldiers in April, particularly those in Haiphong, may have been the work of Revolutionary League members.[149] In late April, French forces exhumed twelve bodies from the basement of the former Revolutionary League headquarters in Hanoi, including two French nationals who had disappeared on 24 December 1945.[150] Hoàng Cừ, a prominent journalist affiliated with the Revolutionary League, was arrested on charges of illegal transport of one hundred tons of salt and sentenced to ten years' hard labor.[151] The

DRV negotiated with a Revolutionary League leader in Lạng Sơn, then drove him across the Chinese frontier in June, only to be compelled to share Lạng Sơn town with the French from 8 July.[152] Revolutionary League adherents in Quảng Yên and Móng Cái appear to have withdrawn across the border in mid-June, along with departing Chinese troops. Hồ Đắc Thành, Revolutionary League deputy from Nam Định, was listed in late May as member of the ICP-inspired broader united front, the Vietnam National Alliance (Hội Liên Hiệp Quốc Dân Việt Nam). The *Đồng Minh* newspaper reported meetings of remaining Revolutionary League branches, and the participation of some League members in the second session of the National Assembly in late October.[153] The police screened documents captured from the Revolutionary League and called in members for interrogation. Henceforth a few compliant League members would help government authorities to project a national front image, while others faced incarceration or flight.

Vietnam Nationalist Party: No Holds Barred

The Nationalist Party group led by Lê Khang that departed Hanoi immediately following Việt Minh seizure of power on 19 August 1945 made its way fifty kilometers northwest to the town of Vĩnh Yên. There the group was greeted by Đỗ Đình Đạo, energetic head of a local youth organization. Together they organized a demonstration of townsfolk that convinced members of the Vĩnh Yên Civil Guard post to join up.[154] Lê Khang did not choose Vĩnh Yên randomly: it was positioned along the Lào Cai–Hanoi rail line that Chinese troops from Yunnan and Nationalist Party exiles would employ to enter Tonkin.

On 29 August, several thousand people from three adjacent rural districts approached Nationalist Party positions at Vĩnh Yên, waving Việt Minh flags and proposing to conduct a "solidarity" demonstration through the town. After being refused, the crowd nonetheless edged closer and some rifle-toting members opened fire. The Nationalists replied with automatic rifles, killing an unknown number, capturing about 150, and causing other panic-stricken demonstrators to drown in the nearby river. Most of the prisoners were released after listening to a Nationalist lecture and agreeing they had been duped into joining the march. In following weeks, opposing leaders exchanged letters concerning prisoner releases, the authority of individuals to parley, and proposals regarding joint local administration. A Việt Minh blockade of food to the town made life difficult. On 18 September a prominent Democratic Party member, Hoàng Văn Đức, arrived from Hanoi with DRV credentials to negotiate. Lê Khang decided instead to launch an attack on Phúc Yên that failed. DRV Liberation Army units then tried unsuccessfully to capture Vĩnh Yên, after which a de facto ceasefire held for several months.[155] The Nationalists do not appear to have contested Việt Minh ascendancy in the countryside, except for occupying Tam Lộng plantation in Vĩnh

Yên province. A substantial Việt Minh assault on Tam Lộng was repulsed in early December.[156]

On the Chinese side of the frontier with Tonkin, Nationalist Party and Việt Minh activists alike proselytized among thirty-two hundred native members of French colonial units that had fled to Yunnan following the 9 March 1945 Japanese coup. Both sides had much more success among the two thousand or so Kinh soldiers than among the ethnic minority elements. In September, Nationalists struck a covert agreement with Captain Nguyễn Duy Viên, whereby his Kinh company of *tirailleurs* would come over to their side en masse at the appropriate moment. However, Nationalist cadres in Kunming suspected Captain Viên (known as Ba Viên for his three officer stripes) as a French double-agent, whose unit would be ordered to eliminate Nationalists after entering Tonkin. During the first week of November, Viên marched his company almost two hundred kilometers from Mengzi to the Hà Giang province seat, where Nationalists met him enthusiastically. Deserters from other colonial units gravitated to Hà Giang town as well, until Captain Viên could claim four hundred men under his command. However, the bad blood between Nationalist and Việt Minh activists was obvious to at least one ordinary citizen, who felt compelled to dispatch a letter to Hanoi pleading for a government plenipotentiary to come and convince everyone to focus on resisting the foreigner.[157] After traveling to Hanoi and meeting Hồ Chí Minh, Viên returned to Hà Giang, began arresting Nationalists, and later executed some prisoners in the nearby hills. On Christmas Day, Viên's unit was enrolled to the DRV National Guard. In April 1946, a Nationalist hit team located Viên in Hanoi, shooting him fatally as he left a restaurant.[158]

ICP leaders judged that the Vietnam Nationalist Party posed a more substantial challenge to them than the Đại Việt parties, Trotskyists, and the Revolutionary League put together. Despite ICP efforts to convince the public that current Nationalist Party leaders had betrayed the noble legacy of Nguyễn Thái Học and other martyrs of 1930, many citizens kept an open mind in late 1945. Besides the units accompanying Chinese forces down the Red River corridor in late September, active Nationalist cells existed in the Indochina Railway Company, the PTT, and at the Cité Universitaire in Hanoi. There were also Nationalist Party veterans recently released from prison, and Đại Việt members eager to affiliate. Nguyễn Tường Tam (Nhất Linh), Vietnam's best known creative writer, editor, and publisher from the 1930s, had the potential to mount a Nationalist Party print media campaign to rival Việt Minh efforts.

In early September 1945, Vũ Hồng Khanh, head of the Nationalist Party organization based in Yunnan, tried unsuccessfully to gain a seat on a Chinese airplane flying into Hanoi, then was prevented by the Chinese commander at Lào Cai from traveling in by road. After his comrade Nghiêm Kế Tổ lobbied Guomindang contacts in Chongqing, Khanh finally arrived in Hanoi 20 October. In his

FIGURE 23. Titled "Việt Minh Resistance Work," this Nationalist Party cartoon depicts Hồ Chí Minh, Võ Nguyên Giáp, and Trần Huy Liệu slinking away, leaving citizens at the mercy of the French. In *Việt Nam* 30 (19 Dec. 1945). Courtesy of Vietnam National Library.

absence a group more willing to identify with the DRV had created a Mobilization Committee to Reorganize the Vietnam Nationalist Party, which Khanh deliberately ignored.[159] Nguyễn Tường Tam chose to remain in Kunming and Chongqing during all of late 1945, trying unsuccessfully to obtain further Chinese and American assistance.[160] Tam's media talents were sorely missed in Hanoi, although his close colleague Trần Khánh Dư (Khái Hưng) edited *Việt Nam*, the principal Nationalist Party newspaper.

First published on 15 November 1945, *Việt Nam* rapidly became the most effective paper opposing the ICP and Việt Minh. Splashed across page one of the first edition was a Nationalist Party declaration which harkened back to the heroic 1930 sacrifices of Nguyễn Thái Học and his comrades, accused Hồ Chí Minh of betraying the 1942–45 united front by taking power unilaterally in August, and claimed that the Nationalist Party could have overthrown the new regime but chose not to in deference to the higher national interest. The Việt Minh had then pursued a mistaken, ineffective policy, losing foreign friends because of its extremism, terrorizing other Vietnamese parties, failing to deal with desperate economic conditions, and passively accepting enemy invasion of the south. The immediate need, according to the Nationalist Party, was for all parties to set aside parochial concerns, form a legitimate government of national union, and mobilize the entire populace to escape slavery and achieve real independence. An article accompanying the declaration urged "revolutionary brothers" in the Việt Minh to acknowledge that their leaders had taken the country down a dangerous road and had used them for selfish, power-hungry purposes.[161]

For the next six weeks *Việt Nam* editors never employed the name "Democratic Republic of Vietnam," except sarcastically or in quotation marks, and they repeatedly rejected the Việt Minh flag and anthem as national symbols. They accused Hồ Chí Minh of being a dictator, referred to the "fascist Hồ Chí Minh gang," and featured a number of disparaging cartoons of Hồ.[162] However, *Việt Nam*'s prime target was the Tổng Bộ Việt Minh, which it routinely labeled fascist for allegedly spreading lies, extorting money, kidnapping opponents, and launching armed assaults on Nationalist Party bureaus. *Việt Nam* traded vitriolic attacks with *Cứu Quốc (National Salvation)*, the Việt Minh's leading daily. It had less to say about the DRV state, except for regularly condemning the Security Service and the Ministry of Information and Propaganda headed by Trần Huy Liệu.[163]

Stories from the provinces soon increased in *Việt Nam*, particularly news that denounced the actions of local Việt Minh groups and people's committees. *Việt Nam* complained often about local authorities seizing copies of its paper. From DRV archival records we know this happened routinely, and indeed individuals sometimes faced arrest for merely possessing a copy of *Việt Nam*. Nonetheless, copies of *Việt Nam* appeared to circulate widely, facilitated by Nationalist Party members or sympathizers inside the PTT and the Indochina Railroad.

Mutual distrust, even outright animosity, did not preclude Việt Minh and Nationalist Party representatives from meeting with each other to discuss differences and even put their names to tactical accords. What remains unclear is whether leaders on either side wanted to achieve a working coalition or were simply going through the motions to avoid Chinese retribution. Already on 29 September, Nguyễn Lương Bằng (Việt Minh) and Chu Bá Phượng (Nationalist Party) agreed to halt violent altercations, release detainees, and cease condemning each other in public.[164] On 19 November, Hồ Chí Minh, Vũ Hồng Khanh, and Nguyễn Hải Thần signed a list of "High Common Principles" intended to guide negotiations towards a "unanimous government" as well as achieve a single army, the ending of interparty struggles, and elimination of "French colonial cabals" that threatened Vietnam's complete independence. On 24 November, the Nationalist Party convened a public meeting in front of its Hanoi headquarters at which speakers from both sides seemed to avoid the ad hominem recriminations found in opposing newspapers. At the end of this meeting, the same three leaders signed a brief memorandum in which the "two sides" promised to stop attacks on one another, to push for unity, and to support the armed resistance in the south.[165]

Within days, however, *Cứu Quốc* editors were taking the 24 November joint memorandum to mean affirmation of an already existing government of national union, to which the Nationalist Party immediately took strong exception.[166] Hồ Chí Minh also hardened his position, informing Nguyễn Hải Thần and Vũ Hồng Khanh publicly that unity was already achieved, national elections would proceed in three weeks, and there was no need for prior reshuffling of the government. The editors of *Việt Nam* now accused Hồ of lacking the qualities of a Confucian gentleman *(quân tử)*, and, together with his communist comrades, employing "terrorist and dictatorial policies."[167]

With both sides refusing to budge, General Xiao Wen and other Chinese officers took a more direct role in deliberations. On 25 December, Hồ conceded formation of a new provisional government of national union prior to convening of the national assembly and accepted a two-week postponement of the elections. On the other side, Vũ Hồng Khanh and Nguyễn Hải Thần accepted Hồ as continuing provisional president, agreed to leave determination of the national flag and emblem *(quốc huy)* to the national assembly, and failed in their bid to gain immediate access to the national army's command or general staff structure. The Nationalist Party was allocated fifty seats and the Revolutionary League twenty seats in the upcoming National Assembly, without members having to stand for election. Although outwardly a Việt Minh concession, this provision affirmed in many people's minds the inability of the opposition to compete for support at the local level. In a clearcut sign of Chinese arbitration, the Chinese language text of the 23 December accord was declared legally binding.[168] Clause 13 of the agreement was not published, probably because it referred to Chinese action in the event of violations. The text did not once mention the name of the country under discussion, since the Nationalist Party had yet to accept the designation "Democratic Republic of Vietnam."

The 23 December 1945 accord also specified a formula for ten ministerial appointments: two Việt Minh, two Democratic Party [also Việt Minh], two Nationalist Party, two Revolutionary League, and two nonparty. However, the Cabinet announced on 1 January 1946 contained fourteen ministers and two deputy ministers, an indication that bargaining was still underway and not likely to be resolved before the 6 January elections to the National Assembly.[169] Hồ Chí Minh was in no hurry to convene the 1 January 1946 Cabinet. The arrival from Chungking of Nguyễn Tường Tam and Nghiêm Kế Tổ on 20 January, both presumably well-informed on the progress of Sino-French negotiations, must have provoked intense discussion within the Nationalist Party about what to do in the event of Chinese troop withdrawals from northern Indochina. At Lai Châu in February, Nationalist Party and DRV National Guard units skirmished separately with the French, the former eventually retreating to Lào Cai, the latter to Sơn La. On 10 February in Hanoi, the Nationalist Party organized the first public commemoration of the 1930 Yên Bái uprising, with a large crowd attending.[170] In Haiphong, however, the commemoration became divisive when some in the audience protested the absence of any red flag with yellow star.[171]

Following the 23 December 1945 accord, central leaders on both sides had dispatched orders to lower echelons to halt physical and verbal attacks on opponents. Some recipients were perplexed. For example, the Hòa Bình province committee reported that ethnic Mường leaders who had been helping to break up Nationalist Party activities now once again expressed doubts about DRV administration. Others, increasingly mindful of the French military threat, supported an end to fratricide. Few were willing to discuss organizational mergers or combined operations, but for the moment each side stopped looking for a fight.[172] Local Chinese commanders sometimes mediated. General Wang, based in Phú Thọ town, brought the two sides together to discuss joint administration, though the discussion was broken off by a shootout in the marketplace. Aggrieved townsfolk now petitioned President Hồ Chí Minh, complaining that both sides had taken many hostages, commerce had collapsed, and neither side was listening to town elders. General Wang apparently facilitated an uneasy truce, which somehow lasted four months.[173]

From mid-February 1946, knowledge of the Sino-French negotiations, the threat of French invasion of the north, and talks between Hồ Chí Minh and Jean Sainteny all served to heighten political anxieties and rekindle verbal hostilities. One nonparty paper chastised both *Việt Nam* and *Cứu Quốc,* saying that their attacks on each other exceeded the bounds of civility and ignored the fact that foreigners too were reading the press. An editorial titled "Who Is Reactionary?" condemned both the Nationalist Party and the Việt Minh for tossing the reactionary epithet around constantly, causing the public much anxiety and jeopardizing preparations to fight the French invaders.[174] A new twist was added when a crowd showed up at Bảo Đại's residence on 20 February, carrying imperial yellow flags and banners inscribed "Support President Vĩnh Thụy," "Down with Pro-French Policy," and "The Fatherland Is in Danger." Three elders were allowed in to urge Bảo Đại to head the new government in place of Hồ Chí Minh. Chinese military police prevented DRV Security Service personnel from forcibly breaking up the crowd. The Việt Minh accused the Nationalist Party of organizing the demonstration.[175]

Now realizing that French forces were coming to the north one way or another, Hồ Chí Minh moved to resolve disputes with the opposition over Cabinet appointments and convening of the National Assembly. He acceded to the Nationalist Party's longstanding requirement that two of the most prominent communists, Võ Nguyên Giáp and Trần Huy Liệu, be excluded from the Cabinet. A joint conference met repeatedly to try to reach agreement on two questions: who among nonparty or neutral Vietnamese would take up the two key portfolios of defense and interior; and how would authority be shared over the National Guard?[176] From the beginning, Phan Anh appeared the likely choice as defense minister, which is rather surprising given his brother's Việt Minh affiliation.[177] Perhaps Nationalist Party leaders, familiar with Phan Anh's credentials as unflinching defense lawyer and energetic minister of youth in the brief Trần Trọng Kim Cabinet, hoped he would resist Việt Minh efforts to monopolize National Guard high command and general staff positions. If so, they soon would be disappointed.

The joint conference considered at least four persons for the interior portfolio: Huỳnh Thúc Kháng, widely respected editor and publisher in Huế; Trần Đình Nam, physician, writer, and minister of interior in the Trần Trọng Kim government; Ngô Đình Diệm, former mandarin and lay Catholic political leader; and Bùi Bằng Đoàn, former mandarin and current head of the DRV investigation commission. It seems that Diệm was set aside due to his well-known anticommunist sentiments, while Đoàn was seen as too close to the Việt Minh. As of 27 February, Nam appeared to be the consensus candidate.[178] However, Hồ Chí Minh decided to apply all his powers of persuasion on Kháng, dispatching emissaries and telegrams to Huế, and refusing to take no for an answer. Kháng reluctantly accepted and was escorted urgently to Hanoi in time for opening of the National Assembly on 2 March.[179] Given Kháng's national reputation, no one could oppose his appointment once he was prepared to serve.

The question of authority over the National Guard was dealt with by formation of a nine-person Resistance Committee (Kháng Chiến Ủy Viên Hội) that apparently was meant to report to the National Assembly rather than to the president or Cabinet.[180] Remarkably, the Nationalist Party accepted Võ Nguyên Giáp to chair this potentially powerful body, despite having denounced him vehemently for months. Vũ Hồng Khanh was made deputy chair of the Resistance Committee, although he could not have been optimistic about exercising much authority. Perhaps he hoped to insert some Nationalist Party cadres with Chinese Army experience within the General Staff of the National Guard, and to insure that his armed units remained intact if formally integrated to the National Guard. Acutely aware that French forces might arrive soon, and that the 28 February Sino-French agreement had thrown his relations with Chinese officials into question, Khanh was in no position to demand chairmanship of the Resistance Committee.

The two principal Nationalist Party leaders, Nguyễn Tường Tam and Vũ Hồng Khanh, appear to have been left out of the hectic trilateral negotiations of 3–6 March 1946 between the DRV, France, and China. As foreign minister in the new DRV Cabinet, Tam should have been at Hồ's side during key meetings with French and then Chinese officials, yet either Hồ chose to continue negotiating alone, or Tam knew enough about the terms not to want to be party to them.

Tam was not present at the Cabinet meeting where Hồ secured agreement to the final text hammered out with Jean Sainteny. He did attend the formal signing ceremony on 6 March, yet still avoided putting his signature on the document.[181] That onerous act fell to Khanh, presumably under Chinese pressure. Attending the Cabinet meeting in his capacity as deputy chair of the Resistance Committee, Khanh reluctantly agreed to sign the accord along with Hồ.[182] Khanh even agreed to join Hồ and Võ Nguyên Giáp in addressing the perplexed crowd in front of the Hanoi Opera House on 7 March, where he said nothing to contradict the other two speakers (see chapter 4).[183]

Many Nationalist Party members were furious at Vũ Hồng Khanh for signing the 6 March Franco-Vietnamese Accord together with Hồ Chí Minh. Students at the Nguyễn Thái Học cadre school in the Hanoi suburbs walked out of classes in protest, and accompanied their principal to party headquarters to interrogate Khanh. At an urgent meeting of the party's central executive committee, some members called Khanh a dictator for taking such an important decision without prior deliberation. Away from Hanoi, some party branches moved to break with the central leadership and mount popular opposition to government collaboration with the foreign enemy. The central executive committee dispatched Lê Khang, one of its most respected members, to localities to try to explain the political circumstances and restore discipline.[184]

In retrospect, early March 1946 was the last opportunity for the Nationalist Party to challenge the ICP and Việt Minh for leadership of the anti-French resistance. If Nguyễn Tường Tam and Vũ Hồng Khanh had used the 2 March opening of the National Assembly to denounce the Hồ Chí Minh–Sainteny negotiations and call for immediate armed struggle, the Franco-Vietnamese talks might have collapsed. If Hồ and Sainteny had still proceeded with the preliminary convention despite public Nationalist Party condemnation, the National Guard might have fractured, as there already was considerable internal opposition to conceding anything significant to the French. The one thing that prevented the Nationalist Party from taking this course of action was opposition from the Chinese occupation command, which was keen to avoid becoming embroiled in Franco-Vietnamese armed conflict, and was indeed pushing both Hồ and Sainteny towards a compromise. Tam and Khanh would have needed suddenly to risk their Chinese connections and, probably, face Chinese retaliation, while trying to put together and lead a new Vietnamese united front against the French. Instead, they chose to remain within the DRV government and look for opportunities down the road—which never came.[185]

Immediately after signing the 6 March Accord, Hồ Chí Minh secured DRV Cabinet approval to dispatch an official delegation to Chongqing to reaffirm Sino-Vietnamese friendship and in particular gain a better view of how Generalissimo Chiang Kai-shek expected relations to develop following the 28 February

Sino-French agreement.[186] Nghiêm Kế Tổ, a Nationalist Party member with extensive connections in China, and currently DRV deputy foreign minister under Nguyễn Tường Tam, was designated to head the delegation, accompanied by two Việt Minh members. The night before these three were due to depart, Hồ suddenly urged Supreme Advisor Vĩnh Thụy (Bảo Đại) to accompany them. Initially both Bảo Đại and Tổ opposed this idea, but following an urgent meeting with Tam and Vũ Hồng Khanh they changed their minds. On 18 March—the same day General Leclerc and his armored column arrived in Hanoi from Haiphong—the delegation plus Bảo Đại flew to Kunming on a Chinese plane.[187] It seems clear that Hồ wanted to preclude General Leclerc trying to recruit Bảo Đại, while Nationalist Party leaders saw the possibility of Bảo Đại becoming part of an alternative Vietnamese government supported by China and perhaps the United States. Bảo Đại was granted an audience and banquet by Generalissimo Chiang, and remained in Chongqing when the DRV delegation returned to Hanoi on 13 April. Two months later he moved to Hong Kong as an ostensible tourist, living in unaccustomed spartan conditions until other Vietnamese exiles joined him in 1947.[188]

Nguyễn Tường Tam took his job as DRV foreign minister seriously, even though Hồ Chí Minh continued to monopolize contacts with French officials and rely mostly on Hoàng Minh Giám for assistance.[189] As we have seen, Tam headed the DRV delegation to Dalat for the first in-depth talks with the French. Although Võ Nguyên Giáp possessed de facto delegation leadership, Tam proved an able spokesperson, and helped to resolve several disputes over negotiating tactics within the delegation. Yet a few weeks later, Tam chose to flee to China rather than head the DRV negotiating delegation leaving Hanoi for Paris. Assuming that Tam's remarks to the delegation in Dalat about solidarity in the face of French threats had been genuine, something must have changed his mind after returning to the capital. I suspect it was the 29 May circulation of a document foreshadowing establishment of a new Vietnam National Alliance, which put the Vietnam Nationalist Party under the same political umbrella as the Việt Minh. Tam was listed as a founding member of the new Alliance, but most likely the ICP instigators put his name down preemptively, and Tam decided that further attempts at coalition government were futile. On 31 May, newspapers announced that Tam was not going to Paris due to "extreme tiredness."[190] Rumors circulated that Tam had absconded with a large quantity of cash meant for delegation expenses in France.[191] It seems highly unlikely, however, that Tam would have been given this particular responsibility.

Tightening the Screws

Meanwhile, suspicions and animosities festered between Việt Minh and Nationalist Party groups in provinces north of the capital. In April, a member of the Northern Region Committee traveled up the Hanoi–Lào Cai railway to sign "unity agreements" with Nationalist representatives at four provincial towns, aimed at forming mutually acceptable DRV administrative committees.[192] The dense bureaucratic verbiage of these texts betrays underlying tensions and lack of trust, however. In early May, the Northern Committee cautioned the Bắc Giang provincial committee to be more flexible with Nationalist Party members, to "maintain an attitude of unity," and to prepare contingency plans to "avoid unusual activities taking place."[193] During this period, Trần Đăng Ninh, ICP security chief, visited Vĩnh Yên under the pretext of discussing dike repairs and was detained by Vũ Hồng Khanh. Ninh and two comrades managed to flee or were allowed to escape, but their experience was used to argue for repressing the Nationalists.[194] In mid-May, the Interior Ministry ordered all public servants currently working in seven province towns north and northwest of Hanoi to evacuate and join alternative committees being formed in new locations. Those who failed to evacuate would be regarded as having lost their status as government employees.[195]

National Guard units patrolled more aggressively around Nationalist Party positions from early May. As Chinese troops withdrew up the railway towards Yunnan, local Việt Minh militia moved to isolate the Nationalist-held towns. During skirmishes around Phú Thọ on 20 May, Nationalists captured and executed a group of Việt Minh adherents, floating some of the bodies down the Red River by way of warning.[196] From 18 June, the National Guard launched a sustained two-pronged attack on Phú Thọ and Việt Trì. Both sides employed machine guns and occasional mortar fire. Nationalists at Phú Thọ ran out of ammunition after four days and were forced to flee upriver. Vũ Hồng Khanh led the defense of Việt Trì with 350 men, including 120 cadets from the Yên Bái military school. After nine days of combat, hearing that Phú Thọ had fallen and comrades at Vĩnh Yên were negotiating terms with the enemy, Khanh and most of his men slipped out of Việt Trì at night and made their way northwest to Yên Bái.[197] Throughout May and June, *Việt Nam*, the Nationalist Party organ in Hanoi, published increasingly plaintive calls for DRV National Guard members to stop attacking compatriots.[198]

In stark contrast to Phú Thọ and Việt Trì, the Nationalist Party leader at Vĩnh Yên, Đỗ Đình Đạo, opened discussions with Việt Minh representatives in mid-June, and both sides found reason to sustain a ceasefire for two months. Đạo eventually agreed to establishment of a joint Vĩnh Yên administrative committee, and accepted terms for integration of his armed contingent within the National Guard. Huỳnh Thúc Kháng issued a unification decree in his capacity as acting DRV president. The political officer of Military Region 1 presided over a ceremony that formally accepted the "Nationalist Army" (Quốc Dân Quân) into the DRV National Guard.[199] Nationalist units were then split up and dispatched to National Guard battalions elsewhere. Đạo and his deputy, Lê Thanh, moved to Hanoi.[200]

In Hanoi at the end of June, Nationalist Party members debated whether to submit to Việt Minh hegemony, to flee towards the border, or try to mount a coup against the DRV central government. Trương Tử Anh, head of the clandestine Đại Việt group affiliated with the Nationalists, made the case for an uprising, possibly beginning with an attack on French soldiers to sow confusion. Also in late June, Võ Nguyên Giáp asked the acting French commander in Tonkin, Colonel Jean Crépin, what the French attitude would be in the event of the DRV escalating operations against the Nationalist Party and Revolutionary League. Crépin replied that French forces "would not interfere in such an internal affair."[201] As the National Guard had already been on the attack for several weeks in the northwest corridor, both Giáp and Crépin probably had Hanoi city in mind. When the French then mooted plans for a military parade around the Hoàn Kiếm Lake, to take place on Bastille Day, 14 July, DRV security services worried this might make a tempting target for antigovernment elements. In the early hours of 12 July, the Công An raided one building and allegedly uncovered a plan signed by Trương Tử Anh to toss grenades into the black African contingent of the French Army's Bastille Day parade, after which Đại Việt or French units would seize ICP and DRV leaders, and Anh would proclaim a new Vietnamese government. Lê Giản, the Công An head, took this document to Acting President Huỳnh Thúc Kháng, who allegedly put on his glasses, read several passages, banged his cane on the floor, and exclaimed, "Destroy them! Wipe out the entire gang! Traitors! Sons of bitches *(Đồ chó má)*." Lê Giản then located Giáp, who gave the order to attack Nationalist Party offices in both Hanoi and the provinces.[202]

Beginning at seven in the morning on 12 July, the Công An, supported by Việt Minh militia, surrounded seven additional buildings in Hanoi. In several cases they were met with automatic weapons fire and proceeded to rain grenades down from surrounding roofs before the occupants surrendered. More than one hundred people were taken away, some never to be seen again. At a house on 7 Ôn Như Hầu Street, police ostensibly found one bound prisoner, a room containing implements of torture, and seven corpses poorly buried in the back yard. As word spread of the corpses, hundreds of people surged onto the premises without police objection—ogling the scene, crying out, or loudly condemning the perpetrators.[203] The authorities briefed journalists, and soon all the raids were being summarized as the "Ôn Như Hầu Affair." In distant Huế, a Việt Minh newspaper headlined: 'Nest of Kidnappers, Extortionists, and Murderers Destroyed."[204] Hanoi's Democratic Party paper, *Độc Lập*, splashed "Công An Locates and Captures Terrorist Nests" across the top, then asserted that police had acted on intelligence about a plot to oppose the government, conduct assassinations, sell out the country, and use extremist slogans to deceive the populace. Police had discovered a printing press, "rebellious leaflets," counterfeit money, firearms, and some individuals being held for ransom. Culprits had been arrested and were being questioned.[205] Probably under orders from the censors, the Nationalist Party was not named in these early articles.

The "Ôn Như Hầu Affair" has never been subjected to serious historical investigation. Lê Giản's insider account leads one to ask if the Công An and some senior ICP leaders wanted to use evidence that Trương Tử Anh was plotting a coup as a pretext to assault and clean up the entire Nationalist Party, thus finessing further French discussions with domestic third parties and increasing ICP control over the government administration and the National Guard.[206] The key document purportedly shown to Huỳnh Thúc Kháng, detailing the attack on the Bastille Day parade, is admitted by Lê Giản to be a "handwritten draft" by Trương Tử Anh, for use within his Đại Việt organization alone.[207] Lê Giản offers no evidence of French collusion in a prospective 14 July coup, other than Sainteny's continuing insistence on a military parade. If the French had decided to mount a coup (a move they had considered and deferred on numerous prior occasions), there is no reason they would have relied on Trương Tử Anh to provide the trigger, much less give him any chance to form a government. The Công An deliberately fudged demarcations between Anh's Đại Việt clandestine organization and groups previously led by Vũ Hồng Khanh and Nguyễn Tường Tam when it targeted the *Việt Nam* newspaper office and other Nationalist Party venues. It is possible that Nationalist cadres had wind of trouble three days before, when the party's central headquarters revealed that its official seal and one belonging to Khanh had been lost. "Concerned that someone will use them improperly, we declare them no longer valid," the party announcement concluded.[208] Following the Công An attacks and jailings, someone in authority tried to limit public condemnations of the Nationalist Party, so that for purposes of united front propaganda the party could be said to remain within the fold. However, the damage had been done and, except for a few figurehead individuals, every citizen in the DRV henceforth dreaded being identified with the Nationalist Party. "Việt Quốc" became synonymous with treason.

On 20 July, the Northern Committee—without once mentioning the Nationalist Party—informed all provinces that the police recently had uncovered serious criminal behavior, including extortion, kidnapping, and counterfeiting, which had to be investigated and prosecuted. The committee specifically instructed local authorities to stop arrests and detentions from degenerating into "terror" *(khủng bố)*.[209] Local administrative committees now had the green light to detain known or suspected Nationalist Party members, while being cautioned about witch-hunts and summary punishments. From available sources it appears that thousands of persons were questioned in the following months, hundreds were imprisoned or sent to deportation camps, and several hundred others dismissed from the public service.[210] Staff of the "political offices" in province-level Công An bureaus subjected suspects to harsh questioning, secured signed statements, and then made recommendations to the province administrative committee for release, trial, or deportation. In Sơn Tây, for example, police obtained a four-page statement from Dương Thể Tú, a twenty-year-old art student, who admitted to Nationalist Party membership and provided information on party activities in Việt Trì town, where he had served in the propaganda and training office. Tú acknowledged to interrogators that he had gone down the wrong path, pleaded forgiveness, and promised henceforth to support the government.[211] Almost surely Tú was sent to a deportation camp.

Although *Việt Nam* ceased publication in late July 1946, its weekly counterpart, *Chính Nghĩa tuần báo (Righteous Cause Weekly),* continued to publish views very different from the now dominant Việt Minh press for another three months. It persisted with a serialized essay condemning communism and Soviet imperialism (also labeled "Red Fascism"), with only light cuts from the censor. *Chính Nghĩa tuần báo* also criticized the DRV's administrative committee system and the government's failure to establish an independent judiciary. President Hồ Chí Minh's diplomatic strategy was questioned. The mere existence of *Chính Nghĩa tuần báo* suggests that some DRV cabinet members were uncomfortable with the push by Trường Chinh to homogenize opinion under the new National Alliance (Liên Việt) banner. If so, this rearguard effort collapsed in late October, when editorials vanished from the paper, followed by all coverage of domestic affairs. Readers were left with snippets of foreign news, anodyne cultural comment, and short stories by Khái Hưng. By early December the neutering of *Chính Nghĩa tuần báo* was so complete that censors did not feel it necessary to remove a single line.

Between July and November 1946, an unknown number among the fifty Nationalist Party members of the DRV National Assembly were arrested. Amidst the 12 July police assaults, Assembly delegate Phan Kích Nam was accused of kidnapping and extortion and jailed immediately.[212] Another delegate, Nguyễn Đồng Lâm, was detained by the Hải Dương police, which proposed he be sent to a deportation camp for two years. The Hải Dương administrative committee agreed, arguing that "local authorities will have a very difficult time working if Mr. Lâm is left outside the law's compass." Lâm had participated in the Nationalist Party uprising of 1930, spent six years in a colonial prison, and only returned to political action in 1944. During late 1945 he had written for *Việt Nam* newspaper, then withdrew to his home village in Hải Dương in early 1946. Lâm's case was sent to the Northern Region Inspectorate on 7 August, and thence to Nguyễn Văn Tố, nonparty chairman of the National Assembly's Standing Committee, who quickly replied that he could not support Lâm's detention. Tố's opinion was upheld unanimously by the full Standing Committee, which requested the inspectorate to order the Hải Dương police to release Lâm. On 21 August, the inspectorate did this, adding that if solid evidence of Lâm's guilt materialized, permission of the Standing Committee could still be sought to rearrest Lâm.[213]

There were many other arrests of Nationalist Party members of the National Assembly that do not appear to have come to the attention of Nguyễn Văn Tố and his Standing Committee. Nationalist Party delegates were also subject to ominous local harassment. Trình Như Tấu petitioned five different government offices after a militia band surrounded his house to demand restitution of a fictional typewriter, threatening violence if he did not comply. Tấu named four offenders and requested protection as a National Assembly member, but apparently received no reply.[214] When the Assembly convened for the second time in late October, no more than a dozen of the fifty Nationalist Party members were present.[215]

From late July 1946 to the end of the year, the majority of persons detained by the Công An for political reasons bore a Nationalist Party label, whether real or assumed. For example, four out of five persons deported by Hà Đông province in July were tagged as Nationalists. Scores of petitions were received in Hanoi from relatives of individuals arrested in Phú Thọ province on charges of Nationalist Party participation.[216] Arrests extended as far as Quảng Nam province in central Vietnam, where an unknown number of alleged Nationalists were deported in September.[217] Not all individuals accepted their detention meekly. Phạm Đức Tuyên, a Thái Bình Catholic, told police he was attracted by Nationalist Party assertions that Hồ Chí Minh was pro-French, and because taxes were too high. It was time to toss out the current government. For this he was recommended for deportation.[218] The Công An reported to the Northern Committee that Phạm Văn Giàu, deported to a camp in Bắc Kạn, had continued to display a very reactionary attitude, getting others to join him in singing Nationalist Party songs, and claiming that former emperors Duy Tân and Bảo Đại had joined with Nguyễn Hải Thần and Nguyễn Tường Tam to form a legitimate Vietnamese government in Nanjing.[219] Giàu was unaware that ex-emperor Duy Tân had perished in an airplane crash in Africa a year earlier, but his assertions about an alternative government in exile were merely premature. Meanwhile, the ICP nursed its own grievances, continuing to interrogate Nationalist Party prisoners about abductions of ICP cadres that had taken place in late 1945. On the morning of 19 December in Hanoi—only hours before hostilities exploded—a police report was forwarded to the Interior Ministry about efforts to ferret out information on the fate of several ICP members believed to have been killed by the Nationalists.[220]

After withdrawing to Yên Bái at the end of June, Vũ Hồng Khanh soon realized that local food supplies could only sustain Nationalist Party military units, not the civilian cadres, students, family members, and sympathizers who were arriving from the Red River delta as well. Attempts at resupply from Lào Cai faltered due to Việt Minh destruction of the rail line. By November, Lào Cai itself was nearly surrounded by the National Guard and food was running short. Khanh ordered evacuation across the river to Yunnan—and the execution of two military academy instructors accused of trying to lead their students in the opposite direction, back towards the delta. In October 1947, when French paratroopers descended on Phú Thọ town, the DRV Công An allegedly killed more than one hundred Nationalist prisoners rather than risk them escaping or falling into the hands of the French.[221]

From Hanoi Central Prison in November 1946, Nguyễn Tường Thụy, former general director of the PTT, sent a long petition to President Hồ asking for his intercession. Being a professional civil servant, Thụy said that he had deliberately eschewed joining the Nationalist Party along with his younger brother Nguyễn Tường Tam, nor had he discussed politics with him. Thụy professed deep respect for "Elder President," adding that he had supervised production of the DRV's very first postage stamp that bore Elder President's image. Apparently Thụy had been arrested in relation to postage stamp proceeds donated to the Defense Fund and Famine Relief Association, but this was surely a pretext. In plaintive conclusion, Thụy promised that not only he, but his white-haired mother, his wife, and their ten children would forever be grateful for Elder President's assistance. Thụy apparently received no response to his petition, and we don't know what happened to him after 19 December.[222]

CATHOLICS: ALLIES OR ENEMIES?

The Catholic Church and Vietnam's Catholic minority posed a very different challenge to Hồ Chí Minh and the DRV compared to the political organizations discussed above. Here was a mature religious establishment with ties to the Vatican and the prior colonial system, yet also fourteen hundred Vietnamese priests plus numerous lay leaders strongly influenced by patriotic currents of the previous two decades, and 1.6 million Catholic believers (about 8.5 percent of Vietnam's population in 1945) living mostly in disciplined rural communities quite capable of being mobilized for specific social or political objectives. During the 1930s, Rome had promoted three Vietnamese priests to the rank of bishop for the first time. Catholic intellectuals joined non-Catholics in a variety of modernizing projects. Catholic youth groups flourished. By the early 1940s, youth leaders and parish priests alike were routinely preaching the compatibility of love of God and love of Fatherland. Very few Catholics appear to have joined Việt Minh associations, partly because of rumors the Việt Minh was dominated by atheistic communists, but also because many Việt Minh adherents viewed Catholics with deep suspicion.[223] Church government was still largely in the hands of one French apostolic delegate, eleven European bishops, and 330 European priests.[224]

Following the 9 March 1945 Japanese coup, Catholics and non-Catholics alike organized big patriotic anticolonial meetings and demonstrations. Foreign priests and nuns were suddenly vulnerable, although the Japanese military often guarded those within range of their bases, and Vietnamese Catholics generally were able to protect foreign clergy remaining in provincial parishes, orphanages, or monasteries. In one notable exception, a mob stormed and pillaged the Catholic orphanage at Kẻ Sở in Nam Định province on 11 August, taking away the French head of mission, Fr. Dupont, and later killing him.[225] In adjacent Ninh Bình province, a group of young Catholics led by Fr. Hoàng Quỳnh had quietly withdrawn to an upland plantation after the Japanese coup in order to organize themselves, learn military skills, and print and distribute patriotic leaflets to the lowlands. Hearing of the Japanese capitulation, and armed with a few rifles, the group marched into Phát Diệm town on 20 August to take power, with Fr. Quỳnh pinning a badge on the bishop designate, Fr. Lê Hữu Từ, containing the words "Việt Minh Bishop," amidst cheers from thousands of people.[226] Five days later, the senior ICP member in the area, Vân Tiến Dũng, ignored Quỳnh's group when announcing a Ninh Bình province revolutionary people's committee, with himself as chairman. In Hanoi, the initial national "Provisional People's Government" announced on 24 August had no Catholic member, but the provisional DRV Cabinet publicized on 27 or 28 August included Nguyễn Mạnh Hà, a former Catholic youth leader and head of the Northern Region Economic Service at the time of the Việt Minh takeover.[227]

Sunday, 2 September, the date chosen by Hồ Chí Minh to declare Vietnam's independence and the establishment of the DRV, was coincidentally the Catholic "Feast of Vietnamese Martyrs" commemorating those who had died for the faith, particularly during the nineteenth century. Early that morning, Hanoi's churches were crowded with people attending Mass. In a move designed to identify the Vietnamese church with the new government, priests led their flocks through the streets to the square where Independence Day ceremonies took place. In Saigon on the same day, events took a very different turn when shots rang out in the vicinity of a large Independence Day crowd gathered in Norodom Square adjacent to the cathedral. Some crowd members, convinced that the firing had come from the upper floor of the cathedral's presbytery, surged onto the grounds to gain revenge. Fr. Tricoire, a bearded prison chaplain quietly respected by many Vietnamese former political prisoners, was shot as he stood at the main door of the building, then left to bleed to death in the garden.[228] In Huế during the first week of September, ICP leaders killed Ngô Đình Khôi, a former royal minister and senior member of the influential Catholic Ngô Đình clan. His brother Ngô Đình Thục, bishop of Vĩnh Long, was then in Hanoi meeting members of the new government.[229] Yet another brother, Ngô Đình Diệm, was under detention outside Hanoi (see below).

As alarming reports of aggressive British actions in Saigon reached northern and central Vietnam in mid-September, Catholics joined non-Catholics in large protest demonstrations. Catholics also scheduled their own protest meetings for

Sunday, 23 September, which turned out to be the day when fighting commenced in Saigon. At the meeting in Hanoi, parish priests stood in front of serried ranks of believers—all loudly proclaiming their patriotic commitment to and confidence in President Hồ Chí Minh.[230] At the Huế meeting, everyone listened to a proclamation which urged men to prepare to go to the battlefront, women to assume supply and medical duties, and both to set aside class differences in favor of national solidarity. Then came a qualification: "However, in regard to Catholics specifically, we must make those contributions on the foundations of our Religion. Anything that has the Lord as its root, we can and will do immediately." At the meeting's conclusion, all yelled, "For Christ, for the Fatherland!" and "Long live a completely independent Vietnam!"[231]

Also on 23 September, Bishop Nguyễn Bá Tòng, in the name of all four Vietnamese bishops, dispatched a message to Pope Pius XII requesting his benediction and prayers for Vietnam's independence, "which has just been gained, and which our people will labor to keep at all cost." Bishop Tòng tried to convey the significance of the 2 September Feast of Vietnamese Martyrs becoming simultaneously the day when "all Annamite people without religious distinction" had demonstrated their patriotism, and had resolved to "guard their government with their own blood." The message concluded by beseeching the pope, the Roman curia, cardinals, archbishops, bishops, and Catholics around the world—especially in France—to "support the decision of our beloved country."[232] We don't know if Bishop Tòng communicated with any member of the DRV provisional government prior to sending this radiogram, but Hồ Chí Minh certainly would have been pleased with the contents. It seems that none of the fourteen foreign bishops then in Vietnam had been consulted.[233] Without questioning the patriotism of Bishop Tòng, we can imagine that at this volatile moment he simultaneously worried about the vulnerability of Catholics to attack by non-Catholics, and concluded that a highly visible commitment to Hồ Chí Minh and the new government was the best available protection for his coreligionists scattered around the country. Six decades prior, Catholics had been subject to horrible pogroms as French forces approached.

From the beginning of September 1945, affiliates of the Vietnam Catholic National Salvation Association began to crop up, sometimes at the initiative of local clergymen, sometimes led by lay youths. Prior to the August insurrection, the Việt Minh had listed the Catholic association on its united front roster, yet this seems to have been only an aspiration, not reality. The association's published bylaws were almost identical to those of other national salvation groups.[234] Now many existing Catholic youth groups simply changed their names, drafted new bylaws, and sought recognition from government authorities.[235] Catholic newspapers reprinted the "Ten Policies of the Việt Minh" and more recent pronouncements.[236] The new national flag was sometimes draped over church entrances,

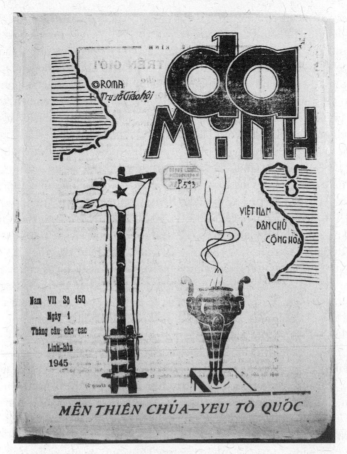

FIGURE 24. Rome and Vietnam are juxtaposed geographically,
Vatican and DRV standards fly side by side, and readers are told
to love both God and the Fatherland. Cover of *Đa Minh* 150
(1 Nov. 1945). Courtesy of Vietnam National Library.

and Việt Minh slogans plastered inside. French missionaries were horrified, but
in no position to react.[237] DRV leaders must have been delighted at these Catholic
Vietnamese identifications with the nation, at a time when the provisional government needed desperately to demonstrate the breadth of its legitimacy to incoming allied forces. On the other hand, ICP organizers probably fretted that
Catholic affiliates to the Việt Minh possessed no party members, which violated
the principle of "united front from below," enunciated since 1941.

A Catholic fortnightly newspaper published in Nam Định conveys the extraordinary mental gymnastics underway in late 1945. Titled *Đa Minh (Dominican)*,

the paper had been circulating since 1939 with sponsorship from the Bùi Chu prelate, Bishop Hồ Ngọc Cẩn. The cover of the 1 September issue bore a bright candle and the small words, "*VIETNAM độc lập*" (Independent Vietnam). The next issue's cover featured a big Việt Minh–DRV flag and the slogan "Long Live the Democratic Republic of Vietnam!!!" Inside there was an article recounting past bloodlettings suffered by Catholics in Vietnam. The 1 November cover contained a highly truncated world map that brought Rome and the DRV in proximity to each other, a flagpole with DRV and Vatican flags side by side, and a large Vietnamese ancestral urn with incense wafting upward. Underneath was the slogan: "Be Devoted to God—Love the Fatherland" *(Mến Thiên Chúa—Yêu Tổ Quốc)*. There were articles justifying Catholic entry in the "national united front," a biography of the new prelate of Phát Diệm, Bishop Lê Hữu Từ, and continuation of the story about persecution of Catholics. References to the Việt Minh declined in subsequent issues. The cover of the Christmas issue contained a shining star designed to represent both the star of Bethlehem and the DRV flag, together with a homily on the redemptive power of Christ's birth and aspirations for peace amidst darkness and anxiety *(thắc mắc)*. Inside there was a plaintive call for unity of non-Catholics and Catholics *(lương giáo)*, and a terse statement from the Nam Định police that charges of foreign missionaries poisoning people had been investigated and found to be unsubstantiated—indeed, they were most likely rumors spread by traitors.[238]

Formal installation of Lê Hữu Từ as bishop of Phát Diệm on 29 October provided an unparalleled opportunity for church and state to meet, sound each other out, and draw lessons for the future. Bishop Tòng and Bishop Cẩn presided over Từ's installation, supported by priests from ten dioceses extending from Lạng Sơn to Huế.[239] None of the foreign bishops were present. The DRV delegation was headed by Supreme Advisor Vĩnh Thụy and included Võ Nguyên Giáp (interior minister), Phạm Văn Đồng (finance minister), and Nguyễn Mạnh Hà (economics minister and prominent lay Catholic)—a remarkable measure of government recognition and attentiveness. Hồ Chí Minh's letter of congratulations to Bishop Từ expressed confidence that he would lead his Catholic countrymen to emulate Christ's example of sacrifice, and "struggle to defend the nation's right to Freedom and Independence." Hồ Chí Minh also invited Bishop Từ to become a supreme advisor, alongside former emperor Bảo Đại. During the midday banquet, Bishop Từ is said to have leaned over to Bảo Đại to offer his services in some new political initiative. After Bảo Đại sighed and conveyed his powerlessness, Bishop Từ replied sharply, "Then you are very mediocre."[240] Bishop Từ relished the cut and thrust of politics, both religious and secular.[241]

At the same banquet, Bishop Từ told Nguyễn Mạnh Hà that he had agreed to Phạm Văn Đồng's proposal to join the Việt Minh's Catholic National Salvation Association. Hà urged Bishop Từ to reconsider this move, which would be opposed by Catholics elsewhere, thus sowing division at a particularly sensitive moment. When Bishop Từ replied that he could not go back on his word, Hà recommended he initiate a second, independent organization as well.[242] In afternoon discussions, when some church participants insisted that the Catholic National Salvation Association not be subject to full Việt Minh integration, Phạm Văn Đồng and Võ Nguyên Giáp conceded that the association could maintain its own parallel hierarchy and liaise laterally with Việt Minh leaders at each level. This "united front from above" formula was duly incorporated in the authorization papers signed by Đồng on behalf of both the government and the Việt Minh. The afternoon concluded with a large parade at the Phát Diệm sports field, complete with patriotic banners and shouting of slogans.[243]

Only that evening did Phạm Văn Đồng and Võ Nguyên Giáp hear of plans to form a second organization, to be called the Vietnam Catholic Federation (Liên Đoàn Công Giáo Việt Nam), which would be more "religious" than the Catholic National Salvation Association, and more subject to church discipline. Đồng and Giáp were said to be furious at Bishop Từ, and they did not speak to Nguyễn Mạnh Hà for a week.[244] At least they could be pleased that the Vietnamese bishops had dispatched a message to the Vatican, London, and Washington, pleading for Catholics across the world to come to the aid of "our invaded country and its children, [who are] animated by pure patriotism and being decimated on the battlefield."[245] Six weeks later in Huế, the apostolic delegate for Indochina, Archbishop Drapier, dissolved the Catholic Federation announced in Phát Diệm and promulgated his own provisional bylaws for an organization of the same name.[246] About the same time a third organization, the National Catholics (Quốc Gia Công Giáo), announced its existence and proceeded to denounce atheistic communism as well as support Vietnam Nationalist Party proposals to establish an anti-Việt Minh national front.[247] From mid-December yet another group published Hồn Công Giáo (Catholic Soul), a Hanoi underground paper which aimed most of its vitriol at Catholics who joined the National Salvation Association, but also criticized National Catholics for lining up with the Nationalist Party. Hồn Công Giáo asserted that the Việt Minh had relied on Japanese fascists to gain power, warned Catholics that the Vatican had forbidden them from allying with communists, and claimed that Bishop Ngô Đình Thục and his brother Ngô Đình Diệm had been detained by the Việt Minh. Both Hồn Công Giáo and Việt Nam reported specific cases of priests being jailed and Vatican flags torn down, especially in central Vietnam.[248]

Nonetheless, at the end of 1945 most Catholics appear to have identified enthusiastically with Hồ Chí Minh and the DRV, while remaining concerned about the ICP and anti-Catholic feelings among some Việt Minh adherents. It was embarrassing to patriotic Catholics that the high commissioner for Indochina, Admiral d'Argenlieu, had been a Carmelite monk before joining General de Gaulle in 1940. In the lead-up to Christmas, with the blessing of Bishop Hồ Ngọc Cẩn, a large meeting and parade was organized in Bùi Chu diocese in support of the government, with church bells pealing and thousands of armed men marching past the dais. A Việt Minh journalist was particularly taken by the unit of armed women, congratulating them for leaving hearth and home to defend Vietnam.[249] In Huế, a writer rejoiced at Vietnam's first independent Christmas; after eighty years of the French pitting Catholics and non-Catholics against each other, people could now emulate Christ's sacrifice to bring liberty, independence, and happiness to humanity.[250]

The imminence of elections to the National Assembly stirred some dioceses to choose priests or lay Catholic leaders to stand as candidates, and to instruct the faithful on voting procedures. Bishop Lê Hữu Từ circulated a pastoral letter on the elections—their political importance, the necessity of skilled Catholic representation, the tactical value of forming a province slate with reliable non-Catholics, and the need to instruct parishioners not to vote for anyone else. He predicted that anti-Catholic delegates to the Assembly would table draft laws detrimental to religion, morality, or church property rights, so that it was essential for the Catholic minority to know how to build a coalition on vital issues.[251]

In Ninh Bình province, four Catholics stood for the 6 January 1946 National Assembly elections, led by Fr. Phạm Ngọc Chi and including Ngô Tử Hạ, owner of a large printing house in Hanoi. Election officials declared only Hạ victorious, whereas the Việt Minh won three seats. Bishop Từ fired off a telegram to the central government claiming election fraud, and threatening to mount a protest demonstration. The government quickly responded that some ballots had been misplaced inadvertently, and that indeed Fr. Chi had won as well. Considering this answer disingenuous, Bishop Từ decided Fr. Chi should decline to join the Assembly.[252] Three Catholic priests from other provinces were elected to the Assembly, and Ngô Tử Hạ was given the honor of chairing the 2 March proceedings (see chapter 2). None of the five Catholic candidates standing in Hanoi city were elected.[253] Clearly Bishop Từ and other Catholic leaders had hoped that the National Assembly would play a pivotal role in DRV politics, finessing communist preferences for dictatorial rule. Their high hopes for the Assembly were soon dashed, and suspicions of communist perfidy reinforced.

In late January, Hồ Chí Minh made a sudden trip to Phát Diệm to confirm Bishop Lê Hữu Từ's appointment as a supreme advisor to the DRV government. The mission's old gatekeeper rushed in to tell the bishop that "some elderly man with a pith helmet, cane, and four-pocket jacket wants to meet your Eminence." Unfazed by this surprise visit from the provisional president, Từ talked with Hồ for an hour while his subordinates organized a formal reception, at which Hồ concluded his remarks by leading the clergy in three cheers of "Long Live Christ!" Everyone then adjourned to the town opera house, where seminarians and youth groups sang praises to President Hồ and the government. Hồ put his hand on Bishop Từ's shoulder and encouraged all present to convey their concerns to the supreme advisor, and together they would find solutions. According to an eyewitness, "Hồ Chí Minh, with his simple garb, self-assured voice, and friendly manner, managed to convert the audience." Several elders were moved to tears when Hồ shook their hands and asked after their health. Within days, Bishop Từ was being addressed as Eminent Advisor *(Đức Cố Vấn)*, and songs were being composed to celebrate his status.[254]

This personal connection between President Hồ and Bishop Từ benefited both the government and Vietnamese Catholics. The DRV needed above all to reduce the chances of French politicians using the Catholic issue as justification for full-scale intervention in Vietnam. Cordial relations with Vietnamese clergy enhanced Hồ's moderate image at home and abroad. Church support for the DRV also made it less likely that local Catholics would collaborate with incoming French forces. The Church was able to use President Hồ's authority and prestige as bulwark against pressures from the ICP and Tổng Bộ Việt Minh to conform on matters of ideology, security, organization, and finances. The dioceses of Phát Diệm and Bùi Chu continued to acquire their own weapons and train paramilitary groups *(nghĩa binh)* without interference from DRV officials. Catholics elsewhere had less protection, although Catholic League branches formed in many provinces as de facto alternatives to Catholic National Salvation groups. Most local attempts to confiscate church property appear to have been blocked by high-level order.

Bishop Từ took his supreme advisor position seriously, forwarding citizen petitions, comments, and proposals to the president's office in Hanoi. In the wake of the 6 March 1946 Preliminary Accords, Bishop Từ came to Hanoi to criticize President Hồ for giving away too much to the French. Hồ is said to have replied: "Our destiny at this moment is to kneel down in order to advance towards independence. Please have faith in me." Bishop Từ remained skeptical, and indeed sent aides to talk with the Nationalist opposition, but found no realistic alternative there.[255] With Hồ's departure for France at the end of May, Bishop Từ's capacity to influence government behavior declined significantly.

Việt Minh newspapers mostly called for solidarity between non-Catholics and Catholics without examining what needed to be done to overcome mutual suspicions and forge a working relationship. An interesting exception appeared in late March 1946 in *Quyết Thắng (Determined to Win)*, the central region Việt Minh weekly published in Huế. According to the author, Tình Sơn, non-Catholics often asserted that Catholics were not true patriots since they believed in a religion imported by the French, thus losing their racial identity *(mất giống nòi)*, and sometimes even collaborating with the enemy. That was the wrong attitude, replied Tình Sơn, because Christianity was a religion like any other, and not specific to any country or people. Having the Vatican located in Italy had not prevented antifascist Italian Catholics from killing fascist Catholics during World War II. In Vietnam there were Catholic and non-Catholic traitors alike. Then Tình Sơn took up Catholic concerns, first dismissing as a "totally outmoded feudal notion" the fear that the nineteenth-century "Kill Heretics" (Sát Tả) movement might resurface. More serious was the fear of communism, with some Catholics claiming that Vietnamese communists aimed to eliminate all Vietnamese Catholics. Here Tình Sơn affirmed the strength and legitimacy of communism, but as based on patriotism and the struggle for national liberation, not any challenge to religion. "Vietnam has never had a religious war, and it won't start now," Tình Sơn concluded.[256]

Such Việt Minh arguments hardly deterred the Catholic hierarchy from building up the Catholic Federation as an alternative to the Catholic National Salvation Association. In May 1946, Archbishop Drapier received Vatican recognition of the Vietnam Catholic Federation as an organization that "meets patriotic aspirations while remaining in accord with Catholic principles of justice and fraternity." Under the federation umbrella, dioceses were instructed to form organizations for youth, women, children, elders, and workers—though often this meant simply renaming existing church groups. In Phát Diệm, however, the "Catholic Labor Union" created thirteen different occupational groups between July and October, with a total of five hundred members.[257] Archbishop Drapier did not bother to send the Catholic Federation application and bylaws to the government until September; the minister of interior, Huỳnh Thúc Kháng, gave his approval the next month.[258] Federation members were permitted to join political parties, "except for any party whose ideology and platform is contrary to Catholic teachings"—an unmistakable reference to the ICP.[259] Phát Diệm and Bùi Chu dioceses continued to pursue a tactic of parallel organization, with their bishops directing both National Salvation Association and Catholic Federation groups. The same may have been true in Nghệ An, where a Catholic Federation meeting in June pledged to be ready to sacrifice for both God and Fatherland, to overcome misunderstandings between non-Catholics and Catholics, and to support President Hồ and the DRV government. However, speakers also expressed concern about "recent antireligious injustices, which have caused temporary suspicions," and stressed the need to protect the faith and mission property.[260]

The continuing presence of foreign prelates and missionaries angered many non-Catholic Vietnamese. By November 1945, most foreign clergy had withdrawn to Hanoi, Huế, or Saigon. Even there, however, foreign priests remained vulnerable without the basic security offered by Vietnamese priests, seminarians, and lay believers. Many Catholics wanted to see foreign clergy replaced by Vietnamese clergy, but not as the result of mob violence. The slogan "Restore Vietnam's Church to Vietnamese priests" could be found on banners hung in and around some churches. Leaflets circulated in Huế, signed allegedly by the Catholic National Salvation Association, denouncing French and Spanish priests as "colonialist reactionaries." Perhaps to balance such generalizations, the same Việt Minh paper which had reprinted that leaflet reported a May Day speech in Vietnamese by a French priest, Fr. Fasseaux, who called for solidarity among both non-Catholics and Catholics in "saving the country," adding that "you are all children of a single Vietnamese father." Fr. Fasseaux concluded by leading everyone in cheers of "Long live independent Vietnam," much to the delight of the audience.[261] Elsewhere, however, an elderly, long-bearded French priest chastised French Army officers for negotiating with "assassins," urging them instead to mount a coup in Hanoi while Hồ Chí Minh was in Paris.[262] Vietnamese Catholic supporters of independence were embarrassed when foreign missionaries started to return to outlying postings under protection of French troops, first in the Mekong delta, then in south-central Vietnam, and then in the Chinese border region. French units also were accompanied by Catholic chaplains in military uniform, several of whom were killed in late 1945 and 1946.[263]

Catholic comment about the DRV government became more critical from March 1946 onward. This was particularly noticeable in *Đa Minh*, published in Bùi Chu. The political catechism column begun in January became more pointed as it explained concepts like "private property," "democracy," "citizens' rights and responsibilities," "equality," "freedom," and "Catholics and politics." Loose use of the "Vietnamese traitor" *(Việt gian)* label was condemned, with the article concluding: "Who is deceitful *(gian)* and who upright *(ngay)* will be answered by time and History." A satirical essay on overuse of the title "comrade" *(đồng chí)* was partly censored, as was a humor column. An article criticizing a Việt Minh propaganda leaflet was eliminated, but then restored two issues later following intervention from the interior minister, Huỳnh Thúc Kháng.[264] Unnamed candidates to a people's council election were accused of allocating rations to those who promised to vote for them. In early August the gloves came off, with a (partially censored) lead article questioning repeated government denials that it was communist, following by long critiques of "Marxist materialism" and the "historical dialectic."

The Catholic Federation organization in Huế was more evangelical than the Phát Diệm–Bùi Chu contingent, and its short-lived newspaper did not bother to mention Hồ Chí Minh or the DRV government at all.[265] *Liên Đoàn Công Giáo Việt Nam (Vietnam Catholic Alliance)* appeared fortnightly from late July with encouragement from Archbishop Drapier. Former empress Nam Phương agreed to be "supreme advisor" to the central region Catholic Federation, which must have angered local DRV authorities. A front-page homily titled "Life, Death" *(Sống, Chết)* suggested that Catholics knew better than anyone else the right way to live and legitimate reasons for sacrificing one's life. Satan received almost as much attention as God. Readers were told to follow the teachings of Pope Pius XII

if they wanted to change society, and Marshal Pétain was quoted as an authority on patriotism (this latter reference being mostly censored). No government that failed to respect beliefs or destroyed religion could last long, another
article intoned. At a Catholic Federation meeting in Huế, attended by forty delegates from most central provinces, an unnamed foreign apostolic visitor condemned the global expansion of materialist doctrine and predicted that, "In the
end, only Catholicism and communism will be left to engage in fierce battle until
just one side is left." A later meeting proclaimed that Vietnam was destined to be
the Vatican's "beloved first child in the Far East." It also condemned the doctrine
of freedom and equality that allegedly had produced the wild killing sprees of
Marrat, Danton, and Robespierre in the French Revolution, followed inevitably by
Marx, Lenin, and Stalin—a continuing "world of bloodletting, evil, and wretched-
ness." By way of doctrinal antidote, a Catholic printing house was to be established
with initial capital of one hundred thousand piastres. The official seal for future
Catholic Federation books would feature a map of Vietnam enclosed by a cross.[266]

Further south, in Saigon and the Mekong delta, the early arrival of British-
French forces in September 1945 had forced Vietnamese Catholics, like other inhabitants, to make quick decisions about whether to stay or flee. Only a minority
of Catholics in the anti-French "maquis" (bưng biển) zones remained for very
long. A few Catholic professionals were assigned positions in the southern DRV
administration, most notably Phạm Ngọc Thuần, a French citizen from a prominent Cochinchina bourgeois family, who became vice-chairman of the Nam Bộ
Resistance and Administrative Committee. When efforts to recruit southerners
to the Catholic National Salvation Association met with scant success, Việt Minh
leaders decided to form another organization. They gave operational responsibility to Nguyễn Thành Vinh, who was a French citizen, Catholic, and previously
senior clerk at the Saigon court of appeals. In May 1946, Vinh managed to gather
together six priests and seventy-four laypersons to establish the Southern Vietnam Catholic Federation (Liên Đoàn Công Giáo Việt Nam Nam Bộ).[267]

Bishop Ngô Đình Thục tried to keep his distance from French officialdom as
well as communist front groups. In Biên Hòa, he warned French interlocutors
that they faced a long, bloody conflict unless they followed the British example
and granted dominion status to Vietnam. He angered Admiral d'Argenlieu when
he evaded French surveillance and returned independently to his Vĩnh Long diocese in early January 1946. Meanwhile, Bishop Thục's younger brother, Ngô
Đình Diệm, had been detained by DRV police in Hanoi in September 1945, kept
under house arrest in an upland village, then escorted back to the Hanoi Redemptorist monastery in late December.[268] Early in 1946, Hồ Chí Minh invited
Diệm to his office for discussion, perhaps to sound him out about participation
in the new DRV Cabinet that would include at least two nonparty members. As
mentioned earlier, Diệm's name was tabled during the late February search for

an interior minister. Undoubtedly Hồ Chí Minh would have liked to include a prominent Catholic in the cabinet, but he was not about to give Diệm control over the DRV police and administrative apparatus, and Diệm was not the type to accept a titular role. Also, Hồ could not depend on Diệm to approve in cabinet the secret deal that Hồ was negotiating with Sainteny and local Chinese commanders.[269]

It seems that Hồ Chí Minh decided to dispatch Ngô Đình Diệm to China rather than rearrest him or allow him to travel southward to Huế. Diệm's younger brother, Ngô Đình Nhu, was able to visit Huế in his capacity as director of the DRV National Archives, only to return to Hanoi convinced that both he and his brother Diệm were in physical jeopardy. In August 1946, French intelligence relocated Diệm in Kunming, where he received twenty thousand piastres from associates in Huế in order to enable him to move to Hong Kong and begin consultations with both Bảo Đại and the French. Also in August, Trần Văn Lý, Diệm's most influential supporter in Huế, chaired the inaugural conference of the Vietnam Catholic Federation, mentioned previously. In early December, Lý was arrested by the Công An, released, and with his family took refuge in the Huế Redemptorist monastery. Former empress Nam Phương joined them just before hostilities broke out in Huế in late December. The attention of the Ngô family now shifted to Saigon and Vĩnh Long, where they took up the formation of a Social Democratic Party dedicated to national independence minus the Communist Party.[270]

The DRV administrative hierarchy dealt infrequently with matters involving Catholics, probably because President Hồ Chí Minh's office took direct responsibility.[271] In early November 1945, a meeting of province committee chairmen with Northern Region officials agreed that religious practice did not require government authorization, yet still needed to be monitored to make sure that no "reactionary political behavior" was involved. Concerning cleavages between non-Catholics and Catholics, the meeting emphasized the need to "find the source of division, sort things out quietly, not resort to force or commands, and avoid any kind of violence."[272] Disputes over property tested this government position. In Hà Nam province, residents of Yên Phú commune had begun their campaign to regain forty-six mẫu (15.3 hectares) of rice land from the Hanoi diocese in May 1945. Beginning in late August they simply changed the date on their petitions from "Twentieth Year of Bảo Đại" to "First Year of the Democratic Republic of Vietnam." A few days later, however, Yên Phú peasants occupied the land unilaterally. The province people's committee now told the peasants that such "land division" was not yet possible, while adding that the DRV government would remember "the interests of the people," and intended to enact a law covering such circumstances. Petitions from both sides now poured in, not least of all from tenants who had been dispossessed. An appeal from the general administrator of the Hanoi diocese stated that the Catholic Church had purchased the land legitimately in the twenty-eighth year of the reign of Tự Đức (1875). A province team reported that Yên Phú residents had never considered the Church acquisition to be legal, and had petitioned for redress three decades into the colonial era. Now they were cultivating the land and were not prepared to move unless given a direct order from the government, although they were willing to release acquired buffaloes, pigs, and farm implements. One year later they were still in possession of the land, and the Church was still demanding they be removed and that ninety thousand piastres compensation be awarded for lost movable property.[273]

I have seen no evidence of the loyalty of Catholic government employees being called into question when Catholic clergy or lay leaders took antigovernment positions. In the National Guard, however, Catholic company or platoon commanders were unlikely to be assigned battalion commands; their opportunities for further promotion were limited to staff positions.[274] In March 1946, fifteen policemen accused the Catholic head of the Phủ Lý (Hà Nam) police bureau of firing them because they were non-Catholic. Three months later the police disciplinary council of Hà Nam province rejected the petition of the dismissed non-Catholics.[275] Catholic clergy occasionally petitioned the central government on behalf of coreligionists in difficulty with local authorities.

Relations between local committees and some Catholic groups appear to have deteriorated starting in late October 1946. Police in Thái Bình arrested one priest and five lay Catholics after finding on their possession copies of *Hồn Công Giáo* newspaper and a book titled *Unmasking the Communist Party*. Under interrogation, one detainee admitted to being sent by the Bùi Chu diocese to Hanoi in February to take a Vietnam Nationalist Party course about Sun Yat-sen's Three Principles of the People, Việt Minh villainy, and techniques for recruiting young activists. Only one of the six detainees repented and sought leniency. The police charged all six with fostering religious division and planning to overthrow the government, then recommended they be sent to a deportation camp away from Thái Bình province.[276] The Công An leadership in Hanoi was looking to accuse some Catholics of allying with remnant antigovernment Nationalists. It was deemed sinister, for example, that copies of Nationalist Party bylaws had been distributed at a Catholic Alliance meeting in Vĩnh Yên province.[277] The DRV propaganda line on Catholics now stated: political maneuvers among Catholics will fail; the government adheres to freedom of religion; the Catholic Church in Vietnam is not under the French church, but communicates directly with the Vatican.[278]

Catholics with grievances continued to send petitions to Hanoi. In early December, Fr. Phạm Bá Trực, a member of the National Assembly Standing Committee, requested that the Interior Ministry investigate serious incidents involving Catholics that had taken place recently in four provinces. On 14 December, he was assured by the Northern Committee chairman, Nguyễn Xiển, that each case was being investigated and would be resolved peacefully.[279] A new weekly newspaper in Hanoi reaffirmed Catholic opposition to materialism, dictatorship, "turning everything upside down," and degrading persons in the name of political necessity. *Nhiệm Vụ tuần báo (Duty Weekly)* denounced communist class struggle for destroying solidarity just at the moment when each and every citizen was needed in the struggle for independence. Yet the paper also insisted that Vietnamese Catholics had an obligation to join Catholic organizations, on the grounds that "Soldiers of Christ must defeat heresy!"[280]

Despite such press commentary, most Vietnamese Catholics in late 1946 did not see themselves as opponents of Hồ Chí Minh or the DRV. They remained fervently anticolonialist and continued to refuse French collaborative approaches. But Catholics also were conscious of their minority status and of non-Catholic suspicions about their loyalty. Tensions rose particularly when non-Catholic police, tax collectors, or Việt Minh recruiters intruded upon long-established procedures in Catholic villages or urban neighborhoods. Hồ was willing to accept a degree of Catholic autonomy in recognition of the greater dangers of overseas Catholics crying persecution or Vietnamese Catholics coming to believe that allegiance to the DRV was incompatible with allegiance to God and the Church.

SILENCED BUT NOT GONE

When full-scale war broke out in late December 1946, much of the DRV security apparatus north of the sixteenth parallel was disrupted, the courts were adjourned, and political prisoners were shifted hastily in various directions. Newspaper offices closed and some printing presses were hauled to the countryside. Anyone who criticized the government now risked summary punishment. Dissidence did not cease, but was driven underground. Surviving Trotskyist and Đại Việt adherents had already been forced down this path in late 1945. Revolutionary League and Nationalist Party representatives existed on the National Alliance roster, but only to be wheeled out by Việt Minh leaders on ceremonial occasions. Other Nationalist Party activists were already in China and Hong Kong talking of an alternative Vietnam government. Many nonparty or independent professionals, writers, and business people fled Hanoi and other towns to seek refuge with rural relatives. Opportunities to debate political options openly would be constrained for decades to come.

The Indochinese Communist Party and the Việt Minh

While the Indochinese Communist Party (ICP) was easily the most significant political organization in Vietnam in late 1945, it did not control the civil administration, most available firearms, or many of the self-styled Việt Minh groups which had sprung up across the country. ICP members did enter state offices in late August and employ the colonial telegraph system to order whoever sat at the other end of the line to declare allegiance to the new Democratic Republic of Vietnam (DRV). Most provinces and districts readily compiled and reported establishment of a revolutionary committee. Some replied that the red flag with yellow star had been hoisted over public buildings, that people were chanting Việt Minh slogans, and that national salvation associations were being formed. Hardly anyone mentioned the ICP. Sometimes this was because local ICP activists understood the party to have subsumed its operations to the Việt Minh Front. Elsewhere it was because non-ICP members had taken power.[1] It would be weeks, in some cases many months, before the ICP general secretary, Trường Chinh, could obtain a rough count of party cells *(chi bộ)* and ascertain how much influence party members exercised over thousands of Việt Minh groups and local government committees around the country.

At this moment the ICP probably possessed no more than five thousand members throughout Indochina, many of them still out of touch with higher echelons of the party.[2] ICP members had managed to initiate a quasi-administration in six upland provinces north of Hanoi, and ICP-led Việt Minh groups moved to take power in many Red River delta towns immediately following Japan's capitulation on 15 August. However, some heavily populated delta districts still had only a single four- or five-person party cell. The key province of Bắc Ninh, across the river from Hanoi, contained only ninety-five ICP members working amidst an estimated three thousand Việt Minh adherents.[3] Down the central coast of Vietnam, there were strong ICP organizations in Huế and in the province of Quảng Ngãi, but elsewhere the party was embroiled in sectarian quarrels or had yet to assert its presence at all. In several central provinces ICP members were powerless to prevent different Việt Minh groups from fighting each other. In southern Vietnam (Nam Bộ), two separate ICP leadership groups continued to undermine each other, even as British-French forces began to arrive on 6 September.[4]

The ICP had been established in 1930 amidst a rising tide of Vietnamese political militancy and French repression. Internal disputes and Sûreté penetration almost destroyed the party in 1931–33, but it revived and flourished during the Popular Front era of 1936–38, reaching out legally to millions of colonial subjects via newspapers, pamphlets, public meetings, and mass demonstrations. These activities were already being curtailed by the colonial authorities before the advent of war in Europe in September 1939, and in the following months thousands of ICP members were thrown into jail. Others returned to a tenuous clandestine existence or fled to China. In late 1940, an ICP uprising in Cochinchina proved so ruinous that survivors found it impossible to renew party activities in the south for four years. In Annam and Tonkin, covert party committees were smashed by the Sûreté, reconstituted, then smashed again. More ICP activity took place behind prison bars than in towns and villages, where simply trying to avoid French capture became the consuming task. Only across the northern frontier, in Guangxi and Yunnan, was it possible for some ICP organizing and training to take place.[5]

In May 1941, a reconstituted central committee met on the Chinese border to redefine ICP revolutionary strategy. A new united front, the Việt Nam Độc Lập Đồng Minh [Vietnam Independence League], or Việt Minh in common parlance, would be formed to attract people from all walks of life to liberate the country from the double yoke of French colonialism and Japanese fascism. Focusing first on ethnic minority hamlets in Cao Bằng province, ICP cadres approached a few individuals in each locality to form a Việt Minh group. Members then began to learn how to read and write, to memorize the basic political platform, undertake military drills, and solicit donations. It was hoped that as the number of participants increased, separate hamlet associations for farmers, youth, women, and elders would be created, with each association electing its own representative to the local Việt Minh committee. ICP cadres would then select the most promising activists to make up the hamlet's first party cell. In practice, French Sûreté operations and military sweeps severely restricted such ICP organizing for three years, but from mid-1944 onward the number of Việt Minh committees in the upland provinces adjacent to China multiplied, and the same process began in the Red River delta following the 9 March 1945 Japanese coup. Simultaneously, hundreds of self-styled Việt Minh groups that lacked any ICP involvement sprung up around the delta and down the central coast.[6] The Vietnam Democratic Party (Việt Nam Dân Chủ Đảng), an affiliate of the Việt Minh, also expanded its membership and activities dramatically in Hanoi and adjacent provinces during July and August 1945.

As a committed Leninist, General Secretary Trường Chinh aimed to extend ICP power over all Việt Minh groups, the nascent DRV state, and "the people" (nhân dân) at large. However, there was no agreed plan for accomplishing this ambitious task. The first list of provisional DRV Cabinet members, published 24 August, was overwhelmingly composed of ICP members. On arrival two days later, Hồ Chí Minh quickly dropped five ICP and National Salvation Cultural Association individuals from the Cabinet in favor of a Catholic intellectual, two Democratic Party members, and two nonparty educators. While Hồ was no less a Leninist than Trường Chinh, his immediate objectives were to widen popular support for the fledgling government and to project himself as a national leader above party, class, or personal interest. More than any other ICP member, Hồ also understood the gravity of the threat posed to the DRV by arriving Chinese and British-French forces—with no prospect that the Soviet Union or the CCP could provide early assistance. In these arduous circumstances, the ICP needed first to get its own house in order, gain authority over disparate revolutionary groups around the country, and not necessarily expect to exercise national power for some time to come. Trường Chinh, however, made no secret of his intention to move Vietnam more quickly towards proletarian dictatorship.

In this chapter I first look at senior ICP members who worked outside the DRV government to enhance party control. I show how the proliferation of local Việt Minh groups created a variety of problems as well as benefits. Then I devote particular attention to Trường Chinh, who set himself the task of analyzing the current reality and promulgating his own findings in both confidential party directives and public periodicals. The auto-dissolution of the ICP in November 1945 did not alter Trường Chinh's modus operandi; he simply changed the name of his periodical and referred to the party as the "Organization" (Đoàn thể). By August 1946, Trường Chinh was ready to publish a revolutionary agenda which influenced the course of Vietnam's history for decades to come. Meanwhile, another ICP group was publishing Cứu Quốc (National Salvation), the principal means by which the party influenced disparate Việt Minh groups in northern and north-central Vietnam. I look particularly at the way Cứu Quốc dealt with highly sensitive Franco-Vietnamese relations, and the manner in which editors used recent history to legitimize both the Việt Minh and the ICP. I then focus on the little-known Democratic Party, demonstrating how it managed to project a separate identity under the Việt Minh umbrella. Simultaneously, the ICP moved against all perceived opposition and tried without much success to create a mega-front, the Liên Việt. Finally, I assess the status of the ICP as of late 1946, at which point it had still not achieved control of the state, yet was in a much better position than it had been fourteen months prior to influence government policy, screen appointments, communicate confidentially with local party cells, and withstand enemy attack.

ICP LEADERS OUTSIDE THE GOVERNMENT

Throughout the Pacific War, Trường Chinh had wielded a sharp pen in underground publications, assessing international and domestic trends, criticizing local party groups for left or right deviations, and forecasting revolutionary opportunities.[7] Immediately after arriving in Hanoi in late August 1945, Trường Chinh located a printing press and expanded publication of *Cờ Giải Phóng (Liberation Flag)*, which the masthead proudly pronounced to be the official organ of the ICP. Now able to reach a much wider audience than before, Trường Chinh reaffirmed the ICP as both the party of workers and the "vanguard leading all the people." The DRV government was "in the hands of the people." Juxtaposing these two statements, readers might well conclude that the ICP controlled the government.[8] By contrast, Hồ Chí Minh insisted repeatedly that his provisional government was subordinate to no party, and was instead eager to involve any group prepared to struggle for Vietnamese independence, freedom, and happiness. In these statements in *Cờ Giải Phóng*, Trường Chinh appeared to contradict the policy enunciated in May 1941 by which the ICP operated from within Việt Minh organizations and kept its own network secret. Ironically he had earlier criticized the southern "Vanguard" group of the party for asserting its ICP identity publicly. Elsewhere this policy difference was being played out with flags: some cells flew the ICP hammer-and-sickle banner side by side with the Việt Minh's yellow star on a red field; others kept the hammer and sickle under wraps, as had been the case in the northern border region and most Red River delta provinces before August. One confidential ICP formulation spoke of the need to demarcate more sharply the responsibilities of comrades working undercover or in public, and admitted that the party had yet to penetrate many Việt Minh groups and government bureaus.[9]

Trường Chinh condemned workers who took direct control of enterprises without authorization, or who agitated for pay hikes to offset rampant inflation. Much additional sacrifice would be required before the revolution brought the "happy rewards of a new life." In particular he threatened, "Don't allow the Trotskyist gang to dupe you into making excessive demands that cannot be resolved yet."[10] In early October 1945, Trường Chinh escalated his attack on alleged Trotskyists, accusing them of wartime collaboration with the Japanese, extreme left opposition to talks with the British in Saigon, and totally unreasonable economic demands in Hanoi. Asserting that "some people" urged cooperation

FIGURE 25. Trường Chinh, ICP
general secretary. Courtesy of
Christophe Dutrône.

with Trotskyists, Trường Chinh instead demanded their elimination.[11] By late
October, ICP "honor squads" were busy killing alleged Trotskyists in Nam Bộ,
including several denounced by name in Trường Chinh's article (see chapter 7).
As for the north, where no one had identified publicly with the Fourth International for years, Trường Chinh used the Trotskyist epithet to menace any other
group which claimed to represent the working class. Young laborers must have
been mystified at being tarred with the name of an assassinated Jewish Ukrai-
nian revolutionary, yet older veterans of 1930s political disputes understood the
gravity of being accused in this way by an ICP that now possessed firearms.

When it became apparent in mid-September that General Douglas Gracey,
the British commander in Saigon, had no intention of recognizing the DRV-
affiliated Southern Provisional Executive Committee, the ICP's entire pro-Allied
strategy was thrown into disarray. Confidentially, Trường Chinh had long predicted that Great Britain would uphold French "reactionary" interests, yet now that
it was happening he was silent on what should be done. After violence exploded
across Saigon on 23 September, Trường Chinh in Hanoi accused the British of
betraying their promises, deceiving the Vietnamese people, and "going contrary to
Allied goals." He concluded: "The Vietnamese people, the Indochinese people,
will sacrifice their last drop of blood to defend the country (đất nước) and defend
the rights to freedom and independence they have so recently won back from the
hands of the Japanese-French fascists."[12]

While Trường Chinh was staking out publicly the vanguard role of the ICP,
other senior members of the party assumed a range of confidential troubleshoot-

ing assignments. Hoàng Quốc Việt went to Saigon to try to resolve party divisions and take part in talks with the British.[13] Nguyễn Lương Bằng, one of Hồ Chí Minh's original recruits in Canton in 1925, took charge of presidential security. Vũ Đình Huỳnh, assistant to the president, had charge of the appointments book, while Bằng's staff tried to conduct prior background checks on visitors, a job rendered more difficult by Hồ's insistence on meeting people from all walks of life. Bằng arranged for Hồ to sleep at multiple buildings around Hanoi, and requisitioned three different automobiles to transport the president.[14] Such precautions were not whimsical, given the covert and sometimes violent struggle taking place between ICP and Vietnam Nationalist Party operatives. Bằng was also senior member of the Tổng Bộ Việt Minh (Việt Minh General Headquarters), and managed ICP finances. Clearly Bằng enjoyed respect inside the ICP for his proletarian origins, his long incarceration, and his personal probity, but he was not known for imagination or intellect.[15]

Trần Đăng Ninh, who had escaped prison alongside Nguyễn Lương Bằng in 1943, led party efforts starting in early September 1945 to reorganize what remained of the colonial Sûreté and to bring under ICP control scores of Việt Minh "honor squads" and self-styled secret investigation units in the north.[16] In November, he was assigned to coordinate political relations with, and undercover operations against, the Nationalist Party. President Hồ also dispatched Ninh to make initial contact with Bishop Lê Hữu Từ in Phát Diệm.[17] Soon Ninh obtained wide powers to investigate other sensitive issues and implement solutions on the spot, in the manner of commissioners of the republic during the French Revolution. He smoked two packs of cigarettes a day, spoke bluntly, was proud of his working-class origins, but defensive about his lack of education. Ninh preferred to function in the background, collecting information tenaciously, which made him both admired and feared among ICP insiders.[18]

Trần Quốc Hoàn, another former organizer inside Sơn La prison, was given the job of building up the ICP's covert intelligence and counterintelligence capacities in the Hanoi area.[19] Beginning with his own Hanoi assassination squad created during the summer of 1945, Hoàn added comrades from prison and some eager teenage volunteers. He also had underworld connections. One of Hoàn's first successes was to recruit female operators at the Hanoi telephone exchange to listen in on conversations and report. Hoàn also convinced an attractive seventeen-year-old member of the Women's National Salvation Association to lure an aide of Nguyễn Hải Thần, head of the Vietnam Revolutionary League, into circumstances where he could be grabbed by male agents and kidnapped. Because the agents failed to administer a sufficient dose of chloroform, the aide escaped, but not before Hoàn's young female spy had made off with his pistol and briefcase full of documents.[20] Hoàn inserted agents among Vietnamese laborers employed by the French military, some of whom were discovered and tortured. The head of

Hoàn's spy ring inside the French-occupied Citadel was run over and killed by a jeep, with the French soldier-driver insisting to authorities that it was an accident. Hoàn developed a reputation for meticulous planning and a fascination with any technology that might serve his operations.[21]

Meanwhile, far to the south, Phạm Hùng was taking up security and investigation responsibilities similar to those of his northern comrades, but in far more chaotic circumstances.[22] Hùng and up to two hundred other ICP inmates had managed to make it from Côn Sơn island prison to Sóc Trăng on the mainland on 23 September 1945, the same day that fighting broke out in Saigon between British-French forces and DRV adherents.[23] A senior southern ICP member, Nguyễn Văn Nguyễn, escorted Hùng to the Saigon suburbs and explained his immediate assignment: to command a regional police group made up of former Sûreté employees, Vanguard Youth, and ICP members dedicated to eliminating alleged counterrevolutionaries but now fragmented and widely disbursed. Hùng recruited some of his Côn Sơn comrades to lead new bureau contingents among young workers and Saigon's underworld, then gradually convinced prior members to accept his authority as well. Lightly armed teams manned checkpoints, issued travel permits, confiscated money, detained suspects, executed condemned prisoners, and undertook assassination missions. A number of prisoners who had been marched out of Saigon were eventually moved to distant Cà Mau peninsula to keep them from French rescue. By late 1946, Phạm Hùng possessed an effective police hierarchy, now titled the Southern Public Security Bureau (Nha Công An Nam Bộ). However, he did not enjoy a monopoly: the Bình Xuyên, Cao Đài, and Hòa Hảo retained their own security units. And Nguyễn Bình, commander of DRV forces in the Military Region 7 (eastern delta), insisted on managing his own security network. Hùng also tried to end the bickering between "Vanguard" and "Liberation" elements of the party, without much success (see below).[24] Hùng and some other Côn Sơn prison returnees accepted the authority of Trường Chinh as ICP secretary general, but this meant little in the absence of a reliable, confidential means of communication with Hanoi.

Lê Đức Thọ, another former inmate of Sơn La prison, took responsibility in Hanoi in early September 1945 for screening the past performance of ICP members and recommending job assignments.[25] Thọ had access to French police files compiled on Vietnamese political prisoners, which probably included reports indicating how much sensitive information ICP detainees had divulged under interrogation and often torture. French files sometimes revealed which ICP members had routinely informed on their comrades, which now made them marked men. On the other hand, comrades who had broken under torture were not necessarily exposed. To do this rigorously would have sparked bitter recriminations and destroyed the myth of heroic refusals even unto death, which already was being projected in party publications. Keeping this information secret also gave

Thọ power over those comrades who feared that their "weakness" might be divulged. Even those who had revealed nothing sensitive under interrogation could not know what other prisoners or informants had said about them to the French.[26] The urgent need to appoint party members to reconstituted provincial ICP committees *(tỉnh uỷ)*, government offices, and provincial administrative committees probably meant that Thọ had no time to scrutinize every relevant French file in advance. It was Thọ who gave Hồ Chí Minh the names of three young ICP members from whom to choose his personal secretary.[27] Background investigations and the practice of compiling personal histories *(lý lịch)* on each party member would soon become ubiquitous. During 1946, Thọ also found time to contribute articles to ICP and Việt Minh periodicals, and to lecture at party training courses.

ICP members possessing recent prison experience were held in awe among the Vietnamese population at large, an awe which the party turned to propaganda advantage beginning with the August 1945 insurrection. Within the party, individuals who had befriended each other behind bars often maintained contact and provided mutual support in later years. Alumni of Sơn La prison became the single most important leadership group within the party for decades to come.[28] In March 1945, the French warden of Sơn La had promoted this concordance when he released two hundred political prisoners before the arrival of a Japanese Army contingent from the delta. Former prisoners of Côn Sơn island became the second most significant leadership group, although many of those arriving on the mainland in late September had to scatter throughout the Mekong delta and fend for themselves for many months.[29] Extended prison experience did not automatically produce party leaders. Some former inmates had been broken physically or mentally. Others found it impossible to shift from a clannish, conspiratorial environment to working with a wide range of people in a relatively open climate of meetings, public speeches, class lectures, and newspaper articles. Still others sought revenge for savageries endured behind bars. With the early outbreak of fighting in the south, these individuals gravitated to security groups scattered around the Mekong delta, where their proclivity for conspiracy and violent retribution often was considered a virtue.

Available sources make no mention of any ICP Standing Bureau meeting in Hanoi during September or October 1945, an extraordinary absence considering the aim of Trường Chinh and others to strengthen party control over the DRV state.[30] There was the problem that Hồ Chí Minh's leadership group from the Việt Bắc hills needed to be represented alongside the existing bureau that Trường Chinh had led for several years in the Red River delta. ICP representatives from central and southern Vietnam would also have to be incorporated. Hồ Chí Minh conducted his activities at the Bắc Bộ Phủ (Northern Region Office), relying on a small team of party and nonparty lieutenants to help him evaluate events, make decisions, and monitor implementation across a wide range of organizations.[31]

Trường Chinh had access to the president's office, but was not involved in day-to-day affairs.[32] He met routinely with senior ICP members active in the central government and provincial party committees. Trường Chinh listened to foreign news broadcasts assiduously, read the daily papers, and factored all this information into his analyses of Vietnam's current circumstances and future prospects. Besides publishing *Cờ Giải Phóng*, he was composing a major ICP policy statement (see below).

THE LIMITS OF SOLIDARITY

While ICP leaders were trying to take control of events from above, at the local level a variety of groups styling themselves ICP or Việt Minh took action on their own volition. Many of these village- and district-level initiatives would assist the fledgling DRV government to consolidate power and foster mass mobilization (see chapter 9). However, other local actions proved quite disruptive, triggering animosities and disputes that persisted for years or decades. Most disturbing was the seizure in August of thousands of alleged traitors, counterrevolutionaries, and reactionaries, who were first held in hundreds of makeshift jails without due process, then executed, deported, or released under local Việt Minh surveillance. Trường Chinh would later complain that not enough enemies had been eliminated in the early days of the revolution. Yet from the explosion of petitions from aggrieved relatives, and the inability of the new administration to deal with more than a small fraction of these cases, we can see why subsequent calls for national solidarity would meet with deep suspicion from those at the receiving end of such violence.

When civil authorities did try to get to the roots of particular killings, local Việt Minh groups pointed to the prerevolutionary offences of the victims, or the risks such persons would have posed to the new order if allowed to live. When such arguments failed to sway government investigators, it was often possible to lobby province-level ICP cadres or simply stall for time. Individuals targeted for killing by Việt Minh groups who managed to escape seldom received legal protection from the state. For example, Nguyễn Quốc Phiên twice escaped being killed in August 1945 by his village Việt Minh group in Hưng Yên province. When he dared to return to the village in September he was seized by the same group, who now controlled the people's committee. A battle of petitions to Hanoi ensued, one side arguing that Phiên was very dangerous, the other urging release of Phiên and punishment of the perpetrators. Although higher authority obtained Phiên's release in November, local national salvation associations continued to protest, leaving one to wonder how long it would be before Phiên either fled the village or was eliminated.[33] I did find one case in which five Việt Minh members arrested for killing a fellow villager during the August insurrection were tried by the Hưng Yên province court, declared guilty, and sentenced to five years' hard labor.[34]

During late 1945, some Việt Minh groups also terrorized landlords, burned down the houses of alleged traitors, extorted money or rice from fellow villagers, reallocated communal land (công điền) without government authorization, and boarded river vessels carrying coal or salt to requisition some of the cargo. In the village of Thái Bình (Hà Đông), the Việt Minh group led by Nguyễn Văn Thế broke into the home of Nguyễn Văn Sinh during the August insurrection, accused Sinh of multiple crimes committed during the colonial era, and took family valuables. Later, Thế did the same at the homes of two other former village notables. When the prefectural judicial officer launched an investigation, he found that systematic extortion of better off families in Thái Bình village was taking place, with Thế convening people's courts, levying fines, and then sharing some of the takings with the poor. Thế and several Việt Minh comrades were arrested in March 1946, sparking a political tussle that eventually reached the Interior Ministry. Thế insisted he was a loyal citizen doing his duty, but the last assessment in the file maintains that "the Thế gang is very cunning, using its [political] power to oppress wealthy members of the village."[35] We don't know if Thế remained in jail, but other case files reveal Việt Minh groups continuing to lobby for release of their comrades.[36] Because most such cases did not get to court, much less result in a judicial decision, the chances of reversing the administrative detentions of Việt Minh adherents were good. Over time, Việt Minh groups learned how to use the administrative system to advantage rather than engage in impulsive violence.

The question of overlap between Việt Minh groups and government committees arose on many occasions, revealing a fundamental ambiguity in the new political system. The DRV central government wanted a demarcation to be observed right down to the commune level, in the first instance to demonstrate to the public that opposition charges that the Việt Minh controlled the government were wrong, but also to satisfy state employees and others who believed in a professional civil service. The ICP was committed to gaining control over all government echelons, but differences of opinion existed over how rapidly this should occur, and by what means. We have already seen how Trần Đăng Ninh, Trần Quốc Hoàn, and Phạm Hùng focused on taking command of police and security, not just by inserting ICP members into existing organizations, but also by building autonomous party secret investigation units. Meanwhile, Lê Đức Thọ was busy inserting party members into central government bureaus and provincial people's committees. ICP members who had already played key roles in seizing power at the province level assigned party comrades to a range of local administrative positions. However, some provincial ICP committees were bedeviled by leadership or doctrinal disputes, Nghệ An being the worst example.

Available archival files are replete with evidence of duplication, contradiction, and occasional conflict between Việt Minh and government organizations. During October 1945, the Haiphong Việt Minh committee forwarded reports directly to the government radio station in Hanoi on rice prices, currency exchange rates, cloth scarcity, and deaths from starvation or disease.[37] A month later, the chair of the Haiphong People's Committee reported that the city's national salvation associations had grown from nothing before the August insurrection to five hundred to six hundred members per association, implying that his committee deserved credit.[38] The Hải Dương province chairman felt it his duty to warn certain youths against "slandering the Việt Minh and people's committee." Villages that failed to delineate the people's committee from the Việt Minh were criticized by the Hưng Yên province chair.[39] Divisions and disputes between local Việt Minh and government committees became a routine entry in provincial periodic reports. As late as December 1945, some village committees were still addressing letters to the "Việt Minh Government" in Hanoi. The Northern Office found it necessary to instruct the Nam Định province committee to "immediately order subordinate committees to destroy all stationery with the heading 'Việt Minh Government,'" and to replace it with "Democratic Republic of Vietnam."[40]

In deliberations leading up to reform of the entire DRV committee hierarchy in November 1945, one unnamed participant tabled a proposal to assign political and military tasks to the Việt Minh Front, leaving "specialized work" to the government committees.[41] This radical proposal was not accepted, yet in following months many Việt Minh groups did acquire a range of quasi-governmental powers. Persons applying for a government firearm permit required a local Việt Minh letter of introduction. The same was true of young men wishing to join the National Guard. National salvation associations collected the highest proportion of donations to government-established patriotic funds, and often kept some portion of the proceeds for their own activities. As inflation eroded salaries, government employees became more dependent on local Việt Minh provision of food. Unpaid Việt Minh members worked side by side with salaried staff. The government's national literacy campaign came to depend on local Việt Minh initiative, since the Department of Popular Study had only a tiny budget. The same applied to public hygiene efforts, as the Health Ministry had barely enough money to print pamphlets. Despite this growing Việt Minh involvement in the business of government, national salvation associations are only mentioned six times in the 1946 *National Gazette*, out of perhaps three thousand entries total.[42] The national government continued to draw a line between the state and popular organizations, even if it meant officially ignoring the myriad overlaps and confusions.

THE ICP DECLARES ITS OWN DISSOLUTION

In late October 1945, as we have seen, Chinese generals in Hanoi increased their pressure on Hồ Chí Minh to accept members of the Vietnam Nationalist Party and Vietnam Revolutionary League into his provisional DRV government. When Hồ's proposals were rejected by the Nationalist Party, he took the extraordinary step of instructing party leaders to announce the dissolution of the ICP. This 11 November ICP resolution began by asserting that Vietnam possessed an opportunity to gain complete independence that "comes only once in a thousand years," a chance which should not be jeopardized by differences of class or political party. To demonstrate that ICP members were "vanguard fighters for the nation" who put the common interest above all, and "to destroy all misunderstandings foreign and domestic" which might hinder the liberation of Vietnam, the Central Executive Bureau had decided "voluntarily to dissolve the ICP." The resolution concluded by inviting "followers of communism wishing to advance their ideological enquiries" to join the Association to Research Marxism in Indochina.[43]

Hồ Chí Minh's immediate objective in securing and publicizing this dissolution resolution was to deflect accusations that his government was run by the ICP. Although Nationalist Party activists soon found and publicized evidence of continuing clandestine ICP operations, Hồ had managed to put them on the defensive in the propaganda contest over forming a national united front to stand up to foreign threats. Independent newspapers had been chiding both sides for their sectarian bickering, and the word "political party" (đảng phái) was taking on negative connotations. The ICP once again subsumed its propaganda to that of the Việt Minh Front. The dissolution resolution was not meant to respond solely to Chinese and opposition challenges, but also to address fears of communism among the general public. Since the early 1930s, landlords, Catholics, government employees, and some entrepreneurs and intellectuals had developed anxieties if not dread at the prospect of communist rule. In November 1945, the DRV government, fearing another terrible famine in the Red River delta, realized that landlords and rich peasants could make or break the next harvest due in May 1946. The harvest proved to be good, Chinese troops were mostly withdrawn by June, and the Nationalist Party position was neutralized by July, yet there was no move by Hồ Chí Minh to bring the ICP back into the light of day. Covert status offered certain operational advantages. Beyond that, I doubt that Hồ wanted an ICP dictatorship any time soon.

Most ICP members were shocked by the 11 November dissolution resolution. There had been no internal discussion, although Trường Chinh is said to have opposed the move.[44] In the north, members soon received confidential instructions to revert to underground operations, not disband. However, many party members in central and southern Vietnam were left confused and demoralized for months. Putative dissolution of the ICP eventually provoked controversy much further away, in Moscow.

SETTING THE LINE

Only two weeks after allegedly dissolving, the ICP Central Executive Bureau issued a long, confidential directive titled "Resistance, Country Building," which made no mention of the 11 November 1945 resolution, as if the author(s) considered it irrelevant to their current outlook or operations.[45] The contents of this directive would presage Vietnamese communist policy for the next three decades. Almost surely written principally by General Secretary Trường Chinh, the directive opened in orthodox Leninist manner by listing a number of international "contradictions" (mâu thuẫn) or oppositions, of which the four most important were: the Soviet Union versus imperialist countries, proletarians versus capitalists, oppressed nationalities versus colonialism, and imperialists versus imperialists. The directive predicted that contradictions between the Soviet Union and the United States would provoke a series of confrontations between progressive peace forces and the forces of reaction, yet not lead to a third world war. In South and Southeast Asia, the fiercest contradiction was between oppressed nationalities and colonialism, and had already sparked liberation wars in Indochina and Indonesia, and bloody demonstrations in India. In Indochina, the fledgling DRV had to contend with British and Chinese intervention, colonial French aggression, serious food shortages, and domestic opponents who relied on the Chinese to demand participation in the government. Characterizing big power policies on Indochina, the directive plaintively complimented Russian newspapers for noting Vietnam's liberation struggle, pointed out that the United States was loaning transport vessels to the invading French military, assessed the British as increasingly disenchanted with French actions, and correctly predicted that Nationalist China would concede northern Indochina to France in exchange for substantial rewards.

Turning to France itself, the 25 November 1945 "Resistance, Country Building" directive highlighted growing strength for the French Communist Party, but then failed to analyze the overall political equation in the métropole, or explain exactly who constituted the "colonial French" enemy. It opined that Paris might recognize Indochinese independence in exchange for economic benefits, yet contained no further discussion of possible Franco-Vietnamese negotiations. Here authors of the directive were probably deferring to President Hồ Chí Minh, who had taken a firm grip on foreign affairs. More fundamentally, many ICP members rejected the idea of making any concessions to the French.

The remainder of the "Resistance, Country Building" directive set forth a host of ICP policies and operational instructions. The party allied itself with the Soviet Union and with workers and progressives around the world who were struggling for peace, freedom, and happiness. It remained focused on the national liberation revolution in Indochina, and exhorted the proletarian class to continue taking the achievement of that revolution seriously.[46] The principal enemy of the revolution was French colonial aggression, against which it was essential to broaden the Việt Minh Front and to construct a Việt-Khmer-Lao united front. Domestic opposition had to be eliminated as well, although in certain cases it might be possible to win over some members, exacerbate divisions, then repress the traitorous elements. DRV military strategy should focus on mobilizing the masses and preparing for protracted resistance. Foreign policy needed to reduce enemies and increase allies. Propaganda had to emphasize national unity, yet reject any unprincipled inclusion of traitors. It should also arouse hatred for French colonialists while avoiding condemnation of France or the French people.

Despite equal weight given to "country building" in the title, the 25 November directive offered readers no coherent economic or social program. For the current antifamine campaign, the directive cited President Hồ's call to "yield food, share clothing" (Nhường cơm, Xẻ áo), then instructed ICP cells to encourage tenants and landlords to make concessions to each other, and convince wealthy citizens to contribute to food relief.[47] Given fears of communism and class struggle among landlords and well-off Vietnamese, such cajolery ought to have been left to DRV administrative committees. Yet the authors of this directive wanted the party to take the lead everywhere. Looking beyond the immediate food crisis, the directive offered a mere shopping list, to include the reopening of factories and mines, creation of cooperatives and stock companies, repair of dikes, establishment of a national bank, release of a national currency, reorganization of taxes, and the compiling of national, regional, and provincial budgets. Without any prioritization, or hint of where resources and expertise could be found to accomplish such monumental tasks, this list revealed both the economic naiveté of Trường Chinh and other ICP leaders, and their grand modernizing ambitions.

The "Resistance, Country Building" directive trod more confident ground when discussing how to strengthen the party and the Việt Minh. In the search for new ICP members, some cadres still adhered to outdated preinsurrection restrictions. On the other hand, being too hasty and inclusive in recruitment would enable "complex elements" (phần tử phức tạp) to penetrate the party.[48] In its only nod to the 11 November dissolution resolution, the directive ordered establishment of Marxist research groups containing both communists and sympathizers. However, organizers of these groups should not allow party members to "contract petty bourgeois habits or catch the disease of openness"—a reference to ICP behavior during the 1936–38 Popular Front period. Simultaneously, the party had to form more cells within the DRV civil administration, the army, and various legally constituted associations, making sure that party secrecy was preserved, and that party cadres functioning in clandestine and open organizations did not come into conflict with each other. The party also needed to distribute more covert printed matter to lower echelons.

Acknowledging current confusion and turmoil, the 25 November directive committed the ICP to building a nationwide Việt Minh Front. Contradictions between local Việt Minh groups and government administrative committees had to be overcome. Disputes between Democratic Party branches and national salvation associations had to be resolved (see below). Salvation associations had to be formed for Catholics, "feudal landlords," and even the Boy Scouts. More priority had to be assigned to creating branches of the Farmers' National Salvation Association. Tổng Bộ functions had to be revamped, enabling it to dispatch instructions to local Việt Minh groups and exercise control over scores of Việt Minh publications. Bylaws of Việt Minh groups needed to be revised to reflect new operational conditions. In the upcoming general election, the directive aimed to have one-third of all candidates to the National Assembly be ICP members and one-third Việt Minh members, leaving one-third for "outsiders"—an unmistakable sign of the party's democratic centralist intentions.

The "Resistance and Country-Building" directive had remarkably little to say about the Franco-Vietnamese hostilities that had broken out nine weeks earlier in Nam Bộ and were already spreading to south-central Vietnam. Accepting as inevitable the evacuation of Vietnamese forces from Saigon and a number of provincial towns, the authors of the directive nonetheless judged resistance morale to be high. No mention was made of the thousands of young men (and some women) in northern and central Vietnam who had already headed south to fight the French. The directive did urge the DRV government to send one or more commissioners southward to "take charge" (điều khiển). Hồ Chí Minh had already dispatched military commanders, but wisely chose not to impose an outsider on the Nam Bộ Resistance Committee. There was no reference to Hoàng Quốc Việt's failed mission in late August to resolve the intra-party dispute in Nam Bộ.

Laos received as much attention as Nam Bộ in the 25 November directive, reflecting the ICP's Indochina-wide concerns. Liberation forces were said to be holding six towns in Laos against enemy assault, although the directive admitted that French units seemed to have free run of the countryside. The directive neglected to mention that ethnic Vietnamese made up the bulk of armed opposition to the French in Laos. It did urge armed propaganda teams to circulate among the Lao "rural masses," creating a Lao-Việt united front to isolate the French and eventually drive them out. Cambodia received only a one-sentence mention in the directive: a Khmer-Vietnamese armed force had to be established "immediately" so that guerrilla operations could spread across the full extent of Indochina. Trường Chinh and comrades in Hanoi possessed only fragmentary information on what was happening in Laos, and they knew almost nothing about events in Cambodia. This led to much wishful thinking, followed by frustration over evident reversals. Nonetheless, the ICP stuck to its grand design for Indochina, in which Vietnamese would lead the backward Lao and Khmer to struggle for independence and freedom.[49]

COMMUNICATING THE LINE

It was not possible for the 25 November 1945 "Resistance, Country Building" directive to be printed and distributed to party committees nationwide. Instead, typescript copies were given to senior party leaders to refer to when addressing confidential gatherings of party members in Hanoi and the provinces. At such meetings, listeners took notes assiduously, and this became the basis for further oral communication to lower echelons. While this system worked reasonably well in the northern delta, it was often unreliable in transmitting the party line to members further afield. Later the party would develop its own covert postal system. Party leaders also aimed to produce ideologically correct periodicals and monographs. The weekly journal *Sự Thật (Truth)* was meant to fulfill this responsibility, yet it seems that only a handful of copies made it beyond northern towns to party members in the countryside or down the central coast. Other Việt Minh newspapers varied in their adherence to any ICP line (see below).

Sự Thật could be purchased on the street in northern towns for 1\$50BIC per issue, or one could pay an annual subscription and receive copies by post. Although the masthead announced that *Sự Thật* was the "propaganda campaign organ of the Association to Research Marxism in Indochina," any Vietnamese old enough to have read Popular Front publications of the late 1930s could easily identify it as a Communist Party paper. Trường Chinh signed many of his own contributions to *Sự Thật,* and clearly controlled overall content. Drawing on his 1927–29 studies in Moscow, Bùi Công Trừng authored articles on the teachings of Marx, Engels, Lenin, and Stalin. Often these essays appeared more theological than practical, with little or no attempt to connect specific ideas to current conditions in Vietnam. Trừng also contributed articles on industry, agriculture, commerce, capital investment, and finance—in each case arguing for Vietnam's commitment to a command economy. Most other contributors to *Sự Thật* employed pseudonyms. The *Sự Thật* editorial office accessed a number of international news services, presumably thanks to a team that monitored shortwave radio broadcasts. Senior cadres of the "underground" ICP routinely visited the *Sự Thật* office, catching up on the news, sharing operational information, and introducing young activists to other persons present.

During its first six months of publication, *Sự Thật* leaned heavily towards general ideological exposition, international commentary, and florid promotion of the ICP's history since 1930. Articles explaining dialectical materialism, Marxist world history, class struggle, and the inevitable victory of proletarian internationalism must have been aimed at the new August 1945 generation of revolutionaries, since the older generation had read it all during the 1930s. *Sự Thật* celebrated the Soviet Army's occupation of Eastern Europe and pictured Moscow as spearheading a new global movement of progressive, democratic, peace-loving peoples. This movement was opposed by reactionary capitalists, remnant fascists, and colonialists who looked increasingly to Washington for leadership. *Sự Thật* was quick to report growing tensions between Moscow and Washington over occupied Germany and Japan, as well as confrontations over Korea, Persia-Iran, and Greece. It condemned Winston Churchill's "Iron Curtain" speech as anti-Soviet, yet agreed with his assessment that the world was quickly dividing into two hostile camps.[50] For readers who wished more detailed explanations of where Vietnam should go in the future, *Sự Thật's* publishing house offered book-length Vietnamese translations from French about Marxist-Leninist ideology, the Soviet Union, and the Communist International. *Sự Thật* also gave prominence to current developments in India, Indonesia, and China, and promoted the idea of an all-Asia anti-imperialist alliance. It did not trumpet its support for the Chinese Communist Party, no doubt for fear of retaliation by Nationalist Chinese occupation authorities, but readers could readily draw their own conclusions.

Sự Thật was monumentally vague when it came to discussing DRV foreign policy, in contrast to its bold, assertive treatment of policies in Moscow, Washington, or London. It of course favored DRV alignment with national liberation movements elsewhere in Asia and solidarity with the "peace-loving French people," but avoided taking a position on relations with the French and Chinese governments. Every issue of *Sự Thật* contained condemnations of "French reactionary colonialists," yet Trường Chinh and other writers chose not to define or explain this epithet. Unlike some other newspapers of the day, *Sự Thật* did not apply the term to individual French leaders like General de Gaulle, Admiral d'Argenlieu, or Commissioner Cédile, although they all undoubtedly met the test in Trường Chinh's eyes. But were Prime Minister Bidault, Minister for Overseas France Moutet, General Leclerc, and Commissioner Sainteny reactionary colonialists too? If so, on what basis could negotiations with France ensue? Were all French civilians resident in Indochina reactionary colonialists? If not, how were readers expected to differentiate between them? These were important questions, but for *Sự Thật* to discuss them would have intruded upon President Hồ Chí Minh's conduct of DRV foreign policy. During the hectic round of DRV-France-China negotiations in late February and early March, Hồ kept matters to himself and a handful of confidents. Trường Chinh probably entertained strong reservations about the results, but he did not use *Sự Thật* to posit a different interpretation from that of his president about what was happening.

On the domestic front, *Sự Thật* routinely castigated the Vietnam Nationalist Party and Vietnam Revolutionary League, yet left it to *Cứu Quốc* to conduct a vitriolic polemic with opposition newspapers. *Sự Thật* had little to say about operations of the DRV civil administration or the nascent army. Topics like education, culture, health, and social welfare received only perfunctory attention. Quite possibly Trường Chinh had been cautioned by Hồ Chí Minh to keep party and state affairs distinct from each other. On the state side of this equation, DRV administrators were under instructions to stay clear of "party politics," the ICP and Việt Minh included. Official correspondence and reports between September 1945 and December 1946 contain only a handful of references to the ICP.[51] It is doubtful that Trường Chinh sought access to government files, although he talked readily with DRV officials who were party members.

In June 1946, *Sự Thật* assumed a more aggressive political position, taking advantage of the withdrawal of most Chinese troops from Indochina and, I would suggest, the departure of Hồ Chí Minh for talks in France. Trường Chinh stated baldly that "all persons worthy of being called Vietnamese" must become members of the new National Alliance (Liên Việt) organization, and warned that "no party calling itself patriotic will be allowed to impede unification of the country's armed forces and civil administration."[52] He also foreshadowed imminent moves to force the Nationalist Party out of positions in the Red River corridor that it had held since September 1945. *Sự Thật* accused "reactionary colonialists" of orchestrating violent altercations between French soldiers and Vietnamese shopkeepers. Any violence instigated by Vietnamese was the work of traitors or "pseudo-patriots" who wanted to undermine DRV authority.[53]

"Our Policy"

On 30 June 1946, Trường Chinh signed and released the ICP's most significant public statement to date. Titled simply "Our Policy," the statement deliberately obfuscated the distinction between party platform and national strategy, in the process taking positions that did not necessarily coincide with DRV government policy.[54] The first section, subtitled "Internal Unity," accused French reactionary colonialists of trying to divide Vietnam between minorities and Kinh, south and north, rich and poor, Catholic and non-Catholic, and traitorous and patriotic political parties. Then, rather than simply dismiss such divisions, Trường Chinh

addressed each of them in turn. He recognized the limited "right of local autonomy" of minorities within the DRV state, mentioning the Mường, "Mọi" and
Thái by name.[55] As for regional differences, Trường Chinh insisted that "Center,
South, and North are three integral parts of Vietnam, like the head, torso, and
legs of the human body." Rich and poor Vietnamese should make mutual concessions and help each other out, in order to resist the common enemy coming
from outside. Then Trường Chinh shifted gears, reaffirming the doctrine of
class struggle, yet arguing that in Indochina's current circumstances, class interests should be subsumed to national interests (quyền lợi dân tộc). On the religious
question, he supported freedom of belief, but also the right to criticize superstition (mê tín). As for contradictions between political parties, Trường Chinh declared ominously that it was time for traitors to be punished.

In a curious paragraph addressed to party members alone, Trường Chinh acknowledged that some comrades accused the Organization (Đoàn thể) of "unprincipled agreements," and of "flattering the bourgeois, landlord, and priestly gangs."
However, these "bombastic criticisms" demonstrated a poverty of reason (lý trí),
according to Trường Chinh. Such comrade-critics lost control when faced with
adversity, allowing sentiment to take over their heads, thus failing to grasp the
tactical imperative of "internal agreement in order to cope with those outside."
We don't know whom Trường Chinh was responding to, but it is notable that he
did not label them "left deviationists" or threaten them with party discipline.[56]
Trường Chinh wanted righteous anger at class enemies to persist, but to be kept
under wraps for release at a later date.

The second section of "Our Policy" was subtitled "Seeking Friends Outside."
Highest priority was assigned to relations with those colonized and semicolo-
nized peoples who also were struggling for freedom and independence, above all
in India, China, and Indonesia. However, Trường Chinh ruled out amity with
unspecified "Indian traitors," as well as with the "die-hard (ngoan cố) Chinese gang
that acted as lackeys of imperialism"—an unmistakable reference to the Chiang
Kai-shek government. This was the ICP's first public condemnation of Nationalist
China since August 1945, and certainly did not reflect Hồ Chí Minh's policy position. Trường Chinh's second friendship priority was the French people, particularly workers, farmers, and the urban petit bourgeoisie, all of whom he asserted
had nothing to gain from French reactionary colonialist assaults on Vietnam. He
castigated those Vietnamese who looked on all "long-nosed, curly-haired French
people" as enemies. Vietnam's third friend was the "loyal and strong Soviet
Union," although the only evidence produced by Trường Chinh for this friendship was Moscow's occasional press criticism of Great Britain and France for actions in Vietnam that violated the United Nations charter. Finally, almost as an
afterthought, Trường Chinh acknowledged as friends the "progressive and
peace-loving forces around the world, even within the most imperialist countries

like Britain and the United States." He then concluded his friendship roster with the words: "We do not struggle alone."

Comparing this 30 June 1946 statement by Trường Chinh with the confidential ICP "Central Executive Bureau" directive of seven months prior, some interesting modifications emerge. Earlier perceived contradictions between imperialist powers had now been replaced by a single imperial system dominated by the United States. Domestic Vietnamese economic and social concerns now received no mention whatsoever, as Trường Chinh focused relentlessly on enforcing national unity and seeking external support for Vietnam's independence struggle. Trường Chinh no longer touted a Việt-Khmer-Lao united front, although doubtless the ambition remained alive. His jibe at Chiang Kai-shek would be noted especially by the overseas Chinese, as they fretted over which way to turn following withdrawal of Chinese troops.

ICP leaders might place great confidence in "the French people," yet their knowledge of current French politics was extremely limited. Vietnamese intellectuals had come to know the France of the 1930s well, but Indochina's 1940–45 isolation left everyone out of date. Until return of the DRV National Assembly delegation in May 1946, the only sources of information on metropolitan politics were shortwave news broadcasts, small French Marxist groups in Hanoi and Saigon, and a few French officials prepared to talk informally with Vietnamese counterparts. The ICP equated the French people with the French Communist Party, a prime example of ideology smothering critical analysis. Sự Thật published speeches by PCF leader Maurice Thorez, highlighted meetings and demonstrations organized by the French General Confederation of Labor, and predicted imminent Communist Party primacy in the French National Assembly. As the summer of 1946 wore on, however, blithe assumptions gave way to plaintive appeals. When commemorating Bastille Day, Sự Thật called on the French people to reaffirm 1789 demands for liberty, equality, and fraternity by joining the Vietnamese people in opposing the reactionary colonialists.[57]

In late July, Sự Thật credited the French people, and notably the French Communist Party, with compelling French negotiators to soften their position slightly at Fontainebleau. However, after the talks stalled a few days later, references to the French people became more muted, and the goodwill of the French government began to be questioned overtly. Sự Thật could not admit that support from the PCF had its limits, nor could it explain why the French people allowed the French delegation to be dominated by "reactionaries." Eventually it quoted l'Humanité to the effect that the French government possessed multiple policies regarding Vietnam, or, more dangerously, no policy at all.[58] At the end of September, Sự Thật published its first analysis of French politics, arguing that General de Gaulle and other reactionaries were using domestic debate over the French Union to take the offensive on the colonial question. The Popular Republican

LIVERPOOL JOHN MOORES UNIVERSITY
LEARNING SERVICES

Movement (MRP) of Georges Bidault was pictured as a spent force, which meant that the Communist and Socialist parties needed to achieve a majority in the next election to be able to turn back the reactionaries.[59]

Trường Chinh's Revolutionary Agenda

On 16 August 1946, Sự Thật began to serialize an essay by Trường Chinh titled "The August Revolution," to commemorate the first anniversary of the nationwide insurrection, which the author declared to be Vietnam's greatest achievement since defeating the Manchus in 1789.[60] Leaving it to others to evoke the heady atmosphere of August 1945, Trường Chinh coolly assessed the results and mapped out his vision of Vietnam's future. He credited the ICP with timing the political takeover to perfection and inducing the great majority of people to rise up, in stark contrast to previous, unsuccessful anticolonial initiatives. Then he proceeded to: criticize August 1945 insurrectionaries for not eliminating more enemies; make the case for proletarian leadership of the ongoing national democratic revolution; insist that the DRV make common cause with the Soviet Union; foreshadow expropriation of property from "feudal landlords"; and argue that Vietnam could advance to socialism without waiting for the "necessary social conditions." "The August Revolution" serialization was edited and released quickly in book form, then republished often in following years, making it the most important statement of ICP outlook and intentions to appear during the resistance era.[61]

In the essay, Trường Chinh's claim that the ICP had mastery over planning and implementation of the August 1945 upheaval compels him to distort the historical evidence. For example, after asserting that the ICP had seized the revolutionary initiative within hours of the 9 March 1945 Japanese coup, he lists events that did not occur until July. He invents attacks on Japanese forces to bolster the Việt Minh's antifascist credentials, and thus the DRV government's right to be taken seriously by the Allies.[62] Trường Chinh regrets that Việt Minh groups did not seize weapons from the Japanese Army immediately following Tokyo's 15 August capitulation, ignoring the continuing discipline that had been displayed by Japanese units, and Allied orders to Japanese commanders to surrender their weapons only to incoming British and Chinese forces. He complains that insurrectionaries did not capture the Bank of Indochina in Hanoi, disregarding the Japanese machine-gun emplacements around the building and tanks on call a few blocks away.[63] Trường Chinh's criticism of August revolutionaries for not killing more Vietnamese traitors and French reactionaries contradicted Hồ Chí Minh's stated policy of leniency, whereby a line was drawn between evil actions committed before 19 August 1945 and malevolent behavior subsequently. Trường Chinh specifically censures uprising leaders in Saigon for talking with the Japanese, being slow to seize power, and failing to wipe out pro-Japanese and pro-French traitors or neutralize the French colonialists. After quoting Lenin to the effect that "a victorious power must be a dictatorial one," Trường Chinh puts his criticisms in historical perspective: "I don't assert that the August Revolution was not heroic, because throughout these events our people spilled a lot of blood. I only wish to say that our August Revolution was not as radical *(triệt để)* and grand as the 1789 French Revolution, the 1917 Russian Revolution, or the recent anti-German uprising in Yugoslavia."[64]

Having established to his own satisfaction that the ICP had led the entire liberation struggle before and during the August Revolution, Trường Chinh states flatly that the party deserves to rule. Furthermore, as sole representative of the proletarian class, it need not share leadership of the national liberation revolution with any other class. However, he criticizes current ICP members for "anarchistic tendencies," and defines both leftist and rightist deviations that must be eliminated. Too many members put compromise ahead of ideological principle. When correcting errors, it is important to remember that "criticism without solidarity is bad, but solidarity without criticism is worse." As a faithful Leninist, Trường Chinh gives detailed attention to the political training of cadres in the party, Việt Minh, army, and DRV government. Pointing out how many workers, peasants, youth, and intellectuals are passionately devoted to the revolution and ready to endure any sacrifice, Trường Chinh then states: "Have confidence in them, employ them boldly, guide them patiently, *but do not forget to control them* [his emphasis]."

Several times in "The August Revolution," Trường Chinh insists that Vietnam must have an "agrarian revolution" that confiscates land held by landlords, although he accepts that in present circumstances it is necessary to win over as many landlords as possible to the anti-imperialist cause. While the August Revolution abolished one facet of the feudal regime—the Huế government and monarchy—Trường Chinh insists that the underpinnings of feudalism remain in current relations between landlords and peasants. As long as the revolution has not completed its antifeudal as well as its anti-imperialist tasks, Vietnam cannot become strong and prosperous. Curiously, Trường Chinh makes no reference to eliminating feudal attitudes among the population at large, an objective dear to the hearts of other ICP leaders (see chapter 9). The issue of when and how to initiate land confiscation would divide the ICP leadership for another decade.

Trường Chinh's image of socialism is sketchy and derivative, based entirely on what he has read or been told about the Soviet Union, where "the socialist state has triumphed." It is the lofty responsibility of the ICP to "complete the task of democratization in order to pave the way to the socialist revolution in the future, which will socialize all means of production and abolish from Vietnam the regime of exploitation of man by man." Here he seems to confuse definitions by Marx of socialist and communist eras. More significantly, Trường Chinh then insists that it is not necessary to complete the national liberation revolution before engineering the agrarian revolution, and then the socialist revolution. Rather, in Vietnam the proletarian class in power can realize a part of the agrarian task during the national liberation revolution and, with support from the growing worldwide socialist revolution, achieve its own socialist revolution before heavy industry has been developed or all forms of "small capitalist exploitation" abolished. This conflation of historical stages became dogma among Vietnamese communists. Trường Chinh does not provide readers with any timetable for these strategic advances, but he would have condemned as "right deviationist" anyone who suggested that his socialist-communist utopia would take fifty or one hundred years to accomplish. Much of what Trường Chinh propounded had little immediate impact on events in Vietnam, but that would change in 1949 as the Chinese Liberation Army swept southward and the prospect of CCP support for the ICP beckoned.

Cứu Quốc: *The Việt Minh Standard-Bearer*

In the absence of a functioning Việt Minh hierarchy in 1945–46, newspapers quickly became the main source of public policy projection, political education, and psychological reinforcement. Both newspaper editors and many readers were resuming habits of the Popular Front era (1936–38), when periodicals often finessed clandestine political behavior. Prior to the August insurrection, *Cứu Quốc (National Salvation)* had circulated underground in the Red River delta.[65] Its volatile editor, Trần Huy Liệu, possessed the most writing and publishing experience of any ICP leader. He was ably assisted by Xuân Thủy, a mild-mannered journalist comrade from the late 1930s. On 20 August 1945, a representative of the Hanoi Uprising Committee located *Cứu Quốc* team members in the countryside and drove them twenty kilometers into the city in style to take control of the most modern publishing plant available. The first capital edition of *Cứu Quốc* appeared four days later, featuring a bright red and yellow flag splashed across the front page, quite a technical accomplishment given wartime disruptions. *Cứu Quốc* was identified on the masthead as "Propaganda and Struggle Organ of the Viet Minh." Articles announced a new "Provisional People's Government," recalled past struggles against foreign aggressors, listed places where revolutionary forces had already seized power, and urged all young men to sign up for the army. On 27 August, Liệu was named minister of information and propaganda in Hồ Chí Minh's provisional DRV government, which meant he had to cease formal connections with *Cứu Quốc*. He continued to set the paper's editorial line, however.

Cứu Quốc was quick to pick up on the emerging crisis in Saigon, criticizing early British actions and publicizing preparations for a Hanoi protest meeting on 14 September. Nonetheless, editors were stunned by the outbreak of fighting in Saigon on 23 September, and continued to hope for British recognition of the

FIGURE 26. Trần Huy Liệu. In *Hồi Ký Trần Huy Liệu* (Hanoi, 1991), facing p. 338. Courtesy of Vietnam National Library.

Nam Bộ Executive Committee. From 9 October, *Cứu Quốc* abandoned that hope completely, calling for full-scale Nam Bộ armed resistance and pledging nation-wide support. Soon it was telling readers that the well organized "Army of Vietnam" had taken the offensive in the south.[66] Thus began months of reporting based on scant information and wishful thinking. Readers must have noticed the contradiction between repeated *Cứu Quốc* assertions of battlefield victory and French occupation of one town after another in the western Mekong delta, the south-central coast, and the central highlands.

Cứu Quốc said far less about Chinese forces occupying Indochina north of the sixteenth parallel, probably because provisional President Hồ Chí Minh had taken personal control of this issue. On arrival of the first Chinese troops in Hanoi in mid-September, *Cứu Quốc* mentioned an altercation at the Return Sword Lake, but then stressed that people were ready to follow government instructions, and predicted that "the spirit of Sino-Vietnamese friendship will last forever." Five days later the lead editorial urged people to avoid any confrontations with the Chinese military, and the next day *Cứu Quốc* tried to rationalize acceptance of grossly inflated Chinese dollars in the marketplace.[67] Official statements by Chinese commanders and President Hồ were printed in full. Vietnamese were encouraged to fly the Chinese flag on "Double Ten" (10 October), anniversary of the 1911 Revolution. Once it became clear that the Chinese authorities were disinclined to overthrow the DRV in favor of a Nationalist Party–Revolutionary

Alliance government, *Cứu Quốc* took the verbal offensive against those parties, and soon each side was accusing the other of treason. Although the Chinese subsequently brokered a government of national union, neither side seriously considered that long-term power sharing was feasible.

In early February 1946, rumors circulated in Vietnam about French negotiations with Nationalist China aimed at reoccupying Indochina north of the sixteenth parallel, as well as secret Franco-Vietnamese talks about averting full-scale conflict. DRV government censors made sure that none of these stories made it into the press, yet when these rumors combined with news of military reversals at Nha Trang to the south and Lai Châu to the northwest, the level of public anxiety escalated dramatically. One *Cứu Quốc* editorial fueled these worries by warning that the French colonialists might be preparing to throw everything into "completing their aggression." To counter this threat, all the nation's strength had to be mobilized for combat, with "every person and every resource placed on a war footing."[68]

The *Cứu Quốc* issue of 20 February captures the ferment of this moment as well as frantic attempts by the DRV government and Việt Minh leaders to ward off panic. A 19 February communiqué signed by President Hồ Chí Minh and Vice President Nguyễn Hải Thần promises that a united resistance government will be formed in a few days and then presented to the National Assembly and the nation. A public meeting at the Hanoi Opera House the same day is featured, starting with a big headline: "Mr. Võ Nguyên Giáp Causes Calm to Return to People's Hearts." Beneath this is a smaller headline: "Even though we stand before a grave situation." Giáp admits that the government kept secret the French entry to Lai Châu, in order to "prepare a response," but chides people for expecting information to be released that would only be useful to the French. He explains that the French strategy is to sow fear and confusion among Vietnamese, "to be able to put us back into slavery." They will fail, Giáp insists, just as the Mongols did in the thirteenth century.

Cứu Quốc then prints what appears to be the full text of Trần Huy Liệu's speech at the same 19 February meeting, in which he describes students abandoning classes, groups volunteering to fight, and popular calls for a general strike, as "anger rises up in the face of foreign invaders coming closer with each hour." Anger is appropriate, Liệu insists, but it must result in "planned, focused action, not confusion, chaos, or anarchy." He reminds everyone of Hồ Chí Minh's pledge on Independence Day the previous September, that no one will become soldiers for the French, work for them, sell them food, or guide them. Liệu concludes: "When the French arrive, we'll show them the heroism of the North, following the lead of the South and the Center. The struggle will be long but the victory will be ours." A *Cứu Quốc* editorial urges readers not to listen to calls for a general strike, citing a similar initiative in Saigon in mid-September that proved disastrous.

Finally, the Ministry of Information and Propaganda issues "factual corrections" about the French advance in the northwest, to refute "rumors spread by French agents" that have put Hanoi public opinion "in an uproar." No mention is made in *Cứu Quốc* or any other newspaper of the negotiations begun in earnest between Hồ Chí Minh and Jean Sainteny four days earlier.

On 22 February, *Cứu Quốc* did print a Reuters story from Paris that Sainteny had met repeatedly with President Hồ, and that the Sino-French talks over Indochina were "proceeding well." Responding to these revelations, a *Cứu Quốc* feature editorial could only bluster: "Our struggle on various fronts is getting stronger every day. When we defeat enemy war efforts, the French bandits will only have recourse to bowing their heads."[69] On 24 February, *Cứu Quốc* ceased publication for three days as punishment for violating censorship regulations. At this point in the final domestic negotiations over forming a Cabinet to present to the National Assembly, the Propaganda Ministry was demoted to an office *(sở)* within the Interior Ministry, meaning that Trần Huy Liệu no longer had a government position. I think Liệu's open opposition to negotiations with the French was seen by Hồ as undermining his authority at this vital juncture. Liệu probably was excluded from top-level deliberations on how to react to Chinese and French moves.

The government did not further muzzle *Cứu Quốc,* but its content quickly became less confident and more garbled. Thus, a 28 February 1946 editorial refused to believe that China would sign an agreement with Paris, citing Generalissimo Chiang Kai-shek's professions of support for Vietnamese independence, and the threat to Chinese security if French forces were stationed in Vietnam. The Sino-French accord was signed that same day in Chongqing, a fact reported by *Cứu Quốc* on 2 March, relying again on Reuters. Only on 2 March did the public learn that French troops would be coming to replace Chinese forces north of the sixteenth parallel, with the Chinese scheduled to be gone by the end of March. *Cứu Quốc*'s lead editorial, still denying that Franco-Vietnamese talks have any chance of success, now advocated a policy of complete noncooperation rather than armed confrontation, to include "destruction of gardens and emptying of houses" *(vườn không nhà trống)* and banning all sale of food to incoming French units.[70]

In following days *Cứu Quốc* made no further editorial comment on the Franco-Vietnamese negotiations, but it did communicate the mood of anxiety and agitation sweeping Hanoi. It vehemently denied rumors that the DRV National Guard was about to assault the Citadel, where Chinese soldiers guarded disarmed French military personnel. The Chinese remained responsible for general security, it added, and China and Vietnam were "two brother countries with close relations for thousands of years." Hanoi's water and electric power went off on 4 March, and people were reported to be fleeing the city. *Cứu Quốc* published rumors that negotiations had collapsed, that French paratroopers had landed in Hải Dương province, and that ten thousand French troops were on their way from Saigon to Haiphong. Only the latter rumor proved correct. Meanwhile, Hồ Chí Minh continued to obfuscate publicly. When reporters asked Hồ about the talks, he replied, "No formal negotiations have begun, so how can they be interrupted?"[71]

On the morning of 7 March, the day after the Franco-Vietnamese Preliminary Accord was signed in Hanoi, Cứu Quốc announced in a big headline that "Vietnamese-French Negotiations Have Begun." Then came three medium headlines: "France Recognizes Vietnam", "Vietnam Temporarily Accepts Some French Troops to Enter the North", and "Agreement to Ceasefire on All Fronts." The main editorial now averred that all types of struggle, including diplomacy, must be employed in the quest for independence. However, if Paris wanted to secure rights for its citizens inside Vietnam, both the French government and French people needed to enhance their understanding of Vietnamese realities. This was the first time that Cứu Quốc editors acknowledged that French nationals might possess legitimate interests in Vietnam, but it was not a topic that would receive much consideration subsequently. The editorial concluded: "We should trust our government, which has at the helm a very clear-sighted leader who has sacrificed so much for the nation (dân tộc)." On 8 March, Cứu Quốc printed the text of the accord in both Vietnamese and French. Rather than offer any editorial comment, it published a communiqué from the Việt Minh General Headquarters that supported the accord for "offering more favorable conditions to struggle (tranh thủ) for complete independence than continuing the resistance." This was quite a climb down from previous Tổng Bộ statements, and represented a complete reversal for the editors of Cứu Quốc. In defense of Việt Minh legitimacy, the communiqué harkened back to alleged leadership of the "victorious August 1945 uprising," and pointed to ongoing commitments to militants at the front and in rear areas. The Tổng Bộ promised to be a "very strong force in the upcoming period of struggle for full independence."[72]

Cứu Quốc editors retained substantial objections to provisions of the 6 March 1946 Accord, yet they could not be seen to challenge President Hồ, or to side with the Vietnam Nationalist Party in opposing the agreement outright. Their first tactic was to print articles by authors, identified only by initials, that rejected the idea of a referendum to decide the future of Nam Bộ and offered historical examples where France had failed to implement signed agreements. Then a series of editorials began to pick apart individual accord clauses, for example questioning French thinking behind the Indochina Federation, objecting to a Nam Bộ referendum on grounds that "the Vietnamese people already decided this issue when they established the DRV on 2 September 1945," and defining état libre to mean nước tự chủ (country self-rule), which came closer to the treasured idea of "independence" (độc lập). Other Cứu Quốc editorials considered fifteen thousand French troops north of the sixteenth parallel to be excessive, asked why the

French did not agree to a DRV delegation going to Nam Bộ to help implement the ceasefire, insisted that the DRV make its own diplomatic postings overseas, and argued that French nationals must obey Vietnamese laws when engaged in economic or cultural activities inside Vietnam. Editors also provided a long criticism of a speech made by Admiral d'Argenlieu on 8 March in Saigon. They condemned Commissioner Jean Cédile's foreshadowing of an autonomous state of Cochinchina, arguing that only Vietnam's National Assembly had the power to grant special status for Nam Bộ.[73] *Cứu Quốc* was undercutting the 6 March Accord from one side while d'Argenlieu and Cédile were doing likewise from the other side. However, *Cứu Quốc*'s negative impact was diffused among Vietnamese readers, whereas the high commissioner had the power to act directly.

Editors of *Cứu Quốc* remained highly skeptical that DRV and French negotiators could achieve a diplomatic settlement that safeguarded core Vietnamese objectives of independence and territorial integrity. They also saw no reason why France or French nationals should receive any preferential treatment in Vietnam. If not prevented by government censors, they would have criticized clauses in the 6 March 1946 Accord concerning the Indochina Federation, French Army command of the combined relief force, and having to wait five years before the last French troops went home. From late May, *Cứu Quốc* began to suggest that French commanders were ordering their troops to stir up trouble. Then came French Army occupation of the former governor general's palace on 25 June, a move which was, according to *Cứu Quốc*, a blatant escalation requiring a more forthright government response. French actions in Lạng Sơn, Bắc Ninh, and Haiphong in July and August saw *Cứu Quốc* chiding the government repeatedly for excessive restraint. Taking the moral high ground, *Cứu Quốc* editors upheld legitimate Vietnamese rights against devious or evil French reactionaries, while intimating that the DRV government was weak in defending the national interest. Yet many readers of *Cứu Quốc* knew that editors and ranking DRV officials alike were ICP members.

When the government was slow to provide the text of the 14 September modus vivendi, *Cứu Quốc* editors employed foreign news sources as the basis for critical response. *Cứu Quốc* complained that the modus vivendi failed to resolve the two vital issues of Vietnam's independence and unity. Provisions for French business and cultural activities were also "too broad," and in any event should not be guaranteed so long as "the reactionaries continued to push" on multiple fronts. By the time President Hồ Chí Minh returned from France on 21 October, *Cứu Quốc* editorials dominated media discourse, while non-Việt Minh newspapers found it ever more difficult to get alternative views past the censor. Armed militia took their cues from *Cứu Quốc* rather than local administrative committee chairmen, who often received outdated government instructions on Franco-Vietnamese matters, or no information at all. As the prospect of war heightened dramatically following the late November French attack in Haiphong, the Tổng Bộ Việt Minh used *Cứu Quốc* to declare that Vietnamese must fight unless they were resigned to losing their country once again. President Hồ's capacity to determine policies of peace or war was progressively eroded. As Hồ tried desperately in mid-December to establish direct contact with the new French premier, Léon Blum, *Cứu Quốc* editors asked rhetorically whether the French Army aimed to provoke a major confrontation in Hanoi.[74] Clearly some ICP leaders believed that the time had come to attack first. Diplomacy had failed, and it was becoming impossible to restrain the militia.

TAKING CHARGE OF HISTORY

Amidst daily events, momentous or trivial, newspaper editors in 1945–46 found space for articles about Vietnamese history, pursuing topics that had exercised intellectuals since the turn of the century. Since the 1920s, a patriotic commemorative calendar had existed that included the mythical founder of the prehistoric Hùng dynasty, the Trưng sisters who had died trying to expel Chinese overlords in the first century A.D., and generals who had managed to defeat or outmaneuver the Chinese on later occasions. In the late 1930s, with colonial censorship relaxed briefly, books and articles appeared on Vietnamese who had fought the French. Other publications denounced Gia Long, founder of the Nguyễn dynasty in 1802, for relying on French mercenaries to gain power.[75] After stringent censorship resumed in 1939, clandestine anticolonial groups printed and distributed occasional broadsides or leaflets commemorating death dates *(giỗ)* of martyrs for their cause. Immediately following the Japanese 9 March 1945 coup, Vietnamese obtained permission to organize anticolonial commemorations, beginning with a mass meeting in Saigon on 18 March that featured the ashes of one martyr being placed before an ancestral altar over which was draped a panel bearing the word "Việt Nam."[76] In June, a number of newspapers commemorated the 1930 execution by guillotine of thirteen Vietnam Nationalist Party activists. Some localities replaced French street signs with ones named after ancient Vietnamese generals or more recent opponents of French colonial rule.[77] During the uprisings of August, people tore down street signs honoring Emperor Gia Long and subsequent Nguyễn dynasty rulers.

Late 1945 saw the much expanded Vietnamese print media commemorating distant and recent heroes alike. On the anniversary of the death of General Trần Hưng Đạo, thirteenth century hero, one newspaper drew the following lesson: "A people *(dân tộc)* who drove away Mongol armies can certainly beat the French colonialists," conveniently ignoring Vietnam's humiliating defeats of the late nineteenth century.[78] At the commemoration one year later, Trần Hưng Đạo's legacy taught Vietnamese that they "must unite and struggle enthusiastically."[79]

Second only to Trần Hưng Đạo was Lê Lợi, who had eventually compelled Ming armies to withdraw and then established his own Lê dynasty (1428–1788). His anniversary in September 1946 was used to remind everyone of the necessity for protracted resistance.[80] Third came Quang Trung Nguyễn Huệ, who had routed Qing dynasty invaders in 1789, and was credited by some historians with reunifying Vietnam after 150 years of partition.[81] With the Trưng sisters providing precedent for remembering heroic failures, two generals who had died in 1873 and 1882 trying to defend the Hanoi Citadel against French assault were now honored as well.[82] The current importance of such heroic stories was captured in a newspaper cartoon showing a frontline Vietnamese combatant dreaming in his sleep of the Trưng sisters and three later generals on elephants or horses, advancing to battle.[83]

Hồ Chí Minh understood well the political value of memorializing the past. During his spare time in the Việt Bắc hills in 1942, Hồ had composed a 208-line narrative poem, "The History of Our Country," beginning with Bronze Age ancestors and ending with a rousing call to take advantage of World War II upheavals to regain Vietnamese independence.[84] After becoming DRV provisional president in late 1945, Hồ was quite selective when it came to participation in commemorations, reflecting the national persona he was crafting for himself. He made a point of visiting the temple dedicated to the mythological Hùng kings. On the anniversary of the founding of the Lý dynasty (1010–1225), Hồ attended the main ceremony at Đình Bảng village (Bắc Ninh province), where he complimented the organizers for simply burning incense at the altar, not slaughtering buffaloes or preparing precisely thirty six hundred glutinous rice cakes as tradition would have dictated. President Hồ invited citizen Vĩnh Thụy (former Emperor Bảo Đại) to accompany him to the Hanoi temple dedicated to Confucius to take part in its annual commemoration, an act that must have upset ICP antifeudalists.[85] Hồ also forwarded his congratulations twice to Generalissimo Chiang Kai-shek on China's "Double-Ten" national day, and he publicly observed the 12 March death date of Sun Yat-sen.[86] Two months later it was time for a new tradition to begin, the celebration of what was said to be President Hồ Chí Minh's birthday on 19 May 1946, complete with special newspaper issues, a reputed flood of congratulatory telegrams, and effusive praise for his sagacious leadership.[87]

During 1945–46, the Vietnam Nationalist Party and the Việt Minh tussled over commemoration of the 9 February 1930 Yên Bái uprising, and particularly the memory of Nguyễn Thái Học, whose charismatic personality had kept followers committed to an increasingly suicidal project. For Việt Nam, the principal Nationalist Party newspaper, Yên Bái had been the most important armed challenge to French colonial rule in sixty years, and the image of Học going to the guillotine, shouting "Vietnam! Vietnam!" resonated with a new generation of young idealists.[88] For Cứu Quốc, Yên Bái was to be incorporated in Vietnam's patriotic legacy and Nguyễn Thái Học remembered as anticolonial martyr, but the Nationalist Party leaders who arrived back in Vietnam in the Chinese baggage train had no claim to this proud tradition whatsoever. When the occasion arrived in February 1946 to commemorate Yên Bái publicly for the first time, both Nationalists and the Việt Minh moved to organize meetings. In Hanoi, a joint meeting appears to have been negotiated, although *Cứu Quốc* subsequently chided unnamed participants for disunity.[89] In Haiphong, the city administrative committee assigned first use of the Opera House on 9 February to the Việt Minh, and second use on 10 February to the Nationalists. The local Việt Minh paper complained that the Nationalists at their Yên Bái commemoration had not flown the DRV flag, and speakers had made "divisive and provocative remarks." On 18 June in Hanoi, a joint Việt Minh/Nationalist Party commemoration of Nguyễn Thái Học's death was organized outside the former Maurice Long Museum, featuring a large portrait of Học behind the altar.[90]

While Việt Minh newspapers nodded respectfully in the direction of patriots of the monarchist and early colonial eras, their real enthusiasm was reserved for Việt Minh activists of more recent years. This was the beginning, in tentative, unsystematic form, of an historiographical campaign to put the ICP at the center of every significant event since 1930. In 1945–46, however, almost nothing was published about the formation of the ICP in 1930, the setbacks of 1931–34, or the public political achievements of 1935–38. The 1930–31 "Nghệ An Soviets" were ignored, perhaps because peasants had killed landlords and redistributed property, contrary to the ICP's united front strategy enunciated in 1941.[91] Later the story of the Nghệ An Soviets would become vital in arguing the ICP's early connection with the peasantry.

The only ICP actions prior to 1941 deemed worthy of current commemoration were two armed uprisings that had taken place in 1940. In late September of that year, six hundred people marched on the Bắc Sơn district seat, one hundred kilometers north of Hanoi, triggering confrontations, capture of a colonial military post, French counterattacks, public executions, and burning of houses and crops. The ICP had been slow to get involved, but amidst the colonial repression succeeded in forming a platoon-size unit optimistically calling itself the National Salvation Army.[92] In late 1945, several Việt Minh newspapers observed the fifth anniversary of the Bắc Sơn uprising, and attention increased for the sixth anniversary.[93] To symbolize the Bắc Sơn experience, one paper featured a woodblock drawing of two severed legionnaire heads.[94] More judiciously, the Tổng Bộ republished a twenty-nine-page booklet on the Bắc Sơn uprising that was half description and half devoted to uncovering operational errors and lessons to be learned.[95]

In southern Vietnam, a much more substantial challenge to French rule had occurred in late 1940, with ICP members leading large crowds of villagers in seizing police posts and administrative bureaus, burning telegraph offices, killing or detaining local collaborators, forming revolutionary committees, and beginning to redistribute land. The French counterattacked ruthlessly, in several cases employing aircraft, armored cars, and artillery to destroy whole villages. At least two thousand people were killed. The ICP in Nam Bộ was in shambles, and it would take four years to regain any momentum.[96] Việt Minh commemorative articles in 1945–46 admitted that the Southern Region Insurrection (Nam Kỳ Khởi Nghĩa) had not been successful, yet offered readers no information on casualties suffered, destruction of ICP leadership, and damage to anticolonial morale. The emphasis was on participation and heroic sacrifice, both particularly relevant when November 1945 commemorations occurred as southern resistance groups faced French attacks deep into the Mekong delta. By the time of the next commemoration, in November 1946, Nam Bộ had become the resistance touchstone for Việt Minh adherents in the north and center of the country, and the territory over which no compromise could be reached between the DRV and France.[97]

Việt Minh efforts during the Pacific War and August 1945 insurrection received significant historiographical attention, although coverage was haphazard, with no sign of a guiding ICP hand. There were colorful stories of life in the Việt Bắc hills, alleged battles with the Japanese, and formation of the first military school.[98] Soon these Việt Bắc stories were being repeated in newspapers down the central coast, alongside vague, almost mystical accounts of clandestine struggles closer to hand.[99] Party martyrs began to appear, for example Tô Hiệu, a Nationalist Party member who had "converted" to the ICP, climbed the ranks rapidly, been arrested at the Haiphong cement plant in December 1939, and died in Sơn La prison in 1943.[100] The martyr who received most devotion was Hoàng Văn Thụ, a member of the Tày minority who had participated in the Guomindang's northern expedition in 1927, joined the ICP, organized cells in southern China during the 1930s, and played a crucial role in reconstituting the ICP's Tonkin network in 1941–43. At the time of his capture in September 1943, Thụ was second only to Trường Chinh in the ICP Standing Bureau. In 1946, a fellow prisoner recounted Thụ's last hours prior to execution on 24 May 1944.[101] Those who had survived French arrest, torture, and incarceration began to publish their stories too.[102] Trần Huy Liệu found time to write a booklet about the March 1945 upheaval at Nghĩa Lộ prison, 160 kilometers northwest of Hanoi, trying to explain to himself, to his party comrades, and to the public at large why events in which he participated had spun out of control and why a large number of inmates were killed while others escaped.[103]

COMMEMORATING THE AUGUST REVOLUTION

How best to celebrate the first anniversary of the August 1945 Revolution and Independence Day became a matter of considerable importance for ICP leaders.

The ICP could not be named publicly, so the objective was to demonstrate pre-eminence of the Việt Minh General Headquarters in events, and hence its right to leadership of the ongoing Vietnamese struggle for full independence. In mid-June 1946, the Finance Ministry allocated twenty thousand piastres for the National Salvation Cultural Association to organize an artistic exhibition in August. However, no one appears to have begun organizing anything until late July, when the Tổng Bộ urgently requested all Việt Minh provincial branches to collect and forward materials for a national exhibition on "Eighty Years of Vietnamese Revolution" to coincide with the 19 August anniversary.[104] Several days later the government's Information and Propaganda Bureau assigned responsibility for conducting the August Revolution commemoration to the National Alliance, with Trần Huy Liệu on the organizing committee.[105] The government declared 19 August to be National Day (Ngày Quốc Khánh). Questions now arose about why the Liên Việt rather than the government was in charge of events, and why 19 August was being highlighted rather than 2 September. At the last minute the government changed the program to put the main emphasis on Independence Day, specifically ordering that the parade and reception for foreign dignitaries be moved to that later date.[106] Commemorative postage stamps featured the image of President Hồ, with special "National Salvation" overprints for buyers wishing to pay extra to the Defense Fund.[107]

Trần Huy Liệu led the push for recognition of ICP hegemony. In mid-August he insisted that the August Revolution had succeeded because of the "existence of a revolutionary organization possessing the correct political path."[108] Although no longer a government minister, Liệu was interviewed by AFP, with *Cứu Quốc* publishing the results.[109] A periodical which Liệu now edited gave voice to a serving army member who stated flatly that "a strong political party *(chánh đảng)* had stood forth to lead the August Revolution," and that the Việt Bắc guerrillas had founded the National Guard.[110] Yet the name of the political party was nowhere printed, and it publicly no longer existed.

Cứu Quốc's special "August Revolution" commemorative issue was an unprecedented sixty pages in length, printed on crisp, imported paper which enabled photographs of historic events to be reproduced with reasonable clarity. The paper's editor, Xuân Thủy, wrote the lead article on the 19 August 1945 insurrection in Hanoi. Tố Hữu contributed an anniversary poem. Tô Hoài and Tố Hữu described the 23 August takeover in Huế, while Trần Huy Liệu recounted how his Hanoi delegation had received the imperial regalia from Bảo Đại one week later. Events in Saigon were depicted by Mai Trang (a pseudonym).[111] The next issue of *Cứu Quốc* reported on 19 August celebrations beyond the capital. In preparation for the 2 September commemoration, *Cứu Quốc* printed a large map of downtown Hanoi that indicated the best streets for crowds to approach the Opera

House venue, and the route to be taken by the subsequent mass march, which a later issue described effusively. People also went to the Children's Pavilion (Ấu trĩ viên) to view the Việt Minh exhibition depicting French colonial exploitation and heroic Vietnamese resistance.[112]

One prominent ICP member absent from *Cứu Quốc*'s "August Revolution" special edition was Võ Nguyên Giáp, who chose instead to write his own fifty-four-page account of Việt Minh activities in the northern hills.[113] Giáp divided his narrative into three periods: preparing the political foundations (1940 to June 1944); moving towards armed struggle (July 1944 to March 1945); and establishment of the liberated zone (March to August 1945). At the end, Giáp offered some Việt Bắc lessons relevant to the present, beginning with effective Việt Minh leadership, the profound impact of liberation ideas on people at large, and having faith in Vietnam's future. He insisted that both politics and revolution were sciences, warned against becoming reckless in victory or demoralized in defeat, and urged comrades to learn from more recent events in southern Vietnam. Indeed, Giáp credited the south as having far more to offer by way of resistance experience than the Việt Bắc. While this seemed to belie the didactic purpose of the essay, it fitted Giáp's incisive character and immediate strategic preoccupations.

In Kiến An, just outside Haiphong, *Quân Bạch Đằng* magazine produced an impressive "August Revolution Special" as well.[114] Văn Cao, creative polymath, provided a vivid woodblock cover drawing of a revolutionary soldier and family, while an article inside recounted his composition of "Tiến Quân Ca" ("Advancing Army"), the DRV national anthem. Numerous essays, memoirs, poems, and short stories described Việt Minh efforts in the lower Red River delta before and during the August 1945 insurrection. However, the editors of *Quân Bạch Đằng* were equally concerned with critiquing activities since then. The magazine's publisher, Lê Quang Hòa, led off with a wide-ranging review of local events. Another contributor urged men to correct citizens who mistakenly called them "Việt Minh soldiers," because the National Guard was under authority of the DRV government of national union, not the Việt Minh Front. To assert the reverse was to fall into the trap set by reactionaries and French colonialists, who wanted to convince people that the National Guard was simply the armed wing of the Việt Minh. Another article unwittingly undermined this statement, however, describing how guardsmen now conducted night classes among villagers to explain the Việt Minh and encourage formation of national salvation associations.

Two weeks later, *Cứu Quốc* produced an "Independence Day" edition that was far less impressive than its "August Revolution" issue.[115] Thus began a subtle historiographical divergence among ICP opinion makers, with some favoring celebration of the exuberant 19 August insurrection in Hanoi, others preferring to highlight the more orderly 2 September declaration of independence and foundation of the DRV. *Cứu Quốc* used the "Independence Day" edition to reprint messages from army and civil organizations to the Tổng Bộ Việt Minh, thanking it for "brilliant leadership of all the people in fighting for total national independence," and for carrying out "glorious military deeds in the national liberation struggle." Several issues later the Haiphong regiment credited the Tổng Bộ with "having led the people to regain Independence for the Fatherland."[116] The public was now expected to pour out its gratitude to the Tổng Bộ, capping the campaign to legitimize the Việt Minh via historical commemorations.

What was the Tổng Bộ? In August 1945, some proclamations by ICP leaders had been signed "Tổng Bộ Việt Minh" (Viet Minh General Headquarters), part of the larger effort to convince people of the existence of a nationwide mass organization linking together all groups calling themselves Việt Minh and featuring the red flag with yellow star. In reality there was no Việt Minh "commander," no functioning headquarters, no hierarchy through which these proclamations could be transmitted and enforced at the district or village level. After establishment of the DRV, Tổng Bộ proclamations persisted. Newspapers were the principal means to reach Việt Minh adherents, gradually supplemented by visits from senior ICP cadres and the convening of brief training courses. As mentioned above, the ICP Standing Bureau in late November wanted to upgrade the Tổng Bộ to a permanent headquarters which would dispatch instructions downward, control local Việt Minh publications, and approve local bylaws. This did not happen, probably because President Hồ Chí Minh and others wanted to strengthen government and military hierarchies, not disperse power to other institutions. Perhaps top leaders also could not agree on who should be put in charge of the Tổng Bộ. Trần Huy Liệu, an obvious candidate, was minister of information and propaganda until February 1946. His occasional public intrusions on President Hồ's foreign policy prerogatives, and especially his open skepticism about any agreement with the French, finished Liệu's career as government minister, but not his capacity to reach the public via Việt Minh newspapers.

Tổng Bộ proclamations continued to appear, sometimes signed by Trần Huy Liệu and other ICP notables, yet no Tổng Bộ chairman was announced and no hierarchy implemented.[117] Trường Chinh may have come to prefer his ICP Standing Bureau assuming direct responsibility for bringing volatile Việt Minh groups into line, rather than having to work through an intermediary Tổng Bộ. The September 1946 publication in *Cứu Quốc* of letters of support for the Tổng Bộ may have been part of a last attempt to give it power. Tổng Bộ proclamations persisted, and Trần Huy Liệu continued to be introduced at meetings as a member of the Tổng Bộ, but his political influence was fading.[118] The Tổng Bộ office remained a useful place for leaders of a formally disbanded organization to meet Việt Minh delegations from afar.

TRƯỜNG CHINH GRAPPLES WITH
THE SOUTHERN ICP

As early as June 1945, Trường Chinh had criticized southern ICP members for failing to comprehend and implement Standing Bureau instructions. He castigated the Vanguard (Tiền Phong) group for trying to "exploit the Japanese to gain government," and reproved the Liberation (Giải Phóng) group for continuing to attack French stragglers. Both groups sent representatives north to make their case, but Trường Chinh had already decided to side with the Liberation group. When Hoàng Quốc Việt was dispatched south in late August, he ordered Trần Văn Giàu and Phạm Ngọc Thạch to disband the Vanguard Youth (Thanh Niên Tiền Phong) apparatus. Giàu argued vehemently against this order, and Thạch told a meeting of five hundred cadres that no one had the authority to dissolve the Vanguard Youth.[119] In October, Giàu and Thạch were directed to go to Hanoi, and in their absence Hoàng Quốc Việt, Tôn Đức Thắng, and Lê Duẩn convened a "southern cadres conference" to assess recent setbacks and restructure ICP operations.[120] However, the meeting could not agree on membership of a new ICP southern region committee to replace the competing Liberation and Vanguard regional committees.

Trần Văn Giàu caused a sensation on his arrival in the north. Always a strong public speaker, audiences responded to his speeches with repeated applause and cries of "Hurrah!" *(Hoan hô!).* In Haiphong, an excited crowd met Giàu in front of the Opera House, then surged into the building to hear his address. According to reporters, Giàu told the audience (incorrectly) that a Russian delegation had arrived in Hanoi. Giàu also dispatched an appeal to British, American, and Soviet foreign ministers then taking part in the Moscow Conference, speaking on behalf of the Nam Bộ Resistance Committee.[121] Trường Chinh now must have considered Giàu a loose cannon, ignoring the chain of command and capable of rousing a crowd at the wrong moment, for the wrong reasons. *Cứu Quốc* had already stopped referring to Giàu as representative of the Nam Bộ Resistance Committee, but rather as a "spokesman for the Information and Propaganda Committee."[122]

Five months later in Hanoi, Trường Chinh brought together selected ICP cadres from the south with Standing Bureau members to tackle continuing organizational chaos. Lê Duẩn, a native of Quảng Trị, but possessing many southern friends from shared prison time on Côn Sơn island, was chosen to return south immediately to form a Committee to Reorganize the Party in Nam Bộ, accompanied by two Liberation members. Committee members would seek out "good comrades" in each locality who would then compile lists of party members to be retained or removed. All vestiges of the Liberation/Vanguard split were to be eradicated. A new provisional Nam Bộ party committee would be set up, leading in due course to an all-region cadres conference that would elect an official committee.[123] Lê Duẩn was given a letter from the Standing Bureau to southern comrades which began by expressing chagrin over reports that Liberation and Vanguard groups were still clashing with and even killing each other. "At a time when communist ranks need to be firmer and more durable than ever, in order to provide good examples to the people, [such clashes] instead foster a bad reputation for the party and for communism," Trường Chinh intoned. He also criticized cadres in the south for allowing "all sorts of opportunists, provocateurs, and persons of complicated background" to enter the party. Southern fighters "still zealous about communism, still passionate about rights for the proletariat, still eager to advance on the road to liberation," should step forward to assist the Reorganization Committee.[124] Six months later, Trường Chinh focused on more immediate priorities, telling southern comrades to make life difficult for the French, to sustain the DRV civil administration, and to unite with Catholic, Cao Đài, and Hoà Hảo adherents.[125] Lê Duẩn eventually made his reputation in southern party building, but progress remained slow. It appears that many Vanguard adherents gravitated to National Guard units under the command of Nguyễn Bình, who was not an ICP member.

THE VIETNAM DEMOCRATIC PARTY

ICP efforts to tighten authority over Việt Minh groups put members of the Vietnam Democratic Party (Việt Nam Dân Chủ Đảng) in an increasingly difficult position. Founded secretly in Hanoi in June 1944 by patriotic intellectuals, students, and clerks in the colonial administration, the Democratic Party soon sought and received affiliation with the Việt Minh Front.[126] Following the 9 March 1945 Japanese coup, Democratic Party groups sprang up in other northern towns, and representatives made further contacts down the central coast. However, it was in Hanoi where hundreds of young men and women signed up for the party, attended meetings, took part in military drills, and formed several armed units that played a key role in seizing power in mid-August. Coordination was poor between Democratic Party and ICP-led national salvation units, which led to some tense encounters and longer-term animosities. Three Democratic Party members were appointed ministers in the DRV provisional government, but not many occupied second echelon positions.[127]

During September 1945 the Democratic Party organized an executive committee, recruited new members, opened literacy classes, began its own newspaper, and debated current developments. General secretary of the party was Hoàng Minh Chính, who ran the Hanoi office, forwarded citizen petitions to relevant government bureaus, and liaised with other political organizations. Other Democratic Party leaders understood Chính to be the principal ICP insertion to the party executive.[128] Đặng Thái Mai was the best known member of the executive committee, having taught literature to a whole generation of students at Thăng Long School in Hanoi and published extensively on modern Chinese history and culture. He was also a member of the ICP-controlled National Salvation Cultural Association (Hội Văn Hóa Cứu Quốc), and in subsequent months became more involved with its fortnightly cultural magazine, *Tiên Phong* (Vanguard). Lê Trọng Nghĩa had led many Democratic Party operations during the August insurrection in Hanoi, but faded from view by late 1946, having been recruited to the National Guard's General Staff.[129] Hoàng Văn Đức took on increasing responsibilities within the party until enrolled as advisor to the DRV diplomatic delegation dispatched to France at the end of May 1946. Đỗ Đức Dục, trained as a lawyer, became the party's most energetic public speaker and a prolific writer on administrative and economic issues. Probably on request, the party executive submitted to the Northern Bureau a list of more than one hundred members currently employed by the government around Hanoi, including pseudonyms where applicable.[130] Clearly the DRV government wanted to know about and implicitly approve any membership by state employees in political parties.

Also in September 1945, the Democratic Party requested a permit to conduct military training at Chu Văn An secondary school (Bạch Mai). Permission came rapidly from the new Hanoi People's Committee, conditional only on party organizers forwarding a copy of their course syllabus.[131] Simultaneously the party requested permits for fifteen firearms, and this was approved immediately by Cù Huy Cận, DRV minister without portfolio, who also happened to be a party member.[132] Some of these sidearms were meant for self-protection, as the threat of political assault or kidnapping persisted in late 1945. Whenever the Vietnam Nationalist Party characterized the Việt Minh as a mere creature of the ICP, Democratic Party leaders argued vehemently to the contrary. On several occasions persons wearing Democratic Party insignia spread anticommunist leaflets around the capital, eventually compelling the party to issue a disavowal, then a condemnation of "saboteurs" *(bọn phá hoại)* who tried to sow division.[133] Hồ Chí Minh, aiming to lower the ICP's profile, selected Hoàng Văn Đức to lead the Việt Minh team in formal meetings with the Nationalist Party and Revolutionary Alliance, where Đức gained the sobriquet of *"l'enfant terrible."*[134]

A serious confrontation between Democratic Party and ICP activists in Hưng Yên province called into question the viability of horizontal membership in the Việt Minh Front. As recounted earlier, ICP members resentful of Democratic Party initiative in the August seizure of power in Hưng Yên had engineered Hanoi's dismissal of the province committee chairman. However, violent altercations persisted, and the authorities in Hanoi were inundated with complaints. The minister of interior, Võ Nguyên Giáp, after excoriating Hưng Yên for producing the most citizen complaints of any province in the country, dispatched a special investigator to ferret out causes.[135] The investigator quickly sided with the National Salvation Youth group, although admitting that it had abrogated powers of the people's committee. A Việt Minh representative arrived from the outside to urge the two sides to stop killing each other and unite. Some fifty individuals remained in the province jail, while others had been dispatched to deportation camps. Even as the investigation proceeded, the province chairman placidly reported to Hanoi that unification had been achieved.[136] For Democratic Party leaders in Hanoi, however, this entire Hưng Yên experience must have highlighted the inferior status of their party within the Việt Minh Front, certainly when it came to organizing in the provinces. Decades later, differences persisted in official publications about the role of the Democratic Party in Hưng Yên, with some praising ICP–Democratic Party cooperation in August 1945, others linking Democratic Party participation to "counterrevolutionary influences" and opposition to the ICP.[137]

In late October 1945, the Democratic Party booked the Hanoi Opera House to introduce itself to the public. Dương Đức Hiền summarized the party's beginnings, affirmed its early partnership with the ICP in the Việt Minh Front, and emphasized its role in the August insurrection and current people's committees. Lê Trọng Nghĩa explained the party's commitment to New Democracy. Đỗ Đức Dục first chastised intellectuals for submissiveness during the colonial era, then challenged them to step forward immediately to "make major contributions to building the nation."[138]

From November 1945, the Democratic Party focused increasingly on the upcoming National Assembly elections. Articles in *Độc Lập (Independence)*, the party newspaper, suggest that leaders saw the National Assembly as the most promising route to popular recognition and policy influence. A number of party members stood as candidates and, within constraints set by the government, tried to campaign seriously. In Nam Định, Lê Trọng Nghĩa told voters that the Democratic Party preferred legislative powers to concentrate largely in the future Standing Committee of the National Assembly, wanted an inspectorate created with sweeping powers to eradicate corruption in local administrative committees, and insisted that more resolute action be taken against traitors. Nguyễn Khoa Diệu Hồng, one of the first female members of the party, reminded voters of her key speech at the Hanoi Opera House on 17 August 1945.[139] Of the 274 persons elected to the National Assembly, some 45 affiliated themselves with the Democratic Party.[140] Five members of the party's executive committee were elected, as well as the three members who had served as ministers in the DRV provisional government. The party executive committee placed notices in newspapers to encourage delegates to arrive in Hanoi a week prior to convocation of the Assembly, so that they could formulate a common position.[141] Clearly party leaders expected the first session of the Assembly to deliberate for some days if not weeks, and may not have been consulted when Hồ Chí Minh reduced the proceedings to a mere matter of hours.

At the National Assembly meeting of 2 March 1946, Đỗ Đức Dục and Cù Huy Cận spoke often from the floor, sometimes questioning the chair's rulings or disagreeing with previous speakers. However, no issue was allowed to take up much time. Top priority was given to approving the machinery of government. In the new DRV cabinet, approved unanimously, there were two ministers from the Democratic Party: Đặng Thái Mai (Education), and Vũ Đình Hòe (Justice). Hoàng Văn Đức and Dương Đức Hiền were appointed to the Assembly's fifteen-person Standing Committee, although they must have been disappointed subsequently when this body met infrequently and was bypassed routinely by the executive branch. Đỗ Đức Dục and Cù Huy Cận were put on the person-person Constitution Drafting Committee, which presented its handiwork to the second sitting of the Assembly in early November.[142] In late March, Đỗ Đức Dục also became education vice-minister, and Cù Huy Cận was named agriculture vice-minister.[143] While these six Democratic Party leaders presumably appreciated being given government positions, it had the effect of making them less available for party building. There was an active Haiphong branch, as when it convened a meeting in April to hear Lê Trọng Nghĩa speak, debate issues, and enjoy the local Catholic band's rendition of the DRV national anthem.[144] In Huế in late May, the separate Central Region Democratic Party was founded, with a platform dedicated to New Democracy, saving and building the country, and unity of Vietnam's three regions.[145] In late June, the second anniversary of the Democratic Party's founding was celebrated in five locations: Hanoi, Haiphong, Kiến An, Nam Định, and Đà Nẵng.[146]

The Democratic Party made a substantial mark via its Hanoi newspaper, *Độc Lập,* which appeared five times a week starting in early September 1945. Politically alert readers routinely compared the content and editorial position of *Độc Lập* with that of *Cứu Quốc,* noting differences amidst the similarities. Both papers treated the armed resistance in south and south-central Vietnam as sacrosanct, and made every effort to mobilize support in the north. Both condemned the Vietnam Nationalist Party at every opportunity. As the DRV entered its most perilous weeks in late February 1946, *Độc Lập* avoided the strident rhetoric of *Cứu Quốc,* notably the latter's assertions that armed conflict was inevitable and imminent in the north.

Throughout the summer of 1946, *Độc Lập* gave more detailed attention to the negotiations in France than did *Cứu Quốc.* In July, *Độc Lập* recalled mention of a French Union in the 6 March Preliminary Accord, then wondered why "it remains only a name without any content."[147] *Độc Lập* then offered readers a serialized history of the British Commonwealth, complete with definitions of "dominions" *(quốc tự chủ)* and "free states" *(quốc gia tự do).* It also brought the

Dutch Union into the conceptual equation. *Độc Lập* was ahead of any other newspaper in Vietnam (or France) when discussing historical precedents and policy options for a French Union. When the Fontainebleau conference was suddenly suspended indefinitely on 10 September, *Độc Lập*'s editorial the next day had fifteen lines blanked out by government censors, perhaps because they questioned the tactics of the Vietnamese delegation. The last lines of the editorial stressed the gravity of the suspension, asking plaintively, "How can the two sides sign together to avoid a war harmful to both sides?"[148] This was precisely the question that motivated Hồ Chí Minh to stay behind in Paris to sign the modus vivendi a few days later. A month later, as the French public went to the polls once again, *Độc Lập* argued that the wording in the 13 October constitutional referendum regarding the French Union represented a step backward compared to the 5 May referendum that had been defeated. *Độc Lập* had lawyers scrutinizing relevant texts and press reports, although the tone of editorials was becoming more pessimistic.[149]

In its international coverage, *Độc Lập* joined *Cứu Quốc* in praising the Soviet Union above all other countries. It repeatedly lauded the heroic struggle of the Soviet people against fascism. Editors translated and serialized an entire Russian novel on the battle of Stalingrad. The Soviet Union's "New Democracy" was presented as Vietnam's prime model. However, *Độc Lập*, unlike *Cứu Quốc*, ignored the Bolshevik Revolution and repeatedly rejected class struggle. As tensions grew between Moscow and Washington, *Độc Lập* applied realpolitik analysis as well as Marxist ideology when trying to explain to readers what was happening. The same realism was evident in *Độc Lập*'s treatment of Nationalist-Communist relations in China.

Độc Lập devoted much more attention to economic questions than *Cứu Quốc*, reflecting the influence of Democratic Party members who had been deliberating Vietnam's development options for years.[150] Readers were given introductions to Vietnam's various economic sectors (agriculture, industry, handicrafts, commerce), but the articles presented no statistics beyond 1940, and content often seemed detached from current conditions. There was consensus that Vietnam needed a command economy, not free market capitalism.[151] Such calls for state economic action were shared across the political spectrum. Nguyễn Văn Luyện, physician and senior public intellectual, asserted provocatively that it had taken the United States eighty years to prosper, Japan forty years, Russia fifteen to twenty years, and Germany only ten years.[152] Luyện's determination to privilege fascist Germany must have upset ICP readers, yet the government censor let it pass. Luyện advised the DRV to seek foreign economic aid, or try to borrow overseas, but if neither of these policies bore fruit then the state plan had to be "very tight, like Germany or Russia." Then Luyện took this logic another step: "The tighter the organization the faster the results, but also the more individual rights have to be restricted."[153] Although *Độc Lập* writers consigned the French and British economies to the historical dustbin of "old capitalism," they sometimes had good things to say about America. President Roosevelt's 1944 proclamation that poor people were not free, while dictatorships produced hunger and unemployment, was rendered entirely in capital letters. Henry Wallace was lauded for promising that the U.S. economy would not go back to being controlled by a rich minority, instead become an economic democracy where everyone had a job, food to eat, and clothing to wear.[154]

The Democratic Party's First National Congress

As the number of Democratic Party local branches increased during the summer of 1946, the need became more pressing for a national meeting to agree on a platform and bylaws, as well as to elect a central committee. In July, the provisional executive told party members to turn in their existing membership cards by the end of August, "in preparation for issuing new 1947 cards."[155] This unusual instruction may have been part of a plan to cull membership, or simply a recognition that cards had been printed at different times and places. Some party branches held preparatory meetings, assessing what they had done so far and where improvements needed to be made. The Haiphong branch was happy with the public talks it had sponsored at the Opera House, and its 2 September 1946 commemorative film screening had proven a big hit. But branch leaders had been deficient in organization, particularly when it came to assigning each member a specific mission.[156] We don't know how delegates to the national congress were selected, but they came from fifty-two branches, including several in central Vietnam and at least one branch in the south. As delegates arrived in Hanoi, *Độc Lập* editors remarked wryly on how many had darker skin than they had before, the result of working outdoors.[157]

The National Congress opened on 15 September 1946 at the Hanoi Opera House, with 235 delegates present. Party chairman Dương Đức Hiền gave the keynote address, followed by a speech from Trần Huy Liệu representing the Tổng Bộ Việt Minh. Đỗ Đức Dục read telegrams of support from around the country. Perhaps about this time in late morning, a news flash arrived from Paris about President Hồ Chí Minh and Prime Minister Moutet signing a modus vivendi of unknown content, which must have thrown the meeting into a flurry. Nonetheless the program went on, with the National Guard band playing the Democratic Party anthem, "Tiếng gọi Thanh Niên" ("Call to Youth"), and delegates then dividing into groups to visit military units, government bureaus, or the Tổng Bộ office (where they were received by Nguyễn Lương Bằng). Late in the afternoon everyone regathered at the Monument for Fallen Combatants (Đài trận Vong Chiến sĩ).[158]

The next day the National Congress moved to the former Masonic Temple, where Nguyễn Thành Lê and Cù Huy Cận delivered extended international and domestic reports. Subsequent discussion from the floor was "lively" according to *Độc Lập,* though it did not divulge the substance.[159] I suspect discussion on the two reports was dislocated by delegates speculating on the contents and likely consequences of the modus vivendi. The absence of any text of the agreement, and the DRV cabinet's failure to release any official statement, meant that delegates could argue almost anything they wished. During the 17 September proceedings, there was further animated discussion, followed by Vũ Đình Hòe describing the "new spirit" among his Justice Ministry subordinates, congress praise for Hoàng Văn Đức's efforts to stave off widespread famine early in the year, congratulations to party members who were leading local literacy campaigns, and regional reports on party activities. Hoàng Minh Chính, party secretary, then criticized himself and the central office for "unscientific methods," failing to release any publications beyond *Độc Lập,* poor liaison, and "individual lack of discipline."[160]

On the fourth day of the congress, delegates began hammering out a party platform. Speaking on behalf of the drafting committee, Đỗ Đức Dục emphasized the party's rejection of "old bourgeois democracy" in favor of New Democracy, wherein "the entire people cooperated from a position of complete equality and freedom without class distinction." No one took exception to this position. From the floor, however, several speakers objected to the draft platform subsuming "national liberation" *(giải phóng dân tộc)* to the objective of "nation building" *(kiến thiết quốc gia).* According to a wry *Độc Lập* journalist, from this moment on "all comrades present seemed to be inhaling fermented rice wine." [Ngô] Xuân Diệu, the poet, argued for separation of the two goals with a metaphor: "When our house is burning and we haven't yet found a way to quench the flames, how is it possible to plan and build a new house?" Comrade Phú Hương was more blunt: "If the country is not liberated, what is there to build?" Scores of delegates wanted to speak on either side of this issue, and many exceeded their time allocation. Our *Độc Lập* reporter did not quote anyone from the nonseparatist side, but presumably they argued that serious efforts in education, health, culture, and material production should not await full independence, and indeed would serve to enhance the prospects of national liberation. Eventually the presiding officer, Hoàng Minh Chính, declared that those wanting to separate national liberation and nation building constituted a majority, and apparently there was no call for a vote.[161] In the context of mid-September 1946, "separatists" wanted to highlight the Democratic Party's readiness to fight for independence, subordinating all other activities.

The other platform topic provoking substantial congress debate concerned the Democratic Party's relationship to progressive forces around the world. Đỗ Đức Dục, presiding officer for this session, urged everyone to focus on immediate strategic priorities, not long-term ideological aspirations. This met with opposition from those who felt the party should affirm support for New Democracy everywhere. Again the debate became heated, leading Dục to call an adjournment so that everyone could cool down. When delegates reconvened, they agreed that Vietnam's independence would not be secure so long as war, fascism, dictatorship, and colonialism persisted internationally.[162] Then Nguyễn Thành Lê asked, "Does this signify internationalism as one finds it among communist parties, or does internationalism simply mean to ally with progressive elements overseas?" The majority eventually agreed to use "alliance" *(liên minh)* rather than any more binding term. A thirteen-person subcommittee was then selected to firm up the platform's wording overnight.

On 19 September the morning newspapers carried Vietnamese translations of the modus vivendi, which provoked further debate at the Democratic Party National Congress about Franco-Vietnamese relations. The party platform was then approved, with the preamble declaring the Vietnamese Revolution to contain three tasks: national liberation, constructing a new country, and struggling for peace and democracy worldwide. These tasks would be implemented following the ideology of New Democracy, which was said to be the product of revolutionary experiences in England (1649), France (1789), China (1911), and Russia (1917), combined with "real conditions" in Vietnam. These specific Vietnamese conditions included a pure *(thuần nhất)* society possessing "few class colorations" and "not too obvious" differences between social strata. Vietnam also had entered a perilous time that required it to "guard constantly against foreign invasion." All the people had to bind together *(đoàn kết)* nationally, and the nation had to cooperate with others internationally. The platform concluded with a rousing modernist credo: "New Democracy is a revolutionary ideology. It demolishes feudal and colonial vestiges and builds a new Vietnam. It relies on both foreign historical experiences and real domestic conditions, operating in accordance with progress *(tiến hóa)* of the Vietnamese people and in harmony with the progressive cadence of humanity."[163]

Finally congress delegates turned their attention to internal party structure and bylaws. A sharp disagreement between proponents of central control and local representation was resolved by compromise wording that favored the latter. Hoàng Minh Chính then summed up what the party had accomplished since its formation in 1944 and tendered the resignation of the entire central executive. Vũ Đình Hòe expressed the membership's gratitude for the executive's efforts, the meeting was wrapped up, and everyone adjourned to an evening banquet.[164] On returning home, delegates had reason to compliment themselves on participation in the most democratic meeting to take place in Vietnam to date. Such an opportunity would not come again. Although the bylaws specified that a new central executive be elected by the full party membership, this does not appear to have happened prior to the outbreak of full-scale hostilities in December.

If war had been averted, the Democratic Party would have played a much more significant role in Vietnam's history than proved to be the case. Although party branches in 1946 were all located in cities and towns, some members had already proven their capacity to reach out to villagers as well. During 1947–49, Democratic Party leaders continued to present opinions that diverged significantly from those enunciated by Trường Chinh and the ICP Standing Bureau, especially on issues of class struggle, land redistribution, and proletarian dictatorship. But with establishment of the CCP-ICP alliance in 1950, the Democratic Party became just window dressing.

THE LIÊN VIỆT: A BRIDGE TOO FAR

In late May 1946, as mentioned earlier, ICP and Việt Minh periodicals announced the formation of a new Vietnam National Alliance (Hội Liên Hiệp Quốc Dân Việt Nam, generally called the Liên Việt), designed to embrace each and every patriotic organization in the country. This was most likely the brainchild of Trường Chinh, designed in the first instance to force the Vietnam Nationalist Party to either accept Việt Minh hegemony or face repression.[165] Employing quasi-fascist rhetoric, *Cứu Quốc* editors insisted that only when all twenty million citizens became members of this single "bloc" or "mass" *(khối)* could Vietnam look optimistically to the future.[166] However, when politically alert readers scanned the list of alleged Liên Việt founders it was obvious that not everyone there had been consulted. Non-Việt Minh newspapers mostly ignored the Liên Việt. One exception was *Dư Luận (Opinion)* in Hanoi, which interviewed two founders, neither of whom proved informative.[167] Most prominent Vietnamese not already affiliated with the Việt Minh realized that the price of joining the Liên Việt was either to mouth the Việt Minh line publicly or passively to allow the organizers to use one's name.

To try to convert the platitudes of the original Liên Việt announcement into some sort of working body, eight meetings were held in June by representatives of the Tổng Bộ Việt Minh, Democratic Party, and Nationalist Party. Following one of those encounters, Võ Nguyên Giáp and two Nationalist Party negotiators, Nguyễn Tường Long and Chu Bá Phượng, met with a foreign reporter from the Associated Press, blithely denying the reporter's information that Việt Minh and Nationalist Party groups were fighting each other. Phượng lied when telling the reporter that Vũ Hồng Khanh was still on a government inspection assignment, and that Nguyễn Tường Tam was "unwell but still working for the DRV cabinet."[168] On 25 June, Nationalist Party representatives reaffirmed their allegiance to the DRV, but a joint statement made no headway on Liên Việt composition. Another statement appeared in early July in the name of the Liên Việt, yet offered no further information about organization or leadership.[169] Only in

Haiphong did Việt Minh leaders move to organize a Liên Việt branch, although their first announcement had five lines blanked out by the censors.[170] Unfazed, the Haiphong Việt Minh committee convened a meeting at the home of a local physician, where a Liên Việt "mobilizing committee" was formed that included representatives from the Việt Minh, Democratic Party, Nationalist Party, and Revolutionary League, as well as a woman, a Catholic priest, a Buddhist monk, and a businessman. Participants anticipated that a provisional Liên Việt committee would be presented to the public "soon," yet for the next fifteen weeks nothing seems to have happened. In mid-October, an announcement signed by the local Liên Việt branch called on all Haiphong residents to observe a one-day general strike, but this patently was a Việt Minh initiative.[171]

The June meetings in Hanoi had involved Nationalist Party representatives who professed acceptance of ICP–Việt Minh supremacy, yet still wanted concessions that might help convince comrades to follow them in abandoning opposition. However, with DRV National Guard units dramatically escalating their attacks on Nationalist Party units in the Red River corridor, followed by Công An and Việt Minh capture of the Nationalist headquarters in Hanoi in mid-July, there was nothing left for either side to negotiate. Nguyễn Tường Long fled to China. Vũ Đình Trí, another Nationalist Party negotiator, was assassinated a few months later. Inclusion of the Nationalist Party name in the Liên Việt became strictly cosmetic.

Organization of the Liên Việt proceeded at glacial pace. On 23 July in Hanoi, a meeting of the "founding committee" talked about a nationwide conference, which did not materialize. Supposedly Liên Việt branches had been formed in "almost all provinces," but no details were provided. It was agreed that the Liên Việt would organize first anniversary commemorations of the August Revolution, yet as we have seen the ICP–Việt Minh took firm control of those proceedings. Trying to camouflage the fact that the Liên Việt was just another front to serve ICP–Việt Minh interests, ICP leaders nudged other groups to request affiliation to the organization before the Việt Minh did likewise. They also wanted the media to "campaign to full extent" for the Liên Việt. Provinces which had already formed branches were instructed to telegraph particulars to the Liên Việt central office in Hanoi.[172]

Another way to try to put life into Liên Việt was to create a new associated party. On 27 July 1946 in Hanoi, twenty-seven individuals put their names to a document establishing the Vietnam Socialist Party (Đảng Xã Hội Việt Nam).[173] During the 1930s, some Vietnamese intellectuals and government employees had joined Hanoi and Saigon branches of the Section française de l'Internationale ouvrière (SFIO). In 1944, as Vietnamese SFIO members sensed independence opportunities for Vietnam they sounded out their French socialist comrades, but found no support for the idea. Following establishment of the DRV in early

September 1945, some French socialists favored early metropolitan recognition of Vietnamese independence, and several of them offered advice and liaison services to DRV negotiators. However, the SFIO (French Socialist Party) participated in governments that reaffirmed French sovereignty over Indochina and allowed High Commissioner d'Argenlieu to use force repeatedly to advance the French position. In this context, French socialist moves to reconstruct SFIO branches in Saigon and Hanoi met with considerable Vietnamese suspicion. Some ICP members may have been keen to reopen the bitter dispute of the 1930s between the Second International and Third International. Instead, the ICP decided to form the Vietnam Socialist Party, "in order to sabotage the French plot to reestablish French Socialist Party (SFIO) branches to attract pro-French Vietnamese members."[174] The 27 July founding document disassociated the new party from the old SFIO branches in Indochina, and by implication from the current French Socialist Party as well.

Độc Lập, the principal Democratic Party newspaper, asked whether the country really needed another political party, and wondered whether the Vietnam Socialist Party might be too influenced by Second International leaders like Léon Blum, Marius Moutet, Clement Atlee, Robert Schuman [sic], and Paul-Henri Spaak. However, after reading the party's founding document, *Độc Lập* editors declared their skepticism to be unwarranted.[175] The most prominent Socialist Party member was Hoàng Minh Giám, former SFIO member, school principal, and beginning in September 1945, Hồ Chí Minh's closest aide on foreign relations.[176] Founders were mostly professionals, government officials, and business people, with only a handful of well-known writers or journalists. A number of founders had stood as nonparty candidates to the National Assembly and been elected in January 1946. On 11 August, Socialist Party founders presented themselves to the public at the Hanoi Opera House, complete with a new flag containing three yellow arrows on a red field. Dr. Trần Hữu Nghiệp opened the proceedings, followed by the provisional general secretary, Phan Tử Nghĩa, and then Mme Phan Thanh (aka Lê Thị Xuyến), one of the best known female political activists of the time.[177] Unlike other political entities, the socialists did not initiate a newspaper until several years later.

Besides finessing the SFIO, another ICP reason for initiating the Vietnam Socialist Party was to head off the Dư Luận (Opinion) group of prominent intellectuals, which was said to be planning to establish its own party.[178] *Dư Luận* had begun in April 1946 as a weekly journal of current affairs and commentary, at one point describing itself ambitiously as "the Voice of nonparty people."[179] Two of its most active participants, Vũ Văn Hiền and Hoàng Xuân Hãn, had served as ministers in the Trần Trọng Kim Cabinet, which had been violently denounced by Trường Chinh during the summer of 1945.[180] By contrast, President Hồ deliberately sought Hãn's political advice in late 1945.[181] *Dư Luận* was most valuable for its incisive analyses of Franco-Vietnamese negotiations, a topic that other non-Việt Minh papers often skirted. In its wider coverage of international affairs, *Dư Luận* took a resolutely realpolitik position, for example when dissecting Yugoslavian and Italian claims to Trieste, describing the contest between Nationalists and Communists in China, or addressing the question "How will the Allies resolve the German problem?" Its serialized history of the June 1944 Normandy invasion, offered counterpoint to Việt Minh preoccupation with Stalingrad. However, *Dư Luận* showed that Vietnamese admiration for the Soviet Union extended well beyond the ICP–Việt Minh. It serialized Mikhail Sholokhov's 1935 novel, *Virgin Soil Upturned: Seeds of Tomorrow*, about collectivization in the Don River area.[182] It praised Soviet youth mobilization, admired the huge state farms, and argued that Vietnam should borrow from Moscow's command economy experience. To help readers catch up with scientific advances worldwide, Hoàng Xuân Hãn wrote essays about radar, German V2 rockets, the atomic bomb, FM radio, and the physics of artillery.

Dư Luận seldom ventured far into domestic politics, and when it did, the censor sometimes blanked out words or whole passages. Thus, when *Dư Luận* responded enthusiastically to the Haiphong Administrative Committee's call for regular public criticism of committee activities, it lost the next forty lines of commentary to the censor's scissors.[183] On the other hand, when Nghiêm Toản mounted a veiled attack on Việt Minh cadres of scant education who employed facile slogans and ideological terms to sneer at people who did not follow them blindly, the censor cut nothing.[184] In early November, *Dư Luận* began a blunt question-and-answer column titled "Anxieties" (*Thắc Mắc*), beginning with issues currently before the second session of the National Assembly. The column's handling of the constitution's clause on equal rights for women provoked vigorous reader response. Then "Anxieties" moved to sensitive matters of peace or war. To the question "What do the French want to accomplish by provoking armed conflict in Haiphong?" *Dư Luận* answered that the French aimed to cut off from the Vietnamese government a substantial source of revenue, "thus making more difficult the work of defending our independence and constructing the nation."[185] Remarkably, the censors left every "Anxieties" column untouched.

It is highly unlikely that the group of prominent intellectuals who published *Dư Luận* ever intended to form a political party, or that ICP leaders believed this to be the case. Rather, the existence of such a lively group, possessing its own newspaper and operating outside the Liên Việt umbrella, was an affront to the ICP's united front strategy, leaving open the possibility that other intellectuals might do the same thing. Following French occupation of Hanoi, some *Dư Luận* participants gravitated towards the Việt Minh, while others moved to Saigon or Paris.

IMPORTING MARXISM-LENINISM

During 1946, at least thirty-five books appeared on Marxist-Leninist subjects, most but not all from ICP or Việt Minh publishers. Some rehashed ideological preoccupations of the 1930s, explaining and upholding dialectical materialism, the historical dialectic, class struggle, European revolutionary history, and the *Communist Manifesto*. Others appeared to be translations of recently acquired French Communist Party publications, for example Lenin on the Paris Commune, Lenin on Engels, a biography of Maxim Gorki, the platform and rules of the Communist International (two volumes), a history of the Bolshevik Party, and treatises on Marxism and political freedoms, Marxism and the individual, and the difference between democracy and fascism.[186] Josef Stalin's *Fundamentals of Leninism* was translated and published in three volumes.[187] Most numerous were books that portrayed the Soviet Union as a shining model for contemporary socialists worldwide. There were books on the Soviet political system, Soviet industrial achievements, life in the Red Army, reasons for the Soviet defeat of Germany, the Soviet socialist economy and the state, the Soviet Union's new constitution, and how the society of the future would emulate Soviet precedent. Publishers made little or no attempt to relate all this foreign information to Vietnamese conditions. Nor were these books part of some grand ICP plan to indoctrinate new or prospective members. Most titles had a print run of only two thousand to three thousand copies. The ICP's principal publishing house, *Sự Thật,* had to request that readers pay for their books by advance money order, "as paper and access to the printer is limited."[188] Nonetheless, from this modest beginning ICP–Việt Minh publishing would grow exponentially in subsequent years, despite wartime obstacles.

Only a handful of 1946 monographs dealt with the Chinese Communist Party or the Chinese Red Army, fewer than had been published in the late 1930s. This did not signify disinterest, however. Books were extremely difficult to acquire from faraway Yan'an, and until June the government censor blocked any manuscript likely to offend Chinese Nationalist generals headquartered in Hanoi.[189] First to break through was *The Chinese Communist Party and Revolutionary War,* with a translator's preface dated 31 May 1946.[190] Trần Huy Liệu lent his name as author on the cover, probably to cow the censor and enhance readership, but otherwise this was a translation of a book published in Shanghai in 1938. In the preface, Minh Tranh stressed the importance of China's experience for the "armed struggle of smaller nationalities determined to recover their country." Minh Tranh also noted that since 1938 the CCP had accomplished a great deal, including successfully defending its liberated zone against Guomindang attack. The translation opened with Stalin being quoted by Mao Zedong to the effect that "revolution must be completely integrated to war, entirely at the service of war." The book concluded with Mao himself hammering home the message for the CCP: "In China, without armed struggle it will not be possible to create a position for the proletarian class, a position for the people *(nhân dân)*, a position for the Communist Party. Without armed struggle we cannot bring about victory for the revolution." If Trần Huy Liệu and Minh Tranh really aimed to apply Stalin's and Mao's words to Vietnam in mid-1946, then any attempt at peaceful settlement with the French was counterrevolutionary. The closer the CCP came to victory in China, the more useful Mao's arguments would become to ICP members in Indochina.

Despite availability of these Marxist-Leninist books and booklets in 1946, there is little evidence that ICP cells or Việt Minh groups employed them extensively in study sessions. The November 1945 proposition to establish an Association to Research Marxism in Indochina seems not to have borne fruit. Some publications were useful to older party members and left intellectuals trying to make up for six years of isolation, eager to be part of what was perceived as an international post-World War advance led by Moscow. Senior party members also drew from these publications when preparing lectures for the short courses which became important to ICP consolidation and expansion. At these classes, listeners kept notebooks to refer to when convening their own classes among subordinates or when making public speeches.

Government administrative staff in Hanoi definitely took advantage of newly available printed matter. Some departments formed their own "clubs" *(câu lạc bộ)*, where members could read newspapers and avail themselves of a modest shelf of books. Thus, Club No. 9 possessed a copy of *The Soviet Political System*, marked with shelf number twenty-one.[191] The Economic Department's club had a book exalting the Soviet Army, which concluded with a call for those "smaller nationalities" that were struggling against imperialism to "believe in the world's liberation force: the Red Army."[192] The *National Gazette* Department had two copies of a late-1945 booklet on social classes, written by a French teacher at the University of Indochina.[193] Someone in the Northern Bureau's directorate had begun to type a manuscript summarizing the history of the Bolshevik Party, followed by expositions on protecting proletarian dictatorship, the "land to the tiller" policy, constructing socialism in one country, and the nationalities question.[194] The Northern Bureau (Bắc Bộ Phủ) was replete with intellectuals and politically alert government employees who would not have been content simply to listen to canned lectures from visiting ICP cadres. Bureau members not only read voraciously but contributed articles to Hanoi periodicals (using pseudonyms).

Northern Bureau personnel did of course attend briefings and lectures, at which they were expected to take detailed notes. Part of one such notebook survives in the archives.[195] Shortly after Hồ Chí Minh signed the 6 March 1946 Accord, this unnamed staff member attended a briefing by an unidentified high level government official; his pen notes are more somber than the ICP directive of that same moment, particularly in regard to international circumstances (see chapter 4). He was told that there was a possibility of war between the Soviet Union and the Allies over Germany, Greece, or Persia, and that such an outcome would not benefit the DRV. Those same Allies were encouraging France to retake Indochina, and Holland to retake Indonesia. Within Vietnam, the "political party question" was still vexatious, the military was not yet unified or trained, and the economy was in shambles. Our staffer then received an analysis of the text of the 6 March Accord, with special attention to the vital Nam Bộ issue. No vision of a longer-term Franco-Vietnamese diplomatic settlement was copied down, simply a recognition that armed struggle was decidedly disadvantageous in current conditions. The government would "continue to prepare its forces, to be able to react *(đối phó)* if France does a volte-face." At a later meeting, our staff member scribbled points about French colonial rule, World War II, the August 1945 insurrection, dialectical materialism, the historical dialectic, and the achievements of the Việt Minh. At other times he was briefed on constitutional precedents, DRV symbols (name of country, flag, anthem, emblem), and democracy as practiced in the Soviet Union. Finally, there were tantalizing notes on how to "rationalize factories" by cutting waste, applying scientific methods, practicing division of labor, and introducing assembly line techniques. Taylorism was alive if not well in Hanoi.

ASSERTING AUTHORITY INSIDE THE ICP

While DRV government personnel were attending periodic briefings, province-level ICP cells received visits from senior cadres and occasionally were called together for larger meetings. One of the first ICP gatherings of this kind took place outside Huế in June 1946, organized by the Central Region Party Committee. Over three days participants discussed global and domestic developments, then engaged in a remarkable round of "self-criticism" *(tự chỉ trích)*. ICP members had terrorized and denigrated petit bourgeois intellectuals, state employees, and shopkeepers, when they should have been winning them over. Former political prisoners continued to demand a "worker-peasant government" rather than the correct "government of all the people." Some members also called wrongly for land redistribution and elimination of traditional customs and religious practices. The meeting characterized ICP–Việt Minh propaganda as full of contradictions, outmoded arguments, and missed opportunities. Some ICP cells were said to be enrolling new members too loosely, others too restrictively. Comrades working inside the government sometimes did not "submit to party discipline." The meeting produced a roster of solutions to these deficiencies, then concluded with a warning that "the national liberation fight will be long."[196]

In late July 1946 in Hanoi, the ICP organized its first Central Cadres Conference, to communicate the current line face to face and to signal a widening of political authority. At the end of the meeting a "resolution" was promulgated.[197] Today the resolution text reads more like a rough set of lecture notes than the product of any conference deliberation, but clearly Trường Chinh wanted to convey the impression that a body larger than his Standing Bureau had met and taken the party to a new institutional level.[198] Given the continuing absence of a properly constituted ICP central committee, this conference resolution, and ones that would emerge from subsequent such meetings, were meant to convince the rank-and-file that decisions were being reached by more than a tiny group around the secretary general.

In the face of considerable evidence to the contrary, this 1 August 1946 ICP conference resolution insisted that the proletarian class had become the "decisive force" in France, the influence of the Soviet Union had "spread around the world," and Indochina was now a vital venue of global revolutionary struggle. Turning to domestic factors, the resolution admitted that the Liên Việt had yet to achieve much. It then condemned "reactionary elements" within the Catholic community, expressed puzzlement that Nationalist Party remnants had yet to accept the "concessions" offered them, and painted a bleak picture of the economy. Remedies to some of these problems were mooted, but none received serious attention. One third of the 1 August resolution dealt with ICP deficiencies and organizational problems. Such matters had been raised in earlier resolutions of the Standing Bureau, but now the leadership had more evidence to make its case. Party members were still too "isolationist, narrow-minded, and leftist," above all in central Vietnam, where some comrades wanted to purge rather than to expand membership, as well as to mount an assault on the "reactionary bourgeoisie." Then the resolution authors targeted "factionalism" (biệt phái), criticizing some ICP cadres for nurturing hatreds dating back to prison life, intellectual and nonintellectual cadres for refusing to acknowledge their respective weaknesses, and old and new members for disputing each other. Party discipline was still weak, important questions received no discussion within party cells, and communication between echelons remained slow. One cause of these shortcomings was singled out: "Party policy cannot be disseminated thoroughly among the majority of cadres." Other sources make it clear that physical communication remained tenuous, especially between Hanoi and ICP units further south than Huế. This problem would persist.

Finally, the ICP 1 August resolution offered a mixed bag of organizational remedies to perceived deficiencies. Each comrade was to nominate one new member to the party within one month of reading the resolution. Higher echelons would open training classes for lower echelons, pamphlets would be printed for cells to use in study sessions, and the party regional committees *(xứ ủy)* for north, center, and south would learn from each other by exchanging reports and other documents. In the party's ongoing mass mobilization efforts, priority would be assigned to workers, women, and youths. The National Salvation Cultural Association had to be revamped, journal articles commissioned to condemn "vagabond, unreal culture," and a national conference of writers and artists convened. ICP resolutions of this type became commonplace in later years, taking on a formulaic or ritual character, yet this early document would have impressed recent party recruits eager in late 1946 to be part of a vanguard, clandestine, yet well connected organization.

In mid-October 1946, Trường Chinh convened the ICP Standing Bureau outside Hanoi to greet Phạm Văn Đồng on his return from Paris, hear his assessment of Franco-Vietnamese relations, and discuss the overall strategic situation. We don't know who else attended this meeting other than Võ Nguyên Giáp and Lê Đức Thọ, who were present when Trường Chinh called in Vương Thừa Vũ to receive command of the Hanoi Special Military Zone.[199] This encounter with Vũ revealed the degree to which the Standing Bureau was now involved in upper-level state assignments. Immediately after the Bureau meeting, Trường Chinh chaired an "All-Country Military Conference" at the same Hà Đông venue. "All-Country" in the title was political hyperbole, as there is no evidence that anyone south of Huế was able to attend. The conference did mark an unmistakable move by the ICP into the realm of defense policy, nonetheless.

Unlike the late July 1946 ICP Central Cadres Conference, discussed above, this October military conference seems to have possessed a firm agenda, opportunities for discussion from the floor, and a set of proposals to be voted upon. Much time was devoted to the question of how to increase ICP control within the National Guard. Although political officers coming from various military zones spoke ecstatically about unit morale and public confidence, the 19 October conference resolution focused soberly on how much remained to be done.[200] The quality of political officers had to be improved, responsibilities delineated, rigorous criticism and self-criticism practiced, individualism stamped out, "collective command" *(tập đoàn chỉ huy)* respected, and instructions from party center obeyed. *Sao Vàng (Yellow Star)*, the weekly periodical of the army's political directorate, needed to be revamped, copies of *Cứu Quốc* and *Sự Thật* distributed, unit libraries established, and sufficient funds allocated for propaganda and education efforts within the military. The conference set a goal of at least one party cell within each National Guard company *(đại đội)* within two months, which would not be achieved until much later. Overall, the tone of this resolution suggests that many commanders and most soldiers were not taking political work very seriously.

By contrast, concluding paragraphs of the 19 October ICP resolution dealing with immediate Franco-Vietnamese interactions probably were read carefully by party members within the military. Small French challenges had to be ignored. Specific French assaults should be defended against resolutely, yet without escalating the confrontation. Additional positions needed to be occupied before the French did so, then not evacuated, even at the cost of all defenders killed. Disseminating such detailed rules of engagement to ICP members without reference to Franco-Vietnamese mixed commission operations, or to the National Guard chain of command, was an audacious power play by Trường Chinh. The resolution also ignored the 30 October ceasefire provision in the 14 September modus vivendi. Indeed, according to the resolution, all thoughts that the modus vivendi meant peace had to be erased. "Sooner or later, the French will attack us and we certainly will have to attack them," the resolution foreshadowed. Significantly, Trường Chinh and other organizers of this ICP meeting felt the need to take a position on the vital issue of war or peace one day *before* President Hồ Chí Minh arrived in Haiphong harbor, after more than four months of overseas diplomatic labors.

REACTING TO FRENCH ATTACKS

Despite predictions in the 19 October resolution of enemy attack north of the sixteenth parallel, the ICP was poorly prepared when the French moved aggressively in Haiphong and Lạng Sơn less than five weeks later. Trường Chinh did not issue another Standing Bureau directive. No new cadre conference was convened. Việt Minh (and other) newspapers expressed outrage at these French attacks, yet editorials lacked analysis, much less policy proposals. Soon, however, ICP leaders were acting with a greater sense of urgency. As we have seen, senior ICP members began to arrange movement of supplies and equipment to the hills. The DRV Northern Committee tried to organize transport of rice stocks down the coast to Thanh Hóa. ICP cadres in the National Guard and Việt Minh militia groups exhorted everyone to heighten combat readiness, maintain discipline, and await new orders.

ICP communications were not up to the tasks at hand. Although the ICP could communicate secretly without state oversight (a privilege not granted to any other group), it still lacked requisite technical capacity compared to the army and the civil administration. Contact with ICP committees in central and southern Vietnam was particularly tenuous. In response to Haiphong events in November, the Saigon ICP committee broadcast a resolution affirming national unity, support for the Hồ Chí Minh government, and commitment to the "realization of socialism." This radio message was picked up in Quảng Ngãi and published locally, but probably never made it to Hanoi.[201] On 16 December, the Standing Bureau transmitted a "flash" message to the ICP Southern Committee, warning that full-scale war was nigh inevitable and ordering southern comrades to put Saigon city "under threat," destroy French military equipment and ammunition dumps, sink transport vessels, and link up secretly with French leftists.[202] Even if this message was received, the Southern Committee was in no position to take any of the actions specified.

As of 12 December, someone inside the ICP Standing Bureau drafted an "All-People's Resistance" platform which summarized the protracted war strategy, specified does and don'ts for civilians and soldiers, and provided thirty propaganda slogans for dissemination.[203] Vietnamese resistance would go through three stages: defense, equilibrium (cầm cự), and a general counteroffensive to "retake the entire country." Civilians were not to become soldiers, guides, or workers for the French, not to reveal information to them, not to pay them taxes, sell them food, or purchase their goods. Soldiers were not to surrender, not to lose their firearms or waste ammunition, not to persecute prisoners of war, and not to violate the life, property, or religious principles of fellow citizens. Resistance would be led by "the organization" (ICP), by the DRV government extending down to the commune level, and by the Liên Việt front. Three days after fighting erupted in Hanoi, the ICP Standing Bureau attached a cover note to this platform urging party members to "discuss and implement immediately," then dispatched copies down the chain of command.

On the night of 18–19 December, an "expanded" meeting of the ICP Standing Bureau took place outside Hanoi to deliberate immediate issues of negotiations and war. It seems likely that President Hồ Chí Minh brought with him to these discussions several noncommunist members of the DRV government, and insisted on continuing attempts to communicate with Premier Blum before any final decision to fight was made. The next day, however, events spun out of control. According to one eyewitness, in the early afternoon of 19 December, President Hồ met with Võ Nguyên Giáp, Trường Chinh, and Lê Đức Thọ, and a decision was reached to attack that evening.[204] Nonetheless, the precise timing and nature of attack remained confused.[205] More days would pass before most people around the country realized that all-out war was underway. For most ICP members there must have been relief that the enemy was now clearly defined and could be targeted at will.

As of late December 1946, the ICP Standing Bureau had achieved only a fraction of the goals it aspired to sixteen months earlier. Party members did occupy key positions in the state apparatus, but they devoted themselves explicitly to civil or military business, seldom liaising with the Standing Bureau, much less taking orders from it. Eventually party members within a given ministry were told to form a confidential group (đảng đoàn) to facilitate control, yet members still tended to relate primarily to their work unit and only occasionally to the ICP. Much the same thing happened in the National Guard. Existing party members were instructed to recruit lots of new members, and by the end of 1946 total

ICP membership may have climbed to thirty thousand, compared to five thousand in August 1945.[206] However, most of this recruitment occurred on a personal, ad hoc basis, with very little organizational vetting or indoctrination. A host of patron-client networks began to form within the party, starting at the top with Lê Đức Thọ's screening of appointments. Meanwhile, the further down the central coast that Standing Bureau members traveled, the more difficulties they encountered, including veteran party activists who continued to contest current ICP policies.

The ICP's major achievement during late 1945–46 was to keep most Việt Minh groups from fighting each other for power or descending into banditry. Local disputes remained to be resolved or sublimated, particularly in Nam Bộ, but in general Việt Minh adherents focused their attention increasingly on the "national resistance and construction" agenda. ICP leaders nursed this transition along, while President Hồ Chí Minh's persistent calls for unity and a blitz of DRV decrees from the capital strengthened the authority of administrative committees. In the south, a decision was made to merge Việt Minh and government bodies into "resistance and administrative committees" (ủy ban kháng chiến hành chánh) at province, district, and commune levels—a policy that would be taken up nationally in late 1947.

By September 1946, Trường Chinh could be satisfied that the Vietnam Nationalist Party and Vietnam Revolutionary League had been neutered, the 1945 August Revolution had been commemorated as an ICP victory, and the ICP call for Vietnam to join the "new democracies" led by the Soviet Union was starting to gain traction among Việt Minh adherents. By the time President Hồ returned from France on 20 October, with only an unpopular modus vivendi to show for it, ICP Standing Bureau pronouncements and cadre conference statements were increasingly influencing state policy. Here we should ask why Trường Chinh did not decide to convene an ICP national congress to select a central committee that would in turn elect a party executive to replace the outmoded Standing Bureau? Admittedly the ICP had been formally disbanded, and events in Haiphong soon made such a meeting impossible to organize. But there were also divisions and disagreements within the ICP that would have been exposed at such a congress. Beyond that, I think President Hồ would have blocked such a meeting going forward. The most senior member of the ICP did not believe in proletarian dictatorship for Vietnam any time soon.

MIXED SIGNALS

Throughout late 1945 and 1946, politically alert Vietnamese continued to debate the question of how much the ICP controlled the DRV state. Most people believed President Hồ Chí Minh when he affirmed and reaffirmed his commitment to a DRV government of national solidarity, above party, class, or special interest. Those citizens fearful of communism noted Hồ's disavowals of ICP control, and the fact that he chose not to accept leadership of the party. However, such evidence was hard to reconcile with articles by Trường Chinh and others that made no secret of the ICP's determination to wield monopoly power. This was borne out within the Công An (Public Security Bureau), where the ICP gained hegemony over central units in April 1946, and moved relentlessly in later months to bring hundreds of local security groups under its authority. The ICP Standing Bureau wanted to do the same with the nascent National Guard, yet it appears the president, the commander (Võ Nguyên Giáp), and the chief of staff (Hoàng Văn Thái) had other ideas, even though all three were party members. The DRV civil administration also functioned distinct from the ICP, although party members at each level undoubtedly shaped the outcomes. Only after establishment of the People's Republic of China in late 1949 did Trường Chinh and others have the opportunity to engineer an ICP takeover of the DRV state.

Before 1945, the ICP might be compared with the very early Christian church, constantly under threat, necessarily clandestine. Then all of a sudden in the summer of 1945, in a wide-open, quickly changing environment, ICP leaders saw the opportunity to take charge of events. Many ICP members were poorly equipped for the job and accomplished little, although the rapid return to clandestinity in Nam Bộ, and later the entire country, would offer them another chance. Meanwhile, other ICP members had moved into government or military positions where obedience to Trường Chinh and the Standing Bureau was not a high priority. Still others worked to bring disparate Việt Minh groups under party discipline. Việt Minh newspapers and Voice of Vietnam radio were used to disseminate the current political line. Senior ICP cadres traveled constantly, assessing conditions, conducting short training sessions, enrolling young Việt Minh activists to the party, and reorganizing local party committees. Communications remained a major problem. Trường Chinh's goal of bringing Vietnam under party control would take much longer than he hoped. Along the way, Trường Chinh became a separate pole of power from President Hồ Chí Minh.

9

Mass Mobilization

During August 1945, Vietnamese participated in an astonishing outpouring of popular exuberance and collective action. Nothing in their own lifetimes offered precedent. There was no certainty that such intense involvement would persist, however. Over the next sixteen months it is possible to delineate three mobilizational patterns. The first was millenarian in character, with citizens called on to sacrifice, to fight, and perhaps die in defense of the sacred Fatherland (Tổ Quốc). I discuss here the highly charged political rhetoric of the day, the emergence of Nam Bộ (southern Vietnam) as resistance trope, and occasional attempts to distinguish patriotism from chauvinism. The second mobilizational pattern was statist and organic in character, with a uniform vision of the body politic, information control, and every citizen assigned functions to be implemented for the greater good. The Ministry of Information and Propaganda took the statist lead, while other organizations promulgated elaborate programs designed to make Vietnam strong and modern. Most of these ambitious plans lacked resources and had to be shelved with the advent of full-scale war, yet they would be dusted off and introduced again in the 1950s. The third pattern was interest-based, accepting that citizens possessed different backgrounds and motivations that needed to be recognized (if not always endorsed) when endeavoring to organize large numbers of people to engage in collective action. The ICP's diverse national salvation associations originated from this interest-based model, which however often seemed to be swallowed up by millenarian or statist preferences. Finally, I look at President Hồ Chí Minh as national icon, and view mobilizing efforts from below.

In previous chapters we have seen how DRV leaders organized a civil administration, army, and security apparatus to achieve national objectives. Simultaneously the ICP Standing Bureau focused on gaining control over Việt Minh groups, enrolling new members to the party, and establishing party cells at each level of the state system. However, such efforts at state and party building could not have been sustained in the face of increasing French pressure without involvement of the vast majority of citizens in local organizations dedicated to upholding the new order. This citizen participation ranged from readiness to commit suicide for the cause to the contribution of time or resources only because one feared the consequences of saying no. In between these two extremes lay a host of other ways to engage and motives for doing so. At the end of 1946, with the central government fleeing to the hills and the machinery of state in disarray, it was the readiness of ordinary villagers to stay involved that warded off collapse.

"INDEPENDENCE OR DEATH"

Blood and death suffused the political idiom of late 1945. "Independence or Death" was the most common slogan to be found on banners hoisted across the street, or daubed on village dwellings. Newspaper editorials, reports of public speeches, and letters from readers were filled with commitments to spill enemy blood, and readiness to shed one's own blood in defense of the nation. As one Huế writer put it, "The key moment has arrived, either independence or extermination, but never again slavery." When addressing an open letter to a friend heading south to fight the French, another writer expressed shame that "My blood will not be mixing with yours to deepen the red on our Fatherland's flag."[1] In Nam Định, a globally-minded writer contrasted his twenty million fellow Vietnamese countrymen now volunteering eagerly to fight, and if necessary die for independence, with the oppressive systems that had dragooned subjects to build the Great Wall of China, the Siegfried Line in Germany, or the Maginot Line in France.[2] In Hanoi, a non-Việt Minh intellectual asked readers what it would be like to have their own children wonder why they had failed to contribute every ounce of energy to "uniting with twenty million countrymen in the People's Revolution of the Year of the Rooster (Ất Dậu)."[3] Government censors in December decided to delete an article that called for an immediate military offensive against the French, and concluded, "Only the road to death will take the Vietnamese people to independence."[4]

Voluntarism overwhelmed all deterministic boundaries in the Vietnamese press of late 1945 and 1946. The Sino-Vietnamese concept of "heart-mind" (tâm), evoking fervor, confidence and willpower, ranked above other personal attributes such as cleverness, knowledge, or objectivity. "Faith is a weapon ten thousand times stronger than guns and bullets," insisted one Hanoi writer. He then offered readers a mélange of true believers: Galileo, Christopher Columbus, Lê Lợi (fifteenth-century liberator from Chinese occupation), Phan Thanh Giản

FIGURE 27. "Revolution: First Destroy . . . In Order to Build." In
Dân Chủ, Tết 1946 special issue. Courtesy of Vietnam National
Library.

(nineteenth-century official who signed away territory to the French and then
committed suicide), and Vietnamese Christians who accepted execution rather
than obey mandarin orders to trample on the cross. Armed with similar faith,
citizens should be totally confident of defeating French forces should they come
northward.[5] Editors occasionally published optimistic letters from the south.
One soldier reported encouragingly that French soldiers, when felled by Vietnamese bullets, "also call out for their father, their mother, or their god." He admitted that French military power was substantial. Yet, in combat his comrades
discovered how to make a tank burn—in the process learning that "courage is
more important than rifles and bullets."[6] Such bravado had roots in Vietnamese
folktales, Chinese kung fu adventures, and more recent Japanese samurai stories.

Although no newspaper spoke of Vietnamese soldiers wearing amulets to ward off bullets, anecdotal evidence suggests this remained common practice.

On the eve of the first independent Tết (Lunar New Year) celebrations in early February 1946, newspaper special editions tried to sum up the popular mood and offer advice to readers. One journalist chose four words to characterize the frame of mind of Hanoi citizens: struggle, victory, endeavor, and determination. Rather than exchanging traditional Tết pleasantries, he heard people talking about revenge and committing themselves to "freedom forever and ever."[7] The principal Việt Minh daily counseled readers that "joy and suffering do not necessarily contradict each other, providing one understands joy as complete belief in progress, no matter what tribulations have to be experienced along the way."[8] The cover illustration of the Tết special issue of *Dân Chủ* (Haiphong) newspaper featured a muscular Vietnamese worker-peasant using a hammer in one hand to smash a house in 1945, and a trowel in the other to build a brick wall in 1946. The caption declared: "Revolution: First Destroy in Order to Construct." [9] Months later, National Guard physicians and medics offered readers the following philosophical platform: "Poor yet cheerful. Cheerful in order to live. Only with joy in life is there faith. Only with faith is victory possible. We will win."[10] A paper claiming to represent young laborers in Haiphong painted a more militantly idealistic picture: "The small and weak are compelled to resist those who are a hundred times more powerful! But with a righteous cause in their hearts they cannot be annihilated. How can the bright sun be afraid of dark clouds?"[11] In Thái Nguyên province, north of Hanoi, the obituary column for locals killed in action was headed: "In life only sacrifice is noble, and the sacrifice of one's life is most noble of all, because it encompasses all other sacrifices."[12]

Among ICP leaders, Trần Huy Liệu was most likely to use millenarian rhetoric in his speeches and essays. We have seen how in mid-February 1946, Liệu promoted heroic armed confrontation with the French, and in August invoked the revolutionary exaltation of one year earlier. In early September, concerned that President Hồ Chí Minh might be giving away too much to the French in faraway Paris, Liệu took the rostrum to argue that war could not be avoided. His tone was apocalyptic: "In this century of 'depression, war, and revolution' through which we are living, no place, no being can hope to find the sheltered conditions of peacetime. All is in motion, rolling over and over." No matter what the French agreed to on paper, Liệu warned they would not leave Vietnam in peace to build the country. More blood had to be spilled.[13] Soon afterward, at a commemoration of the outbreak of fighting in Saigon one year prior, Liệu argued that it was the anti-French resistance in the south that made possible the very mass meeting he was addressing in Hanoi. He insisted that a wide alliance of southerners had put the Fatherland ahead of narrow class interests, and they were not afraid of protracted resistance. "Not to resist is to die," Liệu proclaimed, and three times he repeated the words, "We will never be enslaved again."[14]

NAM BỘ AS RALLYING CRY

People in northern and central Vietnam had been caught unprepared by news of the fighting that broke out in the south on 23 September 1945. Told that the Việt Minh were part of the victorious Allied struggle, and that British and Chinese troops were coming to Indochina simply to take the surrender of Japanese units, most citizens looked forward to peace and to consolidating domestic revolutionary gains. The first sign of trouble came on 13 September, when *Cứu Quốc* urged everyone to take part in a mass demonstration the next day at the Opera House, to protest British Army actions in Saigon.[15] The northern press then shifted its attention to Chinese generals and Chinese units arriving in Haiphong and Hanoi. Then suddenly, on 24 September, *Cứu Quốc*'s big lead headline proclaimed, "The French Colonial Gang Has Carried Out a Surprise Attack on Saigon." A brief, unsigned central government directive *(huấn lệnh)* addressed to countrymen in Nam Bộ stated that "all Vietnamese are moved by your opposition to French Army invaders." It went on, however, to emphasize the gravity of the moment and the importance of following government instructions, "in order to bring our liberation effort to final victory."[16] Not until 26 September did Hồ Chí Minh go on the radio to promise government and popular support for Nam Bộ citizens struggling to defend the nation's independence. He added ominously: "At present, with war just having finished, the French colonial gang reopens conflict either covertly or openly. During the previous four years they sold our country twice. Now they want to dominate our people once again."[17]

Non-Việt Minh newspapers in Hanoi also roundly condemned British-French aggression in Saigon and supported an armed Vietnamese response. *Thời mới (New Times)* printed a special Nam Bộ issue with the huge headline: "Blood Is Spilled in the South! Vietnamese Must Defeat the French Bandits!" The lead article was titled "Swear to Live or Die with Independence." An editorial called on the entire world to bear witness to British-French perfidy, a plea destined to fall on deaf ears. Two weeks later, *Thời mới* quoted Trần Văn Giàu, the southern ICP leader: "Vietnam can only use guns and bullets to talk with the French."[18] *Dân Quốc (People-Country)* published a diagram of Saigon with Vietnamese forces surrounding British-French units on all four sides. It also reported the early October ceasefire discussions in detail, accompanied by a comment from Trần Huy Liệu that people should not be too optimistic. When fighting resumed soon afterward, *Dân Quốc* told readers that the "Vietnam National Army" was preparing to burn Saigon to the ground.[19] *Đồng Minh (Allies)* serialized a southern account of

violent upheavals in Nam Bộ, and made a point of commemorating the one hun-
dredth day since the first soldier had fallen in the south.[20] A Catholic periodical
printed a cartoon of armed Vietnamese in Nam Bộ chasing frightened Frenchmen off a map of Indochina. People would never return to the conditions they
had endured under eighty years of French colonialism, the accompanying editorial emphasized.[21]

Beyond Hanoi, newspapers published by local Việt Minh groups did not wait
for ICP instructions before committing themselves to resisting French aggression in the south. In Huế, the team publishing *Quyết Thắng (Determined to Win)*
relied on brief foreign radio bulletins to inform readers of events in Saigon, accompanied by their own editorials promising Vietnamese victory. The paucity of
hard information did not prevent editors from claiming week-to-week combat
achievements. A poem dedicated to combatants in Nam Bộ concluded: "This land
solely takes red blood; only by coloring the land dark red can we hope to survive."
Tố Hữu, the best known ICP poet, contributed verses suffused with images of
fire, blood, and death.[22] In Nam Định, *Nam Tiến (Southern Advance)* opened its
first issue with an editorial connecting events in the south with local commitments to "eliminate the French invaders" and thus safeguard Vietnam's complete
independence. The next issue described how news of the fighting in Nam Bộ had
caused villagers to take up the unfamiliar term "resistance," to walk long distances
to participate in protest meetings, and to yell "Independence or Death!" with
gusto.[23] One writer described how, at ten in the morning on 5 November 1945, on
"former Route Colonial No. 1," vehicle drivers and pedestrians halted, faced southward, and stood at attention for one minute of silence to honor the Nam Bộ resistance. He then commented: "This did not kill a single additional Frenchman, yet
it had profound emotional meaning. Our hearts and blood were linked to countrymen in the south. Our fate was entwined with theirs."[24]

A combination of meager news sources and editorial wishful thinking gave
northern readers very misleading impressions of what was happening in southern Vietnam. Results of a Vietnamese assault on Saigon's Tân Sơn Nhứt airport
were wildly inflated. Shortly thereafter, a boy was said to have soaked himself in
petrol and become a human torch in order to burn down the oil tanks at the Si-
mon Piétri cement plant. The oil tanks had indeed been destroyed, but the human torch story was fabricated by Trần Huy Liệu in Hanoi, gained nationwide
currency and continued to be used in primary school texts into the 1980s.[25] Over
the next three months, newspapers carried stories of alleged victories at Xuân
Lộc, Phan Thiết, Phan Rang, and Nha Trang, yet anyone looking at a map had to
conclude that Vietnamese resistance was failing to stop the French advance.
Meanwhile the press continued to assert Vietnamese combat triumphs in the
Mekong delta. *Cứu Quốc* carried a report that the commander of British forces,
General Douglas Gracey, had been assassinated by an Indian soldier.[26]

By contrast, shortly after arriving in Hanoi in early November, ICP leader Trần Văn Giàu offered readers a sobering account of conditions in the south. Giàu explained that "at least ten political parties and many religions" had organized their own military and paramilitary groups "before the Việt Minh flag waved freely over the city [Saigon]." When the Nam Bộ Resistance Committee was deliberating in mid-September how to react to British provocations, it was stunned to receive a small box containing twelve pinkie fingers, from a squad demanding authorization to attack. Giàu explained to Hanoi readers that it had been impossible to kill the French without first assaulting Japanese and then Indian forces, so the committee had opted instead for a blockade of the city. The blockade was broken quickly by "British-Indian-Japanese-French forces equipped with tanks, artillery, and aircraft," which then proceeded to seize provincial towns as well. Nonetheless, according to Giàu, villagers had responded by constructing road obstacles, forming guerrilla squads, and mounting ambushes. Young men armed with a single grenade had used it to blow up French soldiers in Saigon as well as themselves. Giàu concluded his article by foreshadowing that the enemy would occupy all twenty-one southern provincial towns, yet would still be in no position to affirm that "Cochinchina has been retaken."[27] Three months later General Leclerc made exactly that claim of Cochinchina reconquest, but by the end of 1946 Giàu's assessment would prove more accurate.

In the same newspaper issue as Trần Văn Giàu's article, Võ Nguyên Giáp gave a more upbeat evaluation to reporters on the fighting in Nam Bộ. Giáp emphasized how townspeople had evacuated to the countryside, buildings had been demolished, the French were being denied food and labor, and small-scale counterattacks were being launched. When a reporter asked Giáp how guerrillas could operate successfully in wide-open expanses of the Mekong delta, his answer was convoluted and unconvincing. Then Giáp was asked whether the war would spread to the north. He replied: "We must plan and prepare for the contingency that the [French] invasion spreads throughout the country, because the ambitions of the imperialist gang are limitless." Vietnam might have to go through a very troubled period of "several or more years," Giáp continued, but that was minor compared to China fighting the Japanese for eight years, or Russia losing more than ten million citizens when defeating the Germans. Giáp even claimed that Yugoslavia had vanquished German occupiers, thanks to a wise political strategy that united all Yugoslavians in the resistance. He clearly wanted to prepare northern citizens for possible French attack, while pointing out that the presence of Chinese troops made this unlikely at the moment. News of the fighting in Nam Bộ and then south-central Vietnam increasingly compelled citizens further north to ponder the personal and familial consequences of war.

For several weeks following the 6 March 1946 Franco-Vietnamese Accord, northern and central Vietnamese newspapers did not discuss the proposed

Cochinchina referendum, as this appeared to concede that Nam Bộ was not yet part of the DRV. The first open comment came in Huế, where a veteran of the fighting in Nam Bộ labeled the referendum a joke, because both sides knew that southerners would vote to join the rest of the country. In the meantime, he asserted, organizations loyal to the DRV administered most of the southern countryside, albeit subject to "French terrorism." Whenever the French tried to install their own Vietnamese village chief, "several days later he's lost his head." Even so, this combatant expressed concern that "protracted war might not be to our advantage," as Vietnamese traitors were "sprouting up like mushrooms."[28] Another Huế reporter interviewed comrades arriving from Nam Bộ about French efforts to establish an autonomous Cochinchina. The group was proud to have killed alleged Cochinchina autonomy adherents and tossed their bodies into the river. When local people captured traitors, they often "requested execution on the spot," rather than delivering culprits to province-level authorities for determination. A member of this Nam Bộ group claimed that traitors marked themselves covertly with the French tricolor, then added, "Even if the flag is on their ass we'll find it."[29] The visiting head of the Mỹ Tho military court described to a Công An audience how the French paid spies by tearing five-hundred-piastre notes in half and presenting them the second part on completion of their mission. Citizens who found individuals in possession of half a five-hundred-piastre note had reacted by cutting the alleged spy in half.[30]

The DRV government established an Office for Nam Bộ in Hanoi in late 1945, but for months it accomplished little beyond offering visitors from the south a place to stay. In mid-March 1946, two familiar southerners, Phạm Ngọc Thạch and Trần Văn Giàu, addressed an Opera House audience while loudspeakers reached a solemn crowd outside. In May 1946, the Nam Bộ office called publicly for contributions of money, medicine, clothing, and printed matter to send south.[31] Cứu Quốc started a column to report local "support Nam Bộ" meetings, demonstrations, and fundraising tallies. Behind the scenes in Hanoi, Nguyễn Thanh Sơn, representing the ICP's Liberation group in the south, focused on acquisition and transport of weapons down the coast to Quảng Ngãi and Tuy Hòa, where they could be used either to outfit units destined to march to Nam Bộ or transshipped by sea to Bến Tre in the Mekong delta.[32] The Việt Minh General Headquarters tried to keep Nam Bộ in the public spotlight, yet it was telling people nothing new. Soon the number of local support meetings dropped off. The Tổng Bộ declared 9 June as Nam Bộ Day. A Class A speaking roster was put together for a meeting in front of the Hanoi Opera House, with Dr. Phạm Ngọc Thạch representing the Nam Bộ Resistance Committee, followed by the acting DRV president, Huỳnh Thúc Kháng, the chair of the National Assembly, Nguyễn Văn Tố, and Trần Huy Liệu for the General Headquarters. However, the absence of published crowd numbers and the lack of followup reporting suggest disappointing public participation. *Cứu Quốc* did assert that 162,953$86BIC had been collected throughout Hanoi on 9 June, but this amount fell well short of similar fundraising efforts in late 1945.[33] Haiphong seems to have ignored Nam Bộ Day entirely. In Huế, it was observed with a march into the city sports stadium by national salvation groups, each contingent wearing a different armband. Following the flagraising ceremony and solemn remembrance of fallen comrades, speakers addressed a crowd of ten thousand, which unanimously affirmed a Nam Bộ support message to be sent to Hanoi.[34]

The 2 July 1946 death in French detention of Albert Thái Văn Lung, a young southern lawyer, French citizen, and member of the DRV National Assembly sparked demonstrations in Saigon that reverberated in Hanoi. On behalf of the National Assembly, Nguyễn Văn Tố sent a protest to the French government, conveying Saigon public opinion that Lung had died under torture. Vietnamese intellectuals convened at the Hanoi Opera House on 20 July to condemn French treatment of Lung. Hoàng Xuân Hãn published a long, angry attack on French behavior, some of which was deleted by DRV censors. *Cứu Quốc* stated that Lung had been commanding a military unit when captured, repeated Associated Press assertions that Lung had been tortured, and printed without rebuttal French claims that Lung had committed suicide.[35] The deaths of Dương Văn Dương, a charismatic Bình Xuyên leader, and Lý Chính Thắng, a Saigon labor union organizer, were reported in the northern press as well.[36] Nam Bộ was providing revolutionary martyrs, whose stories would be repeated and elaborated upon for decades in the Vietnamese press, on the radio, in songs, and in popular dramas.

The first anniversary of the outbreak of fighting in Saigon was commemorated in a number of northern and central localities. In Hanoi on 22 September 1946, a crowd claimed by reporters to number three hundred thousand people listened to speeches and yelled "Nam Bộ is Vietnamese Soil!" *Cứu Quốc* put out a special red-ink issue, with the lead editorial proclaiming "Nam Bộ is our blood and flesh." On 23 September at ten in the morning, citizens faced southward and observed a minute of silence. It was asserted that Hanoi "died for half an hour" in order to remember fallen compatriots in the south. Everyone was called upon to fast during the remainder of the day and to donate the savings to the Resistance Fund. Somehow it was quickly deduced that twenty million citizens around the country had done exactly that.[37] The Vietnam Nationalist Party's weekly paper, which had been heavily cut in previous issues, was allowed by government censors to publish with no blank spaces a lead editorial commemorating one year of Nam Bộ resistance.[38]

In Haiphong, the mass observance began at the Opera House at six thirty in the morning on 23 September, with Catholic priests praying for the souls of soldiers killed in the south. At seven, a siren announced one minute of silence around the city. Children had already posted slogans declaring "Center, South, and North United." There was a commemoration at Haiphong's main Buddhist temple, afternoon speeches, and an early evening gathering on the square in front of the Opera House.[39] In Quảng Ngãi, *Kháng Chiến* published a special 23 September issue which began with a striking cover illustration of the armed Vietnamese masses advancing on the enemy.[40] Overall, however, these first-anniversary Nam Bộ commemorations failed to generate nearly as much enthusiasm or involvement as the National Day ceremonies three weeks prior. Public bewilderment over terms of the Moutet-Hồ Chí Minh modus vivendi, published just at this moment, may have contributed to the decline in participation. Commitment to southern unification with the rest of the country would be tested for the next thirty years.

PATRIOTISM YES, CHAUVINISM NO

While defense of the Vietnamese nation stood above all other values in 1945–46, writers sometimes considered it important to draw a distinction between legitimate patriotism (*chủ nghĩa yêu nước*) and crass chauvinism or antiforeignism.[41] Chauvinists only appreciated their own country and people, disdaining all others or aiming to dominate them. Hitler's Germany and Imperial Japan had demonstrated abundantly the perils of chauvinism.[42] As one newspaper insisted vehemently, "The Vietnamese people's liberation revolution is not antiforeign like fascist Japan or Germans killing Jews; race is not an issue."[43] From this position it followed that patriotic Vietnamese only opposed French colonialists, not the French people. This mantra, which appeared routinely in non-Việt Minh as well as Việt Minh publications, never was subjected to critical analysis, even though it failed to explain French metropolitan politics of the day, and offered no practical guidance on how to deal with ordinary French soldiers and civilians in Vietnam. Meanwhile, newspaper cartoons invariably gave the French long noses and hairy skin, thus reinforcing a Vietnamese stereotype that predated colonial rule. Southern combatants applied the term "French bandits" (*giặc Pháp*) openly and indiscriminately. As French forces advanced northward, this term regained verbal currency throughout the country, although government censors generally kept it out of the media until the outbreak of full-scale war in December 1946. According to one paper, the French Army was afraid of death, enamored of liquor and pretty women, prone to burn, steal, and rape.[44]

When it came to the Lao, Khmer, and various upland groups, the Vietnamese media exhibited decidedly paternalistic tendencies—reflecting centuries of Confucian state disparagement of neighboring "barbarians," and the more recent Social Darwinian demarcation of "advanced" and "backward" peoples.[45] One could still find an otherwise Marxist-Leninist interpretation of the "nationalities question" arguing that "the future of small and weak nationalities will be determined by their capacity to struggle."[46] Vietnamese writers assumed that every "nationality" *(dân tộc)* within Indochina shared an overriding commitment to preventing the return of French colonialism. The media devoted considerable attention to the fighting in Laos without attempting to disguise the high degree of Vietnamese involvement, referring fondly to a Lao-Việt alliance. Northern and central region papers carried practically nothing about Cambodia, except when condemning King Norodom Sihanouk for signing the first "autonomous state" agreement with High Commissioner d'Argenlieu. The term "national minorities" gained currency, usually referring to peoples of the northern hills and central plateau, not yet the overseas Chinese or the Khmer resident in Nam Bô (see below).

Being tagged a "minority" meant, of course, that there existed a "majority," the Kinh or Việt people, who constituted at least 80 percent of the population of the territory claimed by the DRV. On the other hand, the DRV government insisted that all peoples or nationalities within Vietnam were to be treated equally. The DRV constitution of November 1946 would set down the first of many legal formulas for reconciling multiethnicity with unitary citizenship. Meanwhile, members of ethnic minorities who joined the anti-French struggle were referred to as "new Vietnamese" *(người Việt mới)* in many localities, a term considered an honor by Kinh who employed the term, yet carrying distinctly assimilationist overtones.[47]

Much ink would be spilled in subsequent years over the meaning of *Fatherland* or *Nation*. One writer in 1946 cleverly described an exchange about the Fatherland between a village elder and a young intellectual. The elder invoked the communal house *(đình)*, pagoda, church, graves, family, village rice fields, and "all the achievements of my ancestors." The youth scorned this vision as narrow-minded and provincial. "The Fatherland is our mountains and rivers, our cultural inheritance, the history bequeathed by our ancestors," he insisted. To this the elder responded, "Your Fatherland is remote, insipid, lifeless." When the two of them took up for debate Marshal Pétain's recent slogan of "Work, Family, Fatherland," government censors terminated the article in mid-sentence.[48]

THE MINISTRY OF INFORMATION AND PROPAGANDA

In the DRV provisional Cabinet announced in late August 1945, Trần Huy Liệu, minister of information and propaganda, was ranked third in importance, after President Hồ Chí Minh and the interior minister, Võ Nguyên Giáp. This precedence over eleven other ministers reflected both Liệu's national reputation as an anticolonial essayist and speechmaker, and the political priority assigned to mobilizing citizens to support the new regime.[49] Liệu took up his Cabinet portfolio with gusto, issuing press statements, meeting journalists, screening applications for new newspapers, enforcing censorship regulations, and embarking on an ambitious program to train propaganda cadres for assignment to each province and district. It soon became evident that Liệu intended to use his ministry to rationalize and enhance Việt Minh (as distinct from government) propaganda operations. Also, Liệu's role as government spokesman was poorly coordinated with Hồ's responsibilities as head of state and foreign minister.

The first act of the new Information and Propaganda Ministry was to dispatch six Việt Minh slogans to all newspaper editors, "requesting" that they be printed. The next day a stash of musical instruments was located at the former Civil Guard barracks, and quickly acquired by the ministry.[50] The ministry sent telegrams to all town and province committees, urging them to set up local offices of information and propaganda. Five hundred propaganda cadres completed a short course on 20 October, were congratulated by provisional President Hồ at the Opera House, then marched to the Northern Region Office to receive their ID cards and satchels of printed matter.[51] When a Hanoi citizen offered to organize a series of information meetings, he was given thirty-six hundred copies of the prospective national anthem and two thousand copies of a mid-August "Open Letter" from Nguyễn Ái Quốc. The colonial Agence de Presse Indochine (API) had its name changed to Việt Nam Thông Tấn (Vietnam Press).[52] In an administratively gratuitous if politically symbolic act, Trần Huy Liệu signed an order that removed colonial bans on fifteen Vietnamese books, including three of his own publications. Then he proceeded to ban ten other books from the colonial era.[53] Amidst ministry press releases came more political slogans, with instructions to editors to position them prominently on the front page. On 20 November, for example, the ministry sent out for publication the following admonition: "People of conscience (lương tâm) should guard against spendthrift behavior at a time when countrymen are going hungry." Meanwhile, as we have seen, the ministry cooked up black propaganda in the form of fake letters and reports designed to undermine opposition parties, then sent them to trusted Việt Minh editors for publication.

The provisional DRV government retained colonial-era regulations and procedures for supervising the press, including accepting or rejecting applications to publish, prepublication censorship, mandatory deposit of newspaper copies, the power to suspend distribution for due cause, controls over newsprint, and the issuing of ID cards to journalists. Although scores of periodicals had ceased publication between March and August 1945, a few papers persisted and managed to make the transition to DRV requirements. In late August, Việt Minh groups gained control of printing presses in cities and towns for the first time, proceeding to distribute their own newspapers without waiting for government permission. Early September saw scores of applications to publish arriving at both central and provincial government offices. The first formal DRV authorization to publish was obtained by *Cờ Giải Phóng (Liberation Flag)*, the ICP paper begun several months earlier in the countryside north of Hanoi.[54] Next came authorizations for three central-level Việt Minh newspapers.[55] Some non-Việt Minh applicants were told by the Ministry of Propaganda to link up with a national salvation group if they wished to gain approval to publish. Other non-Việt Minh groups began to publish while their applications were still being considered.[56] The most sensitive case involved *Việt Nam* newspaper, organ of the Vietnam Nationalist Party, which started publication on 15 November and received its government permission on 3 December.[57] Throughout late November and December, *Việt Nam* condemned ICP–Việt Minh dominance of the DRV government, often targeting Trần Huy Liệu in particular, yet censors were in no position to retaliate (see below).

The right to censor newspapers and other mass media had been asserted by the provisional DRV government at the 2 September Independence Day meeting in Hanoi. Some colonial-era censors continued to work for the new regime, monitored by Việt Minh adherents with press experience, and of course expected to enforce a different set of content restrictions. During late 1945, outright removal of newspaper articles or cutting of passages was rare. Almost all newspapers offered effusive support to provisional President Hồ Chí Minh and his Cabinet. Editors wishing to criticize a specific policy or action phrased it as a comment or suggestion from sympathetic citizens. In this spirit, censors appeared to overlook some articles that had yet to discard colonial-era terminology or assumptions. They also made no attempt to prevent papers from using a variety of foreign news sources. This latter practice did cause Trần Huy Liệu to issue a warning in October concerning "incorrect or misleading press reports," and to urge all editors to rely on his ministry for accurate information.[58]

The national Propaganda Ministry depended on the Northern Region Bureau of Information and Propaganda for all day-to-day operations in the north. Bureau members much preferred face-to-face discussions with newspaper editors, to "improve their political consciousness" and correct errors, rather than employing scissors on articles. They were concerned about two foreign papers, however. *L'Entente,* produced by a French group in Hanoi, was "potentially dangerous" and ought to be limited to one sheet of news, no commentary, and nothing whatsoever relating to Indochina politics.[59] Editors of a Chinese-language paper, *Youth (Qing Nian)*, were not bringing in text to be checked. With *Youth's* published content ranging from "good" to "disadvantageous," the propaganda official simply recommended encouraging more good articles.[60] When it came to the cinema, the official reported that movie audiences were enjoying American films previously banned by the Japanese. He added that censorship of films was not possible yet. A Hanoi art exhibit had brought in 818$60 piastres for the bureau. A November photograph exhibit had proven very popular, and was therefore being divided up for display in the provinces. Further training classes for local cadres had begun, and forty-six regional propaganda teams had returned to the capital after circulating through northern towns and villages.[61]

The Northern Propaganda Bureau expected provincial cadres not only to disseminate the government's line but also to report regularly on local morals and political behavior in response to a set of questions dispatched from Hanoi. Thái Nguyên province reported eight propaganda cadres making the rounds of villages to promote and help organize voting in the upcoming National Assembly election. Tenants remained "confused" about government policy in relation to landlords. A handful of "reactionaries" had been uncovered. The despised former province mandarin, Cung Đình Vận, had been executed in front of a crowd of ten thousand people (and a photo supplied to Hanoi).[62] About three hundred merchants in Thái Nguyên had little to do. People were upset that an incoming shipment of scarce cloth had been reserved mostly for government employees. Chinese troops had earlier walked through the province but left no garrison behind. Members of the Nùng ethnic minority had chosen to list themselves as Chinese rather than Vietnamese citizens.[63] The morale of local Liberation Army soldiers was said to be "very high," and many noncommissioned officers had entered the military school located in Thái Nguyên.[64]

As the time approached for elections to the National Assembly, some newspaper editors suggested that censorship rules be relaxed in order to promote serious policy discussion and allow voters to see where candidates stood on key issues. Trần Huy Liệu called in newspaper editors to his office, encouraging them to publish all positions and opinions which "do not go contrary to democracy and damage [Vietnam's] independence." More pointedly, Trần Huy Liệu told them that Vietnam did not yet possess freedom of speech. Nor did he alter censorship procedures.[65] As we have seen, opportunities for candidates to communicate with voters, whether via the press, public meetings, or informal encounters, proved quite limited in the weeks leading up to the 6 January 1946 election.

Việt Nam, the newspaper most disliked by the Propaganda Ministry and the Việt Minh General Headquarters, could not be banned or carved up by the censors during the first six months of its existence. Vietnam Nationalist Party editors refused to submit advance copy to the censors, possessed their own printing press, and enjoyed independent access to newsprint. Starting in late June 1946, however, blank spaces did appear in *Việt Nam* issues. Following police assaults on Nationalist Party premises the next month, a different editorial team produced copy much more acceptable to the authorities. *Chính Nghĩa tuần báo (Righteous Cause Weekly),* another Nationalist Party paper, continued to publish virulently anticommunist, anti-Stalinist essays, but by the end of October editorials had vanished, and coverage of domestic affairs disappeared soon after.

Throughout the second half of 1946, the PTT made it difficult, and the Công An dangerous, for individuals in a provincial town or village to obtain copies of any Nationalist Party paper. Catholic papers distributed via the PTT were also "lost" en route, but Catholic priests who carried copies to local parishes were unlikely to be stopped and searched by the police.

Government censors scrutinized middle-of-the-road and Việt Minh publications for unacceptable content as well. *Hà Nội Mới* had the nerve to start serializing a biography of Phạm Quỳnh, who had been killed by ICP members in Huế in late 1945. The censors allowed the biography to proceed for three issues, but decided to chop ninety-six lines from Quỳnh's final testament.[66] *Đồng Minh* lost paragraphs when it wanted to express reservations about the 6 March 1946 Franco-Vietnamese Accord.[67] Some editors were willing to sit down with censors to negotiate content revisions.[68] *Dân Thành (City People)* was shut down for three days for "incorrectly reporting President Hồ's statement to the National Assembly."[69]

One weekly newspaper, *Cấp Tiến (Progressive)*, appears to have been started in early October in anticipation of the second session of the National Assembly, specifically to stimulate debate about the nature of democracy in the DRV. Government censors reacted negatively from the first issue of *Cấp Tiến*, blanking out two articles except for the titles and deleting thirty-four lines from a brief history of democracy since the ancient Greeks.[70] Soon it was obvious the censors aimed to put *Cấp Tiến* out of business (without ordering its closure), chopping whole editorials and multiple articles. An editorial labeled "We Demand the Right of Free Speech" was completely gutted. From what little content survives of this newspaper after censorship, we can deduce that the unnamed individuals behind *Cấp Tiến* wanted to challenge New Democracy, the ideological platform being promoted with increasing vigor by the ICP–Việt Minh. In the context of National Assembly deliberation of the DRV draft constitution, *Cấp Tiến* may also have wanted to promote separation of powers and a multiparty system. However, government censors now had no patience for such ideas, and *Cấp Tiến* closed after eight issues.

After the Ministry of Propaganda was downgraded to a bureau inside the Interior Ministry, the interior minister, Huỳnh Thúc Kháng, appeared determined to treat Việt Minh papers no better than the rest. On 15 April, *Cứu Quốc* lost lines to the censor for the first time, in an article about taxation. Two weeks later an entire article was eliminated. During May the humor column was censored.[71] *Dân Chủ* (Haiphong) found itself in repeated difficulty with the censor over its reports on local French Army activities. When *Dân Chủ* demanded at the end of August that French soldiers withdraw from Haiphong customs houses, only the headline survived.[72] The Democratic Party daily, *Độc Lập*, lost paragraphs repeatedly from articles dealing with Franco-Vietnamese relations. After *Độc Lập* revived the French tradition of publishing court reports, it found those censored on occasion. Thus readers were told of a Sơn Tây province official sentenced to five years prison for detaining citizens illegally and using his position improperly, yet the exact nature of those acts was deleted.[73] Down the coast in Vinh city, *Dân Mới* abruptly stopped a serialized account by an ICP member of three years spent at the Stalin School in Moscow, probably because censors felt it undercut the government's united front policy.[74] In Quảng Ngãi, *Kháng Chiến* apologized for publishing an article "unfair to the Overseas Chinese."[75]

THE RADIO AS MOBILIZING MEDIUM

Most Vietnamese of the 1930s and early 1940s had never listened to a radio. Well-off families might own their own receiver and allow neighbors to join them in listening to music or news bulletins. During the Pacific War, French authorities first ordered registration of private receivers, then impounded some sets. The Japanese confiscated many receivers belonging to French citizens following the 9 March 1945 coup. PTT employees, Indochina Radio Office technicians, plantation managers, and Catholic priests continued to access foreign news broadcasts, thus becoming highly sought-after sources of information. It was they who communicated word of Japan's 15 August capitulation, then news of the French government's appointment of a high commissioner for Indochina, which sparked anticolonial demonstrations. Such momentous radio news spread quickly by word of mouth, and soon afterward daily newspapers accessed foreign bulletins to keep people informed. The radio receiver acquired an almost magical capacity to seize information out of the sky.

Whoever controlled radio transmitters inside Indochina possessed considerable communicative power. From 22 August, Japanese officers in charge of Radio Saigon permitted Vietnamese activists to broadcast a series of vigorous anticolonial statements, heard by incredulous French personnel in faraway Calcutta. Six days later, Dr. Phạm Ngọc Thạch was able to use Radio Saigon to deliver an appeal in French to Allied leaders to recognize the "young Vietnam Democratic Republic." Radio Saigon broadcast lists of Australian POWs which were quickly published in a Melbourne newspaper.[76] In Hanoi, the Japanese turned back the first Việt Minh group seeking to enter the facility of Radio Bạch Mai on 19 August, but ten days later they gave provisional DRV representatives regular access. It was hoped that Hồ Chí Minh's 2 September independence declaration at Ba Đình square could be broadcast live to the country and the world, but this proved impossible. Soon after, a Radio Bạch Mai staff member did read the declaration text over the air, which listeners apparently took to be the voice of the president himself.[77] Groups participating in the August insurrection had taken custody of any radio receiver they could find, tuning in eagerly to foreign stations as well as to Radio Bạch Mai or Radio Saigon.

When the new DRV provisional government wanted to communicate with points distant from Hanoi, the former colonial Radio Office affirmed two-way contact with stations in Saigon, Biên Hòa, Mỹ Tho, Phnom Penh, Huế, Samneua, and Xieng Khoang. However, Samneua station went off the air on 6 September, and soon afterward Xieng Khoang stated that it was subject to French censorship. Radio Saigon stopped transmitting on 24 September, the day following outbreak of hostilities, then resumed broadcasting a few days later under French control. Three weeks later, Hanoi still sustained two-way contact with the Biên Hòa and Mỹ Tho stations, which had been joined by a weaker rural station dependent on Huế to relay messages. By the end of October, however, all three Nam Bộ transmitters had gone silent. In early December, Hanoi exchanged messages with Savannakhet station concerning Việt Kiều eligibility to vote in the upcoming National Assembly elections. The Radio Office also reported that a new French station (FRS2) was transmitting from Phnom Penh. Presumably, operators also tried to establish contacts beyond Indochina, for example with Bangkok, Manila, and New Delhi. However, reports only mention one such contact, with Kunming, where the Chinese authorities on 22 October notified Hanoi that henceforth no DRV press releases would be accepted, and all other messages would need to be paid for and transmitted via the Chinese Army station based at the Albert Sarraut Secondary School in Hanoi.[78]

On 21 November 1945, President Hồ Chí Minh signed a decree placing the Radio Office under the Defense Ministry.[79] This reflected the top priority assigned to building the National Guard, as well as the perceived need to exercise security over all radio transmissions, since enemies would be listening. Nonetheless, the Radio Office maintained its civilian identity and continued to function under the Interior Ministry on logistical and personnel matters. Radio Bạch Mai broadcast both military and civilian traffic, each employing the same wavelengths at different times. Voice of Vietnam, the public component of Radio Bạch Mai, broadcast news bulletins according to a daily schedule, drawing its content from government pronouncements, foreign stations, and the local print media. While voice transmissions reached everywhere in the Red River delta, Morse code proved much more reliable when communicating down the central coast and into Laos. From November, radio staff also began reading selected decrees, edicts, and instructions at slow pace over the airwaves for copying by local administrative committees.[80] In early December, Voice of Vietnam offered to set aside one hour each day for candidates in the National Assembly elections to talk with the electorate, providing they presented themselves first to the Việt Minh's National Salvation Cultural Association headquarters in Hanoi.[81]

It remained unusual for DRV leaders to take to the airwaves. In mid-February 1946, having just returned from the National Guard's serious defeat at Nha

Trang, Võ Nguyên Giáp went on Voice of Vietnam to try to dispel the rumors and incipient panic that threatened the entire DRV cause.[82] Hồ Chí Minh spoke on the radio several times in early 1946. Immediately after the tense public meeting in front of the Hanoi Opera House following announcement of the 6 March Franco-Vietnamese Accord, President Hồ used the radio to particular effect. According to a listener in Huế, President Hồ's brief, easy-to-understand speech had dramatic impact: "For a crowd of people filled with suspicion and indignation, the words of this kind, clear-sighted father (cha) were like a long drought being broken by a refreshing downpour." They especially responded to Hồ saying, "You know I would prefer to die rather than sell our country."[83] The first known audio recording of Hồ Chí Minh occurred in late April. A Paris Radio team visiting Hanoi recorded Hồ's statement, followed by a brief interview, the National Guard band's rendition of the national anthem, and loud cheers of "Long live Hồ Chí Minh!"[84]

Transmitting news items, speeches, declarations, and decrees from Hanoi was one matter, receiving signals locally was another. Circumstantial evidence suggests the existence of two thousand to three thousand radio receivers in Vietnam in September 1945, mostly held by activists who had taken them from private owners or been given them by Japanese personnel (who earlier had confiscated them from French and Vietnamese owners). Most of these sets were of the plug-in electric type, although the search was soon on for wet-cell batteries as backup, or to enable the receiver to be used in the countryside. Generators to charge batteries were highly prized. The extreme scarcity of spare vacuum tubes meant that some sets "died" each month, and indeed this may have been the main reason why local activists gave up radios to administrative committees or National Guard units. Upland provinces sometimes lost telegraph contact, so radio receivers at least enabled committees to be in one-way touch. The Tuyên Quang province committee, 120 kilometers northwest of Hanoi, possessed several receivers and could even boast a portable transmitter, perhaps obtained from the OSS Deer Team in August.[85] Thái Nguyên province, fifty-five kilometers north of the capital, had only one radio receiver and one loudspeaker in October.[86] Ninh Bình, on the southern fringe of the Red River delta, reported one radio receiver belonging to the province committee, adding that districts and villages had to depend entirely on leaflets and roving cadres for information.[87] In late March 1946, the central government instructed local administrative committees to register all radio receivers in their jurisdiction. Trường Chinh complained about a paucity of radio receivers within the ICP.[88]

Every newspaper office seemed to possess at least one radio receiver, in the first instance to copy down the latest international news bulletins. When trying to follow developments in Indonesia, for example, several papers monitored Radio Moscow and the BBC for purposes of comparison. Newspaper editors beyond

Hanoi used news and commentary from Voice of Vietnam extensively. In Huế, *Quyết Thắng* depended on the Voice of Vietnam to provide authorized interpretations of the delicate negotiations between Việt Minh, Nationalist Party, and Revolutionary League representatives in late December. Later a journalist described two hundred people crowding around a single receiver to listen eagerly at scheduled times, "all reacting together, their hearts beating as one." Each radio broadcast constituted a valuable "political class."[89] In Quảng Ngãi, Morse operators copied down Hanoi transmissions and gave them to the two local papers. Newspapers everywhere informed readers of changes by the Voice of Vietnam to its radio frequencies or transmission times. As of February 1946, it was broadcasting in French, English, Esperanto, and Lao as well as Vietnamese.[90]

DRV leaders wanted desperately to find ways to broadcast the government's message to citizens in far-away Nam Bộ. For many months the only reliable means was Morse code transmission, faithfully copied down by operators in the Mekong delta. In March 1946, the French Sûreté noted that not only were Radio Bạch Mai signals reaching Cochinchina, but the news content was reaching the population, and this helped to account for a "resurgence of terrorism" in the region.[91] Soon Hanoi's Radio Bạch Mai featured a Voice of Nam Bộ program each Saturday, which French military intelligence judged to be having "a great influence on the southern population." A proposal to jam the Bạch Mai signal circulated within French offices, but this does not seem to have been attempted.[92]

A stronger southern signal appeared in June 1946, each time opening its broadcast dramatically with, "This is the Voice of Nam Bộ, a voice of suffering, a voice of resentment . . ." These words were followed by the popular marching song, "Call to Youth" *("Tiếng gọi thanh niên"),* by Lưu Hữu Phước. In reality the radio signal was emanating from Quảng Ngãi, and it would take another year before regular voice broadcasts could be organized from within the Mekong delta. A veteran southern ICP activist, Nguyễn Văn Nguyễn, was put in charge of the Quảng Ngãi station, under the authority of General Nguyễn Sơn. Soon a number of southern journalists, musicians, and female vocalists were contributing to the daily programming.[93] The signal reached north as well as south, with one Hanoi newspaper praising the way the Voice of Nam Bộ was able to keep capital listeners informed on "the continuing fight against the reactionary French."[94] On 25 August, first anniversary of the Saigon insurrection, the Voice of Vietnam in Hanoi and the Voice of Nam Bộ in Quảng Ngãi coordinated a day of special programs, including Dr. Phạm Ngọc Thạch and Trần Văn Giàu talking on the 24.26 meter frequency.[95]

The DRV diplomatic delegation that left for France on 31 May did not carry its own radio transmitter, probably expecting to utilize the international cable system. However, High Commissioner d'Argenlieu blocked Vietnamese encrypted cable traffic in either direction, and the French security services disrupted some open messages as well. This compelled the DRV government, press, and radio in Hanoi to rely almost entirely on foreign news agencies (Reuters, United Press, AFP) for information on the negotiations in France. Hồ Chí Minh tried to use his Paris press conferences to inform the Vietnamese public as well as French and international audiences, but of course foreign editors determined the content of dispatches received in Vietnam. For almost four months the Vietnamese public heard no spoken words from their president, and read very few verbatim statements. Then, on 25 September, Voice of Việt Nam listeners were stunned to hear a one-hour recorded talk that President Hồ had given to overseas Vietnamese in Paris, complete with much clapping and cheering from the audience. At the end Hồ called out, and the audience repeated loudly: "Fatherland above all!" "Nation-People above all!" "Unite tightly, respect discipline!" Phạm Văn Đồng then read to the Paris audience letters received from Acting President Huỳnh Thúc Kháng and Military Commissioner Võ Nguyên Giáp. Delegation member Dương Bạch Mai insisted that "Nam Bộ must return to the Fatherland!" and the meeting concluded with a round of patriotic marches and songs.[96] This broadcast was a godsend for the regime at home, given public anxiety surrounding the 14 September modus vivendi.

Radio technicians were the unsung heroes of the expanding network of transmitters and receivers in Vietnam. Very few had formal training. An exception was Trần Văn Có, born in Vĩnh Long in the Mekong delta and beneficiary of courses in electricity and mechanics prior to 1945. Following the outbreak of fighting in late September, Có labored to set up low-output radio communications between several groups in the delta, then was ordered to take one transmitter up the coast to Phan Rang. Có then volunteered to take a transmitter to Ban Me Thuột; when it failed he had to go to Huế to submit a written explanation. Volunteering again to take a transmitter to Nam Bộ, Trần Văn Có was fatally wounded on 11 January 1946.[97] More representative was Nguyễn Văn Hay, who grew up in a Mỹ Tho village devoid of electricity or radios and became fascinated by the large French naval transmitter near his school. He taught himself Morse code, devoured electricity and radio manuals while enrolled at Pétrus Ký College in Saigon, and soldered together his own version of a Schnell receiver just before the August 1945 insurrection.[98]

MEETINGS, DEMONSTRATIONS, AND STRIKES

While perhaps one in ten Vietnamese could read a newspaper in late 1945, and fewer had access to a radio, almost everyone participated in public meetings and demonstrations—on multiple occasions. The model for such mass performances dated back to the Popular Front period (1936–38), complete with temporary speaker's platform, orations, slogans, banners, and a vocally responsive crowd.

Depending on circumstances, the crowd might then march down the street to impress other people and present a list of demands or aspirations to someone in authority. During the summer of 1945, weapons were added to this scenario, possibly a pistol or two displayed by organizers, most often a mélange of swords, machetes, and bamboo spears wielded by a newly formed militia group. Party flags also proliferated, something the French had prohibited earlier. Access to a loudspeaker equipped with microphone and fifty-watt amplifier made a lot of difference. Elsewhere there were megaphones. Big meetings took place in cities and provincial towns, but in August it was the meetings at the village level that brought an important new dimension to politics in Vietnam. Almost invariably young men, not village elders, took the lead in organizing such meetings. Public oratory was still new in the countryside, with young teachers, secondary school pupils, or former political prisoners showing the way. Some people went to meetings filled with eagerness and anticipation, others out of simple curiosity, still others for fear of what neighbors would say if they stayed at home. Once at a meeting, amidst the florid rhetoric, hand clapping, flag waving, and loud repetition of patriotic slogans, many of the curious and fearful found themselves swept up by the exuberance. New friendships were forged, new prospects presented themselves.

Further meetings invariably followed. In Huế, for example, about four thousand Fighting Militia gathered at the sports field on 7 October to swear allegiance to the DRV. Armed almost entirely with spears and machetes, and said to include 1,460 women, the group received from Việt Minh representatives a flag, a sword, and two pistols.[99] While mass meetings persisted, there was also a proliferation of smaller meetings differentiated by age, gender, occupation, education, residence, or personal preference. The groups which took shape owed as much to traditional Vietnamese experience at local organizing as they did to more recent concerns for bylaws, dues, formal reports, minutes, and elections. Nonetheless, self-consciously modern explanations soon appeared in the press about how to organize and conduct different kinds of meetings. When putting together a discussion group, for example, there should be no more than seven or eight participants, a specific topic should be tabled, and towards the end of the meeting the leader should point out strengths and weaknesses, then summarize results.[100] At the larger end of the meeting spectrum, a conference (hội nghị) needed to possess a steering committee, agenda, flag ceremony, election of chairperson, formal reports, resolutions, deliberations, voting, and summary of achievements. Provincial papers published lists of public meetings accomplished.

Not surprisingly, people began to complain about the sheer number of meetings they were expected to attend. Fledgling political officers in the army were criticized for didacticism and long-windedness, so that "calling meetings has become a calamity." The men got bored, and then the political officer became bored as well.[101] When it came to conferences, some people criticized the lack of a prior agenda, or chided chairpersons who failed to maintain order, move the meeting along, and summarize issues prior to voting. Others argued that meetings were too structured, too predictable, and thus too often a waste of time.[102] A Haiphong commentator blasted organizers of mass meetings for not starting on time, for using loudspeakers that only reached a small fraction of the crowd, and for allowing too much posturing by speakers, "as if they were in a movie." Half the audience often departed well before the meeting was declared over.[103] Critiques like this persisted in the press, yet "meeting-itis" became an ever more entrenched characteristic of the Vietnamese revolution.

The provisional DRV government in September 1945 had required anyone wishing to organize a public meeting or conduct a demonstration to obtain a permit twenty-four hours in advance. At some point it even ruled that public speakers must first submit their texts to the censor.[104] In practice, organizers often ignored these regulations, or obtained verbal assent from local administrative committees. However, police officers cited government edicts when warning Nationalist Party or Revolutionary League leaders against conducting a public meeting or demonstration. Opposition leaders pointed to unhindered Việt Minh manifestations, then went ahead with their own plans, including armed guards and prior notification to the Chinese military police. This opposition formula worked in Hanoi and Haiphong, although some citizens stayed away for fear of being harassed by Việt Minh adherents on the fringes of the meeting. Once Chinese units withdrew, however, Nationalist Party orators seldom ventured beyond the loudspeakers in front of their headquarters, where there might now be more Công An agents in the vicinity than members of the public.

One particular type of mass action occasioned considerable debate in Vietnam in 1945–46: the general strike. Vietnamese intellectuals were familiar with earlier European arguments over the capacity of the general strike to achieve political objectives or not. In Saigon in mid-September 1945, as described earlier, the Nam Bộ Administrative Committee declared a general strike, to which the British commander reacted by ordering martial law and seizure of Việt Minh positions downtown, triggering hostilities. For some analysts in faraway Hanoi, the Saigon general strike had foolishly provoked armed conflict at a time when Vietnamese forces were still divided and poorly prepared. This issue was not raised publicly until mid-February 1946, when the Nationalist Party and others called for a general strike to condemn growing French aggression. President Hồ Chí Minh reacted to these calls by insisting that a general strike should only be employed against the enemy, not to divide Vietnamese. He urged everyone to keep working unless told to do otherwise by the government.[105] The principal Việt Minh paper, Cứu Quốc, went further in a feature editorial bluntly titled, "General Strike Encourages Invasion Efforts." The editorial made earlier Saigon

FIGURE 28. A Việt Minh youth group sings patriotic songs to warm up a Hanoi mass meeting at the Cité Universitaire, 14 March 1946. Copyright Imperial War Museums (SE 7016).

FIGURE 29. The female section of a 14 March 1946 mass meeting. The signs say, "Oppose the French colonialist policy of deceit," and "Ready to follow the orders of President Hồ." The solemn faces may reflect awareness that the French Army is coming soon. Copyright Imperial War Museums (SE 7019).

events the principal argument against a general strike in the north, asserting that British troops "had not showed themselves to oppose us," but that when the general strike broke out, "they used it to attack." This charitable interpretation of General Gracey's frame of mind would not appear again in Việt Minh publications. *Cứu Quốc* labeled as "suicidal" any current resort to a general strike.[106] Since French troops had yet to arrive in Haiphong or Hanoi, the only visible target of such a strike would have been French civilians, which might well have jeopardized the secret Hồ-Sainteny negotiations. No strike action materialized.

Only five weeks later, however, a general strike did occur in Hanoi in response to a French military detachment occupying the Finance Ministry building and hauling down the DRV flag. It is unclear why the French Army took this action on 27 March, but it put Hồ Chí Minh in a difficult position, as he had met Admiral d'Argenlieu in Hạ Long Bay only three days earlier. Presumably with Hồ's approval, the Hanoi Việt Minh committee called for general "noncooperation" *(bất hợp tác)* on 29 March, to include closure of government offices, schools, markets, restaurants, and shops. The direct impact on French personnel was minimal, although Vietnamese employed by the French allegedly stood outside their work sites by way of protest, and there were no rickshaws for hire.[107] While the Nationalist Party idea of a general strike in February had been roundly denounced, the Việt Minh sponsored general strike in late March was lauded, even though the Vietnamese public was far more inconvenienced than the French. At best, people felt a momentary sense of solidarity when observing their city come to a halt.

French seizure of the former governor general's palace in Hanoi immediately following the departure of General Lu Han for China on 25 June provoked widespread Vietnamese outrage, and compelled the DRV government and Việt Minh to take counteraction. Again the political weapon of choice was the general strike, designed to protest a range of French violations of the 6 March Accord, of which the palace occupation was the most recent. On the morning of 27 June, streets were empty, shops and markets were closed, and government employees, teachers, and pupils stayed home. Apparently no public meetings or demonstrations took place, probably for fear of crowds getting out of hand, destroying property, and assaulting French nationals. Although some people wanted to continue denying food and other commodities to the French until they relinquished the governor general's palace and ceased their aggression elsewhere, *Cứu Quốc* editors insisted the one-day strike had already made its point. "Now it is time to await the attitude of the French," the editorial concluded lamely.[108]

No general strike was called in Hanoi from July through September, probably because key government ministers doubted the efficacy of shutting down the capital repeatedly. In Haiphong, however, the simmering Franco-Vietnamese dispute over collection of customs duties kept the city on edge, and there were repeated calls for the government to take a more resolute stand. On 9 October,

French soldiers forced their way into several Công An stations, detaining police officers and seizing documents. On 13 October, the Liên Việt branch in Haiphong called a general strike for the next day. According to newspaper reports, from sunrise to noon on 14 October, factories, workshops, markets and stores closed down, traffic disappeared from the streets, the port was silent, and people stayed clear of French bases. Most Indian shops and "some Chinese shops" closed as well. Government offices stayed open, and there was no move to shut down water or electricity, probably on instructions from higher authority in Hanoi. No "unfortunate incidents" materialized.[109] The general strike as a mobilizing device had lost its cachet. It never proved itself as a means to alter French behavior for the better.

French observers were more impressed by participation of ordinary Vietnamese in well organized demonstrations, each complete with cadres, whistles, banners, flags, slogans yelled in unison, and firm march discipline. Jean Julien Fonde in October 1946 watched mass manifestations to protest illiteracy, to receive refugees from the south, and to greet the return of Vietnamese "combatants" from the *métropole*. In Hanoi each morning, Fonde was awoken by a siren calling people in all quarters of the city to engage in physical education and paramilitary drills.[110]

SIGHTS AND SOUNDS

Political imagery, dramatic performances, and music energized Vietnamese during late 1945 and 1946 alongside the print media, radio broadcasts, and meetings. Most compelling of all was the red flag with yellow star, which spread throughout the country in August and September 1945 and came to symbolize the nation for all but a small minority. The Nationalist Party tried to make flag selection a major issue, arguing logically that a banner belonging to a particular self-interested political party (the Việt Minh) ought not be chosen to represent everyone. The provisional DRV government had already decreed otherwise in early September, although not until November 1946 did the National Assembly make the selection legal. Meanwhile, thousands of public meetings had opened with a solemn flag-raising ceremony. At the top, provisional President Hồ Chí Minh and Supreme Advisor Vĩnh Thụy (Bảo Đại) could be seen standing side-by-side as young men or women hoisted the flag or presented the colors. Catholic groups took the flag as national standard from the beginning, despite its Việt Minh origins. *Đa Minh*, the Dominican Catholic periodical, repeatedly featured the flag and flag-raising ceremonies on its cover.

Already in September the government published drawings of the flag that provided precise measurements and a proper shape for the star. The extreme scarcity of cloth posed a challenge for organizations wanting to display a flag, while ordinary citizens had to limit themselves to paper renditions.[111] The government banned DRV flags on civilian autos, presumably so they would not be mistaken for official vehicles.[112] Việt Minh vehicles often ignored the ban, however. The first widespread display of flags by homeowners and shopkeepers came in the leadup to national election day, 6 January 1946. Five months later, military personnel were being given three pages of instructions on how properly to "love and respect the flag."[113] There was popular anger when French troops allegedly seized six flags belonging to people exiting a 2 September 1946 Independence Day commemoration in Bắc Ninh town, just northeast of the capital. *Cứu Quốc* editors labeled this a stupid act, and asked, "Do the French expect us to fear them or despise them?"[114] The Interior Ministry in October instructed citizens not to fly the national flag on ordinary days, only during public holidays and at public ceremonies, a ruling widely ignored.[115] People with no liking for the government still might display the flag as precaution. Many others came to see the red banner with yellow star as a new vital symbol of the Vietnamese people-nation (*dân tộc*). Soldiers in combat sought to protect the flag from capture or dishonor. Yet the flag did not seem to acquire mystical powers. I have found no prayers to the flag, or reliance on it to protect individuals from harm. Nor did the state establish a pledge of allegiance to the flag, as in the United States.

On 10 December 1946, as tensions with the French escalated dangerously, Hồ Chí Minh still found time to compose and dispatch instructions on how properly to salute the flag or national anthem. He had observed three different salutes at public occasions. Henceforth civilians should take off their hats, place both arms alongside, and stand at attention. The raised right arm with clenched fist might be used at demonstrations or in greeting, but was not official. And the right hand salute to the forehead was to be limited to the military. Not to rectify existing confusion meant that foreigners would continue to laugh, Hồ commented.[116]

Material scarcities made it difficult to employ other visual imagery on a large scale. People who prepared banners to hoist across city streets had to write their slogans in water-based paint or use paper cutout letters, so that the valuable cloth background could be reused many times. Efforts to reproduce graphic posters were constrained by low-quality paper, color ink shortages, and the paucity of suitable printing presses. Photo paper was much too expensive to permit organizing regular exhibits of pictures. One professional cameraman, Nguyễn Bá Khoản, created a sensation with his Hanoi exhibition of photos taken during an eventful trip to the south in late 1945. Four days after opening on 18 March, the exhibit mysteriously closed, perhaps due to French complaints about the content.[117] Somewhat later in central Vietnam, an exhibition of photographs, military artifacts, and documents circulated through four towns, attracting large audiences.[118]

Editors of newspapers around the country would have leapt at the chance to publish current photographs, as during the late colonial era, but they lacked the technical means. Only *Thời mới* (Hanoi) possessed this capacity in late 1945, showing it off each week with full front-cover illustrations.[119] After *Thời mới* ceased publication at the end of December, its photo equipment may have been taken over by *Cứu Quốc,* the principal Việt Minh daily. *Cứu Quốc*'s special Tết issue at the end of January featured six pages of photos of President Hồ, the 6 January national elections, successful Việt Minh candidates, and a group picture of the newspaper's staff. However, no further photos appeared in *Cứu Quốc* until May Day, when two images of the mass meeting in Hanoi failed to reproduce properly. By contrast, a small photo of a woman wanted by the police for abducting a four-year-old boy turned out clearly. In late May, *Cứu Quốc* attempted without success to reproduce a photomontage of Paris newspapers which the National Assembly delegation had just carried home.[120] By August the quality of photos in *Cứu Quốc* was improving, although they were still employed sparingly.

Lacking photographs, newspaper editors turned to woodblock prints or pen cartoons to communicate visually. The broad lines produced by woodblock carving withstood even the worst quality newsprint, and the decisive linear cuts fitted the revolutionary mood of the time. In late 1945, *Tương Lai* weekly featured an arresting woodcut on each cover, for example a muscular, axe-wielding Vietnamese peasant threatening a cowering French soldier, a Vietnamese soldier ambushing goateed Frenchmen wearing nineteenth-century uniforms, or a huge hand pouring out a bottle of monopoly alcohol that had reduced Vietnamese (in the background) to abject poverty.[121] By far the most common woodcut motif depicted Vietnamese soldiers lunging forward to battle. For their Lunar New Year (Tết) special editions, however, editors chose colorful woodcuts suggesting peace. Most affirmative was the *Đa Minh* front page portraying the sun rising behind a Catholic church, verdant hills (with rare green ink), spring peach blossoms, and two doves.[122] *Chiến Sĩ* (Huế) presented a Vietnamese soldier and a French soldier, each with fixed bayonet rifles in one hand, but with their free hands placing red flowers on a tree between them.[123] *Quyết Thắng* (Huế) pictured Vietnamese dancing joyfully around an Independence tree, while a tearful French soldier looked on from behind.[124] As 1946 proceeded, the woodcuts became more somber, and images of soldiers were joined by resolute-looking workers, peasants, women, and students.

Cartoons had gained a solid hold in Vietnamese newspapers from the 1930s, with artists and editors employing the medium to considerable critical and satirical effect. Cartoonists developed visual stereotypes to represent the French official, the Vietnamese mandarin, the village headman, the Westernized young woman, the exploited peasant, and many more.[125] This creative opportunity was drastically reduced by censors during the Pacific War, although following the 9 March 1945 Japanese coup it became possible to mock the French colonialists as never before. The French continued as principal object of cartoonist derision

FIGURE 30. A French soldier offers money for information. Vietnamese reply: "Don't know," "Haven't seen them," and "Haven't heard." The slogan: "To Keep Secrets Is to Kill the Enemy." SHD 10H 2369(1). Tous droits réservés.

following the August insurrection. The archetypical French Army officer was unshaven, long-nosed, fat, wore an ill-fitting uniform with epaulettes, and sported big riding boots. Cartoonists generally portrayed French women as long-nosed, overweight, wearing chintz dresses that exposed their legs, and carrying a pinched expression. By contrast, the stereotypical Vietnamese woman was young, slim, demure, and wearing a stylish long tunic (*áo dài*). Cartoonists had yet to agree on the stereotypical Vietnamese man, sometimes giving him the traditional black tunic and turban, sometimes a Western suit and tie. The national independence struggle pushed domestic social satire to the periphery, leaving cartoonists much less room to exercise their talents. Taking aim at the French in cartoon form seldom attracted the censor's scissors, however. Thus *Cứu Quốc* summarized the lack of progress in Franco-Vietnamese negotiations with a feature cartoon that placed an image of the 6 March 1946 Accord on one side of a line, and French tanks running over fleeing Vietnamese civilians on the other.[126]

Professional artists found it difficult to position themselves creatively in Vietnam following the August 1945 insurrection. Most had been trained at the Ecole des beaux-arts d'Indochine in Hanoi, favored European Impressionist or classical Chinese styles, and made their living prior to 1945 doing paintings for wealthy Vietnamese or French patrons.[127] A lively group of art students who earlier had been transferred to Sơn Tây to avoid U.S. air attacks returned in late August to Hanoi, where Việt Minh friends put them to work making traditional woodblock prints on patriotic themes.[128] Several painters were invited to display at a "Culture Week" exhibition organized by the National Salvation Cultural Association in Hanoi in early October.[129] Painters in oil found it increasingly difficult to obtain their colors, while painters on silk could no longer find quality cloth. Meanwhile, Việt Minh writers chided artists for not taking up patriotic themes or failing to immerse themselves in the life of the masses.[130] Artists did make themselves available at Hanoi's Temple of Literature (Văn Miếu) to teach almost eight hundred children how to draw.[131] They also drew propaganda leaflets and sketched caricatures of prominent individuals for the press. Nonetheless, a reporter who interviewed artists at a Nam Định cultural festival found them hesitant, still reliant on prerevolutionary themes, and divided over the meaning of "propaganda" *(tuyên truyền)*.[132] No one had anything good to say about current Vietnamese sculptors. One critic mused, "Perhaps when a new [capital] city is constructed, with public buildings needing commemorative statues, we will be compelled to rely on foreign sculptors?"[133] When one artist commented that putting together a first-year commemorative exhibition might be premature, as independence could not yet be celebrated, he was roundly condemned for making light of what had already been accomplished. More to the point, "Artists should be in the middle of the struggle to make victory, to sacrifice, not just enjoy the fruits later."[134]

A substantial August 1946 fine arts exhibition did go ahead in Hanoi, displaying the work of seventy-four painters and sculptors out of a total of eighty-three applicants. Ordinary people apparently came by the thousands, curious to view what previously had been the preserve of the rich or educated. They praised some creations and criticized others, leading one Việt Minh observer to theorize that the masses and artists were "no longer distant from each other like the sun and the moon."[135] However, when a furor erupted over the display of nudes in the exhibition, this same observer mounted a vehement defense of their inclusion, arguing that "drawing the nude is fundamental to fine art education (painting, sculpture) in all countries." Then he took readers on a quick tour of nudes from ancient Greece and Rome to Rodin in France and Kitagawa Utamaro in Japan (ignoring their absence in the Muslim world or China).[136] Other writers insisted that the techniques and styles of the August exhibition were outmoded, and most of the subject matter irrelevant to present concerns.[137] Tô Ngọc Vân, teacher at the Ecole des beaux-arts prior to the August insurrection, took the lead among painters in trying to make art speak to the masses.[138]

Western drama had attracted attention among urban Vietnamese since the 1900s, and a Vietnamese adaptation of Molière's *Le malade imaginaire* was staged in 1920. In the 1930s, the theater proved well suited to exploring issues of individuality, the family, love, marriage, and morality.[139] In 1945–46, however, dramatists were expected to subsume these topics to the political imperative of fostering patriotic sacrifice and national solidarity. The Vietnam Nationalist Party weekly serialized a play in three acts by Khái Hưng, titled *Unity*.[140] Then Khái Hưng tested the censors with a short play in which a badly injured National Guardsman and a Nationalist Party soldier converse through the night and come to understand each other, only to have the former die of his wounds and the latter be killed by advancing guardsmen.[141] *Tiên Phong*, fortnightly publication of the Việt Minh's National Salvation Cultural Association, printed plays by several young writers.[142] Đặng Thái Mai translated from Chinese and published a play set just prior to the outbreak of the Sino-Japanese War in 1937.[143] During 1946, at least six plays were also published in monograph form.[144] Unfortunately we don't know how many of these published dramas were actually performed. Nguyễn Huy Tưởng's play *Bắc Sơn*, evoking the September 1940 uprising one hundred kilometers north of Hanoi, was staged by Việt Minh groups at a number of venues.[145] In November 1945, a play titled *Raising High the Victory Flag* was performed in Hanoi, climaxing with a scene in which Vietnamese carried the national standard forward against the enemy. When they were cut down, others picked up the flag, until finally it was planted firmly on top of a pile of corpses.[146]

Military units being organized around the country provided a new venue for dramatic performances. Soon theatrical groups were formed within the army, sparked by young intellectuals but recruiting actors from a variety of backgrounds. In December 1945, a new "National Guard Drama Section" was booked to perform at four venues in Huế, with Việt Minh groups selling tickets to the public.[147] The Haiphong Opera House was reserved in August to entertain soldiers with a program that included two plays as well as singers and musicians.[148] Aspiring dramatists and directors within the army were advised on how to choose suitable actors, position lights, and stage the action. They were also urged to provide the vital element of make-believe, not to aim for "total realism."[149] Nonetheless, dramatists had a long way to go from pleasing homesick soldiers to achieving artistic standards set by themselves or literary critics.

Although Vietnam had long indigenous traditions of court and folk music, in 1945 it was Western-style marches that captured people's ears and induced them to memorize and sing the accompanying patriotic lyrics. Musical notation already had been taught in colonial secondary schools, with sheet music readily available in bookshops. Some periodical editors allocated one page in each issue to a song score. Youths who could afford a guitar, mandolin, or harmonica were valued members of singing groups in schools, offices, and organizations like the Boy Scouts and Catholic Youth. The move to marches escalated in 1943–44, especially at the University of Indochina (Hanoi), with student troubadours then taking tunes from one town to the next.[150] In the summer of 1945, the prolific composer, writer, and artist Văn Cao brought the score of "Advancing Army" *("Tiến Quân ca")* to Đỗ Hữu Ích and convinced him to write the lyrics. "Advancing Army" was first sung in public at the 17 August meeting of the General Association of Government Employees in front of the Hanoi Opera House.[151]

In following days and weeks, "Advancing Army" was sung by young choral groups at scores of flag-raising ceremonies around northern and central Vietnam. The former Civil Guard band played "Advancing Army" at the opening of government functions in the capital, while smaller Catholic church bands readily took up this responsibility in Haiphong, Nam Định, and Huế. Already in September, "Advancing Army" was being dubbed the national anthem. Other marching songs too were used at formal occasions, notably "Wipe Out the Fascists" *("Diệt Phát xít")* by Nguyễn Đình Thi, and "Call to Youth" *("Tiếng Gọi Thanh Niên")* by Lưu Hữu Phước.[152] A Japanese observer, Komatsu Kiyoshi, marveled at hearing songs in Hanoi from early morning until late at night. "It seemed as if everybody, old and young alike, kept singing and singing like people intoxicated or suffering from fever," he recalled.[153] In March 1946, Đỗ Nhuận composed a march for the DRV National Guard.[154] Văn Cao even produced a march in honor of the DRV Air Force, which he hoped would be founded soon.[155] "Advancing Army" was employed at the opening of the first National Assembly session in March, and ratified as the national anthem in the DRV constitution approved in early November.[156] Meanwhile, other budding composers tried their hands at patriotic songwriting, with results distributed as sheet music or in periodicals from Hanoi to Quảng Ngãi.

Some composers came to feel that marches were swamping everything else of musical value. In August 1946, Lưu Hữu Phước published an essay extolling musical diversity that encompassed East and West, ancient and modern. He offered readers an eight-part typology of present musical currents, not attempting to define Vietnamese music, simply urging that it not become "rootless" like Filipino music, or "excessively narrow" like Chinese and Japanese music. A few months later, however, Phước shifted position again, praising the role of "struggle music" in the Vietnamese revolution, criticizing divisions among musicians, warning of the seductive influence of American music, and even alleging that reactionaries were buying up scarce instruments—and aiming to buy musicians as well. Given the imminent danger facing Vietnam, musicians had to work together. If not, "Vietnamese music will collapse and Vietnamese musicians will be buried under a pile of bricks and timbers, or be swept away like dry leaves in a whirlwind." To offset this apocalyptic vision, Phước promised another essay about organizing a "Vietnam Music Front," but war intervened.[157]

Far down the coast, in Quảng Ngãi, General Nguyễn Sơn sponsored a musical evening for both soldiers and civilians, with the emphasis on militant optimism. Sơn himself delivered a homily on music and culture, emphasizing the indomitable Vietnamese spirit, yet criticizing composers who went in search of grandiose themes, thus missing the individual heroes whose stories could symbolize something much bigger. Sơn then divided contemporary music into three categories: evocations of insurrectionary glory; petit bourgeois compositions that were half joyous, half sad; and "soft," cowardly works by miserable souls who refused to come alive again with the people-nation.[158] Such remarks certainly put musicians on notice that political and military leaders were watching their every move. As General Sơn had spent more than a decade in revolutionary China, his condemnations of sorrowful "blue" and licentious "yellow" music foreshadowed campaigns that would sweep the DRV later.

LITERACY CAMPAIGNS

Starting in the early twentieth century, educated Vietnamese believed that popular literacy was vital for any country wanting to take the road to modernity. With the colonial education system enrolling less than 10 percent of school-age children, the search was on for ways to teach basic *quốc ngữ* reading and writing skills informally. Illiteracy came to be equated with ignorance *(dốt)* and even stupidity. The struggle to achieve national literacy became a major plank in the Việt Minh program. Hồ Chí Minh's 1945 call to vanquish famine, ignorance, and foreign aggression became his most widely known summary of DRV objectives. As we have seen from his first encounter with the Education Ministry, Hồ wanted the state to assign top priority to mass literacy, yet this was unlikely for an organization composed mostly of former colonial functionaries and senior pedagogues. A separate mass literacy directorate under presidential control would have better met Hồ's unorthodox objectives.[159] The ministry's new Mass Education Bureau had only enough funds to organize ten-day teacher training courses for a total of 291 persons between October 1945 and June 1946.[160] Short of enthusiastic personnel and money, the Education Ministry eventually tried to devolve most of its mass education responsibilities to regional offices, which were expected to "generate the literacy movement, train instructors, provide resource materials (books, leaflets, banners, pictures, songsheets, reporting forms), and inspect classes."[161]

The early September 1945 decree mandating compulsory literacy had nonchalantly made province and commune committees accountable for costs. This clearly did not happen, although many local committees were quick to locate classroom space and encourage citizens to sign up. Unpaid inspectors received a modest six piastres per diem from the ministry when making their rounds.[162] In February 1946, the Interior Ministry ordered regional, province, district, and village committees to take responsibility for opening *quốc ngữ* classes and, together with mass education officials, to achieve the compulsory literacy target set by President Hồ Chí Minh for September. Mass education had to be a regular agenda item at committee meetings, members on tour had to check local literacy efforts, and propaganda sections needed to give literacy higher priority. Villages that possessed communal land *(công điền, công thổ)* were told to set aside some of the income for teaching materials.[163]

In April, citing the Interior Ministry's February order, the director of mass education dispatched a blunt reminder to the Northern Committee to allocate more funds to local committees to fight illiteracy. Eventually the Northern Committee replied simply that it lacked the money. It then lamely told province committees to urge each village to cover the cost of pens, paper, blackboards, and chalk for literacy classes.[164] The Finance Ministry allocated 48,400$BIC per annum to each province to form a mass education management board, yet earmarked nothing for local instruction costs. At this point the Mass Education Bureau warned that if everyone expected the literacy movement to rely solely on volunteers and good intentions, then "the entire effort will collapse, with no way to rescue it."[165] The Interior Ministry weighed in once again in June, telling each commune to allocate at least one thousand piastres from its annual budget for compulsory *quốc ngữ* study. If a commune lacked this amount it would have to levy a small tax on trees, ponds, or community associations *(giáp)*, with the understanding that the tax would be discontinued once all citizens in the commune were literate.[166] Everyone believed in mass education, but no government echelon was willing to give the effort much money. The Mass Education Bureau did locate sufficient funds to publish thirty-four booklets, with a total print quantity of 2.5 million copies. Besides a beginner's alphabet, there were civics primers, patriotic history tales, and basic introductions to science and hygiene.[167]

Finding and retaining instructors was vital to mass education success. A few instructors were indeed public servants transferred to province committee jurisdiction. Some public servants placed on extended leave without pay offered themselves as literacy instructors; they remained technically under government discipline. However, the vast majority of instructors were volunteers and hence could not be ordered around. Vũ Đình Hoè, the education minister, seems to have appreciated this in October 1945 when he warned regional committees not to treat literacy instructors like public servants, subject to standard bureaucratic rewards and punishments. Yet Hoè's only positive suggestion was to put local teams of instructors in direct contact with the Mass Education Bureau in Hanoi.[168] Some individuals volunteered as literacy instructors because they wished to stay clear of overtly political organizations. Others joined in hopes this voluntary service would ameliorate suspicions of neighbors or local committees as to their past colonial affiliations or privileged family backgrounds. The press encouraged readers to step forward as literacy instructors, and meetings of volunteers were organized to give them public recognition and practical advice. In Nam Định by early November, 180 men and women had signed up to be literacy instructors. In Thừa Thiên province six months later, 1,200 literacy instructors convened to share their experiences.[169]

Literacy instructors were not always treated warmly by local authorities, especially if the latter were expected to provide food and shelter. Instructors coming from outside the village also were vulnerable to accusations of improper behavior, disregard of local customs, or even trying to impart dangerous ideas in the classroom. Encouraging young women to study risked the ire of male village leaders. Trương Thị Tặng, native of Công Vụ commune (Hưng Yên), set up several literacy classes at the request of local illiterate women, only to incur the wrath of the commune committee chairman, who is said to have marched in to demand their closure, cursed Mme Tặng, and even hit her with a chair. With her students having fled and afraid to return, Tặng dispatched formal complaints to the province administrative committee and province Việt Minh committee. The dispute went all the way to the central government's Special Inspectorate, with the district chairman eventually negotiating a settlement, and Tặng apparently resuming her classes.[170]

In June and July 1946 there was a surge in high-level attention to mass education, as Hanoi realized the one-year deadline to accomplish nationwide literacy was not far away. Exhortations from the education ministry to administrative committees and mass education offices increased dramatically. Province-level Việt Minh committees stepped up propaganda efforts. A huge census effort began, aimed at collecting the name of every individual who had attended literacy classes, their age category, and the date they had "escaped the calamity of illiteracy" *(thoát nạn mù chữ)*. Statistics on the number of participants and cost of instruction were to be consolidated from commune to central government level during the last two weeks of August, accompanied by public meetings to announce the results and celebrate with torchlight demonstrations, songs, and dramatic performances. Every participant expected to complete class by early September would be deemed literate.[171] At the end of August, the Mass Education Bureau also compiled the numbers of instructors and classes, together with province population figures, to produce impressive charts for northern and central Vietnam.

The chart for northern Vietnam has survived, calculated as of 1 July 1946, wherein 598,766 persons are said to have been taught by 37,358 instructors in 28,231 classes.[172] The highest number of attendees were recorded in Kiến An (83,064), Phú Thọ (52,160), Hải Dương (51,212), and Thái Bình (45,443) provinces, whereas the lowest numbers were from Yên Bái (2,434), Haiphong (3,499) and Phúc Yên (3,835). Statisticians even tried to compare attendees against number of illiterates in each province, declaring that Kiến An had the highest percentage of participants (23 percent) and Quảng Yên the lowest (4 percent). They did not bother to divide total attendees into total illiterate citizens in Bắc Bộ, probably because the figure (14.2 percent) was so far below ambitions stated ten months prior. Only one province (Ninh Bình) seems to have reported how many primary literacy certificates had been issued, which amounted in their case to 5,000 out of 28,281 participants (17.7 percent).[173] If we extrapolate Ninh Bình's certificate percentage to Bắc Bộ at large, then perhaps 106,000 literacy attendees had reached primary proficiency by July 1946. However, this was not the sort of number that higher-level officials wished to communicate. In October, Nguyễn Xiển, chairman of the Northern Region Administrative Committee, told the DRV government that in one year 1,079,688 northerners had been taught by 35,520 instructors in 30,940 classes.[174] The number of attendees reported by Xiển represented a 45 percent increase in less than four months if set beside the 1 July figure cited above; and somehow the cumulative number of instructors had decreased. The Central Region Committee declared that 1,274,550 of its inhabitants had escaped illiteracy between September 1945 and September 1946, with Hà Tĩnh province scoring the highest increase in literacy, from 11 percent to 52 percent.[175] It appears that no literacy statistics arrived from Nam Bộ. In early September, however, the Mass Education Bureau reported that nationwide 2,520,678 persons had been taught in 74,957 classes by 95,665 instructors.[176] This sort of pseudo-scientific precision with big numbers became common in the DRV, sometimes making it impossible for decisionmakers to distinguish wish from reality.

During late August and early September 1946, the current education minister, Ca Văn Thỉnh, toured the provinces of northern and central Vietnam, focusing particularly on literacy efforts. Although he showed more interest in actual reading and writing proficiency than numbers of people sitting in literacy classes, his solutions remained relentlessly bureaucratic—urging the government to train more inspectors, hire clerks, and take over French buildings in the provinces for classrooms and office space. Thỉnh added that such superstructure would enhance the prestige of the Mass Education Bureau and subordinate offices, which remained poor cousins within the state apparatus.[177] In July, the Finance Ministry had finally agreed to allocate 1,000,000$BIC to "supplement" the Trung Bộ budget for mass education, only to reduce this to 672,000$ in October. Bắc Bộ's supplement in October amounted to 1,328,000$.[178] Very little of this money is likely to have reached provincial or district levels before the outbreak of war in December.

Professional educators like Ca Văn Thỉnh failed to appreciate Hồ Chí Minh's utopian vision when it came to mass literacy. In the preface to a 1945 literacy primer, obviously not to be read by beginning pupils, President Hồ Chí Minh sounded the trumpet:

> People who cannot yet read and write must put all their effort into it. If the wife can't read, then the husband should instruct her. If the younger brother can't read, then the elder brother must help. If parents can't read then it is up to the children to teach them. Employers must instruct employees, and the rich must open classes in their homes to teach their unlettered neighbors. Landlords, plantation and mine supervisors, and factory managers must open classes for their tenants and workers. Women especially need to study, since they have been held back so long. Now is the time for you sisters to work to catch up with the men, to demonstrate that you are part of the nation, with the right to elect and be elected. In this entire endeavor I hope that the youth of both sexes will show particular energy and enthusiasm.[179]

In this world portrayed by Hồ, senior or more privileged individuals had an obligation to teach junior or less privileged persons how to read and write. If they could not or would not, then traditional social status was to be cast aside in the interest of citizen equality and national betterment. What Hồ wanted was a mass campaign, with the alphabet and pithy phrases or snatches of poetry expressing basic political points, not another state hierarchy attempting to manage tens of thousands of volunteer instructors.

Some members of Vietnam's modernist intelligentsia took up President Hồ's challenge with enthusiasm. With techniques surpassing Madison Avenue, they promoted a "word forest" that illiterates could not ignore. Slogans proliferated on walls and rock faces, quốc ngữ words appeared on the mud-encrusted flanks of water buffalo, Việt Minh youths tested each individual seeking to enter a market. Everyone was bombarded with messages like "Studying is patriotic," "Eliminate the Ignorance bandit," and "Don't leave any family member illiterate." Songs and drawings supplemented the written word. The image spread of newly independent, barefoot peasants walking to evening class, tiny oil lamp in one hand, battered primer in the other.[180] Classes were held in village communal houses, pagodas, private residences, shops, and offices. Việt Minh writers conveyed the image of three generations of the family sitting side by side, laboriously scratching out the lesson on slate boards or recycled paper. Newspapers carried illustrations of children teaching their parents, and wives teaching husbands. For those who could not or would not attend evening sessions, there were ad hoc classes in the marketplace, in the rice fields, at midday break, and aboard fishing boats or junks. Military units ordered illiterate soldiers to attend classes regularly, and indeed it was most often within the armed forces that instruction persisted long enough for participants to advance to reading newspapers, manuals, and political directives. Already in 1946 there were proposals to organize a primary school curriculum specifically for soldiers, which became reality several years later.[181]

The mass education campaign contained strong elements of psychological pressure and public shaming. This began with the declaration in early September 1945 that all Vietnamese above eight years of age must be able to read and write within one year or they would be fined.[182] The threat to fine illiterates was not repeated as government policy, but individuals unable to read a slogan did find themselves penalized. In June 1946, the Sơn La province committee informed Hanoi that henceforth it intended to tax all illiterates two piastres per month, and from January 1947 it would compel them to wear a "dunce sign" *(thẻ dốt)* as well. "Only that way will people put up with going to study," the committee concluded. The Northern Committee replied that such a tax was beyond the authority of province committees, then urged Sơn La to use more flexible tactics, for example having people read a couple of words before they could pass through a gate, or make them take part in a ten- to fifteen-minute lesson while waiting at a ferry crossing.[183] The Haiphong Administrative Committee, in a communiqué titled "Stupid Persons at the Sắt Marketplace," announced that from 1 July 1946 anyone still unable to read *quốc ngữ* would not be allowed on the market premises.[184] Trương Thị Tặng, whom we encountered earlier complaining about interference by the commune chairman, also revealed that village women had first come to her for literacy instruction because they were prevented from entering the marketplace.

Some local committees went further, for example refusing to allocate communal land to families with illiterate members, or preventing people from signing documents they could not read aloud. Perhaps the most humiliating village practice was to set up a "gate for the blind," through which all illiterates had to pass while children mobilized for the occasion jeered them. Widely circulated poems challenged the old to catch up with the young, wives to surpass husbands, the betrothed to insist that prospective mates learn how to read and write. Worried about the trend towards shaming, the Mass Education Bureau tried to set a limit of five minutes on detaining illiterates for involuntary instruction in public. It also wanted to rule out stopping of soldiers or halting wedding and funeral processions.[185]

Neither the Education Ministry's established pedagogical approach, nor activist techniques of immersion and compulsion came close to achieving the goal of full literacy. A generous estimate would suggest that 20 percent of illiterates in Bắc Bộ and Trung Bộ went to class at some time between September 1945 and December 1946. Others undoubtedly studied at home. Perhaps an additional three hundred thousand citizens could read a newspaper article or leaflet as a result of the mass education campaign. Meanwhile, others were alienated by the petty harassments, or discouraged by how little they had achieved in a class lasting only a short time. None of this would have worried those Việt Minh leaders who gave precedence to mobilizing millions to assimilate the political message embedded in basic lessons and the feeling of taking part in a national effort. The outbreak of full-scale war in December disrupted the literacy campaign for several years, but it also gave time for both the Mass Education Bureau and Việt Minh cadres to reassess and revise their approach without abandoning ultimate objectives. The prime slogan became "We must be literate to emerge victorious in the Resistance."[186]

THE NEW LIFE CAMPAIGN

The new intelligentsia that emerged in Vietnam during the 1920s and 1930s often deliberated how to remake popular attitudes and behavior. Drawing inspiration from sources as diverse as the Confucian *Daxue (Great Learning)*, turn-of-the-century Chinese writers like Liang Qichao, news films of Mussolini's Italy, and left-wing French accounts of life in the Soviet Union, young Vietnamese intellectuals imagined a time when they would convince ordinary peasants of the need for self-improvement, public sensibility, and national discipline. They admired the massive social engineering programs run by communists, fascists, and state capitalists alike. Wanting to be part of this global push to modernity, Vietnamese intellectuals condemned French colonial reactionaries for blocking the way. They also targeted "backward," "uncivilized," or "feudal" characteristics among the populace that impeded progress.[187]

From his mountain hideout during the Pacific War, Hồ Chí Minh promoted a mix of Confucian and modernist values to be assimilated by ICP members and then taught to followers. Within the liberated zone formed north of Hanoi in the summer of 1945, Việt Minh activists warned people to cease gambling, opium smoking, extravagant communal banquets, "superstitious" behavior, and other social evils. During the August insurrection, groups around the country sometimes beat up or fined individuals considered guilty of such vices. The provisional DRV government moved in September to dampen local witch hunts in favor of administrative action, education, and peer pressure.

The Propaganda Ministry under Trần Huy Liệu took responsibility for devising a comprehensive program of social transformation dubbed the New Life Campaign (Vận động Đời sống Mới). The first focused move came in mid-January 1946, when the ministry issued an intricate directive to alter the forms and content of Tết Nguyên Đán (Lunar New Year), the most important annual event in the Vietnamese cultural calendar.[188] This was to be no ordinary New Year, but rather "Independence Tết," celebrated as such by the entire nation and people. Colorful woodblock prints that traditionally featured pigs, ducks, and fish as fertility symbols would instead promote opposition to foreign invaders, famine, and illiteracy. Writers of parallel sentences would discard Confucian homilies in favor of extolling independence, the DRV, and the "spirit of sacrifice and fighting resolve of the entire united citizenry." Parallel sentences would no longer be written in classical Chinese, but instead vertical *quốc ngữ*, which produced some amusing artistic curiosities. The ancient New Year's bamboo pole *(cây nêu)* was to be converted into a DRV flagpole in front of each home. "Superstitious effigies" daubed with lime on building walls were to be replaced by images of the five-pointed star, or drawings of rifles "to ward off the French colonialists."

One week before the New Year, on the day traditionally devoted by families to seeing off the kitchen god *(ông Táo)* amidst flowers, incense and glutinous rice, the Propaganda Ministry told everyone instead to attend public meetings to report accomplishments and to engage in self-criticism. For New Year's Eve, when heads of family beseeched the ancestors in front of a food-laden altar, the ministry instructed citizens to speak entirely in Vietnamese and to announce 1946 as the Second Year of the DRV. When visiting or being visited by relatives and friends in the first days of the New Year, one first had to "wish for the country to be completely independent within this year," and only then offer personal salutations. Use of fireworks was to be minimized, leaving more gunpowder to employ against the enemy.

In unspoken competition to the traditional family orientation of Tết rituals, the Propaganda Ministry called on every city, town, and village to organize mass meetings for the first day of the New Year. Hanoi would take the lead with a gathering at the Opera House, to open at nine in the morning with gongs, drums, and sirens. The ministry promised that these Hanoi proceedings would be broadcast over Voice of Vietnam radio, and urged other cities and towns to connect receivers to loudspeakers so that a wider audience could participate. In villages, everyone should convene in front of a radio receiver, or if that was unavailable then a member of the administrative committee should read to the assemblage President Hồ Chí Minh's New Year's greetings, followed by the independence oath—facing southward to remember combatants—and the shouting of prescribed slogans. People were encouraged to bring Tết gifts to these meetings for distribution to the poor. The ministry urged civilian groups to organize concerts, songfests, plays, and other public amusements during the Tết holidays. Soldiers were the object of special attention, with the ministry calling on groups to bring them Tết gifts, organize amusements, and arrange dinners or invitations to private homes. It was also important to visit families of deceased combatants and wounded soldiers in hospitals.

It is doubtful that many families who read these ambitious propaganda ministry instructions about Tết chose to follow them in any detail. Tết family practices open to public view may have been discontinued by some, for example the wall effigies, the classical Chinese parallel sentences, or the New Year's pole. However, observances inside the house probably remained as before. The ministry did not denounce the eating and drinking vital to Tết family gatherings. Nor did it challenge cockfighting and other traditional gambling opportunities at Tết, merely taking a vague swipe at "immoral and depraved amusements." Meanwhile, the ministry's grandiose attempt at cultural engineering was undercut by Hồ Chí Minh's pre-Tết message, which simply encouraged everyone to share their spring happiness with combatants at the front, families of soldiers, and poorer countrymen.[189] Originators of the Tết directive may have received confidential criticism. A revised text omitted many imperative statements, leaving a much reduced Tết reform agenda. Hồ Chí Minh, Nguyễn Hải Thần, and other provisional unity government members did attend a Tết observance at the Hanoi Opera House, but it contained no hint of propaganda ministry instructions, and could not be hooked up by radio to other gatherings around the country.[190] Nevertheless, the blueprint to redesign Tết remained alive within the ICP–Việt Minh. It would be invoked forcibly with more success in later years.

After Tết was over, a Việt Minh Central Commission to Campaign for the New Life was announced, headed by Trần Huy Liệu, soon to lose his position as propaganda minister.[191] In late April, the commission met to assess opinion, then released a list of eleven personal and twelve group aspirations. *Tiên Phong* devoted an entire issue to New Life issues.[192] In late July the campaign began in earnest, starting with publication of an astonishingly detailed list of 130 slogans approved by the commission.[193] Most slogans were short and pithy, so that they could be displayed on walls, banners, and posters. The list was divided into "Individual Life" and "Common Life," then subdivided meticulously. Individual life maxims dealt with food, clothing, shelter, work, embellishment *(trang súc)*, recreation, consumption, and personal virtues. Under the food category, for example, citizens were told to "Eat fresh products," "Drink boiled water," and "Fill in ponds and dig wells." Then they were warned that "To drink liquor and smoke opium is to commit suicide." Under the category of work, eight mottos emphasized the value of cooperation, planning, persistence, and no shirking. Common life was classified into politics, economy, society, and culture. Political slogans stressed democratizing the state structure, understanding one's responsibilities and rights, and being ready to serve the country according to one's capabilities. One slogan dealing with etiquette *(xã giao)* was subdivided into eight negatives plus one anodyne affirmative, "Be honest and harmonious."

The New Life project dissected "culture" in most detail, with categories for language, the arts, weddings, funerals, votive paper, offerings, mediumship, celebrations, and festivals. On the matter of language, there were slogans about overcoming illiteracy, abandoning classical Chinese, unifying spoken Vietnamese, and promoting a writing style that was "simpler, clearer and easier to understand." Concerning marriage, people ought not look towards money, rank, status, or connections when evaluating possible partners, yet Việt Minh arbiters offered no positive alternative to readers for securing a mate. Funerals were castigated as too elaborate and enveloped with superstition. Ten traditional funeral practices had to be abandoned, starting with astrological determination of the time of burial, and ending with the fifty-day and one-hundred-day feasts following death. Burning of votive paper was to be eliminated. Lunar New Year practices were revisited, shortening the number of days of celebration and urging that children no longer be given envelopes containing money.

Three weeks later, an even longer slate of 241 New Life slogans was published in the *Tiên Phong*.[194] In a brief preface, Ngô Quang Châu stated that he was writing on behalf of a "research board," presumably the same body within Trần Huy Liệu's New Life Central Commission that had produced the earlier list. Châu addressed eight public spaces: train and bus stations, marketplaces, streets, hospitals, schools, government offices, religious temples or pagodas, and latrines (*cầu quán*). At stations, customers were instructed to line up to purchase tickets, not to spit on the floor or throw garbage, not to grab someone else's seat, always to give way to the elderly or infirm, and to assist those with infants. At the market, all commodities should be weighed or measured properly, excessive prices avoided, insulting language banned, and all thieves, beggars, or lepers eliminated. The authentic New Life marketplace must possess a toilet, garbage collection point, pharmacy, information kiosk, people's reading room, and adult education classes. On the street, citizens had to obey the police, who were "friends of the people, not mercenaries with a whip and abusive language." To defecate or urinate in public was "selfish and despicable." When entering government bureaus, citizens should not be fearful or refer to officials as "great-grandfather" (*cụ*) and to themselves as "child" (*con*) or "grandchild" (*cháu*).[195] "Government employees are there to help people, not behave like feudal mandarins," one motto expounded. Bribes must not be offered or received. Other epigrams instructed public servants to be punctual, concise, self-disciplined, patriotic, physically fit, well informed, a member of an organization ("youth, sports, study, etc."), and not use public property for private purposes. As for public latrines, citizens were urged to help maintain them and participate in digging new ones.

Six social aggregations or occasions required New Life attention according to Ngô Quang Châu: villages, cities, enterprises, funerals, weddings, and death-date observances (*ngày giỗ*). A legitimate New Life village had to possess at least one water well, a garbage dump, a club with books and radio receiver, an information office, adult education classes, a pharmacy, a medic and midwife (shared with another village), a cooperative, a drama group, and organizations for children, women, and youth. Funerals must not include sorcerers, amulets, votive paper, hiring of mourners, big banquets, or other ostentatious behavior. Weddings must not involve forced betrothals, numerology, bride price, the red thread ritual (*lễ tơ hồng*), or newlyweds kowtowing to parents and elders. The wedding ceremony had to be kept simple, and the marriage registered with civil authorities. Death-dates must not provide an excuse for drinking, gluttony, gambling, or opium smoking, but instead be simple, dignified commemorations.

Ngô Quang Châu's final and longest set of slogans set down attributes for nineteen categories of person *(hạng người)*. First, however, he admonished everyone to desist with superstitious practices, not to spit, toss garbage, defecate in the wrong places, curse, or insult others. One should keep clean, exercise, speak politely, obey rules, be on time, stand in line, join an organization, seek knowledge, have a recreation, and believe in the democratic system of government. Citizens were then told to be literate, to know the DRV constitution, vote in elections, salute the flag, obey the law, denounce those who did wrong *(làm bậy)*, and enlist in the armed forces. Rural folk should give up wasteful banquets and alcohol so as to be able to feed their family and to purchase a radio, books, and newspapers. They must not be afraid of authority, or resign themselves to being treated badly. Women must become literate, read newspapers and hygiene manuals, learn a self-supporting trade, join an organization, be confident but not impudent, and avoid fortune-tellers. Mothers should not take the side of children when fathers were instructing or punishing them. A wife ought not find a concubine for her spouse; should oppose his smoking opium, gambling, or visiting prostitutes; and should reject being cursed or beaten by him. Masters should attend to the needs of their servants *(đầy tớ)*, make them learn how to read and write, and not permit their own children to strike or use demeaning language towards the servants. Young women should wear simple modern clothing, read newspapers daily, join an organization, and learn how to swim, ride a bicycle, shoot a rifle, and practice first aid. They must not wear a lot of jewelry, become romantic *(lãng mạn)* or dissolute, be too timid, or neglect care of the home. Workers should know that they are making a productive contribution to society, improve their skills, and be willing to put in extra time to help build the nation. They must not allow themselves to be exploited, but also should honor their job and the property of others. Monks and nuns, as part of the nation, were required to take part in social tasks and to fulfill their obligations as citizens. Votive paper burning and fortune-telling represented superstitions not in keeping with Buddhist teachings.

Clearly Việt Minh compilers of these two long lists of New Life slogans aimed to cover just about every realm of the human condition, in keeping with their ambition of transforming the Vietnamese person, family, local community, society, and nation. Nonetheless, certain elements of life were left out. There were no slogans dealing explicitly with sexual relations, merely denunciations of men who frequented prostitutes, and a caution to husbands not to treat their wives as "baby machines." Sex would remain a taboo topic in Việt Minh and DRV propaganda for decades, reflecting both Confucian tradition and revolutionary puritanism. No slogans addressed the social categories of "landlord," "entrepreneur," or "businessperson," probably because differences persisted within the ICP about how to characterize relations with these short-term "friends" but long-term enemies. State laws and the judicial system were barely mentioned. Most notably, there was not a single slogan dealing with ethnic minorities. Minority relations were understood within the ICP to be an important issue, yet public Việt Minh and DRV policy on minorities remained confused (see below). The New Life campaign was addressed solely to the Kinh (ethnic Vietnamese) of Bắc Bộ, ignoring divergent cultural practices among the Kinh of Trung Bộ or Nam Bộ. New Life omissions in 1946 were almost as revealing as the content itself.

Cứu Quốc, the Việt Minh's banner daily, promoted the New Life campaign assiduously, dropping its weekly feature page on workers and peasants in favor of a New Life page that carried upbeat reports from cadres at province, district, and commune levels. "The masses (đại chúng) must change both spiritually and materially to be able to fit the new circumstances created by the August Revolution," a Cứu Quốc editorial intoned.[196] In August 1946, Cứu Quốc published an elaborate diagram of the prospective New Life organizational system, complete with committees at each administrative level, committees for different social groups (youth, children, women, workers, public servants, intellectuals), and associations to tackle specific social or cultural issues.[197] These issue groups were to operate outside the hierarchies and report directly to the central committee. Five issue associations were listed, to oppose alcohol, to oppose opium, to eliminate superstition, to eliminate outmoded customs (hủ tục), and to disseminate hygiene practices. Several empty circles conveyed the central committee's readiness to form additional issue-based associations. Nothing better evokes the hegemonic intentions of ICP leaders than this diagram. Yet the idea of a separate New Life apparatus encompassing the nation was destined to go nowhere. Most other newspapers gave scant attention to the New Life campaign or ignored it entirely.

Việt Minh efforts in 1946 to transform social mores did have some impact nonetheless. When youth teams noticed someone publicly urinating, spitting, or tossing trash they often stepped forward to chastise the person involved. The incidence of such antisocial behavior dropped off dramatically. Families inclined to organize a lavish wedding or funeral cut back their plans after being approached by neighborhood activists. Young women eschewed jewelry, cosmetics, and colorful dresses. Persons in authority learned not to employ a variety of quasi-familial pronouns now denounced as demeaning. Everyone dealing with public money or public grain became fastidious about accounting, down to the last piastre, đồng, or kilogram. It is impossible to know how many people changed internal attitudes, as distinct from those who changed behavior because they worried about being publicly shamed, or worse. Although only a handful of practices were labeled "feudal" (phong kiến), and no negative practice was indicted as "reactionary" (phản động), Việt Minh adherents did apply these terms verbally, with chilling implications for the person being rebuked. The New Life campaign would be revived in the 1950s with many of the same slogans and much more rigorous enforcement.

HEALTH CHALLENGES

The DRV government appreciated the need to tackle epidemics, upgrade the colonial-era medical system, and educate the public on health issues. Given financial stringencies, however, there was no hope soon of the state addressing the ambitious modernizing agenda that Vietnamese health professionals had in mind. Highest priority was assigned to building an army medical corps. Next the Ministry of Health increased vaccine production and inoculation efforts. It also worked to sustain the modest colonial public hospital system and to train more nurses, but had to leave local health clinics to the province administrative committees. Many district and village Việt Minh groups took up the challenge of convincing citizens to improve public hygiene and sanitation.

In October 1945, an outbreak of cholera in the Red River delta severely tested the existing public health system. The Pasteur Institute in Hanoi was commandeered by the new government to produce cholera vaccine, with staff quickly expanding output from twenty to one hundred liters per day. Public health officers from the provinces most affected came to pick up stocks of vaccine in glass ampoules, then supervised free inoculation of at least 160,000 people in a matter of weeks. Incomplete figures from the provinces record 4,375 persons stricken with cholera in Bắc Bộ and 2,864 persons dying before the epidemic faded in late November.[198] Simultaneous arrival of lice-laden Chinese troops was blamed for a smaller outbreak of typhus, and eruption of recurrent fever *(bệnh sốt định kỳ)* several months later. Vaccines and medicines sometimes had to be hidden against the surprise arrival of Chinese Army officers demanding supplies.[199]

When another cholera epidemic threatened the north in March 1946, newspapers were ready with scientific explanations of the disease and instructions to boil drinking water and dispose of garbage properly. Venues were listed where cholera inoculations could be obtained. One paper featured a six-part cartoon labeled "Dead or Alive?" portraying the dire consequences of drinking unboiled water.[200] People seemed to think that independence gave them license to dump garbage anywhere, thus threatening everyone with cholera, one writer complained. "Don't let the French say that their absence causes the natives to live in filth," he concluded.[201] An outbreak of bubonic plague in several central provinces evoked descriptions of the fearful symptoms.[202] A booklet published in April to alert families and traditional healers to deadly epidemics in their midst was titled *Protecting the Race.* One disease after another, the authors addressed incidence, transmission, symptoms, stages, treatments, and ways to avoid becoming ill in the first place.[203]

Anxious to rebuild the stock of smallpox vaccine in order to make possible a major vaccination campaign, health officials reported to government superiors that they could not obtain sufficient numbers of buffalo calves, essential to the production process at the Pasteur Institute. Enough vaccine was available in early 1946 to tell northern urban residents at least where they should go to be vaccinated for smallpox.[204] In newspaper articles, Vietnamese physicians informed readers how modern medicine had developed inoculations against a host of diseases, and urged government authorities to give preference to infants, children, and soldiers. They neglected to mention that most of these shots currently were unavailable.[205] The Pasteur Institute did produce typhoid and rabies injections. A medical student described how two hundred hospital staff members had recently been immunized successfully against typhoid, only to witness nonimmunized friends and several well-known sportsmen die of the disease. People bitten by a dog, cat, or wild animal generally remained unaware of antirabies injections, or chose to heed a traditional healer (ông Lang) who claimed to be able to ward off rabies.[206]

The DRV Ministry of Health and regional health bureaus were supposed to be responsible for public hospitals, provincial clinics, training of staff, control of scarce medicines, and formulation of a long-term health policy, yet resource limits put many of these tasks in jeopardy. The Northern Region Health Bureau was allocated 4,232,346$BIC in the Bắc Bộ budget formulated for 1946, or 20 percent of total regional outlay. Of this amount, 46.1 percent was to go to salaries and supplements for health bureau staff and employees of several Haiphong hospitals. Running costs for the Haiphong hospitals (food, medicines, stationery, burial expenses, laundry, electricity, water) would take 7.1 percent, and provincial hospitals and clinics 40.1 percent.[207] Hanoi's three main hospitals, as well as the Pasteur Institute and the ophthalmology clinic, were regarded as a central government budget obligation, but during 1946 they were transferred to the northern region budget.[208] Đồn Thủy hospital had to accept a Chinese Army contingent on the premises, much to the anguish of its director and members of staff.[209] There were four classes of inpatient at Đồn Thủy, all paying in Chinese "gold dollars." Đồn Thủy offered a total of 107 medical procedures, carefully described in French, although items requiring radiography were in abeyance due to the unavailability of film. Prices ranged from ten Chinese gold dollars to extract a tooth without anaesthetic, to five hundred gold dollars for ten x-ray therapy sessions. In July, Đồn Thủy issued a new price list, now expressed in piastres, and with government employees charged half-rate. The procedures list now included single injections and dressing of wounds, but no further mention of blood transfusions.[210] All procedures were still listed in French, and indeed it would take some years of translation, dissemination, and persuasion before Western medicine was conducted in the Vietnamese language.

Down the central coast, hospitals took in large numbers of wounded and ill soldiers, which must have overwhelmed the Trung Bộ health budget. In Huế, civilians volunteered to wash laundry, catch lice, and bathe six hundred military patients, while barbers came to cut hair for free. Tailors donated five hundred sets of clothing. A worker's group put together individual gift packets of cigarettes, matches, candy, soap, and five piastres of pocket money.[211] A journalist visiting two hospitals in Quảng Ngãi was stunned by the large number of badly wounded soldiers and the debilitated malaria patients. Amidst spartan conditions, doctors and nurses were doing their best, he insisted.[212] Throughout the country, administrative committees tried to ensure that hospitals received periodic allocations of rice and meat to feed patients.[213] However, some hospitals suffered regularly from pilferage of blankets, sheets, mosquito nets, clothing, and even thermometers. The first admonition from the Health Ministry made hospital staff accountable for the losses, suggesting that employees were stealing supplies to supplement their meager salaries. Three more times the authorities sent out lists of compensations demanded for categories of items lost in hospitals, without indicating who the guilty parties were.[214] Such repetitive admonitions amounted to an admission of failure.

During the August 1945 insurrection, thousands of young women around the country had volunteered for nursing or first aid duties, although most lacked prior training. In Hanoi in September, Việt Minh activists and hospital staff organized a crash one-week first aid class for about seven hundred women, which was then followed by a three-month nursing course for two hundred women. Meanwhile, several hundred male nurses and orderlies were being transferred from civilian hospitals and clinics to the nascent armed forces. As of late November, fifty women had volunteered to replace the men in hospitals for no pay. Forty-three first aid stations had been set up in Hanoi, each with a female worker and a few medicines and bandages. In December, a second three-month course began to train more nurses, while another class taught midwives.[215] In mid-1946, however, remaining male nurses resisted being transferred to the National Guard or dispatched to rural districts to establish new dispensaries, citing their age, frail health, or family obligations. This left a number of recently trained female nurses with no paid employment.[216]

Medicines were a constant problem. During the Pacific War, Indochina had been cut off from metropolitan pharmaceuticals, while the Japanese made little effort to provide a substitute supply. Not surprisingly a black market in pharmaceuticals flourished, with insulin, quinine, emetine (for dysentery), and renal medicines going for especially high prices. Soon after the Japanese surrender,

American sulphanilamide and a French sulfamide with the brand name of Dagénan were added to the black-market roster.[217] Dagénan quickly gained a national reputation as all-purpose curative, with men taking it following sex with prostitutes, and middle-class mothers mixing a bit into condensed milk given to their infants. Physicians cautioned the public about misapplication, side effects, and the existence of counterfeit Dagénan.[218] The flood of fake pharmaceuticals marked "Made in the USA" led one Haiphong physician to protest that his city was in danger of being "poisoned, sick, and dead due to American medicines!"[219] Meanwhile, the DRV government reiterated colonial regulations for accreditation of pharmacies, proper labeling of dispensed medicines, and sale according to fixed prices, all to little effect.[220] Many newspapers carried advertisements from pharmacies that made dramatic claims for medicines like "Hepatod," "Diuretana," "Calyptol," "Vitamine B1," and "Gramacidine" (this last allegedly coming from Russia).

Word spread quickly starting in late 1945 about a new miracle medicine called penicillin. Probably first carried into Saigon and Hanoi by Allied medics, penicillin was heralded as a true wonder drug, much more powerful than dagénan. The inspirational story of Alexander Fleming and Howard Florey discovering, isolating, testing, and producing penicillin between 1929 and 1943, in time for use with Allied wounded in the D-Day landings of June 1944, reached Vietnamese by radio and newspaper. For modernizing intellectuals this epitomized the marvel of science in service to humanity. However, Vietnamese physicians soon warned the public that far more counterfeit penicillin was being sold than the real thing, and explained that manufacturing sufficient authentic penicillin for global civilian demand was still some time away.[221] After the French in Hanoi bragged that the *métropole* was producing lots of penicillin, a physician on the Vietnamese negotiating delegation in France discovered that French laboratories were still limited to extracting small amounts of penicillin from the urine of patients treated with the medicine.[222] Another physician urged the DRV government and people to cooperate in international efforts to produce and distribute penicillin, rather than falling back on old Chinese remedies.[223]

During 1946 the dispute between practitioners of Western medicine (*tây y*) and Eastern medicine (*đông y*), which had simmered throughout the 1920s and 1930s, resumed once again. As with prior French colonial authorities, the DRV government favored a system of Western medicines, physicians, surgeons, and nurses, while also being prepared to allow certain kinds of traditional healers to continue practicing subject to regulation. The Northern Region Health Bureau convened a meeting of traditional healers to form a national representative association, and foreshadowed a research council to investigate "Northern medicine" (*thuốc Bắc*) and "Southern medicine" (*thuốc Nam*). Simultaneously, local healers approached province administrative committees for approval to form their own associations and "institutes" *(viện)*.[224] In June 1946, the government approved a new "Vietnam Medical Group" (Việt Nam Y-đoàn) composed entirely of traditional practitioners. This provoked sharp criticism from some Western practitioners, who asked how the authorities were going to draw the line so as to rule out dispensers of snake oil and harmful superstitions. Patients continued to arrive at hospitals too late to be saved because they had gone first to a series of traditional practitioners.[225] However, other physicians pointed out that most villagers lived too distant from any existing hospital, even assuming they knew enough to make a choice for Western treatment. Since the state currently lacked the capacity to confront massive health deficiencies in the countryside, the populace would continue to call upon traditional healers. At best the authorities could urge traditional healers to uphold basic public health principles and to desist from certain harmful treatments.[226]

It remained feasible for the DRV authorities to promote health education, thus continuing the effort begun modestly by the French in colonial schools, the publication of health manuals and family guidebooks in the 1920s and 1930s, and the introduction of health columns in newspapers.[227] Many late 1945 newspapers recruited a Western-trained physician to write a health column, often employing a question-and-answer format. The most ambitious attempt at health education was the fortnightly *Vui Sống (Joy in Life)* newspaper, begun in June 1946 by Western-trained physicians deputized to the National Guard. They deliberately chose to stay clear of politics, diplomacy, or defense in favor of simple explanations of ailments, treatments, preventive health measures, correction of popular misconceptions, and longer-term policy proposals.[228] *Vui Sống* articles were didactic yet seldom patronizing. When discussing fevers, for example, the writer first presented the general belief that fever was caused by bad wind, and that it was not good to drink water when feverish. Then he explained that fever was not an illness but rather a symptom of bacterial infection, and since the fever caused dehydration it was a "major mistake" to desist from taking liquids. On using quinine to treat malaria (dubbed the "deadly ghost of the highlands"), another writer dismissed the popular belief that the drug caused miscarriages and deafness, but then cautioned that quinine was no panacea, and stressed that mosquito nets offered valuable protection.[229] Wives received advice in *Vui Sống* on how many months before and after childbirth they should deny sex to their husbands. A twenty-six-year-old woman who had already given birth to eight children wrote in to ask how she could avoid more. She was advised to use the rhythm method, although it was said to be only 80 percent effective. Men were given advice about wet dreams, premature ejaculation, impotence, and treatments for venereal disease.[230] No other newspaper discussed sex like this. Perhaps the censors deferred to *Vui Sống*'s Defense Ministry sponsorship. On two occasions writers dealt with anxiety and depressive disorders, although the only remedy offered was a facile exhortation: "Don't be defeated!"[231]

Vui Sống printed diagrams showing Vietnam's very high infant mortality rate compared with France and the United States. Although blaming eighty years of colonial rule for holding Vietnam back, the writer did admit that infant mortality had declined from at least four hundred infant deaths per one thousand births in 1925 to about two hundred per one thousand in 1937. To continue this downward trend it was essential to "address poverty, correct wrong attitudes and practices, and organize hygiene and sanitation to prevent diseases occurring." Another contributor described how the Metropolitan Life Insurance Company had distributed four hundred million books and newspapers on hygiene to its twenty-five million customers in the United States and Canada, which helped to reduce mortality by 32 percent between 1911 and 1925, and not incidentally enhanced profits for its owners.[232] Still another writer blithely asserted that 90 percent of deaths due to disease in Vietnam could be prevented by means of immunization and treatment with other Western medicines. Readers were urged to get their children immunized, not "see them die and then say it was fate *(số mệnh)*."[233] None of these authors explained, however, how the DRV in current strained circumstances could take up even a fraction of these policy proposals.

There were remarkable health achievements in 1946 and beyond, but they came mainly as the result of local Việt Minh groups assimilating some of the explanations about hygiene and sanitation, incorporating them into their verbal messages, and cajoling or harassing those individuals who failed to respond appropriately. Traditional six-eight poetic meter familiar to peasants was employed to explain orally the relationship between germs, poor hygiene, unboiled water, and endemic diseases. Poems and ditties targeted the common housefly, rats, lice, and mosquitoes. Women were urged not to wear their hair in a bun, to reduce the chance of lice infestation and hence the danger of typhus. Certain traditional birthing practices were declared harmful. Chewing betel was disparaged as unhygienic and costly. Little was said about parasites, perhaps because public health specialists judged eradication impossible in current socioeconomic circumstances.

When Việt Minh hygiene efforts succeeded it was because they were part of a wider mass mobilization strategy which enabled cadres to link health with patriotism, to employ peer pressure, and to come back again and again to try to ensure compliance. Military units proved most assiduous in boiling drinking water, burying feces, disposing of garbage, treating cuts, and utilizing available medical facilities. Political officers soon were encouraging soldiers to share their basic hygiene knowledge and enthusiasm with nearby civilians. The obstacles were substantial. Even at the Hanoi Opera House, the most important meeting place in the DRV, toilets were reported to be filthy, which *Vui Sống* ascribed to citizens failing to "know and observe their responsibilities."[234] In Haiphong, the city authorities declared 7 June 1946 as "Cleaning Day," aimed at both public and home spaces, but the results only scratched the surface. The following week, the French garrison commander at Haiphong volunteered use of fifteen of his trucks (with drivers and petrol) to collect large accumulations of garbage and then to continue periodic pickups. The Haiphong Administrative Committee accepted the offer, and warned citizens they would be fined twelve piastres if they put garbage out prematurely for collection. The Việt Minh newspaper headlined this story: "Common Hygiene Does Not Distinguish Vietnamese-Chinese-French."[235]

DIKE DEFENSE

From 17 August 1945, rising Red River flows ruptured dikes at 150 or more locations across the Tonkin delta, ruining about one-third of the rice crop meant to be harvested in November. To ward off a similar fate the following year, everyone knew that the dikes needed to be repaired, yet for months nothing was done. In January 1946, President Hồ Chí Minh pinpointed dike dangers in a speech at Nam Định town and secured pledges from local leaders for forty tons of paddy to feed dike workers.[236] Hồ well understood that one of the most ancient tests of political legitimacy in Vietnam was protection of the delta's dike system (*hộ đê*). In addition to dike obligations of ruler, officials, and subjects, the French colonial authorities had inserted a layer of hydraulic engineers and inspectors. They came to rely more on private contractors than province and district mandarins to implement work on the dikes. During the years 1927–33, an impressive twenty-nine million cubic meters of earth was shifted to reinforce Tonkin dikes.[237]

In early 1946, members of the former colonial public works bureau surveyed dike damage, calculated how much earth needed to be moved, how many work hours were required, how much food stockpiled, and what the overall cost was likely to be. Newspapers then published some of these details to support calls for cooperation between government experts and the people.[238] With trucks and fuel in very short supply, most of the earth moving would need to be accomplished by oxcart and carrying pole. A request by the Public Works Bureau to purchase civilian autos to carry inspectors around the delta was rejected by the Finance Ministry, which recommended borrowing bicycles instead.[239] February was taken up negotiating with private contractors and locating rice to feed dike workers, with the Northern Region Committee accepting half the food costs and the twelve involved province committees responsible for the other half.[240] Repair of the important Đáy River dam, twenty-eight kilometers northwest of Hanoi, was delayed first by the Finance Committee and two province committees failing to allocate funds, then by the contractor refusing to accept five-hundred-piastre notes declared void by High Commissioner d'Argenlieu.[241]

Starting in April 1946, the northern dikes finally received serious central government attention. President Hồ Chí Minh and Interior Minister Hùynh Thúc Kháng attended dike construction ceremonies in Hưng Yên and Thái Bình provinces. An interministerial meeting set food payment for workers at five piastres per day, estimated 656,100 work days to complete repairs, and hence labor costs totaling 3,280,500$BIC. Supplies (bamboo, hemp sacks, stones) and equipment (shovels, baskets, vehicles) were expected to cost at least two million piastres. The first meeting of a new Central Dike Protection Committee, chaired by Nguyễn Xiển, head of the Northern Region Committee, heard that some contractors already were operating on trust even though the Finance Ministry so far had allocated only 1.1 million piastres for dike repairs. Đỗ Xuân Dung, senior hydraulic engineer, described which dikes needed the most work. He was especially concerned about the breach at Hưng Nhân (Thái Bình), which would require excavating and reinforcing to a depth of 2.4 meters. With six newspaper editors present, Xiển emphasized that while the central government exercised overall management of dike protection, it was up to province and district committees to recruit laborers.[242] Subsequent meetings agreed upon a dike protection hierarchy, specified that protection posts manned by government employees would be spaced twenty kilometers apart, and approved badges for different ranks. Finally, in late May, President Hồ Chí Minh authorized conscription (trưng tập) of men and women eighteen to fifty-five years old for dike work, and specified rewards and punishments.[243] Not until early August, however, did the Finance Ministry release 4.5 million piastres for northern dike protection.[244]

During June 1946, 515 government employees were redeployed to northern dike protection posts or placed on alert.[245] Each cadre (cán bộ) was given a thirty-two-page booklet containing President Hồ's 22 May decree, a job description, a list of equipment, and six rising water scenarios that might be encountered.[246] It appears these cadres were not meant to engage with private contractors, but rather be in a position to mobilize thousands of additional laborers if and when danger was declared. Hải Dương province, with 187 kilometers of dikes to deal with, calculated that it needed only 13 dike cadres and 38 coolies (phu) in routine circumstances, but as many as 27 cadres, 85 coolie supervisors, and 3,293 coolies whenever the river rose to a threatening level.[247] As most dike posts had no telephone or telegraph connections, cadres were given drum, gong, or fire signals to employ.[248]

Reports circulated of farmers using dikes in ways that jeopardized structural integrity. There was evidence of rampant rodent infestation and water leakage under the dikes. Disturbing reports arrived in Hanoi of villagers making independent preparations to destroy dikes and dams in the event of military conflict.

Confidential messages circulated between the National Guard, Công An, and civil administration committees to try to make sure that such destruction occurred only on orders from the top.[249] In Hanoi, workers were located to fill in former Japanese antiaircraft gun emplacements along the dikes on the east side of the city.[250]

Where was the Việt Minh when it came to dike protection? The Việt Minh General Headquarters never spoke publicly on this topic so far as I can tell. Most Việt Minh newspapers ignored the dikes. Only *Cứu Quốc* eventually offered support, first by reprinting President Hồ's dike decree, then publishing a vigorous editorial headlined "Dike Protection! Dike Protection!" Tô Hoài, prominent member of the National Salvation Cultural Association, reminded readers of the disastrous floods only ten months prior, then pinpointed three weaknesses in current dike reconstruction: too few experienced dike workers involved, not enough food stockpiled, and poor operational coordination. In one village, Tô Hoài claimed, the committee chairman was arrested four times while supervising dike repairs. *Cứu Quốc* dallied another five weeks before publishing a plea to Việt Minh members to lend a hand at the dikes, thus "demonstrating how you can join with the people to take on destiny." The following day a "Việt Minh dike protection youth group" was cheered as it marched to the Hanoi dikes.[251] Meanwhile, Dương Đức Hiền, head of the DRV's Office of Youth and Sports, and founding member of the Democratic Party, was organizing "dike protection youth camps" from among government employees on leave without pay. Soon there were camps in twelve delta provinces, with a total complement of 1,008 dike workers.[252] Hiền, well-known non-ICP member of the Việt Minh, had not given up competing with the Communist Party for young activists.

As Red River water levels climbed ominously in early August 1946, the government issued a general alert, which engaged all reserve personnel. The most worrisome venue remained Hưng Nhân in Thái Bình province, where experts predicted the dike would break if water reached the 12-meter mark. On 5 August at Hanoi, a peak of 10.21 meters was recorded. The next day, Đào Văn Biểu, of the Northern Region Inspectorate, discovered that villagers were refusing to stand guard duty on some dikes, few coolies were working, and the youth camps were not proving very effective.[253] The Central Dike Protection Committee confirmed significant deficiencies in some places, while complimenting work elsewhere.[254] A second alert was declared when the river began rising again, reaching 10.12 meters on 17 August, then ebbing steadily. No serious dike breaches had occurred. Evaluating overall dike protection efforts for 1946, Nguyễn Xiển admitted that relations between the government and private contractors had "not been good"—hardly surprising when contractors had been pushed to perform with no idea when payment would arrive. Nonetheless, two million cubic meters of earth had been shifted and eight million hours of dike labor organized. Total expenses amounted to 11.8 million piastres, half paid by the government, half contributed by the people.[255]

Nguyễn Xiển does not explain how "the people" contributed 5.9 million piastres to dike protection, but it probably involved local administrative committees collecting rice or money, and many coolies being told to bring their own food to worksites. This was uncomfortably close to traditional corvée procedures, and may have been the main reason why most Việt Minh newspapers chose to say nothing about the whole dike repair effort. Some ICP leaders also probably disliked the government relying on private contractors to manage much of the work, particularly when contractors had served the French previously. The party would employ different methods when it took up dike challenges a decade later.

SOCIAL CATEGORIES

If the major chord of the Vietnamese revolution announced national unity and personal sacrifice, a minor chord intoned discreet social identifications and self-interest. The traditional Confucian delineation of scholars, farmers, workers, and merchants (sĩ-nông-công-thương) gave way to a vaguely Marxist class analysis plus acknowledgement that youth, women, and ethnic and religious groups each possessed their own legitimate interests. While the ICP had no monopoly on this construct, its decision in 1941 to foster a range of national salvation associations based on class, age, gender, ethnicity, religion, and occupation put it at the forefront of united front experimentation.

Given the vital role of young men in the August 1945 insurrection, the Youth National Salvation Association seemed the obvious vehicle for perpetuating their revolutionary contribution. However, most young men aspired to join the army. If that was not possible, they favored the militia or the police. The Youth Ministry also recruited personnel to organize sports programs and physical education classes. In March 1946, the Youth Ministry was abolished, probably because it overlapped with Việt Minh youth efforts. The Boy Scouts remained active in late 1945. Some scoutmasters led their scout troops directly into the National Guard, while others wilted under ICP accusations of being too bourgeois or sullied by affiliation with the French scouting movement. ICP maneuvers to subordinate the Hanoi University General Association of Students to the Youth National Salvation Association met opposition from many students.[256] At least five different youth organizations competed for members in Haiphong city until allegedly they agreed to join together under Youth National Salvation auspices in September 1946. That also was the time when Haiphong's Việt Minh committee finally opened a class to instruct young men and women how to run salvation groups.[257] During the late 1940s, two distinct Việt Minh youth group hierarchies continued to function in Bắc Bộ, despite ICP Standing Bureau admonitions that they unite.

Young women wishing to engage wholeheartedly in the revolution faced many more problems than young men. Often they remained under pressure from their families to stay at home, get married, and bear children. Those young women who did "emancipate" *(thoát ly)* themselves from home and village still faced a political culture dominated entirely by men. Although it was impossible for revolutionary males to oppose gender equality in principle, many felt that women were unsuited to leadership positions, that they created problems if put into predominantly male groups, and that they were best directed to nurturing roles.

In the summer of 1945, young women in Quảng Ngãi province had obtained weapons and demonstrated they knew how to use them. That example, together with stories of heroic female soldiers in the Soviet Union and China, was used to argue the case for admitting women to Vietnam's National Guard.[258] Opponents argued the negative consequences of male and female soldiers falling in love with each other. This was said to undermine unit morale and to raise ethical concerns among families and the general public.[259] A survey of one Quảng Ngãi regiment in August 1946 revealed that while sixteen women remained on unit rolls, all now worked in supply, cooking, nursing, or sewing. Several women had been killed while carrying food to units under enemy fire.[260] Trần Độ, a prominent National Guard political officer, admitted that women could be trained to engage in combat, but insisted that they were better suited as medics, hospital nurses, and supply personnel.[261] Young women did remain active in local militia groups, where they took part in drills, guard duty, tactical exercises, and rifle practice. Militia women had already fought in the south, and would do the same throughout the country in following years.

Women of all ages joined the Women's National Salvation Association in order to be able to convene away from men, share experiences, make a public contribution, and, they hoped, carve out some political space for themselves. Association members collected donations, cultivated secondary crops, organized literacy classes, enforced hygiene rules, and assisted families of absent soldiers. They admonished parents who refused to let daughters out of the house, husbands accused of beating their wives, and landlords who demanded sexual favors from tenant girls. Women's committees protested to the authorities when outside groups of young men on work assignments harassed local women and girls.[262] Chairs of women's committees routinely served on Việt Minh committees, interacted with chairwomen in adjacent villages, and took political courses at the district or province level. During 1946, there was a move to allocate communal land *(công điền)* to women as well as men. While women might regard this as an equal right, men only agreed if women made new contributions to public life.[263]

Women's National Salvation Association members in Hanoi and Haiphong came mainly from the urban middle class and intelligentsia. Leaders often were called upon to address Việt Minh audiences, attend government ceremonies, and greet foreign visitors. In November 1945, one thousand Haiphong women converged on the Opera House square to affirm membership in the Women's Association.[264] Most newspaper editors initiated a women's column, and some allocated one page each week or fortnight to women's issues. The press lauded Women's Association members dispatching hundreds of support letters to soldiers at the front, visiting soldiers in hospital, knitting sweaters for the National Guard, and making patriotic offerings at the Trần Hưng Đạo temple in Hanoi. Female writers called for equal rights for women, affirmative education opportunities, a minimum age for marriage, and a ban on prostitution. No one, however, pointed to the absence of any female minister or vice minister in the DRV cabinet or the fact that only eight of the 290 National Assembly delegates who convened in late October 1946 were women.[265] Two of the eighteen members of the National Assembly's Standing Committee were women.[266] Female representation in the higher reaches of the ICP was no better. Women who had committed themselves to the ambitious ICP platform on women publicized during the Popular Front period (1936–38) must have been particularly disappointed.[267] The ICP by late 1946 nonetheless claimed more than one million women in the Women's Association and other Việt Minh affiliates. The Association was renamed the Vietnam Women's Union (Hội Liên Hiệp Phụ Nữ Việt Nam) to suggest wider representation.[268]

Nonrural workers constituted only a small fraction of Vietnam's overall labor force, yet their skills, self-consciousness, and tenuous economic circumstances insured them a place in political affairs of the day. The Pacific War had disrupted many existing enterprises, forcing some workers back to their home villages, and others to eke out a living on part-pay and odd jobs. During the August 1945 insurrection, workers' committees materialized in some enterprises, either asserting control of operations outright or threatening to strike if employers failed to provide better pay and conditions. However, the provisional DRV government refused to recognize most worker takeovers and insisted that employers and employees negotiate wages, rice allowances, and terms of dismissal in good faith. As we have seen, the ICP secretary general, Trường Chinh, warned workers against seizing enterprises without government permission or mounting unauthorized strikes, yet Việt Minh propaganda continued to promise workers shorter working days, more amenable bosses, and lower rice prices. Meanwhile, the Northern Region Labor Inspectorate received scores of petitions each week from worker groups and individuals protesting employer nonpayment of wages, refusal to increase wages or allowances in response to inflation, unfair dismissals, and dismissals with no severance pay.[269] Conditions did not necessarily improve at enterprises controlled by workers' committees. At the AVIAT motor transport company, for example, the workers' committee discovered only three thousand piastres in the office safe, when sixty thousand piastres were needed to meet the monthly payroll for two hundred employees. The AVIAT committee urgently requested and received permission from the government to carry paying passengers and goods to and from Hanoi, Haiphong, and Thanh Hóa.[270]

Dozens of workers' protest demonstrations and strikes went ahead in September and October 1945. "Three piastres a day is not enough!" one Hanoi workers' group summarized.[271] Lê Văn Hiến, minister of labor, called a meeting of three hundred representatives of northern workers at the Hanoi Opera House to try to defuse the situation. President Hồ Chí Minh spoke first, counseling against divisiveness or making "too leftist" requests of the government when the country was in material difficulty. Capitalists and workers alike needed to put national interests above all else, he said. "Do not yet resort to class struggle, but focus instead on safeguarding the independence of the Fatherland," Hồ concluded.[272]

Meanwhile, Việt Minh activists proceeded to form Workers' National Salvation groups at the enterprise level. The new Public Servants National Salvation Association tried to convince members to concentrate on political rather than material concerns. Each member was requested to contribute one piastre per month to a strike fund, to be used only in the event of a general strike.[273] Although government employees no longer dared to call for salary hikes in public, they did continue to petition President Hồ by mail. Several bureau directors told their superiors bluntly that salaries had to increase. Within Vietnam Railways, Việt Minh and Vietnam Nationalist Party cadres competed vigorously for the loyalty of employees. In late June 1946, Workers' National Salvation cadres in Vietnam Railways criticized themselves for "classism," failing to recruit senior staff, and pushing papers rather than making decisions.[274] At the Nam Định textile mill, labor organizers made sure that each day began with a flag-raising and singing ceremony and ended with literacy classes in the evening. In front of the Haiphong Opera House, three thousand people took a pledge of membership in the Workers' National Salvation Association.[275] Nonetheless, many workers remained disappointed at the government's disinclination to stand up for a decent wage.

During 1946, workers found ways to survive and even improve their positions. Some attached themselves to local administrative committees, where they provided services in exchange for monthly rice allocations. Others gravitated to arms facilities being established in many localities. Traditional mutual help associations (hội tương tế) offered job leads and psychological support if not material assistance. In Haiphong, nineteen different occupational groups, from barbers to tanners, cement workers to stevedores, participated in a city competition to "raise production."[276] In Hanoi, a "General Confederation of Workers Cooperative" was established to transport commodities throughout northern and north-central Vietnam. The cooperative delivered rice to Hanoi workers, salt to Tuyên Quang province, and French MIC cigarettes (acquired in Đà Nẵng) to northern smokers.[277] In early December, Huế officials criticized the workers' cooperative for carrying one hundred tons of rice to workers around the central region without first gaining government permission.[278]

Việt Minh propaganda for and about workers focused ever more relentlessly on mass mobilization, not pay and allowances. The Đáp Cầu paper mill northeast of Hanoi was reported to have been transformed from "colonial hellhole to workers' paradise," with women singing "Long live Hồ Chí Minh" and old men learning the alphabet.[279] Strikes were only acceptable if they served political objectives vis-à-vis the French. Thus, there were repeated stoppages at French-controlled coal mines, a walkout by Haiphong power plant workers when French troops searched them and took down a DRV flag, and a strike at the Shell Oil facility in Haiphong after thirteen workers were said to be dismissed unjustly.[280] By contrast, a Việt Minh paper in Huế criticized strikes in the central region as parochial, uncoordinated, and poorly targeted.[281] The biggest strike by far began at the Nam Định textile mill on 13 November 1946, with three thousand workers walking out, allegedly because the mill director, M. Bayle, refused to share increasing company profits with them. Workers' National Salvation leaders predicted the strike could last for months. In subsequent weeks, workers and soldiers as far south as Quảng Ngãi reduced meal portions in order to donate money to feed striking Nam Định workers and their families. The Tổng Bộ Việt Minh sent a support delegation to Nam Định, "because the struggle has political as well as economic characteristics."[282] The Nam Định strike continued into December, but by then it had been overshadowed by the fighting in Haiphong and growing tensions in Hanoi.

Religious Groups

The DRV government had much less success mobilizing religious groups to implement its national agenda than the young men, women, or workers discussed above. Initial enthusiasm of Vietnamese Catholic clergy towards the DRV waned during 1946, although most remained firmly opposed to accepting French authority again. Reform Buddhist Hòa Hảo and Cao Đài organizations recognized DRV legitimacy, but their relations with the Southern Administrative Committee were tenuous at best. As French forces swept across the Mekong delta in late 1945, each southern organization had to fend for itself. Leaders professed commitment to an anticolonial united front, but operational coordination remained a chimera. In June 1946, several Cao Đài leaders joined the French-sponsored "Republic of Cochinchina." News of confrontations between religious and secular powers in the south was censored from newspapers north of the sixteenth parallel in order to protect the image of "Nam Bộ the Bronze Fortress of Resistance."

In central and northern Vietnam, members of the Buddhist sangha celebrated Vietnamese independence and generally supported the new government. However, during August and September 1945, youth groups damaged or defaced some temples, and some local revolutionary committees chose to set up shop inside temple premises. A 20 September DRV decree ordered all citizens not to violate any temple, royal tomb, or church, yet made no mention of punishment.[283] Hồ Chí Minh called often for religious tolerance, and assured Buddhist as well as Catholic faithful that his government would protect their right to worship. In accordance with Buddhist teachings, most monks refused to condone violence, above all between fellow Vietnamese, and expressed hope that war with France could be averted. However, when their fellow countrymen came under French attack, many younger monks wanted to share that suffering directly, not withdraw to pray or meditate.[284] The first Buddhist National Salvation Association in central Vietnam was announced at Huế's Từ Đàm pagoda in early October.[285] Another group met at the Quán Sứ pagoda in Hanoi to establish a national committee of the sangha dedicated to promoting Buddhist doctrine, serving the Fatherland, and coordinating disaster relief efforts. Despite repeated queries from its founders, the Interior Ministry delayed formal approval of this committee.[286]

Perhaps imitating Christian chaplains in Western armies, a few Buddhist clergy were admitted to the National Guard, with Việt Minh editors coyly labeling this "being ordained at the 'Revolutionary temple'".[287] The DRV National Assembly included only one Buddhist monk, from Thừa Thiên province, who took the floor to object to a motion to send a friendly letter to the pope.[288] On the occasion of Buddha's birthday in May 1946, members of the sangha prayed for Vietnam's independence, for world peace, and for the repose of souls of soldiers killed in action. On 23 September, the first anniversary of French assaults in Saigon, separate Catholic, Buddhist, and Việt Minh commemorations were held for all soldiers lost during the previous year.[289]

Many Vietnamese modernists denounced religion. It was said to be feudal or reactionary in character. It fostered dangerous superstitions and diverted people from scientific truth, mass struggle, and linear progress. Like monarchism and landlord exploitation, religion too had to be stamped out if Vietnam was to catch up with advanced countries in the world. Such cultural radicalism was not limited to communists, and it targeted not only the major organized religions. Ancestral temples, family altars, spirit mediums, ghosts, exorcists, and fortune-tellers often received the harshest denunciations. Deep down, some secular modernists envied the capacity of religious leaders to attract and motivate thousands of followers. The challenge was to make national independence and national progress a more compelling message. Meanwhile, however, young radicals alienated religious believers by smashing altars, melting down statues, breaking up death-date observances, and mocking traditional funeral ceremonies. In November 1945, Nguyễn Chí Thanh, representing the Trung Bộ Việt Minh committee, condemned some comrades for thinking that "revolution equals destroying temples and shrines, forbidding all prayers and offerings." Instead, Thanh counseled, they should "encourage a shift of resources from ceremonies and festivals to helping the country, but absolutely not violate freedom of belief in the process."[290] In Hanoi, the city's Buddhist National Salvation branch protested to the Interior Ministry that six local people's committees had seized pagodas, chasing away resident monks or arresting them. "At a time when no orders to liquidate religion have been issued, these [people's committee] fellows are going too far," the letter concluded sardonically.[291] Many religious groups in 1946 endorsed the Việt Minh line of reducing conspicuous consumption on ceremonies in the national interest. Burning of votive paper at funerals became a favorite target.[292]

In May 1946, the Trung Bộ Administrative Committee raised with the Interior Ministry the question of whether Catholic and Buddhist priests and nuns should be required to perform obligatory labor *(tạp dịch)*, stand guard, or perform other citizen duties. The government decided to canvass all province administrative committees on this matter, and received back an impressive range of opinions. At least fourteen northern provinces responded, most supporting exemption of both priests and nuns from obligatory labor, but pointing out that traditionally this meant no right to communal land. Some respondents were concerned that participation of nuns in citizen duties violated traditional separation of the sexes. Others stressed that exemption from obligatory labor should not be extended to tax waivers, particularly in regard to the Defense Fund. Several provinces suggested that priests and nuns should do social work and console families of deceased soldiers, in exchange for exemption from obligatory labor that often involved dike repairs, road construction, or maintenance of public buildings. The Hải Dương committee opposed any exemptions whatsoever, and proposed that priests be armed to kill the enemy like everyone else, thus "putting the interests of the Nation above all theories *(lý thuyết)*," which in this case meant religious beliefs. The Northern Region Committee ignored this radical position when summarizing northern responses to the Interior Ministry, and concluded that excusing all priests and nuns from obligatory labor would demonstrate the government's regard for religion and "prevent our enemies from exploiting the issue." In September, the Interior Ministry instructed all three regional committees to enforce this exemption while also excluding priests and nuns from receiving communal land allocations. A month later priests and nuns were excused from guard duties as well, but made liable for obligatory labor in the event of emergencies such as imminent dike breaches.[293]

Upland Minorities

The DRV government paid little attention to upland minority questions until it became painfully obvious that returning French forces were renewing contacts with local minority leaders in the central highlands (Tây Nguyên) and the northwestern provinces bordering Laos and China. In elections to the new National

Assembly, thirty out of the total of 329 seats were meant to be reserved for minority delegates coming from twenty-three different provinces.[294] However, no practical measures to achieve this quota were promulgated, and only a handful of minority delegates were elected. One hundred other minority representatives were brought to the capital to be greeted by provisional President Hồ, listen to a speech by Võ Nguyên Giáp, and be photographed in front of the Opera House, with minority women in colorful costumes front and center.[295] During the Pacific War, members of the Tày (then known as Thổ) and Dao (Mán) minorities had assisted Việt Minh groups in the northern hills, which led President Hồ to thank them publicly and to promise them arable land and buffaloes once the French threat was gone. A number of Tày men received rapid promotion in administrative committees and the army starting in late 1945. Chu Văn Tấn, of the Nùng minority, brought hundreds of followers from his guerrilla base into the army.[296] However, other Nùng leaders lodged vehement protests when armed Việt Minh cadres rounded up young men involuntarily for military service and required that families supply rice to feed the youths while they were in training camps. When their protests went unheeded, the Nùng leaders approached Chinese officers to intercede, and told Hanoi authorities they might take up Chinese citizenship. This brought matters to the attention of President Hồ, who quickly dispatched an investigation team that brought back conflicting stories, including a prediction from one Nùng leader that "Elder Hồ will not be king (vua) much longer."[297]

Majority Vietnamese (Kinh) generally harbored derogatory views of upland minority peoples, even as they demanded that minorities swear allegiance to the nation of Vietnam. In 1941, the ICP had referred to most ethnic minorities as being at a "low level of existence, dumb and naïve, hence readily deceived." Upland minorities needed Kinh leadership to be able to "advance on the road to genuine civilization".[298] As the French advanced into south-central Vietnam in late 1945, Vietnamese writers tried to convince readers that Rhadé, Bahnar, and other "Mọi" tribes were helping National Guard units to resist the invader by means of poison arrows and tiger traps. Referring to the minorities as "New Vietnamese," journalists portrayed them in patronizing, exotic tones.[299] A Huế editorial declared that majority Vietnamese had to "assist backward ethnic groups to develop politically, economically, and culturally so they can catch up quickly."[300] In the north, meanwhile, DRV administrators adopted some of the same practices as Vietnamese monarchs, dispensing official titles and quantities of salt to minority leaders in exchange for loyalty, and bringing minority groups to the capital to overawe them. Like court mandarins of yore, DRV officials learned to their dismay that local minority leaders (ông Lang; Thổ-ty) knew how to evade or ignore orders as well as to obey them. As before, government officials complained that minority people refused to plan ahead, instead expending their resources on alcohol, parties, ceremonies, and prayer offerings.

From mid-1946 onward, upland minorities received more sustained attention from the government and the press. In June, seventy-one members of the former colonial Highland Affairs branch were located, sixty-two of whom had been born in upland provinces, and forty-seven of whom were currently employed in other government services. A project was mooted to join those individuals with younger Kinh personnel for upland work, but when the latter group insisted on a special hardship allowance and short-term posting, the idea faltered.[301] The Interior Ministry urged relevant province and district chairmen to invite local minority leaders to join their committees. Some chairs saw this merely as a device to keep minority leaders under surveillance and to proselytize, not share powers.[302] Nguyễn Viết Quỳnh, National Assembly delegate from Lào Cai province, and Democratic Party member, submitted a frank report on "the ethnic minority question," which emphasized the strategic and future economic significance of the uplands, and warned of Admiral d'Argenlieu's "dangerous plot" to create a host of minority *pays*. Quỳnh criticized the DRV government's failure to extend its authority to many upland districts, and chided the Tổng Bộ Việt Minh for skimpy political effort except in the former Việt Bắc liberation zone. He concluded by proposing that the government establish a "Council of Nationalities" side by side with the National Assembly.[303] In September, the government announced formation of an Ethnic Minorities Bureau, yet gave it a meager twenty-thousand piastre budget, and delayed appointment of a director for nine weeks.[304] In one of his first acts, the director, Hoàng Văn Phụng, urged renewed harvesting of timber in upland provinces, work which had fallen off because merchants were unable to export via Haiphong. Phụng expected an early renewal of exports— only two weeks before Haiphong was lost to the French.[305] Meanwhile the Defense Ministry sought more upland minority recruits to the National Guard's officer academy, if necessary by relaxing the formal education prerequisite.[306] The Finance Ministry authorized purchase of twenty-five tons of salt for distribution gratis to minority countrymen.[307] Under pressure from a rival contestant for highland loyalties, DRV leaders groped their way towards better minority policies, increasingly aware of the limits of outright coercion.

Kinh and upland minority behavior towards each other was seldom evaluated seriously. The Northern Region Committee did instruct subordinate echelons to stop using the term "New Vietnamese" for upland minorities, because "it implies they only now are becoming citizens, whereas in fact from way back they have been citizens of Vietnam different only in place of residence." This was dubious history, but the purpose was to "avoid offending those who ought better be titled 'minority countrymen' or 'upland countrymen.'"[308] Pejoratives like "Mọi" and

"Thổ" did fade soon from government documents and most newspapers, but not from ordinary Kinh conversation. Whatever upland minorities were named, views about them ranged from blatant racism to hopes of meeting some minority aspirations. A Vietnamese veterinarian portrayed the minorities as doomed to disappear by Darwinian selection, and hinted at eugenic techniques for hastening this extinction.[309] A military analyst predicted that upland minorities (and the Lào) would not be of use to French aggressors because minority culture was so deficient and capacities for development minimal.[310] Another writer insisted that people no longer thought in terms of who was minority, who was majority, but only of "sharing the same blood and flesh within the Great Army Family, the Great Vietnam Family."[311] However, others admitted that the DRV government and army had been much too slow in seeking minority members.[312] Editors now solicited articles or letters from minority readers. A Chàm minority soldier insisted that he had been treated poorly in the French Army compared to current membership in the National Guard.[313] Kinh writers sometimes noted the absence of upland health or education services, while offering no remedies. Sixty-four "New Vietnamese" were brought to Hanoi to be trained to teach the Vietnamese language to their brethren.[314] President Hồ received a series of minority delegations before and after his trip to France. He drank beer with fifty minority members from Tuyên Quang and Hà Giang who brought him yams, corn, honey, cloth, and forest medicines.[315] Such encounters with "Elder Hồ" fostered a personal loyalty to the national leader that civil administrators or Việt Minh cadres could never hope to achieve.

ICP pronouncements now often included a passage assessing interactions with upland minorities and advancing policy improvements. An ICP central region conference resolution admitted that minority groups had "yet to relate earnestly with the new government," due on the one hand to their "very deficient cultural levels," and on the other to current government inability to address their poverty. Also, some young Kinh activists and Kinh traders displayed scornful attitudes and arrogant behavior that angered minority members.[316] In Hanoi, the late July ICP cadre conference came up with ten carrot-and-stick measures to deal with ethnic minorities. Local customs and tales of ethnic heroes should be preserved, more delegations brought to the capital, and taxes reduced or waived in poor districts. Traditional minority headmen should be incorporated within administrative committees, while at the same time identifying younger "progressive persons" to take over subsequently. "Submission" (chinh phục) of minorities could also be achieved through provision of salt, cloth, and matches, and by "combining political persuasion with force of arms." Superstitions had to be combated while simultaneously awarding certificates of merit and promotions to deserving minority members. ICP or Việt Minh cadres needed to focus on neutralizing French divide-and-rule tactics, especially in Lạng Sơn and Sơn La, where French troop numbers were increasing.[317] Later ICP formulations would prove more subtle. Yet patronizing, manipulative attitudes toward upland minority people persisted among the Kinh rank and file.

HỒ CHÍ MINH AS NATIONAL INSPIRATION

For the vast majority of Vietnamese, Hồ Chí Minh came out of nowhere in August 1945. People soon heard that he had devoted his life overseas to gaining his country's independence, yet the fact that Nguyễn Ái Quốc and Hồ Chí Minh were one and the same person was kept out of the press and public speeches.[318] To those who saw him in person, Hồ looked like a traditional village scholar-teacher—thin, simply clothed, poised but approachable. Artists and cartoonists tried with varying degrees of success to capture Hồ's high forehead and cheek bones, bright eyes, prominent ears, and wispy beard. Those who heard Hồ on the radio noted his Nghệ An accent, simple declarative sentences, brevity, and high proportion of Sino-Vietnamese terms. Hồ chose not to publish much during the early months of the DRV. What he did publish was directed at a distinct audience, whether children, elders, southerners, Catholics, entrepreneurs, French nationals in Indochina, graduates of cadre training courses, ethnic minorities, or farmers.[319] On one occasion Hồ addressed a stern message to people's committees at all levels, criticizing them for meting out unjust punishments, being power hungry (cậy thế), and exhibiting depravity (hủ hoá), nepotism, factionalism, and arrogance. Those committee members who failed to mend their ways would "not be forgiven by the Government," a characteristically vague threat. In one of his most widely remembered statements, Hồ then stated, "If the country is independent yet the people enjoy no happiness or liberty, then that independence has no meaning whatsoever."[320]

Despite or perhaps because of his mysterious background, Hồ Chí Minh became the object of intense, unquestioning mass devotion which he did not try to quench, apparently considering it a necessary element in nation-building. There was a religious dimension to popular ways of looking at "Elder Hồ" not as new emperor, but rather as self-abnegating sage who could transform one's life. Hồ was seen to combine moral rectitude with quiet authority and knowledge of the world. Educated Vietnamese considered Hồ the George Washington of their country, defending national independence and promising a brilliant future. Meanwhile, Hồ wanted countrymen to see him as a leader above party affiliation, totally dedicated to the national cause, ready to embrace each citizen regardless of class, ethnicity, region, or religion. Hồ resisted any temptation to become absolute master in the manner of Josef Stalin, which would have required him to eliminate other communists who possessed their own bases of power. This reluctance would result eventually in Hồ being bypassed by those same party leaders, who simultaneously placed him on an ever-higher pedestal for mass adulation.[321]

Hồ Chí Minh cultivated the art of receiving diverse citizen delegations in his Bắc Bộ Phủ office, enquiring about their families and concerns, listening intently, making sure that an aide took notes, delivering a brief homily, and perhaps giving them an autographed photo. If the delegation brought gifts, Hồ would accept them while stating they were to be shared, and perhaps giving the delegation something from previous visitors.[322] The most sensitive delegation meetings occurred following the 6 March 1946 Franco-Vietnamese Accord, when the danger of violent altercations with Chinese or incoming French troops was high. On 8 March, Hồ met a delegation of fifty Hanoi militia members, to whom he emphasized French agreement to troop withdrawals over a five-year period, thus achieving full Vietnamese independence without protracted war. This did not mean a return to attitudes of dependency, Hồ stressed, nor did it preclude improving Vietnam's military capacity and readiness to fight if necessary. A week later Hồ met several score provincial propaganda cadres to explain the accord and urge them to build local support for peaceful implementation.[323]

President Hồ liked getting out of his office to inspect government employees at work, open training courses or conferences, visit literacy classes, and share manual labor for a few minutes with farmers. Government employees dreaded a surprise visit from Hồ, especially if he discovered some of them arriving late to work or absent on second jobs. After one eight in the morning inspection, the interior minister, Võ Nguyên Giáp, ordered every bureau and section to record each tardiness or absence and forward fortnightly reports to him, so he could inform "Elder President Hồ."[324] Concern for Hồ's physical safety restricted his mingling with crowds, but just his presence nearby triggered excitement. When he traveled by auto to a meeting in Hưng Yên province, flags were hoisted along the route in advance, and crowds of people rushed to the roadside to greet Cụ Hồ and yell slogans.[325] People understood that kowtows or other traditional obeisances were unacceptable. During a hectic one-day visit to Nam Định in January 1946, President Hồ met in turn with city committee members, dike workers, and Cub Scouts. When Cubs asked for his autograph, Hồ demurred, saying this was a Western custom, but he did write in their pack notebook, pass out sweets, and have a group photo taken. Proceeding next to a large public meeting, Hồ conveyed his concern about the dikes and the current rice crop, talked about the recently elected National Assembly, urged more help to Nam Bộ, and complemented both Chinese soldiers and Chinese merchants. When young women presented him with flowers, Hồ declared this too was a Western practice to be discarded, but accepted the bouquet. Hồ's last stops were at an orphanage and the local Chinese garrison, where he reviewed the troops.[326]

One of President Hồ's most demanding public performances began on 20 October 1946, when he debarked from a French warship in Haiphong harbor to an uncertain reception, given widespread disappointment over the modus vivendi. Hồ reviewed a National Guard company, discussed the simmering customs dispute with the Haiphong city committee, and assured journalists that Haiphong would become a development model for the rest of the country. Next morning, Hồ visited Haiphong's National Guard garrison with Võ Nguyên Giáp, where the army band played the national anthem at a solemn flag-raising ceremony. Hồ then boarded a special train for the capital and was relieved to see large, friendly crowds at every town and commune along the way. One banner extolled, "The Father of the People-Nation returns in good health to the Homeland." At the Hanoi train station, tens of thousands of citizens cheered Hồ's arrival. Ever the diplomat, Hồ first addressed in French the helmeted French troop contingent present, then turned his attention to the audience. Even the Vietnam Nationalist Party's weekly newspaper complimented the festive atmosphere and warm greetings "appropriate for the presidency of a democratic republic." "Uncle has returned," youths cried out, foreshadowing Hồ's future sobriquet. On 22 October, President Hồ issued an explanation to the country of what needed to be done prior to reopening of Franco-Vietnamese talks in January 1947.[327] Clearly the DRV government and Việt Minh groups had prepared the ground for Hồ's favorable return, but he knew how to seize the occasion to maximum advantage.

Prior to departing Vietnam on 31 May 1946, President Hồ had signed all government decrees (sắc lệnh), and he resumed this procedure on returning in late October. Totaling more than one thousand in number, most decrees were read in the National Gazette by government personnel down to the district level in the north, and selectively transmitted by telegraph or Morse radio down the coast. Decrees reprinted in newspapers often displayed Hồ's unique writing style. Others were composed by Cabinet members or staff, but understood by local committees to carry the authority of the nation's leader. Hồ did not enjoy routine administrative activity, leaving most of it to subordinates. The exceptions were foreign relations and the Special Inspectorate, where Hồ took meticulous interest. Even minor overseas matters attracted Hồ's attention. In November 1946, the mayor of Biarritz wrote to Hồ about disposition of the personal effects of a French friend, formerly head of public works in Vĩnh Yên province. Hồ told his staff to obtain information promptly, as the mayor had been very nice to him during his stay in June, and he wanted to reply personally.[328] At the Special Inspectorate, Hồ monitored the hundreds of citizen petitions coming in each month addressed to him, pinpointing those he wanted to be kept informed about until final disposition. In turn, Inspectorate staff told bureaus and local committees of the president's personal concern. Sometimes interested parties would blitz the president with multiple petitions, hoping to gain his attention. Over a period of ten months, the daughter of Đỗ Đình Thiện petitioned "Elder Government President" repeatedly to help locate her father, a sixty-year-old Hải Dương merchant who had been arrested in December 1945, but then disappeared. Although the Inspectorate file suggests that Thiện was killed in January, as of November 1946, President Hồ was still insisting that the province committee uncover the truth "or be held responsible."[329]

During 1945–46, the public's image of Hồ Chí Minh was still under construction, with no blueprint provided. At one extreme, Nationalist Party newspaper cartoons pictured Hồ as a frail old man with the expression of a stunned mullet, completely out of his depth. In one cartoon a big French soldier put his arm around a fragile, confused Hồ and yelled *"Vive le Viet Minh!"* In another, Hồ held the arm of a blindfolded farmer and promised him food and clothing, while behind the farmer Trần Huy Liệu prepared to chain him, and Võ Nguyên Giáp pointed two pistols, saying "If you're not Việt Minh you are a traitor."[330] At the other end of the political spectrum, adoring citizens carried large portraits of President Hồ in mass processions, like a religious icon.[331] A southern artist used his own blood to paint a portrait of President Hồ.[332] Amidst battle reversals at Nha Trang, one youth cried out "Long live President Hồ!" and then committed suicide.[333] When it came to pronouns, some people wanted to call the president "Father" *(Cha)*. Nationalist Party speakers apparently referred to Hồ with the derogatory pronouns *"thằng"* and *"nó,"* which even members of the anticommunist Revolutionary League found quite unacceptable.[334] Prior to the National Assembly elections there was some disquiet about Hồ having to stand as a candidate like ordinary mortals. After Hồ himself cleared that up, there was worry that voters would eschew writing "Hồ Chí Minh" on their ballots, instead preferring to write "President Hồ" or "Elder Hồ," or even "Hồ Chí Miêng" in conformity with traditional name avoidance principles *(húy tên)* for high dignitaries. Any of those choices would void the ballot.[335] One way or another, however, Hồ was recorded as securing the vote of 97.9 percent of those going to the polls in Hanoi.

As mentioned above, President Hồ gave out autographed copies of his photograph to visitors, and evidenced no reservations about thousands of other photos of himself being distributed nationwide. The Propaganda Ministry expressed displeasure that photos of the president were being sold in shops and market stalls. In October 1945, it tried to monopolize all sales, with proceeds to go to the Independence Fund. This was defeated by the ability of local photo shops to duplicate Hồ indefinitely from a single positive. A Quảng Ngãi newspaper inserted a glossy photograph of the president to each copy, bearing the handwritten inscription "A gift to soldiers. Affectionately, Ho Chi Minh 11–46."[336] In Hanoi, merchants sold large plaster statues of President Hồ for 360$BIC, and small busts for 60$.[337] Images of Hồ were also beginning to circulate on government currency.

In August 1946, a proposal surfaced in Nam Bộ to rename Saigon as Hồ Chí Minh City. Việt Minh papers in Hanoi quickly supported the idea. *Cứu Quốc* declared confidently that "Saigon from now on will change its name to Hồ Chí Minh City"—a prediction that took twenty-nine years to fulfill. On 2 September, a Quảng Ngãi paper affirmed: "One year ago Hồ Chí Minh declared independence in Hanoi; on this first anniversary we give Saigon his name."[338] There were limits emerging, however, on how exactly the president's name could be used. No one appears to have named their child in honor of the president. No village renamed itself Hồ Chí Minh. In November, when word arrived at the Bắc Bộ Phủ that a training class in Hòa Bình had been named after Hồ, the Interior Ministry instructed the Northern Region Committee to implement a policy whereby "the name of President Hồ is not used too often".[339] Meanwhile, ordinary citizens were already helping to determine when Hồ was styled president, when father, and when uncle.

THE VIEW FROM BELOW

It is difficult to draw firm conclusions about what farmers, artisans, or shopkeepers were thinking in 1945–46, given that almost all our available sources were created or compiled by a minority of urban, educated Vietnamese. From a reading of petitions, letters to the editor, and local committee reports, however, it is possible to infer attitudes of ordinary people at particular times and places. Almost all Vietnamese understood that the 9 March 1945 Japanese coup had shattered French colonial rule. Many realized that the mid-August Japanese surrender to the Allies put their own futures in the air. It made no sense to imagine a return to 1940. The subsequent meetings, demonstrations, seizure of government facilities, formation of revolutionary committees, and declaration of independence fostered excitement and enthusiasm even among many Vietnamese who had served the French well. People sensed they were living through momentous times, pregnant with both opportunity and uncertainty, with consequences reaching far beyond themselves, their family and village. At the village level there were festivities, retributions, food shortages, debates over leadership, and initial contacts with the new government hierarchy extending from Hanoi. News of French Army assaults in Saigon heightened attention to militia organization and the search for traitors. During these early months of the Vietnamese revolution, people often responded more to local crowd psychology than in obedience to higher-level instructions.

Also dating from late 1945, ordinary Vietnamese learned how to use positive revolutionary terms like liberation, struggle, progress, sacrifice, comrade, unity, and national front, as well as negative terms such as traitor, counterrevolutionary, reactionary, and exploiter. They had to denounce publicly all aspects of

French rule and hide or destroy evidence of prior participation in the colonial system. Literate individuals sought clues to proper revolutionary behavior in newspapers and leaflets, while illiterates relied on word-of-mouth, activist speech-making, and observing the conduct of visiting cadres. Despite political rhetoric about total transformation, some things remained the same. People tended to seg-ment their thinking and response to events, taking part in mass organizations, employing revolutionary language appropriately, and avoiding dangerous topics, while at the same time concerning themselves with personal, family, and village matters. Balancing these competing needs and desires often provoked anxiety. Social mores did change substantially, whether due to fear of public shaming or to shifts in underlying belief.

Individuals joined revolutionary groups based on geographical proximity, oc-cupation, family links, or sheer accident. Whatever one's inner feelings, it was unwise to be absent from public meetings, or to refuse to donate resources or time to the cause. Some citizens volunteered without being asked, others waited until approached. In either case the desire to take part coincided with trepida-tion over the consequences of staying out. Farming families that survived on very little grain became inured to setting aside a small amount each month for Việt Minh or government collectors. It was hoped that group membership brought protection against inordinate taxation or dangerous accusations. Youths sometimes exited the family circle, living and eating with the new group, perhaps being assigned to missions far beyond the village. Ideology played only a limited role in determining personal behavior during 1945–46. Recruitment locally to the ICP was considered an honor, given the party's history of anticolonial struggle and sacrifice, yet new members hardly altered their outlook as a result. At most they might attend a one-week district training session, learning a list of basic does and don'ts, returning none the wiser concerning party doctrine or structure.

Amidst revolution and war, peer pressure combined with fear and insecurity to lead persons to engage in acts never dreamt of previously. This psychological dynamic produced heroic self-sacrifice at one end of the spectrum, and ruthless treatment of fellow citizens at the other. A spartan image of revolutionary manli-ness influenced youth behavior. People became fastidious about itemizing money or grain received or dispersed, fearing that any mistake invited charges of pecu-lation and harsh punishment. When facing change, human beings often focus more on what they might lose than what they can get. In Vietnam in 1946, some persons undoubtedly did feel the pain of losses, and few enjoyed the pleasure of gains. The most common response was to accept that amidst revolution and war, personal or family gratification had to be deferred.

Under the new state system, people tried to learn what must be obeyed, and what might be ignored, evaded, or even opposed. South of the sixteenth parallel, where French Army units often held the initiative, people could not obey some

DRV government orders and expect to stay alive. The nature of any personal contribution to the national struggle had to change according to time and place. Motives for participation might change as well. Below the sixteenth parallel, the profile of resistance committees, the army, and the police often had to be lower, while the behavioral demands on individuals and the risks of miscalculation were higher. These troubling realities of life in the south would come to everyone north of the sixteenth parallel from late December 1946 onward.

Epilogue

Beginning the night of 19–20 December 1946, DRV forces tried to overwhelm a number of French garrisons before relief could arrive. The small French detachment at Vinh (Nghệ An) capitulated on 21 December. In Hanoi, after six National Guard battalions failed to overrun designated enemy positions, one battalion joined fifteen hundred militia men and women inside the old 36 Street complex to mount a stubborn defense lasting eight weeks. Eighty kilometers south of Hanoi, in Nam Định town, fighting continued for twelve weeks until a large French armored column pushed through from Haiphong. In Huế, repeated Vietnamese assaults on French units holed up in solid colonial buildings were thrown back. When French soldiers and marines debarked subsequently on beaches to the southeast, National Guard commanders ordered defense of the city, but troops panicked under attack and fled in all directions. This enabled the French to advance unopposed up the coast to Quảng Trị and Quảng Bình. Zone 4 authorities, fearing further French advances, ordered destruction of the towns of Hà Tĩnh, Vinh, and Thanh Hóa.

Thousands of DRV civil servants evacuated the capital in late December, mostly lacking instructions on where to go and reliant on daily rumor when trying to grasp the bigger picture. Some personnel had already sent family members to home villages, others left them in Hanoi, still others brought them along to share whatever fate awaited. President Hồ Chí Minh and other cabinet members headed westward towards a planned "safe area" in Sơn Tây and Hòa Bình provinces. In late February, President Hồ visited Thanh Hóa province to consider whether to move the central government down there or not. Thanh Hóa had the merits of large population and extensive rice fields, but any French offensive that forced the government into the hills would have left it vulnerable to enemy attack from Laos. In early March, a French armored sortie from Hanoi westward convinced Hồ to shift the government northward to the Việt Bắc hills. While the Việt Bắc was sparsely populated and a poor food-growing area, it possessed far better defensive terrain than Thanh Hóa. The border with China was both a threat and an opportunity. France might convince Chiang Kai-shek to help throttle the DRV. Or Guangxi and Yunnan generals might continue to cooperate in cross-border trade and DRV arms acquisition.

If the French Army had persisted in attacking west from Hanoi in early 1947 it might have captured or killed several thousand DRV military and civilian personnel making their way laboriously towards the Việt Bắc hills. However, French reserves had been committed to quelling resistance in Hanoi, Nam Định, Huế, and Đà Nẵng. Once those missions were completed, General Valluy had insufficient time before arrival of the monsoon rains in May to organize a campaign upriver to Phú Thọ and Tuyên Quang provinces. Instead, Valluy shifted priority to eliminating the Việt Minh in Cochinchina. The French did win over large numbers of Cao Đài and Hòa Hảo faithful during 1947, yet scores of small National Guard and militia groups in the south continued to mount road ambushes and assaults on dispersed enemy outposts.

During the spring of 1947, neither France nor the DRV ruled out resumption of negotiations. Paris instructed its new Indochina high commissioner, Emile Bollaert, to talk with a wide range of "political and spiritual families," not excluding the Việt Minh. Using the radio, President Hồ affirmed readiness to talk if France recognized the independence and unity of Vietnam. In May, Bollaert dispatched his personal advisor, Paul Mus, to seek out Hồ and present a proposal whereby Vietnamese troops had to assemble at spots designated by the French Army and surrender their arms. Even if the two sides had somehow narrowed the diplomatic chasm and agreed to a ceasefire, many armed Vietnamese groups would have evaded orders. Another seven years of war had to pass before the DRV and France conferred with each other again about a ceasefire.

For the National Guard to endure during the summer of 1947, regiments had to disaggregate to battalions, and commanders often then found it necessary to disperse companies to different districts to obtain food and shelter. Meanwhile, Võ Nguyên Giáp consumed Karl von Clausewitz's On War, especially noting the relatively brief chapter on "Arming the People." Trường Chinh penned a manifesto titled "The Resistance Will Certainly Win," relying on Mao Zedong's 1938 essay "On Protracted War" to argue that Vietnam's strategy must be to prolong the conflict.

In early October 1947, General Raoul Salan began a three-pronged offensive into the Việt Bắc designed to capture or kill the Việt Minh leadership, destroy supply depots hidden in limestone caves, and sever enemy contact with China. Trường Chinh in particular had some anxious hours as he hid underground while French paratroopers moved around above. The French did manage to disrupt central DRV operations substantially and enhance French presence along the Chinese frontier, but after two months they had to withdraw from other advance positions. For the remainder of the First Indochina War, the Việt Bắc would serve as both DRV government headquarters and National Guard command center, supply base, and training ground.

Throughout 1947 most DRV local committees continued to function despite erratic or nonexistent contact with central authorities. They collected taxes and donations, stockpiled food, billeted soldiers, tightened security, and tried to prepare inhabitants against arrival of French troops. Roads were dug up, culverts destroyed, underground caches and hiding places constructed, and scenarios for defense rehearsed. For months the majority of villages north of the sixteenth parallel saw enemy soldiers only at a distance, as General Salan focused on control of urban centers, main roads, and river ways. When French commanders decided to locate a fort or blockhouse at a particular roadside position they dispatched a well-armed unit to the nearest Vietnamese village to demand the "notables" come out to hear what was expected of them. If the local plan was to resist, village women and children would be evacuated and the advancing French fired upon. Far more often, however, administrative committee and Việt Minh cadres made themselves scarce and a preagreed set of elders stepped forward to begin a tenuous relationship with the enemy.

In order to survive, citizens needed quickly to change behavior. Much depended on where one lived. Already in the south three kinds of territory had emerged. In "free zones" (vùng tự do), DRV committees operated openly, crude newspapers circulated, markets convened several times a week, children went to school, and clinics offered basic healthcare. Big propaganda meetings were held at night to avoid enemy air attack. "Guerrilla zones" (vùng du kích) were by definition contested with the enemy, hence most dangerous for inhabitants. Living in "zones temporarily occupied by the enemy" (vùng bị địch tạm chiếm) required DRV adherents to carry French-issued identification papers, to avoid revolutionary language in public, and to stay clear of some old friends. Individuals who crossed routinely from "free" to "occupied" zones and back, for example merchants, boat crews, couriers, and tax collectors, needed to know where and how to shift behavior to avoid detention or worse. Interzone 4 (Liên Khu 4), south of the Red River delta, became the DRV's most populous and successful "free" territory, always facing the possibility of French invasion, but meanwhile absorbing refugees, operating a host of defense ateliers, sending young men to fight in the north, nurturing links with anticolonialist groups in Laos, and building up hospitals, secondary schools, and cultural organizations.

In July 1948, the central government was able to convene a nine-day All-Country Resistance-Administrative Conference that brought together zone and province committee chairmen with DRV ministers and bureau heads to deliberate policy and performance. Every zone in the country was represented except for the three zones in Nam Bộ. Participants discussed civil-military vicissitudes, how to strengthen commune-level committees, how to unify operations inside enemy-controlled areas, and how to overcome food shortages and fight inflation. The justice minister, Vũ Đình Hòe, took up the vexing issue of local arrests and indefinite incarceration without due process. Conference delegates would have known of the public debate then underway between Hòe and one of the editors of *Sự Thật* (ICP) journal over judicial independence, the role of law in society, and whether local committees should decide who were traitors. This conference was the most important DRV national meeting to take place since the National Assembly session of late 1946, designed to demonstrate that the central authorities were once again in touch with localities, and give participants a sense of where Vietnam was heading.

A few weeks later the ICP Standing Bureau convened its own cadres conference, at which Trường Chinh insisted that the time had come for the DRV to line up proudly with Stalin, the Soviet Union, and the "new democracies" of Eastern Europe. Lê Đức Thọ argued the case for immediate introduction of party authority over the National Guard and civil administration. Thọ wanted to move from the current situation, where party members were sprinkled liberally through the state apparatus, to party control of everything. However, the concluding conference statement made no mention of Thọ's sweeping proposals, and Thọ himself was dispatched to faraway Nam Bộ. It would be another two years before the ICP Standing Bureau could move resolutely in the direction advocated by Thọ.

Each year, ICP pundits predicted imminent CCP victory in China, only to be compelled to repeat themselves the next year. In January 1949, however, word arrived in the Việt Bắc that the Liberation Army was at the gates of Beijing, triggering excited discussion about when Vietnam might be able to mount a "general counteroffensive" against the French. Soon ICP cadres were exhorting citizens to heighten production, donate more grain, sew more uniforms, buy more government bonds, go to literacy classes, train more vigorously, and kill more enemy soldiers as preparation for a general counteroffensive. News in April of the Chinese Liberation Army crossing the Yangtze River and seizing Nanjing led some local cadres to drop the word "preparation" in favor of florid images of French soldiers surrendering in droves or being driven into the sea.

By 1949 the DRV central government had overcome 1947 disruptions and was functioning as capably as in 1946, albeit with major wartime changes. With little prospect of the National Assembly convening any time soon, several available members of the Assembly's Standing Committee were called upon to consent to decisions of the government cabinet and be present at anniversaries and other ceremonial occasions. Central authorities interacted most effectively with provinces in the northeast (Interzone 1) and northwest (Interzone 10). Contact with the lower Red River delta region (Interzone 3) was sometimes interrupted by French Army operations, but not for long. Communications with the north-central coast (Interzone 4) were more erratic, while contact with the south-central region (Interzone 5) and Nam Bộ was limited for months at a time to insecure radio transmissions. These disparities became painfully apparent in April when the government convened a second All-Country Resistance-Administrative Conference and no delegates from south of the Red River delta showed up in time.

DRV government finances came under increasing strain. Revenue amounted to only 18 percent of total budget outlays. The Defense Ministry consumed 60 percent of the budget, and the finance minister, Lê Văn Hiến, was shocked in February 1949 when Defense requested three times its 1948 amount. Ever more "Elder Hồ" money was printed and put in circulation. Having obtained a French book which described the collapse of the German mark in the 1920s, Hiến now pondered the consequences of DRV money supply tripling between 1947 and 1949, and possibly expanding to sixteen billion đồng by 1951. The explosion in rice prices made a mockery of DRV attempts at price control. At the end of 1949, the Cabinet accepted Hiến's proposal to collect in kind 6 percent of annual output on all rice land, a tax designed to underpin the issuing of new currency to replace the existing badly devalued notes. Not until 1951 was such an agricultural tax introduced, now closely monitored by Chinese advisors.

Despite material limitations, the National Guard in 1949 demonstrated a capacity to mount successful battalion-size attacks on French forts and convoys. Multi-battalion "campaigns" were also launched in several directions, but their success was limited by problems of supply, transport, communications, and inadequate intelligence on the enemy. In November, President Hồ Chí Minh decreed that all male citizens between fifteen and forty-five years of age had an obligation of two years' military service, and in time of war could be mustered for the duration. President Hồ then ordered mobilization of "all the people's human, material, and financial resources in order to advance to the General Offensive." Punishments awaited those who speculated, hoarded, engaged in black marketeering, or "evaded citizen responsibilities." Clearly the time had come when participation by way of persuasion and encouragement had to be reinforced by compulsory powers of the state. Soon complaints came in from below that Việt Minh cadres were applying too much compulsion and not enough persuasion.

It was at this time that growing numbers of government employees and Việt Minh activists left DRV "free zones" in favor of French-controlled cities and towns. While some were alienated specifically by increased Communist Party assertiveness, others felt that the revolution overall was hardening in ways they could not support, or which left no place for them. Still others bowed to family obligations. The exodus of creative writers, artists, and musicians was particularly telling. Most of these departees tried to assume a neutral or *attentiste* position, rather than affirm allegiance to the new Bảo Đại administration. Some drew on their mass mobilization experiences with the Viet Minh to try to promote a "third force" revolution.

The DRV from its inception in September 1945 had faced the threat of France establishing an alternative state or states. Following the December 1946 flight of the DRV government from Hanoi, Admiral d'Argenlieu's political advisor, Léon Pignon, began assiduously to canvass elite Vietnamese regarding his plan for Bảo Đại to reclaim status as emperor and draw noncommunists into a new relationship with France. The idea of imperial restoration was soon abandoned due to opposition from both French and Vietnamese republicans, but making Bảo Đại head of an associated state remained the heart of Pignon's project. For two years, talks between French officials, Bảo Đại, and interested Vietnamese went in circles, with Bảo Đại's main leverage being his refusal to return to Vietnam until an acceptable accord was signed. The 8 March 1949 Elysée agreement granted independence to the Associated State of Vietnam, yet it soon became clear that France retained important military, diplomatic, economic, and financial powers. When the time finally came in late 1949 to start forming the Associated State Army, its opponent, the DRV National Guard already possessed a seasoned officer corps and battle-hardened battalions moving towards regiment and division-size formations.

In late 1949, the ICP Central Standing Bureau dispatched a letter to Chairman Mao Zedong seeking aid to defeat the French imperialists. Mao agreed in principle, designated a ranking member of the CCP Central Military Commission to liaise, and accepted a request from President Hồ to visit Beijing. The People's Republic of China extended diplomatic recognition to the DRV on 18 January 1950, and the Soviet Union followed suit soon after. When Hồ arrived in Beijing at the end of January he discovered that Chairman Mao and Premier Zhou Enlai had gone to Moscow. Hồ managed to follow them and secure a meeting with Stalin, who told him that Mao had been delegated to deal with Asian communist parties. Traveling back to Beijing with Mao by train, Hồ presumably discussed how much assistance was needed first to clear the Sino-Vietnamese border area of French forces, then to convince Paris of the futility of continuing the war.

Hồ Chí Minh would have understood that Chinese aid, training, and advisors carried important domestic political consequences. Stalin had already criticized Hồ for not implementing radical land redistributions; Chinese advisors would soon be pushing this policy too. High on the agenda as well was a class-based purge of the officer corps and ICP cadres. Because bilateral relations continued to be handled almost entirely on a party-to-party basis, not government-to-government, ICP leaders quickly enhanced their authority throughout the DRV state. President Hồ's preference for keeping the government, army, and party hierarchies functioning in parallel fashion was finessed permanently, although in practice the Communist Party never achieved the total control that Trường Chinh, Lê Đức Thọ, and others desired.

On 16 September 1950, bolstered by Chinese aid, newly commissioned National Guard artillery batteries opened fire on the French post at Đông Khê, astride Route 4 between Lạng Sơn and Cao Bằng. Two days later, two infantry regiments overwhelmed the Foreign Legion defenders. French relief columns advancing from Lạng Sơn and Cao Bằng were blocked, compelled to take to the hills, and there mostly captured or killed. Panic now ensued at French Army command and among the large garrison at Lạng Sơn, where huge quantities of arms, ammunition, gasoline, and food were left intact as troops fled down Route 1 towards Hanoi. The French lost forty-eight hundred dead or missing, perhaps their worst overseas defeat since General Montcalm at Quebec in 1759. Although some National Guard companies had lost up to half their complement, men talked eagerly about liberating Hanoi before Tết in early February 1951. It took two months to reorganize, resupply, and move units into position to mount an offensive in the upper Red River delta (Vĩnh Yên) in mid-January. There Vietnamese soldiers had a terrible encounter with napalm, attacks faltered, and General Võ Nguyên Giáp ordered withdrawal to the hills.

After repeated postponements, the ICP Central Standing Bureau convened a National Congress in February 1951 to elect a Central Executive Committee and resume the party's public persona under the new name of Vietnam Workers' Party (Đảng Lao Động Việt Nam). While Hồ Chí Minh was automatically reaffirmed as party chair, his authority came from being founder and president of the DRV and personification of the Vietnamese nation. Nguyễn Chí Thanh was catapulted to number three in the party hierarchy, perhaps a signal to the CCP that the Workers' Party was serious about using political commissars to "rectify" the military (now renamed the Vietnam People's Army) along Maoist lines. During 1951–53, mounting a general counteroffensive remained the strategic objective, but each campaign into the Red River delta failed with heavy casualties.

In late 1953, General Henri Navarre, faced with collapsing metropolitan support for the war, decided to place some of his best units in the distant mountain valley of Điện Biên Phủ to lure the People's Army to its doom. Vietnamese forces made the long trek, overwhelmed French artillery, neutralized the airstrip, dug a network of siege trenches, and compelled surrender of French survivors on 7 May 1954. Nonetheless, the People's Army was not able to parlay the stunning Điện Biên Phủ victory into a general offensive. Ten weeks later the DRV had to accept an agreement at Geneva which left the country divided.

From 1950 onward Vietnam was intractably embroiled in the Cold War. Some ICP members, as we have seen, had pushed since 1946 to have the DRV declare its allegiance to the clutch of "new democracies" headed by the Soviet Union. Hồ Chí Minh chose instead to cultivate relations as widely as possible. By 1949, however, America's growing support for an alternative Vietnamese state, Thailand's closing down the DRV's regional window in Bangkok, and especially Liberation Army victories in China, led Hồ to abandon his multilateral strategy and seek membership in the communist bloc. While the military benefits were obvious, Hồ still tried to limit or defer some of the domestic political consequences. The high point of the Vietnamese revolution was People's Army units being welcomed as they marched back into Hanoi on 10 October 1954. There followed violent land redistribution, party purges, neutering of private enterprise, and termination of intellectual exploration. As it became clear that the United States intended to sabotage any nonviolent unification of Vietnam, internal party debate centered on how to implement a socialist development agenda in the north while fostering armed liberation of the south. Eventually war imperatives triumphed once again, delaying any kind of economic transformation for another two decades.

Protracted war led to militarization of the Vietnamese revolution and DRV state. The regular army, regional forces, and local militia became the revolution's raison d'être, the prime focus of human and material inputs. War also was the main agent of social mobility, with peasant soldiers becoming squad and platoon leaders, and youths with only a few years of education replacing higher-status company or battalion commanders killed in action or removed for cause. As casualties mounted, the state had to devise ways to deal with maimed soldiers and families of dead and missing combatants. With each year of fighting, more families had reason to nurse grievances and desires for retribution.

No Napoleon emerged from Vietnam's national army. Several charismatic generals did come to prominence by 1950. If President Hồ Chí Minh had been killed, captured, or otherwise removed from power, the DRV might have seen a general replace him. The ICP probably played a key role in the purging or sidelining of several generals in 1950–51. Võ Nguyên Giáp retained his position as army commander, but at the price of sharing authority with two political appointees. Chinese communist advisors helped the ICP to institutionalize party control over the military.

We still know very little about how Hồ Chí Minh felt about all these changes. Party leaders worked to put President Hồ on a pedestal, increasingly removed from day-to-day decisionmaking. Already the public image of "Elder Hồ" was that of a saintly leader above any party affiliation, totally dedicated to the people-nation of Vietnam, anxious to embrace each and every citizen regardless of class, ethnicity, region, or religion. Henceforth the party had the power, the DRV state had the authority, but it was to Hồ Chí Minh that people still looked for legitimacy.

Official history of the 1945–46 era firmed up by the early 1960s in Hanoi, and not much has changed since. Recently some unofficial reassessments have begun to appear, however. The lively role of the Vietnam Democratic Party is attracting new attention. Vietnam's 1946 constitution is being rated favorably compared to the current document. The relative openness of the press in 1945–46 is contrasted with subsequent decades of draconian censorship. The eagerness of young men and women in 1945 to commit themselves to a cause is contrasted with contemporary preoccupations with making money, investing in property, and avoiding political controversy.

There is a dark side to 1945–46 that has yet to be canvassed publicly in Vietnam. With people quick to accuse fellow citizens of treason or reactionary behavior, no proper judicial system emerged to apply due process when deciding guilt or innocence. Proposals for an independent judiciary received short shrift. Today's writers who call for an independent judiciary have no domestic precedents to cite. Communist Party capacity in 1945–46 to operate covertly, kill opponents, and pursue a dictatorial agenda is still transmitted as glorious national history, not to be challenged by anyone inside the country. Today, citizens continue to be detained indefinitely and sometimes tortured by the police.

There is still much to be learned about 1945–46. Above all, we still know little about what ordinary people were thinking and doing. In-depth interviews were conducted recently with several hundred village and district cadres of the resistance era, now in their eighties and nineties. No longer feeling an obligation to hew to the party line, many of these elderly men and women reveal a rich variety of local experience. Some families also possess letters and diaries from this period, yet often remain reluctant to share them with researchers. Then there are the thousands of personal and small-group petitions addressed to "Elder Hồ" or his ministers in 1945–46, and available for reading at the Aix archives. All of these sources, along with district and province files available elsewhere, can be mined for a lively social history of Vietnam during this period.

Comparison of Vietnam's experience in the 1940s with that of other countries during this period has barely begun. Vietnamese sometimes compare their revolution with that of China, yet given major differences of scale and historical timing, this is not particularly rewarding. Preliminary studies comparing Vietnam and Indonesia have appeared, but much more could be done. The obvious pair to compare is Vietnam and Korea, starting with French versus Japanese colonial regimes, then zooming in on August 1945 Allied decisions to assign British and Chinese forces to occupy Indochina, and American and Soviet forces to occupy Korea. As in Vietnam, Japanese officials in Korea had already stirred the pot by allowing some native luminaries to prepare postcolonial alternatives. A congress of representatives met in Seoul on 6 September to form a predominately left-wing provisional government. U.S. General Hodges, landing in Incheon two days later, resolutely refused to meet a Korean delegation, much as British General Gracey had in Saigon. Above the thirty-eighth parallel, Soviet generals allowed a

Committee for Preparation of Korean Independence to continue operating, gradually inserting communists to key positions. The stage was set for de facto partition, confrontation, and eventual war in 1950. While this crude summary of events in Korea suggests parallels to Vietnam, future analysis may find the differences more revealing.

I have been asked by other American veterans what this book can tell us, if anything, about our later debacle in Vietnam. Most of the sources I access here were not available to French decisionmakers at the time, and whatever they learned later was not shared with the Americans who replaced them. The French considered the "Việt Minh" an insurgent threat to legitimate authority, rather than a functioning state. This caused them grossly to underrate their opponents, even after the DRV survived attack, built up its forces, and put the French Army on the strategic defensive. American analysts made much the same mistake, developing an elaborate "counterinsurgency" doctrine and "pacification" plans designed to outmaneuver and defeat the "Việt Cộng." From the point of view of many Vietnamese, the pro-American Republic of Vietnam was the insurgent threat, not the DRV or the National Front for the Liberation of South Vietnam. No CIA-initiated program, be it "civic action," "census grievance," "counterterror," or "political action," managed to overcome this liability. Washington then escalated to search-and-destroy operations, forced urbanization, and bombing the north, greatly increasing the human toll but not reversing the underlying political dynamics.

The DRV state formed in 1945 drew heavily from centralizing Confucian-Legalist and French republican ideologies, yet we have seen how provincial and lower cadres managed to achieve some of their own objectives by indirection or creative obfuscation. Subsequently the ICP/Workers' Party superimposed Leninist-Maoist ideology, and all local leaders became party members. But the party still could not eliminate center/local ambiguities. No one dared to propose a federalist constitution that legitimized local power selectively. More recently, local delegates to the National Assembly have dared to represent the interests of their constituents in a way never possible before. It remains to be seen if Vietnam's legislative branch will stand up to the executive, central or local.

All revolutions end. Paraphrasing the social critic Eric Hoffer, every great cause begins as a movement, becomes an organization, and eventually descends into a racket. By the 1970s, members of Vietnam's revolutionary generation of 1945 were busy passing on perks and power to their children. Nonetheless, Vietnam had changed dramatically from the 1930s, with the fulcrum of those transformations being 1945–46.

With revolution now a distant memory, and war avoided for a quarter century, the Socialist Republic of Vietnam state is the most obvious legacy. If the Communist Party were to fragment or fade away, the state would persist, with the country most likely reverting to the name Democratic Republic of Vietnam.

NOTES

ABBREVIATIONS

AFP	Agence France Presse
ANOM	Archives nationals d'outre-mer (Aix-en-Provence)
BB	Bắc Bộ [Northern Region]
BBP	Bắc Bộ Phủ [Northern Region Office]
BDHV	Bình Dân Học Vụ [Mass Education Bureau]
BIC	Banque de l'Indochine
CB	*Việt Nam Dân Quốc Công Báo* [Vietnam National Gazette]
CCP	Chinese Communist Party
CĐ3	*Chi Đội 3 Giải Phóng Quân Nam Tiến* [Detachment 3 of the Liberation Army Advance South]
CĐ Vi Dân	*Chi Đội Vi Dân* [Detachment Vi Dân]
CMTT	*Cách Mạng Tháng Tám* [August Revolution]
CP	Fonds conseiller politique, ANOM
CQ	*Cứu Quốc* [National Salvation] (Hanoi newspaper).
CTQG	Chính Trị Quốc Gia [National Politics] (Hanoi publishing house)
DC	*Dân Chủ* [Democracy] (Haiphong newspaper)
ĐL	*Độc Lập* [Independence] (Hanoi newspaper)
DOS	Department of State (USA)
DRV	Democratic Republic of Vietnam
GF	Gouvernement de fait (collection), located in ANOM, INDO
HCMTT	*Hồ Chí Minh Toàn Tập* [Complete Works of Ho Chi Minh]
ICP	Indochinese Communist Party
INDO	Fonds Indochine, ANOM
KHXH	Khoa Học Xã Hội [Social Sciences] (Hanoi publishing house)

LSBTTM	*Lịch Sử Bộ Tổng Tham mưu trong kháng chiến chống Pháp* (1945–1954) [History of the General Staff in the Anti-French Resistance (1945–1954)]
LSCKC1	*Lịch Sử cuộc Kháng chiến Chống Thực dân Pháp 1945–1954* [History of Resistance to French Colonialism 1945–1954], vol. 1
LSCKC2	*Lịch Sử cuộc Kháng chiến Chống Thực dân Pháp 1945–1954* [History of Resistance to French Colonialism 1945–1954], vol. 2
MRP	Mouvement Républicain Populaire
NARA	National Archives and Records Administration (USA)
NCLS	*Nghiên Cứu Lịch Sử* [Historical Research] (Hanoi journal)
NĐ	Nghị định [edict]
NTBKC	*Nam Trung Bộ Kháng Chiến, 1945–1975* [South-central Region Resistance, 1945–1975]
NXB	Nhà xuất bản [publishing house]
OSS	Office of Strategic Services (USA)
PCF	Parti Communiste Français
PTNT	*Phong Trào Nam Tiến (1945–1975)* [Southern Advance Movement (1945–1975)]
PTT	Postes, Télégraphes et Téléphones
QĐND	Quân Đội Nhân Dân [People's Army]
SFIO	Section Française de l'Internationale Ouvrière
SHAT	Service Historique de l'Armée de Terre
SHD	Service historique de la Défense (Vincennes) (formerly SHAT)
SL	*Sắc lệnh* [decree]
SRV	Socialist Republic of Vietnam
ST	*Sự Thật* [Truth] (Hanoi newspaper)
TT	Thông tư [communication]
TTTT	Thông Tin Tuyên Truyền [Information and Propaganda]
UBHC	Ủy Ban Hành Chính [Administrative Committee]
UBHCBB	Ủy Ban Hành Chính Bắc Bộ [Northern Region Administrative Committee]
UBND	Ủy Ban Nhân Dân [People's Committee]
UBNDBB	Ủy Ban Nhân Dân Bắc Bộ [Northern Region People's Committee]
VKĐ	Văn kiện Đảng [Party document]
VKĐKC1	*Văn Kiện Đảng về Kháng Chiến Chống Thực Dân Pháp* [Party Documents on Resistance to French Colonialism], vol. 1, *1945–1950*
VKĐTT	*Văn Kiện Đảng Toàn Tập* [Complete Party Documents]
X&N	*Xưa & Nay* [Past and Present] (Hanoi journal)

PREFACE

1. *Vietnamese Anticolonialism, 1885–1925* (Berkeley: University of California Press, 1971)

2. *Vietnamese Tradition on Trial, 1920–1945* (Berkeley: University of California Press, 1981).

3. *Vietnam 1945: The Quest for Power* (Berkeley: University of California Press, 1995).

4. I rhapsodize about my encounters with the GF collection in *Vietnam 1945*, xxii–xxiii.

5. Christopher E. Goscha, *Historical Dictionary of the Indochina War (1945–1954)* (Copenhagen: NIAS Press, 2011), cross-indexes aliases for many of his Vietnamese biographical entries.

INTRODUCTION

1. 21 Dec. 1946 pronouncement, HCMTT 4, 207–10.

2. David G. Marr, *Vietnam 1945: The Quest for Power* (Berkeley: University of California Press, 1995), 382–472.

3. Marr, *Vietnam 1945*, 535–37.

4. Bernard Fall, *The Viet-Minh Regime: Government and Administration in the Democratic Republic of Vietnam* (Ithaca, NY: Cornell University Press, 1954). Fall later published an expanded French version, *Le Viet-Minh: La République Démocratique du Viet-Nam, 1946–1960* (Paris: Colin, 1960).

5. Nguyễn Tố Uyên, *Công cuộc Bảo vệ và Xây dựng Chính quyền Nhân dân ở Việt Nam trong những năm 1945–1946* [Protecting and Constructing People's Government in Vietnam during the years 1945–1946] (Hanoi: NXB KHXH, 1999).

6. An earlier version of this chapter was published in *The First Vietnam War: Colonial Conflict and Cold War Crisis*, edited by Mark Atwood Lawrence and Fredrik Logevall (Cambridge, MA: Harvard University Press, 2007), 74–104.

7. Some of this chapter appeared first in my "Beyond High Politics: State Formation in Northern Vietnam, 1945–1946," in *Naissance d'un État-Parti: Le Viêt Nam depuis 1945/ The Birth of Party State: Vietnam Since 1945*, edited by Christopher E. Goscha and Benoît De Tréglodé (Paris: Les Indes Savants, 2004), 25–60.

CHAPTER 1

1. Members of the provisional government were:

Hồ Chí Minh	President and responsible for foreign affairs	ICP
Võ Nguyên Giáp	Minister of Interior	ICP
Trần Huy Liệu	Minister of Information and Propaganda	ICP
Chu Văn Tấn	Minister of Defense	ICP
Dương Đức Hiền	Minister of Youth	Democratic Party
Nguyễn Mạnh Hà	Minister of National Economy	nonparty
Nguyễn Văn Tố	Minister of Social Relief	nonparty
Vũ Trọng Khánh	Minister of Justice	nonparty
Đào Trọng Kim	Minister of Communications and Public Works	nonparty
Lê Văn Hiến	Minister of Labor	ICP
Phạm Văn Đồng	Minister of Finance	ICP
Vũ Đình Hoè	Minister of National Education	nonparty
Cù Huy Cận	Minister without Portfolio	Democratic Party
Nguyễn Văn Xuân	Minister without Portfolio	ICP

The party identifications in the right column are mine, not present in the *Công Báo*. Four ministers were not present at the first Cabinet meeting: Trần Huy Liệu, Lê Văn Hiến, Phạm Văn Đồng, and Cù Huy Cận. Phạm Ngọc Thạch had been designated minister of health, but this was not announced yet, and he remained in southern Vietnam for two months thereafter; Hoàng Tích Trí served as deputy health minister. *Việt Nam Dân Quốc Công Báo* [Vietnam National Gazette], vol. 1945, 2; hereafter CB 1945. David G. Marr, *Vietnam 1945: The Quest for Power* (Berkeley: University of California Press, 1995), 473–76, 501–07.

2. CB 1945, 4–12. All decrees *(sắc lệnh)* were issued under the title of "President of the DRV Provisional Government," Hồ Chí Minh, but in these early days many were signed by the interior minister, Võ Nguyên Giáp. Each decree specified which ministry or ministries bore responsibility for implementation. Printed copies of decrees were mailed to lower echelons, and in some cases published in daily newspapers. Ministries issued edicts *(nghị định)*, often designed to fulfill a decree.

3. Two additional decrees specified a new inspectorate of education and incorporated museums, public libraries, and l'Ecole française d'Extrême-Orient (Hanoi) to the Ministry of National Education.

4. SL (20 Sept. 1945), in CB 1945, 12. Chapter 2 discusses constitutional deliberations.

5. SL 51 (17 Oct. 1945), in CB 1945, 45.

6. DC 10 (4 Sept. 1945).

7. CQ 38 (9 Sept. 1945).

8. CQ 71 (19 Oct. 1945); DC 52 (24 Oct. 1945).

9. CQ 57 (3 Oct. 1945); 66 (13 Oct. 1945); and 78 (30 Oct. 1945).

10. 6 Sept. 1945 Nội Vụ to all people's committees, via the three regional committees, ANOM, INDO, GF 13. Giáp was overreacting to several French commando probes. More than two hundred neatly bound Northern Region Committee outgoing telegrams from 3 Sept. 1945 onward can be found in GF 58. In all subsequent endnotes citing specific GF cartons I omit "ANOM, INDO."

11. 3 Sept. 1945, chairman UBNDBB to all provinces and bureaus, GF 13.

12. 12 Sept. 1945, Bộ Nội Vụ (Võ Nguyên Giáp) to three regional committees, GF 13. The UBNDBB forwarded this message to all provinces and bureaus the same day.

13. 17 Sept. 1945, UBNDBB to all provinces and bureaus, GF 34.

14. 10 Sept. 1945, Tổng Thư Ký Việt Nam Dân Chủ to UBNDBB, in dossier of Hà Đông petitions, GF 52. The memo is attached to the stack of petitions received from Chính. Decades later, Chính's outspoken behavior would land him in jail repeatedly.

15. 15 June 1945, Gouvernement général personnel rosters, GF 55. Following each employee's name is age, marital status, years in service, rank, current position, and source of funding.

16. Báo cáo tình hình Bắc Bộ [. . .] đến 31–12–45, UBHCBB, 4, in GF 48.

17. SL (3 Oct. 1945), in CB 1945, 33–34. The decree ignores the question of how the Cambodia and Laos responsibilities of the Gouvernement général are to be dealt with.

18. 25 Sept. 1945, Bộ Tài Chính to Bộ Kinh Tế Quốc Gia, GF 3.

19. Undated (Oct. 1945?) personnel roster, GF4. Defense and Finance did not report.

20. 15 Nov. 1945, Danh sách. Interior Ministry outgoing message file, Oct.–Dec. 1945, GF 73.

21. These calculations derive from PTT telegraph bills for the month of September sent to the twelve ministries. Other minimal users of the telegraph included Justice, Communications and Transport, Social Welfare, and Labor. 17 Nov. 1945, Nội Vụ to Tài chính; and 19 Nov. 1945, Nội Vụ to Sở Bưu Điện, in Interior Ministry outgoing message file, Oct.–Dec. 1945, GF 73.

22. Nguyễn Văn Trân was vice chairman of the Northern Region Committee, and there were five ordinary members: Đào Văn Biểu, Phan Tử Nghĩa, Nguyễn Văn Sước, Nguyễn Duy Thân, and Nguyễn Công Truyền. 29 Aug. 1945, Chính Phủ Lâm Thời to all northern people's committees, GF 62. X&N 78 (Aug. 2000): 6–8.

23. Undated (Oct. 1945?) personnel roster, GF 4. The term Bắc Bộ Phủ (BBP) quickly came to refer to the building, which also housed the offices of Hồ Chí Minh and several ministries. Unless otherwise indicated, I will use that meaning of BBP.

24. Almost all members of the Northern Region Office and the eleven bureaus and services came from the former Résidence superieure pour le Tonkin, which a few months prior had numbered 2,266 employees. Undated roster (June 1945?), GF/CR 141.

25. Báo cáo tình hình Bắc Bộ đến 31–12–45, Dec. 1945, 4–7, in GF 48.

26. This account is drawn from handwritten notes of the meeting taken by an unidentified Northern Region Office participant, now located in GF 68. At the time there were twenty-seven provinces in the northern region.

27. Biên bản Hội nghị các chủ tịch ủy ban nhân dân các tỉnh, 1–2 Oct. 1945, GF 68.

28. All province committees had an odd number of members, presumably to avoid tie votes. The majority had five or seven members, but Hòa Bình had nine, Hải Dương eleven, and Thái Nguyên thirteen.

29. Nguyễn Ngọc Minh, "The Birth of an Independent Currency," *Vietnamese Studies* 7 (1965): 200–201.

30. Minutes on this evening discussion are brief and vague. According to a report in CQ 61 (8 Oct. 1945) and CQ 62 (9 Oct. 1945), the discussion of rural administration continued into a third day. See also *Dân Quốc* (Hanoi) 27 (6 Oct. 1945).

31. Marr, *Vietnam 1945*, 442–47.

32. Lê Đức Triêm, et al., *Quân khu 4: Lịch sử kháng chiến chống thực dân Pháp xâm lược (1945–1954)* [Military Zone 4: History of Resistance to French Colonial Aggression (1945–1954)] (Hanoi: NXB QĐND, 1990), 34–35. Trần Hữu Dực, *Bước qua đầu thù* [Stepping over the Enemy's Head] (Hanoi: NXB CTQG, 1996), 250–53.

33. Lê Đức Triêm, 34. "Provisional" was dropped from the title two weeks later, and "Revolutionary" shortly thereafter.

34. Trần Hữu Dực, 253–55. Dực admits to spending his time playing with the bathtub, hot running water, shampoo, bathrobe, and toilet paper, all of which were new to him. The symbolism of taking over the French résident supérieure's bedroom was savored as well.

35. Trần Hữu Dực, 256–67.

36. 10 Sept. 1945, Nội Vụ to UBND Bắc, Trung, Nam Bộ, GF 34.

37. UBHCBB, outgoing message file beginning 1 Jan. 1946, GF 17.

38. The PTT headquarters in Hanoi issued weekly status reports on telegraph and telephone connections nationwide. Some fifty of these reports can be found in GF 71. PTT operations are discussed further in chapter 2.

39. Nguyễn Duy Trinh, a native of Nghệ An, was authorized by Hanoi to make appointments to bureaus and services nominally under ministerial jurisdiction, which meant paying these staff from regional sources as well. 1 Oct. 1946 appointment edict signed by Trinh, GF 72.

40. The regional committee for Nam Bộ went by at least four different names in late 1945. Except where precision is required, I refer simply to the Southern Region Committee.

41. "La Republique Democratique du Viet-Nam," undated but probably early January 1946, in SHD 10H 623, 6–10, 12, 49.

42. Phạm Văn Bạch had received law and literature degrees at the University of Paris, practiced law in Phnom Penh, taught at Cần Thơ college, and been appointed a judge by the Japanese in the summer of 1945.

43. Trần Thị Liên, "Les Catholiques Vietnamiens pendant le guerre d'independence (1945–1954); entre le reconquet colonial et la résistance communiste," (diplôme de doctorat de l'Institut d'études politiques de Paris, 1996), 68–70, 264–67.

44. Christopher Goscha, *Historical Dictionary of the Indochina War* (1945–1954) (Copenhagen: NIAS Press, 2011). Thăng Long, ed., *Nhớ Nam Bộ & Cực Nam Trung Bộ buổi đầu kháng chiến chống Pháp* [Remembering Southern and South-central Vietnam in Early Days of the Anti-French Resistance] (Hồ Chí Minh City: NXB Trẻ, 1999), 99, 106–112, 478–79.

45. Trần Thị Liên, 112–14.

46. SL 63 (22 Nov. 1945), in CB 1945, 85–92. 8 Dec. 1945, Nội Vụ to all provinces and cities, GF 73. Sixty-eight hundred copies of this decree were printed and distributed via official channels, with 23 percent going to the north, 62 percent to the center, and 15 percent to the south (via the Central Region People's Committee). Some newspapers summarized this decree for readers. Nguyễn Tố Uyên, *Công cuộc bảo vệ và xây dựng Chính Quyền Nhân dân ở Việt Nam trong những năm 1945–1946* [Protecting and Building People's Government in 1945–1946] (Hanoi: NXB KHXH, 1999), 145–51, expertly discusses the 22 November decree.

47. 20 Nov. 1945, Thông cáo về việc chấn chỉnh chính quyền nhân dân, GF 73. None of the fifteen members of the drafting committee were from central or southern regions. One month later, a second decree spelled out slightly different administrative provisions for eight cities (Hanoi, Haiphong, Nam Định, Vinh-Bến Thủy, Huế, Đà Nẵng, Dalat, and Saigon) as well as a yet unspecified number of province-level towns *(thị xã)*. SL 77 (21 Dec. 1945); CB 1945, 122–27.

48. Commune people's councils were to elect district administrative committees, and province/city councils were to elect regional committees. Only in the 1959 constitution were districts granted people's councils. In the 1960s, the term "administrative committee" was changed to "people's committee" *(ủy ban nhân dân)*.

49. GF files demonstrate that the change was almost total in northern provinces. Newspapers published in central provinces used the term "administrative committee"

starting in early 1946. Captured Nam Bộ documents in SHD files use the term increasingly during 1946.

50. For example, Thái Nguyên calculated that only 6,374.88$BIC would be left in the province treasury if it honored 19,616.63$BIC in impending salary disbursements. It then respectfully requested Hanoi to "find a way to solve the problem." 29 Oct. 1945, UBND Thái Nguyên to UBNDBB, GF 48.

51. SL 54 (1 Nov. 1945) and Nội Vụ thông tư, in CB 1945, 67–69. 7 Nov. 1945, Bộ Tài Chính to UBNDBB, ANOM, INDO, in CR 141. 13 Nov. 1945, Bộ Tài Chính to UBNDBB, in GF 6. SL 58 (10 Nov. 1945), in CB 1945, 81.

52. Four additional staff members were away on military training, and two had been dismissed.

53. Undated (Dec. 1945?) compilations by Phòng Viên Chức, in GF 53. Police, Customs, the PTT, and two other unnamed units had yet to report.

54. Perhaps half of the northern province committees forwarded personnel rosters to Hanoi at the end of 1945, but often minus key details. Province responses are scattered through some sixty Phòng Viên Chức dossiers in GF 21 and 33.

55. Scores of Interior Ministry responses to employee petitions requesting salary hikes, leave without pay, or retirement with pension can be found in the ministry's outgoing message file for November 1945, GF 73.

56. 24 Dec. 1945, Giám đốc Sở Công Chính Bắc Bộ to UBNDBB, GF 42.

57. 7 Nov. 1945, Nội Vụ thông tư to all ministries and provinces, GF 60.

58. 5 Dec. 1945, Bộ Tài Chính to all ministries and provinces, GF 33; 13 Dec. 1945, UBND Sơn Tây to UBNDBB, GF 33.

59. 26 Dec. 1945, UBNDBB instruction to six offices to submit their end-of-year reports, GF 6; Phòng Viên Chức undated response, GF 6.

60. 24 Oct. 1945, Nội Vụ to UBNDBB, GF 73. The following state employee categories are listed for increases: kitchen staff, houseboys (bồi, a colonial term), laundry workers, manual laborers, and gardeners.

61. January 1946 pay sheets, in "Solde" file, GF 3.

62. Quyết Thắng (Huế) 6 (5 Nov. 1945). Some of his friends had taken up petty commerce.

63. Quyết Thắng 17 (15 Feb. 1946).

64. CQ 154 (29 Jan. 1946). There were subsequent rumors of a planned strike by former colonial employees. Trung Việt Tân Văn (Hanoi) 3 (19 Feb. 1946).

65. CQ 157 (7 Feb. 1946). I have not found evidence that these elections took place, although someone started issuing pronouncements on behalf of the association.

66. Quyết Thắng 37 (4 May 1946).

67. David G. Marr, "A Brief History of Local Government in Vietnam," in Beyond Hanoi: Local Government in Vietnam, edited by Benedict J. Tria Kerkvliet and David G. Marr (Singapore: ISEAS, 2004), 28–38.

68. More than one hundred semi-monthly and monthly reports from northern provinces in late 1945 are scattered through the GF files.

69. 5 Nov. 1945, UBNDBB to UBND Bắc Giang, in Văn Phòng Mật outgoing message file, GF 31.

70. Totalling up numbers from the twelve reporting provinces, we find 183 province office employees before August and 153 afterwards, not a substantial drop. The largest declines were in Thái Bình (28 down to 13) and Quảng Yên (16 down to 9). Undated (early 1946?) list, first bundle, GF 4.

71. Petitions dated between 18 and 21 Sept. 1945, Hưng Yên file, ANOM, INDO, GF 67. About one-third of petitioners affixed thumbprints beside their names rather than signatures.

72. At the subsequent 1–2 Oct. 1945 meeting in Hanoi, discussed earlier, Phạm Quốc Dân is listed as Hưng Yên province chairman, but the minutes do not record him saying anything. He was still chairman in November 1946.

73. 17 Sept. 1945, UBNDBB to UBND Thái Bình, GF 16.

74. 3 Nov. 1945, Giám đốc Ngân khố Quốc Gia to UBNDBB, GF 33; 5 Nov. 1945, UBNDBB to UBND Yên Bái, GF 33.

75. 3 Dec. 1945, BB to UBND Ninh Bình, GF 62.

76. Vấn đề tạp dịch dossier, GF 24.

77. Trợ cấp Vệ Quốc Quân dossier, GF 24.

78. 5 Feb. 1946, Thuế Quan to Tài Chính, with attached correspondence, GF 66. Rice controls are discussed in chapter 6.

79. Early 1946 government coal quotes are in Than máy dossier, GF 72. 23 May 46, UBHCBB to UBHC Hòn Gai, GF 13. See also chapter 6.

80. Bắc Giang transport prices dossier 1946, GF 22.

81. 9 May 1946, UBHCBB (Nguyễn Xiển) to UBHC Hải Dương, outgoing message file, GF 17. Dike repairs are discussed in chapter 9.

82. 11 Sept. 1946, petition and subsequent correspondence, GF 2.

83. Thẻ công dân dossier, GF 22.

84. Grievance petitions, and 18 Jan. 1946 BB to UBHC Nam Định memo, Nam Định dossier, GF 1. Investigation results are unknown.

85. Unsigned 1 Oct. 1946 petition, with province marginalia stating that a secret investigation was launched on 10 Oct. 1946. Nam Định dossier, GF 1.

86. Scores of unresolved cases, with each dossier labeled "Việc xích mích giữa..." (Disagreement between . . .), can be found in GF 16.

87. 17 Oct. 1946, UBHC Bắc Giang to BB, Phòng Kinh tế dossier, GF 48. It is unclear whether the drums had contained oil or not.

88. 5 April 1946, UBHC Hưng Yên (Phan Quốc Dân) to Ban Thanh Tra Đặc Biệt, Phủ Khoái Châu dossier, GF 32.

89. 7 June 1946, memo BB to Bộ Nội Vụ, with attachments, Thái Nguyên dossier, GF 29.

90. Because petitions and petition routing slips are dispersed throughout the seventy-eight GF archive boxes, I did not attempt a full count. I estimate the September 1945–December 1946 files contain at least three thousand petitions and perhaps ten times that number of carbon copies of routing slips. About 95 percent of petitions are handwritten and 5 percent typed), with the latter tending to come from merchants or state employees.

91. A small percentage of petitions were anonymous. Group petitions often included thumbprints, with a literate participant adding the person's name in roman script or

Chinese. Following colonial procedure, petitions were supposed to have tax stamps affixed, but the files contain many exceptions.

92. In some cases, typed copies of the petition were made for internal circulation or action at several locations.

93. A carbon copy of the routing slip was kept on file.

94. Letters of introduction folder, GF 45.

95. Những việc sai lầm của Ủy ban huyện Tam Nông dossier, ANOM, INDO, CR 141.

96. SL 64 (23 Nov. 1945), in CB 1945, 94–95. 7 Dec. 1945, UBNDBB to all northern provinces, GF 29. This decree also authorized formation of a special court to try persons charged by the Special Inspectorate, but I have found no evidence that this court ever convened.

97. 20 Dec. 1945, BB to TTTT, outgoing message file, GF 73.

98. SL 80 (31 Dec. 1945), in CB 1946, 15. Cù Huy Cận was listed initially as minister without portfolio.

99. Stacks of petitions were routed from the Interior Ministry to the Northern Region Committee for action starting in September, but it may have been late December before the Political and Administrative Inspectorate was organized.

100. Family petitions and resulting correspondence extend from February to November 1946, with no indication the case was resolved. An Trí dossier, GF 30.

101. 15 Feb. 1946, Ban Thanh Tra Đặc Biệt (both Cù Huy Cận and Bùi Bằng Đoàn signing) to UBHC Hà Nam, Phủ Lý dossier, GF 1. See also Marr, *Vietnam 1945*, 416.

102. 27 Feb. 1946, UBHCBB to UBHC Hà Nam, Thanh Liêm dossier, GF 1.

103. 31 Oct. 1945, UBND Ngoại Thành Hà Nội, GF 64.

104. 30 Sept. 1945, UBND Hà Đông to BB, Hà Đông file, GF 53.

105. 26 Dec. 1945, UBND Hải Dương to BB, Bưu Điện Dossier, GF 45.

106. 14 March 1946, UBHCBB draft specifications to Nội Vụ, Thành lập Ban Thanh Tra Bắc Bộ dossier, GF 19.

107. 9 May 46, Nghị định (Bộ Nội Vụ), Ban Thanh Tra dossier, GF 40. The *Công Báo* did not publish this edict.

108. 10 Oct. 1946, BB to Nội Vụ, Linh tinh dossier, GF 76.

109. 12 Nov. 1946, complaint from two Northern Region Office typists about increasing workloads, on which their boss penned a note linking this increase to dissolution of the Northern Region Inspectorate, GF 62.

110. The only formal budgetary disbursements to the Special Inspectorate I have found is a mere two thousand piastres for "urgent expenses" in March, recorded in CB 1946, 459.

111. 29 Aug. 1946, nghị định Bộ Tài chính, CB 1946, 495. In Vietnamese the new unit's lofty designation was Nha Thanh Tra Chính Trị Hành Chính Toàn Quốc.

112. Cù Huy Cận is best remembered for his early 1940s poetry (under the pen name of Huy Cận), while Bùi Bằng Đoàn is mostly recalled today as the father of Bùi Tín, ranking Communist Party editor who defected to the West in 1990.

113. SL 51 (17 Oct. 1945), in CB 1945, 41–45. This decree was distributed throughout the civil administration and reprinted in a number of newspapers.

114. These sparsely populated provinces were Lào Cai, Hòa Bình, Lâm Viên (Lâm Đồng), Baria, and Hà Tiên.

115. Đà Nẵng City was given its own seat later, bringing the total to 330. SL 72 (2 Dec. 1945), in CB 1945, 110.

116. Each reserved seat had to be filled by a person from a specified minority, with the following ethnic groups included: Thái đen, Mán (Dao), Nùng, Mường, Mọi, Jarai, Chàm, and Rhadé. Overseas Chinese and Khmer were not recognized. Subsequently the Interior Ministry made it clear that minority individuals could contest nonreserved seats too. No information is available on how province committees were expected to identify the voters permitted to choose from among reserved ethnic candidates on election day.

117. Thông Tư (2 Nov. 1945), in CB 1945, 96–99.

118. *Quyết Thắng* (weekly organ of the Việt Minh Trung Bô, Huế) 10 (2 Dec. 1945).

119. *Chiến Sĩ* (Huế) 5 (14 Dec. 1945).

120. *Chiến Sĩ* 8 (4 Jan. 1946). "Talent and virtue" *(tài và đức)*, a traditional Confucian formula, was used by other editors as well to characterize a good delegate, without applying it to specific candidates.

121. *Thời Mới* (Hanoi) 13 (16 Dec. 1945). Independently published by Nguyễn Văn Luận, as a continuation of *Trung Bắc Chủ Nhật*.

122. SL 75 (18 Dec. 1945), in CB 1945, 122. Newspapers announced the postponement on 19 December.

123. *Dân Quốc* (Hanoi) 88 (17 Dec. 1945); 89 (18 Dec. 1945); and 92 (21 Dec. 1945). DC 97 (15 Dec. 1945); 115 (7 Jan. 1946). Some other figures on candidate/seat numbers: Haiphong 23/3; Quảng Yên 17/3; Vĩnh Yên 15/4; Lạng Sơn 14/3; Phú Thọ 26/5; Thái Nguyên 7/3; and Yên Bái (Kinh 7/1; Thổ [Tày] 4/1). I have not been able to locate a nationwide list of candidates as of election day.

124. Trần Quang Vân, *Dân Quốc* (Hanoi) 87 (15 Dec. 1945).

125. *Dân Quốc* 97 (29 Dec. 1945).

126. *Trung Việt Tân Văn* (Hanoi) 10 (27 Feb. 1946).

127. DC 75 (20 Nov. 1945); 78 (23 Nov. 1945) This paper was also being read in nearby provinces, where the forms would have been even more useful.

128. DC 91 (8 Dec. 1945). The list of twenty-two Haiphong candidates was signed and released by the people's committee chairman, Vũ Quốc Huy, on 11 December.

129. DC 98 (17 Dec. 1945) No estimate of crowd size is given, which suggests it was not large compared to other public meetings that had taken place at Opera House square. Similar meetings took place at about the same time in nearby Quảng Yên province and Hòn Gai town. 23 Dec. 1945 report, Quảng Yên dossier, GF 71.

130. X&N 236 (May 2005): 16.

131. DC 100 (19 Dec. 1945); 101 (20 Dec. 1945); 103 (22 Dec. 1945); 104 (25 Dec. 1945); 107 (28 Dec. 1945); and 109 (31 Dec. 1945). Photos of preelection meetings are reproduced in Hội Khoa Học Lịch Sử Việt Nam, *Ký Ức về những ngày Độc Lập Đầu Tiên 1945–1946* [Memories of the Early Days of Independence 1945–1946] (Hanoi: NXB Thời Đại, 2010), 79–85.

132. *Quyết Thắng* 12 (16 December 1945), reprints a Tổng Bộ Việt Minh instruction that candidates should not list their Việt Minh affiliation.

133. *Nam Tiến* 4 (21 Dec. 1945); 5 (4 Jan. 1946). Biographical sketches of candidates were also printed.

134. Nguyễn Khoa Diệu Hồng, a native of Huế, had vaulted to prominence when she addressed the 17 August 1945 mass meeting in front of the Hanoi Opera House. Marr, *Vietnam 1945,* 386.

135. *Nam Tiến* 5 (4 Jan. 1946). One Nam Định candidate not present was the propaganda minister, Trần Huy Liệu, but a speech he had delivered on 21 December was reported extensively in this issue. The paper also described election activities in adjacent Thái Bình and Ninh Bình provinces.

136. *Tương Lai* (Hanoi) 12 (13 Dec. 1945). Trương Văn Minh was also principal of a private girl's school. A subsequent issue indicates he was elected, but the official roll of National Assembly delegates does not list him. CB 1946, 212–16.

137. *Bạn Gái* (Hanoi), số đặc biệt (late Dec. 1945). Đán was not elected, and the paper appears to have stopped.

138. *Đồng Minh* 5 (18 Dec. 1945); 6 (21 Dec. 1945); 8 (2 Jan. 1946). All four were elected.

139. *Tổng tuyển cử ngày 6-1-1946 . Danh sách và tiểu sử các vị ứng cử ở Hà Nội* [The 6 January 1946 General Election. Roster and Biographies of Candidates in Hanoi] (Hanoi: NXB Viễn Đông, Dec. 1945). The booklet also contains careful instructions on how to cast one's ballot.

140. DC 100 (19 Dec. 1945); 101 (20 Dec. 1945); 103 (22 Dec. 1945); 104 (25 Dec. 1945); 107 (28 Dec. 1945); 109 (31 Dec. 1945); and 115 (7 Jan. 1946). Among the three Kiến An victors on 23 December was Nguyễn Xiển, chairman of the Northern Region Committee.

141. *Dân Quốc* (Hanoi) 88 (17 Dec. 1945). *Đồng Minh* 10 (9 Jan. 1946). *Chiến Sĩ* (Huế) 9 (11 Jan. 1946). Hội Khoa Học Lịch Sử Việt Nam, *Ký Ức,* 86–93.

142. Duong Van Mai Elliott, *The Sacred Willow: Four Generations in the Life of a Vietnamese Family* (New York: Oxford University Press, 1999), 133.

143. *Chiến Sĩ* 9 (11 Jan. 1946).

144. CQ 142 (15 Jan. 1946); 145 (18 Jan. 1946). *Thời Mới* (Hanoi) 13 (16 Dec. 1945).

145. *Dân Quốc* (Hanoi) 93 (22 Dec. 1945). It was said too that Phạm Ngọc Thạch had stood for election in Saigon, and Phạm Văn Bạch in Bến Tre, yet neither is listed in the subsequent official roll of National Assembly delegates. Their names were added later.

146. Nguyễn Tố Uyên, 127. Hồng Thái, "Vài nét về Quốc hội," NCLS 167 (March–April 1976), 27–29.

147. *Chiến Sĩ* 10 (18 Jan. 1946). The article doesn't indicate how the votes were sent to Vietnam and allocated to specific province contests.

148. 8 Jan. 1946, UBHCBB to all provinces, Haiphong, and Nam Dinh city, outgoing message file, GF 17.

149. 8 Jan. 1946, UBHCBB to UBHC Mộc Châu, outgoing message file, GF 17.

150. DC 121 (14 Jan. 1946). When dividing Hồ Chí Minh's vote count into total votes cast the result is 97.9 percent, probably reflecting a small number of informal ballots that had to be subtracted before obtaining the official 98.4 percent figure.

151. DC 123 (16 Jan. 1946). Informal ballots totaled 861. The number of votes for every candidate is listed, although there appears to be at least one misprint. The lowest vote received by a candidate was 26.

152. 26 Jan. 1946, UBHCBB to all provinces and cities, outgoing message file, GF 17. Original government instructions were to conduct runoff elections on 20 January, but this proved impossible.

153. ST, Tết Bính Tuất special issue, late Jan. 1946. *Sự Thật* was the organ of the new Association for Marxist Studies, set up by the officially disbanded ICP. See chapter 8.

154. See, for example, 11 Feb. 1946, UBHCBB to UBHC Lạng Sơn, querying why 100,251 ballots were tallied when only 58,187 voters were registered. Outgoing message file, Văn Phòng Bắc Bộ, GF 17. In this particular case, Hanoi may have been seeking to embarrass a province committees not controlled by Việt Minh adherents. In other cases, no query was sent.

155. Monthly report for Jan. 1946, Directeur de la Police et de la Sûreté Federales en Indochine, CP 186. 17 Feb. 1947 study, in Etude sur le Vietminh dossier, ANOM, CP 128.

156. So far as I know, no scholarly examination of the 6 January 1946 elections has ever been published in the DRV/SRV, perhaps because it would expose the complications outlined here.

157. Philippe Devillers, *Histoire du Viet-nam de 1940 à 1952* (Paris: Editions de Seuil, 1952), 201.

158. Văn Phòng Bắc Bộ Phủ, outgoing message file, GF17; and perusal of incoming messages elsewhere for January–February 1946. CQ 137 (9 Jan. 1946) and 144 (17 Jan. 1946) reprint people's council election procedures in elaborate detail.

159. Tuyên Quang file, GF 75. Probably the file was sent to Hanoi for critical scrutiny.

160. A lot of names and titles are rendered in Chinese rather than *quốc ngữ*, partly reflecting the multi-ethnic character of Tuyên Quang province.

161. 14 Jan. 1946, UBHCBB to UBHC all provinces/cities, outgoing message file, GF 17. The following description is based on the April–May section of the UBHCBB outgoing message file, GF 17.

162. ĐL 161 (12 Feb. 1946); 162 (13 Feb. 1946).

163. *Đồng minh* 17 (16 Feb. 1946).

164. Small deferral notice in ĐL 180 (8 March 1946).

165. DC 139 (12 Feb. 1946); 142 (15 Feb. 1946); 147 (21 Feb. 1946); 148 (22 Feb. 1946); 163 (11 March 1946).

166. CQ 267 (15 June 1946); 269 (18 June 1946); 270 (19 June 1946); 272 (21 June 1946); 274 (24 June 1946); 280 (1 July 1946). ĐL 189 (5 July 1946).

167. CQ 286 (8 July 1946).

168. 29 July 1946, BB to all northern provinces/cities, second folder, GF 69.

169. 26 Aug. 1946, BB to Nội Vụ, second folder, GF 69.

170. 20 Aug. 1946, minutes of UBHCBB meeting, GF 35.

171. *Quyết chiến* (6 May 1946); (10 May 1946); and (11 May 1946).

172. Võ Quang Dụ, *Quyết Thắng* (Huế) 32 (13 April 1946), makes this argument most vehemently.

173. A polemic on this issue was carried out for several months between *Việt Nam* (Nationalist Party) and *Cứu Quốc* (Việt Minh). For a Revolutionary League comment on the argument, see *Đồng minh* 29 (31 March 1946).

174. 29 July 1946, BB to Nội Vụ, second folder, GF 69.

175. 29 Jul 1946, BB to Nội Vụ, second folder, GF 69.

CHAPTER 2

1. SL (9 Jan. 1946), in CB 1946, 42. DC 118 (10 Jan. 1946).

2. *Việt Nam* (Hanoi) 46 (9 Jan. 1946); 50 (12 Jan. 1946); and 51 (13 Jan. 1946). ST 11 (10 Jan. 1946). A number of southern delegates converged on Rạch Gía to prepare to board a boat to Bangkok, and thence travel by ship to Haiphong, but the French captured the boat first. Thăng Long, ed., *Nhớ Nam Bộ & Cực Nam Trung Bộ buổi đầu Kháng Chiến chống Pháp*. [Remembering South and South-central Vietnam in Early Days of the Anti-French Resistance] (Hồ Chí Minh City: NXB Trẻ, 1999), 145.

3. 19 Feb. 1946, Danh sách dân biểu Quốc hội Bắc Bộ, UBHCBB, GF 64.

4. As it happened, the breakthrough encounter between Hồ Chí Minh and Jean Sainteny did not occur until 16 February, and a preliminary accord was only signed on 6 March. See chapter 4.

5. *Nam Tiến* (Nam Định) 6 (28 Jan. 1946).

6. 10 Jan. 1946 Hồ Chí Minh speech, reported in *Nam Tiến* 6 (28 Jan. 1946).

7. *Quyết Thắng* (Huế) 15 (6 Jan. 1946).

8. Văn Phòng Quốc Hội, *Lịch Sử Quốc Hội Việt Nam, 1946–1960* [History of Vietnam's National Assembly, 1946–1960] (Hanoi: NXB CTQG, 1994), 65. Four members belonged to the Việt Minh, one to the Nationalist Party.

9. ST, Tết Bính Tuất special issue, late Jan. 1946.

10. 30 (?) Jan. 1946, UBHCBB to all provinces/cities, outgoing Message File, Văn Phòng BB, GF 17.

11. DC 137 (10 Feb. 1946); 154 (28 Feb. 1946).

12. *Gió Mới* (New Wind) 13 (22 Feb. 1946).

13. Undated (but late February) circular, VKĐTT 8, 409–12.

14. *Trung Việt Tân Văn* (Hanoi) 10 (27 Feb. 1946); 11 (28 Feb. 1946). X&N 236 (May 2005): 16–17. Hội Khoa Học Lịch Sử Việt Nam, *Ký Ức*, 119–22.

15. Quoted in *Lịch Sử Quốc Hội Việt Nam*, 67.

16. Lâm Quang Thự, NCLS 184 (Jan.–Feb. 1979), 8–9.

17. CB 1945, 52. CB 1946, 212–15. I have cross-checked the number of seats allocated in the original election decree with actual National Assembly numbers (present and absent).

18. This description of Assembly proceedings is taken from the official minutes contained in CB 1946, 203–12; and *Lịch Sử Quốc Hội Việt Nam*, 68–79. Most newspapers also carried stories on the 2 March meeting. Photos in Hội Khoa Học Lịch Sử Việt Nam, *Ký Ức*, 123–25.

19. Nguyễn Đình Thi, Assembly delegate from Haiphong, and a key member of the Việt Minh's National Salvation Cultural Association (Hội Văn Hóa Cứu Quốc), had helped to make arrangements for arriving delegates. He also seems to have been assigned responsibility at this meeting for guiding proceedings in the direction desired by ICP leaders.

20. Nguyễn Tường Tam, foreign affairs (Nationalist Party); Huỳnh Thúc Kháng, interior (nonparty); Chu Bá Phượng, economics (Nationalist Party); Lê Văn Hiến, finance (ICP); Phan Anh, defense (nonparty); Trương Đình Tri, society (including health, relief, labor) (Revolutionary League); Đặng Thái Mai, education (Democratic Party); Vũ Đình Hòe, justice (Democratic Party); Trần Đăng Khoa, transport and public works (ICP); Bồ Xuân Luật, agriculture (Revolutionary League).

The party designations for Khoa and Luật are mine, not indicated in the *Công Báo*: both were temporary appointments, pending arrival of unnamed replacements from the south. CB 1946, 206.

21. Nguyễn Đình Thi spoke fifteen times, with no one else contributing more than four times. He may also have been chairing the proceedings, as Ngô Tử Hạ speaks only once at the end.

22. CB 1946, 211.

23. CB 1946, 211.

24. Nguyễn Tố Uyên, 257. Phạm Văn Đồng (ICP) and Cung Đình Quỳ (Nationalist Party) were designated vice-chairs of the bureau, while Hoàng Minh Giám (Việt Minh) and Dương Đức Hiền (Democratic Party) became secretaries.

25. Nguyễn Tố Uyên, 257. These individuals were: Tôn Đức Thắng, Dương Bạch Mai, Nguyễn Ngọc Bích, and Huỳnh Tấn Phát. None of these persons are on the absentee list of National Assembly members tabled 2 March 1946 (CB 1946, 215), which raises questions about how and when they were elected or appointed as delegates.

26. *Lịch Sử Quốc Hội Việt Nam*, 85, illustrations facing 88.

27. Published in DC 176 (27 March 1946).

28. 28 April 1946, Thông tư của Chính phủ, Ban thường trực Quốc Hội can thiệp vào việc hành chính dossier, Phòng Hành Chính, UBHCBB, GF 24.

29. 11 June 1946, UBHC Hải Dương to BB, with attachments; 20 June 1946, memo prepared by Phòng Hành Chính, UBHCBB, GF 24.

30. 11 June 1946, Trưởng Ban Thường Trực Quốc Hội to Nội Vụ, Công Thự 1946 dossier, Văn Phòng, GF 22. From late March, Standing Committee staff were housed at the former Hội Khai Trí Tiến Đức (Association pour la formation intellectuelle et morale des annamites) building adjacent to Hoàn Kiếm lake. CQ 187 (15 March 1946)

31. Correspondence 7–18 May 1946, Ninh Bình dossier, GF 67.

32. Correspondence 7–21 Aug. 1946, Hải Dương (hiện hành) dossier, GF 59. Lâm's case is discussed in chapter 7.

33. 22 July 1946, petition and subsequent correspondence, Khiếu nại tháng 5 năm 1946 dossier, GF 34.

34. ĐL 188 (4 July 1946).

35. ĐL 240 (8 Sept. 1946).

36. 6 Aug. 1946, Trưởng Ban Thường Trực Quốc Hội to UBHCBB and subsequent correspondence, Thứ vị trong nghi lễ 1946 dossier, GF 67.

37. *Tương Lai* (Hanoi) 6 (1 Nov. 1945); 7 (8 Nov. 1945). Several other newspapers published brief comparisons of U.S., British, Soviet, and French constitutions.

38. Full texts of the draft constitution are found in *Dân Quốc* (Hanoi), CQ (Hanoi), DC (Haiphong), and *Đa Minh* (Bùi Chu).

39. V. T., feature article, *Chiến Sĩ* (Huế) 3 (30 Nov. 1945).

40. *Nam Tiến* (Nam Định) 4 (21 Dec. 1945). As seen above, Tứ subsequently criticized President Hồ on the floor of the National Assembly.

41. *Chiến Sĩ* 5 (14 Dec. 1945).

42. Hoàng Gia Linh, *Tương Lai* 12 (13 Dec. 1945).

43. *Chiến Sĩ* 5 (14 Dec. 1945). *Nam Tiến* 5 (4 Jan. 1946).

44. X. X. X., *Tương Lai* 9 (22 Nov. 1945).

45. Tinh Sơn and Hải Sinh, *Quyết Thắng* 13 (23 Dec. 1945). The authors may have been well-known ICP members, using pseudonyms because the party had declared its self-dissolution in late November.

46. *Quyết Thắng* 17 (15 Feb. 1946).

47. DC 150 (24 Feb. 1946).

48. Vũ Bội Tấn, in *Tương Lai* 15 (28 Feb. 1946).

49. *Đồng Minh* 17 (16 Feb. 1946).

50. *Gió Mới* 14 (18 March 1946).

51. Nguyễn Bằng, *Giữ hay bỏ chế độ Ủy ban Nhân dân* [Keeping or Dropping the People's Committee System] (Hanoi: Tự Cường, 1946). Nguyễn Bằng, *Nghị Viện* [Parliament] (Hanoi: Quang Trung Thư Xã, 1946).

52. Nguyễn Bằng, *Nghị Viện*, 11.

53. Nicolas Machiavelli, *Sứ quán,* translated by Nguyễn Bằng (Hanoi: Tân Việt, 1946).

54. I have yet to uncover anything about Nguyễn Bằng's background, affiliation, or subsequent fate.

55. Công Văn đến and Những phiếu gửi, Đổng lý Văn phòng, Nội Vụ Bộ, GF 73. Confidential traffic was handled separately. Early Interior Ministry operation are described in NCLS 346 (3–2005): 3–12.

56. Undated (but probably early May 1946) handwritten notes, GF 40.

57. 4 May 1946, UBHCBB to Nội Vụ; 21 June 1945, UBHCBB to Nội Vụ; 11 July 1946 UBHCBB to Nội Vụ, GF 14.

58. Several dozen such printed forms can be found in GF 22, sometimes with French originals attached.

59. Handwritten receipts for a two-month period found in GF 22.

60. For example, the Economic Bureau of the Northern Region Office routed about one thousand dossiers marked "Urgent" to other internal destinations between 2 January and 18 September 1946. Sở Kinh tế routing ledger, GF 50.

61. 4 April 1946 report, Phòng Viên Chức to Chủ tịch UBHCBB and subsequent correspondence, Phòng Viên chức, GF 3. It id not occur to the report writer that office staff could have carried the stacks back upstairs themselves.

62. Phòng Công Văn work reports, GF 61. 12 Nov. 1946 written complaint from two typists, supported by Chủ Sự Phòng Công Văn, GF 62.

63. Bản Lưu Công Văn đi, Tập 5, Văn Phòng Mật, UBHCBB, GF 31. Confidential outgoing telegraphs had to be encrypted and dispatched separately.

64. 19 Dec. 1946, BB to Sơn Tây, in Bản Lưu Công Văn đi, Tập 5, Văn Phòng Mật, UBHCBB, GF 31.

65. 31 May 1945, Trưởng Ban Công Thự to BB, and subsequent correspondence, Chuyển Ban Bảo Vệ Thành Phố dossier, Văn Phòng BBP, GF 35.

66. The context is sketched in 20 May 1946, Quân Ủy Hội Đặc Phái Viên to Bộ Trưởng Bộ Ngoại Giao (Ngoại Kiều Pháp Vụ), Công Thự, 1946, Văn Phòng BB, GF 22. Chinese authorities had already allowed French Army units to occupy much of the Citadel in late March. The following custody cases are all derived from the same GF 22 file.

67. Phạm Như Thịnh, X&N 93 (June 2001): 7–8.

68. Vũ Đình Hòe, *Hồi ký Vũ Đình Hòe* [Memoirs of Vu Dinh Hoe], vol. 1 (Hanoi NXB Văn Hóa-Thông Tin, 1995), 334–36. NCLS 312 (5–2000): 70–78.

69. Vũ Đình Hòe, *Những Phương pháp Giáo dục ở các nước và vấn đề cải cách Giáo dục* [Educational Methods in Various Countries and the Question of Educational Reform] (Hanoi: Thanh Nghị, May 1945). Hòe also was a member of the *Thanh Nghị* journal group (1941–45), which was well represented in the provisional DRV cabinet.

70. SL 17 and SL 20 (8 Sept. 1945), in CB 1945, 8–9. The mass education campaign is discussed in chapter 9.

71. Nguyễn Văn Huyên achieved a doctorate in history from the Sorbonne in 1934, returning to Hanoi to teach at the École française d'Extrême-Orient. Ngụy Như Kontum obtained his *agrégé de science physiques* at the Sorbonne in 1938, returning to teach at the Lycée Chasseloup-Laubat (Saigon) and then the École du Protectorat (Hanoi).

72. Vũ Đình Hòe, *Hồi Ký*, 336–37. Nguyễn Đình Đầu, X&N 29 (July 1996): 13–14.

73. Vũ Đình Hòe, *Hồi Ký*, 334.

74. Vũ Đình Hòe, *Hồi Ký*, 337.

75. NĐ (21 Sept. 1945), in CB 1945, 21.

76. Decrees and edicts formalizing Education Ministry structure were not issued until July 1946. SL (9 July 1946), in CB 1946, 375–76, 378. NĐ (13 July 1946), in CB 1946, 413–16.

77. NĐ (14 Sept. 1945), (17 Sept. 1945), and (19 Sept. 1945), in CB 1945, 15, 27–28. 15 Sept. 1945 to 15 Dec. 1945, Học vụ monthly reports, GF 38.

78. 24 Dec. 1945, Nội vụ to Tài Chính and UBNDBB; TT (12 Sept. 1945), in CB 1945, 16.

79. SL (10 Oct. 1945), in CB 1945, 37. NĐ (23 Oct. 1945), in CB 1945, 62–63. Nine months later a very similar edict was issued, with some faculties still not functioning. NĐ (25 July 1946), CB 1946, 431–32.

80. NĐ (3 Nov. 1945), in CB 1945, 73–74. NĐ (9 Nov. 1945), in CB 1945, 83. The absence of French is notable. Perhaps it was assumed that enough students were fluent in French already.

81. NĐ (3 Nov. 1945), in CB 1945, 74–76.

82. Nguyễn Kim Nữ Hạnh, *Tiếp bước chân cha: Hồi ký về Giáo sư Nguyễn Văn Huyên* [Following in Father's Footsteps: Memoir on Professor Nguyen Van Huyen] (Hanoi: NXB Thế Giới, 2003), 115–20. Also reported in X&N 158 (Nov. 2002): 7–8. Diplomas were presented to graduating medical students, the first advanced degrees awarded in independent Vietnam. *Tiên Phong* 2 (1 Dec. 1945). *Dân Quốc* 62 (16 Nov. 1945). Hội Khoa Học Lịch Sử Việt Nam, *Ký Úc*, 62–63.

83. Vũ Đình Hòe, X&N 249 (Dec. 2005): 4–7.

84. NĐ (31 Dec. 1945), in CB 1946, 28.

85. NĐ (27 Dec. 1945); NĐ (17 May 1946), in CB 1946, 36, 329–30. The Russian language teacher was Oreste de Pletner, a White Russian émigré. There were three English language instructors: Trịnh Văn Bách, Tạ Quang Bửu, and Nguyễn Khắc Kham. The absence of modern Chinese language is puzzling.

86. NĐ (17 May 1946), in CB 1946, 329. Faculty of Letters: Đặng Thái Mai (Chinese literature), Nguyễn Văn Huyên (history), Nguyễn Thiệu Lâu (geography), Nguyễn Mạnh Tường (Western philosophy), Đào Duy Anh (ancient East Asian history), Hồ Hữu Tường (social science), Cao Xuân Huy (Eastern philosophy), Nguyễn Đức Nguyên (Vietnamese literature; literature and doctrine), Bùi Kỷ (Wang Yang-ming; Nguyễn Trãi's writing), Phạm Duy Khiêm (Greek and Latin literature), Trần Văn Giáp (Chinese literature), and Đỗ Xuân Hợp (anthropology). Three creative writers were listed separately as Vietnamese literature lecturers, to be paid at the rate of ten piastres per hour: Ngô Xuân Diệu, Đoàn Phú Tứ, and Cù Huy Cận.

87. NĐ (8 Feb. 1946); NĐ (21 March 1946), in CB 1946, 125, 195.

88. Tạ Quang Bửu had studied mathematics, physics, and electrical engineering in France and Great Britain. He undertook training at the Boy Scout academy outside London, and in 1937 expanded scouting activities in Annam while teaching at the Institut de la Providence in Huế, run by Canadian priests of the Redemptorist order.

89. NĐ (26 Sept. 1946), in CB 1946, 551–52. NĐ (1 Oct. 1946), in CB 1946, 552.

90. NĐ (24 Oct. 1945); NĐ (5 Nov. 1945), in CB 1945, 69, 76.

91. Ngân sách Bắc Bộ niên khoa 1946, chapter 27, GF 27. The secondary schools listed are Nam Định, Haiphong, Bắc Ninh, Thái Bình, Lạng Sơn, and Phú Thọ.

92. NĐ (13 Dec. 1945); NĐ (28 Jan. 1946); NĐ (13 Feb. 1946), in CB 1946, 18, 92, 123–24.

93. NĐ (5 April 1946); NĐ (13 Sept. 1946), in CB 1946, 254, 537.

94. NĐ (12 Oct. 1946), UBHCBB to Nha Trung Học Vụ, BDHV dossier, GF 24.

95. NĐ (5 Oct. 1946), in CB 1946, 588. Tờ trình Quốc Hội của Bộ Quốc gia Giáo dục, as quoted in Thaveeporn Vasavakul, "The State in Post-colonial Viet Nam: Schools, Economy, and National Culture (1945–1965)" (unpublished paper, Nov. 1995), 46.

96. *Tiến Hóa* 1 (15 Nov. 1946). Lê Hồng Long, founder, also explained how families would need to pay regular tuition.

97. 25 Oct. 1946, Đại diện Hoa kiều Hải Dương to UBHCBB, in BDHV dossier, GF 24.

98. CQ 344 (13 Sept. 1946) announced that the school would open on 16 October.

99. 29 Aug. 1946, Tổng Giám đốc Nha Thanh Niên và Thể Dục quyết nghị, GF 72.

100. Ngân sách Bắc Bộ niên khoa 1946 (chapters 29 and 30), GF 27.

101. Nguyễn Xiển, Báo cáo về tình hình Bắc Bộ, GF 19.

102. "Tờ trình Quốc Hội," as cited in Thaveeporn Vasavakul, 46.

103. NĐ (13 Sept. 1946), in CB 1946, 537.

104. Two SL (10 Aug. 1946), in CB 1946, 443–45.

105. NĐ (10 Sept. 1946), in CB 1946, 561–73.

106. Here it appears that "cooperatives" *(hợp tác xã)* and "New Life" *(Đời sống mới)* were tacked on to the original text to accommodate Việt Minh policies. See chapter 9.

107. SL (13 Sept. 1945), in CB 1945, 18. Subsequent decrees added two more military courts and specified territorial jurisdictions. SL (29 Sept. 1945), in CB 1945, 19–20, 27; and SL (28 Dec. 1945), in CB 1946, 14.

108. Lê Giản, *Những Ngày Sóng Gió: Hồi Ký* [Days of Adversity: Memoirs] (Hanoi: NXB Thanh Niên, 1985), 145–46. Phan Mỹ replaced Trần Độ as presiding judge in January 1946. 18 Jan. 1946, Nội Vụ NĐ, in CB 1946, 50, 161.

109. CB 1946, 219, 328, 448.

110. CB 1946, 44, 115–16, 142–45

111. SL (10 October 1945), in CB 1945, 35–36, 93–94.

112. *Việt Nam* 15 (1 Dec. 1945). CQ 107 (3 Dec. 1945).

113. Vũ Trọng Khánh, "Tờ Trình," attached to SL (24 Jan. 1946), in CB 1946, 64.

114. CQ 146 (19 Jan. 1946).

115. SL (24 Jan. 1946), in CB 1946, 63–71.

116. Five months later, the Northern Region Committee requested subordinate committees to send names of five persons to be people's assessors in criminal cases: one worker; one farmer; one woman; and two "prominent persons" *(nhân sĩ)* or "industrialists" *(kỹ nghệ gia)*. No school diploma or literacy test was required. 17 May 1946, UBHCBB to nine provinces and Haiphong, outgoing message file, GF 17.

117. 15 Jan. 1946, Bộ Tư Pháp to UBHCBB, and subsequent materials, GF 3.

118. 31 Jan. 1946, NĐ Tư Pháp, CB 1946, 152. Vũ Trọng Khánh chaired this committee, with Bùi Bằng Đoàn, Vũ Đình Hoè, Cù Huy Cận, and Hoàng Hữu Nam as members.

119. 13 Feb. 1946, Định Lệnh, CB 1946, 146.

120. CB 1946, 282, 589–91. Only five appointees were former mandarins.

121. CB 1946, 625–30. In Trung Bộ, the number of district magistrates per province ranged from twenty in Thanh Hóa to only one in Phú Yên.

122. Đơn xin đi làm của các viên chức tòa sứ cũ dossier, GF 25. CB 1946, 401, 516.

123. CB 1946, 261, 357, 410–12, 583–84.

124. 15 May 1946, Thông Tư; 1 Aug. 1946, Thống tư, in CB 1946, 323–24, 428.

125. CQ 386 (25 Oct. 1946); 387 (26 Oct. 1946).

126. SL (3 April 1946), in CB 1946, 217–18. I have yet to find information on "special courts."

127. DC 269 (18 July 1946). CQ 295 (18 July 1946). Chu Văn An, thirty years old, had been the object of numerous censorious petitions to the Interior Ministry, yet continued for months to dominate the Ủy Ban Hành Chính Ngoại Thành Hà Nội until his arrest in February. The trial was public and attracted a large audience.

128. Huyện Bình Xuyên (Vĩnh Yên) file, GF 59.

129. *Tương Lai* 8 (16 Nov. 1945); 9 (22 Nov. 1945); and 15 (28 Feb. 1946).

130. July–Sept. 1946, Vấn đề Bộ Tư Pháp/UBHC Hà Đông, GF 47. According to the provincial magistrate, the Hà Đông deputy chairman had intimated to him that Kinh was killed for reasons of state, but the deputy chairman vehemently denied this to the Northern Region Committee. There is no indication that Kinh's killers were ever arrested, much less punished.

131. "Lịch Sử ngành Thông Tin Bưu Điện Việt Nam (Dự thảo)" [A History of the Vietnam Information and Postal Branch (Draft)]. (Hanoi, 1989), 42–48.

132. Hundreds of daily telegraph and telephone operational reports can be perused in GF 53 and 71. Below the sixteenth parallel, PTT members kept much shorter lines functioning in DRV "free zones."

133. The PTT's radio units were placed under the Defense Ministry in late 1945. See chapter 3.

134. DC 50 (22 Oct. 1945). Hồ's message may have been an indirect rebuke to the Vietnam Nationalist Party, which controlled the Lào Cai province seat at that time.

135. Undated (probably May–June 1946), Sổ điện thoại Hà Nội, GF 16. Telephone books dated 1942–44 for Hanoi, Huế, and Haiphong can be found in GF 53.

136. David G. Marr, *Vietnam 1945: The Quest for Power* (Berkeley: University of California Press, 1995), 410, 502.

137. 27 Sept. 1945, Nha Giám đốc Bưu Điện Miền Bắc, Lưu trữ dossier, GF 25.

138. (?) Sept. 1945, Thổng tư, Tổng Giám đốc Bưu Điện Việt Nam, Bưu Điện (linh tinh) 1945 dossier, GF 45.

139. 3 Dec. 1945, Nội Vụ to UBHCBB, dossier 437, GF 73. (?) Dec. 1945, UBNDBB to all provinces, Bưu Điện dossier, GF 40. 14 Jan. 1946, Tổng Giám đốc to UBHCBB, Văn Phòng dossier 296, GF 48.

140. DC 124 (17 Jan. 1946). Why the government should be willing to purchase back the ill-gotten goods is left unexplained.

141. 29 Jan. 1946, UBHCBB to UBHC Hà Đông, outgoing telegraph file, GF 17.

142. 27 April 1946 to 21 May 1946, correspondence, Văn Phòng dossier 294, GF 48.

143. *Hình sự Công báo* (Hanoi) 7 (30 Sept. 1946).

144. (?) Nov. 1946, Nguyễn Tường Thụy petition to President Hồ Chí Minh, Văn Phòng Bộ Nội Vụ petitions dossier, GF 34.

145. CB 1946, 38–39, 60, 107–8, 129–30, and 153–54. No information is provided on PTT personnel below Quảng Nam.

146. Ty Kiểm Duyệt 1946 dossier, GF 12. PTT monitors blocked a few communications, but their main task was to compile fortnightly commodity price and political opinion summaries.

147. CB 1946, 185.

148. 12 Sept. 1946, UBHCBB to Giám đốc Bưu Điện Miền Bắc, GF 38, complains that the telephone repair instruction being given to militiamen is poorly organized.

149. 28 Nov. 1946, UBHCBB to Giám đốc Bưu Điện, GF 16.

150. CB 1946, 60, 129–30, 153–54. Such outright dismissals were rare in most other government bureaus.

151. 14 Jan. 1946, Tổng Giám đốc Bưu Điện to UBHCBB, Văn Phòng dossier 296, GF 48. CB 1946, 255, 521.

152. "Lịch sử ngành Thổng tin Bưu Điện . . . ," 79–80.

153. In late 1945 we observe one clerk itemizing each stamp used over a four-month period, the four-page typescript list totalling 33$60BIC. GF 39.

154. CB 1946, 92–93. *Villes martyres* refers to French towns destroyed in World War I.

155. CB 1946, 257–58, 443. The overprinting included the word *"Dân Sinh"* (People's Livelihood), and the faces of the former emperor and empress were left free of inked words.

156. CB 1946, 472–73. Alexandre Yersin, discoverer of the vaccine against plague, also was selected for overprinting, but unlike the Bishop of Adran his face was left free. Đặng Phong, X&N 135 (March 2003): 27–28, cites Yersin's unblemished face as an example of the August Revolution's refusal to condemn all French influences.

157. By the late 1980s, both cancelled and uncancelled DRV overprinted stamps from 1945–46 could be purchased from street vendors in Saigon and Hanoi.

158. CB 1946, 474–75. Denominations of the Hồ Chí Minh stamp ranged from ten *xu* to 150 *xu* (1.50$BIC), with portions of proceeds from the higher denominations going to the National Defense Fund.

159. I base this mostly on the number of articles written from Laos and mailed to papers in Huế, Vinh, and Hanoi, which also reveal that home periodicals were arriving in Laos via the PTT.

160. CQ 270 (19 June 1946).

161. CQ 363 (2 Oct. 1946). I discuss the modus vivendi in chapter 4.

162. DC 339 (11 Oct. 1946). CQ 372 (11 Oct. 1946). CB 1946, 599.

163. CB 1946, 596. The per diem was forty piastres.

164. See, for example, the Nationalist Party's *Chính Nghĩa tuần báo* (Hanoi) 20 (21 Oct. 1946); 21 (28 Oct. 1946); and the Revolutionary League's *Đồng Minh* (Hanoi) 58 (25 Oct. 1946).

165. DC 353 (28 Oct. 1946).

166. (?) Nov. 1946, Note sur la "Democratie Vietnamienne," Commissariat fédéral aux affairs politiques, Haussaire (Saigon), ANOM, INDO, CP-supplémentaire, box 5.

167. *Dư Luận* (Hanoi) 28 (3 Nov. 1946), partly censored. DC 354 (29 Oct. 1946). *Lịch Sử Quốc Hội Việt Nam*, 94. X&N 251/252 (Jan. 2006): 60–63.

168. DC 355 (30 Oct. 1946). CQ 391 (30 Oct. 1946). A secretariat and an order group (Đoàn trật tự) were also elected. 256 delegates were present for these votes. Phạm Văn Đồng and Trần Hữu Dực ended up chairing most subsequent sittings, not Tôn Đức Thắng.

169. CQ 392 (31 Oct. 1946). Henceforth the Opera House balcony was usually filled with citizens.

170. Nguyễn Văn Tạo, *Bài diễn văn của ông Nguyễn Văn Tạo trước Quốc hội Việt Nam* [Address of Mr. Nguyen Van Tao before the Vietnam National Assembly] (Hanoi: NXB CQ, Nov. 1946), 14.

171. DC 354 (29 Oct. 1946). CQ 391 (30 Oct. 1946). X&N 308 (May 2008): xiii.

172. Stein Tønnesson, *Vietnam 1946: How the War Began* (Berkeley: University of California Press, 2010), 120.

173. *Chính Nghĩa tuần báo* 22 (4 Nov. 1946). CQ 392 (31 Oct. 1946).

174. CQ 392 (31 Oct. 1946). DC 356 (31 Oct. 1946).

175. Observers quickly noted the absence of Defense Minister Phan Anh, about to be replaced by Giáp. Soon it was reported that President Hồ had offered Phan Anh a different portfolio, but Anh felt he could accomplish more for the nation outside the new government. CQ 305 (4 Nov. 1946).

176. CQ 393 (1 Nov. 1946); 394 (3 Nov. 1946). DC 357 (1 Nov. 1946).

177. CQ 394 (3 Nov. 1946). DC 358 (2 Nov. 1946). *Dư Luận* 28 (3 Nov. 1946). "La constitution de la République du Viet Nam," ANOM, INDO, CP- supplémentaire, box 4, 26–32. Thanks to Stein Tønnesson for sharing with me his photocopies of these ANOM documents.

178. CQ 394 (3 Nov. 1946). *Lịch Sử Quốc Hội Việt Nam*, 97–100.

179. CQ 389 (28 Oct. 1946).

180. CQ 395 (4 Nov. 1946). DC 360 (4 Nov. 1946). *Sao Vàng* 23 (7 Nov. 1946). Nguyễn Tố Uyên, 261–62. Phạm Văn Đồng became vice minister of economics, but soon after departed for Quảng Ngãi to lead resistance efforts in south-central Vietnam (Liên khu 5). It is unclear why the position of prime minister *(thủ tướng)* was left unfilled.

181. DC 359 (3 Nov. 1946). CQ 394 (3 Nov. 1946). " La constitution de la Republique . . . ," 36–38. *Lịch Sử Quốc Hội Việt Nam,* 102–3. *Đồng Minh* 59 (4 Nov. 1946).

182. DC 359 (3 Nov. 1946). CQ 394 (3 Nov. 1946). "La constitution de la République . . . ," 39–44. The subcommittee returned four days later to propose that private schools be permitted if they conformed to the government curriculum, and this wording was approved.

183. DC 361 (5 Nov. 1946). CQ 396 (5 Nov. 1946). "La constitution de la République . . . ," 45–48. According to *Kháng Chiến* (Quảng Ngãi) 9 (25 Nov. 1946), sixteen serving military personnel were delegates to the Assembly's second session.

184. The legislature's formal name was Nghị Viện Nhân Dân (People's Parliament), but delegates and journalists continued to use the term Quốc Hội (National Assembly).

185. Đào Trọng Truyền, from Thừa Thiên province, as quoted in DC 361 (5 Nov. 1946). The previous speaker is not named in the article.

186. "La constitution de la République . . . ," 49–50. *Lịch Sử Quốc Hội Việt Nam,* 103–104.

187. "La constitution de la République . . . ," 51–53. DC 362 (6 Nov. 1946). CQ 397 (6 Nov. 1946). For composition of the Standing Committee, see Nguyễn Tố Uyên, 260.

188. La constitution de la République . . . ," 53–67. DC 363 (7 Nov. 1946); 364 (8 Nov. 1946). CQ 398 (7 Nov. 1946); 399 (8 Nov. 1946); 400 (9 Nov. 1946); 411 (20 Nov. 1946). Nguyễn Tố Uyên, 262.

189. Đỗ Đức Dục's speech is reprinted in *Độc Lập Chủ Nhật* (Hanoi) 9 (10 Nov. 1946).

190. DC 365 (9 Nov. 1946). CQ 400 (9 Nov. 1946). "La constitution de la République . . . ," 70–71.

191. DC 371 (16 Nov. 1946).

192. DC 366 (11 Nov. 1946). CQ 401 (10 Nov. 1946); 402 (11 Nov. 1946). "La constitution de la République . . . ," 77. The constitution was published in full in CQ 411 (20 Nov. 1946). *Lịch Sử Quốc Hội Việt Nam,* 110.

193. Tønnesson, *Vietnam 1946,* 92–93.

194. CQ 401 (10 Nov. 1946). HCMTT 4, 486–87.

195. CQ 401 (10 Nov. 1946). "La constitution de la République . . . ," 80. *Nhiệm Vụ Tuần Báo* 4 (10 Nov. 1946).

196. Nguyễn Huy Tưởng, *Tiên Phong* 23 (15 Nov. 1946), 2–3.

197. Oct. 1945–Nov. 1946, Action du Front Viet-Minh contre les parties d'opposition, SHD 10H, 280.

198. Phạm Khắc Hoè, *Từ Triều đình Huế đến Chiến khu Việt Bắc* [From the Hue Court to the Việt Bắc War Zone] (Hanoi: NXB Hà Nội, 1983), 155.

199. This December effort should not be confused with the August–November 1946 shipments of rice to Trung Bộ to ward off famine, discussed in chapter 6.

200. CQ 397 (6 Nov. 1946); 416 (25 Nov. 1946). *Lịch Sử Đảng Cộng Sản Việt Nam: Sơ thảo* [Preliminary History of the Vietnam Communist Party], vol. 1 (Hanoi: NXB ST, 1984), 508–10.

201. CQ 419 (28 Nov. 1946); 420 (29 Nov. 1946). Devillers, *Histoire*, 346.

202. Devillers, *Histoire*, 349.

203. 3 Dec. 1946, UBHCBB to all bureau heads, ANOM, INDO, CR 141.

204. 19 Dec. 1946, Bộ trưởng Bộ Nội vụ to chủ tịch UBHCBB, outgoing message file, Văn Phòng Mật, UBHCBB, GF 31.

205. 19 Dec. 1946, Sở Kinh tế to UBHC Hải Dương, Hồ sơ tiếp tế Trung-Bộ lần thứ hai folder, GF 78.

206. 19 Dec. 1946, Thông Tư UBHCBB to all BBP offices, Phòng Kinh tế folio, GF 50. Also on 19 December, a 16 Dec. 1946 notice made the rounds announcing formation of an Evacuation Protection Association, headed by Mai Văn Hàm.

207. Dossier of Dec. 1946 newspapers, Phòng Báo chí, Bộ Nội vụ, GF 51. Early December papers from Thanh Hóa, Huế, and Quảng Ngãi are filed here as well.

208. 19 Dec. 1946, BBP internal routing slip for Nha Kinh tế Trung Bộ to Bộ trưởng Bộ Canh nông and UBHCBB, Công văn gửi đến, Sở Kinh tế, GF 26.

209. 19 Dec. 1946, UBHCBB to all provinces, Haiphong and Khu đặc biệt Hòn Gai, Bản lưu Công điện, GF 31. 19 Dec. 1946, UBHCBB to UBHC Sơn Tây, Công Văn gửi đi, Văn Phòng Mật, UBHCBB, GF 31.

210. For the most detailed attempt to analyse French and Vietnamese behavior during 19 December 1946, see Stein Tønnesson, 201–29.

211. Phạm Khắc Hòe, 154–57. Hòe and his two teenage sons had previously packed belongings on three rickshaws with plans to evacuate on 20 December.

212. Lê Văn Hiến, *Nhật ký của một Bộ trưởng* [Diary of a Cabinet Minister], vol. 1 (Đà Nẵng: NXB Đà Nẵng, 1995), 1.

213. Phạm Khắc Hòe, 157–59, 163–64. Hòe cellmates were: Đào Trọng Kim, minister of communications and public works in Hồ Chí Minh's first cabinet; three officials from the Trần Trọng Kim government of April–August 1945 (Hoàng Xuân Hãn, Vũ Văn Hiền, and Trần Văn Lai); and Nguyễn Xuân Chữ, a Đại Việt Party leader.

214. Nguyễn Q. Thắng, *Từ điển tác giả Văn Hóa Việt Nam* [Vietnam Culture Dictionary of Authors]. (Hanoi: NXB Văn Hóa, 1999). Trained as a doctor, Luyện died while treating the wounded.

215. Võ Nguyên Giáp, *Chiến đấu trong Vòng Vây* [Fighting while Encircled] (Hanoi: NXB QĐND and NXB Thanh Niên, 1995), 48.

CHAPTER 3

1. The diplomatic dimensions of national defense are discussed in chapter 4, the fragile economic underpinnings of defense in chapter 6, the National Guard's role in suppressing domestic opposition in chapter 7, and the importance of mass mobilization to defense in chapter 9.

2. *Cờ Giải Phóng* (Hanoi) 16 (12 Sept. 1945). HCMTT 3, 386. This is the concluding sentence of Hồ's independence speech.

3. Philippe Héduy, ed., *Histoire de l'Indochine*, vol. 2 (Paris: Société de Production Litteraire/Henri Veyrier, 1983), 285.

4. Nguyễn Việt, *Nam Bộ và Nam Phần Trung Bộ trong hai năm đầu Kháng Chiến (1945–1946)* [Southern and South-central Vietnam in the First Two Years of Resistance (1945–1946)] (Hanoi: NXB Văn Sử Địa, 1957), 34. NCLS 307 (June 1999), 65–71. Unless otherwise indicated, "Saigon" includes the territory of adjacent Chợ Lớn.

5. Nguyễn Việt, 19–20.

6. Nguyễn Tố Uyên, *Công cuộc bảo vệ và xây dựng chính quyền Nhân Dân ở Việt Nam trong những năm 1945–1946* [Protecting and Building People's Authority in Vietnam in 1945–1946] (Hanoi: NXB KHXH, 1999), 236.

7. Nguyễn Việt, 33, 72–73. Nguyễn Tố Uyên, 236. Each "division" probably contained one thousand to two thousand members. A 30 Sept. 1945 Reuters dispatch estimated there were seven thousand Vietnamese with firearms in the Saigon area.

8. Nguyễn Việt, 27.

9. Trần Văn Giàu, ed., *Lịch Sử Sài Gòn-Chợ Lớn-Gia Định Kháng Chiến (1945–1975)* [History of Saigon, Cholon, Gia Dinh Resistance (1945–1975)] (Ho Chi Minh City: NXB Thành Phố Hồ Chí Minh, 1994), 42–43. Trần Văn Giàu, "Hồi ký 1940–1945" [Memoir 1940–1945], *Thời Đại Mới* (Dayton, Ohio) 21 (May 2011): 331–41.

10. Statement reprinted in CQ 54 (29 Sept. 1945).

11. Bui Dinh Thanh, "The First Year of Resistance in South Vietnam," *Vietnamese Studies* (Hanoi) 7 (1965): 69–70.

12. Peter M. Dunn, *The First Vietnam War* (London: C. Hurst & Co, 1985), 237–44, 249–52, 254, 256.

13. Dunn, 253–54, 257–59.

14. Trần Văn Giàu, ed., *Lịch Sử*, 42.

15. Archimedes L. A. Patti, *Why Viet Nam? Prelude to America's Albatross* (Berkeley: University of California Press, 1980), 349.

16. Trần Văn Giàu, *Lịch Sử*, 45. Texts of relevant north-south exchanges have never been published, nor has any memoir revealed the content of Hanoi deliberations of 23–25 September.

17. *Phong Trào Nam Tiến (1945–1946)* [The Southern Advance Movement (1945–1946)] (Hanoi: NXB QĐND, 1997), 36. Henceforth PTNT.

18. CQ 54 (29 Sept. 1945). HCMTT 4, 25–26. VKĐ 1 (1945–50), 23–24.

19. PTNT, 15, 35, 140, 175. For the earlier Quảng Ngãi upheavals, see David G. Marr, *Vietnam 1945: The Quest for Power* (Berkeley: University of California Press, 1995), 102–3, 222–24, 350, 425, 427, 432, 433–35.

20. "Detachments" varied considerably in size, from two hundred to two thousand men. The name was dropped when the National Guard reorganized, starting in July 1946, into regiments, battalions, companies, and platoons.

21. *Chi Đội 3 Giải Phóng Quân Nam Tiến* [Detachment 3 of the Liberation Army Advance South] (Hanoi: NXB QĐND, 1995), 33–34, 38, 41. Henceforth CD3. PTNT, 86–88, 179. Trần Văn Quang, X&N 9 (Sept. 1995): 22–23.

22. CD3, 40, 45, 50–51, 54–55. PTNT, 88–89, 108–10.

23. Dunn, 260–61, 264–67. CD3, 55–58. PTNT, 89–90.

24. CD3, 59–64, 67–8. PTNT, 90–91.

25. Dunn, 263–64, 268. B. Prasad, editor, *Official History of the Indian Armed Forces in the Second World War 1939–1945. Post-War Occupation Forces: Japan and South East Asia* (n.p., 1958), 203. Trần Văn Giàu, ed., 62–66.

26. Dunn, 269–70, 274, 278–79. Prasad, ed., 204–5.

27. PTNT, 81, 91.

28. CD3, 68–81. Detachment Vy was named after its commander, a common practice (see below).

29. CD3, 72–90. Dunn, 271, 279–80, 282–83. CQ81 (3 Nov. 1945) reported Xuân Lộc as a Vietnamese victory.

30. CD3, 88–92. Dunn, 283.

31. CQ 83 (5 Nov. 1945).

32. CD3, 92–111. PTNT, 92–95. Dunn, 271. Nguyễn Phụng Minh, ed., *Nam Trung Bộ Kháng Chiến, 1945–1975* [South-central Region Resistance, 1945–1975] (Hanoi: NXB CTQG, 1995), 79. Hereafter NTBKC. X&N 9 (Sept. 1995): 23.

33. CD3, 10–17.

34. *Chi Đội Vi Dân* (Hanoi: NXB QĐND, 1998), 37, 40–41. Henceforth CD Vi Dân. PTNT, 49–50, 61, 176–77, 300.

35. X&N 279 (March 2001): 13–17.

36. CD Vi Dân, 38–40. CD3, 42–44. PTNT, 47, 49, 59, 61, 75, 114, 118–19, 139, 292–93.

37. CD Vi Dân, 53, 78. PTNT, 127. Such Japanese-Vietnamese exchanges had begun in August in many other locations.

38. Dunn, 282.

39. CD Vi Dân, 28, 33–34, 49, 54. PTNT, 16, 58, 72, 94, 96, 125, 138, 223. Nguyễn Bá Khoản, *Những Khoảnh Khắc Lịch Sử qua ống Kính* [Historical Moments via Nguyen Ba Khoan's Camera] (Hanoi: NXB QĐND, 1997), 52–70.

40. PTNT, 138, 321. Thu Sơn, the detachment commander, had received training at Whampoa Military Academy in China in the 1930s, and participated in early 1945 Liberation Army assaults on French border posts. X&N 34 (Dec. 1996): 15–16.

41. CD Vi Dân, 50. PTNT, 59, 72, 120, 126, 128b, 139, 142, 178. X&N 124 (Sept. 2002): 22, 42.

42. Trần Đăng, in Nguyễn Khắc Viện and Hữu Ngọc, compilers, *Vietnamese Literature* (Hanoi: Foreign Languages Publishing House, 1983), 762–63.

43. PTNT, 41, 123–24, 137, 171, 299, 327. CD3, 37, 41, 101. CD Vi Dân, 85, 87, 92, 103. Hà Văn Lâu had undergone six months Garde Indochinoise training in 1942, and in September 1945 was made commander of a Khánh Hòa province detachment. Trần Công Tấn, *Hà Văn Lâu: Người đi từ bến làng Sình* [Ha Van Lau: The Man from Sinh Village] (Hanoi: NXB Phụ Nữ, 2004), 22, 42–44, 110.

44. CD Vi Dân, 29–30, 45.

45. PTNT, 39, 148–49, 161–63, 291–93.

46. Lê Văn Hiến, *Chuyến Công Cán Đặc Biệt* [Special Official Journey] (Đà Nẵng, 1986), 50, 51, 54, 59. The late Đặng Phong kindly sent me a photocopy of this book. Hiến, a native of Đà Nẵng, and early ICP organizer there, became known nationally due to his 1938 prison memoir *Ngục Kontum* [Kontum Prison]. In March 1946, he would become DRV finance minister.

47. PTNT, 124, 295. CD Vi Dân, 34, 61. For an early published account, see Hoài Tân, *Trung Bộ Kháng chiến* [Central Region Resistance] (Hanoi: NXB Quốc Tế, Jan. 1946).

48. CD3, 34–35, 75, 134. CD Vi Dân, 42–44.

49. CD Vi Dân, 48, 92, 97.

50. CD3, 3, 35, 133–34.

51. Besides the CD3 duo, mentioned earlier, CD Vi Dân sent a four-person delegation to Hanoi in early December. CD Vi Dân, 126.

52. PTNT, 45–46, 51–52. Later operations in Nam Bộ are discussed below.

53. Lê Văn Hiến, 71–77. The Bình Xuyên was a secret society with membership drawn from the Cholon underworld, Mekong River boat crews, and rural day laborers.

54. Trần Công Tấn, 45–46, 51–55, 63–65. Interview with Hà Văn Lâu, Hồ Chí Minh City, 14 Feb. 2001.

55. Nguyễn Việt, 49, 51. PTNT, 95–96, 140–43, 170–73, 182–83. CD3, 113. NTBKC, 76–78. Dunn, 298, 307–8, 310. Trần Công Tấn, 62, 66–93, 97–110. X&N 122 (Aug. 2002): 60–61.

56. Lê Văn Hiến, 59–63.

57. CD Vi Dân, 56–59. PTNT, 119, 129–35, 149, 196. Dunn, 336.

58. Lê Văn Hiến, 65–66. CD3, 120–22. PTNT, 76.

59. PTNT, 78–80. NTBKC, 83–84. Devillers, 176. Adrien Dansette, *Leclerc* (Paris: Flammarion, 1952), 194. Detachment Bắc Bắc had been raised in the provinces of Bắc Ninh and Bắc Giang.

60. CD3, 122–25, 146g. PTNT, 143–44, 173–74. X&N 34 (Dec. 1996): 15–16.

61. Nguyễn Thế Lâm, X&N 125 (Oct. 2002): 7. Lâm was the embarrassed reporting officer.

62. Võ Nguyên Giáp, *Unforgettable Months and Years* (Ithaca, NY: Cornell SEAP, 1975), 70–75. Translation by Mai Elliott.

63. PTNT, 173–74.

64. Trần Công Tấn, 118–19.

65. Võ Nguyên Giáp, *Unforgettable Months*, 75–7.

66. Tân Dân, *Quyết Thắng* (Huế) 17 (15 Feb. 1946).

67. ĐL, 166 (18 Feb. 1946); 167 (19 Feb. 1946); 172 (24 Feb. 1946). DC 144 (18 Feb. 1946). X&N 349–50 (Feb. 2010).

68. *Lịch Sử Quân Đội Nhân Dân Việt Nam* [History of the Vietnam People's Army] (Hanoi: NXB QĐND, 1974), 134–38. Marr, *Vietnam 1945*, 225–27.

69. Captain Vũ Văn Thụ remained as director of the Northern Civil Guard Bureau. In November, Captain Thụ complained officially about being required to move residence three times when space was needed by another bureau. 6 Nov. 1945, Giám Đốc Bảo An Bình Bắc Bộ to BBP, GF 58.

70. Ty Vật Liệu dossier, GF 22. I have found no evidence that such an election was conducted.

71. 28 Aug. 1945, Tuyên Cáo, in CB 1945, 2. Marr, *Vietnam, 1945*, 504–5. Chu Văn Tấn was not yet in Hanoi, but on 10 September he joined Hồ Chí Minh in welcoming General Xiao Wen to the city. Patti, 287–88.

72. Phan Văn Cẩn, ed., *Lịch sử Bộ Tổng Tham mưu trong kháng chiến chống Pháp (1945–1954)* [History of the General Staff in the Anti-French Resistance (1945–1954)]

(Hanoi: Bộ Tổng Tham Mưu, 1991), 6–8. Hereafter LSBTTM. Thái had joined the ICP in 1938 and received some instruction at the Guilin military academy in 1942–43.

73. Trần Ngọc Ngôn, *Lịch Sử Bộ đội Thông tin Liên lạc* [History of Communication Liaison Units], vol. 1 *1945–1954*. (Hanoi: NXB QĐND, 1984), 14.

74. The following examples are taken from: Quốc Phòng (linh tinh) 1945, Văn Phòng dossier 85, GF 38; and early issues of the *Công Báo*.

75. 10 Sept. 1945, Ủy Ban Thái Bình to UBNDBB, in Thái Bình dossier, GF 16. 16 Nov. 1945, Thái Bình to UBNDBB; 31 Dec. 1945, Thái Bình to UBNDBB, in Thái Bình dossier, GF 71.

76. 3 Oct. 1945, Bắc Giang to UBNDBB, GF 45.

77. 29 Nov. 1945, Hòa Bình to UBNDBB, Hòa Bình 1945 dossier, GF 53.

78. 20 Oct. 1945, Ủy Ban Quân Sự Đội Cấn, Thái Nguyên 1945 dossier, GF 71.

79. 5 Dec. 1945, Hà Đông to UBNDBB, GF 53.

80. 1 Nov. 1945, Ngô Quyền (Sơn Tây) to UBNDBB, Sơn Tây dossier; 30 Dec. 1945 Quảng Yên to UBNDBB, Quảng Yên dossier, GF 71.

81. Quốc Phòng (linh tinh) 1945, Văn Phòng dossier, GF 38.

82. (?) Sept. 1945, UBNDBB authorization, Quân Sự (linh tinh) 1945, GF 38. On 25 September, Nguyễn Văn Triệu, representing four hundred armed men in Haiphong, complained in a petition to Hồ Chí Minh that the Haiphong People's Committee showed suspicion towards the group and had refused to assign it a mission. The petition was routed to Vũ Quốc Uy, without comment.

83. 13 Sept. 1945, Trưởng Ban Quân Sự Tán Thuật to Trưởng Ban Quân Sự Hà Nội; and 8 Oct. 1945, UBNDBB to UBND Hưng Yên, in Hưng Yên dossier, GF 67. I have not found any such message sent subsequently to all provinces.

84. Ngô Vi Thiện, et al., *Lịch Sử Hậu Cần Quân Đội Nhân Dân Việt Nam, 1944–1954* [Logistics History of the People's Army of Vietnam, 1944–1954], vol. 1 (Hanoi: NXB QĐND, 1985), 72–74. Hoàng Chí, et. al., *Biên Niên Sự Kiện Lịch Sử Hậu Cần Quân Đội Nhân Dân Việt Nam, 1944–1954* [Chronology of Events in the Logistical History of the People's Army of Vietnam, 1944–1954] (Hanoi: NXB QĐND, 1986), 55–57.

85. 4 Sept. 1945, UBNDBB to Sở Vô Tuyến Điện, and subsequent exchange, Quân sự (linh tinh); 1945 dossier, Văn Phòng, GF 38.

86. Trần Ngọc Ngôn, 10–11, 15–16.

87. 6 Sept. 1945, Bộ Nội vụ nghị định, Nội Vụ, GF 76. Marr, *Vietnam 1945*, 531n.

88. Nguyễn Dực, X&N, 56 (Oct. 1998): 23, 35. Most radio equipment in Indochina in 1945 had been made by Philips during the 1930s, but there were some American Siler and Crosley sets as well.

89. Sở vô tuyến điện dossier, GF 38.

90. In April 1946, Nguyễn Phi Hùng was commended for infiltrating enemy lines to retrieve forty-eight boxes of radio equipment and one 25mm AA gun left behind following the early February defeat at Nha Trang. Hùng was fatally wounded five months later. *Kháng Chiến* (Quảng Ngãi) 7 (5 Nov. 1946).

91. *Sao Vàng* 22 (31 Oct. 1946).

92. Trần Ngọc Ngôn, 18.

93. Trần Ngọc Ngôn, 17–18. Lê Đình Ý, et al., *Lịch Sử Nghành Cơ Yếu Quân Đội Nhân Dân Việt Nam* [History of the Vietnam People's Army Code Branch] (Hanoi: NXB QĐND, 1990), 11–17. This latter book was translated and published by the U.S. National Security Agency under the title *Essential Matters: A History of the Cryptographic Branch of the People's Army of Viet-Nam, 1945–1975* (Washington: U.S. National Security Agency, 1994).

94. Tg décryptés dossier, Viet Minh (Archives politiques), ANOM, INDO, CP 128. The first decryptions in this file date from Dec. 1945.

95. CQ 302 (26 July 1946).

96. Trần Ngọc Ngôn, 27, 30–34, 36–37.

97. 20 Oct. 1945, travel pass, Giấy phép về việc linh tinh, GF 45.

98. A month earlier the Northern Region People's Committee had proposed requisition of the Sitgard auto works, to convert to weapons fabrication. The French owner wanted to dismiss more than one hundred employees. 27 Sept. 1945, UBNDBB to Nội vụ, second folio, GF 69. There is no record of an Interior Ministry response.

99. Ngô Vi Thiện, et al., 80–83. Phạm Như Vưu, et. al., *Lịch Sử Quân Giới Việt Nam Thời kì Kháng Chiến chống Thực Dân Pháp (1945–1954)* [Vietnam Arms History during the Resistance against French Colonialists (1945–1954)] (Hanoi: NXB QĐND, 1990), 20–22.

100. Quốc Phòng (linh tinh) 1945, Văn Phòng dossier, GF 38.

101. 3 March 1947, CSTFEO attaching translated documents from May–June 1946, SHD, dossier 13, carton 10H532. Thanks to Christopher Goscha for sharing his notes.

102. Trần Kháng Chiến ed., *Trần Tử Bình: Từ Phú Riềng Đỏ đến Mùa Thu Hà Nội . . .* [Tran Tu Binh: from Phu Rieng Rubber Plantation to Hanoi in Autumn . . .] (Hanoi: NXB QĐND, 2006).

103. Lê Đình Cẩm, et al., *Lịch Sử Trường Sĩ Quan Lục Quân Trần Quốc Tuấn* [History of the Tran Quoc Tuan Army Officer Academy] (Hanoi: NXB QĐND, 1985), 20–37. Hội Khoa Học Lịch Sử Việt Nam, *Ký Ức*, 46.

104. Lê Đình Cẩm, et. al., *Lịch Sử Trường Sĩ Quan*, 37–43. Hội Khoa Học Lịch Sử Việt Nam, *Ký Ức*, 184–85.

105. 6 Sept. 1946 letter, signed by Trần Tử Bình, Lê Vinh Quốc, Vương Thừa Vũ, Trương Văn Quyền, and Nguyễn Văn Sỹ. *Sao Vàng* 16 (19 Sept. 1946).

106. SL 66 (24 Nov. 1945), in CB 1995, 95. A later edict specified six months' service for physicians, first calling on those with fewer children.

107. Feb. (?) 1946, danh sách Bộ Y-tế, in CB 1946, 133.

108. NĐ (16 July 1946), in CB 1946, 392. Trần Minh Hồng, et al., 77–78.

109. Health Minister Trương Đình Tri responding to a question in the National Assembly, CQ 394 (3 Nov. 1946).

110. *Vui Sống* (Hanoi) 1–11 (June–Nov. 1946). The paper carried regular obituaries for nurses and medics killed south of the sixteenth parallel.

111. Patti, 291–92. I have not been able to find any edict or instruction making this name-change.

112. Patti, 346. Peter Worthing, *Occupation and Revolution: China and the Vietnamese August Revolution of 1945* (Berkeley: University of California Press, 2001), 74–75.

113. Patti, 348–49.

114. Worthing, 76–88.

115. SL (5 Jan. 1946), in CB 1946, 1.

116. Nguyễn Tố Uyên, 255–59.

117. Viện Lịch Sử Quân Sự Việt Nam, *Lịch Sử cuộc kháng chiến chống Thực Dân Pháp 1945–1954* [History of the Anti-French Colonial Resistance], vol. 1 (Hanoi: NXB QĐND, 1994), 105–7. Hereafter LSCKC1. My chapter 7 discusses the bitter contest between the ICP–Việt Minh and opposition political parties.

118. René Charbonneau and José Maigre, *Les parias de la victoire: Indochine-Chine 1945* (Paris: Editions France-Empire, 1980), 382–97. Reports by Lieutenant Colonel Quilichini between January and June 1946, in ANOM, Laos, carton Q4. Worthing, 117–19. Nguyễn Tố Uyên, 190–92, 202–4, 207. LSCKC1, 108–109.

119. Moyens de transport sur l'Indochine, ANOM, INDO, carton 134, dossier 1221.

120. Worthing, 118–20, 126–27. The French also wanted access to airstrips at Điện Biên Phủ and Xieng Khouang.

121. Tønnesson, "La paix imposée," 46. Worthing, 143–44. The planes had to turn back to Pakse airport, but finally delivered their cargo to Hanoi following the 18 March arrival of General Leclerc's column from Haiphong.

122. Ministère de la France d'Outre-mer, *Bulletin hebdomadaire,* 67 (18 March 1946). See chapter 4 for additional discussion of the 6 March Accord.

123. Jean Julien Fonde, *Traitez à tout prix . . . Leclerc et le Vietnam* (Paris: Robert Laffont, 1971), 169–70. Devillers, *Histoire du Vietnam,* 238–39. Vo Nguyen Giáp, *Unforgettable Days* (Hanoi: Foreign Language Publishing House, 1975), 211. At all such ceremonies Giáp continued to wear a civilian suit and tie, plus his signature fedora hat.

124. Philippe Devillers, *Paris-Saigon-Hanoi: Les archives de la guerre 1944–1947* (Paris: Éditions Gallimand/Julliard, 1988), 178–80.

125. Tiểu đoàn thứ 1, Đại đoàn Khu Hà Nội documents, GF 77. Most of this information was recorded on the back of RST/Garde Indigène papers dating back to 1931. Most striking is a one-week Garde Indigène menu, with each of the two meals per day containing 650 grams "1st class" white rice, fish sauce with hot peppers, tea, and a variety of soups, meat, vegetables, and fruit. One imagines the 1946 company clerks wondering when they would be as well fed as this.

126. Tiểu đoàn trưởng, Siêu Hải, messages to all units, GF 77.

127. June 1946, messages in Tiểu đoàn 1 Hanoi dossier, GF 64.

128. July 1946, Tiểu đoàn 1 Hanoi dossier, GF 39.

129. June 1946, Bộ Chỉ Huy Vệ Quốc Đoàn Hà Nội messages, Tiểu đoàn 1 Hanoi dossier, GF 64.

130. 26 June 1946, Bộ Chỉ Huy Vệ Quốc Đoàn Khu Hà Nội, Tiểu đoàn 1 Hanoi dossier, GF 64.

131. 9 July 1946 and 10 July 1946, incoming messages, July 1946 Tiểu đoàn 1 dossier, GF 39.

132. 24 July 1946, Tham Mưu Trưởng to Khu Hà Nội; 26 July 1946, Tiểu đoàn 1 to companies, July 1946 Vệ Quốc Đoàn dossier, GF 64.

133. Undated, Lời Hiệu Triệu signed by Siêu Hải; 13 July 1946, Battalion Political Officer to companies, in July 1946 Vệ Quốc Đoàn dossier, GF 64. As it turned out, both Siêu Hải and Vi Ngô were themselves replaced on 23 Aug. 1946.

134. 27 Aug. 1946, Hoàng Văn Thái to all military regions, Aug. 1946 Vệ Quốc Đoàn dossier, GF 64.

135. 30 Aug. 1946, Tham mưu trưởng to all military regions, Aug. 1946 Vệ Quốc Đoàn dossier, GF 64.

136. SL 33 (22 March 1946), in CB 1946, 177–78. Published in *Chiến Sĩ* (Huế) 21 (17 April 1946). Because the National Guard/People's Army subsequently dropped the *sư đoàn* designation I translate *đại đoàn* as *division* rather than *brigade*.

137. SL 71 (22 May 46), in CB 1946, 437–41. This decree was held back from publication for three months, presumably for security reasons. When published, the first portion of the section on organization was deleted. Drafters of this decree appear to have consulted French, Nationalist Chinese, and Communist Chinese military precedents. In practice, the name National Guard continued to be used widely.

138. SL 124 (19 July 1946), in CB 1946, 383.

139. Lê Văn Hiến, the finance minister, reveals this request in *Việt Nam phải có một Đội Quân Hùng Mạnh* [Vietnam Must have a Strong Army] (Huế [?]: Tuyên Truyền Trung Bộ, July 1946), 3.

140. LSCKC1, 152. The relief force and Vietnamese-French mixed commission are discussed in chapter 4.

141. LSBTTM, 45–48, 69–70.

142. Trần Ngọc Ngôn, 49–53, 60–62. LSBTTM, 48, 50–51.

143. Lê Đình Ý, 20–22.

144. LSCKC1, 150–51. 29 June 1946 continues to be remembered as the Artillery Corps' birthday.

145. Doãn Tuế, et al., *Voi Xung Kích* [Assault Elephants] (Hanoi: NXB QĐND, 1966), 5–15.

146. Tran Dai Nghia, "The First Days of the Armaments Service," *Vietnam Courier* (Hanoi) (Dec. 1980): 23–24.

147. Goscha, "Le contexte asiatique de la guerre franco-vietnamienne: Réseaux, relations et économie (D'août 1945 à mai 1954)," (PhD thesis, Ecole pratique des hautes études, 2000), 359–60.

148. Five regiments were shared by two provinces.

149. LSCKC1, 150. LSBTTM, 66–67

150. Trần Quốc Tuấn, better known as Trần Hưng Đạo, was credited with defeating the Mongol armies of Kublai Khan in the late thirteenth century.

151. "*Trung với Nước, Hiếu với Dân.*" Here Hồ Chí Minh deliberately reworked the Confucian formula of loyalty to the king, and filial piety/gratefulness towards one's parents.

152. Lê Đình Cẩm, et al., *Lịch sử Trường sĩ quan*, 47–56.

153. LSCKC1, 153.

154. *Chiến Sĩ* (Huế) 17 (20 March 1946).

155. *Chiến Sĩ* 10 (18 Jan. 1946).

156. *Chiến Sĩ* 1 (18 Nov. 1945); 10 (18 Jan. 1946). *Sao Vàng* (Hanoi), 9 (25 July 1946); 10 (1 Aug. 1946); 15 (12 Sept. 1946); 23 (7 Nov. 1946). *Quân Bạch Đằng* (Kiến An), 1 (1 July 1946); 9/10 (Oct. 1946).

157. *Quân Bạch Đằng* 4 (19 Aug. 1946). Thảo became a vaunted division commander.

158. *Chiến Sĩ* 23 (8 May 1946).

159. *Quân Bạch Đằng* 1 (1 July 1946); 9/10 (Oct. 1946).

160. *Sao Vàng* 4 (20 June 1946); *Chiến Sĩ* 16 (13 March 1946).

161. *Sao Vàng* 1 (30 May 1946). It cannot be accidental that Liệu published this inflammatory rhetoric the day before Hồ Chí Minh departed for negotiations in France.

162. *Chiến Sĩ* 23 (8 May 1946).

163. *Sao Vàng* 12 (15 Aug. 1946).

164. *Quân Bạch Đằng* 11 (10 Nov. 1946).

165. *Kháng Chiến* 7 (5 Nov. 1946).

166. *Sao Vàng* 5 (7 June 1946). Hải Thanh, *Quân Bạch Đằng* 4 (19 Aug. 1946).

167. Interview by the well-known photographer Nguyễn Bá Khoản, CQ 237 (11 May 1946). Five lines were excised by the censors, unusual for *Cứu Quốc*.

168. *Kháng Chiến,* special anniversary issue, 2 Sept. 1946.

169. According to one course announcement, prospective political officers were simply to be at least eighteen years old and possess a minimum of three years' education. *Chiến Sĩ* 7 (28 Dec. 1945).

170. *Chiến Sĩ* 13 (20 Feb. 1946).

171. *Quân Bạch Đằng* 1 (1 July 1946).

172. *Sao Vàng* 8 (18 July 1946); 24 (14 Nov. 1946). *Chiến Sĩ* 46 (31 July 1946).

173. 17 Oct. 1945, UBNDBB to Ủy Viên Quân Sự, Hội Viên Chức, Quân Sự (linh tinh) 1945 dossier, GF 38.

174. 31 Oct. 1945, Chủ Tịch UBND Ngoại Thành Hà Nội to Bắc Bộ, in GF 64.

175. 5 Oct. 1945, Tự Vệ Cứu Quốc làng Thạch Bích to Ủy Ban Bắc Bộ, in Việc xảy ra tại tỉnh (Hà Đông) dossier, GF 28. "Cứu Quốc" is an assertion of Việt Minh affiliation.

176. November 1945, routing slips in Phủ Hoài Đức dossier, GF 28.

177. As often happened, Hanoi simply routed the petitions to the province committee for action. 15 Jan. 1946, UBNDBB to UBHC Ninh Bình, in Điện tín gửi đi dossier, GF 17.

178. 9 Jan. 1946, Quốc Phòng to Ninh Bình, Bộ đến message book, GF 56.

179. See, for example, *Việt Nam* 150 (17 May 1946).

180. Fonde, 179, 188–89, 204, 223, 242–48, 270. Jean-Etienne Valluy, "Indochine: Octobre 1945–mars 1947," *Revue des Deux Mondes* (15 Nov. 1967): 201–2, 206, 216. The most serious such case, occurring in Bắc Ninh in early August, is discussed in chapter 4.

181. Sûreté federales en Indochine, *Bulletin quotidiene* 92 (10 May 1946); 131 (25 June 1946); 133 (27 June 1946); and 134 (28 June 1946), ANOM, INDO, CP 186.

182. CQ 280 (1 July 1946). As of the end of August, efforts to unify the two largest Hanoi militia groups, the Tự vệ chiến đấu and the Tự vệ Thành, had yet to bear fruit. CQ 332 (30 Aug. 1946).

183. See, for example, the thick dissolution dossier about one militia group that involved officials at Hanoi, province, district, and village levels in May–June 1946. Phú Thọ (các việc lưu) folder, GF 59.

184. Hỏa Xá Việt Nam 1946 dossier, GF 52.

185. Sûreté monthly report, June 1946; Sûreté, *Bulletin quotidiene* 142 (7 July 1946), ANOM, CP 186.

186. Undated nhật lệnh, *Chiến Khu* (Thái Nguyên) (Sept. 1946).

187. *Sao Vàng* 19 (10 Oct. 1946).

188. 19 Sept. 1946, UBNDBB to all provinces, Tự Vệ xung đột với nhân viên nha thuế quan dossier, GF 24. Taxation is discussed further in chapter 6.

189. 11 Nov. 1946, Giám Đốc Nha Thuế Quan và Thuế Giám Thu to Chủ Tịch UBH-CBB; 21 Nov. 1946, UBHCBB to all provinces, Tự Vệ xung đột dossier, GF 24.

190. Nguyễn Xiển, Báo cáo về tình hình Bắc Bộ từ ngày 19–8–1945 đến 20–10–1946, UBHCBB, 7, GF 19.

191. 22 Nov. 1946, Bắc Bộ to Ủy Ban Chấp Hành Đội Tự Vệ, quyển 5, Văn Phòng Mật, GF 31. This is the only mention I have seen of a "Militia Executive Committee."

192. 27 Nov. 1946 and 13 Dec. 1946, Bắc Bộ to Quốc Phòng, quyển 5, Văn Phòng Mật, GF 31.

193. Nam Long, in *Cựu Chiến Binh Trung Đoàn 96* [Veterans of the 96th Regiment] (Đà Nẵng: NXB Đà Nẵng, 1996), 9–12. Nguyễn Sơn occasionally shifted to Chinese to make his points, knowing that Nam Long understood that language.

194. Đoàn Văn Nghệ, in *Cựu Chiến Binh*, 153–54.

195. Anonymous author, *Quyết Thắng* 18 (23 Feb. 1946).

196. NTBKC, 84, 88–89. LSCKC1, 138–39.

197. Hoàng Chí, et al., 75.

198. Thăng Long, ed., *Nhớ Nam Bộ*, 270–81.

199. *Kháng Chiến* (Quảng Ngãi) 7 (5 Nov. 1946); 9 (25 Nov. 1946).

200. LSCKC1, 140–42. *Tướng Nguyễn Sơn*, 82. NTBKC, 90–91. Nguyễn Việt, 92–94.

201. Trần Ngọc Ngôn, 54–55.

202. Christopher E. Goscha, "Le contexte asiatique," 375–84, 399–402.

203. The 1 June 1946 ceremony opening the Trường Lục Quân Trung Học Quảng Ngãi is described in *Chiến Sĩ* (Huế) 29 (19 June 1946).

204. *Tướng Nguyễn Sơn*, 69–71, 74–78, 83–84. *Nguyễn Sơn: Lưỡng Quốc tướng quân* [Nguyen Son: General of Two Countries] (Hanoi: NXB Thông Tấn, 2006), 52–60, 109–20. Goscha, "Le contexte asiatique," 369–72.

205. Nguyễn Lai, in *Cựu Chiến Binh*, 124–25. Lai misremembered the publisher as Hachette.

206. Goscha, "Le contexte asiatique," 370–71, quoting from the notebook of a dead Japanese instructor.

207. Nguyễn Việt, 94.

208. Lê Kích, in *Cựu Chiến Binh*, 60. The cloth for the uniforms came from the Nam Định textile mill.

209. *Cựu Chiến Binh*, 11–12, 15–17, 60–62, 72–73, 115, 138.

210. *Cựu Chiến Binh*, 63–64, 114, 167–68, 171.

211. *Cựu Chiến Binh*, 120, 124–25, 169–70.

212. Nguyễn Bá Phát, in *Khởi Đầu*, 33–37.

213. Devillers, *Histoire*, 349.

214. This is the Ủy Ban Kháng Chiến Miền Nam, not to be confused with the Ủy Ban Kháng Chiến Nam Bộ (Southern Region Resistance Committee), based in the Mekong delta. Phạm Văn Bạch chaired the former committee, based in Phú Yên, until returning to Nam Bộ in 1948.

215. NTBKC, 93.

216. *Lực Lượng Vũ Trang Cách Mạng trong Năm Đầu của Chính Quyền Nhân Dân* [Revolutionary Armed Forces in the First Year of People's Power] (Hanoi: NXB QĐND, 1970), 64. The Central Military Commission was abolished.

217. *Tướng Nguyễn Sơn*, 78, 91–2. *Nguyễn Sơn: Lưỡng Quốc tướng quân*, 69–70.

218. *Lịch Sử Đảng Bộ Đảng Cộng Sản Việt Nam tỉnh Nghệ-Tĩnh* [History of the Vietnam Communist Party Organization of Nghe-Tinh Province], vol. 1, *1925–1954*. (Vinh: NXB Nghệ Tĩnh, 1987), 230, 236.

219. *60 Năm Hoạt Động của Đảng Bộ Đảng Cộng Sản Việt Nam Thừa Thiên-Huế* [Sixty Years Activity of the Vietnam Communist Party Organization in Thua Thien-Hue] (Huế, 1990), 76.

220. Goscha, "Le contexte asiatique," 101–4. Yves Gras, *Histoire de la Guerre d'Indochine*, 2nd ed. (Paris: Denoël, 1992), 55–56, 80–84, 114.

221. See, for example, the reports in *Chiến Sĩ* (Huế) 10 (18 Jan. 1946); 11–12 (Tết 1946); and 13 (20 Feb. 1946).

222. Thus, in Hà Tĩnh, Detachment Phan Đình Phùng organized a ceremony on 3 March for comrades killed in fighting around Napé. *Chiến Sĩ* 21 (17 April 1946). This paper routinely names north-central Vietnamese killed in action at diverse locations, with at least twenty-nine of these being killed in Laos.

223. *Chiến Sĩ* 21 (17 April 1946).

224. LSCKC1, 143–44.

225. *Chiến Sĩ* 1 (16 Nov. 1945); 4 (7 Dec. 1945); 6 (21 Dec. 1945); 7 (28 Dec. 1945); 18 (27 March 1946); 26 (29 May 1946); and 33 (10 July 1946).

226. The editor of *Chiến Sĩ*, Ngô Điền, may already have been proficient in English. He later became a senior DRV diplomat. X&N 52 (June 1998): 13.

227. Devillers, *Histoire du Viet-Nam*, 250.

228. *60 Năm Hoạt Động Thừa Thiên-Huế*, 76, 79–81. Hoàng Quốc Việt attended the July meeting as central representative. The Trần Cao Vân Regiment was named after the leader of an ill-conceived anticolonial coup attempt in Huế in 1916.

229. LSCKC1, 150.

230. *Chiến Sĩ* 2 (23 Nov. 1945); 8 (4 Jan. 1946); 13 (20 Feb. 1946); and 19 (3 April 1946).

231. *Quyết Chiến* (9 May 46). Subsequent issues list hundreds of individual donations to the Association.

232. Gilbert Bodinier, compiler, *La guerre d'Indochine 1945–1954 : Textes et Documents*, vol. 1, *Le retour de la France en Indochine 1945–1946*. (Vincennes: SHAT, 1987), 67–71, 84. Besides "partisans," the French recruited native *"supplétifs"* and civilian *"auxiliaires."* By July, they also had brought from the *métropole* about ten thousand Indochinese military replacements for "Europeans" ending tours of duty. Half of these were "Annamites."

233. Devillers, *Histoire*, 252. Nguyên Hùng, *Nguyễn Bình*, 229–30. A second councillor, Nguyễn Văn Thạch, was shot on 3 May and died in hospital.

234. Christopher E. Goscha, "'La guerre par d'autres moyens': Réflexions sur la guerre du Việt Minh dans le Sud Vietnam (de 1945 à 1951)," *Guerre mondiales et conflits contemporains* 206 (2002), 29–57. Nguyên Hùng, 185–88, 222–26, 231–36. Trần Văn Giàu, ed. *Lịch Sử*, 98–101; 107–09.

235. Devillers, *Histoire*, 253, says the dump contained four thousand tons of explosives. See also the 26 April 1946 report in dossier 4, Terrorisme V.M., ANOM, CP 158. Nguyên Hùng, 288–89.

236. Dossier 2, Activités des Rebelles, ANOM, CP 158.

237. Bodinier, 240–41. Sûreté, *Bulletin quotidian* (Saigon), 88–157 (6 May 1929–July 1946), ANOM, CP 186.

238. Nguyễn Việt, 81.

239. Goscha, "Le contexte asiatique," 215–16. LSCKC1, 76–79.

240. August 1946 report, Directeur de la Police et de la Sûreté Federales en Indochine, ANOM, CP 186.

241. Bodinier, 260, 275, 277.

242. Reprinted in CQ 355 (24 Sept. 1946).

243. *Lịch Sử Bà Rịa-Vũng Tàu kháng chiến (1945–1975)* [History of Ba Ria-Vung Tau Resistance (1945–1975)] (Ho Chi Minh City: NXB QĐND, 1995), 44–57.

244. VKĐTT 8, 98–114. Political dimensions of this meeting are discussed in chapter 8.

245. CQ 335 (4 Sept. 1946).

246. *Kháng Chiến* 3 (23 Sept. 1946).

247. *Sao Vàng* 21 (24 Oct. 1946).

248. "Trường Kỳ Kháng chiến," speech by Liệu, then DRV minister of information and propaganda, reprinted in *Quyết Thắng* (Huế) 4 (22 Oct. 1945).

249. *Chiến Sĩ* 13 (13 March 1946).

250. Stein Tønnesson, *Vietnam 1946: How the War Began* (Berkeley: University of California Press, 2010), 112. Giáp, *Unforgettable Days*, 319, compliments Morlière as "someone who meant well and desired peace."

251. VKĐTT 8, 126–33. Proposals for strengthening party control within the armed forces are discussed in chapter 8.

252. Nguyễn Tố Uyên, 261–62.

253. LSBTTM, 41–42, 67–68, 90.

254. LSBTTM, 15, 20, 69, 88–89.

255. HCMTT 4, 179–81. LSBTTM, 107, reveals that these notes were not circulated in late 1946, only being discovered much later in the archives.

256. Ngô Vi Thiện, et al., *Trần Đăng Ninh: Con Người và Lịch Sử* [Tran Dang Ninh: Character and History] (Hanoi: NXB CTQG, 1996), 24.

257. Lê Văn Hiến, *Nhật Ký của một Bộ Trưởng* [Diary of a Government Minister], vol. 1 (Đà Nẵng: NXB Đà Nẵng, 1995), 2, 5, 9.

258. Ngô Vi Thiện, et al., 148–49.

259. Lê Văn Hiến, *Nhật Ký*, 38–40.

260. Ngô Vi Thiện, et al., 326–27. *Lịch Sử Quân Đội Nhân Dân Việt Nam*, 246.

261. Võ Nguyên Giáp, *Chiến đấu trong vòng vây: Hồi Ức* [Fighting While Encircled: Memoir] (Hanoi: NXB QĐND and NXB Thanh Niên, 1995), 89. 12 Dec. 1946, Thuế Quan BB to Thương Thuyền, Kho muối Văn lý dossier, GF 45. Lê Văn Hiến, *Nhật Ký*, 4.

262. *Biên niên sự kiện Lịch Sử Hậu Cần,* 87–8.

263. Tønnesson, *Vietnam 1946,* 120, 122–28. Võ Nguyên Giáp, *Unforgettable* Days, 373–80. Martin Shipway, *The Road to War: France and Vietnam, 1944–1947* (Providence: Berghahn Books, 1996), 240–42. Franco-Vietnamese encounters over Haiphong are discussed further in chapter 4.

264. CQ 412 (21 Nov. 1946); 413 (22 Nov. 1946); 414 (23 Nov. 1946); 415 (24 Nov. 1946). Nguyễn Kiến Giang, 239–41, 243–44. LSCKC1, 161–62.

265. CQ 416 (25 Nov. 1946); 417 (26 Nov. 1946). LSCKC1, 162. Valluy, 508.

266. Tønnesson, *Vietnam 1946,* 128–33. CQ 413 (22 Nov. 1946). Nguyễn Kiến Giang, 241–42.

267. Võ Nguyên Giáp, *Chiến đấu,* 35.

268. LSCKC1, 150. No date is attached to this list, but the context suggests August or September 1946.

269. 10 Oct. 1946, Note sur l'armée vietnamienne, SHD 10H 530, as cited by Goscha, 58.

270. Bodinier, 84. Three-quarters of these French forces were *"européens,"* and one-quarter *"autochtones."*

271. Traditional accounts speak of almost one million militia being available nationwide in late 1946, but no one has attempted to provide substantiation.

272. LSBTTM, 96–97, 101.

273. Vương Thừa Vũ, 85–90. The Métropole Hotel accommodated French officers and was located right across from the Northern Region Office. Neither building was blown up subsequently.

274. Võ Nguyên Giáp, *Chiến đấu,* 39.

275. Vương Thừa Vũ, 99–101.

276. Vương Thừa Vũ, 92–98. *Lịch Sử cuộc kháng chiến thực dân Pháp 1945–1954* [History of Resistance to French Colonialism 1945–1954], vol. 2 (Hanoi: NXB QĐND, 1986), 13–20. Hereafter LSCKC2. Võ Nguyên Giáp, *Chiến đấu,* 40–41. LSBTTM, 102–5, indicates that final approval was not given until 14 December.

277. Vương Thừa Vũ, 107.

278. LSBTTM, 97–102.

279. Tønnesson, *Vietnam 1946,* 161–80, 195–200, discusses these Franco-Vietnamese interactions in exquisite detail. See also Võ Nguyên Giáp, *Unforgettable Days,* 390–413.

280. LSCKC1, 168–69. Tønnesson, *Vietnam 1946,* 207–8.

281. Võ Nguyên Giáp, *Chiến đấu,* 26. LSCKC1, 169.

282. Võ Nguyên Giáp, *Chiến đấu,* 43. By contrast, LSCKC2, 20, states that it was only the local Hoàn Kiếm lighting facility which was sabotaged.

283. Stein Tonnesson, "The Outbreak of War in Indochina 1946," *PRIO Report* (March 1984): 201. Vương Thừa Vũ, 106–10.

284. Võ Nguyên Giáp, *Chiến đấu,* 44, 48. LSCKC2, 21–22. Two squads at the Hanoi Opera House held off the enemy for a similar period of time before being wiped out.

285. LSCKC2, 19–20. Võ Nguyên Giáp, *Chiến đấu,* 48–9.

286. Vương Thừa Vũ, 111–15. *LSCKC2,* 23–28.

CHAPTER 4

1. Text in *Journal officiel de la République française: Ordonnances et decréts* (Paris, 1945), 1606–7. The background to the 24 March 1945 Declaration is examined meticulously in Martin Shipway, *The Road to War: France and Vietnam 1944–1947* (Providence: Berghahn Books, 1996), 41–125.

2. Philippe Devillers, *Histoire de 1940 à 1952* (Paris: Editions de Seuil, 1952), 144–150. Marr, *Vietnam 1945: The Quest for Power* (Berkeley: University of California Press, 1995), 328, 333–34, 492–93.

3. Messmer would become secretary general of the Comité interministériel de l'Indochine in late 1946, and eventually prime minister of France (1972–74).

4. Marr, *Vietnam 1945*, 481, 520–21. Only in Cambodia did the parachute gambit pay off, with the French team not only transported to the city in style but able to plot the overthrow of the nationalist regime formed two weeks prior.

5. Marr, *Vietnam 1945*, 403, 476–78, 494, 497.

6. 22 Aug. 1945, Leclerc to High Commissioner, ANOM, INDO, CP carton 133, dossier 1211.

7. Peter Worthing, *Occupation and Revolution: China and the Vietnamese August Revolution of 1945* (Berkeley: University of California Press, 2001), 72, 74–75.

8. Worthing, 83–84. Archimedes L. A. Patti, *Why Viet Nam? Prelude to America's Albatross* (Berkeley: University of California Press, 1980), 343–44, 345, 360–62. Philippe Devillers, *Paris-Saigon-Hanoi: Les archives de la guerre 1944–1947* (Paris: Éditions Gallimand/Julliard, 1988), 93, 95.

9. Jean Sainteny, *Histoire d'une paix manquée: Indochine, 1945–1947* (Paris: Fayard, 1953), 15, 27, 37–43, 46–51, 57–59, 67–81, 85–91. Patti, 141–47, 151–58, 171–73, 190–93, 197–98, 201–2, 205–10. Dixie R. Bartholomew-Feis, *The OSS and Ho Chi Minh: Unexpected Allies in the War against Japan* (Lawrence, Kansas: University Press of Kansas, 2006), 227–40.

10. François Missoffe, *Duel Rouge* (Paris: Éditions Ramsay, 1977), 24–27. Devillers, *Paris-Saigon-Hanoi*, 92–93.

11. As quoted in Patti, 299.

12. 19 Sept. 1945 conversation with T. V. Soong, President of China's Executive Yuan, quoted in Institut Charles-de-Gaulle, *Le Général de Gaulle et l'Indochine, 1940–1946* (Paris: Plon, 1982), 68–69.

13. 16 Sept. 1945, de Gaulle to d'Argenlieu, as quoted in Devillers, *Paris-Saigon-Hanoi*, 91–92. Here de Gaulle specifically harkens back to "l'ignoble jeu des Anglais en Syrie."

14. Peter M. Dunn, *The First Vietnam War* (London: C. Hurst & Co., 1985), 149–76. Peter Dennis, *Troubled Days of Peace: Mountbatten and South East Asia Command, 1945–46* (Manchester: Manchester University Press, 1987), 34–39. Daniel B. Valentine, "The British Facilitation of the French Re-entry into Vietnam" (PhD dissertation, University of California Los Angeles, 1974), 258–90. The most vivid Western account of 12–24 Sept. 1945 in Saigon is the diary of Germaine Krull, French war correspondent, a copy of which is in box 2, folder 7 of the Douglas Pike collection, Vietnam Archives, Texas Tech University. Thanks to John Kleinen for sharing his copy with me.

15. During these days, Vietnamese leaders also met repeatedly with Lieutenant Colonel Peter Dewey, head of the American OSS team to Saigon, who strongly urged them to talk rather than attack. See chapter 5.

16. Devillers, *Histoire*, 155–59. Joseph Buttinger, *Vietnam: A Dragon Embattled*, vol. 1, (New York: Praeger, 1967), 321–29. Dennis, 39, 45–48. Valentine, 291–317.

17. Dunn, 184–206. Jacques Le Bourgeois, *Ici Radio Saigon, 1939–45* (Paris: Éditions France-Empire, 1985), 218–25. Jean-Michel Hertrich, *Doc Lap: L'Indépendance ou la mort* (Paris: Jean Vigneau, 1946), 85. Three decades later, Jean Cédile asserted that a maximum of forty native French had been massacred on the night of 24–25 September, adding that no one knew how many naturalized Vietnamese, Eurasians, or *"français de l'Inde"* had suffered the same fate. *Académie des Sciences d'Outre-Mer: Comptes Rendus Trimestriels,* 31, no. 3 (1977?): 410–11.

18. Nguyễn Kỳ Nam, *Hồi ký (1925–1964)* [Memoirs (1925–1964)], vol. 2, *1945–1954* (Saigon: Dân Chủ Mới, 1964), 224–38.

19. Patti, 311, 331–32.

20. H. K. T., "Cuồng vọng của de Gaulle" [The Crazy Ambition of de Gaulle], *Thời Mới* 1 (16 Sept. 1945).

21. Dunn, 230–33. Valentine, 318–46.

22. Dunn, 237–41. Dennis, 63–64. Valentine, 347–68. Exactly who attended the 1 October meeting with Gracey remains unclear, but it surely included Dr. Phạm Ngọc Thạch, a physician specializing in lung disorders who had leaped to prominence in late June 1945 as head of the southern paramilitary Vanguard Youth organization.

23. Dunn, 242–44. Quotations are from Brain's report of the meeting with Thạch.

24. Background on each participant in these talks can be found in Christopher E. Goscha, *Historical Dictionary of the Indochina War (1945–1954)* (Copenhagen: NIAS Press, 2011). Hoàng Quốc Việt had arrived in Saigon in early September, representing the ICP Standing Bureau, with orders to resolve the ongoing dispute between Vanguard Youth and Liberation elements of the Communist Party in the south.

25. Nguyễn Kỳ Nam, 241–43. Dunn, 249–51, 254. Bui Dinh Thanh, "The First Year of Resistance in South Vietnam (1945–1946)," *Vietnamese Studies* (Hanoi) 7 (1965?): 70–72.

26. Dunn, 252–54. Dennis, 165–67. The record apparently does not identify the Vietnamese representatives, nor is there any indication they talked. Dunn says the encounter was "fairly short," and the Vietnamese departure "hasty."

27. Dunn, 254. Unfortunately no date is given for the radio transmission from Hanoi, nor do we know if the message was sent in the clear or in code that was decrypted by the French.

28. Nguyễn Đức Thuận, "Kháng chiến Nam Bộ," *Sinh Hoạt Nội Bộ* 16 (April 1949), as quoted in Nguyễn Việt, *Nam Bộ và Nam Phần Trung Bộ trong hai năm đầu Kháng Chiến (1945–1946)* [Southern and South-central Vietnam in the First Two Years of Resistance (1945–1946)] (Hanoi: NXB Văn Sử Địa, 1957), 39.

29. Dunn, 256–60. Dennis, 68.

30. Nguyễn Kỳ Nam, 243–44.

31. Sainteny, *Histoire*, 163–64. Devillers, *Histoire*, 204, 208. Sainteny met Thần again on 15 October.

32. Hồ had already voiced this concern to Archimedes Patti on 26 August. Patti, 202.

33. Devillers, *Histoire*, 164–65. Dunn, 298, 307–8, 310.

34. By then Japanese personnel had been confined to camps, awaiting transport home.

35. From September 1945, de Gaulle had considered the idea of touring Indochina following a triumphant show of force, accompanied by Prince Vĩnh San, the former boy Emperor Duy Tân (r. 1907–1916), whom the French had banished to Réunion Island, but much later commissioned into the French Army. Vĩnh San died in a plane crash in Africa in late December. Frédéric Turpin, *De Gaulle, les gaullistes et l'Indochine, 1940–1946* (Paris: Les Indes Savants, 2005), 190–94.

36. Christopher Goscha, "Le contexte asiatique de la guerre franco-vietnamienne: réseaux, relations et économie (d'août 1945 à mai 1954)," (Thèse de doctorat, Ecole pratique des hautes études, 2000), vol. 1, 82–100. Yves Gras, *Histoire de la Guerre d'Indochine*, 2nd ed. (Paris: Denoël, 1992), 54–56, 80–84.

37. Institut Charles-de-Gaulle, 34–35.

38. Stein Tønnesson, *Vietnam 1946: How the War Began* (Berkeley: University of California Press, 2010), 40–43, 46. Leclerc's late February–early March target first took account of the need for several months possible combat before the monsoon season, and second the high tides occurring during those specific days.

39. P. M. Dessinges, article in *Résistance* (Paris), as quoted in Devillers, *Histoire*, 204.

40. Worthing, 124–25. Sainteny, *Histoire*, 139. Buttinger, 365–627. Devillers, *Paris-Saigon-Hanoi*, 120–21, 129–30.

41. Françoise Martin, *Heures tragiques au Tonkin (9 mars 1945–18 mars 1946)* (Paris: Berger-Levrault, 1948), 85–90, 102–03, 140–49. Marr, *Vietnam 1945*, 61–68, 144, 233–34.

42. A later French government inquiry calculated twenty-three thousand civilian French inhabitants and twelve thousand disarmed French soldiers in Indochina during the summer of 1945. The study does not say whether naturalized Vietnamese and Indians were included in the civilian figure. My thanks to Eric Jennings for providing this information.

43. Marr, *Vietnam 1945*, 352, 357–58, 387, 438, 445, 461, 474–76, 517–18, 525–28.

44. Hoàng Tùng, "Những kỉ niệm vê Bác Hồ" [Recollections of Uncle Ho], *Diễn Đàn Forum* (Paris) (1 July 2010): 7.

45. Raoul Salan, *Mémoires: Fin d'un Empire*, vol. 1 (Paris: Presses de la Cité, 1970), 202, 205. Seventy-four percent of the civilians and 94% of the soldiers were in Hanoi, the remainder in Haiphong, Vinh, and Huê. Again, it is not clear whether naturalized Vietnamese and Indians from Pondicherry were included.

46. 19 Oct. 1945, d'Argenlieu (Chandernagore) to de Gaulle (no. 220 Cab/Civil/G2), ANOM, INDO, CP 368, dossier 2925. Thanks to Stein Tønnesson for this source.

47. Sainteny, *Histoire*, 137–38. Martin, 195–96, 206–7. Patti, 567.

48. *L'Entente* 105 (10 Feb. 1956); 114 (19 Feb. 1946). Martin, 249–50. CQ 257 (4 June 1946). ĐL 186 (1 July 1946).

49. Sở Công An Bắc Kỳ, *Hình Sự Công Báo* 1 (30 March 1946) to 9 (30 Nov. 1946). ĐL 186 (1 July 1946).

50. Jean Julien Fonde, *Traitez à tout prix . . . Leclerc et le Viet Nam* (Paris: Robert Laffont, 1971), 186. Jean Valluy, "Indochine: Octobre 45–mars 47," *Revue des Deux Mondes* (1 Dec. 1967): 362.

51. Fonde, 239. I have not found evidence of how many French civilians continued to reside in Hanoi into late 1946; it probably did not exceed several thousand.

52. Gilbert Bodinier, ed., *Le retour de la France en Indochine (1945–1946)* (Vincennes: SHAT, 1987), 202–4. Salan, 288–91.

53. Devillers, *Paris-Saigon-Hanoi*, 132–34. Shipway, 132–41, 152–55, offers a fine account of official French meanderings over the word "independence" from August 1945 to February 1946.

54. English translation from Shipway, 168.

55. 10 Dec. 1945, Réponse au général Leclerc, SHD 10H-161, dossier 4, as cited in Alain Ruscio, *1945–1954: La guerre Française d'Indochine* (Brussels: Éditions Complexe, 1992), 58–59.

56. Devillers, *Paris-Saigon-Hanoi*, 138–42.

57. In addition to a brief notice for publication, the government dispatched telegrams to province and city committees which concluded by warning every echelon to "be ready for any eventuality" and to confirm receipt of the message. 27 Feb. 1946, UBHCBB to all provinces and Haiphong, outgoing message file, GF 17.

58. France also relinquished her old concessions in China and agreed to sell the Yunnan railway to China. Roger Lévy, *L'Indochine et ses traités: 1946* (Paris: Hartmann, 1947), 75–82. Worthing, 139–42.

59. See, for example, DC 156 (2 March 1946).

60. Đảng Cộng Sản Việt Nam, *Văn Kiện Đảng về Kháng Chiến Chống Thực Dân Pháp* [Party Documents on Resistance to French Colonialism], vol. 1, 1945–1950 (Hanoi: NXB ST, 1986), 40–46. Hereafter VKĐKC1. Also reproduced in VKĐTT 8, 41–47. It is very doubtful this "Instruction" had time to circulate within the party.

61. The French suffered thirty-four killed and ninety-three wounded. Chinese commanders reported at least thirty killed and wounded. Stein Tønnesson, "La paix imposée par la Chine: l'Accord franco-vietnamien du 6 mars 1946," in *Les Guerres d'Indochine de 1945 à 1975,* edited by Charles-Robert Ageron and Philippe Devillers (Paris: Institut d'histoire du temps présent, 1996), 35–36. Worthing, 135–69. Devillers, *Paris-Saigon-Hanoi,* 143–47. In a memoir late in life, Hoàng Minh Giám confirmed that Chinese pressure was applied on Hồ to reach a deal with the French. X&N 25 (March 1996): 8.

62. Nguyễn Tố Uyên, 128–29.

63. Khanh is identified in the document as "Special Delegate of the Council of Ministers." The DRV minister of foreign affairs, Nguyễn Tường Tam, also of the Nationalist Party, attended the signing ceremony but did not contribute his name. Representatives of the American and British missions in Hanoi attended, as well officers from the Chinese occupation command. Võ Nguyên Giáp, *Unforgettable Months and Years* (Ithaca: Cornell SEAP, 1975), 101–3. Photos in Hội Khoa Học Lịch Sử Việt Nam, *Ký Ức,* 126–27.

64. Ministère de la France d'Outre-mer, *Bulletin Hebdomadaire* 67 (18 March 1946). Lévy, 46–48. Sainteny, *Histoire,* 182–84. Devillers, *Paris-Saigon-Hanoi,* 148–50. Side-by-side French text and (unofficial) Vietnamese translation can be found first in CQ 180 (8 March 1946). DC 160 (9 March 1946), Vietnamese translation. CQ analyses the accord in issues appearing 9–14 March 1946. Nguyễn Kiến Giang, *Việt-nam năm đầu tiên sau Cách Mạng Tháng Tám* [Vietnam's First Year following the August Revolution] (Hanoi: NXB

ST, 1961), 172–74. English translation in Allan W. Cameron, ed., *Viet-Nam Crisis: A Documentary History*, vol. 1 (Ithaca: Cornell University Press, 1971), 77–79.

65. However, two other categories of French troops are specified: (1) those guarding Japanese POWs, expected to complete their mission and depart in ten months or less; and (2) *"les unites chargées de la defense des bases vietnamiennes tiendront garnison,"* probably a deliberately obscure reference to air and naval facilities. See Nguyễn Kiến Giang, 174. Lévy, 48–52. Bodinier, ed., 228–31, reprints Pignon's commentary on military annex discussions.

66. Shipway, 174, contains this quote without saying when or to whom Hồ was speaking.

67. The French version of this proclamation appeared the same day in *L'Entente* (Hanoi) 130 (7 March 1946). It is reprinted in Sainteny, *Histoire*, 247, and in Françoise Martin, *Heures tragiques au Tonkin (9 mars 1945–18 mars 1946)* (Paris: Berger-Levrault, 1948), 271–72. From the tone we can deduce that it was drafted and printed by Sainteny's team without consulting Hồ Chí Minh's office. A Vietnamese version is reprinted in DC 160 (9 March 1946).

68. 6 March 1946, Thông cáo của Chính Phủ Việt Nam, GF 2. The next day, the full French language text of the 6 March Accord was dispatched "most urgently" to localities. 7 March 1946, UBHCBB to all provinces and Haiphong, outgoing message files, GF 17.

69. Here Giáp cited Russian concessions to Germany in the 1918 treaty of Brest-Litovsk, a frightening comparison given how much territory Lenin had given up, and the fact that it had required defeat of Germany by third parties (France, Britain, the United States) to void Russia's commitments.

70. French analysts quickly translated *"Hòa để tiến"* as *"paix pour le progress,"* which misses the tactical emphasis of this policy. The text of Giáp's speech (or someone's shorthand transcription of it) appeared in *Quyết Chiến* (Huế) on 9 March 1946 and 13 March 1946, whereas other newspapers simply summarized the contents. Devillers, *Histoire*, 228–30, contains a French translation.

71. Devillers, *Histoire*, 230, offers only a two-sentence translated quote from Khanh.

72. Devillers, *Histoire*, 230–31.

73. Jean Sainteny, *Ho Chi Minh and His Vietnam: A Personal Memoir* (Chicago: Cowles, 1972), 65–66. Ngô Văn Chiêu, *Journal d'un combatant Viet-Minh* (Paris: Éditions du Seuil, 1955), 68–70, provides another first-hand description of the meeting. See also, Võ Nguyên Giáp, *Unforgettable Days* (Hanoi: FLPH, 1975), 186–90. Hội Khoa Học Lịch Sử Việt Nam, *Ký Úc*, 128–29, contains a panoramic shot of the crowd.

74. Ngô Văn Chiêu, 70–74, describes the bitter arguments that broke out in the Hanoi garrison where he was stationed.

75. Jacques Mordal, *Marine Indochine* (Paris: Amiot Dumont, 1953), 123–34.

76. Võ Nguyên Giáp, *Unforgettable Days*, 194–96. Adrien Dansette, *Leclerc* (Paris: Flammarion, 1952), 205.

77. VKĐKC1, 47–56. Also VKĐTT 8, 48–56. A Tổng Bộ Việt Minh document of 7 March, partially translated and quoted in Devillers, *Histoire*, 231, appears significantly less concessionary than the 9 March Party "Instruction."

78. *Chiến Sĩ* 16 (13 March 1946).

79. *Quyết Thắng* 24 (15 March 1946); 25 (20 March 1946).

80. *L'Entente* (Hanoi) 140 (17 March 1946), devotes its entire front page to this speech.

81. Devillers, *Histoire*, 244–45. Devillers, *Paris-Saigon-Hanoi*, 161–68. Tønnesson, *Vietnam 1946*, 66.

82. CQ 188 (16 March 1946). Hội Khoa Học Lịch Sử Việt Nam, *Ký Ức*, 132–34. Kenneth E. Colton, "The Failure of the Independent Political Movement in Vietnam, 1945–46," (PhD dissertation, American University, 1969), 668–69.

83. Fonde, 157–62. Sainteny, *Histoire*, 139–41. Claude Paillat, *Dossiers secret de l'Indochine* (Paris: Presses de la Cité, 1964), 66–67. Devillers, *Histoire*, 237–38. *Batailles* (Paris), hors-serie no. 1 (2005), 62–63.

84. *L'Entente* 141 (18 March 1946). The next morning's issue was headlined *"Et Voici LE GENERAL LECLERC!"* and included two big Free French crosses, vivid drawings (photo technology was unavailable), an article describing the French Army entry to Hanoi, and a comparison of this event with the triumphant 25 August 1945 entry to Paris.

85. Devillers, *Histoire*, 238–39. Vo Nguyen Giap, *Unforgettable Days*, 211. Fonde, 159, 169–70. Salan, 350–51.

86. CQ 192 (20 March 1946); 200 (28 March 1946).

87. Devillers, *Histoire*, 242–43.

88. 8 March 1946, d'Argenlieu to Cominindo, as cited in Devillers, *Paris-Saigon-Hanoi*, 169. Georges Thierry d'Argenlieu, *Chronique d'Indochine 1945–47* (Paris: Albin Michel, 1985), 199.

89. Devillers, *Paris-Saigon-Hanoi*, 155–56, 169–73. Tønnesson, *Vietnam 1946*, 66–70. Sainteny, 244–46. Claude Paillat, 69–70.

90. *L'Entente* 233 (15 June 1946) and subsequent five issues.

91. *L'Entente* 172 (18 April 1946).

92. *Quyết Thắng* 29 (3 April 1946).

93. *60 Năm Hoạt Động Thừa Thiên-Huế* [Sixty Years Activity in Thua Thien-Huế] (Huế, 1990), 76, 79–81. Most tensions revolved around DRV civil authorities and Việt Minh activists trying to control French access to workers, cyclo drivers, and market stalls.

94. Devillers, *Histoire*, 248. 11 March 1946, Ministry of Interior to Trần Bửu Kiêm Nam Bo Committee, Tg décryptés, Viet Minh (Archives Politiques), ANOM, INDO, CP 128. CQ 180 (8 March 1946); 186 (14 March 1946).

95. Nguyên Hùng, *Nguyễn Bình: Huyền Thoại và Sự Thật* [Nguyen Binh: Myth and Reality] (Hanoi: NXB Văn Học, 1995), 210–14. 11 April 1946, Rapport sur entrevue de Thien Quan, SHD box 10H4088.

96. Annexe I, Rapport sur entrevue de Thien Quan, SHD box 10H4088. At no point did the French grant Nguyễn Bình an official title. The Vietnamese delegation referred to him as "Seventh Zone Commander."

97. Phạm Thiều was a secondary school teacher, publisher of the periodical *Vệ Quốc* (*National Guard*), and member of Nguyễn Bình's staff.

98. Annex II, Rapport sur entrevue de Thien Quan, SHD box 10H4088. The "neutral government" idea may have been tossed in as an afterthought, or it may be another example of resistance leaders in the south thinking for themselves.

99. Rapport sur entrevue de Thien Quan, SHD box 10H4088. Nguyên Hùng, 214–19. 17 April 1946, Ministry of Interior to Nam Bo Committee, Tg décryptés, Viet Minh (Archives Politiques), ANOM, INDO, CP 128.

100. Trần Công Tấn, *Hà Văn Lâu: Người đi từ bến làng Sinh* [Ha Van Lau: The Person from Sinh Village Ferry] (Hanoi: NXB Phụ Nữ, 2004), 137–41.

101. CQ 219 (19 April 1946). Phan Tử Nghĩa, a member of the Northern Region Administrative Committee, had participated in the Hanoi branch of the SFIO, and would be a founding member in July 1946 of the Vietnam Socialist Party. Ngô Tử Hạ, wealthy Hanoi publisher and Catholic lay leader, chaired the DRV National Assembly.

102. 16 April 1946, Instructions pour le delegation française de la Commission mixte d'Armistice pour le Sud-Annam, Annex I, Journal de la Commission d'Armistice du Sud-Annam, SHD box 10H4088.

103. Trần Công Tấn, 141–42. Several other Vietnamese liaison group members were jailed by the French at the end of April, then released by Colonel Penicaut two weeks later.

104. CQ 210 (19 April 1946).

105. Trần Công Tấn, 142–48.

106. Salan, 426–32. Gareth Porter, ed., *Vietnam: The Definitive Documentation of Human Decisions,* vol. 1 (Standfordville, NY: Earl M. Coleman Enterprises, 1979), 98–102. Nguyễn Kiến Giang, 174–75. CQ 209 (8 April 1046). On 20 April 1946, a supplement to the 3 April agreement specified Hanoi venues where a joint guard would be maintained, notably the U.S. and British legations, General Valluy's residence, the Yên Phụ power station, water plant, Long Biên/Doumer bridge, Bank of Indochina, Lanesson hospital, and Hanoi train station. CQ 222 (23 April 1946).

107. 13 May 1946, Thông Tri from Quân Sự Ủy Viên Hội, GF 77. A battalion commander has scribbled on this copy: "French personnel routinely salute our officers, so our responsibility is to reciprocate that custom *(lễ)*."

108. In Vietnamese, the commission was called the Ủy ban Liên lạc và Kiểm soát Quân Sự Việt Pháp Trung Ương, often abbreviated as Liên Kiểm Việt Pháp.

109. Fonde, 171–230.

110. 21 March 1946, Nha Công Chính BB to Bộ Giao Thông Công Chính, GF 46.

111. 21 March 1946, UBHCBB to all provinces and Haiphong, Văn phòng BBP, outgoing message file, GF 17.

112. 27 April 1946, Ty Địa Chính Nam Định to Chánh Giám đốc Địa Chính BB, contracting dossier, GF 33.

113. April 1946 periodic report, Phòng Công Văn dossier, GF 61.

114. 29 March 1946, Fonde to Nam, GF 76. Fonde complained that previous such inquiries had not been answered.

115. Valluy, 35, 202, 365–66. Devillers, *Histoire,* 254, 257, 276. Simpson-Jones was again assailed unsuccessfully on 18 June, with 150 bullet holes counted in his conspicuous amphibious Duck vehicle.

116. 20 May 1946, Hà Đông to Ban Liên Lạc Việt Pháp; 4 July 1946, Capt. De Chatillon to Cdt Bùi Quý, Nạn máy bay dossier, GF 52.

117. 13 Nov. 1946, Haiphong to BB, Sở Kinh tế incoming message file, GF 26.

118. Vũ Hồng Khanh was named a conference delegate too, but did not show up to fly to Dalat.

119. The twelve delegates to the Dalat conference and four advisors are listed in Hoàng Xuân Hãn, "Một vài ký vãng vê Hội Nghị Đà Lạt" [Some Recollections of the Dalat Conference], *La Sơn Yên Hồ Hoàng Xuân Hãn*, vol. 2 (Hanoi: NXB Giáo Dục, 1988), 1501.

120. Messages intercepted and decoded by French intelligence, dossier 4, Terrorisme V.M., ANOM, INDO, CP 158.

121. Nguyễn Kim Nữ Hạnh, *Tiếp bước chân cha: Hồi ký về Giáo Sư Nguyễn Văn Huyên:* [Following in Father's Footsteps: Memoir on Professor Nguyen Van Huyen] (Hanoi: NXB Thế Giới, 2003), 123–25.

122. Hoàng Xuân Hãn, 1502–4. Here Hãn relies on his 1946 notebook for a verbatim quote from Hồ.

123. Nguyễn Kim Nữ Hạnh, 126. In Vietnamese: *"Găng nhưng không được gẫy."*

124. Võ Nguyên Giáp, *Unforgettable Days*, 245.

125. Hoàng Xuân Hãn, 1504–5.

126. Hoàng Xuân Hãn, 1505–8. Nguyễn Kim Nữ Hạnh, 126–27. Võ Nguyên Giáp, *Unforgettable Days*, 245–46.

127. Hoàng Xuân Hãn, 1509–13. Nguyễn Kim Nữ Hạnh, 127–28. Tam had also spoken Vietnamese when meeting d'Argenlieu earlier, with Nguyễn Văn Huyên serving as interpreter. Tam was fluent in French, but the delegation had decided to make a diplomatic point.

128. Hoàng Xuân Hãn, 1513–14.

129. It is thus misleading for Võ Nguyên Giáp to disparage Tam several times for being the only one not present at meetings. Võ Nguyên Giáp, *Unforgettable Days*, 248–50.

130. Nguyễn Kim Nữ Hạnh, 130. Hoàng Xuân Hãn, 1509, 1515–18.

131. By contrast, Nguyễn Văn Sâm analyzed continuing political divisions and suggested that a referendum conducted at that moment in the south might not produce a majority in favor of unification with the center and north. Hoàng Xuân Hãn, 1519–20. Sâm would be assassinated in October 1947.

132. Hoàng Xuân Hãn, 1520–21.

133. Nguyễn Kim Nữ Hạnh, 129–30. Hoàng Xuân Hãn, 1521–24. Võ Nguyên Giáp, *Unforgettable Days*, 250–51. Thạch was released on conclusion of the Dalat conference.

134. Hoàng Xuân Hãn, 1522. Nguyễn Kim Nữ Hạnh, 130–31. Tg décryptés dossier, Viet Minh (Archives Politiques), ANOM, INDO, CP 128.

135. Phan Văn Cẩn, *Lịch Sử Bộ Tổng Tham Mưu trong Kháng Chiến chống Pháp (1945–1954)* [History of the General Staff in the Anti-French Resistance (1945–1954)]. (Hanoi: Bộ Tổng Tham Mưu, 1991), 71.

136. Giáp and Pierre Messmer had particularly long conversations, using the informal *tu* to address each other rather than *vous*. This *tutoiement révolutionnaire* scandalized some former colonial officials, who had long used *tu* to the natives but demanded *vous* in return. Devillers, *Histoire*, 263.

137. Hoàng Xuân Hãn, 1525–38.

138. Hoàng Xuân Hãn, 1543–44.

139. Devillers, *Histoire*, 260–63. Hoàng Xuân Hãn, 1544–50. Bodinier, ed., 247–55.

140. Hoàng Xuân Hãn, 1550–52. Devillers, *Histoire,* 264–66.

141. Hoàng Xuân Hãn, 1554–58. Nguyễn Kim Nữ Hạnh, 133. A well-known poet, Cù Huy Cận had started a poetry capping game on the return flight, but probably felt those couplets too facile to share with the president.

142. *Dân Mới* (Vinh) 1 (1 May 1946).

143. *Le Peuple* (Hanoi) 7 (28 April 1946); 9 (5 May 1946).

144. *Tiên Phong* (Hanoi) 11 (15 May 1946), reprinted in *Tiên Phong* compendium, vol. 1 (Hanoi: NXB Hội Nhà Văn, 1996). Trường Chinh complimented Dalat delegates of diverse background and party affiliation for working together effectively and coming to respect each other more. VKĐTT 8, 427–28.

145. *Gió Mới* (Hanoi) 23 (17 May 1946); and 25 (31 May 1946).

146. The ten members of the National Assembly and five accompanying nonmembers are listed in Sainteny, *Histoire,* 198, and Nguyễn Tấn Gi-Trọng, "Nhật ký ghi chép các sự hoạt động của Phái đoàn Quốc hội Việt Nam đi từ Hà Nội sang Ba Lê" [Diary Recording the Activities of the Vietnam National Assembly Delegation travelling from Hanoi to Paris], in Hoàng Hạnh, et al., eds., *Từ Đà Lạt đến Paris* [From Dalat to Paris] (Hanoi: NXB Hà Nội, 1996), 88–91.

147. Nguyễn Tấn Gi-Trọng, 106, 109, 112–21, 125–26, 129.

148. Nguyễn Tấn Gi-Trọng, 125. Christoph Giebel, *Imagined Ancestries of Vietnamese Communism: Tôn Đức Thắng and the Politics of History and Memory* (Seattle: University of Washington Press, 2004), 43–45. Giebel demonstrates earlier that Thắng could not have been on a French vessel in the Black Sea at the time of the mutiny.

149. Nguyễn Tấn Gi-Trọng, 120–22, 124, 127. Shipway, 190, 194–95. Devillers, *Histoire,* 259.

150. Nguyễn Tấn Gi-Trọng, 104, 106–7, 117, 126. Notes taken by Huỳnh Văn Tiểng are transcribed in X&N 255 (March 2006): 35–36.

151. CQ 215 (15 April 1946). More exactly, the parliamentary delegation carried home donations totaling 10,642,135 francs. X&N 6 (Sept. 1994): 12.

152. Nguyễn Tấn Gi-Trọng, 112–13.

153. Nguyễn Tấn Gi-Trọng, 122–26, 128. Vietnamese soldiers from units in Germany had approached the delegation twice before this trip was arranged

154. DC 222 (22 May 1946); 231 (2 June 1946). *Dân Mới* 4 (15 June 1946).

155. 11 May 1946, Motion reprinted in *Từ Đà Lạt đến Paris,* 180–91. Each person gave in longhand his or her signature, full name, occupation and address, aware that the Sûreté would take note. The original Hanoi message to the people of France and French government, signed by 110 intellectuals, is reprinted in *Le Peuple* 2 (11 April 1946).

156. Nguyễn Tấn Gi-Trọng, 114, 118–22, 126–27, 129–30. Sainteny, *Histoire,* 199. Sainteny mentions only the "Marseillaise" at the airport. Nguyễn Mạnh Hà and Trần Ngọc Danh remained in Paris to prepare for the arrival of Hồ Chí Minh and the DRV negotiating delegation.

157. Nguyễn Tấn Gi-Trọng, 129, 134–35, 137–40. DC 228 (29 May 1946). Hội Khoa Học Lịch Sử Việt Nam, *Ký Ức,* 180–81.

158. "Les fondements du conflit franco-vietnamien," *Les Temps Modernes* 5 (1 Feb. 1946). Jean-Paul Sartre edited this lively journal.

159. This position had been argued by *Gió Mới* as early as its no. 18 (5 April 1946) issue.

160. *Chiến Sĩ* (Huế) 26 (29 May 1946).

161. *Dân Mới* (Vinh) 1 (1 May 1946).

162. This view is best expressed in *Gió Biển* (Haiphong) 4 (1 June 1946).

163. *Dân Mới* (Vinh) 4 (15 June 1946).

164. Sainteny, *Ho Chi Minh*, 69–70, points out that the Sultan of Morocco and Ben Bella of Algeria were arrested in similar circumstances later.

165. Devillers, *Histoire*, 267. Devillers, *Paris-Saigon-Hanoi*, 188. Fonde, 214–15, expresses surprise at Hồ's decision to go, implying that the British intelligence officer Peter Simpson-Jones may have played a role.

166. DC 223 (23 May 1946). The French audience is said to have "applauded vigorously."

167. DC 227 (28 May 1946). I suspect Hồ and Giáp had already agreed that diplomacy was not Giáp's forte.

168. CB 1946, 305. Nguyễn Kim Nữ Hạnh, 134.

169. *Hàng Không Việt Nam* (Hanoi) (August 2003): 41–42. Prior to leaving the Bắc Bộ Phủ for the airport, Hồ read out a formal pledge, then had delegation members raise their hands and join him in swearing to fulfil their duties. CQ 255 (1 June 1946).

170. DC 231 (2 June 1946), special four-page edition in blue ink on better quality paper.

171. *Chiến Sĩ* 29 (19 June 1946). CQ 255 (1 June 1946). Thanks to Cathy Churchman for helping with translation. Sainteny, *Hồ Chí Minh*, 71.

172. Salan, 389. Hồ Chí Minh would not have been entirely surprised. On 26 March, the Cochinchina Council had designated Nguyễn Văn Thinh as president of an autonomous republic. On 18 May, d'Argenlieu told Hồ in person that he was inclined to approve the council's initiative. Tønnesson, *Vietnam 1946*, 72. Devillers, *Paris-Saigon-Hanoi*, 188.

173. Devillers, *Histoire*, 271. D.H., "Nhật ký hành trình của Hồ chủ tịch bốn tháng sang Pháp" [Journal diary of President Ho's four months in France], typescript housed (1988) at the Thư Viện Khoa Học Xã Hội in Hanoi. Hồ may have authored this diary.

174. Sainteny, *Ho Chi Minh*, 71–75, 79–80. Sainteny, *Histoire*, 200, 202.

175. Sainteny, *Ho Chi Minh*, 75–77. D.H., "Nhật ký hành trình."

176. Devillers, *Paris-Saigon-Hanoi*, 193–94. Shipway, 202.

177. Henri Azeau, *Ho Chi Minh, dernière chance: La conférence franco-vietnamienne de Fontainebleau, juillet 1946* (Paris: Flammarion, 1968), 156–57, 166.

178. Azeau, 171–74, reprints this paper. Devillers, *Histoire*, 296, labels it "a new version of the old assimilationist thesis."

179. Text in Azeau, 174–77.

180. D. Bruce Marshall, *The French Colonial Myth and Constitution-making in the Fourth Republic* (New Haven: Yale University Press, 1973), 201–7. Devillers, *Paris-Saigon-Hanoi*, 194–97. Devillers, *Histoire*, 295–97. Nguyễn Kiến Giang, 215–20.

181. Shipway, 205–6, 210–11.

182. George Bidault, *Resistance: The Political Autobiography of George Bidault* (London: Weidenfeld and Nicholson, 1965), 192.

183. Jean d'Arcy, "Confrontation des Thèses Françaises et Vietnamiennes," *Politique Etrangère* (Paris) 12 (July 1947) : 332, 336, 339–41. Trình Quốc Quang, *Hội Nghị Việt Pháp*

Fông-te-nơ-bơ-lô (Fontainebleau) Tháng Bảy Năm 1946 [The Vietnamese-French Conference at Fontainebleau, July 1946] (Hanoi: NXB Văn Hóa, 1949), 22–66. Azeau, 183–93.

184. Turpin, 259–66.

185. 27 July 1946, Telegrammes chiffrés destinés à la Delegation du Viet-Nam, ANOM, INDO, Papiers Moutet P.A. 28, carton 7, dossier 159. The delegation did encode and send by shortwave some messages to Hanoi, which the French were able partially to decrypt. 13 July 1946, Commandant les Transmissions, Section D, SHD 10H1868. Phạm Huy Thông, secretary to President Hồ in Paris, told me in 1980 that Hồ sent typed letters via intermediaries, sometimes in code.

186. Shipway, 211–14. Tønnesson, *Vietnam 1946*, 80–81. Devillers, *Histoire*, 300–2. Devillers, *Paris-Saigon-Hanoi*, 199–206.

187. Délégation française: Séance privée du 25 juillet; and Compte rendu analytique de la séance du 31 juillet (1946), Papiers Monguillot, ANOM, Papiers privée 56-PA6.

188. Shipway, 214–15. R.E.M. Irving, *The First Indochina War* (London: C. Helm, 1975), 5–7, 18–29, offers a trenchant analysis of French politics during the summer of 1946 as they affected Franco-Vietnamese negotiations.

189. Phan Anh conversation with Hoàng Xuân Hãn after returning from France, X&N 82 (Dec. 2000): 17.

190. 3 Sept. 1946, Procès-verbal, Réunion de le Commission restreinte franco-vietnamienne, Papiers Monguillot, ANOM, Papiers privée 56-PA6. Azeau, 227–33

191. Shipway, 217–18.

192. Aubrac's wife, Lucie, was an equally famous Resistance leader. Sainteny, *Hồ Chí Minh*, 85. Goscha, *Historical Dictionary*.

193. Devillers, *Histoire*, 305–7. Devillers, *Paris-Saigon-Hanoi*, 217–19. Shipway, 217–19. Sainteny, *Histoire*, 208–9.

194. The full text of both joint declaration and modus vivendi can be found in: Lévy, 69–72; Sainteny, *Histoire*, 248–52; Azeau, 287–92; and Bodinier, ed., 287–91. English translation in Porter, ed., 116–18; and Cameron, ed., 85–89. For an early interpretation by the head of the French delegation at Fontainebleau, see Max André, "Après l'accord de principe Franco-Vietnamien," *France Illustration*, no. 52 (28 Sept. 1946), 295–96.

195. Devillers, *Paris-Saigon-Hanoi*, 225–27. Tønnesson, *Vietnam 1946*, 93–94.

196. Devillers, *Paris-Saigon-Hanoi*, 227–28. Bodinier, ed., 291–93.

197. Sainteny, *Ho Chi Minh*, 81.

198. Turpin, 257. Sainteny, *Ho Chi Minh*, 79–82, 85–88.

199. A composite print with musical sound track added later can be found at the Vietnam Film Institute archives in Hanoi.

200. Sainteny, *Hồ Chí Minh*, 89–90.

201. Apparently the French government did not offer to fly all or part of the delegation home.

202. Tønnesson, *Vietnam 1946*, 85. 25 Oct. 1946, Schlumberger to Directeur du Cabinet, Haussaire, ANOM, INDO, CP 303.

203. CQ 326 (23 Aug. 1946).

204. Perhaps the most sensitive discussion of property issues can be found in *Chính Nghĩa tuần báo* (Hanoi) 7 (1 July 1946), a weekly published by a Vietnam Nationalist Party

group. By contrast, the Democratic Party's principal newspaper demanded that France compensate Vietnam for eighty years of colonial exploitation. ĐL 203 (21 July 1946).

205. *Dân Mới* (Vinh) 4 (15 June 1946). *Quyết Thắng* (Huế) 56 (20 July 1946). *Dư Luận* (Hanoi) 15 (28 July 1946); 16 (4 Aug. 1946). ĐL 194 (11 July 1946); 209 (28 July 1946); 210 (30 July 1946); 213 (2 Aug. 1946).

206. *Quân Bạch Đằng* (Kiến An) 7 (2 Sept. 1946).

207. *Chính Nghĩa tuần báo* 12 (19 Aug. 1946). Although "Tổ Quốc" has distinct patrimonial origins, hence normally translated as "Fatherland," from the 1930s the image of "mother Vietnam" gained favor as well.

208. CQ 343 (12 Sept. 1946); 344 (13 Sept. 1946). Giáp had largely supplanted Acting President Huỳnh Thúc Kháng as government spokesperson.

209. CQ 345 (14 Sept. 1946).

210. *Độc Lập chủ nhật* 1 (15 Sept. 1946). See also ĐL 243(12 Sept. 1946); 245(14 Sept. 1946).

211. ĐL 244 (13 Sept. 1946).

212. *Dư Luận* 22 (15 Sept. 1946).

213. CQ 349 (18 Sept. 1946). In a rare use of irony, CQ editors credited "our professional brethren at *L'Entente*" for printing the unofficial modus vivendi text.

214. DC 324 (22 Sept. 1946).

215. *Dư Luận* 23 (22 Sept. 1946); 24 (29 Sept. 1946); 25 (6 Oct. 1946).

216. 28 Nov. 1946, French intelligence report, as cited in Tønnesson, *Vietnam 1946*, 87–88.

217. ĐL 253 (27 Sept. 1946). The editors promised an article two days hence on "the sovereignty issue in the modus vivendi," but it seems this entire issue failed to appear.

218. *Chính Nghĩa tuần báo* 17 (23 Sept. 1946).

219. *Kháng Chiến* 4 (30 Sept. 1946); 5 (15 Oct. 1946).

220. CQ 359 (28 Sept. 1946).

221. CQ 369 (8 Oct. 1946).

222. Hoàng Xuân Hãn, X&N 82 (Dec. 2000): 15–17.

223. CQ 251 (28 May 1946); 271 (20 June 1946); 272 (21 June 1946); 275 (25 June 1946); and 283 (4 July 1946).

224. DC 245 (19 June 1946). Valluy, 366.

225. Valluy, 204. Devillers, *Histoire*, 274.

226. CQ 276 (26 June 1946); 277 (27 June 1946). During 1946, *"phần đấu"* meant to struggle short of violence, as distinct from *"tranh đấu."*

227. Devillers, *Histoire*, 287. Valluy, 206. Philippe Héduy, ed., *Histoire de l'Indochine*, vol. 2 (Paris: Société de Production Litteraire/Henri Veyrier, 1983), 287. ĐL 195 (12 July 1946); 212 (1 Aug. 1946). DC 263 (11 July 1946).

228. Tønnesson, *Vietnam 1946*, 129. Devillers, *Histoire*, 283.

229. CQ 302 (26 July 1946); 303 (27 July 1946).

230. 26 July 1946, Tham Mưu Trưởng, July 1946 Vệ Quốc Đoàn dossier, GF 64.

231. 12 Aug. 1946, Historique du Guet-apens de Bac-Ninh le 3 Aout 1946, SHD 10H601. My thanks to Dr. Nguyễn Thanh for locating this report. Phan Mỹ (?), 4 Aug. 1946, Rapport sur la mission au Pont des Rapides, Bacninh, Dapcau, NARA 23, dossier annex VI. CQ 312 (6 Aug. 1946). Fonde, 242–48. Salan, vol. 1, 402.

232. 12 Aug. 1946, Mindef to Lieutenant Colonel Répiton Preneuf, NARA 22, dossier annex VI.

233. Devillers, *Histoire*, 276.

234. Nghị quyết Hội nghị cán bộ Trung Uờng, VKĐKC1, 60. VKĐTT 8, 101.

235. Võ Nguyên Giáp, *Unforgettable Days*, 314–15. CQ 313 (7 Aug. 1946). The Đuồng bridge is only seven kilometers northeast of Hanoi. No French source mentions this altercation.

236. Thanks to our son Danny for providing technical details on each of these vehicles.

237. Võ Nguyên Giáp, *Unforgettable Days*, 315.

238. 6 Aug. 1946, Note from Fonde attached to an 8 Aug. 1946 letter from Colonel Jean Crépin, acting commissioner of the republic for Tonkin and Nord-Annam, to High Commissioner d'Argenlieu in Saigon, CAOM, INDO, CP 301. Copy from Stein Tønnesson.

239. 12 Aug. 1946, Historique du Guet-Apens de Bac-Ninh document, cited above, which contains eighteen pages of text, charts and maps.

240. Jean Crépin, "Rapport sur la situation politique au Tonkin au 12 août 1946," extracted in his unpublished "Souvenirs," 240–41. My thanks to François Guillemot for sharing with me relevant parts of Crépin's memoir.

241. Report for August 1946 of the Directeur de la Police et de la Sûreté Federales en Indochine, second folder, ANOM, INDO, CP 186.

242. 6 Aug. 1946, Fonde Note, ANOM, INDO, CP 301. 8 Aug. 1946, Crépin letter to d'Argenlieu.

243. CQ 314 (8 Aug. 1946); 315 (9 Aug. 1946); and 316 (10 Aug. 1946).

244. CQ 312 (6 Aug. 1946). ĐL 217 (7 Aug. 1946).

245. CQ 313 (7 Aug. 1946); 314 (8 Aug. 1946); 317 (12 Aug. 1946).

246. ĐL 219 (9 Aug. 1946); 222 (14 Aug. 1946).

247. Devillers, *Histoire*, 300–1. Marshall, 205.

248. Crépin, "Rapport," 237–40.

249. Tønnesson, *Vietnam 1946*, 87. Trần Ngọc Danh stayed on in Paris, as nonrecognized representative, mostly interacting with Việt Kiều groups. Dương Bạch Mai, a Fontainebleau delegate, and much more prominent than Danh, also remained active in France until he was arrested in 1947 and deported for trial in Saigon.

250. As quoted in Valluy, *Revue des Deux Mondes* (1 Dec. 1967): 363.

251. Dossier 2, Activités des Rebelles, ANOM, INDO, CP 158. Reports for September and October 1946, Directeur de la Police et de la Sûreté Federales en Indochine, CP 186. Tønnesson, *Vietnam 1946*, 96–97. Bodinier, 293–94, 297–300.

252. Reprinted in CQ 393 (1 Nov. 1946). Nguyễn Việt, 113. Clearly there was no time to distribute this message widely.

253. Valluy, 356. Tønnesson, *Vietnam 1946*, 95. Two weeks earlier d'Argenlieu had released a first batch of eighty-five political prisoners and dispatched them to Hanoi. Fonde, 274.

254. Captured documents SHD 10H 7/06 CD, part 2.

255. DC 363 (7 Nov. 1946). CQ 397 (6 Nov. 1946). CQ 400 (9 Nov. 1946) contains a photo of the two delegations.

256. Valluy, 361–62. Tønnesson, *Vietnam 1946*, 96. CQ 397 (6 Nov. 1946); 401 (10 Nov. 1946).

257. Tønnesson, *Vietnam 1946*, 99. Tønnesson, "The Outbreak," appendix 2, 310–13.

258. Tønnesson, *Vietnam 1946*, 108. Devillers, *Histoire*, 328, 340–41. Valluy, 363. Valluy did not reveal this letter until 1967.

259. Devillers, *Histoire*, 327, 329–30, 340. Tønnesson, *Vietnam 1946*, 103–4, 108, 137–40. Goscha, *Historical Dictionary*.

260. Trần Huy Liệu speech reprinted in *Sao Vàng* 18 (3 Oct. 1946). Fonde, 174, refers to Liệu as "a new Goebbels."

261. *Độc Lập chủ nhật* (Hanoi) 5 (13 Oct. 1946). Devillers *Histoire*, 329.

262. Essay serialized in *Độc Lập chủ nhật*, 7 (27 Oct. 1946); 8 (3 Nov. 1946); and 9 (10 Nov. 1946). Luyện used the term *"trung dung"* to characterize what I translate as "moderate middle," referring back to the Confucian doctrine of the mean.

263. CQ 403 (12 Nov. 1946). DC 368 (13 Nov. 1946).

264. Thanh Thủy, *Độc Lập chủ nhật* 10 (17 Nov. 1946).

265. Tønnesson, *Vietnam 1946*, 82.

266. *Dư Luận* 30 (17 Nov. 1946).

267. *Công An Mới* (Hanoi) 2 (15 Nov. 1946).

268. 24 May 46, UBHCBB to UBHC Haiphong, GF 76.

269. Sûreté *Bulletin* 95 (14 May 1946), ANOM, INDO, CP 186.

270. Devillers, *Histoire*, 288, 314. Valluy, 368. Tønnesson, *Vietnam 1946*, 118–19. CQ 333 (31 Aug. 1946).

271. Tønnesson, *Vietnam 1946*, 119. Turpin, 286–92.

272. DC 339 (11 Oct. 1946); 341 (13 Oct. 1946); 342 (15 Oct. 1946); 344 (17 Oct. 1946).

273. DC 345 (18 Oct. 1946). CQ 380 (19 Oct. 1946).

274. Tønnesson, *Vietnam 1946*, 119–20. Devillers, *Histoire*, 331. Jean Ferrandi, *Les officiers français face au Vietminh 1945–1954* (Paris: Fayard, 1966), 82–96.

275. DC 37 (16 Nov. 1946), Devillers, *Histoire*, 331–32.

276. DC 374 (20 Nov. 1946).

277. 9 Nov. 1946, Fonde to head of Vietnamese delegation to the Mixed Commission, Văn phòng Mật outgoing message file, GF 31.

278. Tønnesson, *Vietnam 1946*, 127–28. Nguyễn Kiến Giang, 238–45. Valluy, 368–75.

279. CQ 412 (21 Nov. 1946) to CQ 419 (28 Nov. 1946). *Cứu Quốc* also translated and published several letters between Hồ Chí Minh and Võ Nguyên Giáp on one side, and General Morlière on the other.

280. *Cấp tiến* 8 (23 Nov. 1946). This appears to be the last issue.

281. *Độc Lập chủ nhật* 11 (24 Nov. 1946).

282. CQ 418 (27 Nov. 1946).

283. *Sao Vàng* 26 (28 Nov. 1946).

284. *Chính Nghĩa tuần Báo*(Hanoi) 27 (9 Dec. 1946).

285. *Nhiệm Vụ tuần báo* (Hanoi) 7 (1 Dec. 1946).

286. *Dư Luận* 32 (1 Dec. 1946); 33 (8 Dec. 1946). X&N 82 (Dec. 2000): 17.

287. *Kháng chiến* 8 (11 Dec. 1946). This undated Tổng Bộ statements appears to have been blocked from publication in northern papers.

288. Tønnesson, *Vietnam 1946*, 161–63. Devillers, *Histoire*, 339, 344, 347.

289. Turpin, 292–305.

290. Tønnesson, *Vietnam 1946*, 191.

291. Tønnesson, *Vietnam 1946*, 194. CQ 440 (18 Dec. 1946) published Hồ's 15 December letter to Blum, adding that the president had just sent Blum a follow-up telegram.

292. Mark A. Lawrence, *Assuming the Burden: Europe and the American Commitment to the War in Vietnam* (Berkeley: University of California Press, 2005), 165.

293. Tønnesson, *Vietnam 1946*, 140–42.

294. *Dân Thành* 385 (18 Dec. 1946).

295. CQ 425 (4 Dec. 1946); 433 (12 Dec. 1946); 434 (13 Dec. 1946); 435 (15 Dec. 1946); 439 (18 Dec. 1946); and 440 (19 Dec. 1946).

296. Tønnesson, *Vietnam 1946*, 223.

297. Tønnesson, *Vietnam 1946*, 235.

298. CQ 440 (19 Dec. 1946). *Dân Quốc* 416 (19 Dec. 1946).

299. Vũ Kỳ, *Tạp chí Lịch sử Quân sự* (Hanoi) 36 (Dec. 1988), 81. Vũ Kỳ, as Hồ's personal secretary, had carried Hồ's letter to Giám, and brought back the bad news.

300. Võ Nguyên Giáp, *Chiến Đấu trong Vòng Vây* [Fighting while Encircled] (Hanoi: NXB QĐND and NXB Thanh Niên, 1995), 26. LSCKC1, 169. Tønnesson, *Vietnam 1946*, 212–15. Giáp does not mention the Blum Cabinet decision to send Moutet.

301. Trần Trọng Trung, *Tạp chí Lịch sử Quân sự* 36 (Dec. 1988): 67–68. Nguyễn Thành, X&N 34 (Dec. 1996): 5. Xuân Thủy was responsible for the call's title when he appended it to *Cứu Quốc* leaflets printed on 20 December. The text is reprinted in HCMTT 4, 202–03.

CHAPTER 5

1. Remarkably, the English-language service of Radio Saigon was used by an Australian national (POW?) for several days in mid-September to transmit news bulletins, personal messages from POWs, and repeated requests to hear back from ABC and BBC counterparts. July 1945 to March 1946, NARA, FBIS transcripts of monitored broadcasts, RG 262, carton Saigon.

2. David G. Marr, *Vietnam 1945: The Quest for Power* (Berkeley: University of California Press, 1995), 476, 489–90, 499–501.

3. Harold R. Isaacs, *No Peace for Asia* (Cambridge: MIT Press, 1967), 170. First published 1947. Isaacs met Hồ Chí Minh in Hanoi, quickly recognizing him as a friend from Shanghai two decades earlier.

4. *Kháng Chiến* 5 (15 Oct. 1946) and continuing.

5. Minh Tranh, *Sao Vàng*, June–July 1946 serialization.

6. *Dư Luận* 16 (4 Aug. 1946) and continuing.

7. *Thời mới* 3 (7 Oct. 1945). *Sao Vàng* 32 (10 July 1946). *Chiến Sĩ* 27 (5 June 1946) and continuing.

8. *Gió Biển* 2 (11 May 1946); 6 (15 June 1946).

9. Tử Luyện, *Thời mới* 3 (7 Oct. 1945).

10. *Thời mới* 6 (28 Oct. 1945).

11. *Chiến Sĩ* 10–12 (số Mùa Xuân). *Quyết Thắng* 16 (số đặc biệt Xuân Bính Tuất).

12. *Đa Minh* (Bùi Chu) 155 (số đặc biệt Xuân Bính Tuất).

13. *Quyết Thắng* 11 (9 Dec. 1945).

14. CQ 122 (20 Dec. 1945); 127 (27 Dec. 1945); and 129 (29 Dec. 1945). *Quyết Thắng* 23 (23 Dec. 1945).

15. *Việt Nam* gave extensive front-page coverage to U.S.-U.S.S.R. relations, Trieste, Egypt, Persia, India, Indonesia, and the UN. Page 2 had long columns devoted to international news briefs, many of them taken from Reuters news agency.

16. *Chính Nghĩa tuần báo* (Hanoi) 9 (29 July 1946).

17. *Tương Lai* 13 (10 Jan. 1946).

18. *Trung Việt Tân Văn* (Hanoi) 11 (28 Feb. 1946).

19. DC 121 (14 Jan. 1946).

20. Ngô Điền, *Chiến Sĩ* 33 (17 July 1946).

21. "Công lý hay Võ lực?" [Justice or Force of Arms?], DC 189 (11 April 1946).

22. Hoàng Xuân Hãn serialization, April 1946; and *Dư Luận* 27 (20 Oct. 1946).

23. CQ 188 (16 March 1946). ĐL 252 (26 Sept. 1946). I have not been able to verify this Stalin quotation.

24. *Viễn đông hôm qua và hôm nay* (Hanoi: Tổng Bộ Việt Minh, August 1946). Minh Tranh was the pseudonym of Khuất Duy Tiến, who worked in the Tổng Bộ training section. X&N 110 (Feb. 2002): 15–16.

25. Minh Tranh chose to ignore dramatically different results in late-nineteenth century Japan.

26. Minh Tranh, 92.

27. Peter Worthing, *Occupation and Revolution: China and the Vietnamese August Revolution of 1945* (Berkeley: University of California Press, 2001), 54–56. Marr, *Vietnam 1945*, 476, 496–97.

28. Marr, *Vietnam 1945*, 418–21.

29. Archimedes L.A. Patti, *Why Viet Nam? Prelude to America's Albatross* (Berkeley: University of California Press, 1980), 281–82, 204–5.

30. Phạm Văn Liễu, *Trả ta Sông Núi* [Return our Rivers and Mountains] (Houston: Văn Hóa, 2002), 93–94.

31. Story recounted to me by Nguyễn Đức Hiệp, teacher at the U.S. Army Language School, Monterey, California, Oct. 1961.

32. For an educated discussion of Chinese troop numbers, see Worthing, 57–58. Other studies assert up to two hundred thousand Chinese soldiers present, without substantiation.

33. Patti, 291–93, 345, 353–54. Worthing, 74–75, 91–92. To further complicate the currency picture, most Chinese troops also carried Central China yuan (CN), which were officially pegged at 20 to 1 CGU.

34. *Dân Quốc* 23 (2 Oct. 1945). DC 34 (3 Oct. 1945).

35. *Thời mới* 3 (7 Oct. 1945).

36. Worthing, 84–87, 89, 123, 124, 126. Lin Hua, *Chiang Kai-shek, de Gaulle contre Ho Chi Minh: Vietnam 1945–1946* (Paris: l'Harmattan, 1994), 122–24.

37. *Quyết Thắng* 5 (29 Oct. 1945).

38. DC 108 (29 Dec. 1945).

39. DC 117 (9 Jan. 1946).

40. 1 Oct. 1945, UBND Thái Nguyên report, Thái Nguyên 1945 folder, GF 71.

41. 27 Sept. 1945, 1 Oct. 1945, and 22 Oct. 1945, correspondence between Sơn La and BB, Sơn La folder, GF 16. 23 Oct. 1945, UBND Sơn La report, Sơn La folder, GF 71. The province committee may have inflated the commandeered figures, as they hoped for recompense from the central authorities.

42. 20 Sept. 1945 and 29 Oct. 1945, reports, second folio, GF 45. As Đèo Văn Trì had died in 1908, these reporters probably meant his son, Đèo Văn Long. See Philippe Le Failler, "The Đèo family of Lai Châu: Traditional Power and Unconventional Practices," *Journal of Vietnamese Studies* 6, no. 2 (Summer 2011): 42–67.

43. DC 23 (19 Sept. 1945). The commander also offered twelve hundred piastres to the three aggrieved families, a sum which was initially refused, then accepted.

44. Undated, Cảnh sát Bắc Ninh report for 18 Sept. 1945 "violent incident," third Phòng Kinh tế folder, GF 47.

45. 1 Nov. 1945, UBND Sơn Tây (Ngô Quyền) to BB, Sơn Tây folder, GF 71.

46. 11 Dec. 1945, Ủy viên Ngoại giao BB to Nội Vụ, Việc xảy ra tại tỉnh lỵ folder, GF 28.

47. 16 Nov. 1945, UBND Phúc Yên to BB, Báo cáo hàng tháng (Phúc Yên) folder, GF 68.

48. DC 8 (1 Sept. 1945); 9 (3 Sept. 1945); 18 (13 Sept. 1945); 24 (20 Sept. 1945); 26 (22 Sept. 1945).

49. 26 Sept. 1945, Ủy ban liên lạc Hoa Việt Hà Nội report, GF 71.

50. Duong Van Mai Elliott, *The Sacred Willow: Four Generations in the Life of a Vietnamese Family* (New York: Oxford University Press, 1999), 131–32. The author's father managed to alleviate depredations by communicating with the unit's commander in Chinese writing.

51. The sixteen-point list of Chinese troop prohibitions was translated and printed in DC 18 (13 Sept. 1945). Stealing, gambling, fornication, and opium smoking were also banned. Execution by fire squad was prescribed for rape, armed robbery, passing counterfeit notes, revealing secrets, killing civilians, fomenting disorder, and hiding weapons.

52. DC 22 (18 Sept. 1945).

53. CQ 30 (27 Aug. 1945). DC 6 (30 Aug. 1945); 11 (5 Sept. 1945). ĐL 4 (14 Sept. 1945).

54. ĐL 3 (11 Sept. 1945); 4 (14 Sept. 1945); 11 (9 Oct. 1945). DC 5 (29 Aug. 1945); 11 (5 Sept. 1945); 17 (12 Sept. 1945).

55. 10 Oct. 1945, report, Bộ Ngoại Giao folder, GF 68.

56. DC 30 (28 Sept. 1945); 31 (29 Sept. 1945).

57. Three Hỏa Xa Việt Điền monthly reports, 15 Sept.–15 Dec. 1945, Báo cáo hàng tháng 1945 folder, GF 38.

58. 5 Nov. 1945, transcript of meeting of representatives from Foreign Affairs, Interior and Transport, GF 36.

59. Giám đốc Viện Thú Y BB to BB, Sở Thú Y 1945 folder, GF 38. The director was especially upset at the loss of two breeding thoroughbreds, Aziza and Ballerine.

60. 21 Sept. 1945, Kinh tế BB to UBNDBB, GF 37.

61. 16 Nov. 1945, Giám đốc Nha Kinh tế BB to UBNDBB, GF 36.

62. 16 Oct. 1945, Société Cotonnière du Tonkin to Service Economique BB, Công Văn Đệ Ký folder, GF 31.

63. Information compiled from Northern Economic Bureau dossiers in GF 34, 37, and 42.

64. 30 Nov. 1945, Ty Vật Liệu to Công Chính BB, GF 52.

65. Giấy thông hành xe hơi của Cảnh bị Trung Hoa phát folder, GF 52.

66. Dec. 1945, S.T.A.I.-UBHCBB-Bộ Ngoại giao correspondence, Autos 1945–1946 folder, GF 64.

67. Marr, *Vietnam 1945*, 96–107, 393–94. Rice is discussed further in chapter 6.

68. 11 Jan. 1946, UB Tiếp tế Haiphong to Nha Kinh tế BB, Phòng Kinh tế BBP folio, GF 46. Jacques Mordal, *Marine Indochine* (Paris: Amiot Dumont, 1953), 118–19. Some later cargoes may have been transshipped to southern China, where there also was a food deficit.

69. DC 28 (26 Sept. 1945); 29 (27 Sept. 1945). 10 Oct. 1945, Ủy Viên tiếp tế Tô Hiệu (Haiphong) to Sở Kinh tế BB, and subsequent correspondence, Service Economique Local folder, GF 41. The piastres to complete these Haiphong transactions had to come from the DRV Finance Ministry in Hanoi.

70. 15 Feb. 1946, Chủ sự Phòng sản xuất report, Phòng Kinh tế BBP folio, GF 46. Worthing, 92–93.

71. DC 55 (27 Oct. 1945).

72. 22 Dec. 1945, UBNDBB to Quốc Phòng, Quân Sự (linh tinh) 1945 folder, GF 38.

73. Hồ Đức Thành, X&N 12 (Feb. 1995): 10.

74. 3 Jan. 1946, UBND Ninh Bình to Nội Vụ, thence to Ngoại giao, interministry message folio, GF 56. 3 Feb. 1946, BB authorization paper, Văn Phòng BB, GF 67.

75. Correspondence March–May 1946, in Việc Ro-Nha (Kiến An) folder, GF 67. CQ 189 (17 March 1946). In a remarkable coincidence, Ms. Oanh Collins, of our former Pacific and Asian History Division, Australian National University, is a distant relative of Diễm. She was able to ascertain that Diễm was released after his family paid the money. Diễm was not married at the time.

76. See, for example, 26 Jan. 1946, UBHCBB to UBHC Hải Dương, Văn Phòng BBP outgoing message file, GF 17.

77. Petitions and correspondence June–Nov. 1946, Kiến An (các việc lưu) folder, GF 11.

78. French intelligence followed Chinese opinion and behavior closely. See the fortnightly and monthly reports of the Sûreté Federales, in ANOM, INDO, CP 186.

79. DC 40 (10 Oct. 1945); 41 (11 Oct. 1945); and 42 (12 Oct. 1945). *Dân Quốc* 30 (10 Oct. 1945).

80. 4 Sept.–6 Oct. 1945 correspondence, in Bảo vệ quyền lợi của Hoa Kiều folder, Văn Phòng BBP, GF 68.

81. UBND Haiphong reports for September and November 1945, GF 53. 30 Nov. 1945, UBNDBB to Thuế Quan, Tuyên Quang folder, GF 16. Correspondence Dec. 1945–Jan. 1946, Salt folder, GF 31.

82. 7 Oct. 1945, Nha Kinh tế BB to UBNDBB, Contrôle 1945 folio, GF 65.

83. Ty Kiểm Duyệt Haiphong report for Nov. 1945, Báo cáo hàng tháng (Hải Phòng) folder, GF 53.

84. 1 Dec. 1945, translation of General Lu Han complaint, Hanoi (việc lưu) 1945 folder, GF 69.

85. "Lòng Trung Người Việt," *Chiến Sĩ* 20 (10 April 1946). *Quyết Thắng* 33 (17 April 1946). The mother was Vietnamese.

86. DC 248 (22 June 1946).

87. Mã Kiến Tăng, *Gió Biển* 4 (1 June 1946).

88. 29 March 1946, chủ tịch UBND Hải Ninh to BB, Tiên Yên folder, GF 54.

89. 12 April 1946, UBHC Hanoi to UBHCBB, Grain output folder, GF 19.

90. 11 June 1946, Thuế Quan Hà Nội to BB; 19 June 1946, UBHCBB to Thuế Quan, Văn Phòng BB folio 1, GF 66.

91. Thus Hải Dương was left with 724,695.97 "tiền tàu," mostly proceeds from selling rice to Chinese Army units. 29 March 1946, Hải Dương to Thanh Tra BB, Hải Dương (hiện hành), GF 59.

92. 3 Dec. 1946, Phòng Kinh tế BB to UBHC Hanoi, Phòng Kinh tế BB outgoing message folder, GF 41.

93. 10 Oct. 1946, Sûreté Federales report for month of September 46, second folio, CP 186. Stein Tønnesson, *Vietnam 1946: How the War Began* (Berkeley: University of California Press, 2010), 118–19.

94. DC 374 (20 Nov. 1946). The lead editorial castigates French pressures on "our Chinese friends carrying on business here."

95. 6 Nov. 1946, chủ nhiệm Ty Hoa-Việt Bộ Nội Vụ to UBHCBB, Văn Phòng Mật outgoing message file, GF 31.

96. Simultaneously, some Nùng were applying to the Chinese Consul General to be Chinese citizens.

97. 13 Dec. 1946, Ty Thông tin Tuyên truyền Lạng Sơn to Giám đốc Thông tin Tuyên truyền BB, Lạng Sơn (việc lưu) folder, GF 11.

98. Marr, *Vietnam 1945*, 164–72, 174.

99. See, for example, Bùi Tiến Cảnh, trans., *Tôn Văn: Học thuyết và đời cách mạng của Tôn Dật Tiên* [The Teaching and Revolutionary Life of Sun Yat-sen] (Hanoi: Tự Cường, 1946). Several booklets containing Chiang Kaishek's teachings also appeared in 1946.

100. Nguyễn Văn Luyện, CQ 166 (18 Feb. 1946).

101. Jean Escarra, *Chính thể Trung Hoa* [China's Form of Government], serialized in *Tương Lai* (Hanoi), Nov. 1945–Jan. 1946. Escarra's original is *La Chine, passé et présent* (Paris, 1937).

102. *Dư Luận*, serialized starting in 24 (29 Sept. 1946).

103. *Gió Mới*, March–April 1946 issues; 29 (19 July 1946). *Dư Luận* 20 (1 Sept. 1946).

104. *Tiên Phong* 4/5 (Tết 1946): 76–80; and 18 (2 Sept. 1946): 15–17. We encountered Học Phi in chapter 1, being removed as Hưng Yên province chairman.

105. *Le Peuple* (Hanoi), serialized in July 1946.

106. Mao Trạch Đông, *Kinh tế và tài chính Diên An* [Yan'an's Economy and Finances] (Hanoi: Tháng Tám, 1946). The ICP only began translating Mao seriously in 1948.

107. *Một tháng ở Diên An* (Hanoi: Tháng Tám, 1946). See also *Tiên Phong* 14 (1 July 1946): 25, 31.

LIVERPOOL JOHN MOORES UNIVERSITY
LEARNING SERVICES

108. *Đi Diên-An về* (Huế) (Sept. 1946).

109. *Đảng Cộng sản Tầu và chiến tranh cách mạng* (Hanoi: ST, 1946).

110. ĐL 206 (25 July 1946) and continuing.

111. *Chiến Sĩ*, serial beginning 24 (15 May 1946).

112. Mai Thủy, in *Thời mới* 2 (30 Sept. 1945); and 6 (28 Oct. 1945).

113. *Gió Biển* (Haiphong) 4 (1 June 1946). *Dư Luận* 9 (16 June 1946); 15 (28 July 1946).

114. *Dân Mới* (Vinh) 3 (1 June 1946). ĐL 195 (12 July 1946). CQ 290 (12 July 1946).

115. CQ 328 (25 Aug. 1946).

116. ĐL 301 (26 Aug. 1946).

117. Minh Tranh, *Viễn đông*, 68–69.

118. The best effort is found in *Dư Luận* 17 (11 Aug. 1946); 18 (25 Aug. 1946).

119. ĐL 253 (27 Sept. 1946). *Độc Lập chủ nhật* 5 (14 Oct. 1946). CQ 372 (11 Oct. 1946). *Dân Quốc* 48 (31 Oct. 1946). *Đa Minh* 6 (24 Nov. 1946).

120. Quotations in Mark P. Bradley, *Imagining Vietnam and America: the Making of Postcolonial Vietnam, 1919–1950* (Chapel Hill: University of North Carolina Press, 2000), 20–22.

121. *Đường Kách Mệnh* [The Road to Revolution], reprinted in HCMTT 2, 190–92.

122. Bradley, 28–29, 117.

123. Dixee R. Bartholomew-Feis, *The OSS and Ho Chi Minh: Unexpected Allies in the War against Japan* (Lawrence: University Press of Kansas, 2006), 144–46, 149, 171, 189.

124. Bartholomew-Feis, 193–94, 202, 208–17. Marr, *Vietnam 1945*, 364–65.

125. Actually Patti held the rank of captain, but at some point began wearing the gold oak leaves of a major. Such "Mexican commissions" to enhance one's status occurred frequently among OSS personnel.

126. Bui Diem and David Chanoff, *In the Jaws of History* (Boston: Houghton Mifflin, 1987), 38. Diễm was nephew to Premier Trần Trọng Kim (May–August 1945), and much later served as Saigon's ambassador to Washington.

127. Bartholomew-Feis, 230–45, 253, 263–64. Bradley, 126, 128–29, 134–36. Marr, *Vietnam 1945*, 485–86, 489–90, 499–500.

128. Patti, 341–46, 353.

129. My April 2004 correspondence with Edward C. Cazier, Jr., U.S. Navy officer aboard the USS Conway (DD507) in the Bay of Tonkin, Oct.–Dec. 1945. U.S. Navy officers also scouted the anthracite coal mines at Hòn Gai, where the local people's committee hosted them to dinner so they would not eat with the French mine employees. 1 Nov. 1945, UBND Hongay to BB, GF 71.

130. Ronald H. Spector, *Advice and Support: The Early Years 1941–1960* (Washington: U.S. Army Center of Military History, 1983), 59–63, 68–71. Worthing, 99–100. See my further discussion in chapter 6.

131. *Dân Quốc* 24 (3 Oct. 1945). Major General McLure was accompanying General He Yingqin, commander in chief of the Chinese Army (see above).

132. Hội Việt-Mỹ Thân Hữu, *Điều Lệ* [By-laws] (Hanoi, Oct. 1945). A partial translation, by Trương Ngọc Bính, is reprinted in Gareth Porter, ed., *Vietnam: The Definitive Documentation of Human Decisions*, vol. 1 (Stanfordville: Coleman Enterprises, 1979),

82–83. A 9 Oct. 1945 American report from Hanoi insisted on calling the organization the *Annamite*-American Friendship Association. Bradley, 238n63.

133. Perhaps picking up on Gallagher's remark, Hồ Chí Minh two weeks later wrote to Secretary of State Byrnes requesting that fifty youths be allowed to come to the United States to study engineering, agriculture, and other specialties. DOS, *United States–Vietnam Relations, 1945–1967,* vol. 1 (Washington: U.S. Government Printing Office, 1971), 90.

134. *Dân Quốc* 28 (8 Oct. 1945).

135. Lê Xuân had been principal ICP–Việt Minh liaison to Patti in late August. He departed with Gallagher in December, and appears to have served both the ICP and American intelligence organizations subsequently.

136. Bartholomew-Feis, 308–09. Bradley, 130–31. Bui Diem, 39.

137. Of the fifteen "Blondie" films released by 1945, the closest title I can locate is "Blondie Goes to College" (1942).

138. Bradley, 131–32.

139. *Tương Lai* 9 (22 Nov. 1945).

140. Bradley, 132. In September 1946, René Defourneaux, member of the July–August 1945 OSS "Deer Team," proposed either to import Vietnamese timber to the United States or start a bus line in Vietnam. Defourneaux's letter to "Ông Hồ" is translated in X&N 15 (May 1995): 6–7.

141. Spector, 58–59.

142. 5 Sept. 1945, BB to Giám đốc Đồn Thủy, Văn Phòng folder, GF 45.

143. 1 Oct. 1945, UBND Hải Phòng report, Báo cáo hàng tháng (Hải Phòng) dossier, GF 53.

144. Patti, 301, 327, 357–58. Chinese guards soon replaced Japanese guards at the Citadel, at which point Chinese officers presumably took over from the Americans control of POW passes.

145. Bartholomew-Feis, 250, 261. Spector, 60. Patti, 239.

146. Patti, 35. Bartholomew-Feis, 250. Hội Khoa Học Lịch Sử Việt Nam, *Ký Ức,* 39.

147. Extracts from translation of Nguyễn Văn Đức notebook, 10 Jan. 1947, BR, Commandant Militaire au Cambodge, SHD 10H 5585. Đức had served as DRV aide to Bảo Đại September–November 1945.

148. 8 Sept. 1945, UBND Hải Phòng to BB; 10 Sept. 1945 reply, Điện Văn folder, Văn Phòng BB, GF 67. The telegraphs do not indicate whether the missing person was believed alive or dead, nor does the file reveal any outcome.

149. 20 Oct. 1945, UBND Đội Cấn (Thái Nguyên) to BB, message attached to Oct. 1945 province report, GF 71. 22 Oct. 1945, UBND Đội Cấn to UBNDBB, folder 37, Văn Phòng BB, GF 15.

150. *Dân Quốc* 96 (28 Dec. 1945).

151. 2 Sept. 1945, (Saigon) Executive Committee of the South, NARA, DOS Special File RG59, box 10, dossier 7, lot file 54-D-190. The committee attached a six-page "report" to the letter of welcome, designed to "show the Fascist attitude of French Colonization in Indochina," to attest Franco-Japanese collaboration, and to prove the Việt Minh's anti-Japanese efforts. Dewey dispatched these documents to Washington on 14 Sept. 1945.

152. Dewey's reports of 7 and 8 Sept. 1945, as described in Patti, 276–77, 298.

153. Dewey apparently also encouraged Bạch to communicate directly with Patti, identified as "Allied Mission Hanoi." Patti, 312.

154. Trần Văn Giàu, "Hồi Ký 1940–1945," Thời Đại Mới 21 (May 2011): 324.

155. Patti, 314, lists the following Vietnamese at this meeting: Trần Văn Giàu, Phạm Văn Bạch, Dương Bạch Mai, Phạm Ngọc Thạch, and Nguyễn Văn Tạo.

156. Patti, 316–18, 326. Bartholomew-Feis, 287–88. George Wickes, "Saigon 1945," unpublished memoir kindly sent to me August 2012. Dewey had given Wickes a "Mexican commission" to second lieutenant, from his actual rank of private first class.

157. Patti, 320.

158. Dewey's father, Charles Dewey, had been a U.S. congressman from Illinois.

159. 29 Sept. 1945 memorandum by General Gallagher on meeting with Hồ Chí Minh the previous evening, reprinted in Porter, vol. 1, 80–81.

160. Bartholomew-Feis, 297–98.

161. X&N 49 (March 1998): 19–20. See also X&N 30 (Aug. 1996): 25–26.

162. 10 May 46, monthly report by Edeleanu to Director SSU, NARA, Records of the OSS Washington Registry SI Field Files, Box 180, RG 226.

163. 17 June 1946, American Consulate General Saigon French Indochina to DOS, "Trends in Indochina," NARA, Records of the OSS, SI Intelligence, box 3, RG 226.

164. George Sheldon, "Status of the Viet Nam," Far Eastern Survey 15, no. 25 (18 Dec. 1946): 373–77.

165. 5 Feb. 1947, Pignon to conseiller Dip du Gov't Féderale, Le Gouvernement Viet Nam dossier, Viet Minh (Archives Politiques), ANOM, INDO, CP 128.

166. 20 Oct. 1945, President Ho Chi Minh to the President, Washington, NARA, DOS Special File, Lot file 54-D-190, box 10, RG 49.

167. Mark Atwood Lawrence, Assuming the Burden: Europe and the American Commitment to War in Vietnam (Berkeley: University of California Press, 2005), 306n68.

168. White's recollections of his meeting with Hồ, written down 22 Jan. 1968 in Saigon, where he was a correspondent for Time-Life. Printed in Causes, Origins, and Lessons of the Vietnam War, hearings before the Committee on Foreign Relations, U.S. Senate, 9–11 May 1972 (Washington: U.S. Government Printing Office, 1973), 155.

169. When White read out this last sentence to a packed Senate committee room in 1972, the stenographer recorded "[Laughter]." Causes, Origins, and Lessons, 150, 155–57.

170. Wickes, "Saigon 1945," 15–17. Georges Wickes, "Hà Nội 1946," X&N 44 (Oct. 1997): 13–14.

171. White, Causes, Origins, and Lessons, 157–58. White apparently departed Hanoi as Hồ was preparing to go to France at the end of May.

172. Patti, 231–33.

173. 17 Oct. 1945, Hồ Chí Minh to Truman, United States–Vietnam Relations, vol. 1, 73–74. Porter, vol. 1, 83–84.

174. 20 Oct. 1945, radio telegram Hồ Chí Minh to Truman, NARA, DOS Special File RG 59, Lot file 54-D-190, box 10.

175. 22 Oct. 1945, Hồ Chí Minh to Byrnes, United States–Vietnam Relations, vol. 1, 80–81. Porter, vol. 1, 84–85.

176. Moffat testimony to Senate Committee on Foreign Relations, 11 May 1972, in *Causes, Origins and Lessons*, 187–88.

177. Lawrence, 74–85, 86–89, 94. Marr, *Vietnam 1945*, 491–93.

178. Lawrence, 100–101. Titled "Between War and Peace," Vincent's October 1945 address dealt with Indonesia as well as Indochina.

179. CQ 73 (22 Oct. 1945).

180. Probably Hồ did not yet know that the ships used to transport the 9th Colonial Infantry Division to Saigon in October were leased from the United States.

181. George McT. Kahin, *Intervention: How America became Involved in Vietnam* (New York: Alfred A. Knopf, 1986), 6–9. As Kahin points out, the United States also knew that some of its financial credits to help rebuild France's war-shattered economy were being used to maintain France's expeditionary force in Indochina.

182. Patti, 83–88.

183. Lawrence, 99–100. Herring, 114.

184. 16 Feb. 1946, Hồ Chí Minh to Truman, *United States–Vietnam Relations*, vol. 1, 95–97. Porter, 95.

185. Lawrence, 120, 131. Bradley, 143.

186. 10 April 1946, Reed to O'Sullivan; 7 Aug. 1946, O'Sullivan to Reed, NARA, RG84, folder 020–127, box 2 (1941–46), Records of the Foreign Service posts of the DOS, Hanoi Consulate. The Chinese would only accept payment in paper "gold units," not piastres, which sent O'Sullivan to the black market.

187. Correspondence in NARA, RG 84, folders 130–800.2 and 8010811.1, box 2.

188. August 1946 report, Tonkin Section, Directeur la Police et de la Sûreté Federales en Indochine, ANOM, INDO, CP 186.

189. NARA, RG 84, folder 020–127, box 2.

190. Correspondence in NARA, RG 84, folder 020–127, box 2; and folder 130–800.2, box 2.

191. 23 Aug. 1946, Bộ Ngoại giao to M. le Consul, NARA, RG 84, folder 801–811.1, box 2.

192. NARA, RG 84, folder 020–127, box 2. The file contains no indication of what happened next. The American unit possessed information that seven or eight bodies of U.S. personnel were located near a particular village on the northern rim of the Mõi Plateaux (Tây Nguyên).

193. NARA, RG 84, folder 020–127, box 2.

194. In Paris in September, for example, Hồ Chí Minh met the U.S. ambassador to France, contrasting French obduracy in Indochina with U.S. granting of independence to the Philippines and British intentions to do likewise in India. *United States–Vietnam Relations*, vol. 1, C41–42, 102–104.

195. DC 183 (4 April 1946).

196. *Quyết Thắng* 44 (29 May 1946).

197. June 1946, Huấn luyện chính trị, Tiểu đoàn 1 Hà Nội (BBP); 13 July 1946, Chính trị viên Tiểu đoàn 1 to companies, GF 64.

198. *Chính Nghĩa tuần báo* (Hanoi) 11 (12 Aug. 1946).

199. CQ 370 (9 Oct. 1946). *Độc Lập chủ nhật* 11 (24 Nov. 1946).

200. 10 Oct. 1946, BB to Chủ tịch UB Viện Thương Mại, Phòng Kinh tế outgoing msgs, GF 77.

201. *Causes, Origins and Lessons of the Vietnam War*, 202.

202. 12 (?) Dec. 1946, Moffat to DOS, *The United States and Vietnam 1944–1947*, appendix II, 42. Porter, vol. 1, 130.

203. Stein Tønneson, *Vietnam 1946: How the War Began* (Berkeley: University of California Press, 2010), 184. Moffat denied having made such a suggestion. The French also protested a 9 December Vietnamese article about Moffat's visit, which led O'Sullivan to complain to the director of the Vietnam Information Service about details in the article. NARA, RG 84, folder 020–127, box 2.

204. 12 (?) Dec. 1946, Moffat to DOS, *The United States and Vietnam: 1944–1947*, appendix II, 41–42. Porter, vol. 1, 129.

205. *Causes, Origins and Lessons of the Vietnam War*, 200–1.

206. 5 Dec. 1946, Acheson to Moffat (Saigon), *United States-Vietnam Relations,* vol. 8, 85–86. Porter, vol. 1, 128–29.

207. Tønneson, *Vietnam 1946*, 184–85.

208. During the Pacific War, and particularly following the 9 March 1945 Japanese coup, Vietnamese had also read occasional Domei News reports about Tokyo-sponsored independence actions elsewhere in Asia.

209. CQ 69 (17 Oct. 1945). *Thời mới* 5 (21 Oct. 1945).

210. *Dân Quốc* 50 (2 Nov. 1945). DC 75 (20 Nov. 1945).

211. Goscha, "Le contexte asiatique de la guerre franco-vietnamienne," (Doctoral thesis, École pratique des hautes études, Nov. 2000), 484–86. *Indonesia* (Ithaca, NY) 49 (April 1990): 141–44. Hồ's letter had been carried to Indonesian leaders by the American journalist Harold Isaacs.

212. *Quyết Thắng* 17 (15 Feb. 1946). See further discussion of the UN below.

213. ĐL 178 (18 April 1946); 186 (1 July 1946). CQ 301 (25 July 1946). DC 254 (1 July 1946); 255 (2 July 1946).

214. *Độc Lập chủ nhật*, 6 (20 Oct. 1946) and subsequent issues. The Dutch resumed military action in July 1947, but under U.S. pressure returned to the negotiating table in 1949 and relinquished sovereignty in 1950.

215. *Cấp tiến* 8 (23 Nov. 1946).

216. *Thời mới* 1 (16 Sept. 1945) and subsequent issues.

217. Leaflet in English found by French, 25 Nov. 1945, Tracts V.M. file, Viet Minh (Archives Politiques), ANOM, INDO, CP 128. CQ 79 (29 Oct. 1945) complimented Nehru for protesting British use of Indian troops in Indochina and Indonesia.

218. CQ 158 (8 Feb. 1946); 198 (24 March 1946); 198 (26 March 1946); and 203 (1 April 1946).

219. Minh Tranh, *Ấn Độ Cách Mạng* [India in Revolution] (Hanoi: Tông Bộ Việt Minh, Oct. 1946).

220. See, for example, CQ 341(10 Sept. 1946); and DC 313 (10 Sept. 1946). A copy of Nehru's letter of invitation to Hồ Chí Minh was intercepted by the British, turned over to the French, and filed away. However, another copy was presented to Hồ in Ceylon, enroute home from France. Goscha, "Le contexte asiatique," 488.

221. Vân Đình (Võ Nguyên Giáp), *Con Đường Chính: Vấn đề dân tộc giải phóng ở Đông Dương* [The Main and Proper Path: The Question of National Liberation in Indochina] (Hanoi: Dân Chúng, 1939), 8–10.

222. *Thời mới* 11 (2 Dec. 1945).

223. *Đa Minh* (Bùi Chu) 167 (21 Jan. 1946).

224. *Quyết Thắng* (Huế) 55 (13 July 1946).

225. Minh Tranh, *Viễn Đông,* 53, 72.

226. Goscha, "Le contexte asiatique," 490–91.

227. *Thời mới* 2 (30 Sept. 1945).

228. Lawrence, 116–17, 143–44.

229. *Kháng Chiến* 1 (2 Sept. 1946); 2 (9 Sept. 1946); and 3 (23 Sept. 1946). Nguyễn Sơn took a direct interest in this newspaper, and may have written the articles.

230. Goscha, "Le contexte asiatique," 101–8, 468–81. After Pridi lost power in Nov. 1947, DRV delegation activities had to be scaled down, and Rangoon took on more importance.

231. Editorial, *Thời mới* 1 (16 Sept. 1945). Nguyễn Khắc Kham wrote on the Russian Revolution in *Thời mới* 1 (16 Sept. 1945) and 6 (28 Oct. 1945).

232. Đỗ Văn Hương, *Tương Lai* 8 (16 Nov. 1945) and continuing.

233. Isaacs, 172–73. From the context it seems Isaacs had these conversations in or near Saigon in early October 1945, during the short truce which collapsed on 10 October.

234. *Quyết Thắng* (Huế) 1 (1 Oct. 1945). The editors urged friendship with the United States and China, while condemning British assistance to the French.

235. Trịnh Văn Hiến, *Có thể mất Nam Bộ được không?* [Can We Lose the Southern Region?] (Hanoi: NXB Tân Quốc Dân, 9 Jan. 1946), 12.

236. I. B. Bukharkin, *X&N* 55 (Sept. 1998): 4–5.

237. Patti, 178–81.

238. Christopher Goscha, *Historical Dictionary of the Indochina War (1945–1954).* (Copenhagen: NIAS Press, 2011).

239. *Quyết Thắng* (Huế) 41 (18 May 46), informs readers that it has received copies of these books. In chapter 8, I canvass the pro-Soviet output further.

240. *Phụ nữ Nga với cuộc cách mệnh Xã Hội* (Hanoi, 1946).

241. *Gió Biển* (Haiphong) 3 (25 May 1946).

242. DC 151 (25 Feb. 1946). *Quyết Thắng* 28 (30 March 1946).

243. *L'Entente* 106 (11 Feb. 1946).

244. DC 198 (22 April 1946); 247 (21 June 1946) and continuing.

245. *Dân Mới* 3 (1 June 1946).

246. "Đây, bọn <Phát xít Đỏ>! Chế độ độc tài trong các tổ chức cổng sản" [Here, the 'Red Fascist' gang! The Dictatorial System within Communist Organizations], *Chính Nghĩa tuần báo* (Hanoi) 6 (24 June 1946) and continuing.

247. *Chính Nghĩa tuần báo* 8 (8 July 1946); and 13 (26 Aug. 1946).

248. *Nhiệm Vụ tuần báo* (Hanoi) 3 (3 Nov. 1946). Nationalist Party and Catholic writings on communism are discussed further in chapter 7.

249. *Sao Vàng* 15 (12 Sept. 1946).

250. CQ 299 (23 July 1946).

251. *Tiến Hóa* 1 (15 Nov. 1946).

252. "Mê Truyện," *Dân Mới* (Vinh) 3 (1 June 1946).

253. *Kháng Chiến* 8 (15 Nov. 1946).

254. DC 369 (14 Nov. 1946).

255. Patti, 102, 144, 244.

256. *Thời mới* 1 (16 Sept. 1945); and 2 (30 Sept. 1945).

257. Nguyễn Tố Uyên, *Công cuộc bảo vệ*, 66.

258. *Đồng Minh* 16 (10 Feb. 1946).

259. ĐL 161 (12 Feb. 1946).

260. DC 144 (18 Feb. 1946).

261. Undated but late Feb. 1946, VKĐTT 8, 410.

262. *Dư Luận* 1 (18 April 1946); and 21 (Sept. 1946).

263. 18 Aug. 1946, *New York Times,* as cited in Kenneth E. Colton, "The Failure of the Independent Political Movement in Vietnam, 1945–46," (PhD dissertation, American University, 1969), 676.

264. 24 Oct. 1946, Sûreté Hanoi to Sûreté Fed Saigon, enclosing a copy of the 22 Oct. 1946 draft, Le Gouvernment Viet Nam dossier, Viet Minh (Archives Politiques), ANOM, INDO, CP 128.

265. *Nhiệm Vụ tuần báo* (Hanoi) 4 (10 Nov. 1946); and 9 (15 Dec. 1946).

CHAPTER 6

1. Pierre Brocheux and Daniel Hémery, *Indochina: An Ambiguous Colonization, 1858–1954* (Berkeley: University of California Press, 2009), 116–80.

2. David G. Marr, *Vietnam 1945: the Quest for Power* (Berkeley: University of California Press, 1995), 229, 370–71.

3. Hồ Chí Minh probably chose Hà more for his links with the Catholic clergy and laity than for his professional background. See chapter 7.

4. Marr, *Vietnam 1945*, 31–32, 74. Some of these "infant industries" would survive in Việt Minh zones after 1946.

5. Marr, *Vietnam 1945*, 32–34, 96–107.

6. SL (5 Sept. 1945), in CB 1945, 6. Provisions of this decree were soon extended to central Vietnam. NĐ (2 Oct. 1945), in CB 1945, 23.

7. SL (22 Sept. 1945), in CB 1945, 19.

8. CB 1945, 21, 23–24, 38–39. Dossier 36, on elimination of *nghiệp đoàn*, in GF 64.

9. Tùng Hiệp interviews, in *Thời Mới* 1 (16 Sept. 1945).

10. Biên bản Hội nghị các chủ tịch ủy ban nhân dân các tỉnh ngày 1 và 2 tháng 10 năm 1945, GF 68. The salt imbroglio is discussed further below.

11. 22 Oct. 1945, UBNDBB to Bộ trưởng Bộ Kinh tế Quốc dân, GF 65.

12. 18 Oct. 1945, Giám đốc Thuế quan và Thuế gián thu to BB, dossier 99, GF 38.

13. Undated, Đại Nam Thương Cục to Nha Kinh tế BB (received 6 Nov. 1945), GF 25.

14. UBND Nam Định report to BB for Sept. 1945, Nam Định dossier, GF 45.

15. SL (9 Oct. 1945), in CB 1945, 48; SL (10 Nov. 1945), in CB 1945, 72.

16. NĐ (9 Nov. 1945), in CB 1945, 83.

17. See for example Nguyễn Mạnh Tử's analysis of commercial practices in Europe and America, serialized in *Tương Lai* (Hanoi) starting with issue 7 (8 Nov. 1945).

18. 3 Dec. 1945, UBNDBB economic report, GF 12. Chứng minh thư dossier, GF 45. Coal operations are discussed below.

19. Undated [Oct. 1945], Tờ trình của Nha Kinh tế BB về nạn lụt vừa qua, Service économique local, dossier KT3, GF 34. Four provinces—Bắc Ninh, Vĩnh Yên, Sơn Tây, and Thái Bình—lost 70 percent or more of their autumn crop.

20. HCMTT 4, 5–7. In late September, President Hồ addressed his fasting proposal to the public, adding that he had already begun to fast himself. CQ 53 (28 Sept. 1945).

21. 3 Sept. 1945, Minister of National Economy to Minister of Health (Phạm Ngọc Thạch, in Saigon), followed by three weeks of urgent cables in both directions, GF 37. 15 Oct. 1945, monthly report, Chủ sự Phòng Kinh tế, GF 36. Riz de Cochinchine dossier, GF 58. Trains stopped just below Vinh because the Giang River bridge had been destroyed by U.S. aircraft.

22. 1 Dec. 1945, UBNDBB monthly report, GF 12. 15 Feb. 1946, Báo cáo về tình hình kinh tế tại Bắc Bộ, GF 46. Limited additional amounts of corn and rice were dispatched north from Quảng Ngãi in January–February 1946.

23. *Thời Mới* 5 (21 Oct. 1945).

24. *Chiến Sĩ* 1 (16 Nov. 1945).

25. 30 (?) Oct. 1945, Nhà Giam Trung Uờng to BB, Hình vụ dossier, GF 38.

26. 31 Oct. 1945 and 27 Nov. 1945, Cứu tế Y tế BB, Cứu tế và Y tế dossier, GF 11.

27. 26 Oct. 1945, UBNDBB to Cụ Hồ, Chủ tịch Chính phủ Lâm thời VN, GF 69.

28. NĐ (30 Oct. 1945), in CB 1945, 70. This edict was repeated in late January 1946. CB 1946, 90.

29. We have only one bit of evidence on mortality: *Văn Mới* (Hanoi) 4 (9 Nov. 1945) reports four hundred persons dying of starvation daily in three specific districts of the lower Red River delta, and a total of 3,325 persons having already died in a fourth district.

30. Nov. 1945–Feb. 1946 files, Phòng Kinh tế dossier, GF 46.

31. HCMTT 4, 64–65. From early December 1945, copies of a *Tấc đất* journal were sent gratis to province, district, and commune people's committees, with a total of fifty thousand copies distributed in four months. Đặng Phong, *Lịch sử Kinh tế Việt Nam* [History of Vietnam's Economy], vol. 1, *1945–1954*. (Hanoi: NXB KHXH, 2002), 132.

32. Bộ Quốc Dân Kinh Tế, Thông tư 26 Oct. 1945, in CB 1945, 76–78; and Thông Tư 16 Nov. 1945, in CB 1945, 100–2.

33. 3 Dec. 1945 report, cited in Đặng Phong, 120.

34. *Việt Nam* 8 (23 Nov. 1945); 9 (24 Nov. 1945); 11 (27 Nov. 1945); 12 (28 Nov. 1945); 21 (8 Dec. 1945); 27 (15 Dec. 1945).

35. *Tương Lai* (Hanoi) 6 (1 Nov. 1945); 7 (8 Nov. 1945); 8 (16 Nov. 1945); 9 (22 Nov. 1945).

36. *Dân Quốc* 69 (29 Nov. 1945).

37. Mai-Thủy, *Thời Mới* 12 (9 Dec. 1945).

38. *Thời Mới* 13 (16 Dec. 1945). Photo by Võ An Ninh, who had come to prominence seven months earlier with images of famine corpses in the streets of Hanoi.

39. Undated, UBND Thái Bình report, received at BB 11 Dec. 1945, Thái Bình dossier, GF 71.

40. The report's calculation was: 0.6 kg *thóc* per day per person=18 kg per month=108 kg for 6 months×one million people=108,000 tons. However, the population of Thái Bình was substantially less than one million at the time. Undated Thái Bình report, in BB rice projection dossier, GF 19.

41. 1 Dec. 1945, UBNDBB monthly economic report, GF 12. Interprovincial committees did not yet exist.

42. 28 May 1946, Chánh Phòng Kinh Tế BB to Chủ tịch Xã Đức Lai, in Phòng Kinh Tế outgoing message file, GF 13.

43. 1 Dec. 1945, UBNDBB monthly economic report, GF 12.

44. 16 Nov. 1945, semimonthly report of UBND Thái Nguyên to UBNDBB, Thái Nguyên 1945 dossier, GF 71.

45. 14 June 1946, UBHCBB complaint to Bộ Quốc Phòng, Văn Phòng dossier 301, GF 15.

46. 20 March 1946, UBHCBB to Bộ Tài Chính, GF 66. The Haiphong restriction came to Finance Ministry attention from 5 Feb. 1946, yet various bureaus denied knowledge for more than a month.

47. For example, Hải Dương's "Special Administrative Account," submitted to the UBHCBB on 29 March 1946, includes 140,000$BIC for rice sold and 1,097,076$BIC for rice purchased. Hải Dương *(hiện hành)* dossier, GF 59.

48. 16 Sept. 1946, UBHC Bắc Giang to UBHCBB, Phòng Kinh Tế outgoing message file, GF 77.

49. 12 April 1946, UBHC Hanoi to UBHCBB, GF 19. Hưng and two other committee members were the only ones authorized to issue Hanoi rice permits.

50. Vũ Hoàng, *Việt Nam* 121 (11 April 1946). CQ 216 (16 April 1946) complained that retail rice prices remained too high.

51. Giám đốc Nha Tiếp tế BB to 4 June 1946 meeting of Hội đồng Chính phủ, GF 19.

52. 25 June 1946, UBHC Hà Nam to BB, rice projection dossier, GF 19. One *mẫu* in northern Vietnam equals thirty-six hundred square meters.

53. 16 Aug. 1946, Bộ Xã hội to UBHCBB; 11 Sept. 1946, repeat proposal; and 2 Oct. 1946, UBHCBB to Bộ Xã hội, GF 12. The UBHCBB response came too late to organize such storehouses for the November 1946 crop.

54. Hoàng Văn Đức, "Comment la révolution a triomphé de la famine," serialized in *Le Peuple* (Hanoi) from 5 (21 April 1946). Republished as pamphlet by the DRV Information Office. See also Đặng Phong, 133–35. The speed with which Hoàng Văn Đức reported these figures, and the absence of any confidential calculations in the GF files, leads me to question their accuracy, but not the essential role of supplementary crops in staving off widespread starvation.

55. If 614,000 tons of yams, corn, and beans equal 506,000 tons of paddy equivalent (as stated by Hoàng Văn Đức), then I calculate: one person needs a minimum of 18 kg paddy/month×5 months=90 kg; 506,000 tons ÷ .09 tons per person=5.62 million people.

56. 30 Aug. 1946, UBHCBB to UBHC các tỉnh and responses, GF 77.

57. The Northern Committee appears never to have requested provinces to supply famine mortality figures for September–December 1945. DRV/SRV official histories do not discuss famine mortality in late 1945 or early 1946, preferring to declare total victory.

58. ĐL 212 (1 Aug. 1946).

59. Assuming twenty-five working days a month, this results in rice incomes of 18.75 kg per month for adults, 15 kg for those fifteen to eighteen years of age, and 11.25 kg for twelve- to fifteen-year-old child laborers. When drafting a decree, wages were expressed in piastres. Minutes of 15 Aug. 1946, BBP meeting, 1946 Hanoi (việc lưu) dossier, GF 69.

60. Đường Sát (Hanoi) 1 (19 Aug. 1946). The article makes no mention of any agreement.

61. 26 Aug. 1946, UBHCBB to UBHC các tỉnh, in rice projection dossier, GF 19. Incoming price reports are scattered through many GF cartons. Merchants probably used these radio reports too when it suited them, although they often possessed more reliable, up-to-date sources.

62. Telegraph requests and responses in GF 77.

63. Thông cáo, reprinted in DC 203 (29 April 1946).

64. Gió Biển (Haiphong) 4 (1 June 1946). Ten lines of this article are censored.

65. DC 239 (11 June 1946).

66. DC 251 (26 June 1946). That same day, the Haiphong Military Court sentenced an exporter of rice to a modest fine and suspended incarceration. DC 252 (27 June 1946).

67. DC 343 (16 Oct. 1946).

68. CQ 408 (17 Nov. 1946), provides some figures on rice harvests by province in Bắc Bộ.

69. 18 Dec. 1946, UBHCBB to UBHC Vĩnh Yên, Phòng Kinh tế outgoing message file, GF 50.

70. 3 Dec. 1946 and 7 Dec. 1946, UBHC Hanoi to UBHCBB, GF 19.

71. 7 Nov. 1946, UBHCBB to Bộ Nội Vụ, Cứu tế và Y tế dossier, GF 12.

72. Undated [probably late Nov. 1946] memo in Cứu tế và Y tế dossier, GF 12.

73. 14 Nov. 1945, Quyết nghị của Hội đồng Chính phủ, CB 1945, 82. Cù Huy Cận already was better known as a poet, under the pen name Huy Cận.

74. SL (1 Dec. 1945), in CB 1945, 109. NĐ (1 Dec. 1945), in CB 1945, 127–30.

75. NĐ (4 Dec. 1945) on organization of Nha Nông Chính, in CB 1945, 129–30. SL (8 May 1946), in CB 1946, 274.

76. NĐ (27 July 1946), in CB 1946, 418. In August, the finance ministry allocated twenty-five hundred piastres to fund a refectory for the committee. NĐ (12 Aug. 1946), in CB 1946, 459.

77. 28 June 1946, Thông tư Bộ Nội Vụ và Canh Nông, CB 1945, 367–68. Villages that did not prevent illegal burning would be punished collectively.

78. 21 Oct. 1946, Nha Nông Nghiệp Tín Dụng to BB, Nông Phố Ngân Qũy dossier, GF 56.

79. 4 Aug. [sic] 1945, Pres. Comité Gouvernement Tonkin à Chef Gouv. Laos, outgoing message file, Kinh tế Cục, GF 37. This remarkable bound folder contains 2,208 fragile sheets dated from 8 August to 28 December 1945.

80. 16 Oct. 1945, Giám Đốc Nha Kinh tế BB to BB, GF 12.

81. NĐ (2 Oct. 1945), in CB 1945, 23–24. Two weeks later, however, slaughter of pigs was restricted to December 1944 levels, CB 1945, 65.

642   NOTES TO PAGES 331–335

82. 3 Dec. 1945, Nha Kinh tế BB report, GF 12. 27 Nov. 1945, UBND Thái Nguyên report, Thái Nguyên dossier, GF 71.

83. 16 Nov. 1945, UBND Thái Bình report, Thái Bình dossier, GF 71.

84. NĐ (27 Dec. 1945), in CB 1946, 20. Pigs, goats, sheep, and dogs could be slaughtered anywhere.

85. SL (30 May 1946), in CB 1946, 306–7. The total slaughter authorization per month for Bắc Bộ was 2,115 buffaloes and 2,019 oxen. Abattoir violators were to be punished with closure (temporary or permanent) or one hundred to five thousand piastre fines.

86. 31 Oct. 1946, Phòng Kinh tế BB to UBHC Hải Dương, outgoing message file, GF 41.

87. Handwritten petition from the farmer's son to the Interior Minister, Bắc Ninh dossier, GF 29. Affixed to the petition is a forty-cent colonial tax stamp.

88. 19 Nov. 1946, UBHC Sơn La to BB, copied 13 Dec. 1946 to Defense and Agriculture ministries, GF 31.

89. October and November petitions routed to Phòng Kinh tế BB, GF/CR 141 and GF 31. 12 Dec. 1946, UBHCBB to Công an BB and UBHC Lạng Sơn, GF 11.

90. 23 June 1946, nghị quyết, VKĐTT 8, 75.

91. 30 May 1945, Chủ sự Sở Địa Chính to Khâm Sai Bắc Kỳ; 17 June 1945, draft instruction; [?] June 1945, Khâm Sai to Nam Định, GF 40.

92. 19 Sept. 1945, Các Bà Phước Việt Nam to Ủy ban Việt Nam Chính phủ Lâm thời, Sơn Tây dossier, GF 16. The nuns complained that local people were taking away cattle and paddy from the plantation.

93. 10 Aug. 1945, Gia Lộc district mandarin to Khâm Sai Phủ, GF 4.

94. Giao Thủy district dossier, GF 1.

95. 11 Dec. 1945 petition addressed to cụ Hồ Chủ tịch, and subsequent correspondence, Phú Thọ (các việc lưu) dossier, GF 59.

96. CMTT 1, 309.

97. 15 Nov. 1945 complaint, Hoà Bình (việc lưu) dossier, GF 11.

98. 23 Sept. 1945 petition, Yên Bái dossier, GF 67. Long had petitioned the Khâm Sai on 18 June 1945, protesting that a government-affiliated youth group had incited villagers to harvest some of his rice crop illegally. Quite possibly the same youths were involved in June and September.

99. 1–2 Sept. 1945, minutes of meeting of provincial committee representatives with central government officials, GF 68.

100. *Cuộc Vận động Cách Mạng Tháng Tám tỉnh Quảng Nam* [The August Revolution in Quảng Nam Province] (Thanh Hóa: Ban Nghiên Cứu Lịch Sử, 1973), 101, 105, 106. CMTT 2, 101–102.

101. Phạm Kiệt, *Từ Núi Rừng Ba Tơ* [From the Ba To Hills] (Hanoi: NXB QĐND, 1977), 112–17.

102. CMTT 2, 279, 358.

103. 30 Aug. 1945, UBNDBB to all province and city UBND, GF 62. 4 Sept. 1945, UBNDBB to all province and city UBND, GF 13.

104. 20 Sept. 1945, Chủ tịch UBNDBB to all province and city UBND, GF 62. I discuss arrests, assaults, and incarcerations in chapter 7

105. 30 Sept. 1945, Hưng Yên monthly report, Hưng Yên dossier, GF 45.

106. Biên bản Hội nghị các chủ tịch UBND các tỉnh 1–20 Oct. 1945, Văn Phòng dossier 51, GF 68.

107. 30 Oct. 1945, UBND Đội Cấn to UBNDBB, Thái Nguyên 1945 dossier, GF 71. Thái Nguyên requested twenty-nine thousand piastres, considerably more than required for twenty-two employees.

108. Nov. 1945 fortnightly reports, UBND Phúc Yên to UBNDBB, Phúc Yên dossier, GF 68.

109. 1 Jan. 1946, UBND Tuyên Quang to UBNDBB, GF 38.

110. NĐ (15 Nov. 1945) and Thông Tư 16 Nov. 1945, in CB 1945, 100–102.

111. *Lịch sử Đảng Cộng Sản Việt Nam: Trích Văn Kiện Đảng* [History of the Vietnam Communist Party: Extracts from Party Documents], vol. 1, *1927–1945.* (Hanoi: NXB ST, 1979), 321, 328, 337.

112. *Quyết Thắng* 9 (25 Nov. 1945); 14 (30 Dec. 1945).

113. *Việt Nam* (Hanoi) 15 (1 Dec. 1945); 17 (4 Dec. 1945); and 27 (15 Dec. 1945).

114. 25–11 Năm Ất Dậu petitions from Trí Trung Xã to Hồ Chủ tịch, Huyện Văn Lâm dossier, Ban Thanh Tra, UBHCBB, GF 32.

115. 12 Feb. 1946, UBHCBB to UBHC Hưng Yên, Văn Phòng BB, outgoing message file, GF 17.

116. 1 Dec. 1945, UBND làng Tạ Xá to Chủ tịch BB, Phủ Kim Động dossier, GF 32.

117. 8 Aug. 1946, UBHCBB to Bộ trưởng Bộ Nội Vụ, Bắc Ninh dossier, GF 29.

118. 27 April 1946, Ban Thanh Tra BB to Nguyễn Văn Tự and file dating back six months, Tuyên Quang dossier, GF 29.

119. 19 Jan. 1946, Bộ Nội vụ to Bộ Canh Nông, Huyện Văn Lâm dossier, GF 32. Đặng Thị Châu was also known as Suzanne Marie Croibier. See below.

120. 2–3 Nov. 1945 meeting at Bắc Bộ Phủ, Văn Phòng dossier 51, GF 68. 16 Nov. 1945 Thái Nguyên report, Thái Nguyên dossier, GF 70.

121. 25–8 Năm Ất Dậu petition, huyện Vân Lâm dossier, Ban Thanh Tra, UBHCBB, GF 32.

122. 5 Dec. 1945, UBND Hà Đông to UBHCBB, Phủ Ứng Hoà dossier, GF 28.

123. 22 May 1946, UBHCBB to UBHC Ninh Bình, Văn Phòng BB outgoing message file, GF 17.

124. 12 Feb. 1946, Bộ Nội vụ to UBHC Yên Bái, with attachments, Yên Bái dossier, GF 29. Apparently Nguyễn Văn Long also was an employee of the Agriculture Ministry.

125. 18 May 1946, Bộ trưởng Bộ Nội vụ, Văn Phòng Kinh tế BB, outgoing message file, GF 13.

126. 19 Oct. 1946, Bộ Nội vụ to BB, forwarded to UBHC Bắc Ninh, GF 29.

127. See examples of compromises reached in Kiến An (việc hiện hành) dossier, GF 11.

128. 4 Dec. 1945, Ty Liêm Phóng Thái Nguyên to UBND Thái Nguyên, Thái Nguyên dossier, GF 29.

129. 19 Nov. 1945, Mme Trimbour to Interior Ministry, Yên Bái dossier, GF 29.

130. Correspondence dating from Sept. 1945 to April 1946, Châu Lạc Thủy (việc lưu) dossier, GF 1.

131. 17 Sept. 1945, UBND Văn Lâm to UBND Hưng Yên, GF 77.

132. 12 June 1946, UBHC Phủ Tứ Kỳ to UBHC Hải Dương, Chuyển dịch bất động sản dossier, GF 24.

133. 2 Oct. 1946, BB to UBHC Hưng Yên, Phủ An Thi dossier, GF 32.

134. 29 Aug.–11 Sept. 1945, Interior Ministry requisition orders,GF 76. 24 Sept. 1945, Interior NĐ, GF 71. CB 1945, 13–14, 20–21.

135. 18 Oct. 1945, Thông Tư BB, Hỏa Xa (linh tinh) 1945 dossier, GF 68.

136. SL (6 Sept. 1945), in CB 1945, 7.

137. Autos 1945–1946 dossier, GF 64.

138. Correspondence in Văn Phòng BB, Công Thự 1946 dossier, ANOM, GF 22. Chương requested and received his villa back in June 1946.

139. 26 Sept. 1945, UBNDBB to UBND Hà Đông, GF 45. 19 April 1946, Kinh tế BB to UBHCBB, KT/2 dossier, GF 77.

140. CB 1946, 163–66.

141. CB 1945, 34.

142. Late 1945 invoice dossier, Phòng Kinh tế BB, GF 41.

143. 24 Sept. 1945, UBNDBB to UBND Đông Anh (Phúc Yên), Phòng Kinh tế dossier, GF 48.

144. CB 1945, 105–7. A distinction was made between requisitioning full ownership (trưng thu) or obtaining usage rights (trưng dụng). Real estate could not be alienated, only subject to taking usage rights. Requisitioning of persons (trưng tập) was also authorized but not spelled out.

145. CB 1946, 25, 383.

146. Information culled from CB issues January to November 1946.

147. Kháng Chiến 6 (25 Oct. 1946).

148. DC 261 (9 July 1946). Statement on the occasion of the first train going all the way from Haiphong to Lào Cai.

149. The Quartermaster Corps had already purchased from De Heulme eight hundred tons of paddy stored from the previous harvest. Correspondence 27 Oct. 1946 to 2 Dec. 1946, Sở Kinh tế incoming message file, GF 26; and Văn Phòng Mật outgoing message file, GF 31. One assumes that De Heulme kept his dealings with Vietnamese authorities secret from the French Army, which would not have been amused.

150. 16 Oct. 1946, Nha Kinh tế Trung Bộ to Bộ trưởng Bộ Canh Nông and UBHCBB, Sở Kinh tế (buồng thứ sáu) incoming message file, GF 26. 19 Dec. 1946, Phòng Kinh tế to Phòng Hành chính BB, Phòng Kinh tế outgoing message file, GF 77.

151. Marr, Vietnam 1945, 207–208, 356, 511. For a succinct description of colonial revenues and expenditures, see Jean-Pascale Bassino, "Public finance in Vietnam under French rule 1895–1954," in Quantitative History of Vietnam, 1900–1990, edited by Jean-Pascale Bassino, et al. (Hitotsubashi University: Hitotsubashi University, 2000), 280–85.

152. This controversial policy was not decreed by provisional President Hồ until 10 Oct. 1945. CB 1945, 35–36.

153. Handwritten notes taken at the 1–2 Sept. 1945 meeting, Văn Phòng dossier 51, GF 68.

154. CB 1945, 7, 10.

155. 1–2 Oct. 1945, Biên bản Hội nghị các chủ tịch UBND các tỉnh, Văn Phòng dossier 51, GF 68.

156. 18 Oct. 1945, Ty Thuế quan và thuế gián thu to UBNDBB; 1 Nov. 1945, UBNDBB to all provinces, Văn Phòng dossier, GF 38.

157. Oct.–Nov. 1945, incoming messages, GF 48. Northern Office administrators replied to these queries in far from uniform fashion.

158. Văn Phòng dossier 99, GF 38. CB 1945, 20.

159. 30 Sept. 1945, Nam Định report, Nam Định dossier, GF 45.

160. 1 Nov. 1945 report, Phúc Yên dossier, GF 68. Phúc Yên chose to ignore the intervening inflation, which made a fifty-piastre fee in late 1945 less than thirteen piastres in 1944.

161. 15 Nov. 1945, Sở Thuỷ Lâm monthly report, Văn Phòng dossier 4, GF 38

162. Tax agents received 20 percent of fines and arrears collected. This practice was later officially terminated for commercial licenses, but may have persisted with other tax collections in arrears. NĐ (1 Sept. 1946), in CB 1946, 494.

163. *Quyết Thắng* 6 (5 Nov. 1945).

164. 16 Nov. 1945, UBND Bắc Kạn to UBNDBB, Bắc Kạn dossier, GF 69.

165. Only two days earlier, the preferred name had been "National Salvation Fund" (Qũy Cứu Quốc), but this was probably discarded as too closely tied to existing Việt Minh terminology. 4 Sept. 1945, Gouv. Provisoire Republique Viet Nam à Ủy Ban Nhân Dân Bắc Bộ (text in French), GF 13. 7 Sept. 1945, UBNNBB to all provinces, Service Economique Local, KT3 dossier, GF 34. CB 1945, 5.

166. 20 Sept. 1945, UBNDBB to Bộ Tài Chính, Quân Sự (linh tinh) 1945 dossier, GF 38.

167. 1–20 Oct. 1945, Biên bản Hội nghị các chủ tịch UBND các tỉnh, GF 68.

168. CQ 61 (8 Oct. 1945), and issues preceding and following. Leaflets also used this image.

169. *Dân Quốc* 30 (10 Oct. 1945).

170. See, for example, 12 Sept. 1945, receipt no. 254 of Ban Lạc Quyên Trung Ương, Qũy Độc Lập, for a total of 879$BIC donated, GF 61. A number of other rosters circulated in the BB, the longest adding up to 2154$BIC in donations.

171. 3 Sept. 1945, Nha Tổng Giám đốc Bưu Điện Điện Thoại Việt Nam contribution list, GF 67. The director's daily salary was 59.10$BIC, so he contributed 60.00$. The lowest paid employee, Bùi Văn Tiết, received 2.60$ daily and donated 3.00$.

172. Sept. 1945, Bảo Anh Binh and Đại Đội III, Khu I, Việt Nam Giải Phóng Quân contribution lists, GF 67. Ty Liêm Phóng Bắc Bộ, Sở Canh Nông, and Viện Viễn Đông Bắc Cổ lists, GF 16.

173. 15 Oct. 1945, Bộ trưởng Bộ Tài Chính to all provinces, GF 16. 22 Nov. 1945, Hải Dương financial report to UBNDBB, Hải Dương dossier, GF 53.

174. 30 Nov. 1945, UBND Hà Đông to UBNDBB, GF 38.

175. 22 May 1946, UBND Hưng Yên to UBHCBB, GF 38.

176. 21 Dec. 1945, Bộ trưởng Bộ Quốc Phòng to các UBND Bắc Bộ và Trung Bộ, GF 16. Donations of precious metals were to be stored as well.

177. Hải Dương, for example, counted 313,971$56BIC in Independence Fund money on its March 1946 financial statement. 29 March 1946, Ủy Viên Tài Chính report, Hải Dương dossier, GF 59.

178. Receipt carbon copies scattered in GF 38. The largest amount from a single village was 1018$BIC.

179. 17 Sept. 1945 and 21 Sept. 1945, UBNDBB to all provinces; 19 Sept. 1945, Bộ Nội vụ to UBNDBB, UBND Trung Bộ và Nam Bộ, GF 16.

180. *Thời Mới* 1 (16 Sept. 1945). The editors offered free subscriptions to anyone who guessed the winner of President Hồ's medal.

181. *Thời Mới* 4 (7 Oct. 1945); 5 (14 Oct. 1945).

182. Đặng Phong, 138. In Haiphong, Mr. Nguyễn Sơn Hà and Mme Nguyễn Thị Năm contributed 105 taels and 100 taels respectively. One tael *(lạng)* equals 37.8 grams.

183. 4 Nov. 1945, Quyết nghị issued by Interior and Finance Ministries following this meeting, Văn Phòng dossier 51, GF 68.

184. 15 Dec. 1945, bimonthly UBND Quảng Yên report, Quảng Yên dossier, GF 71.

185. *Việt Nam* (Hanoi) 160 (28 May 1946).

186. CQ 106 (1 Dec. 1945).

187. Đặng Phong, 139. No citation is provided.

188. See, for example, Nov.–Dec. 1945 issues of *Nam Tiến* (Nam Định) weekly, with each gift list signed by the Tỉnh bộ Việt Minh. *Nam Tiến* 3 (13 Dec. 1945), reported 12,351$BIC in national salvation donations during the previous month.

189. *Chiến Sĩ* 1 (6 Nov. 1945); 2 (23 Nov. 1945). Later there was a request for motorcycle parts.

190. Lists in Oct.–Dec. issues of *Quyết Thắng. Chiến Sĩ* 13 (20 Feb. 1946).

191. *Chiến Sĩ* 7 (28 Dec. 1945); 8 (4 Jan. 1946); 10 (18 Jan. 1946); and 22 (24 April 1946).

192. Nov. 1945 contribution list, GF 69. 15 Dec. 1945, UBND Quảng Yên report, Quảng Yên dossier, GF 71.

193. 28 Dec. 1945, Thông cáo Bộ Nội Vụ to UBMD Bắc Trung Kỳ, Văn Phòng Nội vụ outgoing message file, GF 73.

194. CQ 157 (7 Feb. 1946).

195. Lạc quyên ngày Nam Bộ [và] ủng hộ cuộc Kháng chiến Nam Bộ dossier, Văn Phòng, GF 62.

196. *Việt Nam* (Hanoi) 11 (27 Nov. 1945); 15 (1 Dec. 1945); and 171 (11 June 1946).

197. 26 Oct. 1945, NĐ Bộ Tài Chính, CB 1945, 69. *Dân Quốc* 47 (30 Oct. 1945).

198. 19 Dec. 1945 petition of Trần Phương Thúy to UBNDBB, dossier 93, GF 48. 3 Jan. 1946, Ty Liêm Phóng BB to UBHCBB reports release of Thúy after he signed a promise to repay money owed to the government within one month, or else face rearrest and internal deportation.

199. 20 Nov. 1945, petition and resulting investigation report, Ngoại Thành Hà Nội (các việc lưu) dossier, GF 69.

200. Outgoing telegram file, Văn Phòng BB, GF 17. Together, land taxes and election organizing accounted for almost half of all messages transmitted in January.

201. The collectors had arrived with very detailed earlier plantation tax figures, broken down by family, and evidence that three hamlets *(ấp)* alone had produced 734 tons of paddy in 1945. Đồn điền của Ô. Lê Thuận Quát dossier, GF 12.

202. 31 Jan. 1946, UBHCBB to UBHC Bắc Giang, outgoing telegram file, Văn Phòng BB, GF 17. In this case, tax grain collections appear to have been sold for cash.

203. Report on 20–21 March 1946 inspection visit to Ban Thanh Tra dossier, GF 67.

204. SL (16 May 1946), in CB 1946, 280. CQ 243 (18 May 1946).

205. SL (29 May 1946), in CB 1946, 304–5.

206. 14 May 1946, UBHCBB to UBHC Ninh Bình, outgoing telegram file, Văn Phòng BB, GF 17.

207. 29 Oct. 1946, Nha Thuế Trực thu to BB, Thuế điền thổ dossier, GF 24.

208. Báo cáo về tình hình Bắc Bộ từ ngày 19-8-45 đến 20-10-46, UBHCBB, 7–8, Phòng Chủ tịch dossier, GF 19. Salt, alcohol, and opium monopolies were not included in this collection total.

209. One author was satisfied to estimate DRV land tax revenue as amounting to only 7 percent of colonial land tax income in 1938. CQ 246 (22 May 1946).

210. 30 Nov. 1946, UBHC Bắc Kạn monthly report, GF 13.

211. CQ 147 (21 Jan. 1946); 159 (9 Feb. 1946).

212. Gió Mới 22 (10 May 1946).

213. Gió Biển (2 May 1946). DC 217 (16 May 1946).

214. CQ 263 (11 June 1946); 318 (13 Aug. 1946).

215. Báo cáo về tình hình Bắc Bộ, 7–8, Phòng Chủ tịch dossier, GF 19.

216. SL (10 April 1946), in CB 1946, 277–79. Amended by SL (19 July 1946), in CB 1946, 396–97. See also the appendix in Bùi Thế Văn, Đại Cương về Khoa Học Tài Chính [Outline of Financial Science], vol. 1, Vấn đề Thuế Khóa (Hanoi, July 1946).

217. CQ 213 (12 April 1946); 214 (13 April 1946); and 215 (15 April 1946).

218. A final paragraph appears to have been blanked out by government censors, the first time this happened to Cứu Quốc.

219. DC 209 (7 May 1946). Decree details were published in DC 231 (2 June 1946).

220. Gió Biển 5 (9 June 1946).

221. Dân Mới 2 (15 May 1946); 3 (1 June 1946); and 4 (15 June 1946).

222. Quyết Thắng 41 (18 May 1946); 53 (29 June 1946); 54 (6 July 1946); 55 (13 July 1946); and 56 (20 July 1946).

223. Quân Bạch Đằng 1 (1 July 1946).

224. Việt Nam phải có một Đội Quân Hùng Mạnh [Vietnam Must Have a Powerful Army] (Huế, July 1946), 3–10.

225. Vũ Ngọc Khuê, Vấn đề tài chính của chúng ta [Our Financial Problem] (Hanoi: NXB ST, 1958), 39, as cited in Đặng Phong, 143.

226. CQ 266 (14 June 1946). Xuân Thủy later became DRV foreign minister and participated in negotiations with the United States leading up to the Paris Peace Accords of January 1973.

227. Xuân Thủy followed this up with an editorial on citizen tax responsibilities and a comparison of flat taxes and proportional taxes. CQ 267 (15 June 1946); 272 (21 June 1946).

228. Quân Bạch Đằng 3 (1 Aug. 1946).

229. Sao Vàng 25 (21 Nov. 1946).

230. Vui Sống 2 (16 June 1946); 3 (1 July 1946); 4 (16 July 1946); and 10 (1 Nov. 1946).

231. Quyết Thắng issues between 16 (Tết special) and 56 (20 July 1946).

232. Dân Mới (Vinh) 3 (1 June 1946).

233. Trung Việt Tân Văn (Hanoi) 11 (28 Feb. 1946).

234. Quyết Thắng 43 (25 May 1946).

235. Quân Bạch Đằng 7 (2 Sept. 1946).

236. 29 Oct. 1946, Thông cáo Quân Khu III to all units, in *Quân Bạch Đằng* 11 (10 Nov. 1946).

237. SL (10 Sept. 1945), CB 1945, 10.

238. 29 Sept. 1945, Chỉ thị, in CB 1945, 107–8.

239. 21 Nov. 1945, Ủy Viên Hành chính BB (Đào Văn Biểu) to UBND Hanoi, Việc muối Văn Lý dossier, GF 1. The three smaller salt production sites were located in Thái Bình, Kiến An, and Quảng Yên provinces. CB 1945, 61.

240. During the Pacific War, salt purchased on the Tonkin coast for twenty piastres per kilogram sold for up to fifty times that much across the border in Yunnan, thus earning the sobriquet "white gold." Marr, *Vietnam 1945*, 246. Sea salt contains the iodine which is lacking in rock salt of the uplands, where goiter is a longstanding ailment.

241. 26 Oct. 1945 and 30 Nov. 1945, Sở thuế quan Haiphong to Nha thuế Quan BB, Báo cáo hàng tháng (Haiphong) dossier, GF 53. 22 Jan. 1946, Sở Kinh tế BB, Tư gia dossier, GF 31.

242. 1 Nov. 1945, UBND Hòn Gai to UBNDBB, Quảng Yên province dossier, GF 71.

243. Two NĐ (15 Oct. 1945), in CB 1945, 60–61.

244. 14 Jan. 1946, Bộ trưởng Bộ Nội vụ to UBHC Bắc Bộ, Trung Bộ, and Nam Bộ, Văn Phòng BB, GF 66.

245. Việc muối Văn Lý dossier, GF 1.

246. [?] Jan. 1946, Sở Kinh tế BB to UBHCBB; and 25 Jan. 1946, UBHCBB to all provinces and cities, Groubonnet dossier, GF 65.

247. 11 Feb. 1946, Bắc Ninh to BB; 19 Feb. 1946, BB to Bắc Ninh; 20 Feb. 1946, UBHC Sơn Tây to subordinate districts, Sở Kinh tế dossier, GF 26.

248. NĐ (21 Feb. 1946), in CB 1946, 194. NĐ (22 March 1946), in CB 1946, 183. NĐ (26 June 1946), in CB 1946, 368.

249. NĐ (22 June 1946), in CB 1946, 360. NĐ (4 Oct. 1946), in CB 1946, 550. NĐ (30 Oct. 1946), in CB 1946, 607.

250. 6 Nov. 1946, Nha Kinh tế BB to UBHC Móng Caí, Phòng Kinh tế dossier, GF 41.

251. NĐ (4 Sept. 1946), in CB 1946, 508.

252. Undated [early October] internal fourth-quarter 1946 distribution list, Làm với kho muối Văn Lý dossier, GF 45. 7 Oct. 1946, UBHCBB to each province, Phòng Kinh tế outgoing msg dossier, GF 77.

253. 4 Nov. 1946, UBHCBB to all provinces, Phòng Kinh tế, outgoing message dossier, GF 71.

254. 10 July 1946, Chủ tịch UBHCBB to provinces, Linh tinh dossier, GF 76. Công chức nghiện thuốc phiện dossier, CR 141

255. 6 Nov. 1946 dismissal, Phòng Viên Chức dossier, GF 3.

256. *Quyết Chiến* (29 March 1946). *Quyết Thắng* 32 (13 April 1946). 13 June 1946, Thông Tư, Bộ trưởng Bộ Nội vụ, Thái Bình dossier, GF 16. Huỳnh Thúc Kháng mimeographed his reprimand to distribute to province committees in the north as well.

257. 8 Nov. 1945, UBND Nghệ An to Bộ Nội vụ, outgoing message file, GF 73.

258. Báo cáo hàng tháng (Hải Phòng) dossier, GF 53.

259. [?] Feb. 1946, Thuế Quan to five province UBHC, Thuế Quan và Thuế Gián Thu 1946 dossier, GF 39. Cao Bằng province, for example, was asked to make up its 921,000$BIC salt debt with an unspecified amount of opium.

260. 9 April 1946, Giám đốc Nha Thuế Quan và Thuế Gián Thu to Ty Thuế quan of six provinces; 22 May 1946, UBHC Sơn La to UBHCBB, Thuốc phiện dossier, GF 16. 26 July 1946 authorization papers for Ly Quang Hiou, Các việc năm 1946 dossier, GF 16. It is likely that Chinese Army units were involved in this opium harvest as well.

261. 16 Sept. 1946 court order, Phủ Thanh Đại dossier, GF 18.

262. 12 Dec. 1945, Giám đốc Nha Thuế Quan BB to UBNDBB, and subsequent correspondence, Bắc Ninh dossier, GF 16. Twenty-four boxes of rifle ammunition had also gone missing and were recovered.

263. 27 July 1946, letter of introduction for an Inspectorate member, incoming message dossier, Sở Kinh tế BB, GF 26.

264. 12 June 1946, UBHC Sơn La to UBHCBB; 21 June 1946, UBHCBB to Tài Chính, Hợp tác xã liên đoàn dossier, GF 78. 9 Aug. 1946, Giám đốc Nha Thuế quan to UBHCBB, Kiểm soát hàng nhập cảng dossier, GF 34.

265. 13 Aug. 1946, Thuế Quan to UBHCBB; 10 Sept. 1946, Nội vụ to UBHCBB and UBHCTB; 19 Nov. 1946, UBHC Hà Giang to UBHCBB, Việc giống thuốc phiện dossier, GF 24.

266. 2–3 Nov. 1945 minutes, Hội nghị các chủ tịch UBND 1945 dossier, GF 68.

267. SL (10 Nov. 1945), in CB 1945, 72.

268. 15 Nov.–15 Dec. 1945 report, Sở Kinh tế BB dossier, GF 36.

269. NĐ (21 Dec. 1945), in CB 1946, 18. This edict applied only to Bắc Bộ.

270. Đơn xin phép chế rượu mùi dossier, GF 69.

271. NĐ (5 March 1946), in CB 1946, 148. Prices were also set for soft drinks, carbonated water, and ice.

272. 2 Jan. 1946 permission, Giấy thông hành dossier, GF 45.

273. NĐ (4 Jan. 1946), in CB 1946, 28. Here one wonders if any rice was being used to make auto fuel, as had happened in 1944 and early 1945.

274. 25 Jan. 1946, UBHCBB to UBHC Hải Dương, Văn Phòng BB dossier 390, GF 15.

275. SL (24 May 1946), CB 1946, 303.

276. 26 Aug. 1946, Thuế Quan to BB, Đơn xin phép chế rượu mùi dossier, GF 69. 29 Aug. 1946, UBHCBB to provinces, BBP Phòng Kinh tế outgoing message dossier, GF 77.

277. 5 Oct. 1946, Chủ đồn Thuế Quan Phu-Lô to Chủ sự ty and UBHC tỉnh; 6 Nov. 1946, BB to UBHC Phúc Yên, Rượu và thuốc phiện dossier, GF 24.

278. 10 Nov. 1946, Phòng Kinh tế BB to UBHC Haiphong, BBP Phòng Kinh tế outgoing msg dossier, GF 77.

279. 2 Oct. 1945 minutes of BB meeting, GF 68.

280. 1 Nov. 1945, UBND Hải Dương report, Hải Dương dossier, GF 53.

281. Vũ Văn Hiền, *Tiền vàng và tiền giấy* [Gold Money and Paper Money] (Saigon: Nhà Sách Vỉnh Bảo, 1949). Hiền had a 1939 doctorate in law from the University of Paris.

282. NĐ (17 Oct. 1945), in CB 1945, 49–50. Nguyễn Ngọc Minh, "The Birth of an Independent Currency," *Vietnamese Studies* (Hanoi) 7 (1965): 198–219.

283. Howard A. Daniel III, *The Catalog and Guidebook of Southeast Asian Coins and Currency*, vol. 1, *France* (Portage, Ohio: BNR Press, 1978), 13–14, 58–64.

284. NĐ (1 Dec. 1945), in CB 1945, 110–11. NĐ (21 Jan. 1946), in CB 1946, 84. Trần Quốc Dụ, et al., *Đồng Bạc Tài Chính, Đồng Bạc Cụ Hồ, 1945–1954* [Finance Notes, Elder Ho

notes, 1945–1954] (Hanoi: NXB Tài Chính, 2000), 19. Poor photos of these coins can be found in Lê Hồ, compiler, *Vietnamese Currency* (Ho Chi Minh City: Central State Bank, 1991), 22. See also, Howard A. Daniel III, *The Catalog and Guidebook of Southeast Asian Coins and Currency,* vol. 2, part 3, *Democratic Republic of Viet Nam* (Dunn Loring, Virginia: privately published, 1995), 30–33.

285. Zinc and aluminum coins struck at the Osaka Mint and the Ecole pratique d'Hanoi in 1940–43 continued to circulate to 1945. Daniel, vol. 1, 14, 62–63.

286. Daniel, vol. 1, 66–67.

287. Lê Hồ, compiler, 31–33. Trần Quốc Dụ, et al., 56–63.

288. X&N 314 (Aug. 2008): 6–8.

289. Some of these test notes are reproduced nicely in color in *100 Năm Tiền giấy Việt Nam* [One Hundred Years of Vietnam Paper Money] (Ho Chi Minh City: NXB Trẻ, 1994), 138–39, 142, 144–45, 151–52. They are all signed by Finance Minister Phạm Văn Đồng, who was replaced by Lê Văn Hiến on 2 March 1945.

290. SL (31 Jan. 1946), in CB 1946, 492. This decree was not published until mid-September. See also, Đặng Phong, 156.

291. Trần Quốc Dụ, et al., 93–94. This ceremony took place on the second day of Tết (3 February).

292. NĐ (25 March 1946); NĐ (24 April 1946), in CB 1946, 184, 262. Hoàng Văn Chi was responsible for receiving Treasury checks on behalf of the management committee. Years later he published *From Colonialism to Communism—A Case History of North Vietnam* (London: Pall Mall Press, 1964).

293. Trần Quốc Dụ, et al., 18–19. X&N 65B (July 1999): 18, 37.

294. David Blazer, "Reading the Notes: Thoughts on the Meaning of British Paper Money," *Humanities Research* (Canberra) 1 (1999): 39–52. Not until 1960 did the reigning monarch appear again on British paper currency.

295. SL (10 Sept. 1946), in CB 1946, 502. Daniel, vol. 2, part 3, 34–35.

296. SL (13 Aug. 1946), in CB 1946, 492. ĐL 227 (22 Aug. 1946).

297. July 1946 report of Directeur de la Police et de la Sûreté federales en Indochine, ANOM, CP 186. According to this source, the DRV mint was now printing six hundred thousand đồng per day in notes.

298. CQ 326 (23 Aug. 1946). ĐL 229 (24 Aug. 1946). Currency issued in July and August was in denominations of one, five, twenty, fifty, and one-hundred đồng. Reproductions in *100 Năm Tiền Giấy Việt Nam,* 138, 140, 146–47, 149–50.

299. SL (4 Sept. 1946), in CB 1946, 493. DC 316 (12 Sept. 1946). ĐL 245 (14 Sept. 1946).

300. DC 342 (15 Oct. 1946).

301. *Kháng Chiến* 6 (25 Oct. 1946).

302. DC 364 (8 Nov. 1946); 365 (9 Nov. 1946). CQ 410 (19 Nov. 1946); CQ 414 (23 Nov. 1946).

303. Trần Quốc Dụ, et al., 20.

304. 12 Dec. 1946, Giám đốc Ngân khố Quốc gia to BB, outgoing message file, Văn Phòng Mật, GF 31. Coin consignments up to five hundred thousand đồng in value were ready for each northern province, but transport had yet to be arranged.

305. 6 Nov. 1946, UBHC Bắc Giang to BB, outgoing message file, Văn Phòng Mật, GF 31. 30 Nov. 1946 monthly report, UBHC Bắc Kạn to UBHCBB, GF 13.

306. 5 Dec. 1946, UBHCBB to UBHC Hải Dương; 5 Dec. 1946, BB to Ngân Khố Trung Ương, outgoing message file, Văn Phòng Mật, GF 31. By this time the government was also writing checks made out for DRV rather than BIC amounts of money, to be honored by other government organs in the first instance.

307. *L'Entente* (Hanoi) (15 Dec. 1946). Copy in GF 51.

308. Daniel, vol. 1, 14–15, 66–71, 133–34.

309. Peter Worthing, *Occupation and Revolution: China and the Vietnamese August Revolution of 1945* (Berkeley: University of California Press, 2001), 96–100. King C. Chen, *Vietnam and China 1938–1954* (Princeton: Princeton University Press, 1969), 135–38. Hugues Tertrais, *La piastre et le fusil: Le coût de la guerre d'Indochine 1945–1954* (Paris: Ministère de l'economie, des finances et de l'industrie, 2002), 34–38. CQ 102 (27 Nov. 1945); 105 (30 Nov. 1945). *Dân Quốc* 71 (27 Nov. 1945); 72 (28 Nov. 1945); and 74 (30 Nov. 1945). The BIC's Hanoi branch manager, Pierre Baylin, was murdered on 9 January 1946 while walking home from work.

310. 11 Feb. 1946, *Bulletin quotidiene,* Sûreté Generale Indochine, ANOM, INDO, CP 186.

311. 3 Dec. 1946, petition of typist in the Văn Phòng Mật, BBP, to Ủy viên Bí thư, UBNDBB, GF 53.

312. 23 April 1946, Bộ Nội vụ to UBHCBB, BB incoming message file, GF 56.

313. 26 Feb. 1946, Thủy Nông to Công Chính BB, dike maintenance dossier, GF 47.

314. Public announcements beginning in CQ 158 (8 Feb. 1946) and continuing to CQ 190 (18 March 1946).

315. SL (5 April 1946), in CB 1946, 218–19. NĐ (8 April 1946), in CB 1946, 220. NĐ (18 April 1946), in CB 1946, 252.

316. NĐ (6 July 1946), in CB 1946, 377. *Hình sự Công báo* (Hanoi) 5 (30 July 1946).

317. See, for example, DC 218 (17 May 1946).

318. Trần Quốc Dụ, et al., 97–98.

319. Counterfeit money reports in Khâm Sai Bắc Kỳ dossier, GF 58.

320. 24 March 46, Thông cáo UBHCBB to all provinces, Giấy bạc giả dossier, GF 16.

321. 20 July 1946, UBHCBB to all provinces, Văn Phòng dossier 454, GF 47.

322. See, for example, DC 126 (19 Jan. 1946).

323. 1 May 1946, UBHC Yên Bái to BB, Yên Bái dossier, GF 29. 26 July 1946, UBHC Hà Nam to BB, Huyện Kim Bảng, GF 1.

324. *Hình sự Công báo* 6 (30 Aug. 1946).

325. The following account is derived from multiple Economic Bureau dossiers located in GF 34, 37, and 42.

326. Cloth correspondence dossier, GF 31.

327. 19 Sept. 1945, Hiu Han Yu to BB; and 26 Sept. 1945, Kinh tế BB reply, cloth dossier, GF 47.

328. 26 Sept. 1945, UBND Nam Định report, Báo cáo hàng tháng dossier, GF 45.

329. 12 Sept. 1946, UBHCBB to UBHC Nam Định, Nông phố Ngân quỹ dossier, GF 56.

330. 5 March 1946, Việt Nam Thương Cục to Nha Kinh tế; 15 Feb. 1946, Phòng Tiếp tế report to UBHCBB, Groubonnet dossier, GF 65.

331. 2 Oct. 1946, UBHCBB to Bộ Quốc dân Kinh tế, Phòng Kinh tế outgoing message file, GF 77.

332. 22 Nov. 1946, Bộ Quốc dân Kinh tế to UBHCBB, *Công báo* dossier, GF 61. It is doubtful that any cotton from India was in hand yet.

333. 9 Oct. 1946, UBHC Yên Bái to UBHCBB, Phòng Kinh tế outgoing message file, GF 77.

334. 18 Oct. 1946, UBHCBB to UBHC Nam Định, Phòng Kinh tế outgoing message file, GF 77.

335. 31 Oct. 1946, BB to Bộ Nội vụ, Phòng Kinh tế cloth dossier, GF 48.

336. In the GF files, I estimate one hundred cloth allocation documents for every one document dealing with current or future textile output.

337. 3 Sept. 1945, Sở Công Chính notes, travel permit dossier, GF 16. Đáp Cầu (Bắc Ninh province) possessed a paper mill and iron smelter.

338. 7 Sept. 1945 permit, Kinh tế cục outgoing message dossier, GF 37.

339. Ban Nghiên cứu Lịch Sử Đảng Quảng Ninh, *Lịch Sử Đảng Bộ Tỉnh Quảng Ninh* [History of the Quang Ninh Province Party Apparatus], vol. 1, 1928–1945 (Hanoi, 1985), 187–88.

340. 16 Oct. 1945, monthly report, Nha Kinh tế BB dossier, GF 16.

341. NĐ (26 Nov. 1945), UBHCBB, in CB 1946, 21.

342. 15 Dec. 1945, monthly report of Chủ sự phòng ba, Sở Kinh tế dossier, GF 36.

343. Than máy dossier, Sở Kinh tế GF 72.

344. 1 Nov. 1945, UBND Hòn Gai monthly report, Quảng Yên dossier, GF 71. 27 Nov. 1945, Thái Nguyên monthly report, Thái Nguyên dossier, GF 71.

345. 6 Dec. 1945, petition routed to UBNDBB, Thái Nguyên dossier, GF 29.

346. 15 Dec. 1945, Sở Công Chính monthly report, Báo cáo hàng tháng 1945 dossier, GF 38.

347. Jean Sainteny, *Histoire d'une paix manquée: Indochine 1945–1947.* (Paris: Fayard, 1953), 130–31.

348. 4 June 1946, contract between Nha Kinh tế and Trịnh Văn Yên, translated in 3 March 1947, CSTFEO, EM, SHD 10H532, dossier 13. Thanks to Christopher Goscha for sharing this file.

349. 23 May 1946, Valluy to Hoàng Văn Thái, Hồ Sơ Mỏ than Mao Khê, GF 47.

350. 23 Nov. 1946, Hồ Sơ Mỏ than Mao Khê submitted to UBHCBB, GF 47. M. Richard disappeared in December 1946.

351. Than đá dossier, GF 47.

352. 5 Sept. 1946, Trương Đức Âm to Bộ trưởng Bộ Giao thông Công chính, Service économique local dossier, GF 32.

353. 8 April 1946, Nha Kỹ Nghệ to Phòng Kinh tế BB, Phòng Kinh tế outgoing message file, GF 13, is the first of several such criticisms of Haiphong.

354. 9 Oct. 1946, memo from Thanh Tra Lao Công miền Duyên hải to chủ tịch UBHCBB, Nguyễn Xiển dossier, GF 19.

355. 6 Aug. 1946, salary scales for Cẩm Phả mine, Hòn Gai dossier, GF 54. Workers received daily rice rations at preferential prices.

356. SL (31 Dec. 1945), in CB 1946, 14–15. Two weeks later, ten more individuals were appointed to the Ủy ban Nghiên cứu Kế hoạch Kiến thiết. SL (14 Jan. 1946), CB 1946, 42.

I can identify seven ICP members in the committee. Only two out of fifty members were female, including Mme Vĩnh Thụy (former empress Nam Phương), who was still in Huế,

357. CQ 139 (11 Jan. 1946). Vice President Nguyễn Hải Thần was also present.

358. CQ 200 (28 March 1946). Bình's organizing deputy was Hồ Hữu Tường, who soon left Hanoi for Saigon via Laos. Bình and his brother, Hoàng Cơ Thụy, a prominent lawyer, became noncommunist opponents of Ngô Đình Diệm in Saigon in the late 1950s. Bình spent several years in a reeducation camp after 1975.

359. 7 Oct. 1946, BB to Sở Kinh tế, Phòng Kinh tế outgoing message dossier, GF 77.

360. 13 Feb. 1946 and 17 April 1946, light bulb allocation lists compiled by Vật liệu BBP, GF 35.

361. 25 June 1946 and 14 Oct. 1946, Bộ Quốc dân Kinh tế to BB, tình hình và khả năng kinh tế các tỉnh dossier, GF 53. 1 Oct. 1946, Bắc Giang monthly report, Bắc Giang dossier, GF 72.

362. 5 Oct. 1946, Nha Tiếp tế to UBHC Trung Bộ and UBHCBB, Phòng Kinh tế outgoing message file, GF 77.

363. 13 Sept. 1946, Việt Thương Công ty bylaws, CB 1946, 575–80. These company announcements follow a prior colonial pattern.

364. 2 July 1946, Việt Nam Công Thương Ngân Hàng announcement, CB 1946, 363. 25 Sept. 1946 report, CB 1946, 521–22. Lập hội dossier, GF 77. X&N 72 (Feb. 2000): A–C.

365. 20 July 1946, special meeting of Thái Bình Thương Hội, CB 1946, 421.

366. 31 Oct. 1946, UBHCBB to director of Nam Á Liên Hiệp Công ty, Lập hội dossier, GF 77. The company counted sixteen shareholders contributing a total of 250,000$BIC in capital.

367. Hưng Việt Công ty announcement, CB 1946, 500. 12 Nov. 1946 report, CB 1946, 634.

368. 5 Dec. 1946 and 6 Dec. 1946, UBHCBB to provinces, Phòng Kinh tế outgoing msg file, GF 77.

369. 12 Dec. 1946, Bộ Canh Nông and Bộ Nội vụ to UBHCBB, Phòng Kinh tế BB outgoing message file, GF 26. Outgoing message ledger, GF 50.

370. *Độc Lập chủ nhật* 6 (20 Oct. 1946).

371. *Độc Lập chủ nhật* 8 (3 Nov. 1946); 11 (24 Nov. 1946).

372. *Việt Nam Độc Lập* 174 (11 Sept. 1945), as quoted in Stein Tønnesson, *The Vietnamese Revolution of 1945: Roosevelt, Ho Chi Minh, and de Gaulle in a World at War* (London: SAGE, 1991), 124.

CHAPTER 7

1. Việt Nam DC Cộng Hòa, *Documents* (Hanoi: Oct. [?] 1945), in GF 46. Trần Huy Liệu et al., *Tài Liệu Tham Khảo Lịch Sử Cách Mạng Cận Đại Việt Nam* [Reference Materials on the History of Vietnam's Modern Revolution], vol. 12, (Hanoi: Văn Sử Địa, 1958), 107–19.

2. David G. Marr, *Vietnam 1945: The Quest for Power* (Berkeley: University of California Press, 1995), 532–37.

3. Handwritten notes from 1–2 Sept. 1945 meeting, GF 68. Marr, *Vietnam 1945*, 511–12.

4. 4 Sept. 1945, Việc xử các người bị cản đẩy bị giam từ khi khởi nghĩa, in outgoing message file, GF 13. It is unclear whether this message was actually dispatched.

5. Carbon copy of SL 33D (19 Sept. 1945), GF 64. Not printed in the *Công Báo*.

6. 20 Sept. 1945, UBNDBB to all people's committees, GF 60.

7. *Cờ Giải Phóng* (Hanoi) 18 (20 Sept. 1945); 21 (30 Sept. 1945).

8. Thư gửi các đồng chí tỉnh nhà, 17 Sept. 1945. Reproduced in HCMTT 4, 19.

9. CQ 69 (17 Oct. 1945). Reprinted in HCMTT 4, 36.

10. "Quốc lệnh," 26 Jan. 1946, also lists ten meritorious acts deserving unspecified reward *(thưởng)*. This very traditional pronouncement was reprinted in several periodicals but did not appear in the *Công Báo*. According to the text in *Đa Minh* (Bùi Chu) 156 (20 Feb. 1946), Vice President Nguyễn Hải Thần joined President Hồ in signing. HCMTT 4, 96–97, does not include Thần.

11. Biên bản hội nghị các chủ tịch ủy ban nhân dân các tỉnh ngày 1 và 2 tháng 10 năm 1945, GF 68.

12. *Lịch Sử Công An Nhân Dân Việt Nam (1945–1954): Sơ Thảo* [History of the Vietnam People's Police (1945–1954): Draft] (Hanoi, 1996), 41.

13. Phòng Viên Chức file, GF 44.

14. Marr, *Vietnam 1945*, 234–36, 385–87, 398, 501.

15. Marr, *Vietnam 1945*, 134, 222–24, 459.

16. *Công An Nhân Dân Việt Nam: Lịch Sử Biên Niên (1945–1954)* [Vietnam People's Police: Historical Chronology (1945–1954)] (Hanoi: NXB Công An Nhân Dân, 1994), 30–31.

17. *Lịch Sử Công An*, 41. Similar colonial files seized in Saigon in late August had to be burned soon after to prevent them falling back into the hands of the French.

18. Lê Giản, *Những Ngày Sóng Gió: Hồi Ký* [Days of Wind and Waves: Memoir] (Hanoi: NXB Thanh Niên, 1985), 140–44. Lê Giản had been parachuted by the British into Tonkin in 1944, after being recruited and trained from among young men previously jailed by the French in Madagascar.

19. 24 Sept. 1945, in CB 1945, 20. Given the provisional government's parlous finances, it is unlikely the severance pay ever materialized.

20. Ty Liêm Phóng Bắc Bộ personnel file, GF 14. For correspondence about individual sackings or retirements, see Nội Vụ outgoing message file, GF 73.

21. These two were Nguyễn Tạo (Investigations) and Bùi Đức Minh (Political Affairs). Three apparent former Sûreté members ran the offices for identification, prisons, and (ordinary) crimes. Two former district mandarins were in charge of administration-justice and foreign residents. Lê Giản, 143.

22. 15 Oct. 1945, Trình về công việc của Ty Liêm Phóng, Liêm Phóng file, GF 38.

23. Phạm Hữu Chi and Nguyễn Văn Chính received gun permit numbers 45 and 46. Firearm permits file, GF 16. 27 Aug. 1945, Thông cáo UBNDCMBB, GF 48.

24. (?) Sept. 1945, UBNDBB to Trưởng Ban Trinh Sát, Ty Cảnh Sát Trung Ương, GF 16.

25. 31 Oct. 1945, Ngoại Thành Hà Nội report, GF 64. 8 Oct. 1945, Phú Thọ report, GF 68. 6 Nov. 1945, UBNDBB to Hưng Yên, GF 32.

26. 20 Oct. 1945, Ban Trinh Sát report; September and October reports, Thái Bình file, GF 72.

27. *Lịch Sử Công An,* 84. Trần Đăng Ninh's activities are described in chapter 8.

28. See, for example, 12 Feb. 1946, minutes of meeting of Trinh Sát Liêm Phóng Bắc Ninh, GF 67.

29. 11 July 1946, inventory list of Sở Công An, GF 33.

30. 9 Jan. 1946 petition, Nam Định file, GF 1. May 1946 petitions, Văn Phòng file 409, GF 15.

31. *Việt Nam* 161 (31 May 1946); 174 (14 June 1946).

32. SL (13 Sept. 1945), in CB 1945, 18–19. Following this decree Hanoi Central Prison reported release of 247 inmates, added to the inmates freed soon after Việt Minh takeover. 28 Sept. 1945 note, GF 62.

33. SL 33A (13 Sept. 1945)), in CB 1945, 12. Notifying a court did not equal transferring the person and file, which might occur weeks later.

34. SL 33B (13 Sept. 1945), in CB 1945, 12. The French colonial authorities had maintained a similar system of internal deportation.

35. SL 31 (13 Sept. 1945), in CB 1945, 11.

36. SL (20 Oct. 1945), in CB 1945, 57–58.

37. 28 Nov. 1945, Thông Tư circulated to northern region courts and provincial people's committees, in CB 1945, 113–15. The royal amnesty had been the work of the allegedly pro-Japanese Trần Trọng Kim Cabinet, yet it benefited many anti-Japanese prisoners, including ICP activists.

38. 15 Dec. 1945, Biên bản xử án Cung Đình Vận can tội phản quốc Thái Nguyên dossier, GF 29. As of May 1946, the question of how much of Cung Đình Vận's property was to be left for his wife and children was still undecided.

39. Lăng was shuttled through a series of jails until he reached Thanh Hóa, where General Nguyễn Sơn permitted him to teach literature and then operate a printing house. He was released in 1951, moved to France, and subsequently published a quasi-fictional account of his experiences: *Les Vietnamiens: Les chemins de la revolte: roman* (Paris: Amiot Dumont, 1953). *Nguyễn Sơn: Lưỡng Quốc Tướng Quân* [Nguyen Son: General in Two Countries] (Hanoi: NXB Thông Tấn, 2006), 133, 215–16.

40. *Quyết Thắng* 12 (16 Dec. 1945).

41. SL (14 Feb. 1946), in CB 1946, 115–16. NĐ (24 Feb. 1946) and NĐ (25 Feb. 1946), in CB 1946, 142–45. Most procedural detail appears to be drawn from French precedent.

42. Phú Xuyên district dossier (Hà Đông), GF 28. The prisoner's wife petitioned central authorities repeatedly, but the file does not reveal any military court decision.

43. CQ 257 (4 June 1946).

44. Phủ Lý town dossier, GF 1.

45. *Quyết Chiến* (Huế) (11 July 1946); (15 July 1946).

46. 24 Sept. 1946, Tư Pháp to Nội vụ, GF 28.

47. 24 Nov. 1946, Chánh Giám Thị to Thanh Tra Hành Chính và Chính Trị BB, An Trí dossier, GF 12.

48. 28 Aug. 1946, Tổng Tham Mưu Trưởng to Khu Đặc Biệt Hà Nội, GF 64. Normally National Guard personnel were subject to courts martial (toà án quân đội), not military courts, but here political implications took precedence.

49. Entries in *Hình sự Công báo* (Hanoi) 1 (30 March 1946) to 9 (30 Nov. 1946).

50. Nam Định (hiện hình) dossier, marked "Secret," GF 1.

51. 10 Oct. 1945, Bộ Trưởng Bộ Tư Pháp to Bắc Bộ, Sở Hình Vụ (Linh Tinh) file, GF 68.

52. 15 Sept.–15 Oct. 1945 report, Giám Đốc Đề Lao Trung Uờng, Hình Vụ file, GF 38. Hội Khoa Học Lịch Sử Việt Nam, *Ký Úc*, 57, shows a Central Prison literacy class for inmates, with a portrait of President Hồ above the blackboard.

53. Sở Hình Vụ (Linh tinh) file, GF 68. 1 Nov. 1945, Đề Lao Trung Uờng report, GF 38.

54. 6 Nov. 1945, Lê Văn Ngọ to Bắc Bộ, Sở Hình Vụ (Linh Tinh) file, GF 68. Bắc Bộ passed the request on favorably to the Hanoi People's Committee.

55. 30 Nov. 1945, Giám Đốc Đề Lao Trung Uờng to UBNDBB, Hình Vụ file, GF 38.

56. 15 Dec. 1945, monthly report, Chủ Sự Phòng Nhì, Sở Kinh Tế, GF 36.

57. Undated letter, UBHCBB to Lê Văn Ngọ, Hình Vụ file, GF 38.

58. 29 Sept. 1945, Thái Bình report, Thái Bình file, GF 71. 30 Sept. 1945, Hà Đông report, Hà Đông file, GF 53.

59. 20 Nov. 1945, Hải Dương report, Hải Dương file, GF 53. 23 Oct. 1945, Haiphong to UBNDBB, Công Văn các tỉnh đến ledger, GF 48.

60. 7 Dec. 1945, Hải Dương to UBNDBB; and 10 Dec. 1945, Thái Nguyên to UBNDBB, Công Văn các tỉnh đến ledger, GF 48.

61. Liêm Phóng file (63), GF 68.

62. Đào Duy Anh, *Hán Việt Từ Điển* [Chinese-Vietnamese Dictionary], 3rd ed. (Saigon: Trường Thi, 1957). *"An trí"* literally means "secure deployment."

63. 29 Oct. 1945 report, Phú Thọ file, GF 68.

64. (?) Dec. 1945, UBNDBB to Nội Vụ, GF 40. All individuals appear to be men.

65. 25 Oct. 1945, inspection report prepared by Nguyễn Đức Tố; and 26 Oct. 1945, contract signed by Nguyễn Xiển and Nguyễn Phú Đăng (chủ đồn điền), GF 66.

66. Tập linh tinh của anh Giám đốc Nguyễn Đức Tố giao lại, GF 66. Most Mỏ Chén records were typed or written on the back of 1920s and 1930s colonial arrest forms, prisoner lists and receipts.

67. Mỏ Chén records are scattered through the following GF cartons: 16, 40, 52, 54, 66, and 69.

68. SL (29 March 1946), in CB 1946, 179–81. This decree is discussed further below.

69. NĐ (16 April 1946), in CB 1946, 298. (26 April 1946), CB 1946, 263.

70. An Trí file, GF 12. Bảo vệ tự do cá nhân 1945 dossier, GF 47.

71. 4 April 1946, Công An Phú Thọ to UBHCBB, GF 12. 1 May 1946, UBHC Yên Bái to UBHCBB, GF 29.

72. (?) Sept. 1946, Công An Bắc Bộ to UBHCBB, GF 12.

73. Huyện Mỹ Hào (Hưng Yên), GF 32.

74. 6 Dec. 1946, Bộ Trưởng Bộ Nội Vụ to Chưởng Lý Tòa Thượng Thẩm, GF 19.

75. 3 Dec. 1946, Giám Đốc Công An Bắc Kỳ to UBHC Bắc Kỳ, GF 19.

76. 6 June 1946, pen note on Phạm Lê Bổng file, GF 12. The same inspector opposed release of ten other persons, including an alleged spy for the French, and a man who supposedly had plotted overthrow of the government while a member of the Sơn La People's Committee.

77. Virginia Thompson biographical file, University of California Library (Berkeley).

78. *Việt Nam* 128 (20 April 1946); 139 (5 May 1946); 151 (19 May 1946).

79. *Hình Sự Công báo* 1 (30 March 1946); 4 (30 June 1946); and 9 (30 Nov. 1946).

80. CQ 254 (28 Sept. 1946). All individuals are named.

81. CQ 390 (29 Oct. 1946); 416 (25 Nov. 1946).

82. 2 April 1946, Nội Vụ Thông Tư, CB 1946, 189–90. Emphasis in original.

83. DC (Haiphong) 208 (6 May 1946).

84. Đơn từ file, GF 69. Deportees included Linh Quang Vong, former province head of Lạng Sơn, Nguyễn Tòng, former head of Cao Bằng province, and a number of former district mandarins.

85. 20 May 1946, Ban Thanh Tra Đặc Biệt to Bắc Bộ; 24 May 1946, UBHCBB to all provinces and cities, Bảo Vệ tự do cá nhân file, GF 47.

86. Petitions and statements in Kiến An (việc hiện hành) file, GF 11. As with many such files, there is no document telling us how (or if) the imbroglio was resolved.

87. 1 May 1946, Quốc Phòng Thông Tư, copied to Đại Đoàn Khu Hà Nội, GF 76. Although an experienced lawyer, Phan Anh appears to have said nothing more on detention issues.

88. 19 May 1946, Nội Vụ to Quốc Phòng; 27 May 1946, copied to Đại Đoàn Khu Hà Nội, GF 76.

89. SL 23 (21 Feb. 1946), in CB 1946, 118.

90. Lê Giản, 153–54.

91. SL (22 March 1946), in CB 1946, 173. Nội Vụ NĐ (25 March 1946), in CB 1946, 185. Lê Giản, 155–56.

92. 1 April 1946 and 6 April 1946, UBHCBB to all provinces and cities, GF 17.

93. *Công An Nhân Dân Việt Nam*, 69–71. ICP hegemony of the Công An is described further in chapter 8.

94. Lê Giản, 156–60. Nội Vụ NĐ (9 May 1946), in CB 1946, 275. 9 May 1946, UBHCBB to all provinces and Haiphong, GF 17. Sûreté, *Bulletin quotidien* 65 (8 April 1946); 77 (20 April 1946); 93 (11 May 1946); and 98 (17 May 1946), ANOM, CP 186.

95. *Chiến Sĩ* 6 (21 Dec. 1945); 8 (4 Jan. 1946).

96. CQ 94 (17 Nov. 1945).

97. Trần Huy Liệu press conference, *Thời mới* 13 (16 Dec. 1945).

98. *Quyết Thắng* 11 (9 Dec. 1945); 26 (23 March 1946).

99. CQ 96 (20 Nov. 1945); 198 (24 March 1946).

100. CQ 189 (17 March 1946). See also DC (Haiphong) 169 (18 March 1946).

101. "Thông cáo: Tự chỉ trích," signed by Nguyễn Chí Thanh (ICP), *Quyết Thắng* 8 (19 Nov. 1945).

102. "Ai phản động?" [Who is Reactionary?], *Trung Việt Tân Văn* 9 (26 Feb. 1946).

103. *Việt Nam* 190 (4 July 1946).

104. SL 8 (5 Sept. 1945), in CB 1945, 6–7.

105. These were the Vietnam Nation Building Youth Association (Việt Nam Hưng Quốc Thanh Niên Hội) and the Vietnam Patriotic Youth Association (Việt Nam Thanh Niên Ái Quốc Hội). SL 30 (12 Sept. 1945), in CB 1945, 11.

106. For a richly textured account of these united front efforts in southern China, see Sophie Quinn-Judge, *Ho Chi Minh: The Missing Years 1919–1941* (London: C. Hurst, 2003), 69–115.

107. Daniel Hémery, *Révolutionnaires vietmamiens et pouvoir colonial en Indochine: Communistes, trotskystes, nationalistes à Saigon de 1932 à 1937* (Paris: Maspéro, 1975.)

108. Marr, *Vietnam 1945*, 175–78. During this period, at Chinese insistence, the Nationalist Party and Việt Minh belonged to the Revolutionary League

109. Marr, *Vietnam 1945*, 249–55.

110. François Guillemot, "Au coeur de la fracture vietnamienne: L'élimination de l'opposition nationaliste et anticolonialiste dans le Nord du Vietnam (1945–1946)," in *Naissance d'un État-Parti: Le Viêt Nam depuis 1945*, edited by Christopher E. Goscha and Benoît de Tréglode (Paris: Les Indes Savantes, 2004), 175–182. Hoàng Văn Đào, *Việt Nam Quốc Dân Đảng 1927–1954* [Vietnam Nationalist Party 1927–1954] (Saigon: Nguyễn Hòa Hiệp, 1965), 199–200, 216–17, 222–24. Marr, *Vietnam 1945*, 390–401.

111. 4 Sept. 1945, UBNDCM Ninh Bình to UBNDBB, GF 62. 1 (?) Oct. 1945 and 1 Nov. 1945, Ninh Bình reports to UBNDBB, GF 45.

112. 15 Sept. 1945, UBND Tuyên Quang to UBNDBB, Tuyên Quang file, GF 16.

113. 10 Sept. 1945, UBND Thái Bình to UBNDBB, Thái Bình file, GF 16. 29 Oct. 1945, Phú Thọ to UBNDBB, GF 68.

114. 19 Jan. 1946 petition from her aunt; 13 March 1946, Giám Đốc Sở Liêm Phóng Bắc Bộ to Ban Thanh Tra Bắc Bộ, Mỹ Hào district file (Hưng Yên), GF 32.

115. Quang Minh, *Cách Mạng Việt Nam thời Cận Kim: Đại Việt Quốc Dân Đảng* [Vietnamese Revolution in the Modern Era: Greater Viet Nationalist Party] (Westminster, CA: NXB Văn Nghệ, 2000), 44–49, 143–44.

116. Chương Mỹ district (Hà Đông) file, GF 28.

117. Phục chức file, GF 24.

118. Nguyễn Kỳ Nam, *Hồi Ký, 1925–1964* [Memoirs, 1925–1964], vol. 2, *1945–1954* (Saigon: Dân Chủ Mới, 1964), 224. According to the author, La Lutte members Trần Văn Thạch, Huỳnh Văn Phương, Phan Văn Chánh, and Mme Hồ Vĩnh Ký (Dr. Nguyễn Ngọc Sương) made up the delegation.

119. Ngo Van, *Viêt-nam 1920–1945: Révolution et contre-révolution sous les domination colonial* (Paris: L'insomniaque, 1995), 342–61. Trần Văn Giàu, "Hồi Ký 1940–1945," *Thời Đại Mới* 21 (May 2011): 313–20. Marr, *Vietnam 1945*, 467–69.

120. *Duy Vật Sử quan* (Hanoi, 1945). *Trai Nước Nam với Ông Hoàng Đạo Thúy* (Hanoi, 1945).

121. (3) Sept. 1945, UBND Hải Phòng to UBNDBB, Báo cáo hàng tháng (Hải Phòng) file, GF 53.

122. 31 Oct. 1945 report, Báo cáo hàng tháng (Hưng Yên) file, GF 45. 31 Oct. 1945, UBND Quảng yên to UBNDBB, Quảng Yên file, GF 70.

123. 13 May 1946, Bắc Kạn to UBHCBB (Ban Thanh Tra), An Trí file, GF 12.

124. 16 Dec. 1945, Hải Dương to UBNDBB, Hải Dương file, GF 53.

125. 25 May 1946, petition from Nguyễn Huy Vỹ, Đơn tù file, GF 69.

126. 25 Nov. 1946, biên bản, Thông Tin Tuyên Truyền file, GF 13.

127. CB 1946, 28, 254, 329. Hồ Hữu Tường had travelled north with Tạ Thu Thâu in the summer of 1945, and eventually returned to the south via Laos. Interview with Hồ Hữu Tường, Saigon, 3 March 1967.

128. Peter Worthing, *Occupation and Revolution: China and the Vietnamese August Revolution of 1945* (Berkeley: University of California Press, 2001), 54–56.

129. Marr, *Vietnam 1945*, 420, 498.

130. King C. Chen, *Vietnam and China, 1938–1954* (Princeton: Princeton University Press, 1969), 123. According to a Chinese report, this Revolutionary League unit contained one thousand men with seven hundred firearms.

131. 12 Sept. 1945, Lạng Sơn province to Bắc Bộ, GF 67. On the other hand, Paul Mus, "L'Indochine en 1945," *Politique Etrangère* 11 (1946): 449, reports a Revolutionary League flag with three white stripes on a blue field.

132. In total, the Revolutionary League may have possessed twenty-five hundred armed followers in mid-September, including some with combat experience in China. However, communication between units appears to have been poor.

133. 30 Sept. 1945, Tờ Trình, Liêm Phóng (63) dossier, GF 68.

134. *Đồng Minh* (Hanoi) 1 (6 Dec. 1945). *Ch'ing nien jih pao* (Hanoi) 25 Oct. 1945, as quoted in Chen, 123–24.

135. *Đồng Minh* 1 (6 Dec. 1945); 4 (14 Dec. 1945); and 8 (2 Jan. 1946). Phụng subsequently gained the most Haiphong votes in the National Assembly election, and in November 1946 was identified as member of the National Guard General Staff. *Kháng Chiến* (Quảng Ngãi) 9 (25 Nov. 1946).

136. *Dân Quốc* 65 (20 Nov. 1945), describes the DRV banquet for Đinh Trương Dương prior to his trip southward. *Đồng Minh* 9 (6 Jan. 1946) contains a biography of Dương.

137. Kenneth E. Colton, "The Failure of the Independent Political Movement in Vietnam, 1945–46," (PhD dissertation, American University, 1968), 479, 487. Philippe Devillers, *Histoire du Viet-nam de 1940 à 1952* (Paris: Editions de Seuil, 1952), 195.

138. See, for example, the angry reply in *Việt Nam* 25 (13 Dec. 1945) to Việt Minh assertions of Revolutionary League cooperation with the Việt Minh.

139. Kiểm duyệt 1945 (96) dossier, GF 38. CQ 122 (20 Dec. 1945) and DC 101 (20 Dec. 1945) contain such bogus letters.

140. 15–31 March 1946 case list, Công An Bắc Bộ, GF 12.

141. *Đồng Minh* 6 (21 Dec. 1945). *Dân Quốc* 90 (19 Dec. 1945).

142. 15 Nov.–15 Dec. 1945, Học Vụ report on Lạng Sơn, Yên Bái, Bắc Kạn, and Vĩnh Yên provinces, GF 38.

143. 27 Nov. 1945, Ủy Ban Chấp Hành Trung Ương, Việt Nam Cách Mạng Đồng Minh Hội to Phòng Kinh Tế BB, Outgoing message file, Phòng Kinh tế, GF 41.

144. Chính Phủ Liên Hiệp Lâm Thời Việt Nam Dân-Chủ Cộng Hòa, CB 1946, 1.

145. These twenty Revolutionary League deputies are listed in CB 1946, 216.

146. *Đồng Minh* 6 (21 Dec. 1945). *Nam Tiến* (Nam Định) 4 (21 Dec. 1945).

147. *Đồng Minh* 5 (18 Dec. 1945). CB 1946, 213. Nguyễn Tố Uyên, 258.

148. CB 1946, 206.

149. Devillers, *Histoire du Vietnam*, 254. Jean-Etienne Valluy, "Indochine: Octobre 1945–mars 1947," *Revue des Deux Mondes* (Nov.–Dec. 1967): 366.

150. *Sûreté: Bulletin Quotidiene* 84 (30 April 1946), ANOM, CP 186. All persons exhumed had been tied up.

151. CQ 258 (5 June 1946); 260 (7 June 1946).

152. Nong Quốc Long correspondence with Nguyễn Xiển, chairman of the UBHCBB, Phòng Chủ Tịch dossier, GF 54.

153. *Đồng Minh* 55 (26 Sept. 1946); 58 (25 Oct. 1946); 59 (4 Nov. 1946).

154. Hoàng Văn Đào, 332–34.

155. This brief description is derived from a serialized article beginning in *Việt Nam* 17 (4 Dec. 1945). See also Hoàng Văn Đào, 334–42. Later the Vĩnh Yên Administrative Committee reported that Liberation Army units had lost 80 killed and wounded during the late August–September 1945 confrontations, and that at least 150 civilians were killed. 17 Oct. 1946, UBHC Vĩnh Yên to UBHCBB, GF 19.

156. *Việt Nam* 24 (12 Dec. 1945); 25 (13 Dec. 1945). Tam Lộng plantation may have been owned by Đỗ Đình Đạo's family.

157. 7 Nov. 1945, letter from Lý Tạo to "Chính phủ," Hà Giang dossier, GF 29.

158. CB 209 (8 April 1946); 210 (9 April 1946). Hoàng Văn Đào, 324–31. Nguyễn Tố Uyên, 192. Charbonneau and Maigre, 382–85. X&N 123 (Sept. 2002): 13–14.

159. Hoàng Văn Đào, 240–43. Some members of this Ủy Ban Vận Động Cải tổ Việt Nam Quốc Dân Đảng later split openly from Khang and joined the Việt Minh-dominated Liên Việt.

160. *Việt Nam* 29 (18 Dec. 1945) features an "overseas letter" from Nguyễn Tường Tam.

161. *Việt Nam* 1 (15 Nov. 1945).

162. *Việt Nam* 3 (17 Nov. 1945); 22 (9 Dec. 1945); 23 (11 Dec. 1945); 25 (13 Dec. 1945); 28 (16 Dec. 1945); 29 (18 Dec. 1945); 30 (19 Dec. 1945): and 32 (21 Dec. 1945). The cartoons often put Hồ together with Võ Nguyên Giáp and Trần Huy Liệu, the latter receiving particularly vituperative treatment in articles. *Việt Nam* possessed its own printing press and independent supply of newsprint.

163. As with the Revolutionary League, the Ministry of Information and Propaganda sent fake letters about the Nationalist Party for publication in sympathetic papers. Kiểm duyệt 1945 (96) dossier, GF 38.

164. *Việt Nam* 4 (18 Nov. 1945). The confrontations in Vĩnh Yên province, described above, had led to this meeting.

165. *Việt Nam* 10 (25 Nov. 1945); 19 (6 Dec. 1945). CQ 97 (21 Nov. 1945); 101 (26 Nov. 1945).

166. CQ 104 (29 Nov. 1946). *Việt Nam* 14 (30 Nov. 1945).

167. Nguyễn Tố Uyên, 277–79. *Việt Nam* 19 (6 Dec. 1945).

168. "Biện pháp mười bốn điều và phụ kiện bốn điều," *Việt Nam* 35 (25 Dec. 1945). Also reproduced in Nguyễn Tố Uyên, 279–81.

169. Chính-Phủ Liên-Hiệp Lâm-Thời Việt-Nam Dân-Chủ Cộng-Hòa, CB 1946, 1.

170. Colton, 560–61. Teulieres, 118. CQ 160 (11 Feb. 1946). NCLS, no. 331 (June 2003): 32–37. Hội Khoa Học Lịch Sử Việt Nam, *Ký Úc*, 78–79.

171. DC 139 (12 Feb. 1946).

172. 30 Dec. 1945, UBND Hòa Bình to BB, Hòa Bình 1945 dossier, GF 53. Hoàng Văn Đào, 95–97, 303, 307–08, 349–50, 381. *Nam Tiến* 6 (28 Jan. 1946).

173. 16 Jan. 1946, Liêm Phóng BB to BB; 14 Jan. 1946 petition, Phú Thọ (các việc lưu) dossier, GF 59. Hoàng Văn Đào, 354–55.

174. *Trung Việt Tân Văn* 8 (25 Feb. 1946); 9 (26 Feb. 1946).

175. *Trung Việt Tân Văn* 6 (21 Feb. 1946). CQ 169 (21 Feb. 1946); 170 (22 Feb. 1946). Hội Khoa Học Lịch Sử Việt Nam, *Ký Úc*, 118. Võ Nguyên Giáp, *Những Chặng Đường Lịch Sử* [Historical Paths] (Hanoi: NXB CTQG, 1994), 331. After the demonstrators marched to Hoàn Kiếm Lake, a Việt Minh counterdemonstration arrived, and again the Chinese military police intervened, eventually firing shots in the air to encourage both sides to disperse.

176. *Trung Việt Tân Văn* 9 (26 Jan. 1946), lists Joint Conference (Hội Nghị Liên Tịch) members as: Hồ Chí Minh and Nguyễn Công Truyền (Việt Minh); Đỗ Đức Dục and Hoàng Văn Đức (Democratic Party); Nguyễn Hải Thần and Nguyễn Thước (Revolutionary League); and Nguyễn Tường Tam and Vũ Hồng Khanh (Nationalist Party).

177. Phan Anh's younger brother, Phan Mỹ, was already a valued DRV–Việt Minh trouble-shooter, later becoming DRV minister without portfolio.

178. *Trung Việt Tân Văn* 8 (25 Feb. 1946); 9 (26 Feb. 1946); and 10 (27 Feb. 1946). Interestingly, all four interior minister prospects were from central Vietnam.

179. X&N 207 (March 2004): 6–7.

180. Nguyễn Tố Uyên, 137.

181. Hoàng Văn Đào, 266, and photograph facing 270. As mentioned earlier, Nguyễn Hải Thần vanished during these vital days.

182. Hoàng Văn Đào, 266–67. Nonetheless, Vũ Hồng Khanh avoided being photographed at the formal signing ceremony.

183. Devillers, *Histoire du Viet-nam*, 152. Khanh also accompanied Giáp to Haiphong to address another crowd and to meet with Chinese commanders.

184. Hoàng Văn Đào, 270.

185. Worthing, 143–69, has the best description of Chinese thinking and behavior in early March, but unfortunately says nothing about discussions with Nationalist Party or Revolutionary League leaders.

186. Hồ had dealt only with the Chinese occupation command during the 3–6 March negotiations.

187. Nghiêm Kế Tổ, 95. Hoàng Văn Đào, 272. For a sense of the vivid rumors that surrounded Bảo Đại's sudden departure to China, see Joseph Buttinger, *Vietnam: A Dragon Embattled* (New York: Praeger, 1967), vol. 1, 647–48.

188. Nghiêm Kế Tổ, 96–97. King C. Chen, 148–49.

189. *Đa Minh* (Bùi Chu) 159 (21 March 1946), a Catholic paper, has a complementary woodcut drawing and article on Nguyễn Tường Tam.

190. DC 230 (31 May 1946).

191. Sûreté, *Bulletin quotidiene* 126 (19 June 1946), GF 186. Lê Giản, 161, claims that Tam "stole two million piastres from the Ministry of Foreign Affairs account."

192. Nguyễn Duy Thân trip, April 1946 work report, Phòng Công Văn dossier, GF 61.

193. 4 May 1946, UBHCBB to UBHC Bắc Giang, Ban Thanh Tra dossier, GF 67.

194. Lê Giản, 161–62. Ninh was accompanied by Đặng Việt Châu, a Democratic Party leader, and Đỗ Xuân Dung, a dike engineer. The three were lucky not to be killed subsequently by a Việt Minh militia squad, who considered them Nationalist Party spies until a local Công An officer recognized Ninh.

195. 16 May 1946, Thông Tư, Công chức Vĩnh Yên dossier, GF 40.

196. 12 June 1946, UBHC Sơn Tây to UBHCBB, GF 21, reporting 31 May alert from Phú Thọ and 5 June retrieval of two bodies bound together, one of them Hồ Ngọc Kỳ, former secretary at the French Resident's office at Phú Thọ.

197. Hoàng Văn Đào, 356, 360–63. On 23 June, another Nationalist unit was driven out of Phủ Lạng Tương, seventy kilometers northeast of Hanoi. Ngô Văn Chiêu, *Journal d'un combatant Viet-Minh* (Paris: Éditions du Seuil, 1955), 87–90, provides a vivid description of this short but bloody encounter.

198. *Việt Nam* 145 (11 May 1946); 169 (8 June 1946), 181 (23 June 1946); 186 (29 June 1946). *Việt Nam* showed its first evidence of government censorship in late June, coinciding with withdrawal of most Chinese units from Hanoi.

199. 15 Aug. 1945, BB to Nội Vụ, Phòng Chủ tịch dossier, GF 54. *Chiến Khu* (Thái Nguyên) 2 (1 Sept. 1946). Nguyễn Tố Uyên, 199.

200. Hoàng Văn Đào, 343, 438, 444.

201. Jean Crépin, "Souvenirs d'Indochine," unpublished memoir, SHD, carton T443, 186.

202. Lê Giản, 163–74. Vương Thừa Vũ, 83–84. Hoàng Văn Đào, 277–79. Guillemot, "Au coeur," 193–96.

203. Lê Giản, 174–79. Guillemot, "Au Coeur de la fracture vietnamienne: L'Elimination de l'opposition nationaliste et anticolonialiste dans le Nord du Viet Nam (1945–1946)," in *Naissance d'un État-Parti: Le Viet Nam depuis 1945 / The Birth of a Party-State: Vietnam Since 1945*, edited by Christopher E. Goscha and Benoît de Tréglode (Paris: Les Indes Savantes, 2004), 196–98.

204. *Quyết Thắng* 56 (20 July 1946).

205. ĐL 197 (14 July 1946).

206. Trần Đăng Ninh and Nguyễn Lương Bằng are obvious candidates within the ICP to take such a position.

207. Đại Việt sources insist this document as well as the corpses were planted by the ICP. Quang Minh, 51–52.

208. "Bá Cáo 9-7 VNQDĐ Trung ương Đảng Bộ," *Việt Nam* 195 (10 July 1946).

209. 20 July 1946, BB to all provinces, Việc tầm nả. dossier (454), Văn Phòng, GF 47.

210. My estimate here does not include likely separate detentions and punishments by Việt Minh groups, for which no evidence is available.

211. 18 Aug. 1946, Giấy khai cung, An Trí dossier, GF 30. Attached to the statement are petitions from Tú's mother and other relatives.

212. Lê Giản, 174–76.

213. 7–21 Aug. 1946, Correspondence regarding Lâm, Hải Dương (hiện hành) dossier, GF 59.

214. 28 Sept. 1946, Trình Như Tẩu petition, Hanoi 1946 dossier, GF 69.

215. I base this estimate on a reading of newspaper accounts of the National Assembly's second session. Devillers, *Histoire du Viet-nam*, 313, says "no more than twenty" Nationalist Party and Revolutionary League members combined attended the session.

216. 7 Aug. 1946, UBHC Hà Đông to BB, Việc Xẩy ra tại tỉnh dossier, GF 28. Phú Thọ (các việc lưu) dossier, GF 59.

217. Directeur de la Police et de la Sûreté Federals en Indochine, Sept. 1946 report (Annam section), ANOM, INDO, CP 186.

218. 14 Nov. 1946, UBHC Thái Bình to UBHCBB, Công An dossier, GF 30, enclosing six files on Catholics recommended for deportation beyond province borders.

219. 30 Nov. 1946, (Mật báo) Công An BB to UBHCBB, GF 19.

220. 18 Dec. 1946, Công An BB to BB; 19 Dec. 1946, BB routing to Nội Vụ, outgoing message file, Văn Phòng Mật, UBHCBB, GF 31. One eliminated ICP member, Trần Đình Long, had played a key role in the August 1945 insurrection in Hanoi.

221. Hoàng Văn Đào, 366–72, 382–84.

222. 25 (?) Nov. 1946, Nguyễn Tường Thụy petition to Cụ Chủ-Tịch, Nov. 1946 petitions folder, GF 34.

223. David G. Marr, *Vietnamese Tradition on Trial, 1920–1945* (Berkeley: University of California Press, 1981), 82–88. Charles Keith, "Annam Uplifted: The First Vietnamese Catholic Bishops and the Birth of a National Church, 1919–45," *Journal of Vietnamese Studies* 3, no. 2 (Summer 2008): 128–71. NCLS 322 (March 2002): 23–29.

224. Statistics come from Tran Thi Lien, "Les Catholiques Vietnamiens pendant la Guerre d'independence (1945–1954)," (PhD dissertation, Institut d'études politiques de Paris, 1996), 38, 41, based on information collected by French authorities in Saigon in December 1945. There were also 350 European nuns recorded.

225. A Vietnamese priest was also killed. Marr, *Vietnam 1945,* 358.

226. Đoàn Độc Thư and Xuân Huy, *Giám mục Lê Hữu Từ và Phát Diệm, 1945–1954* [Bishop Le Huu Tu and Phat Diem, 1945–1954] (Saigon, 1973), 38, 55–57.

227. Marr, *Vietnam 1945,* 139, 417, 505n227, 509.

228. Marr, *Vietnam 1945,* 525–26, 529–30. Tran Thi Lien, 50–51.

229. Marr, *Vietnam 1945,* 446, 453. Hoài Tân, *Trung Bộ Kháng chiến* [Central Region Resistance] (Hanoi, Jan. 1946), 15. Khôi's son, Ngô Đình Huân, was also killed.

230. Devillers, *Histoire du Vietnam,* 186.

231. *Quyết Thắng* 1 (1 Oct. 1945). Similar meetings took place in Vinh on 8 October, and two days later in Thái Bình. Devillers, *Histoire du Vietnam,* 186. Trần Tâm Tình, *Dieu et César: Les Catholiques dans l'histoire du Vietnam* (Paris: Sudestasie, 1978), 59.

232. Bernard Fall, *Le Viet Minh, 1945–1960* (Paris: Armand Colin, 1960), 165, citing a 1946 Belgian missionary bulletin. Trần Tâm Tình, 55–56. It is doubtful the other three Vietnamese bishops all saw the message prior to dispatch.

233. Trần Tâm Tình, 58.

234. *Công Giáo Cứu Quốc Hội: Điều Lệ* [Catholic National Salvation Association: Bylaws] (Hanoi, Aug. (?) 1945).

235. *Đa Minh* (Bùi Chu) 149 (1 Oct. 1945) describes establishment of the Phát Diệm Catholic National Salvation group on 5 September 1945. See also the 12 Nov. 1945 letter from Fr. Joseph Quyên to the Interior Ministry requesting to establish a Young Catholic National Salvation group in Hải Dương province. The letter was routed to the Tổng Bộ Việt Minh for an opinion. Những Phiếu Gửi, Nội Vụ Bộ, GF 76.

236. *Đa Minh* 147 (1 Sept. 1945); 151 (15 Nov. 1945).

237. Tran Thi Lien, 51, 127–28. The author points out that the French tricolor had often been hung in church offices during the colonial era.

238. *Đa Minh* 147–153 (1 Sept.–15 Dec. 1945).

239. Bishop Ngô Đình Thục was reported to be in Huế, but by this time he actually was in Biên Hòa, trying to return to his Vĩnh Long diocese.

240. Đoàn Độc Thư and Xuân Huy, 42–45. Fr. Thư was Bishop Từ's personal secretary.

241. Bishop Từ was a Cistercian, one of the most enclosed and contemplative of Catholic monastic orders, which made his political engagements all the more remarkable. Thanks to Fr. Peter Hansen for pointing this out.

242. Tran Thi Lien, 45–46, based on the author's 1989 interview with Nguyễn Mạnh Hà in Paris.

243. Đoàn Độc Thư and Xuân Huy, 45–47, 57–58. Trần Tâm Tinh, 61–64. *Dân Quốc* (Hanoi) 48 (31 Oct. 1945). *Dân Quốc* 60 (14 Nov. 1945) reprints a 29 October pronouncement by the three bishops present.

244. Tran Thi Lien, 46.

245. Paul Isoart, *Le phénomène national vietnamien* (Paris: Librairie Général de Droit et Jurisprudence, 1961), 346n86, quoting *Missi* 184 (Nov. 1954): 296–298. *Dân Quốc* 50 (2 Nov. 1945). Tran Tam Tinh, 57–58. French radio stations picked up this transmission, and within two weeks the content was in tracts distributed at Paris churches.

246. Tran Thi Lien, 65. *Đa Minh* 152 (1 Dec. 1945), reprints the provisional bylaws and platform. See also *Hồn Công Giáo* (Hanoi) 5 (13 Jan. 1946).

247. *Việt Nam* 16 (2 Dec. 1945); 23 (11 Dec. 1945). Not surprisingly, CQ 111 (7 Dec. 1945) condemned National Catholic pronouncements.

248. *Hồn Công Giáo* 1–10 (16 Dec. 1945–31 March 1946), Công An file, GF 30. *Việt Nam* 29 (18 Dec. 1945).

249. *Nam Tiến* (Nam Định) 3 (13 Dec. 1945).

250. *Quyết Thắng* 14 (30 Dec. 1945).

251. Thư Luân Lưu 5 (3 Dec. 1945), reprinted in Đoàn Độc Thư and Xuân Huy, 48–53.

252. Đoàn Độc Thư and Xuân Huy, 62–63.

253. *Quyết Thắng* 23 (13 March 1946). Fr. Phạm Bá Trực (Phủ Lý) soon became the most prominent priest in the Assembly. X&N 87 (March 2001): 9–10. *Dân Quốc* (Hanoi) 97 (29 Dec. 1945). CB 1946, 212.

254. Đoàn Độc Thư and Xuân Huy, 85–87. Thư was present at this meeting, and his assessment is even more significant considering he wrote it in 1973, after almost a quarter-century of anticommunist endeavor. See also the account in *Đa Minh* 155 (Tết 1946).

255. Đoàn Độc Thư and Xuân Huy, 88–90, 93. Phan Phát Huồn, *Việt Nam Giáo Sử* [History of Catholicism in Vietnam], vol. 2 (Saigon: Cứu Thế tùng thư, 1961), 252–53.

256. Tình Sơn, *Quyết Thắng* 28 (30 March 1945).

257. Đoàn Độc Thư and Xuân Huy, 65–66, 90–92. Tran Thi Lien, 80.

258. Reprints are in Đoàn Độc Thư and Xuân Huy, 65–75. A slightly different version of the bylaws can be found in *Liên Đoàn Công Giáo Việt Nam* (Huế) 1 (25 July 1946).

259. Phát Diệm bylaws reprinted in Đoàn Độc Thư and Xuân Huy, 75–84.

260. *Dân Mới* (Vinh) 3 (1 June 1946); 4 (15 June 1946). The Việt Minh editors of this paper blamed "antireligious injustice" on unspecified reactionaries.

261. *Quyết Thắng* 36 (1 May 1946); 38 (8 May 1946).

262. Jean-Julien Fonde, *Traitez à tout prix . . . Leclerc et le Viet Nam* (Paris: Robert Laffont, 1971), 227.

263. Tran Thi Lien, 134–35.

264. *Đa Minh* 163 (21 May 1946); and 166 (11 June 1946).

265. The key organizer appears to have been Fr. J. M. Thích, who had begun publishing attacks on communism in 1927. See Marr, *Vietnamese Tradition*, 84–86.

266. *Liên Đoàn Công Giáo Việt Nam* (Huế) (25 July 1946); 2 (10 Aug. 1946); 3 (25 Aug. 1946); and 4 (1 Sept. 1946).

267. Tran Thi Lien, 55–57, 71–72, 86–91, 94.

268. Edward Miller, "Vision, Power and Agency: The Ascent of Ngô Đình Diệm," *Journal of Southeast Asian Studies* 35, no. 3 (Oct. 2004): 433–38. Tran Thi Lien, 43–44, 67, 108.

269. Nguyễn Mạnh Hà, Catholic participant in the original provisional DRV cabinet, seems to have been ignored in these January–February 1946 discussions.

270. Tran Thi Lien, 67–68, 108–11, 172. Ngô Đình Nhu fled Hanoi for Phát Diệm in December. His younger brother, Ngô Đình Luyện, made it to Saigon.

271. Among seventy-eight GF cartons at the ANOM, I noted only about thirty items dealing specifically with Catholics. Office of the President files seem to have evaded French capture in December 1946.

272. 2–3 Nov. 1945, Quyết Nghị, Hội nghị các chủ tịch UBND 1945 (51) dossier, GF 68.

273. Thanh Liêm district file, Hà Nam (các việc lưu hành), GF 1. The petitions in this dispute number at least fifty, with thousands of signatures in total.

274. Ngô Văn Chiêu, a Nam Định Catholic, realized this no later than March 1946, yet it did not dissuade him from National Guard service until December 1952, when he was badly wounded. Ngô Văn Chiêu, 67.

275. Phủ Lý dossier, Hà Nam (việc lưu), GF 1.

276. 14 Nov. 1946, UBHC Thái Bình to UBHCBB, Công An dossier, GF 30. One individual was also charged with seeking to work for the French.

277. 14 Nov. 1946, UBHCBB to Nội Vụ, Văn Phòng Mật, outgoing message file, GF 31. The bylaws included clauses on military organizing and execution of deviant members, which would not have come from the "tame" Nationalists now part of the Liên Việt.

278. 25 Nov. 1946 report of 15 Nov. 1946 meeting of Information and Propaganda Bureau personnel with provincial propaganda cadres, GF 13.

279. 4 Dec. 1946, BB to Cụ Phạm Bá Trực, outgoing message file, GF 31.

280. *Nhiệm Vụ tuần báo* 3 (3 Nov. 1946); 6 (24 Nov. 1946); 7 (1 Dec. 1946); and 9 (15 Dec. 1946). Office located next to the main Catholic cathedral in Hanoi.

CHAPTER 8

1. David G. Marr, *Vietnam 1945: The Quest for Power* (Berkeley: University of California Press, 1995), 402–72.

2. Ho Chi Minh, "Our Party has struggled . . ." in *A Heroic People: Memoirs from the Revolution* (Hanoi: Foreign Languages Publishing House, 1965), 12. Nguyễn Tố Uyên,

Công cuộc Bảo Vệ và Xây Dựng Chính Quyền Nhân Dân ở Việt Nam trong những Năm 1945–1946 [Protecting and Building People's Government in 1945–1946] (Hanoi: NXB KHXH, 1998), 117, citing *Lịch Sử Đảng Cộng Sản Việt Nam (sơ thảo)*, vol. 1 (Hanoi, 1984), 476.

3. CMTT 1, 252, 253, 331.

4. Marr, *Vietnam 1945*, 520–28.

5. Marr, *Vietnam 1945*, 155–67. William J. Duiker, *The Communist Road to Power in Vietnam* (Boulder: Westview Press, 1981), 45–79.

6. Marr, *Vietnam 1945*, 169–240.

7. Trường Chinh, et al., *Ngọn Cờ Giải Phóng* [Liberation Flag] (Hanoi: NXB ST, 1955); and Trường Chinh, *Cách Mạng Dân Tộc Dân Chủ Nhân Dân Việt Nam* [Vietnam's National People's Democratic Revolution], vol. 1 (Hanoi: NXB ST, 1976), 188–334.

8. *Cờ Giải Phóng* 17 (17 Sept. 1945). Thanks to Ben Kerkvliet for locating and making available to me copies of *Cờ Giải Phóng*.

9. 11 Sept. 1945, Nghị quyết án (Hội nghị cán bộ Bắc Kỳ), VKĐTT 8, 12–13.

10. *Cờ Giải Phóng* 17 (17 Sept. 1945).

11. *Cờ Giải Phóng* 23 (7 Oct. 1945).

12. *Cờ Giải Phóng* 20 (27 Sept. 1945).

13. Hoàng Quốc Việt and other ICP leaders are introduced in Christopher Goscha, *Historical Dictionary of the Indochina War (1945–1954)* (Copenhagen: NIAS Press, 2011).

14. Nguyễn Khánh Hòa, et al., eds., *Anh Cả Nguyễn Lương Bằng* [Eldest Brother Nguyen Luong Bang] (Hanoi: NXB CTQG, 2005), 7–8, 137–39.

15. Nguyễn Lương Bằng later became first director of the Vietnam National Bank, first DRV ambassador to the Soviet Union, and finally DRV-SRV vice president.

16. Ngô Vi Thiện and Nguyễn Hữu Lê, eds., *Trần Đăng Ninh: Con Người và Lịch Sử* [Trần Đăng Ninh: The Person and the History] (Hanoi: NXB CTQG, 1996), 13–20, 52–53, 60–62, 88–124, 134–37, 286–87.

17. X&N 20 (Oct. 1995): 17–18.

18. Ngô Vi Thiện and Nguyễn Hữu Lê, eds., 22, 41–42, 49, 168–69, 297, 312, 317–18, 360, 365, 375.

19. Trịnh Thúc Huỳnh and Lê Văn Đệ, eds., *Đồng chí Trần Quốc Hoàn Chiến sĩ Cách mạng trung kiên của Đảng, Nhà lãnh đạo xuất sắc của Công An Việt Nam* [Comrade Tran Quoc Hoan: Faithful Revolutionary Fighter for the Party, Outstanding Leader of the Vietnam Police] (Hanoi: NXB CTQG, 2006), 7–8, 29–32, 38–42.

20. A year later, Hoàn married the spy. Trịnh Thúc Huỳnh and Lê Văn Đệ, eds., 28, 84, 86, 113–14, 378, 408–12.

21. Trịnh Thúc Huỳnh and Lê Văn Đệ, eds., 54, 85–86, 379.

22. Trịnh Thúc Huỳnh, et al., eds., *Phạm Hùng: Nhà lãnh đạo trung kiên, mẫu mực* [Pham Hung: Faithful and Exemplary Leader] (Hanoi: NXB CTQG, 2003), 44–54, 88–91, 137–42, 324–25, 344–45, 491–97.

23. Other key returnees from Côn Sơn at this time were Lê Duẩn, Tôn Đức Thắng, Lê Văn Lương, Nguyễn Văn Linh, and Mai Chí Thọ. Ban Nghiên Cứu Lịch sử Đảng Đặc Khu Vũng Tàu-Côn Đảo, *Nhà Tù Côn Đảo, 1862–1945* [Con Son Island Prison, 1862–1945] (Hanoi: NXB ST, 1987), 168–78.

24. Trịnh Thúc Huỳnh et al., eds., 92–96, 325–27, 345. Nguyễn Kỳ Nam, *Hồi Ký 1925–1964* [Memoirs 1925–1964], vol. 1, *1945–1954* (Saigon: Dân Chủ Mới, 1964), 294–95.

25. Trần Đình Nghiêm, ed., *Nhớ về anh Lê Đức Thọ* [Remembering Brother Le Duc Tho] (Hanoi: NXB CTQG, 2000), 6, 12, 48.

26. Marr, *Vietnamese Tradition on Trial, 1920–1945* (Berkeley: University of California Press, 1981), 308–15, discusses colonial prison experiences. Trần Đình Nghiêm, ed., 442, refers to French files seized in Quảng Trị. See also, Trần Hữu Dực, *Bước qua đầu thù: Hồi ký* (Hanoi: NXB CTQG, 1996), 277.

27. Hoàng Tùng, *Diễn Đàn* (Paris), 1 July 2010. Tùng says his name was forwarded along with those of Trần Quang Huy and Vũ Kỳ, the latter being selected.

28. Besides Nguyễn Lương Bằng, Trần Đăng Ninh, Trần Quốc Hoàn, and Lê Đức Thọ, introduced above, other influential Sơn La alumni included Trần Huy Liệu, Lê Thanh Nghị, Văn Tiến Dũng, Xuân Thủy, Nguyễn Văn Trân, and Trần Đình Long.

29. Other colonial prisons that socialized ICP members during the early 1940s were: Hỏa Lò (Hanoi), Nghĩa Lộ, and Hòa Bình in Tonkin; Kontum and Lao Bảo in Annam; and Khám Lớn (Saigon) and Tà Lài in Cochinchina. The French practice of shifting inmates around meant that many ICP members came to identify with more than one group.

30. I have yet to find a list of Standing Bureau members among party publications dealing with this period.

31. In late 1945 this team around Hồ included Võ Nguyễn Giáp, Phạm Văn Đồng, Hoàng Hữu Nam, Hoàng Minh Giám, Vũ Đình Huỳnh, and Vũ Kỳ.

32. Archimedes L. A. Patti, *Why Viet Nam? Prelude to America's Albatross* (Berkeley: University of California Press, 1980), 221, 223–24, mentions Trường Chinh's presence at his 29 August 1945 meeting with Hồ Chí Minh.

33. Huyện Phủ Cừ (Hưng Yên) dossier, ANOM, INDO, GF 32.

34. Phủ Khoái Châu (Hưng Yên) dossier, GF 32. Other local Việt Minh members continued to petition for release of their five comrades, but a roving judicial investigator regarded the five-year punishment as lenient.

35. Phủ Ung Hoà dossier, GF 18.

36. 20 Dec. 1945, UBND làng Cốc Lâm (Vĩnh Yên) to BB, Vĩnh Yên dossier, GF 59. 8 Jan. 1946, petition from members of Giai Hê commune (Hưng Yên), incoming message folio, GF 56.

37. 27 Oct. 1945, Lâm Thành Bộ Việt Minh Hải Phòng to Sở Vô Tuyến Điện Hà Nội, dossier 88, GF 48.

38. Late November 1945 report, Báo cáo hàng tháng (Hải Phòng) dossier, GF 53.

39. 20 Nov. 1945 report, Hải Dương dossier, GF 53. 31 Oct. 1945 monthly report, Hưng Yên dossier, GF 45.

40. 10 Dec. 1945, BB to UBND Nam Định, Danh từ công văn dossier, GF 58.

41. Chấn chỉnh các UBHC dossier, GF 19.

42. CB 1946, 206–7, 321, 359, 475, 549, 606. The ICP is not mentioned once.

43. The Vietnamese text of this 11 Nov. 1945 resolution is reprinted in CQ 89 (12 Nov. 1945). See also Nguyễn Kiến Giang, 129–30, and VKĐTT 8, 19–20. A Morse code French version was broadcast by Voice of Vietnam the next day, and printed in *La République* (Hanoi) 7 (18 Nov. 1945). The "Central Executive Bureau" probably did not exist.

44. Hoàng Tùng, *Diễn Đàn* (Paris) (1 July 2010).

45. 25 Nov. 1945 chỉ thị, "Kháng chiến Kiến quốc," reprinted in *Văn Kiện Đảng về Kháng Chiến chống Thực Dân Pháp* [Party Documents on Resistance to French Colonialism], vol. 1, *1945–1950* (Hanoi: NXB ST, 1986), 25–39. Also VKĐTT 8, 21–34. This directive refers to the ICP as "The Party" throughout.

46. The directive makes no further mention of contradictions between proletarians and capitalists, nor does it refer to "socialism" or the "socialist revolution."

47. This is the only time that Hồ Chí Minh is mentioned in the directive.

48. The directive criticizes Quảng Ngãi as well as "many northern provinces" for being too restrictive, and Hà Tĩnh and "many southern provinces" for being too inclusive. According to a much later source, the Party had twenty thousand members by the end of 1945. Nguyễn Tố Uyên, 117, citing *Lịch Sử Đảng*, 476. Enrollment procedures were very lax, as Lê Đức Thọ would point out subsequently.

49. In 1941, central and southern regional committees had been assigned responsibility for building ICP networks in Laos and Cambodia respectively. Marr, *Vietnam 1945*, 180.

50. Churchill gave his famous speech at Fulton, Missouri on 5 March 1946.

51. I base this on perusal of thousands of captured DRV documents in the ANOM's GF file, including many marked "secret" *(mật)*. The files mention the Việt Minh somewhat more often. I have not found a government order which spells out the functional demarcation between the state and political parties, however.

52. ST 38 (4 June 1946): 3. The Liên Việt is discussed below.

53. ST 38 (1 June 1946): 2; and 41 (22 June 46).

54. "Chính sách của chúng ta," ST 42 (30 June 1946); 43 (5 July 1946). Trường Chinh's rhetorical obfuscation took advantage of the technical nonexistence of the ICP, so that "We" could straddle party, state and nation. The text is not included in VKĐTT 8.

55. By contrast, Khmer and Lao peoples enjoyed the "right of self-determination" in Trường Chinh's scheme.

56. My guess is that Trường Chinh was targeting some senior party members in Nam Bộ and Nghệ An province who continued to question his position. However, it is also conceivable that he fabricated doctrinal controversy in order to reinforce his points about rational analysis and internal unity.

57. ST 44 (12 July 1946). According to an accompanying article, the French Revolution remained unfulfilled so long as both the French proletariat and colonial peoples were exploited.

58. Hồng Lĩnh, ST 46 (26 July 1946). Nam Chi, ST 47 (2 Aug. 1946). ST 54 (20 Sept. 1946).

59. Trần Quốc Bảo, ST 55 (27 Sept. 1946).

60. ST 49 (16 Aug. 1946) to 56 (4 Oct. 1946). Other ICP–Việt Minh first-anniversary commemorations are described below. At this time some Việt Minh papers still preferred to call the events of August 1945 an "insurrection" or "uprising" *(khởi nghĩa)*. Trường Chinh eventually enforced the term "revolution" on all state as well as party publications.

61. Trường Chinh, *Cách Mạng Tháng Tám* (Hanoi: NXB ST, Oct. 1946). By 1954, ST Publishing House had reprinted the book three times, and there were two additional

printings in Interzone 4. An English translation appeared in Hanoi in 1962, and this became the first part of Trường Chinh, *Primer for Revolt: the Communist Takeover in Viet-Nam* (New York: Praeger, 1963).

62. In a particularly fanciful passage, Trường Chinh claims that the Vietnamese people fulfilled their international antifascist duties by inhibiting Japanese regional logistics between late 1944 and August 1945.

63. Trường Chinh equates this revolutionary "shortcoming" with the Paris Commune's failure to gain control of the Bank of France in 1871.

64. Trường Chinh's praise of the Yugoslavian partisans was deleted from later editions of this essay to conform with Stalin's condemnation of Tito.

65. Marr, *Vietnam 1945*, 210–11. X&N 141 (June 2003): 4–5.

66. CQ 69 (17 Oct. 1945).

67. CQ 42 (13 Sept. 1945); 46 (18 Sept. 1945); and 47 (19 Sept. 1945).

68. CQ 162 (13 Feb. 1946).

69. CQ 170 (22 Feb. 1946).

70. CQ 175 (2 March 1946)

71. CQ 176 (4 March 1946); and 177 (5 March 1946).

72. CQ 179 (7 March 1946); 180 (8 March 1946).

73. CQ 183 (11 March 1946); 184 (12 March 1946); 185 (13 March 1946); 186 (14 March 1946); and 188 (16 March 1946).

74. CQ 352 (21 Sept. 1946); 418 (27 Nov. 1946); 439 (18 Dec. 1946).

75. Marr, *Vietnamese Tradition on Trial*, 254–87.

76. Nguyễn Kỳ Nam, 151.

77. Marr, *Vietnam 1945*, 121–122.

78. *Thời Mới* (Hanoi) 2 (30 Sept. 1945). On Trần Hưng Đạo's legacy, see also DC 152 (26 Feb. 1946).

79. CQ 346 (15 Sept. 1946).

80. CQ 347 (16 Sept. 1946).

81. Hoàng Xuân Hãn commemorated Quang Trung in *Dư Luận* (Hanoi) 28 (3 Nov. 1946).

82. Nguyễn Tri Phương, wounded and captured by victorious French troops in 1873, is said to have starved himself to death. Hoàng Diệu hung himself in 1882 rather than join his men in fleeing the Citadel under French attack. CQ 210 (9 April 1946). *Gió Biển* (Haiphong) 5 (9 June 1946).

83. *Dân Quốc* (Hanoi) 77 (4 Dec. 1945). While the soldier slept, his comrade manned a light machine gun pointed through sandbags.

84. "Lịch Sử nước ta," HCMTT 3, 210–24.

85. CQ 73 (22 Oct. 1945); 80 (1 Nov. 1945). Hội Khoa Học Lịch Sử Việt Nam, *Ký Úc*, 147.

86. CQ 63 (10 Oct. 1945); 184 (12 March 1946); and 371 (10 Oct. 1946). DC 164 (12 March 1946).

87. The special birthday issue of *Le Peuple* (Hanoi) 12–13 (19 May 1946), is printed on scarce imported paper. DC 220 (19 May 1946) special edition is twice normal size, but Hồ's birthday shares attention with the history of Nam Bộ. Hội Khoa Học Lịch Sử Việt Nam, *Ký Úc*, 178–79.

88. *Việt Nam* 3 (17 Nov. 1945).

89. CQ 160 (11 Feb. 1946). Hội Khoa Học Lịch Sử Việt Nam, *Ký Úc*, 113.

90. DC 136 (9 Feb. 1946); 139 (12 Feb. 1946). Hội Khoa Học Lịch Sử Việt Nam, *Ký Úc*, 198–99.

91. Only one Việt Minh newspaper observed the sixteenth anniversary of the Nghệ An Soviets: *Kháng Chiến* (Quảng Ngãi) 2 (9 Sept. 1946).

92. Marr, *Vietnam 1945*, 158–59,164.

93. See in particular *Quyết Thắng* (Huế) 1 (1 Oct. 1945) and continuing.

94. *Quân Bạch Đằng* (Kiến An) 9/10 (Oct. 1946).

95. Tổng Bộ Việt Minh, *Bắc Sơn Khởi Nghĩa* [Bac Son Uprising], 4th printing (Hanoi: Tủ Sách Cứu Quốc, 1946).

96. Marr, *Vietnam 1945*, 159–63.

97. *Chiến Sĩ* 2 (23 Nov. 1945). *Kháng Chiến* 8 (15 Nov. 1946). *Quyết Thắng* 8 (19 Nov. 1946).

98. See, for example, *CQ* 41 (12 Sept. 1945); 42 (13 Sept. 1945).

99. *Chiến Sĩ* 4 (7 Dec. 1945).

100. DC, special Tết edition (Jan. 1946). The editors mistakenly report Tô Hiệu (1911–43) as dying in 1941. For awhile, Việt Minh groups in Haiphong renamed the city "Tô Hiệu" in their documents and speeches.

101. Trần Các, *Gió Biển* 4 (1 June 1946). See also CQ 247 (23 May 1946).

102. Minh Đệ, *Dân Mới* (Vinh) 2 (15 May 1946) and serialization.

103. Trần Huy Liệu, *Nghĩa Lộ khởi nghĩa, Nghĩa Lộ vượt ngục* [Nghia Lo Uprising, Nghia Lo Escape] (Hanoi: Hội Văn Hóa Cứu Quốc, June 1946).

104. CB 1946, 359. CQ 302 (26 July 1946).

105. CQ 306 (31 July 1946). Ngô Tử Hạ and Tôn Đức Thắng were the two other members.

106. CQ 308 (2 Aug. 1946); 323 (18 Aug. 1946).

107. SL (27 Aug. 1946), in CB 1946, 474–75.

108. Trần Huy Liệu lead editorial, *Sao Vàng* (Hanoi) 12 (15 Aug. 1946). Here Liệu also contrasted Vietnam with Malaya and Burma.

109. CQ 331 (29 Aug. 1946). Liệu is identified as a member of the Tổng Bộ Việt Minh.

110. *Sao Vàng* 13 (29 Aug. 1946). Army policy at this time was to develop a separate identity from the Việt Minh.

111. "Cách Mạng Tháng Tám. Đặc San Cứu Quốc, Tháng Tám 1946" [August Revolution: National Salvation Special Issue, August 1946], *CQ* 19 (Aug. 1946).

112. CQ 325 (22 Aug. 1946); 333 (31 Aug. 1946); 335 (4 Sept. 1946).

113. Võ Nguyên Giáp, *Khu giải phóng* [Liberated zone] (Hanoi: NXB CQ, Aug. 1946).

114. *Đặc San Cách Mạng Tháng Tám. Quân Bạch Đằng* 4 (19 Aug. 1946), 40 pages.

115. "Số đặc biệt 'Ngày Độc Lập,'" CQ 334 (1 Sept. 1946).

116. CQ 341 (19 Sept. 1946).

117. Devillers, *Histoire*, 232, lists eight members of the Tổng Bộ in February–March 1946: Hồ Chí Minh, Võ Nguyên Giáp, Phạm Văn Đồng, Trần Huy Liệu, Nguyễn Lương Bằng, Hoàng Quốc Việt, Trường Chinh, and Hồ Tùng Mậu. However, he offers no citation, nor indication of when this group met.

118. Trần Huy Liệu eventually became head of the Viện Sử Học (Historical Studies Institute) and editor of *Nghiên Cứu Lịch Sử (Historical Research)*. His most influential publication was *Lịch Sử tám mươi năm chống Pháp* [History of Eighty Years Against the French], 2 vols. (Hanoi: NXB Sử Học, 1961).

119. Trần Văn Giàu, "Hồi Ký 1940–1945," *Thời Đại Mới* 21 (May 2011): 320–23. Marr, *Vietnam 1945*, 219–21, 426, 454–55, 523.

120. *Những sự kiện Lịch sử Đảng*, vol. 2, 33–34. Christopher Goscha, "Le contexte asiatique de la guerre franco-vietnamienne: Réseaux relations et économie (d'août 1945 à mai 1954)" (PhD thesis, Ecole pratique des hautes études, 2000) vol. 1, 204.

121. *Dân Quốc* 57 (10 Nov. 1945). CQ 109 (5 Dec. 1945). DC 104 (25 Dec. 1945); and 105 (26 Dec. 1945).

122. CQ 123 (21 Dec. 1945). Giàu was sent to Bangkok in the summer of 1946, and would not be able to return to Nam Bộ until after 1975.

123. 30 May 1946, memo signed by Trường Chinh, VKĐTT 8, 67–68.

124. 30 May 1946 letter, VKĐTT 8, 63–66. Trường Chinh avoided use of the terms "Liberation" and "Vanguard," referring to "Old Việt Minh" and "New Việt Minh" respectively.

125. Việt Nam, Đảng Lao Động, *Văn Kiện Quân Sự của Đảng* [Military Documents of the Party], vol. 2, *1945–1950* (Hanoi: NXB QĐND, 1976), 69–71.

126. Marr, *Vietnam 1945*, 200–1. Under formal Việt Minh provisions, the Democratic Party qualified for horizontal membership on a par with the ICP, whereas national salvation associations functioned under the ICP. In practice the ICP infiltrated the Democratic Party from the beginning, but cannot be said to have controlled it in 1944–46.

127. These ministers were Dương Đức Hiền (youth), Vũ Đình Hòe (national education), and Cù Huy Cận (minister without portfolio). For further information on Democratic Party activities in August 1945, see Marr, *Vietnam 1945*, 365, 374, 383, 386, 388–89, 391, 395, 449, 504–5, and 513.

128. Vũ Đình Hòe, *Hồi Ký Vũ Đình Hòe* [Memoirs of Vu Dinh Hoe], vol. 1 (Hanoi: NXB Văn Hóa-Thông Tin, 1995), 358–62, 366; vol. 2 (Hanoi: Hội Nhà Văn, 2004), 750–56.

129. X&N 5 (Aug. 1994): 4–6; 6 (Sept. 1994): 9–11. In 1950, Lê Trọng Nghĩa was made head of the Army's Bureau of Military Intelligence.

130. 29 Sept. 1945, Dân Chủ Đảng to Bắc Bộ, danh sách các công sở, GF 53. It was common for politically active Vietnamese to have one or more pseudonyms.

131. 7 Sept. 1945, Dân Chủ Đảng to UBND Hà Nội; 13 Sept. 1945 reply, in GF 37.

132. 7 Sept. 1945, Dân Chủ Đảng to CP Việt Nam Dân Chủ Cộng Hòa, firearms dossier, GF 16. The request itemized each firearm by make and serial number.

133. *Việt Nam* 7 (22 Nov. 1945). *Dân Quốc* 68 (23 Nov. 1945).

134. Vũ Đình Hòe, vol. 1, 372–73. Hoàng Văn Đức, trained as an agricultural engineer, had worked in the Tonkin Agricultural Bureau (see chapter 6).

135. 31 Oct. 1945, Hưng Yên monthly report, Hưng Yên dossier, GF 45. 30 Nov. 1945, Bộ Trưởng Bộ Nội Vụ to UBND Hưng Yên, Hưng Yên dossier, GF 32.

136. 30 Nov. 1945 and 3 Dec. 1945 reports, Hưng Yên dossier, GF 32. 1 Dec. 1945, Hưng Yên monthly report, Hưng Yên dossier, GF 45.

137. CMTT 4, 310, compliments ICP–Democratic Party coordination, while Lê Văn Định, et al., *Lịch sử cuộc Kháng chiến chống Pháp trên địa bàn Hải Hưng, 1945–1954* [History of Anti-French Resistance in Hải Hưng, 1945–1954] (Hải Hưng: Bộ Chỉ Huy Quân Sự, 1988), 48–49, affixes the counterrevolutionary and anti-ICP labels to the Democratic Party.

138. CQ 79 (31 Oct. 1946). X&N 32 (Oct. 1996): 10–11.

139. *Nam Tiến* (Nam Định) 4 (21 Dec. 1945). Lê Trọng Nghĩa stood for election under his real name, Đoàn Xuân Tín.

140. Vũ Đình Hòe, vol. 1, 342. The official list of Assembly delegates (CB 1946, 212–16) does not reveal party affiliations, except for the Nationalist Party and Revolutionary League contingents admitted without standing for election.

141. CQ 164 (15 Feb. 1946).

142. CB 1946, 203–12.

143. CB 1946, 216. "Vice-minister" is my rendition of *"thứ trưởng,"* which also can be translated as "permanent secretary."

144. DC 188 (10 April 1946). Not until mid-October did the Haiphong branch elect its nine-person executive committee, which included Vũ Quốc Uy, deputy head of the city's administrative committee. DC 343 (16 Oct. 1946); DC 344 (17 Oct. 1946).

145. 23 May 1946, Tuyên ngôn của Dân chủ đảng Trung Bộ, in *Quyết Thắng* 44 (29 May 1946). A Democratic Party team from Hanoi had earlier addressed a large public meeting in Huế. *Quyết Chiến* (14 May 1946).

146. ĐL 186 (1 July 1946); 187 (3 July 1946). Other party branches probably came to participate in these five commemorations.

147. ĐL 209 (28 July 1946).

148. ĐL 241 (11 Sept. 1946).

149. See in particular T. D., *Độc Lập Chủ Nhật* 5 (13 Oct. 1946).

150. Pierre Brocheux, "La Revue *Thanh Nghị:* Un groupe d'intellectuels Vietnamiens confrontés aux problèmes de leur nation (1941–1945)," *Revue d'histoire moderne et contemporaine* 3 (1987): 317–31.

151. Terminology remained fluid, with authors sometimes advocating in the same article a "command economy," a "planned economy," and a "New Democratic economy."

152. *Độc Lập Chủ Nhật* 1 (15 Sept. 1946) and serialized.

153. *Độc Lập Chủ Nhật* 8 (3 Nov. 1946) and serialized.

154. N. T. L., *Độc Lập Chủ Nhật* 6 (20 Oct. 1946). The author translates from Chinese periodicals appearing one year earlier.

155. ĐL 206 (25 July 1946).

156. DC 315 (12 Sept. 1946).

157. ĐL 246 (17 Sept. 1946). The editors claim one hundred thousand Democratic Party members at this time, but it is doubtful anyone took that figure seriously.

158. ĐL 246 (17 Sept. 1946). Vũ Đình Hòe, vol. 1, 391. I have seen nothing elsewhere about this monument.

159. ĐL 247 (18 Sept. 1946). *ĐL* is reporting Congress proceedings with a one-day delay.

160. ĐL 248 (19 Sept. 1946). Vũ Đình Hòe, vol. 1, 392. The regional reports were given by Nguyễn Đăng (south), Phan Hiến (center), and Lê Trọng Nghĩa (north).

161. ĐL 249 (20 Sept. 1946).

162. It is notable that neither capitalism nor imperialism was included in this list.

163. My description here relies on a "Summary Platform" text published later in *Độc Lập Chủ Nhật* 8 (3 Nov. 1946). By November the party name had undergone a grammatical change to Đảng Dân Chủ Việt Nam.

164. ĐL 250 (21 Sept. 1946); 251 (25 Sept. 1946).

165. ST 38 (1 June 1946).

166. CQ 253 (30 May 1946). Other Việt Minh papers printed the Liên Việt announcement without editorial comment. No one covered the inaugural meeting held at the Hanoi Opera House. Hội Khoa Học Lịch Sử Việt Nam, *Ký Úc*, 189.

167. *Dư Luận* 7 (9 June 1946). The two interviewees were Ngô Tử Hạ, senior lay Catholic representative in the Việt Minh, and Vũ Đình Trí, a Nationalist Party member and National Assembly delegate.

168. *Việt Nam* 176 (16 June 1946). CQ 267 (15 June 1946). Nguyễn Tường Long was better known by his pen name, Hoàng Đạo.

169. CQ 276 (26 June 1946); 285 (6 July 1946).

170. DC 240 (12 June 1946).

171. DC 249 (24 June 1946); 341 (13 Oct. 1946).

172. "Nghị quyết Hội nghị cán bộ Trung Ương, 31 July–1 Aug. 1946," *Văn Kiện Đảng về Kháng chiến*, vol. 1, 66.

173. CQ 307 (1 Aug. 1946). *Tổ Quốc* (Hanoi) (July 1984).

174. VKDTT 8, 105.

175. ĐL 213 (2 Aug. 1946). The Socialist Party founding document is serialized across three issues. Robert Schuman was in the MRP, not the SFIO.

176. Hoàng Minh Giám was in Paris as a member of the DRV negotiating delegation. The new Vietnam Socialist Party soon accredited him to seek DRV supporters in France, especially within the SFIO.

177. CQ 317 (12 Aug. 1946).

178. VKĐTT 8, 105.

179. *Dư Luận* 15 (28 July 1946). *Dư Luận* was seen as successor to *Thanh Nghị*, which had been published during the Pacific War.

180. Phan Anh, another Trần Trọng Kim Cabinet member, also contributed occasional articles to *Dư Luận* in between his duties as DRV defense minister.

181. X&N 88 (March 2001): 10.

182. "Vỡ ruộng," serialized from *Dư Luận* 2 (25 April 1946) onward.

183. *Dư Luận* 18 (25 Aug. 1946).

184. "Giác Ngộ" [Awakening], *Dư Luận* 29 (10 Nov. 1946).

185. *Dư Luận* 32 (1 Dec. 1946).

186. Lists of 1946 titles published and due to be published can be found on the back covers of books now held by the Vietnam National Library.

187. Xít-ta-lin, *Nguyên lý chủ nghĩa Lê-Nin* (Hanoi: NXB ST, 1946).

188. Note on back cover of *Nguyên lý chủ nghĩa Lê-Nin*, vol. 2. Sự Thật books were routinely advertised in *Cứu Quốc*.

189. Several complimentary biographies of Chiang Kai-shek were published.

190. Trần Huy Liệu, *Đảng Cộng sản Tầu và Chiến tranh Cách mạng* (Hanoi: NXB ST, 1946).

191. *Chế độ Chính trị Xô-Viết* (Hanoi: NXB Thế Giới Mới, April 1946). A copy sits in GF 66.

192. *Đời Sống của Hồng Quân Liên Xô* (Hanoi: NXB ST, June 1946), copy in GF 45.

193. Jean Baby, *Les classes sociales: Cours de Marxisme* (Hanoi: Éditions Cờ Giải Phóng, 1945). Công Báo dossier, GF 61.

194. Fifteen-page manuscript (with first page unfortunately missing), Văn Phòng dosser, GF 66.

195. Undated, untitled dossier at the top of GF 76.

196. 23 June 1946, Nghị quyết, VKĐTT 8, 72–97. Although titled a "resolution" this document reads more like a premeeting report modified to take account of subsequent discussion.

197. VKĐTT 8, 98–114.

198. Perhaps somewhere in the still-closed party archives there is a list of conference participants and a copy of minutes taken. The same research void bedevils discussion of later such meetings.

199. Vương Thừa Vũ, *Trưởng Thàng trong chiến đấu* [Maturing in Battle] (Hanoi: NXB QĐND, 1979), 74–78. Vũ entered the room thinking that finally he was going to be dressed down for the failure of the breakout at Nghĩa Lộ prison in March 1945.

200. VKĐTT 8, 126–33.

201. *Kháng Chiến* (Quảng Ngãi), new series, 1 (3 Dec. 1946). The Saigon committee was of course transmitting from outside the city.

202. Gửi Xứ ủy Nam Bộ ngày 16 Dec. 1946, VKĐTT 8, 156.

203. 12 Dec. 1946, Toàn dân Kháng chiến, VKĐTT 8, 150–55. 22 Dec. 1946 cover note, *Văn Kiện Đảng về Kháng chiến*, 88.

204. Vũ Kỳ, *Thư Ký Bác Hồ kể chuyện* [Uncle Ho's Secretary Talks] (Hanoi: NXB Văn Học, 2005), 49–50. Vũ Kỳ first published his account of events in 1988.

205. Nguyễn Thành, X&N 34 (Dec. 1996): 5. Stein Tønnesson, *Vietnam 1946: How the War Began* (Berkeley: University of California Press, 2010), 221–30.

206. The ICP claimed "almost eight thousand" members (including provisionals) in the National Guard at the end of 1946. *Những Sự kiện Lịch Sử Đảng* [Party Historical Events], vol. 2, *1945–1954* (Hanoi: NXB ST, 1979), 51.

CHAPTER 9

1. *Chiến Sĩ* 1 (16 Nov. 1945). Việt Minh adherents immediately fused their own flag with the nation, much to the irritation of some other political organizations.

2. "Thành Trì Xương Máu" [Wall and Moat of Bones and Blood], *Nam Tiến* 2 (8 Nov. 1945).

3. Vũ Bằng, in *Thời mới* 1 (16 Sept. 1945).

4. Text removed from the 5 Dec. 1945 issue of *Tương Lai,* Kiểm duyệt 1945 dossier, ANOM, INDO, GF 38.

5. *Thời mới* 14 (23 Dec. 1945).

6. "Cám ơn các ông Pháp thực dân" [Thank you Mr French colonialists], *Dư Luận* 13 (14 July 1946).

7. Đinh Gia Trinh, in *Tương Lai*, Tết Bính Tuất issue (late Jan. 1946).

8. CQ 149 (23 Jan. 1946).

9. DC số Tết Độc Lập (late Jan. 1946). Woodblock technique in red ink.

10. *Vui Sống* 1 (1 June 1946).

11. "Chính nghĩa" [Righteous Cause], *Gió Biển* 3 (25 May 1946).

12. *Chiến Khu*, special issue (16 Aug. 1946). The men recognized here had died fighting compatriots in the Vietnam Nationalist Party, not the French.

13. *Sao Vàng* 15 (12 Sept. 1946).

14. This fiery 22 September address was reprinted in *Sao Vàng* 18 (3 Oct. 1946), but not given attention elsewhere, a measure of post-modus vivendi sensitivities in Hanoi.

15. CQ 43 (13 Sept. 1945). No description of this demonstration appeared for twelve days, when it was claimed that one million people had participated. CQ 5 (26 Sept. 1945). Archimedes L. A. Patti, *Why Vietnam? Prelude to America Albatross* (Berkeley: University of California Press, 1980), 327, reports five thousand to six thousand participants.

16. CQ 50 (24 Sept. 1945).

17. CQ 54 (29 Sept. 1945). *Cứu Quốc*'s lead editorial the previous day was titled "Determined to Fight."

18. *Thời mới* 2 (30 Sept. 1945); 4 (14 Oct. 1945).

19. *Dân Quốc* 22 (1 Oct. 1945); 23 (2 Oct. 1945); 25 (4 Oct. 1945); 26 (5 Oct. 1945); and 36 (17 Oct. 1945).

20. *Đồng Minh* 1–11 (6 Dec. 1945–13 Jan. 1946).

21. *Đa Minh* (Bùi Chu) 156 (20 Feb. 1946).

22. *Quyết Thắng* 1 (1 Oct. 1945); 2 (8 Oct. 1945); 5 (29 Oct. 1945); 7 (12 Nov. 1945).

23. *Nam Tiến* 1 (29 Oct. 1945); 2 (8 Nov. 1945).

24. Trịnh Văn Hiến, *Có thể mất Nam Bộ được không?* [Can We Possibly Lose Nam Bộ?] (Hanoi: Tân Quốc Dân, Jan. 1946).

25. CQ 70 (18 Oct. 1945); 71 (19 Oct. 1945). Bình Xuyên, *Cậu Bé Sài Gòn: Truyện Nam Bộ* (Hanoi: Hoa Lư, June 1946). Phan Huy Lê, "Về câu chuyện Lê Văn Tám," X&N 340 (Sept. 2009): 8–11.

26. CQ 114 (11 Dec. 1945). Editors did not print a correction.

27. "Anh Trần Văn Giàu người đã kháng chiến viết" [Written by Tran Van Giau, a Resistance participant], CQ 83 (5 Nov. 1945). See also report of a subsequent talk by Trần Văn Giàu, in *Văn Hóa* (Hanoi) 13 (16 Nov. 1945).

28. *Chiến Sĩ* 18 (27 March 1946).

29. *Quyết Thắng* 26 (23 March 1946). This southern group also told the reporter about forty-three traitors executed at one location.

30. CQ 198 (24 March 1946). DC 177 (28 March 1946).

31. Hội Khoa Học Lịch Sử Việt Nam, *Ký Úc*, 130–31, 192–95. CQ 126 (26 Dec. 1945); 247 (23 May 1946).

32. Thăng Long, ed., *Nhớ Nam Bộ & Cực Nam Trung Bộ buổi đầu kháng chiến chống Pháp* [Remembering South and South-Central Vietnam in Early Days of the anti-French

Resistance] (Hồ Chí Minh City: NXB Trẻ, 1999), 157, 273–84, 295–97. Nguyễn Thanh Sơn was earlier known as Nguyễn Văn Tây.

33. CQ 261 (8 June 1946); 262 (10 June 1946); 263 (11 June 1946); and 264 (12 June 1946). Other Hanoi newspapers gave little or no attention to Nam Bộ Day. A separate Nam Bộ meeting was held at the Hanoi cathedral. Hội Khoa Học Lịch Sử Việt Nam, *Ký Ức*, 197.

34. *Quyết Thắng* 46 (5 June 1946); 47 (8 June 1946); and 48 (12 June 1946).

35. ĐL 200 (18 July 1946); 204 (22 July 1946). *Dư Luận* 14 (21 July 1946); 15 (28 July 1946). CQ 294 (17 July 1946). *Kháng Chiến* (Quảng Ngãi) 2 (9 Sept. 1946).

36. *Vui Sống* 5 (1 Aug. 1946). *Sao Vàng* 22 (31 Oct. 1946). Dương had been killed in an ambush 15 Jan. 1946, but this only became public knowledge six months later.

37. CQ 354 (23 Sept. 1946); 355 (24 Sept. 1946). ĐL 251 (25 Sept. 1946).

38. *Chính Nghĩa Tuần Báo*, 18 (30 Sept. 1946).

39. DC 325 (24 Sept. 1946).

40. *Kháng Chiến* 3 (23 Sept. 1946).

41. A few writers translated "chauvinism" as *"chủ nghĩa vị quốc,"* but most retained the French term. "Antiforeignism" was translated as *"chủ nghĩa bài ngoại."*

42. *Chiến Sĩ* 19 (3 April 1946).

43. *Quyết Thắng* 8 (19 Nov. 1946).

44. *Sao Vàng* 22 (31 Oct. 1946).

45. Marr, *Vietnamese Tradition on Trial, 1920–1945* (Berkeley: University of California Press, 1981), 295–300.

46. Quốc Thụy, *Vấn đề Dân tộc* [The Nationality Question] (Hanoi: *Nhà Sách Đại Chúng*, 1946).

47. Commanders also sometimes bestowed Vietnamese surnames on ethnic minority comrades, a tradition of Vietnam's monarchs and mandarins.

48. *Liên Đoàn Công Giáo Việt Nam* (Huế) 2 (10 Aug. 1946).

49. At the ICP–Việt Minh congress convened in the hills two week earlier, Liệu had been named deputy to Hồ in the short-lived National Liberation Committee.

50. Marr, *Vietnam 1945: The Quest for Power* (Berkeley: University of California Press, 1995), 474. Other musical instruments remained in possession of the Civil Guard band, which joined the fledgling Liberation Army. Most newspapers refer simply to the Ministry of Propaganda, a practice I will follow here.

51. CQ 73 (22 Oct. 1945). Hội Khoa Học Lịch Sử Việt Nam, *Ký Ức*, 43.

52. At some point the name was altered to Việt Nam Thông Tấn Xã (Vietnam Press Agency), which remains in operation today.

53. 2 Oct. 1945, Nghị định removing colonial bans; 19 Oct. 1945, Nghị định banning books, Xin phép xuất bản dossier, GF 38.

54. Bộ Nội Vụ NĐ (8 Oct. 1945), in CB 1945, 48–49.

55. These were: *Độc Lập* (Independence), principal organ of the Democratic Party; *Gái Nước Nam* (Vietnamese Female), belonging to the Women's National Salvation group; and *Tiên Phong* (Vanguard), published by the National Salvation Cultural Association. CB 1945, 59–60.

56. Forty-seven additional periodicals received Interior Ministry permission to publish in the first six months of 1946, as recorded in the *Công Báo*. A cross-check of current

Vietnam National Library holdings suggests that many titles either did not materialize or neglected to deposit two copies with the Dépôt Legal.

57. 3 Dec. 1945, Nội Vụ to báo *Việt Nam* Bộ, TTTT Kiểm duyệt 1945 dossier, GF 38. Further Nov.–Dec. 1945 correspondence on seventeen additional applications can be found in Nội Vụ Bộ outgoing message file, GF 73.

58. *Dân Quốc* 45 (27 Oct. 1945).

59. This became the agreed formula for *L'Entente* until March 1946, as discussed in chapter 4.

60. I have not been able to locate any issues of *Qing Nian*.

61. TTTT Bắc Bộ reports for October and November 1945, Báo cáo hàng tháng 1945 dossier, GF 38.

62. Marr, *Vietnam 1945*, 124, 146–47, 518, provides background on this execution.

63. Here an official in Hanoi scribbled on the report's margin: "Influence them; there is no way to purge *(khai trừ)* them at present."

64. 18 Dec. 1945 and 27 Dec. 1945, reports from Ban TTTT Thái Nguyên to TTTT Bắc Bộ, Thái Nguyên 1945 dossier, GF 71.

65. *Thời mới* 13 (16 Dec. 1945).

66. *Hà Nội Mới* 5 (10 July 1946) to 7 (29 July 1946). Văn Tân, in CQ 295 (18 July 1946), reacted to the first installment of the *Hà Nội Mới* article with a vitriolic attack on Phạm Quỳnh and other "feudal remnants."

67. *Đồng Minh* 33 (14 April 1946).

68. *Gió Mới* 18 (5 April 1946).

69. *Dân Thành* 36 (5 Nov. 1946).

70. *Cấp Tiến* (Hanoi) 1 (5 Oct. 1946). In the large blank space left on the front page, the editors substituted a drawing of a boy sowing, with the caption, "The time has arrived for us to cast rice seeds *(gieo mạ)*." All articles were unsigned.

71. CQ 215 (15 April 1946); 229 (1 May 1946); and 245 (21 May 1946). CQ was also closed down for one day in late July. CB 1946, 401.

72. DC 281 (1 Aug. 1946); 305 (30 Aug. 1946).

73. ĐL 271 (20 June 1946).

74. *Dân Mới* 2 (15 May 1946).

75. *Kháng Chiến* 5 (15 Oct. 1946).

76. *The Age* (Melbourne) (3 Sept. 1945); (12 Sept. 1945).

77. Marr, *Vietnam 1945*, 399, 493, 517, 521–22, 531. X&N 5 (Aug. 1994): 7–8; and 56 (Oct. 1998): 23, 35. Many memoirs and official histories continue to insist that Hồ Chí Minh was heard in various localities on 2 September 1945.

78. 15 Sept.–15 Dec. 1945, Sở Vô tuyến điện monthly reports, Vô tuyến điện dossier, Văn Phòng, GF 38.

79. CB 1945, 94.

80. 8 Nov. 1945, Nội Vụ to TTTT, outgoing message file, Văn Phòng, GF 73. Morse versions of such official traffic were copied down in Huế, then retransmitted to listeners further south.

81. *Dân Quốc* 85 (13 Dec. 1945). Nothing seems to have come of this offer.

82. Giáp's radio speech is reprinted in DC 145 (19 Feb. 1946).

83. *Chiến Sĩ* 16 (13 March 1946). It's doubtful that technicians in Hanoi were able to connect the Opera House microphone to Radio Bạch Mai, or that Huế technicians could hook up their main receiver to a loud speaker at the sports stadium. Probably Hồ went to the studio soon after and repeated his talk there.

84. CQ 227 (29 April 1946). It is unclear whether this Paris Radio disk was then played over Radio Bạch Mai.

85. 27 Aug. 1945, Tuyên Quang to Đồng chí Xiển, Tuyên Quang dossier, GF 16.

86. 13 Oct. 1945, Ban Thông Tin to UB Thái Nguyên, Thái Nguyên dossier, GF 71.

87. (?) Sept. 1945, UB Ninh Bình report, Ninh Bình dossier, GF 45. The reporter chose not to mention that the Catholic diocese and most parishes had their own radio receivers.

88. The Haiphong Administrative Committee went further, threatening confiscation if the possessor lacked a certificate of usage for the receiver. DC 177 (28 March 1946).

89. *Quyết Thắng* 15 (6 Jan. 1946); Ngô Hà, *Quyết Thắng* 32 (13 April 1946).

90. ĐL 157 (28 Feb. 1946). Some of these transmissions were in Morse.

91. March 1946 report (dated 13 April), monthly reports of Directeur de la Police et de la Sûreté Federales en Indochine, ANOM, INDO, CP 186.

92. 9 May 1946, 13 May 1946, and 25 Sept. 1946 correspondence, Emission radio VM dossier, ANOM, INDO, CP 128.

93. Mai Văn Bộ, ed., *Đây! Đài phát thanh Tiếng Nói Nam Bộ Kháng Chiến* [Here! The voice of Nam Bộ Resistance Station] (Hồ Chí Minh City, 1995), 7, 13.

94. ĐL 210 (30 July 1946).

95. ĐL 230 (25 Aug. 1946). The editors wanted to leave the impression that the Voice of Nam Bộ was located in the Mekong delta. Shortly thereafter Trần Văn Giàu left Hanoi for Bangkok.

96. ĐL 254 (28 Sept. 1946). The program was repeated on Voice of Việt Nam several times. How this disk recording made it from Paris to Hanoi is not stated, but I suspect it was carried in by a sympathetic French correspondent.

97. "Đài Danh dự" obituary column, *Chiến Sĩ* (Huế) 32 (11 July 1946).

98. Nguyễn Văn Hay, in Mai Văn Bộ, ed., *Đây! Đài Phát thanh*, 28–32.

99. *Quyết Thắng* 3 (15 Oct. 1945).

100. "Tổ chức một cuộc tiểu tổ thảo luận như thế nào" [How to Organize a Small-group Discussion], *Quân Bạch Đằng* (Kiến An) 3 (1 Aug. 1946). See also *Sao Vàng* (Hanoi) 14 (5 Sept. 1946).

101. *Sao Vàng* 24 (14 Nov. 1946).

102. "Tự chỉ trích hội nghị" [Conference Self-Criticism], *Quyết Thắng* 53 (29 June 1946).

103. "Tiến! hay Lùi?: Mit-tinh" [Progress or Step Backwards?: Meetings], DC 179 (30 March 1946).

104. In November 1946, the requirement for prior approval of meetings and demonstrations was reaffirmed, while the rule on censorship of speeches was dropped. *Dân Quốc* 374 (7 Nov. 1946). *Nhiệm vụ tuần báo* 7 (1 Dec. 1946).

105. 19 Feb. 1946 TT, CQ 168 (20 Feb. 1946).

106. CQ 168 (20 Feb. 1946).

107. CQ 201 (29 March 1946); 202 (30 March 1946). Philippe Devillers, *Histoire du Vietnam de 1940 à 1952* (Paris: Editions de Seuil, 1952), 250. Nguyễn Kiến Giang, *Việt Nam năm đầu tiên sau Cách Mạng Tháng Tám* [Vietnam's First Year Following the August Revolution] (Hanoi: NXB ST, 1961), 181–82.

108. CQ 276 (26 June 1946); 277 (27 June 1946); 278 (28 June 1946); and 279 (29 June 1946). Devillers, *Histoire du Vietnam*, 274. There was a supporting strike in Haiphong on 28 June. DC 253 (29 June 1946).

109. DC 339 (11 Oct. 1946); 341 (13 Oct. 1946); and 342 (15 Oct. 1946).

110. Jean-Julien Fonde, *Traitez à tout prix . . . Leclerc et le Viet Nam* (Paris: Robert Laffont, 1971), 267.

111. CB 1945, 5–6. CQ 43 (14 Sept. 1945).

112. *Quyết Thắng* 3 (15 Oct. 1945).

113. *Sao Vàng* 2 (6 June 1946).

114. CQ 338 (7 Sept. 1946).

115. CB 1946, 596.

116. 10 Dec. 1946, Chủ tịch Chính phủ to all ministers, GF 50.

117. CQ 193 (21 March 1946); 194 (22 March 1946). General Leclerc's armored column had arrived in Hanoi on 18 March. The exhibit was routed to the provinces, and subsequently returned to the capital. Nguyễn Bá Khoản, *Những khoảnh khắc Lịch Sử qua Ống Kính Nguyễn Bá Khoản* [Historical Moments via Nguyen Ba Khoan's Camera] (Hanoi: NXB QĐND, 1997), 52–70.

118. *Chiến Sĩ* 38–39 (2 Sept. 1946).

119. The best-known photographer of this time, Võ An Ninh, took many of these *Thời mới* cover images, not all of which reproduced successfully, largely due to poor quality newsprint.

120. CQ 230 (3 May 1946); 234 (8 May 1946); 251 (28 May 1946).

121. *Tương Lai* (Hanoi) 6 (1 Nov. 1945); 11 (6 Dec. 1945); 12 (13 Dec. 1945).

122. *Đa Minh,* Xuân Bính Tuất, 155 (late Jan. 1946).

123. *Chiến Sĩ,* Số mùa Xuân, 11–12 (late Jan. 1946).

124. *Quyết Thắng,* Xuân Bính Tuất, 16 (late Jan. 1946).

125. Nguyễn Văn Ký, *La Société Vietnamienne face à la modernité: La Tonkin de la fin du XIXe siècle à la seconde guerre mondiale* (Paris: Harmattan, 1995), 191–228.

126. CQ 246 (22 May 1946).

127. Nora A. Taylor, *Painters in Hanoi: An Ethnography of Vietnamese Art* (Honolulu: University of Hawaii Press, 2004), 24–41.

128. Phan Kế An, X&N 241 (Aug. 2005): 14–16.

129. *Dân Quốc* 29 (9 Oct. 1945). *Thời mới* 4 (14 Oct. 1945). A similar culture week was staged in Đà Nẵng two months later. *Quyết Thắng* 11 (9 Dec. 1945).

130. Nguyễn Văn Tỵ, *Tiên Phong* (Hanoi) 8 (1 April 1946): 28–31.

131. *Thời mới* 11 (2 Dec. 1945).

132. *Nam Tiến* (Nam Định) 3 (13 Dec. 1945).

133. Nguyễn Văn Tỵ, *Tiên Phong* 15–17 (19 Aug. 1946): 61–65.

134. Đào Kim Thanh, in ĐL 204 (22 July 1946).

135. Nguyễn Văn Tỵ, *Tiên Phong* 18 (2 Sept. 1946): 21–22.

136. Nguyễn Văn Tỵ, *Tiên Phong* 19 (16 Sept. 1946): 28–29; and 20 (1 Oct. 1946): 25–26.

137. See, for example, ĐL 229 (24 Aug. 1946).

138. Taylor, 25–26, 39–41, 43, 47–49.

139. Nguyễn Văn Ký, 171–81.

140. "Đoàn Kết" appeared in the June and July issues of *Chính Nghĩa tuần báo*.

141. "Dưới ánh Trăng" [Under the Moonlight], *Chính Nghĩa tuần báo* 9 (29 July 1946); and 10 (5 Aug. 1946). Censors deleted twenty-nine lines from the play.

142. *Tiên Phong* 4/5 (Tet 1946); 6 (16 Feb. 1946); 7 (15 March 1946); and 15–17 (19 Aug. 1946).

143. "Đêm Trước" [The Night Before], *Độc Lập chủ nhật* (Hanoi), serialized starting with 1 (15 Sept. 1945).

144. Bibliographic details in Võ Quang Uẩn, ed., *Thư mục sách Kháng Chiến 1945–1954* [Catalogue of 1945–1954 Resistance Books] (Hanoi: Thư Viện Quốc Gia Việt Nam, 2002), 223–25.

145. *Tiên Phong* 9 (16 April 1946), reviewed "Bắc Sơn" favorably and reprinted commentary from other periodicals.

146. "Nêu cao cờ chiến thắng," reviewed in *Bạn Gái* (Hanoi) 9 (25 Nov. 1945). No author is given.

147. *Chiến Sĩ* 5 (14 Dec. 1945).

148. *Quân Bạch Đằng* (Kiến An) 3 (1 Aug. 1946). A short play by Hoàng Tuy, "Sống Độc Lập" [Living in Independence], is printed in *Quân Bạch Đằng* 7 (2 Sept. 1946).

149. *Sao Vàng* 11 (8 Aug. 1946).

150. Niels F. Ebbesen, *Music in a Changing City—Hanoi, Vietnam: A Preliminary examination of the History of Modern Vietnamese Music, 1938–1996* (Copenhagen: Danida, 1997), 12–27.

151. *Quân Bạch Đằng* 4 (19 Aug. 1946). Marr, *Vietnam 1945*, 371, 385–87.

152. Jason Gibbs, "The Music of the State: Vietnam's Quest for a National Anthem," *Journal of Vietnamese Studies* 2, no. 2 (2007): 129–74.

153. As quoted in Vĩnh Sinh, "Komatsu Kiyoshi and French Indochina," *Moussons* (Marseille) 3 (June 2001): 80–81.

154. "Vệ Quốc Quân ca," sheet music in *Dân Mới* (Vinh) 1 (1 May 1946).

155. "Chiến Sĩ Không Quân," *Tiên Phong* 15–17 (19 Aug. 1946): 86–87.

156. CB 1946, 203. Article 3 of the 1946 constitution, from the text in Nguyễn Tố Uyên, *Công cuộc Bảo Vệ và Xây Dựng Chính Quyền Nhân Dân ở Việt Nam trong những Năm 1945–1946* [Protecting and Building People's Government in 1945-1946] (Hanoi: NXB KHXH, 1998), 263.

157. *Tiên Phong* 15–17 (18 Aug. 1946): 66–70; 24 (1 Dec. 1946): 15–16, 27. See also Phước's article on music as a means of struggle, in *Độc Lập Chủ Nhật* 9 (10 Nov. 1946); 10 (17 Nov. 1946).

158. *Tiến Hóa* (Quảng Ngãi) 2 (1 Dec. 1946).

159. As noted in chapter 2, Hồ Chí Minh did take this option when establishing his Special Inspectorate.

160. Ngô Văn Cát, ed., *Việt Nam chống nạn thất học* [Vietnam Fights Lack of Education] (Hanoi: NXB Giáo Dục, 1980), 42–45.

161. NĐ (17 July 1946), in CB 1946, 416–17. The regional offices were to be in Hanoi, Huế, and (notionally) Saigon.

162. NĐ (6 Feb. 1946), in CB 1946, 122. This per diem was reduced to four piastres in August, with probationary inspectors receiving only 2$40. NĐ (12 Aug. 1946), in CB 1946, 480. Inspectors also received a pass to travel free on trains, buses, or boats, and a special chop to stamp papers.

163. Nội Vụ NĐ (18 Feb. 1946), CB 1946, 118–19.

164. 13 April 1946, Nha Giám đốc Bình dân Học Vụ to BB; 9 May 1946, BB to Nhá Giám đốc BDHV; 25 May 1946, UBHCBB to all provinces/cities, Học Vụ dossier, GF 67.

165. 16 May 1946, BDHV to BB, BDHV dossier, GF 24.

166. Nội Vụ TT 18 June 1946, CB 1946, 347–48.

167. Ngô Văn Cát, ed., 53–54. The cover of Bình Dân Học vụ, Ngày Hội Lớn [Big Festival Day] (Hanoi: Tủ Sách của Dân Chúng, Dec. 1945), lists ten of these titles "in press."

168. 2 Oct. 1945, Bộ trưởng Bộ Quốc gia Giáo dục to các chủ tịch UB Bắc Bộ, UB Trung Bộ, UB Nam Bộ, 1945 outgoing message file, GF 58.

169. Nam Tiến 2 (8 Nov. 1945). Quyết Thắng 36 (1 May 1946).

170. Aug.–Oct. 1946 petitions of Trương Thị Tặng and official responses, Phủ An Thi (Hưng Yên) dossier, GF 32.

171. 26 July 1946, TT Tổng giám đốc BDHV, CB 1946, 433–34. The age categories were eight to fifteen, sixteen to fifty, and over fifty. Hội Khoa Học Lịch Sử Việt Nam, Ký Ức, 174–77.

172. Bản kế tình hình BDHV tính đến 1-7-46 của các tỉnh Bắc Bộ, attached to 12 Aug. 1946 BDHV to chủ tịch UBHCBB, BDHV dossier, GF 24. Two provinces remained out of contact (Lai Châu and Lào Cai), and six provinces were recorded as "movement still not widespread," hence no figures.

173. 29 July 1946, UBHC Ninh Bình to BB, Cưỡng bách học quốc ngữ 1946 dossier, GF 66.

174. Báo cáo về tình hình Bắc Bộ, phòng chủ tịch dossier, GF 19. Xiển also reported printing of 1,125,530 books and booklets for use in northern literacy classes.

175. Nguyễn Trọng Cổn, NCLS 186 (May/June 1979): 39.

176. Ngô Văn Cát, ed., 58.

177. 10 Sept. 1946, Bộ trưởng Bộ Quốc gia Giáo dục to Bộ Nội Vụ, BDHV dossier, GF 24.

178. NĐ (10 July 1946), in CB 1946, 389. NĐ (14 Oct. 1946), in CB 1946, 598–99.

179. Nha Bình Dân Học Vụ, Vần Quốc Ngữ [The National Alphabet] (Hanoi: Tủ Sách của Dân Chúng, 1945), 1.

180. Ngô Văn Cát, ed., 45–52.

181. Anh Toan and Văn Đoan, "Văn hóa trong bộ đội" [Culture in the Army], Quân Bạch Đằng 11 (10 Nov. 1946). The authors lay out a primary program for soldiers that focuses on citizen's education, history, geography, mathematics, and general science.

182. SL (8 Sept. 1945), in CB 1945, 9.

183. 14 June 1946, Sơn La to BB; 4 July 1946, BB to Sơn La, Cưỡng bách học quốc ngữ 1946 dossier, GF 67.

184. DC 241 (13 June 1946).

185. Ngô Văn Cát, ed., 53.

186. Vũ Huy Phúc, NCLS 30 (Sept. 1961), 33–42.

187. Marr, *Vietnamese Tradition on Trial*, 115–20, 295–300, 315–21, 340–42, 375–78.

188. CQ 141 (14 Jan. 1946); and 142 (15 Jan. 1946).

189. CQ 147 (21 Jan. 1946). Hồ also offered a "self-criticism" and several formal Tết greetings. CQ 153 (28 Jan. 1946); 154 (29 Jan. 1946); and 155 (5 Feb. 1946).

190. CQ 149 (23 Jan. 1946); and 150 (24 Jan. 1946). Hội Khoa Học Lịch Sử Việt Nam, *Ký Úc*, 104–10.

191. Ban Trung Ương Vận động Đời Sống Mới, *Tiên Phong* 6 (16 Feb. 1946): 13–14, 22.

192. *Tiên Phong* 10 (1 May 1946): 2; 12 (1 June 1946). In early May, Trần Huy Liệu addressed a New Life meeting at the Hanoi Opera House standing in front of the slogan "Nationhood, Democracy, Science." Hội Khoa Học Lịch Sử Việt Nam, *Ký Úc*, 172–73.

193. CQ 205 (31 July 1946).

194. *Tiên Phong* 15–17 (19 Aug. 1946): 98–102.

195. Việt Minh social engineers did not yet give their readers new pronouns to use when addressing officials, however.

196. "Trang Đời Sống Mới" [The New Life page], CQ 306 (31 July 1946). This first New Life feature page also reported a "reform marriage ceremony" in the capital, attended by Trần Huy Liệu.

197. CQ 313 (7 Aug. 1946).

198. 25 Nov. 1945, Nha Y tế BB to BB, Cứu tế và y tế dossier, GF 12. The epidemic also spread to Trung Bộ, with seventy mortalities recorded as of 5 Nov. 1945. The glass ampoules had to be returned to the Pasteur Institute for reuse.

199. 25 Feb. 1946, BB to UBHC Hanoi, Y-tế 1946 dossier, GF 67.

200. DC (Haiphong) 177 (28 March 1946); 180 (1 April 1946); and 198 (23 April 1946). *Vui Sống* (Hanoi) 8 (16 Sept. 1946), reports a later outbreak of cholera in Huế.

201. *Quyết Thắng* 24 (16 March 1946).

202. DC (Haiphong) 169 (18 March 1946). Đặng Phong, *Lịch Sử Kinh Tế Việt Nam*, vol. 1, *1945–1954* (Hanoi: NXB KHXH, 2002), 200–203, evokes early DRV health efforts.

203. Nguyễn Bách and Trần Văn Ninh, *Bảo vệ nòi giống* (Hanoi: Quốc Tế, 1946).

204. 25 Nov. 1945, Nha Y-tế BB to BB, Cứu tế và Y tế dossier, GF 12. CQ 146 (19 Jan. 1946). *Trung Việt Tân Văn* (Hanoi) 5 (21 Feb. 1946).

205. Đặng Văn Chung, *Vui Sống* 3 (1 July 1946). Dr. Chung admitted that inoculations had side effects, and were not 100 percent effective.

206. *Vui Sống* 8 (16 Sept. 1946); 4 (16 July 1946).

207. Ngân Sách Bắc Bộ niên khoa 1946, chương 33 and 34, GF 27. The Bắc Bộ Health Bureau probably received only a fraction of this 4.2 million piastre budget projection during the course of 1946.

208. SL (19 July 1946), in CB 1946, 452–53. No allocation figures are available.

209. X&N 65 (July 1999): 12.

210. NĐ (12 Jan. 1946), in CB 1946, 56. NĐ (30 Jan. 1946), in CB 1946, 94–96. NĐ (15 July 1946), in CB 1946, 390–91.

211. *Quyết Thắng* 34 (20 April 1946).

212. Hồ Ngưng, in *Quyết Thắng* 43 (25 May 1946).

213. 15 Dec. 1945, Chủ sự Phòng Nhì monthly report, Sở Kinh tế BB dossier, GF 36. 4 Oct. 1946, BB to Bộ Xã Hội, Phòng Kinh tế outgoing message dossier, GF 77.

214. NĐ (31 Dec. 1945), in CB 1946, 28. CB 1946, 50, 297, 419.

215. 25 Nov. 1945, Nha Y-tế BB report to BB, Cứu tế và Y-tế dossier, GF 12. 17 Oct. 1946, Nha Y-tế BB report to BB, GF 19.

216. 10 Sept. 1946, Giám đốc Nha Y-tế BB to BB, Y-tế dossier, GF 42.

217. Marr, *Vietnam 1945*, 35–36.

218. *Vui Sống* 2 (16 June 1946); 4 (16 July 1946). For some years thereafter the word *"dagénan"* became a Vietnamese metaphor for power and effectiveness.

219. *Vui Sống* 5 (1 Aug. 1946).

220. SL (16 Aug. 1946), in CB 1946, 454, threatens pharmacies with fines up to ten thousand piastres and shop closure. Most northern provinces had only one pharmacy selling "western medicines" *(thuốc tây)*, and some provinces had none. File compiled 24 Nov. 1946, GF 72.

221. Vũ Văn Cẩn, *Vui Sống* 1 (1 June 1946). *Vui Sống* 9 (16 Oct. 1946).

222. *Vui Sống* 3 (1 July 1946). Florey had reached this urine extraction stage prior to linking up with American brewers in late 1941.

223. *Vui Sống* 6 (16 Aug. 1946).

224. 11 Dec. 1945, UBND Phúc Yên to UBND BB; 22 Dec. 1945, Nha Y-tế to BB; 7 Jan. 1946, UBHCBB to UBND Phúc Yên, in first personnel dossier, GF 4. David G. Marr "Vietnamese Attitudes regarding Illness and Healing," in *Death and Disease in Southeast Asia: Explorations in Social, Medical and Demographic History*, edited by Norman G. Owen (Singapore: Oxford University Press, 1987), 162–86.

225. *Vui Sống* 5 (1 Aug. 1946); 9 (16 Oct. 1946).

226. Vũ Văn Cẩn, "Vấn đề y tế thôn quê" [The problem of Rural Health], *Vui Sống* 12 (1 Dec. 1946). See also *Hà Nội Mới* 1 (9 June 1946); and 2 (16 June 1946).

227. Marr, *Vietnamese Tradition on Trial*, 212–13.

228. *Vui Sống* (Hanoi) 1 (1 June 1946). The Hippocratic symbol appears at the top left of each front page.

229. *Vui Sống* 1 (1 June 1946); 8 (16 Sept. 1946); 11 (16 Nov. 1946).

230. Dr. P. N. Khuê serial beginning *Vui Sống* 9 (16 Oct. 1946).

231. *Vui Sống* 3 (1 July 1946); 6 (16 Aug. 1946).

232. *Vui Sống* 6 (16 Aug. 1946); 7 (5 Sept. 1946).

233. "Thuốc tây và người Việt Nam" [Western medicine and Vietnamese people], *Vui Sống* 7 (5 Sept. 1946).

234. *Vui Sống* 5 (1 Aug. 1946).

235. DC 237 (8 June 1946); 241 (13 June 1946).

236. *Nam Tiến* 6 (28 Jan. 1946). Two months later, however, Hanoi was still reminding Nam Định to send this promised grain to Thái Bình. Văn Phòng BBP outgoing message file, GF 17.

237. S. Andrew Enticknap Smith, "Water First: A Political History of Hydraulics in Vietnam's Red River Delta" (PhD dissertation, Australian National University, 2002), 121–27, 196–99.

238. CQ 148 (22 Jan. 1946). DC 132 (26 Jan. 1946).

239. 8 June 1946, Tài Chính to BB, Giao thiệp Bộ Tài Chính dossier, GF 67. Later the Finance Ministry relented to the extent of allocating two hundred thousand piastres for fuel and several vehicle acquisitions.

240. Outgoing message file, Văn Phòng BBP GF 17. In early March, five provinces were criticized for tardy rice deliveries and instructed to buy quickly in the marketplace rather than continue to collect in kind.

241. (?) Feb. 1946, BB to Tài Chính; 26 Feb. 1946, Thủy Nông to Công Chính BB, Hộ đê dossier, GF 47. Collapse of a Đáy River dam sluice gate had contributed to disaster further down the Red River in August 1945. Smith, 198.

242. 25 April 1946, Tờ trình UBHCBB, Bộ Tài Chính dossier, Văn Phòng BBP, GF 52. 12 April 1946 minutes, Hộ đê dossier, GF 35.

243. CB 1946, 302-3. CQ 256 (3 June 1946). Việt Nam 170 (9 June 1946), emphasizes Hồ's warning that a military court awaits anyone jeopardizing the dikes.

244. SL (9 Aug. 1946), Giao thiệp Bộ Tài Chính dossier, GF 67.

245. 7 June 1946 memo and pen attachment, Hộ đê dossier, GF 19.

246. Chống nạn Hồng Thủy ở Bắc Bộ [Fighting Red River Disaster in the North] (Hanoi: Nhà In Rạng Đông, 1946). Copies in GF 35 and 75. One thousand copies were printed, plus three thousand copies of the section on rising water scenarios.

247. Undated, UBHC Hải Dương to BB, Hộ đê dossier, GF 16. Coolies were to receive one kilogram of rice per day, estimated to cost three piastres per kilogram.

248. Chống nạn Hồng Thủy, 12-13. Cadres also had to locate a supply of torches for night work, presumably from nearby villages.

249. Messages exchanged 21 May to 20 June 1946, Hộ Đê dossier, GF 35.

250. June 1946 Hanoi dike inspection, Phòng Hộ đê (1946) dossier, GF 75.

251. CQ 256 (3 June 1946); 262 (10 June 1946); 264 (12 June 1946); 265 (13 June 1946); 297 (20 July 1946); 298 (21 July 1946).

252. 11 July 1946, Tổng Giám đốc Nha Thanh Niên và Thể Dục to BB, GF 53. Early August Trại Hộ đê chart, Văn Phòng BBP, GF 48.

253. 8 Aug. 1946 report after two-day inspection, Phòng Hộ đê BBP dossier, GF 39.

254. 9 Aug. 1946, Hội đồng Trung ương Hộ đê minutes, Hộ đê 1946 dossier, GF 76.

255. Nguyễn Xiển, "Báo cáo về tình hình Bắc bộ," 9, GF 19. I suspect labor hours were not recorded or reported in some localities.

256. Việt Nam 17 (4 Dec. 1945); 23 (11 Dec. 1945). Gió Mới 13 (22 Feb. 1946).

257. DC 334 (5 Oct. 1946). Quân Bạch Đằng 8 (Sept. 1946).

258. A highly complementary account of female guerrillas in Quảng Ngãi is serialized in the February and March issues of Quyết Thắng (Huế). The cover of Tương Lai 7 (8 Nov. 1945), portrays two Nam Bộ women ambushing a French auto. Phụ nữ Nga với cuộc cách mệnh xã hội [Russian Women and the Social Revolution] (Hanoi, 1946).

259. Quân Bạch Đằng 1 (1 July 1946); and 2 (16 July 1946).

260. Kháng Chiến 1 (2 Sept. 1946); 3 (23 Sept. 1946).

261. Sao Vàng 24 (14 Nov. 1946).

262. Hồ sơ các việc năm 1946, Văn Phòng, ANOM, INDO, CR 141. 17 April 1946, BB to Nha Cứu tế TU, Cứu đói dossier, GF 48.

263. DC 211 (9 May 1946). CQ 265 (13 June 1946). The GF files contain some petitions from male villagers protesting communal land for women.

264. DC 73 (17 Nov. 1945).

265. CQ 405 (14 Nov. 1946) does carry a photo of the eight female delegates, all of whom appear to be in their twenties.

266. Lê Thị Xuyến (Mme Phan Thanh) was a full member, and Nguyễn Thị Thục Viên an alternate member. Nguyễn Tố Uyên, 260.

267. On Popular Front discourse over the question of women, see Marr, *Vietnamese Tradition on Trial*, 228–47.

268. Lê Thị Nhâm Tuyết, *Phụ nữ Việt Nam qua các thời đại* [Vietnamese Women across the Ages] (Hanoi: NXB KHXH, 1973), 225–27.

269. Sept.–Dec. 1945 reports, Thanh Tra Lao Động dossier, GF 38. The inspectorate claimed to have resolved more than half of these disputes.

270. 18 Sept. 1945, Ủy Ban Công nhân hãng xe hơi AVIAT to UBNDBB, travel permit dossier, GF 45.

271. 13 Oct. 1945 petition from Một nhóm Công nhân Hoàng Diệu, outgoing file, GF 13.

272. CQ 75 (27 Oct. 1945). Lê Văn Hiến spoke next, followed by an unnamed worker representative, then the formation of a committee and discussion from the floor.

273. 19 Oct. 1945, Ủy ban Trung Ương Tổng hội Viên chức Cứu Quốc to Ủy ban các Sở, Service Economique Local dossier, GF 34.

274. *Quyết Thắng* 49 (15 June 1946).

275. *Nam Tiến* 3 (14 Dec. 1945). DC 81 (27 Nov. 1945).

276. DC 327 (26 Sept. 1946). The total reported increase was not impressive.

277. Hợp tác xã Tổng Liên đoàn Lao động Việt Nam dossier, GF 45.

278. 9 Dec. 1946, Kinh tế Trung bộ to UBHCBB, Phòng Kinh tế outgoing message file, GF 41.

279. *Vui Sống* 2 (16–30 June 1946).

280. DC 202 (25 April 1946); 204 (30 April 1946). *Gió Biển* 2 (11 May 1946).

281. *Quyết Thắng* 25 (20 March 1946).

282. CQ 406 (15 Nov. 1946); 417 (26 Nov. 1946). DC 372 (18 Nov. 1946). *Kháng Chiến* 5 (7 Dec. 1946). The Tổng Bộ also donated ten thousand piastres to the strike fund.

283. CB 1946, 19.

284. Trí Quang Thiền Sư, "Phật giáo với Quốc gia" [Buddhism and the Nation], *Dân Mới* (Vinh) 1 (1 May 1946): 5.

285. *Quyết Thắng* 2 (8 Oct. 1945). It was hoped to extend this organization throughout Trung bộ.

286. 17 Nov. 1945, Ủy ban Chấp hành Tăng già Phật giáo Việt Nam to UBNDBB, Associations dossier, ANOM, INDO, CR 141. 17 Jan. 1946, Ủy ban Tăng già Bắc Bộ to Chủ tịch UBNDBB, GF 65. On 25 March 1946, the Interior Ministry accepted de facto continuation of the committee subject to de jure approval in the future.

287. *Sao Vàng* 2 (6 June 1946).

288. *Quyết Thắng* 23 (13 March 1946). Thích Mật Thể is said to have withdrawn his objections later, and the letter was dispatched.

289. DC 210 (8 May 1946); 325 (24 Sept. 1946).

290. "Thông cáo: Tự chỉ trích," *Quyết Thắng* 8 (19 Nov. 1945).

291. 26 Dec. 1945, Chấp ủy Phật giáo Cứu Quốc Hà Nội to Nội Vụ, 1946 Hanoi (việc lưu) dossier, GF 69.

292. ĐL 215 (4 Aug. 1946).

293. Vấn đề tạp dịch, dossier, GF 24. The many local variations of existing practice were ignored once the state declared a single national policy.

294. Annex to 17 Oct. 1945 decree on election procedures, CB 1945, 45.

295. 3 Dec. 1945, Hội nghị đại biểu dân tộc thiểu số VN dossier, GF 68. *Quyết Thắng* 16 (Tết 1946 issue). *Thời mới* 12 (9 Dec. 1945). Hội Khoa Học Lịch Sử Việt Nam, *Ký Úc*, 66–67.

296. HCMTT 4, 61–62. Marr, *Vietnam 1945*, 179–81.

297. 3 Jan. 1946 petition from Lục Phúc Đồng and subsequent documents, Lạng Sơn (việc lưu) dossier, GF 11.

298. *Lịch sử Đảng Cộng Sản Việt Nam: Trích Văn Kiện Đảng* [History of the Vietnam Communist Party: Extracts from Party Documents], vol. 1, *1927–1945* (Hanoi, 1979), 318–23.

299. *Quyết Thắng* 5 (29 Oct. 1945); 9 (25 Nov. 1945); and 10 (9 Dec. 1945). *Chiến Sĩ* 6 (21 Dec. 1945). *Thời mới* 12 (9 Dec. 1945). *Sao Vàng* 15 (12 Sept. 1946).

300. *Quyết Thắng* 10 (2 Dec. 1945).

301. Ngạch Thượng du (1946) dossier, GF 25.

302. 26 Oct. 1946, UBHC Hòa Bình to BB, dossier 162, GF 67.

303. 18 Aug. 1946, Vấn đề dân tộc thiểu số với đề nghị xin lập bên cạnh Nghị Viện Việt Nam một Hội Nghị các Dân Tộc, GF 67. Quỳnh belonged to a major Thái family in Lào Cai, with one relative chairing the province administrative committee.

304. CB 1946, 495, 525, 599, 625.

305. 8 Nov. 1946, Giám đốc Nha Dân Tộc Thiểu số to ten provinces, outgoing message file, GF 41.

306. 8 July 1946, Quốc Phòng to BB, GF 56.

307. 26 Oct. 1946, BB to Thuế Quan BB, outgoing message file, GF 41.

308. 25 Oct. 1946, UBHCBB to eleven province committees, GF 67.

309. Dr. Phạm Văn Huyên, *Gió Mới* 29 (19 July 1946).

310. Chim Bể, *Quân Bạch Đằng* 7 (2 Sept. 1946).

311. *Sao Vàng* 9 (25 July 1946).

312. *Kháng Chiến* 3 (23 Sept. 1946). *Độc Lập chủ nhật* 7 (27 Oct. 1946).

313. *Dân Mới* (Vinh) 4 (15 June 1946). *Kháng Chiến* 2 (2 Sept. 1946). *Quyết Thắng* 43 (25 May 1946).

314. CQ 279 (29 June 1946). No consideration was given yet to writing and reading in minority scripts.

315. DC 212 (10 May 1946).

316. 23 June 1946, Nghị quyết của toàn kỳ đại biểu Khoách Đại, VKĐTT 8, 77, 82.

317. *Văn Kiện Đảng về Kháng chiến*, vol. 1 *1945–1950* (Hanoi: NXB ST, 1986), 67–68. VKĐTT 8, 107.

318. In May 1947, the DRV Information Bureau in Paris released a French-language pamphlet affirming that Hồ Chí Minh and Nguyễn Ái Quốc were identical, but a similar

pamphlet printed in Nam Bộ the same month omitted that detail. *Le President Ho Chi Minh* and *Tiểu Sử Hồ Chí Minh*, both preserved in the Vietnam National Library collection.

319. HCMTT 4, 10–71.

320. CQ 69 (17 Oct. 1945). 19 Oct. 1945, Thư Chủ tịch Hồ Chí Minh to all committees, GF 76. HCMTT 4, 35–37. This statement also appeared in December in a southern periodical, *Cảm Tử (Death Volunteers)*, according to French intelligence. Propaganda Việt Minh dossier, CP 128.

321. For a well-informed description of Hồ as DRV president, see Pierre Brocheux, *Ho Chi Minh: A Biography* (Cambridge: Cambridge University Press, 2007).

322. President Hồ received from the Northern Region Economic Office significant quantities of rationed soap, which he may have given to visitors and certainly shared with his staff. For example, ten kilograms of soap were provided to Cụ Chủ tịch on 29 Nov. 1946, Phiếu mua hàng do sở Kinh Tế BB kiểm soát, GF 45. Hội Khoa Học Lịch Sử Việt Nam, *Ký Úc*, 72, 171.

323. CQ 181 (9 March 1946); 188 (16 March 1946).

324. 15 Jan. 1946, Nội vụ to all BBP offices, outgoing message file, GF 13. The working day began at seven thirty.

325. 29 April 1946, Hưng Yên to TW, periodic report file, Văn Phòng BB, GF 38.

326. "Hồ Chủ tịch kinh lý Nam Định 10-1-46," *Nam Tiến* 6 (28 Jan. 1946).

327. DC 346 (19 Oct. 1946); 347 (21 Oct. 1946); and 348 (22 Oct. 1946). *Quân Bạch Đằng* 11 (10 Nov. 1946). CQ 382 (21 Oct. 1946); 383 (22 Oct. 1946); 384 (23 Oct. 1946); and 386 (25 Oct. 1946). *Nhiệm vụ tuần báo* 4 (10 Nov. 1946). Fonde, 274–75. Nguyễn Bá Khoản, 42–43.

328. 14 Nov. 1946, BB to UBHC Vĩnh Yên, outgoing message file, Văn Phòng Mật, GF 31.

329. 23 Nov. 1946, UBHCBB to UBHC Hải Dương, plus attachments, An Trí dossier, GF 30.

330. *Việt Nam* 22 (9 Dec. 1945); 23 (11 Dec. 1945).

331. Some participants in the Huế May Day parade questioned this practice. *Quyết Thắng* 38 (8 May 1946).

332. Thăng Long, ed., *Nhớ Nam Bộ*, 517.

333. *Kháng Chiến* 9 (25 Nov. 1946). On the same occasion, an old man cried out, "Elder Hồ! How come you haven't been able to drive them [the French] out?"

334. *Đồng Minh* 19 (24 Feb. 1946).

335. *Dân Quốc* 85 (13 Dec. 1945). CQ 116 (13 Dec. 1946); 118 (15 Dec. 1946). *Chiến Sĩ* 9 (11 Jan. 1946).

336. *Dân Quốc* 30 (10 Oct. 1945); 69 (24 Nov. 1945). *Kháng Chiến* 9 (25 Nov. 1946).

337. *Độc Lập chủ nhật* 5 (13 Oct. 1946).

338. CQ 329 (27 Aug. 1946). ĐL 233 (29 Aug. 1946). *Kháng Chiến* 1 (2 Sept. 1946).

339. 13 Nov. 1946, Bộ Nội vụ to UBHCBB, GF 141. In March 1946, a "Hồ Chí Minh Company" of combatants had been formed in Bến Tre province in the Mekong delta. Thăng Long, ed., *Nhớ Nam Bộ*, 253–58.

SOURCES

ARCHIVES

Archives nationales d'outre-mer, Aix-en-Provence (ANOM)

Fonds conseiller politique (CP)

Fonds du gouvernement de fait (GF). The GF files were seized at the Bắc Bộ Phủ (Northern Region Office) by French forces on 20 December 1946, then eventually made their way to unsorted cartons in the Aix archives. Wherever possible I cite a dossier name as well as carton number. While the GF materials are delightfully rich and diverse, certain topics are seldom encountered, including party politics, foreign relations, ideology, history, religion, and traditional customs.

Indochine nouveau fonds (INDO)

Service historique de la Défense (SHD), Vincennes [Formerly the Service historique de l'Armée de terre (SHAT)]

Fonds 10H Archives de l'Indochine

U.S. National Archives and Records Administration (NARA), Suitland, Maryland

Record Group 59: Department of State Decimal File

OFFICIAL GAZETTES

The *Việt Nam Dân Quốc Công Báo* [Vietnam National Gazette] began publication on 29 September 1945, patterned on the former *Journal officiel de l'Indochine*. Up to sixty-five hundred copies were printed and distributed weekly to central offices, local administrative committees, and National Guard units. Unable to locate more than a sprinkling of original issues of the *Công Báo*, I relied on a 1951 reprinting by the prime minister's office in the Việt Bắc, in which weekly issues have been bound and paginated by year (1945, 1946). Not all decrees and edicts were published in the *Công Báo*.

SERIALS CONSULTED AT VIETNAM NATIONAL LIBRARY, HANOI

Bạn Gái [Women], Hanoi, private
Cấp Tiến [Progressive], Hanoi, private
Chiến Khu [Battle Zone], Thái Nguyên, National Guard
Chiến Sĩ [Combatant], Huế, National Guard
Chính Nghĩa tuần báo [Righteous Cause weekly], Hanoi, Nationalist Party
Cờ Giải Phóng [Liberation Flag], Hanoi, ICP
Công An Mới [New Police], Hanoi, Northern Region Police
Cứu Quốc [National Salvation], Hanoi, Việt Minh
Đa Minh [Dominican], Nam Định, Catholic
Dân Chủ [Democracy], Haiphong, Việt Minh
Dân Mới [New Citizen], Vinh, Việt Minh
Dân Quốc [People-Country], Hanoi, private
Độc Lập [Independence], Hanoi, Democratic Party
Độc Lập chủ nhật [Sunday Independence], Hanoi, Democratic Party
Đồng Minh [Allies], Hanoi, Revolutionary League
Dư Luận [Public Opinion], Hanoi, private
Đường Sắt [Railways], Hanoi, Việt Minh
Gió Biển [Sea Wind], Haiphong, Việt Minh
Gió Mới [New Wind], Hanoi, General Student Association
Hà Nội Mới [New Hanoi], Hanoi, private
Hình Sự Công Báo [Criminal Law Gazette], Hanoi, Northern Region Police
Hướng Đạo Thẳng Tiến [Scouts Advance], Hanoi, Boy Scouts
Kháng Chiến [Resistance], Quảng Ngãi, Southern Resistance Committee
L'Entente, Hanoi, French government
Le Peuple, Hanoi, Việt Minh
Liên Đoàn Công Giáo [Catholic Alliance], Huế, Catholic
Nam Tiến [Southern Advance], Nam Định, Việt Minh
Ngày Mới [New Day], Haiphong, private
Nhiệm Vụ tuần báo [Responsibility weekly], Hanoi, Catholic
Quân Bạch Đằng [Bach Dang Army], Kiến An, National Guard
Quyết Thắng [Determined to Win], Huế, Việt Minh
Sao Vàng [Yellow Star], Hanoi, National Guard
Sự Thật [Truth], Hanoi, ICP
Thời Mới [New Times], Hanoi, private
Tiến Hóa [Progress], Quảng Ngãi, Việt Minh
Tiên Phong [Vanguard], Hanoi, Việt Minh

Trung Việt Tân Văn [China Vietnam News], Hanoi, overseas Chinese
Tương Lai [Future], Hanoi, private
Việt Nam, Hanoi, Nationalist Party
Vui Sống [Joy in Life], Hanoi, Army Medical Corps

REFERENCE WORKS

Bùi Phụng. *Từ Điển Việt-Anh* [Vietnamese-English Dictionary]. Hanoi: Trường Đại Học Tổng Hợp Hà Nội xuất bản, 1986.

Dalloz, Jacques. *Dictionnaire de la Guerre d'Indochine, 1945–1954.* Paris: Armand Colin, 2006.

Đào Duy Anh. *Hán Việt Từ Điển* [Chinese-Vietnamese Dictionary]. Saigon: Trường Thi, 1957.

Goscha, Christopher E. *Historical Dictionary of the Indochina War (1945–1954).* Copenhagen: NIAS Press, 2011.

Nguyễn Đình Hòa. *Vietnamese-English Dictionary.* Saigon: Bình Minh, 1959.

Le Robert & Collins Pratique: Anglais. Paris: Dictionnaires Le Robert, 2004.

Việt Nam, Nước Cộng Hòa Xã Hội Chủ Nghĩa. *Tập Bản Đồ Hành Chính* [Vietnam Administrative Atlas]. Hanoi: NXB Bản Đồ, 2003.

Võ Quang Uẩn, editor. *Thư Mục Sách Kháng Chiến, 1945–1954* [Catalog of Resistance Books, 1945–1954]. Hanoi: Thư Viện Quốc Gia Việt Nam, 2002.

SELECTED BIBLIOGRAPHY

d'Arcy, Jean. "Confrontation des Thèses françaises et vietnamiennes," *Politique Etrangère* (Paris) 12 (July 1947): 322–44.

Azeau, Henri. *Ho Chi Minh, dernière chance : La conférence franco-vietnamienne de Fontainebleau, juillet 1946.* Paris: Flammarion, 1968.

Bartholomew-Feis, Dixie R. *The OSS and Ho Chi Minh: Unexpected Allies in the War Against Japan.* Lawrence: University Press of Kansas, 2006.

Bodinier, Gilbert, compiler and editor. *La guerre d'Indochine, 1945–1954: Textes et documents.* 5 vols. Vincennes: Service Historique de l'Armée de Terre, 1987.

Boudarel, Georges, and Nguyen Van Ky. *Hanoi 1936–1996: Du drapeau rouge au billet vert.* Paris: Les Éditions Autrement, 1997.

Bourdeaux, Pascal. "Approaches statistiques de la communauté du bouddhisme Hòa Hảo (1939–1954)." In *Naissance d'un État-Parti: Le Viet Nam depuis 1945 / The Birth of a Party-State: Vietnam Since 1945,* edited by Christopher E. Goscha and Benoît de Tréglodé, 277–304. Paris: Les Indes Savantes, 2004.

Bradley, Mark Philip. *Imagining Vietnam and America: The Making of Postcolonial Vietnam, 1919–1950.* Chapel Hill and London: University of North Carolina Press, 2000.

Brocheux, Pierre. "L'économie de la résistance vietnamienne, 1945–1954." In *Les Guerres d'Indochine de 1945 à 1975,* edited by Charles-Robert Ageron and Philippe Devillers, 77–92. Paris: Institut d'Histoire du Temps Présent, 1996.

———. "The Economy of War as Prelude to a 'Socialist Economy': The case of the Vietnamese Resistance against the French, 1945–1954." In *Viet Nam Exposé: French Scholarship on Twentieth-Century Vietnamese Society*, edited by Gisele Bousquet and Pierre Brocheux, 313–30. Ann Arbor: University of Michigan Press, 2002.

———. *Ho Chi Minh: Du révolutionnaire à l'icône*. Paris: Editions Payot & Rivages, 2003. Translated by Claire Duiker as *Ho Chi Minh: A Biography*. Cambridge: Cambridge University Press, 2007.

Brocheux, Pierre, and Daniel Hémery. *Indochina: An Ambiguous Colonization, 1858–1954*. Berkeley: University of California Press, 2009.

Bui Dinh Thanh. "The First Year of Resistance in South Vietnam (1945–1946)." *Vietnamese Studies* 7 (1965): 61–97.

Chen, King C. "The Chinese Occupation of Vietnam, 1945–46." *France-Asie/Asia* 196 (first quarter 1969): 3–28.

———. *Vietnam and China, 1938–1954*. Princeton, NJ: Princeton University Press, 1969.

Đặng Phong. *Lịch Sử Kinh Tế Việt Nam 1945–2000* [History of Vietnam's Economy 1945–2000]. Vol. 1, *1945–1954*. Hanoi: NXB KHXH, 2002.

Deroo, Eric, and Christophe Dutrône, *Le Việt-Minh*. Paris: Les Indes Savantes, 2008. Photo compilation.

Desiré, Michel (Commandant). *La Campagne d'Indochine (1945–1954): Bibliographie*. 4 vols. Vincennes: Service Historique de l'Armée de Terre, 1971–77.

Devillers, Philippe. *Histoire du Viet-nam de 1940 à 1952*. Paris: Éditions de Seuil, 1952.

———. *Paris-Saigon-Hanoi: Les archives de la guerre 1944–1947*. (Paris: Éditions Gallimand/Julliard, 1988).

Đinh Thị Thu Cúc, editor. *Lịch Sử Việt Nam* [History of Vietnam]. Vol. 10, *1945–1950*. Hanoi: NXB KHXH, 2007.

Duiker, William J. *The Communist Road to Power in Vietnam*. Boulder, CO: Westview Press, 1981.

———. *Ho Chi Minh: A Life*. New York: Hyperion, 2000.

Dunn, Peter M. *The First Vietnam War*. London: C. Hurst & Co, 1985.

Dương Trung Quốc, Võ Nguyên Giáp, et al. *Tướng Nguyễn Sơn* [General Nguyen Son]. Hanoi: NXB Lao Động, 1994.

Elliott, David W. P. *The Vietnamese War: Revolution and Social Change in the Mekong Delta, 1930–1975*. 2 vols. Armonk, NY & London: M. E. Sharpe, 2003.

Fall, Bernard B. *The Viet Minh Regime: Government and Administration in the Democratic Republic of Vietnam*. Ithaca, NY: Southeast Asia Program, Cornell University, 1954.

———. *Le Viet Minh, 1945–1960*. Paris: Armand Colin, 1960.

Fonde, Jean-Julien. *Traitez à tout prix . . . Leclerc et le Viet Nam*. Paris: Robert Laffont, 1971.

Goscha, Christopher E. *Thailand and the Southeast Asian Networks of the Vietnamese Revolution, 1885–1954*. Richmond, UK: Curzon Press, 1999.

———. "Le contexte asiatique de la guerre franco-vietnamienne: Réseaux, relations et économie (d'août 1945 à mai 1954)." Thèse de doctorate d'histoire, l'Ecole pratique des hautes études, 2000. Two volumes plus index.

———. "'La guerre par d'autres moyens': Réflexions sur la guerre du Viet Minh dans le Sud-Vietnam de 1945 à 1951." *Guerre mondiales et conflits contemporains* 206 (2002): 29–57.

———. "A 'Popular' side of the Vietnamese Army: General Nguyen Binh and the Early War in the South (1910–1951)." In *Naissance d'un État-Parti: Le Viet Nam depuis 1945 / The Birth of a Party-State: Vietnam Since 1945*, edited by Christopher E. Goscha and Benoît de Tréglodé, 325–53. Paris: Les Indes Savantes, 2004.

———. "Intelligence in a Time of Decolonization: The Case of the Democratic Republic of Vietnam at War (1945–50)." *Intelligence and National Security* (Oxfordshire) 22, no. 1 (Feb. 2007): 100–138.

———. *Vietnam: Un État né de la Guerre 1945–1954.* Paris: Armand Colin, 2011. Translated by Agathe Larcher.

Goscha, Christopher E., and Benoît de Tréglodé, editors. *Naissance d'un État-Parti: Le Viet Nam depuis 1945 / The Birth of a Party-State: Vietnam Since 1945.* Paris: Les Indes Savantes, 2004.

Gras, Yves. *Histoire de la guerre d'Indochine.* 2nd ed. Paris: Denoël, 1992.

Guillemot, François. "Vietnamese Nationalist Revolutionaries and the Japanese Occupation: The case of the Dai Viet Parties (1936–1946)." In *Imperial Japan and National Identities in Asia 1895–1945*, edited by Li Narangoa and Robert Cribb, 220–48. London & New York: Routledge Curzon, 2003.

———. "Au Coeur de la fracture vietnamienne: L'Elimination de l'opposition nationaliste et anticolonialiste dans le Nord du Viet Nam (1945–1946)." In *Naissance d'un État-Parti: Le Viet Nam depuis 1945 / The Birth of a Party-State: Vietnam Since 1945*, edited by Christopher E. Goscha and Benoît de Tréglodé, 175–216. Paris: Les Indes Savantes, 2004.

———. *Dai Viêt, indépendance, et révolution au Viêt-Nam: L'échec de la troisième voie (1938–1955).* Paris: Les Indes Savantes, 2012.

Hoàng Hạnh, Triệu Hiền, and Việt Hồng, editors. *Từ Đà Lạt đến Paris* [From Dalat to Paris]. Hanoi: NXB Hà Nội, 1996.

Hoàng Văn Đào. *Việt-Nam Quốc Dân Đảng: Lịch Sử Đấu Tranh Cận Đại 1927–1954* [Vietnam Nationalist Party: History of Struggle 1927–1954]. Saigon: Giảng Dòng Nguyễn Hòa Hiệp, 1964.

Hồ Chí Minh. *Hồ Chí Minh Toàn Tập* [Complete Works of Ho Chi Minh]. Vol. 4, *1945–47.* Hanoi: NXB ST, 1984.

———. *CD-ROM Hồ Chí Minh Toàn Tập* [CD-ROM of Complete Works of Ho Chi Minh]. Hanoi: NXB CTQG, 2001. Also contains video, photos, voice, and music.

Hội Khoa Học Lịch Sử Việt Nam, *Ký Úc về những ngày Độc Lập Đầu Tiên 1945–1946* [Memories of the Early Days of Independence 1945–1946]. Hanoi: NXB Thời Đại and Tạp chí Xưa & Nay, 2010. 177 photographs with captions.

Lawrence, Mark Atwood. *Assuming the Burden: Europe and the American Commitment to the War in Vietnam.* Berkeley: University of California Press, 2005.

———, and Fredrik Logevall, editors, *The First Vietnam War: Colonial Conflict and Cold War Crisis.* Cambridge, MA: Harvard University Press, 2007.

Lê Đình Cẩm, et al. *Lịch Sử Trường Sĩ Quan Lục Quân Trần Quốc Tuấn* [History of the Tran Quoc Tuan Army Officer Academy]. Hanoi: QĐND, 1985.

Lê Giản. *Những Ngày Sóng Gió: Hồi Ký* [Days of Adversity: Memoirs]. Hanoi: NXB Thanh Niên, 1985.

Lê Văn Hiến. *Nhật Ký cuả Một Bộ Trưởng* [Diary of a Government Minister], 2 vols. Đà Nẵng: NXB Đà Nẵng, 1995.

Lévy, Roger. *L'Indochine et ses Traités: 1946.* Paris: Hartmann, 1947.

Lin Hua. *Chiang Kai-shek, de Gaulle contre Ho Chi Minh: Vietnam 1945–1946.* Paris: L'Harmattan, 1994.

Lockhart, Greg. *Nation in Arms: The Origins of the People's Army of Vietnam.* Sydney: Allen & Unwin, 1989.

Marr, David G. *Vietnamese Tradition on Trial, 1920–1945.* Berkeley: University of California Press, 1981.

———. *Vietnam 1945: The Quest for Power.* Berkeley: University of California Press, 1995.

———. "Beyond High Politics: State Formation in Northern Vietnam, 1945–1946." In *Naissance d'un État-Parti: Le Viet Nam depuis 1945 / The Birth of a Party-State: Vietnam Since 1945,* edited by Christopher E. Goscha and Benoît de Tréglodé, 25–60. Paris: Les Indes Savantes, 2004.

———. "Creating Defense Capacity in Vietnam, 1945–1947." In *The First Vietnam War: The First Vietnam War: Colonial Conflict and Cold War Crisis,* edited by Mark Atwood Lawrence and Fredrik Logevall, 74–104. Cambridge, MA: Harvard University Press, 2007.

Martin, Françoise. *Heures tragiques au Tonkin (9 mars 1945–18 mars 1946).* Paris: Berger-Levrault, 1948.

McAlister, John T. *Vietnam: The Origins of Revolution.* New York: Alfred A. Knopf, 1969.

———, and Paul Mus. *The Vietnamese and their Revolution.* New York: Harper & Row, 1970.

Mus, Paul. *Viet Nam: Sociologie d'une guerre.* Paris: Éditions du Seuil, 1952.

Nam Long, et al. *Trung Đoàn 96: Những Năm Tháng Không Thể Nào Quên: Khởi Đầu* [Regiment 96: Unforgettable Months and Years: The Beginning]. Đà Nẵng: NXB Đà Nẵng, 1996.

Ngô Văn Chiêu. *Journal d'un combattant Viet Minh.* Paris: Éditions du Seuil, 1955.

Ngô Vi Thiện, editor. *Lịch Sử Hậu Cần Quân Đội Nhân Dân Việt Nam* [History of Vietnam People's Army Logistics]. Vol. 1, *1944–1954.* Hanoi: NXB QĐND, 1995.

———, et al., editors. *Trần Đăng Ninh: Con Người và Lịch Sử* [Tran Dang Ninh: Character and History]. Hanoi: NXB CTQG, 1996.

Nguyễn Bá Khoản, *Những khoảnh khắc Lịch Sử qua Ống Kính Nguyễn Bá Khoản* [Historical Moments via Nguyen Ba Khoan's Camera]. Hanoi: NXB QDND, 1997. English as well as Vietnamese captions.

Nguyễn Bằng. *Giữ Hay Bỏ Chế Độ Uỷ Ban Nhân Dân* [Keep or Discard the People's Committee System]. Hanoi: Tự Cường, 1946.

———. *Nghị Viện* [Parliament]. Hanoi: Quang Trung Thư Xã, 1946.

Nguyễn Duy Tường and Đỗ Xuân Tuất, editors. *Việt Nam 1945–1946: Thời Điểm Quyết Định Sáng Suốt cuả Đảng* [Vietnam 1945–1946: The Party's Decisive Enlightened Moment]. Hanoi: NXB QĐND, 2005.

Nguyễn Hùng. *Nguyễn Bình: Huyền Thoại và Sự Thật* [Nguyen Binh: Myth and Reality]. Hanoi: NXB Văn Học, 1995.

———. *Nam Bộ: Những Nhân Vật Một Thời Vang Bóng* [Southern Vietnam: Persons in a Vibrant Time]. Hồ Chí Minh City: NXB Công An Nhân Dân, 2003.

Nguyễn Khánh Hòa, et al., editors. *Anh Cả Nguyễn Lương Bằng* [Eldest Brother Nguyen Luong Bang]. Hanoi: NXB CTQG, 2005.

Nguyễn Kiến Giang. *Việt Nam năm đầu tiên sau Cách Mạng Tháng Tám*. [Vietnam's First Year Following the August Revolution]. Hanoi: NXB ST, 1961.

Nguyễn Kỳ Nam. *Hồi Ký 1925–1964* [Memoirs 1925–1964]. Vol. 2, *1945–1954*. Saigon: Dân Chủ Mới, 1964.

Nguyễn Phụng Minh, editor. *Nam Trung Bộ Kháng Chiến 1945–1975* [South Central Region Resistance 1945–1975]. 2nd ed. Hanoi: NXB CTQG, 1995.

Nguyễn Quang Ân, *Việt Nam: Những Thay Đổi Địa Danh và Địa Giới Hành Chính 1945–2002* [Vietnam: Changes in Administrative Names and Demarcations 1945–2002]. Hanoi: NXB Thông Tấn, 2003.

Nguyễn Quốc Dũng and Trần Văn Thức (Viện Lịch Sử Quân Sự). *Chi Đội Vì Dân* [Vi Dan Detachment]. Hanoi: NXB QĐND, 1998.

Nguyễn Tố Uyên. *Công cuộc Bảo Vệ và Xây Dựng Chính Quyền Nhân Dân ở Việt Nam trong những Năm 1945–1946* [Protecting and Building People's Government in 1945–1946]. Hanoi: NXB KHXH, 1998.

Nguyễn Văn Tạo. *Bài Diễn Văn của Ông Nguyễn Văn Tạo trước Quốc Hội Việt Nam* [Address of Mr. Nguyen Van Tao before the Vietnam National Assembly]. Hanoi: NXB CQ, Nov. 1946.

Nguyễn Việt, editor. *Nam Bộ và Nam Phần Trung Bộ trong Hai Năm Đầu Kháng Chiến (1945–1946)* [Southern and south-central Regions in the First Two Years of Resistance (1945–1946)]. Hanoi: NXB Văn Sử Địa, 1957.

Patti, Archimedes L. A. *Why Viet Nam? Prelude to America's Albatross*. Berkeley and Los Angeles: University of California Press, 1980.

Phạm Khắc Hoè. *Từ Triều Đình Huế đến Chiến Khu Việt Bắc* [From the Hue Court to the Viet Bac War Zone]. Hanoi: NXB Hà Nội, 1983.

Phạm Văn Đồng. *Bản Báo Cáo của Ông Phạm Văn Đồng trước Quốc Hội Việt Nam* [Mr. Pham Van Dong's Report before the Vietnam National Assembly]. Hanoi: NXB CQ, Nov. 1946.

Phan Ánh Tuyết, compiler. *Toàn Quốc Kháng Chiến 1946* [All-Country Resistance 1946]. Hanoi: NXB Lao Động, 2009. Photo collection.

Phan Văn Cẩn, editor. *Lịch Sử Bộ Tổng Tham Mưu trong Kháng Chiến Chống Pháp (1945–1954)* [History of the General Staff During Resistance to the French (1945–1954)]. Hanoi: Bộ Tổng Tham Mưu, 1991.

Porter, Gareth, editor. *Vietnam: The Definitive Documentation of Human Decisions*. 2 vols. Stanfordville: Coleman Enterprises, 1972.

Quân Đội Nhân Dân Việt Nam. *Lịch Sử Ngành Cơ Yếu Quân Đội Nhân Dân Việt Nam* [History of the Vietnam People's Army Cryptographic Branch]. Hanoi: NXB QĐND, 1990.

————, (Ban Ký Sự Lịch Sử). *Trận Đánh Ba Mươi Năm: Ký sự Lịch Sử* [Thirty Years of Battle: Historical Recollections]. Vol. 1, *1945–1950*. Hanoi: NXB QĐND, 1983.

————, (Ban Nghiên Cứu Lịch Sử Quân Đội). *Lịch Sử Quân Đội Nhân Dân Việt Nam* [History of the Vietnam People's Army]. Vol. 1, *1930–1954*. Hanoi: NXB QĐND, 1974.

————, (Ban Nghiên Cứu Lịch Sử Quân Đội). *Lực Lượng Vũ Trang Cách Mạng trong Năm Đầu của Chính Quyền Nhân Dân* [Revolutionary Armed Forces in the First Year of the People's Government]. Hanoi: NXB QĐND, 1970.

————, (Tổng Cục Chính Trị). *Tổ Chức Sự Lãnh Đạo của Đảng trong Quân Đội Nhân Dân Việt Nam* [Organizing Party Leadership in the Vietnam People's Army]. Vol 1, *1930–1954*. Hanoi: NXB QĐND, 1994.

————, (Viện Lịch Sử Quân Sự). *Lịch Sử cuộc Kháng Chiến Chống Thực Dân Pháp 1945–1954* [History of Resistance to the French Colonialists 1945–1954]. 6 vols. Hanoi: NXB QĐND, 1985–1993.

————, (Viện Lịch Sử Quân Sự). *Lịch Sử cuộc Kháng Chiến Chống Thực Dân Pháp 1945–1954* [History of Resistance to the French Colonialists 1945–1954]. 2 vols. Hanoi: NXB QĐND, 1994.

————, (Viện Lịch Sử Quân Sự). *Chi Đội 3 Giải Phóng Quân Nam Tiến* [Detachment 3 Liberation Army Southern Advance]. Hanoi: NXB QĐND, 1995(?).

————, (Viện Lịch Sử Quân Sự). *Phong Trào Nam Tiến (1945–1946)* [The Southern Advance Movement (1945–1946)]. Hanoi: NXB QĐND, 1997.

Quang Minh. *Đại Việt Quốc Dân Đảng: Cách Mạng Việt Nam Thời Cận Kim, 1938–1995* [The Greater Vietnam Nationalist Party: The Vietnamese Revolution in Modern Times, 1938–1995]. Westminster, CA: NXB Văn Nghệ, 2000.

Quinn-Judge, Sophie. "Ho Chi Minh and the Making of his Image." In *Naissance d'un État-Parti: Le Viet Nam depuis 1945 / The Birth of a Party-State: Vietnam Since 1945*, edited by Christopher E. Goscha and Benoît de Tréglodé, 159–74. Paris: Les Indes Savantes, 2004.

Ruscio, Alain. *Les Communistes français et la guerre d'Indochine: 1944–1954*. Paris: L'Harmattan, 1985.

————. *La première guerre d'Indochine (1945–1954): Bibliographie*. Paris: L'Harmattan, 1987.

————, compiler. *La guerre «française» d'Indochine 1945–1954: Les sources de la connaissance*. Paris: Les Indes Savantes, 2002.

Sainteny, Jean. *Histoire d'une paix manquée: Indochine, 1945–1947*. Paris: Fayard, 1953.

————. *Ho Chi Minh and his Vietnam: A Personal Memoir*. Chicago: Cowles, 1972.

Salan, Raoul. *Mémoires: Fin d'un Empire*. Vol. 1, *Le sens d'un engagement, Juin 1899–Sept. 1946*. Paris: Presses de la Cité, 1970.

Shipway, Martin. *The Road to War: France and Vietnam, 1944–1947*. Providence: Berghahn Books, 1996.

Smith, Ralph B. "The Work of the Provisional Government of Vietnam, August–December 1945." *Modern Asian Studies* 12, no. 4 (1978): 571–609.

Stowe, Judy. "Money and Mobilisation: the Difficulties of Building an Economy in Time of War." In *Naissance d'un État-Parti: Le Viet Nam depuis 1945 / The Birth of a Party-State: Vietnam Since 1945*, edited by Christopher E. Goscha and Benoît de Tréglodé, 61–70. Paris: Les Indes Savantes, 2004.

Tertrais, Hugues. *La piastre et le fusil: Le coût de la guerre d'Indochine 1945–1954.* Paris: Ministère de l'economie, des finances et de l'industrie, 2002.

Tønnesson, Stein. *1946: Déclenchement de la Guerre d'Indochine.* Paris: L'Harmattan, 1987.

———. "La Paix imposée par la Chine: L'Accord franco-vietnamien du 6 mars 1946." In *Les Guerres d'Indochine de 1945 à 1975,* edited by Charles-Robert Ageron and Philippe Devillers, 35–36. Paris: Institut d'histoire du temps présent, 1996.

———. *Vietnam 1946: How the War Began.* Berkeley: University of California Press, 2010.

Trần Đình Nghiêm, et al., editors. *Nhớ về Anh Lê Đức Thọ* [Remembering Brother Le Duc Tho]. Hanoi: NXB CTQG, 2000.

Trần Huy Liệu, et al., eds., *Cách Mạng Tháng Tám: Tổng Khởi Nghĩa ở Hà Nội và các Địa Phương* [The August Revolution: General Insurrection in Hanoi and Various Localities]. 2 vols. Hanoi: Sử Học, 1960.

Trần Ngọc Ngôn. (Bộ Tư Lệnh Thông Tin Liên Lạc). *Lịch Sử Bộ Đội Thông Tin Liên Lạc* [History of Communications and Liaison Forces]. Vol. 1, *1945–1954.* Hanoi: NXB QĐND, 1985.

Trần Quốc Dụ, et al. *Đồng Bạc Tài Chính Đồng Bạc Cụ Hồ 1945–1954* [Finance Ministry Currency and Elder Ho Currency 1945–1954]. Hanoi: NXB Tài Chính, 2000.

Tran Thi Lien. "Les Catholiques Vietnamiens pendant la guerre d'independence (1945–1954) entre la reconquete coloniale et la resistance communiste." Diplôme de doctorat, l'Institut d'études politiques de Paris, 1996.

———. "Les catholiques et la République démocratique du Viet Nam (1945–1954): Une approche biographique." In *Naissance d'un État-Parti: Le Viet Nam depuis 1945 / The Birth of a Party-State: Vietnam Since 1945,* edited by Christopher E. Goscha and Benoît de Tréglodé, 253–76. Paris: Les Indes Savantes, 2004.

Trần Văn Giàu. "Hồi Ký 1940–1945" [Memoir 1940–1945]. *Thời Đại Mới* (Dayton, Ohio) 21 (May 2011).

Trịnh Thúc Huỳnh, et al., eds. *Phạm Hùng: Nhà Lãnh Đạo Trung Kiên, Mẫu Mực (Hồi Ký)* [Pham Hung: Faithful and Exemplary Leader]. Hanoi: NXB CTQG, 2003.

———. *Đồng Chí Trần Quốc Hoàn: Chiến Sĩ Cách Mạng Trung Kiên của Đảng, Nhà Lãnh Đạo xuất Sắc của Công An Việt Nam* [Comrade Tran Quoc Hoan: Faithful Revolutionary Fighter for the Party, Outstanding Leader of the Vietnam Police]. Hanoi: NXB CTQG, 2006.

Trịnh Văn Hiến. *Có Thể Mất Nam Bộ Được Không?* [Can We Lose the Southern Region?] Hanoi: NXB Tân Quốc Dân, Jan. 1946.

Trường Chinh. *Cách Mạng Tháng Tám* [The August Revolution]. Hanoi: NXB ST, 1946.

———. *Primer for Revolt: The Communist Takeover in Viet-Nam.* New York: Praeger, 1963. Introduction by Bernard B. Fall.

Turpin, Frédéric. *De Gaulle, les gaullistes et l'Indochine.* Paris: Les Indes Savants, 2005.

U.S. Department of State, Bureau of Intelligence and Research. "Political Alignments of Vietnamese Nationalists." OIR Report no. 3708 ("Restricted"). Washington DC, 1 Oct. 1949.

U.S. Senate Committee on Foreign Relations. *Hearings before the Committee on Foreign Relations on the Cause, Origins,* and *Lessons of the Vietnam War.* May 9, 10, and 11, 1972. Washington, DC: Government Printing Office, 1973.

Valentine, Daniel B. "The British Facilitation of the French Re-entry into Vietnam." PhD thesis, University of California Los Angeles, 1974.

Valluy, Jean-Etienne. "Indochine: Octobre 1945–mars 1947." *Revue des Deux Mondes* (1 Nov. 1967; 15 Nov. 1967; 1 Dec. 1967; 15 Dec. 1967).

Việt Nam, Đảng Cộng Sản. *Lịch Sử Đảng Cộng Sản Việt Nam: Trích Văn Kiện Đảng* [History of the Vietnam Communist Party: Extracts of Party Documents]. Vol. 2, *1945–1954*. 2nd ed. Hanoi: NXB Sách Giáo Khoa Mac-Lê-nin, 1979.

———. *Văn Kiện Đảng Toàn Tập* [Complete Party Documents]. Vol. 8, *1945–1947*. Hanoi: NXB CTQG, 2000.

———. *Văn Kiện Đảng về Kháng Chiến Chống Thực Dân Pháp* [Party Documents on Resistance to French Colonialism]. Vol. 1, *1945–1950*. Hanoi: NXB ST, 1986.

———, (Ban Chấp Hành Trung Ương). *Văn Kiện Đảng 1945–1954* [Party Documents 1945–1954]. Hanoi: Ban Nghiên Cứu Lịch Sử Đảng Trung ương xuất bản, 1978.

———, (Ban Nghiên Cứu Lịch Sử Đảng Trung Ương). *Lịch Sử Đảng Cộng Sản Việt Nam: Sơ thảo* [Preliminary History of the Vietnam Communist Party]. Vol. 1, *1920–1954*. 2nd ed. Hanoi: NXB ST, 1984.

———, (Ban Nghiên Cứu Lịch Sử Đảng Trung Ương). *Những Sự Kiện Lịch Sử Đảng* [Historical Events of the Party]. Vol. 2, *1945–1954*. Hanoi: NXB ST, 1979.

Việt Nam, Đảng Lao Động. *Cuộc Kháng Chiến Thần Thánh của Nhân Dân Việt Nam* [The Superhuman Resistance of the Vietnamese People]. 4 vols. Hanoi: NXB ST, 1960. Reprints of articles from Việt Minh newspapers 1945–1954.

———. *Văn Kiện Quân Sự của Đảng* [Military Documents of the Party]. Vol. 1, *1930–1945*. Vol. 2, *2 Sept. 1945–10 Oct. 1950*. Hanoi: NXB QĐND, 1969 and 1976.

Vietnam, Democratic Republic of. *Causes of the Conflict between France and Vietnam.* Paris: Vietnam Delegation in France, 1948.

———. *The Democratic Republic of Vietnam.* Paris: Vietnam Delegation in France, Information Service, 1948.

———. *Struggle Against Illiteracy in Vietnam.* Hanoi: FLPH, 1959.

Việt Nam, Tổng Bưu Điện. *Lịch Sử Ngành Thông Tin Bưu Điện Việt Nam* [History of Vietnam's Communications and Postal Branch]. 2 vols. Hanoi, 1989. Draft.

Việt Nam, Trung Tâm Lưu Trữ Quốc Gia III. *Nam Bộ Kháng Chiến (1945–1954) qua tài liệu Lưu Trữ* [Southern Region Resistance (1945–1954) seen through Archive Documents]. Hanoi: NXB QĐND, 2007.

Việt Nam, Văn Phòng Quốc Hội. *Lịch Sử Quốc Hội Việt Nam 1946–1960* [History of Vietnam's National Assembly 1946–1960]. Hanoi: NXB CTQG, 1994.

Việt Nam, Viện Khoa Học Công An. *Công An Nhân Dân Việt Nam (1945–1954): Sơ Thảo* [Preliminary History of the Vietnam People's Police (1945–1954)]. Hanoi: NXB Công An Nhân Dân, 1996.

Việt Nam, Viện Khoa Học Xã Hội. (Viện Kinh Tế). *Kinh tế Việt Nam từ Cách Mạng Tháng Tám đến Kháng Chiến Thắng Lợi, 1945–1954* [Vietnam's Economy from the August Revolution to Resistance Victory, 1945–1954]. Hanoi: NXB Khoa Học, 1966.

Việt Nam, Viện Sử Học. *Việt Nam: Những Sự Kiện 1945–1975* [Vietnam: Events 1945–1975]. Vol. 1, *1945–1965*. Hanoi: NXB KHXH, 1975.

Võ Nguyên Giáp. *Những Năm Tháng Không Thể nào quên* [Unforgettable Months and Years]. 2 vols. Hanoi: NXB QĐND, 1970. Translated as *Unforgettable Days* (Hanoi: Foreign Language Publishing House, 1975). Translated by Mai Elliott as *Unforgettable Months and Years* (Ithaca, NY: Cornell Southeast Asian Program, data paper 99, May 1975).

———. *Những Chặng Đường Lịch Sử* [Historical Paths]. Hanoi: NXB CTQG, 1994.

———. *Chiến Đấu trong Vòng Vây: Hồi Úc* [Fighting While Encircled: Memoirs]. Hanoi: NXB QĐND and NXB Thanh Niên, 1995.

Vu, Tuong. "From Cheering to Volunteering: Vietnamese Communists and the Coming of the Cold War, 1940–1951." In *Connecting Histories: Decolonization and the Cold War in Southeast Asia,* edited by Christopher Goscha and Christian Ostermann, 172–204. Washington, D.C.: Woodrow Wilson Center Press / Stanford University Press, 2009.

Vũ Đình Hòe. *Hồi Ký Vũ Đình Hòe* [Memoirs of Vu Dinh Hoe]. Vol. 1. Hanoi: NXB Văn Hóa-Thông Tin, 1995.

Vũ Kỳ. "Những Chặng Đường Trường Kỳ Kháng Chiến Nhất Định Thắng Lợi" [The Paths to Certain Victory in the Protracted Resistance]. *Tập Chí Lịch Sử Quân Sự* 36 (Dec. 1988): 72–82.

Vương Thừa Vũ. *Trưởng Thành trong Chiến Đấu: Hồi Ký* [Growing Up in Battle: Memoirs]. Hanoi: NXB QĐND, 1979.

Woodside, Alexander B. *Community and Revolution in Modern Vietnam*. Boston: Houghton Mifflin, 1976.

———. "The Triumphs and Failures of Mass Education in Vietnam." *Pacific Affairs* 56, no. 3 (Fall 1983): 401–27.

Worthing, Peter. *Occupation and Revolution: China and the Vietnamese August Revolution of 1945*. Berkeley: Institute of East Asian Studies, 2001.

Xuân Thủy, et al. *Những Chặng Đường Báo Cứu Quốc: Hồi Ký* [Paths of *National Salvation* Newspaper: Memoirs]. Hanoi: NXB Hà Nội, 1987.

INDEX

Acheson, Dean, 302

Agence France Presse (AFP), 236, 254

Agriculture, 1947 production targets, 381;
harvest statistics, 351; ministry of, 330–333;
supplementary crops, 321–323, 327;
Veterinary Bureau, 332–333; see also
Rice

Aircraft, and modernity, 316; British, 505;
French, 146, 212, 214–215, 227–228, 279;
French air attacks, 130–131, 241–243; French
plan Saigon–Hanoi air route, 300; US, 266,
288–291, 321, 527, 639n21; Vietnamese attack
Cát Bi airfield, 177

Alcohol, 319–320, 322, 363–365, 541, 558–559;
bans on private distilling, 363; monopoly,
363–365; moonshiners vs. revenuers,
364–365

Alessandri, Marcel, 184–185, 286

Allied powers, xiv, 4, 117, 384, 431, 444, 446,
454, 458; China Theater, 184–185; Trotskyist
position regarding, 408; wartime alliance
unraveling, 260–261, 263; see also United
States, Soviet Union, Great Britain, China

Ammunition, xiv, 134, 139–140, 169, 177, 306,
649n262; French dump in Saigon
sabotaged, 219; scarcity of, 141, 164; see also
Firearms

An Khê, 133; battle of, 162–163, 165

André, Max, 215–220, 229–232

Annam. *See* Central region

Anti-colonialism, Asia-wide upsurge, 260–261

Armistice, 205–210; 30 October ceasefire,
245–247; Hồ Chí Minh instructions,
214; in Saigon, 188–189; raised at Dalat
conference, 216–220; specified in modus
vivendi, 234

Artillery, 125, 130–131, 139–140, 153–154, 163,
251

Associated State of Vietnam, 9, 574

Association pour la formation intellectuelle
et morale des Annamites, 340

Atomic bomb, 262–263

Aubrac, Raymond, 233

Australian POWs, 514, 627n1

Bắc Bộ. *See* Northern region

Bắc Bộ Phủ. *See* Northern Region Office

Bắc Giang province, 36, 40, 135, 325–326, 343,
351, 380, 423

Bắc Kạn province, 346, 352, 361, 396, 401, 410

Bắc Ninh province, 339, 359, 391, 524; early
August attack on French convoy, 231,
241–244; ICP presence in, 442–443

Bahnar ethnic group, 558

Ban Mê Thuột town, 140, 518; fighting in and
around, 131–133

Bank of Indochina, xviii, 28, 234, 273–274, 287,
370–371